A Companion to European Union Law and International Law

A Companion to European Union Law and International Law

Edited by

Dennis Patterson and Anna Södersten

WILEY Blackwell

This edition first published 2016

Registered Office
John Wiley & Sons, Ltd, The Atrium, Southern Gate, Chichester, West Sussex, PO19 8SQ, UK

Editorial Offices
350 Main Street, Malden, MA 02148-5020, USA
9600 Garsington Road, Oxford, OX4 2DQ, UK
The Atrium, Southern Gate, Chichester, West Sussex, PO19 8SQ, UK

For details of our global editorial offices, for customer services, and for information about how to apply for permission to reuse the copyright material in this book please see our website at www.wiley.com/wiley-blackwell.

Library of Congress Cataloging-in-Publication Data

A companion to European Union law and international law / Edited by Dennis Patterson and Anna Södersten.
pages cm
Includes bibliographical references and index.
ISBN 978-0-470-67439-0 (cloth)
1. Law–European Union countries. 2. International law. I. Patterson, Dennis M. (Dennis Michael), 1955– editor. II. Södersten, Anna, editor.
KJE947.C6565 2015
341.242′2–dc23

2015026544

A catalogue record for this book is available from the British Library.

Cover image: *Justice Between Force and the Law*, sculpture by Enrico Quattrini, 1902, Palace of Justice, Rome. Photo © Ron Reznick

Set in 10/12pt Minion by SPi Global, Pondicherry, India
Printed and bound in Malaysia by Vivar Printing Sdn Bhd

1 2016

Contents

Contributors

Ari Afilalo is professor of law at Rutgers University School of Law.

Anthony Arnull is Barber Professor of Jurisprudence at University of Birmingham.

Loïc Azoulai is professor of European law at the European University Institute.

Catherine Barnard is professor of European Union law at the University of Cambridge.

Frank S. Benyon is the former principal legal advisor to the European Commission. He is now a senior fellow in the Department of Law of the European University Institute.

Roland Bieber is professor emeritus, former Jean Monnet Chair of European Law, former vice dean, University of Lausanne, and former legal advisor, European Parliament.

Andrea Biondi is professor of European Union law at King's College London.

Djemila Carron is a PhD candidate at the University of Geneva.

Roger S. Clark is Board of Governors Professor at Rutgers University.

Paul Craig is professor of English law at the University of Oxford.

Marise Cremona is professor of European law at the European University Institute.

Deirdre Curtin is professor of European Law at the University of Amsterdam and director of the Amsterdam Center of European Law and Governance.

Mark Dawson is professor of European law and governance at the Hertie School of Governance.

Pedro Caro de Sousa is a lecturer at the University of Reading.

Bruno de Witte is professor of European Union law at the European University Institute.

Michael Dougan is professor of European law and Jean Monnet Chair in EU Law at the University of Liverpool.

Sionaidh Douglas-Scott is professor of European and human rights law at the University of Oxford.

John Erik Fossum is professor at the ARENA Centre for European Studies, Oslo.

Elspeth Guild is Jean Monnet Professor *ad personam* at Queen Mary, University of London and at the Radboud University Nijmegen.

Christian Joerges is a research professor at the University of Bremen and co-director of the Center for European Law and Politics and part-time senior professor for law and society at the Hertie School of Governance in Berlin. He was formerly professor of economic law at the European University Institute.

Jan Klabbers is Martti Ahtisaari Academy Professor at the University of Helsinki.

Maria Lee is professor of law at University College London.

Miguel Poiares Maduro is former director of the Global Governance Program, professor of law at the European University Institute, and Portuguese minister for regional development.

Ravi Mehta is an English barrister practicing at Blackstone Chambers and specializing in European and international law.

Hans-Wolfgang Micklitz is professor of economic law at the European University Institute.

Valsamis Mitsilegas is professor of European criminal law at Queen Mary University of London.

Giorgio Monti is professor of competition law at the European University Institute.

Dennis Patterson is Board of Governors Professor of Law and Philosophy, Rutgers University. chair in legal philosophy and legal theory, European University Institute, chair in jurisprudence and international trade at Swansea University.

Steve Peers is a professor at the University of Essex.

Zane Rasnača is a PhD researcher at the European University Institute.

Allan Rosas is a judge of the Court of Justice of the European Union.

Marco Sassòli is professor of international law at the University of Geneva.

Martin Scheinin is professor of international law and human rights at the European University Institute.

Silvana Sciarra is a judge of the Constitutional Court of Italy.

Sideek M. Seyad is an associate professor at Stockholm University

Piet Jan Slot is professor of European and economic law at the University of Leiden.

Anna Södersten is a lecturer in law at Uppsala University.

Bariş Soyer is professor of law at Swansea University.

Joel P. Trachtman is professor of international law at the Fletcher School of Law and Diplomacy, Tufts University.

Stephen Weatherill is the Jacques Delors Professor of European Law at the University of Oxford.

Ramses A. Wessel is professor of international and European institutional law at the University of Twente.

Katja S. Ziegler is Sir Robert Jennings Professor of International Law at the University of Leicester.

Preface

The essays in this book cover current topics in European Union law and international law. Why a book on both EU law and international law? The European Union is sometimes described as an international organization created by its member states under an international treaty. Under this view, it is the *pacta sunt servanda* formula that explains the source of authority of the Union. However, in the 1960s, the European Court of Justice declared that the European Union was properly conceived as a "new legal order" and, years later, that the EU treaties were a "Constitutional Charter." This evolution suggests that the European Union cannot be understood as a traditional international organization. Although the nature of the Union has not been completely settled, the EU treaties clearly go beyond classic international treaties.

Moreover, EU law and international law undeniably have many points of contact. There is a fair amount of EU legislation that implements (or in other ways is derived from) international law. Further, the European Union is an important actor on the international scene: it takes an active role in the creation and shaping of international law. We believe that one needs to understand international law – or at least have some knowledge of international law – in order to understand EU law.

The central feature of this book is its integration of these fields. While the central focus is the law of the European Union, the international law entries complement and enhance the reader's understanding of EU law. However, this book is not merely about pointing out similarities between these fields; it is equally about pointing out differences. To this end, we have asked the authors – to the extent that it is possible, and where appropriate – to integrate the two areas of law. For some of the topics, we thought it would be more fruitful to have two separate entries: one entry that deals specifically with the EU law aspects of a specific topic and another entry that deals with the international law aspects.

Much has happened since we began working on this book. The effects of the economic and financial crisis (which in Europe turned into a "Eurocrisis") are still felt. The crisis had profound effects on both the EU member states and the European Union. Consequently, many entries include some analysis of the crisis and its effects on law. As we edited this book, there was an occasional sense that little could be expected for the future of European integration.

At the same time, the "dust" from the Lisbon Treaty started to settle. The Lisbon Treaty, which amends the European Union's core treaties, entered into force in 2009. It marked the end of a decade of discussions among the EU member states about how to reform the Union. Legal scholars will continue to analyze the legal implications of the Lisbon Treaty for many years to come; a considerable number of the entries in this volume devote space to these aspects.

The *Companion* is divided into six parts: (I) International Law and EU Law; (II) EU Political Institutions and Decision Making; (III) The Court; (IV) Economic Dimensions of the European Union; (V) The European Union and the External World; (VI) Human Rights, Social Issues, and the Environment. Many entries have overlapping themes; they could fit into more than one part. However, we believe that this arrangement of the entries will facilitate the reader's use of the book. Each part presents a multitude of topics and perspectives to a relatively coherent theme.

We have assembled some of the best scholars in these fields. We asked the authors to survey the topic assigned and, where appropriate, indicate their own view of the questions and issues at stake. The entries cover the key figures, terms, topics, and problems in the field. The collection of the entries took much longer than expected but it was certainly worth the effort; the book displays a diversity, range, and richness of legal scholarship. We wish to thank the authors who have contributed their time and talent to this *Companion*. Many of the entries are remarkable in terms of originality and presentation. We are grateful to Bosko Tripkovic and Sofie Christine Møller for their editorial assistance in preparing this book for publication. We are especially grateful to Felicity Marsh for copy editing that went beyond our expectations. We cannot be emphatic enough in our appreciation for her work on this project.

The *Companion* could serve as a reference work, but it is much more than that; it offers commentaries on the work pursued in each field. It is our hope that the entries are of interest to both beginning students and professionals.

Abbreviations

ATT	Arms Trade Treaty
BAT	best available techniques
BITs	bilateral investment agreements
BREFs	BAT reference notes
CCP	Common Commercial Policy
CEAS	Common European Asylum System
CESL	Common European Sales Law
CERD	Convention for the Elimination of Racial Discrimination
CFSP	Common Foreign and Security Policy
CFI	Court of First Instance
CFR	Common Frame of Reference
CIL	customary international law
CJEU	Court of Justice of the European Union
COREPER	Comité des représentants permanents (Committee of permanent representatives of the member states)
CRC	Convention on the Rights of the Child
CRPD	Convention on the Rights of Persons with Disabilities
CSDP	Common Security and Defence Policy
CT	Constitutional Treaty
DCFR	Draft of a Common Frame of Reference
DSB	Dispute Settlement Body
EAW	European Arrest Warrant
EC	European Community
EC Treaty	Treaty establishing the European Community
ECB	European Central Bank

ECHR	European Convention on Human Rights
ECJ	European Court of Justice
ECS	European Committee for Standardization
ECSC	European Coal and Steel Community
ECtHR	European Court of Human Rights
EDC	European Defence Community
EEAS	European External Action Service
EEB	European Environmental Bureau
EEC	European Economic Community
EEC Treaty	Treaty establishing the European Economic Community
EEZ	Exclusive Economic Zones
EFSF	European Financial Stability Facility
EFSM	European Financial Stabilization Mechanism
ELVs	emission limit values
EMAS	Eco-Management and Audit Scheme
EMU	Economic and Monetary Union
EP	European Parliament
EPC	European Political Community
EPPO	European Public Prosecutor's Office
EQSs	environmental quality standards
ESCB	European System of Central Banks
ESM	European Stability Mechanism
ETUC	European Trade Union Confederation
EU	European Union
Euratom	European Atomic Energy Community
GATS	General Agreement on Trade in Services
GATT	General Agreement on Tariffs and Trade
GBER	General Block Exemption Regulation
GC	General Court
GDP	Gross Domestic Product
GSP+	sustainable development and good governance
ICC	International Criminal Court
ICCPR	International Covenant on Civil and Political Rights
ICESCR	International Covenant on Economic, Social and Cultural Rights
ICN	International Competition Network
ICJ	International Court of Justice
IED	Industrial Emissions Directive
IGC	Intergovernmental Conference

IHFFC	International Humanitarian Fact-Finding Commission
IHL	International Humanitarian Law
IMF	International Monetary Fund
IOM	International Organization for Migration
IPPC	Integrated Pollution Prevention and Control
MARPOL	International Convention for the Prevention of Pollution from Ships
MiFID	Markets in Financial Instruments Directive
MiFIR	Markets in Financial Instruments Regulation
NATO	North Atlantic Treaty Organization
NGO	Non-Governmental Organization
NIAC	non-international armed conflict
OAS	Organization of American States
OECD	Organisation for Economic Co-operation and Development
OIC	Organization of the Islamic Conference
OLAF	European Anti-Fraud Office
OMC	Open Method of Coordination
OPEC	Organization of Petroleum Exporting Countries
OSCE	Organization for Security and Co-operation in Europe
PCIJ	Permanent Court of International Justice
PSC	Political and Security Committee
SEA	Single European Act
SIS	Schengen Information System
TA	Treaty of Amsterdam
TEU	Treaty on European Union
TFEU	Treaty on the Functioning of the European Union
TL	Treaty of Lisbon
TSCG	Treaty on Stability, Coordination and Governance in the Economic and Monetary Union
TWG	Technical Working Group
UN	United Nations
UDHR	Universal Declaration of Human Rights
UNCLOS	United Nations Convention on the Law of the Sea
UNCTAD	United Nations Conference on Trade and Development
UNECE	United Nations Economic Commission for Europe
VCLT	Vienna Convention on the Law of Treaties
VIS	Visa Information System
WHO	World Health Organization
WTO	World Trade Organization

Part I

International Law and EU Law

1

Sui Generis? The European Union as an International Organization

Jan Klabbers

Introduction

The precise status of the European Union in international law has never really been settled, and this applies to its predecessors (the European Economic Community (EEC) and European Community (EC) in particular) as well. What is clear, it seems, is that the Union is not a state as commonly conceived. It lacks its own territory and it lacks a population it can call its own, therewith failing to tick the two formal boxes when it comes to statehood.[1] Moreover, the European Union is not generally recognized as a state, even though its attitudes and legal order sometimes suggest that statehood might be a close and reasonably accurate analogy.

But if the European Union is not a state, then what is it? The most common classification is that it is an international organization, yet this is often accompanied by the caveat that it is an organization unlike any other. Traditionally, this has been captured in a variety of ways. Thus, for some, the European Union is the archetype of a supranational organization. It is held to be a species of the genus "international organization," but one where decision making is more centralized than in others and actually takes place not so much between the member states but above them. This claim is then often accompanied by the statement that there is really only one example of such a supranational organization: the European Union.

Likewise, the European Union is sometimes said to be an international organization *sui generis*, in a class of its own. According to this line of reasoning, while it is an organization, it does not resemble other organizations in all respects and, if the *sui generis* label is taken seriously, may even not be an international organization at all. This label then reveals conceptual paucity: the European Union is placed in a category whose contours are undefined and within which it might not fit that well.

Sometimes the European Union is deemed to be an international organization but one that is of a higher nature than others. This presupposes that there are sliding scales of "organizationhood," with some being more developed than others. Some might constitute merely rudimentary forms of interstate cooperation, but the European Union, so the argument goes, would be at the other end of the spectrum and can be seen as a model for other international organizations to emulate.

A Companion to European Union Law and International Law, First Edition.
Edited by Dennis Patterson and Anna Södersten.

Neither of these labels is very satisfying: they each create a category of one, and if that is the case, then perhaps the category may not be all that well chosen.[2] In this chapter, I will explore a different route. Instead of trying to fit the European Union into an existing category I aim to rethink that category. While one of the brilliant aspects of the Union is that it allows observers to make their own classification (and here it is useful to remember that those versed in domestic law[3] or political science[4] may find yet other ways to characterize the European Union), it does cast some doubt on the wisdom of the enterprise. Maybe the problem is not only that the Union is uncategorizable, maybe it is also that the label "international organization" is not all that well considered to begin with. Maybe the European Union's existence should force the community of international lawyers to rethink both the very concept of international organization and, related to this, the discipline's main theory concerning international organizations: the theory of functionalism. In what follows, I will first address the standard definition of international organizations and the theory of functionalism before discussing why the status of international organization may be deemed attractive. Thereafter, the chapter focuses on the European Union.

Defining International Organizations

There is no airtight definition of "international organization" available in international law, and the concept of international organization comprises an enormous variety of disparate entities. These range from military alliances, such as NATO, to public cartels (OPEC, and also, in their own way, the various commodity organizations) and from financial institutions, such as the various investment banks, to predominantly academic enterprises, such as the European Forest Institute. Likewise, in form these entities can be radically different. The UN, on the one hand, is highly structured, the Council of the Baltic Sea States, on the other hand, is a loose collection of cooperating states which, for want of a better label, is sometimes also considered as an international organization.[5] While lacking some degree of formalism, the various meetings of the parties or conferences of the parties set up under multilateral environmental agreements are sometimes seen as international organizations.[6] A case can be made that simply because some organizations are set up explicitly on the basis of an instrument considered to be nonlegal in nature (such as the Organization for Security and Co-operation in Europe (OSCE)) does not entail that for that reason alone, they ought not to be regarded as international organizations. In short, the concept of an international organization is a broad church accommodating a wide variety of rather different actors. This broad approach owes much to the absence of definition, beyond the purely formal. The literature is united in thinking that there are three, or perhaps four, main elements that are characteristic of international organizations. These elements stem, it seems, from an inductive analysis: scholars have looked at what they held to be international organizations, drawn comparisons, and singled out the elements those entities appear to have in common.[7]

The first of these common elements is that international organizations are created – typically but not invariably – by states. The second, that international organizations are typically set up on the basis of treaties. The third, that, although most will have more, international organizations are generally deemed to possess at least one organ. This serves to distinguish the organization from mere regular interstate meetings: if there is an institutional pattern, then it probably is an international organization.

These three elements are purely formal in nature, and can be verified with relative ease. If two or three states meet, decide to create a common organ, and do so by means of a treaty, the resulting entity will be regarded as an international organization, regardless of what the organization is supposed to be doing or how it will perform its tasks. For this reason, perhaps, some have advocated a fourth element, introducing a more substantive consideration: the organization should possess a will of its own, separate from the will of the member states (a *volonté distincte*). While to some extent this is captured in the element of there being at least one organ, it is nonetheless not quite identical: the idea behind the *volonté distincte* is to make sure that the "proper" organization is differentiated from the state vehicle.

Yet, this is also highly problematic: once thought through it would entail that the only proper organizations are those which can tell member states what to do, even if those member states are unwilling to comply. In other words: it presupposes an organization which is, first, capable of taking decisions binding on the member states, and second, capable of taking such decisions by majority vote (or any other mechanism which does not give each and every member state a veto: hence, unanimity and consensus are disqualifying factors). Thus seen, very few organizations will actually qualify as "proper" organizations: the European Union, part of the UN (the Security Council in particular), perhaps the International Civil Aviation Organization, and maybe a small handful of others. As a result, this fourth element is usually not taken all that literally and functions more as a reminder that organizations are different from regular meetings of states.

Be that as it may, once an international organization exists, it is deemed to operate along functional lines. The powerful theory of functionalism[8] explains that international organizations (lacking territory, after all) are not set up along territorial lines but in order to fulfill certain functions that are delegated to them by their member states. The functions, and the powers necessary to give effect to them, are deemed to be conferred on the organization, and both member states and nonmember states are expected not to interfere with the exercise of these functions and powers.

This finds its normative justification in the thought that the functions of international organizations are generally considered to comprise the global common good. It is this contribution to the common good that justifies, for example, the proposition that international organizations are usually immune from suit and exempt from taxation and that their officers enjoy privileges and immunities as well. In short, the functioning of the organization should not be impeded. Much the same justification applies to the implied powers of organizations: following the International Court of Justice (ICJ) in the classic *Reparation for Injuries* opinion,[9] these have been held justifiable precisely in order to enable the organization to exercise its functions. The theory also comes with limits to what organizations can do. As Bekker put it with brilliant brevity, an international organization "shall be entitled to (no more than) what is strictly necessary for the exercise of its functions in the fulfillment of its purposes."[10]

This is problematic because, if indiscriminately applied, this would mean that even organizations with a nasty purpose should be given free hands.[11] Yet, functionalism has never been able to distinguish properly between "good" and "bad" organizations, as organizations are by its definition meant to contribute to the global good. Where this contribution is substantively doubtful, functionalism can resort to a higher level of abstraction: all organizations embody cooperation between states, and since cooperation between states is generally a good thing, it follows that international organizations are generally a good thing too, no matter how nefarious their purposes may be.

The law and theory relating to international organizations, then, conspire to create a very broad concept of international organization. Some observers denied the organizationhood of the Warsaw Pact and Comecon for largely political (substantive, value-based) reasons, but since an overt political argument is not available, this had to be dressed up: Comecon and the Warsaw Pact were thus sometimes regarded as nonentities because they were dominated by a single member state.[12] Likewise, most works on international organizations have difficulties accommodating the Organization of the Islamic Conference (OIC), set up in 1969 among a number of Muslim countries (currently numbering 57 member states) and dedicated to safeguarding and protecting the interests of the Muslim world.[13]

Functionalism in International Institutional Law

On the explanatory level, functionalism used to pack (and still packs) a powerful punch. Functionalism appears highly plausible when it suggests why international organizations are set up since, obviously, a single state will be unable to guarantee the accurate delivery of mail abroad or provide for collective security. Functionalism appears plausible when it holds that international organizations can only act on the basis of the powers conferred upon them, and it appears plausible when suggesting that organizations are not allowed to act *ultra vires*. And functionalism continues to look plausible when one realizes that the two main global crises of the early twenty-first century (the financial meltdown and the environmental meltdown) concern issue areas in which no comprehensive international organization is active: the environmental regime is characterized by dispersion and fragmentation, and financial regulation is almost entirely left to highly informal gatherings of a limited number of powerful actors, for example, the Basel Committee.[14] Hence, the committed functionalist can easily point to the utility of functionalism: if the WHO has been able to eradicate polio, should not a global financial institution be expected to contribute to global financial health?

Yet, the explanatory force of functionalism also has its limits. As noted above, the very definition of international organization creates problems: to the (considerable) extent that functionalism is based on a principal–agent model (member states create an organization as their agent), the *volonté distincte* of international organizations is more fictitious than real. If an entity truly can give orders to its member states, then it can no longer be said with full conviction that this entity exercises functions delegated by its member states. It is for this reason that functionalism has traditionally had problems incorporating the European Union, since the claim that the Union exercises functions delegated to it by its member states only holds true at an unhelpfully high level of abstraction.

For all its explanatory power, functionalism does have a few black holes, and one of these is the issue of accountability or control. This stems from the fact that functionalism is limited to addressing the relationship between the organization and its member states and has little to say about two other relevant types of relationships: it remains silent on "internal" relations (between organization and staff or between organs of the organization) and it remains silent on "external" relations (the relations the organization may have with the outside world).[15] As a result, the theory does not recognize that organizations can engage in wrongful acts. Organizations, as suggested above, are seen as being created for the common good or, in Singh's famous phrase, the "salvation of mankind";[16] in this light, even their *ultra vires* activities must be considered as beneficial to the world at large. And where organizations do wrong it must be the fault of the member states, for these should have exercised greater control.

The Rules of Attraction

All this raises the question of why entities would desire to be considered international organizations. What makes it attractive (if anything does) to be considered an international organization? The answer consists of various layers. First, there are few if any attractive alternatives. Organizations, obviously, are not states, but neither do they wish to be regarded as anything else. While international law does not offer a systematic legal framework with regard to entities, it does recognize some other classes of actors in one way or another. Thus, there is room in international law for national liberation movements, indigenous peoples, national minorities, and companies, but none of these labels apply with conviction to entities usually considered international organizations. The closest analogy, then, is with the NGO sector and entities such as Greenpeace or Amnesty International, but here, too, awkwardness sets in rapidly. Indeed, the very term "NGO" points to the absence of governmental representation; hence, international organizations by definition cannot be thus classified. For all practical purposes, therefore, this leaves the label "international organization" as the only practically available possibility. Whatever the European Union is, or the WHO, or the Nordic Investment Bank, they are closer to being international organizations than anything else.

But more than this, the legal and political status attached to the label "international organization," with its association with the global good, makes it politically attractive. International organizations are *ex hypothesi* legitimate actors, and legitimacy is a scarce yet highly attractive good.

With this comes the possibility of legal advantages. There is general agreement that international organizations and their staff are entitled to taxation privileges and jurisdictional immunities. While there is no guarantee concerning the precise level of privileges and immunities (these are typically subject to negotiations with the member states, and perhaps the host state in particular), it is generally considered necessary for international organizations to possess at least certain privileges and immunities. This follows from functionalist logic: in order to work for the common good, the organization's work should not be interfered with by petty or obstructive governments, because if that happens, the organization cannot perform its functions. This is a strong incentive: several entities have refashioned themselves into international organizations precisely so as to be able to receive privileges and immunities.

Likewise, as noted above, international law has had a hard time developing rules on the responsibility or accountability of international organizations. Where organizations are hardly controlled by their member states, and hardly deemed subject to a general accountability regime, the result is wide discretionary power. Organizations can do much as they please because there are few or no mechanisms to hold them accountable. To the extent that mechanisms do exist, they may not be the strictest possible: the World Bank, for example, is sometimes considered to be accountable to its major shareholder states but is rarely seen to be accountable to the people living in the states where the bank's projects take place.[17] This is undergoing some change, and perhaps the most eye-catching development is that quite a few organizations have invented mechanisms of self-control, for example, appointing compliance officers or creating internal audit mechanisms. These developments notwithstanding, the point is that control remains limited and self-administered. While this need not necessarily be a cynical ploy, it does remedy the normative gap in functionalism.[18]

The European Union

Now where does this leave the European Union? It is quite uncontested that the European Union can be regarded as possessing international legal personality. The European Communities were all individually granted legal personality, and this was construed as including personality under international law.[19] The Maastricht Treaty, however, contained no separate clause concerning the international legal personality of the new Union. Hence, the theory arose that the drafters had intentionally withheld international personality. But this theory, surely, is untenable. A grant of personality cannot solely depend on the intentions of the creators of an organization (the legal system also might claim a stake) and, surely, it was never plausible to create an entity with treaty-making powers, and even a foreign and security policy, without this entity being a legal person.[20] While legal personality may not be a threshold condition for engaging in legal acts[21] (many legal acts are performed by entities whose personality may be controversial), nonetheless, with respect to the post-Maastricht European Union, its personality should never have been doubted.

But even then, to possess international legal personality is not the same as being an international organization, as other entities too can possess such personality. What makes many think of the European Union as an international organization, then, is that it is endowed with a number of specific powers. Article 5 of the Treaty of the European Union (TEU) holds that the European Union is based on conferred powers (to be governed by the principles of proportionality and subsidiarity), to which Article 4 TEU adds that powers not conferred on the Union remain with the member states.

This is a curious construction, which perhaps ought not be taken too literally: a strict reading would eventually suggest that the European Union is merely the vehicle for its member states, and such a reading would seriously underestimate the independent policy role of the Commission, the relevance of its many agencies and committees, the co-legislative role of the European Parliament, and the possibility of majority voting within the Council – not to mention the important role of the judiciary.[22] Nonetheless, the basic idea is clear enough: the competences of the European Union are not unlimited.

Another implication of a strict reading of the principle of conferred powers would hold that the implied powers doctrine holds little sway within the European Union. It is generally accepted that international organizations may have implied powers: powers that have not been granted expressly but may be necessary to give effect to the tasks of the organization. There is some doubt whether this actually applies to the European Union: while some have explained the Court of Justice of the European Union's (CJEU) finding of external transport powers as an emanation of the implied powers doctrine, others have argued that the Court found the Union to possess such powers not so much to enable it to exercise its functions as to protect "internal" EU law against circumvention by member states. After all, if member states could conclude their own agreements with third states in a field where the European Union has "internal powers" then such separate agreements could depart from EU law, and therewith place its integrity at risk, as such separate agreements would have to be considered binding under public international law and thus, potentially, overrule EU law.[23]

Either way, the powers of the European Union come in various shapes and forms. On some issues (e.g., commercial policy, including investment), it nowadays has exclusive powers. In other fields, powers are shared between the European Union and its member states. In yet other fields, powers are parallel. And on some topics, its powers are merely thought to supplement those of the member states. This is a far cry from the regular situation with respect to international organizations, whose powers typically remain in parallel with those of their member states: while the WHO may have the mandate to eradicate diseases, nothing hinders its member states from doing the same. And while the World Bank can lend money to poor nations, so too can the Bank's individual member states. It is no surprise, therefore, that many observers have held that the European Union is "analytically more similar to the U.S. political system than to other international organizations," in Pollack's words.[24]

Hence, whether the European Union qualifies as an international organization remains an open question. It meets the requirements of international law, but these are so broad as to encompass a wide variety of entities. The possession of international legal personality may well be of relevance, but it does not in and of itself suggest that the European Union is an international organization: such personality is also possessed by, for example, the Holy See. And while the European Union is based on conferred powers, the possibility of member states being preempted from acting makes it different from other organizations as does, arguably, the way the implied powers doctrine is applied by and in the Union.

In this light, it is perhaps interesting to ask how the European Union has characterized itself. The answer cannot but be complicated, if only because the Union does not always speak with one voice. The TEU and the Treaty on the Functioning of the European Union (TFEU) provide some indications that the European Union considers itself a regular international organization; indeed, one of the intergovernmental kind, shedding all ambitions of supranationalism. The claim that the Union is based on conferred powers and the related claim that powers not conferred upon it remain vested in the member states both suggest, if taken literally, firm member state control, and therewith suggest that the European Union is best seen as an international organization of the intergovernmental kind.

On the other hand, the European Union has made it clear within discussions concerning the drafting of a regime on the responsibility of international organizations that it regards itself as "special." Commenting on drafts prepared within the International Law Commission, the EU Commission remarked that

> the International Law Commission should carefully consider the large diversity among international organizations when adapting the articles on State responsibility to the topic of responsibility of international organizations. The European Union and the European Community are themselves testimony to this diversity. In particular, the European Community is an international organization with special features as envisaged in the founding treaties.[25]

And a moment later it explained that "there is a need to address the special situation of the Community within the framework of the draft articles."[26] The main concern, or so it seems, was that the regime on international responsibility should ensure that responsibility and attribution would go hand in hand: the European Union should be held responsible for the behavior of its member states acting *qua* organs of the European Union. Otherwise, the entire EU edifice might start to crumble.[27] In the end, the Commission kept tapping into the special nature of the Union: "there are significant differences between traditional international organizations on the one hand, and organizations such as the European Union."[28]

The CJEU, however, has been less insistent on highlighting the differences with other organizations. In *Van Gend en Loos*, it held that the EEC Treaty "is more than an agreement which merely creates mutual obligations between the contracting states," as was "confirmed more specifically by the establishment of institutions endowed with sovereign rights, the exercise of which affects Member States and also their citizens."[29] Without using the term "international organization," it seems plausible enough that the Court's conception of the EEC went in that general direction: a treaty beyond the mere contractual, creating an entity endowed with institutions.

On one occasion the Court was asked to dig a little deeper into the concept of "international organization," and its reasoning was instructive. The case initially arose before a Belgian court, with a German airline company (SAT) complaining about charges payable to Eurocontrol, an international organization in the field of aviation safety. SAT suggested that Eurocontrol was guilty of abusing a dominant position, which gave rise to the question of whether Eurocontrol should be seen as an "undertaking" within the meaning of EU competition law.[30]

The Court answered in the negative. It argued that though Eurocontrol had as one of its tasks the collection of route charges levied on users of air space it was not in a position to itself decide on these charges: the power, in other words, was delegated, and limited, with the individual member states deciding individually on the appropriate charges. In addition, Eurocontrol played a small role in the operational exercise of air navigation control, but only at the request of some of its member states. Finally, the Court observed that Eurocontrol's expenses are borne by its member states; it does not make a profit. This allowed the Court to hold that "Eurocontrol thus carries out, on behalf of the Contracting States, tasks in the public interest aimed at contributing to the maintenance and improvement of air navigation safety."[31] The charges, moreover, "are merely the consideration, payable by users, for the obligatory and exclusive use of air navigation control facilities and services."[32] In the end, the Court concluded that

> [t]aken as a whole, Eurocontrol's activities, by their nature, their aim and the rules to which they are subject, are connected with the exercise of powers relating to the control and supervision of air space which are typically those of a public authority.[33]

The picture that emerges from *SAT Fluggesellschaft* is, at a minimum, that an entity that exercises delegated powers without much discretion, and does so in the public interest, is, in the eyes of the Court, classified as an international organization.[34] In doing so, the Court confirmed an earlier decision of the Court of First Instance in *Vardakas*,[35] where it held that the European Committee for Standardization (ECS) qualified as an international organization despite having been set up by national standardization bodies instead of member states. What mattered, as the Court noted, was that ECS

> has been recognized by States and by international organizations created by States, such as the European Communities, and has been entrusted with tasks in the public interest by those States and international organizations.[36]

There are few domestic court cases against the European Union, even though it does not enjoy immunity from suit.[37] One case where immunity was explicitly invoked on behalf of the (then) EEC involved the demise of the International Tin Council, a commodity organization of which the EEC was one of the members. Kerr LJ discussed this at some length, only to find the argument wanting: to his mind, the privileges and immunities enjoyed by the EEC did not include "immunity from any legal process."[38]

Functionalism finds its normative justification in the contribution of organizations to the common good, and the CJEU, in similar spirit, has placed considerable weight on the public nature of the tasks of an international organization, both in *SAT Fluggesellschaft* and in *Vardakas*. This raises the question of the extent to which the European Union can itself be deemed instrumental to the common good or the public interest. These are, obviously, different notions, and they cannot be meaningfully discussed without also asking whose common good: one can hold that the European Union contributes to Europe's common good without necessarily also contributing to the global common good. Indeed, this is the picture that emerges from a perusal of the European Union's basic documents.

The Union's overriding aim, according to Article 3 TEU, is "to promote peace, its values and the well-being of its peoples." It "shall offer its citizens an area of freedom, security and justice without internal frontiers" and "work for the sustainable development of Europe" while promoting "economic, social and territorial cohesion, and solidarity among Member States" and ensuring "that Europe's cultural heritage is safeguarded and enhanced." In the same article, paragraph 5 is devoted to the world at large, and this too starts by pointing to internal, domestic interests: "In its relations with the wider world, the Union shall uphold and promote its values and interests and contribute to the protection of its citizens." Only thereafter does the global public interest make a muted appearance, with references to human rights, sustainable development, and the observance of international law. Moreover, the institutional framework of the Union is told to promote the interests of the European Union, its citizens and member states (Article 13 TEU), and the Commission is explicitly instructed to "promote the general interest of the Union," as Article 17 TEU puts it.

This kind of language is rare in instruments establishing international organizations, even regional ones. The Charter of the Organization of American States (OAS), for example, makes repeated reference to what the OAS aims to hold good for the American continent, but in terms radically different from the TEU. One of the "essential purposes" of the OAS is to "strengthen the peace and security of the continent"; another is to "promote, by cooperative action, their [i.e., the members'] economic, social, and cultural development," but even so, the OAS Charter does not draw a sharp line between the wellbeing of its member states and that of the rest of the world. The European Council, by contrast, is instructed to bear in mind the "strategic interests and objectives" of the Union (Article 22 TEU). The very idea of the European Union having strategic interests and objectives distinguishes it from other regional organizations, or, indeed, from international organizations generally.[39]

By Way of Conclusion

So where does this lead? The functionalist theory of international organizations law holds that organizations are created for the common good, and it is this starting point that gives rise to a number of rules and doctrines: ideas about the powers of international organizations, their privileges and immunities, and even their accountability, tend to be informed by the proposition that organizations do not act out of self-interest but in view of the common interest, broadly defined.

The European Union has a difficult time fitting into this framework in that its self-declared mission is mostly limited to the common good of the Union and its member states and citizens rather than aiming at the general or global common good. In this respect, the European Union is difficult to distinguish from other interest groups, and among international organizations perhaps its closest analogue is the OIC: set up to "safeguard and protect the common interests and support the legitimate causes of the Member States" (Article 1 OIC). Like the European Union, the OIC is more in the nature of an interest group, espousing and endorsing the interests of its members and the organization itself. It posits itself as a political actor, much like the European Union, and aims to exercise influence within UN bodies as the largest united bloc of states.[40]

What this boils down to is the observation that the law of international organizations may need a conceptual overhaul. The very concept of "international organization" is so broad as to allow entities to invoke it as they see fit and to use the question of their precise status as a political instrument. The European Union, for one, seems to be doing so, sometimes insisting that it is a regular international organization but sometimes, also, that it is a very special entity. This is not to blame the European Union, of course: it merely utilizes the tools put at its disposal by the international legal order. Hence, it would be for that international legal order to rethink its categories and, with respect to international organizations in particular, to rethink the relationship between organizations devoted to the common good.[41] If the link to the common good can only be established by insisting on a high level of abstraction ("organizations imply interstate cooperation and are thus good") or requires extremely rose-tinted glasses or some sort of *Verelendungstheorie*,[42] then perhaps something is amiss. In much the same way as domestic law recognizes a number of different legal persons (limited liability companies, foundations, associations, partnerships, etc.), so too the law of international organizations may well move towards greater recognition of the diversity of international organizations and create different regimes for different kinds of entities. In order to do so it will have to decide on how the common good can be represented, and that is, of course, no small task. Yet, doing so will not only be analytically helpful but also normatively rewarding. After all, it remains somewhat unsatisfying to treat interest-based entities, such as the European Union, OPEC, the OIC, or the Organisation Internationale de la Francophonie, with their distinct political and economic agendas, in the same way as the WHO or UNICEF.

Notes

1 Statehood is usually thought to depend on at least three factors: territory, population, and effective government. The first two are formal in nature, while the third is substantive. See generally, Jan Klabbers, *International Law* (Cambridge: Cambridge University Press, 2013).

2 For a thoughtful recent contribution, see Bruno de Witte, "The European Union as an International Legal Experiment," in *The Worlds of European Constitutionalism*, ed. Gráinne de Búrca and J.H.H. Weiler (Cambridge: Cambridge University Press, 2012).

3 Note, e.g., Wilhelmsson's idea of the European Union as a "jack-in-the-box" surprisingly popping up in domestic legal settings. See Thomas Wilhelmsson, "Jack-in-the-Box Theory of European Community Law," in *Dialectic of Law and Reality: Readings in Finnish Legal Theory*, ed. Lars D. Eriksson and Samuli Hurri (Helsinki: Forum Iuris, 1999).

4 For a good overview, see Mark A. Pollack, "Theorizing the European Union: International Organization, Domestic Polity, or Experiment in New Governance?" *Annual Review of Political Science* 8 (2005).

5 See Jan Klabbers, "Ostseerat," in *Enzyklopädie zum Europäischen Recht*, ed. Peter Müller-Graff and Armin Hatje (Baden-Baden: Nomos, 2014).

6 See Robin R. Churchill and Geir Ulfstein, "Autonomous Institutional Arrangements in Multilateral Environmental Agreements: A Little-Noticed Phenomenon in International Law," *American Journal of International Law* 94 (2000).

7 See, e.g., Jan Klabbers, *An Introduction to International Institutional Law* (Cambridge: Cambridge University Press, 2009); and H.G. Schermers and Niels M. Blokker, *International Institutional Law* (Leiden: Martinus Nijhoff, 2011).

8 It is perhaps telling that a comprehensive exposition in strictly theoretical terms is missing, although Schermers and Blokker, *International Institutional Law*, is often regarded as the leading functionalist work. The closest thing to a functionalist manifesto is a brief article by Michel Virally, "La Notion de fonction dans la théorie de l'organisation internationale," in *Mélanges offerts à Charles Rousseau: La communauté internationale*, ed. Suzanne Bastid et al. (Paris: Pédone, 1974).

9 See *Reparation for Injuries Suffered in the Service of the United Nations*, advisory opinion, 1949 ICJ REP. 174.

10 See Peter H.F. Bekker, *The Legal Position of Intergovernmental Organizations: A Functional Necessity Analysis of Their Legal Status and Immunities* (Dordrecht: Martinus Nijhoff, 1994), 5.

11 Reportedly, Mussolini presented a draft for an organization made up of the United Kingdom, France, Germany, and Italy to establish a directorate to dominate 1930s Europe – France, however, resisted the temptation. See Remco van Diepen, *Voor Volkenbond en vrede: Nederland en het streven naar een nieuwe wereldorde 1919–1946* (Amsterdam: Bert Bakker, 1999), 143.

12 See Bryan Schwartz and Elliott Leven, "International Organizations: What Makes Them Work?" *Canadian Yearbook of International Law* 30 (1992).

13 See http://www.oic-oci.org/page_detail.asp?p_id=52.

14 A useful overview is Howard Davies and David Green, *Global Financial Regulation: The Essential Guide* (Cambridge: Polity, 2008).
15 See Jan Klabbers, "Theorizing International Organizations," in *The Oxford Handbook of the Theory of International Law*, ed. Anne Orford and Florian Hoffmann (Oxford: Oxford University Press, 2016).
16 See Nagendra Singh, *Termination of Membership of International Organisations* (London: Stevens and Sons, 1958), vii.
17 For a recent ethnography of the World Bank, see Galit A. Sarfaty, *Values in Translation* (Stanford CA: Stanford University Press, 2012).
18 See generally Jan Klabbers, "Self-Control: International Organizations and the Quest for Accountability," in *The International Legal Responsibility of the European Union*, ed. Malcolm Evans and Panos Koutrakos (Oxford: Hart, 2013).
19 See Case 22/70 *Commission v. Council* (ERTA) EU:C:1971:32.
20 See Jan Klabbers, "Presumptive Personality: The European Union in International Law," in *International Law Aspects of the European Union*, ed. Martti Koskenniemi (The Hague: Martinus Nijhoff, 1998).
21 See generally also Jan Klabbers, "The Concept of Legal Personality," *Ius Gentium* 11 (2005).
22 For a fine overview, see Deirdre Curtin, *Executive Power of the European Union: Law, Practices, and the Living Constitution* (Oxford: Oxford University Press, 2009).
23 See generally Jan Klabbers, *The European Union in International Law* (Paris: Pédone, 2012), 28–31.
24 See Pollack, "Theorizing the European Union," 358. Recent theorists have returned to federalism as inspiration for the explanation of the workings of the European Union. See, e.g., Robert Schütze, *From Dual to Cooperative Federalism: The Changing Structure of European Law* (Oxford: Oxford University Press, 2009).
25 See UN Doc A/CN.4/556, 12 May 2005, at 5. See also UN Doc A/CN.4/593, 31 March 2008, 4: the "Commission expresses some concerns as to the feasibility of subsuming all international organizations under the terms of this one draft in the light of the highly diverse nature of international organizations, of which the European Community is itself an example."
26 See UN Doc A/CN.4/556, 6.
27 See UN Doc A/CN.4/582, 1 May 2007, 23.
28 See UN Doc. A/CN.4/637, 14 February 2011, 7.
29 See Case 26/62 *Van Gend en Loos v. Nederlandse Administratie der Belastingen* EU:C:1963:1.
30 Case C-364/92 *SAT Fluggesellschaft mbH v. Eurocontrol* EU:C:1994:7.
31 Ibid., para 27.
32 Ibid., para 28.
33 Ibid., para 30.
34 The CJEU essentially confirmed its position in Case C-113/07 P *Selex Sistemi Integrati SpA v. Commission* EU:C:2009:191, also addressing the position of Eurocontrol in light of EU competition law.
35 See Case T-4/92 *Evangelos Vardakas v. Commission* EU:T:1993:29.
36 Ibid., 47. Note, however, that the CJEU felt compelled to present a broad interpretation of the staff regulations on which Mr. Vardakas relied, so it remains uncertain whether the concept of international organization in *Vardakas* must be seen as the CJEU's general concept, or as a special concept for purposes of the staff regulations.
37 Currently, the matter is governed by Article 343 TFEU and Protocol No. 7 to the Lisbon Treaty. The latter deals with the European Union's privileges and immunities, but it does not include immunity from suit for the European Union itself.
38 See *MacLaine Watson v. Department of Trade*, Court of Appeal, judgment of 27 April 1988, reproduced in 80 *International Law Reports* 47. Kerr's words can be found at 127. While counsel for the EEC made the argument, Kerr LJ did note that the EEC's claim to sovereign immunity was not supported by an "affidavit or other document emanating from the E.E.C. itself" (128).
39 Moreover, this can hardly be a slip of the pen, as the phrase recurs in several other provisions: Articles 26 and 31 TEU.

40 The well-known Non-Aligned Movement never was quite as united and never was considered an international organization to begin with.

41 See Jan Klabbers, "Unity, Diversity, Accountability: The Ambivalent Concept of International Organisation," *Melbourne Journal of International Law* 14 (2013).

42 It has been suggested, not entirely in jest, that OPEC contributes to the common good by indirectly providing the impetus to switch to sustainable energy production and consumption. See Cedric Ryngaert, "Domestic Legal Remedies against OPEC," in *Challenging Acts of International Organizations before National Courts*, ed. August Reinisch (Oxford: Oxford University Press, 2010), 256.

References

Bekker, Peter H.F. *The Legal Position of Intergovernmental Organizations: A Functional Necessity Analysis of Their Legal Status and Immunities*. Dordrecht: Martinus Nijhoff, 1994.

Churchill, Robin R., and Geir Ulfstein. "Autonomous Institutional Arrangements in Multilateral Environmental Agreements: A Little-Noticed Phenomenon in International Law." *American Journal of International Law* 94 (2000): 623–659.

Curtin, Deirdre. *Executive Power of the European Union: Law, Practices, and the Living Constitution*. Oxford: Oxford University Press, 2009.

Davies, Howard, and David Green. *Global Financial Regulation: The Essential Guide*. Cambridge: Polity, 2008.

de Witte, Bruno. "The European Union as an International Legal Experiment." In *The Worlds of European Constitutionalism*, edited by Gráinne de Búrca and J.H.H. Weiler, 19–56. Cambridge: Cambridge University Press, 2012.

Klabbers, Jan. "Presumptive Personality: The European Union in International Law." In *International Law Aspects of the European Union*, edited by Martti Koskenniemi, 231–253. The Hague: Martinus Nijhoff, 1998.

Klabbers, Jan. "The Concept of Legal Personality." *Ius Gentium* 11 (2005): 35–66.

Klabbers, Jan. *An Introduction to International Institutional Law*. Cambridge: Cambridge University Press, 2009.

Klabbers, Jan. *The European Union in International Law*. Paris: Pédone, 2012.

Klabbers, Jan. *International Law*. Cambridge: Cambridge University Press, 2013.

Klabbers, Jan. "Unity, Diversity, Accountability: The Ambivalent Concept of International Organisation." *Melbourne Journal of International Law* 14 (2013): 149–170.

Klabbers, Jan. "Self-Control: International Organizations and the Quest for Accountability." In *The International Legal Responsibility of the European Union*, edited by Malcolm Evans and Panos Koutrakos, 75–99. Oxford: Hart, 2013.

Klabbers, Jan "Ostseerat." In *Enzyklopädie zum Europäischen Recht. Band 1: Europäisches Organisations- und Verfassungsrecht*, edited by Peter Müller-Graff and Armin Hatje, 1163–1172. Baden-Baden: Nomos, 2014.

Klabbers, Jan. "Theorizing International Organizations." In *The Oxford Handbook of the Theory of International Law*, edited by Anne Orford and Florian Hoffmann. Oxford: Oxford University Press, forthcoming.

Pollack, Mark A. "Theorizing the European Union: International Organization, Domestic Polity, or Experiment in New Governance?" *Annual Review of Political Science* 8 (2005): 357–398.

Ryngaert, Cedric. "Domestic Legal Remedies against OPEC." In *Challenging Acts of International Organizations before National Courts*, edited by August Reinisch, 239–257. Oxford: Oxford University Press, 2010.

Sarfaty, Galit A. *Values in Translation*. Stanford, CA: Stanford University Press, 2012.

Schermers, H.G., and Niels M. Blokker. *International Institutional Law*. Leiden: Martinus Nijhoff, 2011.

Schütze, Robert. *From Dual to Cooperative Federalism: The Changing Structure of European Law*. Oxford: Oxford University Press, 2009.

Schwartz, Bryan, and Elliott Leven. "International Organizations: What Makes Them Work?" *Canadian Yearbook of International Law* 30 (1992): 165–194.

Singh, Nagendra. *Termination of Membership of International Organisations*. London: Stevens and Sons, 1958.

van Diepen, Remco. *Voor Volkenbond en vrede: Nederland en het streven naar een nieuwe wereldorde 1919–1946*. Amsterdam: Bert Bakker, 1999.

Virally, Michel. "La Notion de fonction dans la théorie de l'organisation international." In *Mélanges offerts à Charles Rousseau: La communauté internationale*, edited by Suzanne Bastid et al., 277–300. Paris: Pédone, 1974.

Wilhelmsson, Thomas. "Jack-in-the-Box Theory of European Community Law." In *Dialectic of Law and Reality: Readings in Finnish Legal Theory*, edited by Lars D. Eriksson and Samuli Hurri, 437–454. Helsinki: Forum Iuris, 1999.

2

The Nature of International Law

Anna Södersten and Dennis Patterson

This chapter is devoted to the theory of international law. In analytic jurisprudence, at least since the latter half of the twentieth century, the primary debate in general jurisprudence has been between legal positivism and its most ardent critic, Ronald Dworkin. The positivist tradition is represented here by its two most important theorists, Hans Kelsen and H.L.A. Hart. During their careers, Kelsen and Hart clashed over the best understanding of legal positivism. For his part, Dworkin devoted the bulk of his critical attention to Hart's work. In this chapter, we will focus on the way in which each theorist builds his view of international law against the background of a more general jurisprudence.

Kelsen

For Kelsen, the fundamental requisite of a legal order is that it is a "coercive order," that is, "a set of norms regulating human behavior by attaching certain coercive acts (sanctions) as consequences to certain facts, as delicts, determined by this order as conditions."[1] The possibility of sanctions is thus the requisite of a coercive order. In Kelsen's view, such sanctions are available in international law. He identifies them as reprisals and war. These sanctions allow international law to qualify as a legal order and international law is thus "law" in the same sense as national law.

Why are reprisals and war sanctions? Kelsen explains that a state that considers its interests violated by another state is authorized to resort to reprisals or war. They take place against the will of the state that has violated the other state's interests. In normal circumstances, reprisals and war are prohibited under international law: they are only permissible as reactions against violations of international norms. If they are not such reactions, they are by themselves international delicts. This is the principle of *bellum iustum*, or "just war." Kelsen finds this assumption well founded as this doctrine is enshrined in the UN Charter, which is accepted by most states. In Kelsen's view, reprisals and war are thus the appropriate sanctions for violations of international norms. Kelsen explains that the sanctions in international law are no different in content from sanctions of national law. In that sense, international law evinces the same characteristics as national law.

A Companion to European Union Law and International Law, First Edition.
Edited by Dennis Patterson and Anna Södersten.

However, for Kelsen, international law is a primitive legal order. He explains that international law is "in a state of decentralization," which is "only at the beginning of a development which national law has already completed."[2] International law is a primitive legal order because it does not have special organs for the creation and application of its norms. The norms are created by the members of the legal community themselves not by a legislative source. When it comes to the application of norms, it is the state itself that has to decide whether the fact of a delict exists, and there exists no authority to decide the conflict: "[t]he technique of self-help, characteristic of primitive law, prevails."[3] But Kelsen foresees an evolution of international law from this primitive condition. The development is directed towards "centralization," the ultimate goal of which is the emergence of a world state.

Despite these shortcomings, even a decentralized order is a legal order in Kelsen's view. Unlike Austin, Kelsen believed that the lack of specialized organs for implementing the law – the lack of a sovereign – does not preclude the conception of international law as a legal order. For Kelsen, the central element is the existence of rules regarding the exercise of force, codified as the *bellum iustum* doctrine. Therefore, according to Kelsen, rejecting the *bellum iustum* doctrine is equivalent to denying the very legal nature of international law.

Having defined the nature of international law, Kelsen then explicates the relationship between international law and national (municipal) law. In Kelsen's general theory of law, he sees a legal order as a system with hierarchically organized norms. In this hierarchical system, lower-order norms derive their validity from higher-order norms: the entire system is grounded in the "*Grundnorm*." Kelsen advocates a monistic approach: that is, he sees international law and national law as a unity. This means that international law and national law are subject to the same basic norm, which must be found either in international law or in the national legal order.

Kelsen rejects a dualistic construction in which international law is regarded as a system of binding norms, valid but standing beside national law norms (the conventional wisdom). According to Kelsen, the dualistic construction fails in explaining how the norms of international law obligate individuals. In this regard, Kelsen's instincts were good, but he was unable to solve this problem within his own approach.

In establishing his monistic construction, Kelsen first addresses the question of whether there can be an irresolvable conflict between the international legal order and a national legal order. If such conflicts exist, only a dualistic or pluralistic construction would be possible, and a monistic approach would then be rejected. Kelsen explains that insofar as international law is regarded as a system of valid norms (independent of each other in their validity), "the relations could be interpreted only either from the viewpoint of the national legal order or from that of the international legal order."[4]

Kelsen felt that it was erroneous to see national and international law as being in conflict. Seeking unity above all else, he presents two different approaches to the so-called monistic construction of the relationship between national and international law. In establishing the unity of international law and national law, one can start from either international law or national law as a valid legal order. He explains as follows:

> International law must be conceived either as a legal order delegated by, and therefore included in, the national legal order; or as a total legal order comprising all legal orders as partial legal orders, and superior to all of them.[5]

If one starts from the validity of a national legal order, it is within it that the reason for the validity of international law is to be found. According to this view, general international law is valid for a state only if it is recognized by an individual state as binding. International law is then regarded as part of national law, or as a legal order delegated by the national legal order. The representatives of this approach start from the validity of their own national order, which they consider self-evident.

Kelsen is equally open to taking international law as the starting point for validity, thus placing it at the apex of the pyramid in his hierarchical system. From this point of view, the international legal system is characterized as a universal legal order. The international legal system is the "total system," which encompasses all national legal orders, which are merely "partial legal orders." The state is an order delegated by international law in its validity. Kelsen rejects the objection that, historically, the states preceded the creation of general international law and that the individual state therefore cannot be conceived of as an order delegated by international law. He argues that historical and normative–logical relations should not be confounded.

In Kelsen's monistic construction, the content in international law is the same whether the validity of national law or international law takes precedence. The function of international law is thus the same: through the principle of effectiveness, it determines the reason and sphere of validity of national legal orders.

The concept of sovereignty is the heart of Kelsen's monistic construction. Kelsen explains state sovereignty as the decisive factor for assuming the primacy of the national legal order. He writes,

> For a state to be "sovereign" merely means that the establishment of the historically first constitution is presupposed as a law-creating fact without a positive norm of international law taken into account which institutes this fact as a law-creating fact. [6]

In his view, sovereignty is a presupposition of a normative order as the highest order whose validity is not derivable from any other higher order. But the idea of international law as a "universal legal order" is incompatible with this idea of state sovereignty. If one takes international law as the starting point, the concept of sovereignty has to be a different one. Kelsen explains: "[o]nly the international legal order, not the national legal order, is sovereign,"[7] and if states are denominated "sovereign," this means only that they are subject to the international legal order. The concept of "state" cannot be defined without reference to international law.

From a logical point of view, Kelsen sees these two systems – these two different monistic constructions – as "equally correct and equally justified." He explains that it is impossible to decide between them on the basis of law or legal theory alone. Kelsen claims that the decision can only be made on nonscientific, political considerations:

> He who treasures the idea of sovereignty of his state … will prefer the primacy of the national legal order. He who values the idea of legal organization of the world, will prefer the primacy of international law.[8]

And so it is.

Hart

Hart develops his approach to international law in the final chapter of *The Concept of Law*.[9] In Hart's view, international law is "law," but it lacks the main characteristics of a legal system (i.e., secondary rules): a Rule of Recognition, rules of change, and adjudication. Without these features, international law is not a legal system, merely a set of primary rules. He comes to this conclusion by comparing international law and municipal law, finding that they are analogous in content and function, but different in form.

Hart identifies the two main objections (or "sources of doubt") to international law being regarded as law. Both of these objections start from municipal law as the standard example of what "law" is. The first objection is that international law is not binding because it lacks sanctions. As Hart points out, the question "Is international law binding?" expresses a doubt about the general legal status of international law. The second objection is the claim that states are fundamentally incapable of being subject to legal obligations. States cannot both be sovereign and at the same time have obligations under international law. Hart repudiates both of these objections.

Hart identifies the two main objections (or "sources of doubt") to international law being regarded as law. He does not attempt to demonstrate the existence of effective sanctions available to international law; this is not the basis of his argument. In fact, he points out that Chapter VII of the UN Charter cannot answer the objection. As Hart sees it, those international sanctions cannot be equated with the sanctions of municipal law because they are largely inefficient. Whenever their use is of importance, the law-enforcement provisions of the UN Charter are likely to be paralyzed by a veto in the Security Council. Thus, for Hart, international law lacks "real" sanctions. But he rejects the notion that this absence disqualifies international law from being law. Hart explains that the view that international law is not law because it lacks sanctions tacitly accepts the conception of law as a matter of order backed by threats. This is Austin's command theory, which Hart repudiates in his general theory of law. As Hart shows, the command theory is untenable even in the context of municipal law, so this theory cannot possibly disqualify international law from being law.

Hart also provides an additional argument in the same context. While the existence of sanctions might be a necessary condition in municipal law, sanctions might play a different role in international law. He writes: "[i]n societies of individuals, approximately equal in strength and vulnerability, physical sanctions are both necessary and possible."[10] In municipal law, sanctions may be used successfully with small risk, and the threat of them would add much to natural deterrence. But the situation is different in the international context. Hart claims that the organization of international sanctions involves risks, and the threat of them adds little to natural deterrence. The use of violence on the international level is public, which means that there is a risk that third parties will get involved: "[t]o initiate a war is, even for the strongest power, to risk much for an outcome which is rarely predictable with reasonable confidence."[11] On the international level, there is an unequal distribution of power and strength among states, and sanctions do not guarantee that powerful states obey the rules. Hart argues that although sanctions might have different functions in international law from those in municipal law, this is not a reason for depriving international law of its character as law.

The second objection Hart considers is that states are incapable of being subjects of legal obligation, that is, states cannot both be sovereign transnational governance regimes and at the same time have obligations under international law. Hart sees this as a "radical inconsistency."[12] He repudiates the assumption that sovereignty would mean being above the law, a notion associated with voluntarist theories or theories of auto-limitation. These theories claim that international obligations arise from the consent of the party bound. Hart argues that auto-limitation theories fail to explain not only how it is known that states can be bound by self-imposed obligations but also why their absolutist view of sovereignty should be accepted. Hart further argues that not all international obligations are self-imposed. He provides two examples showing that the voluntarist doctrine cannot be correct. The first example is the case of a new state. A new state is bound by the general obligations of international law, including the rules that give binding force to treaties. The second example is the case of a state acquiring territory or undergoing some other change. This, he writes, "brings with it … the incidence of obligations under rules which previously it had no opportunity to observe or break, and … [to which it previously had] no occasion to give or withhold consent."[13]

For Hart, sovereignty means independence. He shows that there are many possible forms and degrees of dependence and independence. For Hart, it is instead the international rules that define the scope of sovereignty: "we can only know which states are sovereign, and what the extent of their sovereignty is, when we know what the rules are."[14]

After having answered two objections to the stature of international law as law, Hart turns to the claim that international law is best understood as morality. This insistence, he argues, is sometimes inspired by the dogmatism that any form of social structure that is not reducible to orders backed by threats can only be a form of "morality." Hart offers some reasons why this is untenable. First, states often reproach one another for immoral conduct or praise themselves or others for living up to a standard of international morality. Hart points out that such appraisals are recognizably different from legal assessments under the rules of international law. When states address one another over disputed matters of international law, they refer to precedents, treaties, and juristic writings, but often no mention is made of morality. Thus, states differentiate between moral and legal assessments.

The second reason why international law cannot be reduced to morality is that the rules of international law (like rules of municipal law) are morally indifferent. Hart explains that unlike morality, legal rules contain much specific detail and draw arbitrary distinctions. He avers, "Regard for forms and detail carried to excess, has earned for law the reproaches of 'formalism' and 'legalism.'"[15] Hart explains that some rules exist only because it is convenient to have some clear fixed rule about the subjects with which it is concerned and not because any moral importance is attached to the particular rule.

The third reason is that, unlike morality, the rules of international law are subject to deliberate change. Morality is conceived of as the ultimate standards by which human actions are evaluated. The notion of a legislature making moral rules is therefore absurd. Hart contrasts this with the situation in international law, where the lack of a legislature is just a defect that might one day be repaired. Hart finally points out that there can be many reasons why states obey international obligations, and moral obligation may be one of them. But it is not a necessary feature of international law.

In the final part of his chapter on international law, Hart explains why international law is not a "legal system." The absence of an international legislature, courts with compulsory jurisdiction, and centrally organized sanctions make international law resemble a simple form of social structure. In Hart's view, international law resembles a simple regime of primary rules in form but not in content. International law resembles a municipal system, but it does so only in function and content, not in form.

Hart explains that in minimizing the formal differences between international law and municipal law some theorists have exaggerated the analogies. The fact that the parties generally follow judgments of the International Court of Justice does not compensate for the lack of a compulsory and comprehensive jurisdiction of any international court. He also considers analogies between the use of force, as a sanction in municipal law, and the "decentralised sanctions" in international law (for example, for Kelsen, the sanctions of international law are war and reprisal). Hart reminds us that there is no international court with a jurisdiction similar to courts in municipal law, and that the law-enforcement provisions under the UN Charter have been paralyzed by veto.

Hart then considers Kelsen's insistence that international law must contain a basic norm (*Grundnorm*), which represents the ground of the validity of all norms and which constitutes the unity in the international legal system. According to Hart, the opposite view is that international law merely consists of a set of primary rules of obligations. Hart reminds us that there have only been fruitless attempts to formulate a unifying basic norm in international law. Thus, the suggestion that the basic norm could be the principle *pacta sunt servanda* is "incompatible with the fact that not all obligations under international law arise from 'pacta.'"[16] Equally untenable is the rule that "states should behave as they customarily behave."[17] Hart sees this as a "useless reduplication" of the fact that the international society observes certain standards of conduct as obligatory rules.[18]

In Hart's view, there is no Rule of Recognition in international law.[19] Since there is no Rule of Recognition, international law cannot be a legal system. It is instead a "set" of rules. But a Rule of Recognition is not a necessity for international rules to be binding. The existence of international rules depends instead on whether they are accepted. International law is thus a set of social rules. In his view, no other social rules are so close to municipal law as those of international law.

Hart argues that the differences between international law and municipal law might eventually be overcome. International law might be in a stage of transition that will bring it nearer in structure to a municipal system. This would be the case if it were generally recognized that multilateral treaties could bind states that are not parties. Such treaties would be legislative enactments. A Rule of Recognition could then be formulated in international law, and international law would then resemble municipal law not only in content and function but also in form.

Dworkin

Ronald Dworkin was the most trenchant critic of legal positivism, especially Hart's positivism. Throughout his career, Dworkin returned again and again to what he perceived to be the central weaknesses of positivism as a theory of the nature of law. From his initial success in showing that Hart failed to take account of the role of principles in law,[20] Dworkin went on to develop his own account of law, grounded in the idea that interpretation is the centerpiece of any conception of law. This account of law, built on the distinction between fit and justification,[21] is today the principal rival to positivism.

For most of his career, Dworkin never wrote about international law. Just before his death, he penned an article on international law that was posthumously published to wide interest. Not surprisingly, his position in this article is a development of his more general jurisprudence.

Dworkin's treatment of international law begins with the observation that "almost everyone assumes that there is international law."[22] Nevertheless, Dworkin seeks to put to rest challenges to international law that have not been properly answered. This article is his answer to anyone skeptical of the bona fides of international law as "law."

Why was anyone ever skeptical that international law was really law? Dworkin lays the blame for this misperception at the feet of legal positivism, the theoretical core of which is the notion that "whether a law exists is fundamentally a question of historical fact."[23] As he did throughout his career, Dworkin uses Hart's positivism as his exemplar for the shortcomings of legal positivism. As mentioned, Hart questioned the status of international law as law owing to its lack of secondary rules. Characterizing this as a "sociological" approach to the question of the nature of law, Dworkin likens Hart's approach to "the recent discussion among astronomers whether it would be sensible to continue to use the word 'planet' in such a way as to make Pluto a planet."[24]

The conventional wisdom – which reaches beyond positivist legal theory – locates the ground of legitimacy for international law in the consent of sovereign nations. The form of consent is the treaty. Dworkin rejects this view, asserting that "consent is neither a necessary nor a sufficient ground of legitimacy."[25] Dworkin argues that in place of the "sociological" conception of law advanced by positivism, a better ground for the legitimacy of law is to be found in a "doctrinal" conception of law which, Dworkin argues, is interpretive in character. This concept is a normative theory, a theory of political morality which provides an account of the grounds of law.[26] As Dworkin puts it, what the law is "depends on a moral theory."[27] Identifying the law of a community is not a matter of sources but is instead found "by asking which rules its citizens or officials have a right they can demand be enforced by its coercive institutions without any further collective political decision."[28]

In these brief passages from Dworkin's article one sees all the elements of his general jurisprudence. Law is a branch of political philosophy. Finding the law is a matter of argument wherein the work of fit and justification is carried out with an interpretive lens, one which seeks to put the practice in its best light. We must start with what everyone agrees on as sources for rights: "the political constitution, legislation pursuant to that constitution, and past judicial decisions."[29] Moreover, law is a matter of justifying coercive state power. As Dworkin argues, this "is a moral question whose answer is a legal judgment."[30] It is in these judgments that "genuine legal rights" are identified.

As mentioned, it is commonplace to see sovereignty as the basis for international law. Sovereign nations bind themselves to one another through the medium of a treaty. As Dworkin sees it, "we cannot take the self-limiting consent of sovereign nations to be the basic ground of international law."[31] He offers several reasons. Treaties are vague and in need of interpretation over time; it is unclear just what states are agreeing to when they sign treaties. Further, in Dworkin's view, it is "unfair" that one generation can bind the next when the consent is the product of different political processes. Dworkin also argues that the logic of consent as the basis for international law is circular. There is no explanation to why states that have not consented to a law may nevertheless be subject to it as "customary" law. Customary law also fails to identify just how many states must adhere to a particular practice before it becomes "customary." In the same vein, consent cannot explain the binding character of peremptory norms (*jus cogens*, i.e., a norm from which derogation is never permitted). Dworkin concludes that this presupposes that there is a more basic principle at work.[32]

Dworkin's approach to international law is motivated by his view that the single most important virtue of a proper jurisprudence of international law is its ability to mitigate the failures of state sovereignty: the risks posed by the "Westphalian system of full sovereign independence."[33] For this, Dworkin proposes the principle of salience, which he describes as follows:

> Coercive government (I include not just traditional "sovereign" states but also any institution or organization claiming coercive authority) has a standing duty to improve its own legitimacy. Each traditional state therefore has a duty to pursue available means to mitigate the failures and risks of the sovereign-state system. That duty of mitigation provides the most general structural principle and interpretive background of international law. But as it stands, it is not sufficiently determinative. In many circumstances, a number of very different regimes of international law would each serve to improve the legitimacy of the international system, were it enacted and enforced, and states may reasonably disagree about which would be best. That obvious fact explains a further fundamental structural principle. This is the principle of salience: If a significant number of states, encompassing a significant population, has developed an agreed code of practice, either by treaty or by other form of coordination, then other states have at least a prima facie duty to subscribe to that practice

> as well, with the important proviso that this duty holds only if a more general practice to that effect, expanded in that way, would improve the legitimacy of the subscribing state and the international order as a whole. [34]

Dworkin maintains that the principle of salience exemplifies his general approach to jurisprudence, that of fit and justification. Salience explains international law as we find it (fit). It does so against a background of interpretive contestation the purpose of which is to mitigate the flaws of the system of state sovereignty.

As previously noted, Dworkin's foray into international law is of recent vintage. As such, sufficient time has not elapsed to attract sustained scholarly consideration of his views. Of course, given the fact that his views on international law closely track his approach to general jurisprudence, the strengths and weaknesses of that approach inform his account of international law. In the fullness of time, we will see the extent to which Dworkin's jurisprudence of international law confirms the enduring quality of his general jurisprudence. We cannot really understand one without the other.

The Status of International Law

It is a commonplace that the status of international law as "law" is a contested matter. Legal philosophers have approached this question from different points of view. Hart famously argued that international law was not comparable to municipal or national (the terms are synonymous) law in that international law lacked secondary rules (e.g., rules of change). International law was simply a "primitive" legal system in that it contained only primary norms. While some have castigated Hart for his "failure" to see the true status of international law, the important point is rather that the question Hart was asking has been taken by many to devolve to a search for the essence of law. Today, some in analytic jurisprudence continue to pursue such a line of inquiry and many have abandoned this methodological approach.

In the discussion of international law, the question of methodology is never raised. Clearly, Kelsen's embrace of a neo-Kantian frame of reference puts him squarely in the camp embracing the idea that the concept of "law" has necessary content. For his part, Hart was certainly interested in identifying the salient features of law, but it is unclear to what degree he took himself to be engaged in an enterprise where the identification of necessary and sufficient conditions is paramount. Dworkin clearly believed in the notion of an "essence" or essential components for law.[35]

The most efficacious treatment of the views of these three theorists would be one where they are joined in direct conversation or debate about the best construction of international law. This is difficult if for no other reason than the fact that they start from very different premises, which are dictated by their general approach to jurisprudence. Hart thought his disagreements with Dworkin were so stark that he concluded they were each engaged in different enterprises. Perhaps this is a topic for another day. We would conclude, however, by noting that Kelsen is the only one of the three with a "unified" (i.e., monistic) view of the relationship between national and international law. A better approach may well be to think of international law not as an appendage to national law but as a body of law that requires its own theorization.

No matter how one approaches these questions, consideration of the views of Kelsen, Hart, and Dworkin are essential for anyone contemplating international law. Despite these impressive interventions in a field dominated by discussions of the varieties of positivism and the merits of interpretivism, far too little attention has been paid to what is surely a central and increasingly important topic of law and legal theory.

Notes

1 Hans Kelsen, *Pure Theory of Law*, trans. Max Knight (Berkeley: University of California Press, 1967), 320.
2 Ibid., 323.
3 Ibid.
4 Ibid., 330.
5 Ibid., 333.
6 Ibid., 335.
7 Ibid., 338.
8 Ibid., 346.
9 H.L.A. Hart, *The Concept of Law*, 2nd ed. (Oxford: Clarendon Press, 1994).
10 Ibid., 218.
11 Ibid., 219.
12 Ibid., 220.
13 Ibid., 226.
14 Ibid., 223.
15 Ibid., 229.
16 Ibid., 233–234.
17 Ibid., 236.
18 Ibid.
19 Hart identified two sorts of rules in modern legal systems: primary and secondary. Primary rules create obligations. Secondary rules are rules about primary rules (e.g., how to change primary rules). The master secondary rule, the Rule of Recognition, is a social practice among officials for what counts as valid sources of law. See ibid., 91–99. The Rule of Recognition is analogous to Kelsen's *Grundnorm*.
20 See Ronald Dworkin, *Taking Rights Seriously* (Cambridge MA: Harvard University Press, 1978), Chap. 2 and 3.
21 Dworkin argued that any theory of law had to explain enough of law as we find it for the explanation to count as an explanation of "law" (fit). But lawyers can agree that more than one theory can fit the law as we find it. Choice among competing principles for the explanation of law requires resort to moral argument (justification). See Ronald Dworkin, *Law's Empire* (Cambridge MA: Harvard University Press, 1986), Chap. 7.
22 Ronald Dworkin, "A New Philosophy for International Law," *Philosophy and Public Affairs* 41 (2013): 2.
23 Ibid., 3.
24 Ibid., 5.
25 Ibid., 11.
26 Ibid.
27 Ibid., 12.
28 Ibid.
29 Ibid.
30 Ibid.
31 Ibid., 10.
32 Ibid., 7–10.
33 Dworkin explicates these risks at ibid., 17–19.
34 Ibid., 19.
35 Dworkin trusts that concepts like "law" and "justice" are analogous to natural kinds, for their meaning is a function of their "deep structure." See Ronald Dworkin, "Hart's Postscript and the Character of Political Philosophy," *Oxford Journal of Legal Studies* 24 (2004): 12–13.

References

Dworkin, Ronald. *Taking Rights Seriously*. Cambridge MA: Harvard University Press, 1978.
Dworkin, Ronald. *Law's Empire*. Cambridge MA: Harvard University Press, 1986.
Dworkin, Ronald. "Hart's Postscript and the Character of Political Philosophy." *Oxford Journal of Legal Studies* 24, no. 1 (2004): 1–37.
Dworkin, Ronald. "A New Philosophy for International Law." *Philosophy and Public Affairs* 41, no. 1 (2013): 2–30.
Hart, H.L.A. *The Concept of Law*. 2nd edition. Oxford: Clarendon Press, 1994.
Kelsen, Hans. *Pure Theory of Law*. Translated by Max Knight. Berkeley, CA: University of California Press, 1967.

3

The Development of European Integration and EU Constitutional Reform

Michael Dougan

The Schuman Plan and the Establishment of the European Coal and Steel Community

Although there was a certain ideological groundswell in favor of a "United Europe" shortly after the Second World War,[1] as evidenced by the call of the 1948 Hague Congress for Western European economic and political union, the first concrete steps towards integration were prompted by the specter of Soviet expansion. Within days of the signature by France and the United Kingdom of the Dunkirk Treaty, providing for mutual assistance in the event of a renewal of hostilities with Germany, the breakdown of the Moscow Conference over the future of occupied Germany was to set the pattern for future strained relations between the Soviet Union, on the one side, and the United States, Great Britain, and France, on the other. Despite the indispensable United States defense commitment affirmed in the North Atlantic Treaty, Western Europe stood divided and vulnerable in the face of a Soviet Union whose wartime military potential had been scarcely diminished by demobilization, and whose political influence had been enhanced by successful Communist Party coups in Bulgaria, Romania, Poland, and Czechoslovakia.[2] It was in this context that Robert Schuman, the French foreign minister, made an historic proposal to a ministerial meeting in London on 9 May 1950.[3] His proposal was for nothing less than the fusion of the coal and steel industries of France and Germany, and any other countries wishing to participate, under a supranational High Authority. Such a pooling of production would not only make future conflict between France and Germany impossible but would also provide a sound basis for economic expansion. The implications of the scheme were clearly far-reaching, constituting, as Schuman himself explained, the first concrete foundation for a European Federation, which is indispensable for the preservation of peace.

The Schuman Plan was enthusiastically endorsed by the Benelux countries, France, Germany, and Italy, but the United Kingdom declined to participate, refusing to accept the supranational role of the projected High Authority. The treaty Establishing the European Coal and Steel Community (ECSC) was signed in Paris on 18 April 1951, and it came into force on 20 July in the following year. It was concluded for a period of fifty years from that date and thus expired in July 2002.[4]

A Companion to European Union Law and International Law, First Edition.
Edited by Dennis Patterson and Anna Södersten.

The strategy of the treaty, inspired by the Schuman Declaration, was to set limited and specific economic objectives as steps towards the long-term political objective of European unity. The preamble to the treaty announced that Europe was to be built "through practical achievements which will first of all create real solidarity, and through the establishment of common bases for economic development." The economic community created pursuant to the treaty was to constitute "the basis for a broader and deeper community among peoples long divided by bloody conflicts," and the foundations were to be laid "for institutions which will give direction to a destiny henceforward shared."

The central economic mechanism of the ECSC was a common market for coal and steel.[5] Article 4 of the treaty thus provided that various measures were to be recognized as incompatible with the common market and should accordingly be prohibited within the Community: for example, import and export duties, or charges having equivalent effect, and quantitative restrictions on the movement of products; measures or practices that discriminated between producers, between purchasers, or between consumers, especially in prices and delivery terms or transport rates and conditions; measures or practices that interfered with the purchaser's free choice of supplier; subsidies or aids granted by member states, or special charges imposed by member states, in any form whatsoever; and restrictive practices which tended towards the sharing or exploiting of markets. Article 4 thus envisaged a Community-wide market for coal and steel free from interference by the member states or by economic operators tending to impede the flow of trade or to distort the play of competition.

The Failure of the Proposed European Defence and Political Communities

Significant as the founding of the ECSC may have been, it contributed little of itself to the increasingly pressing problem of incorporating West Germany into the defense network established by the Brussels and North Atlantic Treaties.

While the United States was enthusiastic for German participation, France was naturally wary of seeing her recently vanquished enemy so soon rearmed. At the instigation of Winston Churchill and Paul Reynaud,[6] the Consultative Assembly of the Council of Europe[7] called for the

> immediate creation of a unified European Army, under the authority of a European Minister of Defence, subject to proper European democratic control and acting in full co-operation with the United States and Canada. [8]

After a French initiative known as the "Pleven Plan," the treaty establishing the European Defence Community (EDC) was signed (subject to ratification) by the Benelux countries, France, Germany, and Italy (the Six).[9] Once again the United Kingdom held aloof. If the ECSC had been calculated to bind Germany to France industrially, the EDC was to provide the framework for German rearmament.

The projected EDC had two significant characteristics. First, it was to be endowed with a supranational institutional structure not unlike that of the ECSC. The EDC Treaty provided for a European army, composed of units placed at the disposal of the Council of Ministers by the member states. A common budget would be drawn up, and an executive body, the "Commissariat," would lay down common programs in the field of armaments, provisioning, and military infrastructure. The objects of the EDC were to be purely defensive, within the context of the North Atlantic Treaty. Secondly, the EDC's statute assumed that it would be of a transitional nature and would give way to some more comprehensive form of federal or confederal European Union. Article 8(2) provided that the institutional structure laid down in the EDC Treaty would remain in force until displaced by the establishment of the federal or confederal organization, as explicitly envisaged under Article 38. The latter Article required the Assembly of the EDC to make proposals to the governments of the member states on the establishment of a directly elected assembly, and the powers it should exercise. Particular regard was to be had to the principle that such a modified parliamentary body should be able to constitute one of the elements in a subsequent federal or confederal structure.

These proposals were to be presented to the governments of the Six after the Assembly of the EDC assumed its functions, but within days of the signing of the EDC Treaty, the Consultative Assembly of the Council of Europe resolved that it would be

> of great advantage if the basic principles of a European supranational political authority and the nature and limits of its powers were defined within the next few months, without waiting for the entry into force of the Treaty instituting the European Defence Community.[10]

Despite the fact that the assembly provided for in Article 38 of the EDC Treaty was not yet in existence, and that the article only referred to the constitution of a future parliamentary body, the foreign ministers of the member states of the ECSC requested the members of the Coal and Steel Community Assembly to co-opt additional members, reorganize the distribution of seats laid down in the Paris Treaty in accordance with that prescribed for the assembly of the proposed EDC, and draw up a draft treaty for a European Political Community (EPC). On 10 March 1953, the "Ad Hoc Assembly" presented the requested draft.[11]

The "European Community" proposed by the Ad Hoc Assembly provided for the extensive political and economic integration of its members. Its aims were: to contribute to the protection of human rights and fundamental freedoms in member states; to cooperate with the other free nations in ensuring the security of member states against all aggression; to ensure the coordination of the foreign policy of member states in questions likely to involve the existence, the security, or the prosperity of the community; and to promote the development of employment and the improvement of the standard of living in member states by means, in particular, of the progressive establishment of a common market. To ensure the protection of human rights in the proposed community, provision was made for the application, as part of the Community Statute, of the provisions of Section I of the European Convention on Human Rights, along with the first protocol to that convention, signed in Paris on 20 March 1952. The institutions of the EPC were to comprise a bicameral legislature, a European executive council, a council of national ministers, a court of justice, and an economic and social council. Financial resources would be derived from a combination of Community taxation and contributions from the member states.

The hopes of those who saw the future of Western Europe in immediate federation were dashed when the French parliament voted against ratification of the EDC Treaty. A change of government in France, and an easing of tension between East and West,[12] contributed to the rejection of the treaty by the combined votes of Gaullists, Communists, Socialists, and radicals.[13] In the event, Germany's participation in the defense of Western Europe was achieved by other means. The Paris Agreements of 23 October 1954 provided for the recognition of the Federal Republic of Germany as a sovereign state and for its subsequent accession to the North Atlantic Treaty.[14]

The Spaak Report and the Two Treaties of Rome 1957

Despite the setback represented by the rejection of the EDC Treaty, the Six were still convinced of the need for closer integration. At a conference held in the Sicilian city of Messina in 1955, the foreign ministers of the ECSC countries expressed the belief that the time had come to make "a fresh advance towards the building of Europe," but that this must be achieved "first of all, in the economic field."[15] Two objectives were agreed: developing atomic energy for peaceful purposes and establishing a European common market. An intergovernmental committee under the chairmanship of the Belgian foreign minister, Paul-Henri Spaak, was entrusted with the task of making proposals to this end. The United Kingdom was invited to participate in the work of the committee, but although a Board of Trade official was initially dispatched, he was recalled after a few weeks. The Spaak Report was published in April 1956.[16] In the light of its conclusions, two new treaties were negotiated, one providing for the establishment of the European Economic Community (EEC) and the other for the establishment of the European Atomic Energy Community (Euratom). The EEC and Euratom Treaties were signed in Rome on 25 March 1957 and came into force on 1 January 1958.

The preamble to the EEC Treaty expressed the determination of the High Contracting Parties "to lay the foundation of an ever closer union among the peoples of Europe." From 1958 to the present day, the treaty (though much amended, not least in its name) has provided the core framework for the process of European integration.

The central mechanism of the original EEC was to create a common market covering all economic sectors other than those falling within the purview of the ECSC Treaty (while it remained in force) or the Euratom Treaty.[17] The construction and maintenance of that common market – the existence, on a Europe-wide scale, of economic conditions similar to those on the market of a single state[18] – remains for many the central responsibility of the modern European Union. The common market, as envisaged by the EEC Treaty, involved the establishment of a customs union through the elimination of all customs duties and quantitative restrictions in trade between the member states and the erection of a common customs tariff, as well as the removal of barriers to the free movement of "the factors of production" (labor, business, and capital). In addition, the EEC Treaty introduced rules designed to prevent competition from being restricted by arrangements between private operators, or by government subsidies or the activities of member state monopolies. Legal machinery was provided for the harmonization of national legislation that may have a bearing on the well-functioning of the common market. Other primordial features of the system were the Common Agricultural Policy and the Common Transport Policy, relating to sectors where a completely free market was thought impracticable, and provisions relating to the Community's external trade and the possibility of creating an "association" with a third country or an international organization.

For these purposes, the EEC Treaty created a set of supranational institutions charged with fulfilling the objectives of the new community: the Council of Ministers, the Commission, the Assembly, and the Court of Justice. The Council of Ministers, composed of a representative from each member state at the ministerial level, was empowered to adopt binding measures. The Commission, appointed by the member states but charged with acting independently in the collective interest, was to be principally responsible for proposing measures to the Council of Ministers and subsequently for implementing Community legislation, while the Assembly, again appointed by the member states, would exercise an essentially consultative role in relation to the Council of Ministers. It was the role of the Court of Justice, composed of judges appointed by the member states, to ensure, within the treaty system, the observance of the rule of law.

Political Stagnation, Legal Transformation

The initial years of the EEC's existence are often downplayed and it is true that, particularly when it came to adopting the implementing measures required for the construction of the common market, the institutions were often characterized by political inertia – thanks not least to the requirement of unanimity among the member states for the purposes of adopting Community legislation within the Council of Ministers. However, the 1960s and 1970s still witnessed significant developments that played a crucial role in shaping the European integration process.

First, the so-called Merger Treaty of 1965 (which entered into force in 1967) sought to promote institutional coherence between the three Communities – ECSC, Euratom, and EEC – by providing that they should be served by a single council and commission. A previous convention between the member states had already provided that the three Communities should be served by a single assembly and court of justice. Thenceforth, the ECSC, the EEC, and Euratom were served by the same set of institutions, whose powers varied depending on the treaty under which they acted for any given purpose.

Secondly, the Assembly was recast as the European Parliament and, in accordance with an act approved by the Council of Ministers in 1976 and ratified by all the member states, held its first direct elections in 1979 – thus injecting an important element of democratic legitimacy into the EEC's institutional framework and strengthening the Parliament's calls for greater input into the Community's decision-making processes.

Thirdly, it was decided in 1974 that the heads of state or government of the member states should begin to meet on a regular basis to discuss matters relevant to the Communities at the highest political level. This gave birth to the European Council, a body which initially lay outside the formal institutions of the modern European Union but which is now acknowledged to be its supreme political organ, responsible for setting the strategic direction and priorities of the European integration process.

Fourthly, the Court of Justice (CJEU) also played an immensely influential role during this period. It was established in rulings such as *van Gend en Loos* that provisions of Community law that are sufficiently clear, precise, and unconditional may have direct effect within the national legal systems, entitling individuals to invoke those treaty-based norms before the domestic courts as an autonomous source of law, even in the absence of implementing measures adopted by the competent domestic authorities for the purposes of transposing Community rules into national law.[19] It was further held in rulings such as *Costa v. Enel* that directly effective rules of Community law must take primacy over any conflicting provisions of national law, so that even national constitutional norms must be set aside in favor of the treaty and all acts of Community secondary legislation.[20] Such rulings laid the foundations for an increasingly integrated relationship between the legal orders of the Community and its member states, whereby Community law could rightly be described as an integral part of the national legal systems and could act as an important font of rights and obligations for individuals and public authorities alike.

Finally, a series of early accession treaties gradually expanded the number of member states of the Communities: the 1972 treaty led to the accession of the United Kingdom, Ireland, and Denmark in 1973; the 1979 treaty led to the accession of Greece in 1981; and the 1985 treaty led to the accession of Spain and Portugal in 1986. By that stage, the EEC therefore comprised twelve member states.

Since the 1980s, the EEC has undergone an even more far-reaching set of transformations. In some respects, the treaties have achieved their goal of creating an ever-closer union among the peoples of Europe; in other respects, the integration process has revealed serious tensions between the Community (now Union) and its member states. Those developments can usefully be charted through the evolution of the primary treaties themselves.

The Single European Act

The Single European Act (SEA) was signed on 17 February 1986 and entered into force on 1 July 1987.[21] Its seemingly odd title is explained by the fact that, within a single legal instrument, there were juxtaposed provisions amending the three Community treaties and provisions organizing cooperation in the intergovernmental sphere of foreign policy.

The amendments to the treaties contained in Title II of the SEA were the most extensive adopted up to that time. They included the introduction of a new "cooperation procedure" giving the European Parliament a significantly enhanced role in the legislative process: although important in the development of the Parliament's power within the European Union, that "cooperation procedure" is now defunct and thus of purely historical interest. One of the principal objectives of the SEA was to ensure the completion of the EEC's internal market by the end of 1992.[22] The SEA also inserted into the EEC Treaty a number of specific new legal bases for Community action: for example, concerning economic and social cohesion,[23] research and technological development,[24] and the protection of the environment.[25]

Title III of the SEA contained the treaty provisions on European cooperation in the sphere of foreign policy, known more shortly as "European Political Cooperation." Those provisions were superseded by the Treaty on European Union (TEU), which continues to provide the legal basis for the common foreign and security policy (CFSP).

The Treaty on European Union

The TEU[26] (often referred to by the name of the Dutch city, Maastricht, where it was signed in February 1992) entered into force on 1 November 1993.

The treaty brought into being a new legal and political entity: the European Union. Article 1 of the TEU as adopted at Maastricht stated that "[t]he Union shall be founded on the European Communities, supplemented by the policies and forms of cooperation established by this Treaty." That wording sought to capture the complex character of the new-born Union and the preponderant influence of the three Communities within it, that is, the ECSC (while it remained in force), Euratom, and what was thenceforth known as the European Community (EC) – the word "Economic" being dropped from the title in recognition of the substantially extended and enhanced role of the Community in various fields of governmental activity. The TEU's clumsy phrase, "policies and forms of co-operation," referred to the legal arrangements provided by Title V and Title VI of the Maastricht Treaty, which organized the activities of the common institutions in two fields of activity that the member states could not agree to bring within the purview of the EC Treaty. Title V concerned the CFSP – broadly covering the *political* aspect of external relations (diplomatic contacts, election monitoring and other forms of political assistance to third countries, security activities such as peacekeeping and peacemaking, prospectively even defense), and thus to be distinguished from external *economic* relations (such as trade, development cooperation, and emergency aid), which fell within the competence of the EC. In the TEU as originally concluded, Title VI grouped together, under the heading "cooperation in the fields of justice and home affairs" (or JHA), a variety of matters concerning the treatment of third country nationals and aspects of law enforcement and the maintenance of public order.

These included: aspects of the free movement of persons, such as asylum policy, the control of the Union's external frontiers, and immigration policy; combating drug addiction and international fraud; and cooperation between the member states' judicial, customs, and police authorities.

The image of a Greek temple facade, with three pillars joined by a pediment, was commonly used to illustrate the constitutional structure that was created by the original TEU.[27] The difference between the "first pillar" (comprising the preexisting Communities) and the "second and third pillars" (respectively, Titles V and VI of the TEU) lay in the much lesser degree to which, in respect of the latter, the sovereign powers of the member states were curtailed. The "pediment" consisted of the elements common to the three components of the Union, notably that they were to be served by a single institutional framework,[28] and that there was common machinery for the amendment of the Treaties,[29] as well as for the enlargement of the Union.[30]

Besides establishing the Union structure, the TEU effected a number of significant reforms within the EC system (the first pillar), two of which may briefly be noted here. First, an effort was made to tackle the problem of the "democratic deficit" in the system by changing the rules on the appointment of the Commission and by introducing a new legislative procedure, commonly referred to as "codecision," both measures being designed to enhance the role of the European Parliament. Secondly, the treaty contained detailed provisions on the organization of economic and monetary union (EMU) and a timetable for its realization in three stages. It was specifically provided that the third stage, involving the introduction of a single currency, must start (at the latest) on 1 January 1999; and so, in the event, it did, with the introduction on that date of the "euro" as the currency of eleven out of the then fifteen member states.

The ratification process of the TEU was thrown off course by the negative outcome of the referendum that was held in Denmark in June 1992. Subsequent referenda in Ireland in June and in France in September 1992 brought votes in favor of ratification, although in the latter case by a narrow margin. Political and economic uncertainty increased as a result of turbulence in the international money markets during the period immediately preceding and following the French referendum, and this led to the suspension by Italy and the United Kingdom of their membership of the exchange rate mechanism of the European Monetary System and to the reintroduction of exchange rate controls by Spain and Ireland. However, at an extraordinary meeting of the European Council in Birmingham on 16 October 1992, the heads of state or government reaffirmed their commitment to the TEU. It was agreed that the Community must develop together, on the basis of the TEU, while respecting, as the treaty did, the identity and diversity of the member states.[31]

That positive development was confirmed by the European Council held in Edinburgh on 11–12 December 1992. Agreement was reached in Edinburgh on texts establishing interpretations of various provisions of the TEU which the Danish authorities announced would make it possible to hold a second referendum, with a good prospect that Denmark would be in a position to ratify the treaty.[32] Nevertheless, there were more alarms and delays during 1993. Ratification of the TEU by the parliament of the United Kingdom was achieved by the narrowest of margins and in Germany the treaty was the subject of a legal challenge before the Constitutional Court.[33] Thus, it was only on 1 January 1993 that the TEU finally entered into force and the European Union appeared as a new player on the international stage.

The Challenge of Enlargement

The TEU was followed in 1994 by the Treaty of Accession for Sweden, Finland, and Austria.[34] Those countries joined the Union in 1995, bringing the total number of member states to fifteen. However, by this date, the Union was facing the prospect of a much more challenging enlargement: the fall of the Berlin Wall and the collapse of the Eastern Bloc meant that many of the former satellites of the ex-USSR were keen to join the Union. As the horrific experience of the disintegration of Yugoslavia illustrated only too well, it was evidently in the Union's own interests to stabilize the region. Participation in the European integration process was a tried and tested instrument for consolidating democratic institutions, enhancing economic prosperity, and resolving conflict by peaceful means.

The Union entered into various agreements and negotiations with the candidate states in central and eastern Europe, intended to prepare them for their eventual adoption of the treaties. Meanwhile, the existing member states concluded two additional reforming treaties between themselves, primarily concerned with the need to reform the Union's own institutional structures with a view to the impending enlargement. While those reforming treaties did not fundamentally alter the structure of the European Union as created by the TEU, they nevertheless introduced many important technical reforms to the Union's institutional framework and substantive powers.

The Treaty of Amsterdam

To some of those who had been involved in the Intergovernmental Conference (IGC) on the TEU, the institutional reforms that were agreed seemed disappointing, and provision was made for a new IGC to be convened as early as 1996, in order to consider further changes.[35] However, the ambition to press ahead with further "deepening" of European integration was overtaken by other aims which became the primary focus of the 1996 IGC: to counteract the alienation of public opinion from the whole EU enterprise, which had become painfully apparent during the process of ratifying the TEU; and to effect the changes in the composition and functioning of the institutions of the Union, necessary in order to pave the way for the enlargements, by then perceived as politically ineluctable, that would bring in many (and eventually perhaps all) the countries of central and eastern Europe, as well as other applicants from the Mediterranean area.[36]

The IGC on the Treaty of Amsterdam (TA) completed its work in June 1997, and the treaty was signed in October of that year.[37] The ratification process went more smoothly than that of the TEU, and the TA entered into force on 1 May 1999.[38]

A major achievement of the TA was the reform of the Community's legislative process – both extending the influence of the European Parliament within the codecision procedure and expanding the range of policies which were subject to that more democratic decision-making process. The TA also brought about a significant shift of matters relating to the treatment of third country nationals from the third pillar to the first pillar: a new Title IV of Part Three of the EC Treaty dealt with "visas, asylum, immigration and other policies related to free movement of persons," while also including provisions relating to cross-border judicial cooperation in civil matters. The reorganized third pillar was thereafter focused on "police and judicial cooperation in criminal matters," with a notable extension in the scope of Union powers to take action in that field. Another reform was the adoption of the principle of "closer cooperation," the idea behind which remains the same today, even if the detailed rules governing its implementation have been much revised: it should be possible for a limited number of member states to establish, within the institutional framework of the Union, rules in relation to a certain matter that will apply only to themselves and not to the nonparticipating member states.

The Treaty of Nice

There were, however, two important issues, regarded as relevant to the impending enlargement of the Union, on which the IGC on the TA was unable to reach agreement: the size and composition of the Commission, and the distribution of votes between the member states when the Council acts by a qualified majority (the so-called weighting of votes in the Council). Those matters, together with a possible extension of the policy areas in which the Council is empowered to act by a qualified majority (rather than by unanimity), were placed on the agenda of a new IGC that completed its work in December 2000. The Treaty of Nice (TN) was signed on 26 February 2001.[39] As with the Maastricht Treaty, the ratification process was thrown off course by a negative referendum result, this time in Ireland, but following a second popular vote in the Irish Republic, the TN finally entered into force on 1 February 2003.[40]

The TN carried through important reforms intended to adapt the institutional functioning of the Union to the challenges of further enlargement: for example, in relation to the scope of both qualified majority voting and the codecision procedure; the provisions on closer (renamed "enhanced") cooperation between groups of member states; and the structure and jurisdiction of the Union courts. Other major issues of institutional concern were also addressed: the size and composition of the Commission; the weighting of votes in Council; and also the composition of the European Parliament. However, since the TN was finalized before it was decided when and in what order the various candidate countries would eventually accede to the Union, many of the relevant provisions on these issues sought merely to establish templates for future reform – the full details of which were subsequently finalized in the Treaties of Accession 2003 and 2005.

Enlargement from Fifteen to Twenty-Eight (Plus ...)

With the Union's own institutional preparations complete, the path was clear for the signing of the Treaty of Accession 2003 with Poland, the Czech Republic, Slovakia, Slovenia, Latvia, Estonia, Lithuania, Hungary, Malta, and Cyprus. They became members on 1 May 2004.[41] This "big bang" enlargement took effect subject to two main sets of legal provisions.[42] In the first place, the Treaty of Accession 2003 contained numerous transitional provisions intended to ensure the smooth assimilation of the new member states into the Union (for example, in the field of the free movement of workers and freedom to provide services), as well as providing a realistic timetable for the full application of Union law within those countries (as with certain aspects of agricultural, environmental, transport, and energy policies). In the second place, the Treaty of Accession 2003 provided for more permanent adjustments to the EU and EC treaties so as to accommodate the new member states: for example, as regards the allocation of seats within the European Parliament, and (as mentioned previously) the weighting of votes within the Council of Ministers.

A further Treaty of Accession, signed on 25 April 2005, provided for the accession of Bulgaria and Romania on 1 January 2007.[43] That brought to twenty-seven the number of member states of the European Union. The 2005 Accession Treaty, like its 2003 predecessor, contained the necessary temporary and permanent adjustments to the existing body of EU law. There were some important differences, however, not least in the way that Bulgaria and Romania were to become subject to more intensive supervision by the Commission for a transitional period following their accession to the Union, in fields such as cross-border criminal cooperation and as regards judicial cooperation in civil matters.[44]

The most recent Accession Treaty – signed on 9 December 2011 – envisaged Croatia's membership of the European Union as from 1 July 2013.[45] However, even that did not represent the end of the Union's enlargement program. In October 2005, accession negotiations were formally opened with Turkey (though they are expected to last a considerable period of time). The Former Yugoslav Republic of Macedonia was officially recognized as a candidate country by the European Council in December 2005. Following the domestic economic instability generated by the world financial crisis which erupted in 2008, Iceland submitted an application for EU membership in July 2009 and was accorded the status of candidate country in June 2010. Formal candidate country status was extended to Montenegro in December 2010 and then also to Serbia in March 2012. Other countries in the Western Balkans are acknowledged to be potential candidates (Albania, Bosnia Herzegovina, and Kosovo), while yet more states (including the Ukraine) have at some stage or another expressed political ambitions towards becoming members of the European Union in the future.

The Treaty Establishing a Constitution for Europe

Even as they concluded the TN in December 2000, the member states decided to adopt a "Declaration on the Future of the Union" highlighting the need for a more thorough reflection upon the European Union's constitutional framework. The Laeken European Council held in December 2001 then agreed a "Declaration on the Future of the European Union" laying down more precisely the parameters for this process of constitutional reflection, and establishing a "Convention on the Future of Europe" charged with preparing proposals for consideration at a future IGC. The Convention – composed of representatives of the member states, the European Parliament, the national parliaments, and the Commission – commenced its work in February 2002 and culminated in the presentation of a draft "Treaty establishing a Constitution for Europe" to the European Council in July 2003.[46] That text provided the basis for further negotiations between the member states, leading eventually to the signature of the treaty establishing a Constitution for Europe (the Constitutional Treaty or CT) on 29 October 2004.[47]

The CT represented a very far-reaching set of proposals for reform of the Union's primary legal instruments. In the first place, the CT would have reconstituted the Union upon an entirely new (and much simplified) set of legal foundations. Most of the existing EU treaties would have been repealed and replaced in their entirety (including the Treaties of Rome, Maastricht, Amsterdam, and Nice). The pillar structure introduced at Maastricht would have been dismantled, and the EC abolished as a distinct legal entity. Instead, there would have been a unitary European Union, based upon a single constitutional treaty, and possessing its own legal personality. In the second place, the CT would also have carried out a multitude of more detailed reforms to many aspects of the Union's functioning and activities: for example, with respect to the structure of and relations between the institutions, the range of competences exercised by the Union, the types of legal instrument available to it, the protection of human rights and fundamental freedoms, and the arrangements for enhanced cooperation between groups of member states.

The Treaty of Lisbon

The CT was to be ratified by the High Contracting Parties in accordance with their respective constitutional requirements, with a view to entering into force on 1 November 2006. At first, ratification by national parliaments (and, in the case of Spain, through a popular referendum) proved unproblematic. However, the ratification process descended into crisis following negative results in popular referenda in France (29 May 2005) and the Netherlands (1 June 2005). In the light of those events, the European Council meeting in June 2005 called for a "period of reflection" across all member states.[48] The outcome of that process was that the European Council, meeting in June 2007 under the presidency of Germany, agreed to declare the CT dead and approved the mandate for another IGC charged with drafting a new "Reform Treaty."[49] This Reform Treaty was to shed the form, language, and symbols of a "European Constitution" in favor of having another amending treaty, similar in nature to the SEA, TA, or TN. With this new garb, the goal was to preserve as many as possible of the technical reforms proposed under the old CT that were intended to improve the Union's effectiveness, efficiency, and accountability.

The IGC itself was convened by the Portuguese presidency in July 2007[50] and reached political agreement on the text in October 2007. The Reform Treaty was then signed by the member states at a ceremony in Lisbon on 13 December 2007. Its contents closely followed the 2007 mandate.[51] In particular, instead of repealing and replacing the existing treaties entirely, the TEU would be extensively revised; the treaty establishing the EC would also be substantially amended and recast as the Treaty on the Functioning of the European Union (TFEU). But the EC would still be abolished as a distinct legal entity and succeeded by a unitary European Union possessed of its own legal personality. In addition, the existing third pillar on police and judicial cooperation in criminal matters would be transferred out of the TEU and incorporated (with certain special provisions) into the TFEU.

The Treaty of Lisbon (TL) was intended to enter into force on 1 January 2009, before the European Parliament elections scheduled for June of that year.[52] However, that timetable was again thwarted when the people of Ireland – the only country to hold a popular referendum on the TL's ratification – voted "no" in June 2008. A fresh period of uncertainty ensued: the Irish government undertook to investigate the reasons behind the negative referendum result;[53] the European Council then agreed on various "guarantees" intended to address the concerns thus identified (though without formally amending the TL, which would have required its re-ratification by the other member states).[54] The most important of those "guarantees" was an agreement by the European Council to exercise its powers under the revised treaties so as to retain the principle that the European Commission should contain one member per country – the potential loss of "Ireland's Commissioner" as a result of a planned reduction in the overall size of the Commission being treated as a major factor behind the TL's unpopularity in that member state. On the strength of the European Council's guarantees, Ireland held a second referendum in October 2009; this time, just over 67 percent of votes cast were in favor of the TL.

However, the Irish referendum saga was not the only hurdle to implementation of the TL. Constitutional challenges to domestic ratification of the TL had been raised (ultimately unsuccessfully) before the supreme courts of several member states.[55] The original Irish "no" vote had also provided a rallying point for Eurosceptic leaders in other countries, particularly Poland and the Czech Republic, to resist formal ratification of the TL.[56] Shortly after the second Irish referendum, the Polish president finally gave up his resistance and signed off the TL. The Czech president, Václav Klaus, held out for longer, though even his bullish opposition eventually yielded after the Czech Constitutional Court reaffirmed the compatibility of the TL with domestic law.[57] That was not before President Klaus had secured the European Council's agreement that a controversial protocol agreed under the TL, seeking to qualify the application of the European Union's Charter of Fundamental Rights within the United Kingdom and Poland, should be extended so as also to cover the Czech Republic.[58]

All final obstacles overcome, the path was cleared for the TL to enter into force on 1 December 2009. Thus, after nearly a decade of complex negotiations and often-bitter disputes, the outcome of the constitutional reform process initiated at Nice and Laeken is that the TEU and the TFEU (as revised by the TL) now provide the fundamental legal framework for the institutions and activities of the European Union.[59]

Yet Further Treaty Reform …

With Lisbon's fate finally settled, many commentators argued that the Union should try to move on from what felt like interminable wrangling about treaty revisions to focus instead on delivering concrete results as regards its substantive policy objectives and on winning back support from an apparently disillusioned and disaffected public.

Nevertheless, further treaty reform remains firmly on the agenda. In the first place, elections to the European Parliament took place in 2009 on the basis of the pre-TL system of 736 MEPs.[60] Yet, the TL itself had envisaged a total of 751 MEPs, with some countries (such as Spain, France, and the United Kingdom) gaining and one state (Germany) losing positions within the Parliament as compared to the 2009 figures.[61] The European Council decided that special provisions were needed to address this situation: all MEPs already elected to the Parliament should remain in office, but the additional MEPs provided for by Lisbon should also be able to take up their posts, thus raising the total number of MEPs to 754, at least for the remainder of the 2009 to 2014 parliamentary term.[62] The amendments to Union primary law necessary to implement this complex solution were agreed upon at a brief IGC held in June 2010,[63] with the changes due to enter into force upon ratification by all twenty-seven member states.[64]

In the second place, the economic turmoil which followed the world financial crisis of 2008 revealed various shortcomings in the existing rules governing the operation of the European Union's single currency – leading to the emergence of deep-rooted sovereign debt problems among several countries that had adopted the euro (such as Greece, Ireland, and Portugal). At its meeting in December 2010, the European Council formally initiated the "simplified" procedure for revising the treaties,[65] so as to provide for the establishment of a permanent crisis fund to assist individual members of the eurozone and thereby guarantee the financial stability of the euro-area as a whole.[66] Additional treaty amendments, containing much more far-reaching reforms to the governance structures of the eurozone, were proposed to the European Council meeting in December 2011. However, the British prime minister controversially vetoed any changes to the existing EU treaties – effectively forcing the other member states to pursue their planned reforms through the medium of an international agreement standing altogether outside the legal order of the Union itself. That "Treaty on Stability, Coordination and Governance in the Economic and Monetary Union" was signed by twenty-five member states (all save the UK and the Czech Republic) in March 2012. This new international agreement raises a host of constitutional problems for EU lawyers – not least, how far it is lawful, or at least desirable, for certain member states to enter into a treaty which is separate from, yet very closely interrelated to, the primary law of the European Union itself, and also to make provision within that international agreement for the participation of EU institutions (such as the Commission and the Court of Justice).[67] It is worth noting, however, that the 2012 treaty explicitly expresses the desire of its signatory states to secure its future incorporation into EU law (if necessary, through amendments to the TEU and TFEU).

Clearly, even in the short term, Lisbon has not proven to be the last word on revision of the European Union's main treaties. Yet, while the recent treaty changes concerning the European

Parliament or the eurozone bail-out fund may seem relatively minor when compared to major overhaul of the Union's constitutional structures contained in the TL, it is worth noting that the ongoing crisis in the single currency continues to exert significant pressure towards a more fundamental change in the trajectory of European integration – perhaps including a much greater degree of economic and political integration among the eurozone countries, thereby implying the emergence of a more formal "two-speed" European Union, in which the rights and obligations of various groupings of member states become even more sharply differentiated than they are at present. Germany, in particular, seems keen to convene a new convention on treaty reform, tasked with drawing up proposals for more extensive political union among the eurozone states.[68] Such a prospect would pose myriad challenges for EU scholars – not least whether, and how to preserve the coherence of the European Union's institutional framework, the integrity of its fundamental constitutional principles, and the notion of equality associated with Union citizenship.

Notes

This chapter draws upon work already published in Alan Dashwood et al., *Wyatt and Dashwood's EU Law* (Oxford: Hart, 2011), Chap. 1.

1 On the historical context, see Alan S. Milward, *The Reconstruction of Western Europe 1945–51* (Berkeley, CA: University of California Press, 1984). On the early history of the European Communities, see Michael Palmer, *European Unity: A Survey of the European Organisations* (London: Allen & Unwin, 1968); Gladwyn, *The European Idea* (New York: Frederick A. Praeger, 1967); Arthur Henry Robertson, *European Institutions* (New York: Praeger, 1973); and Derek W. Urwin, *The Community of Europe: A History of European Integration* (Harlow: Pearson Education, 1995).

2 NATO, *NATO: Facts and Figures* (Brussels: NATO Information Service, 1971), Chap. 1.

3 For the French text, see *Documents on International Affairs* (1949–1950), 315–317. An English translation (from which the quotations in the text are extracted) appears in *Department of State Bulletin* 22 at 936–937.

4 Article 97 ECSC. Since no steps were taken to renew the ECSC Treaty, the coal and steel sectors now come within the purview of the TEU and TFEU.

5 Article 1 ECSC proclaimed that the Community is "founded upon a common market, common objectives and common institutions."

6 Robertson, *European Institutions*, 18.

7 The Council of Europe is an intergovernmental organization established in 1949. Its aim is to achieve greater unity among its members and to this end it seeks agreement on common action "in economic, social, cultural, scientific, legal and administrative matters and in the maintenance and further realisation of human rights and fundamental freedoms."

8 Resolution of the Consultative Assembly of the Council of Europe (11 August 1950); *Documents on International Affairs* (1949–1950), 331. As is clear from the quotation cited in the text, the Council at times interprets the terms of its statute with some liberality. See Robertson, *European Institutions*, 19.

9 27 May 1952. See *Documents on International Affairs* (1952) 116–162. See also Edward Furdson, *The European Defence Community: A History* (Macmillan: London, 1979).

10 Resolution of 30 May 1952. Texts Adopted (1952) and see *Report on the Constitutional Committee instituted to work out a Draft Treaty setting up a European Political Community* (Paris, 20 December 1952), 6.

11 See *Information and Official Documents of the Constitutional Committee of the Ad Hoc Assembly* (Paris, 1953), 53 *et seq.* For a brief but informative account of the events surrounding the preparation of the draft treaty and its ultimate demise, see Richard T. Griffiths, "Europe's First Constitution: The European Political Community, 1952–1954," in *The Construction of Europe*, ed. Stephen Martin (Dordrecht: Kluwer, 1994).

12 Robertson, *European Institutions*, 21.

13 Palmer, introduction to *European Unity*.
14 NATO, *NATO: Facts and Figures*, 35. For the Protocol to the North Atlantic Treaty on the Accession of the Federal Republic of Germany, and the texts known collectively as the "Paris Agreements," see Apps 9 and 10.
15 *Documents on International Affairs* (1950), 163; Cmnd 9525.
16 *Rapport des chefs de délégation aux ministres des affaires étrangères* (Brussels, 21 April 1956). A summarized translation of Part I of the Spaak Report, "The Common Market," was published by *Political and Economic Planning* as Broadsheet No. 405 of 17 December 1956.
17 See ex-Article 305 EC.
18 See the description of the common market in Case 15/81 *Schul v. Inspecteur de Invoerrechten en Accijnzen* EU:C:1982:135.
19 Case 26/62 *Van Gend en Loos v. Nederlandse Administratie der Belastingen* EU:C:1963:1.
20 Case 6/64 *Costa v. Enel* EU:C:1964:66 .
21 The SEA is published at [1987] OJ L169/1.
22 Ex-Articles 14 and 95 EC (see now Articles 26 and 114 TFEU).
23 Ex-Articles 158–162 EC (see now Articles 174–178 TFEU).
24 Ex-Articles 163–173 EC (see now Articles 179–190 TFEU).
25 Ex-Articles 174–176 EC (now Articles 191–193 TFEU).
26 [1992] OJ C191/1. Note that the numbering of the original TEU, like that of the old EC Treaty, was altered by the TA (and again by the TL).
27 The structure created by the TEU was much criticized. See, in particular, Ulrich Everling, "Reflections on the Structure of the Union," *Common Market Law Review* 29 (1992): 1053; and Deirdre Curtin, "The Constitutional Structure of the Union: A Europe of Bits and Pieces," *Common Market Law Review* 30 (1993): 17.
28 See Article 3 of the original TEU (cf. Article 13 TEU as it currently stands).
29 See Article 48 of the original TEU (which remains Article 48 TEU).
30 See Article 49 of the original TEU (which remains Article 49 TEU).
31 See Presidency Conclusions from the Birmingham European Council in October 1992, to which the text of the "Birmingham Declaration" is annexed.
32 See Presidency Conclusions of the Edinburgh European Council in December 1992.
33 See Bundesvervassungsgericht, Judgment of 12 October 1993, 2 BvR 2134 and 2 BvR 2153/92 [1994] 1 CMLR 57.
34 [1994] OJ C241/10.
35 See Article N(2) of the original TEU (deleted by the TA).
36 On the task of the IGC, see Alan Dashwood, ed., *Reviewing Maastricht Issues for the 1996 IGC* (London: Sweet & Maxwell, 1996).
37 See the text of the TA as published in [1997] OJ C340.
38 On the TA, see, e.g., Andrew Duff, *The Treaty of Amsterdam* (London: Sweet & Maxwell, 1997); and Sally Langrish, "The Treaty of Amsterdam: Selected Highlights," *European Law Review* 23 (1998): 3.
39 See the text of the TN as published at [2001] OJ C80.
40 On the TN, see, e.g., Kieran St. C. Bradley, "Institutional Design in the Treaty of Nice," *Common Market Law Review* 38 (2001): 1095; and Alan Dashwood, "The Constitution of the European Union after Nice: Law-Making Procedures," *European Law Review* 26 (2001): 215.
41 See the text of the Treaty of Accession 2003 as published at [2003] OJ L236.
42 For analysis, see Christophe Hillion, "The European Union is Dead. Long Live the European Union … A Commentary on the Accession Treaty 2003," *European Law Review* 29 (2004): 583.
43 See the text of the Treaty of Accession 2005 as published at [2005] OJ L157.
44 For analysis, see Adam Łazowski, "And Then They Were Twenty-Seven … A Legal Appraisal of the Sixth Accession Treaty," *Common Market Law Review* 44 (2007): 401.
45 See the text of the Treaty of Accession 2011 as published at [2012] OJ L112.
46 For analysis, see, e.g., Michael Dougan, "The Convention's Draft Constitutional Treaty: Bringing Europe Closer to its Lawyers?" *European Law Review* 28 (2003): 763; and Juliane Kokott and Alexandra

Rüth, "The European Convention and its Draft Treaty Establishing a Constitution for Europe: Appropriate Answers to the Laeken Questions?" *Common Market Law Review* 40 (2003): 1315.

47 See the text of the CT as published at [2004] OJ C310. For analysis, see, e.g., Alan Dashwood, "The EU Constitution: What Will Really Change?" *Cambridge Yearbook of European Legal Studies* 7 (2004/2005): 33.

48 See the Declaration by the Heads of State or Government of the Member States of the European Union on the Ratification of the Treaty establishing a Constitution for Europe (18 June 2005). The "period of reflection" was extended by the European Council meeting in June 2006 (see Presidency Conclusions of 16 June 2006). Note also the Commission's "Plan D for Democracy, Dialogue and Debate," COM(2005) 494 and COM(2006) 212.

49 See Presidency Conclusions of 23 June 2007.

50 12004/07. The IGC was formally based on a proposal submitted by Germany (11222/07) reproducing the European Council mandate. Note the Commission's generally positive opinion on the IGC mandate (COM(2007) 412 final); as well as the more ambivalent opinion of the European Parliament (Resolution of 11 July 2007).

51 For analysis, see, e.g., Michael Dougan, "The Treaty of Lisbon 2007: Winning Minds, Not Hearts," *Common Market Law Review* 45 (2008): 617; and Paul Craig, "The Treaty of Lisbon: Process, Architecture and Substance," *European Law Review* 33 (2008): 137.

52 See Article 6(2) TL.

53 See, in particular, European Council Conclusions of 19–20 June 2008; and of 15–16 October 2008.

54 See, in particular, European Council Conclusions of 11–12 December 2008; and of 18–19 June 2009. It is envisaged that several of those guarantees will (in due course) be annexed to the treaties in the form of a protocol.

55 E.g., in Germany, the Czech Republic, and Latvia.

56 Even though the TL had already received the necessary parliamentary assents in those member states.

57 See the Czech Constitutional Court's "Second Lisbon Treaty Judgment" of 3 November 2009.

58 See European Council Conclusions of 29–30 October 2009. Such an extension has not (thus far anyway) been further pursued by the Czech Republic.

59 For consolidated texts of the TEU and TFEU (as well as their protocols and declarations), see [2010] OJ C83.

60 In accordance with ex-Articles 189 and 190 EC.

61 See Article 14(2) TEU; Protocol No. 36 on transitional provisions; Declarations No. 4 and 5.

62 See, in particular, European Council Conclusions of 11–12 December 2008 and 18–19 June 2009.

63 Published at [2010] OJ C263/1.

64 See Article 48(4) TEU.

65 See Article 48(6) TEU.

66 See European Council Decision 2011/199 of 25 March 2011 amending Article 136 of the TFEU with regard to a stability mechanism for Member States whose currency is the Euro [2011] OJ L91/1. Note the interim measures provided for, e.g., by Council Regulation (EU) No. 407/2010 of 11 May 2011 establishing a European financial stabilization mechanism [2010] OJ L118/1.

67 See further, e.g., Editorial Comments, "Some Thoughts Concerning the Draft Treaty on a Reinforced Economic Union," *Common Market Law Review* 49 (2012): 1.

68 See e.g., "Merkel wants EU Treaty Convention by end of year" on euobserver.com, 27 August 2012.

References

Bradley, Kieran St. C. "Institutional Design in the Treaty of Nice." *Common Market Law Review* 38 (2001): 1095–1123.

Craig, Paul. "The Treaty of Lisbon: Process, Architecture and Substance." *European Law Review* 33 (2008): 137–166.

Curtin, Deirdre. "The Constitutional Structure of the Union: A Europe of Bits and Pieces." *Common Market Law Review* 30 (1993): 17–69.
Dashwood, Alan, ed. *Reviewing Maastricht Issues for the 1996 IGC*. London: Sweet & Maxwell, 1996.
Dashwood, Alan. "The Constitution of the European Union after Nice: Law-Making Procedures." *European Law Review* 26 (2001): 215–238.
Dashwood, Alan. "The EU Constitution: What Will Really Change?" *Cambridge Yearbook of European Legal Studies* 7 (2004/2005): 33–56.
Dashwood, Alan, Michael Dougan, Barry Rodger, Eleanor Spaventa, and Derrick Wyatt. *Wyatt and Dashwood's EU Law*. Oxford: Hart, 2011.
Dougan, Michael. "The Convention's Draft Constitutional Treaty: Bringing Europe Closer to its Lawyers?" *European Law Review* 28 (2003): 763–793.
Dougan, Michael. "The Treaty of Lisbon 2007: Winning Minds, Not Hearts." *Common Market Law Review* 45 (2008): 617–703.
Duff, Andrew. *The Treaty of Amsterdam*. London: Sweet & Maxwell, 1997.
Editorial Comments. "Some Thoughts Concerning the Draft Treaty on a Reinforced Economic Union." *Common Market Law Review* 49 (2012): 1–14.
Everling, Ulrich. "Reflections on the Structure of the Union." *Common Market Law Review* 29 (1992): 1053–1077.
Furdson, Edward. *The European Defence Community: A History*. MacMillan: London, 1979.
Gladwyn. *The European Idea*. New York: Frederick A. Praeger, 1967.
Griffiths, Richard T. "Europe's First Constitution: The European Political Community, 1952–1954." In *The Construction of Europe*, edited by Stephen Martin, 19–40. Dordrecht: Kluwer, 1994.
Hillion, Christophe. "The European Union is Dead. Long Live the European Union … A Commentary on the Accession Treaty 2003." *European Law Review* 29 (2004): 583–612.
Kokott, Juliane, and Alexandra Rüth. "The European Convention and its Draft Treaty Establishing a Constitution for Europe: Appropriate Answers to the Laeken Questions?" *Common Market Law Review* 40 (2003): 1315–1345.
Langrish, Sally. "The Treaty of Amsterdam: Selected Highlights." *European Law Review* 23 (1998): 3–19.
Łazowski, Adam. "And Then They Were Twenty-Seven … A Legal Appraisal of the Sixth Accession Treaty." *Common Market Law Review* 44 (2007): 401–430.
Milward, Alan S. *The Reconstruction of Western Europe 1945–51*. Berkeley, CA: University of California Press, 1984.
NATO. *NATO: Facts and Figures*. Brussels: NATO Information Service, 1971.
Palmer, Michael. *European Unity: A Survey of the European Organisations*. London: Allen & Unwin, 1968.
Robertson, Arthur Henry. *European Institutions*. New York: Praeger, 1973.
Urwin, Derek W. *The Community of Europe: A History of European Integration*. Harlow: Pearson Education, 1995.

4

The Relationship between EU Law and International Law

Katja S. Ziegler

Introduction

How do EU law and international law interact? Do they relate to one another as general international law and one of its specialized legal regimes? Or does the relationship resemble that between international law and national law, on the basis of claims of autonomy of the EU legal order?[1] Elements of both the international and the constitutional paradigms are reflected in most areas of EU law, but they are particularly prominent when analyzing the relationship between international and EU law,[2] a topic that has enjoyed increasing attention in recent years.[3]

These questions have triggered a wide range of theories, broadly divided into pluralist and constitutionalist approaches, which are often considered to displace the traditional monist and dualist approaches to international law.[4] The European Union is an international organization by birth, but it has become highly constitutionalized. It combines features of both an international organization and a state. Empirically, there is no doubt of the constitutionalization of the EU legal order, although the question of whether specific expressions of constitutionalization are desirable may be controversial. Whether the Union is now still conceived of as a creature of international law (i.e., closer to an international organization) or instead as *sui generis*, because of its advanced constitutionalization, depends on the relative weight and significance attributed to formal and foundational internationalism (i.e., rootedness in international law) on the one hand and substantive constitutionalization of the EU legal order on the other hand.

Differences are also partly dependent on who is conducting the analysis (e.g., an EU lawyer or an international lawyer), to underlying assumptions about what characterizes a legal system, and to the degree of formalism with which the question is approached. Much also depends on one's perspective on international law, the constitutionalization of international law, and an assessment of the uniqueness of the EU legal order. The theoretical question of the international or *sui generis*/constitutional nature of the European Union cannot be answered in this chapter, but it is not merely of academic interest, because it will influence the interpretation of EU law and the standards by which the European Union is, or ought to be, held accountable and evaluated.

A Companion to European Union Law and International Law, First Edition.
Edited by Dennis Patterson and Anna Södersten.

The relationship between EU law and international law is influenced by a number of specific and practical factors:

First, the Court of Justice of the European Union (CJEU)[5] adopts a strong constitutionalist approach which assimilates the relationship between EU law and international law in many respects to the relationship between international law and national law. The Union's approach to international law may be motivated by inward-looking (constitutional) considerations that may be instrumental to its own dynamics, constitutional narrative, and trajectory.

Second, the triangular relationship between EU law, international law, and the EU member states means that the European Union's approach to international law will influence member states' approaches to international law and it will impact – through the prism of EU law – on member states. Such impact and the possible reaction of member states will, in turn, influence the EU's approach to international law.

Third, as with any specialized legal order of international law, there may be conflicts of norms and conflicts between courts and tribunals about jurisdiction and substantive interpretation of rules between EU law and general international law ("fragmentation").

Fourth, general international law benefits from the more evolved, more constitutionalized parts of international law, in particular in the context of an international organization that may be considered as a "laboratory of international law":[6] supranational rule making, compulsory jurisdiction, strong subjectivity of the individual, and strong enforcement mechanisms available in and for EU law mean that it suffers much less from an enforcement deficit. International law benefits from the full range of enforcement mechanisms of EU law where it is directly effective in the EU legal order.

Therefore, the relationship is more than a niche interest of EU lawyers. It is significant both for general international law, which it challenges and shapes (cf. fragmentation discourse), as well as for other specialized or regional legal orders of international law and for questions of intersectionality of legal systems more broadly.

Finally, the question of the relationship is not confined to legal rules and their enforcement (to which this chapter will be limited). The European Union is increasingly an "actor of international law."[7] It has international legal capacity and concludes treaties. It is a member of some international organizations and tries to enhance its status in others. It thus contributes to the shaping of international law.[8]

In this chapter, first, the more formal basis for the relationship between international law and EU law will be considered by looking at the international law framework of EU law. Then, the approach of the EU legal order to international law and the various ways in which the two legal orders interact within the EU legal order will be discussed. The final section will conclude and consider reasons for and implications of the CJEU's approach.

The European Union within the Legal Framework of International Law: Embeddedness

The European Union is an international organization created by treaty. The original Treaty establishing the European Economic Community (EEC Treaty) and the treaties that followed – today the Treaty on the Functioning of the European Union (TFEU) and the Treaty on European Union (TEU), together with the sectoral Euratom Treaty – are the source of all EU law, either directly by their terms or indirectly by providing the mechanisms for autonomous (supranational) EU lawmaking (see, e.g., Article 249 TFEU). Thus, EU law is a branch of international law. The ultimate power to amend treaties or exit from the treaty system, although regulated somewhat in Articles 48 and 50 TEU, still rests with the member states, a characteristic feature of the treaty basis and its rootedness in the international legal order.

The EU Treaty system is embedded in general international law in that secondary norms of international law, for example, rules of interpretation in the law of treaties[9] or the rules of responsibility of states or international organizations,[10] remain applicable where no special rules have been adopted. The European Union has international legal personality (Article 47 TEU) which is derived from the act of transfer of states' sovereignty to the European Union. It is, therefore, on the international plane, bound both by customary international law (CIL) and treaty law,[11] and it must face the consequences of a breach of international law in the law of international responsibility.

International obligations of the European Union may arise from all sources of international law, in particular CIL and treaty law. The Union has the power to conclude treaties (Articles 216(1) TFEU, 37 TEU) where it has competence to act, either explicitly or implicitly: where the Union has internal competences, it is also presumed to have external competence to conclude treaties.[12] It has made widespread use of its competences in the common commercial policy.[13] A special case of treaties in the EU context are so called mixed-agreements, concluded both by the European Union and its member states in areas of shared competence with third states or other subjects of international law.

Traditionally, the European Union's international obligations have also arisen from functional succession into the member states' obligations. This was famously held to be the case for the General Agreement on Tariffs and Trade in the *International Fruit Company* case.[14] However, the CJEU subsequently adopted a very narrow approach allowing for succession into member states' obligations only in case of "a full transfer of the powers previously exercised by the member states to the Community."[15] This virtually rules out succession into international obligations by the member states: the Court has been much criticized for its strict approach.[16]

Furthermore, the European Union is bound by what may be called "objective elements" in international law. Treaties cannot derogate from *ius cogens* rules (Article 53 of the Vienna Convention on the Law of Treaties (VCLT)). The UN Charter is recognized to be a treaty of special universal character capable of creating binding obligations even for nonmembers (states, international organizations, and other nonstate actors). Its special status is expressed in Article 103 of the UN Charter[17] and may be further supported by emerging notions of an international community.[18]

Article 3(5) TEU recognizes the embeddedness and role of the European Union in, and its responsibility towards, international law in the aims of the Union:

> In its relations with the wider world, the Union shall uphold and promote its values and interests and contribute to the protection of its citizens. It shall contribute to peace, security, the sustainable development of the Earth, solidarity and mutual respect among peoples, free and fair trade, eradication of poverty and the protection of human rights, in particular the rights of the child, as well as to the strict observance and the development of international law, including respect for the principles of the United Nations Charter.

A general constitutional openness of the European Union towards international law – emphasized regularly by the CJEU,[19] for example, when referring to international law being an "integral part" of EU law[20] – may be derived from its natural embeddedness in the international legal order and its aims as expressed in Article 3(5) TEU.[21] However, the abstract and general question of the openness of the EU legal order towards international law does not automatically resolve the question of the status international law has *within* the EU legal order: international law itself is traditionally thought not to be normative with respect to its effect within a legal order of states,[22] and insofar as their legal orders are shaped by contracting states, the same is true for international organizations. This is notwithstanding the fact that international organizations will remain bound by international law on the international plane and a resultant interpretative rule: a presumption that member states will not create conflicting obligations which would lead to a breach of international law and expose them or the international organization to (state) responsibility.[23]

Status and Effect of International Law in the EU Legal Order: General Approach

The EU treaties do not lay down explicit rules about the status of international law within EU law. Although Article 216(2) TFEU states that treaties are binding on the institutions of the European Union and the member states, the provision refers to the binding effect of treaties internationally rather than to their effect within EU law.[24] The question therefore needed to be addressed by the CJEU, drawing from states' approaches to the interaction of national and international law but also adapting such approaches to the specific situation of the Union.

Interactions between international law and EU law may be approached from at least two perspectives: from the formal perspective of the sources of international law (treaty or CIL) and/or from a "substantive" perspective of the effect of international law in EU law which cuts across the distinction by source. The CJEU gives effect to international law in at least three ways:

1. Direct effect: international law may enjoy direct effect within EU law, that is, it will apply automatically without an act of transformation into the EU legal order.
2. Consistent interpretation: international law will be relevant in interpreting EU law.
3. "Substantive borrowing": international law (or foreign law) may be used in a nonstructured way where no formal relationship exists. General international law may directly fill gaps in EU law.[25] In addition, it may be relevant in different ways within EU law, ranging from inspiration, persuasive authority, to feeding substance into a formal source of EU law, in particular, general principles of (EU) law.[26] Such substantive interaction is frequently linked to shared values. It is a mechanism which allows for cross-fertilization of legal orders and facilitates coherence. It points to the openness of the EU legal order towards other legal orders, including the international legal order.[27]

Both CIL and treaty law have consistently been considered to be "integral parts" of EU law and at least capable of direct effect.[28] Traditionally this could be interpreted as meaning that, as a rule, both treaty law and CIL were part of the legal order of the European Union and, therefore, directly effective.[29] This is significant because of the consequences both within the legal order of the European Union and for its member states. If international law is directly effective in the EU legal order, it will also have direct effect within the legal orders of all member states and, as EU law, enjoy supremacy over national law.[30] EU law thus acts as a "door opener"[31] for international law in the member states' legal orders and provides an enforcement mechanism and potentially also an hierarchical "boost": international law can be enforced by all mechanisms used to enforce EU law, in particular by national courts, and it will benefit from the doctrine of supremacy of EU law according to which it enjoys a higher rank than member states' constitutions.

In what follows, the interaction between international and EU law will be explored in further detail by source and by effect of international law (direct effect and the principle of conform or consistent interpretation) to assess the extent to which a general presumption for direct effect of international law and openness of the EU legal order can still be assumed.

Customary International Law

Like many national legal systems, the CJEU generally applies CIL directly.[32] Examples are principles of the international law of treaties;[33] the scope of jurisdiction under international law;[34] the international obligation of states to admit their own nationals to their territory;[35] rules on the nationality of persons and ships;[36] and the status/immunities of a head of state under international law.[37] The CJEU has held that CIL, just like treaty law, is a standard of assessment in the review of the validity of EU secondary legislation,[38] thus ranking CIL more highly within the EU legal order than secondary legislation.[39] However, the Court in *Air Transport Association of America* introduced criteria which restrict when individuals may rely on CIL.[40] Its review is also limited to the standard of whether the EU legislative institutions have made "manifest errors of assessment" in applying CIL because "a principle of customary international law does not have the same degree of precision as a provision of an international agreement."[41] To date, there has been no successful challenge of the validity of an EU measure based on CIL. This raises some doubts as to whether the courts would actually be prepared to annul EU secondary legislation which is in conflict with CIL.

International Treaties

Traditionally, the CJEU accorded wide-ranging direct effect to international treaties,[42] subject to them fulfilling three conditions: first, the European Union must be bound by the treaty; second, the relevant treaty provision must be sufficiently clear, precise, and unconditional to be capable of direct application; and third, direct effect must not be precluded by the "nature and structure" or "broad logic" of a treaty.[43] If the provision was capable of direct effect, there was a presumption for its direct effect, consistent with a monist approach.[44] Until 2008, the CJEU had precluded direct effect as being against the nature or logic of a treaty only in one case, considered to be the exception to the rule:[45] the GATT/WTO Agreement, on the basis that its obligations were flexible, subject to negotiation and reciprocity.[46]

However, starting with three judgments in 2008, direct effect of treaties appears to have become more restricted in regard to each of the three requirements. The Court denied direct effect of final decisions of the WTO Dispute Settlement Body (DSB) because of the "nature and structure" of the agreement[47] even in circumstances where there was no scope for considerations of flexibility, reciprocity, and negotiation to justify precluding direct effect. Similarly, the CJEU excluded United Nations Convention on the Law of the Sea (UNCLOS) – frequently called the "constitution of the sea" – from direct effect, invoking the exception of the "nature and structure" of UNCLOS as being primarily state-centered in nature.[48] It also conceived more narrowly the conditions of direct effect: the traditional requirements that a norm had to be clear, precise, and unconditional were not sufficient. The Court required that a higher threshold must be met, namely that a provision must confer a truly subjective/individual right to be capable of direct effect.[49] As with CIL,[50] this raised the threshold for individuals to invoke international law. Moreover, it contrasts with a wider notion of individual rights and direct effect which is applied to EU law. Also, it does not take into account that individual interests frequently are protected by international law in traditional terms of state obligations without being fully fledged subjective rights (e.g., norms of international humanitarian law). Such norms, however, should not be precluded from direct effect.[51]

Direct effect was also denied to the UN Charter in the *Kadi I* case of 2008.[52] (However, the reasoning in *Kadi I* reflects a restrictive approach to international law more generally.) The *Kadi* cases of 2008 and 2013[53] challenged the validity of regulations by which the European Union implemented UN Security Council resolutions imposing sanctions (travel ban and asset freeze) on listed individuals suspected of terrorism. As remedies at the UN Security Council level were insufficient, individuals challenged the implementing legislation on human rights grounds, in particular the lack of judicial protection. The Court excluded any obligations resulting from the UN Charter from application within the EU legal order for three reasons. Each of the reasons would have been sufficient to exclude any international obligations from consideration of the Court and reflects different aspects of the Court's approach to international law. Although the judgment may be considered to rest on the second reason, the reasons will be discussed in their logical order, rather than in the order of their weight in the judgment:

1. Lack of international obligation of the European Union: the Court seems to imply that because the European Union was not party to the UN Charter it was not bound by obligations arising under the charter.[54] This was only implied as an *obiter dictum* because it was not relevant in the light of its dualist approach (see 2): the Court continues its analysis "supposing it to be applicable to the Charter of the United Nations."[55] However, this creates uncertainty about the binding nature of an international obligation at the international level, in this case the UN Charter. Although there might be a superficial logic to the argument, it is problematic as a matter of both international and EU law. It is too simplistic to find that the European Union would not be bound by the charter in a situation where all member states are bound and where the Union implements charter obligations of the member states. A better interpretation would consider the presumption that the member states, when creating the European Union, did not intend to breach Article 103 of the charter, which requires states to give priority to charter obligations. Article 351 TFEU, which respects international obligations of member states predating the European Union, supports this argument from the perspective of EU law.[56] The European Union could have been considered to have functionally succeeded in member states' obligations under the UN Charter to implement antiterrorist sanctions as a matter of EU law,[57] as the Court of First Instance (CFI) had held.[58] Indeed, in other contexts the Court refers to the Union's obligations under the charter, but it does not respond to the CFI's succession argument. The question of the binding nature of the international obligation is not decisive for the outcome of the case. Following the logic of the dualist/constitutional approach of the Court, any international obligations, including Article 103 of the UN Charter, may be excluded from the consideration of the Court.[59] But the CJEU's approach blurs the distinction between the international and the internally binding character of a norm and casts *obiter* at least some doubts on the question of whether the European Union is bound by the UN Charter.

2. Autonomy of the EU legal order based on dualism: the *Kadi I* judgment was grounded in a strong dualist approach to treaties, or possibly international law more widely. Acting like a domestic court, the CJEU emphasized that the European Union was an "internal and autonomous legal order,"[60] and decided the case purely on the basis of reviewing the validity of EU regulations by the (constitutional) human rights standards of EU law. This logically excluded

any possible international obligations from the case,[61] and it categorically ruled out any review of the Security Council Resolutions, even for breaches of *ius cogens*.[62] But the Court strongly upheld human rights in a situation of normative conflict, rooted in constitutional principles of the European Union. The result of the decisions can, therefore, hardly be criticized, and has to be seen in the light of the very thin accountability mechanism at international level and the much reduced accountability of executive power in international affairs. The Court creates such accountability in *Kadi I* and even more so in *Kadi II*[63] and contributed to improving the review mechanism for certain sanctions at UN level. The strongly dualist reasoning, however, is unnecessarily antagonistic to general international law, as manifested in the UN Charter, and to the charter as a treaty of special constitutional significance for the international legal order. It has far-reaching effects on the relationship between EU and international law beyond the case and beyond a more specific restrictive approach to the conditions of direct effect of treaties.

3. Non-derogable nature of fundamental constitutional principles of the European Union: the Court held that there were fundamental constitutional principles of the European Union from which no derogation was allowed: "the principles of liberty, democracy and respect for human rights."[64] This reason was based implicitly on two hypothetical assumptions (i.e., that the charter was binding and that it was binding internally). This substantive argument from a normative hierarchy within EU (and international) law is the most convincing one in *Kadi I* although only an *obiter* in this case. In *Kadi II*, the CJEU seems to have relied more on considerations of hierarchy of constitutional norms than on the logic of autonomy and dualism. Although the CJEU did not revisit the dualist approach explicitly, as requested by Council, Commission, and several interveners (e.g., United Kingdom), it seems to avoid referring to the autonomy of the European Union in *Kadi II* and focuses on the normative hierarchy argument instead.[65] A relationship between EU law and international law which is defined by the hierarchy of specific norms is less antagonistic than the formalistic and strongly dualist premise of autonomy. If the fundamental principles had been raised on an appropriate normative basis and if the CJEU had engaged appropriately with international law in its interpretation, there would be little to object to.

The Hierarchy of International Law within the EU Legal Order

Once international law is directly applicable within the EU legal order it can be a basis for reviewing the validity of legislative acts of the European Union,[66] and therefore must rank more highly than EU secondary legislation. International law, however, generally does not rank more highly than EU primary law (EU Treaty provisions). International law thus ranks between secondary legislation and the "constitution" of the European Union. This is similar to the rank of treaties in some domestic legal systems[67] and amounts to a comparatively open approach to incorporating international treaty law.[68]

There are exceptions to this rule, allowing international law to prevail over primary EU law, in particular, norms of *ius cogens* from which the EU treaties cannot derogate.[69] Within the EU legal order, Article 351 TFEU allows for international obligations predating a member state's joining the Union to prevail, that is, obligations already existing at the inception of the EEC Treaty in 1958 or prior to a later date of accession of a member state. That (new) member states are not forced by EU law to breach existing international obligations, recognizes the interests of third states involved. However, EU law puts the member states under an obligation to "take all appropriate steps" to eliminate incompatibilities. Traditionally, this meant that member states were under an obligation to renegotiate, suspend, or terminate a treaty which conflicted with EU law.[70] Recently, the CJEU has taken a firmer stand in regard to the obligations of (accession) states to eliminate conflicts with other treaty rules. For bilateral investment treaties it has required member states to eliminate not only existing conflicts with EU primary law and secondary legislation but also potential conflicts with future harmonizing (secondary) legislation. Member states are now required to negotiate a special reservation to allow for immediate implementation of future EU law that might clash with a preexisting treaty to preempt a conflict from arising in the first place.[71]

Following the 2008 *Kadi I* judgment (reinforced by the 2013 *Kadi II* judgment[72]), a further hierarchy within EU law has emerged: that between "ordinary" EU primary law and primary law that concerns the "foundations" of the Union, that is, constitutional principles of the European Union from which no derogation is possible, in particular "the principles of liberty, democracy and respect for human rights and fundamental freedoms enshrined in Article [6(3) TEU] as a foundation of the Union."[73] If such a constitutional hierarchy is assumed, it may be logically possible to limit the exception of the application of the "ordinary" treaty rules of Article 351 TFEU and Article 347 TFEU.

Article 347 TFEU provides a sort of "emergency derogation" from EU primary law and lists a number of grounds which may practically or legally affect a member state's ability to comply with the TFEU, including internal disturbances, war, and obligations accepted for the purpose of maintaining peace and security. The later variant may allow international obligations to prevail even over primary EU law.

Consistent (or Harmonious) Interpretation

While direct effect is a more formal, stronger "door opener" for international law in the EU legal order, the potential of the open textured principle of conform, consistent, or harmonious interpretation is not to be underestimated. At times direct effect comes in the disguise of interpretation of an existing EU rule in the light of an international rule.[74] The notions of direct effect and consistent interpretation are particularly blurred with regard to CIL.[75]

If the European Union is party to an international treaty, including a mixed agreement, the CJEU requires that EU secondary legislation is interpreted "as far as possible" in the light of the international obligations of the European Union.[76] According to the hierarchy of norms in EU law, international agreements have primacy over secondary legislation and "interpretation in conformity with international law must be given priority over other methods of interpretation." Conform interpretation is, however, limited by "rules and principles which take precedence over the [Union's] obligations under international law," such as "general legal principles and in particular the principle of legal certainty," which precludes a *contra legem* interpretation."[77]

Even where the CJEU does not consider the European Union to be formally bound by an international treaty concluded by the member states,[78] but where it nevertheless implements aspects of it due to member states' international obligations, it usually applies the principle of conform interpretation. For example, the CJEU held that when interpreting EU regulations implementing UN Security Council resolutions, it must "take due account of the terms and objectives of the resolution concerned and of the relevant obligations under the Charter of the United Nations" as well as the "wording and purpose" of the relevant Security Council Resolution.[79]

From the perspective of EU law, at least, there is an obligation to interpret EU law in the light of the member states' obligations under international law because of the principle of sincere cooperation (Article 4(3) TEU), which requires the Union not to create conflicting obligations for the member states.

Treaties in the area of human rights have enjoyed a relatively strong role within EU law, either by interpretation[80] or by linking them to general principles of law. General principles allow the CJEU to import standards to which the European Union is not formally related (so it is also a form of "substantive borrowing," but through a formal prism of – interpretation of – general principles).[81] This has been most notably the case in regard to the European Convention on Human Rights (ECHR).

Although the principle of consistent interpretation has been widely referred to and applied, more recent case law suggests that it may be subject to the same sorts of rationales as restrict direct effect. In *Intertanko*, the CJEU did not even attempt a consistent interpretation, although the Advocate General had presented an extensive and detailed interpretation of the relevant EU directive in the light of two conventions and CIL and even though the CJEU does not differ in its outcome.[82] Even though the Court may have thought conform interpretation to be impossible,[83] the fact that it does not engage with or take "into account" the extensive arguments of the Advocate General contributes to the impression that the CJEU is reluctant to review an act of the European Union against international law.[84] Furthermore, in contrast to the tradition outlined above,[85] the CJEU has at times also found itself not to be competent even to interpret an international treaty to which the European Union is not a party.[86] Recently in *Qurbani* it denied an instrument as universal as the Geneva Refugee Convention 1951 even a mere interpretive effect.[87] Hence, once more it casts doubts on the actual effect of international law in EU law.

The CJEU construed the conflict of international law (in the form of Security Council resolutions binding the EU member states) and higher-ranking EU fundamental rights as irreconcilable in *Kadi I*. It thus left little scope for a conform interpretation to prevail. Although there are traces of consistent interpretation of the contested EU regulation in the judgment,[88] Article 351 TFEU would still have required an interpretation that the conflict of obligations between EU law and UN law had been regulated in the treaty, in particular in the light of the purposes of Article 351 (one of which is to avoid conflicts of norms for the member states).

Consistent interpretation, harmonious with international law, does not end here and is not a one-way street. The CJEU could eliminate conflict by considering more closely the exact scope and possible limitations of the international obligation. Thus, a consistent or harmonious interpretation would have been possible even in a scenario like that of *Kadi*, where the EU legal order appears to be more "progressive" in protecting human rights than the international one. Consistent interpretation can include the interpretation of the international norm in the light of its limits. Using the example of *Kadi I*, there may be, first, direct limits, even of the UN Security Council, that result from *ius cogens*.[89] Second, inherent limits can be derived from international human rights law which is part of the international legal order and the UN Charter system. It cannot be assumed that the Security Council would deliberately want to bypass such limits when adopting sanctions against individuals. Therefore, a presumption may be said to operate in the light of Article 24(2) of the UN Charter that the Security Council would not act to force member states (and the European Union) to breach fundamental rights[90] and to expose the UN ultimately to international responsibility.

Making full use of interpretation as a tool to avoid conflict does not only benefit a harmonious and more coherent relationship between EU and international law: it is also required by international law, and, as a process of engagement, may contribute to its development. Articles 31(1) and (3)(c) VCLT take a wider, contextual perspective in prescribing interpretation in "good faith," taking into account the context and purpose of the norm and treaty and also the "relevant rules of international law applicable to the parties." From this it may be deduced that one of the rationales for interpretation in Article 31 VCLT, and in particular Article 31(3)(c), the principle of systemic integration, is to avoid conflicts and preserve unity with other areas of international law, or at least reflect respect and comity towards it. From this it follows that international organizations, their courts, and tribunals have a procedural duty to at least engage with other areas of international law and to attempt to avoid conflict in the interpretation of their own constitutional treaties. In other words, the CIL rules of treaty interpretation, as expressed in Article 31 VCLT,[91] oblige international courts and tribunals to pay special regard to international law and the impact of their decisions on international law as a whole when interpreting the rules of partial legal orders of international law. It is not sufficient to adopt whatever is the quickest and easiest solution in a case without regard for the system of which a partial legal order is a part. Such a heightened responsibility makes sense in the light of the special nature of the international legal order, especially regarding the formation of CIL.

Where international obligations and constitutional values are genuinely irreconcilable through "engaged" interpretation, it may be exceptionally justified to depart from obligations under international law on the basis of shared fundamental legal principles, such as the protection of human rights and the rule of law. Such exceptions may lead to breaching one international rule in order to comply with another, but even under this scenario an engagement with the international legal order can and should occur: such a breach may be legally justified as a countermeasure under the law of international responsibility for internationally wrongful acts – if the obligation imposed is breaching international law.[92]

Conclusions: A More Restrictive Approach of the EU Legal Order

The analysis above reveals a tension. On the one hand, the CJEU describes EU law as open and friendly to international law, of which it is considered to be an "integral part." [93] It stresses the strong commitment, in principle, of the European Union to international law, which it "must respect … in the exercise of its powers."[94] On the other hand, in practice and at a specific level of interaction, examples of an instrumental and selective use of international law seem to be on the rise, and these cases question the expressed general approach.

There are at least three respects in which general international law stands weaker in the relationship, despite the more reconciliatory overtone of *Kadi II*.[95] First, in regard to direct effect: the presumption that international law is directly effective in the legal order of the European Union has been weakened considerably by the expansion of the exceptions. Furthermore, the threshold requirements for direct effect of both treaty law and for individuals to invoke customary law in the CJEU became more restrictive. This is the most significant and most far-reaching of several more restrictive approaches which point towards a wider trend. Second, the openness to harmonious interpretation of EU and international law is no longer unequivocal. Third, the recent development of a notion of hierarchy within EU primary law limits the possibility for giving priority to international law. Fourth, the possibility to derogate from EU primary law for pre-accession agreements (Article 351 TFEU) has been reduced considerably.

There are at least two possible sets of reasons for this trend, one relating to the decision in an individual case and the other relating to EU constitutionalism itself. First, very much as at national level, reasons lie in an outcome-oriented, selective use of international law. The CJEU uses reasons which are procedurally or argumentatively easiest to justify and, therefore, most efficient for the Court in a particular case (*FIAMM and Fedon, Intertanko, Kadi, ATAA).* At times, a true concern about the substantive constitutional values (*Kadi*) or about the pursued regulatory goal (*Intertanko, ATAA*) may also be determining. Where openness towards international law is useful for the European Union and supports the claims and enforcement of EU law (as is the case with direct effect of trade and association agreements), the CJEU has adopted – selectively – a more open approach.[96] In contrast, the CJEU has shown itself less willing to be open to international law where international law limits the power of the European Union, for example, as a standard for the validity review of EU acts. A similar observation has to be made where international law exposes the Union to competing dispute settlement fora.[97] The potential influence of an "institutional interest" could already be observed in the past with regard to the European Court of Human Rights[98] and, more recently, in regard to the International Tribunal of the Law of the Sea in the Mox plant dispute.[99] It culminated in Opinion 2/13, in which the CJEU held that the extensively negotiated accession agreement of the European Union to the ECHR was incompatible with EU law, thus delivering a severe setback to the accession process.[100]

Second, an important reason for the CJEU's approach to international law is EU constitutionalism. There are several dimensions to this. A concern for the legitimacy of the European Union may determine substantive constitutionalization in contrast with international law – as in the human rights context in *Kadi I.* Upholding constitutional values will impact the actual and perceived legitimacy of the European Union vis-à-vis individuals and EU member states. In the context of human rights in particular, the CJEU's approach will be influenced by the need to keep the equilibrium it has reached with member states in the struggle for supremacy of EU law. This equilibrium preempts member states' resistance to the European Union but depends on its effective and generally equivalent protection of human rights. Hence, the actual and perceived protection of human rights by the European Union is just as relevant for the legitimacy of the Union as for securing the de facto supremacy of EU law over member states' law.[101] A further shift in approach to international law in the EU legal order is, therefore, one from form to substance or content, which may make the classical monist/dualist distinction ultimately less relevant.

The recent trend of relative closure of the European Union towards international law along a statist-constitutional paradigm is instrumental to the further internal constitutionalization of the EU legal order, but constitutionalization does not depend on it. It is of concern because it unnecessarily heightens the potential for conflicts between different parts of international law. This would lead to a loss of coherence, which ought to be avoided where possible.[102] The CJEU should, therefore, not rely on notions of autonomy and purely internal versions of normative hierarchy when encountering international law. Instead, the CJEU should properly embrace its claim of openness to the international legal order as part of its constitutionalism. In doing so, it should accept an international obligation appropriately, such as one resulting directly or indirectly from the member states' obligations under the charter in *Kadi I*; furthermore, it should adopt a coherent approach to direct effect and interpret international obligations making full use of the canon of interpretation, including consistent and contextual interpretation; and, if necessary, it should engage with the limits of norms resulting both from international and from EU norms of fundamental importance. The fact that international organizations are creatures of international law (treaties) might even justify a stricter requirement of comity towards other parts of international law. In addition, the European Union has a constitutional responsibility to strictly observe and develop international law (Article 3(4) TEU)[103] which is better served by engagement. As the case may be, the principle of sincere cooperation in Article 4(3) TEU may support such a responsibility in order to avoid double-bind situations for the member states.

The wider benefits of an open engagement with international law were demonstrated by aspects of the *ATAA* and *Diakité* cases which may be contrasted with *Intertanko* or *Kadi*: there is a direct, stronger, and possibly quicker contribution to the development of international law. By rigorously engaging with international law, the CJEU was able to offer strong reasons for the compatibility of the European emissions trading scheme with international law. The engagement with international law thus added to the legitimacy of the European Union's emissions trading scheme and might even influence the creation of a worldwide regime.[104] In *Diakité* the CJEU provided a strong teleological interpretation which showed why similarly phrased concepts of "internal armed conflict" in EU refugee law and in international humanitarian law were not to be interpreted identically.[105] In contrast, a purely autonomy-based constitutional approach would simply have posited a result without engagement with international law, and might have set a detrimental precedent for disengagement from, and breach of, international law. International law relies on the reinforcement and affirmation of individual norms to develop and maintain CIL. As a system, it is vulnerable to breaches, which may ultimately undermine not just the individual rule but also the binding nature of international law as such. An engaged, interpretative approach would avoid many of these negative and probably unintended consequences.

Notes

1 Joined Cases C-402/05 P and C-415/05 P *Yassin Abdullah Kadi and Al Barakaat International Foundation v. Council and Commission of the European Union* (Kadi I) EU:C:2008:461, para 317.

2 See also Katja S. Ziegler, "International Law and EU law: Between Asymmetric Constitutionalisations and Fragmentation," in *Research Handbook on the Theory and History of International Law*, ed. Alexander Orakhelashvili (Cheltenham: Edward Elgar, 2011), 268.

3 E.g., Enzo Cannizzaro, Paolo Palchetti, and Ramses A. Wessel, eds., *International Law as Law of the European Union* (Leiden: Martinus Nijhoff, 2011); and Jan Wouters, André Nollkaemper, and Erika De Wet, eds., *The Europeanisation of International Law: The Status of International Law in the EU and its Member States* (The Hague: Asser Press, 2008).

4 Ramses A. Wessel, "Reconsidering the Relationship between International and EU Law: Towards a Content Based Approach?," in *International Law as Law of the European Union*, ed. Enzo Cannizzaro, Paolo Palchetti, and Ramses A. Wessel (Leiden: Martinus Nijhoff, 2011), 7, 10.

5 The post-Lisbon term "CJEU" is used as a generic term for the Court of Justice of the EU (CJEU) and European Court of Justice (ECJ).

6 Christian Walter, "International Law in a Process of Constitutionalization," in *New Perspectives on the Divide between National and International Law*, ed. Janne Nijman and André Nollkaemper (Oxford: Oxford University Press, 2007), 191, 214.

7 See, e.g., Koen Lenaerts and Eddy de Smijter, "The European Union as an Actor in International Law," *Yearbook of European Law* 19 (1999): 95; and Enzo Cannizzaro, ed. *The European Union as an Actor in International Relations* (The Hague: Kluwer Law International, 2002).

8 The actual impact of the European Union has been debated. See Karen E. Smith, "The European Union at the Human Rights Council: Speaking with One Voice but Having Little Influence," *Journal of European Public Policy* 17 (2010); and Jan Wouters, Anna-Luise Chané, and Jed Odermatt,

"Improving the EU's Status in the UN and the UN System: An Objective Without a Strategy?" (working paper no. 133, KU Leuven Centre for Global Governance Studies, March 2014). Cf. Dimitry Kochenov and Fabian Amtenbrink, "The Active Paradigm of the Study of the EU's Place in the World: An Introduction," in *The European Union's Shaping of the International Legal Order*, ed. Dimitry Kochenov and Fabian Amtenbrink (Cambridge: Cambridge University Press, 2013).

9 In particular Article 31 of the Vienna Convention on the Law of Treaties (VCLT) 1155 UNTS 331 (1980).

10 See Draft Articles on the Responsibility of International Organisations of the International Law Commission, UN Doc A/66/10 para 87, *Yearbook of the International Law Commission* 2011, Vol. II, part 2. In detail the contributions to Malcolm D. Evans and Panos Koutrakos, eds., *The International Responsibility of the European Union: European and International Perspectives* (Oxford: Hart, 2013).

11 This has been stressed regularly by the CJEU, see, e.g., Case C-162/96 *Racke v. Hauptzollamt Mainz* EU:C:1998:293, para 55; Case C-286/90 *Anklagemyndigheden v. Poulsen and Diva Navigation Corp* EU:C:1992:453, para 9 f; Joined Cases C-402/05 and C-415/05 *Kadi I*, n 1 this chapter, para 291 ff; and Case C-366/10 *Air Transport Association of America v. Secretary of State for Energy and Climate Change* (ATAA), EU:C:2011:864, para 101.

12 See Piet Eeckhout, *EU External Relations Law* (Oxford: Oxford University Press, 2011), 71 ff.

13 See for more detail, ibid., 11 ff.

14 Joined Cases 21/72 to 24/72 *International Fruit Co. NV v. Produktschap Voor Groenten en Fruit* EU:C:1972:115, paras 110 ff.

15 Case C-308/06 *The Queen, on the application of International Association of Independent Tanker Owners (Intertanko) and Others v. Secretary of State for Transport* EU:C:2008:312, para 49; confirmed in Case C-366/10 *ATAA*, n 11 this chapter, paras 62 ff, 71 and recently in C-481/13 *Mohammad Ferooz Qurbani* EU:C:2014:2101, paras 23 ff.

16 Eeckhout, *EU External Relations Law*, 400; Ziegler, "International Law and EU Law," 289 ff.

17 See Alexander Orakhelashvili, "1969 Vienna Convention. Article 30: Application of Successive Treaties Relating to the Same Subject Matter," in *The Vienna Convention on the Law of Treaties: A Commentary*, ed. Olivier Corten and Pierre Klein (Oxford: Oxford University Press, 2011), 764, para 41 ff.

18 Bardo Fassbender, "The United Nations Charter as Constitution of the International Community," *Columbia Journal of Transnational Law* 36 (1998); Andreas Paulus, "The Emergence of the International Community," in Nijman and Nollkaemper, *New Perspectives*.

19 See n 11.

20 Case 181/73 *Haegeman v. Belgium* EU:C:1974:41, para 5; Case 104/81 *Kupferberg v. Hauptzollamt Mainz* EU:C:1982:362, para 13; Case C-162/96 *Racke*, n 11 this chapter, para 46; Case C-308/06 *Intertanko*, n 15 this chapter, para 38; and Case C-366/10 *ATAA*, n 11 this chapter, paras 73 and 101.

21 Ziegler, "International Law and EU law," 292 ff, with further references. After finalizing this manuscript, however, Opinion 2/13 *ECHR* EU:C:2014:2454, casts a dark shadow over any perceptions of openness, as it is heavily relying on notions of autonomy of the EU legal order (cf. paras 170, 178 ff, 194, 258).

22 For a recent challenge of this traditional view see André Nollkaemper, "The Duality of Direct Effect in International Law," *European Journal of International Law* 25 (2014).

23 Case C-377/98 *Kingdom of the Netherlands v. European Parliament and Council of the European Union* (Directive on Biotechnological Inventions) EU:C:2001:523, para 55.

24 Article 216(2) is generally interpreted as having its principal thrust in making treaties which are concluded by the European Union also binding on the member states (who may not be parties to the treaty), and not as making all treaties directly effective within the EU legal order, Eeckhout, *EU External Relations Law*, 326 ff.

25 See text around n 10.

26 Famously, EU human rights norms were developed in this way by the CJEU, see Andrew Williams, *EU Human Rights Policies: A Study in Irony* (Oxford: Oxford University Press, 2004), 145–157; Philip Alston, ed. *The EU and Human Rights* (Oxford: Oxford University Press, 1999); Bruno de Witte, "International Law as a Tool for the European Union," *European Constitutional Law Review* 5 (2009); and Anne Peters, "Supremacy Lost: International Law Meets Domestic Constitutional Law," *Vienna Online Journal on International Constitutional Law* 3 (2010).

27 See in more detail Ziegler, "International Law and EU law," 308 f.

28 See n 20.

29 This effect is derived either from the automatic incorporation of international law, which seems to be the prevailing opinion following the Court's judgments in Case 181/73 *Haegeman*, n 20 this chapter, and Case 104/81 *Kupferberg*, n 20 this chapter (Christine Kaddous, "Effects of International Agreements in the EU Legal Order," in *EU Foreign Relations Law Constitutional Fundamentals*, ed. Marise Cremona and Bruno de Witte (Oxford: Hart, 2008), 291, 293, 311), or from an unwritten blanket act of transformation which explains better how agreements are fully reviewable as acts of the member states (see Anne Peters, "The Position of International Law within the European Community Legal Order," *German Yearbook of International Law* 40 (1997): 9, 21 ff, esp. 34 f).

30 See Peters, "Position of International Law," 31 ff.

31 Franz C. Mayer, "European Law as Door Opener for Public International Law?" in *Droit International et Diversité des Cultures Juridiques – International Law and Diversity of Legal Cultures* (Paris: Pedone, 2008).

32 Case C-162/96 *Racke*, n 11 this chapter, para 46; Case C-286/90 *Anklagemyndigheden*, n 11 this chapter, para 12 ff; Pieter Jan Kuijper, "Customary International Law, Decisions of International Organisations and Other Techniques for Ensuring Respect for International Legal Rules in European Community Law," in Wouters, Nollkaemper, and de Wet, *The Europeanisation of International Law*, 87.

33 Case C-70/09 *Hengartner and Gassner v. Landesregierung Vorarlberg* EU:C:2010:430, para 36; Case C-386/08 *Brita GmbH v. Hauptzollamt Hamburg-Hafen* EU:C:2010:91, para 44 f; Case T-115/94 *Opel Austria GmbH v. Council* EU:T:1997:3; Case C-162/96 *Racke*, n 11 this chapter.

34 Joined Cases 89/85, 104/85, 114/85, 116/85, 117/85, and 125/85 to 129/85 *Ahlström Oy v. Commission* EU:C:1988:447; Case C-366/10 *ATAA*, n 11 this chapter, para 125 ff (in regard to the exercise of jurisdiction in airspace and flight over high seas and the question of the exclusivity of jurisdiction by the state of registration of aircraft).

35 Case 41/74 *Van Duyn v. Home Office* EU:C:1974:133, para 22.

36 Case C-200/02 *Chen v. Secretary of State for the Home Department* EU:C:2004:639, para 37; Case C-135/08 *Janko Rottmann v. Freistaat Bayern* EU:C:2010:104, paras 39, 48, 53; Case C-286/90 *Anklagemyndigheden*, n 11 this chapter.

37 Case C-364/10 *Hungary v. Slovakia* EU:C:2012:630, para 44.

38 I.e., regulations, directives, and decisions.

39 Case C-162/96 *Racke*, n 11 this chapter, para 46; Case C-366/10 *ATAA*, n 11 this chapter, paras 74, 84, 107.

40 Individuals can only rely on rules or principles of CIL where "first, those principles are capable of calling into question the competence of the European Union to adopt that act … and, second, the act in question is liable to affect rights which the individual derives from European Union law or to create obligations under European Union law in his regard." Case C-366/10 *ATAA*, n 11 this chapter, para 107. Eileen Denza, "International Aviation and the EU Carbon Trading Scheme: Comment on the Air Transport Association of America Case," *European Law Review* 37 (2012): 314, 324 points to the problem with this approach as it potentially precludes relevant CIL which is not directly effective as a standard of assessment of validity. See similar trend in regard to treaties, text around n 49.

41 Case C-162/96 *Racke*, n 11 this chapter, para 52; Case C-366/10 *ATAA*, n 11 this chapter, para 110.

42 Eeckhout, *EU External Relations Law*, 435, 331 ff.

43 Case C-308/06 *Intertanko*, n 15 this chapter, para 45; Joined Cases C-120/06 P and C-121/06 P *FIAMM and Fedon v. Council and Commission* EU:C:2008:476; Joined Cases 21/72 to 24/72 *International Fruit Co. NV*, n 14 this chapter, para 25 ff; Case C-192/89 *Sevince v. Staatssecretaris van Justitie* EU:C:1990:322; Case C-366/10 *ATAA*, n 11 this chapter, para 53 ff.

44 Enzo Cannizzaro, "Neo-Monism and the European Legal Order," in Cannizzaro, Palchetti, and Wessel, *International Law*, 35, 36 ff; cf. Eeckhout, *EU External Relations Law*, 353 (in detail 331 ff); Panos Koutrakos, *EU International Relations Law* (Oxford: Hart, 2006), 251 ff.

45 See n 50 and in favor of this approach, Eeckhout, *EU External Relations Law*, 375 ff (more strongly in favor in the first edition of his book Piet Eeckhout, *External Relations of the European Union* (Oxford: Oxford University Press, 2004), 302 ff); and Marco Dani, "Remedying European Legal Pluralism: The FIAMM and Fedon Litigation and the Judicial Protection of International Trade Bystanders," *European Journal of International Law* 21 (2010).

46 Critical of this restriction: Pieter J. Kuijper and Marco Bronckers, "WTO Law in the European Court of Justice," *Common Market Law Review* 42 (2005); and Steve Peers, "Fundamental Right or Political Whim? WTO Law and the European Court of Justice," in *The EU and WTO*, eds. Gráinne de Búrca and Joanne Scott (Oxford: Hart, 2001).

47 Joined Cases C-120/06 P and C-121/06 P *FIAMM and Fedon*, n 43 this chapter, paras 108 ff, 310, 325.

48 Case C-308/06 *Intertanko*, n 15 this chapter, paras 54, 58, 65. Similarly restrictive in regard the Kyoto Protocol Case C-366/10 *ATAA*, n 11 this chapter, para 75 ff.

49 Case C-308/06 *Intertanko*, n 15 this chapter, paras 59, 61.

50 See text around n 40.

51 Cf. in more detail, Ziegler, "International Law and EU law," 301 ff. In favor of the approach of the CJEU (albeit critical of the narrow interpretation of the subjective rights in Case C-308/06 *Intertanko*, n 15 this chapter, see Eeckhout, *EU External Relations Law*, 382 ff.

52 A similar approach was taken in regard to the Chicago Convention on International Civil Aviation in Case C-366/10 *ATAA*, n 11 this chapter, para 69 ff.

53 Joined Cases C-402/05 and C-415/05 *Kadi I*, n 1 this chapter; Joined Cases C-584/10 P, C-593/10 P, and C-595/10 P *European Commission et al. v. Yassin Abdullah Kadi* (Kadi II) EU:C:2013:518.

54 Similar in regard to the Chicago Convention on International Civil Aviation in Case C-366/10 *ATAA*, n 11 this chapter, para 69 ff.

55 Joined Cases C-402/05 and C-415/05 *Kadi I*, n 1 this chapter, para 306 ff.

56 See text around n 69.

57 As criticized previously, see text near n 16.

58 Case T-315/01 *Kadi v. Council and Commission* (Kadi I (CFI)) EU:T:2005:332, para 192 ff.

59 The international obligation remains relevant in the context of interpretation in conformity with international law.

60 Joined Cases C-402/05 and C-415/05 *Kadi I*, n 1 this chapter, para 317.

61 Peter Hilpold, "EU Law and UN Law in Conflict: The *Kadi* Case," *Max Planck Yearbook of United Nations Law* 13 (2009): 141, 160; Ziegler, "International law and EU law," 289 ff.

62 Joined Cases C-402/05 and C-415/05 *Kadi I*, n 1 this chapter, para 287.

63 Ibid.; and Joined Cases C-584/10 P, C-593/10 P, and C-595/10 P *Kadi II*, n 53 this chapter.

64 See text at n 73.

65 Joined Cases C-584/10 P, C-593/10 P, and C-595/10 P *Kadi II*, n 53 this chapter, para 66. However, autonomy was very much in the foreground again in Opinion 2/13 *ECHR*, n 21 this chapter.

66 Case C-162/96 *Racke*, n 11 this chapter, para 46.

67 For example, in France, Greece, and Spain.

68 It compares favorably with countries that accord incorporated treaties only equal rank with a statute, such as in the United Kingdom (apart from the TFEU), the United States, Germany, and South Africa; Katja S. Ziegler, "Strengthening the Rule of Law, but Fragmenting International Law: The *Kadi* Decision of the ECJ from the Perspective of Human Rights," *Human Rights Law Review* 9 (2009): 295.

69 Article 53 VCLT. Cf. Case T-315/01 *Kadi I* (CFI), n 58 this chapter, para 226 ff – albeit with regard to the review of the UN Security Council.

70 Case C-473/93 *Commission v. Luxembourg* EU:C:1996:263; Case C-62/98 *Commission v. Portugal* EU:C:2000:358.

71 Case C-205/06 *Commission v. Austria* EU:C:2009:118, para 36 ff; see also Case C-249/06 *Commission v. Sweden* EU:C:2009:119; Case C-118/07 *Commission v. Finland* EU:C:2009:715. Critically, Nikolaos Lavranos, "Protecting European Law from International Law," *European Foreign Affairs Review* 15 (2010): 265, 279 ff.

72 See text around n 64.

73 Joined Cases C-402/05 P and C-415/05 P *Kadi I*, n 1 this chapter, para 303. See also paras 282 ff, 304 ff. Ziegler, "Strengthening the Rule of Law," 297.

74 See, e.g., Case C-364/10 *Hungary v. Slovakia*, n 37 this chapter, para 44, where limitations on citizenship are fleshed out by the CIL on the status of heads of states – direct effect or interpretation?

75 The Court has interpreted EU law in the light of CIL and general principles of international law on some occasions, e.g., in regard to the nationality of persons and ships, *pacta sunt servanda*, the *rebus sic stantibus* rule, and interpretation in good faith in the law of treaties. See already discussed in the text around n 32; Case C-308/06 *Intertanko*, n 15 this chapter, paras 51–52; Eeckhout, *EU External Relations Law*, 355 ff; Kuijper, "Customary International Law," 92 ff; and Federico Casolari, "Giving Indirect Effect to International Law within the EU Legal Order: The Doctrine of Consistent Interpretation," in Cannizzaro, Palchetti, and Wessel, *International Law*. On other occasions it used both direct effect of customary law in EU law and the interpretation of EU law (the notion of legitimate expectations) in the light of CIL. See Case T-115/94 *Opel Austria*, n 33 this chapter, paras 90 ff; and Eeckhout, *EU External Relations Law*, 386 ff.

76 Case C-53/96 *Hermès International v. FHT Marketing Choice BV* EU:C:1998:292, para 28; Case C-61/94 *Commission v. Germany* (International Dairy Arrangement) EU:C:1996:313, para 52.

77 Opinion of Advocate General Kokott in Case C-308/06 *Intertanko*, n 15 this chapter, paras 107 ff.

78 See text around n 15 and 58.

79 Joined Cases C-402/05 P and C-415/05 P *Kadi I*, n 1 this chapter, para 296 f. Case C-84/95 *Bosphorus Hava Yollari Turizm ve Ticaret AS v. Minister for Transport, Energy and Communication and Others* EU:C:1996:312, para 13 ff; Kuijper, "Customary International Law," 100.

80 See for the International Covenant on Civil and Political Rights and the Convention on the Rights of the Child: Case C-244/06 *Dynamic Medien v. Avides Media* EU:C:2008:85, paras 39–41; Case C-540/03 *Parliament v. Council* (Family Reunification Directive) EU:C:2006:429, para 37; for the 1951 Refugee Convention: Joined Cases C-175/08, 176/08, 178/08, and 179/08 *Salahadin Abdulla and Others* EU:C:2010:105, para 52 ff; and Case C-31/09 *Bolbol v. Bevándorlási és Állampolgársági Hivatal* EU:C:2010:351, para 38. For the European Convention on Nationality and the Convention on the Reduction of Statelessness and the Universal Declaration of Human Rights, see Case C-135/08 *Janko Rottmann*, n 36 this chapter, para 52 ff. For the International Covenant on Economic, Social and Cultural Rights, see Case C-73/08 *Bressol and Others v. Gouvernement de la Communauté francaise* EU:C:2010:181, paras 85 ff. See in detail Opinion of Advocate General Sharpston, paras 135 ff; and Marco Bronckers, "The Relationship of the EC Courts with Other International Tribunals: Non-Committal, Respectful or Submissive?" *Common Market Law Review* 44 (2007): 602, 610–627.

81 See, e.g., for the Chicago Convention, Case C-366/10 *ATAA*, n 11 this chapter, paras 90 ff, esp. 104. Further details in Ziegler, "International Law and EU Law," 305 ff.

82 Opinion of Advocate General Kokott in Case C-308/06 *Intertanko*, n 15 this chapter, paras 80 ff, esp 93, 96, 101, 111; critically as "excessively charitable towards the drafting of the Directive," Eileen Denza, "A Note on Intertanko," *European Law Review* 33 (2008): 870, 874.

83 Cf. Piet Eeckhout, "Case C-308/06, *The Queen on the application of Intertanko and Others v Secretary of State for Transport*, judgment of the Court of Justice (Grand Chamber) of 3 June 2008," *Common Market Law Review* 46 (2009): 2041, 2056.

84 Case C-308/06 *Intertanko*, n 15 this chapter, para 51.
85 See text around n 78.
86 Case C-533/08 *TNT Express Nederland BV v. AXA Versicherung AG* EU:C:2010:243, para 56, in respect of the Geneva Convention on the Contract for the International Carriage of Goods by Road of 19 May 1956.
87 Case C-481/13 *Mohammad Ferooz Qurbani*, n 15 this chapter, paras 22–24.
88 Joined Cases C-402/05 P and C-415/05 P *Kadi I*, n 1 this chapter, para 296–297.
89 As the CFI had held in Case T-315/01 *Kadi I* (CFI), n 58 this chapter, para 192 f.
90 This was the approach of the European Court of Human Rights in *Al-Jedda v. United Kingdom* Appl no 27021/08 (2011) 53 EHRR 23, para 102. In the same vein Allan Rosas, "International responsibility of the EU and the European Court of Justice," in Evans and Koutrakos, *The International Responsibility of the European Union*, 139, 146.
91 Oliver Dörr, "Article 31: General Rule of Interpretation," in *Vienna Convention on the Law of Treaties*, ed. Oliver Dörr and Kirsten Schmalenbach (Berlin: Springer, 2012), 521, para 6.
92 See n 10. See in detail Antonios Tzanakopoulos, *Disobeying the Security Council: Countermeasures against Wrongful Sanctions* (Oxford: Oxford University Press, 2011), esp. 154 ff.
93 See n 20.
94 Case C-162/96 *Racke*, n 11 this chapter, para 55; Case C-286/90 *Anklagemyndigheden*, n 11 this chapter, para 9 f; Case C-405/92 *Etablissements Armand Mondiet SA v. Armement Islais SARL* EU:C:1993:906, paras 13–15; Case C-308/06 *Intertanko*, n 15 this chapter, para 51; Joined Cases C-402/05 and C-415/05 *Kadi I*, n 1 this chapter, para 291 f; Case C-366/10 *ATAA*, n 11 this chapter, para 101.
95 See text around n 65.
96 Cf. de Witte, "International Law as a Tool for the EU."
97 The case of the WTO DSB has been mentioned earlier in this chapter (Joined Cases C-120/06 P and C-121/06 P *FIAMM and Fedon*, n 43 this chapter), see text after n 47.
98 In Opinion 2/94 *ECHR* EU:C:1996:140 the Court held that the EU did not have competence to accede to the Convention even though it had developed human rights within the EU legal order to limit EU action. See also Sionaidh Douglas-Scott, "A Tale of Two Courts: Luxembourg, Strasbourg and the Growing European Human Rights *Acquis*," *Common Market Law Review* 43 (2006): 629–650 ff, where the author points out that the CJEU only referred to the jurisprudence of the European Court of Human Rights for the first time in 1996 in the Case C-13/94 *P v. S* EU:C:1996:170, whereas it had been referring to the ECHR for over twenty years at the time. Article 6(2) TEU, following the amendments of the Lisbon Treaty, now provides a competence, but the accession process has been slow and cumbersome (see Craig, "EU Accession to the ECHR" for further details), and concerns have been voiced as to how the jurisdiction of the ECHR will work out in practice in a post-accession Europe: Eeckhout, *EU External Relations Law*, 381.
99 Case C-459/03 *Commission v. Ireland* (MOX plant) EU:C:2006:345, albeit facilitated by an escape route in Article 282 UNCLOS; Nikolaos Lavranos, "The Epilogue in the MOX Plant Dispute: An End Without Findings," *European Energy and Environmental Law Reporter* 18 (2009): 117–121, 180–184; Inge Govaere, "Beware of the Trojan Horse: Dispute Settlement in (Mixed) Agreements and the Autonomy of the EU Legal Order," in *Mixed Agreements Revisited: The EU and its Member States in the World*, ed. Christophe Hillion and Panos Koutrakos (Oxford: Hart, 2010).
100 Opinion 2/13 *ECHR*, n 21 this chapter.
101 See in more detail Ziegler, "International Law and EU Law," 278 ff.
102 See, for example, Eeckhout, *EU External Relations Law*, 355.
103 See text of the provision near n 11.
104 Denza, "EU Carbon Trading Scheme," 322. Although these cases may be quoted for the selective use of international law by the CJEU to support outcomes under EU law, it is this mechanism of

engagement that deserves wider consideration. The CJEU, however, has ignored this link between constitutionalization and legitimacy in the form of external human rights control by its parochial focus on autonomy in Opinion 2/13 *ECHR*, n 21 this chapter.

105 Case C-285/12 *Aboubacar Diakité v. Commissaire général aux réfugiés et aix apatrides* EU:C:2014:39, paras 27 ff.

References

Alston, Philip, ed. *The EU and Human Rights*. Oxford: Oxford University Press, 1999.

Bronckers, Marco. "The Relationship of the EC Courts with Other International Tribunals: Non-committal, Respectful or Submissive?" *Common Market Law Review* 44 (2007): 601–627.

Cannizzaro, Enzo, ed. *The European Union as an Actor in International Relations*. The Hague: Kluwer Law International, 2002.

Cannizzaro, Enzo. "Neo-Monism and the European Legal Order." In Cannizzaro, Palchetti, and Wessel, *International Law*, 35–58.

Cannizzaro, Enzo, Paolo Palchetti, and Ramses A. Wessel, eds. *International Law as Law of the European Union*. Leiden: Martinus Nijhoff, 2011.

Casolari, Federico. "Giving Indirect Effect to International Law within the EU Legal Order: The Doctrine of Consistent Interpretation." In Cannizzaro, Palchetti, and Wessel, *International Law*, 395–415.

Craig, Paul. "EU Accession to the ECHR: Competence, Procedure and Substance." *Fordham International Law Journal* 36 (2013): 1115–1150.

Dani, Marco. "Remedying European Legal Pluralism: The FIAMM and Fedon Litigation and the Judicial Protection of International Trade Bystanders." *European Journal of International Law* 21 (2010): 303–340.

Denza, Eileen. "A Note on Intertanko." *European Law Review* 33 (2008): 870–879.

Denza, Eileen. "International Aviation and the EU Carbon Trading Scheme: Comment on the Air Transport Association of America Case." *European Law Review* 37 (2012): 314–326.

de Witte, Bruno. "International Law as a Tool for the European Union." *European Constitutional Law Review* 5 (2009): 265–283.

Dörr, Oliver. "Article 31: General Rule of Interpretation." In *Vienna Convention on the Law of Treaties*, ed. Oliver Dörr and Kirsten Schmalenbach, 521–570. Berlin: Springer, 2012.

Douglas-Scott, Sionaidh. "A Tale of Two Courts: Luxembourg, Strasbourg and the Growing European Human Rights *Acquis*." *Common Market Law Review* 43 (2006): 629–666.

Eeckhout, Piet. *External Relations of the European Union*. Oxford: Oxford University Press, 2004.

Eeckhout, Piet. "Case C-308/06, *The Queen on the application of Intertanko and Others v Secretary of State for Transport*, judgment of the Court of Justice (Grand Chamber) of 3 June 2008." *Common Market Law Review* 46 (2009): 2041–2057.

Eeckhout, Piet. *EU External Relations Law*. Oxford: Oxford University Press, 2011.

Evans, Malcolm D. and Panos Koutrakos, eds. *The International Responsibility of the European Union: European and International Perspectives*. Oxford: Hart, 2013.

Fassbender, Bardo. "The United Nations Charter as Constitution of the International Community." *Columbia Journal of Transnational Law* 36 (1998): 529–619.

Govaere, Inge. "Beware of the Trojan Horse: Dispute Settlement in (Mixed) Agreements and the Autonomy of the EU Legal Order." In *Mixed Agreements Revisited: The EU and its Member States in the World*, edited by Christophe Hillion and Panos Koutrakos, 187–207. Oxford: Hart, 2010.

Hilpold, Peter. "EU Law and UN Law in Conflict: The *Kadi* Case." *Max Planck Yearbook of United Nations Law* 13 (2009): 141–181.

Kaddous, Christine. "Effects of International Agreements in the EU Legal Order." In *EU Foreign Relations Law Constitutional Fundamentals*, edited by Marise Cremona and Bruno de Witte, 291–312. Oxford: Hart, 2008.

Kochenov, Dimitry and Fabian Amtenbrink. "The Active Paradigm of the Study of the EU's Place in the World: An Introduction." In *The European Union's Shaping of the International Legal Order*, edited by Dimitry Kochenov and Fabian Amtenbrink, 1–18. Cambridge: Cambridge University Press, 2013.

Koutrakos, Panos. *EU International Relations Law*. Oxford: Hart, 2006.

Kuijper, Pieter Jan. "Customary International Law, Decisions of International Organisations and Other Techniques for Ensuring Respect for International Legal Rules in European Community Law." In Wouters, Nollkaemper, and de Wet, *The Europeanisation of International Law*, 87–106.

Kuijper, Pieter J. and Marco Bronckers. "WTO Law in the European Court of Justice." *Common Market Law Review* 42 (2005): 1313–1355.

Lavranos, Nikolaos. "The Epilogue in the MOX Plant Dispute: An End Without Findings." *European Energy and Environmental Law Review* 18 (2009): 180–184.

Lavranos, Nikolaos. "Protecting European Law from International Law." *European Foreign Affairs Review* 15 (2010): 265–282.

Lenaerts, Koen and Eddy de Smijter. "The European Union as an Actor in International Law." *Yearbook of European Law* 19 (1999): 95–138.

Mayer, Franz C. "European Law as Door Opener for Public International Law?" In *Droit International et Diversité des Cultures Juridiques – International Law and Diversity of Legal Cultures*, edited by Société Française pour le Droit Internationale, 241–255. Paris: Pedone, 2008.

Nijman, Janne and André Nollkaemper, eds. *New Perspectives on the Divide between National and International Law*. Oxford: Oxford University Press, 2007.

Nollkaemper, André. "The Duality of Direct Effect in International Law," *European Journal of International Law* 25 (2014): 105–125.

Orakhelashvili, Alexander. "1969 Vienna Convention. Article 30: Application of Successive Treaties Relating to the Same Subject Matter." In *The Vienna Convention on the Law of Treaties: A Commentary*, edited by Olivier Corten and Pierre Klein, 764–803. Oxford: Oxford University Press, 2011.

Paulus, Andreas. "The Emergence of the International Community and the Divide between International and Domestic Law." In Nijman and Nollkaemper, *New Perspectives*, 216–249. Oxford: Oxford University Press, 2007.

Peers, Steve. "Fundamental Right or Political Whim? WTO Law and the European Court of Justice." In *The EU and WTO: Legal and Constitutional Issues*, edited by Gráinne de Búrca and Joanne Scott, 111–130. Oxford: Hart, 2001.

Peters, Anne. "The Position of International Law within the European Community Legal Order." *German Yearbook of International Law* 40 (1997): 9–77.

Peters, Anne. "Supremacy Lost: International Law Meets Domestic Constitutional Law." *Vienna Online Journal on International Constitutional Law* 3 (2010): 170–198.

Rosas, Allan. "International Responsibility of the EU and the European Court of Justice." In Evans and Koutrakos, *International Responsibility of the European Union*, 139–159.

Smith, Karen E. "The European Union at the Human Rights Council: Speaking with One Voice but Having Little Influence." *Journal of European Public Policy* 17 (2010): 224–241.

Tzanakopoulos, Antonios. *Disobeying the Security Council: Countermeasures against Wrongful Sanctions*. Oxford: Oxford University Press, 2011.

Walter, Christian. "International Law in a Process of Constitutionalization." In Nijman and Nollkaemper, *New Perspectives*, 191–215.

Wessel, Ramses A. "Reconsidering the Relationship between International and EU Law: Towards a Content-Based Approach?" In Cannizzaro, Palchetti, and Wessel, *International Law*, 7–33. Leiden: Martinus Nijhoff, 2011.

Williams, Andrew. *EU Human Rights Policies: A Study in Irony*. Oxford: Oxford University Press, 2004.

Wouters, Jan, Anna-Luise Chané, and Jed Odermatt, "Improving the EU's Status in the UN and the UN System: An Objective Without a Strategy?" Working paper no. 133, KU Leuven Centre for Global Governance Studies, March 2014.

Wouters, Jan, André Nollkaemper, and Erika De Wet, eds. *The Europeanisation of International Law: The Status of International Law in the EU and its Member States*. The Hague: Asser Press, 2008.

Ziegler, Katja S. "Strengthening the Rule of Law, but Fragmenting International Law: The *Kadi* Decision of the ECJ from the Perspective of Human Rights." *Human Rights Law Review* 9 (2009): 288–305.

Ziegler, Katja S. "International Law and EU Law: Between Asymmetric Constitutionalisations and Fragmentation." In *Research Handbook on the Theory and History of International Law*, edited by Alexander Orakhelashvili, 268–327. Cheltenham: Edward Elgar, 2011.

5

The Effect of EU Law

Anthony Arnull

Introduction

The Court of Justice of the European Union (CJEU) increasingly resembles an aging actor. After a meteoric early career, it finds itself typecast and unable to adapt to changing tastes. Nowhere is this more apparent than in the field considered in this chapter: the effect of EU law in the national courts of the member states and its status vis-à-vis overlapping rules of national law. The basic doctrines crafted by the CJEU marked a significant departure from the standard model of international law and made a major contribution to the early development of the common market. However, the Court has been less successful at accommodating the loss of its role as the leading player on the European legal stage and growing demands for accountability and transparency in the European Union.

Direct Effect and Primacy

The CJEU's big break came in 1963 to 1964 over a period of less than eighteen months. It was triggered by the silence of the Treaty establishing the European Economic Community (EEC) on how conflicts between the treaty and provisions of national law arising in the national courts should be resolved. With the benefit of hindsight, the omission of a provision dealing with the matter seems odd. It is possible that the negotiators could not agree, but perhaps it is more likely that they simply assumed the EEC Treaty was no different from ordinary international treaties and that its effect within the member states would depend on their domestic law.[1] In any event, the issue initially attracted little attention from commentators.[2]

However, two features of the EEC Treaty challenged the conventional wisdom. One was that the achievement of its policy objectives, particularly the establishment of a common market, might have been fatally compromised had the treaty's internal effect differed from member state to member state. Another was that the innovative preliminary rulings procedure allowed national courts to ask the CJEU what effect the treaty had in domestic legal proceedings.

A Companion to European Union Law and International Law, First Edition.
Edited by Dennis Patterson and Anna Södersten.

That question was raised in *Van Gend en Loos v. Nederlandse Administratie der Belastingen*,[3] one of the most momentous cases the CJEU has ever decided. It turned on the question of whether the applicant could rely on Article 12 EEC to challenge an increase in the import duty payable on imports of a chemical from Germany into the Netherlands. Article 12 was addressed to the member states and contained no express reference to the rights of individuals. However, the CJEU ruled, rejecting the advice of Advocate General Roemer, that Article 12 produced direct effect and created individual rights that national courts had to protect. The CJEU observed that the treaty did more than merely create mutual obligations between the contracting states. On the contrary,

> the [Union] constitutes a new legal order of international law for the benefit of which the states have limited their sovereign rights ... and the subjects of which comprise not only Member States but also their nationals ... [Union] law therefore not only imposes obligations on individuals but is also intended to confer upon them rights which become part of their legal heritage.[4]

Article 12, the CJEU noted, contained "a clear and unconditional prohibition."[5] Its implementation was not dependent on further action by the national legislatures. These features helped make it "ideally adapted to produce direct effects in the legal relationship between Member States and their subjects." The fact that the article was addressed to the member states did not, in the CJEU's view, imply that their nationals could not rely on it. Although the treaty contained provisions enabling the Commission or a member state to take action before the CJEU against any member state they considered to be in breach of its treaty obligations, it did not follow that individuals could not rely on such breaches in the national courts. Denying them the possibility of doing so would deprive them of direct legal protection of their rights. Moreover, by enlisting an army of private enforcers it would strengthen the obligations imposed on member states by the treaty.

Article 12 was negative in character, which meant that all a national court had to do was deprive of legal effect a provision which was inconsistent with the treaty. Moreover, the dispute was a vertical one, involving an action by a company against a public authority. It subsequently emerged, however, that neither factor was decisive, treaty provisions also being found to be capable of producing direct effect when positive in character.[6] The CJEU also made it clear that treaty provisions might have that effect in horizontal proceedings between private parties,[7] further evidence of the Union's tendency to push the boundaries of international law.

In *Van Gend* the Court was able, through the preliminary rulings procedure, to lay down a common approach to the internal effect of the treaty rather than leaving it to the national courts to craft their own inevitably divergent approaches.[8] But the CJEU's ruling provided only a partial solution. Although it made it clear that Article 12 could be invoked by the applicant before the referring court, it did not say how that court was to resolve the conflict between Article 12 and the inconsistent provision of Dutch law on which the respondent authority was relying. The referring court did not need to put that question to the CJEU in *Van Gend* because it was resolved by national law, the Dutch Constitution giving directly effective provisions of international agreements primacy over national law.

The primacy question[9] was raised directly in *Costa v. ENEL*,[10] a reference by an Italian judge concerning the compatibility with the EEC Treaty of a 1962 law nationalizing the Italian electricity industry. The issue was potentially difficult. Although the treaty was subject to the established international law principle of *pacta sunt servanda*, that principle applied only to relations between the contracting parties.[11] International law had not previously been thought to impose on national courts a duty to enforce treaty provisions which conflicted with national law.[12]

The CJEU's task was facilitated by its earlier ruling in *Van Gend*, which would have been deprived of much of its impact if a directly effective treaty provision could be overridden by a contrary rule of national law. The CJEU accordingly declared that

> the law stemming from the Treaty, an independent source of law, could not, because of its special and original nature, be overridden by domestic legal provisions, however framed, without being deprived of its character as [Union] law and without the legal basis of the [Union] itself being called into question.
>
> The transfer by the States from their domestic legal system to the [Union] legal system of the rights and obligations arising under the Treaty carries with it a permanent limitation of their sovereign rights, against which a subsequent unilateral act incompatible with the concept of the [Union] cannot prevail ...[13]

The CJEU's reasoning implied that Union law would take precedence regardless of the constitutional status under national law of the conflicting domestic norm and regardless of the date on which that norm was adopted, whether before or after the entry into force of the treaty. That implication was confirmed in *Internationale Handelsgesellschaft v. Einfuhr- und Vorratsstelle Getreide.*[14] In that case, a German court referred to the CJEU two questions on the validity of two regulations. The referring court took the view that the contested measures were incompatible with certain fundamental principles contained in the German Constitution that had to be protected within the framework of the Union.

There were three potentially significant differences between *Costa v. ENEL* and *Internationale Handelsgesellschaft.* In the latter case, the national provisions in dispute were adopted *before* the entry into force of the treaty. Moreover, they had constitutional status. By contrast, the rules of Union law at issue were contained not in the treaty itself but in acts of the Union institutions. None of those factors deterred the CJEU from ruling that

> [r]ecourse to the legal rules or concepts of national law in order to judge the validity of measures adopted by the institutions of the [Union] would have an adverse effect on the uniformity and efficacy of [Union] law. The validity of such measures can only be judged in the light of [Union] law ... Therefore the validity of a [Union] measure or its effect within a Member State cannot be affected by allegations that it runs counter to either fundamental rights as formulated by the constitution of that State or the principles of a national constitutional structure.[15]

For the CJEU to have accepted that the validity of provisions of Union law could be tested against rules of national law, even those of constitutional status, would have been wholly incompatible with the fundamental principles of the Union legal order it was in the process of developing. However, the CJEU sugared the pill of the momentous conclusion it had reached by acknowledging that "respect for fundamental rights ... must be ensured within the framework of the structure and objectives of the [Union]."[16] It concluded that the contested provisions did not infringe fundamental rights. Some national courts were not entirely reassured by the approach of the CJEU, as we shall see.

In several member states, jurisdiction to rule on the constitutionality of a domestic provision belongs not to the ordinary courts but to a special constitutional court. This has given rise to difficulty where a national provision is said to be incompatible with Union law, which may itself have been given effect internally by an amendment to the constitution. The issue arose in *Amministrazione delle Finanze dello Stato v. Simmenthal*, a reference from an Italian court where the Italian Finance Administration argued that an ordinary court could not simply refuse to apply a national law considered to be in conflict with Union law. Until the law in question was amended, the matter had to be brought before the Italian Constitutional Court, which alone had the power to declare the disputed law unconstitutional. The CJEU made it clear that

> a national court which is called upon, within the limits of its jurisdiction, to apply provisions of [Union] law is under a duty to give full effect to those provisions, if necessary refusing of its own motion to apply any conflicting provision of national legislation, even if adopted subsequently, and it is not necessary for the court to request or await the prior setting aside of such [a] provision by legislative or other constitutional means.[17]

It would obviously have been incompatible with the binding force of directly effective provisions of Union law for a national court before which such provisions were invoked to be deprived of jurisdiction to apply them. However, the CJEU was not saying that the national court was expected to quash the inconsistent national provisions, merely that it had to decline to give effect to them in the case pending before it. Those provisions might remain applicable in other cases. The existence of the incompatibility did not in itself render them void.

This was reiterated in *Ministero delle Finanze v. IN. CO. GE.'90 and Others*.[18] In that case, the Commission argued on the basis of *Simmenthal* that a member state had no power to adopt a provision that was incompatible with Union law and that any such provision had to be treated by the national courts as nonexistent. The CJEU expressly rejected that argument, declaring that the national court was merely obliged to "disapply" the inconsistent rule of national law. Be that as it may, the maintenance in force of national rules which are incompatible with provisions of Union law constitutes a breach by the member state concerned of its obligations under the treaty which the Commission is entitled to challenge in infringement proceedings under Article 258 of the Treaty on the Functioning of the European Union (TFEU).[19]

It is not only national courts that must apply the doctrines of primacy and direct effect. Those doctrines also bind national administrative bodies,[20] even though such bodies are not able to seek guidance from the CJEU under the preliminary rulings procedure, which is confined to courts and tribunals of the member states.[21] Primacy and direct effect may even require administrative bodies to reopen decisions which have become final.[22] However, overriding interests such as legal certainty have sometimes led the CJEU to limit the effect of its rulings. In *Defrenne v. SABENA*,[23] for example, it was held that the direct effect of a treaty article on equal pay for men and women could not be invoked in respect of periods which preceded the date of the judgment except where proceedings had already been brought. In *Winner Wetten*,[24] the CJEU even acknowledged the possibility that it might exceptionally postpone the ousting effect of directly effective provisions of Union law until some future date, although it did not consider this justified in the circumstances of that case. However, in *Inter-Environnement Wallonie v. Région Wallonne*[25] the CJEU permitted a national court to preserve temporarily a national measure adopted in breach of a directive on environmental protection where annulment of the measure with retroactive effect would have been more damaging to the environment.

In 1986, Rasmussen argued in his famous book on the CJEU that excessive activism was undermining its authority and legitimacy. He referred to *Costa v. ENEL* as one of a number of cases "in which the Court probably pushed its gap-filling activities beyond the proper scope of judicial involvement in society's law and policy making."[26] However, the absence in the treaty of a provision clearly stating that Union law was to take precedence over inconsistent provisions of national law should not be taken to imply a consensus among the signatories to the treaty that this result was not intended. Once the question was raised by a national court, the CJEU had no choice but to craft an answer that was consistent with the spirit of the treaty. In any event, *Van Gend* and *Costa* attracted no immediate political response.[27]

The practice of consensus which emerged following the Luxembourg Compromise of January 1966 put to rest lingering hopes that the common market might be established by the end of the transitional period.[28] It was in this context that the CJEU applied the doctrine of direct effect in a series of groundbreaking preliminary rulings on fundamental planks of the common market, thereby helping to ensure that the integration process did not lose momentum. The year 1974 was particularly remarkable. In that year, the CJEU delivered several major rulings which would help drive the project forward, holding in particular that the treaty rules on the right of establishment[29] and the freedom to provide services[30] were capable of producing direct effect from the end of the transitional period notwithstanding the Council's failure to adopt the directives envisaged by the treaty.

Direct Effect and Union Acts

The 1970s marked the apogee of the CJEU's influence and prestige and helped create its image as both the architect and the savior of the integration process. Unencumbered by a large body of previous case law and properly functioning political institutions, the CJEU was able to craft a constitutional framework for an enterprise to whose spirit the CJEU itself held the key. Over the next thirty years or so, the institutions and the member states began to play a more active role in the functioning of the Union. At the same time, the inexorable growth in the volume of case law presented the CJEU with new challenges: how to decide cases promptly while at the same time reconciling them with previous decisions. Against that background, much of the case law on direct effect became technical and incoherent. This was almost entirely due to the CJEU's inability to lay down a clear line about the direct effect of a particular type of Union act and then stick to it. The act in question was the directive, which plays such an important role in helping to achieve the policy objectives of the Union.

The directive is one of the three types of binding act described in Article 288 TFEU, the other two being the regulation and the decision.[31] Article 288 describes the regulation as having "general application" and as being "binding in its entirety and directly applicable in all Member States." Although the CJEU sometimes uses the terms "direct applicability" and "direct effect" as if they were interchangeable, the former is better understood as describing the self-executing quality of regulations: they take effect throughout the Union on their own terms as soon as they are adopted. Their provisions are capable of having both vertical and horizontal direct effect in the *Van Gend* sense. As with the treaty, whether particular provisions do so depends on their terms and whether they are unconditional and sufficiently precise. By and large the legal status of regulations has not caused the CJEU much difficulty. The same is true of decisions, the legal effects of which are concisely captured in Article 288. The directive, however, has spawned a vast and meandering case law which can seem to defy understanding even when accompanied by copious supplies of black coffee.

In a paragraph which has never been changed since the signing of the EEC Treaty, Article 288 provides that "[a] directive shall be binding, as to the result to be achieved, upon each Member State to which it is addressed, but shall leave to the national authorities the choice of form and methods." Thus, when a directive is timeously and correctly implemented by its addressee member states, it fades from view and those affected need concern themselves only with the national implementing legislation. But if, as is too often the case, a member state is late in giving effect to a directive or does not do so properly, can an individual intended to benefit from it rely on it directly before the national courts?

In a series of cases decided in the 1970s, the CJEU gave a semi-affirmative answer to that question.[32] In vertical cases where the deadline for giving effect to a directive had passed,[33] it said, it would be incompatible with the binding effect of a directive to rule out the possibility that it might be invoked by individuals in the national courts where its provisions were unconditional and sufficiently precise. If individuals were prevented from doing so, the "useful effect" of the directive would be weakened.[34] A member state could not in such cases be permitted to "rely, as against individuals, on its own failure to perform the obligations which the directive entails."[35]

Rasmussen was highly critical of this case law, arguing that it was not supported by the text of the treaty and declaring, "To many a European lawyer this is revolting judicial behavior."[36] That view was reflected in the decisions of some national courts, notably that of the French Conseil d'Etat in the notorious *Cohn-Bendit* case of 1978.[37] There, in flagrant disregard of the case law of the CJEU, the Conseil d'Etat held that an individual could not rely on a directive to challenge an individual administrative act.[38] National judicial opposition may well have influenced the CJEU when it confronted the question of whether directives could not only confer rights but also impose obligations directly on individuals, in other words, produce horizontal direct effect.

In *Marshall v. Southampton and South-West Hampshire Area Health Authority*,[39] the CJEU appeared to draw a line in the sand. The appellant claimed that her dismissal by the respondent authority was contrary to a Union directive. Having found that the directive precluded the dismissal of someone in the position of the appellant, the CJEU considered whether she could rely on it. The respondent authority had been described by the referring court as an "emanation of the State," but both the authority and the United Kingdom argued that, where the state acted as an employer, it should be treated in the same way as a private employer. Directives, they said, were incapable of imposing obligations directly on private bodies. The CJEU's response was that

> according to Article [288 TFEU] the binding nature of a directive, which constitutes the basis for the possibility of relying on the directive before a national court, exists only in relation to "each Member State to which it is addressed". It follows that a directive may not of itself impose obligations on an individual and that a provision of a directive may not be relied upon as such against such a person.[40]

The CJEU concluded that it was irrelevant whether the state was acting as an employer or a public authority: in either case it was necessary "to prevent the State from taking advantage of its own failure to comply with [Union] law."[41]

Weatherill observed,

> In return for such clarification and such restraint [the CJEU] hoped to gain from the national courts an acceptance of that more restricted notion of direct effect – against the state alone. The tactic seems largely to have worked.[42]

Nonetheless, there were various problems with the CJEU's reasoning. Its emphasis on the wording of Article 288 seemed inconsistent with its approach in *Van Gend* and *Defrenne*, both of which also concerned treaty provisions addressed to the member states. In *Defrenne*, a horizontal case, the CJEU stated,

> the fact that certain provisions of the Treaty are formally addressed to the member states does not prevent rights from being conferred at the same time on any individual who has an interest in the performance of the duties thus laid down.[43]

The importance attached by the CJEU to the notion of "state" meant that a claimant's rights might depend exclusively on the status of the defendant, an apparently arbitrary distinction. The CJEU seemed to be under the mistaken assumption that the boundaries of the state were static and that there was a Union-wide consensus about where they were located. The result was that the enforceability of directives, which are intended to lay down common rules, might paradoxically vary from member state to member state.

Around the early 1990s, a number of advocates general urged the CJEU to reconsider the *Marshall* case law and in *Faccini Dori v. Recreb*[44] the CJEU asked all the member states for their views on the matter. Only one of them favored a departure from *Marshall* and the CJEU rejected the idea, declaring that the effect of extending its case law on the vertical direct effect of directives

> to the sphere of relations between individuals would be to recognize a power in the [Union] to enact obligations for individuals with immediate effect, whereas it has competence to do so only where it is empowered to adopt regulations.[45]

One argument conspicuously absent from the judgment in *Marshall*, but which might have helped justify the outcome, is based on the principle of legal certainty. It is essentially that individuals cannot be expected to compare the applicable national law with relevant Union directives in order to establish their legal obligations. In *Wells*,[46] the CJEU belatedly acknowledged the relevance of the principle of legal certainty in this context, though it perhaps went too far in suggesting that it was the *only* reason why directives do not impose obligations on individuals. In any event, the post-*Marshall* case law had by then introduced so many qualifications to the apparently straightforward rule laid down in that decision that it had begun to seem that legal certainty might be damaged more by denying directives the capacity to create obligations for individuals than by allowing them to do so.

Mitigating factors (1): The meaning of "state"

Ambivalence on the part of the CJEU about the conclusion in *Marshall* was evident from the outset. Its conclusion that the respondent in that case effectively constituted a member state for the purposes of Article 288 was unconvincing. It could not in any sense have been said to be seeking to "take advantage of its own failure" to comply with Union law since it had no responsibility for implementing directives and no jurisdiction to do so. In that respect, its position was indeed analogous to that of a private employer. Subsequent case law was to confirm that it was not only against a member state's central government but also against public bodies more generally, that directives could be enforced in the national courts.[47] Paradoxically, this does not stop a public body from itself relying on a directive in proceedings against the State construed narrowly.[48]

Mitigating factors (2): The duty of consistent interpretation

Further evidence of the CJEU's ambivalence can be found in the duty of consistent interpretation it has imposed on national courts.[49] Based initially on Article 4(3) of the Treaty on European Union (TEU) and now considered inherent in the treaties, the duty originated in a decision which predated *Marshall*[50] but developed fully only after that case had been decided.

When national courts apply domestic law, they are bound to interpret it, so far as possible, in the light of the wording and the purpose of any overlapping directive so that the aim of the directive is achieved.[51] This obligation extends to all provisions of national law, whether adopted before or after the directive in question: it is not confined to national provisions adopted to give effect to it. The duty is subject to certain qualifications. It does not require national law to be interpreted *contra legem*, that is, in a way that is inconsistent with its clear terms. Moreover, it is limited by general principles of law, particularly those of legal certainty and non-retroactivity. This has been important in criminal cases, where the CJEU has held that the duty of consistent interpretation cannot have the effect of determining or aggravating criminal liability.[52] The duty of consistent interpretation does not apply in its full rigor before the deadline for giving effect to a directive has passed. However, from the moment a directive is adopted, national courts

> must refrain as far as possible from interpreting domestic law in a manner which might seriously compromise, after the period for transposition has expired, attainment of the objective pursued by that directive.[53]

This is an application of the rule requiring the member states to which a directive is addressed to refrain as soon as it is adopted from taking any measures liable seriously to compromise the attainment of the result prescribed by it.[54]

The principle of consistent interpretation has a number of advantages. When successfully invoked, it is less intrusive than direct effect because the outcome is determined by national law. It is also more flexible, because the national court enjoys some discretion in determining how far it can legitimately go in interpreting its national law consistently with overlapping directives. However, these features make the principle less effective than direct effect in securing effective judicial protection of the rights individuals are intended to enjoy under Union law. Moreover, by creating doubt about the effect of national law, the principle undermines the objection from legal certainty to the idea of endowing directives with horizontal direct effect.

Mitigating factors (3): Incidental effect

A third principle, sometimes called incidental effect, which may have the effect of mitigating the *Marshall* case law emerged in the 1990s, principally in cases generated by Council Directive No. 83/189/EEC of 28 March 1983 laying down a procedure for the provision of information in the field of technical standards and regulations.[55] The purpose of that directive was to enable preemptive action to be taken to ensure that national technical regulations relating to products did not create unnecessary barriers to trade. The mechanism laid down in the directive involved the notification of national drafts to the Commission and a standstill period, during which adoption of notified drafts had to be postponed to give the Commission and other member states a chance to comment. If the Commission or another member state asked for the draft to be amended to reduce potential barriers to trade, or the Commission said it intended put forward a directive on the subject, the notifying member state was required to postpone the adoption of the draft for between six and twelve months (except in urgent cases). Directive 83/189 did not specify the consequences of noncompliance by a member state with the notification and standstill requirements it laid down. Would it be possible for a technical regulation adopted in breach of those requirements to be invoked before a national court? That question came before the CJEU in *CIA Security v. Signalson and Securitel*.[56]

It seems clear that a national authority could not prevent a business from selling products that did not comply with technical regulations introduced in breach of the procedural requirements of Directive 83/189. Similarly, a business could go to the national courts to challenge national technical regulations introduced in breach of those requirements, even though the consequence might be detrimental to a seller of products that complied with the disputed regulations. In *Wells*, the CJEU made it clear that

> mere adverse repercussions on the rights of third parties, even if the repercussions are certain, do not justify preventing an individual from invoking the provisions of a directive against the Member State concerned.[57]

However, *CIA Security* involved a dispute before a national court between two private parties. The *Marshall* case law might have suggested that this would make a difference, but the CJEU thought otherwise. It observed that the directive was a useful and effective way of protecting the free movement of goods, "one of the foundations of the [Union]."[58] Because a breach of the obligation to notify would weaken the system established by the directive, such a breach rendered national technical regulations inapplicable, with the result that they could not be enforced against individuals. The CJEU applied similar reasoning in *Unilever*, a contractual dispute between private parties. The application of technical regulations adopted in breach of the procedural regime laid down in the directive was liable to undermine the effectiveness of the directive in tackling obstacles to trade. The CJEU concluded that

> a national court is required, in civil proceedings between individuals concerning contractual rights and obligations, to refuse to apply a national technical regulation which was adopted during a period of postponement of adoption prescribed in … Directive 83/189.[59]

In *CIA Security*, Advocate General Elmer denied that this outcome involved endowing Directive 83/189 with horizontal direct effect. He observed that, while the Directive imposed obligations on member states, it did not "aim to impose duties on individuals and therefore no question arises as to whether the Directive should have direct effect as far as individuals' obligations are concerned."[60] In *Unilever*, the CJEU reiterated that argument. Having cited *Faccini Dori*, the CJEU declared,

> Directive 83/189 does not in any way define the substantive scope of the legal rule on the basis of which the national court must decide the case before it. It creates neither rights nor obligations for individuals.[61]

So, if the CJEU was not intending to depart from the *Marshall* case law, how can *CIA Security* and *Unilever* be explained?

In *Océano Grupo Editorial and Salvat Editores*,[62] Advocate General Saggio proposed a distinction between relying on a directive *to exclude* an incompatible national rule and relying on a directive *in substitution for* an incompatible national rule. While the latter involved direct effect in the strict sense, the former was more limited, merely enabling a party to oppose the application of a national provision which was incompatible with a directive. This was an application not of direct effect but of primacy.[63]

Advocate General Saggio referred to the work of several academic writers who had considered such a distinction. It implied a blurring of the boundary between the Union and its member states, even that they together constituted a unitary legal order with federal characteristics.[64] However, the usefulness of the distinction is questionable.[65] While it might account for

CIA Security and *Unilever*, it does not explain several of the leading authorities on direct effect and consistent interpretation. It would mean that *Van Gend* was not about direct effect at all but about primacy, even though the latter doctrine had not yet been formulated by the CJEU. It would mean that the CJEU was wasting its time in *Marshall* by considering whether directives could impose obligations on individuals because the applicant's claim could have been upheld in any event by applying the doctrine of primacy. It would deprive the principle of consistent interpretation of much of its significance in exclusion cases[66] because the provision of national law would simply be displaced if it could not be interpreted consistently with the overlapping directive. The distinction between exclusionary and substitution effect does not therefore involve an application of the doctrine of primacy as currently understood but an extension of it. It is possible that such an extension is desirable, but whether the CJEU now has the legitimacy to effect it is doubtful. It would in any event need to be properly reasoned. Moreover, if such an extension were to take place, it is not clear why it should be confined to cases of exclusion. This would weaken its effectiveness and inevitably give rise to difficulties of classification.[67]

An opportunity for the CJEU to pronounce on the validity of the distinction arose in *Pfeiffer and Others*,[68] a horizontal case in which the applicants invoked a directive to exclude the effect of a derogation from a general rule laid down in the national implementing legislation from which they wished to benefit. The CJEU acknowledged that the relevant provisions were sufficiently precise to produce direct effect but said that they could not do so in these circumstances because the dispute was between private parties. The CJEU proceeded to emphasize the importance of the principle of consistent interpretation. It did not treat as relevant the fact that eliminating the national derogation would have left the case to be resolved on the basis of the general rule, which was consistent with the directive. Its decision seemed to constitute a rejection of the theory of exclusionary and substitution effect and to confirm that the Union remains ultimately an organization of international law, albeit a highly advanced one.[69]

Where does that leave *CIA Security* and *Unilever*? Perhaps the principle underlying those cases is that an individual may not invoke, in domestic legal proceedings against another individual, a breach by a member state of a substantive obligation of a public law character imposed on it by a directive. There is undoubtedly something unsatisfactory in contemplating the possibility that an individual might be able to rely in horizontal proceedings on legislation that the competent national authority could not itself enforce directly. But it cannot be denied that the outcome of those cases was to impose on one of the parties in each a disadvantage derived directly from a directive. And if a substantive obligation is enough to trigger this effect, why not the procedural obligation to implement the directive imposed on member states by the treaty?

Mitigating factors (4): General principles of law

In *Werner Mangold v. Rüdiger Helm*,[70] the CJEU found another way of escaping from the shackles of the *Marshall* case. *Mangold* concerned the interpretation of Council Directive 2000/78/EC of 27 November 2000 establishing a general framework for equal treatment in employment and occupation.[71] That directive was based on what is now Article 19 TFEU. It laid down a general framework for combating discrimination on some of the grounds listed in that article, including age. In *Mangold*, the CJEU was asked for guidance on the effect of the directive in the context of proceedings against a lawyer brought by one of his employees, who claimed he had been discriminated against because of his age.

The CJEU found that the provisions of national law at issue in the main action could not be justified under Directive 2000/78. This might have seemed immaterial, for the dispute was a horizontal one and the deadline for implementing the directive had not expired at the material time. However, the CJEU declared that the source of the principle of equal treatment in the field of employment and occupation was not the directive itself but "various international instruments" and "the constitutional traditions common to the Member States."[72] The principle of nondiscrimination on grounds of age therefore constituted a general principle of Union law. Observance of that principle could not be conditional on the expiry of the deadline for implementing the directive. On the contrary, it was

> the responsibility of the national court to guarantee the full effectiveness of the general principle of non-discrimination in respect of age, setting aside any provision of national law which may conflict with [Union] law.[73]

The CJEU's decision proved highly controversial,[74] with its application in the German courts leading to a complaint to the German *Bundesverfassungsgericht* (ultimately unsuccessful).[75] Later cases established that the Union law prohibition of age discrimination did not have to be applied in cases containing no link with Union law. Such a link might be found where the deadline for the implementation of Directive 2000/78 had expired[76] or the relevant national provisions gave effect to other Union measures, at least where they had some substantive link with Article 19 TFEU. In *Römer*,[77] the CJEU took the same approach in a case involving discrimination on the ground of sexual orientation. It would seem to follow that discrimination on any of the grounds listed in Directive 2000/78, and indeed Article 19 TFEU, will constitute an infringement of the general principle of nondiscrimination.

Mangold has its defenders.[78] The principle of nondiscrimination is well established and is enshrined in Article 21 of the Charter of Fundamental Rights, which now has the same legal status as the treaties.[79] It is right that it should keep pace with contemporary attitudes. On the other hand, general principles of law had not previously been considered directly effective in and of themselves.[80] The principle of nondiscrimination is not an absolute one but may be subject to exclusions and justifications. Their precise scope cannot be deduced from the principle itself but must be spelled out in implementing measures, such as Directive 2000/78.[81] Moreover, the approach of the CJEU subverted the clear intention of the authors of Article 19 TFEU that combating discrimination on the grounds there laid down should be left to the Council.

A sign that the CJEU is becoming wary of extending this approach to other general principles came in *Dominguez v. CICOA*,[82] which involved the right to paid annual leave. Such a right is enshrined in European Parliament and Council Directive 2003/88 concerning certain aspects of the organization of working time[83] and has been described by the CJEU as "a particularly important principle of EU social law."[84] The ruling in *Dominguez* makes it clear that it cannot be applied directly in horizontal proceedings, even though it features in Article 31(2) of the Charter of Fundamental Rights and has a strong claim to be considered a general principle of law.[85]

The Principle of State Liability

The capstone of the edifice the CJEU started to construct in the 1960s was added nearly thirty years later in the landmark case of *Francovich*, where the CJEU held "that the Member States are obliged to make good loss and damage caused to individuals by breaches of [Union] law for which they can be held responsible."[86] That obligation was said to be both "inherent in the system of the Treaty"[87] and included among the "appropriate measures" that member states were required by Article 4(3) TEU to take to ensure performance of their obligations. The CJEU rejected the advice of its advocate general that the temporal effect of any such ruling should be limited because member states might reasonably have thought that only under national law could they incur liability for infringing a rule of Union law. The CJEU presumably felt that it was simply clarifying what was already implicit in earlier case law.[88]

Claims for damages against a member state were to be brought in the national courts, which would have to make available the standard range of remedies to ensure for claimants their right to effective judicial protection. Claimants would have to show that the rule of Union law alleged to have been infringed was intended to confer rights on individuals; that the infringement was sufficiently serious, in the sense that the defendant had manifestly and gravely disregarded the limits on its discretion; and that there was a direct causal link between the infringement and the damage sustained by injured parties.[89] The CJEU later held that such liability could exceptionally result from an infringement of Union law by a national court of last resort.[90]

In *Brasserie du Pêcheur and Factortame*, the CJEU said that, where a member state infringed a directly effective provision of Union law, the right to reparation was "the necessary corollary" of its direct effect,[91] because otherwise "the full effectiveness of [Union] law would be impaired."[92] However, *Francovich*, which involved a directive that was found not to be directly effective, had shown that direct effect was not essential to a finding of state liability. Indeed, it is in cases where the claimant is unable to rely directly on a provision of Union law that the principle of state liability comes into its own. Thus, in *Faccini Dori*[93] the CJEU specifically drew the referring court's attention to the obligation of a member state to make good damage caused to individuals through its failure to transpose a directive.

The CJEU's conclusion that such a far-reaching principle could be deduced from the scheme of the treaty and Article 4(3) TEU was challenged in *Brasserie du Pêcheur and Factortame*[94] by the German government. In rejecting that challenge, the CJEU said that, since the treaty did not deal expressly with the consequences of a breach of Union law by a member state, it was for the CJEU to rule on the matter. It pointed out that, under the second paragraph of Article 340 TFEU, the tortious liability of the Union itself was based on the general principles common to the laws of the member states. That provision reflected, it said, "the general principle familiar to the legal systems of the Member States that an unlawful act or omission gives rise to an obligation to make good the damage caused" and the obligation of public authorities "to make good damage caused in the performance of their duties."[95] The CJEU added, "in many national legal systems the essentials of the legal rules governing State liability have been developed by the courts."[96] The principle of state liability has in practice been applied by the CJEU with restraint.[97]

The Reaction of the National Courts

The national courts now routinely apply the doctrines of direct effect and what de Witte calls "ordinary primacy"[98] (primacy over national legislation and hierarchically inferior national laws). However, the idea that Union law takes precedence over national rules having constitutional status has proved problematic with top national courts, particularly in so-called dualist member states. Unlike monist countries, where treaties take effect internally upon ratification, dualist countries require treaties to be transposed into national law before they can be given internal effect. The domestic status of a treaty will then be determined by the national norm giving effect to it.[99] But in both monist and dualist countries, the internal effect of treaties is determined by national law,[100] of which the ultimate guardians are the top national courts. The standard-bearer for national judicial resistance to the full implications of primacy is the German *Bundesverfassungsgericht,* which has asserted (but not yet exercised) a constitutional power of its own to police the protection of fundamental rights in the Union,[101] ensure respect by the Union institutions for the limits of their powers,[102] and uphold Germany's "constitutional identity."[103] Similar approaches have been taken in other member states, including Denmark, Italy, and the United Kingdom.[104]

What would be the consequence if a national constitutional court refused to apply a norm of European law on the basis that it was inconsistent with a norm of national constitutional law? There would be no possibility of an appeal to the Court of Justice in such circumstances. However, the formal position in Union law is clear. The national court would be acting in breach of its obligations under Union law and creating a situation in the member state concerned that was incompatible with the treaties. As the CJEU made clear in Opinion 1/09,[105] it would be open to any individual who thereby suffered loss to seek damages from that state in its national courts. Moreover, the Commission would be entitled to bring infringement proceedings against the state concerned. These might in theory lead to the imposition of a financial penalty on the offending state. In reality, if that state was not able or willing to resolve the situation on its own, an attempt to find a solution through political dialogue would probably be made. As a last resort, the member state concerned might have to withdraw from the Union, although whether this could be seriously contemplated would depend on the political weight of the state in question and the surrounding circumstances. This scenario has all the elements of a constitutional crisis. It is not therefore surprising that national courts have generally followed MacCormick's advice, avoiding conflict through circumspection and political as much as legal judgment.[106]

A potential threat to this pragmatic standoff came with the inclusion in the treaty establishing a constitution for Europe of a provision which would for the first time have codified the doctrine of primacy. Article I-6 CT provided that "[t]he Constitution and law adopted by the institutions of the Union in exercising competences conferred on it shall have primacy over the law of the Member States." That short provision contained an essential ambiguity: although it referred to the Constitution of the Union, it did not mention the constitutions of the member states. This might have been a deliberate ploy to avoid inflaming the national constitutional courts, but it might also have been interpreted as a dilution of the doctrine of primacy. In the event, the Constitutional Treaty did not enter into force, and the provision on primacy did not find its way into the Treaty of Lisbon. Instead, to avoid giving the impression that primacy had been abandoned, a declaration was made recalling that

> in accordance with well settled case law of the Court of Justice of the European Union, the Treaties and the law adopted by the Union on the basis of the Treaties have primacy over the law of Member States, under the conditions laid down by the said case law.[107]

Although the declaration does not have binding force, it makes it clear that it was not the intention of the member states to abrogate the doctrine of primacy. The absence once again of any reference to the constitutions of the member states is probably deprived of significance by the final clause of the sentence quoted above, referring to the case law of the CJEU.

Although the primacy provision of the Constitutional Treaty did not find its way into the Treaty of Lisbon, a related provision did survive. Article 4(2) TEU, which largely reproduces Article I-5(1) CT, requires the Union to respect the member states' "national identities, inherent in their fundamental structures, political and constitutional … ." This provision has the potential to soften the edges of the primacy doctrine in cases where important national political and constitutional principles are at stake. As we have seen, the German *Bundesverfassungsgericht* has already arrogated to itself the right to protect Germany's "constitutional identity."[108] As a matter of EU law, however, it will be the CJEU which ultimately determines the import of Article 4(2).[109]

A stone was thrown into this murky pond in the "Slovak Pensions" case,[110] where the Czech Constitutional Court described a decision of the CJEU[111] as *ultra vires* on the basis that it exceeded the powers transferred to the Union under the Czech Constitution. It therefore declined to follow the decision, applying instead a constitutional principle and fundamental right of domestic origin. The Czech Republic is not Germany, and the repercussions of the Czech Constitutional Court's decision may prove limited. However, if other national courts follow suit, who knows how far the ripples will spread.

Conclusion

The CJEU's image as the architect and savior of the European Union is based largely on its innovative case law of the 1960s and 1970s, in which it laid down the fundamental doctrines of direct effect and primacy and kept the integration process on track while the Council was operating under the long shadow of the Luxembourg Compromise. The CJEU's deftness deserted it when it was forced to confront the question of whether directives could have horizontal direct effect. Although it ruled out this possibility in the *Marshall* case in 1986, it lacked the courage either to persevere with that line or to abandon it. Instead it sought to qualify it through a range of increasingly technical devices which have threatened the coherence of the case law, with consequent damage to legal certainty. The modern CJEU's inability to provide adequate reasons for some of the twists and turns in its case law threatens to undermine the reputation it built up in the early decades of its existence. If it is to play a starring role once again, the CJEU needs to accept that it can no longer fix everything and should not try to do so.

Notes

1 See Francis Jacobs and Shelley Roberts, eds., *The Effect of Treaties in Domestic Law* (London: Sweet & Maxwell, 1987), xxiv.

2 Bruno de Witte, "Direct Effect, Primacy, and the Nature of the Legal Order," in *The Evolution of EU Law*, ed. Paul Craig and Gráinne de Búrca (Oxford: Oxford University Press, 2011), 323, 324.

3 Case 26/62 *Van Gend en Loos v. Nederlandse Administratie der Belastingen* EU.C.1963.1.

4 Ibid., para 12. Cf. Opinion 1/91 Agreement Creating the European Economic Area [1991] ECR I-6079, para 21, where the Court spoke of the member states having limited their sovereign rights "in ever wider fields."

5 Case 26/62 *Van Gend en Loos*, n 3 this chapter, para 13.

6 Case 57/65 *Lütticke v. Hauptzollamt Saarlouis* EU:C:1966:34; Case 28/67 *Molkerei-Zentrale Westfalen v. Hauptzollamt Paderborn* EU:C:1968:17. See Robert Lecourt, *L'Europe des Juges* (Brussels: Bruylant, 1976), 53–54.

7 Case 127/73 *BRT v. SABAM* EU:C:1974:6; Case 36/74 *Walrave v. Union Cycliste Internationale* EU:C:1974:140; Case 43/75 *Defrenne v. SABENA* EU:C:1976:56; Case C-281/98 *Angonese v. Cassa di Risparmio di Bolzano SpA* EU:C:2000:296; Case C-438/05 *International Transport Workers' Federation and Finnish Seamen's Union* EU:C:2007:772; Case C-341/05 *Laval un Partneri* EU:C:2007:809.

8 See de Witte, "Direct Effect," 327.

9 Commentators (but not the CJEU) sometimes speak of supremacy rather than primacy: see de Witte, "Direct Effect," 323 (n 1). For discussion of whether the distinction is important, see Matej Avbelj, "Supremacy or Primacy of EU law – (Why) Does it Matter?" *European Law Journal* 17 (2011): 744.

10 Case 6/64 *Costa v. ENEL* EU:C:1964:66.

11 See Article 26, Vienna Convention on the Law of Treaties.

12 De Witte, "Direct Effect," 329.

13 Case 6/64 *Costa*, n 10 this chapter.

14 Case 11/70 *Internationale Handelsgesellschaft v. Einfuhr- und Vorratsstelle Getreide* EU:C:1970:114. See also Case 100/77 *Commission v. Italy* EU:C:1978:78; and Case C-285/98 *Kreil* EU:C:2000:2.

15 Case 11/70 *Internationale Handelsgesellschaft*, n 14 this chapter, para 1134.

16 Ibid.

17 Case 106/77 *Amministrazione delle Finanze dello Stato v. Simmenthal* EU:C:1978:49, para 24. Cf. Case C-314/08 *Filipiak* EU:C:2009:719; and Joined Cases C-188/10 and C-189/10 *Melki and Abdeli* EU:C:2010:363.

18 Joined Cases C-10/97 to C-22/97 *Ministero delle Finanze v. IN. CO. GE.'90 and Others* EU:C:1998:498, para 21.

19 See, e.g., Case 167/73 *Commission v. France* EU:C:1974:35.

20 See Case 103/88 *Fratelli Costanzo v. Comune di Milano* EU:C:1989:256.

21 De Witte, "Direct Effect," 333.

22 See Case C-453/00 *Kühne & Heitz* EU:C:2004:17.

23 Case 43/75 *Defrenne*, n 7 this chapter.

24 Case C-409/06, *Winner Wetten* EU:C:2010:503, para 67.

25 Case C-41/11 *Inter-Environnement Wallonie v. Région Wallonne* EU:C:2012:103.

26 Hjalte Rasmussen, *On Law and Policy in the European Court of Justice: A Comparative Study in Judicial Policymaking* (Dordrecht: Martinus Nijhoff, 1986), 28.

27 De Witte, "Direct Effect," 347.

28 See Article 8 EEC. The transitional period ended on 31 December 1969.

29 Case 2/74 *Reyners v. Belgium* EU:C:1974:68.

30 Case 33/74 *Van Binsbergen v. Bedrijfsvereniging Metaalnijverheid* EU:C:1974:131.

31 See also Article 216 TFEU, dealing with international agreements concluded by the Union. On the direct effect of such agreements, see Robert Schütze, *European Constitutional Law* (Cambridge: Cambridge University Press, 2012), 337–343; Trevor Hartley, *The Foundations of European Union Law* (Oxford: Oxford University Press, 2010), 240–243; and de Witte, "Direct Effect," 336–337.

32 See in particular Case 8/81 *Becker v. Finanzamt Münster-Innenstadt* EU:C:1982:7.

33 Case 148/78 *Pubblico Ministero v. Ratti* EU:C:1979:110.

34 See Case 41/74 *van Duyn v. Home Office* EU:C:1974:133, para 12.

35 Case 148/78 *Ratti*, n 33 this chapter, para 22.

36 Rasmussen, *Law and Policy*, 12.

37 *Minister of the Interior v. Cohn-Bendit* [1980] 1 CMLR 543.

38 See Jens Plötner, "Report on France," in *The European Courts and National Courts – Doctrine and Jurisprudence*, ed. Anne-Marie Slaughter, Alec Stone Sweet, and Joseph Weiler (Oxford: Hart, 1998), 41, 48–50; Juliane Kokott, "Report on Germany," in ibid., 77, 116; Pierre Pescatore, "The Doctrine of 'Direct Effect': An Infant Disease of Community Law," *European Law Review* 8 (1983): 155, 169–170; and Hartley, *Foundations*, 271–272.

39 Case 152/84 *Marshall v. Southampton and South-West Hampshire Area Health Authority* EU:C:1986:84.

40 Ibid., para 48.

41 Ibid., para 49.

42 Stephen Weatherill, *Law and Integration in the European Union* (Oxford: Oxford University Press, 1995), 124.

43 Case 43/75 *Defrenne*, n 7 this chapter, para 31.

44 Case C-91/92 *Faccini Dori v. Recreb* EU:C:1994:292.

45 Ibid., para 24. Cf. Advocate General Lenz at 3341–3342; Advocate General Jacobs in Case C-316/93 *Vaneetveld* EU:C:1994:82; and Advocate General Slynn in Case 152/84 *Marshall*, n 39 this chapter, para 734.
46 Case C-201/02 *Wells* EU:C:2004:12, para 56.
47 See, e.g., Case 222/84 *Johnston v. Chief Constable of the Royal Ulster Constabulary* EU:C:1986:206; and Case C-188/89 *Foster and Others* EU:C:1990:313.
48 See Joined Cases 231/87 and 129/88 *Ufficio Distrettuale delle Imposte Dirette di Fiorenzuola d'Arda and Others v. Comune di Carpaneto Piacentino and Others* EU:C:1989:381.
49 See Anthony Arnull, *The European Union and its Court of Justice* (Oxford: Oxford University Press, 2006), 209–225. Although it is in relation to directives that the duty has been most significant, it extends to any provision of Union law: see, e.g., Case 157/86 *Murphy v. An Bord Telecom Eireann* EU:C:1988:62, para 11; and Case C-165/91 *van Munster v. Rijksdienst voor Pensioenen* EU:C:1994:359, para 34.
50 Case 14/83 *Von Colson and Kamann v. Land Nordrhein-Westfalen* EU:C:1984:153.
51 See Joined Cases C-378/07 to C-380/07 *Angelidaki and Others* EU:C:2009:250, paras 197–201.
52 See, e.g., Case 80/86 *Kolpinghuis Nijmegen* EU:C:1987:431. See also Case 14/86 *Pretore di Salò v. Persons Unknown* EU:C:1987:275; Case C-105/03 *Pupino* EU:C:2005:386; and Case C-227/09 *Accardo and Others* EU:C:2010:624.
53 Case C-212/04 *Adeneler* EU:C:2006:443.
54 See Case C-129/96 *Inter-Environnement Wallonie* EU:C:1997:628. That rule applies to all national authorities, including the courts (Case C-212/04 *Adeneler*, n 53 this chapter, para 122).
55 [1983] OJ L 109/8.
56 Case C-194/94 *CIA Security v. Signalson and Securitel* EU:C:1996:172.
57 Case C-201/02 *Wells*, n 46 this chapter, para 57. See also Case 103/88 *Fratelli Costanzo v. Comune di Milano*, n 20 this chapter, Case C-435/97 *WWF and Others v. Autonome Provinz Bozen and Others* EU:C:1999:418, and Case C-127/02 *Waddenvereniging and Vogelsbeschermingvereniging* EU:C:2004:482.
58 Case C-194/94 *CIA Security*, n 56 this chapter, para 40.
59 Case C-443/98 *Unilever* EU:C:2000:496, para 52.
60 Case C-194/94 *CIA Security*, n 56 this chapter.
61 Case C-443/98 *Unilever*, n 59 this chapter, paras 50 and 51.
62 Case C-240/98 to C-244/98 *Océano Grupo Editorial and Salvat Editores* EU:C:2000:346. See also Advocate General Léger in Case C-287/98 *Linster* EU:C:2000:468.
63 See further Michael Dougan, "When Worlds Collide! Competing Visions of the Relationship between Direct Effect and Supremacy," *Common Market Law Review* 44 (2007): 931.
64 See ibid., 943.
65 See Arnull, *Court of Justice*, 239–252.
66 E.g., Case 14/83 *Von Colson*, n 50 this chapter; and Case C-106/89 *Marleasing* EU:C:1990:395.
67 De Witte, "Direct Effect," 338. See, e.g., Case C-91/92 *Faccini Dori*, n 44 this chapter.
68 Joined Cases C-397/01 to C-403/01 *Pfeiffer and Others* EU:C:2004:584. See also Joined Cases C-387/02, C-391/02, and C-403/02 *Berlusconi and Others* EU:C:2005:270; Case C-282/10 *Dominguez v. CICOA* EU:C:2012:33.
69 See de Witte, "Direct Effect," 362; Bruno de Witte, "The European Union as an International Legal Experiment," in *The Worlds of European Constitutionalism*, ed. Gráinne de Búrca and Joseph Weiler (Cambridge: Cambridge University Press, 2012), 19. Cf. Schütze, *European Constitutional Law*, 77–79.
70 Case C-144/04 *Werner Mangold v. Rüdiger Helm* EU:C:2005:709.
71 [2000] OJ L 303/16.
72 Case C-144/04 *Mangold*, n 70 this chapter, para 74.
73 Ibid., para 78.
74 See, e.g., Alan Dashwood, "From *Van Duyn* to *Mangold* via *Marshall*: Reducing Direct Effect to Absurdity?" *Cambridge Yearbook of European Legal Studies* 9 (2006–2007): 81.
75 See *Re Honeywell* [2011] 1 CMLR 33.
76 See Case C-555/07 *Kücükdeveci* EU:C:2010:21.
77 Case C-147/08 *Römer* EU:C:2011:286.
78 Michael Dougan, "In Defence of *Mangold*?" in *A Constitutional Order of States? Essays in EU Law in Honour of Alan Dashwood*, ed. Anthony Arnull et al. (Oxford: Hart, 2011), 219; and Jan Jans, "The Effect in National Legal Systems of the Prohibition of Discrimination on Grounds of Age as a General Principle of Community Law," *Legal Issues of Economic Integration* 34 (2007): 53.

79 Article 6(1) TEU.
80 See Advocate General Sharpston in Case C-427/06 *Bartsch* EU:C:2008:517, 7269 (n 72); and Hartley, *Foundations*, 239.
81 See, e.g., Council Directive 2000/78/EC [2000] OJ L 303/16, Articles 4 and 6.
82 Case C-282/10 *Dominguez*, n 68 this chapter.
83 [2003] OJ L 299/9.
84 See Case C-282/10 *Dominguez*, n 68 this chapter, para 16.
85 See Advocate General Trstenjak in Case C-282/10 *Dominguez*, n 68 this chapter, para 114.
86 Joined Cases C-6/90 and C-9/90 *Francovich* EU:C:1991:428, para 37.
87 Ibid., para 35.
88 See Case 60/75 *Russo v. AIMA* EU:C:1976:9.
89 See Joined Cases C-46/93 and C-48/93 *Brasserie du Pêcheur and Factortame* EU:C:1996:79.
90 See Case C-224/01 *Köbler v. Austria* EU:C:2003:513.
91 Joined Cases C-46/93 and C-48/93 *Brasserie du Pêcheur and Factortame*, n 89 this chapter, para 22.
92 Ibid., para 20.
93 Case C-91/92 *Faccini Dori*, n 44 this chapter.
94 Joined Cases C-46/93 and C-48/93 *Brasserie du Pêcheur and Factortame*, n 89 this chapter.
95 Ibid., para 29.
96 Ibid., para 30.
97 See, e.g., Case C-392/93 *The Queen v. H M Treasury, ex p British Telecommunications* EU:C:1996:131; Case C-319/96 *Brinkmann* EU:C:1998:429; and Case C-424/97 *Haim* EU:C:2000:357.
98 De Witte, "Direct Effect," 350.
99 See Schütze, *European Constitutional Law*, 306–308; de Witte, "Direct Effect," 325.
100 Hartley, *Foundations*, 204.
101 *Internationale Handelsgesellschaft mbH v. Einfuhr- und Vorratsstelle für Getreide und Futtermittel* (Solange I) [1974] 2 CMLR 540; *Wünsche* (Solange II) [1987] 3 CMLR 225.
102 *Brunner v. European Union Treaty* [1994] 1 CMLR 57.
103 *Re Ratification of the Treaty of Lisbon* [2010] 3 CMLR 13.
104 See Christoph Grabenwarter, "National Constitutional Law Relating to the European Union," in *Principles of European Constitutional Law*, ed. Armin von Bogdandy and Jürgen Bast (Oxford: Hart, 2009), 83, 100; and Hartley, *Foundations*, 259–286.
105 On the Proposed Agreement Creating a Unified Patent Litigation System, 8 March 2011, paras 86 and 87.
106 Neil MacCormick, *Questioning Sovereignty: Law, State, and Nation in the European Commonwealth* (Oxford: Oxford University Press, 1999), 119–120. Cf. Advocate General Poiares Maduro in Case C-127/07 *Arcelor Atlantique et Lorraine and Others* EU:C:2008:728.
107 Declaration No. 17 Concerning Primacy.
108 See n 103 this chapter.
109 See Armin von Bogdandy and Stephan Schill, "Overcoming Absolute Primacy: Respect for National Identity Under the Lisbon Treaty," *Common Market Law Review* 48 (2011): 1417.
110 Pl. ÚS 5/12, 31 January 2012. See Robert Zbíral, "A Legal Revolution or Negligible Episode? Court of Justice Decision Proclaimed *Ultra Vires*," *Common Market Law Review* 49 (2012): 1475.
111 Case C-399/09 *Landtová v. Česká správa socialního zabezpečení* EU:C:2011:415.

References

Arnull, Anthony. *The European Union and its Court of Justice*. Oxford: Oxford University Press, 2006.

Avbelj, Matej. "Supremacy or Primacy of EU Law – (Why) Does it Matter?" *European Law Journal* 17 (2011): 744–763.

Dashwood, Alan. "From *Van Duyn* to *Mangold* via *Marshall*: Reducing Direct Effect to Absurdity?" *Cambridge Yearbook of European Legal Studies* 9 (2006–2007): 81–109.

de Witte, Bruno. "Direct Effect, Primacy, and the Nature of the Legal Order." In *The Evolution of EU Law*, edited by Paul Craig and Gráinne de Búrca, 324–362. Oxford: Oxford University Press, 2011.

de Witte, Bruno. "The European Union as an International Legal Experiment." In *The Worlds of European Constitutionalism*, edited by Gráinne de Búrca and Joseph Weiler, 19–56. Cambridge: Cambridge University Press, 2012.

Dougan, Michael. "When Worlds Collide! Competing Visions of the Relationship between Direct Effect and Supremacy." *Common Market Law Review* 44 (2007): 931–963.

Dougan, Michael. "In Defence of *Mangold*?" In *A Constitutional Order of States? Essays in EU Law in Honour of Alan Dashwood*, edited by Anthony Arnull, Catherine Barnard, Michael Dougan, and Eleanor Spaventa, 219–244. Oxford: Hart, 2011.

Grabenwarter, Christoph. "National Constitutional Law Relating to the European Union." In *Principles of European Constitutional Law*, edited by Armin von Bogdandy and Jürgen Bast, 83–129. Oxford: Hart, 2009.

Hartley, Trevor. *The Foundations of European Union Law*. Oxford: Oxford University Press, 2010.

Jacobs, Francis, and Shelley Roberts, eds. *The Effect of Treaties in Domestic Law*. London: Sweet & Maxwell, 1987.

Jans, Jan. "The Effect in National Legal Systems of the Prohibition of Discrimination on Grounds of Age as a General Principle of Community Law." *Legal Issues of Economic Integration* 34 (2007): 53–66.

Kokott, Juliane. "Report on Germany." In Slaughter, Stone Sweet, and Weiler, *The European Courts*, 77–131.

Lecourt, Robert. *L'Europe des Juges*. Brussels: Bruylant, 1976.

MacCormick, Neil. *Questioning Sovereignty: Law, State, and Nation in the European Commonwealth*. Oxford: Oxford University Press, 1999.

Pescatore, Pierre. "The Doctrine of 'Direct Effect': An Infant Disease of Community Law." *European Law Review* 8 (1983): 155–177.

Plötner, Jens. "Report on France." In Slaughter, Stone Sweet, and Weiler, *The European Courts and National Courts - Doctrine and Jurisprudence*, 41–75.

Rasmussen, Hjalte. *On Law and Policy in the European Court of Justice: A Comparative Study in Judicial Policymaking*. Dordrecht: Martinus Nijhoff, 1986.

Schütze, Robert. *European Constitutional Law*. Cambridge: Cambridge University Press, 2012.

Slaughter, Anne-Marie, Alec Stone Sweet, and Joseph H.H. Weiler, eds. *The European Courts and National Courts - Doctrine and Jurisprudence*. Oxford: Hart, 1998.

von Bogdandy, Armin, and Stephan Schill. "Overcoming Absolute Primacy: Respect for National Identity under the Lisbon Treaty." *Common Market Law Review* 48 (2011): 1417–1453.

Weatherill, Stephen. *Law and Integration in the European Union*. Oxford: Oxford University Press, 1995.

Zbíral, Robert. "A Legal Revolution or Negligible Episode? Court of Justice Decision Proclaimed *Ultra Vires*." *Common Market Law Review* 49 (2012): 1475–1491.

Part II

EU Political Institutions and Decision Making

6

EU Competences

Paul Craig

Lisbon Treaty

The general principle has always been that the European Union only has the competence conferred on it by the treaties.[1] However, prior to the Lisbon Treaty it was difficult to determine the limits of that competence.[2] This could only be discerned by paying close attention to the detailed treaty provisions. It could, moreover, be difficult to decide whether competence in a particular area was exclusive or shared.

The scope of EU competence was therefore central to the reform process that culminated in the Lisbon Treaty. There are now categories of competence specified in the Lisbon Treaty: the European Union may have exclusive competence, shared competence, or competence only to take supporting, coordinating, or supplementary action. Legal consequences flow from this categorization. There are, however, certain areas of EU competence that do not fall within these categories. The Lisbon Treaty also makes provision as to whether the competence should be exercised, which is governed by the principle of subsidiarity.

The Lisbon Treaty competence provisions borrowed heavily from those in the Constitutional Treaty. Some provisions are contained in the Treaty on European Union (TEU),[3] but the detailed schema is in the Treaty on the Functioning of the European Union (TFEU). Article 2 TFEU is the foundational provision, setting out the categories of competence and the consequences that flow from them.

Exclusive competence

Article 2(1) TFEU establishes the category of exclusive competence, which carries the consequence that only the Union can legislate and adopt legally binding acts. The member states can only do so if empowered by the Union or for the implementation of Union acts.

The subject matter areas that fall within exclusive competence are set out in Article 3(1) TFEU: customs union; the establishing of the competition rules necessary for the functioning

A Companion to European Union Law and International Law, First Edition.
Edited by Dennis Patterson and Anna Södersten.

of the internal market; monetary policy for the member states whose currency is the euro; the conservation of marine biological resources under the common fisheries policy; and the common commercial policy. This list is limited and reflects the serious consequences in terms of diminution of member state competence that flow from inclusion in this category: the member states have no autonomous legislative competence and they cannot adopt any legally binding act. They can neither legislate nor make any legally binding non-legislative act.

Article 3(2) TFEU states that the Union shall also have exclusive competence for the conclusion of an international agreement when its conclusion is provided for in a legislative act of the Union, or is necessary to enable the Union to exercise its internal competence, or insofar as its conclusion may affect common rules or alter their scope. Article 3(2) TFEU should be read in conjunction with Article 216 TFEU, which is concerned with whether the European Union has competence to conclude an international agreement.

The case law on the scope of the European Union's external competence, and the extent to which it is exclusive or parallel with that of the member states, is complex, which meant that embodying the principles in a treaty article was difficult. The reality is that Article 3(2), read together with Article 216 TFEU, comes close to eliding the Union's power to act via an international agreement with the exclusivity of that power, an issue which preoccupied much of the case law in this area.

Article 3(2) TFEU specifies three situations in which the European Union has exclusive external competence. The first is where conclusion of an international agreement is provided for by a legislative act of the Union. Article 3(2) TFEU is not therefore limited to the situation where a Union legislative act expressly confers exclusive competence. It also covers situations where the conclusion of an international agreement is provided for in a legislative act. Thus, express external empowerment to conclude an international agreement is taken to mean exclusive external competence, with the corollary that member states are preempted from concluding any such agreement independently, from legislating or adopting any legally binding act.

The same elision of external power and exclusive external power is evident in the second situation listed in Article 3(2) TFEU. The European Union has exclusive external competence to conclude an international agreement where it is necessary to enable the Union to exercise its competence internally, irrespective of the type of internal competence it possesses.

The third of the situations mentioned in Article 3(2) TFEU is that the European Union shall have exclusive competence insofar as the conclusion of an international agreement "may affect common rules or alter their scope." This is in accord with prior case law of the European Court of Justice (ECJ). This phrase has been interpreted broadly by the ECJ such that in most instances where the European Union has exercised its power internally it will be held to have an exclusive external competence.

Shared competence

Article 2(2) TFEU defines shared competence. It provides that when the treaties confer on the Union a competence shared with the member states in a specific area, the Union and the member states may legislate and adopt legally binding acts in that area. The member states shall exercise their competence to the extent that the Union has not exercised its competence. The member states shall again exercise their competence to the extent that the Union has decided to cease exercising its competence.

The areas that fall within shared competence are delineated in Article 4 TFEU. Shared competence is the general residual category, since Article 4(1) provides that the Union shall share competence with the member states where the treaties confer on it a competence which does not relate to the categories referred to in Articles 3 and 6 TFEU, which deal respectively with exclusive competence and where the Union is restricted to taking action to support, coordinate, or supplement member state action. This follows also from Article 4(2), which states that shared competence applies in the "principal areas" listed, implying thereby that the list is not necessarily exhaustive. The list of areas to which shared competence applies is as follows: internal market; social policy, for the aspects defined in this treaty; economic, social, and territorial cohesion; agriculture and fisheries, excluding the conservation of marine biological resources; environment; consumer protection; transport; trans-European networks; energy; area of freedom, security, and justice; common safety concerns in public health matters, for the aspects defined in the Lisbon Treaty.

Article 2(2) TFEU stipulates that a member state can only exercise competence to the extent that the Union has not exercised or has decided to cease to exercise its competence within any such area. Member state action is therefore preempted where the Union has exercised its competence, with the consequence that the amount of shared power held by the member state in these areas may diminish over time.

Member states will, however, only lose their competence within the regime of shared power to the extent that the Union has exercised its competence. The scope of the European Union's competence within these areas is determined by considering the detailed provisions that divide power in areas as diverse as social policy, energy, the internal market, and consumer protection. Thus, the real limits on Union competence must be found in the detailed provisions which delineate what it can do in the diverse areas where power is shared.

The preemption will, moreover, only occur to the extent that the European Union has exercised its competence in the relevant area. There are different ways in which the Union can intervene in a particular area.[4] It may choose to make uniform regulations, it may harmonize national laws, it may engage in minimum harmonization, or it may impose requirements of mutual recognition. Thus, for example, where the European Union chooses minimum harmonization, member states will have room for action in the relevant area.[5] It is nonetheless still possible for Union acts to cover the entire area subject to shared power, provided that it could do so under the relevant treaty provisions.

It should also be noted that Article 2(2) TFEU expressly provides for the possibility that the European Union will cease to exercise competence in an area subject to shared competence, the consequence being that competence then reverts to the member states. A declaration attached to treaty[6] specifies different ways in which this might occur.

The final qualification concerns Article 4(3) and Article 4(4) TFEU, which deal respectively with the areas of research, technological development and space, and development cooperation and humanitarian aid. These provisions make clear that the member states can continue to exercise power even if the European Union has exercised its competence within these areas.

Shared competence constitutes the default position in relation to division of competence within the Lisbon Treaty, but that does not mean that the nature of the sharing will be the same in all the areas to which shared competence applies. The reality is that shared competence is simply an umbrella term, with the consequence that there is significant variation as to the division of competence in different areas of EU law. It follows that the precise configuration of power sharing in areas such as the internal market, consumer protection, energy, social policy, the environment, and the like can only be determined by considering the detailed rules that govern these areas, which are found in the relevant provisions of the TFEU.

The sharing of power in relation to, for example, the four freedoms is very different from the complex world of power sharing that operates within the area of freedom, security, and justice. There are, indeed, significant variations of power sharing that operate within the overall area of freedom, security, and justice. This is not a criticism, but rather it is a consequence of the fact that the European Union has been attributed competence in different areas through treaty amendments, coupled with the fact that the precise degree of power it has been accorded differs between these areas. This is recognized by Article 2(6) TFEU, which states that "the scope of and arrangements for exercising the Union's competences shall be determined by the provisions of the Treaties relating to each area."

Supporting, coordinating, or supplementary action

The third general category of competence allows the European Union to take action "to support, coordinate or supplement Member State action, without thereby superseding their competence in these areas, and without entailing harmonization of Member State laws," Article 2(5) TFEU.[7] While the European Union cannot harmonize the law in these areas, it can pass legally binding acts on the basis of the provisions specific to them, and the member states will be constrained to the extent stipulated by such acts. The meaning of such competence, and hence the precise extent of EU power, varies in the different areas listed, but the Union has significant power in these areas, albeit falling short of harmonization.[8]

The areas that fall within such competence are set out in Article 6 TFEU: protection and improvement of human health; industry; culture; tourism; education, vocational training, youth, and sport; civil protection; and administrative cooperation. Article 6 TFEU gives the impression that the list is finite, but this is belied by the fact that when reading the TFEU as a whole, it is clear that there are other important areas in which the European Union is limited, prima facie at least, to supporting, coordinating, or supplementary action, notably in respect to some aspects of social policy[9] and certain facets of employment policy.[10]

The meaning of EU action supporting, coordinating, or supplementing action by the member states varies somewhat in the different areas listed, but the general approach is as follows. Each substantive area begins with a provision setting out the objectives of Union action. Thus, in relation to public health, Article 168 TFEU lists, inter alia, the improvement of public health, prevention of illness, and the obviation of dangers to health. The European Union is to complement national action on these topics. Member states have an obligation to coordinate their policies on such matters, in liaison with the Commission.[11] The Commission can coordinate action on such matters by exchanges of best practice, periodic monitoring, and evaluation.[12] The Union can also pass laws to establish "incentive measures" designed to protect human health and combat cross-border health scourges, subject to the prohibition on harmonization.[13] Thus, while harmonization is ruled out, the European Union still has significant room for intervention through persuasive soft law, in the form of guidelines on best practice, monitoring, and the like, and through legal incentive measures.[14] The same combination of soft law and legal incentive measures falling short of harmonization can be found in the other areas within this category.[15]

The scope of EU power within these areas should not, however, be underestimated. The standard approach under the Lisbon Treaty is for the European Union to be empowered to take measures to attain the objectives listed in that area. The language of the empowerment varies. It is sometimes framed in terms of taking "incentive measures,"[16] on other occasions the language is in terms of "necessary measures,"[17] in yet other instances the terminology is "specific measures."[18]

These measures constitute legally binding acts, normally passed in accordance with the ordinary legislative procedure. The boundary of this EU legislative competence is that such legal acts must be designed to achieve the objectives listed for EU involvement in the area. These objectives are normally set at a relatively high level of generality, with the consequence that the European Union is legally empowered to take binding measures, provided that they fall within the remit of these broadly defined objectives and do not constitute harmonization of national laws.

Article 2(5) TFEU provides that EU action designed to support, coordinate, or supplement member state action does not supersede member state competence. It also states that legally binding acts of the Union adopted on the basis of the provisions specific to these areas cannot entail harmonization of member state laws. Thus, while the European Union cannot harmonize the law in these areas, it can pass legally binding acts on the basis of the provisions specific to these areas. It follows that where the Union passes such legal acts they will bind the member states and the competence of the member states will be constrained to the extent stipulated by the legally binding act. While member state competence is not per se superseded merely because the European Union has enacted legally binding acts, it will be constrained to the degree entailed by the EU legal act. It is clear, moreover, that the Union can pass legislative acts in these areas, provided that they do not entail harmonization and that there is foundation for the passage of such laws in the detailed provisions of the TFEU. It would be for the CJEU to decide whether the contested measure constituted harmonization and was therefore caught by the limit in Article 2(5) TFEU. The line between a legitimate, legally binding act that advances the objectives of the areas covered by this category of competence and illegitimate harmonization of national laws may be a fine one in a particular case.

Economic, employment and social policy

Article 2(3) TFEU states that "the Member States shall coordinate their economic and employment policies within arrangements as determined by this Treaty, which the Union shall have competence to provide." The detailed rules are set out in Article 5 TFEU:

1. The Member States shall coordinate their economic policies within the Union. To this end, the Council shall adopt measures, in particular broad guidelines for these policies.
   Specific provisions shall apply to those Member States whose currency is the euro.
2. The Union shall take measures to ensure coordination of the employment policies of the Member States, in particular by defining guidelines for these policies.
3. The Union may take initiatives to ensure coordination of Member States' social policies.

The explanation for this separate category was political. There would have been significant opposition to the inclusion of these areas within shared competence, with the consequence of preemption of state action when the European Union exercised power within this area, and some felt that the category of supporting, coordinating, and complementary action was too weak. This was the explanation for the creation of a separate category and its placement after shared power but before the category of supporting, coordinating, and supplementary action. There are boundary problems since certain aspects of social policy fall within shared competence, although it is not precisely clear which; other aspects appear to fall within the category of supporting, coordinating, and supplementary action, even though they are not within the relevant list; and there is in addition a separate provision for social policy in the category being considered here.

The treaty schema for competence in Article 2 TFEU is, in general, premised on the ascription of legal consequences for EU and member state power as the result of coming within a particular category. Article 5 TFEU is an exception in this respect, since Article 2(3) TFEU does not spell out the legal consequences of inclusion within this category. The legal consequences of inclusion within this category can therefore only be divined by considering the language of Article 5 TFEU, which is couched largely in terms of coordination, and by considering the detailed provisions that apply to these areas.

Common foreign and security policy and defense

The three-pillar structure that characterized the previous treaty has not been preserved in the Lisbon Treaty. Nonetheless, there are distinct rules that apply in the context of foreign and security policy, and this warrants a separate category of competence for this area. It is set out in Article 2(4) TFEU:

> The Union shall have competence, in accordance with the provisions of the Treaty on European Union, to define and implement a common foreign and security policy, including the progressive framing of a common defence policy.

The rules concerning the Common Foreign and Security Policy (CFSP) are set out in Title V TEU. Decision making in this area continues to be more intergovernmental and less supranational by way of comparison with other areas of Union competence. The European Council and the Council of the European Union (hereafter, the Council) dominate decision making, and the legal instruments applicable to the CFSP are distinct from those generally applicable for the attainment of Union objectives. Article 2(4) TFEU does not specify which type of competence applies in the context of the CFSP. In truth, none of the categories is a good fit. It is clearly not within exclusive competence, since it is not listed in Article 3 TFEU and the substance of the CFSP simply does not accord with the idea of exclusive EU competence. Nor is it mentioned in the list of those areas that are subject to supporting, coordinating, or supplementing member state action in Article 6 TFEU. This would seem to imply that it falls within the default category of shared competence in Article 4 TFEU, even though not mentioned in the non-exhaustive list. The CFSP may not, however, readily fit within the frame of shared administration, insofar as this connotes preemption of member state action when the European Union has exercised its power in the area, nor does this idea cohere with declarations appended to the Lisbon Treaty.[19]

The "flexibility" clause

Article 352 TFEU is the successor provision to Article 308 of the Treaty establishing the European Community (EC), which was long viewed with suspicion by those calling for a clearer delimitation of Community competences and, in particular, by the German Länder. This issue was placed on the post-Nice and Laeken agenda for reform of the European Union. The Laeken Declaration asked whether Article 308 EC ought to be reviewed in light of the twin challenges of preventing the creeping expansion of competences from encroaching on national and regional powers and allowing the European Union to continue to be able to react to fresh challenges and developments and to explore new policy areas. The flexibility clause is now enshrined in Article 352 TFEU:

1. If action by the Union should prove necessary, within the framework of the policies defined in the Treaties, to attain one of the objectives set out in the Treaties, and the Treaties have not provided the necessary powers, the Council, acting unanimously on a proposal from the Commission and after obtaining the consent of the European Parliament, shall adopt the appropriate measures. Where the measures in question are adopted by the Council in accordance with a special legislative procedure, it shall also act unanimously on a proposal from the Commission and after obtaining the consent of the European Parliament.
2. Using the procedure for monitoring the subsidiarity principle referred to in Article 5(3) of the Treaty on European Union, the Commission shall draw national Parliaments' attention to proposals based on this Article.
3. Measures based on this Article shall not entail harmonisation of Member States' laws or regulations in cases where the Treaties exclude such harmonisation.
4. This Article cannot serve as a basis for attaining objectives pertaining to the common foreign and security policy and any acts adopted pursuant to this Article shall respect the limits set out in Article 40, second paragraph, of the Treaty on European Union.

Article 352(1) TFEU is framed broadly in terms of the "policies defined in the Treaties," with the exception of the CFSP. It can therefore serve as the basis for competence in almost all areas of EU law. The unanimity requirement means, however, that it will be more difficult to use this power in an enlarged European Union and Article 352 TFEU also requires the consent of the European Parliament, as opposed to mere consultation as was previously the case under Article 308 EC. The need for recourse to this power will diminish, given that the Lisbon Treaty created a legal basis for action in the areas where Article 308 EC had previously been used.[20] The conditions in Article 352(2) to (4) are novel, including an obligation to draw the attention of national parliaments to use of this power in order that they might contest it on the grounds of subsidiarity.

Subsidiarity

Closely linked to the question of the existence of competence is the principle of subsidiarity, which is intended to regulate the exercise of competence. Subsidiarity was introduced in the Maastricht Treaty and was intended to curb the "federalist" leanings of the Community. The pre-Lisbon formulation was contained in Article 5 EC.[21] The subsidiarity principle has been retained in the Lisbon Treaty. It distinguishes between the existence of competence and the use of such competence, the latter being determined by subsidiarity and proportionality.[22] The principles are embodied in Article 5(3) to (4) TEU:[23]

3. Under the principle of subsidiarity, in areas which do not fall within its exclusive competence, the Union shall act only if and insofar as the objectives of the proposed action cannot be sufficiently achieved by the member states, either at central level or at regional and local level, but can rather, by reason of the scale or effects of the proposed action, be better achieved at Union level.

   The institutions of the Union shall apply the principle of subsidiarity as laid down in the Protocol on the application of the principles of subsidiarity and proportionality. National Parliaments ensure compliance with the principle of subsidiarity in accordance with the procedure set out in that Protocol.
4. Under the principle of proportionality, the content and form of Union action shall not exceed what is necessary to achieve the objectives of the Treaties.

> The institutions of the Union shall apply the principle of proportionality as laid down in the Protocol on the application of the principles of subsidiarity and proportionality.

The Lisbon Treaty contains a Protocol on the Application of the Principles of Subsidiarity and Proportionality,[24] which should be read in tandem with the Protocol on the Role of National Parliaments in the European Union.[25] The Subsidiarity Protocol only applies to draft legislative acts,[26] and does not cover delegated or implementing acts.

The Subsidiarity Protocol imposes an obligation on the Commission to consult widely before proposing legislative acts.[27] The Commission must provide a detailed statement concerning proposed legislation so that compliance with subsidiarity and proportionality can be appraised. The statement must contain some assessment of the financial impact of the proposals, and there should be qualitative and, wherever possible, quantitative indicators to substantiate the conclusion that the objective can be better attained at Union level.[28] The Commission must submit an annual report on the application of subsidiarity to the European Council, the European Parliament, the Council, and to national parliaments.[29] The CJEU has jurisdiction to consider infringement of subsidiarity under Article 263 TFEU, brought by the member state, or "notified by them in accordance with their legal order on behalf of their national parliament or a chamber of it."[30]

The most important innovation in the Protocol on Subsidiarity is the enhanced role accorded to national parliaments. The Commission must send all legislative proposals to the national parliaments at the same time as to the Union institutions.[31] A national parliament or chamber thereof, may, within eight weeks, send the presidents of the Commission, European Parliament, and Council a reasoned opinion as to why it considers that the proposal does not comply with subsidiarity.[32] The European Parliament, Council, and Commission must take this opinion into account.[33] Where noncompliance with subsidiarity is expressed by national parliaments that represent one third of all the votes allocated to such parliaments, the Commission must review its proposal.[34] The Commission, after such review, may decide to maintain, amend, or withdraw the proposal, giving reasons for its decision.[35] Where a measure is made in accord with the ordinary legislative procedure and at least a simple majority of votes given to national parliaments signal noncompliance with subsidiarity, then the proposal must once again be reviewed and, although the Commission can decide not to amend it, the Commission must provide a reasoned opinion on the matter and this can, in effect, be overridden by the European Parliament or the Council. Thus, the European Parliament acting by a majority of votes cast, or 55 percent of members of the Council, can decide that the legislative proposal is not compatible with the principle of subsidiarity and that it should not be given further consideration.[36]

While the protocol imposes obligations on the Commission to ensure compliance with the principles of subsidiarity and proportionality, national parliaments are afforded a role only in relation to the former and not the latter. The reasoned opinion submitted by the national parliament must relate to subsidiarity, but it seems nonetheless that the Commission will take account of opinions that relate in effect to proportionality as well as those relating directly to subsidiarity, more especially because it is difficult to disaggregate the two.

It remains to be seen how subsidiarity operates in practice. It is clear that there will be many areas in which the comparative efficiency calculus in Article 5(3) TFEU favors Union action, particularly in an enlarged European Union. It is equally clear that subsidiarity has impacted on the form of Union action. If EU action is required, the Commission will often proceed through directives rather than regulations, and there has been a greater use of guidelines and codes of conduct.

Time will tell how far the new provisions in the protocol according greater power to national parliaments affect the incidence and nature of EU legislation. Much will depend on the willingness of national parliaments to devote the requisite time and energy to the matter. The national parliament has to submit a reasoned opinion as to why it believes that the measure infringes subsidiarity. It will have to present reasoned argument as to why the Commission's comparative efficiency calculus is defective. This may not be easy. It will be even more difficult for the requisite number of national parliaments to present reasoned opinions in relation to the same Union measure so as to compel the Commission to review the proposal. The Commission is nonetheless likely to take seriously any such reasoned opinion, particularly if it emanates from a larger member state.

The protocol provides for recourse to the CJEU for infringement of subsidiarity under Article 263 TFEU, in an action brought by a member state. The protocol also provides for the action to be notified by the state on behalf of the national parliament. The central issue is the intensity of the judicial review. The indications are that the CJEU will not lightly overturn EU action on the ground that it does not comply with subsidiarity. This is apparent in procedural terms from *Germany v. European Parliament and Council.*[37] The CJEU held that the duty to give reasons did not require that Community measures contain an express reference to the subsidiarity principle. It was sufficient that the recitals to the measure made it clear why the Community institutions believed that the aims of the measure could best be attained by Community action. The difficulty of overturning a measure in substantive terms is apparent from the *Working Time Directive* case.[38] The United Kingdom argued that the directive infringed subsidiarity since it had not been shown that action at Community level would provide clear benefits compared with action at national level. The CJEU disposed of the argument briskly. It was, said the Court, the responsibility of the Council under Article 118a EEC[39] to adopt minimum requirements to contribute to improvement of health and safety. When the Council found it necessary to improve the existing level of protection and to harmonize the law in this area while maintaining the improvements already made, achievement of that objective necessarily presupposed Community-wide action. A similarly "light" judicial approach to subsidiarity review is evident in other cases.[40]

There are difficulties with judicial review in this area. If the CJEU continues with very "light touch" review, it will open itself to the criticism that it is effectively denuding the obligation in Article 5(3) to (4) of all content. If, by way of contrast, the CJEU takes a detailed look at the evidence underlying the Commission's claim it will have to adjudicate on what may be a complex socioeconomic calculus concerning the most effective level of government for different regulatory tasks.

The difficulty of adjudicating on the substantive issue of comparative efficiency would be alleviated if the Union courts were to require more from the Commission in procedural terms. The obligation to give reasons could be used to require the Commission to disclose the qualitative and quantitative data that is meant to inform its reasoning pursuant to the protocol. The development of Impact Assessment[41] is significant in this context. It includes the subsidiarity calculus, with a specific section devoted to verification of the European Union's right of action in terms of subsidiarity. The very fact that there is a framework within which these issues are considered is a positive step that facilitates scrutiny as to the nature of the justificatory arguments and their adequacy.

Subsidiarity has always been an emotive subject, ever since its introduction in the Maastricht Treaty. Lawyers have criticized, with justification, the low intensity judicial review undertaken by EU courts when dealing with subsidiarity claims. There have been more far-reaching critiques,[42] to the effect that the subsidiarity inquiry is misplaced and the focus should rather be on whether the challenged EU legislation is disproportionate by intruding too far into member state values in relation to the objective sought to be attained by the EU legislation. There are, however, real difficulties with this latter view.[43] Moreover, it should also be noted that there have been few legal challenges based on subsidiarity since its introduction into the treaty, roughly one real challenge per year, and it is by no means clear that the CJEU's decisions in these cases were wrong, or that they would have been different if judicial review had been more intensive.

Notes

1 Article 5(1) EC, Article 7(1) EC, Article 5(2) TEU.

2 Alan Dashwood, "The Limits of European Community Powers," *European Law Review* 21 (1996): 113; Armin von Bogdandy and Jürgen Bast, "The European Union's Vertical Order of Competences: The Current Law and Proposals for its Reform," *Common Market Law Review* 39 (2002): 227; Paul Craig, "Competence: Clarity, Conferral, Containment and Consideration," *European Law Review* 29 (2004): 323; and Robert Schütze, *From Dual to Cooperative Federalism, The Changing Structure of European Law* (Oxford: Oxford University Press, 2009).

3 Articles 4–5 TEU.

4 Stephen Weatherill, "Beyond Preemption? Shared Competence and Constitutional Change in the European Community," in O'Keefe and Twomey, *Legal Issues of the Maastricht Treaty*, Chap. 2; and Michael Dougan, "Minimum Harmonization and the Internal Market," *Common Market Law Review* 37 (2000): 853.

5 The member states were nonetheless sufficiently concerned as to the possible preemptive impact of Article 2(2) TFEU as to press for the inclusion of the Protocol (No 25) on Shared Competence, which seeks to reinforce the point made in the text.

6 Declaration 18.

7 Robert Schütze, "Co-operative Federalism Constitutionalized: The Emergence of Complementary Competences in the EC Legal Order," *European Law Review* 31 (2006): 167.

8 See, e.g., Article 167 TFEU, culture; Article 168 TFEU, public health; and Article 173 TFEU, industry.

9 Article 153 TFEU.

10 Article 147 TFEU.

11 Article 168(2) TFEU.

12 Article 168(2) TFEU.

13 Article 168(5) TFEU.

14 There are also aspects of public health that come within the shared power, where the scope for EU intervention is greater, Article 4(2)(k), Article 168(4) TFEU.

15 Article 165(4), Article 166(4) TFEU, education and vocational training; Article 167 TFEU, culture; Articles 173(2)–(3) TFEU, industry; Article 195 TFEU, tourism; and Article 196 TFEU, civil protection.

16 Article 165(4), Article 166(4) TFEU, education and vocational training; Article 167(5) TFEU, culture; and Article 168(5) TFEU, public health.

17 Article 196(2) TFEU, civil protection.

18 Article 195(2) TFEU, tourism; Article 173(3) TFEU, industry.

19 Declarations 13 and 14 on the CFSP.

20 See, e.g., Energy, Article 194(2) TFEU; Civil Protection, Article 195(2) TFEU; and Economic Aid to Third Countries, Article 209(1), 212(2) TFEU.

21 Akos Toth, "A Legal Analysis of Subsidiarity," in O'Keeffe and Twomey, *Legal Issues of the Maastricht Treaty*, 39–40; Josephine Steiner, "Subsidiarity under the Maastricht Treaty," in O'Keeffe and Twomey, *Legal Issues of the Maastricht Treaty*, 57–58; Nicholas Emiliou, "Subsidiarity: Panacea or Fig Leaf?" in O'Keeffe and Twomey, *Legal Issues of the Maastricht Treaty*, Chap. 5; Nicholas Emiliou, "Subsidiarity: An Effective Barrier Against the 'Enterprises of Ambition'?" *European Law Review* 17

(1992): 383; and Antonio Estella, *The EU Principle of Subsidiarity and its Critique* (Oxford: Oxford University Press, 2002).

22 Article 5(1) TEU.

23 Jean-Victor Louis, "National Parliaments and the Principle of Subsidiarity: Legal Options and Practical Limits," in Pernice and Tanchev, *Ceci n'est pas une Constitution – Constitutionalization without a Constitution?*, ed. Ingolf Pernice and Evgeni Tanchev (Berlin: Nomos, 2009); and George Bermann, "National Parliaments and Subsidiarity: An Outsider's View," in Pernice and Tanchev, *Ceci n'est pas une Constitution*, ed. Pernice and Tanchev.

24 Protocol (No 2) On the Application of the Principles of Subsidiarity and Proportionality.

25 Protocol (No 1) On the Role of National Parliaments in the European Union.

26 Protocol (No 2) On the Application of the Principles of Subsidiarity and Proportionality, Article 3.

27 Ibid., Article 2.

28 Ibid., Article 5.

29 Ibid., Article 9.

30 Ibid., Article 8.

31 Ibid., Article 4.

32 Ibid., Article 6.

33 Ibid., Article 7(1).

34 Ibid., Article 7(2). This threshold is lowered to one quarter in cases of acts concerning the area of freedom, justice, and security that are based on Article 76 TFEU.

35 Ibid., Article 7(2).

36 Ibid., Article 7(3).

37 Case C-233/94 *Germany v. European Parliament and Council* EU:C:1997:231.

38 Case C-84/94 *United Kingdom v. Council* EU:C:1996:431, paras 46–47, 55.

39 Now Article 154 TFEU.

40 Case C-377/98 *Netherlands v. Parliament and Council* EU:C:2001:523; Case C-491/01 *The Queen v. Secretary of State for Health, ex p. British American Tobacco (Investments) Ltd and Imperial Tobacco Ltd* EU:C:2002:741; Case C-210/03 *R v. Secretary of State for Health, ex p. Swedish Match* EU:C:2004:802; Joined Cases C-154/04 and 155/04 *The Queen, on the application of Alliance for Natural Health and Nutri-Link Ltd* v. *Secretary of State for Health* EU:C:2005:449; Case C-103/01 *Commission v. Germany* EU:C:2003:301, paras 46–47; Case T-168/01 *GlaxoSmithKline Services Unlimited v. Commission* EU:T:2006:265; Case T-326/07 *Cheminova A/S v. Commission* EU:T:2009: 299 ; and Case C-58/08 *The Queen, on the application of Vodafone Ltd v. Secretary of State for Business, Enterprise and Regulatory Reform* EU:C:2010:321.

41 Impact Assessment, COM(2002) 276 final; Impact Assessment: Next Steps, SEC(2004) 1377; Better Regulation and Enhanced Impact Assessment, SEC(2007) 926; and Impact Assessment Guidelines, SEC(2009) 92.

42 Gareth Davies, "Subsidiarity: The Wrong Idea, in the Wrong Place at the Wrong Time," *Common Market Law Review* 43 (2006): 63.

43 Paul Craig, "Subsidiarity: A Political and Legal Analysis," *Journal of Common Market Studies* 50 (2012): 72.

References

Bermann, George. "National Parliaments and Subsidiarity: An Outsider's View." In Pernice and Tanchev, *Ceci n'est pas une Constitution*, 155–161.

Craig, Paul. "Competence: Clarity, Conferral, Containment and Consideration." *European Law Review* 29 (2004): 323–344.

Craig, Paul. "Subsidiarity: A Political and Legal Analysis." *Journal of Common Market Studies* 50 (2012): 72–87.

Dashwood, Alan. "The Limits of European Community Powers." *European Law Review* 21 (1996): 113–128.

Davies, Gareth. "Subsidiarity: The Wrong Idea, in the Wrong Place at the Wrong Time." *Common Market Law Review* 43 (2006): 63–84.

Dougan, Michael. "Minimum Harmonization and the Internal Market." *Common Market Law Review* 37 (2000): 853–885.

Emiliou, Nicholas. "Subsidiarity: An Effective Barrier Against the 'Enterprises of Ambition'?" *European Law Review* 17 (1992): 383–407.

Emiliou, Nicholas. "Subsidiarity: Panacea or Fig Leaf?" In O'Keefe and Twomey, *Legal Issues of the Maastricht Treaty*, 65–83.

Estella, Antonio. *The EU Principle of Subsidiarity and its Critique*. Oxford: Oxford University Press, 2002.

Louis, Jean-Victor. "National Parliaments and the Principle of Subsidiarity: Legal Options and Practical Limits." In Pernice and Tanchev, *Ceci n'est pas une Constitution*, 131–154. Berlin: Nomos, 2009.

O'Keefe David, and Patrick Twomey, eds. *Legal Issues of the Maastricht Treaty*. London: Chancery Law Publishing, 1994.

Pernice Ingolf, and Evgeni Tanchev, eds. *Ceci n'est pas une Constitution - Constitutionalization without a Constitution?* Berlin: Nomos, 2009.

Schütze, Robert. "Co-operative Federalism Constitutionalized: The Emergence of Complementary Competences in the EC Legal Order." *European Law Review* 31 (2006): 167–184.

Schütze, Robert. *From Dual to Cooperative Federalism: The Changing Structure of European Law*. Oxford: Oxford University Press, 2009.

Steiner, Josephine. "Subsidiarity under the Maastricht Treaty." In O'Keefe and Twomey, *Legal Issues of the Maastricht Treaty*, 49–64.

Toth, Akos. "A Legal Analysis of Subsidiarity." In O'Keeffe and Twomey, *Legal Issues of the Maastricht Treaty*, 37–48.

von Bogdandy, Armin, and Jürgen Bast. "The European Union's Vertical Order of Competences: The Current Law and Proposals for its Reform." *Common Market Law Review* 39 (2002): 227–268.

Weatherill, Stephen. "Beyond Preemption? Shared Competence and Constitutional Change in the European Community." In O'Keefe and Twomey, *Legal Issues of the Maastricht Treaty*, 13–33.

7

The Decision-Making Process

Bruno de Witte

Introduction

This chapter comprises four sections. In the first section, the general *evolution* of the European Union's decision-making regime will be traced in broad outline. In the second section, EU *legislative* decision making will be examined in greater detail, followed, in the third section, by *administrative* rule making by the EU institutions. A brief concluding section will complete the overview by describing *other* relevant forms of decision making in the European Union. The analysis is focused on the process of lawmaking, with limited attention given to other forms of political decision making that do not take create legal rules.

The Evolution of the EU Decision-Making Process: Institutional Balance and Policy-Related Variation

The pattern of EU decision making has traditionally varied across policy fields to a degree that is unknown in the national constitutional law of its member states, where laws and administrative rules are usually made according to fairly standard procedures covering all policy areas. Such policy-related variation has been a constant feature throughout the history of European integration. Even though in the early days of their existence the European Communities were engaged in far fewer policy fields than today's European Union, the institutional functioning of the Communities was already different from one sector to another. Indeed, the decision taken in 1957 by the original six member states to set up two new Communities alongside the existing European Coal and Steel Community (ECSC), rather than establishing a broader multipurpose organization, was primarily inspired by the governments' view that institutional rules appropriate for regulating the coal and steel markets were not suitable for the much broader multisector European Economic Community (EEC). In particular, when setting up the EEC, the member states granted to the Commission more limited independent decision-making powers than the Commission's equivalent – the High Authority – had possessed under the ECSC Treaty.

A Companion to European Union Law and International Law, First Edition.
Edited by Dennis Patterson and Anna Södersten.

Within the EEC itself, different legal instruments and different decision-making rules were used in the main policy fields as they were at the time – agriculture, competition, and harmonization of national laws for the purpose of creating a common market. The main embodiment of this institutional variation was – and still is – the *legal basis* requirement. Whereas federal constitutions usually list the broad policy domains attributed to either the federal or member state level, the Community treaties operated a much more detailed division of competences between the Communities and their member states by specifying at great length *what* the European Community (EC) could do, and *how*. Every legal act of Community law had to find a basis in a specific article of the treaties, spelling out not only the policy domain in which the Community could act but also the policy objectives it had to pursue, the legal instruments that could be used for that purpose, the institution that could adopt those instruments, and the decision-making rules that should be followed. So, for example, the chapter on competition law specified from the start that both the Council and the Commission had a lawmaking role (although different ones), and that the legal instruments to be used in this area were to be, essentially, the regulation and the decision; whereas harmonization of national laws, when needed for a better functioning of the common market, could be done either by means of directives adopted by the Council acting unanimously on a proposal of the Commission, or by means of conventions concluded directly between the member states.

This fragmented institutional reality did not prevent legal authors and the Court of Justice from trying to identify some overall institutional features of the Community legal order and crosscutting institutional principles. The most commonly prescribed legislative decision-making process was termed the "Community method." It involved the European Commission making a fully fledged proposal for legislation that was to be adopted by the Council acting by qualified majority or by unanimity, depending on the subject matter, although the Council informally sought to achieve an overall consensus among the national delegations on all pieces of legislation. The European Parliament played a merely consultative role without any major impact on policy outcomes.

As for the overarching principles, a central role was given to the concept of *institutional balance* (in French: *équilibre institutionnel*), which was used by the European Court of Justice already during the 1950s, in the context of the ECSC Treaty, and could be found rather regularly in its later case law. In fact, the concept played a mostly declaratory role, since the Court used the term "institutional balance" as convenient shorthand for the set of treaty rules that happened to apply to the particular institutional dispute under consideration. In several cases, the Court firmly rejected arguments that the specific treaty rules on the division of powers between the institutions should, if necessary, be disregarded in view of an unwritten higher principle of institutional balance. It did so most clearly in an action for annulment brought in the early 1980s by several member states against a Commission directive on the transparency of financial relations between the member states and their public undertakings. It was argued on behalf of the applicants that the Commission's power to adopt directives, under the (then) Article 90(3) EEC, should not be interpreted as giving this institution an original lawmaking power as that would be contrary to the general principles governing the division of powers between the institutions. The Court of Justice replied that

> the limits of the powers conferred on the Commission by a specific provision of the Treaty are to be inferred not from a general principle, but from an interpretation of the provision in question, in this case Article 90, analysed in the light of its purpose and its place in the scheme of the Treaty.[1]

As the Court observed in another of those interinstitutional disputes, "the powers of the institutions ... are not always based on consistent criteria,"[2] and the Court refused to establish institutional consistency across policy sectors when the drafters of the treaties had chosen not to be consistent.

The Maastricht Treaty (1992) added a large number of new policy domains to those which the European Communities had previously included, but it also – and at the same time – strongly increased the existing institutional fragmentation. To some extent, this was the almost mathematical consequence of the addition of new policy fields. Since the legal basis requirement retained the pivotal role that it had had prior to Maastricht, and since there was a significant increase of the number of legal bases, there was a concomitant increase in variation of decision-making rules. However, the Maastricht Treaty added a new dimension to this variation by the creation of an entirely new legislative decision-making mechanism, which was colloquially called "codecision." It was cautiously introduced in only a limited number of policy fields, whereas other legal bases continued to require the so-called cooperation procedure (which is now defunct) and others still the "old-fashioned" procedure whereby the Council could decide after simple consultation of the European Parliament. After Maastricht, there was thus no longer a mainstream "Community method" but rather three principal legislative procedures whose use depended on the particular policy domain involved.

But the Maastricht Treaty also increased institutional fragmentation in another way. It transferred to the European level three important new policy domains that were subject to wholly idiosyncratic institutional rules for which there was no precedent in Community law. One such domain, namely the Economic and Monetary Union (EMU), was encapsulated within the EC Treaty[3] as an – institutionally speaking – alien object, whereas the other two domains, Common Foreign and Security Policy (CFSP) and Justice and Home Affairs (JHA), were conceived so differently from the rest – again, institutionally speaking – that the member states enacted a wholly new treaty (the Treaty on the European Union (TEU)) and established a new organization (the European Union) to accommodate them, so as to emphasize that "normal" Community law mechanisms should not apply to them.

The EMU was given a very specific decision-making structure, or rather two very different substructures: for the monetary union, the central decision-making power shifted to a newly created supranational institution, the European Central Bank (ECB), whereas the economic union branch of the EMU was marked by a very complex and cautious mechanism of coordination of national policies, with little or no room for binding acts to be adopted by the Community institutions.

As for CFSP and JHA, those new policy fields were marked, in legal terms, by the deliberate rejection of some of the key legal characteristics undergirding the Community legal order, such as Commission initiative for legislation; full judicial review; and primacy and direct effect in the domestic legal orders. All power was, rather, concentrated in the hands of the Council, the institution representing the member states, with only marginal roles given to the supranational institutions (Commission, Parliament, and Court of Justice).

Finally, the Treaty of Maastricht also loosened the unity of the European legal order by allowing some member states not to participate at all, or to participate in limited ways, in crucial areas of Community law such as the EMU and social policy. Later on, the Treaty of Amsterdam (1999) would also create an opt-out regime for immigration policy. The United Kingdom, in particular, was given an opt-out from all those areas. This meant that the Council, when acting in those fields, operated (or at least voted) in a reduced composition.

Since that period of the early 1990s, we have seen further major evolutions in the macro-institutional landscape, mainly through the work of the Convention on the Future of the Union, meeting in 2002 to 2003, and the reflection of that work in first the Constitutional Treaty (2003) and later the Lisbon Treaty (2007). The institutional "bits and pieces" created by the Maastricht Treaty[4] have been put together into a relatively more coherent whole. In particular, the Lisbon Treaty led to the formal absorption of the former intergovernmental pillars of CFSP and JHA into the common regime of competences, legal instruments, decision making, judicial review, and legal effect. In reality, whereas JHA has been almost completely absorbed within the Union's common decision-making regime, CFSP remains a very distinct institutional field which, as Article 24(1) of the TEU quaintly states, is "subject to specific rules and procedures," marked by the continuing predominance of the Council over the other institutions and the continuing reliance on unanimity as the main decision-making mode.

Accordingly, with the entry into force of the Lisbon Treaty in December 2009, the organizational dichotomy created at Maastricht was terminated. The Lisbon Treaty left in existence two separate treaties, the TEU and the Treaty on the Functioning of the European Union (TFEU) – the successor of the EC Treaty – but only one single organization: the European Union.[5] The "two-treaties-for-one-organization" idea was rendered as follows in the new Article 1(3) TEU:

> The Union shall be founded on the present Treaty and on the Treaty on the Functioning of the European Union (hereinafter referred to as "the Treaties"). Those two Treaties shall have the same legal value. The Union shall replace and succeed the European Community.

Alongside the merger of the pillars, the Lisbon Treaty introduced the concept of the *ordinary legislative procedure* as the new label for what used to be known as codecision. The use of the new term is justified by the fact that the vast majority of legal bases allowing for EU legislative acts now, since the Lisbon Treaty reform, point to codecision as the applicable decision-making method. So, there is once again a predominant "Community method"[6] for adopting legislation, but it is very different from its first pre-Maastricht version: whereas the Commission has maintained its power of legislative initiative, the adoption of legislation is now entrusted to the Council and the Parliament acting together (rather than the Council on its own), and the decision-making mode in the Council is now firmly that of qualified majority[7] rather than unanimity, despite a lingering practice of seeking the overall consensus of all delegations whenever possible. Despite these important steps towards greater institutional uniformity across policy domains, the central role of the legal basis requirement was not affected. One still needs to turn to one of the myriad legal provisions in the two treaties (and their protocols) to find out how precisely the European Union is supposed to act, with which instruments, by means of which institutions, and according to which procedures, for the particular purposes defined in that legal basis provision.

In contrast with this reduction of cross-policy variation in decision making, the Lisbon Treaty also entrenched the practice of *differentiated lawmaking*[8] by retaining the existing opt-out mechanisms in the policy domains of EMU and immigration policy and by adding a major new opt-out regime in the field of police cooperation and criminal justice. In return for the introduction of the "Community method" in that policy area, the United Kingdom obtained an opt-out from future developments and even a right to unilaterally pull out from *existing* criminal justice instruments by which the United Kingdom is bound.[9]

Legislative Decision Making

After the sketch of the historical evolution in the preceding section, this section examines in further detail the current rules and practice of legislative decision making in the European Union, and in particular the role played therein by the Commission, the Council, and the European Parliament.

EU legislation can roughly be described as acts of EU law that have an abstractly and generally formulated content and that are adopted directly on the basis of an article of the treaty.[10] The main instruments of EU legislation are *regulations* and *directives*. A formal description of the concept of legislation by reference to the use of these two legal instruments would, however, not be correct. Some directives and many regulations are administrative rather than legislative acts. There is, however, an alternative formal criterion for the identification of a "legislative act" in EU law that is not based on the form of the act but rather on the procedure of decision making. According to Article 289(3) TFEU, "legal acts adopted by legislative procedure shall constitute legislative acts," and the use of a legislative procedure is, in turn, prescribed in the treaty article that serves as the legal basis of the act.

No single institution can claim the title of "the Union's legislative branch" for itself. EU legislation results from the cooperation and interaction between three institutions, essentially: the Commission, the Council, and the European Parliament. This interaction is not structured uniformly across all policy fields, but – as was mentioned above – depends on the treaty article which forms the legal basis of the legislative act. Compare, for example, the following two treaty articles, which provide for very different decision-making regimes.

Article 46 TFEU:

> The *European Parliament and the Council* shall, acting in accordance with *the ordinary legislative procedure* and after consulting the Economic and Social Committee, issue directives or make regulations setting out the measures required to bring about freedom of movement for workers, as defined in Article 45 …

Article 86(1) TFEU:

> In order to combat crimes affecting the financial interests of the Union, the *Council*, by means of regulations adopted *in accordance with a special legislative procedure*, may establish a European Public Prosecutor's Office from Eurojust. *The Council shall act unanimously after obtaining the consent of the European Parliament.*

Thus, the legal basis articles now make a formal distinction, which was introduced by the Lisbon Treaty reforms, between "the" ordinary legislative procedure and "a" special legislative procedure. The choice of different adjectives underscores the fact that there is one single ordinary procedure but a number of different special procedures. The domains in which a special legislative procedure applies are usually the typically "intergovernmental" ones, in which the member states seek to control the legislative process: the Council is the sole author of legislation (as it used to be in *all* policy areas in pre-codecision days) and/or the Council must act by unanimity rather than qualified majority.[11]

The vast majority of legal bases currently prescribe the use of the *ordinary legislative procedure*. This is its formal denomination in the text of the treaties, although it is still commonly called the codecision procedure. The steps in the decision-making process are described in great detail in Article 294 TFEU, and this detailed description makes it seem cumbersome and time consuming. In practice, though, the EU institutions have adopted a number of informal rules and arrangements that make the procedure more manageable than it would seem.

The Treaty of Maastricht introduced codecision in order to make the Parliament a more or less equal partner with the Council in the Community legislative process, at least in a small number of policy areas. The procedure was simplified somewhat by the Treaty of Amsterdam, and certain inequalities between the Council and Parliament were further leveled out;

moreover, the number of policy areas to which this procedure applied was increased. The same happened with the Treaty of Nice and the Treaty of Lisbon, and the coining of the term "ordinary legislative procedure" by the latter treaty is fully warranted, since codecision nowadays is used for approximately 90 percent of all EU legislative projects.

The equality of the Parliament and the Council is expressed at the beginning and end of the process. At the beginning, the Commission submits its legislative proposal not just to the Council but also to the European Parliament. And at the end, the EU regulations, directives, or decisions adopted in accordance with this procedure are signed by the president of the European Parliament and by the president of the Council[12] and are entitled "Directive [or regulation, or other type of act] of the European Parliament and of the Council."

The codecision procedure thus starts with the submission of the Commission proposal to the Parliament and the Council. The Parliament, in a plenary session, adopts its opinion on the proposal on the basis of a report by the appropriate standing committee. At the same time, the Council prepares its own position, on the basis of the preparatory work by national civil servants meeting in Brussels within Council working groups and by the Committee of Permanent Representatives (grouping the member states' diplomatic representatives posted in Brussels), whereas the ministers themselves are "flown in" from their respective capitals to formally adopt the Council's position and/or to discuss controversial points that their civil servants and diplomats have not been able to solve on their own. If the Parliament and the Council agree on a common text during this *first reading*, the legislative act can already be adopted at this stage of the ordinary legislative procedure. If, however, the two institutions disagree (for example, the Parliament may adopt amendments to the Commission's text which are not to the Council's liking, or vice versa), then the file moves to the so-called *second reading*.

In that case, the Council's version of the text (called its "position at first reading") is communicated to the Parliament, which must also be informed fully by the Council of the reasons that led it to adopt the common position and by the Commission of its own views on the evolution of the file. The Parliament then has three months in which to react; this stage is known as the second reading in the Parliament. If, within this period, the Parliament approves the Council's position or fails to take a decision, the act in question "shall be deemed to have been adopted in the wording which corresponds to the position of the Council" (Article 294(7)(a) TFEU), that is, the regulation or directive is then enacted without the Council needing to consider it anew.

If instead, within that three-month period, the Parliament – by an absolute majority of its component members (which is significantly more than the majority of votes cast!) – rejects or amends the Council's position, then the proposed act is not adopted. In that case, the Council examines the proposals in its *second reading*. The Council may – within a period of three months, and by qualified majority – accept all the amendments proposed by Parliament, and in that case the act is adopted in the version proposed by the Parliament. The Council may also, though, stick to its earlier views, or at least fail to reach the required qualified majority to accept all the amendments proposed by Parliament; in that case, a Conciliation Committee is convened, which consists of twenty-eight members of the Council (each representing one state) and an equivalent number of members of the European Parliament.

The *conciliation procedure* (Article 294(10) TFEU) which is thus initiated aims to reach a compromise which is acceptable to both institutions by means of direct negotiation between the Council and Parliament. The Conciliation Committee has six weeks in which to do this. Within the Committee, a double majority rule applies: the draft text must be approved by a majority of the representatives of the Parliament (so, at least fifteen) and a qualified majority of the representatives of the Council in the Committee (with the same weighting of votes as for the decision making in the Council itself). If such a joint text is approved, then the Parliament and the Council both have six weeks during which they must endorse the text or reject it (this is called their *third reading*).

It is clear that the influence of the Parliament on legislative decision making has increased substantially thanks to the codecision procedure. On the other hand, this growing role of the European Parliament has led to a gradually more complex behind-the-scenes coordination between key actors of the three institutions. This takes the form of the so-called *trialogues*, that is, informal meetings of just a few key representatives of Council, Commission, and Parliament who seek to reach compromises which can then be presented and approved in the formal meetings. This phenomenon characterizes the different stages of the codecision procedures and not just the final phase of conciliation. So, whereas the text of Article 294 TFEU seems to point to a process whereby the Council and Parliament act *consecutively* and react thereby to each other's moves, the political reality is one where their consecutive moves are coordinated a priori by means of trialogue compromises. This has led to a clear prevalence of *first reading adoptions*. This does not denote a spontaneous commonality of views between Council and Parliament but instead shows that the informal method of reaching a compromise works rather well. There is, however, a price to be paid in terms of transparency and accountability. Both within the European Parliament and within the Council, this informal practice has increased the power of key players to the detriment of the institution as a whole, leading to what has been called "secluded decision-making."[13]

Following this discussion of the codecision procedure, three general features of the legislative decision-making process are worth highlighting.

First, as a consequence of the continuing plurality of legislative procedures (the ordinary one and the special ones), there are still occasions, although fewer than before, for legal basis disputes between the institutions, or between the institutions and some member states, since the choice of a treaty basis for a given measure will trigger a particular lawmaking procedure and therefore also a particular balance between the institutions.

Second, one thing the various procedures have in common is the *Commission's right of legislative initiative*, which is an original but still crucial feature of the European Union's decision-making process. The Council and the European Parliament simply cannot adopt legislation on their own initiative without a formal proposal by the Commission. There are only few exceptions to this rule. The proposal from the Commission is a fully fledged draft legislative act that forms not only the formal starting point but also the substantive basis on which the Council and Parliament then start working. The Commission's exclusive right of initiative also entitles it to determine whether and at what time it will submit a proposal. In political practice, though, this right of initiative is not the Commission's exclusive preserve. Before making its proposals, the Commission tends to sketch the outlines of a new policy through communications, reports, or Green Papers in order to gauge the views of the other institutions and of relevant stakeholders. For some years now, the Commission has also carried out *impact assessments* of many of its draft legislative texts. These assessments explore the economic, social, and environmental consequences of the adoption of the proposed legislation and follow a standard methodology. There is often also a very informal process of "pre-negotiation" with member state experts even before a formal draft is tabled by the Commission. Moreover, in relation to important questions of policy, the real political initiative often comes from the European Council. This institution, composed of the heads of government of the member states, does not play a formal role in the legislative process but, according to Article 15(1) TEU, it has the task of laying down "the general political directions and priorities" of the European Union, and this role obviously extends to the Union's legislative process.[14] Sometimes, it gives quite specific indications as to the kind of legislative enactments it would like to see, although the actual proposals still need to be adopted by the Commission – which can be politically pressured but not legally compelled to act in a certain way. Finally, the Commission's right of initiative is further qualified by the fact that much of its legislative work, nowadays, consists of updating existing legislation in the light of technical changes or the Court's case law and that many legislative initiatives consist in implementing international agreements which the European Union has concluded with third countries. The role of the Commission, though, is not limited to making the formal proposal: it continues to sit at the negotiation table throughout the procedure, during Council sessions or at trialogue meetings, where it can use its technical expertise to help the other institutions in defining a workable compromise text.

Third, in addition to the four most important political institutions (Commission, Council, European Council, and Parliament), a number of other bodies play a role in legislative decision making. The Economic and Social Committee and the Committee of the Regions are consulted on proposals for legislation in all cases where consultation is required under the legal basis of the proposed legislation; their advisory opinions are not binding on the other institutions and their policy impact is limited. The ECB is an important actor in the area of monetary legislation. National parliaments, in addition to their "ordinary" role of exercising political control on their government's European policy, have been given a "special" and direct role in the EU legislative process. The treaty protocol on subsidiarity allows the national parliaments of the twenty-eight member states to scrutinize Commission proposals of legislation for their compatibility with the principle of subsidiarity. If a sufficient number of national parliaments express their opposition to the draft, a "yellow card" is shown to the Commission which must respond to the objections and explain better if and why it wants to maintain its draft.[15] In addition to these bodies and organs which have a formal role in the legislative process, recognized in the treaties, there are of course numerous informal actors, in particular interest groups, which may exert considerable influence on the decision-making process.[16]

Administrative Rule Making

Administrative rule making by the European Union takes a number of different forms, which will be briefly discussed in this section: autonomous executive action by either the Council or the Commission; implementation of legislation by the Council, or by the Commission through delegated and implementing acts; and rule making by independent EU agencies.

First, there are processes of administrative rule making that are independent of a preexisting piece of legislation and, rather, seek to implement directly a mandate conferred on the institutions by the treaty text. A policy area where this typically happens is CFSP. The TEU states that, in this domain, both the Council and the European Council have the power to adopt decisions, but it adds that "the adoption of legislative acts shall be excluded" (Article 24(1) TEU). So, CFSP decisions are binding legal instruments but not legislative acts; they are not implementing measures either, since the power to adopt them is given directly by the treaty rather than by a legislative act. A prominent category among them is the trade sanctions and other restrictive measures adopted by the Council against third countries.[17] Similarly, the Commission adopts autonomous administrative rules based directly on an empowerment by the treaty text, most notably in the important area of competition and state aid law.[18]

Second, the European Union is generally empowered to adopt administrative rules for the further implementation of EU legislation. The use of that power is subject to the general but rather empty condition that "uniform conditions for implementing legally binding Union acts are needed."[19] Indeed, the main principle remains that EU legislation is to be implemented and applied by the member states according to the rules and procedures of their own systems of administrative law. Still, it happens very frequently that European legislation provides for its implementation at the European level by the EU institutions themselves.

This task may occasionally be attributed to the Council, which is rather curious from a separation of powers perspective, since the Council is the (co)author of the legislative act which it then sets out to implement. This mechanism is, actually, rather uncommon, but the option is explicitly acknowledged in Article 291(2) TFEU. One important area where this occurs is in the adoption of antidumping measures in international trade (although the Council's decisions depend on an antidumping investigation being initiated by the Commission). In the vast majority of policy areas, however, the Commission is the institution entrusted with a "derivative" administrative role assigned in a specific legislative act. In the exercise of this executive task, the Commission is obliged in most cases to consult other bodies in its decision making, in particular committees consisting of national civil servants from the member states. For the Council, these procedures provide a solution to the dilemma that it faced originally when it was still the sole European legislator: either reserving the implementation entirely to itself, which is impractical and sometimes de facto impossible, or leaving the implementation entirely in the hands of the Commission, which it found to be politically undesirable. Such control procedures on the Commission's executive role make sense in that the application of Union law "on the ground" eventually involves the national governments and their civil services, so that one may as well consult them before enacting the rules. The name commonly used to refer to this system is "comitology." Its role has been very prominent for many years in all sorts of policy areas where EU law is being implemented through common European rules (particularly in the area of agriculture and fisheries, food quality, and structural funds).[20]

The Lisbon Treaty introduced a differentiation within that system, by laying down a principled distinction between *delegated acts* and *implementing acts*. Those two categories of administrative rules are both to be adopted by the Commission, according to its own internal decision-making rules,[21] but the distinction is relevant in terms of the control mechanisms imposed on the Commission when it enacts such measures. In the case of implementing acts, the Commission's power is subject to the newest version of the comitology system,[22] whereby committees composed of member state experts are required to give their opinion before the Commission adopts the rules; in some limited cases, the committee can force the Commission to withdraw or reconsider its draft decision. In the case of delegated acts, which amend or "supplement" (rather than "implement") legislative acts, the Commission acts more freely but under potentially stricter control. Indeed, the delegated acts must not be scrutinized by a committee of national officials, but both delegators (the European Parliament or the Council) have the power to either revoke the delegation or object to the entry into force of the delegated act if they are not happy with the Commission's text. The limited practice since the creation of this bifurcated regime shows among other things[23] that delegated acts are much fewer in number than implementing acts and that the delegators rarely if ever formulate objections to the Commission's decisions (also because the Commission makes sure to conduct informal consultations in the politically more delicate cases).

A *third*, and very different, mode of administrative rule making is by means of the now numerous EU *agencies*. There are now approximately thirty-five regulatory agencies[24] exercising a number of different functional roles, including information gathering, providing scientific expertise, and actual decision making in individual cases. Administrative rule making is also increasingly entrusted to agencies, most prominently so for the supervision of financial institutions.[25] Each of these agencies acts as a "mini-executive," with its own decision-making procedure and its own mechanisms allowing for monitoring and control by the European Union's main institutions.[26]

Other Forms of Decision Making

Although legislative and administrative rule making constitute the bulk of the European Union's decision-making activity, some other forms of decision making should be mentioned very briefly for the sake of completion.

First, and most important, is *revision of the Treaties* (meaning the TEU and TFEU), since this legal instrument changes the rules of the EU game and therefore may also modify the legislative and administrative decision-making rules themselves. We have seen repeatedly, in the previous pages, how successive revisions of the European treaties (Single European Act, Treaty of Maastricht, Treaty of Amsterdam, Treaty of Nice, and Treaty of Lisbon, to mention only the main ones) have incrementally modified the decision-making regime of the European Union. Treaty revision itself takes the form of an international agreement concluded between the EU member states and not that of an EU law instrument, except in some cases of so-called simplified revision, when a unanimous European Council decision is enough to modify a particular treaty provision.[27] In all cases, though, the actual revision is decided by unanimous agreement of all the member state governments and subject to the approval of their parliaments. Although the EU institutions play a certain role in the negotiation process leading up to the revision treaty, they do not decide the final outcome. Treaty revision is therefore a confirmation of the leading role of the European Union's member states, as "masters of the Treaties" who continue to steer the overall institutional evolution of the Union.[28]

Second, another, increasingly important, form of lawmaking is the conclusion of *external agreements*, that is, treaties between the European Union and third countries (or international organizations). The European Union can conclude such treaties in all areas of its competence, ranging from international trade to environment, to immigration, to transport, and so on. The involvement of third parties in the lawmaking process makes that process, naturally, very different from internal EU legislation. The process is composed essentially of a negotiation phase, which is conducted by the Commission under more or less strict instructions of the Council, and a conclusion phase, where the outcome of the negotiations is approved and ratified (or not) by the Council. The European Parliament used to play a marginal role, but the Lisbon Treaty has upgraded its powers. Basically, the European Parliament now has to give its consent to the conclusion of all external agreements in policy areas in which internal legislation is adopted through codecision; in addition, the European Parliament also has the same power of consent for international trade agreements for which there is no "internal" counterpart.[29]

Third, there are forms of decision making that do not lead to the adoption of *legal rules*. In a number of, sometimes important, policy areas, the European Union acts in a *coordination* mode. Lawmaking powers remain firmly in the hands of the member states, but the EU institutions conduct a process of governance whereby those autonomous national policies are being steered through procedures taking place at the European level. Although such coordinating mechanisms have existed since the start of the European integration process, they rose to greater prominence with the Maastricht Treaty, which introduced a mechanism of coordination of the *fiscal and macroeconomic policies* of the states,[30] and some years later with the Treaty of Amsterdam, which introduced a similar coordination regime for the member states' *employment policies*.[31] In both cases, there is a process of ongoing interaction between the member states, the Commission, and the Council during which, in mutual consultation, annual guidelines are established at the European level for the relevant national policy. This procedure departs sharply from the traditional legislative procedure since the Commission does not have the formal right of initiative but acts as a "process manager," and also because the end product is not formal EU legislation but soft law instruments that do not formally bind the member states.

Under the name of "open method of coordination," this approach was later introduced in other policy domains in which the European Union has only very limited legislative competences, and in which, therefore, the development of an EU policy requires the "cooptation" of the relevant national authorities – in particular, in the fields of social policy and education policy.[32] Whereas the term "open method of coordination" was coined by the European Council at its meeting in Lisbon in 2000 (and thus became part of the "Lisbon agenda"), it was not incorporated in the text of the treaties. A description of a method of action which corresponds to the open method of coordination – but without using the term – was included in the articles by the Lisbon Treaty dealing with the policy areas of public health, industry, and research, though not in other fields where it is also used.[33] In addition, the existing and differently formulated references to policy coordination were kept for the areas of economic policy and employment. Yet, as a result of the euro crisis, the system of economic governance was recently strengthened into a hybrid regime of coordination-with-teeth, in which member states must abide by the guidelines decided at the European level if they do not wish to incur financial sanctions.[34]

A final form of EU decision making is *appointments* to key positions in the EU institutional world. Separate rules are laid down in the treaties regarding the selection and appointment of members of the European Commission and of the Court of Justice, as well as the Presidents of the European Council and of the ECB, to name only the main ones. All those appointments used to be made in a classic "diplomatic" way, that is, by common accord of all the member state governments. Here as well, successive treaty revisions have introduced some new rules, the most important change probably being that the president and members of the European Commission must now be appointed with the joint approval of the European Council (acting by qualified majority rather than by common accord) and the European Parliament.[35] Lastly, the president of the European Council is elected by the members of that institution by qualified majority rather than by the traditional common accord rule.[36]

Notes

1 Joined Cases 188/80 to 190/80 *France, Italy and UK v. Commission* EU:C:1982:257, para 6.

2 Case 242/87 *Commission v. Council* EU:C:1989:217, para 13.

3 The Maastricht Treaty renamed the European Economic Community into "European Community" (hence, also, "EC Treaty" instead of "EEC Treaty") in recognition of the fact that the attribution of a number of new policy competences in noneconomic fields had made the term "Economic" obsolete.

4 The reference here is to a well-known article of Deirdre Curtin describing the institutional reforms enacted by the Maastricht Treaty in rather negative terms: Deirdre Curtin, "The Constitutional Structure of the Union: A Europe of Bits and Pieces," *Common Market Law Review* 30 (1993).

5 The EC disappeared as an organization by being absorbed within the European Union. Therefore, one of the unavoidable amendments of the EC Treaty made by the Lisbon Treaty was to change its name into the TFEU.

6 That term is still commonly used in EU parlance, despite the fact that the "Community," which gave its name to the method, no longer exists since its merger with the Union in 2009.

7 Qualified majority voting in the Council was based on a system of weighted votes attributed to each member state in rough accordance with its population. A total number of 352 votes were thus allocated to the twenty-eight member states and Council decisions were adopted if at least fifteen states voted in favor and if they, together, had 260 votes, i.e., approximately 74 percent of the total number of weighted votes. As of 1 November 2014, this system was replaced by a more rational and simple one whereby a qualified majority requires the votes of 55 percent of the number of states (i.e., sixteen out of twenty-eight), on condition that they also represent at least 65 percent of the total EU population. See Article 16(4) and (5) TEU.

8 For the use of that expression and a short description of its various forms, see Damian Chalmers, Gareth Davies, and Giorgio Monti, *European Union Law – Text and Materials* (Cambridge: Cambridge University Press, 2014), 135–143.

9 See Steve Peers, "In a World of Their Own? Justice and Home Affairs Opt-Outs and the Treaty of Lisbon," *Cambridge Yearbook of European Legal Studies* 10 (2007–2008).

10 The latter characteristic distinguishes them from EU administrative acts, which are themselves based on a legislative act and thus only indirectly on the treaties themselves, although there are some exceptions to this: see the section on administrative rule making later in the chapter.

11 Treaty articles providing for the use of a special legislative procedure can be found all over the text of the TFEU. They include among others: tax harmonization, antidiscrimination policy, and certain kinds of measures in the field of energy, social security, family law, police cooperation, etc. For a complete list, see Koen Lenaerts and Piet Van Nuffel, *European Union Law* (London: Sweet & Maxwell, 2011), 673.

12 Article 297(1) TFEU (the president of the Council means the president-in-office of the Council in the relevant configuration; for example, a directive on environmental protection adopted during the six-month presidency of Italy will be signed by the Italian minister of the environment).

13 Christine Reh et al., "The Informal Politics of Legislation: Explaining Secluded Decision-Making in the European Union," *Comparative Political Studies* 46 (2013). For a comprehensive assessment of the political reality of codecision, see the contributions to "Twenty Years of Legislative Codecision in the European Union," special issue, *Journal of European Public Policy* 20 (2013).

14 See the recent assessment by Pierre Bocquillon and Mathias Dobbels, "An Elephant on the 13th Floor of the Berlaymont? European Council and Commission Relations in Legislative Agenda Setting," *Journal of European Public Policy* 21 (2014).

15 On the role of national parliaments in the EU legislative process, see Chalmers, Davies, and Monti, *European Union Law*, 127–135; and Ian Cooper, "A Virtual Third Chamber for the European Union? National Parliaments after the Treaty of Lisbon," *West European Politics* 35 (2012).

16 There is extensive political science literature on their role. See, e.g., Heike Klüver, *Lobbying in the European Union: Interest Groups, Lobbying Coalitions, and Policy Change* (Oxford: Oxford University Press, 2013); and Rainer Eising and Sonja Lehringer, "Interest Groups and the European Union," in *European Union Politics*, ed. Michelle Cini and Nieves Pérez-Solórzano Borragán, (Oxford: Oxford University Press, 2010).

17 See, e.g., Council Decision 2014/512/CFSP of 31 July 2014 concerning restrictive measures in view of Russia's actions destabilizing the situation in Ukraine [2014] OJ L 229/13. This decision's legal basis is Article 29 TEU, which refers in very general terms to the Council's power to "adopt decisions which shall define the approach of the Union to a particular matter of a geographical or thematic nature."

18 An example of a general administrative measure of the Commission adopted directly on the basis of the treaty is Commission Regulation 1407/2013 of 18 December 2013 on the application of Articles 107 and 108 TFEU to *de minimis* aid [2013] OJ L 352/1.

19 Article 291(2) TFEU.

20 See in particular Thomas Christiansen and Torbjörn Larsson, eds., *The Role of Committees in the Policy-Process of the European Union* (Cheltenham: Edward Elgar, 2007); Paul Craig, *EU Administrative Law* (Oxford: Oxford University Press, 2012), Chap. 5; and Adrienne Héritier et al., *Changing Rules of Delegation – A Contest for Power in Comitology* (Oxford: Oxford University Press, 2013).

21 Internal decision making within the Commission takes place, formally speaking, by a simple majority vote of its members, although in practice an overall consensus is sought for all decisions and votes are exceedingly rare. In routine matters, decision making is often delegated to the Commission's civil service.

22 That newest version is contained in Regulation 182/2011 laying down the rules and general principles concerning mechanisms for control by member states of the Commission's exercise of implementing powers [2011] OJ L 55/13.

23 For a study of the incipient practice, see Thomas Christiansen and Mathias Dobbels, "Non-Legislative Rule Making after the Lisbon Treaty: Implementing the New System of Comitology and Delegated Acts," *European Law Journal* 19 (2013).

24 See a list with a nutshell description of the tasks of each of them in Michelle Everson, Cosimo Monda, and Ellen Vos, eds., *European Agencies in between Institutions and Member States* (Alphen: Kluwer Law International, 2014), Annex I. Note that there is no treaty list nor a treaty definition of agencies and some of the bodies listed as agencies are not actually called "agency" but "centre," "authority," or "office."

25 See Madalina Busuioc, "Rule-Making by the European Financial Supervisory Authorities: Walking a Tight Rope," *European Law Journal* 19 (2013).

26 There is a burgeoning literature on agencies. See, among others, Paul Craig, *EU Administrative Law*, Chap. 6; and Everson, Monda, and Vos, *European Agencies*.

27 See Articles 48(6) and (7) TEU for the hypotheses in which treaty revision can be decided by a European Council decision rather than a formal international treaty.

28 For more detailed analysis of the legal regime of treaty revision after its reform by the Lisbon Treaty, see Steve Peers, "The Future of EU Treaty Amendments," *Yearbook of European Law* 31 (2012); and Bruno de Witte, "Treaty Revision Procedures after Lisbon," in *EU Law after Lisbon*, ed. Andrea Biondi, Piet Eeckhout, and Stefanie Ripley (Oxford: Oxford University Press, 2012).

29 The details of the decision-making process are quite complex. See further discussion in Chapter 25 in this volume.

30 See Imelda Maher, "Economic Governance: Hybridity, Accountability and Control," *Columbia Journal of European Law* 13 (2007).

31 See Diamond Ashiagbor, *The European Employment Strategy: Labour Market Regulation and New Governance* (Oxford: Oxford University Press, 2005).

32 For a scholarly evaluation of its operation in the field of social policy, see Egidijus Barcevicius, J. Timo Weishaupt, and Jonathan Zeitlin, eds., *Assessing the Open Method of Coordination: Institutional Design and National Influence of EU Social Policy Coordination* (Basingstoke: Palgrave Macmillan, 2014).

33 The three identically phrased references to the method, in relation to public health, industry, and research, can be found in Articles 168, 173, and 179 TFEU.

34 See, for a synthesis of this recent evolution, Chalmers, Davies, and Monti, *European Union Law*, 745–752.

35 Article 17(7) TEU.

36 Article 15(5) TEU.

References

Ashiagbor, Diamond. *The European Employment Strategy: Labour Market Regulation and New Governance*. Oxford: Oxford University Press, 2005.

Barcevicius, Egidijus, J. Timo Weishaupt, and Jonathan Zeitlin, eds. *Assessing the Open Method of Coordination: Institutional Design and National Influence of EU Social Policy Coordination*. Basingstoke: Palgrave Macmillan, 2014.

Bocquillon, Pierre, and Mathias Dobbels. "An Elephant on the 13th Floor of the Berlaymont? European Council and Commission Relations in Legislative Agenda Setting." *Journal of European Public Policy* 21 (2014): 20–38.

Busuioc, Madalina. "Rule-Making by the European Financial Supervisory Authorities: Walking a Tight Rope." *European Law Journal* 19 (2013): 111–125.

Chalmers, Damian, Gareth Davies, and Giorgio Monti. *European Union Law – Text and Materials*. Cambridge: Cambridge University Press, 2014.

Christiansen, Thomas, and Mathias Dobbels. "Non-Legislative Rule Making after the Lisbon Treaty: Implementing the New System of Comitology and Delegated Acts." *European Law Journal* 19 (2013): 42–56.

Christiansen, Thomas, and Torbjörn Larsson, eds. *The Role of Committees in the Policy-Process of the European Union*. Cheltenham: Edward Elgar, 2007.

Cooper, Ian. "A Virtual Third Chamber for the European Union? National Parliaments after the Treaty of Lisbon." *West European Politics* 35 (2012): 441–465.
Craig, Paul. *EU Administrative Law*. Oxford: Oxford University Press, 2012.
Curtin, Deirdre. "The Constitutional Structure of the Union: A Europe of Bits and Pieces." *Common Market Law Review* 30 (1993): 17–69.
de Witte, Bruno. "Treaty Revision Procedures after Lisbon." In *EU Law after Lisbon*, edited by Andrea Biondi, Piet Eeckhout, and Stefanie Ripley, 107–127. Oxford: Oxford University Press, 2012.
Eising, Rainer, and Sonja Lehringer. "Interest Groups and the European Union." In *European Union Politics*, edited by Michelle Cini and Nieves Pérez-Solórzano Borragán, 189–206. Oxford: Oxford University Press, 2010.
Everson, Michelle, Cosimo Monda, and Ellen Vos, eds. *European Agencies in between Institutions and Member States*. Alphen: Kluwer Law International, 2014.
Héritier, Adrienne, Catherine Moury, Carina S. Bischoff, and Carl Fredrik Bergström. *Changing Rules of Delegation - A Contest for Power in Comitology*. Oxford: Oxford University Press, 2013.
Klüver, Heike. *Lobbying in the European Union: Interest Groups, Lobbying Coalitions, and Policy Change*. Oxford: Oxford University Press, 2013.
Lenaerts, Koen, and Piet Van Nuffel. *European Union Law*. London: Sweet & Maxwell, 2011.
Maher, Imelda. "Economic Governance: Hybridity, Accountability and Control." *Columbia Journal of European Law* 13 (2007): 679–704.
Peers, Steve. "In a World of Their Own? Justice and Home Affairs Opt-outs and the Treaty of Lisbon." *Cambridge Yearbook of European Legal Studies* 10 (2007–2008): 383–412.
Peers, Steve. "The Future of EU Treaty Amendments." *Yearbook of European Law* 31 (2012): 17–111.
Reh, Christine, Adrienne Héritier, Edoardo Bressanelli, and Christel Koop. "The Informal Politics of Legislation: Explaining Secluded Decision-Making in the European Union." *Comparative Political Studies* 46 (2013): 1112–1142.
"Twenty Years of Legislative Codecision in the European Union." Special issue, *Journal of European Public Policy* 20 (2013).

8

The European Union and Executive Power

Deirdre Curtin

Bits and Pieces

The scope and nature of executive power in a given political system is difficult to define in substantive and normative terms. This may have something to do with the fact that "the" executive power is rarely fixed and determinate but evolves over time, shaped by social and political circumstances as well as by the letter of a constitution. Scholars argue that the contemporary executive branch of government can be considered as "the most dangerous branch"[1] compared to the legislative and judicial branches.[2] Since 9/11 in particular, we have seen both in the United States and in Europe the consolidation of an executive power that subsumes much of the traditional tripartite structure of government.[3] More recently in Europe, this preexisting trend has been confirmed in unprecedented and very dynamic political and legal practices, instruments, and (new) institutions erected in response to the financial crisis.[4] The incoherence of the contemporary executive is fed by multiple, overlapping structures and networks at different governance levels.

Can we really speak of an executive power in a political system that does not have a unitary government – in the sense that we know it from state systems – existing alongside legislative and judicial power? As originally designed, executive power was never meant to reside at the European level. To the extent that it did, only the Commission was originally given tasks of an actual executive nature. Nowadays, executive power is also exercised by supranational actors such as the European Council, the Council, the European Central Bank, and even European agencies such as Europol.[5] But in the eurozone, at any rate, executive power is exercised also in *new* international organizations and through executive agreements that deliberately avoid supranational actors, such as the Commission and the European Parliament, as well as national parliaments, to a very considerable extent.[6]

In Europe the emergence of a common but accumulated "executive order" stresses the changing nature of executive power in a manner that captures both the political level and the administrative level of power.[7] The compound nature of executive power in Europe entails both a horizontal dimension (EU institutions and actors) and a vertical dimension (involvement of

A Companion to European Union Law and International Law, First Edition.
Edited by Dennis Patterson and Anna Södersten.

national institutions and actors in EU institutions and postnational networks), which may at times conflict with one another.

The fragmentary and disaggregated character of contemporary government is accentuated and intensified by internationalization, in one form or another, of the tasks of small "g" government[8] and has quite dramatically affected the manner of interaction with both the legislative and the judicial powers. Beyond the state, greatly expanded rule making in one form or another and its interaction – express or implied – with formal government powers has contributed to the structural opacity and incoherence of the contemporary executive. Executive power leaks out of the state, but it also leaks in (from the global, international, or European levels). Widespread and increasing postnational rule making by entities loosely associated with (administrative) executive power affects the manner in which authority is exercised and its locus in a novel way that defies, to a large extent, existing categorizations and understandings.[9] Such a layered and accumulated executive order is largely "in shadow," and this lack of visibility of basic structure, organization, layers, and types of actors complicates considerably the discussion on the manner of holding a de facto expanding executive power to account or in check in a meaningful manner.

Executive power in the European Union consists of various bits and pieces that have been cobbled together across a spectrum of institutions, sub-actors, and policy areas. No fewer than three institutions of the European Union and its predecessors can claim to exercise executive (in both its political and administrative components) authority within the Union, albeit to varying degrees and with varying emphasis: the Commission, the Council, and the European Council. In addition, there are a number of "satellite" actors who have in a variety of ways had executive powers delegated to them but whose role is even more "in shadow."[10] This chapter provides a brief overview of the three core executive institutions, followed by a discussion on recent executive constructions outside the EU legal framework, and it highlights the pressing need for accountability mechanisms on *all levels* of Union governance.

The "Normalized" Executive

The Commission can be described as the "core executive" of the Union.[11] Its tasks gel remarkably well with what Craig described as the central executive tasks in any political system: it initiates legislation, and thus, up until recently, was the only agenda setter in the EU context; it is the most important executive actor when it comes to implementation of legislation and delegated rule making; and it has a leading role in external relations and is responsible for drawing up and accounting for the Union budget.[12] Unlike national administrations, it is not in the business of service delivery, and it only has a limited "direct administration" (e.g., in the fields of competition policy). Much of its focus is on policy making and regulation. It depends heavily on national administrations in respect of service delivery and enforcement. In the words of one scholar,

> [t]he European Commission is one of the most unusual administrations ever created. It was born as a body that would perform both mundane administrative and overtly political tasks. It has always found it difficult to perform them simultaneously and well.[13]

The precursor of the Commission, the High Authority in the European Coal and Steel Treaty, was designed in such a way that politics was effectively organized out. The Commission was designed as a technocratic body composed of independent experts to propose solutions to policy problems, to broker deals, to constitute the "motor of integration," and to be the guardian of the common European interest. In the words of Wille, the integration and mediating function of the Commission

> was to be guided by the judgment of a technocratic elite rather than by political judgment since politicians are bound to be short-sighted and self-seeking, as they are subject to electoral mechanisms. It would make for better governance to take the impartial, the overall and long-term view of the "technocrat" as a guardian of the European interest. The Commission's role would hence depend on its expertise and its credibility as an impartial mediator between political views, conflicting national interests and interest group pressures.[14]

Yet the Commission is best understood in its contemporary form if compared with a national executive:

> The Commission consists of a set of executive politicians who are in charge of various administrative services. Similar to national executives, the Commission is authorized to initiate and formulate policy proposals and to implement policies or, more commonly, to monitor their implementation.[15]

In other words, the Commission has in several respects become "normalized" as a political executive.[16] A clearer demarcation now exists between the political top and the administrative body, both in terms of recruitment and of decision making. The Commission focuses more than it did in the past on what it perceives to be its core political tasks, delegating away or contracting out other nonpolitical tasks to outside bodies and an elaborate network of agencies, both Community level and national. However, the Commission does not represent a kind of parliamentary government, even if there are clear signs that the College of Commissioners is gradually becoming more and more dependent on the European Parliament. This is especially the case with regard to new provisions of the Lisbon Treaty providing for the election of the Commission president by the European Parliament. These new provisions stem essentially from an effort to enhance the democratic legitimacy of the Commission; in particular, the belief is that increasing the "politicization" of the Commission in this manner will attenuate – in one respect – the "democratic deficit" of the Union.

The Commission has "normalized" in the sense that it acquired many of the organizational features and behavioral patterns that are highly typical of the "normal" executives in national settings.[17] This normalization process was taken a step further in various measures that were adopted in the context of crisis management. In particular, the role and power of the Commission regarding the content of national budgets within the framework of the so-called European Semester has enhanced its executive powers vis-à-vis the member states. In this context, its accountability must be both European and national. The Commission must engage in an "economic dialogue" with the Economic and Monetary Affairs Committee of the European Parliament and inform it in an ongoing, iterative process.[18] In fact, the Commission has suggested establishing a special "euro committee" within the European Parliament that might then develop "a special relationship of confidence and scrutiny" with the Commission Vice President for Economic and Monetary Affairs.[19]

The "In-Between" Executive

Executive power also shifted to the more *political level* with the Treaty of Maastricht twenty years ago. This changed in a significant way the nature of the intergovernmental Council of Ministers, traditionally the main decision maker. The Council of Ministers acquired in 1993 tasks of an "operational" nature that in many ways parallel those of the Commission in the Community areas but expanded to the newer "sensitive" policy areas of foreign policy and justice and home affairs. The structures of the Council itself, in particular the Council General Secretariat, acquired a powerful role in these years. These executive powers were in addition to its normal legislative task.

The Council of Ministers is not only to be understood as a profoundly political organ, with the member states de facto in the driver's seat, but also as an EU executive institution which has gained (oversight over) not insignificant administrative and even operational-type powers since roughly the turn of the millennium.[20] This belies a purely intergovernmental reading of the Council of Ministers, but it is not widely understood in such terms in the legal or political science literature. In other words, the Council of Ministers also acquired what can be called *an autonomous executive* role. This is true at various levels.

In terms of the more *administrative* part of executive power, a considerable expansion in tasks and responsibilities has taken place as part of a process of a "living institution" that develops in legal and institutional practices. When the administrative part of the Council of Ministers – the General Secretariat – was originally created, it was designed to fulfill the classic intergovernmental functions of conference organization and committee servicing. The Council of Ministers can thus arguably also be analyzed in terms of a politics–administration dichotomy in the sense that the level of the ministers is the obvious political (and intergovernmental, albeit qualified with the advent of widespread qualified majority voting) level, and the administration is the General Secretariat of the Council of Ministers that for a long time was considered to be merely a supporting secretariat, as found in many international organizations.

The Council has, in fact, two different types of bureaucratic support or input into its political decisions. First, like the Commission, it has a (much smaller) staff of European civil servants, responsible for "public administration" largely in its General Secretariat. In the past decades, however, a considerable expansion in its tasks and responsibilities has taken place. In recent years, the role of the Secretariat has evolved to the point where it has assumed significant tasks in policy making and implementation that would traditionally have been carried out by the Commission as an executive actor in other (Community) policy fields.[21]

Second, the system of working parties and committees that participate in formulating and sometimes finalizing the contents of its (political) decisions is also "administrative" in the sense of being populated by national civil servants. The Council of Ministers is indeed a more "chameleon-like" institution[22] than the Commission since it also houses within it committees, working groups, and so on, which are populated by national civil servants acting, presumably, within the web of national politics and not European politics. The Commission knows its functional equivalent in the area of implementation of EU legislation: the comitology committees that carry out rule-making functions under the auspices of the Commission (with powers delegated to it by the Council). These committees are populated by both national civil servants and (independent) "scientific" experts.

With the Treaty of Lisbon in 2009, many of the executive powers of the Council shifted elsewhere, and its core role since then has been as a legislative body. The Council of Ministers shares legislative power with the European Parliament. The fact remains that its composition is of national ministers and, at the lower levels, national civil servants. It still behaves as if legislation is largely a matter of "diplomatic" negotiation behind closed doors among representatives of the member states. As a result, it is impossible for national parliaments and the public to know the input of national representatives into a legislative process that replaces a national legislative process.

The "Dominant" Executive

With the Lisbon Treaty, the European Council formally became an institution of the Union subject to its rules, rather than floating outside it, and its powers were explicitly stated to be non-legislative. Its powers are executive in the substantive sense of agenda setting, steering, and at times operational tasks. The European Council (and its euro area counterpart – the Euro Summit) is the top-level political "leader" of the European Union as such. It has seen its executive powers consolidated and even expanded in processes of incremental institutionalization, first, in layers of legal and institutional practices and, more recently, in formal treaty provisions after the Lisbon Treaty. The introduction at that time of the position of a full-time European Council president reinforced the autonomy of the European Council as an institution with non-legislative powers. This marked a change in the collective face of the European Council and its ability to interact as such with the other institutions and be included in existing interinstitutional accountability mechanisms (legal, financial).

In practice, the European Council is the default crisis manager of the European Union, handling events such as the constitutional crisis of 2005 and the economic crisis of 2008 and onwards.[23] Having that role in a political system that tends to find itself in a more or less perpetual crisis makes for a strong concentration of executive power. In addition, further institutionalization at the supranational level helps that concentration process. The European Council has, since the Treaty of Lisbon, a permanent president elected for a term of two-and-a-half years, renewable once. The president has his own cabinet and is supported by the Council services. This professionalization of the support of the European Council has meant that it has been able to increase greatly the frequency with which it meets, over and above the normal twice a year dictated by the rotating Council presidency.

The permanent presidency of the European Council plays a fundamental role in enabling it to play its role as the agenda setter and effective coordinator and power broker of Union institutions and the member states. These tasks belonged in the past to the Commission, but the latter has seen its position progressively weakened over the years as bit-by-bit powers of agenda setting and political initiative moved to the European Council.

The European Council has gradually reinforced its own role, becoming in effect the most important agenda setter of the larger developments of the European Union, in spite of the Commission's monopoly of legislative initiative.[24] In fact, empirical evidence points to a "progressive erosion" of the Commission's power of initiative and a much more pronounced role of the European Council in setting the legislative agenda despite its lack of formal legislative powers.[25] An example of this shift in the balance of legislative power is the strongly worded resolution of the European Parliament, which stressed "that any further initiative … must imperatively be established in accordance with the Community method."[26] It called upon the European Council "to stop instructing the Commission on the form and/or content of any further legislative initiative," emphasizing in this respect that "[the European Council] does not have any Treaty-based prerogative of legislative initiative."[27]

At the national level, as it has become increasingly apparent that significant power has shifted, both in law and in practice, to the European Council, some national parliaments engage in a more intensive fashion with their own government than was previously the case.[28] Those national parliaments that had already been given significant rights on EU affairs in general tend to be the ones leading the way regarding parliamentary engagement with European Council meetings post crisis. There is a certain leapfrog effect of "best practices" discernible among national parliaments, and they are on the whole trying hard to "catch up" with the new and shifting institutional and policy realities.[29]

Individual national parliaments can never hold the collective decision making by the European Council or the Euro Summits to account. They can only hold their individual prime minister or minister to account. Only another actor at the *same governance level*, the supranational level, can hold the European Council to account. This means the *European Parliament* or a new parliament beyond the state (a eurozone parliament?). *De jure* the traditional accountability arrangement for the European Parliament was very limited pre-crisis.[30] The debate suffered from the strict format of plenary sessions.[31] But there have been some *de jure* developments in some of the (legislative) measures adopted to combat the crisis, providing inter alia for the president of the European Council to come before a committee of the European Parliament, in particular the Committee on Economic and Monetary Affairs, and to inform it and engage in an "economic dialogue."[32] This is not mandatory but rather facilitative. There is certainly more likely to be a real dialogue in committees rather than in plenary meetings. This would seem to indicate an evolving accountability relationship in practice. In addition, Article 12 (5) TSCG provides that the president of the European Parliament may be invited to be heard by the Euro Summit (as opposed to full European Parliament participation). This, however, is an autonomous decision of the summit; the European Parliament does not have a "right" to be heard.[33]

Non-EU Executive Constructions

If it needs to (because of a veto) the European Council changes hats at times and converts itself into another entity with fewer participants, or it may otherwise adopt decisions outside the European Union. It does this, as the French say, largely *en marge* of a European Council meeting. A variety of clever legal constructions are used that are tailor-made to each situation and have the specific object of avoiding EU rules and constraints. These decisions are binding under international law and are subject to even less parliamentary control than if taken within the EU system and to no judicial control. It is an illusion to imagine that multilateral arrangements are subject to more scrutiny, democratic or otherwise, than EU ones. This is patently not the case.

If this is the fire brigade of a more politically integrated future for the European Union, it is one that is even more executive dominated than the core Union and the traditional Community method of lawmaking. Like the Schengen Treaty, initially outside the treaties but now completely absorbed into them, the chances are that this avant-garde, even if it is still fragmented, will function as a type of a Trojan Horse within the old-style European Union.

There are three examples of such "beyond the EU" constructions that do not use the special provisions that the treaties contain to enable what is known as "enhanced cooperation" by less than the full number of member states. Instead, they borrow executive institutions of the European Union to do the implementation and blindside the parliaments at all levels.[34]

First, the *European Financial Stability Facility* was adopted outside the EU legal framework. In the margins of a meeting of the ministers of economy or finance, the so-called ECOFIN Council, the members of the Council from the seventeen euro area countries "switched hats" and transformed themselves into representatives of their states at an intergovernmental meeting. They established the European Financial Stability Facility as a private company established under Luxembourg law of which the seventeen euro states are the only shareholders. By using a curious mixture of public international law and private law, a large part of the Council parted company with the Commission and the European Parliament.

Second, the *European Stability Mechanism*, the permanent successor of the temporary European Financial Stability Facility was established by means of a fully fledged treaty between the seventeen euro member states even though an EU legal instrument could well have been used. The European Stability Mechanism was established as a separate international organization rather than as an EU agency.

Thirdly, the *Fiscal Compact* is an international agreement concluded by twenty-five member states outside the context of the EU institutional framework. Most of what it contains in terms of economic governance at the European level could have been adopted through EU legislation or by means of a modification of Protocol No. 12 on the excessive debt procedure.

The effect is a Europe of "bits and pieces" of much more structural proportions than was the case at the time of the Maastricht Treaty. Executives operate – seemingly at will – beyond the reach of national and European democracies to an even greater extent than under the existing EU system. Rather than reducing the existing democratic deficit, such legal maneuvering creates in effect a new and more intense democratic deficit than that which existed already.

Beyond Accountability?

The nature and scope of executive power in a given political system remains difficult to define in substantive terms. It seems that, nowadays, it is the executive branch that may be "everywhere extending the sphere of its activity and drawing all power into its impetuous vortex."[35] At the same time, the executive power can be considered in structural terms "in shadow."[36] In the political system of the European Union this may be aggravated by the fact that the legislative and executive functions are so mixed together – more so than in the political systems of the constituent member states where the legislative power will basically be exercised by a directly elected parliament (with input into the system by the executive power in terms of an often nonexclusive power of legislative initiative).

The problem is fundamentally one of democratic accountability of the executive. If it is not clear *who* makes the decisions, *how*, and *where*, then how can the executives be held to account in a manner that makes allowance for democratic representation at the national level or at the European level? Political actors may adopt decisions at one level with no accountability forum able to deliberate on their actions, either politically, as in a parliament or election procedure, or legally, as in a court. That gap in accountability may infiltrate other levels of governance such as the European level and, subsequently, the national level. This raises sensitive questions about which actors should be held accountable: holding governments to account may no longer be enough and will need to be complemented with mechanisms and forums that focus both on the accountability of supranational executive bodies as well as national agencies and agents with dual loyalties (national and European).

Notes

1 Martin S. Flaherty, "The Most Dangerous Branch," *Yale Law Journal* 105 (1995–1996).

2 Alexander Hamilton wrote in The Federalist Papers that the judiciary was "the least dangerous" branch. See Alexander Hamilton, "Essay No. 78," in *The Federalist*, Alexander Hamilton, James Madison, and John Jay, ed. Benjamin F. Wright (Cambridge, MA: Harvard University Press, 1961), 490.

3 On the United States, see Symposium 2006, "The Most Dangerous Branch? Mayors, Governors, Presidents, and the Rule of Law: A Symposium on Executive Power," *Yale Law Journal* 115 (2005–2006). On the European Union, see Deirdre Curtin, *Executive Power of the European Union: Law, Practices, and the Living Constitution* (Oxford: Oxford University Press, 2009).

4 See Deirdre Curtin, "Challenging Executive Dominance in European Democracy," *The Modern Law Review* 77 (2014).
5 See further Curtin, *Executive Power of the European Union*, and Curtin, "Challenging Executive Dominance."
6 See Bruno de Witte, "Using International Law in the Euro Crisis: Causes and Consequences," ARENA Working paper no. 04/2013.
7 Deirdre Curtin and Morten Egeberg, "Tradition and Innovation: Europe's Accumulated Executive Order," *West European Politics* 31 (2008).
8 Eoin Carolan, *The New Separation of Powers: A Theory for the Modern State* (Oxford: Oxford University Press, 2009), 257.
9 Jürgen Habermas, *Zur Verfassung Europas Ein Essay* (Berlin: Suhrkamp, 2011).
10 See further Curtin, *Executive Power of the European Union.*
11 Simon Hix, *The Political System of the European Union* (Basingstoke: Palgrave Macmillan, 2005), 32.
12 Paul Craig, "The Constitutional Treaty: Legislative and Executive Power in the Emerging Constitutional Order," EUI Working paper, Law, no. 2004/7, 7–8.
13 John Peterson, "The Santer Era: The European Commission in Normative, Historical and Theoretical Perspective," *Journal of European Public Policy* 6 (1999): 60.
14 Anchrit C. Wille, "Bridging the Gap: Political and Administrative Leadership in a Reinvented European Commission" in *Institutional Dynamics and the Transformation of Executive Politics in Europe*, ed. Morten Egeberg (Mannheim: CONNEX, 2007), 13. See also Anchrit C. Wille, *The Normalization of the European Commission: Politics and Bureaucracy in the EU Executive* (Oxford: Oxford University Press, 2013).
15 Morten Egeberg, "The European Commission – the Evolving EU Executive," ARENA Working paper, 30/2002.
16 See Wille, *The Normalization of the European Commission.*
17 Ibid., 2.
18 Cristina Fasone, "European Economic Governance and Parliamentary Representation. What Place for the European Parliament?" *European Law Journal* 20 (2014): 176.
19 Communication from the Commission "A blueprint for a deep and genuine economic and monetary union: Launching a European Debate," COM(2012) 777 final, 38.
20 See Fiona Hayes-Renshaw and Helen Wallace, *The Council of Ministers* (Basingstoke: Palgrave Macmillan, 2006).
21 See further Thomas Christiansen, "Out of the Shadows: The General Secretariat of the Council of Ministers," *Journal of Legislative Studies* 8 (2006); Thomas Christiansen and Sophie Vanhoonacker, "At a Critical Juncture? Change and Continuity in the Institutional Development of the Council Secretariat," *West European Politics* 31 (2008).
22 See Helen Wallace, "The Council: An Institutional Chameleon?" *Governance: An International Journal of Policy, Administration, and Institutions* 15 (2002).
23 Daniel Naurin, "Representation in the Council of the EU," in *Political Representation in the European Union: Still Democratic in Times of Crisis?* ed. Sandra Kröger (London: Routledge, 2014).
24 See further Pierre Bocquillon and Mathias Dobbels, "An Elephant on the 13th Floor of the Berlaymont? European Council and Commission Relations in Legislative Agenda Setting," *Journal of European Public Policy* 21 (2014).
25 Paolo Ponzano, Costanza Hermanin, and Daniela Corona, *The Power of Initiative of the European Commission: A Progressive Erosion?* (Paris: Notre Europe, 2012). http://www.eng.notre-europe.eu/011-3068-The-Power-of-Initiative-of-the-European-Commission-A-Progressive-Erosion.html.
26 European Parliament Resolution of 12 June 2013 on strengthening European democracy in the future EMU (2013/2672 (RSP)), point 3.
27 Ibid.
28 See Wolfgang Wessels et al., *Democratic Control in the Member States of the European Council and the Euro Zone Summits* (Brussels: Directorate General for Internal Policies Study requested by the Constitutional Affairs Committee of the European Parliament, 2013). http://www.notre-europe.eu/media/democraticcontrol-rozenberg-kreilinger-et-al-ne-jdi-tepsa-mar13.pdf?pdf=ok; House of

Commons European Scrutiny Committee, *Reforming the European Scrutiny System in the House of Commons: Twenty-Fourth Report of Session 2013–14* (London: The Stationary Office Limited, HC 109-I, 2013). http://www.publications.parliament.uk/pa/cm201314/cmselect/cmeuleg/109/109.pdf. See also Marianne van de Steeg, "The European Council's Evolving Political Accountability," in *The Real World of EU Accountability: What Deficit?* ed. Mark Bovens, Deirdre Curtin, and Paul 't Hart (Oxford: Oxford University Press, 2010).

29 See Curtin, "Challenging Executive Dominance," 25 *et seq*.

30 Article 15(6)(d) TEU.

31 van de Steeg, "The European Council's Evolving Political Accountability," 129.

32 Fasone, "European Economic Governance and Parliamentary Representation," 176.

33 Ibid., 179.

34 See, in greater detail, de Witte, "Using International Law in the Euro Crisis."

35 These are the words originally used by James Madison to describe the "legislative department." See Madison, "Essay No. 48," in Hamilton, Madison, and Jay, *The Federalist*, Alexander, 343. See also http://thomas.loc.gov/home/histdox/fedpapers.html.

36 Terence Daintith and Alan Page, *The Executive in the Constitution: Structure, Autonomy and Internal Control* (Oxford: Oxford University Press, 1999), 2.

References

Bocquillon, Pierre, and Mathias Dobbels. "An Elephant on the 13th Floor of the Berlaymont? European Council and Commission Relations in Legislative Agenda Setting." *Journal of European Public Policy* 21 (2014): 20–38.

Carolan, Eoin. *The New Separation of Powers: A Theory for the Modern State*. Oxford: Oxford University Press, 2009.

Christiansen, Thomas. "Out of the Shadows: The General Secretariat of the Council of Ministers." *Journal of Legislative Studies* 8 (2006): 80–97.

Christiansen, Thomas, and Sophie Vanhoonacker. "At a Critical Juncture? Change and Continuity in the Institutional Development of the Council Secretariat." *West European Politics* 31 (2008): 751–770.

Craig, Paul. "The Constitutional Treaty: Legislative and Executive Power in the Emerging Constitutional Order." EUI Working paper, Law, no. 2004/7.

Curtin, Deirdre. *Executive Power of the European Union: Law, Practices, and the Living Constitution*. Oxford: Oxford University Press, 2009.

Curtin, Deirdre. "Challenging Executive Dominance in European Democracy." *The Modern Law Review* 77 (2014): 1–32.

Curtin, Deirdre, and Morten Egeberg. "Tradition and Innovation: Europe's Accumulated Executive Order." *West European Politics* 31 (2008): 639–661.

Daintith, Terence, and Alan Page. *The Executive in the Constitution: Structure, Autonomy and Internal Control*. Oxford: Oxford University Press, 1999.

de Witte, Bruno. "Using International Law in the Euro Crisis: Causes and Consequences." ARENA Working paper no. 04/2013.

Egeberg, Morten. "The European Commission – the Evolving EU Executive." ARENA Working paper no. 30/2002.

Fasone, Cristina. "European Economic Governance and Parliamentary Representation. What Place for the European Parliament?" *European Law Journal* 20 (2014). 164–185.

Flaherty, Martin S. "The Most Dangerous Branch." *Yale Law Journal* 105 (1995–1996): 1725–1839.

Habermas, Jürgen. *Zur Verfassung Europas – Ein Essay*. Berlin: Suhrkamp, 2011.

Hamilton, Alexander. "Essay No. 78." In Hamilton, Madison, and Jay, *The Federalist*, 489–496.

Hamilton, Alexander, James Madison, and John Jay. *The Federalist*. Edited by Benjamin F. Wright. Cambridge, MA: Harvard University Press, 1961.

Hayes-Renshaw, Fiona, and Helen Wallace. *The Council of Ministers*. Basingstoke: Palgrave Macmillan, 2006.

Hix, Simon. *The Political System of the European Union*. Basingstoke: Palgrave Macmillan, 2005.

House of Commons European Scrutiny Committee. *Reforming the European Scrutiny System in the House of Commons: Twenty-Fourth Report of Session 2013–14*. London: The Stationary Office Limited, HC 109-I, 2013. Accessed 3 June 2015. http://www.publications.parliament.uk/pa/cm201314/cmselect/cmeuleg/109/109.pdf.

Madison, James. "Essay No. 48." In Hamilton, Madison, and Jay, *The Federalist*, 343–347.

Naurin, Daniel. "Representation in the Council of the EU." In *Political Representation in the European Union: Still Democratic in Times of Crisis?* edited by Sandra Kröger, 69–85. London: Routledge, 2014.

Peterson, John. "The Santer Era: The European Commission in Normative, Historical and Theoretical Perspective." *Journal of European Public Policy* 6 (1999): 46–65.

Ponzano, Paolo, Costanza Hermanin, and Daniela Corona. *The Power of Initiative of the European Commission: A Progressive Erosion?* Paris: Notre Europe, 2012. Accessed 4 June 2015. http://www.eng.notre-europe.eu/011-3068-The-Power-of-Initiative-of-the-European-Commission-A-Progressive-Erosion.html.

Symposium 2006. "The Most Dangerous Branch? Mayors, Governors, Presidents, and the Rule of Law: A Symposium on Executive Power." *Yale Law Journal* 115 (2005–2006): 2218–2643.

van de Steeg, Marianne. "The European Council's Evolving Political Accountability." In *The Real World of EU Accountability: What Deficit?* edited by Mark Bovens, Deirdre Curtin, and Paul 't Hart, 117–149. Oxford: Oxford University Press, 2010.

Wallace, Helen. "The Council: An Institutional Chameleon?" *Governance: An International Journal of Policy, Administration, and Institutions* 15 (2002): 325–344.

Wessels, Wolfgang, Olivier Rozenberg, Mirte van den Berge, Claudia Hefftler, Valentin Kreilinger, and Laura Ventura. *Democratic Control in the Member States of the European Council and the Euro Zone Summits*. Brussels: Directorate General for Internal Policies Study requested by the Constitutional Affairs Committee of the European Parliament, 2013. Accessed 4 June 2015. http://www.notre-europe.eu/media/democraticcontrol-rozenberg-kreilinger-et-al-ne-jdi-tepsa-mar13.pdf?pdf=ok.

Wille, Anchrit C. "Bridging the Gap: Political and Administrative Leadership in a Reinvented European Commission." In *Institutional Dynamics and the Transformation of Executive Politics in Europe*, edited by Morten Egeberg, 7–41. Mannheim: CONNEX, 2007.

Wille, Anchrit C. *The Normalization of the European Commission: Politics and Bureaucracy in the EU Executive*. Oxford: Oxford University Press, 2013.

9

New Modes of Governance

Mark Dawson

Introduction

Writing a chapter on new modes of governance (hereinafter NMG) in the European Union confronts a pressing initial challenge. While all of the subjects covered in this volume raise complicated legal issues, most have the advantage of carrying a basic conceptual clarity. To take one issue discussed – direct effect – while there are different interpretations of the scope of this doctrine, there is at least one authoritative actor – the Court of Justice of the European Union (CJEU) – that has set the basic parameters for what this particular term means (even if subsequent actors have contested its definition).

"New modes of governance," by contrast, is not only an unclear phrase in itself but largely a combination of other vague or contested terms. By defining themselves as "new," NMG seem to contrast themselves with the old without specifying what form of "old governance" they seek to critique or replace. Worst of all, by centering on "governance," NMG are associated with one of the most contested social science concepts of all.[1] It is no surprise that, when discussing NMG, academics and institutional actors have often been talking past one another, basing their debates on entirely different starting points as to what "governance" in the European Union means. NMG have the capacity not only to attract interest but also to engender considerable confusion.

The challenge of defining and understanding NMG has been in focus since 2010. Certainly the academic excitement surrounding new governance methods has waned significantly since the early 2000s. Many of the hopes surrounding their participatory and social potential have faded through the confrontation of NMG with a number of skeptical academic and institutional appraisals.[2]

In spite of this skepticism, however, every attack on NMG seems to do little to check their progress. The agreement of the European Union's legislative "six-pack" in response to the euro crisis is the latest round of expansion and duplication of new governance procedures, each of which seems to differ markedly from one policy field to the next.[3] This simultaneous disenchantment, expansion, and fragmentation seems to create an even greater need to clarify what NMG, as a category of EU lawmaking, really entails.

A Companion to European Union Law and International Law, First Edition.
Edited by Dennis Patterson and Anna Södersten.

This chapter will approach NMG with the task of clarity in mind. Its essential function will be first to map the dominant conceptions of NMG that frame existing institutional and academic discourse; second to analyze the strengths and weaknesses of NMG as an alternative means of delivering EU law and policy; and finally to consider the future prospects of NMG in a political context (the euro crisis) that both challenges and reinforces their institutional relevance. As we will see, while the effectiveness and legitimacy of new governance methods have been justly questioned, the ability of such methods to forge a middle path between central coordination and intergovernmental bargaining has made NMG an almost immovable plank of EU policy making. As such, pinning NMG down as a legal or political concept is a tricky, yet important, task.

What are "New Modes of Governance" and What is their Relationship to EU Law?

In broad terms, there may be two ways of considering NMG at a definitional level. One is to see NMG as a series of mechanisms and procedures. Advancing the debate at this level, academics have, for example, argued about which particular facets of EU policy making ought to fit within the NMG label. To give one particular example, academics have disagreed about whether or not both the social dialogue and the model of the EU agency ought to be considered as part of NMG given that the former may result in binding hierarchical legislation while the latter is often legally subordinated underneath the umbrella of the European Commission.[4]

A second definitional approach (and one that will be followed here) is to see NMG not as a set of procedures alone but as an overarching philosophy of governing, or as a legal or decision-making paradigm. According to this level of analysis, NMG is, for better or worse, a new way of imagining EU law without the hierarchical and formal strictures of "traditional" EU law. In the words of Jonathan Zeitlin and Charles Sabel, NMG are not a series of "modes" at all but part of a broader "architecture" of rule distinctly suited to a postnational setting.[5] While this involves an exercise in simplification, it may be useful to chart three different and evolving attempts to conceptualize NMG in this way.[6]

The first of these has been to characterize NMG largely in terms of their departure from or opposition to traditional forms of EU law.[7] In 2001, the Commission produced its White Paper on Governance,[8] an attempt to provide a conceptual and operational framework for methods of governing going well beyond traditional modes of Community law. A year later, 2002 saw the publication by Joanne Scott and David Trubek of a highly influential paper that sought to make sense of emerging alternatives to hierarchical forms of EU law, mapping their principal features.[9]

While these two papers differed markedly in their audience, they both made a similar conceptual move. For both, the definition of NMG rested on an explicit contrast with traditional forms of law. This traditional paradigm was represented by the Community method: a form of producing EU law that allowed for the involvement on equal terms of the three main EU institutions. This method involves the creation of relatively uniform legal standards, the dual legitimation of EU law through central political institutions like the Council and European Parliament, and the hierarchical application of binding rules within the member states. To understand NMG, or what brought different NMG processes together, one had to consider them as contrasting explicitly with one or all of these features.

The Open Method of Coordination (OMC) – established through the European Employment Strategy – provides a useful example. The OMC rejects or modifies all of the above features. Rather than uniform standards, the OMC offers broad guidelines to be incorporated differently according to the distinct social structures of each member state. Instead of seeking legitimation through official EU institutions, OMC procedures tend to reject parliamentary involvement entirely, legitimating themselves through alternative means, such as their openness to civil society. Finally, rather than act through hierarchical and binding rules, OMC standards are nonbinding, with practice in the member states "feeding into" future guidelines and rules. To understand NMG, we had to see it as "outside" or external to "normal" EU law. If the Community method was Mars, NMG, according to this view, was Venus; EU law's softer, and more plural, cousin.[10]

While Scott and Trubek's careful analysis has been highly influential, it already spoke to some of the problems with the "outside" definition. In truth, many new modes had hierarchical or binding elements. Equally, "traditional" EU law was not always as hard, binding, or hierarchical as the initial accounts of NMG had made out.[11] Multiple norms of EU law – from treaty provisions to directives – have a vague or "framework" character, leaving the process of elaborating precise norms to other more local actors. This may be (in the case of the treaty) national and EU courts or (in the case of directives or delegated legislation) national and EU administrative actors, who must "flesh out" basic principles established in the legislative text itself.[12]

At the same time, processes labeled under the heading of NMG have always carried "hard" elements. An example is the corrective arm of the excessive deficit procedure – while it is monitored through an OMC procedure (the Broad Economic Policy Guidelines), its normative benchmarks are adopted though a binding decision of the Council. Noncompliance with the Commission's recommendations may lead to significant sanctions.[13] The definition of NMG as "external to law," as much as it may have provided clarity, fell down against the evidence of strong interaction and continuities between supposedly "traditional" EU law on the one hand and supposedly "new" or "soft" forms of governance on the other.

The characterization of "traditional" EU law and NMG as in a relationship of continuity, however, provided a new starting point. This second approach has often been considered under the term "transformation." In keeping with prior vocabulary, let us consider it as the "inside" approach.[14] Under this view, NMG are not external to traditional EU law but part of how EU law is transforming in novel directions. NMG are themselves emblematic of a shift in EU law and policy from hierarchical models of rules adapted from the national context to a more experimental, deliberative, or reflexive paradigm of lawmaking.

Understanding this inside approach requires engagement with theory. The most influential of these theories has, perhaps counter intuitively, come from the US context. In an influential essay from 2008 (building from earlier work) Jonathan Zeitlin and Charles Sabel have associated the development of NMG with a shift in the European Union towards "democratic experimentalism."[15] The experimentalist model is based on skepticism that contemporary regulatory problems can be solved by central actors.

> The possibility conditions for experimentalist governance are arguably quite minimal: strategic uncertainty, meaning that policy-makers recognize that they cannot rely on their strategic dispositions (e.g. more market vs. more plan) to guide action in a particular domain (or equivalently that they do not know *how* to achieve their declared goals) and a multi-polar or polyarchic distribution of power, in which no single actor has the capacity to impose their own preferred solution without taking into account the views of others ... Together, these conditions open up the possibility for transforming distributive bargaining into deliberative problem-solving through the institutional mechanisms of experimentalist governance.[16]

Under these conditions, there may be a considerable advantage to delegating the ability to solve common problems to local actors provided both that their performance is monitored and evaluated and that these actors continuously report both to the "center" and each other on what they have done. Under this system, NMG represent a form of law and policy making that not only accommodates diversity but celebrates it, using "local" practice to redesign more efficient and responsive strategies for the (EU level) community as a whole.[17]

Sabel and Zeitlin's view of NMG as part of a broader change in how EU law is conceived is reflected in other approaches which characterize NMG as representing a shift towards a "procedural" view of EU law and politics.[18] Whereas conventional forms of EU law tend to focus on the elaboration of a common EU model able to harmonize national policy, the development of directives for "minimum harmonization" suggest that EU integration may occur in the context of lasting regulatory divergences or even "competition" between the member states.[19]

In this context, NMG has been seen by some as part of a "proceduralization" or "reflexive" stage of EU law, whereby common standards of expertise, transparency, or participation are established at the EU level while the elaboration of detailed substantive standards is left to national actors or to functional experts. While this procedural approach gives courts and hierarchical actors a more central role, it follows Sabel and Zeitlin in seeing NMG not as external to law but as part of a new stage of European lawmaking. Under both of these readings, law and governance are not separated but merged into one another.[20]

While the inside approach also provides an original view, it has provoked much skepticism. The first problem is the shear obstinacy of "traditional" EU law. For all the talk of the development of an overarching "governance" architecture, there is little indication that the volume of traditional hierarchical legislation in the European Union is decreasing, even in areas (such as employment) where new governance structures are prevalent.[21] In this regard, one has to consider the heavily prescriptive nature of many directives on the internal market, which continue to contain detailed rules, as well as the propensity of the CJEU to interpret exceptions to free movement principles contained in legislation narrowly. A much discussed example of this is the *Laval* line of cases, where the CJEU employed an approach to the balance between market freedoms and national social objectives that was far from "procedural" in nature.[22] Much of the law of the European Union – including in the social domain – remains both heavily prescriptive and broadly harmonizing in character.

The second problem is the failure of "inside" approaches to translate theory into practice. It is one thing to hail the merits of a procedural or experimental approach to policy making but it is quite another to demonstrate that reflexive links between central policy making and local deliberation actually exist. As will be explored in later sections of this chapter, the greatest obstacle to the inside view is the resolute failure of many NMG processes to actually display the features of bottom-up and experimental rule which theorists like Sabel and Zeitlin attribute to them. To go back to the fabled example of the OMC, numerous studies have demonstrated the depressing tendency of OMC procedures to descend into a form of "executive politics" with policy input restricted to administrative actors rather than the broad church of regional administrations, NGOs, and others that "inside" approaches envisage.[23] Experimentalism's attractive normative conceptualization of NMG may be of limited use given its failure to describe adequately how new governance processes operate.

Recent years have seen the academic and institutional development of a third approach, one which both accepts and rejects many of the assumptions of the two prior conceptions. Principally, this approach rejects the notion that NMG and law are competitors – or that one is historically destined to succeed and marginalize the other – while still accepting the idea that law and new governance carry distinct operative logics. A third approach is to see NMG and law as two distinct systems but systems that can usefully complement and supplement each other.[24]

This "complementarity" thesis refers to a reciprocal contribution. From the perspective of new governance, legal institutions are not simply bodies associated with "hard law" but carry a surrounding procedural infrastructure that can contribute to the effectiveness and legitimacy of new governance processes. Law can be seen not just as an external element to new governance but rather as a means either to provide participation and other rights to excluded participants[25] (a strong critique as we will see of present NMG processes), or to improve new governance's credibility among actors who would otherwise deem its norms too "soft" and "weak" to be worthy of serious consideration.

NMG, though, also has something to contribute to law.[26] If the legal critique of new governance has often focused on its "weakness," new governance's own critique of law (demonstrated under the first two approaches) was that it was too static and politically blind to deal with rapidly changing and complex political issues. NMG may also, under this view, offer EU law a route to ensuring that its rules are based on a sufficiently rich understanding of both the national systems into which EU rules must "fit" and the complex fields of policy (from environmental protection to social inclusion and poverty) that EU law must regulate. By this view, far from displacing "traditional" EU law, the reflexive loop envisaged by the experimentalist model between central rules and local experiences can itself engender a European legal order that is both more responsive and more readily complied with at the national level.

As is already clear, this final "complementarity" approach – like its predecessors – is both an attempt to describe the relationship between NMG and law as well as a normative account. The institutional and academic debate about NMG has always been as much an attempt to defend or critique the move towards nonhierarchical modes of rule in the European Union as it has been about understanding the reasons for NMG's emergence. In the following section, we will place this normative debate in a more explicit focus.

The Normative Debate: Strengths and Opportunities

The fact that the birth of new governance procedures engendered considerable optimism and excitement has already been mentioned. What was the basis of that optimism, and to what extent have NMG delivered on their initial promise? This promise might be said to be associated with three broad narratives about the desirability of NMG.

The first is a social promise. Critical assessments of the process of EU integration – as prevalent today as ever – frequently find that it carries a distinct market bias.[27] By this view, while the CJEU has gradually constitutionalized a set of market freedoms that have broken down barriers to cross-border trade, the social dimension to integration has lagged decisively behind. This "gap" has been exacerbated by two factors: first, the increasing tendency of internal market law to breach the walls of the welfare state, that is, to reorganize otherwise national social policies to ensure their "proportionality" vis-à-vis the internal market, and, second, the strict limitations on EU legislative competence in the social field, which makes legislation on employment, welfare, and other social matters thin or fragmented.[28]

The dawn of the OMC in particular was celebrated in part because it was seen as an instrument capable of addressing this asymmetry. As recognized by the extraordinary Lisbon European Council in 2000, if the European Union was to achieve its goal of becoming "the most dynamic economic area in the world," reform in areas like education and labor markets (that were not matters of strong EU competence) was necessary.[29] The advantage of the OMC was that – as a nonbinding process of guideline setting and mutual learning – it could be deployed in areas of policy making where legislative action was impossible. The flexible nature of OMC guidelines – their ability to be translated differently in different national contexts – was a further bonus given the significant divergences between European "welfare families," each of which delivered core social services in distinct ways (and with different resources).[30] The social hope of new governance was thus that it could build a more social Europe not through a single legislative blueprint but through a common agenda of reform, implemented flexibly across the European Union as a whole.[31]

The second promise of new governance, and one upon which the social promise is in part predicated, is a promise of effectiveness; of building a more responsive system of EU policy making. Traditional and hierarchical EU regulation may have been suitable for the European Union's early years but as the Union has expanded – both territorially and into more complex and sensitive areas of policy – hierarchical governance may be simply unable to achieve important public policy objectives; "social" or otherwise. In particular, hierarchical actors may either lack knowledge of how local levels of governance will apply centrally agreed rules or may not carry the expertise necessary to frame effective central rules in the first place. Alternatively, decision makers may simply disagree on how best to tackle a particular problem, either deferring a legislative decision for the future or agreeing to monitor the problem through a decentralized framework.[32]

NMG can be seen as an answer to this dilemma of transnational regulation. Bodies like agencies and expert committees have been designed by the Union precisely to effectively bridge the knowledge gap, justifying transnational regulation on the basis of the superior information and expertise that they hold.[33] At the same time, OMC-style reporting mechanisms may also bridge the gap to lower levels of governance, allowing the flexible implementation of rules where complete agreement is impossible, or using lower levels of governance as laboratories for policy solutions that can "feed up" to inform central decision making.[34]

A useful practical example of some of these features is the new approach to technical harmonization adopted by the Commission in 1985.[35] The new approach was adopted as a practical solution to the need to harmonize product standards under the internal market without going through a burdensome legislative process. Under this approach, the EU institutions adopt minimum standards by way of legislation yet entrust the setting of technical specifications to specialized and private standard-setting bodies. The standards produced are voluntary yet conformity with them establishes a presumption for the producer of compliance with the directives. This system illustrates some of the advantages in terms of effectiveness that NMG can bring – the new approach allows the European Union to regulate an area of policy where central actors may have significant knowledge gaps, or may not agree on detailed legislation, by drawing on knowledge that only private actors hold. At the same time, overall control of the policy-making process at the EU level is formally retained.

Finally, an important part of NMG's effectiveness promise rests on its ability to induce mutual learning and review. Various processes considered under the new governance umbrella – from comitology committees to the OMC – have been defended in terms of their ability to encourage the actors involved to share information and best practice.[36] In the case of comitology, for example, a well-established insight of committee governance in the EU context has been that national officials may not only seek to "control" delegation to the Commission in comitology committees but have often used their expertise to qualitatively deliberate upon and improve secondary legislation.[37] In the case of the OMC, its peer review processes have also been cast as an opportunity for national officials to learn from the practices of their peers, adapting to examples of good practice and "naming and shaming" poor performers as an incentive to them to do better.[38] Under both of these examples, the rise of NMG seeks to relocate the very meaning of policy effectiveness. Compliance and effectiveness may be secured not only through hierarchical obligation and coercion but also through mechanisms that seek to persuade lower actors of the benefits of transnational coordination and review.

The last promise of new governance is the most explicitly normative: it is a democratic promise. The early wave of optimism about the development of mechanisms like the OMC was not about creating "effective" transnational policies alone but also about establishing a new form of law and policy making, one that could make up for the European Union's democratic shortcomings. Certainly, the birth of the NMG debate coincided with the rising chorus of academic writing (reflected in the discussions of the 2003 constitutional convention) on participatory democracy in Europe.[39] If EU law could only ever be partially legitimated through sparsely attended European parliamentary elections and the negotiations of heads of government, perhaps it could be legitimated through the direct involvement of EU citizens in the policies that most affected them?[40]

This possibility was not only an academic idealization but a hope recognized by the Commission itself. Among the five "principles of good governance" elaborated by the Commission in its 2001 Governance White Paper, the Commission also promised that,

> at EU level, the Commission should ensure that regional and local knowledge and conditions are taken into account when developing policy proposals. For this purpose, it should organize a systematic dialogue with European and national association of regional and local government, while respecting national constitutional arrangements.[41]

This systemic dialogue was to be mainstreamed into all of the European Union's governance instruments, not least the social dialogue and OMC, where national reporting on reforms was explicitly designed to include the views of civil society organizations as well as regional and local government.[42] In this sense, NMG was seen as part of a benevolent circle, where greater participation and greater effectiveness were to go hand in hand. Just as local participation was needed to ensure more effective transnational policies, so also it could render those policies more readily acceptable to EU citizens, who had themselves played a role in their creation.

The Normative Debate: Weaknesses and Pitfalls

If these three stories were the "promise" of NMG, to what extent were these promises fulfilled? This requires us to engage with a debate that has been raging between proponents and critics of new governance methods since the mid-2000s. While this debate is far from resolved, its empirical evaluations and normative assessments reveal significant shortcomings in terms of each of the three promises outlined above. In the following section, I would like to outline four main critiques that this literature has presented to NMG's initial institutional and academic proponents (three of them following the three promises outlined above as well as one further, overarching, critique).

The first is a "social" critique; one that directly answers the social promise mentioned earlier. The association of new governance with the Lisbon Agenda was an ambiguous portent for NMG's social aspirations.[43] While the agenda indeed set social priorities, these were often cast as subordinate to a larger economic goal: increasing the European Union's competitiveness. From the establishment of OMC processes in social fields such as employment and social inclusion in the early 2000s, many have argued that the true agenda of these processes has not been to build a more "social Europe" but instead to ensure that national social policies better reflect the demands of an integrated and competitive internal market. According to this reading, NMG are, at their best, a red herring; insufficiently strong and robust to offset the domineering reach of the market freedoms.[44] At their worst, methods like the OMC have often been seen not as vehicles for social policy but as a Trojan Horse designed to reorganize national social policies to better meet the demands of the internal market.[45]

The empirical assessment of NMG's social potential has been more mixed. While, on the one hand, empirical appraisals, including those of the author, have indicated the ability of methods like the OMC to move social protection issues up the national and European agendas, economic policy coordination processes have tended to predominate.[46] Thus, while economic criteria – such as limiting budget deficits – have often constrained domestic reforms under processes like the OMC, there is little indication that social concerns – such as the need to limit income inequality or promote social cohesion – have significantly informed mechanisms of economic policy coordination (a problem that – see the next section – the response to the euro crisis may only exacerbate).

This empirical black mark has been most pronounced in terms of the second critique of NMG: the effectiveness critique. For all the hope of NMG creating a more effective and informed basis for EU policy making, the loudest objections against NMG methods have come from those disputing their ability to promote meaningful policy changes at the national level at all. This claim resonates across different NMG mechanisms. In the case of the social dialogue, for example, the significant advances in social policy via the dialogue in the late 1990s have been followed by legislative inertia in the decade from 2000. Faced with a largely voluntary process, European business in particular has decided its interests lie in refusing to cooperate, or doing so only through limited voluntary arrangements.[47]

Similarly, in the OMC case, numerous empirical studies, including by some OMC "proponents," have lambasted its failure to induce meaningful policy change.[48] Even the claim that NMG can produce secondary effects, like the promotion of mutual learning and exchange, is contested by the many who have questioned the extent to which committee structures genuinely engage in peer review rather than a mere reporting of existing achievements.[49] This poor implementation record was institutionally recognized in the 2010 review of the Lisbon Strategy which lay many of the strategy's failures to achieve its headline targets at the door of weak and ineffectual new governance instruments.[50] Given that NMG are largely a bundle of voluntary and nonbinding standards, to what extent do they create meaningful incentives for national actors to comply with them, particularly when obligations run contrary to a perceived national interest? For many, NMG has simply been a rhetorical device, "cheap talk" that was never designed or intended to be a genuine engine of political reform.[51]

The "cheap talk" criticism resonates when we move to the final "democratic" story of NMG's development.[52] The democratic promise was predicated upon the structural openness of new governance to civil society involvement, with principles of participation, peer review, and transparency substituting for the (anyway often defunct) role of parliaments in holding fast-moving regulatory processes accountable.[53] Again, here, empirical accounts have cast heavy doubt on the idea that NMG have been any better than more "traditional" EU lawmaking methods in reaching out to an emerging pan-European civil society.

The metaphor of a free-flowing deliberative process was always an uneasy one when applied to the model of the EU Committee. As has long been observed by the European Parliament, comitology committees are marked by their relative lack of transparency: few documents are made publicly available and the precise remit and number of committees is often obscure.[54] Similar skepticism has been applied to OMC processes. In spite of their image of decentralized participation, many have seen reporting under the OMC as a process controlled largely by executives, with NGO actors included at the whim of national and EU administrations.[55] To take one specific example, the author's own study of one OMC process – the OMC in social inclusion and protection – indicated that most NGO participants in OMC procedures received funding from the European Commission itself (thus casting doubt on the notion that such organizations could hold administrations, such as the Commission, accountable for their activities).[56] The problem here is less the ideal of democratic participation than the absence of the necessary incentives and structures to make participatory governance under NMG a reality.

The notion of executive control under NMG feeds into a final criticism. This criticism is based on the attitude of NMG processes to basic constitutional and legal values; what one might call the "rule of law" challenge to new governance's development.[57] In many ways, this is an overarching criticism, one that combines social, democratic, and policy-related concerns.

The first aspect of the rule of law objections concerns the exclusion by NMG of institutions and principles upon which the European Union – as a community integrated through law – is based.[58] OMC procedures, for example, habitually exclude the European Parliament from having any significant say over their overall guidelines and objectives. At the same time, these procedures – by operating in areas where EU competences are limited – seemingly override the system of conferred powers.[59] It is difficult to refute this objection on the basis that OMC standards are nonbinding – after all, if OMC objectives have no influence or constraining power on national policy at all, then why establish a system of open coordination in the first place? This objection was put forcefully by the European Parliament itself in a 2007 resolution on the use of soft law in the European Union.

> The use of soft law is liable to circumvent the properly competent legislative bodies, may flout the principles of democracy and the rule of law under Article 6 of the EU Treaty, and also those of subsidiarity and proportionality … Soft law tends to create a public perception of a "super-bureaucracy" without democratic legitimacy, not just remote from citizens, but actually hostile to them, and willing to reach accommodations with powerful lobbies which are neither transparent, nor comprehensible to citizens.[60]

On this view, soft law methods are both a direct contravention of the European order's most basic constitutional principles and "bad political business," entrenching ever further the idea of the European Union as a distant and nontransparent regulator.

The rule of law objection is more, however, than an exclusion of particular institutions but also an exclusion of law itself.[61] It is an exclusion by new governance of particular features that are central to the very notion of governing a polity "by rules." Central to many traditional ideas of the rule of law, for example, is the notion of relative stability in lawmaking as well as the idea that a clear distinction should be drawn between those (like parliaments) who make rules and those (like police and judges) who apply them in concrete circumstances.[62] These guarantees are designed to limit the arbitrary use of legal power.

In new governance, these distinctions are broken down. Bodies like regulatory agencies, as well as OMC procedures, develop rules that are constantly changing to keep up to date with new circumstances. They speak in an opaque technical language that citizens are likely to find lacking in clarity. They create standards that are rarely the final word but instead are intended as open-ended, to be flexibly implemented later on in different ways according to the needs and preferences of different member states.[63] While all of these features may be intrinsic to NMG, they all flout the idea of a polity governed by stable rules that are to be applied according to prior, politically agreed-upon, standards. According to this view, NMG are not creating a new "experimental" form of rule but are "bringing the law to trial"; they are doing no less than threatening the very centrality of law to the EU integration project.[64]

What are we to make of these criticisms? Certainly they cannot all be accepted. One of the distinguishing features of many critiques of NMG is their ability to work against one another. How, for example, can methods like the OMC and social dialogue be a Trojan Horse undermining the foundations of the welfare state (or the legal state) while simultaneously being ineffective? There is a marked tendency among critical accounts (just as there is among NMG's proponents) either to exaggerate the significance of new methods (and thereby their threat) or to downplay and ignore the effects of new governance methods entirely.

A better approach may be to view NMG as an imperfect model but one that is still in a state of evolution and that should only ever be seen as one mode of EU lawmaking among others. At the very least, the idea of NMG as an archetype to which EU law *as a whole* would gradually converge seems wildly out of step with the failure of new governance methods to reach into national policy and with their uninspiring record in meeting standards of accountability, transparency, and participation.[65]

Decline or Reemergence? New Modes of Governance and the Euro Crisis

Given these shortcomings, what does the future hold for NMG? Certainly one cannot contemplate this question without seeing it in the context of the current (at the time of writing, unending) euro crisis. This crisis seems both to present a solid critique of NMG, one that builds on the criticisms developed above, and to suggest the continued centrality of NMG to the EU's policy-making architecture.

The critique element can be seen most clearly when considering some of the institutional causes of the euro crisis.[66] Just as NMG have been criticized throughout their existence for being ineffective – or being the mere plaything of "power politics" – so a much vaunted weakness of European Monetary Union has been the perceived lack of strength and credibility of its monitoring and corrective mechanisms. At least part of this weakness can be attributed to NMG processes such as the Broad Economic Policy Guidelines, which failed (arguably as a matter of explicit institutional design) to monitor fiscal risks, particularly those arising in the private sector. A second problem the crisis has exposed is the reliance of the Excessive Deficit Procedure on soft "naming and shaming" methods when eurozone states failed to meet fiscal targets, with sanctions applied too haphazardly (and being prone to political manipulation). Consequently, the institutional setup of the eurozone has consistently lacked credibility (with the confidence of consumers and investors declining rapidly as the first signs of trouble emerged).

As a result of these criticisms, the default response to the crisis has been both a diagnosis that the eurozone's existing governing instruments are too "weak" and a desire to reassert central control. This has resulted in the strengthening of central institutions, particularly the Commission, as well as the creation of further processes of coordination on top of existing NMG processes for economic policy. In the future, the Commission will in future be able to issue semiautomatic recommendations for sanctions against member states that breach the European Monetary Union's 3 percent deficit and 60 percent debt targets, which can be overturned by the Council only through a qualified majority.[67] At the same time, a new macroeconomic imbalances procedure (which includes a sanctioning mechanism) will monitor national budgets, including within its ambit many risks (such as through private debt or unsustainable pension programs) missed by the Broad Economic Policy Guidelines.[68] Much of this program seems to seek to centralize the coordination of fiscal policy; is it not, therefore, a step back from the "flexible" and decentralizing vision of NMG?

This conventional story of the crisis, however, glosses over the extent to which institutional reforms do not so much replace new governance methods as expand and consolidate them.[69] One must keep in mind that Commission sanctions under the Excessive Deficit Procedure themselves can only be imposed after following a long period of monitoring and review, with recommendations, reporting, and benchmarking preceding any formal sanctioning decision.[70] Furthermore, what is the macroeconomic imbalances procedure but another variety of OMC, and what is, one whose substantive content is likely to overlap significantly with existing OMC procedures?

The creation of new fiscal surveillance procedures in this sense seems less a departure from than a return to NMG, albeit a variety where bilateral relations between the Commission and the member states replace horizontal peer review, and where tougher sanctions for default are an increasingly prominent element. One might associate the new model, for example, with an idea often mooted by political scientists such as Fritz Scharpf, who advocated "governance in the shadow of hierarchy," that is, the establishment through hard law of a dissuasive institutional framework with coordination remaining as a means of monitoring compliance and encouraging agreement around common fiscal standards.[71]

The reforms made in the wake of the euro crisis illustrate the stubborn obstinacy of NMG. Even after a crisis that displayed many of their most prominent weaknesses, new governance continues to be a set of mechanisms to which EU leaders turn. As when they originated, NMG are seen by decision makers as offering an attractive middle path between the need for more central control and the need to deliver central coordination in a decentralized Union where only the member states carry the resources and institutions that can fully realize common European goals. Jonathan Zeitlin has dubbed this *via media* a "constitutional compromise": the ability of new governance to bridge the gap between federalist visions of the EU polity on the one hand and the reality of national control over many core areas of policy on the other.[72] The compromise embodied by NMG seems likely to ensure their survival and even multiplication in the coming decade.

Notes

1 Christoph Möllers, "European Governance: Meaning and Value of a Concept," *Common Market Law Review* 43 (2006); Markus Jachtenfuchs, "The Governance Approach to European Integration," *Journal of Common Market Studies* 39 (2001).

2 As well as further references below, see Adrienne Héritier and Martin Rhodes, eds., *New Modes of Governance in Europe: Governing in the Shadow of Hierarchy* (London: Palgrave Macmillan, 2010); and Sandra Kröger, ed., "What We Have Learnt: Advances, Pitfalls and Remaining Questions in OMC Research." Special Issue, *European Integration Online Papers* 13 (2009).

3 On fragmentation in NMG, see Mark Dawson, "Transforming into What? New Governance and the Managerial Sensibility in Modern Law," in "New Governance and Transformation of Law." Special Issue, *Wisconsin Law Review* 2 (2010).

4 Contrast, e.g., Edoardo Chiti's account of the agency as an example of legalized procedural cooperation between national and EU administrations with the incorporation of agencies within early NMG literature (e.g., by Scott and Trubek). Edoardo Chiti, "Decentralisation and Integration into the Community Administrations: A New Perspective on European Agencies," *European Law Journal* 10 (2004).

5 Charles Sabel and Jonathan Zeitlin, "Learning from Difference: The New Architecture of Experimentalist Governance in the EU," *European Law Journal* 14 (2008).

6 I have elsewhere described this as three "waves" in considering the relationship between governance and law. See Mark Dawson, "Three Waves of New Governance in the European Union," *European Law Review* 36 (2011).

7 As well as Joanne Scott and David Trubek, "Mind the Gap: Law and New Approaches to Governance in the European Union," *European Law Journal* 8 (2002), see the definition offered by Craig and de Búrca: "when it comes to the concrete question of what is distinctive about certain forms of EU governing when compared to others, we suggest that the core of the debate on new governance concerns a move away from hierarchical forms of governing." Paul Craig and Gráinne de Búrca, *EU Law: Text, Cases and Materials* (Oxford: Oxford University Press, 2011), 159.
8 European Commission, *European Governance: A White Paper*, COM(2001) 428 final.
9 Scott and Trubek, "Mind the Gap."
10 See also the contrast drawn by Gráinne de Búrca between NMG and the constitutional project in de Búrca, "The Constitutional Challenge of New Governance in the European Union," *European Law Review* 28 (2003).
11 David Trubek and Louise Trubek, "Hard and Soft Law in the Construction of Social Europe: The Role of the Open Method of Co-ordination," *European Law Journal* 11 (2005): 355–361.
12 Kenneth Armstrong, "The Character of EU Law and Governance: From 'Community Method' to New Modes of Governance," *Current Legal Problems* 64 (2011): 185–187.
13 On new governance in fiscal policy, see Waltraud Schelkle, "EU Fiscal Governance: Hard Law in the Shadow of Soft Law?" *Columbia Journal of European Law* 13 (2007).
14 See, e.g., Gráinne de Búrca and Joanne Scott, introduction to *Law and New Governance in the EU and US* (Oxford: Hart, 2006); "New Governance and Transformation of Law." Special Issue, *Wisconsin Law Review* (2010); and Mark Dawson, *New Governance and Transformation of European Law* (Cambridge: Cambridge University Press, 2011), 92–101.
15 Charles Sabel and Jonathan Zeitlin, *Experimentalist Governance in the European Union: Towards a New Architecture* (Oxford: Oxford University Press, 2010).
16 Sabel and Zeitlin, "Learning from Difference," 271.
17 Ibid., 274.
18 See Dawson, *New Governance and Transformation of European Law*, 105–120; Claudio M. Radaelli and Anne C.M. Meuwese, "Hard Questions, Hard Solutions: Proceduralisation through Impact Assessment in the EU," *West European Politics* 33 (2010); and Jacques Lenoble, "OMC and the Theory of Reflexive Governance," in *Social Rights and Market Forces: Is the Open Coordination of Employment and Social Policies the Future of Social Europe?* ed. Simon Deakin and Olivier de Schutter, (Brussels: Bruylant, 2005).
19 Simon Deakin, "Regulatory Competition after Laval," in *Cambridge Yearbook of European Legal Studies* 10 (Oxford: Hart, 2008).
20 Neil Walker and Gráinne de Búrca, "Reconceiving Law and New Governance," *Columbia Journal of European Law* 13 (2007); the "absorption" thesis.
21 See, e.g., the mix of legislative and non-legislative measures proposed in the Commission's 2008 Social Agenda, *A Renewed Social Agenda: Opportunities, Access and Solidarity in 21st Century Europe* (Communication) COM(2008) 412 final.
22 Case C-341/05 *Laval un Partneri Ltd v. Svenska Byggnadsarbetareförbundet* EU:C:2007:809.
23 See, e.g., Sandra Kröger, "The End of Democracy as We Know it? The Legitimacy Deficits of Bureaucratic Social Policy Governance," *Journal of European Integration* 29 (2007) and Milena Büchs, "How Legitimate is the Open Method of Coordination?" *Journal of Common Market Studies* 46 (2008).
24 See David Trubek and Louise Trubek, "New Governance and Legal Regulation: Complementarity, Rivalry and Transformation" *Columbia Journal of European Law* 13 (2007) and Claire Kilpatrick, "New EU Employment Governance and Constitutionalism," in de Búrca and Scott, *Law and New Governance in the EU and US*.
25 Joanne Scott and Susan Sturm, "Courts as Catalysts: Re-Thinking the Judicial Role in New Governance," *Columbia Journal of European Law* 13 (2007).
26 Tamara Hervey, "'Adjudicating in the Shadow of the Informal Settlement?': The Court of Justice of the EU, 'New Governance' and Social Welfare," *Current Legal Problems* 63 (2010).
27 See, e.g., Wolfgang Streeck, "Neo-Voluntarism: A New European Social Policy Paradigm?" in *Governance in the European Union*, ed. Gary Marks et al. (London: Sage, 2006).

28 Fritz Scharpf, "The European Social Model: Coping with the Challenges of Diversity," *Journal of Common Market Studies* 40 (2002).
29 European Council, Presidency Conclusions, 23–24 March 2000, para 5.
30 Jonathan Zeitlin, "Social Europe and Experimentalist Governance: Towards a New Constitutional Compromise?" in *EU Law and the Welfare State: In Search of Solidarity*, ed. Gráinne de Búrca (Oxford: Oxford University Press, 2005).
31 Jonathan Zeitlin, "Strengthening the Social Dimension of the Lisbon Strategy," *Belgian Review of Social Security* 2 (2007).
32 Radaelli and Meuwese, "Hard Questions, Hard Solutions"; Rik de Ruiter, "Developing Multilateral Surveillance Tools in the EU," *West European Politics* 31 (2008).
33 See, e.g., the justification for the establishment of executive EU agencies in the preamble to Council Regulation (EC) 58/2003 of 19 December 2002 laying down the statute for executive agencies to be entrusted with certain tasks in the management of Community programmes [2003] OJ L 11/1.
34 Sabel and Zeitlin, "Learning from Difference."
35 See European Commission, *Technical Harmonisation and Standardisation: A New Approach* (Communication) COM(1985) 19.
36 See, e.g., Joao Rodrigues, "The Open Method of Coordination as a New Governance Tool," in "L'evoluzione della governance europea," ed. Mario Telò, Special Issue, *Europa Europe* 2–3 (2001): 96; and Christian Joerges and Jürgen Neyer, "From Intergovernmental Bargaining to Deliberative Political Processes: The Constitutionalisation of Comitology," *European Law Journal* 3 (1997).
37 Joerges and Neyer, "From Intergovernmental Bargaining to Deliberative Political Processes."
38 See, e.g., Tanja Börzel's characterization of the OMC as "governance by competition": "European Governance: Negotiation and Competition in the Shadow of Hierarchy," *Journal of Common Market Studies* 48 (2010).
39 See, e.g., Erik Eriksen and John Fossum, "Democracy through Strong Publics in the European Union," *Journal of Common Market Studies* 40 (2002); and Agustin Menendez, John Fossum, and Erik Eriksen, "The Constitution's Gift? A Deliberative Democratic Analysis of Constitution Making in the European Union," *European Law Journal* 11 (2005).
40 See the reflections in Kenneth Armstrong, "Rediscovering Civil Society: The European Union and the White Paper on Governance," *European Law Journal* 8 (2002).
41 COM(2001) 428 final, 13.
42 See, e.g., the explanations provided in the preamble to the Council Recommendation SEC(2010) 488 of 27 April 2010 on *Broad Guidelines for the Economic Policies of the Member States*, i.e., the Europe 2020 Integrated Guidelines that guide the employment OMC.
43 Mark Dawson, "The Ambiguity of Social Europe in the Open Method of Coordination," *European Law Review* 34 (2009).
44 See Scharpf, "The European Social Model."
45 Claus Offe, "The European Model of Social Capitalism: Can it Survive European Integration?" *European Journal of Political Philosophy* 11 (2003); and Christian Joerges and Florian Rödl, "'Social Market Economy' as Europe's Social Model?" (working paper, Law, no. 8, European University Institute, Florence, 2004).
46 Dawson, *New Governance and Transformation of European Law*, 215–221.
47 Armin Schäfer and Simone Leiber, "The Double Voluntarism in EU Social Dialogue and Employment Policy," in "What We Have Learnt: Advances, Pitfalls and Remaining Questions in OMC Research," ed. Sandra Kröger, Special Issue 1, *European Integration Online Papers* 13, Art. 9 (2009), DOI: 10.1695/2009009; and Berndt Keller and Sabrina Weber, "Sectoral Social Dialogue at EU Level: Problems and Prospects of Implementation," *European Journal of Industrial Relations* 17 (2011).
48 See, e.g., Sandra Kröger, "The Effectiveness of Soft Governance in the Field of European Anti-poverty Policy: Operationalization and Empirical Evidence," *Journal of Comparative Policy Analysis* 11 (2009). For a more positive yet still critical account, see Martin Heidenreich and Jonathan Zeitlin, introduction to *Changing European Employment and Welfare Regimes: The Influence of the Open Method of Coordination on National Reforms*, ed. Martin Heidenreich and Jonathan Zeitlin (Abingdon; New York: Routledge, 2009).

49 Martin Lodge, "Comparing Non-Hierarchical Governance in Action: The Open Method of Coordination in Pensions and Information Society," *Journal of Common Market Studies* 45 (2007), 348.

50 See European Commission, *Lisbon Strategy Evaluation Document* (Commission Staff Working Document) SEC(2010) 114 final, at 21.

51 Susana Borras and Claudio Radaelli, "Recalibrating the Open Method of Coordination: Towards More Diverse and Effective Usages," *SIEPS Report* 7 (2010).

52 See, e.g., Yanas Papadopoulos, "Problems of Democratic Accountability in Network and Multi-level Governance," *European Law Journal* 13 (2007).

53 See, e.g., Zeitlin's skepticism of parliamentary involvement in NMG in Jonathan Zeitlin and Phillipe Pochet, *The Open Method of Coordination in Action: The European Employment and Social Inclusion Strategies* (Brussels: Peter Lang, 2005), 488.

54 Gijs Brandsma, Deirdre Curtin, and Albert Meijer, "How Transparent are Comitology Committees in Practice?" *European Law Journal* 14 (2008). On the historical struggle between the Parliament and Council over transparency and accountability in comitology, see Kieran Bradley, "Halfway House: The 2006 Comitology Reforms and the European Parliament," *West European Politics* 31 (2008).

55 See, e.g., Kröger, "What We Have Learnt"; Mark Dawson, "EU Law 'Transformed'? Evaluating Accountability and Subsidiarity in the 'Streamlined' OMC for Social Inclusion and Social Protection," in "What We Have Learnt: Advances, Pitfalls and Remaining Questions in OMC Research," ed. Sandra Kröger, Special Issue 1, *European Integration Online Papers* 13, Art. 8 (2009), DOI: 10.1695/2009008.

56 Dawson, *New Governance and Transformation of European Law*, 198.

57 See Mark Dawson, "Soft Law and the Rule of Law in the European Union: Revision or Redundancy?" in *The European Legal Field*, ed. Bruno de Witte and Antoine Vauchez (London: Hart, 2012).

58 See Vassillis Hatzopoulos, "Why the Open Method of Coordination in Bad for You: A Letter to the EU," *European Law Journal* 13 (2007).

59 Article 5 TEU.

60 European Parliament, *On the Institutional and Legal Implications of the Use of Soft Law Instruments* (Resolution) 2007/2028(INI), Point Y.

61 Christian Joerges, "Integration through De-Legislation?" *European Law Review* 33 (2008).

62 Lon Fuller, *The Morality of Law* (Yale: Yale University Press, 1969), Chap. 1.

63 This also, of course, potentially leads to contradiction, i.e., dual standards in the member states, each of which is equally "valid." See, e.g., the varying policy responses accepted (and even commended) in the 2008 *Joint Report on Social Inclusion and Social Protection* (Office for Official Publications of the EC, 2008), 8–12.

64 Christian Joerges, "What is Left of the European Economic Constitution" (working paper, Law, no. 13, European University Institute, Florence, 2005), 25.

65 On my own suggestions for reform, see Dawson, *New Governance and Transformation of European Law*, 235–310.

66 For a summary of institutional causes, see House of Lords (EU Committee), *The Future of Economic Governance in the EU*, 12th Report of Session 2010–2011. Available at: http://www.publications.parliament.uk/pa/ld201011/ldselect/ldeucom/124/124.pdf.

67 Council Regulation (EU) No 1173/2011 of 16 November 2011 on the effective enforcement of budgetary surveillance in the euro area [2011] OJ L 306/1, Article 5.

68 Council Regulation (EU) No 1174/2011 of 16 November 2011 on enforcement measures to correct excessive macroeconomic imbalances in the euro area [2011] OJ L 306/8.

69 See Armstrong, "The Character of EU Law and Governance," 10.

70 See the procedure established in Council Regulation (EC) 1466/97 of 7 July 1997 on the strengthening of the surveillance of budgetary positions and the coordination of economic policies, [1997] OJ L 202/36, Articles 5 and 6.

71 Scharpf, "The European Social Model," 5.

72 Zeitlin, "Social Europe and Experimentalist Governance."

References

Armstrong, Kenneth. "Rediscovering Civil Society: The European Union and the White Paper on Governance." *European Law Journal* 8 (2002): 102–132.

Armstrong, Kenneth. "The Character of EU Law and Governance: From 'Community Method' to New Modes of Governance." *Current Legal Problems* 64 (2011): 179–214.

Borras, Susana, and Claudio Radaelli. "Recalibrating the Open Method of Coordination: Towards More Diverse and Effective Usages." *SIEPS Report* 7 (2010).

Börzel, Tanja. "European Governance: Negotiation and Competition in the Shadow of Hierarchy." *Journal of Common Market Studies* 48 (2010): 191–219.

Bradley, Kieran. "Halfway House: The 2006 Comitology Reforms and the European Parliament." *West European Politics* 31 (2008): 837–854.

Brandsma, Gijs, Deirdre Curtin, and Albert Meijer. "How Transparent are 'Comitology' Committees in Practice?" *European Law Journal* 14 (2008): 819–838.

Büchs, Milena. "How Legitimate is the Open Method of Coordination?" *Journal of Common Market Studies* 46 (2008): 765–786.

Chiti, Edoardo. "Decentralisation and Integration into the Community Administrations: A New Perspective on European Agencies." *European Law Journal* 10 (2004): 402–438.

Craig, Paul, and Gráinne de Búrca. *EU Law: Text, Cases and Materials*. Oxford: Oxford University Press, 2011.

Dawson, Mark. "The Ambiguity of Social Europe in the Open Method of Coordination." *European Law Review* 34 (2009): 55–79.

Dawson, Mark. "EU Law 'Transformed'? Evaluating Accountability and Subsidiarity in the 'Streamlined' OMC for Social Inclusion and Social Protection." In "What We Have Learnt: Advances, Pitfalls and Remaining Questions in OMC research," edited by Sandra Kröger. Special issue 1, *European Integration Online Papers* 13 (2009): 8–11. DOI: 10.1695/2009008.

Dawson, Mark. "Transforming into What? New Governance and the Managerial Sensibility in Modern Law." In "New Governance and Transformation of Law." Special Issue, *Wisconsin Law Review* No. 2 (2010): 389–440.

Dawson, Mark. *New Governance and Transformation of European Law*. Cambridge: Cambridge University Press, 2011.

Dawson, Mark. "Three Waves of New Governance in the European Union." *European Law Review* 36 (2011): 208–225.

Dawson, Mark. "Soft Law and the Rule of Law in the European Union: Revision or Redundancy?" In *The European Legal Field*, edited by Bruno de Witte and Antoine Vauchez. London: Hart, 2012.

Deakin, Simon. "Regulatory Competition after Laval." *Cambridge Yearbook of European Legal Studies*, 10 (2008): 581–609.

de Búrca, Gráinne. "The Constitutional Challenge of New Governance in the European Union." *European Law Review* 28 (2003): 814–839.

de Búrca, Gráinne, and Joanne Scott, eds. *Law and New Governance in the EU and US*. Oxford: Hart, 2006.

de Ruiter, Rik."Developing Multilateral Surveillance Tools in the EU." *West European Politics* 31 (2008): 896–914.

Eriksen, Erik, and John Fossum. "Democracy through Strong Publics in the European Union." *Journal of Common Market Studies* 40 (2002): 401–424.

Fuller, Lon. *The Morality of Law*. Yale: Yale University Press, 1969.

Hatzopoulos, Vassillis. "Why the Open Method of Coordination in Bad for You: A Letter to the EU." *European Law Journal* 13 (2007): 309–342.

Heidenreich, Martin, and Jonathan Zeitlin. Introduction to *Changing European Employment and Welfare Regimes: The Influence of the Open Method of Coordination on National Reforms*, edited by Martin Heidenreich and Jonathan Zeitlin. Abingdon; New York: Routledge, 2009.

Héritier, Adrienne, and Martin Rhodes, eds. *New Modes of Governance in Europe: Governing in the Shadow of Hierarchy*. London: Palgrave Macmillan, 2010.

Hervey, Tamara. "'Adjudicating in the Shadow of the Informal Settlement?': The Court of Justice of the EU, 'New Governance' and Social Welfare." *Current Legal Problems* 63 (2010): 92–152.
Jachtenfuchs, Markus. "The Governance Approach to European Integration." *Journal of Common Market Studies* 39 (2001): 245–264.
Joerges, Christian. "Integration through De-Legislation? "*European Law Review* 33 (2008): 291–312.
Joerges, Christian. "What is Left of the European Economic Constitution." Working paper, Law, no. 13, European University Institute, Florence, 2005.
Joerges, Christian, and Jürgen Neyer. "From Intergovernmental Bargaining to Deliberative Political Processes: The Constitutionalisation of Comitology." *European Law Journal* 3 (1997): 273–299.
Joerges, Christian, and Florian Rödl. "Social Market Economy as Europe's Social Model?" Working paper, Law, no. 8, European University Institute, Florence, 2004.
Keller, Berndt, and Sabrina Weber. "Sectoral Social Dialogue at EU Level: Problems and Prospects of Implementation." *European Journal of Industrial Relations* 17 (2011): 227–243.
Kilpatrick, Claire. "New EU Employment Governance and Constitutionalism." In de Búrca and Scott, *Law and New Governance in the EU and US*, 121–152.
Kröger Sandra. "The End of Democracy as We Know it? The Legitimacy Deficits of Bureaucratic Social Policy Governance." *Journal of European Integration* 29 (2007): 565–582.
Kröger, Sandra. "The Effectiveness of Soft Governance in the Field of European Anti-poverty Policy: Operationalization and Empirical Evidence." *Journal of Comparative Policy Analysis* 11 (2009): 197–211.
Kröger Sandra., ed. "What We Have Learnt: Advances, Pitfalls and Remaining Questions in OMC Research." Special issue 1, *European Integration Online Papers* 13 (2009).
Lenoble, Jacques. "OMC and the Theory of Reflexive Governance." In *Social Rights and Market Forces: Is the Open Coordination of Employment and Social Policies the Future of Social Europe?* edited by Simon Deakin and Olivier de Schutter. Brussels: Bruylant, 2005.
Lodge, Martin. "Comparing Non-Hierarchical Governance in Action: The Open Method of Coordination in Pensions and Information Society." *Journal of Common Market Studies* 45 (2007): 343–365.
Menendez, Agustin, John Fossum, and Erik Eriksen. "The Constitution's Gift? A Deliberative Democratic Analysis of Constitution Making in the European Union." *European Law Journal* 11 (2005): 380–440.
Möllers, Christoph. "European Governance: Meaning and Value of a Concept." *Common Market Law Review* 43 (2006): 313–336.
"New Governance and Transformation of Law." Special Issue, *Wisconsin Law Review* (2010).
Offe, Claus. "The European Model of Social Capitalism: Can it Survive European Integration?" *European Journal of Political Philosophy* 11 (2003): 462–466.
Papadopoulos, Yanas. "Problems of Democratic Accountability in Network and Multi-level Governance." *European Law Journal* 13 (2007): 469–486.
Radaelli, Claudio M., and Anne C.M. Meuwese. "Hard Questions, Hard Solutions: Proceduralisation through Impact Assessment in the EU." *West European Politics* 33 (2010): 136–153.
Rodrigues, Joao. "The Open Method of Coordination as a New Governance Tool." In "L'evoluzione della governance europea," edited by Mario Telò. Special issue, *Europa Europe* 2–3 (2001).
Sabel, Charles, and Jonathan Zeitlin. "Learning from Difference: The New Architecture of Experimentalist Governance in the EU." *European Law Journal* 14 (2008): 271–327.
Sabel, Charles, and Jonathan Zeitlin. *Experimentalist Governance in the European Union: Towards a New Architecture*. Oxford: Oxford University Press, 2010.
Schäfer, Armin, and Simone Leiber. "The Double Voluntarism in EU Social Dialogue and Employment Policy." In "What We Have Learnt: Advances, Pitfalls and Remaining Questions in OMC Research," edited by Sandra Kröger. Special issue 1, *European Integration Online Papers* 13 (2009): DOI: 10.1695/2009009.
Scharpf, Fritz. "The European Social Model: Coping with the Challenges of Diversity." *Journal of Common Market Studies* 40 (2002): 645–670.
Schelkle, Waltraud. "EU Fiscal Governance: Hard Law in the Shadow of Soft Law?" *Columbia Journal of European Law* 13 (2007): 705–732.

Scott, Joanne, and Susan Sturm. "Courts as Catalysts: Re-Thinking the Judicial Role in New Governance." *Columbia Journal of European Law* 13 (2007): 565–594.

Scott, Joanne, and David Trubek. "Mind the Gap: Law and New Approaches to Governance in the European Union." *European Law Journal* 8 (2002): 1–18.

Streeck, Wolfgang. "Neo-Voluntarism: A New European Social Policy Paradigm?" In *Governance in the European Union*, edited by Gary Marks et al. London: Sage, 2006.

Trubek, David, and Louise Trubek. "Hard and Soft Law in the Construction of Social Europe: The Role of the Open Method of Co-Ordination." *European Law Journal* 11 (2005): 343–364.

Trubek, David, and Louise Trubek. "New Governance and Legal Regulation: Complementarity, Rivalry and Transformation." *Columbia Journal of European Law* 13 (2007): 539–564.

Walker, Neil, and Gráinne de Búrca. "Reconceiving Law and New Governance." *Columbia Journal of European Law* 13 (2007): 519–537.

Zeitlin, Jonathan. "Social Europe and Experimentalist Governance: Towards a New Constitutional Compromise?" In *EU Law and the Welfare State: In Search of Solidarity*, edited by Gráinne de Búrca, 213–242. Oxford: Oxford University Press, 2005.

Zeitlin, Jonathan. "Strengthening the Social Dimension of the Lisbon Strategy." *Belgian Review of Social Security* 2 (2007): 459–473.

Zeitlin, Jonathan, and Phillipe Pochet. *The Open Method of Coordination in Action: The European Employment and Social Inclusion Strategies*. Brussels: Peter Lang, 2005.

10

The European Union and Democracy

John Erik Fossum

Introduction

European integration is widely referred to as "integration through law." This is a process whereby law is also programmed to serve democracy. An important assumption that has long given impetus and credence to the integration process is that there is a close and positive link between integration and democratization. Thus, the European Union is the most prominent effort to develop a system of democracy beyond the nation state, at the supranational level. In that connection it is interesting to note that many scholars point to the experimental character of EU democratization, in lieu of the unprecedented nature of the EU experience.[1] Other scholars downplay its novelty. They underline that European integration is taking place in a context of democratic nation states where the member states' central input into (and steering of) the process entails that EU democratization takes on traits of copying and emulating legally entrenched systems of representative democracy from the level of the nation state to the EU level.[2]

How we understand the European Union – as a genuine democratic experiment or as a more mundane copying exercise – has bearings on the prospects for law shaping democracy, and vice versa, in a transnational context. But whereas analysts would disagree on the form of democratization, most would agree that the European Union suffers from a democratic deficit. They would not share the same view of the precise nature of the deficit. We therefore need to take a step back and look at what is meant by a "democratic deficit."

Democratic deficit refers to a gap between democratic aspirations (as reflected in a given set of democratic standards) and democratic realities. Establishing that there is a gap or a shortfall requires knowledge of both standards and practice. We need to know against what democratic standards the European Union is to be measured, which in turn requires knowledge of the type of political formation or political order the Union is. Acknowledging that the European Union suffers from a democratic deficit is akin to acknowledging that it is something more than, and different from, an ordinary international organization.[3]

A Companion to European Union Law and International Law, First Edition.
Edited by Dennis Patterson and Anna Södersten.

This chapter has three aims. The first aim is to clarify what the democratic deficit is, and to consider whether and to what extent the European Union labors under a democratic deficit. This includes spelling out the implicit assumptions or standards of evaluation on which such an assessment can be justifiably based. It also includes, as we shall see, specifying the form of democracy (participatory, representative, or deliberative) in which EU democratization resides and the type of polity within which these processes unfold. Since both (form of democracy and type of polity) are matters of controversy, it is necessary to present the different positions and to justify the choices that are made here. The second aim is to consider possible remedial measures: can the democratic deficit be remedied? In today's context that must include paying attention to the European crisis, which is here understood as a composite financial, fiscal, institutional, and constitutional crisis. The third and final aim is to examine the effects of the crisis on the prospects of remedying the European Union's democratic deficit. Of particular importance is establishing whether the crisis appears to be redefining the relationship between integration and democratization. Obviously, given that this chapter is written while we are still in the midst of crisis, we can only point to tendencies and general directions of change.

Contending Conceptions of Democracy in Europe

When we consider the contending conceptions of democracy in Europe we need to keep in mind that there also are analysts who disagree that the European Union suffers from a democratic deficit. The counterargument is that, however exceptional, it is ultimately an international arrangement and therefore it cannot be evaluated by traditional standards of representative democracy. It makes no sense to discuss the democratic quality of international systems because such systems are made up of, and must respond to, the real repositories of democratic values: the nation states. That, in effect, means that international organizations should be evaluated by means of standards of legitimacy or accountability that are different from and less demanding than the ones we apply to democratic nation states.[4] The upshot is that the discussion of the European Union's democratic deficit is the wrong debate: what is necessary is to establish which standards of legitimacy and accountability we may justifiably apply to international organizations.

One important assumption underlying this line of reasoning is that globalization and Europeanization have not fundamentally altered the nature of national democracy. What we see instead is a widening gap between those decisions that affect a state and that state's ability to control the decisions; the main challenge for national systems is to restore national control of these processes by extending their international reach. That does not require any fundamental restructuring of national democracy, however.

The more widely shared view is that European integration restructures national democracies. The result is that the integration process now affects national democratic arrangements so much and so directly that it is no longer possible to establish the quality of national democracy without taking the European level explicitly into account. But how the European dimension is to be taken into account is a matter of contention. Some see the European Union mainly as a destructive force, one that undercuts national representative systems of government and does not come up with anything convincing in its stead.[5] To Dieter Grimm, for example, it makes no sense to try to democratize the European Union because there is no European democratic demos, and the European Union is not a kind of political entity that lends itself to democratization.[6] This position shares with the first one a deep skepticism about integration's relationship with democratization: it is difficult to see it as anything but negative because it is very hard, or next to impossible, for the Union to develop the necessary democratic requirements.

Other analysts take a more optimistic view and think that integration may be compatible with democratization. Among commentators, precisely how this is to occur varies considerably, however. One line of argument understands European integration as a novel and experimental process that, as part of a transnationalization of politics, compels us to reconsider democracy itself along transnational deliberative democratic lines. James Bohman argues that, in today's interdependent world, "[t]he main issue is not the real or supposed democratic deficit, but the democratic criterion itself . . . ."[7] The upshot is that we need to rethink the meaning of democracy, in particular the presumption that democracy requires a single demos. Bohman's alternative, transnational conception of democracy is based on multiple demoi. To Bohman, deliberative democracy, when properly institutionalized within a decentered reflexive system, can serve as a democratically viable near-substitute for representative democracy. The democratic quality of the system does not hinge on the quality of a vertically structured system of representation that enables a people to authorize a set of leaders and to hold them to account in regular elections. Rather, the European Union's democratic deficit is better understood in terms of a "deliberative deficit about the ends of the polity."[8]

Another line of argument focuses on the European integration experience as novel in the sense of instituting democracy at the supranational level but conventional in the choice of form, namely that of representative democracy. The focus is on the increased power of the European Parliament (EP) and the reprogramming of national representative systems to accommodate the new European level. Here the argument is that the democratic deficit resides in deficient representative-democratic arrangements. The new institutions that have been established at the European level, most notably the EP, are deficient and unable to compensate for the weakening of national (and regional) representative systems that the European integration process has brought about.[9]

There are more positions in the debate, and positions are more nuanced than what comes across in the broad-brush picture provided here.[10] But what this brief overview highlights is that the debate is about fundamentals; it revolves around the two core components of the democratic deficit: what are the appropriate standards, and what kinds of practice do the standards refer to? The positions do not share a common understanding of democracy. The disagreement is three-dimensional: it is over the relevant form of democracy; the relevant level of locating democracy (national, supranational, or global); and the type of polity (what kind of political entity the European Union is).

Ultimately, this debate comes down to one's underlying conception of democracy and what one understands the basic democratic requirements to be. Does democracy require the "state form," or is it compatible with a much broader range of political arrangements? Does democracy require a common identity or *demos*? In order to shed light on this debate, it is necessary to start by defining democracy.

Democracy must be understood foremost as a higher-order legitimation principle. As such, it is a principle that spells out the requisite conditions for justification. Laws must be justified to those affected by them. Democracy thus serves as a critical standard with conditions for how to get things right in the political sphere of action. That places deliberation at the center of democracy; deliberation is necessary to get political results right. It does not exclude the use of voting; it underlines that the relevance of such decision-making procedures must be explained and justified.

The two core criteria of democracy can be said to be *autonomy* and *accountability*.[11] Autonomy refers to the notion that those who are affected by laws should be authorized to make them. Accountability is both about making an account and holding to account. It is about a justificatory process that rests on a reason-giving practice, wherein the decision makers can be held responsible to the citizenry, and where, in the last resort, it is possible to *dismiss* incompetent rulers.[12] These principles require representative democratic arrangements and explicit sanctioning mechanisms.

The two core criteria of democracy require institutions and procedures, which must ensure that citizens will be able to affect lawmaking processes and which also provide citizens with opportunities for evaluating whether they find the justifications behind the laws and decisions to be acceptable. In that sense democracy in the deliberative trapping that I espouse here presupposes a set of arrangements that include: (1) a constitution with a set of inalienable rights; (2) forums for public debate; and (3) institutional mechanisms that are capable of transforming political initiatives into collective commitments in a representative manner.[13]

It follows from the above that whereas democracy is fundamentally a legitimation principle, in the modern state context it has developed into a distinct institutionalized arrangement that comes with explicit presuppositions for how human beings should relate to each other and how they should address problems and issues that concern them all, individually and collectively. Democracy is associated with a conception of the relevant community, or *demos*; there are, therefore, also associated presuppositions of membership (and citizenship), that is, of who is part of the community and of how and in what sense they are part; of identity (people need to identify with the community for this to make up a community in the first place); and of legitimacy, as people must believe that the community's basic norms are just and valid for this to make up a democracy. Such additional presuppositions are necessary, for at the core of democracy there is a fundamental ambiguity: democracy cannot itself determine the *demos*; that is, spell out precisely who the people shall be. Thus, whereas democracy requires other additional arrangements to establish the specific popular make-up, it not only depends on but also places particular – democratic – requirements on identity, membership status (citizenship) in a given community, and legitimacy.

At the same time, precisely because democracy is essentially a justification principle, all the criteria for establishing the demos have to be open to constant contestation. That means that a central precondition for a democratic order is a viable public sphere – namely, a communicative space (or spaces) in which relatively unconstrained debate, analysis, and criticism of the political order can take place.[14] It also means that democracy is not strictly tied to the state form. The state form has been able to deliver arrangements that can sustain democracy within a given territory. At the same time, the state plays a central role in sustaining a profound paradox in today's world, namely that the successful entrenchment of democracy in the internal affairs of states is coupled with "a lust for power [that] marks the relations among countries in which the stronger dominate the weaker."[15]

With these kinds of reflections on the nature of democracy, what are we to make of the European Union's democratic deficit?

The European Union's Democratic Deficit

If we consider the EU treaties, EU level democratization is foremost a matter of installing a system of representative democracy at the EU level, with pronounced deliberative features (cf. Article 11 of the Treaty on European Union (TEU)). The provisions on representative democracy are most explicitly spelled out in Article 10 TEU:

1. The functioning of the Union shall be founded on representative democracy.
2. Citizens are directly represented at Union level in the European Parliament. Member States are represented in the European Council by their Heads of State or Government and in the Council by their governments, themselves democratically accountable either to their national Parliaments, or to their citizens.

A literal reading of this provision suggests that EU-level democracy is embedded in two distinct channels of representation that address citizens in their capacity as individual members of a European constituency and in their capacity as members of the European Union through their respective national constituencies. This gives the impression of a rather conventional two-channeled structure of representation – similar to the kind of structure we find in federal states such as Germany. The provision gives credence to the notion of EU democratization as a process that has taken strong cues from the context in which it unfolds, a setting of already existing democratic states (which vary considerably in the manner in which representation is structured). The problem with such a reading is that it only considers how the context of existing democratic states shapes the European Union without at the same time taking properly into account how that very context of existing states is also, in turn, being shaped and altered by EU integration and democratization.

In the following, I will first briefly assess the European Union against the two criteria of autonomy and accountability, in order to get a clearer sense of the Union's democratic deficit, which then appears as a representative-democratic deficit. It is readily apparent that when we compare the Union to a fully fledged parliamentary system, the system of representation we find at the EU level is not only incomplete, it also holds important defects, both in terms of autonomy and accountability. In the famous Lisbon Treaty ruling, the German Constitutional Court noted that the European Union:

> cannot support a parliamentary government and organize itself with regard to party politics in the system of government and opposition in such a way that a decision on political direction taken by the European electorate could have a politically decisive effect.[16]

The European Union's representative-democratic structure fails to offer the measure of electoral accountability that we associate with representative government. Elections to the EP are frequently referred to as "second-order elections." This entails that voters primarily pass judgments on their *national leaders* rather than on the EU leaders.[17] European political parties are still organizationally tied to the nation-state level and have not developed Europe-wide party organizations.[18] The party constellations that are formed in the EP after each election are rooted in a fragmented, and not transnational, party structure. Member states' party systems exhibit a limited degree of organizational adaptation to the European Union's increased influence and presence.[19] Citizens' sense of disconnect from the EU level shows up in a steady turnout decline in EP elections, with the European average now well below 50 percent.[20]

Within what was generally known as the Community system, the independent European Commission holds the exclusive right to present legislative and policy proposals; these will be adopted by the EP and the Council; and the European Court of Justice maintains the institutional balance.[21] The fact that there is no directly elected body at the EU level that can propose legislation, and that everything has to go through the nonelected Commission, is an important defect in autonomy. The Commission (generally portrayed as the European Union's key executive) is appointed by the member states and approved by the European Council (through qualified majority) and the EP. The ordinary legislative procedure (earlier named "codecision") is a complex procedure for consensus formation through interinstitutional deliberation and interaction. In practice, however, there is an increasing trend towards informal Commission, EP, and Council "trialogues" that effectively short-circuit parliamentary handling of legislative proposals in the sense that deals are struck in secret among a limited number of actors.[22]

The EP's ability to hold the Commission to account has gradually increased, but the system still falls well short of the core parliamentary principle whereby the government derives from the parliament. Consider the manner in which the Commission as the European Union's main executive is selected. The president and members of the Commission are drawn from national lists of candidates proposed to the European Council and elected by the EP.[23] This cumbersome procedure reflects how the selection of the Union's main executive agent first activates the agents of the national constituencies before the proposal is put to the body in charge of representing the European constituency. The process is marked by a joint, yet sequential, activation of constituencies. This stands in marked contrast to federal states where subunits have no direct say in the process of selecting the central executive.

It is important to underline that the Council also carries executive functions, notably within foreign and security policy. In that regard, it does not respond to a European constituency, because the EP's role is merely consultative in that field. Thus, albeit such matters are increasingly handled at the EU level, the Europe-wide representative body, the EP, is unable to legislate.

The EP, though directly elected by the EU's citizens, has a weak ability to hold the executive to account. It can approve or reject the Council's suggestions for Commissioners, but it cannot on its own determine the Commission's composition. It can, however, force the Commissioners (as a collective) to resign. As noted, this produces an awkward structuring of the accountability relation – the forging of the new Commission involves both the collective of national constituencies and the European constituency in the decision.

Further, as the Union's main legislative and most powerful body, the Council is made up of elected member state representatives with relatively weak lines of accountability back to the national constituencies. It could also be argued that the Council increases executive actors' legislative power at the expense of elected legislators. As Joseph Weiler has noted:

> Community and Union governance perverts the balance between the executive and legislative organs of the state. The executive branch, government ministers, are reconstituted in the Community as the principal legislative organ with ... an ever widening jurisdiction over increasing areas of public policy.[24]

The Council is internally composed of government ministers and well over 250 working parties and committees that are made up of national officials and diplomats.[25]

Until recently, the Council's deliberations were closed, even when operating as a legislative body. Even now, when performing its executive functions, the Council is not subject to the transparency provisions.[26] The Union's complex system of implementation (which also plays an important role in policy initiation), its *comitology* underbelly, is notoriously opaque and weakly accountable.

A closely related aspect of the European Union's democratic deficit refers to the strong technocratic imprint on EU policy making. This on the one hand relates to the fact that the EP does not control all aspects of relevant policy making at the EU level and on the other hand to the presence of exceptionally strong or impervious technocratic bodies. For instance, Fritz Scharpf has noted that the "European Court of Justice (ECJ) is more immune from political correction than the constitutional court of any democratic state."[27]

The final aspect of the democratic deficit that I will briefly point to here can be traced directly to the distinctive nature of the European Union. The point is that European citizens have no directly elected body at the European level with a formal role in the procedure to alter the constitutional arrangement. The Intergovernmental Conference is the formal procedure for treaty change. Its core agent, the European Council, is – democratically speaking – a *second-order* European constitutional agent.[28] The leaders who occupy the European Council are democratically elected by, and are directly accountable to, their national constituencies. They can therefore not claim to be democratically authorized to speak on behalf of the collective of European citizens, understood as the European constituency. In contrast, the EP, which is directly elected by the EU constituency, plays no direct role in the process making or amending treaties.[29]

This brief assessment provides us with the unsurprising conclusion that the European Union suffers from a representative-democratic deficit, in terms of both autonomy and accountability. The assessment so far has been conducted against two criteria, each of which has built into it a set of implicit institutional and procedural arrangements that are attuned to the institutional and procedural conditions we are accustomed to from the democratic constitutional state. In other words, the assessment has taken for granted that the logic of copying national arrangements to the European Union level is such a pervasive feature of the process that we can use the same standards and the assumptions of representative democracy as exist in democratic nation states. Simply doing that would, however, be to overplay the element of copying at the behest of several important novel and distinctive features that the EU integration process has brought about. One important point is that European integration is a *process*, where the endpoint is not established but is subject to constant contention and discussion. In that sense, James Bohman[30] is correct in noting that there is a "deliberative deficit about the ends of the polity." But as has been shown above, the European Union's deficient representative-democratic arrangement must figure centrally in the reading of its democratic deficit, which is therefore of an institutional-constitutional nature.

What is particularly important is that the specific conditions under which European integration takes place – establishing supranational democracy in a context of already existing democratic states – also gives a distinct twist to this very process. The process by which EU democratization is accomplished is different from the way in which democracy develops within a state. A democratic system does not unfold for the European Union simply as an endogenous process (within a given and established entity) but rather develops as a system of states and, as a process, which is itself an intrinsic element in the creation of the democratic entity. In effect, then, democratization is part of what we may term the endogenization of a system of rule at the European level. It is not a matter of democratizing an already existing system but of establishing and democratizing a supranational system that is solidly anchored in the member states. This is at the core of the Europeanists' assumption about a positive relationship between integration and democratization. But it also highlights something that has often been overlooked in the integrationist literature, namely how dependent this process is on the combination of a horizontal (all member states) and vertical (EU level) anchoring in institutions and processes. How this combination plays itself out is more complex and composite than is generally thought. It gives a distinct and peculiar twist to the character and workings of representative democracy in the European Union.

What is then also important to recognize is that these features give the European democratization process a certain experimental quality. They make it more difficult to establish the precise nature and quality of EU democracy and also, therefore, to establish precisely what is the nature of the democratic deficit. Because the European integration process takes place in a setting of extant states, and the process is one of bringing states together in order to hold the system together, there is an important horizontal (cross-national) dimension to the process. This is even more so because of the way the integration process is structured: it is a matter of fusing levels (European Union and member state) and sharing competencies more than one of singling out a distinct European level of government with exclusive competencies.[31] The assessment of the European Union brought this out very clearly. Consider the example of how the Commission is democratically authorized (through the sequential activation of multiple constituencies) or how the European Council effectively operates as a "second-order" constitutionalizing agent.

The imbricated nature of this system and the fact that it is rooted in the member states is readily apparent in the very process of EU democratization. Consider the case of the EP, which was initially composed of national parliamentarians. Since direct EP elections were instituted and the EP took on a more independent shape, there has nevertheless also been a gradual increase of interparliamentary coordination (generally but not always including the EP). Thus, as will be spelled out in more detail below, the process of EU democratization was never only one of forging a vertical system of representation at the EU level, operating between the European Union and member states. Since Maastricht, it has taken on a distinct shape that is both vertical and (working across member states) horizontal lines.

The question we turn to now is whether any of the conclusions pertaining to the democratic deficit change when we bring into closer relief the more innovative features of the European Union's process of democratization and the effects of the crisis.

Interparliamentary Coordination: Relation to the European Union's Democratic Deficit?

The argument thus far is that EU democratization has proceeded through representative-democratic means but is shaped by the particular challenges facing the European Union and by the distinct structure within which it is unfolding. Simply put, the interstate structure adds an important horizontal dimension to the vertical process of establishing a European parliament. This horizontal dimension manifests itself in a distinctive system of interparliamentary coordination and cooperation. What has become increasingly apparent since the Maastricht Treaty is that EU democratization through representation has been taking place through two imbricated tracks. These are, on the one hand, the vertical process that has given rise to the EP as the world's first supranational parliamentary arrangement, with the EP being directly elected by EU citizens, and, on the other hand, a more horizontal process that has instituted a range of measures that foster closer relations of cooperation, information exchange, and learning across member state parliaments – often also including the EP. The upshot is the emergence of a system of representation that is quite different from the two channels of representation that we normally associate with multilevel federal systems.[32]

Perhaps the best way of conceiving of this system is as a fledgling so-called Multilevel Parliamentary Field.[33] A field is a set of "institutions that, in the aggregate, constitute a recognised area of institutional life," with some element of connectedness and structural equivalence.[34] This notion implies that parliamentary systems share certain structural similarities and are connected across states and levels of governance. They have the same overarching function, namely to represent their citizens. The notion of a parliamentary field picks up on the fact that there is an ever-tightening web of arrangements that link parliaments at both the national and EU level.[35] Each parliament becomes an intrinsic part of the other parliaments' operating environment, and the patterns of representation that link state and society in each member state open up and take on a more horizontal logic as the representative structures of the member states interact and coordinate with each other. Such a field structures parliamentary relations in distinctive manners, which differ from what we are used to in federations. Federations normally contain two vertical channels of representation that connect citizens to their two main levels of government, the federal and the sub-level (US: state, Canada: province), respectively. The notion of a Multilevel Parliamentary Field is different: it combines vertical and horizontal patterns of interaction.

What does this structure do to the European Union's democratic deficit? Does it weaken or strengthen it? It is clear that the structure complicates representative relationships. Precisely because the European integration process is a matter of establishing a European-level constituency on top of already existing national ones, the process is one of working out who represents whom where. We might say that the process is a complex blend in which the construction of an EU constituency is combined with the re-construction of (national and regional) constituencies. When these are imbricated through the field structure, the net effect is greater uncertainty in terms of constituency bounds. On the one hand, it heightens uncertainty as to the nature and the character of the relevant democratic constituency – the represented – to which each representative body speaks. On the other hand, it also would seem to give representatives from European, national, and regional levels greater leverage in constructing – in substantive and symbolic terms – their respective constituencies, that is, *who* they represent and *in what sense* they represent them. There is clearly considerable scope for symbolic and substantive manipulation and credit and blame shifting across levels and constituencies. The strong executive presence in the European Union would appear to amplify this because the executives have access to power both at the EU level and at the national level. We see frequent examples of how executives claim national credits when it benefits them and shift the blame to the EU level when that benefits them.

An obvious implication is that this complex structure amplifies problems of accountability, making it less obvious whose accounts we should rely on when actors at several levels are involved in the policy-making process. That, in turn, raises the question of whom to hold to account. But it should also be added that the multiple accountability inherent in this structure could compensate for its greater lack of clarity. The point is that actors in one setting can refer to other settings, and what transpires there will more easily be considered as relevant and pertinent to the issue at hand in this complex structure. The multiplication of liable actors can also serve accountability in the sense that accounts may be more credible. It is thus possible to argue that the field improves accountability in terms of account making; the field can serve as an important "external check" on what transpires within one given democratic setting. It might also be added that the field as a site for improving learning and exchange of best practices can serve accountability and democracy. At the same time, the field renders the process of holding a specific set of actors to account more difficult because the potential for blame-shifting is higher.

Two points need to be added here. First, the democratic quality of the member states varies considerably, and the EP is not capable of fulfilling a complete coordinating role because it lacks access to key decision-making areas such as foreign and security policy. These deficiencies have negative implications for the democratic operation of the field. Second, problems of accountability will likely be exacerbated if the system solidifies through tighter linkages among national parliaments and the EP.

The final question to which we now turn is that of what the crisis context has done to this structure.

The Crisis and Europe's Conundrum

There is no doubt that the crisis and how it has been handled to date has had negative implications for EU democracy. The EP has noted that "the democratic credibility of European integration has suffered enormously from the manner in which the euro crisis has been dealt with to date."[36] In what sense is that the case, and what are the broader implications?

The answer is necessarily shaped by how we understand the crisis: as a mere response to an externally generated problem in the global financial markets or as a reflection of deeper structural faults in construction of the Union. The crisis has elements of both. It has not only exposed but also exacerbated deep structural flaws in the EU construction. On balance, the European Union's handling of the crisis[37] has aggravated, not ameliorated, the democratic problems.

First, the crisis has in many instances weakened the role and political influence of parliamentary assemblies, notably, but far from exclusively, in the eurozone. The pattern is, however, far from even across member states: it is clearly more so in debtor than in creditor countries.[38] Several debtor countries have seen technocrats temporarily taking over governments. Eurozone debtor countries' parliaments, especially those needing bailouts, are subject to very stringent EU and troika demands for budget cutbacks and deeply unpopular fiscal restraint measures. The economic philosophy underpinning much of the crisis management coupled with the lopsided monetary union generate policies with strong distributional effects (wage, welfare, and pension reductions). All member states are subject to strict budget requirements that constrain their leverage, place strong constraints on budgetary policy, and subject them to sanctions in case of noncompliance. This system is now coordinated at the EU level under the so-called European Semester procedure. The European Union and the eurozone coordinate their budgetary and economic policies *ex ante* and, based on this, specific policy recommendations are issued to each state. This has reduced the budgetary scope for national parliaments. The EP's role in this system is quite marginal. The onus on instituting constitutional spending brakes, if necessary, at the national level is also a major imposition.

A second and closely related point is a relative strengthening of executives and experts at the behest of legislatures. That includes weakening the integrity of the European Union's supranational apparatus. There is also a general relative strengthening of the European Council, coupled with a strong compulsion towards handling the crisis through intergovernmental means (the so-called Merkel method[39]), including fashioning intergovernmental treaties (e.g., the Treaty on Stability, Coordination, and Governance in the Economic and Monetary Union) and striking informal intergovernmental bargains through extensive summitry (including bilateral meetings between Germany and France).[40] This has negative implications for the EP but also for national parliaments. When much of the crisis is handled through intergovernmental bargains – either to deal with issues that are outside of the treaties or to manage situations where the treaties are not considered helpful to fashion adequate responses and are therefore effectively violated – law's bite is reduced. This has implications for the rule of law and for the continued embedding of integration in legal provisions.

This intergovernmental turn has in many instances been a second best, a matter of moving forward when certain member states (notably the UK) veto treaty changes. It exposes a structural problem, a clear discrepancy between the problem structure and the decision structure. Simply put, the seventeen-member eurozone relies on the twenty-eight-member EU institutions to foster binding decisions. It raises the question of how and in what respect non-euro member states should participate in decisions pertaining to the euro, by which they will clearly be affected but differently from the manner in which euro countries will be affected. One problem is how to sort out what are common concerns and what are concerns specifically pertaining to the eurozone. Another is that of representation: how to devise a democratic decision-making structure that can accommodate these different concerns.

A third and related aspect of the crisis is how supranational institutions and arrangements are made to serve the emerging, more informal, intergovernmental approach to crisis handling. One aspect is the sidelining of the EP and another is a certain tendency for the supranational structure to be increasingly transgovernmentalized. "Transgovernmental"

> connotes the greater intensity and denser structuring ... where EU member governments have been prepared cumulatively to commit themselves to rather extensive engagement and disciplines, but have judged the full EU institutional framework to be inappropriate or unacceptable, or not yet ripe for adoption.[41]

In previous instances, such as the Schengen Accord, transgovernmentalization exhibited a centripetal logic that served integration, whereas in the crisis a more centrifugal logic was at work, weakening the credibility and legitimacy of the supranational structure and making it easier for certain core member states to carry out their particular conceptions of how the crisis should be dealt with. It exposes the Commission, which is attributed with a very salient role, including instituting sanctions (according to the undemocratic reverse quality majority voting system[42]).

A fourth and readily apparent element is the great increase in citizens' distrust of political leaders and rising opposition to European integration.[43] As part of this we see a rise in extreme left- and right-wing populism. The upshot can be a situation wherein representative democracies find themselves enmeshed in a highly toxic mixture of market-oriented technocracy and extreme populism.

The fifth and final point is that, even before the crisis, the Lisbon Treaty increased uncertainty and ambiguity as to the European Union's constitutional nature and status.[44] This has arguably made it easier for leaders to either violate or sidestep legal provisions in their efforts to handle the crisis. That, combined with the intergovernmental way of handling the crisis and the general trend towards transgovernmentalization of the European Union structure, is altering the European Union's constitutional construct. With specific reference to the economic constitution, Christian Joerges has aptly noted that

> [w]hat we see emerging is a new mode, a de-legalized economic constitution, which is dedicated to balanced budgets and seeks to ensure compliance with that objective through a regulatory machinery with comprehensive supervisory powers and the means to ensure compliance with its evaluation.[45]

These are tendencies, not certainties. They can be reversed and negative effects can be mitigated. There are proposals for further measures in the pipeline, including treaty changes. Politicization can foster progress but time does not seem to be on the side of Europe's leaders.

Conclusion

Prior to the crisis (considered here as a composite of financial, fiscal, institutional, and constitutional crises) the general assumption was one of a clear "positive sum" relationship between integration and democratization. With the crisis, in particular, there are grounds to question the continued veracity of this assumption. The crisis can foster disintegration, which in turn can undermine democracy. There is, however, no assurance that the rolling back of integration will aid democracy, not least because disintegration will be stimulated by narrow nationalism and populism. The crisis can also give rise to further integration but will not necessarily do so with an attendant democratization. Integration can stimulate technocracy and democracy may not be able to catch up.

This conundrum underlines that the crisis is ultimately of a political and constitutional nature. It has brought to a head the question of what the Union is for. It has also, as we see in many places, opened up more space for technocracy and populism, and for the prospect of a toxic mixture of the two. The rise of technocracy poses a challenge to the credibility and legitimacy of democratic arrangements and feeds citizens' alienation. The rise of extreme populism poses challenges to the representative and decision-making ability of existing parliamentary-representative arrangements and brings forth demands for direct democracy or "strong men." This two-pronged attack on representative democracy can weaken or undermine parliaments' unique deliberative qualities; it can also render politics and policy susceptible to populist whims – of an ethnonationalist and exclusivist bent. Vicious circles may occur where solidarity and trust weaken, the political system's credibility and legitimacy erodes, and the leaders' leverage to come up with lasting solutions to the crisis is significantly reduced.

Thus far it is not clear if these developments have moved beyond the point of no return. Most citizens are still exhibiting restraint and there appear to be further crisis handling measures in the pipeline. There is focus on the need for political union and growth stimulating measures. Many of the proposals for further changes underline the need to strengthen democracy, including measures to reinforce interparliamentary coordination and cooperation. Such horizontal measures may work but they do not substitute for vertical deficiencies. Increased interparliamentary coordination, as such, cannot do away with the autonomy and accountability defects in the current role of the EP.

In the postwar period, Europeans have taken many important measures to improve the future of democracy and address the structural limitations in state-based democracy. This crisis is putting this important undertaking to its hardest test thus far.

Notes

1 James Bohman, *Democracy across Borders: From Dêmos to Dêmoi* (Cambridge: MIT Press, 2007); Joshua Cohen and Charles F. Sabel, "Directly-Deliberative Polyarchy," *European Law Journal* 3 (1997); Joshua Cohen and Charles F. Sabel, "Sovereignty and Solidarity: EU and US," in *Governing Work and Welfare in the New Economy: European and American Experiments*, ed. Jonathan Zeitlin and David M. Trubek (Oxford: Oxford University Press, 2003); Charles F. Sabel and Jonathan Zeitlin, "Learning from Difference: The New Architecture of Experimentalist Governance in the EU," *European Law Journal* 14 (2008); and Charles F. Sabel and Jonathan Zeitlin, eds., *Experimentalist Governance in the European Union: Towards a New Architecture* (Oxford: Oxford University Press, 2010).

2 John Erik Fossum and Agustín J. Menéndez, *The Constitution's Gift – A Constitutional Theory for a Democratic European Union* (Boulder: Rowman and Littlefield, 2011).

3 In comparison to an international organization, it would be more sensible to talk about the European Union as having a "democratic surplus," see, e.g., Erik O. Eriksen and John Erik Fossum, eds., *Democracy in the European Union: Integration through Deliberation?* (London: Routledge, 2010); and Agustin J. Menéndez, "The European Democratic Challenge: The Forging of a Supranational Volonté Générale," *European Law Journal* 15 (2009).

4 Robert A. Dahl, "Can International Organizations be Democratic? A Skeptic's View," in *Democracy's Edges*, ed. Ian Shapiro and Casiano Hacker-Cordón (Cambridge: Cambridge University Press, 1999); Robert Keohane, *Power and Governance in a Partially Globalized World* (London: Routledge, 2002); and Andrew Moravcsik, "In Defence of the 'Democratic Deficit': Reassessing Legitimacy in the European Union," *Journal of Common Market Studies* 40 (2002).

5 This is a standard Eurosceptic position. See, e.g., the contributions in Martin Holmes, ed. *The Eurosceptical Reader* (Houndmills: Macmillan, 1996).

6 Dieter Grimm, "Does Europe Need a Constitution?" *European Law Journal* 1 (1995).

7 Bohman, *Democracy across Borders*, 10. Proponents of directly deliberative polyarchy (see Cohen and Sabel, "Directly-Deliberative Polyarchy" and Cohen and Sabel, "Sovereignty and Solidarity") also embrace a transnational notion of democracy but are less comprehensive than Bohman on the need to revise existing conceptions.

8 Bohman, *Democracy across Borders*, 135.

9 See, e.g., Andreas Føllesdal and Simon Hix, "Why There is a Democratic Deficit in the EU: A Response to Majone and Moravcsik," *Journal of Common Market Studies* 44 (2006).

10 For a selection of what is now a very comprehensive body of literature, see David Beetham and Christopher Lord, *Legitimacy and the European Union* (London: Longman, 1998); Erik O. Eriksen, ed., *Making the European Polity: Reflexive Integration in Europe* (London: Routledge, 2005); Erik O. Eriksen, *The Unfinished Democratization of Europe* (Oxford: Oxford University Press, 2009); Eriksen and Fossum, *Democracy in the European Union*; Erik O. Eriksen and John Erik Fossum, *Rethinking Democracy in the European Union* (London: Routledge, 2012); Michael Th. Greven and Louis W. Pauly, eds., *Democracy beyond the State? The European Dilemma and the Emerging Global Order* (Toronto: Toronto University Press, 2000); Jürgen Habermas, *The Postnational Constellation: Political Essays* (Cambridge: Polity Press, 2001); Jürgen Habermas, *Europe: The Faltering Project* (Cambridge: Polity Press, 2011); Jürgen Habermas, *The Crises of the European Union: A Response* (Cambridge: Polity Press, 2012); Catherine Hoskyns and Michael Newman, *Democratizing the European Union: Issues for the Twenty-First Century* (Manchester: Manchester University Press, 2000); Christopher Lord, *A Democratic Audit of the European Union* (Basingstoke: Palgrave, 2004); Christopher Lord and Erika Harris, *Democracy in the New Europe* (Basingstoke: Palgrave Macmillan, 2006); Giandomenico Majone, *Dilemmas of European Integration: The Ambiguities and Pitfalls of Integration by Stealth* (Oxford: Oxford University Press, 2005); Glyn Morgan, *The Idea of a European Superstate: Public Justification and European Integration* (Princeton: Princeton University Press, 2005); John Pinder, *Foundations of Democracy in the European Union: From the Genesis of Parliamentary Democracy to the European Parliament* (Basingstoke: Palgrave Macmillian, 1999); Berthold Rittberger, *Building Europe's Parliament Democratic Representation beyond the Nation State* (Oxford: Oxford University Press, 2005); Fritz W. Scharpf, *Governing in Europe: Effective and Democratic?* (Oxford: Oxford University Press, 1999); Vivien A. Schmidt, *Democracy in Europe: The EU and National Polities* (Oxford: Oxford University Press, 2006); Philippe C. Schmitter, *How to Democratize the European Union – and Why Bother?* (Oxford: Rowman & Littlefield, 2000); and Larry Siedentop, *Democracy in Europe* (London: Penguin Books, 2000).

11 Eriksen and Fossum, *Democracy in the European Union*; Eriksen and Fossum, *Rethinking Democracy in the European Union*.

12 David Held, *Democracy and the Global Order: From the Modern State to Cosmopolitan Governance* (Cambridge: Polity Press, 1995), 16; and Mark Bovens, "New Forms of Accountability and EU-Governance," *Comparative European Politics* 5 (2007): 107. For a comprehensive empirical assessment of EU accountability, see Mark Bovens, Deirdre Curtin, and Paul 't Hart, eds., *The Real World of EU Accountability: What Deficit?* (Oxford: Oxford University Press, 2010).

13 For more details on this institutional version of deliberative democracy, see Erik O. Eriksen and John Erik Fossum, "Representation through Deliberation: The European Case," *Constellations* 19 (2012).

14 Jürgen Habermas, *The Structural Transformation of the Public Sphere* (Cambridge, MA: MIT Press, 1989). For an assessment of the EU's public sphere, see, e.g., John Erik Fossum and Philip R. Schlesinger, eds., *The European Union and the Public Sphere: A Communicative Space in the Making?* (London: Routledge, 2007).

15 Daniele Archibugi, *The Global Commonwealth of Citizens: Toward Cosmopolitan Democracy* (Princeton: Princeton University Press, 2008), at xiii.

16 The German Constitutional Court's ruling on the Lisbon Treaty, press release no. 72/2009 of 30 June 2009, Judgment of 30 June 2009 – 2 BvE 2/08, 2 BvE 5/08, 2 BvR 1010/08, 2 BvR 1022/08, 2 BvR 1259/08, and 2 BvR 182/09.

17 Karlheinz Reif and Hermann Schmitt, "Nine Second-Order National Elections: A Conceptual Framework for the Analysis of European Election Result," *European Journal of Political Research* 8 (1980).

18 Simon Hix, Abdul G. Noury, and Gérard Roland, *Democratic Politics in the European Parliament* (Cambridge: Cambridge University Press, 2007), 39.

19 Thomas Poguntke et al., *The Europeanization of National Political Parties: Power and Organizational Adaptation* (London: Routledge, 2007). "The selection of candidates, the arguments of the campaign, electoral success or failure, and the label under which an MEP is elected are ... governed by domestic party politics ... ." Quoted from Simon Hix and Christopher Lord, *Political Parties in the European Union* (New York: St. Martin's Press, 2007), 84.

20 Turnout percentages in the 2009 EP elections in a select number of the member states are: Denmark 59.54; France 40.63; Germany 43.3; Italy 65.05; Netherlands 36.75; Poland 24.53; Spain 44.9; and the UK 34.7. EU average was: 43. Source: European Election Database. From the same source, we see that turnout in a select number of member state parliamentary elections was: Germany (2009) 69.57; Denmark (2011) 86.9; UK (2010) 65.1.

21 Majone, *Dilemmas of European Integration.*

22 Adrienne Héritier and Henry Farrell, "The Invisible Transformation of Codecision: Problems of Democratic Legitimacy" (Report No.7, Swedish Institute for European Policy Studies, 2003); and Anne E. Stie, *Democratic Decision-Making in the EU: Technocracy in Disguise?* (London: Routledge, 2012).

23 Article 17.7 TEU.

24 Joseph H.H. Weiler "Legitimacy and Democracy of Union Governance," in *The Politics of European Treaty Reform: The 1996 Intergovernmental Conference and Beyond*, ed. Geoffrey Edwards and Alfred Pijpers (London: Pinter, 1997), 274.

25 For a thorough assessment of the ministers' influence over decision making in the Council, see Frank M. Häge, *Bureaucrats as Law-Makers* (London: Routledge, 2013).

26 Deirdre Curtin, *Executive Power of the European Union: Law, Practices and the Living Constitution* (Oxford: Oxford University Press, 2009).

27 Fritz W. Scharpf, "Legitimacy in the Multilevel European Polity," *European Political Science Review* 1 (2009): 176.

28 Fossum and Menéndez, *The Constitution's Gift.*

29 Under the ordinary revision procedure, Article 48(3) TEU includes provisions for a Convention with EP participation, but the Convention's role is only preparatory.

30 Bohman, *Democracy across Borders.*

31 The theory of institutional fusion brings this out very clearly. See Wolfgang Wessels, "An Ever Closer Fusion? A Dynamic Macropolitical View on Integration Processes," *Journal of Common Market Studies* 35 (1997); and Wolfgang Wessels and Dieter Rometsch, eds., *The European Union and Member States: Towards Institutional Fusion?* (Manchester: Manchester University Press, 1996).

32 Federations (at the central level) generally include one body that represents the people directly (e.g., US House of Representatives or German Bundestag) and a body that represents them through their states (e.g., US Senate or German Bundesrat). The US Senate differs from the German Bundesrat, in that the former consists of directly elected representatives whereas the latter is made up of elected executives from the Länder.

33 Ben Crum and John Erik Fossum "The Multilevel Parliamentary Field – A Framework for Theorising Representative Democracy in the EU," *European Political Science Review* 1 (2009); and Ben Crum and John Erik Fossum, eds., *Practices of Inter-Parliamentary Coordination in International Politics – The European Union and Beyond* (Essex: ECPR Press, 2013).

34 Walter Powell and Paul DiMaggio, eds., *The New Institutionalism in Organizational Analysis* (Chicago: Chicago University Press, 1991).

35 There are formal structures linking the parliaments, including institutionalized meeting places; important support structures that stimulate interaction, specific systems of information generation and exchange, such as IPEX and the European Centre for Parliamentary Research and Documentation; and legal arrangements such as the Early Warning Mechanism. For overviews of these consult, for instance, Karl-Heinz Neunreither, "The Democratic Deficit of the European Union: Towards Closer Cooperation between the European Parliament and the National Parliaments," *Government and Opposition*, 29 (1994); Crum and Fossum "The Multilevel Parliamentary Field"; and contributions in Crum and Fossum, *Practices of Inter-Parliamentary*

Coordination. Ian Cooper argues that the Early Warning Mechanism can be understood as a kind of "virtual third chamber" for the European Union. Ian Cooper "A 'Virtual Third Chamber' for the European Union? National Parliaments after the Treaty of Lisbon," *West European Politics* 35 (2012).

36 European Parliament 2011/2071[INI] of 15 November 2011, Report on the European Semester for Economic Policy Coordination.

37 Many of the measures are set out in the intergovernmental Treaty on Stability, Coordination, and Governance T/SCG/en 1 of 2 March 2012 and the so-called Six-Pack, a bundle of five regulations and one directive that cover fiscal surveillance and macroeconomic surveillance under the new Macroeconomic Imbalance Procedure.

38 Arthur Benz, "An Asymmetric Two-Level Game: Parliaments in the Euro Crisis," in Crum and Fossum, *Practices of Inter-Parliamentary Coordination in International Politics*.

39 See "Phoenix Europe: How the EU Can Emerge from the Ashes," Spiegel International, 18 November 2011. http://www.spiegel.de/international/europe/phoenix-europe-how-the-eu-can-emerge-from-the-ashes-a-797626.html.

40 For an overview of types and frequency, see Desmond Dinan, "Governance and Institutions: Impact of the Escalating Crisis," *Journal of Common Market Studies* 50 (2012).

41 Helen Wallace, "An Institutional Anatomy and Five Policy Modes," in *Policy-Making in the European Union*, ed., Helen Wallace, William Wallace, and Mark Pollack (Oxford: Oxford University Press, 2005).

42 "RQMV implies that a recommendation or a proposal of the Commission is considered adopted in the Council unless a qualified majority of member states votes against it." European Commission, Economic and Financial Affairs, 2013. "Six-pack? Two-pack? Fiscal compact? A short guide to the new EU fiscal governance." http://ec.europa.eu/economy_finance/articles/governance/2012-03-14_six_pack_en.htm.

43 José Manuel Durão Barroso, "State of the Union 2012 Address," Speech/12/596 Plenary session of the European Parliament/Strasbourg, 12 September 2012.

44 Fossum and Menéndez, *The Constitution's Gift*.

45 Christian Joerges, "The European Economic Constitution and its Transformation through the Financial Crisis," Chap. 18, this volume.

References

Archibugi, Daniele. *The Global Commonwealth of Citizens: Toward Cosmopolitan Democracy*. Princeton: Princeton University Press, 2008.

Beetham, David, and Christopher Lord. *Legitimacy and the European Union*. London: Longman, 1998.

Benz, Arthur. "An Asymmetric Two-Level Game: Parliaments in the Euro Crisis." In Crum and Fossum, *Practices of Inter-Parliamentary Coordination in International Politics*, 125–140.

Bohman, James. *Democracy across Borders: From Dêmos to Dêmoi*. Cambridge, MA: MIT Press, 2007.

Bovens, Mark. "New Forms of Accountability and EU-Governance." *Comparative European Politics* 5 (2007): 104–120.

Bovens, Mark, Deirdre Curtin, and Paul 't Hart, eds. *The Real World of EU Accountability: What Deficit?* Oxford: Oxford University Press, 2010.

Cohen, Joshua, and Charles F. Sabel. "Directly-Deliberative Polyarchy." *European Law Journal* 3 (1997): 313–342.

Cohen, Joshua, and Charles F. Sabel. "Sovereignty and Solidarity: EU and US." In *Governing Work and Welfare in the New Economy: European and American Experiments*, edited by Jonathan Zeitlin and David M. Trubek, 33–58. Oxford: Oxford University Press, 2003.

Cooper, Ian. "A 'Virtual Third Chamber' for the European Union? National Parliaments after the Treaty of Lisbon." *West European Politics* 35 (2012): 441–465.

Crum, Ben, and John Erik Fossum. "The Multilevel Parliamentary Field – A Framework for Theorising Representative Democracy in the EU." *European Political Science Review* 1 (2009): 249–271.

Crum, Ben, and John Erik Fossum, eds. *Practices of Inter-Parliamentary Coordination in International Politics – The European Union and Beyond*. Essex: ECPR Press, 2013.

Curtin, Deirdre. *Executive Power of the European Union: Law, Practices and the Living Constitution*. Oxford: Oxford University Press, 2009.
Dahl, Robert A. "Can International Organizations be Democratic? A Skeptic's View." In *Democracy's Edges*, edited by Ian Shapiro and Casiano Hacker-Cordón, 19–36. Cambridge: Cambridge University Press, 1999.
Dinan, Desmond. "Governance and Institutions: Impact of the Escalating Crisis." *Journal of Common Market Studies* 50 (2012): 85–98.
Eriksen, Erik O., ed. *Making the European Polity: Reflexive Integration in Europe*. London: Routledge, 2005.
Eriksen, Erik O. *The Unfinished Democratization of Europe*. Oxford: Oxford University Press, 2009.
Eriksen, Erik O., and John Erik Fossum, eds. *Democracy in the European Union: Integration through Deliberation?* London: Routledge, 2010.
Eriksen, Erik O., and John Erik Fossum. "Representation through Deliberation: The European Case." *Constellations* 19 (2012): 325–339.
Eriksen, Erik O., and John Erik Fossum. *Rethinking Democracy in the European Union*. London: Routledge, 2012.
Føllesdal, Andreas, and Simon Hix. "Why There is a Democratic Deficit in the EU: A Response to Majone and Moravcsik." *Journal of Common Market Studies* 44 (2006): 533–562.
Fossum, John Erik, and Agustín J. Menéndez. *The Constitution's Gift – A Constitutional Theory for a Democratic European Union*. Boulder: Rowman and Littlefield, 2011.
Fossum, John Erik, and Philip R. Schlesinger, eds. *The European Union and the Public Sphere: A Communicative Space in the Making?* London: Routledge, 2007.
Greven, Michael Th., and Louis W. Pauly, eds. *Democracy beyond the State? The European Dilemma and the Emerging Global Order*. Toronto: Toronto University Press, 2000.
Grimm, Dieter. "Does Europe Need a Constitution?" *European Law Journal* 1 (1995): 282–302.
Habermas, Jürgen. *The Structural Transformation of the Public Sphere*. Cambridge, MA: MIT Press, 1989.
Habermas, Jürgen. *The Postnational Constellation: Political Essays*. Cambridge: Polity Press, 2001.
Habermas, Jürgen. *Europe: The Faltering Project*. Cambridge: Polity Press, 2011.
Habermas, Jürgen. *The Crises of the European Union: A Response*. Cambridge: Polity Press, 2012.
Häge, Frank M. *Bureaucrats as Law-Makers*. London: Routledge, 2013.
Held, David. *Democracy and the Global Order: From the Modern State to Cosmopolitan Governance*. Cambridge: Polity Press, 1995.
Héritier, Adrienne, and Henry Farrell. "The Invisible Transformation of Codecision: Problems of Democratic Legitimacy." Report No.7, Swedish Institute for European Policy Studies, 2003.
Hix, Simon, and Christopher Lord. *Political Parties in the European Union*. New York: St. Martin's Press, 2007.
Hix, Simon, Abdul G. Noury, and Gérard Roland. *Democratic Politics in the European Parliament*. Cambridge: Cambridge University Press, 2007.
Holmes, Martin, ed. *The Eurosceptical Reader*. Houndmills: Macmillan, 1996.
Hoskyns, Catherine, and Michael Newman. *Democratizing the European Union: Issues for the Twenty-First Century*. Manchester: Manchester University Press, 2000.
Keohane, Robert. *Power and Governance in a Partially Globalized World*. London: Routledge, 2002.
Lord, Christopher. *A Democratic Audit of the European Union*. Basingstoke: Palgrave, 2004.
Lord, Christopher, and Erika Harris. *Democracy in the New Europe*. Basingstoke: Palgrave Macmillan, 2006.
Majone, Giandomenico. *Dilemmas of European Integration: The Ambiguities and Pitfalls of Integration by Stealth*. Oxford: Oxford University Press, 2005.
Menéndez, Agustin J. "The European Democratic Challenge: The Forging of a Supranational Volonté Générale." *European Law Journal* 15 (2009): 277–308.
Moravcsik, Andrew. "In Defence of the 'Democratic Deficit': Reassessing Legitimacy in the European Union." *Journal of Common Market Studies* 40 (2002): 603–624.
Morgan, Glyn. *The Idea of a European Superstate: Public Justification and European Integration*. Princeton: Princeton University Press, 2005.

Neunreither, Karl-Heinz. "The Democratic Deficit of the European Union: Towards Closer Cooperation between the European Parliament and the National Parliaments." *Government and Opposition*, 29 (1994): 299–314.

Pinder, John. *Foundations of Democracy in the European Union: From the Genesis of Parliamentary Democracy to the European Parliament.* Basingstoke: Palgrave Macmillian, 1999.

Poguntke, Thomas, Nicholas Aylott, Elisabeth Carter, Robert Ladrech, and Kurt R. Luther. *The Europeanization of National Political Parties: Power and Organizational Adaptation.* London: Routledge, 2007.

Powell, Walter, and Paul DiMaggio, eds. *The New Institutionalism in Organizational Analysis.* Chicago: Chicago University Press, 1991.

Reif, Karlheinz, and Hermann Schmitt. "Nine Second-Order National Elections: A Conceptual Framework for the Analysis of European Election Result." *European Journal of Political Research* 8 (1980): 3–44.

Rittberger, Berthold. *Building Europe's Parliament Democratic Representation beyond the Nation State.* Oxford: Oxford University Press, 2005.

Sabel, Charles F., and Jonathan Zeitlin. "Learning from Difference: The New Architecture of Experimentalist Governance in the EU" *European Law Journal* 14 (2008): 271–327.

Sabel, Charles F., and Jonathan Zeitlin, eds. *Experimentalist Governance in the European Union: Towards a New Architecture.* Oxford: Oxford University Press, 2010.

Scharpf, Fritz W. *Governing in Europe: Effective and Democratic?* Oxford: Oxford University Press, 1999.

Scharpf, Fritz W. "Legitimacy in the Multilevel European Polity." *European Political Science Review* 1 (2009): 173–204.

Schmidt, Vivien A. *Democracy in Europe: The EU and National Polities.* Oxford: Oxford University Press, 2006.

Schmitter, Philippe C. *How to Democratize the European Union – and Why Bother?* Oxford: Rowman & Littlefield, 2000.

Siedentop, Larry. *Democracy in Europe.* London: Penguin Books, 2000.

Stie, Anne E. *Democratic Decision-Making in the EU: Technocracy in Disguise?* London: Routledge, 2012.

Wallace, Helen. "An Institutional Anatomy and Five Policy Modes." In *Policy-Making in the European Union*, edited by Helen Wallace, William Wallace, and Mark Pollack, 49–90. Oxford: Oxford University Press, 2005.

Weiler, Joseph H.H. "Legitimacy and Democracy of Union Governance." In *The Politics of European Treaty Reform: The 1996 Intergovernmental Conference and Beyond*, edited by Geoffrey Edwards and Alfred Pijpers, 249–287. London: Pinter, 1997.

Wessels, Wolfgang. "An Ever Closer Fusion? A Dynamic Macropolitical View on Integration Processes." *Journal of Common Market Studies* 35 (1997): 267–299.

Wessels, Wolfgang, and Dieter Rometsch, eds. *The European Union and Member States: Towards Institutional Fusion?* Manchester: Manchester University Press, 1996.

Part III

The Court

11

EU Procedural Law

Andrea Biondi and Ravi Mehta

Introduction

EU procedural law is a potentially vast and heterogeneous area which has been the subject of considerable academic analysis.[1] It is particularly difficult to delimit the scope of our inquiry since the concept of a "procedural" rule is in itself difficult to define,[2] and a study of the area could potentially encompass many different legal principles and mechanisms. When taking a broad view of the topic, however, there are striking features. The first is that it is torn between contrasting dynamics: its genesis is driven by very different processes (sometimes legislative or proactive, sometimes judicial or responsive) and its underlying philosophy is often inspired by heterogeneous national legal systems. For instance, the approach to the rights of defense in competition procedures elicits various responses from common law and civil law countries. The second is that – now, more than fifty years since *Van Gend en Loos* [3] – there is a high level of integration at the procedural level between EU and national law which, at times, has wrought significant changes on national procedures.[4]

Like Magritte's famous surrealist depiction of a pipe, this chapter will begin by identifying what it is *not* about. We will not consider: (1) the procedural rules in the area of EU criminal law; (2) harmonization initiatives adopted since the early 2000s; (3) so-called substantive procedural rules (such as the quantification of damages[5]); or (4) rules applicable to the EU institutions, for example, interim relief against an EU institution. While undoubtedly important, these initiatives are often sectorally specific and remain the exception to the rule that national systems are the implementers of EU law.

Instead, in this chapter, we would like to reexamine the case law of the Court of Justice of the European Union (CJEU) through the prism of the modern structure of the foundational treaties of the European Union: the Treaty on European Union (TEU) and the Treaty on the Functioning of the European Union (TFEU).

Traditionally branded as "national procedural autonomy,"[6] EU remedies law has engendered significant scholarship and case law for many decades[7] and is often explored through a "core

A Companion to European Union Law and International Law, First Edition.
Edited by Dennis Patterson and Anna Södersten.

narrative" (as Michael Dougan calls it[8]). Professor Dougan's chapter provides an elegant and compelling account of that history and the determining features of this area.

We believe, however, that the treaty structure recasts this debate. In our view, such a structure provides three "focal points" through which to view the core principles on a spectrum of analysis of the interrelationship between national procedures and EU law. While we accept that this is not a "bulletproof" model explaining every case or context-specific result, we believe it to be the most coherent way in which to approach the underlying principles that have emerged over time. Moreover, it accurately expresses three key new features of this area: (1) the calibration of the general framework to different substantive fields; (2) its reconceptualization as a facet of EU fundamental rights protection; and (3) the potential for substantive regulation of national procedures at the EU level. Ultimately, this variability reflects the inherent nature of procedural law in national legal systems – sensitive to the context and interests at play. However, it is important to identify the different and often opposing interests involved rather than conflate them. We will conduct a concrete study of the interaction between national *res judicata* principles and EU law as an illustration of the challenges and limitations of the current framework.

All Roads Lead to Lisbon: Three Gateways for a Common Framework

The Lisbon Treaty has reshaped the structure of the positive law of the European Union, "mark[ing] a new stage in the process of creating an ever closer union" (Article 1, second indent TEU). For EU procedural law, this has led to the formal establishment of three focal points which reflect the issues involved:

At one extreme, are general principles of EU law, which have "constitutional status"[9] including the general principle of "effective judicial protection." These are often described as "filling the gaps," amorphous and even hierarchically superior to the provisions of the treaty.[10] Relevant general principles are also expressly acknowledged in the treaty, for instance in Article 6(3) TEU. They arguably establish the outer limits within which national procedures must remain.

In the middle of our spectrum are two provisions which recognize the balancing of national and EU interests required at the procedural level:

1. Article 4(2) TEU recognizes the respect which the Union must give to the "national identities" of the member states, including their "constitutional" structures. This would logically include national procedural systems. Article 4(3) TEU then sets out the duty of "sincere cooperation" incumbent on member states as a corollary to that diversity. This includes a duty to (1) "take any appropriate measure, general or particular, to ensure fulfilment of the obligations arising out of the treaties or resulting from the acts of the institutions of the Union" (second indent) and (2) to "facilitate the achievement of the Union's tasks and refrain from any measure which could jeopardize the attainment of the Union's objectives" (third indent). Article 4 TEU is, therefore, a schizophrenic provision which requires a balancing of competing interests;
2. Article 19(1), second indent TEU is a new provision which specifically states that "Member States shall provide remedies sufficient to ensure effective legal protection in the fields covered by Union law." Its placement in the general provision that concerns the functions of the CJEU illustrates the vision of member state remedies as a tool for the implementation of EU law.

Finally, the treaties recognize the possibility for substantive regulation at the EU level:

1. Article 47 of the Charter of Fundamental Rights (incorporated by Article 6(1) TEU) recognizes an individual's "right to an effective remedy" wherever member states are implementing

EU law. While this cannot be said to create "new" rights, its influence arguably requires greater intervention by the EU courts in a substantive assessment of national procedures;

2. The TFEU goes further, explicitly recognizing competences to harmonize procedural law in the areas of judicial cooperation (Articles 81 and 82 TFEU), the creation of sanctions for so-called Euro crimes (Article 83(1) TFEU), police cooperation (Article 87 TFEU), language arrangements and rules governing the creation of European intellectual property rights (Article 118 TFEU), administrative cooperation (Article 197(1) to (2) TFEU), and combating fraud (Article 325(4) TFEU). As we will note briefly later in the chapter, there has been a substantial proliferation of harmonization measures in recent years.

So much for our cardinal "focal points." We do not suggest that they are unrelated – this will turn on the facts before a court. Indeed, the Explanations to the Charter expressly link Article 47 to the concept of effective judicial protection.[11] However, we suggest that they express the different tensions which this area of law raises: (1) the basic protections guaranteed within the context of EU law; (2) the flexibility for national legal systems to retain their internal logic; and (3) the desire to establish EU standards of procedural protection.

Interestingly, the CJEU appears to approach this tripartite structure as a distinction without a difference, entering all three gateways to arrive at the same destination. Perhaps the best illustration of this is the most recent authoritative exposition in the Grand Chamber's judgment in *Unibet*:

> 38. Under the principle of cooperation laid down in Article 10 EC, it is for the Member States to ensure judicial protection of an individual's rights under Community law … .
>
> 39. … in the absence of Community rules governing the matter, it is for the domestic legal system of each Member State to designate the courts and tribunals having jurisdiction and to lay down the detailed procedural rules governing actions for safeguarding rights which individuals derive from Community law … .
>
> 40. Although the EC Treaty has made it possible in a number of instances for private persons to bring a direct action, where appropriate, before the Community Court, it was not intended to create new remedies in the national courts to ensure the observance of Community law other than those already laid down by national law … .
>
> 41. It would be otherwise only if it were apparent from the overall scheme of the national legal system in question that no legal remedy existed which made it possible to ensure, even indirectly, respect for an individual's rights under Community law … .
>
> 42. Thus, while it is, in principle, for national law to determine an individual's standing and legal interest in bringing proceedings, Community law nevertheless requires that the national legislation does not undermine the right to effective judicial protection … .
>
> 43. … the detailed procedural rules governing actions for safeguarding an individual's rights under Community law must be no less favourable than those governing similar domestic actions (principle of equivalence) and must not render practically impossible or excessively difficult the exercise of rights conferred by Community law (principle of effectiveness) …[12]

While the CJEU treats our three focal points as facets of a common principle, we will explore how the treaty structure seems to reflect distinct considerations and tendencies.

Exploring the Gateways

The general principle of "effective judicial protection" was first recognized in the *Johnston*[13] case as a corollary to Articles 6 and 13 of the European Convention on Human Rights (ECHR). It reflects "an irreducible core of protection"[14] for a party by means of access to a judicial process, that is, where an individual has no remedy at all, EU law will step in to provide one. On a number of occasions, the Court has clearly stated that this principle exists independently of considerations of the "effectiveness" of remedies.[15]

The principle is best illustrated by *Johnston* and *Unibet*. In *Johnston*, an employee could not bring a claim for sex discrimination in an Industrial Tribunal because a national provision allowed the Secretary of State to certify – conclusively – that her case concerned national security and that derogations from the principle of nondiscrimination were therefore justified. In stark terms, the CJEU characterized such a rule as "depriv[ing] an individual of the possibility of asserting by judicial process the rights conferred by the directive" (paragraph 20) and therefore falling afoul of the general principle. In contrast, in *Unibet* it was held that the principle did not require national law to create a freestanding action for the enforcement of EU law if other effective legal remedies – no less favorable than those governing similar domestic actions – achieved the same result. Similarly, in cases where national law has vested jurisdiction to resolve disputes concerning EU rights in specifically designated tribunals or specific procedures,[16] there is no vacuum which requires the creation of a remedy to ensure the effective protection of EU rights.

Other examples of judicial responses to a vacuum include the creation of new EU remedies, "such as damages liability of the Member States or of a private party."[17] Thus, the CJEU created the principle of state liability in the absence of an explicit textual basis in the treaties.[18] It has required the creation of an interim remedy, even where none had previously existed in national law, in order to ensure the effective protection of EU rights.[19] It also recognized the possibilities for horizontal actions between private parties on the basis of a breach of competition law.[20]

We see this as distinct from the other "focal points" we have identified. It is clear that the principle does not bite where national law merely imposes preconditions on the access to a court, such as requiring the parties to submit to a prior mandatory settlement procedure.[21] Commentators – and, it appears, advocates general – have approached the principle of effectiveness and the principle of effective judicial protection as expressions of each other.[22] However, this dilutes the strength of the latter principle and mischaracterizes its object – which is to step in where there is a right without a remedy. Properly construed, many of the cases where the CJEU has referred to that principle have not really engaged it at all since there was no absence of a remedy for it to address. A proper example was *Kadi I*, albeit in the context of *EU procedures*, in which the Court found a breach of the general principle since individuals had no means of making any representations to the body that listed them for the UN's asset freezing.[23] Whether other aspects of EU procedural law are also engaged in a given case may calibrate the standard of review applied and shift the case along the spectrum of analysis, but this should not change the principle's purity as one of the "focal points."

A useful way of testing this is to examine the adjacent "focal point" on the spectrum – the most prolific in terms of the case law. The treaty provisions following the Lisbon Treaty (Articles 4 and 19 TEU) demonstrate the careful balancing act that is needed between expectations of "cooperation" from the member states and the autonomy given to national systems within EU law.

One of the distinguishing features of the EU system (in contrast, for instance, to federal models) is that national courts are co-opted to be the frontline enforcers of EU law. Like every good story, the procedural narrative between EU and national legal systems began with a couple – here the *Rewe*[24] and *Comet*[25] cases – which established the two requirements now reflected in the treaties. The decentralized enforcement of Union law requires that (1) rules governing EU-based claims cannot be less favorable than those relating to similar domestic actions ("equivalence") and (2) they cannot make it impossible in practice or excessively difficult to exercise EU rights ("effectiveness"). Some commentators have emphasized the cooperative nature of this framework, in contrast to – for instance – the "conflict-oriented" model in cases such as *Simmenthal*.[26]

The key features of this extensive case law are threefold. First, the minutiae, as well as control over the basic tenets of the domestic legal system and the role of a given national procedural rule within that system, are left in the hands of national legal orders.[27] As such, they are empowered to be the ones to enforce EU law, the latter only creating new remedies where there is a lacuna at the national level (the first "focal point" above).

Second, the assessment of equivalence and effectiveness provides robust latitude for member states, and EU courts will often cede the difficult balancing act between competing substantive interests to the national legal order. An illustration of this is the Court's cautious case law on limitation periods, which has for some time allowed significant margins to member states when identifying what a "reasonable" period would be.[28] The CJEU in many ways keeps an "escape route" for itself to step in where the imbalance is clear, but otherwise it remains above the fray.[29] This is more likely to be triggered in cases where secondary legislation has already incited national legal systems to provide "penalties [which are] effective, proportionate and dissuasive."[30] Given the widespread use of this vague terminology in directives[31] and the absence of guidance as to the meaning of those terms, it would appear that litigation is likely to arise on the question of the necessary remedies at the national level.[32]

Third, over time the Court's approach has matured to allow for corrective mechanisms to address some of the potential inconsistencies of its logic. For instance, it has recognized the ability of national legal systems to enforce principles such as "abuse of rights" to stop parties relying upon EU law in a manner contrary to its underlying objectives.[33] Moreover, the Court has insisted that the natural logic of the principle of equivalence is that there should be an internal consistency between remedies for EU rights *inter se*.[34]

This nuanced framework is a classic creature of EU law, incorporating the tensions at play between legal orders and respecting the autonomy of national systems within the European Union. In light of the features above, the intervention of EU law is likely to occur only where there is either a clear difference between national procedures and those for enforcing EU rights or where there are clear obstacles placed in the path of persons relying on those rights which have no corollary in the underlying secondary EU legislation, which is the origin of the EU rights.

Thus far, the "focal points" we have considered appear limited in nature, either biting only where there is a vacuum to be filled or where there are clear obstacles strewn across the path of those relying on EU rights. However, two developments have heralded a substantive regulation of national procedures: (1) the emphasis on the individual rights of parties to an effective remedy and (2) efforts to harmonize procedural standards at the EU level.

As to the first development, Article 47 of the Charter of Fundamental Rights contains a number of guarantees. However, in general terms, the CJEU's approach to that provision appears to be quite limited in the context of procedural law. Indeed, the Third Chamber recently stated that "Article 47 of the Charter … constitutes a reaffirmation of the principle of effective judicial protection."[35] This would suggest that it does little more than reflect our first "focal point." However, in our view this statement and the judicial approach which consists of limiting Article 47 to other principles has been adopted in specific circumstances where the particular complaint is analogous to that which is the focus of the general principle of effective judicial protection. The Explanations of Article 47 make clear that it is not *solely* concerned with that general principle. Instead, Article 47 recognizes the importance of a separate interest – that of individual parties to an "effective remedy" where their rights have been infringed. This is an individual right rather than a systemic principle. It appears that the judiciary takes a similar view, as noted recently by a member of the Court.[36]

A powerful example of this shift in philosophy is *DEB*.[37] DEB was a German company which applied for legal aid in support of its claim for state liability against the German State for delay in its transposition of two directives. German law effectively precluded it from bringing this claim as it (1) required the company to make an advance payment to the court in respect of the costs of the proceedings and be represented by a lawyer (things it could not afford as it was out of funds) and (2) imposed restrictions on legal persons from applying for legal aid. The CJEU was specifically informed by the referring court that the *Bundesverfassungsgericht* had not taken issue with this restriction under the German Basic Law (paragraph 24). However, the CJEU noted the "right of a legal person to effective access to justice and … the general principle of effective judicial protection" (paragraph 29) and "recast the question referred so that it relates to the interpretation of the principle of effective judicial protection *as enshrined in Article 47 of the Charter*" (paragraph 33). It then examined at length the case law of the European Court of Human Rights on legal aid under Article 6(1) ECHR and concluded that "it is not impossible for legal persons to rely upon [Article 47]" (paragraph 59). It went on to set out a framework of analysis for the national court (paragraphs 60 to 62). While the Court referred to case law under the second "focal point" and the "virtually impossible or excessively difficult" formula, this was arguably a substantial interference with the rules of national law and may herald an increased willingness to enforce substantive guarantees where parties allege that their fundamental right under Article 47 has been infringed.

The second development of note is the proliferation of positive harmonization measures, which have had the direct consequence of calibrating the test applied by the Court when examining national procedural rules. The EU legislator has been busy: as has been noted elsewhere,[38] measures have been introduced in areas ranging from public procurement to sex discrimination, consumer protection, environmental protection, and the enforcement of intellectual property rights. Furthermore, extensive rules concerning civil and criminal justice have been adopted.[39] This legislative activity, in our view, explains the variations in the case law which are context-specific. For instance, in the field of consumer law the Court has repeatedly insisted, in contrast to its more general case law, that national judges raise *ex officio* questions of EU law which arise in a case.[40] In the area of intellectual property law, the CJEU has lent the weight of its authority to the idea of a pan-European injunction against infringements of Community trademarks.[41] Similarly, in the area of environmental protection the Court has intervened to generate new remedies where necessary.[42] Finally, its case law in the field of employment has placed particular duties on national courts to ensure respect of EU law,[43] as well as to guarantee the existence of effective sanctions.[44] The Court has also adopted a more interventionist view of limitation periods to that alluded to above.[45]

Somewhere "In-Between": the Court's Treatment of *Res Judicata*

As soon as academic hubris tempts one towards systematizing, the question of hard cases which fall "in-between" quickly rears its head. For instance, can the three "focal points" explain the way in which EU law deals with one of the most sacred principles of procedural law: *res judicata*? Delivery of justice within a society requires finality in litigation, despite the possibility that mistakes, new facts, and other events might emerge in the future. In recent years, several cases raised the question of whether EU law requires national courts to ignore the finality of their previous judgments in order to provide for an effective judicial remedy to breaches of an EU right. The conflict is there to be seen: in one corner, respect for the principle of *res judicata* ensures legal certainty and closure within the national legal order (and engages the flexibility of our second focal point); in the other, the *vulnus* to an EU right would be left unhealed without a remedy (suggesting the need for intervention to protect the core guarantees of our first focal point and to ensure consistent EU-wide standards under our third). The CJEU's initial reaction fell into our second "focal point": thus in *Kapferer*, the Court ecumenically recognized the fundamental importance for both the EU[46] and national legal orders of the principle of *res judicata*. It concluded that

> Community law does not require a national court to disapply domestic rules of procedure conferring finality on a decision, even if to do so would enable it to remedy an infringement of Community law by the decision at issue. [47]

A few months later, however, in the *Lucchini* judgment, the CJEU found that Italian provisions ensuring the principle of *res judicata* must not be applied in so far as their application prevented the exercise of an EU right – in that case the recovery of state aid granted in breach of EU law.[48] Finally in *Olimpiclub*, although the Court confined *Lucchini* to the specific area of exclusive EU competences – such as state aid control – it still went on to hold that the Italian Supreme Court's interpretation of the principle of *res judicata* in tax disputes would lead to results incompatible with EU VAT law and thus it had to be set aside.[49] In all these cases, the national procedural system in question was supposed to have functioned properly as the appeals process, counter claims, evidence, opportunity to raise new pleas, and so on were all in place. There was no vacuum to be filled by looking through our first focal point. Moreover, no legal system provides for an absolute bar to reopening proceedings, thus a mere application of the equivalence test should have sufficed. Instead in *Lucchini* and *Olimpiclub* the CJEU substantially intervened to overturn what it perceived to be flawed national adjudications. In the first case the Italian court had disregarded a previous Commission decision, and in the second the Court resisted a certain reading of the *res judicata* principle that would have meant applying an incorrect interpretation of VAT law in all future cases related to the same taxpayer or taxable entity, although for different tax years. These rulings are therefore more related to the preservation of the coherence and exclusive competences of the EU legal system as a whole rather than being concerned with a remedial outcome. When faced with these types of fundamental tensions between legal orders, the Court's results shade between the protection of national autonomy and interventionism. As now candidly admitted by the Court itself, ultimately it all depends on "the particular features of the situations and interests at issue."[50]

Conclusion

Where does this leave us? We have tried to recast the extensive developments to date through the use of a conceptual framework which mirrors the foundational treaties. We consider this reformulation to be an important clarification, given that the case law of the Court so often confuses and combines different concepts in its search for a fair result in a given case. In our view, that methodology fails in two respects. First, it does not clearly identify what the Court is doing when faced with particular facts – a particularly important exercise when it is concerned, as here, with the outsourcing of justice to national legal orders. This makes it difficult to discern clear principles from the case law or to predict which principles the Court will invoke when resolving a dispute. Second, by doing this the Court risks diluting the effect of each notion or giving the impression that a given concept is more limited than it was initially designed to be. For instance, the general principle of effective judicial protection is rarely infringed given that it is invoked in cases where there is no vacuum to fill. When left with an analytical framework such as that in *Unibet*, it is hard to expect more than a form of balancing between national and EU interests. This is only supposed to occur within the context of our second "focal point" on the spectrum, that is, where there is no underpinning secondary EU legislation in the area, no vacuum without remedies, and the rights of the individual party are not jeopardized so as to require active intervention. The structural guidance in the treaties may be a more constructive way to measure out the different weights placed on the balance.

Notes

1 See, for a general overview, e.g., Koen Lenaerts, Ignace Maselis, and Kathleen Gutman, *Procedural Law of the European Union*, ed. Janek Tomasz Nowak (Oxford: Oxford University Press, 2014).

2 See, e.g., Pekka Haapaniemi, "Procedural Autonomy: A Misnomer?" in *The Europeanization of Procedural Law*, ed. Laura Ervo et al. (Groningen: Europa Law Publishing, 2009), 87–121; Claire Kilpatrick, "The Future of Remedies in Europe," in *The Future of Remedies in Europe*, ed. Claire Kilpatrick, Tonia Novitz, and Paul Skidmore (Oxford: Hart, 2000), 1, 4; and the "working definition" proposed by Advocate General Van Gerven in "Of Rights, Remedies and Procedures," *Common Market Law Review* 37 (2000): 501.

3 Case 26/62 *Van Gend en Loos (NV Algemene Transporten Expeditie Onderneming) v. Nederlandse Administratie der Belastingen* EU:C:1963:1.

4 A process described as "hybridization" by Norbert Reich in "Horizontal Liability in EC Law: Hybridization of Remedies for Compensation in Case of Breaches of EC Rights," *Common Market Law Review* 44 (2007): 707.

5 Consider most recently the adoption of Directive of the European Parliament and of the Council on certain rules governing actions for damages under national law for infringements of the competition law provisions of the member states and of the European Union on 17 April 2014, following Case C-453/99 *Courage* EU:C:2001:465, para 29 and Joined Cases C-295/04 to C-298/04 *Manfredi* EU:C:2006:461, para 62.

6 A term endorsed on occasion by the CJEU, see, e.g., Case C-550/07 P *Akzo Nobel Chemicals Ltd and Akcros Chemicals Ltd v. European Commission* EU:C:2010:512, para 114.

7 See, e.g., Paul Craig and Gráinne de Búrca, *EU Law: Text, Cases & Materials* (Oxford: Oxford University Press, 2011), Chap. 8; Takis Tridimas, *The General Principles of EU Law* (Oxford: Oxford University Press, 2007), Chap. 8; Michael Dougan, *National Remedies Before the Court of Justice: Issues of Harmonisation and Differentiation* (Oxford: Hart, 2004); and Andrea Biondi and Julian Lonbay, *Remedies for Breach of EC Law* (London: Wiley, 1997).

8 Michael Dougan, "The Vicissitudes of Life at the Coalface: Remedies and Procedures for Enforcing Union Law Before the National Courts," in *The Evolution of EU Law*, ed. Paul Craig and Gráinne de Búrca (Oxford: Oxford University Press, 2011). See also Anthony Arnull, "The Principle of Effective Judicial Protection in EU Law: An Unruly Horse?" *European Law Review* 36 (2011).

9 Case C-101/08 *Audiolux SA e.a v. Groupe Bruxelles Lambert SA (GBL) and Others and Bertelsmann AG and Others* EU:C:2009:626, para 63.

10 Alan Rosas and Lorna Armati, *EU Constitutional Law: An Introduction* (Oxford: Hart, 2010), 47, claim that certain general principles may in fact be "super-primary" law. They point to Joined Cases C-402/05 P and C-415/05 P *Yassin Abdullah Kadi and Al Barakaat International Foundation v. Council and Commission* (Kadi I) EU:C:2008:461 as an example of the provisions of the treaties being subject to general principles (see paras 308 and 326).

11 *Explanations relating to the Charter of Fundamental Rights* (2007/C 303/02), OJ C303/17, 14 December 2007, at 29.

12 Case C-432/05 *Unibet (London) Ltd and Unibet (International) Ltd v. Justitiekanslern* EU:C:2007:163.
13 Case 222/84 *Johnston v. Royal Ulster Constabulary* EU:C:1986:206.
14 Michael Dougan, "The Vicissitudes of Life at the Coalface," 431.
15 Most recently, Case C-12/08 *Mono Car Styling SA v. Dervis Odemis and Others* EU:C:2009:466, para 49.
16 See, e.g., Case C-268/06 *Impact* EU:C:2008:223 and *Mono Car*, n 15, para 51.
17 Dorota Leczykiewicz, "Effective Judicial Protection of Human Rights after Lisbon," *European Law Reivew* 35 (2010): 333.
18 Joined Cases C-6/90 and C-9/90 *Francovich* EU:C:1991:428; and Joined Cases C-46/93 and C-48/93 *Brasserie du Pêcheur and Factortame* EU:C:1996:79.
19 Case C-213/89 *The Queen v. Secretary of State for Transport, ex parte: Factortame Ltd and others* EU:C:1990:257, para 21.
20 See Case C-453/99 *Courage*, n 5, and Joined Cases C-295/04 to C-298/04 *Manfredi*, n 5.
21 Joined Cases C-317/08 and C-320/08 *Alassini* EU:C:2010:146
22 See Arnull, "The Principle of Effective Judicial Protection in EU Law," 55, referring critically to Advocate General Kokott in Case C-75/08 R *(on the application of Mellor) v. Secretary of State for Communities and Local Government* EU:C:2008:252 .
23 See Joined Cases C-402/05 P and C-415/05 P *Kadi I*, n 10 this chapter, paras 322–324.
24 Cases 33/76 *Rewe-Zentralfinanz eG and Rewe-Zentral AG v. Landwirtschaftskammer für das Saarland* EU:C:1976:188, para 5.
25 Case 45/76 *Comet BV v. Produktschap voor Seirgewassen* EU:C:1976:191, paras 13–16.
26 Case 106/77 *Amministrazione delle Finanze dello Stato v. Simmenthal SpA* EU:C:1978:49. See Haapaniemi, "Procedural Autonomy," 96.
27 See, e.g., Case C-312/93 *Peterbroeck v. Belgian State* EU:C:1995:437, para 14; Joined Cases C-430/93 and Case C-431/93 *Van Schijndel and others* EU:C:1995:441, para 18; and Case C-261/95 *Rosalba Palmisani v. Istituto nazionale della previdenza sociale* (INPS) EU:C:1997:351, para 27.
28 See, e.g., Case C-445/06 *Danske Slagterier v. Bundesrepublik Deutschland* EU:C:2009:178, para 32 and the case law cited there; and Case C-542/08 *Friedrich G. Barth v. Bundesministerium für Wissenschaft und Forschung* EU:C:2010:193, para 28.
29 Andrea Biondi, "The Impact of EU law on National Procedural Law," in *Civil Procedure Reform in Comparative Perspective*, ed. Niccolo Trocker and Vincenzo Varano (Turin: Turin Giappichelli, 2005), 231.
30 Case C-271/91 *Marshall v. Southampton and South-West Hampshire Area Health Authority* (Marshall II) EU:C:1993:335, para 38; Case C-63/08 *Pontin v. T-Comalux SA* EU:C:2009:666.
31 For recent examples, see, e.g., Directive 2013/30/EU of the European Parliament and of the Council of 12 June 2013 on safety of offshore oil and gas operations and amending Directive 2004/35/EC, [2013] OJ L 178/66, Article 34; and Directive 2012/27/EU of the European Parliament and of the Council of 25 October 2012 on energy efficiency [2012] OJ L 315/1, Article 13.
32 Consider a recent example in the reference by the UK Supreme Court to the CJEU in *R* (on the application of ClientEarth) *v. The Secretary of State for the Environment, Food and Rural Affairs* [2013] UKSC 25.
33 Case C-206/94 *Paletta II* EU:C:1996:182, paras 24–25; Case C-367/96 *Kefalas* EU:C:1998:222, para 28; and Case C-110/99 *Emsland Stärke* EU:C:2000:695, paras 51–54.
34 Case C-460/06 *Paquay* EU:C:2007:601, para 52; and the comments related to that case in Michael Dougan, "The Vicissitudes of Life at the Coalface," 423–424.
35 Case C-93/12 ET *Agrokonsulting-04-Velko Stoyanov v. Izpalnitelen direktor na Darzhaven fond "Zemedelie" – Razplashtatelna agentsia* EU:C:2013:432, para 59.
36 Marek Safjan, "A Union of Effective Judicial Protection: Addressing a Multi-Level Challenge through the Lens of Article 47 CFREU," Keynote lecture at the Annual Conference of the Centre for European Law at King's College, London, February 2014, pp. 3, 7, 10–12, available at www.kcl.ac.uk/cel.
37 Case C-279/09 *DEB Deutsche Energiehandels- und Beratungsgesellschaft mbH v. Bundesrepublik Deutschland* EU:C:2010:811.

38 See Dougan, "The Vicissitudes of Life at the Coalface," 435–437; and Arnull, "The Principle of Effective Judicial Protection in EU Law," 63–68.
39 See, e.g., Eva Storskrubb, "Civil Justice – A Newcomer and an Unstoppable Wave?" in Craig and de Búrca, *The Evolution of EU Law*, 309–321; and Dougan, "The Vicissitudes of Life at the Coalface," 436.
40 Compare Case C-618/10 *Banco Español de Crédito SA v. Joaquín Calderón Camino* EU:C:2012:349, to Joined Cases C-222/05 to C-225/05 *van der Weerd* EU:C:2007:318.
41 Case C-235/09 *DHL Express v. Chronopost* EU:C:2011:238.
42 See, e.g., its creation of an "altruistic group action" for judicial review by an environmental NGO, Case C-115/09 *Bund für Umwelt und Naturschutz Deutschland, Landesverband Nordrhein-Westfalen e. V. v. Bezirksregieruna Amsberg* EU:C:2011:289.
43 See Case C-144/04 *Mangold* EU:C:2005:709 and Case C-555/07 *Kücükdeveci v. Swedex GmbH & Co. KG* EU:C:2010:21.
44 See, e.g., Case C-63/08 *Pontin v. T-Comalux SA* EU:C:2009:666, paras 74–75.
45 Ibid., paras 62–63.
46 See Case C-462/05 *Commission v. Portugal* EU:C:2008:337, para 23; and more recently Case C-529/09 *Commission v. Spain* EU:C:2013:31.
47 Case C-234/04 *Kapferer v. Schlank & Schick* EU:C:2006:178; see also Case C-2/06 *Willy Kempter KG* EU:C:2008:78.
48 Case C-119/05 *Ministero dell'Industria, del Commercio e dell'Artigianato v. Lucchini SpA, formerly Lucchini Siderurgica SpA* EU:C:2007:434.
49 Case C-2/08 *Fallimento Olimpiclub* EU:C:2009:506. It would appear that similar motivations have driven the Court's recent case law on the scope of EU law. See Case C-617/10 *Åkerberg Fransson* EU:C:2013:105; Case C-418/11 *Texdata Software* EU:C:2013:588; and Case C-206/13 *Siragusa* EU:C:2014:126.
50 Case C-249/11 *Hristo Byankov* EU:C:2012:608, para 77 and cases cited.

References

Arnull, Anthony. "The Principle of Effective Judicial Protection in EU Law: An Unruly Horse?" *European Law Review* 36 (2011): 51–70.

Biondi, Andrea. "The Impact of EU Law on National Procedural Law." In *Civil Procedure Reform in Comparative Perspective*, edited by Niccolo Trocker and Vincenzo Varano, 231–250. Turin: Turin Giappichelli, 2005.

Biondi, Andrea and Julian Lonbay. *Remedies for Breach of EC Law*. London: Wiley, 1997.

Craig, Paul and Gráinne de Búrca. *EU Law: Text, Cases & Materials*. Oxford: Oxford University Press, 2011.

Craig, Paul and Gráinne de Búrca. *The Evolution of EU Law*. Oxford: Oxford University Press, 2011.

Dougan, Michael. *National Remedies Before the Court of Justice: Issues of Harmonisation and Differentiation*. Oxford: Hart, 2004.

Dougan, Michael. "The Vicissitudes of Life at the Coalface: Remedies and Procedures for Enforcing Union Law Before the National Courts." In *The Evolution of EU Law*, 412–421.

Haapaniemi, Pekka. "Procedural Autonomy: A Misnomer?" In *The Europeanization of Procedural Law*, edited by Laura Ervo et al., 87–121. Groningen: Europa Law Publishing, 2009.

Kilpatrick, Claire. "The Future of Remedies in Europe." In *The Future of Remedies in Europe*, edited by Claire Kilpatrick, Tonia Novitz, and Paul Skidmore, 1–34. Oxford: Hart, 2000.

Leczykiewicz, Dorota. "Effective Judicial Protection of Human Rights after Lisbon." *European Law Review* 35 (2010): 326–348.

Lenaerts, Koen, Dirk Arts, and Ignace Maselis. *Procedural Law of the European Union*. Edited by Janek Tomasz Nowak. Oxford: Oxford University Press, 2014.

Reich, Norbert. "Horizontal Liability in EC Law: Hybridization of Remedies for Compensation in Case of Breaches of EC Rights." *Common Market Law Review* 44 (2007): 705–742.
Rosas, Alan and Lorna Armati. *EU Constitutional Law: An Introduction*. Oxford: Hart, 2010.
Safjan, Marek. "A Union of Effective Judicial Protection: Addressing a Multi-Level Challenge through the Lens of Article 47 CFREU." Keynote lecture at the Annual Conference of the Centre for European Law at King's College, London, February 2014.
Storskrubb, Eva. "Civil Justice – A Newcomer and an Unstoppable Wave?" In *The Evolution of EU Law*, 299–321.
Tridimas, Takis. *The General Principles of EU Law*. Oxford: Oxford University Press, 2007.
Van Gerven, Walter. "Of Rights, Remedies and Procedures." *Common Market Law Review* 37 (2000): 501–536.

12

The Court of Justice of the European Union as a Self-Made Statesman

Loïc Azoulai and Zane Rasnača

Modest Origins and Excessive Promises

In the Schuman Declaration of 9 May 1950, which forms the basis for the establishment of the European Communities, no mention was made of a judicial body. It provided for the institution of a "High Authority" that then became the "European Commission," an international body independent of the member states and responsible for the supervision and regulation of the common market in coal and steel. This organ was to exercise considerable powers, taking decisions that would bind the member states and would be directly enforceable in these countries. Concerning judicial aspects it was simply stated that "appropriate measures will be provided for means of appeal against the decisions of the authority." One of the draft versions of the declaration was more explicit and referred to the possibility of appealing decisions of this new supranational authority to the Permanent Court of International Justice established five years earlier in The Hague.[1] This reference was later taken out as doubts arose regarding the suitability of externalizing judicial resources to an international institution composed of judges from other countries rather than the member states of the European Communities. However, when it eventually came to the drafting of the original treaties, the decision was taken to provide the European Communities with a proper system of judicial review. Thus, a permanent and supranational Court called the "Court of Justice" was established. In doing this, the EU system departed from the classic architecture of international organizations not only through its unprecedented transfer of powers to an independent executive body – what has been called, suggestively, "a transfer of sovereign rights" – but also because of the establishment of this unique judicial mechanism.

It is clear, however, that the framers of the European treaties did not intend to establish a constitutional court charged with protecting human rights, preserving the balance of powers within the new European institutional system, and furthering the cause of a supranational Europe. In correspondence with the American lawyer Donald Swatland dating back to 1957 the head of the legal service of the High Authority, Michel Gaudet, once recognized that it is

A Companion to European Union Law and International Law, First Edition.
Edited by Dennis Patterson and Anna Södersten.

"difficult to get the European minds to accept the idea that a Court must be a 'statesmanlike job'" which, however, was the role he expected the Court to assume.[2]

The reasons that prompted the drafters of the first treaties to propose the creation of a supranational judicial body, and the signatory countries to accept it, were rather narrow. First, the High Authority's discretion was feared by the member states. European integration was originally thought of as a "partial integration."[3] This meant that the High Authority should refrain from intruding in those sectors that did not come within the province of the Community. The Court was to be the protector of these boundaries. It was entrusted with the task of policing misuse of powers on the part of the High Authority. To this end, it was granted the power to review the legality of the Community measures. Herein lies the origin of the action of annulment under what is now Article 263 of the Treaty on the Functioning of the European Union (TFEU), the plea of illegality under Article 277 TFEU, and the preliminary rulings procedure established by Article 267 TFEU, which allows national courts to raise questions on the validity of Union acts.

Second, the Court was seen as a mechanism to ensure that member states would respect their commitments made under the treaties. Ensuring the credibility of legal commitments is a traditional motive for establishing international courts.[4] Accordingly, the Court was granted international jurisdiction with the power to decide on disputes arising between the member states and to ensure that they would respect the obligations arising from the treaties. The power to review member states' fulfillment of their obligations is ensured by the so-called infringement procedure, which is usually triggered by the Commission according to Article 258 TFEU.

A final motivation behind establishing the Court was the vague idea of protecting the rule of law.[5] Since the Community enjoyed an unprecedented capacity of action in both breadth and depth, it was deemed necessary to ensure that private parties directly affected by its activities would be judicially protected.[6] Hence, it was made possible for individuals to gain access to the Court through the action for annulment. This gave rise to great expectations in terms of legal protection. However, from the outset, the treaties imposed strict procedural constraints upon these potential litigants. While EU institutions and the member states are privileged in their access, individuals can rarely reach the Court directly; they have to fulfill the still very strict requirements of *locus standi*.[7] This may have prompted the Court to encourage individuals to seek justice via national courts and indirectly cause the development of the preliminary ruling procedures mechanism. Through this mechanism, national courts may or should refer to the Court questions concerning the interpretation of EU law and, ultimately, the compatibility of national provisions with EU law.[8] Nevertheless, the preliminary reference mechanism is by no means a functional substitute for direct access to the Court for individuals as in any case the request for a reference from any of the parties in the proceedings is not binding upon the national courts. This division of labor is now reflected in Article 19 of the Treaty on European Union (TEU), according to which the Court is charged with ensuring the observance of the law, whereas national courts are to ensure "effective legal protection in the fields covered by Union law."

Taking a broad view of international courts and tribunals, Robert Keohane, Andrew Moravcsik, and Anne-Marie Slaughter have distinguished two ideal types of international dispute resolution: interstate and transnational.[9] Interstate dispute is present in the EU system: under Article 259 TFEU, the member states can sue each other for breaches of the treaties, even though this rarely happens in practice. The Court is certainly much closer to the transnational dispute resolution mechanism where both access to courts and the subsequent implementation of their decisions are insulated from the will of national governments. Although this category may well account for the original position of the Court stipulated by the original treaties, it does not completely fit the dynamics of the EU judicial system.

One essential aspect of the system is the central role the Court and judicial actors more broadly have been able to confer upon themselves in the context of the integration process. Technically, this was made possible through the system of preliminary rulings. Under Article 267 TFEU the Court was endowed with the power to assist national courts in ensuring the correct application of EU law. The drafters of the treaties may not have foreseen the great potential of this mechanism. By enabling domestic courts (upon being confronted with a problem involving the dimension of EU law) to refer to the Court of Justice of the European Union (CJEU) any questions of validity or interpretation they deem fit to ask, they allowed for the establishment of a special connection between domestic judicial organs and the Court. Through this channel, national courts acquired extraordinary powers within the domestic setting in their capacities as "Union courts,"[10] while the Court became able to interfere directly with national proceedings, to the point that it takes on the function of a higher ranking "domestic court."[11] In its first years of activity, the Court spared no effort to win national courts' confidence, be it by patiently explaining what it expected them to do or by cultivating court-to-court dialogue. There is no doubt that, in so doing, the Court committed itself to ensuring the uniform application of EU law and to furthering the progress of integration.

To be sure, the CJEU has powers that in several respects go well beyond those of "ordinary" international tribunals. However, these powers are far from unlimited. Its jurisdiction, even though vastly broadened over the years, is still restricted not least by the limits of EU competences.[12] Its human and material resources are limited as well.[13] Moreover, there is no established hierarchy between the Court and national authorities: their relationship is governed by a regime of clear separation of powers and of functions.[14] The EU treaties in no way set the Court "above the national judicial system."[15] The Court does not have the formal authority to determine the validity of national law and it does not possess hierarchical authority over national courts. Although the EU judicial system promises justice and protection on paper, it is bound by constraints that make it difficult to provide them in practice. As a result, much of its efficiency depends on the cooperation of national actors. It relies on the motives of individual national judges, the voluntary submissions of lower courts driven by a promise of emancipation within the domestic system, or a transfer of loyalty towards what is viewed as a new center of power and interest. On the whole, national courts, especially lower courts, have joined in "the Euro-law game" with enthusiasm.

The Architecture of the Court and "Judicial Self-Government"

The CJEU has some basic structural features similar to that of most judicial bodies. According to the treaties, the members of the Court are chosen from individuals whose independence is beyond doubt and who possess the ability required for appointment to higher judicial offices. Collegiality and deliberation secrecy are ensured. Incompatibilities with the office of judge and immunities are laid down in the Court's internal regulations. With respect to its composition, however, the Court departs from its domestic counterparts. Formally, the members of the Court are appointed by the common accord of the governments of the member states for renewable six-year terms. According to Article 19(2) TEU, "the Court of Justice shall consist of one judge from each Member State." Although this does not require that the judge is necessarily a national of the member state, as a matter of fact, each member state is to be "represented" by one national judge.

With respect to international courts, the emphasis is on the equal representation of quarrelling states on the bench as much as on the need for impartiality. The usual justifications for introducing an element of representation into an essentially independent and non-majoritarian judicial system are the following: first, it must be ensured that such a supranational judicial body properly understands the national context of the cases that come before it; second, governments and their electorates must be able to trust that their legitimate concerns will be taken into account in the process of implementation and interpretation of common EU rules; third, the fact that different national legal cultures are represented within the Court may make "the national courts abide more closely by the Court's case-law."[16]

However, in the EU context, two problems remain. On the one hand, as a consequence of successive enlargements of the European Union, the number of members has considerably increased. One must not ignore the impact this may have on the consistency of deliberation and the coherence of case law. On the other hand, this allows each government to choose "its" judge, keeping an eye on him or her, and possibly renewing him or her.[17] The discretion given to the member states in choosing the judges is one of the most criticized structural aspects of the CJEU. To address this issue, the Lisbon Treaty has introduced a new appointment procedure. Article 255 TFEU states that appointment shall take place only after obtaining an opinion of a panel on the suitability of the nominees. The panel consists mainly of previous judges of the CJEU and members of national supreme courts. Although this panel is confined to giving an opinion, its negative opinions have so far always been followed by the member states and rejected candidates have been withdrawn.[18] An important side effect of this procedural change is that many member states have set up new procedures in order to improve the quality of the national process of candidate selection. Interestingly, there seems to be a certain pressure on the member states to follow Recommendation (94)12 of the Venice Commission stating that the authority taking the decision on the selection of judges should be independent of governments and administrations, and that the task should be entrusted to a "judicial council." This reflects a trend toward self-empowerment of the judiciary in Europe.

The role of the president of the Court is particularly essential in shaping the architecture of the Court. Unlike the president of many constitutional courts and the chief justice of the US Supreme Court, the president is elected by his or her peers for a three-year term with a possibility of being reelected. The involvement of the Court and its president in the most important reforms of the European Union's judicial architecture in recent years is a striking feature which may be called "judicial self-government."[19] Of course, the member states and EU-level political actors are involved, and the Court's interventions are not always decisive. Yet, Vassilios Skouris, president of the Court from 7 October 2003 to 6 October 2015, openly recognized the central role played by the Court in these reforms, stating that "the Court has recently submitted a series of proposals to the legislative authorities of the Union."[20] Thus, to respond to the ever-growing competences of the Court instigated by treaty amendments that confer new competences on the European Union, the creation of an EU system for protection of fundamental rights, and the enlargements, a series of reforms in the judicial architecture have been adopted. First, as a result of these reforms, the institution called the Court of Justice of the European Union today consists of the Court of Justice, the General Court, and specialized courts – at present only the Civil Service Tribunal. Second, changes were introduced in the Court's working methods: for example, the formation of chambers, election of the presidents of the chambers, and the possibility of issuing a judgment without the opinion of the advocate general.[21] The question of whether these reforms are enough still remains, especially in light of the caseload of the EU courts and the doubts about the efficiency of its management this has created.[22]

The prospect of a forthcoming accession of the Union to the European Convention on Human Rights has triggered further concerns within the Court. Remarkably, the Court dared to intervene in what is essentially a political decision-making process by issuing a discussion document expressing its opinion on various substantial points regarding the accession.[23] One of the Court's main fears is that its judgments will be subjected to another judicial authority and that it will thus lose the last word on the compliance of EU law with human rights standards.[24] It seems that a large part of the agenda of organizational design and procedural reforms nowadays is shaped by the Court itself.[25]

The Court's Authority in Question

International courts today go well beyond their traditional role of settling disputes. They develop forms of legality and both control and legitimize authority exercised by other actors.[26] They have shifted away from being principally committed to dispute settlement towards pursuing other goals, such as advancing international norms and facilitating cooperative international arrangements.[27] Legalization beyond mere dispute settlement is taking place. This is true for the CJEU as well.

Nevertheless, the Court differs from classic international courts in two ways. While for the international courts legalization remains in some sense a hidden agenda and they tend to represent themselves as mere applicators of the law, the CJEU is more open about its creative role.[28] As its central task, the Court has assumed the elaboration on and protection of "the spirit" of the treaties.[29] Far from keeping to the real or supposed intention of the contracting parties, the Court has frequently drawn inspiration from the ultimate objective of integration.[30] Moreover, its enterprise is one of constitutionalization beyond one of legalization. As the Court famously stated in the *Van Gend en Loos* ruling of 1963, "the Treaty is more than an agreement which merely creates mutual obligations between the contracting parties."[31] This means, first, that the treaty gives rise to an objective legality to which the member states and all other institutional players are uniformly bound. The EU legal order does not allow for mechanisms of reciprocity. The member states cannot unilaterally adopt corrective or retaliatory measures to compensate for other member states' failure to comply with the treaties and neither can it deter them from doing so.[32] As the Court has framed it, the EU legal order is alien to any attempt to resurrect the intersubjective mechanisms enshrined in public international law.[33] Second, this means that rights and obligations are not merely attributed to member states but to individuals as well. The treaty is not only about organizing the relations between member states in a coherent and objective manner but is also about empowering and protecting peoples. In many ways, the Court has framed the EU treaties as a basis for establishing a "'social contract' among the nationals of those states."[34]

This constitutional role has been central to the self-perception of the Court. It comes to light most illustratively in three of its endeavors. First, the CJEU has been actively involved in the construction of the EU legal order. The well-known judgments of the Court in *Van Gend en Loos, Costa/ENEL,*[35] *Simmenthal,*[36] and *Francovich*[37] guaranteed the effective incorporation of Union rules in the national legal orders and, by affirming the principle of the primacy of EU law, granted them the status of higher law. As a consequence, they created the basis for a "quasi-federal" legal order. These cases are also famous for their proclamation of the autonomy of the EU legal order and the direct relationship it establishes with individuals. In coming to its judgments in these cases, the Court vested in individuals' rights emerging directly from the EU legal order that it had to guarantee and protect itself. Basically, all the interpretative work of the Court had as its aim the creation of a "European system of guarantees" that protects EU law and the individual rights stemming from that law against dissolution into the various national legal orders. In constitutionalizing EU law, the Court sought to protect EU standards from state contestations and all the bureaucratic complexities that EU texts are likely to encounter when they enter the domestic arena. This case law greatly strengthened the authority of EU law, while at the same time giving the Court absolute control over this new legal order.

Second, the Court shaped, and still actively shapes, the European political sphere. It has managed to ensure that any actor hoping to matter in the sphere of European politics must join the legal battles that take place before it and are to a large extent framed by it.[38] The European institutions and the national governments see the Court as a forum for furthering, or at least safeguarding, their own interests. The Commission in particular appreciated the potential of the Court from the very beginning and has evolved the practice of intervening in all cases before the Court. This also explains the elevated interest with which the European Parliament, which at the outset had only limited access to the Court, fought for its prerogatives to be extended. The Court has become not only central for the development of EU law but also one of the most important arenas for institutional interaction. The political actors benefit from a reciprocal empowerment that results from this interaction, the Court being one of the main arenas where this interaction takes place. This central role has allowed the Court to contribute to the development of the EU institutional system by fashioning key doctrines such as the rule that common action by the member states can only be taken within the institutional framework of the European Union, the notion that EU institutions are "Community institutions" and not to be used by a group of states to further their interests, or the principle that member states are bound to adopt an attitude of sincere cooperation and full mutual respect. These doctrines have contributed to tying the Union and its main players to a particular institutional and legal culture. This culture is, however, being questioned by some recent developments emerging from the euro crisis.[39]

Third, the Court perceived a constitutional role for itself in responding to external forces and competing concerns within the European Union. This was the case with the incorporation of fundamental rights from both national and international systems in the EU legal order (the European Convention on Human Rights especially). When demands concerning the protection of fundamental rights first appeared before the Court, they were entirely ignored by the Community's legal order. However, once upheld by the German and Italian constitutional courts and supported by domestic doctrines, the Court could not ignore them. These demands threatened the autonomy of the Community and its legal order. Integrating the substance of fundamental rights into European Community (EC) law was the answer, giving them an apparently common foundation among the member states (the general principles of EC law derived from the "constitutional traditions common to the Member States"[40]) while simultaneously maintaining the formal neutrality of EC law regarding any foreign source, even if that source was constitutional. This move enabled the Court to conserve a significant freedom of appreciation when it came to the definition and scope of these rights. As a result, instead of being paralyzed by the pressure, it turned it into a useful means of action. What was a threat and could have been a defeat to the Court was turned into a powerful instrument with which to enlarge its jurisdiction. Now, the potential constraint conveyed by the application of fundamental rights is no longer directed against European institutions, rather it emanates from EU law and is directed against member states' actions.[41] Equally remarkable is the intro duction of elements of social justice into the construction of the internal market.[42] Ultimately, the effect of such incorporations has been to imbue the EU legal order with a system of values similar to those of national constitutional orders. The famous *Kadi* judgment is a good illustration of affirmation by a powerful judicial actor of an inalienable constitutional identity that it is keen to define by itself.[43] Not by chance, the Court presents itself as being an integral part of this identity.

How is one to explain the central role occupied by the Court in the European integration process? It is true that the Court's influence may have varied over time, affected as it was by many events. The stalemates, such as the Luxembourg crisis, of the past might have served as a catalyzer for judicialization.[44] It is likewise true that particular actors and individuals have differentially affected the process of building and facilitating the CJEU's power. Nevertheless, the Court has always been able to rely on three series of factors. First, its institutional position has favored the enhancement of its role. As provided for in Article 13 TEU, the Court is part of the Union's institutional framework "which shall aim to promote [the] values [of the Union], advance its objectives, serve its interests." The Court is on a par with the other EU institutions, tasked with ensuring that in the interpretation and application of the treaties the law is observed. This position inevitably turns it into an overseer, helping it not only to ensure the rule of law but also to create a new legal, economic, and social order that corresponds to the establishment of the Union. Moreover, the Court is relatively insulated against the political and legal mechanisms that could be employed to discipline it or to rectify its case law. This is true in particular for amendments to the treaties owing to the complex procedure, as well as the unanimity required for such revisions. But the same can be said of the legislative procedure. The diversity of preferences among member states next to the many flaws of the Union decision-making process lead to compromise texts filled with broad clauses or general principles that by their nature reempower the judicial process.

Second, the jurisprudence of the Court reflects a general commitment to market integration principles that have been broadly agreed among member states, even when the application of these principles in individual cases conflicted with their self-interest, narrowly conceived. It is remarkable that, despite occasional rumbles, the Court has not experienced systematic resistance from the governments and has never faced serious attempts to curtail its powers. It may be that the Court tends to calculate how far it can go without causing too costly a reaction from the political actors. Oreste Pollicino has argued that the Court is very careful to "not overstep the threshold of tolerability."[45] It may also be that the context of the first decades of integration explains why the Court's innovative jurisprudence did not meet with stronger resistance: the relative paralysis of the Council following the Luxembourg compromise; the pro-integration stance of a majority of national governments; and the existence of a wide (even if shallow) support for integration within public opinion all concurred to facilitating acceptance of the "constitutionalization" of the Community's legal order.[46]

Third, what has sustained the Court's authority in the European context is certainly also linked to the construction and dominance of a narrative privileging legal discourse and independent organs as the best triggers for the establishment of a new social order. This narrative has been able to rely on the active support of a set of actors who constituted a strong community of belief in the European integration project.[47]

These days, however, none of these factors seem to hold any longer. The Court finds itself under greater public scrutiny. Its moment of splendid isolation has come to an end. Not only lawyers but also many politicians and even judges of the most powerful constitutional courts in the member states have openly questioned the Court's judgments.[48] Noncompliance may become a clever strategy for a constitutional court to establish its position vis-à-vis the Court.[49] Moreover, support from member state governments is no longer guaranteed. This is mainly because of the intrusion of EU law into sensitive areas of national policy which were previously considered as part of member states' retained powers. In judgments like *Metock*, where the Court granted the right of residence for third-country family members who had not previously lived in another member state, the very core of state competences is concerned, namely the conduct of immigration policy. Nor are any long-term benefits related to the construction of the internal market clearly discernible here. Unsurprisingly, this ruling caused uproar.[50] Judgments such as *Ruiz Zambrano*,[51] *Mangold*,[52] *Viking Line*,[53] and *Laval*[54] similarly illustrate the extensive reach of the Court into areas of national policy and the controversy this can bring. The permissive consensus on furthering European integration seems not to hold anymore. Finally, legal formalism seems to have lost its strength in the enlarged and much more conflictual context of today's Europe – weakened by the economic crisis and the rise of value conflicts in an enlarged Europe. The Court has to cope with a new set of problems such as the recognition of legal, social, moral, and ethical diversity for which the traditional doctrines establishing its constitutional authority are of little use.[55]

Current Challenges

There are two main challenges the Court faces today. One concerns the European Union's internal dimension, the other the external one. The first relates to the rise of claims for the protection of local identities within Europe, whether national, constitutional, or regional in nature, and the need to take these into account and accommodate them. The second is the reality of the fragmentation of the international arena and the need to account for the proliferation of international judicial institutions that produce an ever-growing set of norms. In both cases, the Court's authority is challenged by conflicting obligations to which national actors feel bound.

While at the EU level the Court's decisions meet little resistance, at the national level a court may find it hard to implement EU law in cases where national constitutional provisions are challenged. The domestic courts often find themselves in a balancing act between the EU and national legal and constitutional values to which they are still bound. The Court has long ignored the challenge by simply maintaining the authority of EU law and its formal indifference regarding any foreign source. Recently, the vigorous reactions to this approach of some higher courts willing to acknowledge the existence of this conflict has attracted much attention. The decision of the German Federal Constitutional Court on the Lisbon Treaty, for instance, was a clear warning that further erosions of Germany's constitutional identity would not be tolerated. However, the very same court has recently, and for the first time in its remarkable history, referred a preliminary reference to the CJEU.[56] This is a groundbreaking development. For the CJEU, this is not only a challenge but also an opportunity to strengthen its relationship with one of the most powerful of Europe's constitutional courts.

The external dimension presents the Court with even more of a challenge as it cannot rely on established coordination mechanisms, like the preliminary reference procedure, when it interacts with systems of international law. The Court has long maintained an attitude of insulation from this development. The *Mox Plant* decision is a case in point: according to the Court's interpretation, EU law precluded Ireland from initiating proceedings before the United Nations Convention on the Law of the Sea Arbitral Tribunal because this "involves a risk that a judicial forum other than the Court will rule on the scope of obligations imposed on the Member States pursuant to Community law."[57] In general, the Court suggested that it does not wish to tolerate a possibility that EU law will be in any way considered in a foreign forum. In reality, this is a train long gone. Other international courts and tribunals have for years dealt with EU law more or less directly, especially when member states invoke EU law as a justification for their noncompliance with the requirements of international law.[58] This may lead to a friendly and hands-off attitude to the EU law, as in the *Bosphorus*[59] decision of the European Court of Human Rights, or it may lead to more critical stances, as with the International Labour Organization's Committee of Experts on the Application of Conventions and Recommendations in a report dealing with the CJEU's *Laval* judgment.[60] While the Court theoretically can ignore such developments, the national courts, the traditionally willing and necessary collaborators of the Court, have been put in a more difficult situation. In an extreme case, this could cause them to turn their back on the CJEU.

The reinforcement of the cooperation of the Court with national courts on the one hand, and with international courts and tribunals on the other, is one of the great current challenges facing the Court. For a long time, the Court was struggling for the recognition of the main stakeholders of European integration – hence the keenness to avoid conflicts as well as the reluctance to engage in a genuine judicial dialogue. In the present context, the fact of being challenged is not to be feared. Only through contestation and the ensuing possibility of a constructive dialogue will it be able to establish its position in a fragmented and complex world where layers of legal intervention at the transnational and national levels are constantly increasing and interacting. But for that to happen, the Court needs a free hand. It is certain that the recent development in the wake of the euro crisis of a set of international agreements concluded among the member states outside the institutional framework of the Union (European Financial Stability Fund, Treaty on the European Stability Mechanism, "Fiscal Compact," Euro Plus Pact) questions the position of the Court as a central actor of the EU political and legal system.

Notes

1 Anne Boerger-De Smedt, "La Cour de Justice dans les négociations du Traité de Paris instituant la CECA," *Journal of European Integration History* 18 (2008): 10.

2 See the correspondence between Michel Gaudet and Donald Swatland presented by Julie Bailleux, "Correspondence between Michel Gaudet and Donald Swatland," *Common Market Law Review* 50 (2013): 371.

3 See Case 30/59 *De Gezamenlijke Steenkolenmijnen in Limburg v. High Authority* EU:C:1961:2; and Pierre Pescatore, *The Law of Integration: Emergence of a New Phenomenon in International Relations, Based on the Experience of the European Communities* (Leiden: A.W. Sijthoof, 1974).

4 Ingo Venzke, "Understanding the Authority of International Courts and Tribunals: On Delegation and Discursive Construction," *Theoretical Inquiries in Law* 14 (2013): 390.

5 During the negotiations Germany fought for making the court more "constitutional." The introduction of a preliminary reference mechanism was a compromise in this regard. See Anne Boerger-De Smedt, "Negotiating the Foundations of European Law, 1950–57: The Legal History of the Treaties of Paris and Rome," *Contemporary European History* 21 (2012): 344.

6 Which was later on made clear in Case 294/83 *Les Verts v. Parliament* EU:C:1986:166.

7 The traditional requirement for *locus standi* under Article 263 TFEU for individuals is direct and individual concern. After the Lisbon Treaty the requirements have been relaxed when the action is brought regarding a regulatory act not entailing implementing measures. See for interpretation, Case C-583/11 P *Inuit Tapiriit Kanatami and Others v. Parliament and Council* EU:C:2013:625.

8 The national courts have discretion concerning whether to refer. The national courts of last instance have an obligation to refer under Article 267 TFEU.

9 Robert O. Keohane, Andrew Moravcsik, and Anne-Marie Slaughter, "Legalized Dispute Resolution: Interstate and Transnational," in *International Law and International Relations*, ed. Beth A. Simmons and Richard H. Steinberg (Cambridge: Cambridge University Press, 2006), 132.

10 Opinion 1/09 EU:C:2011:123, para 80.

11 See Gaetano Morelli, "La Cour de justice des Communautés européennes en tant que juge interne," in *Studi sul processo internazionale*, ed. Gaetano Morelli (Milan: Giuffrè Editore, 1963), 93.

12 See Loïc Azoulai, ed., *The Question of Competence in the European Union* (Oxford: Oxford University Press, 2014).

13 Damian Chalmers, "The Dynamics of Judicial Authority and the Constitutional Treaty," in *The EU Constitution in a Contextual Perspective* (Jean Monnet working paper no. 5/04, 25).

14 In Case 6/64 *Costa v. ENEL* EU:C:1964:66, para 593 the Court speaks of "a clear separation of functions."

15 Case 6/60 *Humblet v. Belgian State* EU:C:1960:48, para 572.

16 European Commission, "Report by the Working Party on the Future of the European Communities' Court System," January 2000, http://ec.europa.eu/dgs/legal_service/pdf/due_en.pdf, 46.

17 Jean-Victor Louis, "The Court in the Constitution: How Federal?" in *The Future of the European Judicial System*, ed. Ingolf Pernice et al. (Baden-Baden: Nomos Verlag, 2006), 135.

18 Niilo Jääskinen, "Through Difficulties towards New Difficulties – Wandering in the European Judicial Landscape" (lecture, King's College London, 15 February 2013).

19 The expression is borrowed from Tomáš Dumbrovský, Bilyana Petkova, and Marijn Van Der Sluis, "Judicial Appointments: The Article 255 TFEU Advisory Panel and Selection Procedures in the Member States," *Common Market Law Review* 51 (2014): 481.

20 Vassilios Skouris, "The Evolution of the Judicial Architecture of the European Union and its Procedural Implications," in *Of Courts and Constitutions*, ed. Kieran Bradley, Noel Travers, and Anthony Whelan (Oxford: Hart, 2014), 10.

21 Good overview of the reforms concerning the architecture of the CJEU can be found in Skouris, "The Evolution of the Judicial Architecture of the European Union and its Procedural Implications."

22 With regards to the question of noncompliance, please see Geoffrey Garrett, R. Daniel Kelemen, and Heiner Schultz, "The European Court of Justice, National Governments, and Legal Integration in the European Union," *International Organization* 52 (1998).

23 Court of Justice of the European Union, "Discussion Document of the Court of Justice of the European Union on Certain Aspects of the Accession of the European Union to the European Convention for the Protection of Human Rights and Fundamental Freedoms," 5 May 2010, http://curia.europa.eu/jcms/upload/docs/application/pdf/2010-05/convention_en.pdf.

24 See Opinion 2/13 EU:C:2014:2454.

25 See Juliane Kokott et al., *The Future of the European Judicial System in a Comparative Perspective* (Baden-Baden: Nomos Verlag, 2006).

26 Venzke, "Understanding the Authority of International Courts and Tribunals," 382.

27 Yuval Shany, "No Longer a Weak Department of Power? Reflections on the Emergence of a New International Judiciary," *The European Journal of International Law* 20(1) (2009): 76.

28 For a brief overview concerning interpretation in international law, see Michael Waibel, "Demystifying the Art of Interpretation," *The European Journal of International Law* 22 (2011).

29 Case 26/62 *Van Gend en Loos* EU:C:1963:1; Case 283/81 *CILFIT v. Ministero della Sanità* EU:C:1982:335.

30 Albertina Albors Lorens, "The European Court of Justice, More than a Teleological Court" *Cambridge Yearbook of European Legal Studies* 2 (1999): 373.

31 Case 26/62 *Van Gend en Loos*, n 29 this chapter, para 12.

32 Case 232/78 *Commission v. France* EU:C:1979:215, para 9.

33 See *contra* Bruno Simma, "Self-Contained Regimes," *Netherlands Yearbook of International Law* 16 (1985): 111 and Dirk Pulkowski and Bruno Simma, "Of Planets and the Universe: Self-Contained Regimes in International Law," *The European Journal of International Law* 17 (2006): 483.

34 J.H.H. Weiler, "To be a European Citizen: Eros and Civilization," *Journal of European Public Policy* (1998): 510.

35 Case 6/64 *Costa v. ENEL*, n 14 this chapter.

36 Case 106/77 *Amministrazione delle finanze dello Stato v. Simmenthal* EU:C:1978:49.

37 Case C-6/90 *Francovich and Bonifaci v. Italy* EU:C:1991:428.

38 See Loïc Azoulai and Renaud Dehousse, "The European Court of Justice and the Legal Dynamics of Integration," in *The Oxford Handbook of the European Union*, ed. Erik Jones, Anand Menon, and Stephen Weatherill (Oxford: Oxford University Press, 2013).

39 Editorial Comments, "Union Membership in Times of Crisis," *Common Market Law Review* 51 (2014).
40 Case 29/69 *Stauder* EU:C:1969:57; Case 11/70 *Internationale Handelsgesellschaft mbH v. Einfuhr- und Vorratsstelle für Getreide und Futtermittel* EU:C:1970:114, para 4.
41 See Loïc Azoulai, "The Case of Fundamental Rights: A State of Ambivalence" in *The European Court of Justice and the Autonomy of the Member States*, ed. Hans-Wolfgang Micklitz and Bruno de Witte (Cambridge: Intersentia, 2012).
42 Starting with Case 43/75 *Defrenne v. SABENA* EU:C:1976:56.
43 Joined Cases C-402/05 P and C-415/05 P *Kadi and Al Barakaat International Foundation v. Council and Commission* EU:C:2008:461.
44 Suzanne Katzenstein, "In the Shadow of Crisis: The Creation of International Courts in the Twentieth Century," *Harvard International Law Journal* 55 (2014): 151.
45 Oreste Pollicino, "Legal Reasoning of the Court of Justice in the Context of the Principle of Equality between Judicial Activism and Self-Restraint," *German Law Journal* 5 (2004): 317.
46 J.H.H. Weiler, "The Community System: The Dual Character of Supranationalism," *Yearbook of European Law* 1 (1981): 267.
47 Antoine Vauchez, *L'Union par le droit: l'invention d'un programme institutionnel pour l'Europe* (Paris: Presses de Sciences Po, 2013).
48 Probably the most popular attack has been that made by Lüder Gerken and Roman Herzog, "Stop the European Court of Justice," English translation of an article published in *Frankfurter Allgemeine Zeitung* (8 September 2008) to be found in *EU Observer* (10 September 2008) http://euobserver.com/opinion/26714.
49 Arthur Dyevre, "The German Federal Constitutional Court and European Judicial Politics," *West European Politics* 34 (2011): 357.
50 Case C-127/08 *Metock and Others* EU:C:2008:449.
51 Case C-34/09 *Ruiz Zambrano* EU:C:2011:124.
52 Case C-144/04 *Mangold* EU:C:2005:709.
53 Case C-438/05 *International Transport Workers' Federation v. Viking Line ABP* EU:C:2007:772.
54 Case C-341/05 *Laval un Partneri Ltd v. Svenska Byggnadsarbetareförbundet* EU:C:2007:809.
55 Floris de Witte, "Sex, Drugs & EU Law: The Recognition of Moral and Ethical Diversity in EU Law," *Common Market Law Review* 50 (2013): 1545.
56 German Federal Constitutional Court, "Principal Proceedings ESM/ECB: Pronouncement of the Judgment and Referral for a Preliminary Ruling to the Court of Justice of the European Union," available on the Court's website.
57 Case C-459/03 *Commission v. Ireland* EU:C:2006:345, para 174. See also para 173.
58 Matthew Parish, "International Courts and the European Legal Order," *European Journal of International Law* 23 (2012): 148.
59 *Bosphorus Airways v. Ireland* (2006) 42 EHRR 1.
60 International Labour Organization, "Report of the Committee of Experts on the application of Conventions and Recommendations," 2013, http://www.ilo.org/wcmsp5/groups/public/---ed_norm/---relconf/documents/meetingdocument/wcms_205472.pdf, 178.

References

Albors Lorens, Albertina. "The European Court of Justice, More Than a Teleological Court." *Cambridge Yearbook of European Legal Studies* 2 (1999): 373–399.

Azoulai, Loïc. "The Case of Fundamental Rights: A State of Ambivalence." In *The European Court of Justice and the Autonomy of the Member States*, edited by Hans-Wolfgang Micklitz and Bruno de Witte, 207–218. Cambridge: Intersentia, 2012.

Azoulai, Loïc, ed. *The Question of Competence in the European Union*. Oxford: Oxford University Press, 2014.

Azoulai, Loïc, and Renaud Dehousse. "The European Court of Justice and the Legal Dynamics of Integration." In *The Oxford Handbook of the European Union*, edited by Erik Jones, Anand Menon, and Stephen Weatherill, 350–364. Oxford: Oxford University Press, 2013.

Bailleux, Julie. "Correspondence between Michel Gaudet and Donald Swatland." *Common Market Law Review* 50 (2013): 359–382.

Boerger-De Smedt, Anne. "La Cour de Justice dans les négociations du Traité de Paris instituant la CECA." *Journal of European Integration History* 18 (2008): 7–33.

Boerger-De Smedt, Anne. "Negotiating the Foundations of European Law, 1950–57: The Legal History of the Treaties of Paris and Rome." *Contemporary European History* 21 (2012): 339–356.

Chalmers, Damian. "The Dynamics of Judicial Authority and the Constitutional Treaty." In *The EU Constitution in a Contextual Perspective*, edited by Joseph H.H. Weiler and Christopher L. Eisgruber, 3–35. Altneuland: Jean Monnet working paper no. 5/04.

de Witte, Floris. "Sex, Drugs & EU Law: The Recognition of Moral and Ethical Diversity in EU Law." *Common Market Law Review* 50 (2013): 1545–1578.

Dumbrovský, Tomáš, Bilyana Petkova, and Marijn Van Der Sluis. "Judicial Appointments: The Article 255 TFEU Advisory Panel and Selection Procedures in the Member States." *Common Market Law Review* 51 (2014): 455–482.

Dyevre, Arthur. "The German Federal Constitutional Court and European Judicial Politics." *West European Politics* 34 (2011): 346–361.

Editorial Comments, "Union Membership in Times of Crisis." *Common Market Law Review* 51 (2014): 1–12.

Garrett, Geoffrey, R. Daniel Kelemen, and Heiner Schultz. "The European Court of Justice, National Governments, and Legal Integration in the European Union." *International Organization* 52 (1998): 149–176.

Gerken, Lüder, and Roman Herzog. "Stop the European Court of Justice." Original article in *Frankfurter Allgemeine Zeitung* (8 September 2008). English translation in *EU Observer* (10 September 2008). Accessed 3 June 2015. https://euobserver.com/opinion/26714.

Jääskinen, Niilo. "Through Difficulties towards New Difficulties – Wandering in the European Judicial Landscape." Lecture presented at Kings College, London, 2013.

Katzenstein, Suzanne. "In the Shadow of Crisis: The Creation of International Courts in the Twentieth Century." *Harvard International Law Journal* 55 (2014): 151–209.

Keohane, Robert O., Andrew Moravcsik, and Anne-Marie Slaughter. "Legalized Dispute Resolution: Interstate and Transnational." In *International Law and International Relations*, edited by Beth A. Simmons and Richard H. Steinberg, 131–156. Cambridge: Cambridge University Press, 2006.

Kokott, Juliane, Julia Mall, Ingolf Pernice, Cheryl Saunders, and Patricia Stöbener, eds. *The Future of the European Judicial System in a Comparative Perspective*. Baden-Baden: Nomos Verlag, 2006.

Louis, Jean-Victor. "The Court in the Constitution: How Federal?" In *The Future of the European Judicial System*, edited by Ingolf Pernice, Patricia Stöbener, Juliane Kokott, Julia Mall, and Cheryl Saunders, 135–142. Baden-Baden: Nomos Verlag, 2006.

Morelli, Gaetano. "La Cour de justice des Communautés européennes en tant que juge interne." In *Studi sul processo internazionale*, edited by Gaetano Morelli, 93–101. Milan: Giuffrè Editore, 1963.

Parish, Matthew. "International Courts and the European Legal Order." *European Journal of International Law* 23 (2012): 141–153.

Pescatore, Pierre. *The Law of Integration: Emergence of a New Phenomenon in International Relations, Based on the Experience of the European Communities*. Leiden: A.W. Sijthoof, 1974.

Pollicino, Oreste. "Legal Reasoning of the Court of Justice in the Context of the Principle of Equality between Judicial Activism and Self-Restraint." *German Law Journal* 5 (2004): 283–317.

Pulkowski, Dirk, and Bruno Simma. "Of Planets and the Universe: Self-Contained Regimes in International Law." *The European Journal of International Law* 17 (2006): 483–529.

Shany, Yuval. "No Longer a Weak Department of Power? Reflections on the Emergence of a New International Judiciary." *The European Journal of International Law* 20(1) (2009): 73–91.

Simma, Bruno. "Self-Contained Regimes." *Netherlands Yearbook of International Law* 16 (1985): 111–136.

Skouris, Vassilios. "The Evolution of the Judicial Architecture of the European Union and its Procedural Implications." In *Of Courts and Constitutions*, edited by Kieran Bradley, Noel Travers, and Anthony Whelan, 1–11. Oxford: Hart, 2014.

Vauchez, Antoine. *L'Union par le droit: l'invention d'un programme institutionnel pour l'Europe.* Paris: Presses de Sciences Po, 2013.

Venzke, Ingo. "Understanding the Authority of International Courts and Tribunals: On Delegation and Discursive Construction." *Theoretical Inquiries in Law* 14 (2013): 381–409.

Waibel, Michael. "Demystifying the Art of Interpretation." *The European Journal of International Law* 22 (2011): 571–588.

Weiler, J.H.H. "The Community System: The Dual Character of Supranationalism." *Yearbook of European Law* 1 (1981): 267–306.

Weiler, J.H.H. "To be a European Citizen: Eros and Civilization." *Journal of European Public Policy* 4 (1997): 495–519.

13

The Preliminary Rulings Procedure

Allan Rosas

Introduction

The EU legal order of today exhibits many constitutional features.[1] This is mainly because of

1. its effects in the legal orders of the member states (primacy, direct applicability, and direct effect);
2. its internal hierarchy of norms and institutional system, including assigning tasks to subcomponents of the member states such as national parliaments;
3. the legislative, regulatory, and other decision-making powers based on majority decision making appertaining to Union institutions; and
4. a comprehensive system of judicial and other legal controls.

It should be noted that the EU constitutional order is in many ways highly decentralized. The main burden of applying and implementing Union law lies with the authorities and courts of the member states.

As far as the judicial system is concerned, the legal actions that can be brought before the Union courts – the Court of Justice, the General Court, and specialized courts[2] – do not provide for a comprehensive system of procedural remedies. Direct actions, such as actions for annulment and actions for damages, can be brought before these courts only with respect to acts or omissions of Union institutions, bodies, offices, or agencies, not in order to challenge measures taken at the member state level. True, infringement actions may be brought by the European Commission or a member state for failure by another member state to fulfill its obligations under Union law – and the actions brought by the Commission are usually inspired by complaints made by individuals or groups of individuals – but the decision to bring an action is at the discretion of the Commission (or, as the case may be, the member state concerned), and there is no judicial remedy available to individuals by which they could challenge the decision not to bring an infringement action against a member state.[3]

A Companion to European Union Law and International Law, First Edition.
Edited by Dennis Patterson and Anna Södersten.

The main route available to individuals or other persons who wish to challenge acts or omissions at the national level that they consider to be in contravention of Union law is thus to make their case before a *national court* of the member state concerned. This can be done either by initiating an action (as a plaintiff, applicant, or otherwise) or by using Union law as a defense in proceedings (criminal, civil, administrative, or otherwise) brought against a physical or legal person. As such, national proceedings can concern the application and interpretation of Union law, including questions relating to its validity. There could be variations in the interpretations arrived at by national courts at different levels and/or in different member states and so the uniform application of Union law would be at risk.

The main procedural remedy to address this problem is the *preliminary ruling procedure*, which enables all national courts, and obliges some of them, to suspend the main proceedings before it and refer questions concerning the interpretation and validity of Union law to the Court of Justice for a binding ruling.[4] The procedure was already introduced, albeit in a somewhat limited way, by the Treaty establishing the European Coal and Steel Community (ECSC) of 1952.[5] It is today mainly regulated in Article 267 of the Treaty on the Functioning of the European Union (TFEU), which, with the entry into force of the Treaty of Lisbon on 1 December 2009, has replaced Article 234 of the Treaty establishing the European Community (EC), Article 23 of the Statute of the Court of Justice of the European Union, and Articles 93 to 118 of the new Rules of Procedure of the Court of Justice, which were adopted on 25 September and entered into force on 1 November 2012.[6]

All requests for preliminary rulings are dealt with by the Court of Justice, not the General Court. It is true that Article 256(3) TFEU provides that the General Court shall have jurisdiction to hear and determine questions referred for a preliminary ruling under Article 267 TFEU "in specific areas laid down by the Statute." No such delegation of jurisdiction has taken place, however. Transferring a part of the preliminary ruling cases to the General Court would not make much sense under current circumstances, as the General Court is faced with a much more difficult situation than the Court of Justice as regards the backlog of pending cases and the duration of the proceedings.[7] That said, the number of references for preliminary rulings brought before the Court of Justice has been on a more or less constant rise. For instance, the number of new references introduced during 1971 was thirty-seven, whereas the corresponding figures for 1981, 1991, 2001, and 2011 were 108, 186, 237, and 423, respectively.[8] For 2013, there was a further increase to 450 incoming requests for preliminary rulings.[9]

The *Raison d'Être* of the Preliminary Ruling Procedure

The function of the preliminary ruling procedure as a mechanism to ensure the uniform application of Union law is brought out, inter alia, in the Recommendations addressed by the Court of Justice to national courts and tribunals in relation to the initiation of preliminary ruling proceedings, as amended in October 2012 in order to reflect the new rules of procedure of the Court, which entered into force on 1 November 2012.[10] In their opening paragraph, the recommendations state that

> [t]he preliminary ruling system is a fundamental mechanism of European Union law aimed at enabling national courts and tribunals of the Member States to ensure uniform interpretation and application of that law within the European Union.

This observation draws upon the Court's case law. For instance, in a case concerning a limitation on its jurisdiction contained in the ECSC Treaty which, while attributing to the

Court the sole jurisdiction to rule on the validity of acts of the then High Authority (later the Commission), did not provide for the possibility of preliminary rulings on questions of interpretation, the Court had the following to say: it would be "contrary to the objectives and the coherence of the Treaties" if the Court of Justice were the ultimate arbiter on questions of interpretation of the treaty establishing the then European Economic Community (EEC, later to become the EC) and the European Atomic Energy Community (EAEC) but such jurisdiction in respect of the ECSC Treaty were to belong exclusively to the national courts, "whose interpretations might differ," and so the Court of Justice "were to have no power to ensure that such rules were given a uniform interpretation."[11]

The Court of Justice has also referred to the preliminary ruling procedure as a mechanism to fill in the gaps and ensure respect for the principle of effective judicial protection when acknowledging that such gaps may exist with regard to the right, under Article 263 TFEU, to bring actions of annulment, which is circumscribed by some rather strict conditions. The Court, in the context of the control of the validity of Union acts, has stated, inter alia, that "requests for preliminary rulings, like actions for annulment, constitute means for reviewing the legality of acts of the Community institutions."[12] Further, when in 2002 upholding a rather strict interpretation of Article 230(4) EC (now Article 263 TFEU) concerning the right of private persons to bring actions for annulment, the Court hastened to add that there were other remedies and procedures available, including the possibility to plead the invalidity of Community acts before the national courts and ask them to make a reference to the Court of Justice for a preliminary ruling on validity. It was thus up to the member states to establish a system of legal remedies and procedures which ensure respect for the right to effective judicial protection.[13] In accordance with this view, Article 19(1) of the Treaty on European Union (TEU), as amended by the Treaty of Lisbon, now provides that "Member States shall provide remedies sufficient to ensure effective legal protection in the fields covered by Union law."

To mention another example, in a more recent case where the Court had to deny the admissibility of actions for damages under the then "third pillar" of the Union, and more precisely, Article 35 EU contained in Title VI EU (police and judicial cooperation in criminal matters),[14] the Court found solace in the preliminary ruling procedure, which "is designed to guarantee observance of the law in the interpretation and application of the Treaty." It would, according to the Court, run counter to that objective if the then Article 35(1) EU, which provided for the availability of preliminary rulings only under some conditions, were to be given a narrow interpretation. And so the right of a national court to make a reference to the Court of Justice existed "in respect of all measures adopted by the Council, whatever their nature or form, which are intended to have legal effects in relation to third parties,"[15] including measures that, according to their title and the wording of the Treaty, would have fallen outside the preliminary ruling procedure.

This emphasis on the role of the national judicial system and the preliminary ruling procedure as a key component of the EU judicial system as a whole was brought into sharp focus in an opinion the Court of Justice gave on the compatibility with Union law of the envisaged new judicial system for a European uniform patent system.[16] There was a proposal to create an international court with participation also of non-EU states, excluding the corresponding right (and in some cases duty) of the national courts of the EU member states to request preliminary rulings. The Court of Justice held such a system, which would have meant an "outsourcing" of the judicial functions of the EU national courts under Union law to international courts going beyond the EU framework, incompatible with the Union legal order. The main reason was that the proposed system would, without a basis in Union primary law, have deprived the national courts of the member states from their constitutional right (and duty) to function as EU courts. The Court of Justice stated that the Union courts in Luxembourg and the national courts fulfill a "duty entrusted to them both" of ensuring that in the interpretation and application of the treaties the law is observed. The Court added that the tasks attributed not only to the Union courts but also to the national courts are "indispensable to the preservation of the very nature of the law established by the Treaties."[17]

It is not easy to detect this fundamental role of the national courts in the EU judicial system in the Statute of the Court of Justice of the European Union.[18] The statute seems to be based primarily on the idea of direct actions such as infringement actions and actions for annulment, and it includes appeals from decisions of the General Court rather than requests for preliminary rulings.[19] Until recently, the same bias existed in the Court's rules of procedure.[20] When the Court began preparing a recast of these rules, it was from the outset clear that the preliminary rulings procedure had to be given pride of place. The new rules of procedure have been completely restructured as compared to the previous rules, which were focused on actions for annulment and other direct actions, and now provide for more detailed rules on references for preliminary rulings contained in Title III, which precedes Title IV on direct actions and Title V on appeals from the General Court.[21]

The Main Features of the Procedure

According to Article 267(1) TFEU, the Court of Justice shall have jurisdiction to give preliminary rulings concerning: (1) the interpretation of the treaties and (2) the validity and interpretation of acts of the institutions, bodies, offices, or agencies of the Union. This provision thus makes a distinction between questions of *interpretation*, which can concern both primary ("the Treaties") and secondary law (such as legislative, delegated, and implementing acts adopted by the Union institutions), and questions of *validity*, which in the provision are limited to acts of secondary law.

The Court of Justice is thus supposed not to enter into questions of the validity of primary law, which, in principle, is at the discretion of the "Masters of the Treaties," in other words, the member states. The Court has, in fact, held that it has no jurisdiction to consider the legality of provisions of primary law.[22] There may today be some caveats to this observation. Thus, in a fairly recent case which concerned the legality of using the so-called simplified revision procedure, provided for in Article 48(6) TEU, for adding to Article 136 TFEU (and thus for amending primary law) an explicit authorization to establish a stability mechanism to support financially weak eurozone member states, the Court examined whether the conditions for applying the simplified revision procedure were fulfilled (the Court answered in the affirmative).[23]

As to questions of interpretation, a distinction has to be made between interpretation and application. To cite the aforementioned recommendations addressed to national courts and tribunals,[24] the role of the Court of Justice is "to give an interpretation of European Union law … not to apply that law to the factual situation underlying the main proceedings, which is the task of the national court." Neither is it the task of the Court of Justice to decide issues of fact raised in the main proceedings before the national judge or to resolve differences of opinion on the interpretation and application of rules of national law.[25] These distinctions are not always easy to make in concrete cases. The borderline between application and interpretation is particularly fluid. To determine that it is a question of application may require a certain degree of interpretation, and an interpretation *in abstracto*, without any regard for the application of the norm as interpreted to the facts at hand, may be difficult and even undesirable.[26]

Article 267 TFEU endows all courts and tribunals of the member states with the competence ("may") to request the Court of Justice to give a ruling on the aforementioned questions of interpretation and validity if they consider that a decision on the question is necessary to enable them to give judgment in cases before them. This right of national courts is a right directly attributed by Union law (notably Article 267 TFEU) and it cannot be limited by national law to certain courts or certain cases only.[27]

According to Article 100(1) of the new Rules of Procedure of the Court of Justice of 2012, the Court shall remain seized of a request for a preliminary ruling for as long as it is not withdrawn by the court or tribunal which made that request to the Court.[28] The Court of Justice has held that in cases involving a separate appeal against the decision of a lower court to make a reference to the Court of Justice, while the case remains pending before the lower court, an appellate court cannot prevent the lower court from exercising the right, conferred on it by the treaty, to make a reference to the Court of Justice. This Court must abide by the decision to make a reference,

> which must have its full effect so long as it has not been revoked or amended by the referring court, such revocation or amendment being matters on which that court alone is able to take a decision.[29]

The Court of Justice has further held that ordinary national courts cannot, by virtue of national constitutional law obliging them to submit questions of constitutionality to a national constitutional court, be prevented from referring questions of EU law to the Court of Justice and this, if need be, before submitting the question of constitutionality to the constitutional court.[30]

This right, conferred directly by EU law and Article 267 TFEU in particular, and the obligation, in principle, of the Court of Justice to rule on the questions put by the national judge, does not imply that the Court of Justice is hindered to control that the conditions of Article 267 are fulfilled. Not only should the questions referred concern the validity or interpretation of EU law and not national law but the body making a reference must be a "court or tribunal" and this court or tribunal must "consider that a decision on the question is necessary to enable it to give judgment."

As to the notion of *court or tribunal*, there is extensive case law from the Court of Justice which cannot be analyzed in greater detail here.[31] Suffice it to note that the Court has emphasized that this question is governed by Union law alone and has summarized some of the factors to be taken into account in the following way:

> the Court takes account of a number of factors, such as whether the body is established by law, whether it is permanent, whether its jurisdiction is compulsory, whether its procedure is *inter partes*, whether it applies rules of law and whether it is independent.[32]

The Court of Justice has also specified that the courts and tribunals envisaged in Article 267 TFEU must be courts or tribunals of the member states, not international courts or courts of third states (but a court entitled to use Article 267 may be a court common to a number of member states[33]).[34]

As to the requirement that a preliminary ruling is necessary to enable the national court to give a judgment, the Court of Justice has specified that the ruling must be necessary in order to give a judgment in a real case pending before the national court. The questions should thus not be hypothetical, and the Court's answer should be necessary to enable the national court to give a judgment, meaning that the interpretation of Union law sought should not be unrelated to the actual facts of the main action or to its purpose.[35] The case before the national court should be real and not purely fictitious.[36] As explained in greater detail later in the chapter, the order for reference should also, in order to be admissible, contain a certain minimum degree of information concerning the case pending before the national judge, including a statement of the reasons that prompted the referring court to inquire about the interpretation or validity of provisions of Union law.

This information is important not only for the Court of Justice but also for the interested persons who, according to Article 23 of the Statute of the Court of Justice of the European Union, have the right to participate in the written and oral parts of the procedure by submitting statements and observations (notably the parties to the main proceedings, the member states, and the European Commission). Their statements and observations will be based mainly on the decision of the national judge to request a preliminary ruling and, as will be explained, it is only this decision, not the national files that accompany it, which is translated by the translation services of the Court of Justice into all the official languages of the European Union and served on the interested persons in their respective language.

When is There an Obligation to Refer?

While (according to Article 267(2) TFEU) national courts and tribunals "may" request the Court of Justice to give a ruling on questions concerning Union law raised before them, the third paragraph of this article provides that they "shall" do so if they constitute courts or tribunals "against whose decisions there is no judicial remedy under national law."

This obligation, in principle, to refer a case to the Court of Justice thus presupposes that it is a national court of last instance (which is not necessarily a supreme court, as certain judgments of, say, appellate courts may be final). The Court of Justice has sometimes had to take a position as to whether a national court belongs to this category. The Court has held, for instance, that the decisions of an appellate court that can be challenged before a supreme court are not decisions of a court of last instance even if the examination of the merits of the appeal is subject to a prior declaration of admissibility by the supreme court.[37]

A textual reading of Article 267(3) TFEU could lead to the conclusion that a court of last instance is always obliged to refer any question concerning the interpretation of Union law to the Court of Justice. Such an unconditional obligation could soon lead the docket of the Court to explode, and the Court would be unable to give rulings within a reasonable time frame. Already at the beginning of the 1980s the Court, by referring to an older judgment from the 1960s, had occasion to reaffirm that the obligation to refer would not apply, neither to situations of application rather than interpretation nor to situations where the question of interpretation raised before the national court "is materially identical with a question which has already been the subject of a preliminary ruling in a similar case."[38] The Court then added that the same effect, as regards the limits set to the obligation laid down by Article 267(3), may be produced "where previous decisions of the Court have already dealt with the point of law in question, irrespective of the nature of the proceedings which led to those decisions," and "even though the questions at issue are not strictly identical."[39] The latter type of situation is thus one where the answer to the question can be inferred from the Court's case law rather than following directly from an earlier case concerning an identical question.

The Court did not stop there, however, but introduced also a third category of situations, which have been called actes clairs: the correct application of Union law "may be so obvious as to leave no scope for any reasonable doubt as to the manner in which the question raised is to be resolved."[40] Some caveats were, on the other hand, attached to this possibility. The national judges should use the *acte clair* possibility only if they are convinced that the matter is equally obvious to the courts of the other member states and to the Court of Justice. In such an assessment, the characteristic features of Union law and the particular difficulties to which its interpretation gives rise should be taken into account. The Court recalled that Union legislation is drafted in several languages, that legal concepts do not necessarily have the same meaning in Union law and in national law, and that Union law must be placed in its broader context (contextual interpretation) and account taken of its objectives (teleological interpretation).[41]

These so-called *CILFIT* criteria are also reflected in Article 99 of the Rules of Procedure of the Court of Justice.[42] According to this provision, the Court may, in certain cases, decide to rule by reasoned order instead of a judgment. This option will imply a simplification of the procedures in that there will be no oral hearing and no opinion of an advocate general (although the advocate general must be heard before the decision to rule by order is taken). Article 99 lists three situations which enable a reasoned order: where a question referred to the Court "is identical to a question on which the Court has already ruled," where the reply to such a question "may be clearly deduced from existing case-law," and finally where the answer to the question "admits of no reasonable doubt." It can thus be generally assumed that where the Court gives an order instead of a judgment, the referring judge would have been authorized not to refer his case at all but instead could have ruled himself in application of the *CILFIT* criteria.

The foregoing discussion concerns matters of interpretation (of norms of Union law). As to questions of validity, the situation is somewhat different. In a judgment rendered a few years after its *CILFIT* decision, the Court of Justice held that if a national court has doubts about the legality of an act of the Union, the national court may not itself decide that the act is invalid but must seek a ruling on its invalidity from the Court of Justice in order to be able to set the act aside.[43] If the national judge has serious doubts about the legality of the Union act, it is arguable that the "may" expressed in Article 267(2) TFEU becomes a "shall."[44] In any case, while being able to determine that the act is valid (if he does not have serious doubts about its legality), the national judge may never decide that the act is invalid. This does not, according to the case law of the Court of Justice, prevent the national court from suspending, as a matter of interim relief, the application of the contested act until the Court of Justice has given a ruling.[45]

What is Required of a Request for a Preliminary Ruling?

In its previous information note on references from national courts for a preliminary ruling, the Court of Justice laid down some recommendations, based on past experience, for the drafting of a decision referring matters of Union law to the Court. The main part of these recommendations has now been elevated to a provision of the new rules of procedure.[46] Article 94 of the rules, entitled "Content of the request for a preliminary ruling," contains a list of matters which, in addition to the actual questions posed to the Court, should be included in the order of reference. The request shall thus contain

1. a summary of the subject matter of the dispute and the relevant findings of fact as determined by the referring court or tribunal, or, at least, an account of the facts on which the questions are based;
2. the tenor of any national provisions applicable in the case and, where appropriate, the relevant national case law; and
3. a statement of the reasons that prompted the referring court or tribunal to inquire about the interpretation or validity of certain provisions of European Union law, and the relationship between these provisions and the national legislation applicable to the main proceedings.

It should be underlined that this list now contains legally binding requirements, and that referrals that do not comply with them may lead to a decision on inadmissibility by the Court of Justice.

Among other matters that the referring court may wish to include in the order of reference, which are also mentioned in the rules of procedure, are the following: requesting that one or more persons or entities concerned by the case be rendered anonymous (Article 95(2)); informing the Court of Justice that a new party has been admitted to the main proceedings (in which case this party may, from that moment on, participate in the proceedings) (Article 97(2)); and requesting that the case be dealt with pursuant to an expedited procedure or under an urgent procedure (Articles 105 and 107).

The new recommendations to national courts and tribunals, which replace the previous information note mentioned earlier,[47] provide in addition that the Union law provisions relevant to the case "should be identified as accurately as possible in the request for a preliminary ruling," which should also contain, "if need be, a brief summary of the relevant arguments of the parties to the main proceedings" (paragraph 23). Moreover, the recommendations instruct the national court, "if it considers itself able to do so," to "briefly state its view on the answers to be given to the questions referred for a preliminary ruling," as such information "may be useful to the Court, particularly where it is called upon to give a preliminary ruling in an expedited or urgent procedure" (paragraph 24).

Procedural Issues

Article 23 of the statute[48] provides that after the national court or tribunal has notified to the Court of Justice that it has suspended its proceedings and that it is referring the case to the Court of Justice, the registrar of the Court shall notify the decision of the national court to the parties to the main proceedings, to the member states, to the Commission, and to the institution, body, or agency of the Union that adopted the act of which the validity or interpretation is in dispute. Within two months of this notification, these interested persons are entitled to submit written observations to the Court of Justice. Article 96(2) of the Rules of Procedure[49] spells out that nonparticipation in the written part of the procedure does not preclude participation in the oral part. In fact, if an interested person has not participated in the written part, Article 76(3) of the Rules of Procedure provide that the discretion granted to the Court of Justice in Article 76(2) as to whether an oral hearing is necessary does not apply to requests for a hearing submitted by an interested person who has not participated in the written part of the procedure; in such a case, the oral hearing has to be granted, provided that the request is reasoned.

According to Article 23 of the Statute and Article 96 of the Rules of Procedure, also nonmember states that are parties to the Agreement on the European Economic Area, that is, Iceland, Liechtenstein, and Norway, and the European Free Trade Association Surveillance Authority may submit observations where a question concerning one of the fields of application of the European Economic Area Agreement has been referred to the Court of Justice for a preliminary ruling. Moreover, nonmember states that are parties to other agreements concluded with the European Union may, if the agreement so provides, submit observations if a question falling within the scope of that agreement has been referred to the Court of Justice.

At the request of the referring court or tribunal or, exceptionally, at the Court of Justice's own motion, the Court[50] may decide that a reference for a preliminary ruling is to be determined pursuant to an expedited procedure or, alternatively, if the reference raises questions in the areas covered by Title V of Part Three of the TFEU (the area of freedom, security, and justice), an urgent procedure.[51] In the expedited procedure, the time limit for written observations, which will be fixed by the president of the Court, may be considerably shorter than the normal two months (although Article 105(3) of the Rules of Procedure of the Court of Justice prescribes that it may not be shorter than fifteen days).

In the urgent procedure, the time limit, which will be fixed by a designated chamber of the Court consisting of five judges,[52] may be even shorter. In the urgent procedure, the right of the member states to submit written observations is limited to the member state from which the reference is made. The decision to deal with a reference under the urgent procedure is taken by the designated chamber, which will normally also rule on the substance of the case (but the designated chamber may decide to sit in a formation of three judges and also request the Court to assign the case to a formation composed of a greater number of judges). In cases of "extreme urgency," the designated chamber may, according to Article 111 of the Rules of Procedure, decide to omit the written part of the procedure (this has so far never happened in practice).

The request for a preliminary ruling (the decision of the national court) shall be served on the member states (and, as the case may be, certain nonmember states) in the original version, but accompanied by a translation made by the translation services of the Court of Justice into the official language of the member state to which they are being addressed (or one of the official languages of the European Union chosen by an addressee nonmember state). If the request for a preliminary ruling is lengthy (in practice more than twenty pages), the translation may, according to Article 98(1) of the Rules of Procedure, be replaced by the translation of a summary of the request. The written observations of the interested persons are based on the decision of the national court so translated and notified. The oral hearing, if it is being organized (which is normally the case as far as preliminary ruling procedures are concerned), will provide the first and only opportunity for the interested persons to make observations on the written observations submitted by other interested persons.

In all proceedings before the Court of Justice, whether preliminary ruling procedures or not, the Court may (according to Article 61 of the Rules of Procedure) invite the interested persons to answer certain questions in writing or at the oral hearing and may also invite the participants in the oral hearing to concentrate in their oral pleadings on one or more specified issues. In addition, the judge-rapporteur and the advocate general may request the interested persons to submit information and documents, and they may also send to them questions to be answered at the hearing. Moreover, Article 101 of the Rules of Procedure provides that in preliminary ruling procedures, the Court may request clarification from the referring court or tribunal within a time limit prescribed by the Court. Such requests for clarification, which may address issues concerning, for instance, relevant national law or the facts of the case, are quite rare in practice.[53]

In line with what has been said previously about the exclusive competence of the referring court or tribunal to decide whether to refer a case and whether to maintain a referral, Article 100(1) of the Rules of Procedure of the Court of Justice states that the Court shall remain seized of a request for a preliminary ruling for as long as it is not withdrawn by the court or tribunal which made the request. If, on the other hand, the request is withdrawn, the Court of Justice is no longer competent to give a ruling. Article 100(1), second sentence, however, adds a minor exception to this rule: the withdrawal may no longer be taken into account by the Court of Justice after notice of the date of delivery of the judgment has been served on the interested persons.

The Ruling Given by the Court of Justice

A decision of the Court of Justice is normally given in the form of a judgment. According to Article 87 of the Rules of Procedure,[54] all judgments should contain, inter alia, a summary of the facts, the grounds for the decision, and the operative part of the judgment. In preliminary ruling procedures, the operative part will attempt to provide an answer to the questions as they have been put by the national judge. As was noted previously, the Court may also reply by reasoned order if one of the three conditions of Article 99 of the Rules of Procedure is fulfilled.

A judgment is as a rule preceded by an opinion of an advocate general. The advocates general are members of the Court who give an independent opinion on how the questions referred should, in their view, be answered. As they are not judges, they do not take part in the deliberations on judgments and orders. Pursuant to Article 20(5) of the statute, the Court, after having heard the advocate general, may, if it considers that the case "raises no new point of law," decide that the case can be determined without an opinion from an advocate general. Nor will there be such an opinion if the Court, after having heard the advocate general, decides to reply by reasoned order. If a request for a preliminary ruling is dealt with under an expedited procedure or under an urgent procedure, there will be no formal opinion of an advocate general but the advocate general will always be heard, which in practice implies that he or she will put forward his or her views normally in an abridged (although written) form and that these views will be rendered public.

According to Article 102 of the Rules of Procedure of the Court of Justice, it shall be for the referring court or tribunal to decide as to the costs of the preliminary ruling proceedings. As is set out in Articles 115 to 118, however, this does not prevent the Court of Justice from granting legal aid to a party to the main proceedings who is wholly or in part unable to meet the costs of the proceedings before the Court of Justice. If the applicant has already obtained legal aid before the referring court or tribunal, he shall produce the national decision and specify what is covered by the sums already granted.

Clerical mistakes, errors in calculations, and obvious inaccuracies in judgments or orders may, according to Article 103 of the Rules of Procedure, be rectified by the Court of Justice of its own motion or at the request of an interested person made within two weeks after delivery of the judgment or the service of the order. Article 104 of the Rules of Procedure makes it clear that the general possibility, pursuant to Article 158 of the Rules of Procedure, to request an interpretation of judgments and orders does not apply to preliminary ruling proceedings. Instead, the referring court or tribunal may, if it considers that a preliminary ruling does not provide sufficient guidance, decide to make a further reference to the Court of Justice. Such requests for clarification are rare but they do take place from time to time.[55]

It follows from the case law of the Court of Justice that rulings given by the Court of Justice are not only binding on the referring court or tribunal but also decide questions of validity and interpretation of Union law in a manner binding, in principle, on the courts and authorities of all member states and with effect *ex tunc* (retroactively) and not only as from the delivery of the judgment or service of the order.[56] However, legal security may require that national judgments and decisions that have become final are not reopened, despite a subsequent ruling from the Court of Justice suggesting that they were not in conformity with Union law as interpreted by the Court.[57] Moreover, the Court of Justice may under exceptional circumstances decide to limit the effects of the judgment in time.[58]

Final Observations

When introduced in the early 1950s, the preliminary ruling procedure constituted a radical novelty in the context of international organizations. Over the years, it has become a well-established and even crucial part of the EU legal order and judicial system in particular. It has also in quantitative terms become the most important category of cases the Court of Justice has to deal with. While the statute of the Court still reflects this procedure rather inadequately, case law and the new Rules of Procedure of the Court of 2012 have brought a number of precisions to its contours, conditions, and procedural modalities. Within the context of the constitutionalization of the EU legal order in general, the preliminary ruling procedure has come to underline the constitutional role of the national courts of the EU member states *as* EU courts and the powers they enjoy, in direct application of Union law, to be in direct dialogue with the Court of Justice, without undue interference from national governments, parliaments, or other national courts. At the same time, the developments outlined above have put the focus also on the responsibility of national courts to contribute to the smooth functioning of the system and, in particular, to provide, by their requests for preliminary ruling, a good legal and factual basis for the Court of Justice in order to enable it to give a useful answer to the questions put to it. Perhaps there will come a day when the number of such requests will be so high that some filtering mechanism has to be envisaged. In any case, we are not there yet, and for the time being, insisting on the existing requirements stemming from Article 267 TFEU, Article 94, and other provisions of the Rules of Procedure of the Court, read in junction with the recommendations addressed to national court and tribunals and the case law of the Court of Justice itself, should by and large suffice to meet the challenges of today and of the near future.

Notes

1 Allan Rosas and Lorna Armati, *EU Constitutional Law: An Introduction* (Oxford: Hart, 2012), esp. Chap. 1–6.

2 See Articles 13(1) and 19(1) of the Treaty on European Union (TEU), Articles 251–281 of the Treaty on the Functioning of the European Union (TFEU) and the Protocol (No 3) on the Statute of the Court of Justice of the European Union annexed to the TEU and the TFEU. The only specialized court that exists at the time of writing is the EU Civil Service Tribunal. The official name of the institution which encompasses all three courts is the "Court of Justice of the European Union."

3 On the judicial system of the European Union more generally and the procedural remedies available under that system see, e.g., Henry G. Schermers and Denis F. Walbroeck, *Judicial Protection in the European Union*, 6th ed. (The Hague: Kluwer Law International, 2001); Koen Lenaerts, Dirk Arts, and Ignace Maselis, *Procedural Law of the European Union* (London: Sweet & Maxwell, 2006); and Pascal Cardonnel, Allan Rosas, and Nils Wahl, eds., *Constitutionalising the EU Judicial System: Essays in Honour of Pernilla Lindh* (Oxford: Hart, 2012).

4 On the preliminary ruling procedure in general see, e.g., Lenaerts, Arts, and Maselis, *Procedural Law of the European Union*, 36–82, 174–199, and 353–368; Schermers and Walbroek, *Judicial Protection in the European Union*, 218–307; Caroline Naômé, *Le Renvoi préjudiciel en droit européen: Guide pratique* (Brussels: Éditions Larcier, 2010); Morten Broberg and Niels Fenger, *Preliminary References to the European Court of Justice* (Oxford: Oxford University Press, 2014); and Georges Vandersanden, *La Procédure préjudicielle devant la Cour de justice de l'Union européenne* (Brussels: Bruylant, 2011).

5 Article 41 ECSC. The ECSC ceased to exist in 2002, when its assets were transferred to the (then) European Community (EC). See Rosas and Armati, *EU Constitutional Law*, 11.

6 On the Statute, see n 2. The new Rules of Procedure of the Court of Justice, which constitute a recast of the previous Rules of Procedure, were published in [2012] OJ L 265/1.
7 At the end of 2011, there were 849 cases pending before the Court of Justice and 1,308 cases pending before the General Court. The average duration of proceedings before the Court of Justice as far as preliminary rulings were concerned was 16.4 months, whereas the average duration of proceedings before the General Court, excluding appeals from the Civil Service Tribunal, varied between 20.3 and 50.5 months, depending on the nature of proceedings (20.3 months stood for actions concerning intellectual property and 50.5 months actions in the area of competition law). See Court of Justice of the European Union, *Annual Report 2011* (Luxembourg: Publications Office of the European Union, 2012), 95, 110, 193, and 201, http://curia.europa.eu/jcms/upload/docs/application/pdf/2012-06/ra2011_version_integrale_en.pdf.
8 Ibid., 115–116.
9 Ibid., 2013, 84.
10 Recommendations to national courts and tribunals in relation to the initiation of preliminary ruling proceedings [2012] OJ C 338/1. These recommendations replace the information note on references from national courts for a preliminary ruling (for the latest version of this information note see [2011] OJ C 160/1).
11 Case 221/88 *Busseni* EU:C:1990:84, para 16.
12 Case 314/85 *Foto-Frost* EU:C:1987:452, para 16.
13 Case C-50/00 P *Unión de Pequeños Agricultores* EU:C:2002:462, paras 40–41.
14 The Treaty of Lisbon has replaced Title VI EU (the "third pillar") with new provisions mainly to be found in the TFEU, although some decisions taken under this title may still be applicable during a transitional period.
15 Case C-355/04 P *Segi and Others* EU:C:2007:116, para 53. See also Case C-354/04 P *Gestoras Pro Amnistía and Others* EU:C:2007:115, para 53.
16 Opinion 1/09 (The Draft Agreement on the European and Community Patents Court) EU:C:2011:123. See also Allan Rosas, "The National Judge as EU Judge: Opinion 1/09," in Cardonnel, Rosas, and Wahl, *Constitutionalising the EU Judicial System*, 105–121.
17 Opinion 1/09, n 16 this chapter, paras 69 and 85.
18 On the Statute, see n 2 this chapter.
19 The only clear exception is Article 23 of the statute, which sets out some basic rules relating to the preliminary ruling procedure. Article 23a refers to the possibility of an urgent procedure concerning references for a preliminary ruling relating to the area of freedom, security, and justice. Some other provisions of the statute may be relevant for the preliminary rulings procedure as well, at least *mutatis mutandis*.
20 The original Rules of Procedure were adopted on 4 March 1953. A new version, which remained fundamentally unchanged in structure, was adopted on 19 June 1991 (Consolidated Version of the Rules of Procedure of the Court of Justice [1991] OJ L 176/7) and was subsequently amended on several occasions. For the latest modifications, see Amendments to the Rules of Procedure of the Court of Justice [2011] OJ L 162/17.
21 See n 6 this chapter.
22 Joined Cases 31/86 and 35/86 *LAISA and CPC España v. Council* EU:C:1988:211.
23 Case C-370/12 *Pringle* EU:C:2012:756. One of the issues raised in this case is whether the amendment to Article 136 TFEU will increase the competences conferred on the Union in the treaties. The simplified revision procedure provided for in Article 48(6) TEU cannot be used to amend the treaties in such a way that the competences of the Union are increased. See also Rosas and Armati, *EU Constitutional Law*, 38–39.
24 See n 10.
25 Recommendations, n 10 this chapter, para 7.
26 See, e.g., Case 283/81 *CILFIT* EU:C:1982:335, Opinion of Advocate General Capotori and Case C-338/95 *Wiener* EU:C:1997:552, Opinion of Advocate General Jacobs, paras 12–13.
27 See, e.g., Case C-210/06 *Cartesio* EU:C:2008:723, paras 88 and 93; Joined Cases C-188/10 and C-189/10 *Melki* and *Abdeli* EU:C:2010:363, paras 40–45, and the case law cited in these judgments.

28 See n 6 this chapter. Article 100(1) adds that the withdrawal of a request may be taken into account until notice of the date of delivery of the judgment has been served on the interested persons.
29 Case 210/06 *Cartesio*, n 27 above, paras 88–98, quotation from para 97. Cf. the Order of 4 June 2009 in Case C-129/08 *Cloet and Cloet* EU:C:2009:347, paras 8–11. See also the Order of the Court in Case C-525/06 *Nationale Loterij* EU:C:2009:179, para 11.
30 Joined Cases C-188/10 and C-189/10 *Melki and Abdeli*, n 27 this chapter, paras 45–47; Case C-112/13 *A v. B and Others* EU:C:2014:2195.
31 The case law of the Court concerning the notion of court or tribunal is presented and discussed, e.g., in the Opinions of Advocates General Sharpston (in Case C-363/11 *Elegktiko Synedrio*, EU:C:2012:825, paras 5–48) and Kokott (in Case C-394/11 *Belov* EU:C:2013:48, paras 24–50). See also, e.g., Naômé, *Le Renvoi préjudiciel*, 94 et seq; Broberg and Fenger, *Preliminary References to the European Court of Justice*, 59–104.
32 See, e.g., Case C-210/06 *Cartesio*, n 27 this chapter, para 55; Case C-196/09 *Miles and Others* EU:C:2011:388, para 37.
33 Case C-337/95 *Parfums Christian Dior* EU:C:1997:517, para 21; Opinion 1/09, n 16 this chapter, para 82.
34 Case C-196/09 *Miles and Others*, n 32 this chapter, paras 38–42; Opinion 1/09, n 16 this chapter, para 80.
35 See, e.g., Case C-83/91 *Meilicke* EU:C:1992:332; and Case C-210/06 *Cartesio*, n 27 this chapter, para 67. See also Naomé, *Le Renvoi préjudiciel*, 113–122; Broberg and Fenger, *Preliminary References to the European Court of Justice*, 164–211.
36 See, e.g., Case 104/79 *Foglia* EU:C:1980:73.
37 Case C-99/00 *Lyckeskog* EU:C:2002:329, paras 14–16. See also Case C-210/06 *Cartesio*, n 27 this chapter, paras 75–79.
38 In Case 283/81 *CILFIT*, n 26 this chapter, para 13, the Court is in this regard citing Joined Cases 28/62 to 30/62 *Da Costa* EU:C:1963:6.
39 Case 283/81 *CILFIT*, n 26 this chapter, para 14.
40 Ibid., para 16.
41 Ibid., paras 17–20.
42 See n 6 this chapter.
43 Case 314/85 *Foto-Frost*, n 12 this chapter.
44 Rosas and Armati, *EU Constitutional Law*, 275.
45 Joined Cases 143/88 and C-92/89 *Zuckerfabrik Süderdithmarschen* and *Zuckerfabrik Soes* EU:C:1991:65, paras 16–21. See also Case C-466/93 *Atlanta Fruchthandelsgesellschaft* EU:C:1995:370, para 22; and Case C-68/95 *T. Port* EU:C:1996:452, para 49.
46 See n 6 this chapter.
47 See n 10 this chapter.
48 See n 2 this chapter.
49 See n 6 this chapter.
50 The decision is taken either by the president of the Court (concerning expedited procedures) or by a designated chamber of the Court (concerning urgent procedures).
51 On the expedited and urgent procedures see, e.g., Naômé, *Le Renvoi préjudiciel*, 143–148; Broberg and Fenger, *Preliminary References to the European Court of Justice*, 385–395. On the urgent procedure, initiated in 2008, in particular see, e.g., Allan Rosas, "Justice in Haste, Justice Denied? The European Court of Justice and the Area of Freedom, Security and Justice," *The Cambridge Yearbook of European Legal Studies* 11 (2008–2009); and Antonio Tizzano and Bruno Gencarelli, "La Procédure préjudicielle d'urgence devant la Cour de Justice de l'Union européenne," in *Chemins d'Europe: Mélanges en l'honneur de Jean Paul Jacqué* (Paris: Dalloz, 2011), 647.
52 That the designated chamber is a chamber of five judges is clear from Article 108(1) in combination with Article 28(2) of the Rules of Procedure. It is in practice designated for a period of one year, after which the responsibility for dealing with urgent cases will be transferred to another chamber (at the time of writing, there are five chambers consisting of five judges).
53 For an example, see Case C-476/01 *Kapper* EU:C:2004:261, para 26.

54 See n 6 this chapter.
55 See, e.g., Naômé, *Le Renvoi préjudiciel*, 291–296.
56 See, e.g., Case C-262/96 *Sürül* EU:C:1999:228, para 107; Naômé, *Le Renvoi préjudiciel*, 274–276; and Broberg and Fenger, *Preliminary References to the European Court of Justice*, 431–445.
57 See, e.g., Case C-453/00 *Kühne & Heitz* EU:C:2004:17; Joined Cases C-392/04 and C-422/04 *I-21 Germany and Arcor* EU:C:2006:586; Case C-2/06 *Kempter* EU:C:2008:78; and Naômé, *Le Renvoi préjudiciel*, 276–278.
58 See, e.g., Case C-308/93 *Cabanis-Issarte* EU:C:1996:169, paras 46–48; and Broberg and Fenger, *Preliminary References to the European Court of Justice*, 445–457.

References

Broberg, Morten, and Niels Fenger. *Preliminary References to the European Court of Justice*. Oxford: Oxford University Press, 2014.

Cardonnel, Pascal, Allan Rosas, and Nils Wahl, eds. *Constitutionalising the EU Judicial System: Essays in Honour of Pernilla Lindh*. Oxford: Hart, 2012.

Court of Justice of the European Union. *Annual Report 2011*. Luxembourg: Publications Office of the European Union, 2012. Accessed 3 June 3 2015. http://curia.europa.eu/jcms/upload/docs/application/pdf/2012-06/ra2011_version_integrale_en.pdf.

Lenaerts, Koen, Dirk Arts, and Ignace Maselis, eds. *Procedural Law of the European Union*. London: Sweet & Maxwell, 2006.

Naômé, Caroline. *Le Renvoi préjudiciel en droit européen: Guide pratique*. Brussels: Éditions Larcier, 2010.

Rosas, Allan. "Justice in Haste, Justice Denied? The European Court of Justice and the Area of Freedom, Security and Justice." *The Cambridge Yearbook of European Legal Studies* 11 (2008–2009): 1–13.

Rosas, Allan. "The National Judge as EU Judge: Opinion 1/09." In Cardonnel, Rosas, and Wahl *Constitutionalising the EU Judicial System*, 105–121.

Rosas, Allan, and Lorna Armati. *EU Constitutional Law: An Introduction*. Oxford: Hart, 2012.

Schermers, Henry G., and Denis F. Walbroeck, *Judicial Protection in the European Union*. The Hague: Kluwer Law International, 2001.

Tizzano, Antonio, and Bruno Gencarelli. "La Procédure préjudicielle d'urgence devant la Cour de justice de l'Union européenne." In *Chemins d'Europe: Mélanges en l'honneur de Jean Paul Jacqué*. Paris: Dalloz, 2011.

Vandersanden, Georges. *La Procédure préjudicielle devant la Cour de justice de l'Union européenne*. Brussels: Bruylant, 2011.

Part IV

Economic Dimensions of the European Union

14

The Construction of the Internal Market

Catherine Barnard

Introduction

The creation of a common market lay at the heart of the original European Community (EC) project; it has been the single EU policy which has commanded universal support from the member states. Article 2 EC (now repealed) said that the (then) Community had as its task the establishment of a common market (Article 3(3) of the Treaty on European Union continues to provide that "The Union shall establish an internal market"), and one of the activities of the Community listed in Article 3 EC (now repealed) was the creation of "an internal market characterized by the abolition, as between Member States, of obstacles to the free movement of goods, persons, services and capital" (now replicated in Article 26 of the Treaty on the Functioning of the European Union (TFEU)). The idea underpinning the original treaty was that "eliminating the barriers which divide Europe" (i.e., by facilitating free trade between states) would "ensure the economic and social progress of their countries by common action" with "the essential purpose of constantly improving the living and working conditions of their peoples."[1]

Views as to how the single market is to be achieved have varied over time, as have the various techniques used to achieve it; but attainment of the single market continues to lie at the forefront of the European Union's policy agenda, albeit that it no longer enjoys the preeminent position it once did. This chapter will first outline the three main phases of the development of the single market, together with the impetus and philosophy underpinning it; it will then examine some of the challenges facing the single market.

The Creation of the Single Market

Phase one: Tolerance of the single market

The idea behind the original EEC Treaty was simple: barriers to free movement of goods, persons, services, and capital would be removed through the use of treaty provisions that prohibited obstacles to free movement.[2] In exceptional cases (e.g., public policy, security, and

A Companion to European Union Law and International Law, First Edition.
Edited by Dennis Patterson and Anna Södersten.

health) prescribed by, for example, Article 36 TFEU on free movement of goods and Article 58 TFEU on free movement of capital, national rules would be allowed to stand; otherwise, they should be abolished. This approach, based on *negative* integration was always intended to be supplemented by *positive* integration: EU legislation adopted under prescribed legal bases, notably Articles 115 and 352 TFEU. These legal bases required unanimous voting in Council, which limited their utility, a problem exacerbated by the French "empty chair policy" of the 1960s. Further, the legislation that was adopted tended to be exhaustive in nature, thereby leading to a protracted negotiation process that tended to choke attempts at reform. It was also politically unpopular, particularly when it came to food. The idea of a "Euro-sausage," much caricatured in the Euroskeptic press, might have been the product of this centralized approach.

In fact, while quotas and customs duties levied on products imported from other member states were successfully abolished according to the timescale laid down by the Treaty of Rome, lack of political will more generally stymied the achievement of the full potential of the common market, and it took the Court of Justice to step in and inject some momentum into the project. This it did with its ruling in *Cassis de Dijon*,[3] where it said that the principle of mutual recognition underpinned Article 34 TFEU. This meant that goods lawfully produced in one member state should be admitted to another member state, without restriction, unless there were good "mandatory requirements" why not. The principle of mutual recognition was rapidly taken up and exploited by the Commission, which used it to underpin some of its legislative proposals, not only in the field of goods but also in respect of free movement of natural and legal persons, especially in respect of recognition of qualifications and financial services.

The significance of the decision in *Cassis de Dijon* cannot be overstated. First, it established the idea that, in principle, all national regulatory standards were equal, and so goods made according to the standards of state A could be freely imported into other member states. This anticipated a high degree of trust between states – easier when there were only nine states than with twenty-eight. Second, and implicitly, *Cassis de Dijon* introduced the idea of home state control: this meant that it was the home state's responsibility to ensure compliance with its rules in respect of goods aimed at both the domestic and export market. Third, it allowed for regulatory diversity: each state could have its own rules on, for example, the production of sausages, which proved legally and politically more popular.

Thus, the effect of *Cassis de Dijon*, together with the Commission's adoption of the mutual recognition principle as a basis for legislative proposals, marked a sea change from a centralized model with the EU institutions in the driving seat to a decentralized model with a much greater role for the states. However, the principle of mutual recognition came at a price for market integration, namely the development of mandatory requirements. Host member states often had good reasons for adopting national rules (e.g., environmental and consumer protection), reasons which were not covered by the treaty derogations. Recognizing this, the Court developed the concept of mandatory requirements, now better known as public interest requirements, in parallel to the express derogations. These public interest requirements allow host states to justify more of their national rules, provided the measures taken by the states are proportionate. Thus, the model of home state control envisaged by *Cassis de Dijon* has always been tempered by host state control, albeit that host states usually face an uphill battle to justify their rules under the mandatory requirements/public policy route.

Where host states do successfully invoke one of the public interest requirements/express derogations, for example, in the field of tobacco control, this has the effect of partitioning the EU market on national lines. This may necessitate EU action to harmonize the rules. However, harmonization requires a more robust legal basis than the original EEC Treaty provided. This was eventually resolved by the Single European Act 1986, the key achievement of Phase Two.

Phase two: Determination to deliver a real single market

By the mid-1980s, Euro-sclerosis had set in and the failure of the common market was plain for all to see. In 1985 Jacques Delors, then president of the European Commission, responded with his ambitious plan for the single market. A White Paper, *Completing the Internal Market*,[4] was drawn up under the direction of the British commissioner, Lord Cockfield, which focused on removing barriers that continued to prevent free movement.[5] It identified three principal obstacles to the completion of the single market:

1. physical barriers to trade – for example, intra-EU border stoppages, customs controls, and associated paperwork;
2. technical barriers to trade – for example, meeting divergent national product standards adopted for health and safety reasons or for consumer and environmental protection, other technical regulations, conflicting business laws, entering nationally protected public procurement markets;[6]
3. fiscal barriers to trade – especially differing rates of VAT and excise duties.

The Cecchini Report on the Cost of Non-Europe[7] anticipated that the growth resulting from the single market would put between four and seven percentage points on the Union's domestic product and the creation of between two and five million new jobs.

The White Paper then identified 300 measures (the final count was 282) necessary to complete the single market. The Single European Act 1986, the first significant treaty amendment after the Treaty of Rome, gave the necessary means to achieve these objectives. It introduced a new legal basis, Article 114 TFEU, which provided for qualified majority voting when enacting measures for the approximation of member states' laws that have as "their object the establishment and functioning of the internal market." The introduction of Article 114 TFEU emphasized that the single market was essentially a lawmaking project. A number of major pieces of legislation have been adopted under this basis, including the Tobacco Advertising Directive 98/34,[8] which we consider in the section Tensions Underlying the Single Market. The SEA also introduced Article 100b EEC into the Treaty of Rome. This required the Commission, together with each member state, to draw up an inventory of national measures which fell under Article 100a EEC (now Article 114 TFEU) and which had not been harmonized. The Council could then decide whether the provisions in force in a member state could be recognized as being equivalent to those in another member state. This power was not used, and Article 100b was abolished by the Amsterdam Treaty.

For presentation purposes, the SEA repackaged the four freedoms into the renamed "internal" or "single" market and, in Article 7a EEC (now Article 26 TFEU), set a new deadline by which they were to be achieved: 31 December 1992.[9] While the deadline was psychologically and politically significant, it had no legal effect.[10] The name change, from "common" to "single" or "internal" market, also had little effect. In reality, the realization of the single market was, and is, dependent on further policy action in an ever-wider range of fields, including competition and social policy.[11]

The legislation adopted in this period also differed from Phase One in that it tended to involve directives, rather than regulations, creating more space for member states to act, and it often set minimum standards on which member states were free to improve. This appeared to create the optimal position of an exhaustively harmonized minimum floor of rights combined with freedom for member states to experiment above that floor. The Commission also experimented with the so-called new approach directives, most famously on toy safety.[12] These directives set out general principles rather than detailed rules, leaving wide latitude for interpretation,[13] and they relied on private bodies to set voluntary standards.

Phase three: Market making, and the european union's response to the crisis

Although the deadline for the completion of the single market was 1992, in fact the single market is not yet – and will probably never be – complete. As the Commission puts it, creating a genuinely integrated market is not a finite task but rather an ongoing process requiring constant effort, vigilance, and updating. With technological and political developments, the environment in which the single market functions is changing all the time. Although many obstacles have been removed, others come to light and will continue to do so and need to be addressed.

That said, the period starting with the late 1990s and onwards has been characterized by "market making": an emphasis on ensuring that EU rules are actually implemented and applied by member states and enforced by the users. There has been a veritable tsunami of Commission documents emphasizing the importance of market making, the most important of these being, in recent years, the Monti Review of May 2010. Monti recognized "integration fatigue," an erosion of the appetite among citizens for a *single* market, and "market fatigue," a reduced confidence in the role of the market. His report was followed up with a relaunch of the single market in spring 2011, grandly named the Single Market Act (SMA) I. This identified "Twelve Levers to boost growth and strengthen confidence"[14] accompanied by fifty complementary actions. These levers included Lever 2, "Citizens mobility," modernizing the rules for the recognition of professional qualifications and improving the portability of pensions, and Lever 5, "services," revising legislation on European standardization and ensuring the implementation of Services Directive 2006/123. With services now occupying over 70 percent of GDP, it is this area that is now attracting the most attention.

Despite all the fanfare surrounding the launch of the SMA I, within eighteen months the Commission felt obliged to issue the SMA II[15] in order to inject some fresh impetus into the program. As the Commission noted, eleven of the twelve key action proposals had not been agreed by the European Parliament and Council. The SMA II largely reiterates the content of SMA I, but it returns to a familiar theme:

> The success of this endeavor will depend on whether Single Market rules are applied on the ground efficiently, in a predictable and reliable manner. To this end, the transposition and day-to-day implementation of Single Market rules by authorities in Member States is of paramount importance. The Commission will devote all its attention to this challenge.[16]

This idea of a "coordinated and cooperative approach" between the Commission and the member states with a "common objective of improved transposition, application and enforcement of single market rules"[17] has been described by Weatherill as "market management."[18] In fact, the program is more far reaching than this. It requires simplification/improving the quality of legislation, as well as implementation and enforcement. In respect of *improving* the quality of draft legislation, the "Better Lawmaking" program,[19] now replaced by the Better Regulation for Growth and Jobs Agenda,[20] requires the screening of *pending* legislative proposals to ensure their consistency with the objectives of the revised Lisbon Strategy, the simplification of *existing* legislation,[21] and improving the quality of *new* Commission proposals, in particular through the systematic use of impact assessment[22] and public consultation.[23] These different strands now fall under the umbrella title of "smart regulation"[24] and form part of the Commission's program on better governance for the single market.[25]

Despite all these initiatives, the problem remains that legislation, like the Services Directive,[26] adopted under the codecision procedure (now the ordinary legislative procedure) is the result of a large-scale political compromise which inevitably means that there are provisions whose meaning is not clear. This makes implementation difficult. Nevertheless, the Commission has improved its practice here too: it produces handbooks, guidelines, and other resources to help steer correct *implementation*.[27] Further, in a strategy described as preventive, the Commission now tries to work with the member states as partners in the implementation process. This includes regular consultation between member state officials negotiating a directive and those (later) responsible for implementation and enforcement, as well as consultation with the Commission officials concerned during the implementation process.

At a more formal level, Directive 98/34[28] requires draft technical standards in the field of goods and information society services to be notified to the Commission in advance of their adoption. With the help of the Court of Justice, which has ruled that unnotified technical standards are unenforceable,[29] this directive has proved its worth in keeping off the statute books of the member states some hundreds of technical standards that would create unjustified obstacles to trade. Lighter versions of the notification procedure can also be found in the Services Directive.

When national rules interfering with the single market do nevertheless get onto the statute book, they can be challenged by individuals through the national courts, by the Commission using the enforcement procedure, and more informally through the SOLVIT network, an online network for settling cross-border disputes informally over the incorrect and inaccurate application of the single market rules.

These steps to ensure the effective operation of the single market are seen as part of the European Union's response to the crisis. In the opening paragraphs of the Commission's communication on better governance for the single market, the Commission says

> The crisis has shown that the EU needs to act to improve its economic model and restore competitiveness. This requires a mix of sound public finances, deep structural reforms and targeted investment. Europe 2020 is the EU's strategy to boost sustainable growth and the creation of jobs and the Single Market has a key role to play in this. The Single Market is a key driver for economic growth. However, to reap the benefits it brings, its rules must be properly implemented and enforced.[30]

While some might doubt whether the effective enforcement of existing rules will be sufficient to provide the boost for growth that the European Union needs, the European Council's emphasis on investments in digital infrastructure and the accelerated deployment of new technologies and its commitment to completing a consumer- and business-friendly Digital Single Market by 2015 do seem to be a step in the right direction.

Other aspects of the single market have also been reformed following the crisis, notably financial services. The new financial services and banking rules that have been adopted since the crisis have abandoned the idea of home country control that predominated in Phase Two but were found to be wanting in the crisis, and moved to a centralized approach with a single rulebook. Further, the legislature is increasingly moving towards the use of regulations, rather than directives, to ensure greater uniformity and maximum as opposed to minimum harmonization to remove the possibility of national variation.

Tensions Underlying the Single Market

The previous section focused on the process of constructing the single market; this section looks at some of the tensions and challenges experienced by the legislature and courts in the integration process. Those challenges essentially concern questions of competence, sovereignty, and effectiveness. In essence, member states are keen to allow their exporters to export but generally want to preserve their national markets for national goods/people/capital. How far can/should the European Union intervene? As the previous section has shown, the approach adopted by the legislature and the Court has varied over time.

There are two main approaches to attaining a common market: (1) the decentralized model, underpinned by the principles of nondiscrimination, market access, and the concept of competitive federalism; and (2) the centralized model, which concerns harmonization. The essence of the decentralized model is that states retain the freedom to regulate matters as diverse as product standards, qualifications to practice, and employment law as long as those national rules do not interfere with key principles of "federal" law. In the early days of the European Union, the key principle was nondiscrimination on the grounds of nationality, requiring host states to treat out-of-state goods, persons, services, and capital in the same way as their in-state equivalents.

The advantage of the nondiscrimination model is that it does not interfere with national regulatory autonomy. This creates space for member states to develop rules best suited to the needs of the state and its people. States can also experiment with rules in order to remain attractive to citizens and to become attractive to other citizens/goods/capital. This model, under which states can experiment with laws with a view to producing "better" laws than other states, is referred to as competitive federalism. The only restriction laid down by EU law is that the regulation must apply equally to home and host state goods or persons. So, national rules which are genuinely nondiscriminatory are lawful. However, if there is (unjustified) discrimination, Union law requires the discriminatory element of the national measure to be set aside, but the substance of the national rule remains intact. So if State A sets the standards for widgets but requires State B's producers to satisfy higher standards than State A's producers, State A is therefore directly discriminating against goods from State B. The application of the nondiscrimination principle means that State A can continue to set quality standards for widgets but that the widgets produced in State B must be subject to the same treatment as those produced in State A. This example shows that the nondiscrimination model says nothing about the level at which the standards should be set, merely that the imported and domestic goods must be treated in the same way. The result is that the diversity of national rules is preserved, which, as we saw earlier when discussing sausages, is often politically popular and democratically justified.

However, while the discrimination test has a number of advantages, there are drawbacks too, in particular that it allows barriers to movement to remain because it permits the host state to impose its own rules on imported goods/migrants provided those rules apply equally to domestic goods/persons. For this reason, the Court has moved towards applying a broader market access test. This provides that national rules preventing or hindering market access are unlawful, irrespective of whether they actually discriminate against imports or migrants on the grounds of their nationality. The market access approach therefore looks at the national rule solely from the perspective of the (usually out-of-state) claimants: does the national rule prevent or hinder their market access?[31] This test has proved somewhat illusive in practice.[32] The advantages and disadvantages of this model are the converse of what has already been discussed: the market access test provides an effective challenge to more national rules than the nondiscrimination model but it is also more damaging to national regulatory autonomy. Most (in)famously the Court has ruled that strike action taken lawfully under national law can nevertheless interfere with an employer's access to the market in another member states.[33]

While the Court has tried using a variety of techniques to limit the reach of the market access approach none has proved entirely satisfactory, so member states have had to rely on public interest requirements to justify their rules and hope that the Court finds the measure proportionate. However, the more member states invoke public interest requirements to protect national interests, the more the market is partitioned, and the more there is the need for EU legislation (centralization). The main legal basis for that is Article 114 TFEU.

Article 114(1) TFEU provides, "[s]ave where otherwise provided in the Treaty" the European Parliament and Council, acting in accordance with the ordinary legislative procedure, are to adopt "measures" (not just directives) "for the approximation of the provisions laid down by law, regulation, or administrative action in Member States which have as their object the establishment and functioning of the internal market." Given the potential breadth of the single market, this legal basis might indicate almost unlimited competence for the European Union, contrary to notions of conferral of powers. However, the Court signaled that there were limits on the use of Article 114 TFEU in the leading case of *Tobacco Advertising I*.[34] The Court said that where the Union measure was genuinely[35] intended to improve the conditions for the establishment and functioning of the internal market,[36] and actually had that effect,[37] then Article 114(1) TFEU could be used in two, alternative,[38] situations: (1) where the legislation contributes to the elimination of likely obstacles to the exercise of fundamental freedoms; (2) where the legislation contributes to the removal of appreciable distortions of competition that are likely to arise from the diverse national rules. On the facts of the case, certain of the provisions in the Tobacco Advertising Directive 98/34 on, for example, the ban on advertising on parasols could not be justified on either of these grounds and so the directive was annulled. In subsequent cases the Court has shown itself willing to accept the use of Article 114 TFEU as a legal basis for a wide range of measures including, in *Swedish Match* and *Arnold André*,[39] a total ban on the marketing of oral tobacco products such as snuff (finely ground tobacco consumed by placing it between the gum and the lip), even though a *ban* might appear to fly in the face of a single market in goods.[40] And in *Österreichischer Rundfunk*[41] the Court said that the Data Protection Directive could be adopted under Article 114 TFEU even though it applied to a wholly internal situation. The Court said that

> recourse to Article [114 TFEU] as a legal basis does not presuppose the existence of an actual link with free movement between Member States in every situation referred to by the measure founded on that basis.

Articles 114(4) to (5) TFEU make express provision for member states to derogate from a measure adopted under Article 114(1) TFEU. This was the price for the introduction of QMV into Article 114(1) TFEU. Article 114(4) TFEU concerns preexisting national measures. It says:

> If, after the adoption of a harmonisation measure by the European Parliament and the Council, by the Council or by the Commission, a Member State deems it necessary to maintain national provisions on grounds of major needs referred to in Article 36, or relating to the protection of the environment or the working environment, it shall notify the Commission of these provisions as well as the grounds for maintaining them.

Article 114(5) TFEU concerns new measures. It allows a member state "to introduce national provisions based on new scientific evidence … on grounds of a problem specific to that Member State arising after the adoption of the harmonisation measure." This scientific evidence – which must be both new and raising a problem specific to the applicant member state – can relate only to the protection of the environment or the working environment. Thus, unlike Article 114(4) TFEU, the grounds listed in Article 36 TFEU (public policy, security, health, etc. – considered earlier in this chapter) cannot be invoked to justify a national derogation under Article 114(5) TFEU. This is because, as the Court explained in *Commission v. Denmark*[42] in respect of Article 114(4) TFEU, the EU institutions already know of the national provisions but choose not to take them into account, while the adoption of new national legislation under Article 114(5) TFEU is more likely to jeopardize harmonization. For this reason the grounds under which Article 114(5) TFEU can be invoked are more limited. The procedure for applying for a derogation is spelled out in Articles 114(6) to (9) TFEU. While there was concern in the early days that this provision would be used to drive a coach and horses through the single market, in fact little use has been made of this possibility, suggesting that member states are able to have their interests accommodated in the negotiation process rather than waiting to use the opt-out.

Conclusion

The single market has been the European Union's success story. Like the member states, the Union continues to experiment with what works and what does not. And it has been forced to adapt to the changing times. Some of its experiments have proved successful (e.g., the new approach directives), others less so (e.g., minimum standards). Some of its approaches have withstood the crisis and continued to provide a safety net for the its citizens (e.g., social policy, consumer protection), others have not (e.g., mutual recognition, better known as passporting, in respect of financial services). The European Union does have the tools at its disposal to make changes. But this takes time – which is not necessarily on the Union's side: some EU citizens blame the European Union and the single market for breaking down barriers, allowing foreigners (who are in fact other EU citizens) to work in their countries, and thus creating domestic unemployment. The solidarity between EU citizens, created by the internal market, is only skin deep. The crisis has shown this most starkly.

Notes

1 Preamble to the EEC Treaty.

2 The relevant treaty provisions are: Articles 28–30 TFEU on customs duties, Article 110 TFEU on taxation, Articles 34–35 TFEU on goods, Article 45 TFEU on workers, Article 49 TFEU on establishment, Articles 56–57 TFEU on services, and Article 63 TFEU on capital.

3 Case 120/78 *Rewe v. Bundesmonopolverwaltung für Branntwein* EU:C:1979:42.

4 COM(85) 310.

5 Lord Cockfield, *The European Union: Creating the Single Market* (Chichester: Wiley Chancery, 1994), 39.

6 Paolo Cecchini, *The European Challenge 1992: The Benefits of a Single Market* (Aldershot: Wildwood House, 1988), 4. These problems persist: see the Commission's Internal Market Package (COM(2007) 35).

7 Ibid., xvii–xviii.

8 [1998] OJ L 204/37.

9 The deadline is merely noted in Case C-9/99 *Echirolles Distribution SA v. Association du Dauphiné* EU:C:2000:532. The deadline of 31 December 1992 has been removed from Article 26 TFEU. See generally, David Edward, "The Impact of the Single Act on the Institutions," *Common Market Law Review* 24 (1987); Pierre Pescatore, "Some Critical Remarks on the Single European Act," *Common Market Law Review* 24 (1987); and J.W. De Zwann, "The Single European Act: Conclusion of a Unique Document," *Common Market Law Review* 23 (1986).

10 The declaration attached to the article by the SEA said that the participants expressed their "firm political will" to complete the internal market before 1 January 1993 but that setting the date of 31 December 1992 did not create "an automatic legal effect."

11 The terminology of "single market" has in fact been used by the Court since the early 1960s. See, e.g., Case 32/65 *Italy v. Council and Commission* EU:C:1966:42; and Case 15/81 *Gaston Schul* EU:C:1982:135, para 33.

12 Directive 2009/48 of 18 June 2009 on the Safety of Toys [2009] OJ L 170/1.

13 Noreen Burrows and Hilary Hiram, "Legal Articulation of Policy in the EC," in *Implementing EC Law in the UK: Structures for Indirect Rule*, ed. Terence Daintith (Chichester: Wiley, 1995), 45.

14 COM(2011) 206.

15 COM(2012) 573.

16 Commission Communication, "Single Market Act II: Together for new growth," COM(2012) 573 final.

17 COM(2007) 724. See also Commission in its Recommendation 2009/524/EC on measures to improve the functioning of the single market [2009] OJ L 176/17.

18 Stephen Weatherill, "New Strategies for Managing the EC's Internal Market," *Current Legal Problems* 53 (2000): 595, 598.

19 COM(96) 559. See also the Commission's Action Plan, "Simplifying and Improving the Regulatory Environment" (COM(2002) 278) followed up by the Commission's Communication, "Updating and Simplifying the Community *Acquis*" (COM(2003) 71). See also the Inter-Institutional Agreement on Better Law-Making [2003] OJ L 321/1, 4.

20 Commission Communication, "Better Regulation for Growth and Jobs in the European Union" COM(2005) 97.

21 This strand builds on the earlier "SLIM" (Simpler Legislation for the Internal Market) initiatives and has now been rejuvenated via the REFIT (Regulatory Fitness and Performance) program where the Commission sets out, by policy area, where it will take further action to simplify or withdraw EU laws: COM(2013) 685.

22 See the Commission's *Impact Assessment Guidelines* (SEC(2005) 791).

23 Commission, "Towards a Reinforced Culture of Consultation and Dialogue – General Principles and Minimum Standards for Consultation of Interested Parties by the Commission" (COM(2002) 704).

24 http://ec.europa.eu/smart-regulation/.

25 COM(2012) 259.

26 Directive 2006/123 of 12 December 2006 on services in the internal market [2006] OJ L 376/36.

27 See, e.g., the Handbook on the Implementation of the Services Directive http://ec.europa.eu/internal_market/services/docs/services-dir/guides/handbook_en.pdf.

28 OJ [1998] L 204/37.

29 Case C-194/94 *CIA Security* EU:C:1996:172.

30 Commission Communication, "Better Governance for the Single Market," COM(2012) 259 final.

31 Case C-55/94 *Gebhard v. Consiglio dell'Ordine degli Avvocati e Procuratori di Milano* EU:C:1995:411, para 37, citing Case C-19/92 *Kraus v. Land Baden-Württemberg* EU:C:1993:125, para 32; Case C-76/90 *Sager v. Dennemeyer & Co. Ltd* EU:C:1991:331, para 12; and Case C-110/05 *Commission v. Italy* EU:C:2009:66, para 50.

32 Jukka Snell, "The Notion of Market Access: A Concept or a Slogan?" *Common Market Law Review* 47 (2010): 437.

33 Case C-438/05 *International Transport Workers' Union Federation et al. v. Viking Line ABP et al.* EU:C:2007:772.

34 Case C-376/98 *Germany v. European Parliament and Council* (Tobacco Advertising I) EU:C:2000:544; and Case C-74/99 *R v. Secretary of State for Health and others, ex p. Imperial Tobacco* EU:C:2000:547.

35 Case C-376/98 *Tobacco Advertising I*, n 34 this chapter, para 84.

36 Ibid., para 83.

37 Although not very clearly stated in *Tobacco Advertising I*, it can be seen in paras 84, 102, 104, and 107–108.

38 Case C-380/03 *Germany v. European Parliament and Council* (Tobacco Advertising II) EU:C:2006:772, para 67.

39 Case C-210/03 *Swedish Match* EU:C:2004:802; and Case C-434/02 *Arnold André* EU:C:2004:800.

40 See also Regulation (EC) No 1007/2009 of 16 September 2009 on Trade in Seal Products [2009] OJ L 286/36, which essentially banned the import of seal products.

41 Case C-465/00 *Österreichischer Rundfunk* EU:C:2003:294, para 41; and Case C-101/01 *Lindqvist* EU:C:2003:596, paras 40–41.

42 Case C-3/00 *Commission v. Denmark* EU:C:2003:167, para 57.

References

Burrows, Noreen, and Hilary Hiram. "Legal Articulation of Policy in the EC." In *Implementing EC Law in the UK: Structures for Indirect Rule*, edited by Terence Daintith, 29–47. Chichester: Wiley, 1995.

Cecchini, Paolo. *The European Challenge 1992: The Benefits of a Single Market*. Aldershot: Wildwood House, 1988.

Cockfield, Lord. *The European Union: Creating the Single Market*. Chichester: Wiley Chancery, 1994.

De Zwann, J.W. "The Single European Act: Conclusion of a Unique Document." *Common Market Law Review* 23 (1986): 747–765.

Edward, David. "The Impact of the Single Act on the Institutions." *Common Market Law Review* 24 (1987): 19–30.

Pescatore, Pierre. "Some Critical Remarks on the Single European Act." *Common Market Law Review* 24 (1987): 9–18.

Snell, Jukka. "The Notion of Market Access: A Concept or a Slogan?" *Common Market Law Review* 47 (2010): 437–472.

Weatherill, Stephen. "New Strategies for Managing the EC's Internal Market." *Current Legal Problems* 53 (2000): 595–619.

15

The Free Movement of Goods

Miguel Poiares Maduro and Pedro Caro de Sousa

Introduction

One of the greatest objects of judicial activity and academic commentary in EU law has been the free movement of goods. Few topics have given rise to so many cases and scholarly works. In spite of all this intellectual and judicial attention, the free movement of goods continues to generate intense debates because it is at the intersection of complex and difficult choices between public regulation and market freedom, on the one hand, and EU and state powers on the other. This chapter will provide an overview of such debates and how they affected the development of EU law on the free movement of goods. Given that these debates are not specific to the European Union but are inherent to any trade system, the General Agreement on Tariffs and Trade (GATT) will be used to identify some specificities of the European system.

The Free Movement of Goods in International Economic Law and in European Law

When reviewing state measures that affect trade, courts and dispute resolution bodies decide on the limits of state powers and impact on the degree of regulation in a market. The extent of regulatory powers that can still be exercised by states depends largely on the interpretation given to the free movement provisions, which in turn affects the regulation of the market. In the European Union, the interpretation of these provisions implies choices regarding the division of competences between the member states and the Union, but it also requires choices concerning the limits of state intervention in the market. It is this underlying tension requiring courts to undertake a difficult balance between conflicting legitimate goals that is often reflected in the debates surrounding the interpretation and application of these rules.

The EU treaties stipulate that the European Union shall have an internal market. Several rules in the treaties are charged with the promotion of this objective, but of paramount importance,

A Companion to European Union Law and International Law, First Edition.
Edited by Dennis Patterson and Anna Södersten.

in this regard, are the free movement provisions concerning goods, workers, services, establishment, and capital, alongside the rules on competition. The free movement of goods, in particular, is regulated in the Union by a number of directly effective provisions in the treaties, which broadly correspond to measures found in international economic law precluding pecuniary and nonpecuniary restrictions to trade.[1]

In adopting the distinction between pecuniary and nonpecuniary restrictions, as in other respects, the provisions in the EU treaties concerning the free movement of goods are comparable to the GATT provisions.[2] As regards nonpecuniary restrictions, the GATT forbids national measures from being "applied to domestic and imported products so as to afford protection to domestic production" (Article III) and proscribes prohibitions or restrictions on the importation and exportation (or sale for export) of goods between contracting parties, "other than duties, taxes or other charges, whether made effective through quotas, import or export licences or other measures" (Articles XI), unless justified under Article XX. In the European Union, Articles 35 to 37 of the Treaty on the Functioning of the European Union (TFEU) prohibit all quantitative restrictions on imports and exports, and all measures having an equivalent effect, unless they are justified. Concerning pecuniary restrictions, both the GATT and the EU treaties have provisions related to customs and to discriminatory internal taxation.

Despite these similarities, there are significant differences between the European Union and GATT. Some relate to drafting. For example, the GATT has different provisions for those nonpecuniary restrictions that take place at the border and those that are the result of national regulation, whereas the TFEU adopts a unified approach to potentially restrictive regulations in this respect, while distinguishing between imports and exports. Also, while European law completely bans customs within the internal European market, Article I GATT merely seeks to ensure the application of the most-favored-nation principle and to gradually lower customs through subsequent rounds of negotiations.

However, the main differences between the European Union and the GATT stem from the fact that they ultimately have different purposes, have quite different constituencies, and have evolved differently.[3] While the World Trade Organization (WTO) system is focused on trade liberalization between states, Article 3(1)(c) of the Treaty establishing the European Community sets the more ambitious goal of creating "an internal market characterised by the abolition, as between Member States, of obstacles to the free movement of goods, persons, services and capital." Though the Lisbon Treaty has repealed this article, Article 26 TFEU still holds that the "Union shall adopt measures with the aim of establishing or ensuring the functioning of the internal market," meaning "an area without internal frontiers in which the free movement of goods, persons, services and capital is ensured."

The result of this is that, albeit both EU and GATT provisions on the free movement of goods interfere with the powers of sovereign states, the EU provisions have a much greater impact on state sovereignty. This is a consequence of the different interpretations to which these provisions are subject and of the different mechanisms in place to enforce them in the Union and in the international sphere. This is particularly evident in the regulation of nonpecuniary restrictions in the European Union.

The Evolution of European Case Law

To a certain extent, the dilemmas inherent in the free movement and interstate commerce rules have been pointed out, in the EU context, by Advocate General Tesauro in his Opinion in *Hünermund*:

> Is Article [34] of the Treaty [the provision that defines what constitutes a restriction to the free movement of goods] a provision intended to liberalize intra-Community trade or is it intended more generally to encourage the unhindered pursuit of commerce in individual Member States?[4]

In this sentence, the Advocate General identified a question of constitutional dimension for the interpretation of the free movement of goods: is the purpose of this provision simply to prevent protectionist policies, or does it also aim to promote economic integration beyond protectionist concerns – or, as some have argued, does it even aim to promote and protect a particular economic model of open markets and free competition?

In the context of the European Union, there have been many tests proposed to determine what ought to be considered restrictions on free movement, from classic nondiscrimination tests to pure balancing, passing through intensity tests (*de minimis*), tests focusing on certain categories of state measures, and market access tests. In part, these tests reflect different conceptions of what is sometimes called the "economic constitution" of the European Union. From another perspective, they attempt to provide an answer to the specific challenges that arise in the application of these rules, in particular regarding the search for legal certainty.

In the early stages of European integration, the provisions on the free movement of goods were applied in a broadly similar manner to those in the GATT, with decisions being adopted on physical barriers to trade and discriminatory rules. While the removal of physical barriers to goods is a precondition to the marketing of foreign products, prohibiting states from discriminating on grounds of nationality is the traditional tool advocated by antiprotectionist theories and used by trade liberalization instruments.

Nevertheless, it is often not easy to identify clear differences on the impact that adopting a different approach would have in the review of state measures. Consider, for example, the adoption of a nondiscrimination or antiprotectionist criterion. In order to escape the usual criticisms that such a criterion can "too easily be circumvented by legislation which is on its face applicable to domestic and imported products alike,"[5] or be dragged into endless, esoteric discussions of protectionist purpose and intent, antiprotectionist theories have developed criteria of discriminatory impact or protectionist effects. If state measures place a heavier burden on imports than they do on home products they are considered to be materially discriminatory, thus having protectionist effects. As such, they are considered prima facie inadmissible.[6] It so happens that a higher burden imposed on imports may not be so much a direct result of the legislation as of the different presence or forms of access of national and imported products in the market or of the existence of national legislative disparities. In this instance, nondiscrimination tests become quite similar to market access tests, and even to an economic freedom test, since the borderline between securing access to state markets and simply promoting access to that market is often thin and difficult to establish.[7]

Under the GATT, discrimination tests are preceded by a market equivalence analysis of the relevant products, requiring an economic and empirical analysis of the market prior to determining whether the products are subject to differentiated treatment. This is understood to be a difficult exercise and, as such, a variety of different criteria (e.g., objective standards (physical characteristics, tariff classification, end uses, or even the act of exportation) and economic standards (market definition)) have been used.[8] In EU law, however, the approach is not quite so structured, and the Court appears not to be so empirically minded, with the consequence that its case law seems to face a greater risk of spilling over into an approach protecting market access or economic freedom even if the Court were to ostensibly adopt a protectionist-based approach.[9]

In any event, in its landmark *Dassonville* judgment of 1974, the Court made it clear that indistinctly applicable national measures were also prohibited. The fact that it was sufficient for a measure to be "captured" by Article 34 for it to be "capable of hindering directly or indirectly, actually or potentially, intra-community trade," seemed to mean that not only protectionist or discriminatory measures were subject to review under Article 34.[10]

The Court built on *Dassonville* in its decision in *Cassis de Dijon*, which stated that obstacles resulting from disparities between national laws must be accepted only in so far as they are necessary to satisfy mandatory requirements.[11] The case concerned a legislative disparity between the French and German rules on alcoholic beverages that required *Cassis de Dijon* producers to adapt to the German national requirements, therefore imposing on their products a double burden to which, arguably, the German domestic products would not be subject to.

How to deal with double burdens resulting from legislative disparities remains an eternal question in the area of free movement: is the double burden to which products or persons are subject when having to comply (and therefore adapt) to the laws of another member state a form of discrimination since it tends to protect those already in that domestic market? Or does it promote further market integration beyond that which a nondiscrimination test would engender? This question is important because the answer determines the borderline between what are to be treated as legitimate legislative disparities between states and what constitutes an unlawful exercise of state regulatory power, infringing upon the free movement rules.

The difficulty in identifying this borderline was evident in *Oosthoek's*,[12] a case dealing with national rules that prohibited a certain method of sales. The Court stated that to compel a producer either to adopt advertising or sales promotion schemes that differ from one member state to another or to discontinue a scheme he considers particularly effective may constitute an obstacle to imports even if the legislation in question applies to domestic and imported products without distinction.[13] It could be argued that in this judgment the Court merely extended the idea of double burden, advanced in *Cassis de Dijon* for rules governing the characteristics of products, to other types of measures such as those regulating sales methods, since foreign producers will suffer an additional burden when they are not allowed to use marketing strategies and methods allowed in other member states. However, if it means that requiring a producer to discontinue a scheme he considers particularly effective suffices for a finding of restriction on free movement, the case could be interpreted as meaning that the free movement of goods has a broader reach in reviewing the exercise of a state's regulatory powers.

That the scope of the free movement of goods extended beyond purely protectionist grounds was made clear in *Cinéthèque*.[14] The case concerned French legislation that prohibited the commercial exploitation of cinematographic works in recorded form, mainly videocassettes, before the end of a set time limit. The Court concluded that while this system did not have the purpose of regulating trade patterns or the effect of favoring national production as against products of other member states,

> *[n]evertheless*, the application of such a system may create barriers to intra-Community trade … . In those circumstances a prohibition of exploitation laid down by such system is not compatible with the principle of free movement of goods provided for in the Treaty unless [justified].[15]

The outcome of these developments in the Court's case law was that a broad set of regulatory measures became susceptible to review under the free movement of goods.[16] But while the Court's adoption of a broad concept of restriction to the free movement of goods was essential to market integration, it was increasingly liable to place a heavy burden on the Court's resources – particularly because the Court developed a power to interfere with national regulatory systems that was much more intense than anything that ever existed under the GATT. Since findings of restriction require the Court to pursue balancing exercises under a proportionality test,[17] the more situations in which the Court (and national courts) are required to pursue such a balancing, the more they become responsible for national regulatory policy. The Court found itself having to answer an increasing number of questions – for example, should there be regulation? If so, who should regulate? What are the substantive limits that any regulation may prescribe? – requiring value judgments on broad policy questions not necessarily related to market integration.[18] Advocate General Van Gerven expressly identified these problems. Referring to the broad approach the Court had adopted, the advocate general stated,

> [T]he Court will inevitably have to decide in an increasing number of cases on the reasonableness of policy decisions of Member States taken in the innumerable spheres where there is no question of direct or indirect, factual or legal discrimination against, or detriment to, imported products. The question may arise whether excessive demands would not then be put on the Court, which would be confronted with countless new mandatory requirements and grounds of justification.[19]

The subsequent decision in *Keck and Mithouard*[20] has been seen as an attempt to address these problems. In *Keck*, the Court revisited and partially reversed its approach to the concept of restriction to the free movement of goods. Its stated purpose was to discourage

> the increasing tendency of traders to invoke Article [34] of the Treaty as a means of challenging any rules whose effect is to limit their commercial freedom even where such rules are not aimed at products from other Member States.[21]

To this end, the Court started by reinterpreting *Cassis de Dijon* in a way that restricted its application to product requirements (i.e., rules that regulate the characteristics of products):

> It is established by the case law beginning with "Cassis de Dijon" that, in the absence of harmonisation of legislation, measures of equivalent effect prohibited by *Article [34] include obstacles to the free movement of goods where they are the consequence of applying rules that lay down requirements to be met by such goods* (such as requirements as to designation, form, size, weight, composition, presentation, labelling, packaging) *to goods from other Member States where they are lawfully manufactured and marketed*, even if those rules apply without distinction to all products unless their application can be justified by a public-interest objective taking precedence over the free movement of goods.[22]

Thus, measures laying down product requirements are submitted to the proportionality test even if they are nondiscriminatory. However, the same is not the case with regard to "national provisions restricting or prohibiting certain selling arrangements."[23] In the case of such measures, the Court decided to reverse the interpretation given to *Dassonville* in subsequent decisions. It held that

> contrary to what has previously been decided, the application to products from other Member States of national provisions restricting or prohibiting certain selling arrangements is not such as to hinder directly or indirectly, actually or potentially, trade between Member States within the meaning of the Dassonville judgement, provided that those provisions apply to all affected traders operating within the national territory and *provided that they affect in the same manner, in law and in fact*, the marketing of domestic products and of those from other Member States.
>
> Provided that those conditions are fulfilled, the application of such rules to the sale of products from another Member State meeting the requirements laid down by that State is not by nature such as *to prevent their access to the market or to impede access any more than it impedes the access of domestic products*. Such rules therefore fall outside the scope of Article 30 of the Treaty.[24]

In other words, measures prohibiting or restricting certain selling arrangements that discriminate in law or in fact against imported products infringe upon the free movement of goods because they unduly restrict market access.

This link between discrimination and market access, however, founders on the difficulty of distinguishing between a measure that aims to protect state operators from foreign competition and a measure that protects certain operators established on the national market from foreign and domestic potential competition. As already discussed, a state measure that protects certain domestic operators from internal competition often also protects them from external competition by protecting the status quo of the market and, therefore, makes it more difficult for new economic operators to access it. Furthermore, measures reducing the economic attractiveness of pursuing a given activity will tend to have a detrimental effect on the pursuit of cross-border activities in that field, making it very difficult to differentiate between those measures that pose obstacles to trade prohibited under the treaty from those that merely regulate economic activity. That explains why measures restricting economic freedom in national markets may incidentally restrict the access of external operators to this market – and why the opening up of national markets by free movement provisions can, incidentally, have the effect of liberalizing national economies.

Ultimately, the case law of the Court reflects both the difficulties in finding a clear and indisputable criterion by which to identify inadmissible national rules and the Court's need to constantly refine its approach in the light of the challenges that the cases, and the economic realities they express, raise. It will perhaps be difficult for the Court to provide lawyers and scholars with an "ideal" test; instead, what the case law reveals is a careful balancing of pragmatism and concerns for legal certainty alongside attempts simultaneously to articulate a clearer normative foundation for the rules on the free movement of goods. Rather than the provision of a – highly elusive – clear-cut test to determine what measures constitute free movement restrictions or an undue burden on commerce, this area of the law is dominated by the identification of the normative concerns that can more easily provide courts (including national courts) with the guidance necessary to decide hard cases.

The case law kept developing after *Keck*, to the point where at least three criteria – and some underlying normative concerns – can be identified.[25] First, any discrimination based on nationality, whether direct or indirect, is prohibited. A good example is a publicity campaign promoting the purchase of national products.[26] Secondly, it is established that any state measure imposing an additional burden or supplementary costs on goods in circulation in the European Union, or on traders carrying out a cross-border activity, creates a barrier to trade that needs to be duly justified. This, as stated earlier, raises the difficult problem of distinguishing such situations from costs that arise from simple disparities in the laws of the member states. It would appear that a decisive criterion in this respect is whether that additional cost is a result of the fact that the state rules did not take into account the particular situation of the imported products and, in particular, the fact that those products already had to comply with similar rules in their state of origin. As a consequence of this, it can be stated that free movement rules require more than equal treatment under national laws – they require equal consideration of out-of-state interests by the national laws. Thirdly, any measure that amounts to a barrier on access to the market is usually considered to be a measure restricting the free movement of goods. That appears to be the case where such a measure protects the acquired positions of certain economic operators on a domestic market,[27] or where it makes intra-Community trade more difficult than trade within the national market, even if the measure concerns selling arrangements.[28] In the Italian "trailers case," after having restated *Keck and Mithouard*, the Court stated that

> measures adopted by a Member State *the object or effect of which is to treat products coming from other Member States less favourably* are to be regarded as measures having equivalent effect to quantitative restrictions on imports within the meaning of Article [34] EC, as are [product requirements]. Any other measure which *hinders access of products originating in other Member States to the market of a Member State* is also covered by that concept.[29]

It should be noted that the market access test was imported from the GATT, but in quite a different form: with the GATT, market access applies only to measures applicable to imports at the border – that is, it corresponds to the prohibition of physical barriers, custom duties, and equivalent measures.[30] In the European Union, on the other hand, this test extends to market regulations that prevent new operators from entering the market, even if such measures can affect national operators.

From this analysis, it follows that the fundamental objective of the free movement of goods is to ensure that producers are put in a position to benefit from the right to carry out their activity at a cross-border level, while consumers are put in a position to access goods from other member states in the same conditions as domestic products – that is, to ensure market access to producers and consumers alike, and then guaranteeing that foreign and domestic producers and consumers are treated the same in law and in fact. This goes beyond the mere promotion of interstate trade: it is also a reflection of the status conferred on European citizens by the treaties. In addition to guaranteeing that there will be no discrimination based on nationality, this status requires member states to take into account the effect of the measures they adopt on European citizens asserting their rights to economic free movement. As the Court has pointed out, this requires national legislation to take into consideration a broader scale than a strictly national context.[31]

Judicial Tests and National Autonomy

By requiring states to take out-of-state interests into account, the free movement of goods interferes with state autonomy. While this interference occurs at both the GATT and EU level, the EU free movement of goods interferes with national sovereignty much more than the free movement provisions in the GATT.[32]

When the Court decides that a national rule falls within the scope of the free movement of goods, it is effectively making an institutional choice: it takes control over the legitimacy of that rule away from the ordinary national legislative processes and subjects it to the jurisdiction of the judiciary (particularly of the Court, which may, by means of a proportionality test, determine whether the manner in which a state protects its public interests is acceptable). Additionally, in certain cases – namely concerning justifications not provided for by the treaties – the Court may even determine what public interests a state can legitimately pursue. This means that even if a prima facie restrictive measure is deemed justified, by finding that the measure is restrictive, the Court arrogates to itself ultimate authority regarding its validity, thereby removing ultimate control from the member state and leading to the judicial centralization of such control at EU level.

In addition to its centralizing effect, the free movement of goods has an impact on the very content of market regulation, setting substantive limits to the exercise of legislative powers at both the national and EU levels.[33] The result is that a member state loses part of its autonomy to legislate, and that member states other than the state subject to the Court's decision (but with similar measures in place) will find themselves under the "shadow of the law" and under pressure to amend out-of-step rules in accordance with the Court's case law.[34] This has a much deeper impact on state sovereignty than the GATT – with its focus on most-favored-nation status, and without mechanisms ensuring the direct effect of its provisions on internal legal orders – has ever had.

However, the EU treaties also provide for compensatory mechanisms to this interference that do not exist at the GATT level by providing for the adoption of harmonizing European legislation. In addition to the promotion of economic integration through free movement rules (which is frequently referred to as "negative integration"), Articles 114 to 118 TFEU and several other "sectorial" provisions empower the European Union to adopt legislative measures for the establishment and functioning of an internal market (also referred to as "positive integration").

A number of consequences arise from the interaction of negative and positive integration. The first is that the provisions on the free movement of goods have an inherently deregulatory effect, since the Court can strike down legislative measures but cannot legislate itself – in other words, the greater the degree of judicial centralization (via the free movement rules), the greater the prospect of deregulation of national markets. On the other hand, the free movement of goods also allows for the activation of the EU political process, so that the prospect of reregulation at EU level also increases.[35] Positive integration in the form of reregulation affects national sovereignty as much as, if not more than, negative integration. While national markets avoid automatic deregulation under positive integration, they will be subject to European rules that will differ from the original national rules. This is a result of the participants in the EU political process being more numerous and diverse – in particular by including previous market outsiders – than the participants in national political processes. As a result, reregulation at EU level can differ from national regulation in both regulatory goals and methods.

The practical impact of the treaty provisions on free movement of goods, however, can only be assessed by reference to the specific institutional context in which they produce their effects. When the Court replaces the parameters of acceptability of a certain regulatory scheme, this will have a mainly deregulatory effect if the possible options for reregulation – particularly at the EU level – are blocked (as commonly occurred prior to the adoption of the Single European Act). If this is not the case, and the reregulatory channels are open, a prima facie deregulatory decision may well have preponderantly reregulatory effects.

In any event, the effects of the free movement of goods are even more complex than this suggests. It happened in a context where the political process at EU level was unable to replace European legislation for national legislation struck down by the Court that the Court developed a tool then unknown at the GATT level – but which has since become a common presence in bilateral trade treaties – to remove obstacles to trade without directly striking down national regulations: mutual recognition. Mutual recognition is the flipside of the double burden issue first raised in *Cassis de Dijon*. As we have seen, national measures imposing product requirements may infringe upon the free movement of goods unless justified. However, the outcome of this is not pure deregulation: it is merely that goods can only be subject to the rules on technical standards of their home state, even when marketed in a different state, thereby being freed from the onus of having to comply with two or more sets of rules. Mutual recognition can be thought of as a contract between governments mandating the transfer of regulatory authority from one jurisdiction to another: all member states must mutually recognize the regulatory authority of the state of origin as regards product requirements being in principle equivalent to their own.[36]

By mandating that standards of a home state be accepted as functionally equivalent to those of a host state, the Court replaced the deregulatory effects of the free movement of goods by the imposition of a different regulatory standard.[37] Since different member states can have different degrees of protection of public interests, the determination of the level at which equivalence takes place is a prerequisite for mutual recognition to occur, with this determination requiring the Court to balance how much the regulatory autonomy of a member state must be sacrificed for the sake of the functioning of the internal market.[38] This effectively substitutes a European value assessment for a national one and imposes the Court's evaluation of what level of protection is sufficient. Mutual recognition still implies a loss of regulatory autonomy for the member state, by delinking the exercise of sovereign power from its territorial anchor through a reciprocal allocation of jurisdictional authority to prescribe and enforce laws.[39] But it is a European middle way, less intrusive than outright deregulation or harmonization, which respects state autonomy while simultaneously ensuring that member states take into account considerations beyond the purely national sphere.

Notes

1 Goods are material objects: they can be valued in money as well as form the subject of, or move across frontiers for the purposes of, commercial transactions. See Jukka Snell, *Goods and Services in EC Law: A Study of the Relationship between the Freedoms* (Oxford: Oxford University Press, 2002), 4–5. The free movement of goods applies both to products originating in member states and to those from nonmember countries that are in free circulation.

2 J.H.H. Weiler, "Epilogue: Towards a Common Law of International Trade," in *The EU, the WTO, and the NAFTA: Towards a Common Law of International Trade?*, ed. J.H.H. Weiler (Oxford: Oxford University Press, 2000), 205–207. On the impact of the GATT 1947 on the drafting of the Rome Treaty, see Eric White, "In Search of the Limits to Article 30 of the EEC Treaty," *Common Market Law Review* 26 (1989): 239.

3 Tamara Perisin, "Balancing Sovereignty with the Free Movement of Goods in the EU and the WTO – Non-Pecuniary Restrictions on the Free Movement of Goods," *Croatian Yearbook of European Law and Policy* 1 (2005): 3.

4 Case C-292/92 *Hünermund* EU:C:1993:932, Opinion of Advocate General Tesauro.

5 Lawrence Gormley, "Actually or Potentially, Directly or Indirectly? Obstacles to the Free Movement of Goods," *Yearbook of European Law* 9 (1989): 198. See also, e.g., Alfonso Mattera, *Le Marché unique européen, ses règles, son fonctionnement* (Paris: Jupiter, 1988), 191–192; Michel Waelbroeck, *Les Réglementations nationales de prix et le droit communautaire* (Brussels: Editions de l'Université de Bruxelles, 1975), 27 ff.

6 Alan O. Sykes, "Regulatory Protectionism and the Law of International Trade," *University of Chicago Law Review* 66 (1999): 16–23; and Gráinne de Búrca, "Unpacking the Concept of Discrimination in EC and International Trade Law," in *The Law of the Single European Market*, ed. Catherine Barnard and Joanne Scott (Oxford: Hart, 2001), 187–188.

7 For a critique of the protectionist effects test, see Donald Regan, "The Supreme Court and State Protectionism: Making Sense of the Dormant Commerce Clause," *Michigan Law Review* 84 (1986): 1130 ff.

8 Nicolas Diebold, "Standards of Non-Discrimination in International Economic Law," *International and Comparative Law Quarterly* 60 (2011): 835–837.

9 Daniel Wilsher, "Does Keck Discrimination Make Any Sense? An Assessment of the Non-discrimination Principle within the European Single Market," *European Law Review* 33 (2008): 18–20.

10 Case 8/74 *Dassonville* EU:C:1974:82, para 5.

11 Case 120/78 *Rewe-Zentral AG* (Cassis de Dijon) EU:C:1979:42. These are Court-made justifications that have to a large extent been incorporated in Article 36 TFEU. "Obstacles to the movement within the Community resulting from disparities between national laws … must be accepted in so far as those provisions may be recognized as being necessary in order to satisfy mandatory

requirements relating in particular to the effectiveness of fiscal supervision, the protection of public health, the fairness of commercial transactions and the defence of the consumer."

12 Case 286/81 *Oosthoek's* EU:C:1982:438.
13 Ibid., para 15.
14 Joined Cases 60/84 and 61/84 *Cinéthèque* EU:C:1985:329.
15 Ibid., paras 21 and 22, emphasis added.
16 Illustrative examples include price regulations (Case 229/83 *Leclerc* (Prix du Libre) EU:C:1985:1) and prohibition on Sunday trading or on employing workers on Sundays (Case 145/88 *Torfaen* EU:C:1989:593; Case C-312/89 *Conforama* EU:C:1991:93; Case C-332/89 *Marchandise* EU:C:1991:94; and Case C-169/91 *Stoke-on-Trent* EU:C:1992:519).
17 On the proportionality test, see one of the authors' Opinion in his capacity of Advocate General in Case C-434/04 *Leppik v. Virallinen syyttäjä* EU:C:2006:609, para 23 ff.
18 With potential consequences to its legitimacy as well. See Miguel Poiares Maduro, "Reforming the Market or the State? Article 30 and the European Constitution: Economic Freedom and Political Rights," *European Law Journal* 3 (1997): 55–57.
19 Case C-145/88 *Torfaen*, Opinion of Advocate General Van Gerven, n 16 this chapter, para 25.
20 Joined Cases C-267/91 and C-268/91 *Keck and Mithouard* EU:C:1993:905.
21 Ibid., para 14.
22 Ibid., para 15, citation omitted and emphasis added.
23 Ibid., para 16.
24 Ibid., para 16, citation omitted and emphasis added.
25 See the Opinion by one of the authors in his capacity of Advocate General in Joined Cases C-158/04 and C-159/04 *Trofo Super-Markets* EU:C:2006:562.
26 Case 249/81 *Commission v. Ireland* EU:C:1982:402.
27 See, e.g., Case C-442/02 *CaixaBank France* EU:C:2004:586, para 13.
28 See, e.g., concerning the freedom to provide services, Case C-70/99 *Commission v. Portugal* EU:C:2001:355, paras 25–27; and Case C-92/01 *Stylianakis* EU:C:2003:72, para 26.
29 Case C-110/05 *Commission v. Italy* EU:C:2009:66, para 37 (emphasis added). See also Case C-142/05 *Mickelson and Roos* EU:C:2009:336, para 24.
30 Jukka Snell, "The Notion of Market Access: A Concept or a Slogan?" *Common Market Law Review* 47 (2010): 439–443.
31 Case C-322/01 *Deutscher Apothekenverband* EU:C:2003:664, paras 73 and 74.
32 Gregory Shaffer, "A Structural Theory of WTO Dispute Settlement: Why Institutional Choice Lies at the Centre of the GMO Case," *New York University Journal of International Law and Politics* 41 (2008): 4.
33 Michael Schillig, "The Interpretation of European Private Law in the Light of Market Freedoms and EU Fundamental Rights," *Maastricht Journal of European and Comparative Law* 15 (2008): 285.
34 James Caporaso and Alec Stone Sweet, *From Free Trade to Supranational Polity: The European Court and Integration* (Oxford: Oxford University Press, 1998), 128. While EU legislation can be assessed as to its conformity with the substantive orientation of the market freedoms, this has only seldom occurred and even more rarely resulted in a finding of incompatibility. See Piet Eeckhout, "The European Court of Law and the Legislature," *Yearbook of European Law* 18 (1998): 12–14.
35 Subject to the assembly of the required support among the EU's lawmaking institutions.
36 Kalypso Nicolaïdis, "Globalization with Human Faces: Managed Mutual Recognition and the Free Movement of Professionals," in *The Principle of Mutual Recognition in the European Integration Process*, ed. Fiorella Kostoris and Padoa Schioppa (Basingstoke: Palgrave Macmillan, 2005), 133.
37 Kalypso Nicolaïdis, "Mutual Recognition of Regulatory Regimes: Some Lessons and Prospects" (Jean Monnet working papers no. 7/97 (1997): 2–14). This may, occasionally, lead to harmonization through regulatory competition. See Miguel Poiares Maduro, "So Close and Yet So Far: The Paradoxes of Mutual Recognition," *Journal of European Public Policy* 14 (2007): 814.
38 Nicolaïdis, "Globalization with Human Faces," 144–146; and Markus Möstl, "Preconditions and Limits of Mutual Recognition," *Common Market Law Review* 47 (2010): 411.

39 Kenneth Armstrong, "Mutual Recognition," in Barnard and Scott, *The Law of the Single European Market*, 232; Möstl, "Preconditions and Limits of Mutual Recognition," 407; and Kalypso Nicolaïdis, "Trusting the Poles? Constructing Europe through Mutual Recognition," *Journal of European Public Policy* 14 (2007): 691.

References

Armstrong, Kenneth. "Mutual Recognition." In Barnard and Scott, *The Law of the Single European Market*, 225–268.

Barnard, Catherine, and Joanne Scott, eds. *The Law of the Single European Market*. Oxford: Hart, 2001.

Caporaso, James, and Alec Stone Sweet. *From Free Trade to Supranational Polity: The European Court and Integration*. Oxford: Oxford University Press, 1998.

de Búrca, Gráinne. "Unpacking the Concept of Discrimination in EC and International Trade Law." In Barnard and Scott, *The Law of the Single European Market*, 181–196.

Diebold, Nicolas. "Standards of Non-Discrimination in International Economic Law." *International and Comparative Law Quarterly* 60 (2011): 831–865.

Eeckhout, Piet. "The European Court of Law and the Legislature." *Yearbook of European Law* 18 (1998): 1–26.

Gormley, Lawrence. "Actually or Potentially, Directly or Indirectly? Obstacles to the Free Movement of Goods." *Yearbook of European Law* 9 (1989): 197–208.

Maduro, Miguel Poiares. "Reforming the Market or the State? Article 30 and the European Constitution: Economic Freedom and Political Rights." *European Law Journal* 3 (1997): 55–82.

Maduro, Miguel Poiares. "So Close and Yet So Far: The Paradoxes of Mutual Recognition." *Journal of European Public Policy* 14 (2007): 814–825.

Mattera, Alfonso. *Le Marché unique européen, ses règles, son fonctionnement*. Paris: Jupiter, 1988.

Möstl, Markus. "Preconditions and Limits of Mutual Recognition." *Common Market Law Review* 47 (2010): 405–436.

Nicolaïdis, Kalypso. "Mutual Recognition of Regulatory Regimes: Some Lessons and Prospects." Jean Monnet working paper no. 7/97 (1997).

Nicolaïdis, Kalypso. "Globalization with Human Faces: Managed Mutual Recognition and the Free Movement of Professionals." In *The Principle of Mutual Recognition in the European Integration Process*, edited by Fiorella Kostoris and Padoa Schioppa, 129–189. Basingstoke: Palgrave Macmillan, 2005.

Nicolaïdis, Kalypso. "Trusting the Poles? Constructing Europe through Mutual Recognition." *Journal of European Public Policy* 14 (2007): 682–698.

Perisin, Tamara. "Balancing Sovereignty with the Free Movement of Goods in the EU and the WTO – Non-Pecuniary Restrictions on the Free Movement of Goods." *Croatian Yearbook of European Law and Policy* 1 (2005): 1–30.

Regan, Donald. "The Supreme Court and State Protectionism: Making Sense of the Dormant Commerce Clause." *Michigan Law Review* 84 (1986): 1091–1287.

Schillig, Michael. "The Interpretation of European Private Law in the Light of Market Freedoms and EU Fundamental Rights." *Maastricht Journal of European and Comparative Law* 15 (2008): 285–321.

Shaffer, Gregory. "A Structural Theory of WTO Dispute Settlement: Why Institutional Choice Lies at the Centre of the GMO Case." *New York University Journal of International Law and Politics* 41 (2008): 1–90.

Snell, Jukka. *Goods and Services in EC Law: A Study of the Relationship between the Freedoms*. Oxford: Oxford University Press, 2002.

Snell, Jukka. "The Notion of Market Access: A Concept or a Slogan?" *Common Market Law Review* 47 (2010): 437–472.

Sykes, Alan. "Regulatory Protectionism and the Law of International Trade." *University of Chicago Law Review* 66 (1999): 1–46.

Waelbroeck, Michel. *Les Réglementations nationales de prix et le droit communautaire*. Brussels: Editions de l'Université de Bruxelles, 1975.

Weiler, J.H.H. "Epilogue: Towards a Common Law of International Trade." In *The EU, the WTO, and the NAFTA: Towards a Common Law of International Trade?* edited by J.H.H. Weiler, 201–232. Oxford: Oxford University Press, 2000.

White, Eric. "In Search of the Limits to Article 30 of the EEC Treaty." *Common Market Law Review* 26 (1989): 235–280.

Wilsher, Daniel. "Does Keck Discrimination Make Any Sense? An Assessment of the Non-discrimination Principle within the European Single Market." *European Law Review* 33 (2008): 3–22.

16

Freedom of Establishment

Frank S. Benyon

Introduction

Other chapters in this volume have described how the European Union's internal market was constructed based upon the four fundamental freedoms of movement of goods, persons, services, and capital. The internal market rules were applied vigorously by the European Court of Justice and developed in amending treaties, notably the Single European Act; the Maastricht Treaty, introducing full freedom of movement for capital and payments; and the Lisbon Treaty, with its provisions on foreign direct investment, important for the capital and establishment freedoms. It is in this context that this chapter will consider the establishment freedom, concentrating on three aspects where recent Court decisions have appeared to enlarge its scope but have also left unsolved questions on particular aspects.

First, we shall look at the nature of the establishment freedom, distinguishing it from the other freedoms, in particular the right to provide services and free movement of capital.

Second, we shall examine who are the beneficiaries of the right of establishment and, in particular, the position of legal persons, companies, where harmonization of member states' company laws has achieved results but has not solved all problems.

Last, we shall address the question of which parties are obliged by the treaty to respect the right of establishment and consider a 2007 judgment, *Viking*, which, with the *Laval* decision concerning services,[1] caused much criticism. They ruled that the treaty also prohibits measures taken unilaterally by trade union organizations, thus allowing enforcement of the freedoms between private parties.

The Nature and Extent of the Right of Establishment

In Chapter 2 of Title IV of Part Three of the Treaty on the Functioning of the European Union (TFEU) we find Article 49 (formerly Article 43 of the Treaty establishing the European Community (EC)), which foresees that

A Companion to European Union Law and International Law, First Edition.
Edited by Dennis Patterson and Anna Södersten.

> restrictions on the freedom of establishment of nationals of a Member State in the territory of another Member State shall be prohibited. Such prohibitions shall also apply to restrictions on the setting up of agencies, branches or subsidiaries by nationals of any Member State established in the territory of any Member State.

Articles 50 and 53 TFEU foresee the adoption of directives to facilitate the exercise of the freedom. These provisions have become less necessary since direct effect of the freedom was established by the Court; nevertheless, we should note paragraph (g) of Article 50, pursuant to which a large number of directives have been adopted concerning company law, and Article 53 and the directives adopted to facilitate the recognition of diplomas in, for example, the medical professions, which harmonization has allowed the Court to be strict with regard to member states' restrictions regarding citizens seeking healthcare abroad.

Before the provisions of Article 49 can be applied in a particular situation, it is essential to ascertain whether an EU national should be seen as established in a member state or whether he or she is simply providing cross-border services into that member state. For this purpose, one can do no better than look at the Court's landmark judgment in *Gebhard*.[2]

Mr Gebhard, a German lawyer (Rechstanwalt), had been employed in an Italian law firm in Milano for over ten years, resided in Italy with an Italian wife and family, and paid taxes there. In 1989, he set up his own chambers, using the title "avvocato." The Bar Council instigated a disciplinary proceeding against him for having a permanent office and using the title avvocato, which was prohibited by the Italian legislation transposing Directive 77/249 on lawyers' activities pursued by way of providing services. In reply to questions put to the Court on the meaning of the directive and the difference between the notions of establishment and of services, the Court stated that the situation of a Community national who moves to another member state to pursue an economic activity is governed by the treaty chapter on workers, establishment or services, these being mutually exclusive.

It confirmed that in order to have a subsidiary or branch – a secondary establishment – clearly one needed to have a primary establishment and, thus, confirmed that one could be established in two member states at the same time.

It then set out the now classic definition of establishment as follows:

> 25 The concept of establishment within the meaning of the Treaty is therefore a very broad one, allowing a Community national to participate, on a stable and continuous basis, in the economic life of a Member State other than his State of origin and to profit therefrom, so contributing to economic and social interpenetration within the Community in the sphere of activities as self-employed persons.

This was to be contrasted with the notion of services, where activities were carried out on a temporary basis, in order to decide on that

> 27 … the temporary nature of the activities in question has to be determined in the light, not only of the duration of the provision of the service, but also of its regularity, periodicity or continuity. The fact that the provision of services is temporary does not mean that the provider of services within the meaning of the Treaty may not equip himself with some form of infrastructure in the host Member State (including an office, chambers or consulting rooms) in so far as such infrastructure is necessary for the purposes of performing the services in question.
>
> 28 However, that situation is to be distinguished from that of Mr Gebhard who, as a national of a Member State, pursues a professional activity on a stable and continuous basis in another Member

> State where he holds himself out from an established professional base to, amongst others, nationals of that State. Such a national comes under the provisions of the chapter relating to the right of establishment and not those of the chapter relating to services.

The Court then took up the issue of requirement of membership of the national bar and other requirements enacted in the general good, and these will be considered later.

Since the *Gebhard* judgment brings out clearly the difference between the treaty right of establishment and that of the free provision of services, let us now consider that freedom.

Chapter 3 of Title IV provides in its Article 56 TFEU (previously Article 49 EC) that:

> [w]ithin the framework of the provisions set out below, restrictions on freedom to provide services within the Union shall be prohibited in respect of nationals of Member States who are established in a Member State other than that of the person for whom the services are intended.

Article 57 lists examples of services activities, Article 59 foresees harmonizing directives, and Article 62 provides for the application to services of the provisions of Articles 51 to 54 (of the establishment chapter) which confirm member states' powers to adopt restrictions for reasons of public policy, public security, and public health as well as clarifying the status of companies. Thus, a service provider may provide services on his home state conditions and does not have to respect the conditions of the host state (the recipient state of the services), unless such conditions, where restrictive, can be shown to be pursuing an objective of public health, public policy, or public security, or another essential objective of public interest (justification "imported" from the jurisprudence on the free movement of goods) and that the restriction in question is necessary for, and proportionate to, the attainment of the said objective.

The *Gebhard* judgment also established that the notion of a "restriction" in ex Article 49 EC covers any measure liable to hinder establishment by making "less attractive" the exercise of fundamental freedoms guaranteed by the treaty. Subsequent judgments have applied this appreciation widely to cover numerous disincentives. One recent judgment, which concerns the ongoing pursuit or management of a business establishment (referred to in the second paragraph of Article 49), is illustrative. The case of *CaixaBank*[3] concerned a Spanish company that had established a subsidiary in France. The subsidiary was fined by the French authorities for offering current accounts with interest, in conflict with a general French law prohibiting them. The Court noted that subsidiaries of foreign companies would be deprived of the ability to compete more effectively with traditionally established banks, which were in a more favorable position on the national market and that this constituted a "serious obstacle to the pursuit of their activities via a subsidiary, affecting their access to the market." The Court concentrated on credit institutions that were subsidiaries of banks established in other member states, looking at their effective means of competition, an examination that seemed to recall state aid decisions rather than an internal market freedom.

The Court's approach has been much discussed. Some see the rapid examination of whether an obstacle exists and the declarations on competitive methods without any examination of classic competition law arguments, or any reference to the national court, as surprising.[4] Nevertheless, the result is consistent with previous broad interpretations of the nature of a restriction on the establishment freedom.

More evidence of the Court's wide interpretation is to be found in decisions where it had been submitted that the establishment rules should not apply for reasons relating to the application of other treaty rules, including the *Open Skies* cases and *Viking*.

The *Open Skies* cases[5] were infringement proceedings brought against a number of member states that had concluded agreements on liberalizing air transport services with the United

States. A major claim was that the provisions in the agreements, which restricted the grant of flight rights to airlines of that member state's nationality, were in breach of Article 49 TFEU (second paragraph) in relation to airlines of other member states established there. An argument in the UK case that air transport services to third countries had not yet been liberalized under the transport chapter and that Article 49 did not apply because of the provisions of Article 58(1), which provides that "freedom to provide services in the field of transport shall be governed by the provisions of the title relating to transport" was rejected by the Court, interpreting textually the exclusion in this article limiting it to the services freedom only. The UK's international law obligations under its agreement with the United States did not excuse the breach either.

Viking[6] arose from a dispute between Viking, a Finnish ferry company, and the International Transport Workers Federation when the latter issued instructions to its union members to boycott Viking and its ship, *Rosella*, which wished to flag out such ferries to Estonia via a subsidiary there (thus an establishment), in order better to compete with Estonian ferries. Of the numerous questions posed by the national court, one relates to the scope of application of Article 49 in relation to trade unions. Did it apply in this "special" area? First, the Court rejected an argument that the application of the establishment freedom was excluded by Article 153(5) TFEU which precludes EU legislation on the right of association, since member states are obliged to respect treaty freedoms even in areas where they remain competent, as previous rulings in the areas of healthcare and of taxation show. It had also been submitted that the right to strike was excluded from Article 49 as it constitutes a fundamental right, part of the European Social Charter. The right to take collective action was indeed accepted by the Court as being a fundamental right, forming part of the general principles of EU law, respect of which had to be ensured by the Court. However, the restriction inherent therein had to respect EU law and, thus, pass the tests of pursuit of overriding requirements, necessity, and proportionality. It thus concluded that "in principle, collective action introduced by a trade union … is not excluded from the scope of Article 43."[7]

A more difficult question concerns whether it is the establishment rules which should be applied to a specific restriction or whether another freedom's rules should be applied. We have seen in *Gebhard* that a member state national cannot, at the same time, benefit from the establishment and the services freedoms. In contrast, the freedom of establishment and of capital movements may both be relevant to the same member state restriction.

This was made clear in a Commission Communication of 1997[8] in relation to restrictions in the acquisition of shares in companies being privatized by member states. The Commission's Communication described two types of measures often applied in member states' privatizations, usually by way of a Golden Share. The first being those requiring an authorization for the acquisition of shares above a certain amount and the second giving rights to the national authorities to veto certain major decisions of the privatized company. It explained which freedom could be concerned by such arrangements. It stated that Article 63 TFEU covers direct investment, namely that defined in a 1988 directive on capital movements,[9] as "direct links between the person providing the capital and the undertaking" and "investments of all kinds … which serve to establish or maintain lasting economic links."

But the Communication went on to state,

> At the same time, the acquisition of controlling stakes in an EU company by an EU investor, in addition to being a form of capital movement, is also covered under the scope of the right of Establishment. In this sense, Article 43 of the Treaty [now Article 49 TFEU], governing the right of establishment provides that restrictions on the right of establishment shall be abolished.

However, since the Maastricht Treaty, capital freedom has a scope much wider than establishment freedom as it concerns capital movements and payments irrespective of the nationality of the parties as well as movements between member states and third countries. In subsequent infringement procedures, the Court followed the Commission's approach as to the notion of "restriction" and the limited scope for exemptions, giving a wide interpretation to the freedom. In these decisions, the Court considered the restrictions either under the establishment freedom or capital freedom or a combination of the two, often depending upon how these had been argued. These initial cases did not cause problems as they concentrated on the position of member state nationals and frequently centered on the capital provisions. Dealing in the Belgian *Golden Share* case[10] with the Commission's request for declaration of a breach also of the establishment article, the Court stated that since both freedoms contained a justification for public security reasons, the restriction would be considered in the same way and dismissed the application under that chapter too.

In subsequent decisions, the Court considered the Article 49 or 63 question in more detail. In Case C-207/07,[11] Spain questioned the alleged infringement of Article 63 TFEU (capital), arguing that the requirement of consent for an acquisition of more than 10 percent of an energy company's shares would only concern purchasers wishing to acquire a certain influence over the company and thus Article 49 (the establishment freedom) was implicated. Referring to earlier decisions, in particular *Fidium Finanz*, the Court stated that it was necessary to consider the object of the national legislation. Since it was not certain that in every case the acquisition of 10 percent of the share capital would allow a purchaser to exercise a "certain influence," it found that the Spanish provision breached both Article 49 and Article 63 TFEU. In Case C-326/07,[12] decided the year after the Spanish case, the Court introduced a refinement in finding that a power of the Italian authorities to oppose share transfers of at least 5 percent of the share capital could fall not only under Article 63 but also under Article 49 if the shareholdings were very widely distributed (allowing a 5 percent shareholder to "exercise a definite influence," no doubt!).

If there had been a third country element in these two cases, problems could have arisen. A third country investor would have been able to ask the member state to justify its restriction under the capital chapter, whereas the establishment chapter gives him no such rights. Assistance on how to solve such a dilemma may come from the area of the freedom to provide services, the subject of the Court's judgment in *Fidium*.[13] That case concerned the requirement by Germany for a Swiss finance company to obtain authorization in order to offer loans from Switzerland to German nationals. Stating that, in principle, the Court would consider a measure only in relation to one freedom and noting that loan activities are not only found in the list of capital movements in Directive 88/361 but also in directives on the provision of financial services, it found that granting a credit "concerns in principle both … Articles 43 and 56" (now Articles 49 and 63 TFEU). In order to conclude, it referred to the purpose of the national legislation, there the supervision of the provision of financial services, thus leaving *Fidium*, a non-EU national, with no rights.

If a similar rationale were to apply to conflicts between the establishment and capital freedoms, would there not be problems? Can one allow the member state alone to determine the objectives of its restrictive legislation? Furthermore, would a claim to apply only Article 49 not lead to questions as to what number of shares allowed an investor to exercise a "decisive influence," with references to the Court involving the examination of factual situations? But now that the subject of foreign direct investment has been incorporated by the Lisbon Treaty into the European Union's common commercial policy,[14] can one not expect that the extent of third country investors' rights will form part of a harmonized EU approach in new EU agreements with those countries, leaving the only area where member states might still act to be the establishment freedom?

Finally, let us consider perhaps the most important subject of every debate before the Court, namely whether, and how, a restriction on the establishment freedom can be justified.

Article 52 TFEU foresees that

> [t]he provisions of this Chapter ... shall not prejudice the applicability of provisions laid down by law, regulation or administrative action providing for special treatment for foreign nationals on grounds of public policy, public security or public health.

For another ground of justification of a restriction, "the general good," one can do no better than to cite *Gebhard* again:

> 35 However, the taking-up and pursuit of certain self-employed activities may be conditional on complying with certain provisions laid down by law, regulation or administrative action justified by the general good, such as rules relating to organization, qualifications, professional ethics, supervision and liability (see Case 71/76 *Thieffry v. Conseil de l'Ordre des Avocats à la Cour de Paris* [1977] ECR 765, para 12). Such provisions may stipulate in particular that pursuit of a particular activity is restricted to holders of a diploma, certificate or other evidence of formal qualifications, to persons belonging to a professional body or to persons subject to particular rules or supervision, as the case may be. They may also lay down the conditions for the use of professional titles, such as *avvocato*.
>
> 36 Where the taking-up or pursuit of a specific activity is subject to such conditions in the host Member State, a national of another Member State intending to pursue that activity must in principle comply with them. It is for this reason that Article 57 provides that the Council is to issue directives, such as Directive 89/48, for the mutual recognition of diplomas, certificates and other evidence of formal qualifications or, as the case may be, for the coordination of national provisions concerning the taking-up and pursuit of activities as self-employed persons.
>
> 37 It follows, however, from the Court's case-law that national measures liable to hinder or make less attractive the exercise of fundamental freedoms guaranteed by the Treaty must fulfil four conditions: they must be applied in a non-discriminatory manner; they must be justified by imperative requirements in the general interest; they must be suitable for securing the attainment of the objective which they pursue; and they must not go beyond what is necessary in order to attain it (see Case C-19/92 *Kraus v. Land Baden-Württemberg* [1993] ECR I-1663, para 32).

Subsequent judgments concerning "essential reasons of general interest" and "general good" have confirmed that the requirements of necessity, suitability, and proportionality – of not going beyond what is needed to achieve the stated objective – apply across the board, including thus public security and public health reasons.

The public security exception has often been raised in relation to network industries, especially security of energy supply. An exception on this ground was admitted in relation to the free movement of goods in the case of *Campus Oil*,[15] when it was found that a requirement for importers of oil into Ireland to refine part of such imports at the only refinery operating in Ireland was a measure necessary for the public security of a small country wholly dependent upon imports of this energy resource. The privatization judgments concerning the establishment and capital freedoms led to different results since, although the Court clearly admitted that the security of energy supply is part of public security, it could not see how controlling the identity of future shareholders or the amount of shares that could be purchased was a necessary or appropriate measure to ensure such security.[16] However, on one occasion the Court approved a measure in this area, since it accepted that a limited power for the member state to intervene after any decision by a gas company to dispose of its pipelines, in accordance with published criteria, was a necessary and appropriate measure to ensure security of gas supply.[17]A similar approach is seen for other network industries: the 2010 judgment against Portugal concerning privatization in the telecommunications sector is an illustration.[18]

The story is not, however, the same with respect to public health. Here a clear distinction needs to be made between healthcare claims by EU nationals under the services freedom and under the establishment freedom. For services, in the late 1990s, the Court rejected refusals by member state healthcare bodies to reimburse expenses incurred by their citizens to obtain healthcare[19] or health-related products, spectacles, and so on, in another member state. It pursued this approach in relation to type of illness or waiting-list restrictions concerning health services[20] and rejected any need to discuss the noneconomic nature under Article 57 of a national health service which has no payment mechanisms by simply concentrating on the patient's payment for the relevant service in the member state where care took place.[21] The patient is, thus, free (in broad terms) to obtain healthcare services in any member state and to be reimbursed by his or her member state of affiliation.

For a healthcare provider in one member state to establish in another, the situation is not the same, as two judgments illustrate. The judgment in *Sodemare*[22] concerned Italian rules reserving to non-profit-making organizations the right to participate in the running of its social welfare system, thus excluding a Luxembourg company which had set up profit-making subsidiaries in Italy in order to run old people's homes. The Court found that EU law does not detract from the powers of member states to organize their social security systems and that these are based on the principle of solidarity.[23] It stated that a member state may, in the exercise of the powers it retains to organize its social security system, consider that this necessarily implies a non-profit-making requirement. This rule did not discriminate between non-profit-making companies from Italy and those from other member states, so it concluded that there was no breach of Articles 59 or 65 TFEU. How does this decision sit with other rulings? In *Viking*, the Court stated that even in areas where member states retained competence, in social matters in that case, they had to respect the treaty freedoms. The Court did not, as it did in *Caixa Bank*, consider the measure from the point of view of a restriction, instead it simply found that it did not discriminate. This favorable approach is seen in a 2009 judgment against Italy,[24] concerning rules preventing nonpharmacists from owning or having stakes in pharmacies. The Court's approach differed from that in *Sodemare*. It began by recalling that although the treaty does not detract from member states' powers to organize their health systems, they have to comply with the freedoms when doing so.[25] It then found that both Articles 49 and 63 were concerned, establishment and capital, since the rules prevented total or partial ownership equally, and that such prevention constituted a restriction. The main debate thus concerned justification. The protection of public health was accepted as an overriding interest able to justify the restriction; essentially, the Court found that a pharmacist "is presumed to operate the pharmacy not with a purely economic objective, but also from a professional viewpoint"[26] and that other persons would be likely to have, rather, a profit motive. Although real proof of the Court's assumptions is lacking, the Commission's application was dismissed.

The health sector is, thus, a special sector, a sensitive sector, where, after the initial *Sodemare* approach, the debate concerning establishment will center on questions of justification, with significant discretion as to necessity and proportionality for the member state.

The Beneficiaries of the Right of Establishment

While Article 49 TFEU grants the right of establishment to "nationals of a Member State," thus, natural persons, Article 54 TFEU[27] provides in relation to legal persons, that

> [c]ompanies or firms formed in accordance with the laws of a Member State and having their registered office, central administration or principal place of business within the Union, shall, for the purposes of this Chapter, be treated in the same way as natural persons who are nationals of Member States.

The national laws to which the article refers differ, with each member state having its own idea of what obligations are to be imposed in return for the privilege of limited liability. The rules on raising capital, voting, protection of creditors or minority shareholders, or the place where the company must be managed differ, and this hinders cross-border establishment by companies. The definition in Article 54 does, however, have a Union-wide dimension since the link – registered office, place of business, and so on – simply needs to be in the Union and not limited to the member state of incorporation. Further, the nationality of the shareholders is irrelevant.

With respect to the establishment, the Court has had to evaluate the obstacles that can arise when a company wants to move its business abroad. The first such case concerned the refusal by the UK authorities, for fiscal reasons, to allow Daily Mail,[28] a UK company, to transfer its central management and control to the Netherlands, notwithstanding the fact that UK law allows such transfer without the loss of the company's legal personality. The Court found that companies were creatures of national law and that member states' legislation differed widely as to the requisite "connecting factor" to the national territory (registered office, central administration, and so on) and as to the possibility to change that factor.[29] A similar situation came before the Court twenty years later concerning the refusal by Hungarian authorities to allow Cartesio, a Hungarian company, to move its company seat to Italy in circumstances where Hungarian company law required the company seat to be in the place where the company's central administration was situated. In its 2008 judgment,[30] the Court found that, in the absence of an EU definition of the companies enjoying the right of establishment on the basis of a single connecting factor, the question of whether Article 49 applies to a company seeking to rely on the establishment freedom – like the question of whether a natural person is a national of a member state,[31] can only be resolved by national law. Advocate General Maduro expressed a different view, essentially seeing the Hungarian rule as a restriction, and inquiring whether it could be justified on grounds of general public interest, such as the prevention of fraud or protection of creditors or minority shareholders. He rejected the total prohibition as excessive. This judgment has been criticized, especially in the light of intervening decisions which took a different view with regard to restrictions introduced by a member state on a company of another member state wishing to establish a branch or simply wishing to move its place of business. In its 1999 *Centros* decision,[32] the Court considered that the refusal of the Danish authorities to register a branch of a UK company formed by two Danish nationals expressly to do business in Denmark and avoid Denmark's minimum capital requirements, was a breach of the establishment freedom since the treaty specifically intended to enable companies established in one member state to establish an agency, branch, or subsidiary in another. Such a process "cannot in itself constitute an abuse of the right of Establishment."[33] *Inspire Art*, decided in September 2003,[34] concerned a requirement by the Dutch authorities that a UK company wishing to register a branch there describe itself as a "formally foreign company," pay up extra capital, and oblige its directors to assume personal liability. The Court examined all the directives harmonizing aspects of company law and concluded that the Eleventh Directive concerning publicity for foreign branches was exhaustive, ensured total harmonization, and so did not allow extra restrictive provisions. *Überseering*[35] differed from the two other cases as it concerned a German judge's refusal to allow an action to be brought by a Dutch company with its registered office in the Netherlands without reconstituting itself as a German company, where that company had removed its actual central administration to Germany following the acquisition of all its shares by German nationals residing in Germany. The Court did, however, leave a small opening for some requirements:

> It is not inconceivable that overriding requirements relating to the general interest, such as the protection of the interests of creditors, minority shareholders, employees and even the tax authorities, may in certain circumstances and subject to certain conditions, justify restrictions on the freedom of Establishment.[36]

The Court did not specify what such measures could be. Rather it stated that such objectives cannot justify denying legal capacity to a foreign company as this would be tantamount to an outright negation of the freedom of establishment of companies.

These decisions, with one rule for "emigrants" and another for "immigrants," have been criticized, but they perhaps find their foundation in a literal reading of Article 54 TFEU, where the first line refers to national law, according to which one may choose one of the article's three connecting factors.

Total harmonization of company laws could solve these problems, but this has not proven possible. The intention of EU harmonization was initially to impose rules at EU level gradually unifying company law. But a total coordination has not been possible as member states have such different views of what a company is and how it should act, for example, with or without worker participation, according to the "real seat theory" in which the business is run in the jurisdiction where it is incorporated or according to the "registered office theory," where legal provisions and practical management do not need to cohabit. EU action has therefore moved towards the introduction of an EU-wide company vehicle, the "Societas Europea," and to measures which do not necessarily prejudice the underlying national rules, namely the Merger Directive and the Take-Over Bids Directive.

The Merger Directive[37] and the Take-Over Bids Directive,[38] both based on the establishment chapter's harmonization article, do not go very far in dismantling obstacles. Although the former sets out in detail the procedural steps involved in a merger, it permits member states not only to apply nondiscriminatory restrictive measures but also allows special rules, thus discriminatory rules, for cross border situations.[39] Whether these latter would comply with basic EU law is not clear. The judgment in *Sevic Systems*,[40] given only months after adoption of the directive in a similar situation, would seem to confirm such doubts.[41] The Take-Over Bid Directive was intended to facilitate this increasingly common method of cross-border establishment by ensuring equal treatment of shareholders by requiring a purchaser to make a bid once a certain number of shares had been acquired, a restrictive framework for pre- and post-bid defensive measures by a target company (no poison pills), and a "breakthrough" rule, namely a clear power for the bidder, once a certain number of shares had been acquired, to set aside obstacles on acquiring the rest, such as share transfer restrictions, multiple voting rights, and so on.

The Commission's 1989 proposal[42] encountered countless problems with the lawmakers; thus the resulting 2004 Directive contains numerous references to nonharmonized national laws, weakens the defensive measures rules, is unclear as to the breakthrough and, worse, in its Article 12, entitled "Optional Arrangements," gives powers to member states not to require their companies to respect the rules on defensive measures or breakthrough. Yet, in a 2012 report on the operation of the directive, the Commission finds that this seems to be satisfactory,[43] but it points out some areas for improvement.[44] Hopefully the Court will be able to rule on this secondary legislation and render a verdict consonant with the treaty which envisages harmonization as a way of facilitating exercise of the establishment freedom and not the contrary.[45]

Which Parties Must Respect the Freedom of Establishment?

But how is the Court to rule on these questions? Who can allege in court a breach of the establishment freedom?

The Court has found that fundamental freedoms bind not only member states, but also entities that have rule-making powers, in particular in the employment sector.[46] Whether the establishment freedom in Article 49 TFEU was also such as to confer rights on a private undertaking that may be relied on against a trade union was another of the questions posed in the *Viking* case.

In reply, the Court, recalling its jurisprudence on measures "resulting from the exercise, by associations or organizations not governed by public law, of their legal autonomy," *Walrave* and *Koch, Bosman, Deliege, Angonese, Wouters* and others, and its *Defrenne* decision concerning "agreements intended to regulate paid labour collectively,"[47] stated that those decisions "must also apply to Article 43 EC."[48]

The Court found that in the case at hand, the collective trade union action was aimed at the conclusion of an agreement meant to regulate the work of Viking's employees collectively. This clearly extends the scope of the earlier decisions since the treaty prohibition will now cover preliminary and inconclusive acts of only one party to any agreement. The Court took comfort in its approach[49] by referring to its *Strawberries* and *Schmidberger* decisions.[50] However, these cases concerned member states' responsibilities in relation to collective boycotts and not responsibilities of private parties for their actions. The *Strawberries* case concerned the failure by France to prevent destruction of imports by protesters and the *Schmidberger* case, the legality of Austria's decision to allow a particular road-blocking demonstration. The responsibility of the private parties, of the protesters, was not the object of either of those cases. In the *Viking* case, there was no failure to act by Finland, whose trade union law expressly required any action to conform to EU law. But the Court refused to limit its earlier jurisprudence to rule-making bodies only; rather it found that trade unions participate in the drawing up of agreements intended to regulate paid work collectively.[51] It thus concluded that "Article 43 EC is capable of conferring rights on a private undertaking which may be relied on against a trade union."[52]

Conclusion

The treaty article prohibiting restrictions on the freedom of establishment has been given wide application by the Court with no sector excluded, covering thus those within member state competence such as healthcare and taxation. The notion of "restriction" covers every measure capable, rendering the exercise of the right less attractive, every competitive disadvantage for an investor coming from another member state. Overlaps between the establishment and capital freedoms may cause problems to non-EU nationals, but these can be solved, since Lisbon, by EU common commercial policy agreements. The categories of parties obliged to respect the freedom now include private bodies with no rule-making powers, permitting, thus, horizontal application of the rule – at least where working conditions are concerned. Some nondiscriminatory restrictions may, however, be applied if they pursue an acceptable objective and use means necessary for, and proportionate to, attainment of that objective. In the area of public security of energy supply, and in public health, the acceptability of restrictions is not always easy to foresee.

While sketching out the contours of the establishment freedom, this chapter has tried to point to areas which are sensitive – legally, economically, and thus politically – such as energy, healthcare, and cross-border investment into "National Champion" companies, and to flag up Court decisions which have not solved all problems, and this with the intention of stimulating further debate and research into these important questions.

Notes

1 Case C-438/05 *International Transport Workers Federation and Finnish Seamans Union v. Viking Line* EU:C:2007:772; and Case C-341/05 *Laval un Partneri Ltd v. Svenska Byggnadsarbetareförbundet, Svenska Byggnadsarbetareförbundets avdelning 1, Byggettan and Svenska Elektrikerförbundet* EU:C:2007:809.

2 Case C-55/94 *Reinhard Gebhard v. Consiglio dell'Ordine degli Avvocati e Procuratori di Milano* EU:C:1995:411.

3 Case C-442/02 *CaixaBank France v. Ministère de l'Économie, des Finances et de l'Industrie* EU:C:2004:586.

4 Eleanor Spaventa, "Case C-442/02, *Caixa-Bank France v. Ministère de l'Économie, des Finances et de l'Industrie*," *Common Market Law Review* 42 (2005).

5 Case C-466/98 *Commission v. United Kingdom* EU:C:2002:624; Case C-467/98 *Denmark* EU:C:2002:625; Case C-468/98 *Sweden* EU:C:2002:626; Case C-469/98 *Finland* EU:C:2002:627; Case C-471/98 *Belgium* EU:C:2002:628; Case C-472/98 *Luxembourg* EU:C:2002:629; Case C-475/98 *Austria* EU:C:2002:630; Case C-476/98 *Germany* EU:C:2002:631.

6 Case C-438/05 *Viking*, n 1 this chapter.

7 Now Article 49 TFEU, see para 55.

8 Communication of the Commission on certain legal aspects concerning intra-EU investments (97/C 220/06).

9 Council Directive 88/361/EEC of 24 June 1988 for the implementation of Article 67 of the Treaty [1988] OJ L 178/5.

10 Case C-503/99 *Commission v. Belgium* EU:C:2002:328. This is the only case where the Commission's infringement procedure was dismissed by the Court. See also Case C-483/99 *Commission v. France* EU:C:2002:327; Case C-367/98 *Commission v. Portugal* EU:C:2002:326; C 98/01 *Commission v. United Kingdom* EU:C:2003:273; and C-112/05 *Commission v. Germany* EU:C:2007:623.

11 Case C-207/07 *Commission v. Spain* EU:C:2008:428.

12 Case C-326/07 *Commission v. Italy* EU:C:2009:193.

13 Case C-452/04 *Fidium Finanz AG v. Bundesanstalt für Finanzdienstleistungsaufsicht* EU:C:2006:631.

14 Article 207 TFEU.

15 Case 72/83 *Campus Oil v. Minister for Industry and Energy* EU:C:1984:256.

16 See in particular Cases C-326/07 *Commission v. Italy*, n 12 this chapter; and C 207/07 *Commission v. Spain*, n 11 this chapter.

17 Case C-503/99 *Commission v. Belgium*, n 10 this chapter.

18 Case C-171/08 *Commission v. Portugal* EU:C:2010:412.

19 Case C-120/95 *Decker* EU:C:1998:167; and Case C-158/96 *Kohll* EU:C:1998:171.

20 Case C-173/09 *Elchinov v. Natsionalna zdravnoosiguritelna kasa* EU:C:2010:581.

21 Case C-372/04 *Watts v. Bedford Primary Care Trust* EU:C:2006:325.
22 Case C-70/95 *Sodemare spa et al v. Regione Lombardia* EU:C:1997:301.
23 This, surely, is also the case for the UK National Health Service, but in the *Watts* case, no such discussion took place.
24 Case C-531/06 *Commission v. Italy* EU:C:2009:315.
25 Recitals 35–36.
26 Recitals 58–61.
27 Also applicable to the services chapter, see Article 62 TFEU.
28 Cases 81/87 *The Queen v. HM Treasury and Commissioners of Inland Revenue ex parte Daily Mail and General Trust plc.* EU:C:1988:456.
29 Recitals 22–24.
30 Case C-210/06 *Cartesio Oktato es Szolgaltato bt* EU:C:2008:723.
31 Case C-369/90 *Micheletti v. Delegación del Gobierno in Cantabria* EU:C:1992:295.
32 Case C-212/97 *Centros Ltd v. Erhvervs- og Selskabsstyrelsen* EU:C:1999:126.
33 Para 27.
34 Case C-167/01 *Kamer van Koophandel en Fabrieken voor Amsterdam v. Inspire Art Ltd* EU:C:2003:512.
35 Case C-208/00 *Überseering BV v. Nordic Construction Company Baumanagement Gmbh* EU:C:2002:632.
36 Recital 92. There is some similarity to Advocate General Maduro's Opinion in Case C-210/06 *Cartesio*, n 30 this chapter.
37 Directive 2005/56/EC of the European Parliament and of the Council of 26 October 2005 on cross-border mergers of limited liability companies [2005] OJ L 310/1.
38 Directive 2004/25/EC of the European Parliament and of the Council of 21 April 2004 on takeover bids [2004] OJ L 142/12.
39 Articles 4(1)b and 4(2).
40 Case C-411/03 *Sevic Systems AG v. Amtsgericht Neuwied* EU:C:2005:762.
41 See also Case C-210/06 *Cartesio*, n 30 this chapter, para 111 and 112.
42 COM(1990) 416 final.
43 Commission Staff Working Document of 21 February 2007 SEC (2007) 268.
44 COM(2012) 347 final.
45 See, e.g., Case E-1/10 *Periscopus AS v. Oslo Bors ASA and Erik Must AS.*
46 E.g., Case C-281/98 *Roman Angonese v. Cassa di Risparmio di Bolzano* EU:C:2000:296 .
47 Recitals 57 and 58.
48 Recital 59.
49 Recital 62.
50 Case C-265/95 *Commission v. France* EU:C:1997:595; and Case C-112/00 *Eugen Schmidberger, Internationale Transporte and Planzüge v. Austria* EU:C:2003:333.
51 Recital 65.
52 Recital 66.

Reference

Spaventa, Eleanor. "Case C-442/02, *Caixa-Bank France v. Ministère de l'Économie, des Finances et de l'Industrie.*" *Common Market Law Review* 42 (2005): 1151–1168.

17

Free Movement of Capital

Sideek M. Seyad

Introduction

The constitutional provisions dealing with the four economic freedoms constituting the single market of the European Union had been subject to different degrees of change by successive amendments to the European treaties to strengthen, deepen, and widen the integration process. Such changes introduced to the rules on the free movement of goods, persons, services, and the right of establishment were, however, relatively trivial compared to the radical changes introduced to the rules on the free movement of capital.

Unlike the other economic freedoms, most of the subsequent amendments introduced to the original Treaty of Rome, 1958, had a direct impact on the rules on the free movement of capital. The most far reaching of all such amendments were those introduced by the Maastricht Treaty in 1993, which completely repealed and replaced the original rules on the free movement of capital. Even the Lisbon Treaty, which entered into force in December 2009, introduced more changes to the capital rules than the other economic freedoms.

This chapter will examine the progressive nature of liberalization of the free movement of capital supported by reference to the relevant treaty provisions, secondary legislation, and case law of the Court of Justice of the European Union (CJEU). Such an approach will highlight the significance of the capital freedom to the single market and the extent to which its legal framework has changed dramatically over the years. It will clearly highlight the monopolistic competence of the member states in matters relating to exchange and investment controls at the time of the inception of the common market and the gradual but progressive erosion of such competence over the years. There are also more exceptions to the exercise of this freedom than the other economic freedoms, which will also be examined.

Since the free movement of capital is an integral part of the single market and forms an essential pillar of the legal foundation of the financial market, it is also useful to highlight its relations to the free movement of services and establishment. The free movement of capital is closely associated with the single currency of the European Union, the euro; consequently, this chapter will also briefly examine the current reform measures introduced for its effective management.

A Companion to European Union Law and International Law, First Edition.
Edited by Dennis Patterson and Anna Södersten.

Aim and Scope of Application of Article 67 EEC

The aim of the Treaty of Rome was to create the European Economic Community (EEC), within which the four economic freedoms were to be liberalized in order to create a market common to all its member states. The rules on the free movement of capital were set out in Articles 67 to 73 EEC with the aim of facilitating the liberalization of the capital movements between the member states. However, this aim was frustrated when the CJEU refused to confer direct effect to this freedom.[1]

Capital Directive 88/361/EEC

After the CJEU declared Article 67 EEC to have no direct effect, there was hardly any progress made in the field of financial integration until the Treaty of Rome was amended by the Single European Act in 1985. One of the major objectives of this treaty amendment was to facilitate and expedite the process of financial integration by means of simplifying the lawmaking procedure in this sector.

The treaty amendment facilitated the adoption of several secondary legal measures in the financial sector. Apart from facilitating the launch of the internal market on 1 January 1993 as mandated in the Single European Act, it also provided a sound legal foundation to liberalize the free movement of capital and to realize the objective of creating a single market in financial services.

The problem left behind by the CJEU in *Casati* was rectified by the adoption of Capital Directive 88/361, the aim of which was to completely liberalize the free movement of capital between the member states. Article 1 of this directive was carefully formulated to ensure its direct effect. It simply declares that all member states shall remove the restrictions to cross-border movements of capital. In *Aldo Bordessa*,[2] a dispute involving the compatibility of the Spanish exchange control legislation requiring prior authorization to export large sums of money with EU law on the free movement of capital, the CJEU declared that Article 1 should have direct effect.

The Maastricht Treaty and the Free Movement of Capital

Even though the Capital Directive 88/361/EEC coupled with the judgment in *Aldo Bordessa* provided for liberalization of capital movements, it did not provide sufficient legal certainty to the exercise of this economic activity. The reason for this legal uncertainty is that a treaty provision such as Article 67 EEC, which the CJEU declared not to have direct effect, is (in terms of legal hierarchy) superior to secondary legislation such as the Capital Directive 88/361/EEC. It was partly to remove this legal uncertainty that the Maastricht Treaty repealed and replaced the original rules on the free movement of capital effective from 1 January 1994.

Among the objectives of the Maastricht Treaty were the creation of a clear legal framework for deepening of the single market, establishment of the Economic and Monetary Union (EMU), and further strengthening of the legal foundation on financial integration. In order to achieve these diverse but interrelated objectives, the amending treaty sought to provide constitutional protection to the free flow of capital and payments across the borders within and beyond the European Union. As such, the Maastricht Treaty completely repealed Articles 67 to 73 EEC and replaced them with a new set of rules, namely Articles 73b–h of the Treaty establishing the European Community (EC) (subsequently renumbered as 56 to 60 EC by the Amsterdam Treaty); under the Lisbon Treaty they became Articles 63 to 66 and 75 TFEU respectively.

Unlike the previous European treaties, the Maastricht Treaty brought about radical changes to the constitutional structure of the European Union. It introduced a complex three-pillar structure, which constitutionalized a multispeed Europe, thereby enabling some member states to move towards closer integration faster than others. The precedent created by the Maastricht Treaty allowing a series of derogations and opt-outs in favor of some member states has since been followed in all subsequent treaty amendments, including the Lisbon Treaty. Such derogations and opt-outs are, however, not applicable to the single market, including the rules on the free movement of capital. If there were any such derogation, it would be only for a limited period of time.

The *Sanz de Lera* Case

The scope of application of Article 56 EC, which now reads as Article 63 of the Treaty on the Functioning of the European Union (TFEU), formed the key provision on capital movements and was subject to judicial review in *Sanz de Lera*.[3] The case involved the criminal prosecution of individuals who allegedly attempted to smuggle a sum of money in excess of the prescribed limits without authorization out from Spain to Turkey and Switzerland. Since Article 63 TFEU is formulated in a clear, precise, and unambiguous language without any conditions attached to its implementation, the CJEU had no difficulty in declaring it as providing direct effect. The CJEU therefore declared that national laws prohibiting the export of currency without prior authorization were contrary to European Community law.

Articles 63 to 66 and 75 TFEU and the judgment in *Sanz de Lera* warrant closer and critical examination. Article 63 TFEU is unique in so many ways compared to the corresponding rules on the free movement of goods, persons, services, and establishment.

Globalization of Capital Freedom

Article 63 TFEU provides that member states shall remove the barriers to the free movement of capital not only between themselves but also towards third countries. This is in contrast with the other economic freedoms, which operate mainly within the territorial limits of the European Union; these may be labeled "Union freedoms." In contrast, as confirmed in *Sanz de Lera*, the enjoyment of capital freedom is not limited to the EU territory but also extends its benefits to third countries, and as such, it may be declared a global freedom.

The unilateral extension of the capital freedom to countries outside the European Union may provoke mixed reactions. The widening and deepening of the Union had been carried out by strengthening its external borders with non-EU countries such as the Schengen visa-free area within its territory excluding the United Kingdom and Ireland. The European Union had also been criticized as mounting trade barriers, particularly towards developing countries. The judgment in *Sanz de Lera* to some extent may be used as a defense to repel such criticism.

The judgment should also be viewed in light of the launching of the euro as the single currency of some of the member states of the Union in 1999. Even though the Lisbon Treaty does not expressly declare that the euro shall be developed as an international and competitive currency, the European Union plays a major role in international politics and trade and, to that extent, it would like to use its currency as a bargaining tool in such areas. The euro cannot develop into an international currency if the free movement of capital is to be limited to the geographical limits of the European Union.

The extension and the scope of the free movement of capital to third countries are, however, subject to various qualifications. As far as movements of capital within the Union are concerned, all member states are legally bound to adhere to the general principle of nondiscrimination. There is no need for reciprocity within an integrated financial market as all member states are bound by the same set of rules and regulations. There are no similar legal rules to regulate the Union's financial and monetary relations with third countries.

It is thus desirable to limit the scope of the judgment in *Sanz de Lera* strictly to the facts of the case, namely the removal of exchange controls such as free movement of banknotes, and not to extend the freedom automatically to abolition of all forms of capital controls. The European Union should have the bargaining power not only to ensure that its financial operators are not subject to any form of discrimination in a third country but also to ensure that its nationals receive reciprocal treatment in such countries.

The Union has some legal instruments at its disposal to secure reciprocity from third countries in relation to capital movements. The general policy of the Union in relation to financial integration is to extend its benefits to third countries as well. At the same time, it has retained certain control measures to ensure that its financial institutions receive equal and nondiscriminatory treatment in third countries.[4] The new chapter on capital and payments has laid down certain rules to ensure that the capital moves smoothly not only within the European Union but also beyond its boundaries; indeed, most of them are directed towards third countries.

Treaty Exceptions to the Free Movement of Capital

The general principle is that all four economic freedoms shall be completely liberalized. At the same time, there are also provisions in each chapter dealing with these freedoms which authorize the member states to restrict the exercise of such freedoms. The free movement of goods may be restricted by member states on grounds of public morality, public policy, or public security; and likewise there are various grounds recognized in the treaty allowing member states to limit the free movement of workers, services, and establishment.[5]

As far as the free movement of capital is concerned, on the one hand, the level of liberalization is much greater than other freedoms as the exercise of this freedom is extended to third countries as well. On the other hand, the scope of recognized exceptions to the exercise of this freedom is also much wider.

Article 63 TFEU is the key treaty provision on the free movement of capital not only between the member states but also towards third countries. All the provisions following this treaty provision form an exception to the general rule on free movement of capital. However, only Article 65 TFEU applies to movements of capital between the member states, whereas all treaty provisions, including Article 65 TFEU, apply to third countries.

Under Article 64 TFEU member states enjoy the right to enforce certain restrictions on capital movements that existed under their national law and Community law as at 31 December 1993 in relation to direct investment – including investment in real estate – establishment, the provision of financial services, or the admission of securities to capital markets. After the Lisbon Treaty the relevant date on which national restrictive measures may be maintained is given an extended time framework effective from 31 December 1999 in favor of Bulgaria, Estonia, and Hungary respectively. The objective of this article was to keep intact restrictions on capital movements in relation to the right of establishment and provision of financial services until the European Union adopts liberalizing measures and not to extend a blank check unilaterally to third countries to enter the EU's financial market.

Article 65 TFEU is the most comprehensive exception to the general principle of free movement of capital, both between the member states and towards third countries. This treaty provision authorizes member states to derogate from their obligations if freedom of capital movements comes into conflict with the national tax administration, public policy matters, prudential supervision of financial institutions, and the right of establishment. It may appear at a glance that Article 65 TFEU extends a wide scope of discretion to member states to invoke this exception. However, Article 65(3) TFEU seems to dispel such fears as it provides that restrictions permitted under this article must not constitute an "arbitrary discrimination or a disguised restriction" on the free movement of capital and payments.

An amendment introduced to Article 65 TFEU by the Lisbon Treaty further strengthens the competence of member states in relation to tax matters. According to Article 65(4) TFEU, if the European Commission fails to take tax measures towards third countries as envisaged in Article 65(3) TFEU, a member state may be authorized to adopt restrictive tax measures towards one or more third countries.

The exceptions enumerated in Article 65 TFEU closely resemble a counterpart on free movement of goods found in Article 36 TFEU. The latter article is subject to a similar limitation, namely that prohibitions or restrictions shall not constitute a means of arbitrary discrimination or a disguised restriction on trade between member states. Since Article 36 TFEU has been subject to extensive judicial review, the principles developed in this context would be useful to ascertain the scope of Article 65 TFEU.

The CJEU has consistently maintained that member states cannot avoid their treaty obligations by pleading economic difficulties that may have been caused by the dismantling of barriers to intra-Community trade.[6] Applying a similar judicial yardstick, it might well be that the control measures envisaged in Article 65 TFEU should be strictly confined to the effective administration and enforcement of the tax system and the effective supervision of financial institutions rather than to matters of economic policy.[7]

Another judicial innovation relevant in this context is that national measures authorized under a treaty exception cannot be invoked to matters that are sufficiently dealt with by EU law.[8] The application of this principle to capital movements is more distinct. The periodical liberalization of capital movements by means of Council directives[9] reduces proportionately the right of member states to apply national laws to those categories of capital movements that have been completely liberalized.

A member state that seeks to invoke an exception in order to derogate from a treaty obligation must ensure that it does not adopt any national measures that may amount to arbitrary discrimination.[10] Applying the same philosophy to Article 65 TFEU, member states will be required to show that effective measures are taken internally to deal with tax laws, the prudential supervision of financial institutions, or other perceived problems contained in Article 65 TFEU.

Any measures adopted in terms of Article 65 TFEU may still be deemed to be a disguised restriction if such measures exceed the need to protect a particular national interest. Article 65 TFEU will not protect a member state that adopts measures in pursuance of this treaty provision if the same objective could be achieved by other means less restrictive on inter-Community trade.[11]

These judicial principles should form a rich source of guidelines to interpret and apply the restrictions in Article 65 TFEU and should help to ease the burden imposed on the free circulation of capital.

Capital Movements and Monetary Union

After the Maastricht Treaty, the relevance of the free movement of capital has shifted from its traditional link to the single market to the establishment of the EMU. The creation of the EMU is a well-entrenched treaty objective which was achieved in three stages.[12] The majority of the member states of the European Union have joined the EMU at different intervals, and all other member states, except the United Kingdom and Denmark, will follow suit as soon as they fulfill the entry requirements.[13]

Before the introduction of the euro there had been several instances of monetary turbulence within the European Union, caused largely by external factors, but the Union had no legal instrument at its disposal to deal with a crisis. This legal vacuum was filled by Article 66 TFEU, which forms one of the exceptions to Article 63 TFEU. In terms of this treaty provision, if movements of capital to or from third countries cause, or threaten to cause, serious difficulties for the operation of the EMU, the European Union can take safeguard measures to deal with the situation. Such measures can be taken only against third countries, only in exceptional circumstances, and furthermore, within a definite time limit – a maximum of six months. The treaty is not specific about the grounds on which such safeguard measures may be invoked, but it is likely that such measures may be invoked, for example, in cases involving purely speculative movements of capital destabilizing the euro.

Free Movement of Capital and an Area of Freedom, Security, and Justice

Apart from EMU, the Maastricht Treaty also laid the foundation for the European Union to develop two other policy areas, namely a common foreign and security policy and justice and home affairs, which after the Amsterdam Treaty came to be known as freedom, security, and justice. It is significant to note that the European Union frequently invokes the rules on the free movement of capital as one of its legal tools to develop other policy areas.

Before the Lisbon Treaty, Article 60 EU, which formed one of the exceptions to the free movement of capital, was linked to the provisions on the Common Foreign and Security Policy (CFSP). The European Union and its member states may, under Article 60 EU, interrupt or reduce economic relations with third countries, including the terminating or suspending capital movements. The reservation of these powers should be viewed in the light of the provisions concerning the CFSP. The significance of the reference to CFSP in Article 60 EU is that the Union has the legal means to impose economic embargoes against third countries, including restrictions on financial transactions, such as freezing of the financial assets.

After the Lisbon Treaty, Article 60 EU was replaced by Article 75 TFEU: it now refers to an area of freedom, security, and justice. Article 75 TFEU specifically refers to Article 67 TFEU, which deals with an area of freedom, security, and justice. An objective of Article 75 TFEU is to facilitate the implementation of one of the objectives in Article 67 TFEU, namely to develop an area of freedom, security, and justice. In order to prevent and combat terrorism and related activities, an objective covered by Article 67 TFEU, Article 75 TFEU provides

> a framework for administrative measures with regard to capital movements and payments, such as the freezing of funds, financial assets or economic gains belonging to, or owned or held by, natural or legal persons, groups or non-State entities.

The Link between the Free Movement of Capital and Other Economic Freedoms

The free movement of capital is closely associated with the right of establishment and the freedom to provide services. The right of establishment is broadly defined to cover both primary and secondary establishment and also includes both natural and legal persons.[14] Similarly, "services" covers not only to "provide services" but also to "receive services."

Before the CJEU declared the rules on free movement of capital as directly effective, it resolved disputes arising out of a pure capital transaction by reference to the rules on establishment or services. For example, in *Luisi and Carbone*,[15] which involved export of banknotes from Italy to Germany and France to pay for medical services and for purposes of tourism, the CJEU resolved the dispute by reference to the rules on services rather than capital.

This judicial approach changed after the CJEU declared that free movement of capital is a directly effective freedom. Since then, even disputes where the transaction appears to be more connected to establishment and services rather than capital have been resolved by invoking the rules on free movement of capital.

Trummer and Mayer[16] involved a real estate transaction where the property was located in Austria. The owner of the property lived in Germany and the buyer in Austria. A dispute arose over the registration of a mortgage bond relating to this property. When the dispute reached the CJEU, it declared that the cross-border transaction is covered by the rules on the free movement of capital. In this case, the CJEU gave a broad interpretation as to what constitutes movement of capital, declaring that money realized by the liquidation of an investment in real estate constitutes movement of capital. This was contrary to the interpretation given by the national court, which came to the finding that the disputed transaction did not constitute capital movements.[17]

André Ambry[18] is a case in which the national court in its preliminary reference asked the CJEU about the compatibility of a national law with the rules on the free movement of services and capital. In this case, the CJEU declared the French law to be contrary to the rules on free movement of services and decided not to examine its compatibility with the rules on free movement of capital. The dispute involved a financial guarantee provided by an applicant in France for a travel agency license. One of the requirements to secure the license is that a bank, insurance company, or financial company should provide a financial guarantee. The relevant French authority rejected the application on grounds that the financial security was provided by a company based in Italy and that it was not supplemented by a company based in France.

Free Movement of Capital and Company Law

A new generation of case law in the field of free movement of capital has emerged known as the "special rights" or "golden shares" cases. These cases involve especially sensitive sectors where some member states felt the need to retain control of privatized companies and thus resorted to holding on to special rights in them. The origin of this line of cases may be traced back to the pre-EMU period during which many member states embarked on a massive privatization program of state enterprises, such as those dealing in energy, oil, gas, petroleum, telecommunication, and so on. These member states had difficulties meeting the fiscal criteria to join the monetary union. They privatized the state enterprises, and with the proceeds they managed to reduce their budgetary deficits to the prescribed limits to join the EMU.

In these cases, the European Commission brought action against the member states for seeking to control the privatized enterprises, alleging that such control measures form a serious obstacle to the free movement of capital. The main argument adduced by the Commission was that the member states, by retaining management control by holding minority shares, were discouraging foreign investors to participate in such enterprises. Such national measures limiting or preventing cross-border investment in companies may also be treated as an obstacle to the cross-border right of establishment. However, in most of the cases, the Commission based its line of action on Article 63 TFEU.

A brief reference to one of the cases decided by the CJEU sheds more light on the nature of golden shares some countries sought to enjoy even after privatizing such state property. In *Commission v. Germany*,[19] the case involved the compatibility of the German "Volkswagen law" with the EU rules on the free movement of capital. The Volkswagen law was passed by Germany to protect the Volkswagen car company from takeover by any foreign competitors. The German government and the relevant state where the company is located retained about 20 percent of the shares even after its privatization. Under the law's provisions, any major management decision, such as mergers or selling of assets, could be taken only with over 80 percent of votes. In other words, no major management decision could be taken without the consent of the state. The Commission successfully challenged this law on the basis that the relevant law forms an obstacle to cross-border investments and thereby is in breach of the rules on the free movement of capital.

Free Movement of Capital beyond the Lisbon Treaty

The 2008 global financial crisis and the 2011 fiscal crisis within the eurozone give some indication as to the future direction which the free movement of capital should take, not only for the survival of the euro but also to preserve the stability and good reputation of the single market. As both these crises made abundantly clear, there is no nation or regional organization that is immune from such crises, even though the source of the financial and fiscal crisis may be traced to the United States and the European Union respectively.

The impact of these crises has been felt in different degrees across the globe. This is a price that had to be paid with the international liberalization of the free movement of capital. The solution is, however, not to reintroduce capital controls but to look into the causes that created the crises and take remedial action. It is against this background that we have to explore the extent to which the Lisbon Treaty should be amended or protective and preventive measures adopted so that in the future the European Union should be able to eliminate, or at least minimize, the risk of another round of financial and fiscal crisis developing within its territory.

Capital Movements and Banking Union

As the preceding discussion highlights, free movement of capital does not operate in isolation. The freedom of capital is an indispensable requirement for the proper and efficient exercise of the other freedoms, such as the right of establishment and free movement of financial services.

The line between the free movement of capital and the free movement of financial services is rather thin. As the case law makes abundantly clear, the same transaction may constitute either a capital movement or a banking transaction. In view of this inextricable link between these freedoms, it is essential that they should operate interdependently in order to ensure the proper functioning of the internal market in financial services.

One of the factors internal to the European Union that partly contributed to the financial crisis was the inadequacy in the banking sector. There is legislation adopted to liberalize the banking market but it is not sufficient to ensure the smooth cross-border flow of capital.[20] Since the banking sector is fully liberalized, the national banks operate at the European level freely lending and accepting deposits from their customers across the borders. If the free flow of cross-border capital is to function harmoniously, it is essential that the European Union identify the shortcomings in its single market in banking services and develop it into a fully fledged banking union.

In previous work, I have strongly stressed that a European banking system should be supported by a central authority similar to the European Central Bank (ECB) for effective supervision.[21] As the recent financial crisis exposed, one of the contributing factors was the shortcomings in the home country control system prescribed to supervise the banking system.[22]

Soon after the financial crisis, the European Union established various authorities to supervise its financial market. There are three separate authorities created to supervise the banking, securities, and insurance markets, and these are supported by a body known as the European Systematic Risk Board for macroprudential purposes.[23] The powers of the authorities are limited to overseeing the functioning of the national supervisory system.

At the recently concluded meeting of the European Council, it was decided that at least the member states of the eurozone should move towards the creation of a banking union.[24] One of the proposals discussed in this context is to elevate the post-crisis financial authorities into a pan-European body. This proposal has emerged in the light of the serious banking crisis that developed in some of the eurozone member states, which in turn is threatening the stability of the euro.

In this context, it is suggested that a powerful pan-European body should be created to jointly supervise the banking and securities market. These two segments of the financial market have reached a high level of liberalization in providing their services across borders. The legal instruments adopted to liberalize these financial services have provided the financial institutions with a European "passport" with a wide range of financial products to market across the borders. The kind of financial services offered by these financial institutions often overlap with each other. As such, it is appropriate that they are subject to unified supervision by a single authority.

The Lisbon Treaty envisages that at some point the ECB should be delegated the authority to supervise institutions providing banking and securities services.[25] Since the monetary policy for the eurozone countries are exclusively vested in the ECB, it is also appropriate that the same institution should be given the task of monitoring and supervising the banking and securities market.

Pan-European Deposit Guarantee Scheme

At the height of the financial crisis, several depositors across the European Union began to withdraw their savings, fearing collapse of their financial institutions. The existence of the deposit guarantee scheme created by European legislation did not provide them with sufficient confidence of the safety of their deposit.[26] At the time of the crisis, the deposit guarantee schemes gave protection to a maximum amount of €20,000.

In order to generate confidence and to prevent large-scale withdrawals, the European Union amended the existing directive.[27] The aim of this amendment was to increase coverage and to facilitate the depositors recovering money within a short span of time.[28] These emergency measures acted, at least temporarily, to restore depositor confidence in the banking system.

There are risks that the deposit guarantee scheme in a particular member state may not be sufficient to cover all their depositors in case of more than one financial institution becoming unable to pay back their depositors. It is unlikely that a deposit guarantee scheme from another member state could come to the rescue owing to fear of spread of contagion risk, which is a phenomenon in the banking sector. As such, it is suggested that the deposit guarantee schemes should be elevated to a pan-European mechanism, which should be in a better position to deal with a major European banking crisis. This is one of the proposals that emerged at the European Council as part of the package to move towards banking union. Since the banks are operating at the European level through their branches and agencies, it is desirable that the bank depositors are protected by a European deposit guarantee scheme, as it will be better equipped, especially financially, to deal with a banking crisis.[29]

Capital Movements and Fiscal Union

The aim of liberalizing the free movement of capital was to facilitate the transfer of capital from one member state to another; thereby, the financial resources could be used in a productive manner. Such transfer of capital should facilitate individuals and companies to start new businesses or expand existing economic activities. Such an investment climate should enhance efficiency and generate competition, which is one of the objectives of the creation of the single market.

The creation of the single currency – the euro – was a logical consequence of the free movement of capital. In order to achieve the goal of generating competition and enhancing efficiency in the single market, the European Union decided to merge the different national currencies into a single monetary unit, and this objective was achieved by the introduction of the euro.

The recurring fiscal crisis within the eurozone clearly indicates that the EMU is an incomplete and imperfect project. Following the Lisbon Treaty some legislative measures have been adopted to strengthen the euro by way of enforcing stricter fiscal discipline among the member states by amending and widening the scope of application of the Stability and Growth Pact.[30]

An amendment to the Lisbon Treaty known as the European Stability Mechanism was created to make the existing European Financial Stability Facility a permanent bailout mechanism in order to prevent the debt crisis that developed in Greece from spreading to the other member states.[31] The aim of this treaty is to facilitate the application of stricter rules to ensure fiscal discipline and provide sanctions for countries that breach the fiscal rules. The overall aim of this treaty, which will later be incorporated into EU law, is to strengthen the economic pillar of the EMU, a missing link in its current legal framework.

At the June 2012 European Council summit it was also decided to gradually move the monetary union into a fiscal union. The EU leaders approved a roadmap for building a more integrated eurozone, with the ultimate objective to create a fiscal union. As a counter to future Greek-style debt crises it also includes plans for issuing of eurobonds and mutualization of eurozone debts.

If all these measures are put in place, it should guarantee the stability of the euro and the eurozone. If the monetary union is supplemented by a fiscal union, this should guarantee, at least within the eurozone, that there will be smooth and harmonious cross-border flow of capital.

Conclusion

In the European single market, the free movement of capital was confined to the slow track towards liberalization. Even though this freedom developed at a very gradual pace, its final destination was beyond that of the other economic freedoms. On the one hand, it facilitated to complete the single market of the European Union by enabling the financial resources to be freely moved across its internal borders. On the other hand, it also set a precedent to the trading partners of the Union to liberalize the international movements of capital.

The legal and judicial involvement to remove all restrictions and uncertainties surrounding the free movement of capital is a timely intervention to facilitate the Union's task of achieving its objective of full integration of the European financial market and carrying the European Union forward towards a zone of financial and monetary stability.

The legal framework prior to the Maastricht Treaty governing capital movements was characterized by a contradiction between Article 67(1) EEC, which the CJEU declared not to be directly effective, and Article 1 of Capital Directive 88/361/EEC, seeking to completely liberalize this freedom, which was declared to be directly effective. The conflict between the treaty provision and its implementing legislation was one of the contributory factors to the complete replacement of the chapter on capital.

The change of the legal foundation of the free movement of capital after the Maastricht Treaty has created some degree of uncertainty over the legal status of Capital Directive 88/361/EEC as it owes its existence to the repealed Article 67 EEC. Since the treaty basis of this directive is repealed and Article 63 TFEU now forms the supreme law governing the free movement of capital, the secondary legal instrument has lost its legal significance. However, since Article 63 TFEU (following the pattern of its preceding Article 67 EEC) failed to define what constitutes capital movements, it is desirable to retain this directive as a source of guidelines to ascertain what constitutes capital and capital movements. It is noteworthy that the directive contains a long list of capital transactions that should be treated as capital.

The debt crisis has threatened the stability of the euro. There had been large outflows of capital from southern member states to their northern counterparts, where the fiscal conditions were considered to be sound and safe to park the money. Such movements of capital will not facilitate achieving the objective of the Lisbon Treaty of ensuring the smooth and harmonious development of the single market as a whole. In order to reverse this trend, the European Union has taken emergency measures, and hopefully fiscal stability should return to the Union and thereby a stable and dynamic internal market within which the capital could flow smoothly and without any distortion.

Notes

1 Case 203/80 *Casati* EU:C:1981:261.
2 Joined Cases C-358/93 and C-416/93 *Aldo Bordessa* EU:C:1995:54.
3 Case C-163/94 *Sanz de Lera* EU:C:1995:451.
4 Council Directive 89/646/EEC of 15 December 1989 on the coordination of laws, regulations, and administrative provisions relating to the taking up and pursuit of the business of credit institutions and amending Directive 77/780/EEC [1997] OJ L 311/42.
5 Articles 45, 52, and 62 TFEU respectively.
6 Case 7/61 *Commission v. Italy* EU:C:1961:31.
7 John A. Usher, *The Law of Money and Financial Services in the European Community* (Oxford: Oxford University Press, 1994), 36.

8 Case 28/84 *Commission v. Germany* EU:C:1985:386.
9 First Council Directive, 11 May 1960 as amended in 1962 and Directive 86/566/EEC, 17 November 1986.
10 Case 4/75 *Rewe* EU:C:1975:98.
11 Case 25/88 *Wurmser* EU:C:1989:187.
12 Seyad M. Sideek, "Sweden and the European Economic and Monetary Union," *European Financial Services Law* 2 (1995): 289.
13 Protocols No. 15 and 22 respectively.
14 Article 49 TFEU.
15 Case 286/82 *Luisi and Carbone* EU:C:1984:35.
16 Case C-222/97 *Manfred Trummer and Peter Mayer* EU:C:1999:143.
17 Paragraphs 6, 7, and 8 of the judgment.
18 Case C-410/96 *André Ambry* EU:C:1998:578.
19 Case C-112/05 *Commission v. Germany* EU:C:2007:623.
20 Directive 2000/12/EC of the European Parliament and of the Council of 20 March 2000 relating to the taking up and pursuit of the business of credit institutions [2000] OJ L 126/1.
21 Sideek M. Seyad, "A Single Regulator for the EC Financial Market," *Journal of International Banking Law* 16 (2001): 208.
22 Sideek M. Seyad, "A Critical Evaluation of the Causes and Remedies to Global Financial Crisis with Special Reference to the European Union," *European Policy Analysis* (Stockholm: Swedish Institute for European Policy Studies, May 2009).
23 The new European Supervisory Authorities are the European Securities and Markets Agency, the European Banking Agency, and the European Insurance and Occupational Pensions Authority. They replace the "Level 3 Committees" (also known as "Lamfalussy"): Committee of European Banking Supervisors; Committee of European Securities Regulators; and Committee of European Insurance and Occupational Pensions Supervisors.
24 Conclusions of the European Council, Brussels, 28–29 June 2012.
25 Article 127(6) TFEU.
26 Council Directive 94/19/EC of 30 May 1994 on deposit guarantee schemes [1994] OJ L 135/5.
27 Council Directive 2009/14/EC of 11 March 2009 amending Council Directive 94/19/EC on deposit guarantee schemes as regards the coverage level and the payout delay [2009] OJ L 68/3.
28 Sideek M. Seyad, "Protection of EU Bank Depositors after the 2008 Global Financial Crisis," *Europarättslig Tidskrift* 15 (2012): 69.
29 Ibid., 74.
30 Sideek M. Seyad, "A Critical Evaluation of the Revised and Enlarged European Stability and Growth Pact," *Journal of International Banking and Regulation* 27 (2012): 202.
31 Sideek M. Seyad, "A Legal Analysis of the European Financial Stability Mechanism," *Journal of International Banking Law and Regulation* 26 (2011): 421.

References

Seyad, Sideek M. "Sweden and the European Economic and Monetary Union." *European Financial Services Law* 2 (1995): 288–295.

Seyad, Sideek M. "A Single Regulator for the EC Financial Market." *Journal of International Banking Law* 16 (2001): 203–212.

Seyad, Sideek M. "A Critical Evaluation of the Causes and Remedies to Global Financial Crisis with Special Reference to the European Union." *European Policy Report*. Stockholm: Swedish Institute for European Policy Studies, May 2009.

Seyad, Sideek M. "A Legal Analysis of the European Financial Stability Mechanism." *Journal of International Banking and Regulation* 26 (2011): 421–433.

Seyad, Sideek M. "Protection of EU Bank Depositors after the 2008 Global Financial Crisis." *Europarättslig Tidskrift* 15 (2012): 55–78.

Seyad, Sideek M. "A Critical Evaluation of the Revised and Enlarged European Stability and Growth Pact." *Journal of International Banking Law and Regulation* 27 (2012): 202–211.

Usher, John A. *The Law of Money and Financial Services in the European Community*. Oxford: Oxford University Press, 1994.

18

The European Economic Constitution and its Transformation Through the Financial Crisis

Christian Joerges

Scope and Structure of the Argument

In early 2012, the state of the European Union and the prospects of its further development were not yet perceived as particularly disquieting. Subsequent developments gave rise to one of the most dramatic crises that the integration project has experienced: it has become impossible not to consider the impact and risks to which the Union, its economy, and its constitution are now exposed. Europe's "economic constitution" is obviously affected in a very fundamental way. Tellingly enough, this notion which, notwithstanding its Germanic origin, appeared fairly well established both in scholarly discussions and beyond the academy, is at present not even mentioned by the European Commission in its presentation of efforts to explain current challenges and to design a better future.

The vocabulary of "crisis" has been in flux for quite some time; now, however, economic governance has emerged as the most widely used term and concept. As defined by the Commission, economic governance comprises the idea of "fiscal coordination" and strategies that are intended to "prevent and correct macroeconomic and competitive imbalances."[1] It is immediately apparent to anyone who is even vaguely familiar with the concept of the economic constitution that both the objectives and the measures now envisaged are at odds with two key characteristics that have always been associated with the economic constitution: first, contrary to the limited scope and objectives of the economic constitution, the range of economic governance is unlimited in that it can affect every conceivable policy field of the European body politic; second, contrary to the economic constitution's commitment to the rule of law and the guidance of economic policy by justiciable criteria, economic governance can resort to any conceivable means in the pursuit of political priorities and enjoys wide margins of discretion. This terminological shift from "constitution" to "governance" is neither new nor surprising. The most instructive precedent, which deserves to be recalled here, stems from the proceedings of the European Convention in 2002. The Convention had established a "Working Group on Economic Governance."[2] The translation service still recalls the ferocity with which

A Companion to European Union Law and International Law, First Edition.
Edited by Dennis Patterson and Anna Södersten.

the German delegation taking part in the preparation of the Maastricht Treaty defended their idea of *Ordnungspolitik*. In order to please the Germans and avoid a similar experience, the Convention's notion of "economic governance" mutated to "*Ordnungspolitik*" in the German documents – not even the German Chairman of the Working Group objected.[3]

This little incident is not so much amusing as revealing. *Ordnungspolitik* is what an economic constitution, in the German understanding of the notion, is to enable and ensure. If such a message gets lost in translation and is replaced by a notion without any legal confines, we are likely to witness a structural change of fundamental importance. But do we? There is every reason to depart from an historical reconstruction of the origins of the "economic constitution" in the early 1920s, to consider its remarkable renaissance in postwar Germany, and to explore against this background its emigration to the European level of governance as well as its development and metamorphosis in the integration process. A separate section will be dedicated to the Economic and Monetary Union (EMU), which, once hailed as the crowning achievement of Europe's market building and the precursor of a more truly political Union, has become the epicenter of the present crisis. The practices of Europe's crisis management and the specifics of the governance modes that they are generating will be discussed in the final section, and alternative institutional prospects will be briefly sketched out in an epilogue.

Origins

The notion of the economic constitution originated in the social turmoil and intellectual laboratory of Weimar. Anxieties about the economic downfall and social tensions of post-First World War and post-monarchic Germany were threatening to grow out of control. The new republic was a democracy facing strong antidemocratic opponents, both on the radical Right and the radical Left. Doubts as to the strength and determination of the new parliament were widespread and were nurtured by renowned teachers of public law who lacked a democratic parliamentarian mindset.[4] Ordoliberalism suggested a new mode of liberal response. This answer distanced itself from laissez-faire ideas, which Alexander Rüstow notably belittled as "*paläo*-liberal."[5] Two foundational ordoliberal manifestos were published at the peak of the crisis in 1932: Walter Eucken's "Staatliche Strukturwandlungen und die Krise des Kapitalismus" ("Structural Transformations of the State and the Crisis of Capitalism")[6] and Alexander Rüstow's *Interessenpolitik oder Staatspolitik* (roughly: "Defending Interests or Striving for the Common Good").[7] Other subsequently famous protagonists followed suit in the same year.[8] Franz Böhm's seminal monograph on *Wettbewerb und Monopolkampf* (roughly: "Competitive Order or Monopoly Struggle") followed just one year later.[9] The thrust of these works was liberal in their rejection of the two state-fixated contemporary competitors, the Historic School of Economics, on the one hand, and socialist ideas as propagated by the labor movement, on the other.[10] It was post laissez-faire in that it assigned the task of ensuring the *ordo* of the economic sphere to the state. Walter Röpke used the oxymoron "liberal interventionism" to characterize this function.[11]

Ordoliberalism is a very widely discussed tradition, but only quite recently has Philip Manow, in a series of fascinating studies,[12] explored its early religious underpinnings. The notorious "social question" that generated so much unrest in early capitalism was a challenge to which the Christian Church sought to respond. This is not major news as far as Germany's political Catholicism is concerned. But Manow's account of the importance of social *Protestantism* is new.[13] *Ordo* is a Catholic notion. Yet, the ordoliberals who embraced it – Walter Eucken, Alexander Rüstow, Wilhelm Röpke – were all strongly linked to Protestantism.[14]

What both Protestants and Catholics sought was a third way between capitalism and socialism – and this alliance was the underpinning of Germany's postwar social market economy; this was their ecumenical project which politically united Protestants and Catholics in the Christian Democratic Union.

No period in Germany's history has been more intensively studied and discussed than the twelve years of the Third Reich. Ordoliberals were not only prodded to explain their advocacy of a "strong state" but also suspected or accused of intellectual partisanship or collaboration. It is true, and, indeed, it is no coincidence, that the school flourished in the mid-1930s. The 1937 monograph of its leading legal scholar, Franz Böhm, which outlined the ideas of the *Freiburg School* programmatically,[15] pleased contemporary academic partisans of the Nazi Party, and not just for its somewhat pathetic title. But the school was to survive untainted. The categorical difference between authoritarian dictatorship and "authoritarian liberalism"[16] resides in the primacy of the political for the former and commitment to the rule of law of the latter.[17]

Postwar Renaissance and Early Schisms

The concept of the economic constitution was not generated in a social and political vacuum. The vocation which both its founding fathers had attributed to it in the 1920s and which their heirs sought to defend during the Nazi period was a great asset. But this legacy was an insufficient basis for defining the ordoliberal position in Germany's new democratic order. Article 20(2) of the Basic Law articulated a new self-understanding that had a basis in the constitutional theory of Hermann Heller, an early critic of ordoliberalism: as that article proclaims, postwar Germany is "a democratic and social federal state." The weight of the commitment to the social state was underlined by the so-called eternity clause, which provided that constitutional amendments that would affect the principles laid down in Article 20 are "inadmissible." The commitment to "the social" had a much broader backing than that of mainstream constitutionalism. It allied the Social Democratic Party, the Christian church, and the trade unions, as well as the left-leaning factions of the Christian Democratic Party. For all these reasons, one-dimensional economic constitutionalism was not a real option for a school of thought which was prepared to play a leading role in Germany's new political life. The need to integrate "the social" into the ordoliberal worldview was irresistible and did, in fact, occur.

Postwar ordoliberalism and the social market economy

One theoretically elegant response was found by none other than the economic head of the Freiburg School, Walter Eucken, with his theory of "interdependent orders."[18] The economic order was restricted to commodity and service markets. It was complemented by a set of other orders, each organized by specific patterns. Thus, the *Arbeitsverfassung* acknowledged that labor must not be subjected to the regular discipline of markets and should, instead, profit from a system of industrial relations with strong trade unions; a *Sozialverfassung* organized social welfare entitlements; and even agriculture was granted a *Sonderweg*.[19] The "theory of the social market economy," through which Alfred Müller-Armack had started to develop his vision independently from the group in Freiburg in the 1930s, was much more prominent than these conceptual endeavors.[20] He elaborated it, in close contact with the Freiburg School, into a comprehensive program after the war.[21] His work gained an "official" status when he served as the head of the *Grundsatzabteilung* (again a very ordoliberal, and hence hardly translatable, term), a section of officials in the Ministry of Economic Affairs that was entrusted with the task of elaborating the principles upon which policy making should be based. Müller-Armack was then promoted to the position of a *Staatssekretär* under the Minister for the Economy, Ludwig Erhard, the most influential defender of ordoliberal positions in the Adenauer era, remaining keen to stay on good terms with Freiburg. He often underlined the compatibility of his concepts with ordoliberal principles but was equally keen to emphasize the social dimension of the social-market economy in his pleas for a "system of social and societal measures," which the state was to provide,[22] while his minister held the view that a strong antitrust law would be the best conceivable social policy.[23]

The comeback of the corporatist tradition

Ordoliberalism and the social-market economy managed to coexist peacefully and dominated public opinion. The early 1950s, however, witnessed the return of an old opponent, ironically thanks to American pressures. The US had urged Germany to support – through governmental action – their economic policies in the Korean War. Ludwig Erhard was not ready to betray his anti-interventionist principles, but he did tolerate a reestablishment of Germany's corporatist traditions. This was a legacy reaching back to the era of "organized capitalism" in the nineteenth century and the "organized economy" of the Weimar Republic.[24] These traditions were anathema to the ordoliberal school. However, once reestablished, they did not go away.[25] From this time forward, Germany played "Dr Jekyll and Mr Hyde" – it preached *Ordnungspolitik* but practiced corporatism – a German *Lebenslüge*, to be sure, albeit one that proved to be an economically successful and socially beneficial arrangement.[26]

Emigration to the European Economic Community

In its preparatory stages and years, European integration was by no means an uncontested project in the ordoliberal school.[27] One important reason for this was the universalism of its principles and orientation, which leading exponents have always defended.[28] Some uneasiness about the strength of the social state in the social-market economy, and more serious concerns about the renaissance of the anticompetitive corporatist traditions in the Federal Republic, seemed to have led to a conversion.[29] It was Alfred Müller-Armack who represented the German Federal government as its chief negotiator for the Treaty of Rome. Thus, it is no small wonder that the European Economic Community (EEC) received a significant ordoliberal imprint.

The freedoms guaranteed in the EEC Treaty the opening up of national economies, the antidiscrimination rules, and the commitment to a system of undistorted competition – could be, and were in fact, interpreted as a "decision" to support an economic constitution that established the framework conditions for a market economic system (at least to the degree that the many departures from the market economy might be classified as exceptions). The fact that Europe had started down its integrationist path as a mere economic community lent plausibility to ordoliberal arguments – and even required them: in the ordoliberal account, the Community acquired a legitimacy of its own by interpreting its pertinent provisions as prescribing a law-based order committed to the guaranteeing of economic freedoms and the fostering of competition by supranational institutions. This legitimacy was independent of democratic constitutional institutions. By the same token, it imposed limits upon the Community: discretionary economic policies seemed illegitimate and unlawful.[30]

However, one must not forget that what looked like a splendid success was not widely seen as such. Within Germany, the ordoliberal idea of an economic constitution suffered a serious setback when, in a judgment of 20 July 1954,[31] the Constitutional Court rejected a complaint against interventionist policy making and explained that Germany's Basic Law was not legally committed to an order which relied exclusively on procompetitive regulation. Equally importantly, most of the scholars of the ordoliberal school worked in the fields of private and "economic" law (again, a notion with connotations specific to German traditions) and resorted almost exclusively to a "private-law" movement. It had only few adherents in "public law," which was feeding the new discipline of European law. Last, but not least, the translation of the economic constitution to the European level of governance created a twofold tension. One aspect concerned the dedication to Ordnungspolitik, a concept hardly understood beyond the German borders,[32] let alone appreciated by its neighbors, especially on the other side of the Rhine. The second concerned the social embeddedness of the economic constitution, which, at national level, was conceptualized in the theorem of interdependent orders or in the social politics of the "social market economy."

The birth of a dilemma

This second issue is of general importance. Markets do not operate like machines; a broad spectrum of approaches in economic sociology has made us aware of their "social embeddedness."[33] This insight concerns the whole range of institutions on which the operation of market economies relies, most notably "money" and "labor." We will return to the monetary *problématique* in some detail later in the chapter. The institutionalization of "labor" is, of course, the most important dimension of the European welfare state traditions.

This is why Fritz Scharpf has good reasons for his characterization of the European Economic Constitution as a project that has "decoupled" social and economic policy.[34] Legally speaking, his observation is correct; sociologically speaking, it is less convincing. The competencies in the fields of social policy and industrial relations conferred to the EEC were marginal indeed. "Social Europe" was instead constituted by the ensemble of the member states and their welfare state commitments and strategies. This, however, did not seem as disquieting as it looks in hindsight. Eminent economists with social democratic credentials expected very positive effects from an opening of national *Volkswirtschaften*;[35] eminent political scientists provided the notion of "embedded liberalism,"[36] which was characterized by a sustainable coexistence of market integration and national welfare systems.

The completion of the internal market as a disembedding exercise

The equilibrium between the supranational economic constitution and national social orders seemed stable for a considerable period of time. The optimistic expectations of the formative period were merely irritated by the stagnation of the integration process and the still-national economies of the member states. It was the Commission's charismatic president Jacques Delors who managed to break this impasse. His 1985 White Paper on Completion of the Internal Market[37] carefully designed the objectives and means for Europe's renewal. Integration through market building now credibly promised to strengthen Europe's competitiveness as a whole. The economic constitution was affected subtly but deeply. The German Weberian sociologist M. Rainer Lepsius[38] has analyzed this move as the institutionalization of economic rationality.

He sees it as the guiding orientation of the integration project. What he captures with this notion is a reconfiguration of the relations between law, politics, and the economy – and this is precisely the transformative move which the ordoliberal tradition advocated at this stage of the integration process. This mutation had started at national level with the move of Friedrich August von Hayek from Chicago to Freiburg, where he soon found strong support for a change of paradigmatic dimensions in the ordoliberal conceptual edifice. His notion of "competition as a discovery process" replaced the orthodox commitments to law-controlled competitive conditions.[39] This shift has led the "second generation" of ordoliberal scholars to redefine the objectives and the methods of national and European competition law dramatically. From this time onward, their focus was on critiques of anticompetitive state activities and regulatory practices and the promotion of entrepreneurial freedom rather than the control of economic power.

The internal market was by no means the deregulatory exercise that so many of its proponents had presented it as, or would have liked to conceptualize it as. The program was about the kind of market building which modern economies requires. Hence, it understood market building as an exercise in regulatory politics – to such a degree that Giandomenico Majone, who had pioneered the turn of European research to the study of regulation, came to characterize Europe as a "regulatory state."[40] Consumer protection, safety at work, and environmental protection were the focus of these new activities, which led to the establishment of irresistibly expanding institutional machinery. The ordoliberal school, however, turned a blind eye to all this. The school remained true to its tendency not to take into account what was not foreseen in its conceptualization.[41] However, in the case of European regulatory politics, a more positive attitude would have been conceivable. Europe's new regulatory politics were not anticompetitive; they could be understood as compensating for market failures through a "sustained and focused control … over activities that are socially valued,"[42] and hence as premised on market governance and aiming at an improvement and defense of its functioning. This accomplishment could indeed be conceptualized as a "regulatory state."

Two renowned political scientists have recently argued[43] that the regulatory restructuring of the internal market and the jurisprudence accompanying it encompassed a "countermovement" in the terms described by Polanyi. This reading is hardly plausible.[44] The establishment of markets has always – and this is the core message of Polanyi's reconstruction of the development of industrial capitalism – been accomplished through political planning. The challenge to this planning stems from its disembedding of the economy and its markets from political, social, and cultural contexts. This is the type of query which Fritz Scharpf raised when diagnosing the "decoupling" of the economic constitution from its national contexts, which included the institutions of welfare states and modes of political accountability that cannot be ensured at European level. In the sphere of labor law, these disembedding processes have become plainly visible in the heavily criticized jurisprudence of the Court of Justice of the European Union (CJEU), which has ascribed primacy to the economic freedoms of the Treaty establishing the European Community (EC) over national labor law, thereby suspending the emancipation of labor law from the kind of discipline that governs commodity markets.[45] During the present crisis, the pressure exerted by European authorities on national welfare state entitlements and labor law has become much more intense. However, these recent developments must not be read as a final victory of the "economic constitution." Quite the contrary: what is at stake today is not just the survival of welfare state traditions but also the economic constitution itself. An analysis of these dynamics and their impact is a matter separate from the establishment of the EMU.

Economic and Monetary Union as a Pyrrhic Victory of Ordoliberalism

The introduction of a common European currency had been considered for more than two decades before the outlines of the present EMU were laid down in the 1992 Treaty of Maastricht. The reasons for this breakthrough were manifold but will not concern us here. Our focus will instead be on the specific shape of the EMU and its apparent ideal fit with the theoretical premises of the economic constitution. These affinities became extremely close after the von Hayekian conversion of ordoliberalism, which was accompanied in Germany by a move away from the Keynesian dimensions of German macroeconomic politics in favor of a monetarist program that encompassed monetary autonomy and a politically influential Bundesbank bringing to bear all its prestige in endorsing this reorientation.[46] The ensuing configuration seemed logical: EMU was understood as a political project, albeit one that was to be shielded strictly from the influence of daily politics and entrusted instead to the medium of law and to a strictly politically independent institution.

On closer inspection, however, what was widely perceived as the crowning achievement of the internal-market project and an irrevocable institutionalization of economic rationality as Europe's core constitutional value proved to be a less than robust construction, being established on politically contested and conceptually shaky premises. Tellingly enough, the opposition to EMU was very considerable precisely in the country that had exerted so much pressure on its legal design. The controversy was fought out before the German Constitutional Court in proceedings that attracted much public attention and led to a highly contested judgment.[47] The economic constitution, with its material and institutional substitution of legal rules for politics, was of key importance: according to the Court's reasoning, nothing less than a *sine qua non* for German participation within EMU. This assertion was made in the course of a curious chain of reasoning. The Court first addressed the arguments of the main plaintiffs, in particular, the argument that the European Union possessed such wide-ranging competences that nation states could no longer take action with regard to their own "fundamental" tasks. Such a situation, it was argued, endangered the future of *democratic statehood*, in particular with regard to monetary policy. The Court nonetheless demurred, arguing that law had endowed the EMU with a democratic political structure of its own. Law had made of ordoliberal and monetarist theorems instruments of its own, or had given them a "democratized" legal form: economic integration, so it was maintained, was an autonomous and *apolitical* process, which might and, indeed, must, take place beyond the reach of member state political influence. By virtue of a constitutional commitment to price stability and rules that guarded against inappropriate budgetary deficits, the EMU was correctly structured as a "stability community." Accordingly, all doubts about the democratic legitimacy of economic integration could be denied.[48]

As puzzling as this type of reasoning is, one wonders about the expectations which the Court may have had about the effects of the provisos that it has articulated in its acceptance of EMU. Could these judges, having heard so many experts, really assume that the rules of the EMU would be respected and that, if this should not be the case, Germany would retreat from it? Ernst-Wolfgang Böckenförde, one of those judges, has indicated in a comment on Europe's crisis management in a leading Swiss newspaper[49] that the judges were indeed fully aware of the fragility of the new edifice. He went on to explain that the Court had expressed its doubts as to the wisdom of EMU in the most drastic way conceivable with the following warning:

> The decision to agree on a monetary union and put it into operation without a simultaneous or immediately subsequent political union is a political one, for which the institutions with competence on the matter must take political responsibility.[50]

It is possible to interpret this passage as Böckenförde suggests it should be understood. It is also true that it had "been pointed out by important contributors to the debate," including the president of the Bundesbank,

> that a currency union, especially between States which are oriented towards an active economic and social policy, can ultimately only be realized in common with a political union (embracing all essential economic functions) and cannot be realized independently thereof or as a mere preliminary stage on the way to it.

This kind of skepticism was simply not taken seriously "in the culture of total optimism" that prevailed at the time.[51] More tragically for the law and its guardians, there is virtually no legal means available to exert control over this species of politics. This point will be explored further in the following section.

The Economic Constitution in Default

The confidence in the orderly functioning of the EMU was of short duration. Germany, France, the Netherlands, and others, failed to respect the rules of the stability pact. The Commission's much vaunted efforts to take action against deficits dwindled to nothing. Why did this happen? The German case is particularly instructive. The country was in serious economic difficulties after its unification. It simply could not afford to play the rules of the game and was not willing to comply. How much blame does it deserve? The "3 percent ceiling," commented Barry Eichengreen, who had studied the EMU since its inception, "is at best silly and at worst perverse."[52] The German situation was unique.

The one-size-fits-all philosophy of EMU and the Stability Pact was a gross error because it failed to acknowledge Europe's diversity. By now, the assessment of the skeptics has become the *communis opinio*. However, the insights into the construction failures have not led to a consensus about its cure. What we observe, instead, are turbo-speed legislative activities that are accompanied by hectic political activities and a fundamental transformation of the economic constitution.

The output is documented on the Commission's website, and is certainly impressive: "Strategy Europe 2020" (March 2010), "European Semester" (May 2010), "European Financial Stability Facility" (June 2010), "Euro-Plus-Pact" (March 2011), "Six-Pack" (December 2011), "Two-Pack" (proposed in November 2011), "European Stability Mechanism" (February 2012), "Treaty on Stability, Co-ordination and Governance in the Economic and Monetary Union" (TSCG) (signed in March 2012), Amendment of Article 136 TFEU (January 2013, Council Decision of March 2011). Legal problems with all this abound. Two issues deserve particular attention in the present context: the first is the transformation of the economic constitution; the second is the potential of judicial supervision.

The new patterns

The new regimes deploy a three-dimensional, at first sight somewhat contradictory, yet (on closer inspection) ultimately quite coherent, pattern. One lesson learned from the shortcomings of the EMU and the Stability Pact is the need to specify the targets that member states have to meet. The overall objective is a balanced budget with a tolerance of a structural deficit of, in principle, just 0.5 percent of the gross domestic product (Article 3(1)(b) TSCG). Compliance is ensured at domestic level "through provisions of binding force and permanent character, preferably constitutional" (Article 3(2)). The request for a balanced budget exceeds the competences of the Union – hence, the resort to a new treaty. This is how the old "Community Method" is complemented and replaced by what Chancellor Merkel has famously called the "Union Method." The third dimension of the new pattern becomes visible particularly clearly in the "Six Pack." Among its instruments are Regulation 1176/2011 on the prevention and correction of macroeconomic imbalances[53] and Regulation 1174/2011 on enforcement measures to correct excessive macroeconomic imbalances in the euro area.[54] Regulation 1176/2011 provides for systematic information of and in-depth review by the Commission for each member state and an evaluation of whether there are imbalances of an "excessive" nature. If these are detected, the Commission will develop recommendations of which it will inform the Council, the European Parliament, and the Eurogroup. All of the measures provided for in Regulation 1176/2011 are nonbinding. This is where Regulation 1174/2011 takes the next step. It empowers the Council, "acting on recommendation from the Commission," to impose sanctions such as an "interest-bearing deposit" or "an annual fine" on member states in cases where recommendations based upon Regulation 1176/2011 have been disregarded. It is worth noting that recommendations from the Commission can be rejected by the Council only by qualified majority (Regulation 1174/2011, Article 5 – so-called reversed qualified-majority voting).

This third dimension of crisis management is the most delicate one for three interdependent reasons: first, through the supervision and control of imbalances, it disregards the principle of enumerated powers, and, by the same token, disrespects the democratic legitimacy of national institutions, in particular the budgetary powers of parliaments; second, in its departure from the one-size-fits-all philosophy of the old EMU, the new regime arrives at highly individualized measures that are oriented only by necessarily indeterminate general clauses; third, the machinery that it establishes is regulatory in its form[55] but does not respect the limits which, for example, Giandomenico Majone has defined in his conceptualization of the "regulatory state" with the explicit exemption of distributive politics from European social regulation.[56] In Majone's diagnosis, Europe, with its crisis management, is moving "from the democratic deficit to a democratic default."[57]

A union of unequals: The judgment on the Greek rescue package

It seems obvious that the new crisis management, including the activities of the European Central Bank, could be questioned with good prospects before the CJEU under the procedures of Article 263. It is highly unlikely, however, that any of the privileged plaintiffs named in Article 263(2) will make use of this provision. To date, only the constitutional courts of the member states have been the *fora* of pertinent litigation.[58] The German court was in the forefront at various instances in the past and has already been in action four times in the current crisis.

The judgment of 7 September 2011 on the Greek rescue package is the first of these,[59] although it is not the most elegant one of them. But it does illustrate best the intricacies of these controversies and the difficulties the Court encounters in its efforts to find a path through legal, political, economic, national, and European territories.

The Court was confronted with complaints from a group of five professors against the aid granted to Greece, and by a member of the Bundestag against the Euro Rescue Package. The procedural specifics of the Federal Constitutional Court Act need not concern us here. However, the substantive principles which the Court has established are certainly instructive – and so are their limits. Three times the Court has defined such principles and has underlined their importance; three times the Court has gone on to explain why it can and should refrain from intervening.

1. The core argument concerns the budgetary power and responsibility of the Bundestag, clearly an essential feature of any representative democracy, because "the decision on public revenue and public expenditure is a fundamental part of the ability of a constitutional state to democratically shape itself" (47, para 122). The Bundestag must "retain control of fundamental budgetary decisions even in a system of intergovernmental administration" (48, para 124). However, "in establishing that there is a prohibited relinquishment of budget autonomy with regard to the extent of the guarantees given, the Federal Constitutional Court must restrict itself to manifest violations" and must with regard to the risks incurred "respect a latitude of assessment of the legislature" (51, para 130).

2. Recalling the Maastricht judgment and its warning that Germany will not comply with European legislative acts where the order of competences has not been respected ("*ausbrechende Rechtsakte*"), the Court states bravely, "In this connection, particular mention should be made of the prohibition of direct purchase of debt instruments of public institutions by the European Central Bank, the prohibition of accepting liability (bail-out clause) and the stability criteria for sound budget management" (50, para 129). Was all this respected? The German Court has only recently in its *Mangold/Honeywell* jurisprudence taken a big step back from the pronouncements of the Maastricht judgment, promising that it would focus on evident violations of great importance, and that it would ask the CJEU for a preliminary ruling before declaring an act *ultra vires*.[60] In the present case, a detailed examination is not essential, even though it is "possible to derive" from Articles 123 to 126 and 136 TFEU that these provisions presuppose the autonomy of national budgetary powers and that hence an "acceptance of liability for decisions of other Member States with financial effect which overstretches the basis of legitimation of the association of sovereign states (*Staatenverbund*) – by direct or indirect communtarisation of state debts – is to be avoided" (50, para 129).

3. The Basic Law protects the citizen against "a loss of substance of their power to rule by far-reaching … transfers of duties and powers of the Bundestag to supranational institutions" (39, para 98). However, the acts complained against here were "not sovereign acts of German state authority" which may be challenged under the Federal Constitutional Court Act (46 to 47, para 116).

All this is opaque, to be sure. Is there, hence, a kernel of truth in J.H.H. Weiler's remark on the dog that barks and then never bites?[61] This is the prevailing reaction to the judgment of the German Constitutional Court of 12 September 2012 on the Treaty Establishing the European Stability Mechanism (ESM Treaty) and the Fiscal Compact, in which the Court raised no principled objections against these agreements and only underlined the upper limits of Germany's liability and the right of the Bundestag to be involved in the financial operations under the new regime.[62] As the European Central Bank had announced almost simultaneously that it was ready to launch an open-ended and unlimited bond-buying program to help the indebted eurozone countries, "the markets" did, indeed, send a signal of relief. However, the kind of judicial restraint which the German court has exercised is very ambivalent. To be sure, the Court gave the green light to extensive endebtment of the Federal Republic. But it conditioned its *placet*. The constitutional weight of the budgetary powers of the Bundestag requires that the German parliament retains the power to determine the most important conditions for future successful demands for capital disbursements.[63] The judgments of the Karlsruhe Court on European issues tend to provoke harsh criticism in Germany's European law community. The critique has so far neglected an issue of fundamental importance. Why is budgetary autonomy not understood as a common European constitutional legacy? The one-sidedness of this argument is all the more disappointing as the Court, in an earlier paragraph of its judgment, had opened another and more constructive perspective: departing from its much criticized decontextualized reading of the "eternity clause" (Article 79 of the Basic Law), the Court now explained that "Article 79(3) seeks to protect those structures and procedures which keep the democratic process open."[64] This type of reasoning suggests that a resolution of the conflict between the exercise of budgetary powers must not be sought in prescriptions by an economic hegemon. The Court's reasoning instead leads to petrifying a link between economic stability and social austerity. This kind of judicial self-restraint seems even more questionable in the light – or even the shadow – of the Maastricht judgment discussed earlier. In that judgment, the Bundesverfassungsgericht had conditioned the participation of Germany in the EMU on the European-wide acceptance of Germany's economic and institutional philosophy. This move is now repeated and modified significantly. While the Maastricht judgment assumed that Europe's economic constitution could be an essentially legal project, the new judgment is moving from law to governmental and executive managerialism, with requirements defined by Germany and its northern allies.

This implication is not just deplorable but also illustrates – by the same token – the severe institutional deficits of the Union. The Bundesverfassungsgericht did not pursue such objectives deliberately. It realized that it could not comply with the black letter of the law because that law is one of the causes of our present troubles; the Court also realized that it was not entitled to act as the guardian of Europe. It was its effort to remain, at the very least, the guardian of the German constitution that generated its one-sided decision. This, however, is not yet the dilemma in its entirety. As indicated, the CJEU will not be confronted with complaints by the privileged plaintiffs. Even if this did occur, the European Court would not be legitimated to overrule the essentials of Germany's Basic Law or the equivalents of the constitutions of other member states. We must sadly conclude that what was once understood as a European economic constitution has been transformed, in the crisis, into general mandatory commitments to budgetary discipline within the eurozone space of the Union. However, these commitments can only be laid down in general clauses which will then have to be substantiated according to the varying exigencies of the particular situation. This type of regime cannot be enforced by conventional legal techniques; it requires a managerial supervisor with discretionary powers who can try to control the unruly interdependencies which we are witnessing and to which we are exposed. This type of arrangement has nothing in common with the ordoliberal vision of an economic constitution. What we see emerging is a new mode, a delegalized economic constitution, that is dedicated to balanced budgets and seeks to ensure compliance with this objective through regulatory machinery with comprehensive supervisory powers and which commands the means to ensure compliance with its evaluations. The management of this delegalized new constitutional condition is not amenable to jurisdictional adjudication as we know it. It is all the more remarkable that increasing numbers of commentators discern a strong ordoliberal imprint in Europe's crisis management.[65]

Where the law ends: The Outright Monetary Transactions controversy

The involvement of the European judiciary promises to become a story of considerable length with a still uncertain end and unpredictable effects. This is a foreboding that the judgment handed down by the CJEU (sitting as Full Court, with all twenty-seven judges) on 17 December 2012 in the case of Thomas Pringle,[66] and the order of Germany's Federal Constitutional Court of January 24,[67] have not dissolved. To be sure, all of Mr Pringle's complaints were rejected, and the reasons given by the CJEU met with wide approval in European law scholarship,[68] and the judgment helped to calm down politics and markets. It is also true that Karlsruhe has for the first time ever made use of the reference procedure. But the German Court made its own views unmistakably clear. The Outright Monetary Transactions program, including the announced buying of state bonds of the "countries in financial difficulties" in unlimited amounts, is encroaching on the fiscal and economic policy powers of Germany; the European Central Bank is thereby acting beyond its mandate, which is restricted to monetary policy; the program is incompatible with the prohibition of state financing (Article 123 TFEU) and exposes the German taxpayer to risks that are far beyond the amount consented to in the ESM Treaty. It is less clear how the CJEU will respond, and difficult to understand what motivated Karlsruhe to underline that it is not necessarily prepared to accept that response. The stakes, however, are high. The praxis of Europe's crisis management amounts to a profound transformation of Europe's constitutional constellation. Who is constitutional guardian for that change? Two of the judges of the Bundesverfassungsgericht have delivered dissenting opinions, with objections against the admissibility of the complaints. Could it be that the majority felt that such restraint would have left too much room for maneuver to Luxemburg? Be that as it may: both courts are involved in matters of highest political sensitivity. None of them can know what it really takes to ensure Europe's financial stability and to "resolve" the crisis. Such a pronouncement might accomplish what the Second Senate failed to accomplish through the reserves articulated in its Maastricht judgment.[69] Is it conceivable the CJEU will refuse to conceal political responsibilities with a veneer of legality?

Epilogue: Are There No Alternatives?

As articulated in the introductory section, the financial crisis has had a strong impact on the argument that is now submitted. What I intended to address as a core problem, namely, the tension between "the economic" – institutionalized at European level – and "the social" – institutionalized in the member states – did not disappear: it has merely changed its form; what could be analyzed as a common, albeit eroding, European postwar legacy is now transforming itself into a new social divide of Europe, with a small number of northern European states getting through the crisis while societies in the south endure a dramatic worsening of social conditions thanks to European and transnational machinery imposing austerity measures of uncertain economic and dreadful social effects.

Two alternatives are, nevertheless, conceivable. One is best represented by the most ardent defender of the European project among Europe's intellectual elite, namely Jürgen Habermas, acting evermore impatiently in his capacity as a political philosopher and in the role of a political citizen. "The crisis can be turned into a democratising constitutional moment" – this is his core message of countless public interventions,[70] and of his latest essay on Europe.[71] Habermas has now responded to what nonbelievers felt was unsociological voluntarism. Following an invitation by the leaders of Germany's Social Democratic Party to substantiate his *monita*, he now pleads for public referenda on a nonfederal political union and a new conventional assembly.[72] He not only identifies a state of exception in which an unbound executive has come to power, he also insists that the way out of the crisis into a new constitutional condition must be of a different democratic quality than permanent intergovernmental management and even treaty amendments as we know them.

It is difficult to believe that it will be possible in the near future to present a constitutional proposal to the citizens of Germany which they will consider to be so attractive that they will be prepared to give up essential elements of their Basic Law and that other European nations will follow suit. It seems much more likely that Europe's citizens will witness more of the kind of transnational management of fiscal discipline as Europe's new economic "constitution," with austerity as the price to pay for budgetary balance and competitiveness.

The present dilemmas are likely to persist. The governments of the member states will be expected to act as servants of two categorically different masters, namely the expectation of their citizens that they will defend their institutions and respect democratic processes on the one hand, and the macroeconomic imperatives as defined by a supranational regulatory machinery on the other. Somewhat paradoxically, the quest for a pan-European budgetary discipline will undermine the rule of the unitary currency and inexorably force the economies of the member states apart.

Under such conditions it would seem outright irresponsible *not* to search and consider what might be done if no kind of "big bang" will bring about radical change for the better and an ongoing postdemocratic crisis management fails. "Unity in diversity," the fortunate motto of the otherwise unfortunate Draft Constitutional Treaty of 2003, should not be forgotten, and we should try to make sense out of it. Europe could be better off if it ceased to strive for more uniformity and more centralization and, instead, focused on the establishment of legally structured cooperative arrangements and the civilized responses to its conflicts. This type of modesty may well be incompatible with global political ambitions, but it might make Europe more attractive for its citizens.[73]

Notes

1 See the explanation by the European Commission at http://ec.europa.eu/economy_finance/economic_governance/index_en.htm.

2 For its mandate and proceedings, see http://european-convention.europa.eu/EN/doc_register/doc_registerfa73.html?lang=EN&Content=WGVI; the Final Report of Group VI is available at http://european-convention.europa.eu/pdf/reg/en/02/cv00/cv00357.en02.pdf.

3 For the German version of the mandate with an explicit reference to "*Ordnungspolitik*" see http://european-convention.europa.eu/pdf/reg/de/02/cv00/cv00076.de02.pdf.

4 Most famously, Carl Schmitt, *Die geistesgeschichtliche Lage des heutigen Parlamentarismus* (Berlin: Duncker & Humblot, 1923). Translated by Ellen Kennedy as *The Crisis of Parliamentary Democracy* (Cambridge, MA: MIT Press, 1988).

5 Alexander Rüstow, "Paläoliberalismus, Kollektivismus und Neoliberalismus in der Wirtschafts- und Sozialordnung," in *Christentum und Liberalismus: Studien und Berichte der Katholischen Akademie in Bayern*, vol. 13, ed. Karl Forster (Munich: Zink, 1960), 149–178; and Alexander Rüstow, "Freie Wirtschaft: starker Staat," in *Deutschland und die Weltkrise, Schriften des Vereins für Socialpolitik*, ed. Franz Böse (Munich: Duncker & Humblot, 1932), 62–69.

6 Walter Eucken, "Staatliche strukturwandlungen und die Krise des Kapitalismus," *Weltwirtschaftliches Archiv* 36 (1932).

7 Alexander Rüstow, "Interessenpolitik oder Staatspolitik," *Der Deutsche Volkswirt* 7 (1932).

8 Alfred Müller-Armack, *Entwicklungsgesetze des Kapitalismus: Ökonomische, geschichtstheoretische und soziologische Studien zur modernen Wirtschaftsverfassung* (Berlin: Duncker und Dünnhaupt, 1932).

9 Franz Böhm, *Wettbewerb und Monopolkampf* (Berlin: Heymann, 1933).

10 Werner Abelshauser, *Kulturkampf: Der deutsche Weg in die neue Wirtschaft und die amerikanische Herausforderung* (Berlin: Kadmos, 2003), 158ff.

11 See Wilhelm Röpke, *German Commercial Policy* (London: Longmans Green, 1934), 40ff. See also, Wilhelm Röpke, *Die Lehre von der Wirtschaft* (Vienna: Springer, 1937). On Röpke, cf., Maurice Glasman, *Unnecessary Suffering: Managing Market Utopia* (London: Verso, 1996), 52ff.

12 Philip Manow, "Modell Deutschland as an Interdenominational Compromise" (working paper no. 003/2001, Minda De Gunzburg Centre for European Studies, Harvard University, 2001); Philip Manow, "Ordoliberalismus als ökonomische Ordnungstheologie," *Leviathan* 29 (2001).

13 "New" is, of course, a relative concept. In the core Chapter 3.5 on "Social Protestantism and the Redefinition of Social Reforms" Manow points not only to primary sources but also to an impressive range of historical studies.
14 Philip Manow, "Ordoliberalismus," 180.
15 Franz Böhm, *Die Ordnung der Wirtschaft als geschichtliche Aufgabe und rechtsschöpferische Leistung* (Stuttgart: Kohlhammer, 1937).
16 Hermann Heller, "Autoritärer Liberalismus," *Die Neue Rundschau* 44 (1933).
17 See Werner Abelshauser, *Deutsche Wirtschaftsgeschichte: Von 1945 bis zur Gegenwart* (Munich: Beck, 2011), 87ff. For further references, see Christian Joerges, "Europe a Großraum? Shifting Legal Conceptualisations of the Integration Project," in *Darker Legacies of Law in Europe: The Shadow of National Socialism and Fascism over Europe and its Legal Traditions*, ed. Christian Joerges and Navraj S. Ghaleigh (Oxford: Hart, 2003). For a thorough portrayal of Franz Böhm, see Rudolf Wiethölter, "Franz Böhm (1895–1977)," in *Juristen an der Universität Frankfurt a.M.*, ed. Bernhard Diestelkamp and Michael Stolleis (Baden-Baden: Nomos, 1989), 215ff.
18 See Walter Eucken, *Grundzüge der Wirtschaftspolitik* (Tübingen: Mohr/Siebeck, 1990[1952]), 180ff. On the interdependence theorem, see Milène Wegmann, *Früher Neoliberalismus und europäische Integration: Interdependenz der nationalen, supranationalen und internationalen Ordnung von Wirtschaft und Gesellschaft (1932–1965)* (Baden-Baden: Nomos, 2002), 369ff. For a confirmation, albeit only implicit, of the topicality of Eucken's interdependence theorem, see Kaarlo Tuori, "The Many Constitutions of Europe," in *The Many Constitutions of Europe*, ed. Kaarlo Tuori and Suvi Sankari (Farnham: Ashgate, 2009).
19 See the illuminating remarks in Michel Foucault, *Geschichte der Gouvernementalität II: Die Geburt der Biopolitik* (Frankfurt a.M.: Suhrkamp Verlag, 2004), 199–201.
20 See Alfred Müller-Armack, *Staatsidee und Wirtschaftsordnung im neuen Reich* (Berlin: Junker and Dünnhaupt, 1933).
21 Starting with Alfred Müller-Armack, *Wirtschaftlenkung und Marktwirtschaft* (Hamburg: Verlag für Wirtschaft und Sozialpolitik, 1947).
22 See Alfred Müller-Armack, "Die Wirtschaftsordnungen sozial gesehen," in *Wirtschaftsordnung und Wirtschaftspolitik: Studien und Konzepte zur sozialen Marktwirtschaft und zur europäischen Integration* (repr. Freiburg i. Br.: Verlag Rombach, 1966[1948]); and Alfred Müller-Armack, "Die Soziale Marktwirtschaft nach einem Jahrzehnt ihrer Erprobung," reprinted in *Wirtschaftsordnung und Wirtschaftspolitik: Studien und Konzepte zur sozialen Marktwirtschaft und zur europäischen Integration*, (repr. Freiburg i. Br., Verlag Rombach, 1966[1959]), 251–265. For further references, see Christian Joerges and Florian Rödl, "The 'Social Market Economy' as Europe's Social Model?" in *A European Social Citizenship? Preconditions for Future Policies in Historical Light*, ed. Lars Magnusson and Bo Stråth (Brussels: Lang, 2005). For a comprehensive account, see, more recently, Christian L. Glossner, *The Making of the German Post-war Economy: Political Communication and Public Reception of the Social Market Economy after World War II*, (London: I.B. Tauris, 2010), 47ff.
23 Abelshauser, *Deutsche Wirtschaftsgeschichte*, 190.
24 For a discussion of these concepts and their historical background, see Gert Brüggemeier, *Entwicklung des Rechts im organisierten Kapitalismus*, 2 vols (Frankfurt a.M.: Syndikat, (1977–1979); Knut Wolfgang Nörr, *Zwischen den Mühlsteinen: Eine Privatrechtsgeschichte der Weimarer Republik* (Tübingen: Mohr, 1988); and Knut Wolfgang Nörr, *Die Republik der Wirtschaft. Teil I: Von der Besatzungszeit bis zur Großen Koalition* (Tübingen: Mohr, 1999).
25 See Abelshauser, *Deutsche Wirtschaftsgeschichte*, 163–172.
26 Well documented in Werner Abelshauser, *Die Langen Fünfziger Jahre: Wirtschaft und Gesellschaft in Deutschland 1949–1966* (Düsseldorf: Schwann, 1987).
27 See Wegmann, *Früher Neoliberalismus und europäische Integration*, 297ff. and 351ff.
28 See, e.g., Wolfgang Fikentscher, "Wirtschaftskontrolle und Weltinnenpolitik," *Gewerblicher Rechtsschutz und Urheberrecht/ Internationaler Teil* 28 (1973): 543–585. Out of the work of Ernst-Ulrich Petersmann, see, e.g., "Constitutional Economics, Human Rights and the Future of the

WTO," *Aussenwirtschaft* 58 (2003); and "Welthandelsrecht als Freiheits- und Verfassungsordnung," *Heidelberg Journal of International Law (ZaöRV)* 65 (2005).

29 See Wegmann, *Früher Neoliberalismus und europäische Integration*, 24ff., 392ff., and 419ff.

30 See, for illuminating, if reconstructivist, accounts, Ernst-Joachim Mestmäcker, "Macht-Recht-Wirtschaftsverfassung," *Zeitschrift für das gesamte Handelsrecht und Wirtschaftsrecht* 137 (1973); Josef Drexl, "Wettbewerbsverfassung," in *Principles of European Constitutional Law*, ed. Armin von Bogdandy and Jürgen Bast (Oxford: Hart, 2011); and Armin Haltje, "The Economic Constitution within the Internal Market," in von Bogdandy and Bast, *Principles of European Constitutional Law*.

31 BVerfGE 4, 7 – Investitionshilfegesetz.

32 But see, for a fascinating analysis, Foucault, *Geschichte der Gouvernementalität II*, in particular, the lecture of 7 February 1979, 148–184, and that of 14 February 1979, 185–224 – the most profound analysis of ordoliberalism I have become aware of.

33 For an elaboration, see Christian Joerges, Bo Stråth, and Peter Wagner, eds., *The Economy as Polity: The Political Constitution of Contemporary Capitalism* (London: UCL Press, 2005); and Christian Joerges and Josef Falke, eds., *Karl Polanyi, Globalisation and the Potential of Law in Transnational Markets* (Oxford: Hart, 2011).

34 Fritz W. Scharpf, "The European Social Model: Coping with the Challenges of Diversity," *Journal of Common Market Studies* 40 (2002): 646.

35 See, most notably, the "Ohlin Report": International Labour Organisation, "Social Aspects of European Economic Co-Operation: Report by a Group of Experts," *International Labour Review* 74 (1956): 99–123.

36 John G. Ruggie, "International Regimes, Transactions and Change: Embedded Liberalism in the Postwar Economic Order," *International Organization* 36 (1982).

37 European Commission, White Paper to the European Council on Completion of the Internal Market, COM(85) 310 final.

38 See M. Rainer Lepsius, "The European Union as a Sovereignty Association of a Special Nature," in *What Kind of Constitution for What Kind of Polity? Responses to Joschka Fischer*, ed. Christian Joerges, Yves Mény, and J.H.H. Weiler (Florence: EUI, 2000). The theoretical basis is more comprehensively elaborated in M. Rainer Lepsius, "Institutionalisierung und Deinstitutionalisierung von Rationalitätskriterien," in "Institutionenwandel," ed. Gerhard Göhler, special issue *Leviathan* 16 (1996) (Wiesbaden: Westdeutscher Verlag, 1997).

39 See the report on the Walter-Lippmann Symposium in Paris back in 1939 in Foucault, *Geschichte der Gouvernementalität II*, 188ff. The differences between the ordoliberalism of the Freiburg school and the Austrian neoliberalism as represented by von Hayek became already apparent.

40 Starting with Giandomenico Majone, "Regulating Europe: Problems and Prospects," *Jahrbuch zur Staats- und Verwaltungswissenschaft* 3 (1989).

41 See Christian Joerges, "What is Left of the European Economic Constitution? A Melancholic Eulogy," *European Law Review* 30 (2005): 461–489.

42 Philip Selznick, "Focusing Organizational Research on Regulation," in *Regulatory Policy and the Social Sciences*, ed. Roger G. Noll (Berkeley, CA: University of California Press, 1985), 363–364.

43 James Caporaso and Sydney Tarrow, "Polanyi in Brussels: European Institutions and the Embedding of Markets in Society," *International Organization* 63 (2009).

44 Martin Höpner and Armin Schäfer, "Polanyi in Brussels? Embeddedness and the Three Dimensions of European Economic Integration" (MPIfG discussion paper no. 10/ 8, Max Planck Institute for the Study of Societies, Cologne, 2010).

45 See the infamous series of CJEU judgments: Case C-438/05 *International Transport Workers' Federation, Finnish Seamen's Union v. Viking Line ABP, OÜ Viking Line Eesti* EU:C:2007:772; Case C-341/05 *Laval un Partneri Ltd v. Svenska Byggnadsarbetareförbundet, Svenska Byggnadsarbetareförbundets avdelning 1, Byggettan und Svenska Elektrikerförbundet* EU:C:2007:809; and Case C-346/06 *Rechtsanwalt Dr. Dirk Rüffert v. Land Niedersachsen* EU:C:2008:189.

46 See Fritz W. Scharpf, "Monetary Union, Fiscal Crisis, and the Pre-emption of Democracy" (MPIfG discussion paper no. 11/11, Max Planck Institute for the Study of Societies, Cologne, 2011).

47 See *Brunner v. European Union Treaty*, 89 *BVerfGE* 155 and 1 *CMLR* 57 (1994). On the following, Christian Joerges, "States without a Market: Comments on the German Constitutional Court's Maastricht-Judgment and a Plea for Interdisciplinary Discourses" (NISER working paper, NISER, Utrecht, 1996).

48 In the broad and fierce critical debate which the Maastricht judgment has provoked this surprising segment of the Court's reasoning was hardly ever addressed. The critique focused, instead, upon the Court's description of democracy as requiring a "relatively homogeneous people"; the Court's announcement that Germany does not need to comply with an *ultra vires* act; and its resort to the term "*Staatenverbund*" instead of Community. See J.H.H. Weiler, "Does Europe Need a Constitution? Reflections on Demos, Telos and the German Maastricht Decision," *European Law Journal* 1 (1995).

49 See Ernst-Wolfgang Böckenförde, "Kennt die europäische Not kein Gebot? Die Webfehler der EU und die Notwendigkeit einer neuen politischen Entscheidung." *Neue Züricher Zeitung*, 21 June 2010.

50 *Brunner v. European Union Treaty*, n 47 this chapter, para 93.

51 See Giandomenico Majone, *Rethinking the Union of Europe Post-crisis: Has Integration Gone Too Far?* (Cambridge: Cambridge University Press, 2014), 58ff.

52 See Barry Eichengreen, "Gibt es Alternativen zum Stabilitätspakt? Drei Experten antworten" No. 49/27, *Die Zeit*, 20 November 2003.

53 Regulation (EU) No. 1176/2011 of the European Parliament and of the Council of 16 November 2011 on the prevention and correction of macroeconomic imbalances [2011] OJ L 306/25.

54 Regulation (EU) No. 1174/2011 of the European Parliament and of the Council of 16 November 2011 on enforcement measures to correct excessive macroeconomic imbalances in the euro area [2011] OJ L 306/8.

55 Damian Chalmers, "The European Redistributive State and the Need for a European Law of Struggle," *European Law Journal*, 18 (2012): 667–693.

56 Giandomenico Majone, *Regulating Europe* (London: Routledge, 1996).

57 Giandomenico Majone, "Rethinking European Integration after the Debt Crisis" (UCL working paper no. 3/2012, 19ff.).

58 There is not yet any overview available. It seems, however, simply inconceivable that the practices we are witnessing will remain unchallenged. Supranational powers have never been as uncontroversial as European constitutionalism tends to present as being the case. See, for recent accounts, Peter L. Lindseth, *Power and Legitimacy: Reconciling Europe and the Nation-State* (Oxford: Oxford University Press, 2010), 166–188; and Darinka Piqani, "Supremacy of EU Law and the Jurisprudence of Constitutional Reservations in Central Eastern Europe and the Western Balkans: Towards a 'Holistic' Constitutionalism" (PhD dissertation, European University Institute, Florence, 2012). The Pringle case – Irish Supreme Court, judgment of 31 July 2012 [2012] IESC 47 – *Thomas Pringle v. The Government of Ireland, and the Attorney General* – was not challenging European law (Case C-370/12 *Pringle* EU:C:2012:756).

59 The English translation is available in Edoardo Chiti, Agustín Menéndez, and Pedro Teixeira eds., "The European Rescue of the European Union? The Existential Crisis of the European Political Project" (RECON report no. 19, Oslo: RECON, 2012, 447–501).

60 See BVerfGE 126, 286, available at: http://www.bverfg.de/entscheidungen/rs20100706_2bvr266106.html.

61 J.H.H. Weiler, "The 'Lisbon *Urteil*' and the Fast Food Culture," *European Journal of International Law* 20 (2009): 505–509, commenting on *Bundesverfassungsgericht*, judgment of 30 June 2009, available at: www.bundesverfassungsgericht.de. English translation at: http://www.bundesverfassungsgericht.de/entscheidungen/es20090630_2bve000208en.html.

62 Available at: http://www.bundesverfassungsgericht.de/entscheidungen/rs20120912_2bvr139012en.html.

63 Para 274; this section is not yet translated. It reads in the German original: "Da der Bundestag durch seine Zustimmung zu Stabilitätshilfen den verfassungsrechtlich gebotenen Einfluss ausüben und Höhe, Konditionalität und Dauer der Stabilitätshilfen zugunsten hilfesuchender Mitgliedstaaten mitbestimmen kann, legt er selbst die wichtigste Grundlage für später möglicherweise erfolgende Kapitalabrufe nach Art. 9 Abs. 2 ESMV."

64 Para 206 in the English extract, para 222 in the German original.
65 See the widely cited paper by Ulrike Guérot and Sebastian Dullien, 'The Long Shadow of Ordo-Liberalism: Germany's Approach to the Euro Crisis', available at www.ecfr.eu/page/-/ECFR49_GERMANY_BRIEF_AW.pdf.
66 Case C-370/12 *Pringle*, n 58 this chapter.
67 BVerfG, Case 2 BvR 2728/13 et al. *OMT*, order of 14 January 2014, translation available at: www.bundesverfassungsgericht.de/en/decisions/rs20140114_2bvr272813en.html.
68 But see Michelle Everson, "An Exercise in Legal Honesty: Re-Writing the Court of Justice and the Bundesverfassungsgericht," Institute for Advanced Studies, Vienna, Political Science Series, 136/2014.
69 See n 50 this chapter.
70 Jürgen Habermas, "Bringing the Integration of Citizens into Line with the Integration of States," *European Law Journal* 18 (2012): 485–488.
71 Jürgen Habermas, "The Crisis of the European Union in the Light of a Constitutionalization of International Law," *European Journal of International Law* 23 (2012).
72 See Peter Bofinger, Jürgen Habermas, and Julian Nida-Rümelin, "The Case for a Change of Course in European Policy," *Social Europe Journal*, 9 August 2012.
73 See, for an elaboration, Christian Joerges, "Unity in Diversity as Europe's Vocation and Conflicts Law as Europe's Constitutional Form," in *The Changing Role of Law in the Age of Supra- and Transnational Governance*, ed. Rainer Nickel and Andrea Greppi (Baden-Baden: Nomos, 2012).

References

Abelshauser, Werner. *Die Langen Fünfziger Jahre: Wirtschaft und Gesellschaft in Deutschland 1949–1966*. Düsseldorf: Schwann, 1987.

Abelshauser, Werner. *Kulturkampf: Der deutsche Weg in die neue Wirtschaft und die amerikanische Herausforderung*. Berlin: Kadmos, 2003.

Abelshauser, Werner. *Deutsche Wirtschaftsgeschichte: Von 1945 bis zur Gegenwart*. Munich: Beck, 2011.

Böckenförde, Ernst-Wolfgang. "Kennt die europäische Not kein Gebot? Die Webfehler der EU und die Notwendigkeit einer neuen politischen Entscheidung." *Neue Züricher Zeitung*, 21 June 2010.

Bofinger, Peter, Jürgen Habermas, and Julian Nida-Rümelin. "The Case for a Change of Course in European Policy." *Social Europe Journal*, 9 August 2012.

Böhm, Franz. *Wettbewerb und Monopolkampf*. Berlin: Heymanns, 1933.

Böhm, Franz. *Die Ordnung der Wirtschaft als geschichtliche Aufgabe und rechtsschöpferische Leistung*. Berlin: Kohlhammer, 1937.

Brüggemeier, Gert. *Entwicklung des Rechts im organisierten Kapitalismus*. 2 vols. Frankfurt a.M.: Syndikat, 1977–1979.

Caporaso, James, and Sydney Tarrow. "Polanyi in Brussels: European Institutions and the Embedding of Markets in Society." *International Organization* 63 (2009): 563–620.

Chalmers, Damian. "The European Redistributive State and the Need for a European Law of Struggle." *European Law Journal* 18 (2012): 667–693.

Chiti, Edoardo, Agustín Menéndez, and Pedro Teixeira, eds. "The European Rescue of the European Union? The Existential Crisis of the European Political Project." RECON report no. 19, Oslo 2012.

Drexl, Josef. "Wettbewerbsverfassung." In von Bogdandy and Bast, *Principles of European Constitutional Law*, 659–698.

Eichengreen, Barry, "Gibt es Alternativen zum Stabilitätspakt? Drei Experten antworten" No. 49/27. *Die Zeit*, 20 November 2003: 24.

Eucken, Walter. "Staatliche strukturwandlungen und die Krise des Kapitalismus." *Weltwirtschaftliches Archiv* 36 (1932): 297–321.

Eucken, Walter. *Grundzüge der Wirtschaftspolitik*. Tübingen: Mohr/Siebeck, 1990. First published 1952.

Everson, Michelle. "An Exercise in Legal Honesty: Re-Writing the Court of Justice and the Bundesverfassungsgericht," Institute for Advanced Studies, Vienna, Political Science Series, 136/2014.

Fikentscher, Wolfgang. "Wirtschaftskontrolle und Weltinnenpolitik." *Gewerblicher Rechtsschutz und Urheberrecht/Internationaler Teil* 28 (1973): 478–486.

Foucault, Michel. *Geschichte der Gouvernementalität II: Die Geburt der Biopolitik*. Frankfurt a.M.: Suhrkamp Verlag, 2004.

Glasman, Maurice. *Unnecessary Suffering: Managing Market Utopia*. London: Verso, 1996.

Glossner, Christian L. *The Making of the German Post-war Economy: Political Communication and Public Reception of the Social Market Economy after World War II*. London: I.B. Tauris, 2010.

Guérot, Ulrike, and Sebastian Dullien. "The Long Shadow of Ordo-Liberalism: Germany's Approach to the Euro Crisis." Accessed 11 June 2015. www.ecfr.eu/page/-/ECFR49_GERMANY_BRIEF_AW.pdf.

Habermas, Jürgen. "The Crisis of the European Union in the Light of a Constitutionalization of International Law." *European Journal of International Law* 23 (2012): 335–348.

Habermas, Jürgen. "Bringing the Integration of Citizens into Line with the Integration of States." *European Law Journal* 18 (2012): 485–488.

Haltje, Armin. "The Economic Constitution within the Internal Market." In von Bogdandy and Bast, *Principles of European Constitutional Law*, 589–629.

Heller, Hermann. "Autoritärer Liberalismus." *Die Neue Rundschau* 44 (1933): 289–298.

Höpner, Martin, and Armin Schäfer. "Polanyi in Brussels? Embeddedness and the Three Dimensions of European Economic Integration." MPIfG Discussion paper no. 10/8, Max Planck Institute for the Study of Societies, Cologne, 2010.

International Labour Organisation. "Social Aspects of European Economic Co-Operation: Report by a Group of Experts." *International Labour Review* 74 (1956): 99–123.

Joerges, Christian. "States without a Market: Comments on the German Constitutional Court's Maastricht-Judgment and a Plea for Interdisciplinary Discourses." NISER working paper, NISER, Utrecht, 1996.

Joerges, Christian. "Europe a Großraum? Shifting Legal Conceptualisations of the Integration Project." In *Darker Legacies of Law in Europe: The Shadow of National Socialism and Fascism over Europe and its Legal Traditions*, edited by Christian Joerges and Navray S. Ghaleigh, 167–191. Oxford: Hart, 2003.

Joerges, Christian. "What is Left of the European Economic Constitution? A Melancholic Eulogy." *European Law Review* 30 (2005).

Joerges, Christian. "Unity in Diversity as Europe's Vocation and Conflicts Law as Europe's Constitutional Form." In *The Changing Role of Law in the Age of Supra- and Transnational Governance*, edited by Rainer Nickel and Andrea Greppi, 99–133. Baden-Baden: Nomos, 2012.

Joerges, Christian, and Josef Falke, eds. *Karl Polanyi, Globalisation and the Potential of Law in Transnational Markets*. Oxford: Hart, 2011.

Joerges, Christian, and Florian Rödl. "The 'Social Market Economy' as Europe's Social Model?" In *A European Social Citizenship? Preconditions for Future Policies in Historical Light*, edited by Lars Magnusson and Bo Stråth, 125–158. Brussels: Lang, 2005.

Joerges, Christian, Bo Stråth, and Peter Wagner, eds. *The Economy as Polity: The Political Constitution of Contemporary Capitalism*. London: UCL Press, 2005.

Lepsius, M. Rainer "Institutionalisierung und Deinstitutionalisierung von Rationalitätskriterien." In "Institutionenwandel," edited by Gerhard Göhler. Special Issue, *Leviathan* 16 (1996): 57–69. Wiesbaden: Westdeutscher Verlag, 1997.

Lepsius, M. Rainer. "The European Union as a Sovereignty Association of a Special Nature." In *What Kind of Constitution for What Kind of Polity? Responses to Joschka Fischer*, edited by Christian Joerges, Yves Mény, and J.H.H. Weiler, 203–222. Florence: EUI, 2000.

Lindseth, Peter L. *Power and Legitimacy: Reconciling Europe and the Nation-State*. Oxford: Oxford University Press, 2010.

Majone, Giandomenico. "Regulating Europe: Problems and Prospects." *Jahrbuch zur Staats- und Verwaltungswissenschaft* 3 (1989): 159–177.

Majone, Giandomenico. *Regulating Europe*. London: Routledge, 1996.

Majone, Giandomenico. "Rethinking European Integration after the Debt Crisis," UCL working paper no. 3/2012.

Majone, Giandomenico. *Rethinking the Union of Europe Post-crisis: Has Integration Gone Too Far?* Cambridge: Cambridge University Press, 2014.
Manow, Philip. "Modell Deutschland as an Interdenominational Compromise." Working paper no. 003/2001, Minda De Gunzburg Centre for European Studies, Harvard University, 2001.
Manow, Philip. "Ordoliberalismus als ökonomische Ordnungstheologie." *Leviathan* 29 (2001): 179–198.
Mestmäcker, Ernst-Joachim. "Macht-Recht-Wirtschaftsverfassung." *Zeitschrift für das gesamte Handelsrecht und Wirtschaftsrecht* 137 (1973): 97–111.
Müller-Armack, Alfred. *Entwicklungsgesetze des Kapitalismus: Ökonomische, geschichtstheoretische und soziologische Studien zur modernen Wirtschaftsverfassung*. Berlin: Duncker und Dünnhaupt, 1932.
Müller-Armack, Alfred. *Staatsidee und Wirtschaftsordnung im neuen Reich*. Berlin: Junker and Dünnhaupt, 1933.
Müller-Armack, Alfred. *Wirtschaftlenkung und Marktwirtschaft*. Hamburg: Verlag für Wirtschaft und Sozialpolitik, 1947.
Müller-Armack, Alfred. "Die Soziale Marktwirtschaft nach einem Jahrzehnt ihrer Erprobung." In *Wirtschaftsordnung und Wirtschaftspolitik: Studien und Konzepte zur sozialen Marktwirtschaft und zur europäischen Integration*, 251–265. Freiburg im Breisgau: Verlag Rombach, 1966. First published in 1959.
Müller-Armack, Alfred. "Die Wirtschaftsordnungen sozial gesehen." In *Wirtschaftsordnung und Wirtschaftspolitik: Studien und Konzepte zur sozialen Marktwirtschaft und zur europäischen Integration*, 171–199. Freiburg im Breisgau: Verlag Rombach, 1966. First published in 1948.
Nörr, Knut Wolfgang. *Zwischen den Mühlsteinen: Eine Privatrechtsgeschichte der Weimarer Republik*. Tübingen: Mohr, 1988.
Nörr, Knut Wolfgang. *Die Republik der Wirtschaft. Teil I: Von der Besatzungszeit bis zur Großen Koalition*. Tübingen: Mohr, 1999.
Petersmann, Ernst-Ulrich. "Constitutional Economics, Human Rights and the Future of the WTO." *Aussenwirtschaft* 58 (2003): 49–91.
Petersmann, Ernst-Ulrich. "Welthandelsrecht als Freiheits- und Verfassungsordnung." *Heidelberg Journal of International Law (ZaöRV)* 65 (2005): 543–585.
Piqani, Darinka. "Supremacy of EU Law and the Jurisprudence of Constitutional Reservations in Central Eastern Europe and the Western Balkans: Towards a 'Holistic' Constitutionalism." PhD diss., European University Institute, Florence, 2012.
Röpke, Wilhelm. *German Commercial Policy*. London: Longmans Green, 1934.
Röpke, Wilhelm. *Die Lehre von der Wirtschaft*. Vienna: Springer, 1937.
Ruggie, John G. "International Regimes, Transactions and Change: Embedded Liberalism in the Postwar Economic Order." *International Organization* 36 (1982): 375–415.
Rüstow, Alexander. "Freie Wirtschaft: starker Staat." In *Deutschland und die Weltkrise, Schriften des Vereins für Socialpolitik*, edited by Franz Böse. Munich: Duncker & Humblot, 1932.
Rüstow, Alexander. "Interessenpolitik oder Staatspolitik." *Der Deutsche Volkswirt* 7 (1932): 169–172.
Rüstow, Alexander. "Paläoliberalismus, Kollektivismus und Neoliberalismus in der Wirtschafts- und Sozialordnung." In *Christentum und Liberalismus: Studien und Berichte der Katholischen Akademie in Bayern*. Vol. 13, edited by Karl Forster. Munich: Zink, 1960.
Scharpf, Fritz W. "The European Social Model: Coping with the Challenges of Diversity." *Journal of Common Market Studies* 40 (2002): 645–670.
Scharpf, Fritz W. "Monetary Union, Fiscal Crisis, and the Pre-emption of Democracy." MPIfG discussion paper no. 11/11, MPIfG, Cologne, 2011.
Schmitt, Carl. *Die geistesgeschichtliche Lage des heutigen Parlamentarismus*. Berlin: Duncker & Humblot, 1923. Translated by Ellen Kennedy as *The Crisis of Parliamentary Democracy*. Cambridge, MA: MIT Press, 1988.
Selznick, Philip. "Focusing Organizational Research on Regulation." In *Regulatory Policy and the Social Sciences*, edited by Roger G. Noll, 363–367. Berkeley, CA: University of California Press, 1985.
Tuori, Kaarlo. "The Many Constitutions of Europe." In *The Many Constitutions of Europe*, edited by Kaarlo Tuori and Suvi Sankari, 3–30. Farnham: Ashgate, 2009.

von Bogdandy, Armin, and Jürgen Bast. *Principles of European Constitutional Law*. Oxford: Hart, 2011.

Wegmann, Milène. *Früher Neoliberalismus und europäische Integration: Interdependenz der nationalen, supranationalen und internationalen Ordnung von Wirtschaft und Gesellschaft (1932–1965)*. Baden-Baden: Nomos, 2002.

Weiler, J.H.H. "Does Europe Need a Constitution? Reflections on Demos, Telos and the German Maastricht Decision." *European Law Journal* 1 (1995): 219–258.

Weiler, J.H.H. "The 'Lisbon Urteil' and the Fast Food Culture." *European Journal of International Law* 20 (2009): 505–509.

Wiethölter, Rudolf. "Franz Böhm (1895–1977)." In *Juristen an der Universität Frankfurt a.M*, edited by Bernhard Diestelkamp and Michael Stolleis, 208–252. Baden-Baden: Nomos, 1989.

19

European Private Law

Hans-Wolfgang Micklitz

Introduction

Lawyers around the world roughly agree on the meaning of "private law." Whatever their national origins, they will point to contract and tort and identify their roots in the national private law order. Understanding *European* private law requires clarification of each of the three composite elements: (1) "Europe" is not a state but a quasi-state with a multilevel governance structure; (2) the law is not only "private" (freedom of contract, private autonomy) but also has a strong "regulatory" (public) dimension; and (3) "law" cannot be equated with codified (secondary EU) law but has a multifaceted character – ranging from private regulation within a public regulatory frame to contract governance and self-regulation.

Understanding European private law means understanding its transnational character. The disembedding of private law from its nation-state origin and its reembedding into European statehood requires clarification of the "constitutional framework" in which European private law must be located. As the European Union is not a state and will never resemble a nation-state, it is insufficient to equate European private law with the perspective of a European civil code of which the Draft Common Frame of Reference (DCFR), the Feasibility Study on a Common Sales Law, and the proposed Optional Instrument (Common European Sales Law (CESL)) are understood as building blocks. Quite to the contrary, European private law should be conceived of as a genuine legal order that remains largely distinct from the national private law orders – an order that is autonomous in its "own right" and self-standing. This private law is understood as economic law,[1] covering not only contract and tort – systematically speaking the continental codifications – but also public and private regulation of the economy. At the forefront is the regulation of services, such as telecommunications, postal services, energy, transport, and financial services. In that respect, the new path of European Regulatory Private Law is inherently linked to the European Union understood as a market state.

A Companion to European Union Law and International Law, First Edition.
Edited by Dennis Patterson and Anna Södersten.

European Statehood and European Private Law

The debate about European statehood started in the 1970s with the ordoliberal concept of the European Union understood as an economic constitution (see Chapter 18 in this volume). From that perspective, the economic freedoms and competition law rules in the European Economic Community treaty set the frame within which the "private law society" (Privatrechtsgesellschaft) may operate. Freedom of contract and private autonomy are regarded as "constitutionally guaranteed." The European economic constitution differs from national economic constitutions in that private law is instrumentalized for the completion of the internal market.[2] The strong instrumental character is equally reflected in the notion of freedom of contract and private autonomy. The premise of European private law is not freedom of contract or private autonomy as a self-standing concept but rather "instrumentalized" and "regulated" freedom of contract and private autonomy.[3]

After the fall of the Berlin Wall in 1989, the member states began to debate the transformation of the European legal order into a constitution. The deliberations initiated in 2001 on the feasibility of a European civil code must be regarded as a second major pillar in the then-envisaged EU statehood building. Both "big" projects – the European constitution and the European civil code – failed. Neither a European constitution nor a European civil code can be built after the nation-state model. This is the lesson to be learned from these two grand failures. The European Union as it stands is much closer to the idea of a market state.[4]

I will use "competence" to highlight the constitutional intricacies of European civil code building and economic freedoms/fundamental rights to demonstrate the particularities of the "constitutional charter" which has been designed by the Court of Justice of the European Union (CJEU).[5] The European Union is built on the concept of enumerated powers. The first question is then whether the Union has competence at all to legislate on private law issues or whether the regulation of private law remains in the hands of the member states. This is not only a technical legal question. Private law forms an integral part of a society and a community. Those who have the power to legislate on private law have the means to influence the way in which a society and a community is built.

European Civil Code Building and the Paradigmatic Importance of Legislative Competence

So far, the competence for the adoption of private law measures has had to be "borrowed" from Article 114 of the Treaty on the Functioning of the European Union (TFEU), previously Article 100a of the Treaty establishing the European Economic Community (EEC) and Article 95 Treaty establishing the European Community (EC). The CJEU has by and large accepted the use of Article 114 TFEU with regard to status-related (consumer law) or sector-related (market bound) secondary community law measures.[6] Elaborating a European civil code would go beyond this and one might wonder whether and to what extent a European civil code would require an explicit competence in the treaty – not just the rather shaky one of Article 114 TFEU. However, even the boldest draft of a European constitution left private law competences unaffected. We might ask why this is so? Two positions compete with each other. Hugh Collins[7] argues in favor of a European private law to be developed bottom-up on the basis of an emerging European civil society: he is not the only one advancing this view. Walter van Gerven[8] with the Ius Commune Project and Jan Smits[9] promoting "Law 2.0." have taken a similar position. Although each of the three starts from different premises, they are united in the conviction that European private lawmaking is not a matter of competence but a matter of societal integration. It is for citizens and market participants to use freedom of contract and party autonomy to develop private regulation which reaches beyond the national territorial boundaries and which sets standards for the European Union as a whole (Collins and Smits). Similarly, it is for national courts to develop a common European doctrine on contract and tort through a judicial dialogue with other national and European courts (Gerven).[10]

Now to the European institutions. They cannot act *without* competence. European integration remains bound to legal integration. From such a perspective, shaping European statehood exemplifies a top–down approach. A European civil code, if it existed, would promote societal integration. When the European Commission launched the debate on a European civil code in its 2001 Communication, it deliberately avoided impinging upon the politically sensitive issue of competence. Digging deeper into competence would have made it necessary to reflect on the particularities of a European private law order, which is not nation-state bound but is bound to the completion of the internal market. It would have made it necessary to engage in a debate about the relationship between the then still envisaged European constitution and the feasibility of a European civil code. Therefore, the European Commission was advised not to discuss and not to propose a particular competence – otherwise the whole exercise of studying the feasibility of a European civil code might never have occurred.

The 2011 Proposal of the European Commission on a Regulation of a Common European Sales Law[11] remains far behind the original ambitions – in particular, those of the European Parliament, which was advocating the elaboration of a fully fledged European civil code in parallel with the then envisaged European constitution. Despite its modest outlook, seven member states are challenging the use of Article 114 TFEU (majority principle) as the appropriate basis. They would prefer Article 352 TFEU (unanimity principle). Using Article 352 TFEU would take away the risk of being outvoted. It would guarantee each and every member state – regardless of its seize – the right to veto the adoption of a common European sales law and to bring the process within the European Commission and the European Parliament to a halt.[12] The struggle over the correct legal basis – that is, Article 114 TFEU (majority principle) or Article 352 TFEU (unanimity principle) – underpins the "constitutional" dimension of sales law, which forms an integral part of the (national) civil codes. Member states are not ready to accept a silent transformation of the Internal Market on a quasi-constitutional legal basis.

Constitutionalization of European Private Law through Economic Freedoms and Fundamental Rights

The political resistance to overt constitution building through the adoption of a European civil code cannot hide the covert constitutionalization of European private-law building via the CJEU's use of economic freedoms and fundamental rights. Constitutionalization refers to a process in which private law is submitted to constitutional values. In the European Union, the constitutional values can be found in the economic freedoms and, since 2000, also in the Charter of Fundamental Rights. The question remains – what private law? The private law of the member states or European private law – and if European private law, what kind of European private law? In two landmark decisions of the early 1990s – *Alstom Atlantique*[13] and *CMC Motorradcenter*[14] – the CJEU made it abundantly clear that it was not ready to use the treaties (*primary* community law) to rule on the substance of national private law. However, largely unnoticed until recently,[15] the CJEU has used the economic freedoms to engage in a kind of European private-law building via development of an autonomous understanding of the key concepts underpinning private law. There are plenty of cases that affect the concept of contract, of property, unjust enrichment, tort, state liability, prescription periods, and procedural rules. The so-called general principles of civil law[16] could then be understood as just giving explicit expression to a development that started implicitly decades ago. The academic discussion and the research to be undertaken are still in their infancy.

The second strand of constitutionalization goes back to the Charter of Fundamental Rights, which was made legally binding by the Treaty of Lisbon. Constitutionalization of private law through the increasing use of fundamental rights and human rights ranks high on the political, judicial, and academic agendas. However, most of the research deals with the constitutionalization of national private law via national fundamental rights.[17] The parallel process of constitutionalization at the EU level has attracted much less attention. The case law of the CJEU illustrates the impact of fundamental rights on economic freedoms and on secondary EU law. In labor law, social security law, immigration law, and even in consumer law there is a certain tendency to apply the charter outside an economic and market-driven context. The overarching tendencies are sometimes interpreted as constitutionalization of the European Union beyond the internal market logic, which would mean a development towards a genuine European statehood.[18] However, in the core of private law relations, contract and tort – "traditional private law" – the instrumental market-driven use of economic freedoms and fundamental rights clearly dominates.

The Traditional Variant – Civil Code Building as State Building

The traditional national private law orders, with their focus on contract and tort, represent the *state nation* and later the *nation-state variant of private law*. They emerged from and are deeply rooted in the state nation and nation-state building process of the eighteenth and nineteenth centuries in continental Europe. The actors are private individuals – private economic actors originally and primarily operating within the territorial boundaries of the state. The states claim the authority to adopt private law rules in their territory. Local law and *droit commun* should no longer be applicable side-by-side. Private law became nationalized. The grand codifications of the early and late nineteenth century were meant to overcome the informal authority of private law as it stood in the seventeenth and eighteenth centuries. The result was an enormous increase of economic efficiency and legal coherence. Savigny's *International Private Law* provided the conceptual answer to the building of national private law orders as a means and technique to decide on the applicable law in cross-border transactions.[19]

From Coordination of Member States' Private Law Orders to a European Civil Code

The Treaty of Rome did not affect national private law orders. The 1980 Brussels Convention on jurisdiction and the 1980 Rome Convention on the applicable law were based on traditional mechanisms of international lawmaking. The conventions were bound to Europeanize or harmonize the national international private law rules with the particularity that the CJEU was given the ultimate authority to interpret the conventions[20] after the Brussels Convention was transformed into Regulation 44/2001/EC on jurisdiction and the Rome Convention was transformed in Regulation 593/2008/EC on the applicable contract law (supplemented by Regulation 423/2007/EC on tort law). The two Conventions, as well as the three Regulations that were adopted later, left the national private law orders intact, although the CJEU took a very active stand in the interpretation of the Brussels Convention and developed its own understanding of the parties to the contract, of the concept of contract, of *res judicata*, and so on.

The next step was the discovery of consumer law, triggered by the adoption of two unanimously agreed consumer policy programs in 1976 and 1981. While the member states of the Union had begun in the late 1960s, but particularly in the 1970s, to react to the rise of the consumer society by adopting laws on consumer credit, consumer safety, and unfair terms, it took the European Union to boost the development of consumer law as a means to complete the internal market.[21] For nearly twenty-five years – until the adoption of Directive 99/44/EC on consumer sales in 1999 – the building of a European consumer contract law remained largely unnoticed. It remained a domain for consumer lawyers around the globe that was not really taken seriously by private law scholars. It was seen as a kind of "bastard," an illegitimate child in the private law domain. After 1999, the European scene changed dramatically. Academics and politicians began to realize that the Europeanization of consumer law had led to a growing body of rules that steadily and ever more intrusively affected national private law orders – much more than did the Brussels and Rome Conventions – and that did not infringe on the integrity of national private law orders as a whole.

Being pushed into action by the European Parliament,[22] which clearly linked the European civil code project to the building of a European constitution, the European Commission adopted its 2001 Communication on Contract Law.[23] The Communication defined four different options – the idea of a European civil code was one of them – which were phrased in rather cautious terms. Based on the feedback from stakeholders, the European Commission then launched the project on the development of a common frame of reference, which was put into the hands of the Study Group on a European Civil Code and the Acquis Group by the European Commission. The Study Group continued the comparative research started by Professor Ole Lando at the University of Copenhagen,[24] which eventually led to the adoption of the Principles of European Contract Law. The Acquis Group, which was established by the European Commission, had to analyze the *acquis communautaire* of European private law. The 2001 document of the European Commission listed European international private law and consumer contract law directives, but it ignored the impact of primary community law and the Charter of Fundamental Rights on private law. The large set of rules that the European Union has adopted in the field of services in order to build a European market (financial services) or to transform public services into competitive markets (energy, telecommunication, postal services, transport, health care, education) were similarly excluded from the stocktaking, with far-reaching consequences, as will be shown later in the chapter.

The European Commission set the tone, defined the agenda, and supervised the activities of the Study Group and the Acquis Group. The merging of the two initiatives brought together roughly two hundred academics from around Europe, mainly from the old member states. In only four years the two groups of academics presented what the authors called the Academic Draft of a Common Frame of Reference (Academic DCFR). The merging of the freestanding Study Group and the Acquis Group brought new dynamics into the drafting process. Together, the two distilled out of the comparative analysis and the *acquis communautaire* a set of principles that looked like a fully fledged European civil code. This was possible as the two groups of academics enjoyed freedom to decide on the scope and the content of the codification project. Under the auspices of the then newly elected Commissioner Reding (Directorate-General for Justice), the civil code project returned to the political agenda. First, the Academic DCFR was transformed into a Political Common Frame of Reference (CFR) in 2011[25] and then into the draft Regulation of the European Commission, proposing a Common European Sales Law.[26]

This major conceptual move was the result of a reduction of a fully fledged European civil code to a set of rules governing transborder sales in B2B (business-to-business) and B2C (business-to-consumers) relations only. However, the basic concept, laid down in the DCFR, survived the political process. Translated into the narrative of the nation-state versus the market state, the CESL still bears the flavor of a body of rules that provides for a building block in the elaboration of a European civil code.

The Making and the Role of Academics

The Study Group and the Acquis Group were dominated by traditional nation-state private lawyers. There was obviously no preparedness on the side of the European Commission to take professors of EU law, EU constitutional law, or of energy, telecommunications, transport, Internet law, or financial services law on board. Services were included in the codification project at all stages, but they were not the services for which the European Union had most actively changed the legal rules and which form the core of "European Regulatory Private Law."[27] *Summa summarum* the merger of the two groups even strengthened the nation-state understanding of a future European private law. The suggested fully fledged European civil code was built after the master print of the grand codifications of civil law in Austria, France, Germany, and Italy. Implicitly, it was understood that the envisaged European civil code would become an integral part of the then still pending European constitutional project. The overall group of academics was rather homogeneous – all trained in their respective nation-state private law orders. The internal homogeneity finds its counterpart in the external pressure from those of the private law community who were not involved in the drafting process and who had raised critique against the whole exercise. This could be either from the point of view of a traditional private lawyer who defended the integrity of the national private law order or from the point of view of all those who argued that such an undertaking – the elaboration of a European civil code – would have to be linked to the overall status of the European Union and its quasi-state character, which might result in a different perspective on private law codification in the twenty-first century. The Study Group and the Acquis Group had to demonstrate the feasibility of a European civil code shaped along the lines of nation-state private law orders, thereby respecting the *droit commun*.[28] Inside and outside pressure favored a monistic view on private law – one where a European civil code is designed after nineteenth-century national codifications. While there was certainly no agreement within the two groups on the relationship between the proposed European civil code and the national private law orders, between the so-called Academic DCFR and national codifications or common law, the idea of a fully fledged European civil code promoted the idea that a European civil code in a fully integrated European Union might replace national and nation-state private law orders – at least in the long run. There was a strong idealistic momentum behind the concept of a European civil code that revitalized the early ideas of a European state in the aftermath of the Second World War.

Conceptual Deficits in the DCFR/CFR/CESL

The rather backward-looking concept of the DCFR/CFR/CESL may be demonstrated by looking at the understanding that underpins the notion of contract in the work of the Study Group and the way in which it is conceived. For decades contract lawyers across Europe have been discussing new modes of contract that are not regulated in the old codifications but which determine economic transactions. The drafters did not take these new modes of contract into consideration, although the question was raised early enough to allow for a redesign of the project.[29]

A first category concerns *relational contracts*,[30] where the parties engage in long-term commitments in contrast to one-shot transactions. Relational contracts merit a different contractual design, which takes into account the fact that parties are willing to or must continue to cooperate even in times of conflict, such as distribution agreements.[31] A second category constitutes *network contracts*, where more than two parties are involved. Network contracts appear in various industrial sectors. They play a dominant role in the energy, telecommunications, transport, and financial services sectors.[32] One of the key issues for network contracts is how to shape rights and duties and, in particular, how to assign responsibilities between parties to the contract.[33] A third category is *contract governance*, which should not be confused with corporate governance. Contract governance transfers the governance debate that arose in the area of public law to the private-law forum. It cuts across relational and network contracts; it even affects traditional bilateral contracts and searches for new modes of contractual management that meet the standards of accountability, transparency, and legitimacy.[34]

There are more questions to be raised with respect to the concept of contract as it stands and as it has been used in the DCFR/CFR/CESL. The proposed mechanism integrates mandatory consumer law into the body of rules. This seems to be very much in line with the German approach, where the legislator decided in the Law on the Modernization of the Civil Code to insert consumer law into the German civil code. This is contrary to the French and Italian approach, where consumer law rules are codified in a separate piece of legislation that stands side-by-side with the *codice civile* and the *code civile*. However, just as in German law, it remains to be seen whether and to what extent there are different concepts of contract behind consumer law and civil law – concepts which do not fit together.

Similar conceptual deficits can be identified with respect to tort law. This is worth mentioning even if tort law has been excluded from the draft Regulation on CESL, although the Study Group and the Acquis Group have spent time and energy on this building block of the envisaged European Civil Code. Book VI of the Academic DCFR competes with the Principles of European Tort Law, published in 2005 and elaborated by a group of tort lawyers, joined together in the European Centre of Tort and Insurance Law. The conceptual question is whether liability in tort should be based on personal responsibility alone or whether outside and beyond personal responsibility a new category is needed that recognizes the modern forms of organizations in the economy and society – organizational liability or enterprise liability.[35] While the Principles of European Tort Law deal with these new forms of liability, at least in a rudimentary form, the Academic DCFR fully relies on personal liability as the starting point for assigning responsibilities. This does not make the concept enshrined in the Academic DCFR immune to the criticism that the envisaged rules are opening up the floodgates to court litigation that aims to make the wrongdoer liable beyond all boundaries.[36]

Collective Private Regulation

The DCFR/CFR/CESL is designed to operate in a framework based on conventional actors: individual private parties, judges, and the legislator. Collective actors are out of the picture. They could be trade organizations, chambers of commerce, or even public regulators, which in practice play a key role in the drafting of private or semiprivate regulation. A theory of sources that would be able to incorporate these forms of collective private regulation is absent.

This approach fails to reflect the evolution of European private law as a multilevel system.[37] Private lawmaking contributes to the creation of the internal market and, in a complementary fashion with public regulation, to address market failures. It influences contract, property, civil liability, unfair competition, and many other areas of legislation. Examples range from the euro payment system to technical standardization, from environmental to food law, from advertising to warranties. Private regulation includes both pure self-regulation and different forms of co-regulation – from delegation of regulatory tasks to private bodies to *ex post* approval.

Private regulation constitutes a multilevel system articulated in different ways depending on whether it is promoted by associations or by market players.[38] Often when trade associations draft regulatory principles there is coordination between the state and the European level at which these associations operate. Self-regulation operates mainly in the field of contract standardization, but also in unfair trade practices, for example, in deceptive advertisement law and in civil liability both in the area of professional malpractice and in that of product liability. Co-regulation, where private actors operate within a public frame, is emerging in many fields. Co-regulation is well established in the field of technical standards, but from there it is increasingly intruding into more fields of private law. Co-regulation is eroding some of the spaces traditionally occupied by self-regulation and results in an increasing degree of public legislation, especially at the EU level, but it also covers fields earlier occupied by legislation and command and control regulation (see below).

The New Path – European Regulatory Private Law as Market State Building

Consumer law is also regulatory law. Its purpose and outlook comply with old political, theoretical, and doctrinal claims to introduce a social element into the formalistic private law orders rooted in nineteenth-century thinking. While it is true that consumer law saw a dramatic transformation when transferred from the nation-state level to the European level,[39] the integration of the social remains an "old" and "established" normative claim, going back to *ius aequum* in the Roman times, equity in the common law systems or good faith or fair dealing requirements in the continental private law systems.

The second less visible and more covert path of European regulatory private law relates to vertical sector-related rules on telecommunication, energy, transport, and financial services, where the European Union makes an attempt to establish markets where none existed before, or where markets were compartmentalized, and where it intends to establish a true European market where there were national ones. Here we can observe a much deeper transformation of private law – one in which the European Union takes the lead in challenging established social welfare paradigms and where private law and private-law means are just one facet of a much larger process of societal change, where the it turns into a market state, following the market dicta in taking over the task to set the appropriate conditions that allow for the establishment of competitive market structures.

The Innovative Character of European Regulatory Private Law

Private law – excluding family law – is easily associated with economic transactions. In European private law, the European Union appears as a *regulator* – through the CJEU, which is challenging national economic rules that hinder free trade of products, services, capital, or persons, and through the EU legislator, which is adopting horizontal or vertical market-related rules on private transactions, often by way of new modes of governance.[40]

This regulatory private law, in its negative variant through the impact of the four freedoms on the private law and in its positive variant[41] through the bulk of EU rules that have been adopted in the aftermath of the Single European Act, is consistent with the *modern variant of the European Union as a market state*. This private law takes its form, procedure, and content from being instrumentalized for building and shaping markets,[42] yielding its own pattern of justice, called *access justice* (*Zugangsgerechtigkeit*). It covers the setting of the regulatory frame through the EU institutions, the EU-driven creation of new market surveillance authorities, the fine tuning of the rules through intermediary forms of cooperation between European Union and member states institutions – be they called comitology, Lamfalussy, Open Method of Coordination – the development of new substantive legal mechanisms that reach beyond traditional private law rules and, last but not least, the enforcement of the self-standing rules through sectorial regulatory agencies and through new forms of alternative dispute settlement mechanisms.[43]

There is an obvious argument against the distinction between *nation*-states being equated with contract and tort law, with freedom of contract and private autonomy, and *European* private law which is regulatory in nature and meant to design markets. Regulation in private law is a matter that has been discussed already for more than one hundred years.[44] However, in comparison to the beginning of the twenty-first century there are major differences in terms of substance and in terms of institutions that justify maintaining the equation that nation-states equal the traditional concept of private law (contract and tort law (common law and/or codifications)) and the European Market State equals the modern concept of private law (European regulatory private law).

Regulatory law at that time was mainly labor and social law, which was kept outside the big codifications. Today's regulatory private law cuts across all sectors of the economy and policies. Two phenomena stand out. First and foremost, there is antidiscrimination law, which started in employment law and social security Directives 75/117/EEC and 76/207/EEC (now 2006/54/EC), but which entered into the private law domain via Directives 2000/43/EC, 2000/78/EC and 2004/113/EC, to the dismay of parts of the legal academia though largely supported by politics. Today, antidiscrimination turns into a common European value that cuts across all areas of the law – a process that was enabled by the decline of the nation-state.[45]

The second phenomenon concerns the vast array of secondary community law on financial services, telecommunications, energy (electricity, gas), transport (rail, ship, road, air), (the increasingly privatized) healthcare services, and more and more on educational services. Services account for 70 percent of the gross income in the European Union. The driving force behind all these rules that aim mainly at opening up markets, establishing competition, liberalizing former public services, and promoting privatization in former areas of public services, is undoubtedly the European Union – more precisely, the European Commission. "Regulatory" should not be equated with rules that restrict private autonomy and freedom of contract. Its instrumental character prevents it from being easily classified. Regulatory private law contains two constitutive elements, establishing market freedoms, therefore increasing private autonomy, while at the same time providing for rules that set boundaries to the newly created competitive market autonomy.

About one hundred years ago, the regulator was the nation-state, which used regulation to shape national markets for national economies. This is particularly true for the then emerging new industries, such as the chemical industry and, in today's terminology, the telecommunications industry. At that time, however, the firms were national – they were deeply anchored in the nation-state, both economically and culturally.[46] The establishment of the European Economic Community in 1957 changed the economic, political, and social environment. All the European Commission needs is a competence in the treaty and a majority in the European Parliament and the Council. There are only a few examples where the European Commission suffered from a severe setback, such as the legislative history of Service Directive 2006/123/EC. In most cases the European Commission managed to gain the necessary support at all institutional levels to implement its policies to complete the internal market, even in the sensitive area of healthcare. It then remains for the member states to implement and enforce what has been decided at the EU level. Differences remain, linked to the evolutionary path of the member states.[47]

The Substance of European Regulatory Private Law

Four areas of European regulatory private law can be distinguished: (1) network markets and network law; (2) commercial practices and contract law; (3) competition law, state aid, and public procurement; and (4) health, food safety, and regulation of services. These four areas of European private law create new principles, new modes of contract conclusion, new remedies, new forms of contractual standard setting, and new liability standards. This overview aims to demonstrate the vast areas of regulatory private law that are shaped by the European Union and that are normally ignored in the analysis of European private law. It is here that the clash between the traditional concept of private law and the modern market state concepts is most visible. It is also here where more research is needed to develop a deeper understanding of how private law is transforming, whether this new law can be systematized at all, and what its links are with traditional private law – either at the EU or at the national state level.

Regulated Markets

Network markets and network law: The privatization (liberalization) of former state monopolies in the sector of telecommunication (Directives 2009/22/EC and 2009/136/EC), energy (2007/92/EC and 2007/93/EC), and transport (passenger rights Regulation 261/2004 air; Regulation 137/2007 rail; Regulation 1177/2010 ship; Regulation 181/2011 bus) has raised the importance of contract law.[48] The overwhelming bulk of the literature dealing with network law ignores the contractual dimension – whether it is B2B or B2C.[49] It focuses on the public law side, that is, on the concept – the regulatory devices are meant to open up markets and to establish a competitive structure – as well as on the availability of an appropriate decentralized enforcement structure. This may be explained by the fact that the different set of EC directives deal only to a very limited extent with private law relations. In fact, contract law is turned into a device to serve the overall purpose of liberalization and privatization of former public services.[50] The concept of universal services implants new principles and new legal concepts into private law relations which may serve as a nucleus for a genuine social European private law.[51]

Insurance law (which is usually regarded as its own subject)[52] and capital market law (investor protection law), in both[53] policy and regulatory technique – the emphasis on establishing the market via public-law regulations – resemble the approach chosen in the field of telecommunications, energy, and transport. However, the regulatory approach is different. Directive 2004/39/EC on Markets in Financial Instruments – the so-called MiFID – lays down a broad framework that aims to establish a coherent European capital market within Level 1 of the Lamfalussy approach. After the financial crisis, the MiFID II (Directive 2014/65/EU), which repeals the MiFID I, and the MiFIR (Regulation (EU) 600/2014) have been enacted in order to make financial markets more efficient, resilient, and transparent. Moreover, the MiFIR entrusts European and national supervisory authorities with the power to temporarily prohibit or restrict certain financial instrument activities when there is a significant investor protection concern or a threat to the orderly functioning and integrity of financial markets or to the stability of the financial system in the Union. In line with the Lamfalussy procedure, two levels of law have been adopted: Directive 2006/73/EC on organizational requirements and operating conditions for investment firms and the implementing Regulation 2006/1287/EC. These directives and regulations establish a dense network of rules that contain strong links to contractual relations, where a professional or a private investor engages with his or her investment firm. The third level rules to be developed by national regulatory agencies are of primary concern for a deeper understanding of the transformation of private law rules.[54]

Company and capital market law: There are two dominant perspectives at the member state level which clash in the harmonization efforts of the European Community. There are those member states where company law is in essence regarded as dealing with the inner organization and the correct shaping and sharing of responsibilities; there are others where company law is seen as forming an essential part of capital market law. Last but not least, because of the failure of the European Commission to merge the two conflicting perspectives, the CJEU has become the key actor in deregulating national company law.[55] The possible impact of the CJEU's case law, as well as the few directives and regulations that have been adopted to give shape to European company law, in particular Directives 77/91/EEC on the formation of public limited companies, 78/855/EEC on mergers of public limited companies, 82/891/EEC on the division of public limited companies, 89/666/EEC on disclosure requirements, 89/667/EEC on single member private limited companies, 2001/86/EC Statute for a European Company with the involvement of employees, 2005/56/EC on cross-border mergers of limited liability companies, and Regulations 2137/85/EC European economic interest groups, and 2157/2001 Statue for a European Company, has not yet been analyzed with regard to its possible effects on private law, for example, on the concept of natural persons and legal persons.

Commercial Practices, Contract Law, Consumer Law

Commercial practices law: This is a field where the CJEU set the tone in numerous judgments in which it has analyzed the compatibility of national commercial practices (trading rules or marketing practices rules) with market freedoms – in particular the concept of misleading advertising.[56] It is here that the CJEU has developed the notion of "the average consumer."[57] Commercial practices law is heavily regulated by secondary law. The most important rules are Directive 2005/29/EC on unfair commercial practices dealing with B2C relations and Directive 2006/114/EC on misleading and comparative advertising in B2B relations. Again the CJEU seems ready to set the benchmarks.[58] The e-commerce Directive, 2000/31/EC, Directive 99/44/EC on consumer sales, and Directive 2011/83/EU on consumer rights (outside business premises and distant selling) affect the modalities under which a contract is concluded – the pre- and postcontractual stage (disclosure of information, role of third parties). What we can observe in European regulation is the disappearance of well-established boundaries between (public) regulation of commercial practices and private law.[59]

Consumer contract law: Over the last twenty-five years the European Union has created a dense net of consumer law rules that is similar to a consumer law code.[60] EU consumer law can be broken down into a general part formed by Directive 93/13/EEC on the control of unfair terms in consumer contracts and Directive 2011/83/EU on the modalities of contract conclusion (see the preceding paragraph above); a specific part on particular types of consumer contracts and on product liability: Directive 90/314/EC on package tours, Directive 99/44/EC on consumer sales, Directive 2008/48 on consumer credit, Directive 2008/122/EC on time sharing, Directive 2014/17/EU on mortgage credit; and an enforcement part: Directive 2009/22/EC on injunctions, Regulation 524/13/EU on Online Dispute Resolution, Directive 2013/11/EU on Alternative Dispute Resolution, Recommendation 2013/396/EU on common principles for injunctive and compensatory collective redress mechanisms.

Intellectual property rights: Intellectual property rights law is subject to control under the competition rules of the treaty, in particular Article 102 TFEU.[61] More important in our context is the EU policy to extend the existing intellectual property rights law and give it a European outlook coupled with appropriate legal redress mechanisms to sanction violations of property rights (Directive 2004/48/EC). The considerable expansion[62] of intellectual property impacts users' rights.[63] These exclusive rights are enforced via contract law, often via standard terms that form part of the license contract, the user concludes often via the Internet.[64]

Competition Law, State Aids, and Public Procurement

Private competition law (*Kartellprivatrecht*)[65] is another neglected domain. Block exemptions are a well-established means used by the European Commission to control vertical agreements by means of competition law. The diverse regulations on exclusive and selective distribution, the umbrella Regulation 330/2010, Regulation 461/2010 on the car sector, and Regulation 772/2004 on technology transfer (under revision) intervene indirectly in contract making. This impact is indirect because the parties to the vertical agreement are free to define their contractual relations. However, in practice, the content of the rights and duties in vertical agreements is determined to a large extent by block exemptions. The parties will often literally copy the articles of the block exemptions into their contracts to avoid discrepancies between EU rules and contractual rights. This is particularly true with regard to "hard core restrictions."

State aid law: State aid is submitted to control by Articles 107 *et seq.* of the TFEU. The huge bulk of case law constitutes a prominent field of research in order to investigate the indirect effects of primary EU law on contractual relations.[66] The new economic approach has led to the adoption of the *de minimis* Regulation 1998/2006. European state aid law may be divided into a substantive and a procedural part. The terminology differs – sometimes procedural law is dealt with under the heading of "remedies,"[67] while it can also simply be called procedural rules on state aid.[68] What really matters is the possible consequences of illegal state aid – the question of repayment of unlawful state aid and the possible remedies of third parties.[69]

Public procurement law: Public procurement affects market freedoms. It is heavily regulated by secondary law. As early as 1971, the EC adopted Regulation 1182/71. The two major pieces of EU law which have determined public procurement law since they have come into force on 31 January 2006 are Directive 2004/17/EC, dealing with procurement procedures of entities operating in the water, energy, transport, and postal services, and Directive 2004/18/EC on the coordination of the procurement procedure on public works contracts, public supply contracts, and public services contracts. The emphasis in academic research has been on competition and market freedoms.[70] While the purpose of these directives is clearly to enhance competition and strengthen market freedoms, at the same time they shape contractual relations.[71] This is particularly true with regard to appropriate remedies.[72] Recently, the CJEU held, in a landmark decision, that a member state is obliged to cancel contracts that have been concluded in violation of EU procurement obligations.[73] This judgment challenges the principles of *pacta sunt servanda* and legitimate expectation (*Vertrauensschutz*) and establishes a new understanding of the concept of contract.

Health, Food Safety, and the Regulation of Services

Product safety and food safety law: Directive 2001/95/EC on product safety enhances the role of contract law as a means to shape contractual relations.[74] Even more interesting are liability rules hidden in various fields of food law.[75] This is particularly true with regard to liability rules, which may be found in the Feed Hygiene Regulation 183/2005, the Food Hygiene Regulation 852/2004, the Regulation on Official Feed and Food Controls 882/2004, and Regulation on Food Law 178/2002.[76]

Consumer law and services: The so-called Services Directive 2006/123/EC enhances the elaboration of "technical standards" by the European standard bodies CEN/CENELEC as well as by national standards bodies that come near to some sort of standard contract conditions with a rather unclear legal status.[77] These technical standards are developed within and under the Service Directive, which defines a fully harmonized frame for the regulation of services. However, technical standards are generally not directly binding. What happens if these technical standards contravene national unfair contract terms legislation? So far it is even unclear whether technical standards come within the scope of application of Directive 93/13/EEC on unfair contract terms.

New Forms of Rule/Lawmaking

Shifting the focus to the new European regulatory private law requires a deeper look into new lawmaking procedures. The EU directives and regulations do not provide for a comprehensive picture of the new rules which might affect private law. A common regulatory technique in European private law is co-regulation.[78] European secondary law sets the statutory frame, which is then completed by nonbinding rules that are either developed by private bodies (comitology, e.g., European and national standard bodies) or by European and national enforcement authorities (Lamfalussy procedure). Whether and to what extent these rules affect private law is mainly a matter of empirical research. Little research has been done in this field until now – perhaps with the exception of the Open Method of Coordination.[79] There is a strong governance dimension in that these new processes of law and rule making are developed outside legal procedures – whether they are quasi-constitutional, quasi-administrative, or entirely self-organized.

New Devices of Private Law Enforcement

From a traditional perspective, it is for the private party concerned to defend their rights in and out of courts. In regulatory private law, the perspective changes from individual rights to collective enforcement via courts or administrative authorities.[80] Under the EU treaties, enforcement lies in the hands of the member states authorities, courts, and regulatory agencies. However, this does not mean that the European Union has not adopted directives and regulations in the field of private law enforcement. Of particular relevance are the developments in the enforcement of intellectual property rights (Directive 2004/48), in consumer law (Directives 2009/22/EC on injunctions, Regulation 524/2013 on online dispute resolution, Directive 2013/11/EU on alternative dispute resolution), and more recently in competition law (Directive 2014/000/EU on antitrust damages actions).

The national and European courts are tied together via the preliminary reference procedure (see Chapter 13 in this volume). The shift towards administrative enforcement stimulates new forms of governance between national administrative enforcement authorities and newly emerging European regulatory agencies. EU law does not contain a fully fledged procedural law dealing with rights, procedures, and remedies. This is the background to the doctrine of procedural autonomy of member states in procedural law. However, the CJEU has developed two powerful instruments on the basis of primary EU law and by referring to human rights: the principle of effectiveness and the principle of equivalence. These are not only applicable to "procedure" but also to "remedies." They are applied to constantly narrow down the autonomy of member states by an increasing body of case law.[81] The principles of effectiveness and equivalence are applied through the holders of enforceable rights granted by primary and secondary EU law.

The interplay of national and EU rules with respect to rights, remedies, and procedure gains importance with regard to both procedure *and* remedies. A prime example to demonstrate the power of the effectiveness doctrine in the field of "procedure" is the *Claro* case,[82] in which the CJEU argued that member states' courts have to exercise control over contract terms *ex officio* – a doctrine which belongs now to the *acquis communautaire*.[83] In the field of consumer law "remedies," *Aziz*[84] introduced injunctive relief in the execution procedure to prevent unfair terms. *Courage*[85] and *Manfredi*[86] prepared the ground for the Directive on Antitrust Damages Actions. *Reich* has called the interplay of national procedural law (including remedies) and the arising EU procedural law "hybridization"[87] to emphasize that neither of the two legal orders is standing alone. Hybridization is then a "double-headed federalist approach" whereby the European Union and the member states both have constitutional responsibilities. Despite some fundamental differences – the US legal system provides for fully fledged procedural law at both the federal and the state level – research comparing the European Union and the United States with regard to rights, procedure, and remedies provides helpful insights in how a "federal" structure might be shaped with regard to effective legal protection.[88] Elements of hybridization can also be found in administrative enforcement – in particular, in the numerous directives dealing with privatization of former state monopolies. They have established precedents in the way in which public authorities are to be shaped.[89] These initiatives have had a spillover effect on private law.

There is a similar impact on the distinction between judicial and administrative enforcement. European regulatory private law is characterized by combining administrative enforcement and judicial enforcement – to an increasing extent via collective judicial enforcement. The more strongly the European Union intervenes in the various fields of the visible private law, the more the competence balance is shifted away from the member states to the European level. This does not mean that enforcement is centralized at the EU level, although the Union has established European regulatory agencies in all regulated markets (Regulation 1211/2009 telecom, Regulation 713 and 714/2009 energy). These agencies differ considerably in their outlook, their independence, and their regulatory competences. What might be even more important than the degree of centralization is the shift from judicial enforcement to administrative enforcement. This implies a stronger need to coordinate administrative enforcement via new modes of governance.

The Going Together of the Old and the New Private Law

So far, nation-state private law and the new regulatory private law have appeared as two distinct disciplines. It remains to be seen whether and to what extent the new European regulatory private law will turn into a self-standing autonomous legal order and what remains for the nation-state private law systems. The double transformation process, at the national and at the EU level, requires careful attention. For years to come, European private law could well be at the center of the stage – not only in academic research but also on the political agenda.

Notes

The research leading to these results has received funding from the European Research Council under the European Union's Seventh Framework Programme (FP/2007–2013) / ERC Grant Agreement n. [269722].

1 Heinz-D. Assmann et al., *Wirtschaftsrecht als Kritik des Privatrechts: Beiträge zur Privat- und Wirtschaftsrechtstheorie* (Königstein: Athenäum, 1980).
2 See Stefan Grundmann, "The Concept of the Private Law Society: After 50 Years of European Law and European Business Law," *European Review of Private Law* 16 (2008). A nice account of the European economic constitution in its influence on (European) private law is given by Sabine Frerichs and Teemu Juutilainen, "Rome under Seven Hills? An Archeology of European Private Law" (Legal Studies Research Paper Series, no. 32, University of Helsinki, Faculty of Law, 2014).
3 Hanoch Dagan, "Autonomy, Pluralism and Contract Law Theory," *Law and Contemporary Problems* 76 (2013); and Guido Comparato and Hans-Wolfgang Micklitz, "Regulated Autonomy between Market Freedoms and Fundamental Rights in the Case Law of the CJEU," in *General Principles of EU Law and European Private Law*, ed. Ulf Bernitz, Xavier Groussot, and Felix Schulyok (Alphen aan den Rijn: Kluwer Law International, 2013). In the same direction, see Norbert Reich, *General Principles of EU Civil Law* (Cambridge: Intersentia, 2013).
4 Ari Afilalo and Dennis Patterson, "Statecraft and the Foundations of European Union Law," in *Philosophical Foundations of European Union Law*, ed. Julie Dickson and Pavlos Eleftheriadis (Oxford: Oxford University Press, 2012).
5 Since 26 September 1984, Case 294/83 *Parti écologiste Les Verts* EU:C:1986:166, para 23.
6 With the exception of Case C-436/03 *European Parliament v. Council* EU:C:2006:277.
7 Hugh Collins, *The European Civil Code: The Way Forward* (Cambridge: Cambridge University Press, 2008).
8 The different *Casebooks* on Tort Law, Private Law, Consumer Law, Anti-Discrimination Law (Oxford: Hart).
9 Jan Smits, "Private Law 2.0: On the Role of Private Actors in a Post-National Society" (inaugural lecture as Maastricht-HiiL Chair on the Internationalisation of Law, 30 November 2010, The Hague: Eleven International, 2011).
10 In that direction, Giovanni Comandé, "The Fifth European Union Freedom: Aggregating Citizenship ... around Private Law," in *Constitutionalization of European Private Law*, ed. Hans-Wolfgang Micklitz (Oxford: Oxford University Press, 2014), 61.
11 COM(2011) 635 final.
12 On the importance of political consensus for European integration, see J.H.H. Weiler, "The Transformation of Europe," *Yale Law Journal* 100 (1991).

13 Case C-339/89 *Alsthom Atlantique SA v. Compagnie de construction mécanique Sulzer SA* EU:C:1991:28.

14 Case C-93/92 *CMC Motorradcenter GmbH v. Pelin Baskiciogullari* EU:C:1993:838.

15 Ernst Steindorff, *EG-Vertrag und Privatrecht* (Baden-Baden: Nomos, 1996); Christoph Schmid, *Die Instrumentalisierung des Privatrechts durch die Europäische Union* (Baden-Baden: Nomos, 2010); Arthur S. Hartkamp, *European Law and National Private Law* (Deventer: Kluwer, 2012); and Arthur S. Hartkamp and Leen Keus, *The Influence of EU Private Law on National Private Law* (Deventer: Kluwer, 2014).

16 Case C-412/06 *Hamilton* EU:C:2008:215; Case C-489/07 *Messner* EU:C:2009:502; Case C-101/08 *Audiolux* EU:C:2009:626.

17 Olha Cherednychenko, *Fundamental Rights, Contract Law and the Protection of the Weaker Party: A Comparative Analysis of the Constitutionalisation of the Contract Law with Emphasis on Risky Financial Transactions* (Munich: Sellier, 2007); Chantal Mak, *Fundamental Rights in European Contract Law: A Comparison of the Impact of Fundamental Rights on Contractual Relationships in Germany, the Netherlands, Italy and England* (Alphen aan den Rijin: Kluwer, 2008); Gert Brüggemeier, Giovanni Comandé, and Aurelia Colombi Ciacchi, eds., *Fundamental Rights and Private Law in the European Union*. 2 vols. (Cambridge: Cambridge University Press, 2010).

18 See the contributions of Collins, Comandé, Colombi Ciacchi, Bell, Cherednychenko, Godt, and Mak in Hans-Wolfgang Micklitz, ed., *Constitutionalisation of European Private Law* (Oxford: Oxford University Press, 2014).

19 Although von Savigny was referring to the law of princedoms that should be connected. He rejected the idea of elaborating a civil code for Germany. Friedrich Carl von Savigny, *International Private Law: A Treatise on the Conflict of Laws and the Limits of Their Operation in Respect of Place and Time*, trans. William Guthrie (Edinburgh: T & T Clark Law, 1869).

20 There are differences between the two. It is only after the Lugano Convention had been transformed into Regulations Rome I and Rome II that the Court of Justice started to play a role.

21 Stephen Weatherill, *EU Consumer Law and Policy* (Cheltenham: Edward Elgar, 2005).

22 [1989] OJ C 158, 400; [1994] OJ C 205, 518.

23 COM(2001) 398 final.

24 See http://www.sgecc.net/.

25 European Commission, "A European Contract Law for Consumers and Businesses: Publication of the Results of the Feasibility Study Carried Out by the Expert Group on European Contract Law for Stakeholders' and Legal Practitioners' Feedback" (Brussels, 2011).

26 COM(2011) 635 final.

27 See below in the same text.

28 See Horst Eidenmüller et al., "The Common Frame of Reference for European Private Law: Policy Choices and Codification Problems," *Oxford Journal of Legal Studies* 28 (2008).

29 Stefan Grundmann, "European Contract Law(s) of What Colour?" *European Review of Contract Law* 1 (2005): 187; and Fabrizio Cafaggi, ed., *The Institutional Framework of European Private Law* (Oxford: Oxford University Press, 2006).

30 Stewart Macaulay, "Non-Contractual Relations in Business: A Preliminary Study," *American Sociological Review* 28 (1963): 55.

31 Christian Joerges, ed., *Franchising and the Law: Theoretical and Comparative Approaches in Europe and the United States* [Das Recht des Franchising: Konzeptionelle, rechtsvergleichende und europarechtliche Analysen, Schriftenreihe der Gesellschaft für Rechtsvergleichung] (Baden-Baden: Nomos, 1991), 153.

32 Gunther Teubner, *Networks as Connected Contracts* (Oxford: Hart, 2008); Fabrizio Cafaggi, "Contractual Networks and the Small Business Act," *European Review of Contract Law* 4 (2008): 493; and Marc Amstutz and Gunther Teubner, *Networks: Legal Issues of Multilateral Co-operation* (Oxford: Hart, 2009).

33 On credit financed consumer investments, see Hans-Wolfgang Micklitz, "The Relationship between National and European Consumer Policy – Challenges and Perspectives," in *Yearbook of Consumer Law*, ed. Christian Twigg-Flesner et al. (Aldershot: Ashgate, 2008), 35.
34 Fabrizio Cafaggi and Horatia Muir Watt, eds., *Making European Private Law* (Cheltenham: Edward Elgar, 2008); and Stefan Grundmann, Florian Moslein, and Karl Riesenhuber, eds., *Contract Governance: Dimensions in Law and Interdisciplinary Research* (Oxford: Oxford University Press, 2015).
35 For a modern concept of liability in tort, see Gert Brüggemeier and Zhu Yan, *Entwurf für ein Chinesisches Haftungsrecht, Text und Begründung: Ein Beitrag zur internationalen Diskussion um die Reform des Haftungsrechts* (Tübingen: Mohr Siebeck, 2009).
36 Horst Eidenmüller et al., "Der Gemeinsame Referenzrahmen für das Europäische Privatrecht – Wertungsfragen und Kodifikationsprobleme," *Juristenzeitung* 63 (2008): 529.
37 Fabrizio Cafaggi and Horatia Muir Watt, eds., *The Regulatory Functions of European Private Law* (Cheltenham: Edward Elgar, 2009).
38 Fabrizio Cafaggi, "Private Law-Making and European Integration: Where Do They Meet, When Do They Conflict?" in *The Regulatory State: Constitutional Implications*, ed. Dawn Oliver, Tony Prosser, and Richard Rawlings (Oxford: Oxford University Press, 2010).
39 Hans-Wolfgang Micklitz, "Do Consumers and Business Need a New Architecture for Consumer Law? A Thought Provoking Impulse," *Yearbook of European Law* 32 (2013): 266.
40 Cafaggi and Muir Watt, *Making European Private Law* and *The Regulatory Functions of European Private Law*.
41 Fritz W. Scharpf, "Negative and Positive Integration in the Political Economy of European Welfare States," in *Governance in the European Union*, ed. Gary Marks et al. (London: Sage, 1996).
42 Private law as economic law, *Privatrecht als Wirtschaftsrecht*. See, for Europe, Schmid, *Die Instrumentalisierung des Europäischen Privatrechts durch die Europäische Union*.
43 Hans-Wolfgang Micklitz, "The Visible Hand of European Private Law," *Yearbook of European Law* 28 (2010).
44 Otto von Gierke, *Die Soziale Aufgabe des Privatrechts* (Berlin: Springer, 1889), 13.
45 Richard Münch, *European Governmentality: The Liberal Drift of Multilevel Governance* (London: Routledge, 2010), 28 *et seq*.
46 Cornelius Torp, "Von Junkern und Schlotbaronen: Zur Interpretation des deutschen Protektionismus vor 1914," *Saeculum* 60 (2010).
47 Sven Steinmo, *The Evolution of Modern States: Sweden, Japan, and the United States* (Cambridge: Cambridge University Press, 2010).
48 Jürgen Keßler and Hans-Wolfgang Micklitz, *Kundenschutz auf den liberalisierten Märkten für Energie, Telekommunikation, Personenverkehr/Eisenbahn* (Baden-Baden: Nomos, 2008).
49 Peter Cameron, *Legal Aspects of EU Energy Regulation* (Oxford: Oxford University Press, 2007).
50 Serge Gijrath and Jan Smits, "European Contract Law in View of Technical and Economic Regulation," in *The Future of European Contract Law*, ed. Katharina Boele-Woelki and Willem Grosheide (Alphen aan den Rijn: Wolters Kluwer, 2007), 53; and Giuseppe Bellantuono, *Contratti e regolazione nei mercati dell'energia* (Bologna: Molino, 2009).
51 Peter Rott, "A New Social Contract Law for Public Services? Consequences from Regulation of Services of General Economic Interests in the EC," *European Review of Contract Law* 1 (2005): 323; and Hans-Wolfgang Micklitz, "Universal Services: Nucleus for a Social European Private Law?" in *Market Integration and Public Services in the European Union*, ed. Marise Cremona (Oxford: Oxford University Press, 2011), 63.
52 Jürgen Basedow, Till Fock, and Dorothée Janzen, eds., *Europäisches Versicherungsvertragsrecht*, vol. 3. (Tübingen: Mohr Siebeck, 2003). Vols. 1 and 2 show the particularities of EC insurance law.
53 Klaus J. Hopt and Hans-Christoph Voigt, eds., *Prospekt-und Kapitalmarktinformationshaftung: Recht und Reform in der Europäischen Union, der Schweiz und den USA*, vol. 79. (Tübingen: Mohr Siebeck, 2005).

54 Eva Ruffing, *Die europäische Wertpapierregulierung zwischen Input- und Output-Legitimität: Das Lamfalussy-Verfahren* (Baden-Baden: Nomos, 2011); Guido Ferrarini, "Contract Standards and the Markets in Financial Instruments Directive (MiFID): An Assessment of the Lamfalussy Regulatory Architecture," *European Review of Contract Law* 1 (2005). On the relationship between the public and the private in the EU rules on financial services, see the special issue of the *European Review of Contract Law* 4/2014 with contributions from Olha Cherednychenko, Annetje Ottow, Yane Svetiev, Heikki Marjosola, and Federico della Negra.

55 Case C-212/97 *Centros* EU:C:1999:126; Case C-208/00 *Überseering* EU:C:2002:632; Case C-167/01 *Inspire Art* EU:C:2003:512; and Case C-210/06 *Cartesio* EU:C:2008:723.

56 Bert Keirsbilck, *The New European Law of Unfair Commercial Practices and Competition Law* (Oxford: Hart, 2011).

57 Stephen Weatherill, "Who is the Average Consumer?" in *The Regulation of Unfair Commercial Practices under EC Directive 2005/29*, ed. Stephen Weatherill and Ulf Bernitz (Oxford: Hart, 2007), 115.

58 Joined Cases C-261/07 and C-299/07 *VTB-VAB* EU:C:2009:244; Case C-540/08 *Mediaprint Zeitungs- und Zeitschriftenverlag* EU:C:2010:660; and Case C-304/08 *Plus Warenhandelsgesellschaft* EU:C:2010:12.

59 Simon Whittaker, "Form and Substance in the Reception of EC Directives into English Contract Law," *European Review of Contract Law* 3 (2007).

60 For details, Hans-Wolfgang Micklitz et al., *European Consumer Law* (Cambridge: Intersentia, 2014).

61 Case C-418/01 *IMS Health* EU:C:2004:257.

62 Reto M. Hilty, "Entwicklungsperspektiven des Schutzes geistigen Eigentums," in *Stand und Perspektiven des Schutzes geistigen Eigentums*, ed. Peter Behrens (Baden-Baden: Nomos, 2004).

63 Lucie M. C. R. Guibault et al., *Digital Consumers and the Law: Towards a Cohesive European Framework* (Alphen aan den Rijn: Wolters Kluwer, 2013).

64 Till Kreutzer, *Verbraucherschutz bei digitalen Medien* (Berlin: Berliner Wissenschafts-Verlag, 2007).

65 Stefan Grundmann, *Europäisches Schuldvertragsrecht: das europäische Recht der Unternehmensgeschäfte* (Berlin: de Gruyter, 1999).

66 See the list of cases in Hernst-Joachim Mestmäcker and Heike Schweitzer, *Europäisches Wettbewerbsrecht* (Munich: Beck, 2004), 1177.

67 Saša Beljin, "Rechtsprechung ('leading cases')," in *Europarecht: Handbuch für die deutsche Rechtspraxis*, ed. Reiner Schulze and Manfred Zuleeg (Baden-Baden: Nomos, 2006).

68 Mestmäcker and Schweitzer, *Europäisches Wettbewerbsrecht*, paras 42–47.

69 Hanna Schebesta, "Towards an EU Law of Damages: Damages Claims for Violations of EU Public Procurement Law before National and European Judges." (PhD diss., European University Institute, Florence, 2013).

70 See Mestmäcker and Schweitzer, *Europäisches Wettbewerbsrecht*, para 36; Rainer Noch, "Öffentliches Auftragsrecht," in Schulze and Zuleeg, *Europarecht: Handbuch für die Rechtspraxis*.

71 References may be found in Mestmäcker and Schweitzer, *Europäisches Wettbewerbsrecht*, no. 172 *et seq*.

72 Sue Arrowsmith, ed., *EU Public Procurement Law: An Introduction*, The EU Asia Inter University Network for Teaching and Research in Public Procurement Regulation, 2011.

73 Case C-503/04 *Commission of the European Communities v. Federal Republic of Germany* EU:C:2007:432.

74 Fabrizio Cafaggi, "A Coordinate Approach to Regulation and Civil Liability in European Law: Rethinking Institutional Complementarities," in *The Institutional Framework of European Private Law*, ed. Fabrizio Cafaggi (Oxford: Oxford University Press, 2006), 191.

75 Jürgen Basedow, "EC Regulation in European Private Law," in *Private Law in the International Arena. From National Conflict Rules towards Harmonization and Unification – Liber Amicorum Kurt Siehr*, ed. Jürgen Basedow et al. (The Hague: T.MC. Asser Institute, 2000), 17.

76 Civic Consulting, "Liability in the food and feed sector," 50. Study prepared for DG SANCO, Financial Guarantees in the Feed Sector, SANCO/2004/D1/SI2.398887, Final Report, Berlin, 6 September 2005, unpublished.

77 Hans-Wolfgang Micklitz, "Service Standards: Defining the Core Consumer Elements and their Minimum Requirements" (study commissioned by ANEC, the European Voice in Standardisation, 2007).
78 See earlier in the chapter under collective private regulation.
79 Jonathan Zeitlin, in *The Open Method of Coordination in Action: The European Employment and Social Inclusion Strategies*, ed. Jonathan Zeitlin and Philippe Pochet (Brussels: PIE-Peter Lang, 2005); and Stijn Smismans, *Civil Society and Legitimate European Governance* (Cheltenham: Edward Elgar, 2006).
80 Christofer Hodges, *The Reform of Class and Representative Actions in European Legal Systems: A New Framework for Collective Redress in Europe* (Oxford: Hart, 2009).
81 Michal Bobek, "Why there is No Principle of 'Procedural Autonomy' of the Member States," in *The ECJ and the Autonomy of the Member States*, ed. Hans-Wolfgang Micklitz and Bruno de Witte (Cambridge: Intersentia, 2012), 305; and Michal Bobek, *Comparative Reasoning in European Supreme Courts* (Oxford: Oxford University Press, 2013).
82 Case C-168/05 *Elisa Maria Mostaza Claro v. Centro Movil Milenium SL* EU:C:2006:675.
83 Case C-40/08 *Asturcom Telecomunicaciones* EU:C:2009:615; Case C-618/10 *Banco Español* EU:C:2012:349.
84 Case C-415/11 *Mohamed Aziz* EU:C:2013:164; Hans-Wolfgang Micklitz, "Unfair Contract Terms: Public Interest Litigation before European Courts Case C-415/11 *Mohamed Aziz*," in *Landmark Cases of EU Consumer Law: In Honour of Jules Stuyck*, ed. Veerle Colaert and Evelyn Terryn (Cambridge: Intersentia, 2013), 615.
85 Case C-453/99 *Courage Ltd v. Bernard Crehan* EU:C:2001:465.
86 Case C-295/04 *Vincenzo Manfredi v. Lloyd Adriatico Assicurazioni SpA* EU:C:2006:461.
87 Norbert Reich, "Horizontal Liability in EC Law: Hybridization of Remedies for Compensation in Case of Breaches of EC Rights," *Common Market Law Review* 44 (2007).
88 See Johan Lindholm, *State Procedure and Union Rights: A Comparison of the European Union and the United States* (Uppsala: Iustus Förlag, 2007).
89 Yane Svetiev, "W(h)ither Private Law in the Face of the Regulatory Deluge," in *A Self-Sufficient Private Law – A Viable Concept?* ed. Hans-Wolfgang Micklitz and Yane Svetiev (EUI-ERPL working paper no. 2012/31, 26).

References

Afilalo, Ari, and Dennis Patterson. "Statecraft and the Foundations of European Union Law." In *Philosophical Foundations of European Union Law*, edited by Julie Dickson and Pavlos Eleftheriadis, 275–303. Oxford: Oxford University Press, 2012.

Amstutz, Marc, and Gunther Teubner. *Networks: Legal Issues of Multilateral Co-operation*. Oxford: Hart, 2009.

Arrowsmith, Sue, ed. *EU Public Procurement Law: An Introduction*. The EU Asia Inter University Network for Teaching and Research in Public Procurement Regulation, 2011.

Assmann, Heinz-D., Gert Brüggemeier, Dieter Hart, and Christian Joerges. *Wirtschaftsrecht als Kritik des Privatrechts: Beiträge zur Privat- und Wirtschaftsrechtstheorie*. Königstein: Athenäum, 1980.

Basedow, Jürgen. "EC Regulation in European Private Law." In *Private Law in the International Arena: From National Conflict Rules towards Harmonization and Unification – Liber Amicorum Kurt Siehr*, edited by Jürgen Basedow, Isaak Meier, Anton K. Schnyder, Talia Einhorn, and Daniel Girsberger, 17–31. The Hague: T. M C. Asser Institute, 2000.

Basedow, Jürgen, Till Fock, and Dorothée Janzen, eds. *Europäisches Versicherungsvertragsrecht*. Vol. 3. Tübingen: Mohr Siebeck, 2003.

Beljin, Saša. "Rechtsprechung ('leading cases')." In Schulze and Zuleeg, *Europarecht: Handbuch für die deutsche Rechtspraxis*, 1224–1225.

Bellantuono, Giuseppe. *Contratti e regolazione nei mercati dell'energia*. Bologna: Molino, 2009.
Bobek, Michal. "Why there is No Principle of 'Procedural Autonomy' of the Member States." In *The ECJ and the Autonomy of the Member States*, edited by Hans-Wolfgang Micklitz and Bruno de Witte, 305–323. Cambridge: Intersentia, 2012.
Bobek, Michal. *Comparative Reasoning in European Supreme Courts*. Oxford: Oxford University Press, 2013.
Brüggemeier, Gert, Giovanni Comandé, and Aurelia Colombi Ciacchi, eds. *Fundamental Rights and Private Law in the European Union*. 2 vols. Cambridge: Cambridge University Press, 2010.
Brüggemeier, Gert, and Zhu Yan. *Entwurf für ein Chinesisches Haftungsrecht, Text und Begründung: Ein Beitrag zur internationalen Diskussion um die Reform des Haftungsrechts*. Tübingen: Mohr Siebeck, 2009.
Cafaggi, Fabrizio. "A Coordinate Approach to Regulation and Civil Liability in European Law: Rethinking Institutional Complementarities." In *The Institutional Framework of European Private Law*, edited by Fabrizio Cafaggi. Oxford: Oxford University Press, 2006.
Cafaggi, Fabrizio, ed. *The Institutional Framework of European Private Law*. Oxford: Oxford University Press, 2006.
Cafaggi, Fabrizio. "Contractual Networks and the Small Business Act." *European Review of Contract Law* 4 (2008): 493–539.
Cafaggi, Fabrizio. "Private Law-Making and European Integration: Where Do They Meet, When Do They Conflict?" In *The Regulatory State: Constitutional Implications*, edited by Dawn Oliver, Tony Prosser, and Richard Rawlings, 201–228. Oxford: Oxford University Press, 2010.
Cafaggi, Fabrizio, and Horatia Muir Watt, eds. *Making European Private Law*. Cheltenham: Edward Elgar, 2008.
Cafaggi, Fabrizio, and Horatia Muir Watt, eds. *The Regulatory Functions of European Private Law*. Cheltenham: Edward Elgar, 2009.
Cameron, Peter. *Legal Aspects of EU Energy Regulation*. Oxford: Oxford University Press, 2007.
Cherednychenko, Olha. *Fundamental Rights, Contract Law and the Protection of the Weaker Party: A Comparative Analysis of the Constitutionalisation of the Contract Law with Emphasis on Risky Financial Transactions*. Munich: Sellier, 2007.
Civic Consulting. "Liability in the Food and Feed Sector." Study prepared for DG SANCO, *Financial Guarantees in the Feed Sector*, SANCO/2004/D1/SI2.398887, Final Report, Berlin, 6 September 2005, unpublished.
Collins, Hugh. *The European Civil Code: The Way Forward*. Cambridge: Cambridge University Press, 2008.
Comandé, Giovanni. "The Fifth European Union Freedom: Aggregating Citizenship … around Private Law." In *Constitutionalization of European Private Law*, edited by Hans-Wolfgang Micklitz, 61–101. Oxford: Oxford University Press, 2014.
Comparato, Guido, and Hans-Wolfgang Micklitz. "Regulated Autonomy between Market Freedoms and Fundamental Rights in the Case Law of the CJEU." In *General Principles of EU Law and European Private Law*, edited by Ulf Bernitz, Xavier Groussot, and Felix Schulyok, 121–154. Alphen aan den Rijn: Kluwer Law International, 2013.
Dagan, Hanoch. "Autonomy, Pluralism and Contract Law Theory." *Law and Contemporary Problems* 76 (2013): 19–38.
Eidenmüller, Horst, Florian Faust, Hans Christoph Grigoleit, Nils Jansen, Gerhard Wagner, and Reinhard Zimmermann. "Der Gemeinsame Referenzrahmen für das Europäische Privatrecht – Wertungsfragen und Kodifikationsprobleme." *Juristenzeitung* 63 (2008): 529–550.
Eidenmüller, Horst, Florian Faust, Nils Jansen, Hans Christoph Grigoleit, Gerhard Wagner, and Reinhard Zimmermann. "The Common Frame of Reference for European Private Law: Policy Choices and Codification Problems." *Oxford Journal of Legal Studies* 28 (2008): 659–708.
Ferrarini, Guido. "Contract Standards and the Markets in Financial Instruments Directive (MiFID): An Assessment of the Lamfalussy Regulatory Architecture." *European Review of Contract Law* 1 (2005): 19–43.

Frerichs, Sabine, and Teemu Juutilainen. "Rome under Seven Hills? An Archeology of European Private Law." Legal Studies Research Paper Series, no. 32, University of Helsinki, Faculty of Law, 2014.

Gijrath, Serge, and Jan Smits. "European Contract Law in View of Technical and Economic Regulation." In *The Future of European Contract Law*, edited by Katharina Boele-Woelki and Willem Grosheide, 53–90. Alphen aan den Rijn: Wolters Kluwer, 2007.

Grundmann, Stefan. *Europäisches Schuldvertragsrecht: das europäische Recht der Unternehmensgeschäfte*. Berlin: de Gruyter, 1999.

Grundmann, Stefan. "European Contract Law(s) of What Colour?" *European Review of Contract Law* 1 (2005): 184–210.

Grundmann, Stefan. "The Concept of the Private Law Society: After 50 Years of European Law and European Business Law." *European Review of Private Law* 16 (2008): 553–581.

Grundmann, Stefan, Florian Moslein, and Karl Riesenhuber, eds. *Contract Governance: Dimensions in Law and Interdisciplinary Research*. Oxford: Oxford University Press, 2015.

Guibault, Lucie M. C. R., Natalie Helberger, Marco Loos, Chantal Mak, Lodewijk Pessers, and Bart van der Sloot. *Digital Consumers and the Law: Towards a Cohesive European Framework*. Alphen aan den Rijn: Wolters Kluwer, 2013.

Hartkamp, Arthur S. *European Law and National Private Law*. Deventer: Kluwer, 2012.

Hartkamp, Arthur S., and Leen Keus. *The Influence of EU Private Law on National Private Law*. Deventer: Kluwer, 2014.

Hilty, Reto M. "Entwicklungsperspektiven des Schutzes geistigen Eigentums." In *Stand und Perspektiven des Schutzes geistigen Eigentums*, edited by Peter Behrens, 139–188. Baden-Baden: Nomos, 2004.

Hodges, Christofer. *The Reform of Class and Representative Actions in European Legal Systems: A New Framework for Collective Redress in Europe*. Oxford: Hart, 2009.

Hopt, Klaus J., and Hans-Christoph Voigt, eds. *Prospekt-und Kapitalmarktinformationshaftung: Recht und Reform in der Europäischen Union, der Schweiz und den USA*. Vol. 79. Tübingen: Mohr Siebeck, 2005.

Joerges, Christian, ed. *Franchising and the Law: Theoretical and Comparative Approaches in Europe and the United States* [Das Recht des Franchising: Konzeptionelle, rechtsvergleichende und europarechtliche Analysen, Schriftenreihe der Gesellschaft für Rechtsvergleichung]. Baden-Baden: Nomos, 1991.

Keirsbilck, Bert. *The New European Law of Unfair Commercial Practices and Competition Law*. Oxford: Hart, 2011.

Keßler, Jürgen, and Hans-Wolfgang Micklitz. *Kundenschutz auf den liberalisierten Märkten für Energie, Telekommunikation, Personenverkehr/Eisenbahn*. Baden-Baden: Nomos, 2008.

Kreutzer, Till. *Verbraucherschutz bei digitalen Medien*. Berlin: Berliner Wissenschafts-Verlag, 2007.

Lindholm, Johan. *State Procedure and Union Rights: A Comparison of the European Union and the United States*. Uppsala: Iustus Förlag, 2007.

Macaulay, Stewart. "Non-Contractual Relations in Business: A Preliminary Study." *American Sociological Review* 28 (1963): 55–70.

Mak, Chantal. *Fundamental Rights in European Contract Law: A Comparison of the Impact of Fundamental Rights on Contractual Relationships in Germany, the Netherlands, Italy and England*. Alphen aan den Rijin: Kluwer, 2008.

Mestmäcker, Hernst-Joachim, and Heike Schweitzer. *Europäisches Wettbewerbsrecht*. Munich: Beck, 2004.

Micklitz, Hans-Wolfgang. "Service Standards: Defining the Core Consumer Elements and their Minimum Requirements." Study commissioned by ANEC, the European Voice in Standardisation, 2007.

Micklitz, Hans-Wolfgang. "The Relationship between National and European Consumer Policy – Challenges and Perspectives." *Yearbook of Consumer Law*, edited by Christian Twigg-Flesner, Deborah Parry, Geraint Howells, and Annette Nordhausen, 35–65. Aldershot: Ashgate, 2008.

Micklitz, Hans-Wolfgang. "The Visible Hand of European Private Law." *Yearbook of European Law* 28 (2010): 3–59.

Micklitz, Hans-Wolfgang. "Universal Services: Nucleus for a Social European Private Law?" In *Market Integration and Public Services in the European Union*, edited by Marise Cremona, 63–102. Oxford: Oxford University Press, 2011.

Micklitz, Hans-Wolfgang. "Do Consumers and Business Need a New Architecture for Consumer Law? A Thought Provoking Impulse." *Yearbook of European Law* 32 (2013): 266–367.

Micklitz, Hans-Wolfgang. "Unfair Contract Terms: Public Interest Litigation before European Courts Case C-415/11 *Mohamed Aziz*". In *Landmark Cases of EU Consumer Law: In Honour of Jules Stuyck*, edited by Veerle Colaert and Evelyn Terryn, 615–634. Cambridge: Intersentia, 2013.

Micklitz, Hans-Wolfgang, ed. *Constitutionalisation of European Private Law*. Oxford: Oxford University Press, 2014.

Micklitz, Hans-Wolfgang, Norbert Reich, Peter Rott, and Klaus Tonner. *European Consumer Law*. Cambridge: Intersentia, 2014.

Münch, Richard. *European Governmentality: The Liberal Drift of Multilevel Governance*. London: Routledge, 2010.

Noch, Rainer. "Öffentliches Auftragsrecht." In Schulze and Zuleeg, *Europarecht: Handbuch für die Rechtspraxis*, 1302–1361.

Reich, Norbert. "Horizontal Liability in EC Law: Hybridization of Remedies for Compensation in Case of Breaches of EC Rights." *Common Market Law Review* 44 (2007): 705–742.

Reich, Norbert. *General Principles of EU Civil Law*. Cambridge: Intersentia, 2013.

Rott, Peter. "A New Social Contract Law for Public Services? Consequences from Regulation of Services of General Economic Interests in the EC." *European Review of Contract Law* 1 (2005): 323–345.

Ruffing, Eva. *Die europäische Wertpapierregulierung zwischen Input- und Output-Legitimität: Das Lamfalussy-Verfahren*. Baden-Baden: Nomos, 2011.

Scharpf, Fritz W. "Negative and Positive Integration in the Political Economy of European Welfare States." In *Governance in the European Union*, edited by Gary Marks, Fritz W. Scharpf, Philippe C. Schmitter, and Wolfgang Streeck, 15–39. London: Sage, 1996.

Schebesta, Hanna. "Towards an EU Law of Damages: Damages Claims for Violations of EU Public Procurement Law before National and European Judges." PhD diss., European University Institute, Florence 2013.

Schmid, Christoph. *Die Instrumentalisierung des Privatrechts durch die Europäische Union*. Baden-Baden: Nomos, 2010.

Schulze, Reiner, and Manfred Zuleeg. *Europarecht: Handbuch für die Rechtspraxis*, Baden-Baden: Nomos, 2006.

Smismans, Stijn. *Civil Society and Legitimate European Governance*. Cheltenham: Edward Elgar, 2006.

Smits, Jan. "Private Law 2.0: On the Role of Private Actors in a Post-National Society." Inaugural lecture as Maastricht-HiiL Chair on the Internationalisation of Law, delivered on 30 November 2010. The Hague: Eleven International, 2011.

Steindorff, Ernst. *EG-Vertrag und Privatrecht*. Baden-Baden: Nomos, 1996.

Steinmo, Sven. *The Evolution of Modern States: Sweden, Japan, and the United States*. Cambridge: Cambridge University Press, 2010.

Svetiev, Yane. "W(h)ither Private Law in the Face of the Regulatory Deluge." In *A Self-Sufficient Private Law – A Viable Concept?* edited by Hans-Wolfgang Micklitz and Yane Svetiev, 26–44. EUI-ERPL working paper 2012/31.

Teubner, Gunther. *Networks as Connected Contracts*. Oxford: Hart, 2008.

Torp, Cornelius. "Von Junkern und Schlotbaronen: Zur Interpretation des deutschen Protektionismus vor 1914." *Saeculum* 60 (2010): 143–170.

von Gierke, Otto. *Die Soziale Aufgabe des Privatrechts*. Berlin: Springer, 1889.

von Savigny, Friedrich Carl. *International Private Law: A Treatise on the Conflict of Laws and the Limits of Their Operation in Respect of Place and Time*. Translated by William Guthrie. Edinburgh: T & T Clark Law, 1869.

Weatherill, Stephen. *EU Consumer Law and Policy*. Cheltenham: Edward Elgar, 2005.

Weatherill, Stephen. "Who is the Average Consumer?" In *The Regulation of Unfair Commercial Practices under EC Directive 2005/29*, edited by Stephen Weatherill and Ulf Bernitz, 115–138. Oxford: Hart, 2007.

Weiler, J.H.H. "The Transformation of Europe." *Yale Law Journal* 100 (1991): 2403–2483.

Whittaker, Simon. "Form and Substance in the Reception of EC Directives into English Contract Law." *European Review of Contract Law* 3 (2007): 381–409.

Zeitlin, Jonathan, and Philippe Pochet, eds. *The Open Method of Coordination in Action: The European Employment and Social Inclusion Strategies*. Brussels: PIE-Peter Lang, 2005.

20

Consumer Protection

Stephen Weatherill

Introduction

Consumer protection is a competence that is *shared* between the European Union and its member states according to Article 4(2)(f) of the Treaty on the Functioning of the European Union (TFEU). But what does this mean, and what should it mean? How are the tasks of consumer protection shared, on what basis, and with what consequences? Important though its detailed rules are for the specialist in the field, EU consumer law and policy deserves wider attention for how it illuminates key questions of regulatory design in the internal market. Of course, consumer law is important in the European Union more generally and, in particular, for what it reveals about the sharing of responsibility between member states and the Union – the vertical issue – and between the Union's judicial institutions (the Court of Justice of the European Union and its national counterparts) and its political institutions – the horizontal issue.

Moreover, the original Treaty of Rome only tangentially noticed the "consumer," and an explicit legislative competence in the field was added to the European Union's legislative armory as late as 1993, on the entry into force of the Maastricht Treaty. Even that, in the form now found in the TFEU since the entry into force in 2009 of the Lisbon Treaty, offers a slender basis for EU legislative action. Most of the European Union's activity that affects the consumer has been conducted in the name of the construction of the internal market, a project that is certainly ultimately designed to benefit the consumer but is not systematically connected to the consumer interest, still less driven by any notion of a voice that represents the consumer. So how has EU law that controls national measures of consumer protection that hinder the construction of the internal market and EU law that establishes common EU-wide standards of consumer protection developed a notion of the "consumer" against this unhelpful treaty background? What vision of the consumer is found in the construction of the internal market, and has EU law developed an understanding of the consumer interest which goes beyond the economic project of market making? The purpose of this chapter is to expose the tensions that afflict the shaping of EU consumer law and policy and, in particular, to demonstrate that the relationship between EU and national consumer law is dynamic and not always coherent.

A Companion to European Union Law and International Law, First Edition.
Edited by Dennis Patterson and Anna Södersten.

Free Movement in the Internal Market

The Court of Justice's famous ruling in *Cassis de Dijon* applied EU free movement law to national (*in casu*, German) technical standards governing the composition of a product (*in casu*, the amount of alcohol required in blackcurrant liqueur).[1] It insisted that in so far as such technical standards impeded the importation of products from other member states where technical standards were simply different, the local rules could be applied only if shown to pursue a matter in the general interest such as to prevail over the interest in cross-border trade and integrated markets. No such justification was forthcoming in the case – Germany had to accept the appearance on its market of new and differently constituted products, apt to compete with local products and to widen consumer choice. EU law, in effect, puts the local rulebook, incrementally written over centuries, to the test.

The Court's readiness to exercise supervision of national technical standards pursuant to Article 34 TFEU (the treaty provision on the free movement of goods) greatly reduced the need to intervene by legislative act to harmonize such diverse technical standards at EU level. Article 34's vigor as an instrument of market integration was dramatically increased by *Cassis de Dijon* and so too was the judicial role, at the expense of the legislative role, in the making of the internal market. These institutional implications were rapidly perceived. The Commission promptly published an interpretive notice stating that goods lawfully manufactured in one member state are in principle to be admitted to the markets of other member states, which may rely on their distinct regulatory traditions to exclude imports only if able to show a justification for such impediment.[2] Additionally, the rule of conditional mutual recognition shaped by the Court was placed by the Commission at the heart of the 1985 White Paper on Completing the Internal Market, which set out its politically vigorous plan for completing the internal market by the end of 1992.[3] The enduring significance of *Cassis de Dijon* is visible in Regulation 764/2008 laying down procedures relating to the application of certain national technical rules to products lawfully marketed in another member state,[4] which in its Preamble declares,

> The principle of mutual recognition, which derives from the case-law of the Court of Justice of the European Communities, is one of the means of ensuring the free movement of goods within the internal market.

Cassis de Dijon was not only a case about the internal market: it was also a case about consumer law – in fact, it was a case about consumer *laws*. The Court was forced to assess the value of German conceptions about the need for minimum alcohol requirements to protect consumers in the relevant product market against the interest in free movement of goods, intensified cross-border competition, and wider choice for consumers expressed through the application of what is today Article 34 TFEU. This is national consumer law *versus* EU consumer law! The economic project of market making has long been seen as a means to grander political ends. This is, and has always been, reflected in the treaties, but the means are supposed to be advantageous to the consumer, as the winner from the more competitive market that should be created.

In this vein, the Court has declared that the legislation of a member state must not "crystallize given consumer habits so as to consolidate an advantage acquired by national industries concerned to comply with them."[5] So the dynamic of market integration is *itself* a form of consumer policy. In *Mars* the Court concluded that a marketing practice concerning product packaging that would not mislead a "reasonably circumspect" consumer cannot be forbidden in so far as it impedes cross-border trade.[6] The consumer is used as a lever to open up national markets to out-of-state competition – and it is the alert and attentive consumer on whom EU law relies to dismiss attempts to justify national intervention in the market.

In *Commission v. France*, the Court was asked to rule on the compatibility with EU law of national rules requiring that tourist guides possess locally authenticated qualifications. As in *Cassis de Dijon*, so here, the consequence of such a measure was to exclude operators originating in another jurisdiction where the applicable rules are simply different – though, whereas *Cassis* concerns goods markets, this case applies the same principles to service markets. The Court's judgment is unusually open in its preference for market solutions and consumer choice over local regulation:

> [A] licence requirement imposed by the Member State of destination has the effect of reducing the number of tourist guides qualified to accompany tourists in a closed group, which may lead a tour operator to have recourse instead to local guides employed or established in the Member State in which the service is to be performed. However, that consequence may have the drawback that tourists who are the recipients of the services in question do not have a guide who is familiar with their language, their interests and their specific expectations. Moreover, the profitable operation of such group tours depends on the commercial reputation of the operator, who faces competitive pressure from other tour companies; the need to maintain that reputation and the competitive pressure themselves compel companies to be selective in employing tourist guides and exercise some control over the quality of their services.[7]

There is space for national measures designed to protect the consumer only where they are shown to be of sufficient value to prevail against the interest in market integration. *A-Punkt Schmuckhandels* concerned Austrian rules prohibiting parties in the home at which jewelry was sold.[8] Assuming this was an obstruction to interstate trade in jewelry (a matter for the national court to decide), the Court of Justice exhibited receptivity to the justification of such market regulation. It noted the potentially higher risk of the consumer being cheated because of a lack of information, the impossibility of comparing prices, the provision of insufficient safeguards as regards the authenticity of that jewelry, and the greater psychological pressure to buy where the sale is organized in a private setting. The referring national court would have the final say – but there is plainly space allowed by EU law to apply such a prohibition despite its trade-restrictive effect.

A-Punkt Schmuckhandels provides a good example of what it means to treat consumer protection as a shared competence. EU free movement law confines trade-restrictive national measures to the area within which they can be justified, but it does not insist on their inevitable elimination. It does, however, require the excavation of specific and detailed reasons to justify the national rule – bland, untargeted intervention of the type condemned as unjustified "over-regulation" in *Cassis de Dijon* and *Mars* is typically skeptically treated. The structural consequence of this approach is that the more generous the Court is in finding sufficient justification for trade barriers, the more generous it is to local regulatory autonomy. In so far as it finds an admitted trade barrier to be justified, it acknowledges persisting regulatory diversity among the member states – and it defers to the possibility of legislative harmonization as the way to advance market integration. It is to legislative harmonization that we now turn.

Consumer Law – The Legislative Dimension

According to Article 5 of the Treaty on European Union (TEU), the European Union possesses only the competence conferred on it by its treaties, and the inquisitive consumer lawyer accordingly turns the pages to Title XV of the TFEU where Article 169 TFEU is entitled "Consumer Protection." This provision (in its original guise) was inserted into the treaty with effect from 1993 as a result of the entry into force of the Maastricht Treaty. It commits the Union to

> contribute to protecting the health, safety and economic interests of consumers, as well as to promoting their right to information, education and to organize themselves in order to safeguard their interests.

Further, Article 169 confers a legislative competence on the European Union – to be exercised in accordance with the ordinary legislative procedure – to contribute to the attainment of these objectives through "measures which support, supplement and monitor the policy pursued by the Member States." This, then, is a rather weak competence, placing the European Union in a position subordinate to its member states. The fruits of this, frankly uninspiring provision are correspondingly tasteless. Article 169 or its predecessors provide the basis for very few measures. Its use as the legal basis for the creation of a "stakeholder dialogue group" in the area of public health and consumer protection is helpfully illustrative.[9] Not unimportant in a narrow sense, such an initiative is nevertheless unlikely to grab the attention of a scholar not already immersed in the intricacies of consumer policy.

EU consumer policy in its legislative dimension is predominantly the product of Article 114 TFEU, which succinctly deals with harmonization. Here, by contrast to Article 169, there is rich material that discloses vigorous reliance on and shaping of the consumer interest in the making of the internal market, and which demands attention from beyond the narrow world of consumer law. Moreover, the "sharing" of competence between the European Union and its member states, which applies once harmonized standards have been established, has become a deeply contested matter.

Article 114 is not sector-specific. *Any* national measure may be subjected to the discipline of harmonization – provided only that variation in national practice causes harm to the functioning of the Union's internal market. Consumer protection is one of the areas in which some manifestations of national regulatory variation have been replaced by a harmonized EU regime. In so far as national measures of consumer protection serve to impede interstate trade but are considered justified according to the standards recognized by the Court, it falls to the legislature to intervene and select the techniques of consumer protection that shall be applied across the territory of the European Union. This is where deregulation ends and reregulation begins; this is where member state action controlled by EU free movement law ends and where harmonization intrudes; here the Court's role is exhausted and the EU legislature takes over. Establishing harmonized rules by EU legislative act involves *both* setting a common standard for commercial activity in the European Union and *also* making politically sensitive choices about the content and technique of that common standard. The key to this shared regulatory endeavor is that there is no sustainable divide between the member states' role in regulating markets and the Union's in integrating them: the European Union must engage in (re) regulatory choices because its role is to react to national public authorities' long-term assertion of a commitment to legislative consumer protection.

Article 114(3) recognizes this association between market making and the quality of the regulatory environment that underpins that market. It provides that

> [t]he Commission, in its proposals envisaged in paragraph 1 concerning health, safety, environmental protection and consumer protection, will take as a base a high level of protection, taking account in particular of any new development based on scientific facts.

This constitutional linkage is supplemented by the additional direction in Article 114(3) that "[w]ithin their respective powers, the European Parliament and the Council will also seek to achieve this objective." Article 169(1) provides that

> [i]n order to promote the interests of consumers and *to ensure a high level of consumer protection*, the Union shall contribute to protecting the health, safety and economic interests of consumers, as well as to promoting their right to information, education and to organise themselves in order to safeguard their interests. (emphasis added)

And Article 38 of the Charter, binding since the entry into force of the Lisbon Treaty in 2009, mandates that "Union policies shall ensure a high level of consumer protection."

There is, therefore, ample evidence that EU consumer law and policy is driven by strong expressions of the need to secure a high level of consumer protection. However, what really counts in practice is the detailed legislative articulation of this vision of the consumer. What sort of protection is envisaged? What sort of "market" is being built by the legislative harmonization that provides the bulk of the relevant texts of EU consumer law and policy?

A batch of EU directives affects aspects of the formation of particular consumer contracts. By way of example, one may mention Directive 90/314 on package travel, package holidays, and package tours,[10] Directive 2008/48 on credit agreements for consumers,[11] Directive 2008/122 on timeshares,[12] and Directive 2011/83 on consumer rights,[13] which, despite its vainglorious title, is largely concerned only with the formation of contracts concluded on the doorstep and at a distance. The chosen technique at the heart of these measures of harmonization involves mandatory precontractual disclosure of information to consumers plus a chance to think again after the fact and to withdraw if on reflection dissatisfied with the deal. A benevolent interpretation of this approach is that it improves market transparency and emphasizes the power of the informed consumer in the market. However, these measures are vulnerable to the criticism that they make unrealistic assumptions about consumer capability – some, perhaps most, consumers simply do not process such information and are likely in practice to be much less well informed than the "law on paper" suggests they should be. So the laws will not work properly.[14] This is a thematically analogous anxiety to that aimed at the Court's treatment of *national* laws that impede cross-border trade – that the existence of the alert consumer is exaggerated in order to find a basis for shifting responsibility for the development of the market out of the grip of the regulator and into the hands of private traders and consumers. Deeper still, one may be fearful that emphasis on economic growth may subvert hard-fought adjustments in national contract law that have promoted the protection of groups such as consumers (but also workers and tenants) under an assumption that such economically disadvantaged parties are deprived of a genuine right of self-determination in an unregulated market.[15]

These criticism are not without force. They are, however, mitigated, first by appreciation that the majority of these measures set minimum standards, and so do not preclude member states from applying more protective rules provided they comply with the demands of free movement law, and second by the existence in the legislative *acquis* of directives that reflect a significantly more interventionist instinct towards the vulnerability of the consumer in modern markets.

Directive 93/13 prohibits unfair terms in consumer contracts.[16] Article 3(1) of the directive provides that

> [a] contractual term which has not been individually negotiated shall be regarded as unfair if, contrary to the requirement of good faith, it causes a significant imbalance in the parties' rights and obligations arising under the contract, to the detriment of the consumer.

Such "unfair" terms are not binding on the consumer. According to the Court,

> the system of protection introduced by the Directive is based on the idea that the consumer is in a weak position via-a-vis the seller or supplier, as regards both his bargaining power and his level of knowledge.[17]

And so the directive aims to replace the formal balance that the contract establishes between the rights and obligations of the parties with an effective balance that reestablishes equality between those parties.[18] Directive 99/44 on the sale of consumer goods similarly extends beyond a paradigm of consumer information by importing standards of required product quality into consumer contracts.[19] So, aspects of the legislative *acquis* do not conform to an understanding that the consumer is robust enough to take care of him- or herself by exploiting mandatory transparency in the market to choose and buy rationally. Instead these two directives rule out use of unfair terms and impose certain quality standards under an assumption that the consumer lacks the economic power to negotiate such basic protection. The breadth of EU consumer law and policy in its legislative dimension embraces not only the technique of information disclosure but also *some* substantive regulation of the bargain struck.

The legislative assumption that consumers require protection from particularly pernicious marketing practices is also visible in the EU *acquis* affecting contract law. Harmonized administrative regulation requires the suppression of misleading advertising.[20] Directive 2007/65 on Audiovisual Media Services locates, within a regime designed to integrate the market for such services (inter alia), a harmonized prohibition on advertising tobacco products by audiovisual communication, sponsorship, or product placement.[21] The assumption underpinning such EU measures is that diverse national regulatory responses to such ills tend to fragment the market along national lines and so harmonization is called for – but then the EU standard reflects the several treaty commitments to a high standard of protection and it is no charter for aggressive deregulation. In the same vein, Directive 2005/29 requires the suppression of unfair business-to-consumer practices, which are defined in the directive with special reference to misleading and aggressive practices.[22] Additionally, the Court has insisted that pursuit of a high level of consumer protection is a reason to avoid a restrictive interpretation of Directive 2005/29.[23]

The impression made by the map of the legislative *acquis* is disconcertingly random. It is driven by the momentum of the internal market project – as is constitutionally required under Article 114 TFEU – but the areas that have been the subject of legislative intervention by the European Union are puzzlingly diverse.[24] Part of the story is institutional fragmentation: consumer policy has been scattered over time within the Commission, and today three directorates general (SANCO, Internal Market, Justice) hold relevant responsibilities. The directives are largely the product of periodic political opportunism and fleeting fashion. The effect of EU initiatives is to reshape – perhaps to misshape – existing national structures, but only bit by bit, not systematically. Yet, for all the admitted eccentricity of a list that flits from timeshare to package travel to unfair terms, thematic connections binding together the *acquis* may be excavated. The emphasis on (precontractual) mandatory disclosure of information combined with the grant to the consumer of a chance to think again after the fact reveals a preference for transparency in the market and a belief in the virtue of the "informed consumer." The European Union is not exclusively driven by a paradigm of information disclosure and transparency: it does envisage more vulnerable consumers who require sheltering from, for example, unfair terms and unfair commercial practices. Social justice is a contested concept in EU law – but it is not wholly absent.[25]

The Relationship between EU and National Consumer Law

EU consumer law and the project of market integration are intimately connected. Indeed, market integration is intended to yield beneficial effects for the consumer by improving competition and widening choice. The case has been argued already in this chapter that aspects of EU consumer law transcend an understanding of consumer interest that is targeted only at open borders – the Court is receptive to some national measures of consumer protection that restrict trade provided they are adequately explained and justified, whereas some parts of the legislative *acquis* reveal a readiness at EU level to treat the consumer as in need of a more intense form of protection than is available under a model of information disclosure. However, crucial to the assessment is the relationship between EU legislative measures and residual national competence to protect the consumer. If one is highly skeptical of the virtues of EU rulemaking – for example, fearing it imposes a model of consumer rationality that fails adequately to cater for vulnerable or deprived consumers – then what really matters in practice is whether the EU rules preclude member states from choosing more protective regimes within the areas touched by the legislative *acquis*. If the EU rules do have that preemptive effect, then for the critic the matter is truly alarming.

For measures adopted pursuant to Article 169 TFEU, the matter is straightforward and it is *not* alarming. Article 169(4) makes explicit that member states may maintain or introduce more stringent protective measures, provided that such measures are compatible with the treaties and that the Commission be notified of them. But Article 169 is not the engine of EU consumer law and policy. Article 114 is. Further, Article 114 does not explicitly dictate the consequence for national regulatory autonomy of the adoption of measures of legislative harmonization.

Legislative practice reveals that much of the harmonized *acquis* pertaining to the protection of the economic interests of consumers is built on an assumption that minimum harmonization shall be the norm. Minimum directives do not set a single rule as both a floor and a ceiling but rather only as a floor. Member states may maintain stricter rules, up to the ceiling set by primary law. Minimum harmonization promotes the integration of markets while also preserving regulatory diversity, and it ensures space for expression for cultural particularity. Both the European Union and the member states retain competence to protect consumers even after the Union has intervened by way of secondary legislation.

However, the long-standing political preference favoring minimum harmonization in this field is under attack. Beginning in 2001, the Commission initiated a wide-ranging debate about the proper role of the European Community, now the European Union, in the field of contract law. The Commission's July 2001 Communication on European Contract Law declared that

> [t]he Commission would like to find out if the co-existence of national contract laws in the Member States directly or indirectly obstructs to the functioning of the internal market, and if so to what extent. If such obstacles do exist, the European Institutions may be called upon to take appropriate action.[76]

This agenda is not confined to *consumer* contract law, but that is the source of most of the European Union's legislative activity touching contract law.

The anxiety is that the Commission's inquiry depicts diversity between national laws as a problem for the internal market, neglecting the several other functions of contract law in society. This sense that the Commission was intent on treating the perfection of the internal market as the exclusive standpoint for viewing national (consumer) contract law tradition was strengthened by the revelation of Commission's increasing distaste for the preexisting preference for minimum harmonization in the field. Its Consumer Policy Programme for 2002 to 2006 advocated a "move away from the present situation of different sets of rules in each Member State towards a more consistent environment for consumer protection across the EU."[27] Importantly, this means maximum, not minimum, harmonization. In the February 2007 Green Paper on the Review of the Consumer Acquis the orthodox model of minimum harmonization was not even allowed as a possible option for the future.[28]

The Commission's preferences require alignment with a sufficient majority in the Council and Parliament for the shift to maximum harmonization to take legislative effect. Directive 2005/29 on unfair commercial practices demonstrated the political wind was favorable.[29] It is a "maximum" measure. What counts as "unfair" is determined according to the standards set out in the directive: a member state *must* suppress unfair practices that fall within the scope of application of the directive but *may not* suppress such practices that are as a matter of EU law not unfair. This represents a radical vertical shift in regulatory responsibility: the European Union (and in contested cases its Court) decides what is permissible market conduct and alternative national approaches are ruled out. This is dramatically different from the shared model of rule-making that prevails in cases of minimum harmonization. Directive 2011/83 on consumer rights is also a maximum measure.[30] In fact, it recasts two preexisting measures of minimum harmonization (on doorstep selling and on distance selling) into maximum form, thereby centralizing the regulation of such practices at EU level under a thematically familiar model based largely on mandatory information disclosure to the exclusion of diverse national preferences.

However, Directive 2011/83 in fact offers an insight into the vigor of this debate. In October 2008 the Commission had adopted a proposal for a directive on consumer rights that would have established a maximum measure of harmonization in replacement for not only the directives on doorstep selling and distance selling but also the infinitely more important directives on unfair terms and consumer sales and guarantees.[31] Switching the regulation of these practices to a maximum model was simply not politically acceptable – barring space for national choices was judged too brutal. In consequence, the finally adopted text is shorn of its more ambitious material scope.[32] And Directives 93/13 and 99/44 survive as measures that lay down minimum rules governing unfair terms and consumer sales. Competence remains shared between the European Union and member states.

The core sensitivity flowing from a shift from minimum to maximum harmonization is the empowerment of the Union to the exclusion of state-level variation. The particular case of (what was finally adopted as) Directive 2011/83 attracted deep concern that the Commission's proposed model would exert a depressive effect on existing levels of consumer protection in some member states and that it would create an area of law placed beyond national-level adaptation and open to reform by the European Union alone.[33] But the challenge at stake in choosing between minimum or maximum approaches is much broader in its application. Ruling out space for stricter national rules brings benefits consequent on the uniformity promoted at EU level. Indeed that is the "harmony" located within the label harmonization and one can readily understand that pursuit of an integrated market for the European Union tends to be coupled to a thirst for maximum harmonization. It is increasingly clear that this is the Commission's preference. By the same token, the shift to maximum harmonization involves a significant choice in favor of a priority for market making to the exclusion of local regulatory autonomy. It asserts a single notion of regulatory protection when in fact preferences, tastes, and capabilities of consumers in particular, and citizens more generally, differ in Europe. Selection of which model to prefer calls for economic analysis,[34] but here, too, lie deep political anxieties. A maximum model suppresses diversity and experimentation. Additionally, it locks in choices: a maximum measure effects a *complete* transfer of regulatory responsibility from member states to the European Union that is unalterable and irreversible, except where an adequate consensus can be achieved through the complex EU legislative process to change it. An alternative vision promotes minimum harmonization as an embrace of diversity and differentiation as in themselves valuable within a European Union dedicated to more than economic growth and consumer empowerment.[35]

Conclusion

EU consumer law and policy has no single vocation. It aims to integrate markets – while also paying attention to the merits of regulation of those markets, both at national level (as viewed from the perspective of free movement law) and at EU level (in setting harmonized standards). Its treatment of national measures of consumer protection that impede cross-border trade is driven by a visible intolerance rooted in expectation that typical consumers can and should look after their own economic interests. Only where the national measure seeks to protect a defined group of vulnerable consumers does the Court tend to accept that it is of sufficient weight to prevail over the interest in intensified trade integration. Where the European Union acts as a lawmaker in fields affecting the consumer, its primary role is to harmonize national laws, and this leads it to pursue both integration and market *re*regulation. Parts of this legislative *acquis* reveal a clear concern to protect vulnerable consumers from the potentially detrimental impact of integrated markets in Europe; other parts, especially the emphasis on mandatory information provision and market transparency as a technique, suggest an uncomfortably heavy emphasis on the alert and confident consumer as the paradigm case.

EU consumer law cannot be understood in isolation from national consumer law. EU law does different things *via* free movement law (testing the regulatory virtue behind national trade restrictions) and harmonization (setting common standards at EU law in partial or total or replacement for diverse national rules) and it does them *to national law*. The strongest argument against maximum harmonization is that it chokes off the potentially dynamic and mutually reinforcing relationship between EU consumer law – largely, but not entirely, driven by a market-making ethos – and national consumer law, which should be allowed space to develop more sensitive, locally shaped initiatives to protect atypical, often vulnerable types of consumer. Maximum harmonization asks the European Union, and the European Union alone, to find the answers to problems confronted by consumers in the internal market. It cannot do so. The Commission Proposal for a Regulation on a Consumer Programme 2014 to 2020, published in November 2011, declares "the general objective of future consumer policy placing the empowered consumer at the centre of the Single Market."[36] This explicit connection of the consumer interest to economic growth is consistent with long-standing understandings of the place of the consumer interest in the European Union. But it is important that it not be forgotten that there is more to consumer protection than empowerment and growth, and that there is more to consumer lawmaking in the European Union than consumer lawmaking by the European Union. National law matters as well.

Notes

1 Case 120/78 *Rewe-Zentrale AG v. Bundesmonopolverwaltung für Branntwein* EU:C:1979:42.
2 [1980] OJ C 256/2.
3 COM(85) 310.

4 [2008] OJ L 218/21.
5 Case 178/84 *Commission v. Germany* EU:C:1987:126, para 32.
6 Case C-470/93 *Verein gegen Unwesen in Handel v. Mars GmbH* EU:C:1995:224, para 24.
7 Case C-154/89 *Commission v. France* EU:C:1991:76, paras 19–20.
8 Case C-441/04 *A-Punkt Schmuckhandels GmbH v. Claudia Schmidt* EU:C:2006:141.
9 Commission Decision 2007/602/EC of 5 September 2007 setting up the stakeholder dialogue group in the areas of public health and consumer protection [2007] OJ L 234/13, amended in 2011 ([2011] OJ C 299/6).
10 [1990] OJ L 158/59.
11 [2008] OJ L 133/66.
12 [2009] OJ L 33/10.
13 [2011] OJ L 304/64.
14 Geraint Howells, "The Potential and Limits of Consumer Empowerment by Information," *Journal of Law and Society* 32 (2005); Franziska Rischkowsky and Thomas Döring, "Consumer Policy in a Market Economy: Considerations from the Perspective of the Economics of Information, the New Institutional Economics as well as Behavioural Economics," *Journal of Consumer Policy* 31 (2008); and Christopher Willett and Martin Morgan-Taylor, "Recognising the Limits of Transparency in EU Consumer Law," in *European Consumer Protection: Theory and Practice*, ed. James Devenney and Mel Kenny (Cambridge: Cambridge University Press, 2012).
15 Study Group on Social Justice in European Private Law, "Social Justice in European Contract Law: A Manifesto," *European Law Journal* 10 (2004); Martijn Hesselink, "European Contract Law: A Matter of Consumer Protection, Citizenship, or Justice?" *European Review of Private Law* 15 (2007); and Hans-Wolfgang Micklitz, "The Expulsion of the Concept of Protection from the Consumer Law and the Return of Social Elements in the Civil Law: A Bittersweet Polemic," *Journal of Consumer Policy* 35 (2012).
16 [1993] OJ L 95/29.
17 Cases C-240/98 to C-244/98 *Océano Grupo Editorial and Salvat Editores* EU:C:2000:346.
18 E.g., Case C-618/10 *Banco Español de Crédito v. Joaquín Calderón Camino* EU:C:2012:349, paras 40 and 63.
19 [1999] OJ L 171/12.
20 Directive 2006/114 of 12 December 2006 concerning misleading and comparative advertising, [2006] OJ L 376/21.
21 [2007] OJ L 332/27.
22 [2005] OJ L 149/22.
23 E.g., Case C-122/10 *Ving Sverige AB* EU:C:2011:299, paras 29 and 39.
24 Esther van Schagen, "More Consistency and Legal Certainty in the Private Law *Acquis*: A Plea for Better Justification for the Harmonization of Private Law," *Maastricht Journal of European and Comparative Law* 19 (2012).
25 Hans-Wolfgang Micklitz, ed., *The Many Concepts of Social Justice in European Private Law* (Cheltenham: Edward Elgar, 2011).
26 COM(2001) 398, para 23.
27 COM(2002) 208, para 11.
28 COM(2006) 744.
29 See n 22 this chapter.
30 See n 13 this chapter.
31 COM(2008) 614.
32 Stephen Weatherill, "The Consumer Rights Directive: How and Why a Quest for 'Coherence' has (Largely) Failed," *Common Market Law Review* 49 (2012).
33 Hans-Wolfgang Micklitz and Norbert Reich, "Crónica de una Muerte Anunciada: The Commission Proposal for a Directive on Consumer Rights," *Common Market Law Review* 46 (2009).
34 Fernando Gomez and Juan Jose Ganuza, "An Economic Analysis of Harmonization Régimes: Full Harmonization, Minimum Harmonization or Optional Instrument?" *European Review of Contract Law* 7 (2011).

35 Nina Boeger, "Minimum Harmonisation, Free Movement and Proportionality," in *The Judiciary, the Legislature and the EU Internal Market*, ed. Phil Syrpis (Cambridge: Cambridge University Press, 2012); and Stephen Weatherill, "Maximum versus Minimum Harmonization: Choosing between Unity and Diversity in the Search for the Soul of the Internal Market," in *From Single Market to Economic Union: Essays in Memory of John A Usher*, ed. Niamh Nic Shuibhne and Lawrence Gormley (Oxford: Oxford University Press, 2012).

36 COM(2011) 707.

References

Boeger, Nina. "Minimum Harmonisation, Free Movement and Proportionality." In *The Judiciary, the Legislature and the EU Internal Market*, edited by Phil Syrpis, 62–91. Cambridge: Cambridge University Press, 2012.

Gomez, Fernando, and Juan Jose Ganuza. "An Economic Analysis of Harmonization Régimes: Full Harmonization, Minimum Harmonization or Optional Instrument?" *European Review of Contract Law* 7 (2011): 275–294.

Hesselink, Martijn. "European Contract Law: A Matter of Consumer Protection, Citizenship, or Justice?" *European Review of Private Law* 15 (2007): 323–348.

Howells, Geraint. "The Potential and Limits of Consumer Empowerment by Information." *Journal of Law and Society* 32 (2005): 349–370.

Micklitz, Hans-Wolfgang, ed. *The Many Concepts of Social Justice in European Private Law*. Cheltenham: Edward Elgar, 2011.

Micklitz, Hans-Wolfgang. "The Expulsion of the Concept of Protection from the Consumer Law and the Return of Social Elements in the Civil Law: A Bittersweet Polemic." *Journal of Consumer Policy* 35 (2012): 283–296.

Micklitz, Hans-Wolfgang, and Norbert Reich. "Crónica de una Muerte Anunciada: The Commission Proposal for a Directive on Consumer Rights." *Common Market Law Review* 46 (2009): 471–520.

Rischkowsky, Franziska, and Thomas Döring. "Consumer Policy in a Market Economy: Considerations from the Perspective of the Economics of Information, the New Institutional Economics as well as Behavioural Economics." *Journal of Consumer Policy* 31 (2008): 285–323.

Study Group on Social Justice in European Private Law. "Social Justice in European Contract Law: A Manifesto." *European Law Journal* 10 (2004): 653–674.

van Schagen, Esther. "More Consistency and Legal Certainty in the Private Law *Acquis*: A Plea for Better Justification for the Harmonization of Private Law." *Maastricht Journal of European and Comparative Law* 19 (2012): 37–62.

Weatherill, Stephen. "The Consumer Rights Directive: How and Why a Quest for 'Coherence' has (Largely) Failed." *Common Market Law Review* 49 (2012): 1279–1317.

Weatherill, Stephen. "Maximum versus Minimum Harmonization: Choosing between Unity and Diversity in the Search for the Soul of the Internal Market." In *From Single Market to Economic Union: Essays in Memory of John A Usher*, edited by Niamh Nic Shuibhne and Lawrence Gormley, 175–199. Oxford: Oxford University Press, 2012.

Willett, Christopher, and Martin Morgan-Taylor. "Recognising the Limits of Transparency in EU Consumer Law." In *European Consumer Protection: Theory and Practice*, edited by James Devenney and Mel Kenny, 143–163. Cambridge: Cambridge University Press, 2012.

21

The Economic and Monetary Union

Roland Bieber

Economic and Monetary Union as a Process within Differentiated Legal Regimes

Under Article 3(4) of the Treaty on European Union (TEU) "[t]he Union shall establish an economic and monetary union whose currency is the euro." The establishment of an economic and monetary union between the (now twenty-eight) member states of the European Union, together with a common foreign and security policy, is the most ambitious project of European integration. Its origins date back to the early years after the Second World War.[1] Although originally founded on theories of economic integration,[2] economic and monetary union is first and foremost a political project that was consolidated by the Treaty of Maastricht of 7 February 1992.

Like the entire project of European integration (conceived as a "process of creating an ever closer union among the peoples of Europe"[3]), economic and monetary union, as part of the European Union, was not established in a single act or by a single instrument. Economic and Monetary Union (hereafter EMU) is supposed to result from an open-ended process consisting in the promotion of certain aims (e.g., the "strengthening of its economic, social and territorial cohesion"[4]), the observance of certain principles (e.g., "an open market economy with free competition"[5]), and the implementation of a set of rules laid down in the Treaty on the Functioning of the European Union (TFEU) and in several protocols annexed to the treaties.

EMU is a constitutive element of the Union and is therefore applicable to all member states. However, not all member states meet the economic requirements for introducing the common currency. Moreover, some member states who would qualify in economic terms for membership do not wish to join the common currency. Therefore, different legal regimes are applicable for the nine (in 2015) member states outside the euro area and for the nineteen member states of the euro area.

The introduction of the common currency throughout the Union took longer than was initially expected. The main reason for the delay was the accession of several new member states from Central and Eastern Europe in 2005 and 2007. Three other member states (the United Kingdom, Sweden, and Denmark) chose, for political reasons, to remain outside the

A Companion to European Union Law and International Law, First Edition.
Edited by Dennis Patterson and Anna Södersten.

euro area. As a consequence of this continuing dual legal regime, the euro area has increasingly become consolidated as a permanent and separate entity within the European Union. To this end, specific provisions have been introduced by the Lisbon Treaty (Articles 136 and 137 TFEU and Protocol No 14 to the TEU).

Detailed rules for economic and monetary policy are laid down in Articles 119 to 144 TFEU and in several protocols annexed to the EU treaties:

1. Protocol No 4 on the Statute of the European System of Central Banks (ESCB) and of the European Central Bank (ECB);
2. Protocol No 12 on the excessive deficit procedure;
3. Protocol No 13 on the convergence criteria;
4. Protocols Nos 15 to 18 concerning specific problems of individual member states (United Kingdom, Denmark, France).

The legal regime of the EMU is differentiated in two ways. While the rules on economic union apply with few exceptions to all member states, most Treaty provisions on monetary union are applicable only to those member states that have introduced the common currency (nineteen member states in 2015). In certain cases the Union's competences in monetary matters may extend to member states that have not introduced the euro (see Article 141 TFEU). Moreover, competences of the European Union in matters of monetary policy with regard to the nineteen euro area member states are *exclusive*; in matters of economic policy they are, however, *shared* between the Union and the member states.

Notwithstanding the differences in their legal regimes, from an economic and social perspective the areas are closely interconnected. In a formal sense, the interconnection becomes apparent in Title VIII TFEU, which reads "Economic *and* Monetary Policy." The establishment of the Monetary Union brought about a transfer of hitherto national competences for monetary and exchange-rate policy to the Union once a country had introduced the euro. As a consequence, those member states lost influence over some of the traditional tools for an autonomous economic policy, namely the possibility of devaluing the national currency in order to stimulate export of goods and services. On the other hand, member states retain margins of maneuver in matters of social and economic policy which, in turn, influence the common monetary policy. Since 2009, an increasing tension has become apparent between a centralized monetary policy in a large part of the Union and a decentralized economic policy, leading to asymmetric economic evolution within the European Union. As of 2015, it is still not clear whether the present structure of the treaties will be capable of absorbing shocks resulting from this growing asymmetry within the Union.

A first attempt towards a reform of the EMU's foundations was made in 2011 by an amendment to Article 136 TFEU authorizing extra-EU Treaty arrangements of a legally binding character for the establishment of a stability mechanism aimed at granting financial assistance to member states and imposing stricter rules for national budgetary policies.[6] Within a few months two treaties were concluded: the European Stability Mechanism (ESM), a treaty between the euro area member states, signed on 2 February 2012, which replaced a provisional instrument established in 2010, the European Financial Stability Facility (EFSF), and the Treaty on Stability, Coordination and Governance in the Economic and Monetary Union ("Fiscal Pact"), signed by twenty-five member states on 2 March 2012.

None of those texts effect an additional transfer of competences to the European Union. The ESM is entirely controlled by the euro area member states.

A System of Overlapping Competences Shared between the European Union and its Member States

The TFEU establishes a system of "overlapping competences" consisting primarily of measures adopted by the member states. Article 119 TFEU states:

> [t]he activities of the Member States and the Union shall include, as provided in the Treaties, the adoption of an economic policy which is based on the close coordination of Member States' economic policies, on the internal market and on the definition of common objectives …

In its initial phase, the European Union's predecessor, the European Economic Community (EEC), was competent only for specific areas of economic policy (agriculture, transport) or for "horizontal" issues such as the establishment of the single market. Also, after the launch of the EMU in 1991 by the Treaty of Maastricht, general economic policy remains within the realm of the member states. They are, however, obliged to "regard their economic policies as a matter of common concern" and are to coordinate them in accordance with the procedure laid down in Article 121 TFEU. This requires compliance with the principles of an open market economy with free competition, stable prices, sound public finances and monetary conditions, and a sustainable balance of payments (Article 119 TFEU). Moreover, member states are subject to the EU Council's monitoring of their economic developments and of the consistency of their economic policies with "broad guidelines," adopted by the Council.

Member states are also committed to budgetary discipline, as defined in Article 126 TFEU and in Protocol No 12 on the excessive deficit procedure. On the one hand, those provisions prohibit certain categories of financial assistance to member states (Articles 123 to 125 TFEU) but, on the other hand, they authorize assistance in exceptional circumstances (Article 122 TFEU). Furthermore, the Union is empowered to adopt sanctions and to intervene directly if a member state fails to act, once it has been established that an excessive deficit exists in that state. Those measures are, however, authorized only with regard to euro area member states (see Article 139(2)(b) TFEU).

The Union's competences encompass the following activities:

The EU Council may adopt (by way of nonbinding recommendations) the "broad guidelines" of the economic policies of the member states and of the Union. The Council and the Commission are also competent *to monitor the consistency* of economic policies with the broad guidelines ("multilateral surveillance procedure," Article 121(3) TFEU). Furthermore, the European Parliament and the Council may exercise *legislative powers*

- to adopt detailed rules for the multilateral surveillance procedure (Article 121(6) TFEU);
- for the definition of the prohibitions referred in Articles 123 to 125 (e.g., overdraft facilities; Article 125(2) TFEU);
- for the definition of implementing rules in respect of Protocol No 12 on the excessive deficit procedure (Article 126(14) TFEU).

The Council may adopt *specific measures* aimed at reducing excessive government deficits (Article 126(9) TFEU). It may, under exceptional circumstances, *grant assistance* to a member state and it may lay down *conditions* for this assistance. Finally, the Council may impose *sanctions* on member states which fail to comply with the provisions on excessive deficit (Article 126(11) TFEU).

Those competences vary in scope according to whether a member state is within or outside the euro area. Hence, the "broad economic policy guidelines" (Article 121 TFEU) distinguish between euro area member states and member states "with a derogation" (Articles 136(1)(b) and 139(2)(a) TFEU). Equally, coercive means of remedying excessive deficits (Article 126(9) and (11) TFEU) cannot be imposed on member states outside the euro area. Any accession to the Monetary Union therefore implies a shift of economic policy competences to the Union (see Articles 139(2)(a) and (b) and 136 TFEU).

The economic policy coordination provided for in Article 120 TFEU does not result primarily from the adoption of legal acts binding upon the member states, for example, the setting of minimum standards. The "common" policy is supposed to result from indirect intervention, consisting in the definition of general objectives and from peer pressure to comply therewith. Since the outbreak of the financial crisis in 2010, a strong tendency towards a "hierarchization" of the coordination process has been evident. As a result member states are increasingly subject to compliance with common rules and to sanctions in case of failure to comply.

The centerpiece of the coordination process consists of "broad guidelines" for national economic policy that are decided on by the EU institutions (Article 121(2) TFEU). Although not legally binding, a set of instruments has been introduced by way of legislation that aims to ensure conformity of national policies with those guidelines.

As a first step in the formal procedure for adopting the guidelines, the Commission presents a draft to the Council. The latter reports its findings on the draft to the European Council, which adopts a conclusion, pursuant to which the Council formally adopts a recommendation setting out the broad guidelines.[7] Subsequently, member states are subject to "multilateral surveillance" by the Commission and the Council. Several implementing regulations were issued in 1997 and during the financial crisis in 2011; these laid down detailed reporting requirements for the member states aimed at the prevention and correction of macroeconomic imbalances.[8] A failure to comply does not, however, change the distribution of competences between the European Union and the member states. Hence, the Union cannot adopt economic policy decisions in place of a member state. If member state's policies are not consistent with the broad guidelines, "warnings" and "recommendations" may be addressed by the Commission and the Council to the member state in question (see Article 121(4) TFEU). After the full consequences of different economic policies within the euro area became apparent during the financial crisis, the possibility of sanctions was introduced against member states of the euro area that did not comply with the broad guidelines.[9] Such sanctions may consist of compulsory interest-bearing deposits or fines.

It is questionable whether the EU mechanism for achieving a common economic policy and sound public finances is an efficient tool that will work in all circumstances. Especially in situations of low economic growth, when public revenue declines, the system is too rigid. It offers only a choice between weak preventive and harsh *ex post* measures. Sanctions in such a situation are likely to aggravate the financial problems of a member state.[10] From the beginning of the EMU, solidarity between the member states (Article 3(3) TEU) should have required member states together with the EU institutions to take an active and continuing interest in each state's capacity to achieve the common objectives. Only after severe problems occurred were appropriate procedures for close scrutiny of national economic and fiscal policies introduced.

In 2011, the EU institutions formally admitted to shortcomings in the economic governance of the European Union. They declared:

> (4) Experience gained and mistakes made during the first decade of the economic and monetary union show a need for improved economic governance in the Union, which should be built on stronger national ownership of commonly agreed rules and policies and on a more robust framework at the level of the Union for the surveillance of national economic policies. …

> (6) In particular, surveillance of the economic policies of the Member States should be broadened beyond budgetary surveillance to include a more detailed and formal framework to prevent excessive macroeconomic imbalances and to help the Member States affected to establish corrective plans before divergences become entrenched and before economic and financial developments take a durable turn in an excessively unfavourable direction. Such broadening of the surveillance of economic policies should take place in parallel with a deepening of fiscal surveillance.[11]

Subsequently an attempt to improve the instruments was made by the adoption of a legislative package imposing more stringent reporting requirements on member states and sharpening the sanctions for failure to comply with the "broad guidelines" for economic policy (Article 121(2) TFEU).

The most important – and most controversial – tool of macroeconomic policy at Union level has consisted of five mechanisms aimed at strict control of public expenditure in the member states and within the Union:

- the enjoining of member states to "avoid excessive government deficits" (Article 126(1) TFEU);
- the procedure for the detection and prevention of excessive government deficits (Article 126(2) to (14) and Protocol No 12 on the excessive deficit procedure;
- the prohibition of overdraft facilities with the ECB or with central banks of the member states and of privileged access to financial institutions in favor of EU institutions, central governments, and other regional, local, or other public authorities;
- the prohibition against the Union's assuming the commitments of central governments, regional, local, or other public authorities in the member states ("no bail-out") (Article 125 TFEU);
- an obligation on the European Union to keep its annual budget within the limits of its own resources (Article 310(1) and (4) TFEU).

According to Article 1 of Protocol No 12 on the excessive deficit procedure, an "excessive deficit" exists if one of the two following reference values is transgressed:

- 3 percent for the ratio of the planned or actual government deficit to gross domestic product at market prices
- 60 percent for the ratio of government debt to gross domestic product at market prices.

If the Commission finds that a member state is failing to meet the requirements of one or both of these criteria, a procedure, which has various stages, is set in motion and can ultimately result in sanctions pursuant to Article 126(11) TFEU.

The details of the procedure for monitoring national budgets are laid down in Articles 126(3) to (13) TFEU, Regulation No 1467/97,[12] and Directive 2011/85.[13] The latter lays down detailed rules aimed at transparency and approximation of national budgetary rules and procedures.

On a proposal of the EU Commission, the EU Council is to decide whether an excessive deficit exists within a member state.[14] This decision is adopted by qualified majority and the member state to which the decision will be addressed does not take part in the vote (Article 126(13) TFEU). If such a decision has been taken, the member state must bring the situation to an end within a given period. The Council may also decide that payments from the EU budget to the member state in question may be suspended as long as the excessive deficit persists.[15]

If a member state that belongs to the euro area fails to put into practice the recommendations of the Council, the latter may, pursuant to Article 126(9) TFEU, give notice to the member state to take, within a specified time limit, "measures" for the deficit reduction.

Article 136(1) TFEU provides an additional and more flexible instrument for imposing further obligations concerning national budgetary policy on member states showing an excessive government deficit. The latter instrument was used for the first time in 2012 in order to urge Spain to adopt more stringent measures for the consolidation of the national budget.[16]

Little attention has been paid in the past to forestalling problems in national budgetary policies. The inadequacy of the preventive instruments (and their implementation) is shown by the fact that, in 2012, twenty-three of the then twenty-seven member states were found to have an "excessive government deficit" within the meaning of Article 126 TFEU.

Article 126(9) TFEU was used for the first time in 2010 with regard to Greece.[17] By 2012 the measures initially adopted had been expanded and amended several times.[18] Those measures are binding under Article 288 TFEU on all Greek institutions (parliament, government, administration, courts). They constitute the most drastic intervention in a member state's economic and social policy ever decided by the European Union. Greece was required to "put an end to the present excessive deficit situation" and to adopt a set of measures, most of which concerned national social and labor legislation. The Union under normal circumstances has no legislative competences in those areas. Similar obligations were imposed on Portugal in 2011.[19]

Just a year before, in June 2009, the message had been very different. As part of the "economic policy recommendations" regularly addressed to the member states under Article 121(2) TFEU the Council recommended that Greece

> pursue fiscal consolidation in the medium term and improve the efficiency of primary expenditure, speed up ongoing reforms in tax administration and the budgetary process, reduce the debt-to-GDP ratio, and further proceed with the implementation of the pension reform as rapidly as possible.[20]

The astonishing leap from friendly counsel to peremptory command illustrates the extremes of the European Union's competence in the field of economic policy and points to its weaknesses, in particular, the lack of differentiated policy instruments.

In addition to EU Treaty-based measures, a separate "Treaty on Stability, Coordination and Governance in the Economic and Monetary Union" (TSCG, "the Fiscal Compact") was signed by the representatives of twenty-five of the then twenty-eight member states[21] (the United Kingdom and the Czech Republic did not sign, Croatia was not yet a member). The fiscal pact aims "to strengthen the economic pillar of the economic and monetary union" (Article 1). The contracting parties agree to introduce into their national law "provisions of binding force and permanent character, preferably constitutional, or otherwise guaranteed to be fully respected and adhered to throughout the national budgetary process." According to those provisions the budgetary position of the central government of a Contracting Party "shall be balanced or in surplus" (Article 3, Fiscal Compact). Complaints concerning compliance with this commitment may be submitted to the European Court of Justice (Article 8), which may ultimately impose a fine if a member state does not comply with an initial judgment of the Court finding a member state in breach of its obligations under the Fiscal Compact.

The treaty furthermore provides for "economic partnership programmes" to be established by the Commission and the Council with regard to member states which are subject to an excessive deficit procedure (Article 5).

The treaty entered into force on 1 January 2013. Although the procedure of Article 329 TFEU was not followed, this treaty represents a special case of "enhanced cooperation" within the European Union.

The TFEU in Articles 122(1), 122(2), and 143(3) provides for three exceptional tools for EU macroeconomic governance in the form of financial assistance to individual member states. In addition instruments have been created outside the framework of the TEU and TFEU; they are, however, closely connected to these treaties.

Pursuant to Article 122(1) TFEU an unspecified form of assistance may be granted to member states, in particular if severe difficulties arise in the supply of certain products (e.g., energy). As of 2015 this provision has not been used.

Moreover, the Council may, in exceptional circumstances and under certain conditions, grant financial assistance to a member state (Article 122(2) TFEU). This legal basis was used for the first time during the financial crisis in 2010 in order to establish the "European financial stabilization mechanism" (EFSM).[22] It was meant to be used in favor of Greece, Ireland, and Portugal but was worded in general terms. It is, therefore, applicable to member states within and outside the euro area. This mechanism is aimed at "preserving the financial stability of the European Union."[23] It establishes

> the conditions and procedures under which Union financial assistance may be granted to a Member State which is experiencing, or is seriously threatened with, a severe economic or financial disturbance caused by exceptional occurrences beyond its control.[24]

The assistance consists of a loan or a credit line granted to the member state concerned. Since the EU budget does not provide for expenditure to this end the Commission is empowered, on behalf of the European Union, to contract borrowings on the capital markets or with financial institutions (Article 2(1) of Regulation No 407/2010). The decision to grant a loan is to contain *inter alia* "general economic policy conditions with a view to re-establishing a sound economic or financial situation in the beneficiary Member State." These conditions will be defined by the Commission, in consultation with the ECB (Article 3(3), Regulation No 407/2010).

The granting of assistance from the EU budget under Article 122(2) TFEU derogates from the "no-bailout" clause in Article 125 TFEU. It is therefore not surprising that its first use was highly controversial. The main argument against the legality of that instrument was its use in favor of member states with an excessive public deficit that resulted from poor governance, while Article 122(2) restricts its applicability to "severe difficulties caused by natural disasters or exceptional occurrences beyond its control."[25] Given the extraordinary situation in 2010 on the global financial markets, it could, however, be argued that the constitutional principle of solidarity between member states[26] justifies a restrictive reading of the "no-bailout" clause and a corresponding broad reading of Article 122(2) TFEU. Member states receiving assistance from the ESM are subject to "enhanced surveillance" by the EU institutions. This implies inter alia the obligation to adopt measures aimed at addressing the sources or potential sources of their financial difficulties.[27]

The EFSM has been used in favor of Ireland[28] and of Portugal.[29] In both cases, detailed conditions concerning economic policy reforms in those member states were imposed.

In addition, a member state outside the euro area that is suffering difficulties as regards its balance of payments may be granted "mutual assistance" in accordance with Article 143 TFEU. The assistance may include the granting of limited credits by the Union[30] or by other member states, subject to their agreement. Moreover, the Union has established a facility providing medium-term financial assistance for member states' balances of payments.[31] The activation of the assistance is made conditional on the implementation of economic policy requirements, set out by the Commission. The facility was used, for example, in favor of Romania in 2011.[32]

It was already the case that the financial assistance necessary to help Greece effectively in 2010 could not be financed within the limits of the European Union's own resources. Therefore, in parallel with the EFSM, the (then) sixteen euro area member states agreed to establish a private company between them ("*société anonyme*" incorporated in Luxembourg): the EFSF.[33] The EFSF finances loans which are backed by irrevocable and unconditional guarantees of the euro area member states. The EFSF is governed by a board of directors consisting of representatives of the euro area member states. The Commission is given the task of carrying out certain duties and functions, in particular the fixing of the conditions of loans. The EFSF was established for a period of three years and was subsequently replaced by the ESM.

In March 2011, the European Council adopted the following amendment to Article 136 TFEU:

> The Member States whose currency is the euro may establish a stability mechanism to be activated if indispensable to safeguard the stability of the euro area as a whole. The granting of any required financial assistance under the mechanism will be made subject to strict conditionality.[34]

Anticipating this amendment entering into force, the euro area member states agreed, on 2 February 2012, to a "Treaty establishing the European Stability Mechanism."[35] The ESM may provide "stability support" if indispensable to safeguard the financial stability of the euro area as a whole and of its member states. The initial maximum lending volume is set at €500,000 million. The amount can be increased by the Board of Governors of the ESM. This treaty is a permanent instrument.

Answering to a request for a preliminary ruling, the Court of Justice of the European Union (CJEU) has examined the European Council Decision amending Article 136 TFEU and the ESM. The Court found that the ESM does not infringe the provisions of the TFEU relating to economic and monetary policy.[36]

Receiving financial assistance under the ESM is conditional on the ratification of the Treaty on Stability, Coordination, and Governance ("Fiscal Compact") of 2 March 2012.

The TFEU enables the Council to set up "conditions," when a member state is receiving assistance from the Union pursuant to Articles 122(2) and 143(2). Since the financial crisis, this power has increasingly been used in order to impose comprehensive and detailed measures to be adopted by the member state in question.[37] Meanwhile the principle of conditionality has become a generalized treaty notion. According to the amendment to Article 136 TFEU assistance under this new mechanism will be subject to "strict conditions."[38] The ESM, which was adopted subsequently, stresses, in Article 12, that support to a member state can be provided "subject to strict conditionality."

In practice, it is clear that conditions laid down in this context come close to "measures" imposed on a member state pursuant Article 126(9) TFEU. Compliance with those "conditions" and "measures" is normally assessed by the European Commission.

Conditionality generates a new pattern of extensive intervention in national economic and social policy founded exclusively on decisions taken by executive bodies (the EU Council and the EU Commission). No parliamentary participation in those decisions is envisaged. This raises questions as to the legitimacy of this form of economic governance.

Since 2009, in the course of the financial crisis, the impact of private actors (viz., banks) on macroeconomic policy in the European Union has become visible. Member states had to intervene in the banking sector in order to maintain a functioning capital market. The Union tried to gain control over this situation by enacting measures intended to establish macroprudential oversight of the financial system and to prevent the accumulation of excessive risks within the various financial sectors, thus ensuring the functioning of the internal market. To that end, three European Supervisory Agencies were established: the European Banking Authority,[39] the European Insurance and Occupational Pensions Authority,[40] and the European Securities and Markets Authority.[41]

Pursuant to Article 127(6) TFEU, the ECB was given specific tasks concerning policies relating to the prudential supervision of credit institutions[42] and the task of coordinating the three authorities within the framework of a European Systemic Risk Board.[43]

A structural design fault in the TFEU's economic policy provisions is the fact that neither national parliaments nor the European Parliament are involved in the shaping of and the decision on recommendations for economic policy. The European Parliament is only informed *ex post facto* of the recommendations and decisions adopted by the Council under Articles 121(2) and (4), 122, and 126(9) and (11). Precluding any involvement by the body charged with the direct representation of citizens at European level (Article 10(2) TEU) considerably diminishes the legitimacy of any such measures. Here the most serious paradox of the present instruments for the achievement of EMU becomes apparent: the most draconian intervention into hitherto national responsibilities that the treaty authorizes enjoys the least legitimacy.

Such arrangements flout the principle of democracy – postulated in Article 2 of the Treaty on European Union (TEU) as one of the values on which the Union is founded.

Circumventing the European Parliament might well prove exceptionally dangerous to the European Union's legitimacy if the populations of the member states concerned were to engage in large-scale resistance to EU intervention, causing internal political crises with unforeseeable consequences, precisely because no politically responsible institution is visible.

Monetary Union – History and Problems of a Common Currency for Nineteen EU Member States

A common currency facilitates the functioning of an internal market, both with respect to transactions in goods and services and the free movement of capital and payments.[44] Furthermore, it is a powerful symbol of a common political and legal order.[45]

During the initial phase of the EEC, exchange-rate fluctuations or flexible exchange rates obstructed the development of a workable capital market. They also deterred economic actors from regarding the data of the common market as reliable factors on which to base cross-border transactions. The achievement of a common monetary policy in parallel with the establishment of the common (later "internal") market was therefore considered an essential part of European integration (see Article 2 EU).

The Treaty of Lisbon provides that the European Union is to establish a monetary union whose currency is the euro (Article 3(4) TEU). The common currency was introduced in stages.[46] On 1 January 1999 the common currency, provisionally called the "ECU," was substituted for the national currencies of the member states which had accepted the common currency. From that moment on, the ECU became a currency in its own right and the single currency of those member states (Article 109 l(4) of the Treaty establishing the European Community (EC)). The new currency was officially named the "euro."[47] Since 1 January 2003, the euro has had the status of exclusive legal tender in the participating member states.[48] Monetary policy is entrusted to the Union as an exclusive competence in respect of those member states which have introduced the common currency (Article 3(1)(c) TFEU).

The TFEU provides for institutional and procedural mechanisms aimed at protecting the stability of the common currency. The most important institutional guardian of the currency is the ECB, which exercises its mandate jointly with the national central banks. The ECB and national central banks enjoy a status of guaranteed independence from other EU institutions and from national governments.

With the common currency, European integration has acquired a new character. It has become a tangible and visible experience for the individual citizen. Since its introduction the euro has achieved a reputation as one of the leading stable currencies of the world. Yet, the consequences of monetary integration became evident only gradually. Obviously the margin for autonomous action by national governments in matters related to economic, social, and monetary policy had been reduced. However, the expected approximation of national economic and social policy did not come about smoothly. Since differences in economic performance between the member states could no longer be compensated for by alterations in the exchange rate, speculation against the coherence of the euro area began when the global financial crisis erupted in 2009. The heads of state and government of the euro area member states stressed their support for the common currency: "We affirm our strong commitment to do what is necessary to ensure the financial stability of the euro area ..."[49]

To that end, various instruments for the protection of the common currency have been created. Their effect in periods of economic crisis and growing concern among European peoples is, however, uncertain.

The project to transform the EEC, established by the Treaty of Rome (1957), into an economic and monetary union took shape at the political level when the heads of state and government of the member states of the EEC agreed, on 1 and 2 December 1969, to the drawing up of a plan for the attainment, in stages, of that project. Subsequently, such a plan was prepared under the chairmanship of the then prime minister of Luxembourg Pierre Werner.[50]

The plan had to reconcile the opposing concepts of French and Belgian economists on the one hand and German and Dutch economists on the other. The former expected accelerated monetary integration to lead to pressure for the economic and social approximation of the member states and for stronger integration of the other tools of economic policy. The latter warned that contagious high inflation rates were a risk and that horizontal financial transfers might be needed should differences in economic policy structures between the member states persist. Efficient coordination of fiscal and growth policies would therefore be a prerequisite for monetary integration.

In a Resolution of 22 March 1971, the Council and the Representatives of the member states agreed "to establish an economic and monetary union" and initiate a first stage planned to last three years, ending in December 1974.[51]

The decline of the Bretton Woods system of fixed exchange rates in 1972 and the subsequent economic crisis slowed down this plan. Only in 1979 was the project relaunched with the creation of the European Monetary System, whereby the fluctuations of exchange rates between the member states were reduced and monetary policy coordination was tested. A treaty amendment of 1986 ("the Single European Act") inserted a new Article 102a into the Treaty establishing the European Economic Community (EEC Treaty), in which member states were urged to cooperate in order to ensure the convergence of economic and monetary policy.[52]At its meeting on 28 June 1988, the European Council stated that "in adopting the Single Act, the member states of the Community confirmed the objective of progressive realization of economic and monetary union." It mandated a committee, chaired by the then President of the European Commission, to study and propose concrete stages leading towards this union. The report was presented in April 1989.[53] Despite reservations on the part of the prime minister of the United Kingdom, the plan was approved by the European Council in June 1989.

According to the Delors plan, economic and monetary union would imply "complete freedom of movement of persons, goods, services and capital, as well as irrevocably fixed exchange rates between national currencies and, finally, a single currency. This, in turn, would imply a common monetary policy and require a high degree of compatibility of economic policies and consistency in a number of other policy areas, especially in the fiscal field."[54] A three stage process towards economic and monetary union was proposed. The first stage began on 1 July 1990 with the coming into force of legislation enabling free movement of capital and payments.[55]

The definition and timetable of the second and third stages required substantive amendments to the EEC Treaty. They form part of the Maastricht Treaty of 7 February 1992. After that treaty entered into force, the second stage could begin on 1 January 1994, lasting until the beginning of the final stage with the introduction of the common currency, set for 1 January 1999.

The activities of the Union and the member states in matters of monetary policy

> shall include a single currency, the euro, and the definition and conduct of a single monetary policy and exchange-rate policy the primary objective of both of which shall be to maintain price stability and, without prejudice to this objective, to support the general economic policies in the Union, in accordance with the principle of an open market economy with free competition. (Article 119(2) TFEU)

Detailed rules for the conduct of monetary policy are laid down in Articles 127 to 144 TFEU. Articles 127 to 133 cover the legal status and the tasks of the ESCB and of the ECB. Articles 134 and 135 concern further institutional details, that is, the setting up of an Economic and Financial Committee (Article 134 TFEU). Provisions specific to member states whose currency is the euro are to be found in Articles 136 to 138 TFEU. Articles 139 to 144 settle the status of member states which have not yet adopted the euro and the procedure for doing so. Additional institutional details regarding the ESCB and the ECB are spelled out in Articles 282 to 284 TFEU. Those provisions are supplemented by several protocols annexed to the TEU/TFEU (Protocols Nos 4, 13, 14 to 18). The rules on the conduct of monetary policy are closely connected with the treaty provisions on free movement of capital and payments between the member states and between the member states and third countries (Articles 63 to 66 TFEU).

The monetary policy of the Union is conducted by the Eurosystem, consisting of the ECB[56] and the central banks of the member states whose currency is the euro (Article 282(1) TFEU). The central banks of all member states and the ECB together form the ESCB.

The ECB has legal personality of its own and is independent in the exercise of its powers and in the management of its finances (Article 282(3) TFEU). The scope of action of that legal personality is determined by the treaties and the specific functions assigned therein to the ECB. Hence, the ECB is subject to judicial review by the European Court of Justice (Article 263 TFEU). Equally the ECB can be subject to investigation by the European Anti-Fraud Office (OLAF).[57]

The decision-making bodies of the ECB are the Governing Council and the Executive Board (Article 283(1) and (2) TFEU). The Executive Board is composed of the president, the vice-president, and four other members of the ECB, who are appointed by the European Council for a term of office of eight years that is not renewable. The Governing Council comprises the members of the Executive Board and the governors of the national central banks whose currency is the euro (in 2015 this totaled twenty-five members).

The Governing Council is to adopt the Rules of Procedure determining the internal organization of the ECB and its decision-making bodies (Article 12.3 ESCB Statute).[58] The ECB has its seat in Frankfurt am Main, Germany.[59]

The ECB has an initial capital of €5,000 million. The national central banks are the sole subscribers to and holders of the capital of the ECB according to a key which takes into account the share of the member state in question in the population and in the GDP of the Union. The capital may be increased by a decision of the Governing Council (Articles 28 and 29 ESCB Statute). Central banks of member states with a derogation are to contribute only on specific conditions to the operational cost of the ECB (Article 47 ESCB Statute).[60]

The Eurosystem is governed by the decision-making bodies of the ECB (Article 129 TFEU). Its tasks are divided between the Governing Council and the Executive Board as follows (see Article 12 ESCB Statute):

- The Governing Council is to formulate the monetary policy, adopt decisions relating to intermediate monetary objectives, key interest rates, and the supply of reserves in the Eurosystem. It is to adopt guidelines for their implementation.
- The Executive Board is to implement monetary policy in accordance with the guidelines and decisions, laid down by the Governing Council. It may also exercise powers delegated by the Governing Council.

Members of the decision-making bodies of the Eurosystem enjoy a status of complete independence. Institutions and other bodies of the European Union and the governments of the member states undertake to respect that principle and not to influence the members in the performance of their duties (Article 130 TFEU).

Advisory and preparatory tasks are carried out by an Economic and Financial Committee provided for in Article 134 TFEU. It delivers opinions at the request of the Council or the Commission or on its own initiative and it keeps under review the economic and financial situation of the member states and of the Union. It examines, on a regular basis, the situation regarding the free movement of capital and payments as they result from the application of Articles 63 to 66 TFEU. The Committee is composed of two appointees from each member state and a further two each from the Commission and the ECB.[61]

The primary task of the Eurosystem is to maintain price stability. It is, in addition, to support the general economic policies in the Union (Article 127(1) TFEU).[62] More specifically, the Eurosystem defines and implements the monetary policy of the Union by open market and credit operations in the financial markets (Article 18 ESCB Statute),[63] by requiring credit institutions established in the member states to hold minimum reserve on accounts with the ECB (Article 19 ESCB Statute)[64] and ensuring efficient clearing and payment systems (Article 22 ESCB Statute).[65] It holds and manages the official foreign reserves of the member states (Article 127(2) TFEU; Article 3(2) ESCB Statute) and it conducts jointly with the Council foreign exchange operations (Articles 127(2), 219 TFEU) and participates in international monetary institutions (Article 138 TFEU; Article 6(2) ESCB Statute).

The ECB has the exclusive right to authorize the issue of euro banknotes and to approve the issuing of euro coins by the member states (Article 128 TFEU). The ECB also exercises advisory functions in accordance with Article 4 ESCB Statute.

The ECB may be entrusted by the Council to perform specific tasks concerning the prudential supervision of credit institutions (Article 127(6) TFEU). On this basis, in 2010 specific tasks were conferred upon the ECB concerning the functioning of the European Systemic Risk Board.[66]

In order to carry out its tasks the ECB may adopt legal acts (Article 132 TFEU) as defined in Article 288 TFEU (binding regulations and decisions, nonbinding recommendations and opinions). The ECB may also adopt "guidelines" (Articles 12(1), 14(3) ESCB Statute), which are binding upon those to whom they are addressed.

As far as possible and appropriate, the ECB is to have recourse to the national central banks to carry out operations which form part of the tasks of the Eurosystem.

The ECB is prohibited from purchasing debt instruments directly from EU institutions or national governments, regional, local, or other public authorities (Article 123 TFEU; Article 21 ESCB Statute). In the context of the financial crisis of Greece and other member states the ECB, on the basis of Article 127(2) TFEU, adopted an "exceptional measure" relating to the eligibility of marketable debt instruments issued or guaranteed by the Greek government[67] and a "Securities markets programme" intended to address the malfunctioning of securities markets.[68] The compatibility of those measures with the spirit of Articles 123 TFEU and 21 ESCB Statute is moot. They can be justified in the light of the extraordinary situation and the resulting risks for monetary stability in the euro area. In 2014 the German Constitutional Court submitted a request to the CJEU for a preliminary ruling[69] on the compatibility of those measures with the EU treaties.[70]

The introduction of the euro as a common currency is subject to a decision taken by the EU Council on a proposal from the Commission after consulting the European Parliament and after discussion in the European Council (Article 140(2) TFEU). This decision further requires a recommendation of a qualified majority of those member states whose currency is the euro. The decision refers to the fulfillment of four cumulative criteria, set out in Article 140(1) TFEU and specified in detail in Protocol No 13 on the convergence criteria:

- the achievement of a high degree of price stability;
- the sustainability of the government financial position (government debt not exceeding 60 percent of GDP; planned or actual government deficit not exceeding 3 percent of GDP);
- normal fluctuation margins within the exchange-rate mechanism of the European Monetary System[71] for at least two years, without devaluing against the euro;
- the durability of convergence, reflected in the long-term interest-rate levels.

Member states which do not yet fulfill those criteria are referred to by the treaty as "Member States with a derogation" (Article 139(1) TFEU). Provisions of the treaty which specifically refer to the euro area do not apply to member states with a derogation (Article 139(2) to (4) TFEU). Nor are sanctions in a case of an excessive deficit or noncompliance with the broad economic policy guidelines applicable.

At least every two years or at the request of a member state with a derogation the Commission and the ECB are to report on the achievement "of a high degree of sustainable convergence."

At the end of the second stage of EMU, in 1998, of the (then) fifteen member states only Greece and Sweden did not fulfill the convergence criteria. Subsequently the Council decided on transition to the common currency for eleven member states.[72] After fulfilling the criteria, Greece was admitted to the euro area in 2001, Slovenia in 2007, Cyprus and Malta in 2008, Slovakia in 2009, Estonia in 2011, Latvia in 2014, and Lithuania in 2015. In 2015 the euro area comprises nineteen member states.

Since the provisions on EMU came into effect, the United Kingdom and Denmark have had a special status by virtue of Protocols No 15 (United Kingdom) and Nos 16 and 17 (Denmark). Those two countries did not wish to participate in the third stage of economic and monetary union and introduce the common currency. They may do so at a later stage and may request that the Article 140 TFEU participation procedure be applied to them.

Until the euro is introduced, Denmark enjoys the status of a "Member State with a derogation" (see Article 139(1) TFEU). For the United Kingdom, specific provisions and derogations have been laid down in Protocol No 15, points 4 to 8.

Sweden enjoys an intermediate status. The economic situation that, in 1998, prevented its adoption of the euro has changed. Sweden has long been eligible to join the euro area. However, in a referendum held in 2003, the Swedish people rejected the introduction of the euro. Therefore, the admission procedure of Article 140 TFEU remains suspended in respect of Sweden, which continues to have the status of a member state with a derogation.

The Treaty of Lisbon consolidated the institutional structure between the member states whose currency is the euro. Two new Articles (136 and 137) were inserted in the TFEU and a Protocol No 14 on the Eurogroup was annexed to the TEU/TFEU. Those provisions authorize specific legislation for the euro area concerning the coordination and surveillance of budgetary discipline and the adoption of specific economic policy guidelines. The Eurogroup has been given a separate institutional structure consisting of a "euro summit" and a special meeting of the euro area finance ministers. Presidents of those meetings are appointed for a period of two and a half years (Articles 1 and 2 of Protocol No 14; Article 12 of the Treaty on Stability, Coordination and Governance in the Economic and Monetary Union).

With its increasing autonomy, the Eurogroup has become an example of "enhanced cooperation" between a core of member states within the Union capable of preserving the initial concept of an economic and monetary union. The price for this internal flexibility is, however, a growing and persistent divide between the EMU on the one hand and the European Union on the other.

Concluding Remarks: Horizontal and Vertical Division of Competences – A Fragile Albeit Courageous Experiment

The establishment of an economic and monetary union within the European Union is far from accomplished. Although nineteen of the twenty-eight member states have introduced the common currency, the euro, and have therefore abandoned their monetary sovereignty in favor of a common monetary policy, some member states continue to prefer staying outside of the euro area (e.g., the United Kingdom). Others do not yet fulfill the economic and monetary requirements. Hence "the road to (a full) Monetary Union in Europe" is leading to a destination of which the ultimate form is still unknown.[73]

The uncertainty about the outcome of the ambitious project is aggravated by the even greater difficulty of acknowledging the existence of twenty-eight nation's separate macroeconomic policy concepts and traditions while aiming at bringing them together within the framework of a (single) economic (and monetary) union.

The legal instruments and the institutions conceived for those tasks have proven effective in the monetary field for the euro area. The euro has become a stable and internationally recognized currency. In matters of economic policy, however, the existing instruments and procedures could not bring about a harmonious economic development in the Union. Substantial disparities among member states persist. The contradiction between the centralized monetary policy and the essentially decentralized economic policies appears to be the most important obstacle to the transformation of the European Union into a full economic and monetary union as intended by the EU Treaty.

The economic crises of recent years brought to the forefront the shortcomings of the present treaty provisions on economic and monetary union and of their underlying assumption of mutual solidarity among member states. It is unlikely that all of the present member states would join in to adopt reforms of the EU treaties, necessary for the achievement of a true economic and monetary union among all member states. Such a union is probably better achieved instead among a smaller group of the present member states, which in turn would put at stake with the foundations of the existing European Union.

Notes

1 See Jacques Pelkmans, *European Integration, Method and Economic Analysis* (Harlow: Pearson Education, 2006),15; and Jean-Victor Louis, *L'Union Européenne et sa monnaie* (Brussels: éditions de l'Université de Bruxelles, 2009), 9.

2 Jan Tinbergen, *International Economic Integration* (Amsterdam: Elsevier, 1954); and Fritz Machlup, *A History of Thought on Economic Integration* (London: Macmillan, 1977), 39.

3 Article 1 TEU.

4 Article 174(1) TFEU.

5 Article 119(1) TFEU.

6 European Council Decision (EU) No 2011/199 of 25 March 2011 amending Article 136 TFEU with regard to a stability mechanism for Member States whose currency is the euro [2011] OJ L 91/1.

7 See, e.g., Council Recommendation (EU) No 2010/410 of 13 July 2010 on broad guidelines for the economic policies of the Member States and of the Union [2010] OJ L 191/28.

8 Council Regulation (EC) No 1466/97 of 7 July 1997 on the strengthening of the surveillance of budgetary positions and the surveillance and coordination of economic policies [1997] OJ L 209/1, as last amended by Regulation (EU) No 1175/2011 of the European Parliament and of the Council of 16 November 2011 amending Council Regulation (EC) No 1466/97 on the strengthening of the surveillance of budgetary positions and the surveillance and coordination of economic policies [2011] OJ L 306/12; Regulation (EU) No 1176/2011 of the European Parliament and of the Council of 16 November 2011 on the prevention and correction of macroeconomic imbalances [2011] OJ L 306/25.

9 Regulation (EU) No 1174/2011 of the European Parliament and of the Council of 16 November 2011 on enforcement measures to correct excessive macroeconomic imbalances in the euro area [2011] OJ L 306/8.

10 See Damian Chalmers, Gareth Davies, and Giorgio Monti, *European Union Law* (Cambridge: Cambridge University Press, 2014), 740.

11 Recitals 4 and 6 in the preamble to Regulation (EU) No 1174/2011, see n 9.

12 Council Regulation (EC) No 1467/97 of 7 July 1997 on speeding up and clarifying the implementation of the excessive deficit procedure [1997] OJ L 209/6, as last amended by Council Regulation (EU) No 1177/2011 of 8 November 2011 amending Regulation (EC) No 1467/97 on speeding up and clarifying the implementation of the excessive deficit procedure [2011] OJ L 306/33.

13 Council Directive 2011/85/EU of 8 November 2011 on requirements for budgetary frameworks of the Member States [2011] OJ L 306/41. Cf. also Regulation (EU) No 473/2013 of the European Parliament and of the Council of 21 May 2013 on common provisions for monitoring and assessing draft budgetary plans and ensuring the correction of excessive deficit of the Member States in the euro area [2013] OJ L 140/11.

14 On the margin of discretion of the Council with regard to the procedure, see Case C-27/04 *Commission v. Council* [2004] ECR I-6649, paras 70–90.

15 See Article 4 of Council Regulation (EC) No 1084/2006 of 11 July 2006 establishing a Cohesion Fund and repealing Regulation (EC) No 1164/94 [2006] OJ L 210/79. This provision was used for the first time in 2012 with regard to Hungary, see Council Implementing Decision (EU) 2012/156 of 13 March 2012 suspending commitments from the Cohesion Fund for Hungary with effect from 1 January 2013 [2012] OJ L 78/19.

16 Council Decision (EU) 2012/443 of 23 July 2012 addressed to Spain on specific measures to reinforce financial stability [2012] OJ L 202/17.

17 Council Decision (EU) 2010/320 of 10 May 2010 addressed to Greece with a view to reinforcing and deepening fiscal surveillance and giving notice to Greece to take measures for the deficit reduction judged necessary to remedy the situation of excessive deficit [2010] OJ L 145/6.
18 Last amendment by Council Decision (EU) 2012/211 of 13 March 2012 amending Decision 2011/734/EU addressed to Greece with a view to reinforcing and deepening fiscal surveillance and giving notice to Greece to take measures for the deficit reduction judged necessary to remedy the situation of excessive deficit [2012] OJ L 113/8.
19 Council Implementing Decision (EU) 2011/344 of 30 May 2011 on granting Union financial assistance to Portugal [2011] OJ L 159/88.
20 See Council Recommendation (EC) 2008/390 of 14 May 2008 on the broad economic policy guidelines for the Member States and the Community (2008–2010) [2008] OJ L 137/13.
21 Published on the website of the European Council.
22 Council Regulation (EU) No 407/2010 of 11 May 2010 establishing a European financial stabilization mechanism [2010] OJ L 118/1.
23 The (equally binding) German version of this text reads: "Um die Stabilität, Einheit und Integrität der Europäischen Union zu wahren" (In order to preserve the stability, unity, and integrity of the European Union). The other language versions correspond to the English text.
24 Article 1, Regulation No 407/2010.
25 See Jean-Victor Louis, "Guest Editorial: The No Bailout Clause and Rescue Packages," *Common Market Law Review* 47 (2010); and Martin Seidel, "Die 'No Bail-Out' Klausel des Art. 125 als Beistandsverbot," *Europäische Zeitschrift für Wirtschaftsrecht* (2011).
26 See Malcolm Ross and Yuri Borgmann-Prebil, eds., *Promoting Solidarity in the European Union* (Oxford: Oxford University Press, 2011); and Roland Bieber and Francesco Maiani, "Sans solidarité point d'Union européenne," *Revue Trimestrielle de Droit Européen* 48 (2012).
27 Regulation No 472/2013 of the European Parliament and of the Council of 21 May 2013 on the strengthening of economic and budgetary surveillance of Member States in the euro area experiencing or threatened with serious difficulties with respect to their financial stability [2013] OJ L 140/1.
28 Council Implementing Decision (EU) 2011/77 of 7 December 2010 on granting Union financial assistance to Ireland [2011] OJ L 30/34.
29 Council Implementing Decision 2011/344, see n 19.
30 E.g., Council Decision (EU) 2011/289 of 12 May 2011 granting mutual assistance for Romania [2011] OJ L 132/18.
31 Council Regulation (EC) No 332/2002 of 18 February 2002 establishing a facility providing medium-term financial assistance for Member States' balances of payments [2002] OJ L 53/1.
32 Council Decision (EU) 2011/288 of 12 May 2011 providing precautionary EU medium-term financial assistance for Romania [2011] OJ L 132/15. This assistance was granted in addition to that mentioned in n 30.
33 Decision of the Representatives of the Governments of the Euro Area Member States Meeting within the Council of the European Union, Council Document No 9614/10 of 10 May 2010.
34 European Council Decision 2011/199, see n 6.
35 See website of the European Council http://.european-council.europa.eu/eurozone-governance/esm-treaty-signature?lang=en.
36 Case C-370/12 *Pringle v. Government of Ireland* EU:C:2012:756.
37 E.g., Spain, Decision 2012/443, see n 16; Portugal, Decision 2011/344, see n 19; Ireland, Decision 2011/77, see n 28.
38 European Council Decision 2011/199, see n 6.
39 Regulation (EU) No 1093/2010 of the European Parliament and of the Council of 24 November 2010 establishing a European Supervisory Authority (European Banking Authority), amending Decision No 716/2009/EC and repealing Commission Decision 2009/78/EC [2010] OJ L 331/12.

40 Regulation (EU) No 1094/2010 of the European Parliament and of the Council of 24 November 2010 establishing a European Supervisory Authority (European Insurance and Occupational Pensions Authority), amending Decision No 716/2009/EC and repealing Commission Decision 2009/79/EC [2010] OJ L 331/48.
41 Regulation (EU) No 1095/2010 of the European Parliament and of the Council of 24 November 2010 establishing a European Supervisory Authority (European Securities and Markets Authority), amending Decision No 716/2009/EC and repealing Commission Decision 2009/77/EC [2010] OJ L 331/84.
42 Council Regulation (EU) No 1024/2013 of 15 October 2013 conferring specific tasks on the European Central Bank concerning policies relating to the prudential supervision of credit institutions [2013] OJ L 287/63.
43 Regulation (EU) No 1092/2010 of the European Parliament and of the Council of 24 November 2010 on European Union macro-prudential oversight of the financial system and establishing a European Systemic Risk Board [2010] OJ L 331/1; and Council Regulation (EU) No 1096/2010 of 17 November 2010 conferring specific tasks upon the European Central Bank concerning the functioning of the European Systemic Risk Board [2010] OJ L 331/162.
44 Paul de Grauwe, *Economics of Monetary Union*, 9th ed. (Oxford: Oxford University Press, 2014), 57–105; Louis, *L'Union européenne et sa monnaie*, 39–70; and Tommaso Padoa-Schioppa, *The Road to Monetary Union in Europe* (Oxford: Clarendon Press, 1994), 50–67.
45 Tommaso Padoa-Schioppa, *The Road to Monetary Union in Europe*, 1–31 and 185–191.
46 See Article 109 l EC Treaty, as applicable in 1999. This provision has been deleted by the Treaty of Lisbon as from 1 December 2009 [2010] OJ C 83/1.
47 Article 2, Council Regulation (EC) No 974/98 of 3 May 1998 on the introduction of the euro [1998] OJ L 139/1, later confirmed in Article 3(4) of the EU Treaty.
48 Articles 10 and 11 Regulation No 974/98, see n 47.
49 Euro Area Summit Statement, Brussels, 29 June 2012, published on the website of the European Council: http://consilium.europa.eu/uedocs/cms_data/docs/pressdata/en/ec/131359.pdf.
50 [1970] OJ C 136/19.
51 Résolution du Conseil et des Représentants des Gouvernements des Etats Membres du 22 mars 1971 concernant la réalisation par étapes de l'union économique et monétaire dans la Communauté [1971] OJ C 28/1 (no official English translation available).
52 [1987] OJ L 169/1.
53 Jacques Delors, *Report on Economic and Monetary Union in the European Community* (Brussels: European Commission, 1989).
54 Delors, *Report on Economic and Monetary Union*, 13.
55 Council Directive (EEC) 88/361 of 24 June 1988 for the implementation of Article 67 of the Treaty [1988] OJ L 178/5.
56 On the ECB, see René Smits, *The European Central Bank* (The Hague: Kluwer Law International, 1997).
57 Case C-11/00 *Commission v. ECB* EU:C:2003:395.
58 Rules of Procedure of the ECB: Decision of the European Central Bank (ECB/2004/2) of 19 February 2004 adopting the Rules of Procedure of the European Central Bank [2004] OJ L 80/33, as last amended by Decision of the European Central Bank (ECB/2009/5) of 19 March 2009 amending Decision ECB/2004/2 of 19 February 2004 adopting the Rules of Procedure of the European Central Bank [2009] OJ L 100/10.
59 Article 1(c) of Protocol No 6 on the Location of the Seats of the Institutions and of certain Bodies, Offices Agencies and Departments of the European Union annexed to the TEU/TFEU [2010] OJ C 83/265.
60 See Decision (ECB/2010/28) of the European Central Bank of 13 December 2010 on the paying-up of the European Central Bank's capital by the non-euro area national central banks [2011] OJ L 11/56.
61 In 2015: 28 x 2 + 2 x 2 = 60 members. See Council Decision (EC) 98/743 of 21 December 1998 on the detailed provisions concerning the composition of the Economic and Financial Committee

[1998] OJ L 358/109 and Council Decision 1999/8 of 31 December 1998 adopting the Statutes of the Economic and Financial Committee [1999] OJ L 5/71.

62 This task is stressed again twice at treaty level, see Article 282(2) TFEU and Article 2 ESCB Statute.

63 See Guideline ECB/2011/14 of the European Central Bank of 20 September 2011 (recast) on monetary policy instruments and procedures of the Eurosystem [2011] OJ L 331/1.

64 See Regulation (EC) No 1745/2003 of the European Central Bank of 12 September 2003 on the application of minimum reserves [2003] OJ L 250/10, as last amended by Regulation (EU) No 1358/2011 of the European Central Bank of 14 December 2011 amending Regulation (EC) No 1745/2003 on the application of minimum reserves [2011] OJ L 338/51.

65 See Guideline ECB/2012/27 of the European Central Bank of 5 December 2012 on a Trans-European Automated Real-time Gross settlement Express Transfer system (TARGET2) [2013] OJ L 13/1.

66 Regulation No 1096/2010 [2010] OJ L 331/162, see n 43.

67 Decision (ECB/2010/3) of the European Central Bank of 6 May 2010 on temporary measures relating to the eligibility of marketable debt instruments issued or guaranteed by the Greek Government [2010] OJ L 117/102.

68 Decision (ECB/2010/5) of the European Central Bank of 14 May 2010 establishing a securities markets programme [2010] OJ L 124/8. See also Guideline ECB/2012/18 of the European Central Bank of 2 August 2012 on additional temporary measures relating to Eurosystem refinancing operations and eligibility of collateral and amending Guideline ECB/2007/9 [2012] OJ L 218/20; and Guideline ECB/2012/23 of the European Central Bank of 10 October 2012 amending Guideline ECB/2012/18 on additional temporary measures relating to Eurosystem refinancing operations and eligibility of collateral [2012] OJ L 284/14.

69 Cf. Article 267 TFEU.

70 Case C-62/14 *Gauweiler* EU:C:2015:400.

71 Agreement of 16 March 2006 between the European Central Bank (ECB) and the national central banks of the Member States outside the euro area laying down the operating procedures for an exchange rate mechanism in stage three of Economic and Monetary Union (2006/C 73/08) [2006] OJ C 73/21.

72 Council Decision (EC) 98/317 of 3 May 1998 in accordance with Article 109j(4) of the Treaty [1998] OJ L 139/30 (admitting Austria, Belgium, Finland, France, Germany, Ireland, Italy, Luxembourg, the Netherlands, Portugal, and Spain).

73 Padoa-Schioppa, *The Road to Monetary Union in Europe*.

References

Bieber, Roland and Francesco Maiani. "Sans solidarité point d'Union européenne." *Revue Trimestrielle de Droit Européen* 48 (2012): 295–327.

Chalmers, Damian, Gareth Davies, and Giorgio Monti. *European Union Law*. Cambridge: Cambridge University Press, 2014.

de Grauwe, Paul. *Economics of Monetary Union*. 9th ed. Oxford: Oxford University Press, 2014.

Delors, Jacques. *Report on Economic and Monetary Union in the European Community*. Brussels: European Commission, 1989.

Louis, Jean-Victor. *L'Union Européenne et sa monnaie*. Brussels: éditions de l'Université de Bruxelles, 2009.

Louis, Jean-Victor. "Guest Editorial: The No Bailout Clause and Rescue Packages." *Common Market Law Review* 47 (2010): 971–986.

Machlup, Fritz. *A History of Thought on Economic Integration*. London: Macmillan, 1977.

Padoa-Schioppa, Tommaso. *The Road to Monetary Union in Europe*. Oxford: Clarendon, 1994.

Pelkmans, Jacques. *European Integration, Method and Economic Analysis*. Harlow: Pearson Education, 2006.

Ross, Malcolm and Yuri Borgmann-Prebil, eds. *Promoting Solidarity in the European Union*. Oxford: Oxford University Press, 2011.
Seidel, Martin. "Die 'No Bail-Out' Klausel des Art. 125 als Beistandsverbot," *Europäische Zeitschrift für Wirtschaftsrecht* (2011): 529–534.
Smits, René. *The European Central Bank*. The Hague: Kluwer Law International, 1997.
Tinbergen, Jan. *International Economic Integration*. Amsterdam: Elsevier, 1954.

22

EU Competition Law in a Global Context

Giorgio Monti

Introduction

EU competition law enforcement has "a sort of rock-star status."[1] In other policy fields, the Union's competences are limited to proposing legislation and, occasionally, monitoring member state compliance with EU law. In the field of competition law, the Commission instead functions as a supranational authority with police-like powers to act against firms and also against member states that infringe treaty obligations. These vast powers have been a source of contestation within the European Union, and the global effects of competition law enforcement have, at times, risked trade wars.

This chapter provides an overview of the key EU competition law provisions, focusing on their impact on the global economy and how this impact is managed. We begin by considering the main transnational themes that arise. The first is the age-old question of the extent to which national law applies across its borders: can EU competition law stretch to acts carried out abroad that have harmful effects within its territory? The second is the question of externalities, which has two ramifications. The first is an economic one, whereby the concern is that the enforcement of competition law in one jurisdiction may have negative repercussions in others, reducing global welfare. The second branch is political in character and arises when the enforcement of competition law in one jurisdiction harms the economic interests of firms abroad. A third theme, which arises in response to the first two issues, is collaboration among agencies in the context of global anticompetitive conduct (cartels and mergers). This serves to reduce the externalities noted above, to mitigate the controversies over extraterritoriality, and may even render enforcement more effective. A fourth theme is hypocrisy: while countries purport to believe in competition as a virtue, and cooperate to stop certain global risks, they also sponsor export cartels. These issues are obviously not novel but their impact increases the more that states adopt competition laws, and the more global trade expands. More thorough global policy responses may be necessary. While this has been recognized since the mid-twentieth century, the world trading system lacks a global antitrust authority. In its stead, networked governance has emerged, principally via the International Competition Network (ICN): the potential of this

A Companion to European Union Law and International Law, First Edition.
Edited by Dennis Patterson and Anna Södersten.

approach merits close attention, and this is our fifth theme. We explore these aspects in turn, but before doing so we provide a sketch of how competition policy became the European Union's first supranational policy.[2]

The Evolution of EU Competition Law

Competition law was destined to be in the Treaty establishing the European Economic Community (EEC) of 1957: the Americans wanted the introduction of antitrust rules, and so did an influential group of scholars whose work had begun to inform West German politics immediately after the war. It was conceded that the earlier toleration of cartels had been a failure and that competitive markets should be introduced.[3] However, competition rules were introduced gradually. In the Treaty of Rome (1957) the member states agreed only upon rules prohibiting cartels (Article 101 of the Treaty on the Functioning of the European Union (TFEU)) and abuses of dominance (Article 102 TFEU). Provisions regulating mergers were not agreed until 1989.[4] At first this was because it was felt that mergers should be facilitated to allow firms to reach a minimum efficient scale of production, and also to help markets integrate. However, the delayed introduction of merger rules was also caused by member state resistance: merger policy serves political ends, so having the power to authorize or block mergers in one's country can be a convenient industrial policy tool. And even today the Commission only has powers to review very large mergers – the rest remain within the jurisdiction of the member states.[5]

EU competition law also addresses the conduct of member states. The Treaty of Rome has always included a provision prohibiting subsidies and similar forms of governmental assistance (Article 107 TFEU), but the Commission wisely delayed implementing this seriously for some decades, allowing time for states to come into compliance with the provision of their own accord without its having recourse to the full measure of enforcement possible to it.[6] It has then used the budgetary discipline brought about as a result of economic and monetary union to press member states to reduce spending on the one hand, and has used its powers of review to redirect state expenditure to projects of European interest on the other.[7] Furthermore, neither the Treaty of Rome nor subsequent revisions addressed the risks posed by state-owned enterprises in a particularly clear way (see Article 106 TFEU). It was a combination of economic necessity of member states (which led to privatizations), technological evolution, and strategic enforcement by the Commission that together led to the liberalization of state-controlled monopolies in fields like telecommunications, postal services, and energy markets. However, a number of other markets remain subject to restrictive regulation at the national level. To a certain extent, anticompetitive state action can also be kept in check by the application of the so-called fundamental freedoms (viz. free movement of goods, services, workers, and capital), but the absence of centralized enforcement in this sphere has led to haphazard steps in spite of continued advice for a more strategic approach.[8] What emerges, then, is an economy that is largely based upon market principles but has pockets of resistance.[9]

In the beginning, enforcement of antitrust rules was centralized in the hands of the Commission. After some quiet decades, the Commission launched its modern, aggressive enforcement policy in the 1980s. Retrospectively its strategy was wise: it utilized the early years to secure knowledge of the development of European industry, and its infrequent enforcement actions allowed it and the Court of Justice to develop practices and precedents that legitimated competition law enforcement and established key procedural safeguards. Perhaps the most salient example for present purposes is the way the Court supported the Commission's choice to ground its enforcement strategy in deterrence in 1983.[10] Subsequent changes in fining policy have also been supported by the Court and facilitated the Commission's anticartel policy.

EU competition law also served to render inconsistent national law inapplicable: once the Commission had prohibited conduct under its rules, the parties could not rely on national law to justify their practices.[11] This led many member states to align national competition law with the EU model, since the national variations had less and less bite. In some cases, like that of Italy, national competition law is inapplicable once EU competition law is found to apply.[12] In other, like that of the United Kingdom, national competition law is to be applied in a manner consistent with EU competition law.[13] New member states have also opted to model national competition after the EU rules. However, the Commission considered that alignment was insufficient and that antitrust enforcement would become more effective if it were decentralized. That is to say, if national courts and national competition authorities could also enforce EU competition law.[14] The domestic reforms noted above were helpful in this respect because they showed that member states had already accepted the supremacy of EU competition law and the advantage of a single approach to competition problems. Antitrust enforcement was formally decentralized by Regulation 1/2003, which obliges national competition authorities to apply EU competition law when the practice in question has an effect on trade among member states.[15]

Given this new enforcement structure, it would have been reasonable to assume that if, say, the UK competition authority took up the prosecution of a cartel with effects in other jurisdictions, then it would have the powers not only to seize what evidence was available in the other countries but also to impose a fine for the effects caused by the infringement, if this was proved. Insofar as evidence gathering is concerned, Regulation 1/2003 has created a mechanism to facilitate the exchange of information and also to allow for other authorities to carry out inspections on behalf of the authority that is carrying out the investigation, all while safeguarding the rights of the parties. These provisions have functioned well, but they have been utilized only a few times.[16] In terms of fines, it seems that many competition authorities are reluctant to impose fines for the effects of anticompetitive conduct overseas. For example, the UK competition authority indicates that it requires the consent of the other member state or that state's competition authority. Other competition authorities are equally reluctant.[17] This is quite puzzling because it frustrates the main purpose for decentralizing enforcement: it means that when there are transnational cartels then either the Commission acts and imposes a fine for the effects felt across the European Union or multiple member states take action against the same cartel. Both solutions thwart the principal objectives underpinning the policy to decentralize enforcement: to multiply enforcement of EU competition law by harnessing national competition authorities and to allow the Commission to focus on major cases.

Similarly, it seems that not all countries have yet adjusted their legislation to facilitate actions for damages. In a recent dispute, when a UK plaintiff sought damages from a French defendant, the latter claimed that French law prohibited them from making available evidence to the UK courts, making such acts a criminal offence both for the defendant releasing that information as well as for the party requesting that information. The UK Court of Appeal gave this argument short shrift, noting that the supremacy of EU law meant that French law could not be used to protect the defendant.[18] This suggests that some law reform efforts are necessary at the domestic level to remove enforcement barriers. In this respect the recent initiative by the

Commission to harmonize certain aspects of private enforcement is to be welcomed as a timid first step into dangerous territory as states are keen to retain the integrity of their national private law systems.[19]

This brief account of how EU competition law has become a supranational policy should not be interpreted as intimating policy failure. On the contrary, the Commission, accompanied by the Court, has used its powers to create legitimate regulatory space for a competition policy that, judged by global standards, is highly successful. The systemic difficulties averred to above are the result of the continued powers member states exercise to retain competence over sensitive policy domains.

Extraterritoriality

We now turn to consider how far EU competition law might catch anticompetitive conduct carried out overseas that damages the EU market. In considering the extraterritorial reach of laws it is customary to distinguish between subject-matter jurisdiction (does the Commission have the power to find that certain acts are in breach of competition law?) and enforcement jurisdiction (does the Commission have the power to enforce its rules?).

In terms of subject-matter jurisdiction, it would appear that Articles 101 and 102 TFEU allow for extraterritorial application because of the requirement that the practice in question has an effect on trade between member states. It would seem that this put in statutory form the effects-test that is applied in US antitrust law whereby conduct abroad is susceptible to US law when it has an effect on the US markets or US traders.[20] However, the Court has resisted following this literal interpretation, in part, probably, because of the controversial consequence of the effects-test, which is perceived to afford excessive powers to foreign laws to interfere in the activities in other countries.[21] Instead the Court has managed to impose penalties on foreign firms by imaginative techniques: in an early cartel decision the Commission stated that the non-EU firms had acted in the European Union through their wholly owned subsidiaries and so the Commission could apply Article 101 to non-EU firms simply by dint of the presence of subsidiaries. This approach also makes it easy to assert enforcement jurisdiction because the decision may be sent to the EU subsidiary and fines may be enforced against it.[22]

In *Wood Pulp*, the Court of Justice was called upon to consider whether Article 101 could apply to foreign firms that had no presence in the European Union by way of subsidiaries. While the advocate general advised that the European Union could assert subject-matter jurisdiction using an effects-test, the Court of Justice held otherwise and found that foreign firms could be caught because the agreement was implemented in the Union and so no extraterritorial theory was needed. The Court held that an infringement of Article 101 can be subdivided into two parts: its formation and its implementation. Provided goods subject to the agreement are sold in the European Union, the agreement could be said to be implemented in the European Union.[23] Unfortunately, the question of what counts as the implementation of an agreement in the European Union has not been clarified further: sales in the European Union count, while a boycott of the EU market by foreign firms is probably not implemented in the Union.[24]

This absence of clarity has not been helped by the Commission, which in the *Gas Insulated Switchgear* cartel decision deployed another legal technique to rein in conduct that appeared to have no territorial connection with the European Union: this cartel was in large part designed to keep Japanese suppliers out of the European Union and EU suppliers out of Japan. The

Commission did not even discuss the question of extraterritoriality (nor did any of the parties question it). Instead it used the notion of a single infringement to find that the agreement with the Japanese firms whereby they would limit their sales in the Union should be read in the wider context of the global cartel. Aspects of the cartel had been implemented in the European Union, and Japanese firms were aware of and had taken part in it, for example, by notifying their European partners of offers they received from clients in the European Union.[25] In other words, Japanese companies that had sold their goods in the European Union pursuant to an agreement not to do so can be prosecuted for breach of Article 101 because their actions were intimately connected with a conspiracy to affect the EU market, which was implemented in Europe by European firms.

When we turn to Article 102 decisions, the Court's refusal to acknowledge an effects test begins to look even more odd: one only needs to refer to the *Microsoft* decision where the firm's refusal to disclose interoperability information to competitors was prosecuted even if the firm was situated outside the European Union. It is not implausible to suggest that this practice could have anticompetitive effects in the European Union (if successful in excluding competitors, Microsoft would be able to raise prices there), but it is hard to come up with an explanation of how this refusal was implemented in the Union.[26]

Similar puzzles emerge when we turn to merger control. Here the jurisdiction of the Commission is slightly different: the EU Merger Regulation provides that a proposed merger must be notified if the parties to the merger have a combined worldwide turnover in excess of €5,000 million and at least two undertakings have a turnover of at least €250 million in the European Union. Such turnover is established by sales within the European Union.[27] This allows the Commission to require notification of many transactions that are highly unlikely to have anticompetitive effects in the European Union. When this point was considered by the then Court of First Instance (now named the General Court), the judges were careful to explain that satisfying the thresholds is not sufficient to establish jurisdiction. While the thresholds may be a good indicator that the merger has effects on the EU market, these effects would have to be established separately.[28] This is simply a means of saying that the implementation doctrine can be read in an elastic way but this is consistent with international law.[29]

Of course subject-matter jurisdiction is unhelpful if the other country refuses to cooperate. However, the Court of Justice has facilitated enforcement by allowing the decision to be served to a subsidiary in the European Union.[30] Moreover, the Court of Justice has allowed the Commission to impose mandatory injunctions on foreign firms.[31] These orders can be imposed once the firm does business in the Union. However, without a territorial link the Commission cannot take formal steps to demand documents or hear witnesses based on the powers it has. The best it can do is act through diplomatic channels.

One of the results of the US asserting extraterritorial jurisdiction actively since the 1970s has been the enactment of legislation to protect national businesses from the excesses of the US system, especially in light of the treble damages that are awarded to winning plaintiffs.[32] For example, French law makes it a criminal offence to "request, seek, or disclose" evidence that may lead to foreign proceedings.[33] In Australia, legislation allows persons situated in Australia who have been ordered to pay antitrust damages on the basis of foreign law to recover the full amount from the successful plaintiff.[34]

It is no exaggeration to conclude that use of extraterritoriality as an approach to handling the global impact of anticompetitive conduct has proved to be problematic.[35] An aggressive approach to police anticompetitive conduct abroad leads to other states trying to frustrate such efforts, while a less determined approach (like that in the European Union) is likely to be received with less hostility, but its effectiveness and clarity are questionable. Below, we will explore certain avenues that competition authorities and states have utilized to escape the enforcement impasse, but it must be recalled that all of the measures discussed only rein in public enforcement by competition authorities; they have not been used to put an end to the use of US antitrust law by private parties to seek punitive damages.

Negative Externalities

Restrictive practices

For several decades, the major negative externalities of the interpretation and application of competition law were suffered by foreign firms selling in Europe, which in the 1970s and 1980s were mostly US and Japanese firms. For instance, distribution agreements, which are subjected to very light touch control in the United States, were controlled vigorously by the Commission. Practitioners remained generally puzzled by the prescriptive nature of the EU rules in comparison to those in the United States, where, provided you had no market power, almost any form of distribution agreement was tolerated.[36] Nor was Article 102 enforced with any less vigor. United Brands, exporting bananas into Europe and trying to defend its falling market share from other players, was fined for terminating one of its dealers for prohibiting distributors from exporting bananas into other countries and for selling bananas at a lower price in Ireland than in Germany.[37] In *Commercial Solvents* a US firm was condemned for refusing to supply a small Italian firm when there was little proof that its exclusion would cause any harm to the market.[38] (And a number of large firms were fined for entering into distribution agreements when they promised the distributor discounts if it sold more of their goods, again frustrating what appears at first blush to be procompetitive: giving distributors an economic incentive to market goods aggressively).[39] In these episodes, the Court and the Commission appeared more concerned with protecting small and medium-sized undertakings, for ensuring fairness, and for what US commentators said was a penchant for protecting competitors, not competition.[40]

Since the mid-1990s, the Commission has reconsidered its formalistic, aggressive stance and embraced a more economics-based approach under which only behavior likely to cause economic harm is punished.[41] In the context of distribution agreements this has resulted in a block exemption regulation that allows firms that lack market power to enter into almost any sort of distribution agreement they wish: only a small set of contract clauses are forbidden explicitly. While this approach is still unnecessarily aggressive (for absence of market power means incapacity to cause harm), parties now have a good degree of legal certainty.[42] In the context of Article 102, the Commission was less successful in its reform effort because it was unable to legislate to exempt firms and was bound by its case law. The result is a strangely titled document: Guidance on its Enforcement Priorities in Applying Article 82 of the EC Treaty to Abusive Exclusionary Conduct by Dominant Undertakings.[43] In brief, this guidance provides that the Commission will only exercise its prosecutorial discretion when it considers that the dominant firm's conduct is likely to cause harm to a competitor who is as efficient as the dominant player. There is also more scope for the dominant firm to explain that its seemingly exclusionary conduct is efficient. This might serve to relax the hold that Article 102 has on dominant firms, but the evidence from recent jurisprudence is mixed: in some cases it has supported a more restrictive view,[44] in others it has gone back to its earlier approach,[45] and in the first judgment after the publication of the guidance, it indicated that the role of the rules on competition in the treaty was "precisely to prevent competition from being distorted to the detriment of the public interest, individual undertakings and consumers, thereby ensuring the well-being of the European Union."[46] This broad approach appears to go against the Commission's wish to narrow the scope of the abuse doctrine.

In spite of the fact that Article 102 has been applied fairly infrequently, the aggressive stance taken by the Commission has led some to claim that this has significant negative repercussions globally. The point may be extended to all types of antitrust enforcement, where we might see two harmful effects. One is a global decrease in efficiency because a prohibition in one jurisdiction damages the behavior of those firms that operate globally. For example, if it is too easy to condemn a firm for refusing to license its intellectual property rights in one jurisdiction, then this reduces the global incentive to innovate. A second risk is that a jurisdiction that has strict rules may see a fall in investment, which also has repercussions globally.[47] This line of argument is applicable to any rule of law, and seems to disregard any legitimate interest that countries may have in enforcing law to suit national interests. Of course, a synonym of national interest is protectionism, so there is a difficult line to draw between allowing entities like the European Union to enforce competition laws more aggressively than others because of the belief that this is preferable for welfare[48] and raising concern that the enforcement stance harms global welfare.

The other major kind of conduct against which the Commission proceeds is cartels. Here the Commission's approach is in line with what commentators consider normal: it has strong powers of investigation, a working leniency policy, and it may impose large fines on those who collude, thus hopefully deterring cartels. Controversy over the Commission's cartel policy has two sources: first, it is not particularly clear how far the policy serves to deter future cartels; second, many question the extent to which the procedures comply with fundamental rights. The first point is actually of global concern. The theory of deterrence that is used by all competition authorities is that the expected gains from a cartel should be less than the expected losses that competition law enforcement can yield. The evidence shows that the expected gains far exceed the expected losses even in jurisdictions like the United States where there is a potent mix of public criminal enforcement and punitive damages are awarded in courts.[49] This should put in some perspective the continuous complaints about the fairness of the Commission's procedures. It is true that the Commission prosecutes and judges, subject to appeal to a general Court whose depth of review seems to vary from case to case. It may also be argued that this system is not wholly respectful of the fundamental rights of the defendants, and furthermore that the system is problematic because of a confirmation bias (in other words, once the prosecutor starts, it has few incentives to drop a case halfway through and will instead seek to prove its case).[50] Nevertheless, in cartel cases, the procedural complaints should be read together with the weakness of the enforcement system. Moreover, there is a wider issue about how to secure compliance by corporate actors, and, because of the way people engage with the legal system, the deterrence model used might be inadequate even with significantly higher fines.[51]

In sum, the negative externalities imposed by EU competition law today have been reduced as a result of the deployment of a more economics-based approach. While the effectiveness of the Commission's cartel policy might be questioned, here the Commission contributes to the global battle against cartels, and its enforcement policy should not be seen in isolation: the more jurisdictions pursue global cartels, the more likely it is that the accumulation of fines deters anticompetitive conduct.

Mergers: Commission veto power

Merger control is, in many jurisdictions, an exercise in ex ante review: parties are required to give notification of a planned merger, and it is the role of competition authorities to explore whether the merger is likely to have anticompetitive effects. Potentially, every competition authority with jurisdiction over a merger has veto power. For example, in *Gencor/Lonrho*, the South African government favored the deal, but its wishes were confounded by the European Commission ruling that the merger would have anticompetitive effects in the European Union.[52] In these circumstances the merger cannot be consummated: if the parties were to ignore the decision of the Commission they would be subjected to penalties and their assets in the Union would be used to satisfy these claims. Doing business globally requires regulatory approval by all major competition authorities. Obviously, when a less economically significant national competition authority purports to block a merger, there are ways of circumventing that jurisdiction by not engaging in business there, which would in turn make those agencies more compliant since losing business would be worse than tolerating an anticompetitive merger. As a matter of EU law, the Commission may take into consideration the opinions of the merger held by other agencies (and it did so in the *Gencor* decision) but it is not bound to desist in its enforcement because the merger would favor the economy of another country. Again here, veto power creates the power to impose negative externalities globally when the veto player miscalculates the welfare effects.

The Commission's de facto veto power has led to some very tense moments in cases where the United States granted regulatory clearance and where the European Union was more skeptical about the benevolent effects of certain mergers. In *Boeing/McDonnell Douglas* a merger between two US-based aircraft manufacturers was waved through in the United States for what might appear industrial policy considerations, and the Commission only relented after significant political pressure.[53] However, in *General Electric/Honeywell*, the Commission stood its ground and blocked a merger between two US firms that had been approved by the US authorities. This was in the face of intense lobbying efforts of private players and politicians. There followed a public spat between authorities on both sides, with the Department of Justice accusing the Commission of protecting competitors, not consumers, and the European Commissioner for Competition denying the absence of a well-worked-out theory of harm.[54] This is an odd pair of cases because, if anything, there appeared to be stronger economic grounds for objecting to the first merger, indeed on an appeal brought by General Electric the General Court went on to dismiss most of the objections of the Commission.[55] These two spats have led to some literature exploring to what extent the Commission's merger enforcement is protectionist, but the evidence is mixed.[56] As we will see below, the intense degree of cooperation that is normally found in mergers affecting both the US and the EU markets appear to limit the actual possibility of engaging in protectionist policies.

Interjurisdictional Cooperation

In two types of enforcement fields (cartels and mergers) the European Union cooperates with other competition authorities. At the time of writing there are four bilateral agreements specifically devoted to competition law enforcement and nearly thirty trade agreements with competition provisions.[57] The latter may be read as devices for exporting the EU model of competition law to other countries, a matter which we return to later. Presently we outline the main features of bilateral agreements.

The agreement with the United States, which is also the one that has been used most often, provides a good example of the principal features of these agreements.[58] First, the two sides agree to facilitate coordinated enforcement. To this effect, the parties will exchange information about investigations that affect each other's interests (so, for example, a merger of two US firms notified in the European Union would be brought to the attention of the US agency, and a cartel prosecution started in the United States would be notified to the European Union when European firms are involved). Second, the agreement has provisions to minimize conflict: each will have regard to the important interests of the other party, and there are ad hoc as well as regular consultations that are designed to try and resolve conflicts or just inform each other of the policy approaches they take. Third, the agreement contains a positive comity provision, which was extended in 1998:[59] one side may ask the other to enforce the law when conduct in that state's territory has harmful effects in the requesting side's territory. This avoids extraterritorial enforcement based on the effects test, but it relies on the other side's willingness to spend resources for conduct of which it might even tacitly approve. In 2011, after twenty years of cooperation, there was a further burst of cooperation, with the agencies issuing revised Best Practices on Cooperation in Merger Investigations. These guidelines cement the cooperation structures that have been put into place. In particular, they emphasize the need for early discussion on remedies and the importance of encouraging parties to the merger to waive confidentiality so more information may be shared.

The result of these provisions has been to diffuse tensions by allowing the two sides to have a formal channel of communication; it has also been helped by the greater convergence in enforcement priorities and substantive approaches by the two agencies.[60] For instance, in a number of merger cases, the two authorities have agreed on the assessments and have notified each other of specific competition concerns.[61] This secures benefits for the parties as well because remedies (e.g., divestitures of assets) are coordinated. Similarly, in the ongoing Google investigation, the US and EU agencies cooperated, even if it appears that the latter will seek more far-reaching remedies than the former. Of course, informed divergence will not suffice if either agency acts against a national champion of the other, for example, a number of congressmen, in a letter to the Federal Trade Commission, reported their concerns over a "troublesome trend in Europe towards regulatory protectionism" when the Commission imposed a substantial fine on Intel.[62] However, *Intel* is a decision where the Commission applied its new economics-based approach, seeking to establish that Intel's discount schemes would likely have excluded rivals as efficient as Intel. It is likely that the political opposition merely stems from a feeling that since in the United States Intel escaped with mild antitrust intervention, the EU approach seems excessive.[63] Indeed, it appears that occasionally informed divergence between the two authorities is exploited for political motivations.[64] Conversely, there remain rumors that some Commission decisions are informed by the reluctance to contradict the approach taken by the US authorities. Political pressure by large countries is inevitable, and the task for authorities is to manage the delicate task of maximizing enforcement while minimizing political fallout.[65]

Cartel Hypocrisy

Sometimes when you need a cartel the government can help. In 1994 there was a glut of aluminum as a result of the collapse of the Soviet Union, and the price plummeted. Western corporations, with the help of the US government, orchestrated a cartel whereby output was reduced (and the US government gave Russia a promise of financial help in return for also cooperating in this arrangement). The cartel was allowed to overcharge customers worldwide, and was not prosecuted, not even by the European Commission, which could not have been unaware of the cartel as it collaborated in its formation.[66] This episode suggests that competition law can take second place even in states where the antitrust rules are said to have constitutional value.

The more widespread example of cartel hypocrisy, however, is the tolerance of export cartels. These are agreements that coordinate export trade, either fixing prices or dividing markets. The creation of these cartels is expressly provided for in some jurisdictions, where export cartels may be registered.[67] Under EU law, there is no legislative instrument that expressly allows export cartels, but they are implicitly excluded because they do not affect trade between member states. The issue was touched upon in *Javico v. YSL*, which concerned an agreement for the sale of perfumes in territories outside the European Union, and where the distributor was forbidden from reimporting them into the European Union. This was designed to facilitate the penetration of foreign markets and the Court held that normally this arrangement would not affect trade within the Union unless specific circumstances showed the opposite to be the case, such as higher prices in the Union which would be reduced by reimports from outside.[68] Transposed to export cartels, one would have to examine how far an export cartel prevented improved conditions of competition in the European Union. It is likely that this would be the case only if there were also a cartel within the European Union, so a pure export cartel would cause harm (if any) only outside EU territory. This implicit tolerance of export cartels makes it harder to discover them.[69] The consequence of this is that when these cartels export to states with weak or no antitrust law enforcement, then the anticompetitive conduct may be carried out with impunity.[70] Even with an active competition authority abroad, securing evidence of the cartel may be problematic because the relevant evidence is likely situated in the export state, and unless there are bilateral agreements to facilitate discovery then it is impossible to prove the existence of the export cartel.[71] Moreover, a competition authority acting against an export cartel risks retaliatory measures: the exporting state may direct its competition authority to act against an export cartel of the other.[72]

Some claim that export cartels may enhance efficiency: exporters pool resources to target new markets more effectively and, absent the cartel, there would be no exports or higher prices. However, it is difficult to justify penalizing domestic cartels as hardcore restraints while remaining unconcerned about export cartels: at the very least, members of an export cartel should have the burden of showing the countervailing efficiencies that result from their agreements. On the other hand, while export cartels may damage importers, a number of developing countries rely on export cartels, sometimes with state support, as a necessary means to secure export markets. This suggests that diplomatic rather than antitrust enforcement may be a more delicate means of addressing export cartels.

Global Initiatives

It was at the League of Nations Economic Conference in 1927 that the importance of global control of anticompetitive conduct was first mentioned in the modern era; however, attempts to establish binding rules have so far not yielded any tangible result.[73] Between 1995 and 2004 the European Union and the United States (the principal global players in antitrust enforcement) pursued two different agendas to resolve some of the problems we have already noted. The European Union wished for competition law to be incorporated into the World Trade Organization (WTO) Agreement. The WTO would not be turned into a global antitrust agency, but there would be an agreement whereby contracting parties would implement an agreed competition law at national level.[74] However the United States opposed this for two reasons: first, that any global code would be the result of compromise and so be a watered-down version of the US rules; second, that transferring enforcement to a new body was inappropriate given the existing mechanisms of enforcement found at national level.[75] In spite of these objections, a WTO working group to study this issue was established. However, in 2004 the WTO's General Council agreed not to put this issue on the trade agenda. Indeed, the initiative was resisted by a number of WTO members, in particular developing countries that considered that the costs of setting up competition authorities would be too high and that the requirement to apply these rules would be too inflexible and not suit their national industrial policies.[76] The US strategy instead was: first, to engage in bilateral cooperation with other states and establish agreements to cooperate in enforcing law in discrete cases; second, to develop soft laws under the auspices of the Organisation for Economic Co-operation and Development, which resulted, for example, in a *Recommendation Concerning Effective Action Against Hard Core Cartels* in 1998;[77] third, it backed the creation of a global network of competition authorities.[78] This resulted in the establishment of the ICN in 2001,[79] the major site for antitrust global governance today.[80]

In the first ten years, the major tasks of the ICN were broadly in line with those envisaged by the United States, in particular it was based upon resolving practical problems through convergence in procedure and substantive law. One issue it tackled early on was streamlining merger notifications and assessment: it is well known that large mergers require vetting by many agencies, and the work effort here was designed to minimize the burdens firms faced. Since 2004, it has also worked on strengthening cartel enforcement. Here the aim is to identify best practices to strengthen national competition authorities. In both of these policy fields, the ICN published guidance notes or best practice guidelines. These documents are prepared by taking into consideration the input of its members. Nothing is binding, however, as with any network, the expectation is that members of this kind of club should follow the recommendations set. One criticism that may be leveled at the ICN is that it focuses more on the interests of firms (facilitating merger notifications) and not enough on the interests of the majority of its members, which are developing countries. In response it may be noted that the ICN has, from the start, worked on competition advocacy, that is, developing ideas on how the competition authorities may best advise the government of the anticompetitive effects of its legislation, and how the authority can work towards explaining to the public the benefits of its actions. However, again, one might be critical of these efforts as merely being designed to facilitate investment by firms in developing countries, and not being about linking competition enforcement and development.[81]

More recently, the ICN has shifted its priorities slightly and, to some extent, this may play into the hands of the European Union.[82] First, it has sought to achieve greater convergence in the regulation of unilateral conduct. Here the permissive attitude of US antitrust (evidenced both by the absence of prosecutions and by the rulings of the Supreme Court that show a reluctance to read the monopolization provision of the Sherman Act expansively) is at odds with the more interventionist stance taken by many other jurisdictions. The extent to which the best practices diverge from the US approach will serve as a litmus test for the collegial nature of the network; whether the United States will be convinced to modify its approach remains a different question altogether. However, some of the highly technical discussions on predatory pricing may well be lost on agencies that lack the resources and the skills to implement such advance methods of enforcement.[83] Second, the ICN has more recently begun to tolerate some informed divergence among its members.[84] However, this is hard to reconcile with the mission of the ICN, which is "to advocate the adoption of superior standards and procedures in competition policy around the world, [and to] formulate proposals for procedural and substantive convergence."[85] Finally, the ICN has sought to facilitate cooperation among members, not only by dint of regular meetings whereby officials can build working relationships but also more formally by trying to replicate, at a less intense and formal level, the kind of cooperation we noted in bilateral agreements. This begun with cartel enforcement in 2007 and may also spill over into other fields of enforcement.[86]

Conclusions

It is a paradox that while there is substantial agreement over the content and purpose of competition law, there has been no agreement to establish a global antitrust authority or even formulate globally applicable rules.[87] In the European Union, supranational competition law enforcement was probably achieved by accident in that the expectations of robust antitrust enforcement by the Commission were low in the 1950s.[88] However, now the Union has exclusive competence in the field of competition law and Regulation 1/2003 creates a framework to control the decentralized application of competition law by national competition authorities.[89] In Europe, as elsewhere, competition policy has become a technocratic enterprise: the political repercussions of competitive markets have been sidelined in favor of an approach that relies on identifying harm to economic welfare and is enforced by expert bodies. It remains to be seen whether in the present economic climate this trend is countered by more political oversight in the regulation of markets. At the time of this writing, the view that more competitive markets are a way out of the crisis still has a sufficient hold on policymakers.[90]

Turning to the global, the sources of conflict have been numbed by bilateral agreements and by the ICN. However, enforcement that harms national interests of other countries remains risky, and no amount of cooperation can minimize the politicization of decisions one side sees as legitimate and the other as going beyond what competition law is all about. With a less negative perspective, one may observe how political disagreement is usually followed by deeper cooperation among agencies: solidarity among agencies is further entrenched by the work of the ICN and other networks.

Generally speaking, the European Union is perceived to be a weak global player, and its failure to secure agreement to have competition part of the WTO agreement might be said to evidence this. However, the Union has been successful in exporting its brand of competition law enforcement in a number of countries through trade agreements. This means that a not insignificant portion of members of the ICN will look to the European Union for examples of good practices; furthermore, as the ICN develops further into a transnational governance forum,[91] the result may be not so different from what the Commission wished for.

Notes

1 R. Daniel Kelemen, *Eurolegalism: The Transformation of Law and Regulation in the European Union* (Cambridge, MA: Harvard University Press, 2011), 143.

2 For a general overview, see Stephen Wilks, "Competition Policy: Towards an Economic Constitution?" in *Policy-Making in the European Union*, ed. Helen Wallace, Mark A. Pollack, and Alasdair R. Young (Oxford: Oxford University Press, 2010).

3 David J. Gerber, *Law and Competition in Twentieth Century Europe* (Oxford: Oxford University Press, 1998), Chap. 9; and Harm G. Schröter, "Cartelization and Decartelization in Europe, 1870–1995: Rise and Decline of an Economic Institution," *Journal of European Economic History* 25 (1996).

4 See Leon Brittan, *Competition Policy and Merger Control in the Single European Market* (Cambridge: Grotius, 1991), recalling the negotiations he conducted.

5 Council Regulation (EC) 139/2004 of 20 January 2004 on the control of concentrations between undertakings [2004] OJ L 24/1. For possible solutions to national protectionism, see Damien Gerard, "Protectionist Threats against Cross-Border Mergers: Unexplored Avenues to Strengthen the Effectiveness of Article 21 ECMR," *Common Market Law Review* 45 (2008).

6 See Leigh Hancher, Tom Ottervanger, and Piet Jan Slot, *EU State Aids* (London: Sweet & Maxwell, 2012) for a general overview.

7 Michael Blauberger, "Of Good and Bad Subsidies: European State Aid Control through Soft and Hard Law," *West European Politics* 32 (2009).

8 Mario Monti, *A New Strategy for the Single Market: At the Service of Europe's Economy and Society*, Report to the President of the European Commission José Manuel Barroso, 9 May 2010.

9 In addition, among some scholars there is a resistance to the kind of capitalism being promoted by competition law enforcement. Hubert Buch-Hansen and Angela Wigger, *The Politics of European Competition Regulation: A Critical Political Economy Perspective* (Abingdon: Routledge, 2011).

10 Joined Cases 100/80 to 103/80 *Musique diffusion française and Others v. Commission* EU:C:1983:158, paras 105–109.

11 Case C-344/98 *Masterfoods Ltd v. HB Ice Cream Ltd* EU:C:2000:689. However, stricter national competition law could apply.

12 Article 1 of Law of 10 October 1990, n 287, Gazzetta Ufficiale del 13 Ottobre 1990, n 240.

13 Competition Act 1998, s 60.

14 EU Commission White Paper on Modernisation of the Rules Implementing Articles 81 and 82 of the EC Treaty (formerly Articles 85 and 86 of the EC Treaty) [1999] OJ C 132/1. See Rein Wesseling, *The Modernization of EC Antitrust Law* (Oxford: Hart, 2000) for a critique.

15 Council Regulation (EC) No 1/2003 of 16 December 2002 on the implementation of the rules on competition laid down in Articles 81 and 82 of the Treaty [2003] OJ L 1/1. For background and an assessment, see Wouter P.J. Wils, "Ten Years of Regulation 1/2003 – A Retrospective," *Journal of European Competition Law and Practice* 4 (2013).

16 Commission staff working paper accompanying the Communication from the Commission to the European Parliament and Council – Report on the functioning of Regulation 1/2003 SEC(2009) 574 final.

17 Office of Fair Trading's guidance as to the appropriate amount of a penalty (OFT 423, September 2012), para 2.10. For Germany, see Christof Vollmer in Günter Hirsch, Frank Montag, and Franz Jürgen Säcker, eds., *Münchener Kommentar zum Europäischen und Deutschen Wettbewerbsrecht (Kartellrecht)*, vol. 2 (München: C.H. Beck, 2008), section 81, para 128, taking the view that only effects in Germany may be taken into account when imposing a fine. The Commission reports of a cartel case where the Belgian and German competition authorities imposed fines with reference to the effects in their respective territories (Commission staff working paper accompanying the Communication from the Commission to the European Parliament and Council – Report on the functioning of Regulation 1/2003 SEC(2009) 574 final, para 223).

18 *Secretary of State for Health & Ors v. Servier Laboratories Ltd & Ors* [2013] EWCA Civ 1234.

19 Proposal for a Directive on certain rules governing actions for damages under national law for infringements of the competition law provisions of the member states and of the EU, COM(2013) 404 final. Anneli Howard, "Too Little, Too Late? The European Commission's Legislative Proposal on Anti-Trust Damages Actions," *Journal of European Competition Law and Practice* 4 (2013).

20 *Hartford Fire Insurance Co. v. California* 509 US 764 (1993).

21 Indeed, it has even been used by the United States to demand reforms of national laws abroad when this restricted market access for US goods, especially against Japan. See Department of Justice Antitrust Enforcement Policy Regarding Anticompetitive Conduct that Restricts US Exports (3 April 1992, available at: http://www.justice.gov/atr/public/press_releases/1992/211137.htm). For discussion, see Hiroko Yamane and Shingo Seryo, "Restrictive Practices and Market Access in Japan – Has the JFTC Been Effective in Eliminating Barriers in Distribution?" *World Competition* 22 (1999); and Hiroshi

Yamada, "Japanese Antitrust Law: Recent Developments and an Agenda for the Years Ahead," *Journal of European Competition Law and Practice* 2 (2011).

22 Case 48/69 *ICI v. Commission* (Dyestuffs) EU:C:1972:70, paras 130–141.

23 Joined Cases 89/85, 104/85, 114/85, 116/85, 117/85, and 125/85 to 129/85 *Ahlström Osakeyhtiö and others v. Commission* EU:C:1988:447.

24 For further criticism of this kind of formalism, see Florian Wagner-von Papp, "Competition Law and Extraterritoriality," in *Research Handbook on International Competition Law*, ed. Ariel Ezrachi (Cheltenham: Edward Elgar, 2012), 43–47.

25 Case COMP/F/38.899 *Gas insulated switchgear* (decision of 24 January 2007).

26 COMP/C-3/37.792 *Microsoft* (decision of 24 March 2004) paras 990–993 on the effect on trade between member states. While there were Microsoft subsidiaries established in the European Union, it is not clear that the abuse in question emanated from there.

27 Council Regulation (EC) No 139/2004 on the control of concentrations between undertakings [2004] OJ L 24/1, Article 1.

28 Case T-102/96 *Gencor v. Commission* EU:T:1997:82, para 90. The Court's judgment leaves some uncertainty about the specific nature of these effects.

29 Bruno Zanettin, "The Evolution of EC International Competition Policy," in *EC Competition Law: A Critical Assessment*, ed. Giuliano Amato and Claus-Dieter Ehlermann (Oxford: Hart, 2007), 762–763.

30 Case 48/69 *Dyestuffs*, n 22 this chapter.

31 Joined Cases 6/73 and 7/73 *Istituto Chemioterapico Italiano and Commercial Solvents v. Commission* EU:C:1974:18.

32 John Griffin, "Foreign Governmental Reactions to US Assertions of Extraterritorial Jurisdiction," *European Competition Law Review* 19 (1998).

33 Article 1 bis, Law No 68-678 of 26 July 1968, as modified by Law No 80-538 of 16 July 1980. For discussion, see B.C. Toms, "The French Response to the Extraterritorial Application of United States Antitrust Laws," *International Lawyer* 15 (1981).

34 Foreign Proceedings (Excess of Jurisdiction) Act 1984, s 10.

35 Douglas E. Rosental and William M. Knighton, *National Laws and International Commerce: The Problem of Extraterritoriality* (London: Routledge & Kegan Paul, 1982).

36 Damien Neven, Pénelope Papandropoulos, and Paul Seabright, *Trawling for Minnows: European Competition Policy and Agreements between Firms* (London: Centre for Economic Policy Research, 1998).

37 Case 27/76 *United Brands v. Commission* EU:C:1978:22.

38 Joined Cases 6/73 and 7/73 *Istituto Chemioterapico Italiano*, n 31 this chapter.

39 John Kallaugher and Brian Sher, "Rebates Revisited: Anti-Competitive Effects and Exclusionary Abuse under Article 82," *European Competition Law Review* (2004).

40 Eleanor M. Fox, "We Protect Competition, You Protect Competitors," *World Competition* 26 (2003).

41 Generally, see David J. Gerber, "Two Forms of Modernization in European Competition Law," *Fordham International Law Journal* 31 (2008).

42 Commission Regulation (EU) No 330/2010 of 20 April 2010 on the application of Article 101(3) of the Treaty on the Functioning of the European Union to categories of vertical agreements and concerted practices [2010] OJ L 102/1.

43 [2009] OJ C 45/7. For discussion, see Liza Lovdhal Gormsen, *A Principled Approach to Abuse of Dominance in EC Competition Law* (Cambridge: Cambridge University Press, 2012).

44 Notably in Case C-209/10 *Post Danmark A/S v. Konkurrencerådet* EU:C:2012:172.

45 Case C-549/10 P *Tomra and others v. Commission* EU:C:2012:221.

46 Case C-52/09 *Konkurrensverket v. TeliaSonera Sverige AB* EU:C:2011:83, para 22.

47 Michal S. Gal and A. Jorge Padilla, "The Follower Phenomenon: Implications for the Design of Monopolization Rules in a Global Economy," *Antitrust Law Journal* 76 (2010).

48 Josef Drexl, "Real Knowledge Is to Know the Extent of One's Own Ignorance: On the Consumer Harm Approach in Innovation-Related Competition Cases," *Antitrust Law Journal* 76 (2010).

49 John M. Connor and Robert H. Lande, "Cartels as 'Rational Business Strategy: Crime Pays,'" *Cardozo Law Review* 34 (2012).
50 Ivo van Bael, *Due Process in EU Competition Proceedings* (The Hague: Kluwer, 2011).
51 Christine Parker, "The War on Cartels and the Social Meaning of Deterrence," *Regulation & Governance* 7 (2013).
52 Case IV/M.619 *Gencor/Lonrho* [1997] OJ L 11/30.
53 Case M 877 [1997] OJ L 336/16. For comment, see William Kovacic, "Transatlantic Turbulence: The Boeing–McDonnell Douglas Merger and International Competition Policy," *Antitrust Law Journal* 68 (2001).
54 For an excellent account, see Eleanor M. Fox, "GE/Honeywell: The US Merger that Europe Stopped – A Story of the Politics of Convergence," in *Antitrust Stories*, ed. Eleanor M. Fox and Daniel A. Crane (New York: Foundation Press, 2007).
55 Case T-210/01 *General Electric v. Commission* EU:T:2005:456.
56 Compare Nihat Aktas, Eric de Bodt, and Richard Roll, "Is European M&A Regulation Protectionist?" *The Economic Journal* 117 (2007), with Tomaso Duso, Klaus Gugler, and Burchin Yurtoglu, "How Effective is European Merger Control?" *European Economic Review* 55 (2011).
57 For a thorough assessment, see Anestis S. Papadopolous, *The International Dimension of EU Competition Law and Policy* (Cambridge: Cambridge University Press, 2010), Chap. 4 and 5.
58 Agreement between the Government of the United States of America and the Commission of the European Communities regarding the application of their competition laws [1995] OJ L 95/47.
59 Agreement between the European Communities and the Government of the United States of America on the application of positive comity principles in the enforcement of their competition laws [1998] OJ L 173/26.
60 For a good account, see Zanettin, "The Evolution of EC International Competition Policy," 770–780.
61 E.g., Case No COMP/M.6381 *Google/Motorola*, decision of 13 February 2012; Case M.6541 *UTC/Goodrich*, decision of 26 July 2012.
62 Editorial, "Microchips and Monopoly," *New York Times*, 27 October 2009. See also, Keith N. Hylton, Geoffrey A. Manne, and Joshua D. Wright, "US Antitrust Becomes More European," *Forbes*, 18 May 2009.
63 Case COMP/C-3/37.990 *Intel* (Summary Decision) [2009] OJ C 227/13; The FTC settled in 2010: Intel Docket No. 9341 (4 August 2010).
64 See also Zanettin, "The Evolution of EC International Competition Policy," 776–777, noting that the Boeing/MDD merger was one where the two agencies cooperated while politicians used the more populist language of conflict.
65 Alasdair Roberts, *The Logic of Discipline* (Oxford: Oxford University Press, 2010), Chap. 6.
66 Joseph Stiglitz, *Globalisation and Its Discontents* (London: Penguin, 2002), 173–176. For more detail, see Frédéric Jenny, "Competition Law and Policy: Global Governance Issues," *World Competition* 26 (2003).
67 Margaret C. Levenstein and Valerie Y. Suslow, "The Changing International Status of Export Cartel Exemptions," *American University International Law Review* 20 (2005).
68 Case C-306/96 *Javico International and Javico AG v. Yves Saint Laurent Parfums SA* EU:C:1998:173.
69 Levenstein and Suslow, "The Changing International Status of Export Cartel Exemptions."
70 Aditya Bhattacharjea, "Export Cartels: A Developing Country Perspective," *Journal of World Trade* 38 (2004).
71 Cf. the UK/US Mutual Legal Assistance Treaty, Cm5375 (2001).
72 Frédéric Jenny, "Export Cartels in Primary Products: The Potash Case in Perspective," in *Trade, Competition and the Pricing of Commodities*, ed. Simon J. Evenett and Frédéric Jenny (London: Centre for Economic Policy Research, 2012).
73 Gabrielle Marceau, *Anti-Dumping and Anti-Trust Issues in Free-Trade Areas* (Oxford: Clarendon, 1994); and David J. Gerber, *Global Competition: Law, Markets and Globalisation* (New York: Oxford University Press, 2010).

74 The key document is European Commission, *Towards an International Framework of Competition Rules*, COM(1996) 284 final.

75 Joel Klein, "Anticipating the Millennium: International Antitrust Enforcement at the End of the Twentieth Century," in *Annual Proceedings of the Fordham Corporate Law Institute: International Antitrust Law and Practice*, ed. Barry Hawk (Yonkers, NY: Juris, 1998), 9.

76 A good overview is in the report of the meeting of the Working Group on the Interaction between Trade and Competition Policy (9 July 2003, WT/WGTCP/M/22).

77 C(98)35/final.

78 International Competition Policy Advisory Committee to the Attorney General and Assistant Attorney General for Antitrust, *Final Report* (2000).

79 Paul Lugard, ed., *The International Competition Network at Ten: Origins, Accomplishments and Aspirations* (Cambridge: Intersentia, 2011).

80 Imelda Maher and Anestis Papadopolous, "Competition Agency Networks around the World," in Ezrachi, *Research Handbook on International Competition Law*, review all other networks.

81 For an elegant critique, see Katrhyn McMahon, "Competition Law and Developing Economies: Between 'Informed Divergence' and International Convergence," in Ezrachi, *Research Handbook on International Competition Law*, and generally, see Richard Whish and Christopher Townley, eds., *New Competition Jurisdictions: Shaping Policies and Building Institutions* (Cheltenham: Edward Elgar, 2012).

82 Here I do not follow the position of the ICN, which has set out what it has achieved in its first decade and now has a plan for the second decade. (See the documents relating to the ICN's "second decade project" at http://www.internationalcompetitionnetwork.org/second-decade.aspx). Ten-year planning is desirable from the network's perspective, but it hides continuity and incremental change.

83 Giorgio Monti, "Unilateral Conduct: The Search for Global Standards," in Ezrachi, *Research Handbook on International Competition Law*.

84 Brendan Sweeney, "International Competition Law and Policy: A Work in Progress," *Melbourne Journal of International Law* 10 (2009): 63.

85 This is set out on the home page of the ICN: http://www.internationalcompetitionnetwork.org/.

86 ICN Cartels Working Group, *Cooperation between Competition Agencies in Cartel Investigations* (May 2007).

87 Daniel Crane, *The Institutional Structure of Antitrust Enforcement* (Oxford: Oxford University Press, 2011), Chap. 12.

88 Ernst J. Mestmacker, "Towards a Concept of a Workable European Competition Law: Revisiting the Formative Period," in *The Historical Foundations of EU Competition Law*, ed. Kiran K. Patel and Heike Schweitzer (Oxford: Oxford University Press, 2013).

89 For discussion on what exclusive competence might mean, see Giorgio Monti, "Legislative and Executive Competences in Competition Law," in *The Question of Competence in the European Union*, ed. Loïc Azoulai (Oxford: Oxford University Press, 2014).

90 Damian Chalmers, Gareth Davies, and Giorgio Monti, *European Union Law – Text and Materials* (Cambridge: Cambridge University Press, 2014), Chap. 22.

91 Marie-Laure Djelic, "International Competition Network," in *Handbook of Transnational Governance: Institutions and Innovations*, ed. Thomas Hale and David Held (Cambridge: Polity Press, 2011).

References

Aktas, Nihat, Eric de Bodt, and Richard Roll. "Is European M&A Regulation Protectionist?" *The Economic Journal* 117 (2007): 1096–1121.

Bhattacharjea, Aditya. "Export Cartels: A Developing Country Perspective." *Journal of World Trade* 38 (2004): 331–359.

Blauberger, Michael. "Of Good and Bad Subsidies: European State Aid Control through Soft and Hard Law." *West European Politics* 32 (2009): 719–737.
Brittan, Leon. *Competition Policy and Merger Control in the Single European Market*. Cambridge: Grotius, 1991.
Buch-Hansen, Hubert, and Angela Wigger. *The Politics of European Competition Regulation: A Critical Political Economy Perspective*. Abingdon: Routledge, 2011.
Chalmers, Damian, Gareth Davies, and Giorgio Monti. *European Union Law – Text and Materials*. Cambridge: Cambridge University Press, 2014.
Connor, John M., and Robert H. Lande. "Cartels as 'Rational Business Strategy: Crime Pays.'" *Cardozo Law Review* 34 (2012): 427–490.
Crane, Daniel. *The Institutional Structure of Antitrust Enforcement*. Oxford: Oxford University Press, 2011.
Djelic, Marie-Laure. "International Competition Network." In *Handbook of Transnational Governance: Institutions and Innovations*, edited by Thomas Hale and David Held, 80–88. Cambridge: Polity Press, 2011.
Drexl, Josef. "Real Knowledge Is to Know the Extent of One's Own Ignorance: On the Consumer Harm Approach in Innovation-Related Competition Cases." *Antitrust Law Journal* 76 (2010): 677–708.
Duso, Tomaso, Klaus Gugler, and Burchin Yurtoglu. "How Effective is European Merger Control?" *European Economic Review* 55 (2011): 980–1006.
Ezrachi, Ariel, ed. *Research Handbook on International Competition Law*. Cheltenham: Edward Elgar, 2012.
Fox, Eleanor M. "We Protect Competition, You Protect Competitors." *World Competition* 26 (2003): 149–165.
Fox, Eleanor M. "GE/Honeywell: The US Merger that Europe Stopped – A Story of the Politics of Convergence." In *Antitrust Stories*, edited by Eleanor M. Fox and Daniel A. Crane, 331–360. New York: Foundation Press, 2007.
Gal, Michal S., and A. Jorge Padilla. "The Follower Phenomenon: Implications for the Design of Monopolization Rules in a Global Economy." *Antitrust Law Journal* 76 (2010): 899–928.
Gerard, Damien. "Protectionist Threats Against Cross-Border Mergers: Unexplored Avenues to Strengthen the Effectiveness of Article 21 ECMR." *Common Market Law Review* 45 (2008): 987–1025.
Gerber, David J. *Law and Competition in Twentieth Century Europe*. Oxford: Oxford University Press, 1998.
Gerber, David J. "Two Forms of Modernization in European Competition Law." *Fordham International Law Journal* 31 (2008): 1235–1265.
Gerber, David J. *Global Competition: Law, Markets and Globalisation*. New York: Oxford University Press, 2010.
Griffin, John. "Foreign Governmental Reactions to US Assertions of Extraterritorial Jurisdiction." *European Competition Law Review* 19 (1998): 64–73.
Hancher, Leigh, Tom Ottervanger, and Piet Jan Slot. *EU State Aids*. London: Sweet & Maxwell, 2012.
Hirsch, Günter, Frank Montag, and Franz Jürgen Säcker, eds. *Münchener Kommentar zum Europäischen und Deutschen Wettbewerbsrecht (Kartellrecht)*. Vol. 2. Munich: C.H. Beck, 2008.
Howard, Anneli. "Too Little, Too Late? The European Commission's Legislative Proposal on Anti-Trust Damages Actions." *Journal of European Competition Law and Practice* 4 (2013): 455–464.
Hylton, Keith N., Geoffrey A. Manne, and Joshua D. Wright. "US Antitrust Becomes More European." *Forbes*, 18 May 2009.
Jenny, Frédéric. "Competition Law and Policy: Global Governance Issues." *World Competition* 26 (2003): 609–624.
Jenny, Frédéric. "Export Cartels in Primary Products: The Potash Case in Perspective." In *Trade, Competition and the Pricing of Commodities*, edited by Simon J. Evenett and Frédéric Jenny, 99–132 (London: Centre for Economic Policy Research, 2012).
Kallaugher, John, and Brian Sher. "Rebates Revisited: Anti-Competitive Effects and Exclusionary Abuse under Article 82." *European Competition Law Review* (2004): 263–285.

Kelemen, R. Daniel. *Eurolegalism: The Transformation of Law and Regulation in the European Union*. Cambridge, MA: Harvard University Press, 2011.

Klein, Joel. "Anticipating the Millennium: International Antitrust Enforcement at the End of the Twentieth Century." In *Annual Proceedings of the Fordham Corporate Law Institute: International Antitrust Law and Practice*, edited by Barry Hawk, 1–12. Yonkers, NY: Juris, 1998.

Kovacic, William. "Transatlantic Turbulence: The Boeing–McDonnell Douglas Merger and International Competition Policy." *Antitrust Law Journal* 68 (2001): 805–873.

Levenstein, Margaret C., and Valerie Y. Suslow. "The Changing International Status of Export Cartel Exemptions." *American University International Law Review* 20 (2005): 785–828.

Lovdhal Gormsen, Liza. *A Principled Approach to Abuse of Dominance in EC Competition Law*. Cambridge: Cambridge University Press, 2012.

Lugard, Paul, ed. *The International Competition Network at Ten: Origins, Accomplishments and Aspirations*. Cambridge: Intersentia, 2011.

Maher, Imelda, and Anestis Papadopolous. "Competition Agency Networks around the World." In Ezrachi, *Research Handbook on International Competition Law*, 60–88.

Marceau, Gabrielle. *Anti-Dumping and Anti-Trust Issues in Free-Trade Areas*. Oxford: Clarendon Press, 1994.

McMahon, Katrhyn. "Competition Law and Developing Economies: Between 'Informed Divergence' and International Convergence. " In Ezrachi, *Research Handbook on International Competition Law*, 209–237.

Mestmacker, Ernst J. "Towards a Concept of a Workable European Competition Law: Revisiting the Formative Period." In *The Historical Foundations of EU Competition Law*, edited by Kiran K. Patel and Heike Schweitzer, 191–206. Oxford: Oxford University Press, 2013.

Monti, Giorgio. "Unilateral Conduct: The Search for Global Standards." In Ezrachi, *Research Handbook on International Competition Law*, 345–368.

Monti, Giorgio. "Legislative and Executive Competences in Competition Law." In *The Question of Competence in the European Union*, edited by Loïc Azoulai, 101–124. Oxford: Oxford University Press, 2014.

Neven, Damien, Pénelope Papandropoulos, and Paul Seabright. *Trawling for Minnows: European Competition Policy and Agreements between Firms*. London: Centre for Economic Policy Research, 1998.

Papadopolous, Anestis S. *The International Dimension of EU Competition Law and Policy*. Cambridge: Cambridge University Press, 2010.

Parker, Christine. "The War on Cartels and the Social Meaning of Deterrence." *Regulation & Governance* 7 (2013): 174–194.

Roberts, Alasdair. *The Logic of Discipline*. Oxford: Oxford University Press, 2010.

Rosental, Douglas E., and William M. Knighton. *National Laws and International Commerce: The Problem of Extraterritoriality*. London: Routledge & Kegan Paul, 1982.

Schröter, Harm G. "Cartelization and Decartelization in Europe, 1870–1995: Rise and Decline of an Economic Institution." *Journal of European Economic History* 25 (1996): 129–153.

Stiglitz, Joseph. *Globalisation and Its Discontents*. London: Penguin, 2002.

Sweeney, Brendan. "International Competition Law and Policy: A Work in Progress." *Melbourne Journal of International Law* 10 (2009): 58–69.

Toms, B.C. "The French Response to the Extraterritorial Application of United States Antitrust Laws." *International Lawyer* 15 (1981): 585–614.

van Bael, Ivo. *Due Process in EU Competition Proceedings*. The Hague: Kluwer, 2011.

Wagner-von Papp, Florian. "Competition Law and Extraterritoriality." In Ezrachi, *Research Handbook on International Competition Law*, 21–59.

Wesseling, Rein. *The Modernization of EC Antitrust Law*. Oxford: Hart, 2000.

Whish, Richard, and Christopher Townley, eds. *New Competition Jurisdictions: Shaping Policies and Building Institutions*. Cheltenham: Edward Elgar, 2012.

Wilks, Stephen. "Competition Policy: Towards an Economic Constitution?" In *Policy-Making in the European Union*, edited by Helen Wallace, Mark A. Pollack, and Alasdair R. Young, 133–155. Oxford: Oxford University Press, 2010.

Wils, Wouter P.J. "Ten Years of Regulation 1/2003 – A Retrospective." *Journal of European Competition Law and Practice* 4 (2013): 293–301.

Yamada, Hiroshi. "Japanese Antitrust Law: Recent Developments and an Agenda for the Years Ahead." *Journal of European Competition Law and Practice* 2 (2011): 165–169.

Yamane, Hiroko, and Shingo Seryo. "Restrictive Practices and Market Access in Japan – Has the JFTC Been Effective in Eliminating Barriers in Distribution?" *World Competition* 22 (1999): 1–39.

Zanettin, Bruno. "The Evolution of EC International Competition Policy." In *EC Competition Law: A Critical Assessment*, edited by Giuliano Amato and Claus-Dieter Ehlermann, 759–96. Oxford: Hart, 2007.

23

EU State Aids Law

Piet Jan Slot

Introduction

State aids law has become a major subject in its own right.[1] Massive amounts of state aid are granted by member states eager to protect the worldwide competiveness of their industries. In the European Union, state aid is also an important element in furthering social and regional objectives. The apogee of this development is now reflected in the recent spectacular Commission decisions in the banking sector. Large amounts of state aid have been authorized by the Commission, sometimes in less than a week.[2] The Commission provides an annual overview of the state aid by member states.[3]

Article 107 of the Treaty on the Functioning of the European Union (TFEU), which lays down the substantive rules on state aid, and Article 108 TFEU, which provides for the procedural rules, form part of the treaty chapter on competition. The guiding concept of the rules on state aids is found in Protocol (No 27) to the Treaty of Lisbon on the internal market and competition (the text of this Protocol is identical to former Article 3(1)(g) of the Treaty establishing the European Community (EC)) – a system ensuring that competition in the internal market is not distorted. This is reflected in the case law of the Court of Justice of the European Union (CJEU) and in numerous Commission decisions. Unlike the provisions on competition (Articles 101 and 102 TFEU), the rules on state aid have taken shape only slowly. Until the end of the 1990s, the major developments took place in the decisional practice of the Commission and in the case law of the Community courts, the Court of Justice and the General Court (GC), rather than in the form of legislation: indeed, there was very little legislation in the state aid field.[4]

However, there are now several important pieces of legislation. The first is Council Regulation 994/98/EC, which applies Articles 107 and 108 TFEU.[5] The gist of the regulation is that the Commission is authorized to adopt block exemptions for certain categories of aid. On this basis, the Commission has adopted a number of regulations, which will be discussed later in the chapter. The most important Council regulation is Regulation 659/99/EC, which lays down detailed rules for the application of Article 108 TFEU.[6] The regulation is largely a codification of the case law of the Court of Justice and the GC. The substantive rules have been

A Companion to European Union Law and International Law, First Edition.
Edited by Dennis Patterson and Anna Södersten.

developed over recent years in the case law, as well as in a number of Commission documents called guidelines, frameworks, notifications, or communications.[7] These rules have been further developed in the many decisions given by the Commission in individual cases.

Material Principles

The structure of Article 107 TFEU is not unlike that of Article 101 TFEU. Therefore, a systematic analysis of the different elements contained in this article will be useful, as it is for Article 101 TFEU. The following four criteria must be satisfied if the prohibition of Article 107 TFEU is to have bite: the existence of "state aid" must be shown, it must operate in a "selective" manner, and there must be an effect both upon competition and trade between the member states. We will now examine each of these criteria in turn.

The concept of "state aid"[8]

The treaty is silent on the matter of definition, but the case law of the Court of Justice has made it clear that the concept of "aid" is wider than that of a subsidy.[9] The definition is in fact very wide. The outer limit was defined in *Sloman Neptune*:[10] only benefits granted directly or indirectly out of state resources are to be regarded as state aid. In its *PreussenElektra* judgment, the Court held that the charges levied by the state on private companies in order to finance environmental objectives were not to be treated as state aid measures.[11] Nevertheless, this still leaves a broad range of benefits covered by the scope of Article 107 TFEU: direct subsidies, interest subsidies, low interest, interest-free loans, capital injections, grants, asset revaluation, compensation for government-imposed financial burdens, the foregoing of recovery of sums due, preferential terms, price reductions, public supply contracts, reduction in social security charges, state guarantees,[12] state participation in capital tax concessions, and the foregoing of state revenue.

The Court's case law in this area has undergone a further development as a result of the *Altmark* judgment.[13] In this judgment, the Court ruled that compensation for public services does not constitute state aid provided certain conditions are met.

The aid must be effected by a member state or through state resources. An example of the latter is the preferential tariff accorded to the fertilizer industry by the Dutch gas company, Gasunie.[14] In the *Stardust Marine* case, the Court of Justice held that although the French government owned 80 percent of the shares of the company, the Commission should in addition establish that the actions of the company could be imputed to the government. Since this was not the case, the transfers from the company could not be assessed under the state aid rules.[15]

Selectivity

The prohibition of Article 107 TFEU does not apply if all undertakings within a member state benefit from assistance without any distinction being made between them. General measures of economic policy, such as the lowering of the tax rate applicable to corporate profits, fall outside the scope of Article 107 TFEU.

The distinction between general and specific measures is not always easy to apply. Thus, the Italian reduction in the rate of social security contributions was deemed to constitute a state aid because it specifically benefited the Italian textile industry.[16] The Italian government claimed that the reduction was only restoring the competitive position of the textile industry because the industry employed a very high percentage of female workers, which created a situation whereby the contributions for the social security system exceeded the benefits.[17] The concept of selectivity is particularly difficult to apply to tax measures.[18] According to the case law, there is no selective advantage when tax measures differentiate between undertakings except when that differentiation arises from the nature and general scheme of the system of which they form part. In the reform of the Gibraltar corporate tax case, the governments of Gibraltar and the United Kingdom argued that the new payroll tax based on the number of employees employed in Gibraltar was not selective because every employer was liable to pay the tax. The choice of the tax base consisting of the number of persons employed in Gibraltar was, according to the governments, a natural consequence of their fiscal sovereignty.[19] The CJEU held that the UK government had not adduced any justification for the selective advantage.[20] In the *Azores* case, the Portuguese government claimed that there was no selectivity because the Azores autonomous region was, also in tax matters, independent from the central government and thus could set its own tax rates different from those of Portugal. The Commission claimed that the selectivity should be assessed according to the national tax system. The CJEU accepted Portugal's argument in principle, but it ruled that the degree of autonomy of the Autonomous Region of the Azores is in fact limited. Therefore, it upheld the Commission's decision.[21]

Effect upon competition and trade between member states

The granting of benefits must result in a distortion of competition in order to actuate Article 107(1) TFEU. For this purpose, it is necessary to consider whether the aid strengthens the position of the beneficiary enterprise compared with other enterprises operating in the same line of trade.[22] It is not, however, necessary for the Commission to produce a fully fledged analysis of the relevant product and geographical market along the lines of the analysis required by Article 101 and especially Article 102 TFEU. Nevertheless, the Commission must produce something more than a statement that competition has been or may be distorted.[23] In practice this requirement is easily met. The CJEU has so far not endorsed a "*de minimis* rule." Nevertheless, the Commission will have to show that the aid will have an impact on trade between the member states.[24]

In its guidelines on state aids for small and medium-sized enterprises, the Commission has taken the view that while all financial assistance affects competitive conditions to some extent, not all aid has a perceptible impact on trade and competition between member states. This is so especially for aid provided in very small amounts, mainly though not exclusively to small and medium-sized enterprises, and often under schemes run by local or regional authorities.

The *de minimis* rule has its legal basis in Article 2 of Regulation 994/98/EC and in the block exemption regulation on *de minimis* aid.[25]

It should further be noted that, in practice, the effects on competition and those on trade between the member states will almost always coincide. It is, therefore, common practice to employ these two concepts interchangeably even though there is a theoretical difference between them (although this should not lead one to assume that there will never be differences between the two concepts in practice).

The "market economy investor principle"

An important concept to enable the Commission to distinguish between benefits granted by governments that are prohibited by Article 107(1) TFEU and those that are not is the "market economy investor principle."[26] The concept was specially developed in the context of government participation in the capital of enterprises.[27] According to this principle, government actions that take place under market conditions and terms do not give rise to the application of Article 107(1) TFEU. If the provision of funds by the state has been made subject to certain conditions that would also have been required by a private investor, such action will not be considered to amount to a grant of aid. The Commission has also consistently applied this principle in the context of the review of tariffs of public enterprises. In a Decision of 7 December 1993 concerning the price paid for gas by household consumers and, as a raw material, by industry,[28] the Commission stated,

> If Gasunie has agreed temporarily to grant the above-mentioned discounts, it is clearly in its commercial interests to do so. Given the prospects for the relevant industry, Gasunie would not wish to lose an important group of customers which in the Netherlands buys approximately one third of its supplies to industry. It is also in Gasunie's interest that the relevant industry should survive in the countries to which it exports gas. The Commission notes that the export prices fixed by Gasunie enable distribution companies in the importing countries, namely Belgium, France and Germany, to apply pricing policies similar to its own policy in the Netherlands ... In its examination of the decision by Gasunie to grant the discounts in question, the Commission has been unable to detect any behaviour on the part of the Dutch authorities that went beyond that of a private shareholder. In view of the situation on the ammonia and nitrogenous fertiliser market, the Commission considers that, in providing support for an important group of customers whose survival is manifestly in jeopardy, Gasunie has acted out of purely commercial considerations.
>
> The Commission has accordingly decided that the temporary and limited price concessions that Gasunie plans to grant to Dutch ammonia producers do not constitute State aid within the meaning of Article 107(1) TFEU Treaty.

The market economy investor principle has become an important instrument to discriminate between lawful and unlawful governmental assistance. The Commission has provided useful guidance in the Transparency Directive.[29] It is not the intention of the Commission to replace the investor's judgment. It recognizes that the investor has a wide margin of judgment. Only when there are no objective justifications for the investment will the Commission consider Article 107(1) TFEU to be applicable. In the *Chronopost* judgment, the Court held that where the principle is applied to a company that performs services of public importance, the relevant comparison that must be made is with the cost price of the performance of those services by *that* company, not with that of a company in the market sector.[30] The Commission applies a similar test, the private creditor test, that is, when a government provides loans on terms that are more favorable than those given by banks.[31] In the *ING* judgment the GC applied the principle to answer the question of whether an amendment to the repayment terms of an aid measure constitutes state aid.[32]

In the *Bank Burgenland* case, the question was whether the Austrian government had acted in accordance with private vendor test. The Commission as well as the CJEU ruled that Austria, by attaching unlawful conditions to the tender, failed this test.[33]

Exceptions

Once a government measure granting certain benefits meets the conditions of Article 107(1) TFEU, it is incompatible with the common market. It can then only be exempted by the provisions of Article 107(2) or 107(3) TFEU or the provisions of Articles 93 or 106(2) TFEU.

The *Altmark* case[34] and a Commission decision[35] have made it clear that in some cases the provision of financial compensation for the performance of public services is not to be regarded as state aid. The Court ruled in *Altmark* that, where the criteria laid down in that judgment are satisfied, such compensation for the provision of public services did not fall under the scope of the prohibition of Article 107(1) TFEU. In such a case, Article 106(2) TFEU is also inapplicable, and there is also no obligation to notify such a regime. Thus, this reasoning process incorporates the "exception"-style analysis within the notion of what counts as "state aid" in the first place. Functionally, however, the analysis is one that exempts such payments from the standstill obligation and is thus properly treated here.

Assuming that the financial benefit in question does qualify as state aid, there are still means to exempt such aid from the prohibition of the TFEU, which we discuss in the following sections.

The exemptions from the prohibition of Article 107(1) are:

(1) Aid that is compatible with the Common Market, Article 107(2) TFEU

This condition provides for three categories of aid which shall be compatible with Common Market:

1. aid having a social character, granted to individual consumers, provided that such aid is granted without discrimination related to the origin of the products concerned;
2. aid to make good the damage caused by natural disasters or exceptional occurrences;
3. aid granted to the economy of certain areas of the Federal Republic of Germany affected by the division of Germany, in so far as such aid is required in order to compensate for the economic disadvantages caused by that division. Five years after the entry into force of the Treaty of Lisbon, the Council, acting on a proposal from the Commission, may adopt a decision repealing this point.

The word "shall" is taken to imply that the Commission does not enjoy discretion to decide whether or not the exemption applies. Similar wording is used in Article 93 TFEU. Of the three categories, category (c) is by far the most important. This provision allows for aid granted to the economy of the Federal Republic of Germany affected by the division of Germany. The interpretation of this provision has been hotly debated ever since the reunification of Germany. The Commission has adopted a restrictive interpretation that has been endorsed by the Community courts.[36] According to this interpretation, if general disadvantages in East Germany cannot be cured through the application of this exemption, they should be dealt with as exceptions under Article 107(3)(a) and (c) TFEU. There are only few exemption decisions based on this provision.

(2) Aid that may be compatible with the Common Market, Article 107(3) TFEU

According to this provision the following categories of aid may be exempted:

1. aid to promote the economic development of areas where the standard of living is abnormally low or where there is serious underemployment, and of the regions referred to in Article 349, in view of their structural, economic, and social situation;
2. aid to promote the execution of an important project of common European interest or to remedy a serious disturbance in the economy of a member state;

3. aid to facilitate the development of certain economic activities or of certain economic areas, where such aid does not adversely affect trading conditions to an extent contrary to the common interest;
4. aid to promote culture and heritage conservation, where such aid does not affect trading conditions and competition in the Union to an extent that is contrary to the common interest;
5. such other categories of aid as may be specified by decision of the Council on a proposal from the Commission.

It is important to note that the application of this provision is subject to the Commission's discretion. Furthermore, as an exemption from the general principles of the treaty, it has been interpreted in a restrictive manner. Thus, in its judgment in *Philip Morris*,[37] the Court of Justice supported the Commission's interpretation according to which state aids can only be allowed to the extent that they are necessary for the achievement of objectives accepted under Article 107(3) TFEU.

In summary, the requirements are as follows: (1) the aid must promote or further a project that is in the Community interest as a whole; (2) the aid must be necessary for the achievement of this result, and the objective could not have been obtained in the absence of this measure; and (3) the duration, intensity, and scope of the aid must be proportionate to the importance of the intended result.[38]

The second element has been specified by the Commission as follows.

> State aids are in principle incompatible with the common market. The discretionary power of the Commission should only be exercised when the aids proposed by Member States contribute to the achievement of the Community objectives and interest set out in Article 107(3) TFEU. The national interest of a Member State or the benefits obtained by the recipient of the aid in contributing to the national interest do not by themselves justify the positive exercise of the Commission's discretionary powers.[39]

The Court of Justice accepted the validity of the compensatory justification principle in its *Philip Morris* judgment.[40] These principles of interpretation have strengthened the Commission's hand considerably.

The Community courts have stressed that the Commission has broad discretion in applying the provisions of Article 107(3), the exercise of which involves economic assessment that must be made in a European Union context.[41] Article 107(3)(a) is the basis for Commission decisions on regional aid in areas where there is serious unemployment or a very low standard of living, or where the per capita income does not exceed 75 percent of the average in the European Union. Thus, according to the accession treaties for the new member states, the whole territory is eligible for state aid under this provision. A similar provision was included in the Accession Treaty for Greece.

Article 107(3)(b) was for all practical purposes a dead letter until the Commission started applying it to assess aid to the financial sector. Article 107(3)(c) is applied for state aid to less disadvantaged regions. The disadvantage relates to disparities between regions at the national level. As a result, poor regions in wealthy member states, for example, the former DDR regions in Germany, qualify for state aid. The Commission's regional policy was developed in the 1980s through guidelines. Article 107(3)(c) is also the legal basis for rescue and restructuring aid. This type of aid played a major role in the restructuring of the east Bundesländer (the former DDR) industry. The policy in the area has been defined since the 1970s. The Commission published its first guidelines in 1994.

Block exemptions and guidelines

As the EU state aid policy developed and matured, block exemptions have been enacted and guidelines published to clarify the above outlined treaty exemptions. As the term indicates, block exemptions exempt certain categories of aid from the prohibition of Article 107(1) TFEU. The foundation for this policy is found in Regulation 994/98/EC, applying Articles 107 and 108 TFEU, which authorizes the Commission to adopt block exemptions for certain categories of aid.[42] Until the 2014 reform, some 65 percent of state aid cases were block exempted. The major 2014 reform of the General Block Exemption Regulation (GBER) will increase this percentage substantially. Together with the *de minimis* regulation it will raise the level of block exempted aid to about 90 percent. This reform de facto creates a system of *ex post* state aid control whereas until now it was largely an *ex ante* system. The important consequences of this revision of the system will be discussed below. The extension of the GBER allows the Commission to devote more time and resources for the novel and hard cases, such as the massive aid to the financial sector.

The following block exemptions are presently in force:[43]

- Commission Regulation (EC) No 1407/2013 of 18 December 2013 on the application of Articles 107 and 108 of the Treaty on the Functioning of the European Union to *de minimis* aid[44]
- Regulation 1370/2007 of 23 October 2007 on public passenger transport services by rail and by road and repealing Council Regulations 1191/69 and 1107/70[45] and
- Commission Regulation (EC) No 800/2008 of 6 August 2008 declaring certain categories of aid compatible with the common market in application of Article 87 and 88 of the Treaty (GBER).[46]

Regulation 1407/2013 exempts aid of no more than €200,000 over a three-year period from the prohibition. Such aid need not be notified. Article 1 excludes aid to certain sectors, such as agriculture, fisheries, road transport, and aid for exports to third countries. According to Article 6(4) of the regulation, member states shall record and compile all the information regarding the application of this regulation. Such records shall contain all information necessary to demonstrate that the conditions of this regulation have been complied with. The regulation will expire on 31 December 2020.

Regulation 1370/2007 of 23 October 2007 provides special rules for public passenger transport services by rail and by road. Such rules are necessary because

> many Member States have enacted legislation providing for the award of exclusive rights and public service contracts in at least part of their public transport market, on the basis of transparent and fair competitive award procedures. As a result, trade between Member States has developed significantly and several public service operators are now providing public passenger transport services in more than one Member State. However, developments in national legislation have led to disparities in the procedures applied and have created legal uncertainty as to the rights of public service operators and the duties of the competent authorities. … The Community legal framework ought therefore to be updated.[47]

The GBER consolidated and amended five previous block exemptions.[48] It expired on 30 June 2014 when the new regulation came into force.[49] Article 1 excludes, in a very unintelligible manner, several types of aid. Therefore, it should be read very carefully. The GBER does not apply to agriculture, fisheries, and aquaculture, nor to regional aid schemes that are targeted at specific sectors. The GBER further excludes ad hoc aid to large enterprises. According to Article 3, aid schemes that satisfy the conditions mentioned therein are exempted and do not have to be notified. Chapter 2 exempts a large number of aid schemes and individual aid measures.

In order to provide guidance on how to apply Article 107(1) and the exemptions of Article 107(3) TFEU, as well as the block exemptions, the Commission has published guidelines, codes, frameworks, communications, and notices. Although the designations are not consistent, these instruments all serve the same purpose. The Court of Justice has held that such rules cannot be regarded as rules of law; nevertheless, they form rules of practice from which the Commission may not depart in an individual case without giving reasons that are compatible with the principle of equal treatment.[50]

Important guidelines, presently in force, are:[51]

- Communication from the Commission – Criteria for the compatibility analysis of state aid to disadvantaged and disabled workers subject to individual notification;[52]
- Communication from the Commission – Criteria for the compatibility analysis of training state aid cases subject to individual notification;[53]
- Guidelines on national regional aid for 2007 to 2013;[54]
- Communication of the Commission on the review of the state aid status and the aid ceiling of the statistical effect regions for the period 1 January 2011 to 31 December 2013;[55]
- Communication from the Commission concerning the criteria for an in-depth assessment of Regional aid to large investment projects;[56]
- Community Framework for State Aid for Research and Development and Innovation;[57]
- Community guidelines on state aid for environmental protection;[58]
- Prolongation of Community guidelines on state aid for rescuing and restructuring firms in difficulty;[59]
- Community guidelines on state aid for rescuing and restructuring firms in difficulty.[60]

Procedural Rules, Article 108 TFEU and Regulation 659/99/EC

Introduction

The basic procedural rules are found in Article 108 TFEU. This article provides for a system of *ex ante* control of new state aid. This system is not unlike the system as it was applied in Regulation 17 for agreements prohibited under Article 85 of the Treaty establishing the European Economic Community (EEC; now 101 TFEU). It should be noted, however, that the recent changes in the legislation have fundamentally altered the previously existing *ex ante* system for the control of state aid. The 2014 GBER now covers a major part of all state aids. It is estimated that together with the *de minimis* rule some 90 percent of cases are now block exempted. This means that the present system can be characterized as an *ex post* control system. Under this system, which is outlined in the GBER, it is the responsibility of the member states to supervise the granting of state aid. This is done largely through obligations on the member states to play by the rules of the GBER and to keep records of the state aid that they have been granting under the block exemptions. Furthermore, member states have an obligation to report to the Commission. The Commission in turn will supervise the member states.

All aid measures not exempted under the block exemption remain subject to notification. The rules described below are therefore meant to control the nonexempted aid measures.

An important role in the new system is for the national courts, which have to apply the directly effective rules of the block exemptions in addition to the control exercised on the basis of Article 108 TFEU and the procedural regulations.

As has been observed already, the procedural rules are embodied in Regulation 659/99/EC.[61] Implementing rules are laid down in Regulation 794/2004/EC. The latter regulation includes a notification form for new aid. Regulation 659/99 was amended in 2013.[62] First of all, Regulation 659/99/EC provides a set of definitions. Chapter 2 provides the procedure for notified aid. Chapter 3 deals with unlawful aid, that is, aid that has been put into effect without respecting the obligation to notify. Chapter 4 lays down rules for the misuse of aid, that is, where aid has not been implemented in accordance with conditions set out by the Commission or specified by the member state. Chapter 5 provides the procedure for existing aid. Chapter 6 defines the rights of interested parties, including (among others) the intended beneficiaries and complainants, which will usually be competitors of each other. Chapter 7 gives the Commission powers to conduct on-site monitoring and obliges member states to submit annual reports on all existing aid schemes. Chapter 8 deals with the publication of decisions, professional secrecy, and other matters.

Article 108 TFEU reads as follows:

1. The Commission shall, in cooperation with Member States, keep under constant review all systems of aid existing in those States. It shall propose to the latter any appropriate measures required by the progressive development or by the functioning of the common market.
2. If, after giving notice to the parties concerned to submit their comments, the Commission finds that aid granted by a State or through State resources is not compatible with the common market having regard to Article 107, or that such aid is being misused, it shall decide that the State concerned shall abolish or alter such aid within a period of time to be determined by the Commission. If the State concerned does not comply with this decision within the prescribed time, the Commission or any other interested State may, in derogation from the provisions of Articles 258 and 259, refer the matter to the Court of Justice direct.

   On application by a Member State, the Council may, acting unanimously, decide that aid which that State is granting or intends to grant shall be considered to be compatible with the common market, in derogation from the provisions of Article 107 or from the regulations provided for in Article 109, if such a decision is justified by exceptional circumstances. If, as regards the aid in question, the Commission has already initiated the procedure provided for in the first subparagraph of this paragraph, the fact that the State concerned has made its application to the Council shall have the effect of suspending that procedure until the Council has made its attitude known.

   If, however, the Council has not made its attitude known within three months of the said application being made, the Commission shall give its decision on the case.
3. The Commission shall be informed, in sufficient time to enable it to submit its comments, of any plans to grant or alter aid. If it considers that any such plan is not compatible with the common market having regard to Article 107, it shall without delay initiate the procedure provided for in paragraph 2. The Member State concerned shall not put its proposed measures into effect until this procedure has resulted in a final decision.
4. The Commission may adopt regulations relating to the categories of State aid that the Council has, pursuant to Article 109, determined may be exempted from the procedure provided for in paragraph 3 of this Article.

It is of the utmost importance for an understanding of this area of law to draw a distinction between *existing aid* and *new aid*. Control of existing aid takes place *ex post*, while new aid, which is not block exempted, is controlled *ex ante*.

Existing aid

"Existing aid" is defined in Article 1 of the regulation. The most important categories are aid that has been authorized by the Commission and aid applied in a member state before the entry into force of the EEC Treaty[63] or before accession of a new member state. Only existing aid schemes can be challenged. According to Article 108(1) TFEU, as well as Article 17 of Regulation 659/99, existing aid schemes[64] in member states must be kept under constant review by the Commission. According to Article 18 of the regulation, the Commission proposes measures to the member states if the aid is not or is no longer compatible with the Common Market. Member states shall be bound by the Commission's proposals if they accept them. If the member state does not accept the proposals, the Commission is entitled to proceed with the formal examination procedure of Article 108(2) TFEU. Article 1 of the regulation defines aid schemes as any act on the basis of which, without further implementing measures being required, individual aid awards may be made to undertakings defined within the act in a general and abstract manner and any act on the basis of which aid which is not linked to a specific project may be awarded to one or several undertakings for an indefinite period of time and/or for an indefinite amount.

Existing aid, whether it is an existing aid scheme or an individual aid, cannot be challenged in national courts. However, existing aid schemes can be challenged by bringing a complaint to the Commission. The Commission may take action on the basis of Articles 18 and 19 of Regulation 659/99. If the Commission finds that such aid is incompatible with the common market it may propose appropriate measures. If member states accept these they shall bind them. Otherwise the Commission shall initiate the formal procedure which may lead to the adoption of a decision prohibiting the aid. The acceptance by the member state as well as the decision pursuant to Article 19(2) of Regulation 659/99 shall be binding upon them. Their binding force can be enforced by national courts because they have direct effect.

The distinction between the two types of aid is not always straightforward. In the *AEM* case,[65] the applicant, relying on the *Namur-Les Assurances* judgment,[66] sought to argue that measures introduced in Italy before the entry into force of the EEC Treaty would qualify as measures under this provision. The GC dismissed the argument noting that the measures were substantially different from the original ones.

New aid

New aid, that is, any plans to grant or alter aid, must, under Article 108(3) TFEU, be notified to the Commission in sufficient time to enable the Commission to communicate its comments. Regulation 794/2004/EC (referred to as "the Regulation" in what follows) includes in its Annex I the necessary notification form.[67] Its Article 4 also provides that:

> An alteration to existing aid shall mean any change, other than modifications of a purely formal or administrative nature which cannot affect the evaluation of the compatibility of the aid measure with the common market. However, an increase in the original budget of an existing aid scheme by up to 20% shall not be considered an alteration to existing aid.

As a result, such small changes need no longer be notified as "new" aid. Article 4 goes on to subject alterations to existing aid outside this definition to a simplified notification procedure (using the form included in Annex II of the Regulation). These aids concern budget increases over 20 percent, the prolongation of an existing aid scheme by up to six years, and any tightening of the criteria for application of an authorized aid scheme.

The preliminary examination procedure

On the basis of Article 108(3) TFEU and Article 4 of Regulation 659/99, the Commission may, after summary examination, either conclude that the aid is compatible with the Common Market or open the procedure provided for in Article 108(2) TFEU and Article 6 of Regulation 659/99. This is called the "preliminary examination procedure" and is specified in Article 4 of the Regulation. New aid that has been notified may, according to the last sentence of Article 108(3) TFEU, not be put into effect until this procedure, that is, the procedure in Article 108(3) TFEU and Article 4 of Regulation 659/99 and/or Article 108(2) TFEU and Article 6 of Regulation 659/99, has resulted in a final decision. This is called the "standstill clause."

The last sentence of Article 108(3) TFEU and the similarly worded Article 3 of Regulation 659/99 have direct effect. New aid within the scope of the block exemptions referred to above does not have to be notified and is not subject to the standstill clause.

Under the preliminary procedure, the Commission has a period of two months to make up its mind. If it finds that the aid is compatible with the Common Market, it will inform the member states concerned accordingly. Such a decision may be reviewed the GC.[68] Judgments of the GC may be appealed to the CJEU on points of law only.

If the Commission is of the opinion that it needs more time to complete the review of the state aid, it must open the procedure of Article 108(2) TFEU. The decision to open the Article 108(2) TFEU procedure is a contestable act within the meaning of Article 263 TFEU.[69]

If the Commission fails to act, the member state concerned may, according to Article 4(6) of the Regulation, implement the aid, after giving notice to the Commission. The aid then becomes an existing aid.[70]

The formal investigation procedure

The Article 108(2) TFEU procedure is detailed in Articles 6 and 7 of the Regulation. It is called the "formal investigation procedure." It is a contentious procedure, which means that the parties concerned may submit comments. The Commission will publish a notice in the C-series of the Official Journal of the European Union, describing the aid plans and inviting comments. In practice, it is quite common for member states, beneficiaries, and interested parties, competitors as well as trade associations, to provide comments. Such comments strengthen the hand of the Commission considerably. The comments will be submitted to the member state concerned for comments.

According to Article 7(6) of the Regulation, the Commission has eighteen months to adopt a decision. If that period has lapsed, the member state concerned can request the Commission to take a decision within two months. This brings the total time for the Commission under this procedure to twenty months. The combination of the two procedures, Article 108(3) and 108(2) TFEU, leads to a maximum of twenty-two months.

After completing the Article 108(2) TFEU procedure, the Commission may either: (1) declare the aid compatible with the Common Market, with or without conditions; or (2) declare it incompatible with the Common Market. Either decision may be subject to review by the General Court with a possibility of appeal to the Court of Justice on points of law.

A final positive decision ends the operation of the standstill clause of Article 108(3) TFEU and Article 3 of the Regulation. A positive decision may be accompanied by conditions which should alleviate the effect on competition.[71] The Commission's decision in the *Air France* case provides a good example of this practice.[72] In this case, the Commission imposed a series of conditions that included the requirement that Air France was not to use any of the aid received for the purpose of increasing its aircraft fleet. A positive decision may also approve the aid in successive tranches, whereby the approval of the next tranche is subject to the satisfactory implementation of a restructuring program.

In the case of a negative final decision, the standstill clause (contained in the last paragraph of Article 108(3) TFEU) does *not* lapse after the Commission concludes the Article 108(2) TFEU procedure; instead, the standstill obligation is henceforth based on the negative decision.

The simplified procedure

In 2009, the Commission introduced a simplified procedure in an effort to streamline the notification process.[73] According to the Commission this procedure is intended "for measures which only require the Commission to verify that the measure is in accordance with existing rules and practices without exercising any discretionary powers." "Other aid measures will be subject to the appropriate procedures and normally to the Code of Best Practices."[74] According to Section 2 of the notice, the procedure can be used for three categories of aid: (1) aid measures falling under the "standard assessment" sections of existing frameworks or guidelines; (2) aid measures corresponding to well-established Commission decision-making practice and; (3) prolongation or extension of existing schemes.

Section 3 outlines the elements of the procedure. According to the Commission, prenotification contacts with the notifying member state are beneficial. Such contacts allow identification at an early stage of the relevant Commission instruments or precedent decisions, the degree of complexity that the Commission's assessment is likely to involve, and the scope and depth of the information required for the Commission to make a full assessment of the case.

The member state is invited to submit a draft notification form with the necessary supplementary information sheets. In simple cases, a draft notification is not necessary.

In addition, the best practices code published by the Commission explains and further facilitates the procedure. The code also stresses the importance of prenotification meetings.

The position of complainants

Complainants have, according to Article 20 of the Regulation, a right to inform the Commission of any alleged unlawful aid or the misuse of aid. Complainants can bring an action under Article 265 TFEU if the Commission fails to act.[75] Furthermore, as the Court of Justice observed in the *Sytraval* judgment, complainants, as third parties that are "directly and individually concerned," have a right to challenge state aid decisions addressed to governments of member states.[76] The Court also pointed out that, although the Commission is not obliged to hear complainants, it must nevertheless respond to facts and points of law raised by the complainant. The procedural regulation 659/99 has, in 2013, been amended with the purpose of improving the handling of complaints.[77]

Unlawful aid

Unlawful state aid – that is, aid that has not been notified – is not automatically incompatible with the Common Market. The Commission is under a duty to review such aids.[78] According to Article 13(2) of the Regulation, the Commission shall not be bound by the normal time limits in this case. It also has powers to issue injunctions to suspend or provisionally recover the unlawful aid (Article 11 of the Regulation). As explained in the next section, national courts have an important role in preventing unlawful aids being implemented before the Commission has reached a decision on the compatibility of the aid.

The role of national courts

Because of the direct effect of the last sentence of Article 108(3) TFEU and Article 3 of the Regulation, national courts have an important role in enforcing the procedural requirements of the EU state aid regime. Increasingly, national courts also have an important role in applying the block exemptions. The application of the substantive requirements, other than the rules of the block exemptions, remains the exclusive power of the Commission. National courts enforce the standstill clause. National courts can also award damages in cases of unlawful aid[79] and grant injunctions. Such remedies may be of vital importance in aid cases where the timing is often a crucial element in rescue operations. The role of national courts has been stressed in a Commission Communication on the cooperation between national courts and the Commission in the field of state aids.[80] This is a useful document explaining the respective roles and the methods of cooperation. This role was originally highlighted in the judgment of the CJEU in the *SFEI* case.[81] The CJEU held that national courts seized of a request relating to an infringement of Article 93(3) EC (now Article 108(3) TFEU), in case of an aid that is also under review by the Commission, are not required to declare that they lack jurisdiction or stay the proceedings until such time as the Commission has adopted a position. The *CELF* judgments, as well as the *Residex* judgment, now provide detailed rules.[82] Therefore, the rules explained in the Commission notice on the enforcement of state aid law by national courts will need updating.

National courts may provide several remedies. First, national courts have to order the aid recipient to pay interest in respect of the period of unlawfulness of the aid.[83] Second, national courts have an obligation to adopt safeguard measures where three conditions are satisfied. These conditions are set out in paragraph 36 of the *CELF 2* judgment.[84] Such remedies may be of vital importance in aid cases where the timing is often a crucial element in rescue operations. If these conditions have not been met, the national court must dismiss the application for such remedies. According to the *Residex* judgment, national courts have jurisdiction to cancel a guarantee in a situation in which unlawful aid was implemented by means of a guarantee provided by a public authority.[85] The guarantee was provided in order to cover a loan granted by a finance company to an undertaking that would not have been able to secure such financing under normal market conditions. National courts are required to ensure that the aid is recovered and, to that end, they can cancel the guarantee, in particular where, in the absence of less onerous procedural measures, that cancellation is such as to lead to or facilitate the restoration of the competitive situation that existed before that guarantee was provided. Third, national courts may also award damages in cases of unlawful aid.[86]

In case of doubt about the question of whether a measure constitutes an aid in the sense of Article 107(1) TFEU, national courts may refer a question to the Court of Justice or consult the Commission. The Commission may also be consulted on matters of procedure.

Other procedural issues

The second paragraph of Article 108(2) TFEU states that the Commission or an interested member state may bring an action before the CJEU in derogation of the provisions of the Articles 258 and 259 TFEU[87] if the member state concerned does not comply with the Commission's decision.[88]

According to the third paragraph of Article 108(2) TFEU, the Council, acting unanimously, may on an application by a member state decide that an aid shall be considered compatible with the Common Market if such a decision is justified by exceptional circumstances.[89] However, the Council lacks the competence to approve an aid after the Commission has prohibited it.[90]

Recovery[91]
According to Article 14 of the Regulation, the Commission has the power to order recovery of illegally implemented aid.[92] The Commission may also order recovery of interest advantages where unlawful aid has been implemented prior to Commission approval.[93]

When ordered to recover aid, a member state cannot invoke a rule of domestic law to oppose recovery orders.[94] In this context, it is important to note that the Commission has, for many years, when publishing notices under the Article 108(2) TFEU procedure, warned the enterprises concerned that illegally implemented aid can be recovered.

Commission decisions ordering recovery of illegally implemented aids normally require the member states concerned to report to the Commission what measures have been taken to implement the decision. Commission decisions ordering recovery do not normally indicate the exact amount to be recovered. Thus, in the case of the electricity power purchase agreements, the Hungarian government had to calculate the exact amount to be recovered.[95] This practice often gives rise to lengthy discussions between the Commission and the member state about how to calculate the exact amount.

Sometimes it is difficult to identify the company that should pay back the aid. This is particularly the case when a company has sold subsidiaries that benefitted from the aid. As was noted above, national courts may in such a situation use their discretion to determine the amounts to be repaid.[96]

By way of an example, in his speech of 23 February 2012, Commissioner Almunia mentioned that the Commission ordered Germany and Belgium to recover the amount of aid that exceeded the level of compensation for the provision of services of general economic interest.[97]

State Aid to the Financial Sector[98]

Introduction

The collapse of Lehman Brothers in the United States in September 2008 led to a major, worldwide crisis in the banking sector.[99] The EU economy was faced with a steep downturn of a level not seen since the 1930s. As a result, many member states in the European Union resorted to massive state aid to prevent their banks from failing. The Commission approved some €4,506 billion state aid.[100] The EU Commission was flooded with notifications that, as a result of the extreme urgency of the crisis, had to be handled with the greatest possible speed. Often decisions were taken during the weekend in order to avoid a run on the particular bank. Only by approving very substantial aid packages before the opening of the stock exchanges worldwide on Monday could the confidence be restored.

The European Council of 15 October 2008 endorsed the Commission's application of the state aid rules and asked for speedy and flexible action. Initially, the Commission followed the rules for rescue and restructuring aid as laid down in the 2004 Guidelines.[101]

The commission communications

As from October 2008, the Commission issued guidance to member states and financial institutions on the conditions that would need to be met for the state aid granted in response to the financial crisis to be considered compatible with the Treaty.[102] Between October 2008 and July 2009 it published four communications setting out the principles that it would apply to state guarantees for bank liabilities, recapitalizations, impaired asset relief, and restructuring aid. In January 2009, it issued a communication providing for further possibilities for member states to support companies in the real economy during the crisis and the conditions such support should satisfy. The latest measure is the Communication from the Commission on the application, from 1 August 2013, of state aid rules to support measures in favor of banks in the context of the financial crisis ("Banking Communication").[103] This communication withdraws the 2008 Banking Communication and amends the Impaired Assests and Restructuring Communication.

The Banking Communication[104] was the first instrument to set out the general principles to be applied, namely: nondiscrimination,[105] the need for the aid to be clearly defined and limited in time and scope, adequately paid for by the beneficiaries that should bring an appropriate contribution, and subject to behavioral constraints so as to prevent any abuse of the state support, such as aggressive expansion on the back of a state guarantee. That first Communication already emphasized the need for structural adjustment measures for the financial sector as a whole and for restructuring individual financial institutions that benefited from state intervention. In this communication, the Commission explained that it was confronted with a systemic crisis, and, therefore, the application of Article 107(3)(b) was called for. According to paragraph 94 of the 2013 Banking Communication, the 2008 communication is withdrawn with effect from 31 July 2013.

Building on these principles, the *Recapitalisation Communication*[106] provided additional detailed guidance on how it would assess recapitalization measures specifically. In particular, it established detailed principles for the remuneration of the injections of capital made by states into banks, which should reflect the price that a normally functioning market would require for the relevant capital.

The Impaired Asset Communication[107] in turn provided guidance for aid linked to "relieving" banks from assets that were broadly considered as "toxic" or "impaired."[108] Many banks had a substantial portfolio of such assets. According to paragraph 95 of the 2013 Banking Communication point 47 and Annex 5 are withdrawn.

The Restructuring Communication[109] set out in more detail the Commission's approach to the conditions as to when banks needed to submit a restructuring plan and what measures such a plan should include in order to meet the Commission's approval. In particular, it stipulated that banks in need of substantial amounts of aid must, in return for the aid, demonstrate strategies to remedy unsustainable business models and achieve long-term viability without state support under adverse economic conditions. The 2013 Banking Communication amends the Restructuring Communication on several points.

Finally, a *Communication on a Temporary Framework of Aid to the Real Economy*[110] was adopted to promote companies' access to finance and to support the production of green products. Under these rules, member states could grant a maximum of €500,000 aid, €300,000 more than under the *de minimis* guidelines. The aid has been applied to small and medium-size enterprises. According to the Commission's own evaluation, the latter instrument "has allowed a coordinated response to tackle companies' difficulties in accessing finance during the crisis."[111]

The above instruments have been extended and amended by fresh Commission communications.[112]

The Communications have extended the scope for rescue aid for large firms and they have allowed rescue aid for more than six months. They have also extended the requirements for restructuring aid to a period of up to five years. The Commission's approach based on the above communications consists of a first stage approval of rescue aid and a second stage approval of restructuring aid. The first stage approval is subject to the condition that the member state will submit a restructuring plan within six months from the approval. The second stage approval is often subject to extensive conditions that, as can be gleaned from the example of aid to ING discussed below, can be quite onerous for the financial institution involved. The 2013 Banking Communication embodies the latest round of amendments. According to paragraph 23 of the communication:

> This Communication establishes the principle that recapitalisation and impaired asset measures will be authorised only once the bank's restructuring plan is approved. This approach ensures that the amount of aid is more accurately calibrated, that the sources of the bank's problems are already identified and addressed at an early stage and that financial stability is assured. Guarantee schemes will continue to be available in order to provide liquidity to banks. Such schemes can, however, only serve as a means to provide liquidity to banks without a capital shortfall as defined by the competent supervisory authority.

As can be seen this is a new approach: under the old rules aid could be authorized subject to the condition that a restructuring plan was submitted within six months.

During the period of October 2008 to December 2010, the Commission adopted more than two hundred decisions. During 2010, the number of decisions decreased substantially. However, most of the measures approved in the past are still operational. The majority of the decisions were adopted under a very short time frame, in particular in the few weeks following the bankruptcy of Lehman Brothers. The first schemes notified by member states in the course of October 2008 were, for instance, approved by the Commission in less than ten days.

The vast majority of the decisions adopted by the Commission were decisions not to raise objections because the proposed state aid could be approved on the basis of Article 107(3)(b) TFEU in light of the principles set out in the communications. exchanges between the Commission and member states after the notification of state aid were essential in ensuring that the proposed aid measure would be approved by the Commission. The Commission only adopted one negative decision,[113] with recovery of the aid, concerning aid to the financial sector throughout the crisis. So far, three decisions have been appealed by parties.[114] A final judgment was given by the CJEU in the ING case, the Court dismissed the appeal confirming the partial annulment by the GC.[115]

The enforcement of the state aid rules by the Commission has been essential in containing the crisis. The Commission efforts have been supplemented by the policies of the European Central Bank, which provided "enhanced credit support."

Notes

1 Cf. Martin H. Heidenhain, *Handbuch des Europäischen Beihilfenrechts* (Munich: C.H. Beck, 2003); Wolfgang Mederer, Nicola Pesaresi, and Marc Van Hoof, *State Aid*, vol. 4 of *EU Competition Law* (Leuven: Claeys & Casteels, 2008); Gil Carlos Rodriguez Iglesias, et al., eds., *EC State Aid Law: Liber Amicorum Francisco Santaolalla Gadea* (Alphen aan den Rijn: Wolters Kluwer Law, 2008); and Leigh Hancher, Tom Ottervanger, and Piet Jan Slot, eds., *EU State Aids* (London: Sweet & Maxwell, 2012).

2 A very useful overview is provided in the European Commission, "The Effects of Temporary State Aid Rules Adopted in the Context of the Financial and Economic Crisis" (Commission staff working paper SEC(2011) 1126 final, Brussels, 2011).

3 See the State Aid score board COM(2011) 848. See also European Commission, "Facts and Figures on State Aid in the EU Member States" (Commission staff working paper SEC(2011) 1487 final, Brussels, 2011).

4 The only legislation was in the field of shipbuilding, where there have been several directives succeeded by Council Regulation (EC) 1540/98 of 29 June 1998 establishing new rules on aid to shipbuilding [1998] OJ L 202/1.

5 [1998] OJ L 141/1. Amended by Regulation 733/2013 [2013] OJ L 204/1.

6 [1999] OJ L 83/1. Amended by Regulation 734/2013 [2013] OJ L 204/15.

7 Cf. European Commission, *Competition Law in the European Communities: Rules Applicable to State Aids* (Luxembourg: Office for Official Publications of the European Union, 2014). The terminology is not very consistent. The central feature of all of these rules is that they are not adopted on the basis of an article in the treaty or secondary legislation.

8 An extensive analysis of this concept is provided by Luca Rubini, *The Definition of Subsidy and State Aid: WTO and EC Law in Comparative Perspective* (Oxford: Oxford University Press, 2009).

9 Case 30/59 *De Gezamenlijke Steenkolenmijnen in Limburg v. High Authority of the ECSC* EU:C:1961:2, para 19, confirmed in Case C-387/92 *Banco de Crédito Industrial SA, now Banco Exterior de España SA v. Ayuntamiento de Valencia* EU:C:1994:100.

10 Joined Cases C-72/91 and C-73/91 *Sloman Neptune* EU:C:1993:97.

11 Case C-379/98 *PreussenElektra AG v. Schleswag AG* EU:C:2001:160. The interesting thing about this judgment is that the Court's decision would probably have been different had the undertakings concerned been owned by the state.

12 In Case C-559/12 P *France v. Commission* EU:C:2014:217 the CJEU ruled that a presumption exists that the implied unlimited guarantee granted by the French State in favor of La Poste constitutes state aid.

13 Case C-280/00 *Altmark Trans GmbH v. Nahverkers-gesellschaft* EU:C:2003:415.

14 Case 67/85 *Kwekerij Gebroeders van der Kooy BV and others v. Commission* EU:C:1988:38.

15 Case C-482/99 *Commission v. France* EU:C:2002:294.

16 Case 173/73 *Italy v. Commission* EU:C:1974:71.

17 The benefits of the Italian social security were based on the needs of the family of the worker, and the contributions were levied on the basis of the wage costs of each company. The Italian textile sector had a disproportionately low percentage of male workers, who could claim such benefits as head of a family. As a result, the textile industry was paying substantially more to the system than its male workers received in benefits.

18 See, e.g., Wolfgang Schön, "State Aid in the Area of Taxation," in Hancher, Ottervanger, and Slot, *EU State Aids*; and Dimitris Triantafylloou, "La Fiscalite faconnee par la discipline des aides d'Etat," in Rodriguez Iglesias et al., *EC State Aid Law: Liber Amicorum Francisco Santaolalla Gadea*. See also the older Commission notice on the application of the state aid rules to measures relating to direct business taxation [1998] OJ C 384/3.

19 Joined Cases C-106/09 P and C-107/09 P *Commission v. Gibraltar and the United Kingdom* EU:C:2011:732, para 145 with further citations of this principle.

20 Ibid., para 149.

21 Case C-88/03 *Portugal v. Commission* EU:C:2006:511.

22 Case 730/79 *Philip Morris Holland BV v. Commission* EU:C:1980:209.

23 Joined Cases 296/82 and 318/82 *The Netherlands and Leeuwarder Papierfabriek BV v. Commission* EU:C:1985:113, para 24.

24 See, e.g., Case T-274/01 *Valmont v. Commission* EU:T:2004:266. This case concerned the purchase of a plot of land of three hectares for approximately €400,000. The Commission was of the view that provincial government enabled Valmont to buy the land too cheaply and took a decision prohibiting the alleged aid. The striking feature of this case is that none of the parties raised the question of whether this transaction could have an effect on trade between the member states.

25 Commission Regulation (EU) No 1407/2013 of 18 December 2013 on the application of Articles 107 and 108 of the Treaty on the Functioning of the European Union to *de minimis* aid [2013] OJ L 352/1.

26 For trenchant criticism of this principle and its application, see Matthew Parish, "On the Private Investor Principle," *European Law Review* 28 (2003): 70–89. See further, Nicholas Khan and Klaus-Dieter Borchart, "The Private Market Investor Principle: Reality Check or Distorting Mirror?" in Rodriguez Iglesias et al., *EC State Aid Law: Liber Amicorum Francisco Santaolalla Gadea*. The draft

Commission Notice on the notion of state aid pursuant to Article 107(1) TFEU (2014) provides, in section 4.2, a useful summary of this principle.

27 Joined Cases 296/82 and 318/82 *Leeuwarder Papierwarenfabriek v. Commission*, n 23 this chapter.

28 [1994] OJ C 35/6.

29 Directive 2006/111 of 16 November 2006 on the transparency of financial relations between Member State and public undertakings as well as on financial transparency within certain undertakings [2006] OJ L 318/17.

30 Joined Cases C-83/01 P, C-93/01 P, and C-94/01 P *Chronopost SA v. Ufex* EU:C:2003:388.

31 Joined Cases T-267/08 and 279/08 *Région Nord-Pas-de-Calais and Communauté d'agglomération du Douaisis v. Commission* EU:T:2011:209. The appeal against the judgment has been denied C-389/11P EU:C:2012:408.

32 Joined Cases T-29/10 and 31/10 *Netherlands and ING v. Commission* EU:T:2012:98. Appealed as Case C-224/12 P EU:C:2014:213. The Court of Justice dismissed the appeal by judgment of 3 April 2014.

33 Joined Cases C-214/12P, C-215/12P, and C-223/12P EU:C:2013:682.

34 Case C-280/00 *Altmark-Trans*, n 13 this chapter. For a helpful discussion of this case, see Andreas Bartosch, "Clarification or Confusion? How to Reconcile the ECJ's Rulings in *Altmark* and *Chronopost*?" (CLaSF working paper no. 02, October 2003); and Frédéric Louis and Anne Vallery, "*Ferring* Revisited: The *Altmark* Case and State Financing of Public Services Obligations," *World Competition* 27 (2004).

35 Commission Decision of 20 December 2011 on the application of Article 106(2) of the Treaty on the Functioning of the European Union to state aid in the form of public service compensation granted to certain undertakings entrusted with the operation of services of general economic interest [2012] OJ L 7/3.

36 In Case C-156/98 *Germany v. Commission* EU:C:2000:467, the CJEU held (paras 52–55): "the phrase 'division of Germany' refers historically to the establishment of the dividing line between the two occupied zones in 1948. Therefore, the economic disadvantages caused by that division can only mean the economic disadvantages caused in certain areas of Germany by the isolation which the establishment of that physical frontier entailed, such as the breaking of communication links or the loss of markets as a result of the breaking off of commercial relations between the two parts of German territory. By contrast, the conception advanced by the German Government, according to which Article 92(2)(c) of the Treaty permits full compensation for the undeniable economic backwardness suffered by the new Länder, disregards both the nature of that provision as a derogation and its context and aims. The economic disadvantages suffered by the new Länder as a whole have not been directly caused by the geographical division of Germany within the meaning of Article 92(2)(c) of the Treaty. It follows that the differences in development between the original and the new Länder are explained by causes other than the geographical rift caused by the division of Germany and in particular by the different politico-economic systems set up in each part of Germany." See further, Heidenhain, *Handbuch de Europäischen Beiheilfenrechts*, 188 *et seq*.

37 Case 730/79 *Philip Morris*, n 22 this chapter.

38 See the Commission's 12th Report on Competition Policy (1983), para 160.

39 The 12th Report on Competition Policy, n 38 above, para 160.

40 Case 730/79 *Philip Morris*, n 22 this chapter, para 16.

41 Case C-290/07 P *Commission v. Scott* EU:C:2010:480, para 64.

42 The regulation has been amended by Regulation 733/2013, [2013] OJ L 204/11.

43 Readers should consult the website of the Directorate-General for Competition for the actual rules in force. Commissioners have a tendency to constantly revise the rules.

44 [2013] OJ L 352/1.

45 [2007] OJ L 315/1. Commission Regulation 1191/69 was the subject of Case C-280/00 *Altmark*, n 13 this chapter.

46 [2008] OJ L 214/3.

47 Paragraph 6 of the preamble.

48 Article 43 of the Regulation. See Koen Van de Casteele, "General Block Exemption Regulation," Hancher, Ottervanger, and Slot, *EU State Aids*, Chap. 11.03. See also Recital 68 of the Preamble.

49 Please consult the website of the Directorate-General for Competition.

50 Joined Cases C-106/09 P and C-107/09 P *Commission v. Gibraltar and the United Kingdom* n 19 this chapter, para 128.
51 This list excludes the guidelines in the financial sector. A complete overview can be found on the website of the Directorate-General for Competition.
52 [2009] OJ C 188/6.
53 [2009] OJ C 188/1.
54 [2006] OJ C 54/13.
55 [2010] OJ C 222/2.
56 [2009] OJ C 223/3.
57 [2006] OJ C 323/1.
58 [2008] OJ C 82/1.
59 [2009] OJ C 156/3.
60 [2004] OJ C 244/2.
61 Last amended by Regulation 1147/2008 [2008] OJ L 313/1.
62 Regulation 734/2013 [2013] OJ L 204/15. According to press release IP 13/728, "The reform improves the handling of complaints, leading to a swifter, more predictable and more transparent investigation of complaints. It ensures that the Commission is provided from the start with all the information necessary to investigate complaints, and clarifies the requirements to lodge them. New tools for gathering information directly from market participants and for conducting sector inquiries will allow the Commission to obtain all necessary information to adopt well-reasoned decisions. This is expected to significantly reduce the duration of the investigation in complex cases. The codification of the cooperation with national courts will ensure a coherent application of state aid rules across Member States. Together, these elements will improve the efficiency and effectiveness of state aid control, allowing the Commission to concentrate its resources on the most important cases, where distortions of competition are most significant, and to adopt faster and better decisions."
63 An example can be found in Case C-44/93 *Namur-Les Assurances du Crédit SA v. Office National du Ducroire and Belgium* EU:C:1994:311. This case also demonstrates how difficult it can be to draw the distinction between the two categories.
64 Article 108(1) TFEU uses the term "aid system" whereas the Regulation in Articles 1, 17, and 18, uses the term "aid schemes."
65 Case T-301/02 *AEM v. Commission* EU:T:2009:191, para 126. The appeal Case C-320/09 P EU:C:2011:858 was denied. In the same vein, Case T-297/02 *ACEA v. Commission* EU:T:2009:189, para 123; and Case T-222/04 *Italy v. Commission* EU:T:2009:194, para 99.
66 Case C-44/93 *Namur-Les Assurances* n 63 this chapter.
67 The regulation was amended by Commission Regulation 1125/2009 of 23 November 2009 as regards Part III.2, Part III.3, and Part III.7 of its Annex I.
68 As well as the member state, the intended beneficiary of the aid or a competitor that has manifested itself clearly may also lodge the appeal, Case C-198/91 *William Cook plc. v. Commission* EU:C:1993:197. Until April 2004, appeals by member states were reviewed by the Court of Justice.
69 Cases C-312/90 *Spain v. Commission* EU:C:1992:282 and C-47/91 *Italy v. Commission* EU:C:1992:284.
70 Case 120/73 *Gebrüder Lorenz GmbH v. Germany* EU:C:1973:152.
71 According to Article 107(3)(c) and (d) TFEU, "such aid should not affect trading conditions and competition in the Community to an extent that it is contrary to the common interest."
72 [1994] OJ L 254/73.
73 Commission Notice on a simplified procedure for the treatment of certain types of state aid [2009] OJ C 136/3.
74 Commission Notice on a Best Practices Code on the conduct of state aid control proceedings [2009] OJ C 136/13.
75 Case T-95/96 *Gestevision Telecinco SA v. Commission* EU:T:1998:206.
76 Case C-367/95 P *Commission v. Chambre Syndicale* (Sytraval) EU:C:1998:154.
77 Regulation 734/2013. See further n 62 this chapter.
78 Case 301/87 *France v. Commission* (Boussac) EU:C:1990:67.

79 Case C-354/90 *Fédération Nationale du Commerce Extérieur des Produits Alimentaires and Syndicat National des Négociants et Transformateurs de Saumon v. France* EU:C:1991:440.

80 Commission notice on the enforcement of state aid law by national courts [2009] OJ C 85/1.

81 Case C-39/94 *Syndicat Français de L'Express International (SFEI) and others v. La Poste and others* EU:C:1996:285.

82 Case C-199/06 *Centre d'exportation du livre Français and Ministre de la Culture et de la Communication v. Société internationale de diffusion et d'Edition* (CELF 1) EU:C:2008:79; Case C-1/09 *Centre d'exportation du livre Français and Ministre de la Culture et de la Communication v. Société internationale de diffusion et d'Edition* (CELF 2) EU:C:2010:136. See Christopher Vajda and Paul Stuart, "Effects of the Standstill Obligation in National Courts – All Said after CELF? An English Perspective," *European State Aid Law Quarterly* (2010): 629 *et seq.*; and Case C-275/10 *Residex Capital IV v. Gemeente Rotterdam* EU:C:2011:814.

83 The German Supreme Court (Bundesgerichtshof) has applied this rule in an interesting judgment concerning a dispute between Deutsche Lufthansa and Ryanair, I ZR 136/09, of 10 February 2011.

84 "There is an obligation to adopt safeguard measures only if the conditions justifying such measures are satisfied, namely, that there is no doubt regarding the classification as State aid, that the aid is about to be, or has been, implemented, and that no exceptional circumstances have been found which would make recovery inappropriate. If those conditions are not satisfied, the national court must dismiss the application."

85 Case C-275/10 *Residex*, n 82 this chapter, para 49 states, "in order to cover a loan granted by a finance company to an undertaking which would not have been able to secure such financing under normal market conditions. National courts are required to ensure that the aid is recovered and, to that end, they can cancel the guarantee, in particular where, in the absence of less onerous procedural measures, that cancellation is such as to lead to or facilitate the restoration of the competitive situation which existed before that guarantee was provided."

86 Case C-199/06 *CELF 1*, para 53; Case C-354/90 *Fédération Nationale du Commerce Extérieur*, n 79 this chapter.

87 This means that the Commission does not have to give a reasoned opinion, as required by Articles 258 and 259 TFEU. Therefore, the procedure of Article 108(2) TFEU is much more expedient.

88 The Commission followed this procedure in Case 70/72 *Commission v. Germany* (Kohlegesetz) EU:C:1973:87; Cases 31/77 R and 53/77 R *Commission v. United Kingdom* EU:C:1977:86; Case 203/82 *Commission v. Italy* EU:C:1983:218; Case 52/83 *Commission v. France* EU:C:1983:328; Case 93/84 *Commission v. France* EU:C:1985:114; Case 52/84 *Commission v. Belgium* EU:C:1986:3; Case 213/85 *Commission v. Netherlands* EU:C:1988:39; and Case C-5/89 *Commission v. Germany* EU:C:1990:320.

89 For an example of such a Council decision, see Case C-122/94 *Commission v. Council* EU:C:1996:68. Advocate General Cosmas reports that there had been no such decision from 1960 till 1967 and only fourteen between 1967 and 1983. However, there were twenty-three such decisions between 1984 and 1994.

90 Case C-110/02 *Commission v. Council* EU:C:2004:395.

91 Recovery notice Commission Notice Towards an effective implementation of Commission decisions ordering Member States to recover unlawful and incompatible State aid [2007] OJ C 272/4. See Elisabetta Righini, "Godot is Here: Recovery as an Effective State Aid Remedy," in Rodriguez Iglesias et al., *EC State Aid Law: Liber Amicorum Francisco Santaolalla Gadea*. The handbooks listed in n 1 of this chapter all provide extensive treatment of the subject.

92 Case 70/72 *Commission v. Germany*, n 88 this chapter.

93 Case 310/85 *Deufil GmbH & Co KG v. Commission* EU:C:1987:96.

94 Case 94/87 *Commission v. Germany* EU:C:1989:46; and, in particular, Case C-24/95 *Land Rheinland-Pfalz v. Alcan Deutschland GmbH* EU:C:1997:163. See also Case C-527/12 *Commission v. Germany* EU:C:2014:2193, according to the advocate general the question in this case is "May the recovery of aid found incompatible with the internal market be rendered absolutely impossible because of the

obligation to respect the right to effective judicial protection enjoyed by the recipient of that aid and, if so, in what circumstances and for how long?"

95 Article 4 of Commission Decision 2009/609 [2008] OJ L 225/53. See also Joined Cases T-80/06 and T-182/09 *Budapesti Eromu Zrt. v. Commission* EU:T:2012:65, para 21.

96 Case C-69/13 *Mediaset SpA v. Ministero dello Sviluppo economico* EU:C:2014:71.

97 Speech 12/117, dated 23 February 2012; "Here my example is very recent; only last month the Commission ordered Germany and Belgium to recover part of the aid granted to their postal operators over the years. Deutsche Post and the Belgian Post had received an amount of aid that exceeded the level of compensation required for the provision of the Service of General Interest that public authorities had entrusted them with. Therefore, we decided that the extra aid was incompatible since it put the companies in a better position than their competitors in commercial activities beyond their public service mandate." Case SA.17653, decision of 25 January 2012.

98 For an overview, see Francois-Charles Laprévote, "Selected Issues Raised by Banking Restructuring Plans under EU State Aid Rules," *European State Aid Law Quarterly* (2012). This section contains literal quotes and other data from the useful and comprehensive Commission staff working paper, "The effects of temporary State aid rules adopted in the context of the financial and economic crisis."

99 Victoria Ivashina and David Scharfstein, "Bank Lending during the Financial Crisis of 2008," *Journal of Financial Economics* 97 (2010).

100 EU Commission State Aid Scoreboard 2013, http://ec.europa.eu/competition/state_aid/scoreboard/financial_economic_crisis_aid:en.html.

101 [2004] OJ C 244/2.

102 Commission staff working paper, "The effects of temporary state aid rules adopted in the context of the financial and economic crisis," 10.

103 [2013] OJ C 216/1.

104 Communication from the Commission on the application of state aid rules to measures taken in relation to financial institutions in the context of the current global financial crisis [2008] OJ C 270/8.

105 Initially Ireland provided aid only to Irish banks and not to banks from other member states.

106 Communication from the Commission on Recapitalisation of financial institutions in the current financial crisis: limitation of the aid to the minimum necessary and safeguards against undue distortions of competition [2009] OJ C 10/2.

107 Communication from the Commission on the Treatment of Impaired Assets in the Community Banking sector [2009] OJ C 72/1.

108 According to the Commission staff working paper, "The effects of temporary State aid rules adopted in the context of the financial and economic crisis," the notion of "impaired asset" has broadened over time. Initially, impaired assets were understood as (1) assets whose intrinsic value is perceived to lie significantly above their market value, possibly because of failing or missing markets (owing to massive asymmetric information and valuation uncertainty). However, over time, impaired assets are also understood as including (2) assets that incorporate relatively high expected losses, and even (3) long-term assets without high expected losses ("good safe assets") but that still need to be hived off the balance sheet because the banks that carried them faced sharply higher funding costs that led them to record continuing losses over the lifetime of the assets.

109 Communication from the Commission on the return to viability and the assessment of restructuring measures in the financial sector in the current crisis under the State aid rules [2009] OJ C 195/9.

110 Communication from the Commission, "Temporary Community framework for State aid measures to support access to finance in the current financial and economic crisis" [2009] OJ C 16/9.

111 The Commission staff working paper, "The effects of temporary State aid rules adopted in the context of the financial and economic crisis," 6.

112 Communication from the Commission on the application, from 1 January 2011, of state aid rules to support measures in favour of banks in the context of the financial crisis [2010] OJ C 329/07; and

Communication from the Commission on the application, from 1 January 2012, of state aid rules to support measures in favour of banks in the context of the financial crisis [2011] OJ C 356/7.

113 Case C-33/2009 *Restructuring of BPP* [2011] OJ L 159/95. The Commission ordered the recovery by Portugal of the state aid granted to BPP.

114 See cases *ING*, *WestLB*, and *ABN AMRO*. The decisions under appeal are: Commission Decision of 18 November 2009 on state aid C 10/09 (ex N 138/09) implemented by the Netherlands for ING's Illiquid Assets Back Facility and Restructuring Plan [2010] OJ L 274/139; Commission Decision of 12 May 2009 on state aid which Germany proposes to grant towards the restructuring of West LB AG (C 43/08 (ex N 390/08)) [2009] OJ L 345/1; and C 11/2009 (not yet published). In Case T-319/11 *ABN-AMRO* EU:T:2014:186, the GC rejected claims that the Commissions had wrongly applied the Rescue and Restructuring Communication by imposing a ban on new acquisitions.

115 Case C-224/12 P *Commission v. Netherlands and ING Groep* EU:C:2014:213. In its judgment of 2 March 2012 the General Court annulled in part the contested decision, holding, inter alia, that the Commission was required to assess the economic rationality of the amendment to the repayment terms in the light of the private investor test. In order to determine the advantage conferred in the case of a capital injection, that test requires the difference in the terms under which the state has granted the injection and the terms under which a private investor would have done so to be taken into account. The Commission did not have to reexamine the amendment to repayment terms following the judgment of the Court of Justice because it had already taken a fresh decision following the view of the GC Commission decision of 12 May 2012, Decision C(2012) 3150 final.

References

Bartosch, Andreas. "Clarification or Confusion? How to Reconcile the ECJ's Rulings in *Altmark* and *Chronopost*?" CLaSF working paper no. 02, 2003.

European Commission. "Facts and Figures on State Aid in the EU Member States." Commission staff working paper SEC (2011) 1487 final, Brussels, 2011.

European Commission. "The Effects of Temporary State Aid Rules Adopted in the Context of the Financial and Economic Crisis." commission staff working paper SEC (2011) 1126 final, Brussels, 2011.

European Commission. *Competition Law in the European Communities: Rules Applicable to State Aids*. Luxembourg: Office for Official Publications of the European Union, 2014.

Hancher, Leigh, Tom Ottervanger, and Piet Jan Slot, eds. *EU State Aids*. London: Sweet & Maxwell, 2012.

Heidenhain, Martin H. *Handbuch des Europäischen Beihilfenrechts*. Munich: C. H. Beck, 2003.

Ivashina, Victoria, and David Scharfstein. "Bank Lending during the Financial Crisis of 2008." *Journal of Financial Economics* 97 (2010): 319–338.

Khan, Nicholas, and Klaus-Dieter Borchart. "The Private Market Investor Principle: Reality Check or Distorting Mirror?" In Rodriguez Iglesias, Van Miert, Monti, and Kroes, *EC State Aid Law: Liber Amicorum Francisco Santaolalla Gadea*, 109–125.

Laprévote, Francois-Charles. "Selected Issues Raised by Banking Restructuring Plans under EU State Aid Rules." *European State Aid Law Quarterly* (2012): 93–112.

Louis, Frédéric, and Anne Vallery. "*Ferring* Revisited: The *Altmark* Case and State Financing of Public Services Obligations." *World Competition* 27 (2004): 53–74.

Mederer, Wolfgang, Nicola Pesaresi, and Marc Van Hoof. *State Aid*. Vol. 4 of *EU Competition Law*. Leuven: Claeys & Casteels, 2008.

Parish, Matthew. "On the Private Investor Principle." *European Law Review* 28 (2003): 70–89.

Rigihini, Elisabetta. "Godot is Here: Recovery as an Effective State Aid Remedy." In Rodriguez Iglesias, Van Miert, Monti, and Kroes, *EC State Aid Law: Liber Amicorum Francisco Santaolalla Gadea*, 265–288.

Rodriguez Iglesias, Gil Carlos, Karel Van Miert, Mario Monti, and Neelie Kroes. *EC State Aid Law: Liber Amicorum Francisco Santaolalla Gadea*. Alphen aan den Rijn: Wolters Kluwer Law, 2008.

Rubini, Luca. *The Definition of Subsidy and State Aid: WTO and EC Law in Comparative Perspective.* Oxford: Oxford University Press, 2009.

Schön, Wolfgang. "State Aid in the Area of Taxation." In Hancher, Ottervanger, and Slot, *EU State Aids*, 321–362.

Triantafylloou, Dimitris. "La Fiscalite faconnee par la discipline des aides d'Etat." In Rodriguez Iglesias, Van Miert, Monti, and Kroes, *EC State Aid Law: Liber Amicorum Francisco Santaolalla Gadea*, 409–424.

Vajda, Christopher, and Paul Stuart. "Effects of the Standstill Obligation in National Courts – All Said after CELF? An English Perspective." *European State Aid Law Quarterly* (2010): 629–636.

Van de Casteele, Koen. "General Block Exemption Regulation." In Hancher, Ottervanger, and Slot, *EU State Aids*, 363–378. London: Sweet & Maxwell, 2012.

24

Statecraft, States, and the Regulation of Commerce

Ari Afilalo*

Introduction

Over the course of the past several hundred years, Europe has produced principles of international law and theory that have become cornerstones of international legal constructs. Much as the Arab world invented universally recognized numbers with which we still count, Europe has produced essential language and points of reference broadly used in today's international practice. This chapter reviews Europe's contributions to basic assumptions made in international law and governance. I examine the internal legal models that Europe created and that became foundational blueprints for modern liberal democracies (redistributive justice in one form or another, state interventionist to shore up economic borders, the right to elect a government, etc.). I also focus on international legal structures that were designed to operate in a manner consistent with the domestic European model (e.g., liberalization of trade, legal protections for foreign investors, or uniform codes of commercial law for international transactions).

Europe invented and exported a liberal democratic architecture to various destinations around the world that the French have aptly dubbed the *Etat providence*. The state's job is indeed "to provide," and it has done so generously throughout the Western world since 1945. The *Etat providence* redistributes assets. It guarantees its nationals a share of the collective resources. The bundle of rights includes instruments that range from transportation vouchers to complex health insurance schemes, all designed to further the overarching state commitment to provide a safety net for its subjects. Towards that end, the made-in-Europe Provider State created a complex administrative apparatus regulating industry, commerce, and virtually all other areas of societal activities. The state's hand in that model is in everything, and everyone has a stake in how the hand is dealt. The state protects workers against loss of livelihood. It regulates industries' potential infringement on the integrity of air, water, or other collective resources. It falls to the state to stabilize markets as it is the state alone that has the requisite tools. In crisis or in daily routine, the economic life of a mass of subjects affiliated with a given state look to it, and judge its legitimacy, based on how well it performs its function of providing welfare.

A Companion to European Union Law and International Law, First Edition.
Edited by Dennis Patterson and Anna Södersten.

The victors of the Second World War squarely embraced this worldview. The United States, while slower to develop its administrative state and less interventionist than Europe overall, nevertheless subscribed to the European model and even surpassed Europe in many tactical aspects of its modern liberal democratic strategy. The United States allowed its common law roots to flourish into an astonishingly complex judicial system dedicated to protecting its markets, people, and resources. The United States experimented with a federal system that, while constantly struggling with the proper allocation of powers among states and central decision making, still managed to innovate with nationwide administrative agencies that have been the cutting edge of their respective fields. America created securities laws that employed a massive bureaucracy that protected investors, produced rules of unfair competition as well as a wide array of common law redress for injury to person, property, and intangible rights. In turn, Europe followed American strategies and thinking in several of these areas. Altogether, though, at its roots, the system of regulatory welfare originated from the European legitimization of the state by reference to its provider function.

The post-Second World War regulation of commerce and livelihood in the European statecraft model came hand-in-hand with the protection of personal rights. The modern liberal democratic state derived its legitimacy from management of a social and political structure that bettered the material lot of its nationals. The state protected personal autonomy, in a variety of forms. Included here were lofty constitutional principles such as freedom of speech or of religion, and the checks on the state's power to police, investigate, or imprison its subjects. The regulatory space around personal rights also secured basic property and contract expectations. It established norms in a wide array of fields, from medical practice to car tires. At every level of government, the state molded a social context in which the "modern citizen" could safely seek happiness.

The right to vote and choose the government of the state became an inalienable pillar of modern liberal democracies. Along with it came the constitutional mandate to shelter discrete minorities from the majority's tyranny. The modern liberal democracies operated in well-entrenched physical borders associated to a substantial extent with the nation that formed the human basis for the state. The plurality and diversity of the ethnic, religious, or other components of the national collectivity necessitated some checks on the state's power for universal voting. Those included equal protection, freedom of religious practice, and welfare systems that in Europe tended to favor larger families and by demographic extension a relatively well-represented segment of immigrant populations. While the nation could determine its laws and preferences, it had to respect the basic rights of the population strata that did not have the same power and participatory rights as the core classes of the nation.

Given the powerful theoretical and rhetorical appeal of a system "for the people, by the people," it is no wonder that prominent Western thinkers posited that we reached the "end of history."[1] Yet, while they introduced systems and models of supposedly universal applicability and benefit, the made-in-Europe ideas have by-and-large failed spectacularly in the wider field of international application. Europe's failures in its international tests arose from the same stubborn refusal to let go of obsolete theories that profoundly harmed European states themselves. European intellectual history alternately produced creative boldness and breakthrough legal and political theories, on the one hand, and stubborn adherence to obsolete or misfit models of governance on the other. Today, Europe continues to insist on obsolete modalities of statecraft.

In this chapter, my goal is to identify, as relates principally to the business-oriented subject matter areas I focus on, the most damaging mistakes in statecraft, uncover the historical patterns that have led to them, and propose alternative courses of action to isolate the key elements of the European legal and political legacies and suggest applications for today's systems.

Nation-State Class Logic in the Age of the Cross-Border Classes

International legal norms and institutions operate under principles developed from European roots in and for another age. The international system that we regularly call upon to resolve intricate social, political, and financial problems has become structurally incapable of addressing today's challenges. Yet, our thinkers and policymakers continue to operate without even the language necessary to articulate the issues relevant to a foundational adjustment of the system's basic architecture. Instead, they insist on applying old formulas and fighting obsolete and pointless battles, hoping that more of the same in greater doses will accomplish their goals. They keep failing, not because they do not apply enough medication but because they have the wrong vial.[2]

The root cause of the problem lies in European-created theories of statecraft to which mainstream political theory has ascribed universal and timeless value. The twentieth-century European states fought for domination of the nation-state model, and the modern liberal democracies emerged victorious. They won not only militarily but also in the moral and legal battlefields. The European system prided itself on the universalization of voting and the power to self-govern. The consent of the governed, an optional consideration for the monarch, emperor, or other absolute ruler, became the cornerstone of the democratic state. At the same time, the governed would respect limits on the power to regulate over the objections of the minority. A system of individual rights protected individuals and social groupings against excessive control or abuse by the voting majorities.[3] An independent judiciary, obeyed by an executive branch with a "habit of compliance," guarded the effective operation of the rule of law.[4]

Post-Second World War European statecraft judged legitimacy not only in relation to the consent of the governed and the protection of the minority but also on the extent of a state's commitment to protect its nationals' financial security and to support market conditions meeting basic expectations of stability and growth. Economic and financial welfare, designed to secure minimal standards of living, became the subject of intense state intervention. The state shifted an unprecedented volume of resources from one class of citizens to the next; to do so it built massive administrative institutions.[5] The provider state regulated virtually all areas of social life, including labor, commercial, competition, environmental, worker safety, health, and countless other subject matter areas, with a view to establishing minimum standards of protection.[6]

Social security offices administered health or retirement systems of general reach. Labor bureaucracies gave employees access to judicial redress that protected workers and their unions' rights. Securities agencies oversaw markets. Generally, the state acted as the overseer and financial benefactor of a collective of nationals qualifying for citizenship and membership in the nation. The administrative state, a change so profound that eminent thinkers of the West evoked a de facto amendment of constitutionally established structures, became a mainstay of the *Etat providence*.[7]

The modern liberal democracies that won the Second World War, or joined the victors (the ultimate defeaters of Communism), took diverse approaches to their overall provider ethos. Britain chose the "cradle-to-grave" system, where the state defined the essential needs of each life stage and assisted its nationals with healthcare, childcare, education, housing, and other basics. Continental European systems also provided, as part of social safety nets, extensive regulation of the well-being of workers. In contrast to the United States, which followed an at-will common law default employment status, Europe viewed the relationship of employer and employee as a matter of public concern and mandatory law. The state itself designated the essentials of a contract that in many ways was thought of as replicating the social contract among working and high-income classes. The market would be respected, but the stake of the working class in the global pool would be secured. In Japan, the government worked with industry to create large companies' commitment to lifelong worker welfare.

These diverse economic and social projects shared an essential hallmark of legitimacy: the state's basic commitment to guarantee its subjects' economic well-being and its markets' stability. Competition, intellectual property, consumer protection, and other legal fields of extensive reach sought to achieve those twin goals. Direct intervention in the form of monetary policy or aid to industry or other commercial sectors (such as subsidies) was the tool designed to further the state's mission.[8] Not surprisingly, the international legal system was designed to operate in tandem with the domestic structures, and it followed the European model of statecraft in its theoretical assumptions. The international norms and institutional arrangements respected the basic assumption that each state had the freedom to establish and manage its own "provider system" as it saw fit. The nation-state's foundational hallmark of legitimacy was the concept of "national sovereignty," which, despite its definitional vagueness, animated the institutional and normative foundations of international law. The nation-state order relied on and operated in a world divided into "black box" states that the international collective had a habit of recognizing as distinct, sovereign entities.[9]

Sovereignty meant many things, but fundamentally it translated into the principle that the default locus of power lies within the state. Unless the state relinquished power to an international institution, and even then with the caveat that the national government could always select a regulatory space that it would still control notwithstanding international law to the contrary, the state had virtually unfettered power over the individuals, businesses, assets, and land located within its boundaries. States were associated with a distinct, national identity, reified in the United Nations, and no international organization could dictate the policies or strategies of a state, or otherwise interfere with its internal affairs.[10] The United Nations Charter recognized the inviolability of a state's boundaries, allowing interference only in self-defense or in defense of a treaty partner.[11] While international courts and international law flourished, the legitimacy of the international system depended on its respect for the states' domestic authority. The international commercial system followed suit.

Respect for the state's work in the financial and economic fields sheltered the contracting parties' internal regulation under the General Agreement on Tariffs and Trade (GATT) as initially written. The GATT succeeded in liberalizing trade and introducing comparative advantage as the animating norm of international commerce, instead of mercantilism, precisely because it set out to end discriminatory treatment of foreign goods, services, capital, and labor, without threatening redistributive justice choices. The GATT does not in theory mandate any particular system of taxation or of redistribution. It only prohibits discriminatory taxation and regulation, mandating instead "national treatment." While of course the field of trade witnessed fierce clashes between free movement and domestic regulation of commerce, the GATT, like most international treaties, gave its members a wide margin of "selective exit,"[12] the ability of a state to reject its obligations under the international system when it deemed its national interests to be unduly burdened.[13] Indeed, we can see the wisdom of the system at work in the bailout packages crafted by various GATT members. Those emergency monies to revive stalled economies contained large numbers of performance requirements and requirements that the funds target nationals only, which no state bothered to challenge.[14]

This balanced cooperation over the enforcement of international law was defined by the concept of sovereignty. "Rational choice theory" described the process by which officials from different states selected the disputed issues to press with their treaty partners, mindful of their own violations of international law and the need to balance enforcement of norms with limiting the general reach of international law.[15] Virtually all major states shared a common interest in checking and restraining international law, with various degrees of tolerance for its displacement of domestic norms but with a uniform commitment to leaving states masters of the boundaries of national sovereignty. States, in a virtually uniform course of practice, did not allow the international judicial system to empower individuals to pursue their international legal rights. The states' control over collective judicial systems allowed for their respective balancing of the public policy issues involved in a given dispute, including both national and international considerations, free of the individual interests of constituent groups who would assert international law without proper consideration of the systemic consequences.[16]

The geographical boundaries of each state determined the extent of its authority. The boundaries were difficult to cross. In addition to preserving regulatory choices, international law also deferentially left internal security and policing matters to the exclusive province of the states. No matter how brutal the regime, foreign intervention would run afoul of international law. Regardless of how poor a country was, its government had the inalienable right to continue to apply wrongheaded economic policies or to loot the public coffers. The persona of a state was almost likened to that of an individual. One state, one vote, was the rule at the United Nations (although influence over others, wealth, and other factors gave some votes more impact). Unless subject to aggression or defending an ally suffering aggression, the collective of states would not allow a violation of sovereign borders.[17]

This is, then, the model that arose after the Second World War as the universal blueprint for statecraft. It showed such promise that some saw it ushering in the "end of History." This is the model that the West sought to export to the newly independent former colonies of Africa, Asia, and the Americas. And yet, at a time of great strife, the European model of statecraft is experiencing another rupture at a crucial crossroads of strategic and historical profound significance. Much as it failed to recognize after the Second World War that the time had come to abandon the protectionist and noninterventionist policies that had been in line with statecraft in a consolidating stage of their history, the European statecraft model insists on retaining the essentials of modern liberal democratic governance. Despite their familiarity and profound humanity, principles like voting, universal economic security within a "nation," and other staples of the last century must go in order for the modern liberal democracies to evolve successfully and adapt to new circumstances. For this to happen, we must identify the parts of the European model that can be retained, and those that should be abandoned for the sake of graduating to the next era of statecraft.

La Raison du Plus Fou est Toujours la Meilleure

"The law of the most insane is always the best," La Fontaine could have said of today's debates.[18] Another genius, Albert Einstein, famously remarked that insanity is best defined as the repetition of the same pattern of behavior with the expectation of a different outcome.[19] By this definition, most Western governments are populated by not quite sane graduates of prestigious political science schools and constitutional law professors. For good reasons, modern liberal democracies have profound attachment to their essential norms regarding voting rights, civil rights, and state commitment to preserve the economy, these must be retained at all costs in the face of crises. This mode of governance and its assumptions, however, means that the European statecraft model animates political and legal life without taking into account the patterns of history that brought us to where we are and that teach us where statecraft should be going.

The starting point of the analysis must be an understanding of Europe's evolutionary state at the onset of the First World War. At that time, Europe was made up of states with boundaries that grew out of a historical process coinciding roughly with the Industrial Revolution and the advent of market-based capitalism. The European powers had emerged from successive historical phases where power and wealth had concentrated at the top of a society that was sharply class based. Serfs, peasants, servants, and other subordinates had little opportunity to break out of their defined roles in society and to bridge the gap separating them from the nobility and other privileged echelons of society.[20]

The European States' central objective during that period was self-strengthening. Colonial resources were appropriated by force. States sought to maximize exports and minimize imports. At times they resorted to protectionist legislation to shield domestic markets from foreign competition. They seldom resorted to state interventionist action in the national market that later became the staple of the administrative state. The growing markets were as a general rule thought to be too fragile to withstand socioeconomic regulation raising the cost of doing business. States did not yet have a vision of the massive protective social nets of the twentieth century, and instead they held back during cycles of boom and bust that accompanied industrialization, despite widespread economic suffering during recessions.[21]

As Europe transformed its basic mode of statecraft into modern liberal democracies, agrarian economies transformed into increasingly urban-based capitalistic markets. A sharp distinction between workers ("proletariat") and the stakeholders in the capital ("bourgeois," "capitalists," etc.) pool prevailed. The state tended to allow the boom-and-bust cycles to operate unhindered by state intervention in order to accumulate capital and consolidate the economy. Struggle over the allocation of resources took a central part in the historical evolution of statecraft during that era, but the state did not see itself as unconditionally committed to ensuring rights and financial welfare until the beginning of the twentieth century. It was only then that a consolidating "national economy" could sustain the high degree of regulation that came to characterize modern liberal democracy.[22]

European states' external enterprises before the First World War were consistent with their internal constitutional guidelines. The European states sought to consolidate their internal power by drawing on as many resources as they could. The colonization enterprise embodied this model as well. Europeans fought among themselves to carve out African, Asian, and American colonies that they viewed as sources of strength to bolster the "center." International commerce was a zero-sum game because collaboration conflicted with the consolidation ethos. International legal institutions had little place in the system, whereas power, both of gunboat and of economic might, accorded with the consolidation project.[23]

The historical process of formation of the European nation-states' geographical map created blocs that had clear boundaries associated with national identity. Of equal importance were the clear lines of demarcation among internal subgroups on which the state relied when doing its entitlements and regulatory work. The working classes, managerial classes (*le patronat*), unions, and other major actors graduated into a relatively cohesive and definable aggregation of shared interests. Those became the state's principal interlocutors when European statecraft evolved into the age of the nation-state. The state's legitimacy lay in its intervention to balance the allocation of resources among these newly created classes.[24]

This is what transformed statecraft into a modern liberal democratic nation-state model. Making the right to vote universal broke away from the concentration of governance and economic power in the few. The gradual reallocation of shares in the collective pool became a foundational necessity. The consolidating state no doubt could have done more to alleviate the extreme circumstances of working classes, well known from literary testimony of the likes of

Zola or Sinclair. It could have conditioned grants of commercial privileges on a greater extension of rights, and prodded the private sector to give this goal greater priority. It could have gradually allocated sufficient resources to accomplish its welfare goals.

The modern liberal democratic states learned the evolving lessons of statecraft slowly and after suffering existential strategic crises. The deep integration-seeking enterprise of the European Union did not come until after the Second World War. In Robert Schuman's famous words, war was already "unthinkable," and the integration of Europe into interdependent states would also make it "materially impossible." The trade-liberalizing project that started with the GATT did not come about until after modern liberal democracies, stubbornly insisting on protectionist principles that made sense in the consolidating age, fought trade wars as they prepared to fight totalitarianism.

Today, Europe is repeating the historical pattern of seeking to ascribe universal and timeless values to its evolving models. The United States, distinctive but at its roots an adherent to modern liberal democratic statecraft, has followed suit. Internally, the reallocation of resources that characterized the nation-state continues to dominate political theory notwithstanding the new reality of globalized markets. Manuel Valls, the evidently gifted prime minister of France, is leading a government that reacted to a stinging defeat in mid-term elections with a vehement affirmation that better collection of delinquent taxes and more effective systems to combat tax evasion will lead to the recovery of the dwindling *Etat providence* in France. In the United States, we have seen higher minimum wages becoming the focus of old battles between the Right and the Left. Blaming the stock market and banks has become the rallying cry of movements driven by economic and social malaise.

More redistributive justice within the boundaries of the state, however, will not resolve any of today's issues in a world where economic and social actors operate outside of the framework of the nation-state. In a sense, we are experiencing the consolidating process that made the nation-states, except it is happening across borders. Markets are integrating throughout the world. Businesses are demanding, and obtaining, judicially enforceable rights to minimal economic security. They have the right to sue governments and each other in a richly evolving arbitral system. Jobs are being outsourced with little or no regulation from the countries at issue. Ownership of assets has become so associated with cross-border partnerships and virtually "a-national" business interests as to make it extremely difficult for states to control reallocation or interventionist policies.

This process may be conceptualized as a "delocalization" from the national locus of statecraft. States themselves are becoming *apatride*, another useful French concept that denotes the lack of a nation to which belonging may be claimed. Formerly used in reference to refugees and other individuals, the term has now been extended to cover the state: the *apatride patrie*. This is a state no longer associated solely with its nation, its national classes, its redistribution of wealth amassed among a privileged few over the years, and its black box ability to regulate and to control a defined territory. A state could host an exceedingly important economic asset that is controlled in its entirety from another state. It could allow into its markets products and services from another state that were made in violation of its policy choices because required to do so under international trade law. The very same state could have enacted wage and labor legislation yet, at the same time, be home to principally outsourcing enterprises. In all of these cases, the state has no compelling interest in doing what legitimated its existence in the waning age: redistributing wealth and regulating social life in order to shore up and give economic balance to less privileged classes operating in well-defined boundaries.

Indeed, more of the same, without an in-depth assessment and upgrade of the architecture of legal and political systems, will not begin to solve today's problems. Wages of $10 or even

$12 instead of $9 per hour will not eliminate poverty and the discomfort many feel with the international system. Raiding all Swiss banks every morning to unearth hidden money will not bail out the provider state. Occupying every cubicle on Wall Street, or even shutting down Goldman Sachs, will not make our society any less inequitable that it is now. Rather, the focus must be on how to best enable economic opportunity for those who are losing in the international market consolidation process. Free trade posited that the state would provide for the nationals who fared less well in the comparative advantage competitive market. This function was supposed to be part of the providing, welfare-generating ethos of the nation-state. But without classes, without defined groups to support, and without tools of regulation like monetary policy that the international markets have commodified, the redistributive justice system should operate on different essential strategic assumptions than in the waning nation-state order.

This conclusion can be drawn even more sharply when we take into account the consolidating or broken states outside of Europe, which the European-made statecraft continues to insist should follow our modern liberal democratic blueprint. While states like China may achieve a rapid consolidation that will bring their economy into a group resembling the conditions in the European market, other states have no chance of meaningfully participating in the international system unless their boundaries are redrawn fundamentally. Nigeria, for example, follows the classical African pattern of a state with an Islamic north and Christian or (although declining rapidly) animist south. The north has become fractured between the traditional tribal chiefs who would agree to retain the Nigerian construct inherited from the British, and groups like Boko Haram (standing for "the practice of the West is sinful") who would take over and eradicate democracy or secede. The struggle among Boko Haram and other caliphate visionaries and the Nigerian state à la European statecraft is bound to produce yet another catastrophic civil war, much like Biafra's secessionist struggle, which tore to pieces the newly independent Nigeria.

The European model's failure is the result of its continued insistence on treating constitutional systems of statecraft as timeless and universal, instead of recognizing that they are rooted in a specific historical cyclical evolution and may have a certain shelf expiration date. European-born statecraft treats a system that rejects the right to vote, the separation of religion and state, or a commitment to some form of redistributive justice, as heresy. For example, on 3 July 2013, the Egyptian military overthrew President Mohamed Morsi, who emerged from the Muslim Brotherhood movement to become Egypt's first freely elected president following the end of Hosni Mubarak's thirty-year rule in February 2011. In October 2013, the United States decided to cut off foreign aid to Egypt because its military had removed an elected president, even though he was aiding and abetting a global terrorist movement and may never have held elections again.[25]

Endless movements of protests, together with strong expectations of state financial welfare commitment, have created a negative image of freedom of economic activities associating the unprecedented liberalization and expansion of commerce through social strata and groups with inequalities and oppression. In the European marketplace of ideas, the imagery and arguments used stay the same as they were in the last century. The Left wants more entitlements. The Right wants to expand the free market. Both deconstruct and reconstruct the other, and, in the end, they make the same mistake of searching for a single truth that will transcend time and subject matter to provide the ideal mode of government. The "single truth habit," that some have argued is traceable to the appropriation of legitimacy from a single heavenly voice by church and kings, led Europe to retain obsolete systems, impose them on others by force or persuasion, and change only after great damage has been wrought. This happened in the twentieth century, in the *entre-guerre* age of darkness after euphoria, and it is happening now.

The French concept of *acquis social*, discussed earlier, posits a gradual improvement of modes of governance prying away power from the narrowest of circles, the monarchs and their courts, to the widest possible "national tent." The vision of this approach is one in which every regulatory structure makes better provision for the people in an acquired gain from the classes of the "haves." The very language of "reactionary" and "progressive" encapsulates the viscerally averse reaction of European statecraft to a new system of governance that does not hold as sacrosanct existing legitimacy hallmark icons of the Western world such as voting, respecting state boundaries, redistribution of assets across classes to achieve social justice, or other lofty goals that we all have come to know and love – and if not love, at least respect.

The urgent priority facing those who seek in good faith to provide good government is to accept the challenge to the continued adequacy of these notions, however profoundly humane they are. The state is gradually evolving into a new foundational mode of governance that does not legitimize itself by redistributing among classes within nations. The reason for this evolution is, quite simply, that the international and the internal organizational structures of the nation-state no longer exist. The classes have fragmented into loose groups that cut across borders and seek a stake in a collective pool that is no longer coextensive with the nation. Industrial undertakings and assets are owned by diverse groups, and the globalization of trading markets has generated an inevitable wave of company consolidations, joint ventures, and transactions across borders made desirable by the greater market.

Tools of policy such as monetary intervention and exchange rate controls have become commodified by the market to such an extent that governments have little power to intervene in a meaningful way. The market, not the government, fixes trading rates for currencies. The factors of production are so diffuse and loosely interconnected that regulation and state spending no longer have a discernable target group of beneficiaries within the nation. Instead, with outsourcing, interloped ownership of business groups, and the general spillage above and across borders, a US bailout plan may wind up helping Chinese manufacturers more than the Michigan enterprises the Congress has in mind. What was good and true at the end of the consolidating age is no longer a social basis to regulate.

This means that European statecraft must accept that the state can no longer be responsible for redistributing assets in the manner it did in the twentieth century. The state has neither the structure, nor even the means today, to guarantee entitlements. We find ourselves, interestingly, at the transformative beginning of another consolidating age. This time, however, the breaking collective of state is consolidating not around a nation but into some international groupings that are currently in the making and that have no immediate goal other than strengthening themselves.

The new collective of states will first have to redraw geographical boundaries that came out of another age. It will have to accept that voting is not a fundamental element of the liberalized trade if it results in the election of murderous enemies of pluralism and personal autonomy. Boundaries created by colonial powers have clearly failed Africa, the Middle East, and other conquered lands. Ironically, the savviest interpreters of statecraft are radical Islamic movements like Daesh (Islamic State), Boko Haram, or Al-Qaeda in the Maghreb. Those movements recognize the void created by the end of the nation state, and instead of heeding the Western insistence that Sunnis and Shiites should just get along in one central government in Baghdad, they are spreading their own view of the state to territories that have been left in a massive power vacuum.

Just as the state of the Industrial Revolution could not be the provider, there is no international institution or collective of states, despite the "networks" of officials and other international phenomena at work, that can regulate the vast market in a way that replicates on the international plane the welfare mode of the nation-state. However, this does not mean that the states cannot do more than repeat the same governance patterns (higher minimum wage, more redistribution, or less depending on political outlook) and ignore the reality that these methods are not working.

The new collective of states will ultimately transform its legitimating ethos from guaranteeing a safety net for its nations to doing all it can to shore up its markets within the larger globalized whole. This will mean looking at legislation in a different way. For example, if the United States opens up more of its resources to fracking, then the new statecraft architectural mode of legislating would raise the question of how to secure the United States market's meaningful participation in an enterprise that is bound to be multinational. It would make complete sense for the United States to condition the grant of permits or other right to participate in the business on the employment of US nationals or the use of US subcontractors. This would require, in turn, a major overhaul of international trade and international investment law to eliminate national treatment rules that, in this context, would not fulfill their original purpose.

The theoretical work is crucial to this enterprise. From the standpoint of commerce and trade, the foundational model of trade including national treatment, tariffication, and deference to national sovereignty, no longer does the job. National treatment has to be reevaluated in a world where the state cannot tie its hands with a nondiscrimination pledge when virtually every measure shoring up its economy and the opportunities it produces will entail special burdens on foreign businesses. The limits of the state will have to be examined without any "accrued progress" shields. Of course the state will not withdraw overnight from its entitlements programs. That would ensure market collapse instead of incentivizing activities. But the inquiry will require balancing programs against their costs in light of a defined goal that is no longer based on people's rights but on the maximization of economic opportunities.

If states had collaborated more to protect the rising classes as their economy consolidated, then the Industrial Revolution period would have still produced cycles of boom and bust that were difficult to weather but the pain of the business would have been attenuated. Not everyone could come within the cycle of entitlements until enough consolidation created classes and resources to reallocate, but the upward slope of progress could have started much earlier. This is the situation we face today. We must be prepared to accept that some will be facing such dire conditions with the consolidation of the global markets as to evoke Zola's and Sinclair's worlds. To those, perhaps, we should start working on international welfare and entitlements, but we should also be understanding and mindful that there will not be international welfare for all for a few more generations.

This should replicate a rethinking of boundaries and of the universality of voting. It is of course heartening to see a successful birth of a democratic system in a country like Tunisia. But voting and consent of the governed is not an end in itself. If voting brings about the Muslim Brotherhood, then it should give way to more achievable hallmarks of democracy in a country like Egypt: personal security, right to engage freely in livelihood, engagement with the international markets, and so on. If Kurdistan is a country that is viable under these principles, then we should support its birth wholeheartedly without any concern for a broken Iraq. The void of the Sunni areas is like the void of the Malian Sahara or of the Algerian desert land: it will be filled by one state or the next, and our strategic alignment will fare much better with carving Kurdistan out of Iraq than waiting for the Shiite prime minister who will finally erect the tent big enough to welcome the Sunni rebels.

It was not any less difficult for the statesmen and stateswomen of the twentieth century to reject the notion that the "business of America is business," that isolationism was the true protector of American values, or that commerce was a game to win by selling more than the neighbor rather than specializing. We have reified the system that followed the mercantilist, consolidating world with a timeless understanding of comparative advantage, nondiscrimination against foreigners' economic interest, voting for one's own government, and the provider state. It will be difficult to reject those principles, in part because of how lofty and constitutionally sound they have been for so long. However, this choice must be made and, unless we do so proactively now, we will be thinking again about the issues in five or ten years, at the end of the first globalized conflict of the age when fractured democracies will learn in blood the lessons that they could already draw from our past with experience and common sense.

Notes

* The author thanks Yuval Nir for his invaluable contribution, and Dennis Patterson and Anna Södersten for their outstanding editorial support and insights. Throughout this chapter, I use the word "state" to designate the abstract entity that takes various forms such as state nation, nation-state, and market state. A particular state is referenced as, for example, "the French state."

1 Francis Fukuyama, "The End of History?" *The National Interest* (Summer 1989): 3.

2 While this chapter focuses on the commercial and trade international legal fields, my basic conclusions extend generally to the many legal fields (e.g., constitutional protections of discrete minorities) that are shaped by statecraft architecture.

3 "Democracy attaches itself to a form of government: liberalism, to liberty and guarantees of liberty .... The freedom of worship, the freedom of education, and the freedom of the press are derived the most directly from the freedom to think." John Joseph Lalor, *Cyclopædia of Political Science, Political Economy, and of the Political History of the United States* (New York: Maynard, Merrill, & Co., 1899), 760.

4 The "habit of compliance" or "habit of obedience" of the European, American, and other modern liberal democratic governments, arises out of a culture that prides itself on governance through law rather than the arbitrary and unpredictable decisions of government officials: "The compliance pull of law in liberal Western democracies does not rest on the gun and coercion; it rests on a political culture which internalizes, especially public authorities, obedience to the law rather than to expediency. Though not perfect, one good measure of the rule of law is the extent to which public authorities in a country obey the decisions, even uncomfortable, of their own courts." J.H.H. Weiler, "Van Gend en Loos: The Individual as Subject and Object and the Dilemma of European Legitimacy," *International Journal of Constitutional Law* 12 (2014): 100–104.

5 Steffen Mau and Benjamin Veghte, *Social Justice, Legitimacy and the Welfare State* (Aldershot: Ashgate, 2007); and Steffen Mau, "Welfare Regimes and the Norms of Social Exchange," *Current Sociology* 52 (2004).

6 Michael Mandelbaum, *The Ideas That Conquered the World: Peace, Democracy, and Free Markets in the Twenty-First Century* (New York: Public Affairs, 2002), 34–36.

7 So broad and extensive was the power of the administrative state that it led scholars like Bruce Ackerman to argue that its rise amounted to a de facto constitutional amendment creating a "fourth branch" of government. See Bruce A. Ackerman, "The Storrs Lectures: Discovering the Constitution," *Yale Law Journal* 93 (1984): 1053–1055.

8 For further discussion about the type of social welfare that has succeeded in the United States see, e.g., Margaret Weir, Ann Shola Orloff, and Theda Skocpol, eds., *Politics of Social Policy in the United States* (Princeton, NJ: Princeton University Press, 1988); and Ellen Immergut, "Institutions, Veto Points, and Policy Results: A Comparative Analysis of Health Care," *Journal of Public Policy* 10 (1991). For Continental Europe, see Thomas Ertman, *The Birth of the Leviathan: Building States and Regimes in Medieval and Early Modern Europe* (Cambridge: Cambridge University Press, 1997). For the United Kingdom, see Rodney Lowe, *Welfare-State-Britain since 1945* (New York: St. Martin's Press, 1999). For Japan, see Taro Miyamoto, "Dynamics of the Japanese Welfare State in Comparative Perspective: Between 'Three Worlds' and the Developmental State," *The Japanese Journal of Social Security Policy* 2 (2003).

9 Ann Marie Thomson and James L. Perry, "Collaboration Processes: Inside the Black Box," *Public Administration Review* 66 (2006).

10 Ari Afilalo and Dennis Patterson, *The New Global Trading Order: The Evolving State and the Future of Trade* (Cambridge: Cambridge University Press, 2008), 55–56.

11 UN Charter Article 2(7) lays down the general principle of nonintervention by the United Nations and directs the organs of the United Nations to respect domestic affairs of states.

12 J.H.H. Weiler, "The Transformation of Europe," *Yale Law Journal* 100 (1991): 2411–2412.

13 John Ruggie called the delicate understanding that the major players of the trading system finally reached the "embedded liberalism" bargain. See John G. Ruggie, "Embedded Liberalism and the Postwar Economic Regimes," in *Constructing the World Policy: Essays on International Institutionalization* (London: Routledge, 1998).

14 The most well-known US protectionist measure during this period was the American Recovery and Reinvestment Act from February 2009, which included the "Buy American" provision. This provision imposed a general requirement that any public building or public works project funded by the new stimulus package must use only iron, steel, and other manufactured goods produced in the United States. The Buy American provision was later expanded further, for example, with The Consolidated Appropriations Act of 2010 (Public Law 111–117), which forbid Amtrak from issuing "contracts [for] ... services provided at or from any location outside the United States" (Sec. 152).

15 Jack L. Goldsmith and Eric A. Posner, *The Limits of International Law* (New York: Oxford University Press, 2005).

16 Anne-Marie Slaughter frequently discussed the concept of a network of decision makers being the new locus of decisional authority under international law and the efficiencies provided by government networks, particularly regulatory networks. See, e.g., Anne-Marie Slaughter, "Government Networks: The Heart of the Liberal Democratic Order," in *Democratic Governance and International Law*, ed. Gregory Fox and Brad Roth (Cambridge: Cambridge University Press, 2000), 214, 217, 223–224.

17 For further related reading on the process of how sovereignty and balance of powers is gradually replaced by a horizontal playing field created by the continued rise of a global trading class spread across borders in light of the diffuseness that characterizes the global marketplace, see Peter F. Drucker, "The Age of Social Transformation," *Atlantic Monthly* (November 1994). See also Robert Cooper, "The Breaking of Nations: Order and Chaos in the Twenty-First Century," *Atlantic* (2003).

18 Jean de la Fontaine was a famous French fabulist and poet. I based my assumption on his rendition of Aesop's well-known fable, "Le Loup et l'agneau" ("The Wolf and the Lamb"). This fable including a translated version can be found at http://www.jdlf.com/lesfables/livrei/leloupetlagneau.

19 *North American Wildlife and Natural Resources Conference* (Vol. 71, Wildlife Management Institute, 1975), 54.

20 Michael Mann, *The Sources of Social Power*, vol. 1 of *The Rise of Classes and Nation-States, 1760–1914* (Cambridge: Cambridge University Press, 1993).

21 Max Weber, "The Nation State and Economic Policy," in *Political Writings*, ed. Peter Lassman and Ronald Speirs (New York: Cambridge University Press, 1994).

22 On the notions of the "market-state" and the "nation-state," see Philip Bobbitt, *The Shield of Achilles: War, Peace and the Course of History* (London: Penguin, 2003), 213–242; Andrew Gamble, "Two Faces of Neo-Liberalism," in *The Neo-Liberal Revolution: Forging the Market State*, ed. Richard Robison (Basingstoke: Palgrave Macmillan, 2006); and Adrian Pabst, "The Crisis of Capitalist Democracy," *Telos* (Fall 2010).

23 Theda Skocpol, "Bringing the State Back In: Strategies of Analysis in Current Research," in *Bringing the State Back In*, ed. Peter B Evans, Dietrich Rueschemeyer, and Theda Skocpol (Cambridge: Cambridge University Press, 1985), 3. See also Philip Bobbitt, *The Shield of Achilles*, 96. For further reading regarding the process by which postmodern states started to accept, to various degrees, sharing control over domestic matters with supranational or global regimes and institutions, see

Robert Cooper, "The Breaking of Nations"; and Robert Kagan, *Of Paradise and Power: America and Europe in the New World Order* (New York: Random House, 2003).

24 See, e.g., Simon Clarke, *Keynesianism, Monetarism, and the Crisis of the State* (Aldershot: Edward Elgar, 1988), explaining how political stability depended on the development of a constitutional form adequate to the universalistic claims of the liberal state.

25 Elise Labott, "U.S. Suspends Significant Military Aid to Egypt," CNN, available at http://edition.cnn.com/2013/10/09/world/meast/us-egypt-aid/.

References

Ackerman, Bruce A. "The Storrs Lectures: Discovering the Constitution." *Yale Law Journal* 93 (1984): 1013–1072.

Afilalo, Ari, and Dennis Patterson. *The New Global Trading Order: The Evolving State and the Future of Trade*. Cambridge: Cambridge University Press, 2008.

Bobbitt, Philip. *The Shield of Achilles: War, Peace and the Course of History*. London: Penguin, 2003.

Clarke, Simon. *Keynesianism, Monetarism, and the Crisis of the State*. Aldershot: Edward Elgar, 1988.

Cooper, Robert. "The Breaking of Nations: Order and Chaos in the Twenty-First Century." *Atlantic* (2003): 27–44.

Drucker, Peter F. "The Age of Social Transformation." *Atlantic Monthly* (November 1994): 72–73.

Ertman, Thomas. *The Birth of the Leviathan: Building States and Regimes in Medieval and Early Modern Europe*. Cambridge: Cambridge University Press, 1997.

Fukuyama, Francis. "The End of History?" *The National Interest* (Summer 1989): 3–18.

Gamble, Andrew. "Two Faces of Neo-Liberalism." In *The Neo-Liberal Revolution: Forging the Market State*, edited by Richard Robison, 20–35. Basingstoke: Palgrave Macmillan, 2006.

Goldsmith, Jack L., and Eric A. Posner. *The Limits of International Law*. New York: Oxford University Press, 2005.

Immergut, Ellen. "Institutions, Veto Points, and Policy Results: A Comparative Analysis of Health Care." *Journal of Public Policy* 10 (1991): 391–416.

Kagan, Robert. *Of Paradise and Power: America and Europe in the New World Order*. New York: Random House, 2003.

Lalor, John Joseph. *Cyclopædia of Political Science, Political Economy, and of the Political History of the United States*. New York: Maynard, Merrill, & Co., 1899.

Lowe, Rodney. *Welfare-State-Britain since 1945*. New York: St. Martin's Press, 1999.

Mandelbaum, Michael. *The Ideas That Conquered the World: Peace, Democracy, and Free Markets in the Twenty-First Century*. New York: Public Affairs, 2002.

Mann, Michael. *The Sources of Social Power*. Vol. 1 of *The Rise of Classes and Nation-States, 1760–1914*. Cambridge: Cambridge University Press, 1993.

Mau, Steffen. "Welfare Regimes and the Norms of Social Exchange." *Current Sociology* 52 (2004): 53–74.

Mau, Steffen, and Benjamin Veghte. *Social Justice, Legitimacy and the Welfare State*. Aldershot: Ashgate, 2007.

Miyamoto, Taro. "Dynamics of the Japanese Welfare State in Comparative Perspective: Between 'Three Worlds' and the Developmental State." *The Japanese Journal of Social Security Policy* 2 (2003): 12–24.

North American Wildlife and Natural Resources Conference (Volume 71, Wildlife Management Institute, 1975).

Pabst, Adrian. "The Crisis of Capitalist Democracy." *Telos* (Fall 2010): 44–67.

Ruggie, John G. "Embedded Liberalism and the Postwar Economic Regimes." In *Constructing the World Policy: Essays on International Institutionalization*. London: Routledge, 1998.

Skocpol, Theda. "Bringing the State Back In: Strategies of Analysis in Current Research." In *Bringing the State Back In*, edited by Peter B. Evans, Dietrich Rueschemeyer, and Theda Skocpol, 3–38. Cambridge: Cambridge University Press, 1985.

Slaughter, Anne-Marie. "Government Networks: The Heart of the Liberal Democratic Order." In *Democratic Governance and International Law*, edited by Gregory Fox and Brad Roth, 199–236. Cambridge: Cambridge University Press, 2000.

Thomson, Ann Marie, and James L. Perry. "Collaboration Processes: Inside the Black Box."*Public Administration Review* 66 (2006): 20–32.

Weber, Max. "The Nation State and Economic Policy." In *Political Writings*, edited by Peter Lassman and Ronald Speirs, 1–28. New York: Cambridge University Press, 1994.

Weiler, J.H.H. "The Transformation of Europe." *Yale Law Journal* 100 (1991): 2403–2483.

Weiler, J.H.H. "Van Gend en Loos: The Individual as Subject and Object and the Dilemma of European Legitimacy." *International Journal of Constitutional Law* 12 (2014): 94–103.

Weir, Margaret, Ann Shola Orloff, and Theda Skocpol, eds. *Politics of Social Policy in the United States*. Princeton, NJ: Princeton University Press, 1988.

Part V

The European Union and the External World

25

EU External Relations and the Law

Marise Cremona

The Constitutional Framework for the European Union's External Relations

What is EU external relations and why is it suitable for inclusion in a companion to EU and international law? External relations is the term most commonly used to describe the policies of the European Union that have a dimension external to the European Union, including those policies which are inherently external such as external trade and development cooperation, as well as the external aspects of other policies such as environmental protection, migration, or transport. Traditionally "external relations" was used to refer to the external policies of the former European Community (EC), as distinguished from the Common Foreign and Security Policy (CFSP) of the European Union, which was based in the Treaty on European Union (TEU). These "external relations" policies thus tended to have a sectoral nature, although they included such generalized external provisions as the power to conclude association agreements, international agreements that are capable of including all the fields covered by the treaty.[1] The Treaty of Lisbon has subsumed the EC and its powers into the European Union, and the EU treaties[2] now bring together the external relations of the former EC and the CFSP under the general heading of "the Union's external action."[3]

We might also wonder what role law (European or international) plays in the European Union's external relations: foreign relations are after all regarded as highly political and it is unusual for national courts to have much to do with foreign policy. National parliaments are involved primarily as a matter of political control of government, rather than in their legislative, lawmaking capacity.[4] When we examine the external relations of the European Union, however, we find law playing an important role, and the contributions made by the European Court of Justice have been crucial to the development of the European Union as an international actor – possibly even influencing the type of international actor that the European Union is. In this chapter, we will examine the role of law in EU external relations from two perspectives. First, we will examine the European Union as a *rule-based (international) actor*. Law – and here we will focus mainly on EU law – governs both the extent of the European Union's external powers

A Companion to European Union Law and International Law, First Edition.
Edited by Dennis Patterson and Anna Södersten.

and their exercise: what are the constitutional foundations of EU external relations and how have the legal principles that govern external action been developed? Second, we will briefly turn to the European Union's characteristic use of law as an instrument and objective of its foreign policy, the European Union as a promoter of a *rule-based international order*.[5] It is not simply that law shapes the institutional framework within which EU external policies are formed; the European Union characteristically shapes its external relationships through legal instruments and the promotion of a rule-based approach to international relations is threaded through its treaty-based external objectives. With varying degrees of success, it increasingly seeks to play a part in the development of international law, through the United Nations and in multilateral negotiations.[6]

We first address the role of law in governing the constitutional framework within which the European Union defines and exercises its external policies. The European Union is, of course, created by legal instrument (the EU treaties) and possesses only those powers granted by those treaties, extensive though they may be.[7] As the Court once put it, the treaty (now treaties) is a constitutional charter based on the rule of law.[8] Thus, unlike a state, the Union has no inherent internal or external power flowing from its very existence; its capacity to enter into international legal relations flows from its legal personality (Article 47 TEU), but it derives its "actorness" – its ability to act in specific fields – from its conferred powers. The principle of conferral as stated in Article 5(2) TEU reminds us not only that the Union may only act within the limits of the competences conferred on it by the member states but also that competences not conferred upon the Union in the treaties remain with the member states. In terms of external policy this has the important consequence that the Union and its member states will often – in practice normally – be acting side by side. The European Union's international legal capacity does not displace that of the member states, and the Union's system of international relations includes the member states as well as EU institutional actors. In practice, the extent to which, and the conditions under which, member states' external competence is constrained by EU competence and its exercise are among the most difficult and contentious in EU external relations law.

If the capacity of the European Union as an international actor is shaped – empowered but also constrained – by rules and principles ultimately derived from the treaties which we may call constitutional, where are these to be found and what are they?

Although we may sense that some treaty rules are more fundamental than others, the treaties themselves do not establish a formal hierarchy. The pre-Lisbon Treaty structure was based on a legal prioritization of the EC Treaty over the other Union fields of action.[9] However, the Lisbon Treaty reform explicitly gives the TEU and the TFEU equal legal status.[10] There are no explicitly entrenched provisions; all provisions of the treaties are primary law and take precedence over secondary laws.[11] Although when the EEC Treaty was first drafted it included a very limited number of explicit provisions dealing with external relations (trade agreements and association agreements), they have expanded over the generations of treaty revision and we can now identify a large number of provisions on external action: substantive provisions that establish policies, set objectives, and confer decision-making and treaty-making powers, with related procedural provisions; and provisions that confer jurisdiction on the Court of Justice in respect of interpretation and enforcement of the law. Although now somewhat more concentrated than under the pre-Lisbon regime, they are still dispersed both between the treaties and within each treaty. The increase in quantity of treaty provisions on external action has come about not only as a result of decisions to expand the EC and then the European Union's international activity but also as a result of a desire on the part of the member states to define ever more closely the scope and objectives of new (and old) policy fields. In addition, the attempted strengthening of the emergent European Political Cooperation and then the CFSP through successive treaty innovations and amendments has led to an increased institutionalization of EU foreign policy. We can point as a result to an increasing legalization in the evolution of EU external relations, across all policy fields.[12] The European Union's constitutional rules relating to external action are characterized by their volume and their complexity, especially in comparison with the constitutional provisions of the member states themselves: as de Witte points out, national constitutions are typically rather brief in their provisions on foreign relations.[13]

A further factor contributes to this complexity: many of the constitutional principles governing Union external action were not originally expressly stated in the treaties but have been derived directly or indirectly from the founding treaties by the Court of Justice and have emerged through practice: the principles of implied powers, of exclusivity and preemption, rules governing the relationship between international law and the Union legal order, and so on. The Treaty of Lisbon, drawing on the nonratified Constitutional Treaty, attempted to codify many of these rules and principles, especially those concerned with competence, a clarification of competence being one objective of the constitutional reform process that started with the Laeken Declaration.[14] Success in achieving the Laeken goals of greater clarity and simplicity has been mixed. While overall clarity has improved, some issues, such as the management of mixed agreements, where the European Union and the member states participate in treaties alongside each other, are omitted altogether. At the same time, the attempt to codify the case law of the Court of Justice to give expression in the treaties to its *jurisprudence constante*, has led to interpretive difficulties and obscurities, particularly with respect to the relationship between preemption (Article 2(2) TFEU), the exclusivity of Union external competence (Article 3(2) TFEU), and the European Union's general treaty-making competence (Article 216(1) TFEU).[15]

Given the unusual degree of constitutionalization of EU external relations powers, what do these provisions address? We can identify a number of characteristic issues: the definition of the European Union's external powers and their impact on the powers of the member states; the setting of objectives and principles guiding the European Union's external action; the respective powers of the EU institutions in external policy fields; judicial and parliamentary accountability; and the effects of international law within the EU legal order.[16] They have in common a concern with the Union's relationship with, on the one hand, its member states (and their constitutional orders) and, on the other, international law and the global legal order. The Union must look both to its member states and to international law for its international capacity as an actor separate from its member states, and much of the effort of the Court of Justice has been directed at preserving the Union's policy space and delineating the principles governing relations between the institutional and state actors responsible for defining that policy.

Since the Union's international capacity has not deprived the member states of their sovereign capacity as states, Union law regulates the relative powers of these international legal persons. This issue relates not only to the extent of Union powers (competence) but also to the degree to which member states are bound by that exercise of power (primacy) and the extent to which the exercise or sometimes simply the possession of Union powers precludes continuing member state action (preemption, exclusivity). It also encompasses the loyalty principle, or what the Lisbon Treaty calls the principle of sincere cooperation, which governs cases where the Union and member states share competence as well as applying more broadly to the member states in the exercise of their retained foreign relations competences. The questions raised are large and we cannot do justice to them here;[17] instead we will draw attention to some significant trends.

Express and Implied Powers

We shall first consider the relationship between express and implied external relations powers. From the key *ERTA* judgment in 1971, the Court of Justice has argued that the Union's external competence derives not only from express treaty provisions but may also be implied.[18] In the words of a recent restatement by the Court:

> The competence of the Community to conclude international agreements may arise not only from an express conferment by the Treaty but may equally flow implicitly from other provisions of the Treaty and from measures adopted, within the framework of those provisions, by the Community institutions (see *ERTA*, paragraph 16). The Court has also held that whenever Community law created for those institutions powers within its internal system for the purpose of attaining a specific objective, the Community had authority to undertake international commitments necessary for the attainment of that objective even in the absence of an express provision to that effect (Opinion 1/76, paragraph 3, and Opinion 2/91, paragraph 7).[19]

Thus, in ERTA itself, the inclusion in the treaty of provision for the Council to adopt rules relating to international transport and the adoption of internal rules allowed the Court to hold that the Community (as it then was) had the power to enter into an international agreement on road transport on the issues covered by those rules. This principle has now been effectively codified in Article 216(1) TFEU:

> The Union may conclude an agreement with one or more third countries or international organisations where the Treaties so provide or where the conclusion of an agreement is necessary in order to achieve, within the framework of the Union's policies, one of the objectives referred to in the Treaties, or is provided for in a legally binding Union act or is likely to affect common rules or alter their scope.

We may thus derive a treaty-making power where the conditions of Article 216(1) TFEU are satisfied, despite the absence of an express provision to that effect. Perhaps ironically, this is still the case for treaties covering international transport since the treaties do not grant express external powers in this field. This is also true of recognition and enforcement of judgments in civil and commercial matters, the subject of the agreement at issue in Opinion 1/03, cited above. However, and although there are still some important "implied powers" of this kind, practice since the coming into force of the Lisbon Treaty seems to point to a trend in a different direction: towards the development of a few broadly defined express powers, which between them may cover the majority of the Union's external action. These external policy fields include the Common Commercial Policy (CCP; Article 207 TFEU), Development Cooperation Policy (Article 208 TFEU), and the CFSP (Article 24 TEU), together with broad treaty-making competences to conclude association agreements (Article 217 TFEU) and cooperation agreements (Article 212 TFEU).

The Lisbon Treaty extended the scope of the CCP. A number of cases have since demonstrated that the coverage of the CCP over trade in services and intellectual property rights is such that the use of a legal basis implied from the internal market provisions in the treaties will rarely be necessary.[20] Development cooperation has as its primary objective the reduction and, ultimately, the eradication, of poverty (Article 208 TFEU) but may cover a wide variety of topics. A Joint Statement on European Union Development Policy by the Council, the member states, the European Parliament and the Commission, entitled "The European Consensus on Development,"[21] stated that there can be no sustainable development and eradication of poverty without peace and security and that the pursuit of the objectives of the Community's development policy necessarily proceeds via the promotion of democracy and respect for human rights.[22] The European Union's Development Cooperation Policy is thus not limited to measures directly related to the campaign against poverty, although "it is none the less necessary ... that it contributes to the pursuit of that policy's economic and social development objectives."[23]

The inherent breadth of the European Union's CFSP (it covers "all areas of foreign policy and all questions relating to the Union's security"[24]) renders the task of establishing its boundaries potentially difficult. The task is none the less necessary given the "specific rules and procedures" governing the CFSP,[25] and the requirement that the implementation of the CFSP is not to affect the application of the Union's other competences (and vice versa).[26] In the words of Advocate General Bot,

> despite the formal disappearance of the pillars the entry into force of the Treaty of Lisbon has not obviated the need to delimit the respective scopes of the Union's different policies. ... [T]he specific nature of the CFSP compared with the Union's other policies ... is characterised, in particular, by the limited role played by the European Parliament in the CFSP. From this point of view, setting clear criteria to define the scope of that policy in relation to the other fields of the Union's external action represents a certain constitutional challenge.[27]

Pragmatic Solutions to Competence Distribution[28]

It is possible to identify two somewhat opposing tendencies that have emerged since the mid-2000s. On the one hand, the Lisbon Treaty attempts to clarify competences, to codify the Court of Justice case law. As a result, types of competences and their implications *should* be clearer and more distinct. On the other hand, institutional practice – and also decisions of the Court – have tended to undermine rigid distinctions between exclusive and shared competence in the interest of pragmatic solutions. This "blurring" tends to occur in the context of the *exercise* of competence, as opposed to its existence. What is interesting about this practice is, first, that the flexibility concerns exclusive as well as shared competences, and, secondly, that it operates in both directions, that is, both as reticence in insisting on the exercise of EU powers even where they are exclusive and as willingness on the part of member states to see the European Union exercise external powers alone even where competence is shared.

On several occasions during those years, the Council has adopted a procedural framework within which the member states are authorized to continue to exercise a competence which has become exclusive to the Union. The first followed the *Open Skies* cases in which the Court held that certain aspects of air services agreements being concluded with third countries by individual member states fell within exclusive competence.[29] In addition, the Court found that the ownership and control clauses in the bilateral agreements infringed Article 43 EC (now Article 49 TFEU) and there was therefore a need to renegotiate a large number of them. Since the Union was not able or willing to enter immediately into negotiations for replacement agreements, it was decided to authorize member states, under certain conditions, to maintain existing and even conclude new agreements, "without prejudice to the division of competences between the Community and Member States."[30] Alongside this regulation, the member states also agreed that the Union should negotiate, effectively on their behalf, amendments to some of their existing bilateral air transport agreements with third countries so as to bring them into compatibility with the EU *acquis* (so-called horizontal agreements) while also negotiating new EU agreements with strategic countries.[31]

As a consequence of Opinion 1/2003,[32] in which the Court held that conclusion of the Lugano Convention on jurisdiction and the recognition and enforcement of judgments in civil and commercial matters was within the exclusive competence of the Community, two regulations were adopted in 2009, one on the law applicable to contractual and noncontractual obligations[33] and one on the jurisdiction and recognition of judgments in matrimonial matters.[34] In both cases their scope of application is linked to specific internal EU legislation on the same subject matter, and thus to areas of competence where an "*AETR*-effect" and therefore preemption – or now Article 3(2) TFEU – applies.[35] These regulations follow a similar procedural pattern of notification and authorization of member state bilateral agreements, the Commission having the option to propose negotiating guidelines or to request the inclusion of specific clauses.

The third example – that of bilateral investment agreements (BITs) – is striking because it arises not in the context of preemption but within the framework of the CCP. The Lisbon Treaty both confirmed that the CCP is a matter of exclusive competence and brought foreign direct investment within its scope.[36] Bearing in mind the 1,200 existing member state BITs, a regulation was adopted which authorizes the member states, under certain conditions, to maintain in force and amend their existing BITs and to conclude new BITs while requiring them to eliminate incompatibilities between bilateral BITs and EU law.[37] As the preamble to the regulation recognizes, the interests of legal certainty made it important that both member states and investors confirm the continued existence of these member state BITs unless and until such time as they could be replaced by Union agreements. The negotiation and conclusion of new BITs are subject to notification and authorization by the Commission, which may refuse authorization where the Union has decided to conclude a BIT with that third country, or on grounds of incompatibility with EU law, or inconsistency with the Union's principles and objectives for external action as set out in the TEU.

These initiatives have been agreed between the member states and the institutions within the legislative process, and they have not yet come under the Court's scrutiny. There may be some question as to the extent to which the institutions should be able to reauthorize the member states to act where competence is exclusive. The Air Services Regulation is designed, with other measures such as the horizontal agreements mentioned earlier, to manage a transitional phase. Both the Air Services Regulation and the regulations related to civil justice (private international law) address a situation where one aspect of EU competence which has become exclusive via preemption impinges on legislative fields where the Union's *acquis* is currently limited and international agreements are likely to contain provisions falling within both exclusive and shared competence. The BITs Regulation touches upon a competence which is exclusive independently of the existence of the EU *acquis*, and might thereby be distinguished from the other two examples, but it is clearly presented as a transitional measure. The formal requirements of exclusivity may have been preserved but the result is a highly pragmatic solution that allows both the Union and member states to play their part while preserving an overall unity and common interest.

The previous examples of practice have focused on maintaining a role for the member states even where it might not be strictly necessary in legal terms, or even where EU competence is exclusive. However, we can also find examples of cases where the member states are happy to let the Union act alone, although competence is shared. Somewhat paradoxically perhaps, this seems particularly to be the case in those former second and third pillars, the CFSP and the Area of Freedom, Security, and Justice, where the member states are ostensibly most protective of their prerogatives. Despite the clearly nonexclusive nature of CFSP competence,[38] almost all international agreements concluded under CFSP powers have been concluded by the European

Union alone.[39] Mixed agreements are rare in the Area of Freedom, Security, and Justice field, and even agreements on sensitive issues such as migration, for example readmission agreements[40] and agreements involving criminal justice,[41] are concluded by the European Union alone.

Accepting Mixity

"Mixity" refers to the joint exercise of competence by the Union and its member states in concluding an international agreement. Despite the widening extent of EU external powers, now also covering the broader aspects of foreign policy in the CFSP, mixed agreements remain widely used. This is true of the wide-ranging modern partnership and association agreements with a political dimension but also of multilateral sectoral agreements, such as environmental agreements, where competence is shared. There are cases – particularly where agreements are politically important, where they represent an element in a broader policy framework towards a third country, or are seen as a significant part of the global governance of important issues – where the unity of the European Union is served not by the participation of the Union alone (even where this would be possible) but rather by the joint participation of the Union and all its member states, with the powerful signal of concerted action that this sends.

It is notable that the Lisbon Treaty says nothing about this very central aspect of EU external relations practice, either in the provision dealing with the negotiation and conclusion of agreements (Article 218 TFEU) or in any other provision. The fact that a proportion of the most important external agreements are mixed is simply ignored. Although it is true that the principles underlying the Union law obligations of the member states and the institutions in the context of mixed agreements are derived from general principles which appear in the treaties, in particular the principle of sincere cooperation in Article 4(3) TEU, some recognition of the phenomenon, especially at the procedural level, would have assisted transparency. However, it must be said that one of the attractions of mixed agreements for the Union and the member states is that it may not be necessary to identify the precise delimitation of competence between Union and member states, and alterations in the distribution of competence do not call the agreement into question. Even the "declarations of competence" that are sometimes required as the price of joint EU–Member State participation do not really illuminate the distribution of competence; they mainly serve to put the other parties on notice that competence is shared.[42]

The Principle of Sincere Cooperation

This pragmatic approach to the exercise of competence brings to the fore the importance of the principle of sincere cooperation, as expressed in Articles 4(3), 13(2), and 24(3) TEU. The application of this principle by the Court of Justice, in particular via Article 4(3) TEU, is central to the management of ongoing joint participation in multilateral agreements (and organizations) where the European Union and member states continue to act side by side as parties or members.[43] As Christophe Hillion says, "[t]his cooperation jurisprudence suggests a growing [acceptance by the Court] of the plurality that characterises the EU system of external relations."[44] However, the key role played by the duty of sincere cooperation in managing the exercise of competence creates its own difficulties. It is used as a basis for a range of obligations: the primacy of EU law, exclusivity, preemption, and to define the parameters within which the member states may exercise their competence to act. The precise nature of the duty in these different situations is not always clear, leading to a blurring of the distinction between them.[45]

How should we define the nature of this duty so that it is effective in furthering the Union interest and still ensure that both EU and member state powers are respected? The Court in the *PFOS* case employed a logic based on the duty of cooperation to govern the exercise of shared competence, arguing that once the Union has decided how to act the member states cannot depart from this even where no legislative preemption has taken place.[46] It held that where a member state dissociates itself from "a concerted common strategy" so as to act unilaterally this

> is likely to compromise the principle of unity in the international representation of the Union and its Member States and weaken their negotiating power with regard to the other parties to the Convention concerned.[47]

This was a breach of Article 10 EC (now Article 4(3) TEU). The case illustrates the difficulties that arise where there are no clear rules, especially in deciding at what point the member states become "free" to act alone because there is no EU position and the difficulty of deciding whether the situation is one of "no decision" by the European Union or of "a decision not to act."[48] Under what circumstances must the member states refrain from acting except through, or in accordance with, positions adopted by the Union, as opposed to seeking as far as possible to achieve a common position?[49] And under what circumstances is it necessary for a Union objective – to which member state loyalty is owed under Article 4(3) TEU – to be formulated through a formal act adopted on an identified legal basis?[50]

There is also the problem of finding a way to present to third parties the common position of the European Union and member states, and especially the collective position of the member states. An attempt at simplification of the international representation of the Union – the removal by the Lisbon Treaty of a formal role for the rotating presidency in foreign affairs – has instead created more difficulty since the member states have lost a collective representative and have been unwilling to see either the high representative or the Commission taking on that role. After some difficulty the Council arrived at an agreement on the representation of EU positions in multilateral organizations,[51] which makes it clear that the European Union can only present a position where it is competent and there is an agreed position, and also that arrangements for coordination and representation do not affect competences. The document refers to "EU Actors," and explains that

> [t]he term EU actor is used to denote those actors competent to represent the Union as provided in the Treaties, i.e. the President of the European Council, the Commission, the High Representative and EU Delegations.

Member states will decide case by case how to coordinate and who will represent them: this could be an "EU Actor" or a member state ("notably the Member State holding the rotating Presidency of the Council"). The member states undertake to ensure and promote possibilities for the "EU Actors" to deliver statements on behalf of the European Union. The duty of cooperation may facilitate plurality but does not mean that questions of competence have become irrelevant.

Accountability to Courts and Parliament

The foregoing has exemplified, as a corollary to the centrality of law in defining and shaping EU external relations, the important role played by the Court of Justice of the European Union, through judicial review of EU acts, opinions requested on the compatibility of international agreements with EU law, and enforcement actions against member states. Judicial review may be concerned both with legality (enforcing both the vertical division of power and the horizontal balance of power) and with protecting and enforcing constitutional principles, including individual rights. As the Court said in *Les Verts*,

> the European Community is a Community based on the rule of law inasmuch as neither its member states nor its institutions can avoid a review of the question whether the measures adopted by them are in conformity with the basic constitutional charter, the Treaty.[52]

This applies to acts concluding international agreements,[53] as well as to measures adopted to implement international obligations: treaties concluded by the European Union are binding on the EU institutions (Article 216(2) TFEU) but this primacy over secondary Union law does not extend to primary treaty law.[54] The extent of, and possible limitations to, judicial review in cases involving security (e.g., counterterrorism measures) has been the subject of considerable debate, Advocate General Maduro arguing that within the Union system review based on fundamental rights should always be available even in such "political" cases:

> The claim that a measure is necessary for the maintenance of international peace and security cannot operate so as to silence the general principles of Community law and deprive individuals of their fundamental rights.[55]

The Court of Justice in the same case held that

> the obligations imposed by an international agreement cannot have the effect of prejudicing the constitutional principles of the EC Treaty, which include the principle that all Community acts must respect fundamental rights, that respect constituting a condition of their lawfulness.[56]

The possibility of judicial review at Union level of CFSP restrictive measures against natural or legal persons was introduced by the Lisbon Treaty as a limited exception to the exclusion of the Court of Justice from jurisdiction in relation to the CFSP.[57]

In contrast to the important role played by the Court in defining the scope and nature of Community competence and the legal effect of international obligations, the Court is reticent (noninterventionist) as regards the substantive policy choices of the European Union's institutions in external relations.[58] It has not been a driving force behind the formation of an external policy agenda in the same way that the creation of the single market has influenced its approach to substantive treaty provisions on discrimination, competition policy, or free movement. The nature of the treaty provisions on external action, a weaker set of policy objectives and fewer substantive legal obligations on the member states, has left much to the agenda-setting of the political institutions. The Union's external policy objectives are nonteleological, nonprioritized, open-ended, and concerned more with policy orientation than goal-setting. They are defined at a number of levels (general treaty objectives, general external objectives, sectoral objectives, and institutional or legislative objectives). The Court has tended to focus more on institutional/legislative objectives and uses them in the context of defining competences and distribution of powers, for example in decisions on legal basis.[59] In its focus on institutional objectives it has not sought to (re)define them or to impose overriding treaty-based objectives or priorities; it has tended to accept at face value the objectives as expressed by the legislature or institutions[60] and has stressed the need for the institutions to retain their policy discretion, their room for maneuver.[61]

The reticence of the Court when it comes to external policy choices has traditionally left space for the Commission, the Council, and the European Council. In recent years, external policy formation has been altered by two significant developments. The first is the creation of the European External Action Service (EEAS), staffed by members of the Council Secretariat and the Commission alongside staff seconded from national diplomatic services. The EEAS's function is to assist the High Representative for Foreign Affairs and Security Policy in each of her three institutional roles: in fulfilling her mandate to conduct the CFSP and ensure coherence of EU external action,[62] in her capacity as chair of the Foreign Affairs Council, and in her capacity as vice-president of the Commission.[63] The creation of this new body (it is described not as an institution but as a "functionally autonomous body"[64]) has proved challenging, and the EEAS, which has recently undergone a first review,[65] is still too young to be able to assess its real impact.[66] As one commentator points out, while internal improvements to the functioning of the EEAS can certainly be made, progress "depends as least as much on whether and how the EU institutions and the Member States wish to see the Service develop."[67]

The second major change is the expansion by the Lisbon Treaty of the European Parliament's powers, particularly in the adoption of trade policy instruments and in the conclusion of international agreements. The Parliament has been using these new powers both to exercise real control over the conclusion of international agreements[68] and to influence legislation in external fields such as trade policy.[69] In creating a degree of parallelism between internal legislative procedures and external treaty making, the Treaty of Lisbon moved decisively away from what had been the classic balance of power in EU international treaty negotiations, between the Commission as negotiator and the Council as the institution that concludes the treaty. Under Article 218(6)(a)(v) TFEU the conclusion of a treaty by the Council requires the consent of the European Parliament, inter alia, where the agreement covers fields to which the ordinary legislative procedure applies. These fields range from regulation within the internal market to trade policy. In order to deliver on its policy priorities, the Commission thus has to convince not only its negotiating partners, not only the member states in the Council, but also the European Parliament. In fact, the conclusion – and not only the implementation – of an international treaty becomes subject to a legislative process. At the same time its negotiation at the international level, especially in the case of multilateral treaties, is still subject to the conventions of classic treaty making – especially confidentiality and intergovernmental bargaining. And although parliamentary consent in a sense "parallels" the ordinary legislative procedure, it is a blunt instrument in comparison. A consent procedure with its "take it or leave it" dynamic, even where Parliament is kept informed, offers less scope for debate and adjustment or the accommodation of different interests; this has already taken place at the international level and is difficult to replicate within the European Union.

The role of the Parliament in the conclusion of international treaties, which are often regulatory or quasi-legislative in character, brings us to the final theme of this contribution: the role played by law as both an instrument and a goal of EU foreign policy.

The European Union's Use of Law as an Instrument and Objective of its Foreign Policy

Despite some rather general references in the Treaty of Rome to cooperative relations with the United Nations and the Council of Europe, the external relations of the European Communities were historically centered on the conclusion of treaties with external partners. More recently, with the development of the CFSP, the European Union has engaged in both more traditional diplomacy and in operational civil and military missions, but treaty making is still a central part of EU external relations. One feature of the European Union's approach is the way that it structures its relations with third countries through different types of international agreement. The EU treaties themselves, of course, envisage agreements falling within different specific competences such as trade, development cooperation, the CFSP, the environment, association and other forms of cooperation agreement. But in addition to this, the European Union has developed "models" or paradigmatic agreements for specific groups of third countries that contain varying combinations of provisions on trade, development, regulatory cooperation, and political dialogue. Examples include the "Europe Agreements" concluded in the 1990s with the countries of Central and Eastern Europe that are now all EU member states; the "Stabilisation and Association Agreements" with the countries of the Western Balkans that the European Union identified as "potential candidates" for EU membership (not a formal legal category but a political determination); the "Euro-Mediterranean Agreements" with the countries of the southern Mediterranean that now form part of the European Neighbourhood Policy; the "Partnership and Cooperation Agreements" with the countries of the former Soviet Union (also now, with the exception of Russia, forming part of the European Neighbourhood Policy); the "Economic Partnership Agreements" with the developing countries that are party to the Cotonou Convention;[70] and the "deep and comprehensive free trade agreements" being negotiated with the Union's "strategic partners."[71]

This network of agreements through which the European Union structures its external relationships is one dimension of its more general commitment to promoting a "rule-based international order."[72] In economic terms, the European Union seeks to ensure that its trade policy supports EU exporters of goods and services and that internal regulatory policy does not put EU enterprises at a disadvantage on third country markets. These goals have led to an emphasis on extending the regulatory dimension of trade agreements, on regulatory cooperation, the promotion of existing international standards, and EU leadership in developing new international standards that are at least consistent with EU standards. In a more political context, the European Union seeks to promote international norms on a variety of issues from nonproliferation to "decent work." The treaties make explicit the importance of international law and multilateralism to the Union's external policy:

> The Union's action on the international scene shall be guided by the principles which have inspired its own creation, development and enlargement, and which it seeks to advance in the wider world: … [including] respect for the principles of the United Nations Charter and international law. The Union shall … promote multilateral solutions to common problems, in particular in the framework of the United Nations.[73]

Thus, EU foreign policy does not simply use international legal instruments as a policy tool; it affirms its mission to contribute to the development of international law, spearheading or influencing the production of new norms, their adoption, interpretation, and enforcement through diplomacy and participation in international organizations and agencies, including the United Nations.[74] This involves a variety of activities beyond treaty making in the strict sense: consensus building among member states, candidates, and potential candidates and neighbors; the formation of EU strategies and common positions; also negotiation, decision making, and treaty making, including within international organizations. It needs to be said that this dimension of EU action, being often informal and hard to document, is necessarily hard to assess concretely; it is also difficult to be sure what influence the European Union as such has had on the development of an international norm.

An important aspect of the European Union's strategy in norm building is the building of policy consensus. This starts with the member states, facilitating the convergence of member state policies through the formation of strategies, common positions, Council conclusions, and by less formal means. A CFSP common position may seek to build consensus at a number of levels. In addition to the consensus among the member states themselves, necessary for its adoption, the Union may invite other countries to associate themselves with a particular common position; this includes but is not limited to candidate states.[75]

To illustrate these processes we will consider two examples. First is the European Union's campaign for a consensus on the abolition of the death penalty, which has been well documented, Ian Manners using this as a prime example of what he termed "normative power Europe."[76] The Guidelines on the Death Penalty, originally adopted in 1998 as the European Union's first set of Human Rights Guidelines and revised in 2008 and then in 2013,[77] state that the EU objectives are (inter alia):

> To work towards universal abolition of the death penalty as a strongly held policy agreed by all EU member states. Where the death penalty still exists, the EU will advocate the immediate establishment of a moratorium on the use of the death penalty with a view to abolition; call for its use to be progressively restricted, including by reductions in the number of offences for which the death penalty will be implemented; advocate that it be applied respecting the minimum standards as set out in these Guidelines.

The European Union's campaign against the death penalty has been carried out at both bilateral and multilateral levels. Initiatives include declarations and *démarches* on the death penalty in international fora, raising it in dialogues with third countries, as well as *démarches* in specific cases where the use of the death penalty violates international commitments or internationally recognized minimum standards; the use of the death penalty is included in the European Union's human rights reports. The guidelines thus serve two purposes: they are intended to ensure consistency in EU policy on a specific issue where the Union has clear objectives; they also serve as a public statement of those objectives, in itself a policy tool.

The Union's policy has specific practical consequences too: extradition of a suspect to a requesting jurisdiction may be blocked if there is a real risk that he or she may be subject to the death penalty,[78] and the extradition treaty between the United States and the European Union contains a clause permitting the requested member state to make nonapplication of the death penalty a condition of extradition.[79] The Agreement between the European Union and Mauritius establishing the conditions under which persons suspected of piracy and detained by EU Naval Force, the European Security and Defence Policy operation off the coast of Somalia, may be transferred into custody and tried in Mauritius stipulates among other criminal process guarantees that

> No transferred person shall ... be charged with an offence that carries the death penalty, be sentenced to death or be the subject of an application of the death penalty.[80]

Trade in goods that have no practical use other than for capital punishment is prohibited, and export controls exist for goods which can be used for the purposes of capital punishment, including drugs that may be used for lethal injection.[81]

At the multilateral level we can clearly see the European Union seeking to secure universal standards with respect to the death penalty and its eventual universal abolition. Since 1999 the Union has regularly proposed resolutions in the UN General Assembly calling for a moratorium on the use of the death penalty, Resolution 62/149 eventually being adopted in December 2007, followed by a series of updates.[82] In a Joint Declaration by the European Union and Council of Europe on the World Day Against the Death Penalty in October 2013, the Union welcomed

> the extraordinary efforts of the cross-regional alliance that successfully led and guided the adoption, with an unprecedented number of votes, in December 2012, of the UN General Assembly Resolution on a Moratorium on the use of death penalty

as well as committing the European Union to "continue to work closely with all interlocutors, governmental and civil society, with a view to developing synergies towards universal abolition."[83] In addition, the guidelines propose minimum standards for the imposition of the death penalty, including rights to a fair trial, right of appeal, the prohibition of the death penalty on minors and the insane, and the prohibition of public executions.[84] As well as issuing public statements calling for adherence to these minimum standards, the Union filed *amicus curiae* briefs in two US Supreme Court appeals against the death penalty in cases involving juveniles and mentally challenged offenders.[85]

Our second example of the European Union's involvement in shaping the development of new international norms is its campaign for an Arms Trade Treaty (ATT), which finds its impetus in the European Security Strategy as part of the Union's policy on disarmament and small arms and light weapons (SALW),[86] and its own code of conduct on arms exports.[87] The action was launched by the European Union in 2005, with Council Conclusions affirming EU support for an international treaty to be negotiated under the aegis of the United Nations with a view to establishing common standards for the global trade in conventional arms (the initiative was the United Kingdom's).[88] Since then the Council has regularly reverted to the issue, its conclusions timed to coincide with developments within the United Nations,[89] and all member states have voted in favor of UN General Assembly resolutions which made gradual progress towards the start of negotiations in 2012. A text was agreed in March 2013 and adopted by UN General Assembly Resolution in April 2013.[90]

A number of features of the European Union's campaign are worth noting. First, it held out its own arms export control mechanisms as an example of

> the feasibility of agreeing on an instrument without depriving States of their national prerogative to license or deny individual exports, and … the effectiveness and efficiency of a multilateral export control mechanism.[91]

Second, it has included the ATT among its priorities in the UN General Assembly.[92] Third, it has used its regular meetings with third countries to reaffirm its support for the ATT process,[93] and it has included the ATT in joint action programs such as the Association Agenda for Ukraine adopted in June 2013.[94] Fourth, it adopted a series of decisions aimed at promoting the ATT process.[95] Fifth, after the adoption of the ATT by the UN General Assembly in April 2013, the European Union has supported ratification and implementation of the ATT through assistance to third countries in strengthening their arms transfer control systems.[96]

My purpose here is not to assess the actual impact of the European Union's support for and sponsorship of the progress towards an ATT, but rather to draw attention to the way in which consciously seeking to further the development of new international norms in multilateral fora such as the United Nations has become a recognized part of EU foreign policy. Somewhat ironically, perhaps, it should be noted that the European Union itself is not able to become a party to the ATT, which is open only to states. As aspects of the treaty are covered by exclusive EU competence, the Council has adopted decisions authorizing the member states to sign, and then to ratify, the ATT in the interests of the Union;[97] a reminder, if one were needed, that the ability of the European Union to exercise its external competences depends on the international environment in which it operates.

Notes

1 Case 12/86 *Demirel* EU:C:1987:400, para 9. See now Article 217 TFEU.

2 The Treaty of European Union (TEU) and the Treaty on the Functioning of the European Union (TFEU). The Euratom is in a somewhat anomalous position, no longer referred to expressly in the EU treaties but, on the other hand (as provided in the revised Euratom Treaty itself), sharing the same institutional provisions. Since it has a separate legal personality, its external relations can be treated separately from those of the EU.

3 See TEU Title V (General provisions on the Union's external action and specific provisions on the CFSP) and TFEU Part Five (External action by the Union). As convenient shorthand, in what follows we refer to the pre-Lisbon and post-Lisbon regimes to indicate the treaties before and after this significant watershed. Since there is another contribution in this companion on the CFSP (Ramses A. Wessel, Chapter 26 of this volume), we will here focus mainly on non-CFSP external policies.

4 Daniel Thym, "Parliamentary Involvement in European International Relations," in *EU Foreign Relations Law: Constitutional Fundamentals*, ed. Marise Cremona and Bruno de Witte (Oxford: Hart, 2008).

5 European Security Strategy, adopted by the European Council in 9–10 December 2003.

6 Frank Hoffmeister, "The Contribution of EU Practice to International Law," in *Developments in EU External Relations Law*, ed. Marise Cremona (Oxford: Oxford University Press, 2008).

7 The EU treaties have a number of references to the principle of conferral, including Articles 4(1), 5(1), and 5(2) TEU. According to Article 3(6) TEU, "The Union shall pursue its objectives by appropriate means commensurate with the competences which are conferred upon it in the Treaties."

8 Opinion 1/91 EU:C:1991:490; Joined Cases C-402/05 P and C-415/05 P *Yassin Abdullah Kadi and Al Barakaat International Foundation v. Council and Commission* EU:C:2008:461, para 281.

9 The pre-Lisbon EU Treaty required the Union to "maintain in full" and "build on" the *acquis communautaire* (Article 2 EU) and the provisions in the TEU establishing the second and third "pillars" of the Union (CFSP and Police and Judicial Cooperation in Criminal Matters) were not to "affect" the EC Treaty (Article 47 EU).

10 According to Article 1 TEU, "The Union shall be founded on the present Treaty and the Treaty on the Functioning of the European Union (hereinafter referred to as "the Treaties"). Those two Treaties shall have the same legal value." Article 1(2) TFEU is to the same effect. See further Marise Cremona, "The Two (or Three) Treaty Solution: The New Treaty Structure of the EU," in *European Union Law after the Treaty of Lisbon*, ed. Andrea Biondi and Piet Eeckhout (Oxford: Oxford University Press, 2012).

11 For an indication that some principles may be protected as "constitutional principles of the Treaty," "the principles that form part of the very foundations of the Community legal order" see Joined Cases C-402/05 P and C-415/05 P *Kadi and Al Barakaat*, n 8 this chapter, paras 285 and 304.

12 Marise Cremona, "External Relations and External Competence," in *The Evolution of EU Law*, ed. Graínne de Búrca and Paul Craig (Oxford: Oxford University Press, 2011); and Bruno de Witte, "Too Much Constitutional Law in the European Union's Foreign Relations?" in Cremona and de Witte, *EU Foreign Relations Law: Constitutional Fundamentals*.

13 Bruno de Witte, "Too Much Constitutional Law." National constitutions are not, however, generally devoid of such provisions: for a comparative analysis of national constitutional provisions on foreign relations, see Joris Larik, "Worldly Ambitions: Foreign Policy Objectives in European Constitutional Law" (PhD thesis European University Institute, 3 June 2013).

14 Laeken Declaration on the Future of the European Union, annexed to the Presidency Conclusions, Laeken, 14 and 15 December 2001.

15 See further Marise Cremona, "Defining Competence In EU External Relations: Lessons from the Treaty Reform Process," in *Law and Practice of EU External Relations: Salient Features of a Changing Landscape*, ed. Alan Dashwood and Marc Maresceau (Cambridge: Cambridge University Press, 2008).

16 See Bruno de Witte and Marise Cremona, "Introduction," in Cremona and de Witte, *EU Foreign Relations Law: Constitutional Fundamentals.*

17 See further Geert de Baere, *Constitutional Principles of EU External Relations* (Oxford: Oxford University Press, 2008); Piet Eeckhout, *External Relations of the European Union* (Oxford: Oxford University Press, 2011); Panos Koutrakos, *EU International Relations Law* (Oxford: Hart, 2006); Daniel Thym, "Foreign Affairs," in *Principles of European Constitutional Law*, ed. Armin von Bogdandy and Jurgen Bast (Oxford: Hart, 2011); and Robert Schütze, *Foreign Affairs and the European Constitution: Selected Essays* (Cambridge: Cambridge University Press, 2014).

18 Case 22/70 *Commission v. Council* EU:C:1971:32.

19 Opinion 1/03 EU:C:2006:81, para 114.

20 Case C-414/11 *Daiichi Sankyo* EU:C:2013:520; and Case C-137/12 *Commission v. Council* EU:C:2013:675. In contrast, when the EEC concluded the World Trade Organization Uruguay Round agreements, the decision had to be based on Articles 43, 54, 57, 66, 75, 84(2), 99, 100, 100a, 113, and 235 EC, as well as procedurally on Article 228 (3) EC Treaty (Council Decision 94/800/EC of 22 December 1994 concerning the conclusion on behalf of the European Community, as regards matters within its competence, of the agreements reached in the Uruguay Round multilateral negotiations (1986–1994) [1994] OJ L 336/1).

21 [2006] OJ C 46/1.

22 See further Cases C-268/94 *Portugal v. Council* EU:C:1996:461; C-403/05 *Parliament v. Commission* EU:C:2007:624; C-91/05 *Commission v. Council* EU:C:2008:288; and C-377/12 *Commission v. Council* EU:C:2014:1903, Opinion of Advocate General Mengozzi.

23 Case C-91/05 *Commission v. Council*, n 22 this chapter, para 67.

24 Article 24(1) TEU.

25 Article 24(1) TEU.

26 Article 40 TEU.

27 Case C-658/11 European Parliament v. Council EU:C:2014:2025, Opinion of Advocate General Bot.

28 This section draws upon Marise Cremona, "EU External Relations: Unity and Conferral of Powers," in *The Question of Competence in the European Union*, ed. Loic Azoulai (Oxford: Oxford University Press 2014).

29 See, e.g., Case C-476/98 *Commission v. Germany* EU:C:2002:631.

30 Regulation 847/2004/EC of 29 April 2004 on the Negotiation and Implementation of Air Service Agreements between Member States and Third Countries [2004] OJ L 157/7.

31 For an example of such a horizontal agreement, see the Agreement between the European Community and Ukraine on certain aspects of air services [2006] OJ L 211/24. EU agreements have been negotiated with the USA, Canada, and Brazil and are under negotiation with Australia and New Zealand.

32 Opinion 1/03, n 19 this chapter.

33 Regulation 662/2009/EC of 13 July 2009 establishing a procedure for the negotiation and conclusion of agreements between Member States and third countries on particular matters concerning the law applicable to contractual and non-contractual obligations [2009] OJ L 200/25.

34 Regulation 664/2009/EC of 7 July 2009 establishing a procedure for the negotiation and conclusion of agreements between Member States and third countries concerning jurisdiction, recognition and enforcement of judgments and decisions in matrimonial matters, matters of parental responsibility and matters relating to maintenance obligations, and the law applicable to matters relating to maintenance obligations [2009] OJ L 200/46.

35 Regulation 662/2009, n 33 this chapter, is linked to the scope of application of Regulation 593/2008/EC of 17 June 2008 on the law applicable to contractual obligation (Rome I) [2008] OJ L 177/87, and Regulation 864/2007 of 11 July 2007 on the law applicable to non-contractual obligations (Rome II) [2007] OJ L 177/40; Regulation 664/2009/EC, n 34 this chapter, is linked to the scope of

Regulation 2201/2003/EC of 27 November 2003 concerning jurisdiction, recognition and enforcement of judgments and decisions in matrimonial matters, matters of parental responsibility [2003] OJ L 338/1 and Regulation 4/2009/EC of 18 December 2008 on jurisdiction, applicable law, recognition and enforcement of decisions and cooperation in matters relating to maintenance obligations [2009] OJ L 7/1.

36 Articles 3(1) and 207(1) TFEU.

37 Regulation 1219/2012/EU of 12 December 2012 establishing transitional arrangements for bilateral investment agreements between Member States and third countries OJ [2012] L 351/40. For an example of incompatibility between a member state BIT and EU law see Case C-118/07 *Commission v. Finland* EU:C:2009:715.

38 CFSP competence is not defined in Article 2(4) TFEU as exclusive, shared, or complementary. The provisions on the CFSP emphasize the role of the member states: see, e.g., Articles 24, 32, and 42(1) TEU.

39 Admittedly these agreements have been relatively limited in character: status of forces agreements, agreements with third states participating in EU crisis management missions, and on the exchange and protection of classified information. Where more general political or foreign policy issues are covered in broader agreements, these, as we have seen, tend to be mixed. The Treaty of Amity and Cooperation in Southeast Asia, to which France is a party alongside the EU, is based as far as the EU is concerned on both CFSP and non-CFSP powers: Council Decision 2012/308/CFSP [2012] OJ L 154, p. 1, based on Article 37 TEU and Articles 209 and 212 TFEU.

40 Article 79(3) TFEU.

41 E.g., the Agreement between the EU and Australia on the processing and transfer of EU-sourced passenger name record (PNR) data by air carriers to the Australian customs service [2008] OJ L 213/49; Agreement between the EU and the United States of America on the processing and transfer of Financial Messaging Data from the EU to the United States for the purposes of the Terrorist Finance Tracking Program [2010] OJ L 195/5.

42 See Andres Delgado Casteleiro, "EU Declarations of Competence to Multilateral Agreements: A Useful Reference Base?" *European Foreign Affairs Review* 17 (2012): 491.

43 See Ruling 1/78 EU:C:1978:202; Opinion 2/91 EU:C:1993:106 ; Case C-25/94 *Commission v. Council* EU:C:1996:114; Case C-266/03 *Commission v. Luxembourg* EU:C:2005:341; Case C-433/03 *Commission v. Germany* EU:C:2005:462; Case C-246/07 *Commission v. Sweden* EU:C:2010:203; Federico Casolari, "The Principle of Loyal Cooperation: A 'Master Key' for EU External Representation?," in *Principles and Practices of EU External Representation*, ed. Steven Blockmans and Ramses Wessel (CLEER working papers no. 2012/5); Eleftheria Neframi, "The Duty of Loyalty: Rethinking its Scope through its Application in the Field of EU External Relations," *Common Market Law Review* 47 (2010): 323; and Marise Cremona, "Defending the Community Interest: The Duties of Cooperation and Compliance," in Cremona and de Witte, *EU Foreign Relations Law: Constitutional Fundamentals*.

44 Christophe Hillion, "Mixity and Coherence in EU External Relations: The Significance of the 'Duty of Cooperation,'" in *Mixed Agreements Revisited: The EU and its Member States in the World*, ed. Christophe Hillion and Panos Koutrakos (Oxford: Hart, 2010), 232.

45 Andres Delgado Casteleiro and Joris Larik, "The Duty to Remain Silent: Limitless Loyalty in EU External Relations," *European Law Review* 36 (2011): 524.

46 Case C-246/07 *Commission v. Sweden*, n 43 this chapter.

47 Ibid., para 104.

48 Marise Cremona, "Case C-246/07 *Commission v Sweden*, judgment 20 April 2010 (Grand Chamber)," *Common Market Law Review* 48 (2011): 1639; and Geert de Baere, "'O, Where is Faith? O, Where is Loyalty?' Some Thoughts on the Duty of Loyal Cooperation and the Union's External Environmental Competences in the Light of the *PFOS* Case," *European Law Review* 36 (2011): 405.

49 Compare Case C-246/07 *Commission v. Sweden*, n 43 this chapter (shared competence), with Case C-45/07 *Commission v. Greece* EU:C:2009:81 (exclusive competence).

50 For a case contesting the substantive legal basis of a Council decision on the position to be taken by the EU in the framework of an international agreement, see Case C-431/11 *UK v. Council* EU:C:2013:589.

51 General arrangements for EU statements in multilateral organizations, Council doc. 15901/11, 24 October 2011.
52 Case 294/83 *Les Verts* EU:C:1986:166, para 23.
53 E.g., Joined Cases C-317/04 and C-318/04 *European Parliament v. Council* EU:C:2006:346.
54 Joined Cases C-402/05 P and C-415/05 P *Kadi and Al Barakaat*, n 8 this chapter, paras 306–308. The extent to which the obligations in international treaties binding on the EU may prevail over secondary Union law will depend on the nature of the treaty as a whole and on the specific provision in question: Case C-308/06 *Intertanko* EU:C:2008:312.
55 Joined Cases C-402/05 P and C-415/05 P *Kadi and Al Barakaat*, n 8 this chapter, Opinion of Advocate General Maduro, para 34.
56 Joined Cases C-402/05 P and C-415/05 P *Kadi and Al Barakaat*, n 8 this chapter, paras 282 and 285.
57 Article 275 TFEU.
58 See further Marise Cremona, "A Reticent Court? Policy Objectives and the Court of Justice," in *The European Court of Justice and External Relations Law: Constitutional Challenges*, ed. Marise Cremona and Anne Thies (Oxford: Hart, 2014).
59 For recent examples, see nn 20 and 22 this chapter.
60 E.g., Case C-411/06 *Commission v. European Parliament & Council* EU:C:2009:518.
61 E.g., Case C-149/96 *Portugal v. Council* EU:C:1999:574, paras 40 and 46.
62 On the High Representative's mandate as regards coherence, see Article 21(3) TEU.
63 Article 27(3) TEU; Council Decision 2010/427/EU of 26 July 2010 establishing the organization and functioning of the European External Action Service [2010] OJ L 201/30. See Steven Blockmans and Christophe Hillion, eds., *EEAS 2.0: A Legal Commentary on Council Decision 2010/427/EU Establishing the Organisation and Functioning of the European External Action Service* (EUI AEL working papers no. 2013/03).
64 Council Decision 2010/427/EU, n 63 this chapter, Article 1(2). Bart Van Vooren, "A Legal-Institutional Perspective on the European External Action Service" (CLEER working papers no. 2010/07).
65 This review by the high representative is mandated by Council Decision 2010/427/EU, n 63 this chapter, Article 13(3) and was published in July 2013. See http://eeas.europa.eu/library/publications/2013/3/2013_eeas_review_en.pdf.
66 See, e.g., Sophie Vanhoonacker and Natasja Reslow, "The European External Action Service: Living Forwards By Understanding Backwards" *European Foreign Affairs Review* 15 (2010): 1; Antonio Missiroli, "The EU 'Foreign Service' Under Construction," EUI RSCAS policy papers 2010/04; Steven Blockmans, "The European External Action Service One Year On: First Signs of Strengths and Weaknesses" (CLEER working papers no. 2012/2); and Steven Blockmans and Christophe Hillion, eds., *EEAS 2.0: Recommendations for the Amendment of Council Decision 2010/427/EU Establishing the Organisation and Functioning of the European External Action Service*, CEPS Special Report, 13 November 2013.
67 Simon Duke, "Reflections on the EEAS Review," *European Foreign Affairs Review* 19 (2014): 43.
68 Marise Cremona, "International Regulatory Policy and Democratic Accountability: The EU and the ACTA," in *Reflections on the Constitutionalisation of International Economic Law: Liber Amicorum Ernst-Ulrich Petersmann*, ed. Marise Cremona et al. (Leiden: Brill, 2013); and Marise Cremona, "Justice and Home Affairs in a Globalised World: Ambitions and Reality in the Tale of the EU–US SWIFT Agreement" (Austrian Academy of Sciences Institute for European Integration Research, working paper no. 04/2011).
69 David Kleimann, "Taking Stock: EU Common Commercial Policy in the Lisbon Era" (CEPS working papers no. 345, April 2011); and Roberto Bendini, "The European Union's Trade Policy, Five Years after the Lisbon Treaty," European Parliament DG EXPO/B/PolDep/Note/2014_76, March 2014.
70 See generally Marc Maresceau, "Bilateral Agreements Concluded by the European Community," *Recueil des Cours de l'Académie de Droit International* 309 (2006): 125.
71 Including the Transatlantic Trade and Investment Partnership agreement under negotiation with the USA, the Comprehensive Economic and Trade Agreement with Canada, the free trade agreement with South Korea, and free trade agreements under negotiation with Singapore, Mercosur, and Japan.

72 European Security Strategy, n 5 this chapter, 9–10.
73 Article 21(1) TEU.
74 See further Marise Cremona, "Values in EU Foreign Policy," in *Beyond the Established Orders: Policy Interconnections between the EU and the Rest of the World*, ed. Malcolm Evans and Panos Koutrakos (Oxford: Hart, 2011).
75 The eastern European Neighbourhood Policy partners have been invited, on a case-by-case basis, to align themselves with EU declarations, *demarches*, and CFSP common positions: Ukraine since February 2005, Moldova since June 2005, Armenia, Azerbaijan, and Georgia since June 2007.
76 Ian Manners, "Normative Power Europe: A Contradiction in Terms?" *Journal of Common Market Studies* 40 (2002): 235.
77 "EU *demarches* on the issue of the death penalty – Declaration" in Conclusions of the General Affairs Council, 29 June 1998; EU Guidelines on the Death Penalty, 5 June 2008, Council doc. 10015/08; revised EU Guidelines on the Death Penalty, Council doc. 8416/13, 12 April 2013.
78 Article 19(2), Charter of Fundamental Rights. All EU member states are party to ECHR Protocol 13, which provides for the complete abolition of the death penalty; EU candidate states are required to abolish the death penalty.
79 Agreement on extradition between the United States and the EU [2003] OJ L 181/27, Article 13.
80 Agreement between the European Union and the Republic of Mauritius on the conditions of transfer of suspected pirates and associated seized property from the European Union-led naval force to the Republic of Mauritius and on the conditions of suspected pirates after transfer [2011] OJ L 254/3, Article 5.
81 Council Regulation 1236/2005/EC of 27 June 2005 concerning trade in certain goods which could be used for capital punishment, torture or other cruel, inhuman or degrading treatment or punishment [2005] OJ L 200/1; for a proposal to amend the regulation see COM(2014) 01 final.
82 UNGA Resolution 62/149 on a Moratorium on the use of the death penalty, 18 December 2007, reaffirmed in Resolution 63/168 and again in Resolutions 65/206 and 67/176.
83 Joint Declaration by Thorbjørn Jagland, Secretary General of the Council of Europe, and Catherine Ashton, European Union High Representative for Foreign Affairs and Security Policy, on the European and World Day against the Death Penalty, 10 October 2013, Council doc. 14670/13, PRESSE 408.
84 EU Guidelines on the Death Penalty, n 77 this chapter, 10–13.
85 US Supreme Court, *Atkins v. Virginia*, 536 US 304 (2002), in relation to a mentally retarded offender; US Supreme Court, *Roper v. Simmons*, 2004 WL 1619203 (US), in relation to juvenile offenders; see further Hoffmeister, "The Contribution of EU Practice to International Law," 115–117.
86 EU Strategy to combat illicit accumulation and trafficking of SALW [Small Arms and Light Weapons] and their ammunition adopted by the European Council 15–16 December 2005, Council doc 5319/06; Council Joint Action 2002/589/CFSP on the European Union's contribution to combating the destabilising accumulation and spread of small arms and light weapons [2002] OJ L 191/1; Council Decision 2013/698/CFSP in support of a global reporting mechanism on illicit small arms and light weapons and other illicit conventional weapons and ammunition to reduce the risk of their illicit trade [2013] OJ L 320/34.
87 The 1998 Code of Conduct on Arms Exports was replaced in 2008 by Council Common Position 2008/944/CFSP defining common rules governing control of exports of military technology and equipment [2008] OJ L 335/99. See also Council Joint Action 2008/230/CFSP on support for EU activities in order to promote the control of arms exports and the principles and criteria of the EU Code of Conduct on Arms Exports among third countries [2008] OJ L 75/81; Council Decision 2009/1012/CFSP [2009] OJ L 348/16; and Council Decision 2012/711/CFSP [2012] OJ L 321/62.
88 Council Conclusions of 3 October 2005, Council doc 12529/05.
89 Council Conclusions of 11 December 2006, welcoming the formal start of the process towards the elaboration of a legally binding international Arms Trade Treaty through the adoption of UN General Assembly Resolution 61/89, "Towards an arms trade treaty: establishing common international standards for the import, export and transfer of conventional arms" on 6 December 2006, Council doc 16692/06; Council Conclusions of 17–18 June 2007, Council doc 10605/07; Council Conclusions of

10 December 2007, Council doc 15850/07. The UN General Assembly Resolution 64/48 of 2 December 2009 announced the convening of a UN Conference on the Arms Trade Treaty in 2012.
90 Resolution A/RES/67/234 B of 2 April 2013.
91 Council Conclusions 17–18 June 2007, Council doc 10605/07.
92 See, e.g., the EU priorities for the 64th United Nations General Assembly, adopted by the Council 15 June 2009, Council doc 10809/09.
93 E.g., in the Final Communiqué of the 15th ECOWAS–EU Ministerial Troika Meeting held in Luxembourg, 16 June 2009, Council doc 11146/09; the European Union's position for the EU–Egypt Association Council's fifth meeting, 27 April 2009, para 68, Council doc 8725/1/09 REV 1; and the EU–US Summit in Washington, 3 November 2009, Declaration on Non-Proliferation and Disarmament, Council doc 15351/1/09, REV 1; Roadmap 2014–2017 adopted by the Fourth EU-Africa Summit, 2–3 April 2014; Joint Press Statement, 22nd EU-Japan Summit, 7 May 2014, Council doc 9577/14.
94 The EU–Ukraine Association Agenda endorsed by the EU–Ukraine Cooperation Council, 24 June 2013 includes cooperation on arms exports and "in jointly supporting the process of ratification and implementation of the Arms Trade Treaty," para 2.3(ii).
95 Council Decision 2009/42/CFSP on support for EU activities in order to promote among third countries the process leading towards an Arms Trade Treaty, in the framework of the European Security Strategy [2009] OJ L 17/39. See also Council Decision 2010/336/CFSP [2010] OJ L 152/14; and Council Decision 2013/43/CFSP [2013] OJ L 20/53.
96 Council Decision 2013/768/CFSP on EU activities in support of the implementation of the Arms Trade Treaty, in the framework of thc European Security Strategy [2013] OJ L 341/56.
97 Council Decision 2013/269/CFSP authorizing Member States to sign, in the interests of the European Union, the Arms Trade Treaty [2013] OJ L 155/9; Council Decision 2014/165/EU authorizing Member States to ratify, in the interests of the European Union, the Arms Trade Treaty [2014] OJ L 89/44.

References

Bendini, Roberto. "The European Union's Trade Policy, Five Years after the Lisbon Treaty." European Parliament DG EXPO/B/PolDep/Note/2014_76, 2014.

Blockmans, Steven. "The European External Action Service One Year On: First Signs of Strengths and Weaknesses." CLEER working papers no. 2012/2.

Blockmans, Steven, and Christophe Hillion, eds. *EEAS 2.0: A Legal Commentary on Council Decision 2010/427/EU Establishing the Organisation and Functioning of the European External Action Service.* EUI AEL working papers no. 2013/03.

Blockmans, Steven, and Christophe Hillion, eds. *EEAS 2.0: Recommendations for the Amendment of Council Decision 2010/427/EU Establishing the Organisation and Functioning of the European External Action Service.* CEPS Special Report, 13 November 2013.

Casolari, Federico. "The Principle of Loyal Cooperation: A 'Master Key' for EU External Representation?" In *Principles and Practices of EU External Representation*, edited by Steven Blockmans and Ramses Wessel. CLEER working papers no. 2012/5.

Cremona, Marise. "Defending the Community Interest: The Duties of Cooperation and Compliance." In Cremona and de Witte, *EU Foreign Relations Law: Constitutional Fundamentals.*

Cremona, Marise. "Defining Competence in EU External Relations: Lessons from the Treaty Reform Process." In *Law and Practice of EU External Relations: Salient Features of a Changing Landscape*, edited by Alan Dashwood and Marc Maresceau. Cambridge: Cambridge University Press, 2008.

Cremona, Marise. "Case C-246/07 *Commission v Sweden*, judgment 20 April 2010 (Grand Chamber)." *Common Market Law Review* 48 (2011): 1639–1666.

Cremona, Marise. "External Relations and External Competence: The Emergence of an Integrated Policy." In *The Evolution of EU Law*, edited by Gráinne de Búrca and Paul Craig. Oxford: Oxford University Press, 2011.

Cremona, Marise. "Justice and Home Affairs in a Globalised World: Ambitions and Reality in the Tale of the EU–US SWIFT Agreement." Austrian Academy of Sciences Institute for European Integration Research, working paper no. 04/2011.
Cremona, Marise. "Values in EU Foreign Policy." In *Beyond the Established Orders: Policy Interconnections between the EU and the Rest of the World*, edited by Malcolm Evans and Panos Koutrakos. Oxford: Hart, 2011.
Cremona, Marise. "The Two (or Three) Treaty Solution: The New Treaty Structure of the EU." In *European Union Law after the Treaty of Lisbon*, edited by Andrea Biondi and Piet Eeckhout. Oxford: Oxford University Press, 2012.
Cremona, Marise. "International Regulatory Policy and Democratic Accountability: The EU and the ACTA." In *Reflections on the Constitutionalisation of International Economic Law: Liber Amicorum Ernst-Ulrich Petersmann*, edited by Marise Cremona, Peter Hilpold, Nikos Lavranos, Stefan Schneider, and Andreas Ziegler. Leiden: Brill, 2013.
Cremona, Marise. "A Reticent Court? Policy Objectives and the Court of Justice." In *The European Court of Justice and External Relations Law: Constitutional Challenges*, edited by Marise Cremona and Anne Thies. Oxford: Hart, 2014.
Cremona, Marise. "EU External Relations: Unity and Conferral of Powers." In *The Question of Competence in the European Union*, edited by Loic Azoulai. Oxford: Oxford University Press, 2014.
de Baere, Geert. *Constitutional Principles of EU External Relations*. Oxford: Oxford University Press, 2008.
de Baere, Geert. "'O, Where is Faith? O, Where is Loyalty?' Some Thoughts on the Duty of Loyal Cooperation and the Union's External Environmental Competences in the Light of the *PFOS* Case." *European Law Review* 36 (2011): 405–419.
Delgado Casteleiro, Andres. "EU Declarations of Competence to Multilateral Agreements: A Useful Reference Base?" *European Foreign Affairs Review* 17 (2012): 491–510.
Delgado Casteleiro, Andres, and Joris Larik. "The Duty to Remain Silent: Limitless Loyalty in EU External Relations." *European Law Review* 36 (2011): 524–541.
de Witte, Bruno. "Too Much Constitutional Law in the European Union's Foreign Relations?" In Cremona and de Witte, *EU Foreign Relations Law: Constitutional Fundamentals*.
de Witte, Bruno, and Marise Cremona, eds. *EU Foreign Relations Law: Constitutional Fundamentals* (Oxford: Hart, 2008).
Duke, Simon. "Reflections on the EEAS Review." *European Foreign Affairs Review* 19 (2014): 23–44.
Eeckhout, Piet. *External Relations of the European Union*. Oxford: Oxford University Press, 2011.
Hillion, Christophe. "Mixity and Coherence in EU External Relations: The Significance of the 'Duty of Cooperation.'" In *Mixed Agreements Revisited: The EU and its Member States in the World*, edited by Christophe Hillion and Panos Koutrakos. Oxford: Hart, 2010.
Hoffmeister, Frank. "The Contribution of EU Practice to International Law." In *Developments in EU External Relations Law*, edited by Marise Cremona. Oxford: Oxford University Press, 2008.
Kleimann, David. "Taking Stock: EU Common Commercial Policy in the Lisbon Era." CEPS working papers no. 345, April 2011.
Koutrakos, Panos. *EU International Relations Law*. Oxford: Hart, 2006.
Larik, Joris. "Worldly Ambitions: Foreign Policy Objectives in European Constitutional Law." PhD thesis, European University Institute, 3 June 2013.
Manners, Ian. "Normative Power Europe: A Contradiction in Terms?" *Journal of Common Market Studies* 40 (2002): 235–258.
Maresceau, Marc. "Bilateral Agreements Concluded by the European Community." *Recueil des Cours de l'Académie de Droit International* 309 (2006): 125–451.
Missiroli, Antonio. "The EU 'Foreign Service' Under Construction." EUI RSCAS policy papers 2010/04.
Neframi, Eleftheria. "The Duty of Loyalty: Rethinking its Scope through its Application in the Field of EU External Relations." *Common Market Law Review* 47 (2010): 323–359.
Schütze, Robert. *Foreign Affairs and the European Constitution: Selected Essays*. Cambridge: Cambridge University Press, 2014.

Thym, Daniel. "Parliamentary Involvement in European International Relations." In Cremona and de Witte, *EU Foreign Relations Law: Constitutional Fundamentals.*
Thym, Daniel. "Foreign Affairs." In *Principles of European Constitutional Law*, edited by Armin von Bogdandy and Jurgen Bast. Oxford: Hart, 2011.
Vanhoonacker, Sophie, and Natasja Reslow, "The European External Action Service: Living Forwards By Understanding Backwards." *European Foreign Affairs Review* 15 (2010): 1–18.
Van Vooren, Bart. "A Legal-Institutional Perspective on the European External Action Service." CLEER working papers no. 2010/07.

26

Common Foreign, Security, and Defense Policy

Ramses A. Wessel

Introduction

For decades, the Common Foreign and Security Policy (CFSP) of the European Union has been the "odd one out." It emerged in an incremental, pragmatic fashion in the beginning of the 1970s, when it became clear that a coordination of the different foreign policies of the member states was helpful, and occasionally even necessary, for the European Community to pursue its goals.[1] These days the CFSP objectives are an integral part of the overall objectives of the European Union and the policy area has developed from a purely intergovernmental form of cooperation in the days of the European Political Cooperation to an area in which the member states have increasingly accepted new forms of institutionalization.[2]

The integration of external policy goals is visible in Article 3(5) of the Treaty on European Union (TEU):

> In its relations with the wider world, the Union shall uphold and promote its values and interests and contribute to the protection of its citizens. It shall contribute to peace, security, the sustainable development of the Earth, solidarity and mutual respect among peoples, free and fair trade, eradication of poverty and the protection of human rights, in particular the rights of the child, as well as to the strict observance and the development of international law, including respect for the principles of the United Nations Charter.

Yet, as laid down in Article 24(1) TEU, "[t]he common foreign and security policy is subject to specific rules and procedures." Indeed, in many aspects the nature of the CFSP still differs from other "common" policies, such as the Common Commercial Policy or the Common Agricultural Policy. Over the years, member states have shown a willingness to cooperate but have remained reluctant to actually transfer competences.[3] This makes it difficult to establish the type of competence the European Union has under the CFSP. Article 2(4) of the Treaty on the Functioning of the European Union (TFEU) merely states that "[t]he Union shall have competence, in accordance with the provisions of the Treaty on European Union, to define and

A Companion to European Union Law and International Law, First Edition.
Edited by Dennis Patterson and Anna Södersten.

implement a common foreign and security policy … ." Whereas this provision indicates that the CFSP moved beyond intergovernmentalism (as the competences as such is laid in the hand of the Union), the nature of the competence remains unclear. The CFSP is not mentioned in Articles 3 to 6 TFEU under either of the categories: exclusive competences, shared competences, or supporting, coordinating, or supplementing competences. It would probably come closest to the shared competences:[4] both the Union and the member states have roles to play. Yet it remains questionable to what extent activities of the Union would preempt member state action.

The different nature of the CFSP is usually related to a number of elements that are lacking when compared to most other Union policy areas: the different roles of the European Commission and the European Parliament in the decision-making process, the impossibility of the Court of Justice of the European Union to rule on most CFSP decisions and treaty provisions, the different effects of CFSP decisions in the domestic legal orders of the member states, and the different nature of the instruments themselves.[5]

Member States' Obligations under the CFSP

The "systematic cooperation" referred to in the list of CFSP means in Article 25 TEU is to be established in accordance with Article 32, which contains the actual procedural obligations. In principle, the scope of issues to which the systematic cooperation applies is not subject to any limitation regarding time or space: "Member States shall inform and consult one another within the European Council and Council on any matter of foreign and security policy … ." Nevertheless, Article 32 immediately fills this lacuna in adding the words "of general interest." The European Council has not provided a strict definition of "general interest" in Article 32. This seriously limits the information and consultation obligation in the first part of this article. On the one hand, member states are obliged to inform and consult one another, whereas on the other hand they are given the individual discretion to decide whether or not a matter is of "general interest." The principle of conferral (Article 5 TEU) implies that whatever has not been attributed to the organization remains with the member states.

Nevertheless, one may say that through the information and consultation obligation the member states have indeed obliged themselves to inform and consult one another as one of the means to attain the CFSP objectives in Article 11. The procedures stipulated in Article 32 only reflect the methods by which the member states implement the CFSP. Moreover, as we have seen, the content of the norm does not provide any other conditions than that the issue should be of general interest.

Taking into account the nature of the information and consultation obligation, it is rather unfortunate that the treaty does not further define the obligation. Yet, there is no reason to assume that the notion of consultation as used in Article 32 deviates from these general definitions, which leads us to conclude that the EU member states are to refrain from making public national positions on CFSP issues of general interest before they have discussed these positions in the framework of the CFSP cooperation.

Informing and consulting one another should take place "within the European Council and the Council." The requirement of *systematic* cooperation should not be interpreted as applying only within those institutions. Cooperation within the preparatory organs (Political and Security Committee, COREPER (Comité des représentants permanents) and working parties – *infra*), as well as bilateral and multilateral consultations, are equally covered by this obligation. In fact, as we will see, it is in these bodies that the actual systematic cooperation takes place. A second reason not to limit the cooperation to meetings of the member states in the Council may be found in Article 34. According to this provision, member states shall coordinate their action in international organizations and at international conferences as well. Even when not all member states are represented in an international organization or an international conference, those that do participate are to keep the absent member states informed of any matter of common interest.

It has been said that, over the years, CFSP cooperation at all levels has become more intense, automatic, and systematic. The "European reflex" has become part of the decision-making culture in national ministries; traditional national reservations (*domaines réservés*) have decreased in number as well as in intensity; and new issues have become part of the CFSP agenda (such as developments and actions in Africa). The flipside, however, is that the larger member states in particular tend to ignore the information and consultation procedures whenever sensitive policy issues are at stake. In cases like these they take individual positions and diplomatic initiatives or opt for cooperation in the framework of another international organization. This paradoxical situation reveals that CFSP has become part of the day-to-day policymaking in the national ministries as well as in Brussels but that important or sensitive issues may also still be being dealt with nationally or in other fora.

CFSP Decision Making and the Role of the Institutions

The institutions responsible for the CFSP do not differ from those in other policy areas. Indeed, the preamble of the TEU refers to a "single institutional framework" and Article 13 TEU on the institutions does not exclude any policy area. Yet, the role of the institutions is clearly different, and a number of organs are specifically relevant for the CFSP.

The provision in Article 24 TEU that "the adoption of legislative acts shall be excluded," implies that CFSP decisions are not adopted on the basis of the legislative procedure, which is, inter alia, characterized by a Commission initiative, codecision by the European Parliament, and qualified majority voting. As we will see, neither of these elements form part of CFSP decision making.

The European Council

Apart from its general role described in Article 15 TEU, the European Council has a leading role in the formulation of the CFSP. According to Article 22 TEU "the European Council shall identify the strategic interests and objectives of the Union." It

> shall act unanimously on a recommendation from the Council, adopted by the latter under the arrangements laid down for each area. Decisions of the European Council shall be implemented in accordance with the procedures provided for in the Treaties.

Article 216 TFEU adds that

> [t]he European Council shall identify the Union's strategic interests, determine the objectives of and define general guidelines for the common foreign and security policy, including for matters with defence implications. It shall adopt the necessary decisions.

The competences of the European Council in implementing the CFSP are thus indirect: they make possible or facilitate the decision making by the Council of Ministers. Its decisions form the basis for the CFSP decisions taken by the Council and the existence of Common Strategies may allow for different voting procedures in the Council.

The permanent president of the European Council was introduced by the Lisbon Treaty and

> shall, at his level and in that capacity, ensure the external representation of the Union on issues concerning its common foreign and security policy, without prejudice to the powers of the High Representative of the Union for Foreign Affairs and Security Policy. (Article 15(6) TEU)

He or she may convene an extraordinary meeting of the European Council in order to define the strategic lines of the Union's policy if international developments so require (Article 26(1) TEU).

The Council

The Council can be regarded as the main CFSP decision-making institution. Apart from the general rule in Article 26(2) TEU that

> [t]he Council shall frame the common foreign and security policy and take the decisions necessary for defining and implementing it on the basis of the general guidelines and strategic lines defined by the European Council,

more concrete provisions (Articles 28 and 29) stipulate that "[t]he Council shall adopt decisions." Moreover, the Council decides on the voting procedures, and it reviews the principles and objectives of the decisions in order to allow for possible national derogations. Usually CFSP decisions will be taken by the General Affairs Council, consisting of the ministers for foreign affairs of the member states.

Unanimity continues to form the basis for CFSP decisions, "except where the Treaties provide otherwise" (Article 24(1) TEU). In that respect, it is interesting that, apart from the previously existing possibilities for qualified majority voting under CFSP,[6] it is now possible for the Council to adopt measures on this basis following a proposal submitted by the high representative (Article 31(2) TEU). Such proposals should, however, follow a specific request by the European Council, in which, of course, member states can foreclose the use of qualified majority voting. In addition, qualified majority voting may be used for setting up, financing, and administering a start-up fund to ensure rapid access to appropriations in the Union budget for urgent financing of CFSP initiatives (Article 41(3) TEU). This start-up fund may be used for crisis management initiatives as well, which would potentially speed up the financing process of operations.[7] Overall, however, it is clear that any action on the part of the European Union will in the end continue to depend on the consent of its member states.

In most cases, CFSP decisions are adopted without any debate in the Council; they have been prepared by the Council's subsidiary organs, and a consensus has already been established between the representatives of the ministers for foreign affairs. When decisions are taken by the General Affairs Council, the issues do not appear on the agenda out of the blue. In most cases the draft decisions have thus already followed a long path through the various subsidiary organs of the Council.

Some of the preparatory and implementing organs have a direct treaty basis, others are set up by the Council itself. According to Article 240 TFEU, COREPER is responsible for preparing the work of the Council and for carrying out the tasks assigned to it by the Council. Regardless of the fact that COREPER is nowhere explicitly mentioned in the CFSP provisions, its competences in this area are beyond any doubt, since Article 38 TEU provides that the PSC shall act "without prejudice to Article 240 TFEU."

Over the years, the PSC has developed into the key preparatory and implementing organ for the CFSP and Common Security and Defence Policy (CSDP).[8] During the period of the European Political Cooperation, a "Political Committee" was created.[9] This committee consisted of the political directors of the national foreign ministries. The current PSC is a standing committee composed of representatives from the member states. Its remit is to

> monitor the international situation in the areas covered by the common foreign and security policy and contribute to the definition of policies by delivering opinions to the Council at the request of the Council or of the High Representative of the Union for Foreign Affairs and Security Policy or on its own initiative. It shall also monitor the implementation of agreed policies, without prejudice to the powers of the High Representative. (Article 38 TEU)

The PSC is also a key actor in the Union's security and defense policy (discussed later in the chapter).

As in all other areas, CFSP decisions are prepared in working groups or working parties (composed of representatives of the member states and the Commission). The preparatory bodies are installed by the Council[10] and have an important function during the first phase of the decision-making process. According to Article 19(3) of the Council's Rules of Procedure, the main task of the working groups is to carry out certain preparatory work or studies defined in advance. These may include all possible "CFSP output," ranging from *démarches* to decisions in the form of joint actions. The secretariat prepares reports of the discussions of the working group meetings that are circulated to all delegations through the Coreu network. On all CFSP matters the working groups report to the PSC.

The high representative of the Union for Foreign Affairs and Security Policy and the Commission

Unlike other Council configurations, in its configuration as "Foreign Affairs Council" the Council is chaired not by member state representatives but by the high representative (Article 18(3) TEU). Indeed, the original key role of the member states in the CFSP is put into perspective on a number of occasions. Before Lisbon, most proposals in the area of the CFSP came from member states, with the presidency having a particularly active role. Article 30(1) TEU lays down the new general rule that

> [a]ny Member State, the High Representative of the Union for Foreign Affairs and Security Policy, or the High Representative with the Commission's support, may refer any question relating to the common foreign and security policy to the Council and may submit to it initiatives or proposals as appropriate.

In particular, it is this new role of the Commission that may trigger new possibilities for the European Union in its external affairs. Whereas the Commission has so far largely refrained from making use of its competence to submit proposals on issues in the area of foreign, security, or defense policy (Article 22 TEU), the creation of the competence to submit joint proposals with the high representative may enhance its commitment to this area.

This is strengthened by the fact that the person holding the position of high representative at the same time acts as a member (and even as a vice president) of the Commission (Article 17, paras 4 and 5). This combination of the functions of high representative and vice president of the Commission is, without doubt, one of the key innovations of the Lisbon

Treaty.[11] The potential impact of this combination on the role of the European Union in international affairs lies in the fact that there could be a more natural attuning of different external policies, in particular where borders between policies are fuzzy, such as in crisis management. At the same time – as indicated above – the continued separation between CFSP and other Union issues may very well lead to a need for different legal bases for decisions, and hence for the use of distinct CFSP and other Union instruments. This holds true not only for the outcome of the decision-making process but also for the process itself, in which sincere cooperation between the Council and the Commission, supported by the high representative/vice president and the new and hybrid European External Action Service,[12] will remain of crucial importance.Indeed, a successful CFSP depends on successful leadership. The position of the high representative has clearly been strengthened by the last treaty modification. The name change reflects the fact that it has become clear that the role is indeed one of representing the Union and not the (collective) member states. The competences of the incumbent are clearly laid down in the EU Treaty and form part of the institutional framework. Although the term "foreign minister," which was used in the Constitutional Treaty, has been abandoned, the new provisions make clear that the high representative will indeed be the prime representative of the Union in international affairs. Even the president of the European Council (note: not the European Union) exercises that position's external competences "without prejudice to the powers of the High Representative of the Union for Foreign Affairs and Security Policy" (Article 15, para 6(d)). The high representative is appointed by the European Council (with the agreement of the president of the Commission) by qualified majority voting. This again underlines the representative's role as a person who can act on behalf of the Union and who is perhaps competent to act even in the absence of a full consensus among the member states. He or she is to "conduct" the Union's foreign, security, and defense policy, contributing proposals to the development of that policy, and presiding over the Foreign Affairs Council (Article 18 TEU). In addition, the high representative's de facto membership of the European Council is codified in Article 15 TEU (although strictly speaking it is stated that he or she only "takes part in the work" of the European Council). The high representative is to assist the Council and the Commission in ensuring consistency between the different areas of the Union's external action (Article 21 TEU), and together with the Council, ensures compliance by the member states with their CFSP obligations (Article 24(3) TEU). All in all, the position has been upgraded to allow for stronger and more independent development and implementation of the Union's foreign, security, and defense policy, which – potentially – allows for a more coherent and more effective role for the European Union in the world.

The role of the European Parliament: A democratic deficit in CFSP?

Article 36 TEU provides,

> The High Representative of the Union for Foreign Affairs and Security Policy shall regularly consult the European Parliament on the main aspects and the basic choices of the common foreign and security policy and the common security and defence policy and inform it of how those policies evolve. He shall ensure that the views of the European Parliament are duly taken into consideration.
>
> Special representatives may be involved in briefing the European Parliament.
>
> The European Parliament may address questions or make recommendations to the Council or the High Representative. Twice a year it shall hold a debate on progress in implementing the common foreign and security policy, including the common security and defence policy.

Here too, the differences with respect to most other Union policy areas are obvious. The main difference lies in the fact that with regard to the CFSP parliamentary influence is not directed towards a concrete decision (as is the case in other procedures) but only towards "the main aspects and the basic choices" of the CFSP. Moreover, it is not the institution which actually takes the decision that is ordered to consult the European Parliament, but the high representative. The formal influence of the European Parliament is therefore limited to the general policy lines and does not include influence on the actual decisions which are their result. The obligation of the Commission to regularly inform the European Parliament is of course put into perspective when the modest involvement of the Commission in CFSP is taken into consideration.

The Court of Justice of the European Union

Limited parliamentary control may to some extent be compensated for by judicial control. With respect to the CFSP, however, the powers of the Court of Justice are largely excluded by the treaty provisions. Obviously some member states argued that they would rather be safe than sorry, which resulted in a denial of the Court's competences in this area in both treaties. Article 24 (1) TEU provides:

> The Court of Justice of the European Union shall not have jurisdiction with respect to these provisions, with the exception of its jurisdiction to monitor compliance with Article 40 of this Treaty and to review the legality of certain decisions as provided for by the second paragraph of Article 275 of the Treaty on the Functioning of the European Union.

And, indeed, Article 275 TFEU states,

> The Court of Justice of the European Union shall not have jurisdiction with respect to the provisions relating to the common foreign and security policy nor with respect to acts adopted on the basis of those provisions.
>
> However, the Court shall have jurisdiction to monitor compliance with Article 40 of the Treaty on European Union and to rule on proceedings, brought in accordance with the conditions laid down in the fourth paragraph of Article 263 of this Treaty, reviewing the legality of decisions providing for restrictive measures against natural or legal persons adopted by the Council on the basis of Chapter 2 of Title V of the Treaty on European Union. [the specific provisions on].

This is not to say that the CFSP provisions are not at all relevant for the European Court of Justice.[13] The treaty provisions indicate a role for the Court in relation to Article 40 TEU. As indicated before, this provision calls for a balanced choice for either a CFSP or another legal basis of decisions. Conflicts on this issue can be brought before the Court, and the predecessor of Article 40 (Article 47) has indeed been used by the Court.[14] These observations underline that the Court of Justice is the ultimate arbiter to decide where the line of demarcation between the Union's issue areas lies.

Apart from Article 40 situations and general constitutional issues, such as access to documents, the treaty now provides for an additional situation in which the Court enjoys jurisdiction in relation to CFSP. The Court is competent to rule on proceedings, brought in accordance with the conditions laid down in the fourth paragraph of Article 263 TFEU, reviewing the legality of decisions providing for restrictive measures against natural or legal person. This is the result of the proliferation of sanctions targeted at individuals in the (global) fight against terrorism. The implication is that, even if the restrictive measures are only laid down in CFSP measures,[15] the Court has jurisdiction once the plaintiff is directly and individually concerned.

While recent case law indicates that the Court of Justice is increasingly seen as the Court of the European Union, it remains clear that the current regime regarding legal protection reveals a number of shortcomings. The most obvious lack of judicial control is apparent when competences and decision-making procedures *within* the CFSP legal order are at stake. In that case, there are no possibilities for the Court to scrutinize either the decision-making procedures or the legal basis chosen for a CFSP decision. This means, for instance, that neither the Commission nor the European Parliament can commence a procedure before the Court in cases where the Council has ignored their rights and competences in CFSP decision-making procedures in a situation where CFSP as a legal basis is not disputed. As far as the legal basis for decisions is concerned, there are no possibilities for the institutions or the member states to request the opinion of the Court. It is important to note that this brings about a situation in which the interpretation and implementation of the CFSP provisions (including the procedures to be followed) is left entirely to the Council. Keeping in mind their preference for "intergovernmental" cooperation where CFSP is concerned, it may be understandable that member states at the time of the negotiations had a strong desire to prevent a body of "CFSP law" coming into being by way of judicial activism on the part of the European Court of Justice, but it is less understandable that they were also reluctant to allow for judicial control of the *procedural* arrangements they explicitly agreed upon (although it is acknowledged that it may be difficult to unlink procedures and content).

The CFSP Instruments

Article 26(2) TEU entails a general competence for the Council to

> frame the common foreign and security policy and take the decisions necessary for defining and implementing it on the basis of the general guidelines and strategic lines defined by the European Council.

A combination of this provision and the more specific legal bases allows for the Council to adopt different CFSP legal and political instruments. One political instrument is the declaration. Declarations are usually issued by the high representative on behalf of the European Union and may concern all areas of CFSP where a political statement is needed towards third states.

On the basis of Article 25 TEU

> The Union shall conduct the common foreign and security policy by:
>
> (a) defining the general guidelines;
> (b) adopting decisions defining:
> (i) actions to be undertaken by the Union;
> (ii) positions to be taken by the Union;
> (iii) arrangements for the implementation of the decisions referred to in points (i) and (ii); and by
> (c) strengthening systematic cooperation between Member States in the conduct of policy.

The *general guidelines* are adopted by the European Council to lay down the strategies of the Union in relation to a particular third state, region, or theme (Article 26(1) TEU). On the basis of the same provisions, decisions may also be adopted by the European Council,[16] but in relation to CFSP issues these usually take the form of "conclusions."

Informal instruments

Although they lack a specific legal basis, the Council confirmed that the political impact of declarations may go beyond that of formal decisions. The difference with some generally phrased decisions is not always easy to establish. On the other hand, although declarations may be used for policy orientations vis-à-vis a third state, they lack an operational framework, which ultimately calls for a formal legal act to implement that policy.

In practice, CFSP systematic cooperation has also proved important with regard to the so-called political dialogues with third countries. Political dialogues as such cannot be found in the TEU, but they are established on the basis of general association treaties, decisions, declarations, or simply on the basis of an exchange of letters. Political dialogues take place in the framework of CFSP.

Dialogue meetings can take place at different levels. The highest level is that of the high representative or the presidency (together with the president of the Commission). Lower levels are the ministerial level, the level of political directors, the senior official or expert level, and the parliamentary level. Owing to difficulties in scheduling dialogue meetings at times suitable to all of the higher-ranking appointees, there is a growing tendency to send lower deputies to dialogue meetings. Thus the ministers often send junior ministers, and political directors increasingly send deputy political directors or even more junior officials.

Legal acts

CFSP legal acts cannot be adopted in the form of regulations or directives but only as "decisions." This is again a striking difference compared to other Union policy areas. At the same time, the CFSP "decisions" are not to be equated with the "decisions" in Article 288 TFEU. Although they are qualified as "legal acts" (or *actes juridiques* in, for instance, the CFSP Annual Reports) they have not been adopted on the basis of the legislative procedure. Article 25 TEU makes a distinction between decisions defining: "(i) actions to be undertaken by the Union; and (ii) positions to be taken by the Union." Hence, both actions and positions can be laid down in the form of a CFSP decision. At the same time decisions can be used for "(iii) arrangements for the implementation of the decisions referred to in points (i) and (ii)." Again this follows the practice that all implementing, modifying, or repealing decisions take the shape of a CFSP decision.

When we take a first look at the contents of CFSP decisions, the main objectives seem to be "political" (reinforcing democracy and respect for human rights) and "diplomatic" (preventing and solving conflicts, coordinating emergency situations). In addition, "economic" objectives (support of economic reforms, regional development) and "legal" objectives (supporting the development of the rule of law and good governance) can be discovered.

These established characteristics of the CFSP decisions certainly clarify its nature to some extent. The question, however, is whether an analysis of the *procedure* to adopt joint actions may shed some additional light on the nature of the *instrument*.

From the outset, the binding nature of CFSP decisions has puzzled academics and practitioners alike.[17] The main reason would be the very limited role of the Court of Justice of the

European Union in relation to adopted CFSP decisions. Yet – and apart from the indeed limited legal supervision – the obligatory force of CFSP decisions can clearly be derived from Article 28(2) TEU: "Decisions referred to in paragraph 1 shall commit the Member States in the positions they adopt and in the conduct of their activity." Hence, CFSP decisions actions, once adopted, limit the freedom of member states in their individual policies. Member states are not allowed to adopt positions or otherwise to act contrary to the decisions. They have committed themselves to adapting their national policies to the agreed decisions. It is tempting to make comparisons with EU regulations, which also demand the unconditional obedience of member states once they are adopted. But the treaty text alone does not support reading the CFSP decisions along the same lines as the instruments used in Article 288 TFEU – in particular where the addressees of the obligations or the direct applicability are concerned. A comparison with the legal instrument of "directives" equally reveals glaring differences, for example regarding the implementation period of directives.

The nature of Article 29 decisions as concrete norms of conduct demanding a certain unconditional behavior from the member states is underlined by the strict ways in which exceptions are allowed. A first possibility to depart from adopted joint actions is offered by Article 28(1), which is similar to, but at the same time clearly departs from, the *rebus sic stantibus* rule as presented in Article 62 of the Vienna Convention on the Law of Treaties.[18] Article 28(1) provides that even if the original circumstances constitute an essential basis of the consent of the parties to be bound, or the effect of the change is radically to transform the extent of obligations still to be performed, member states may not invoke the change in circumstances as a ground for not living up to the particular decision. In that sense the CFSP provision cannot be regarded as a *clausula rebus sic stantibus*. Instead, it is provided that

> [i]f there is a change in circumstances having a substantial effect on a question subject to such a decision, the Council shall review the principles and objectives of that decision and take the necessary decisions.

Hence, even a change in circumstances may not be invoked by the member state as a reason to neglect the adopted decision. It is up to the Council to decide on possible modifications. Pending the decision of the Council, no deviations from the decision are allowed.

The idea that CFSP decisions, which are adopted by the Council, can only be modified or terminated by that institution, is furthermore emphasized by the subsequent paragraphs of Article 28. Paragraph 3 reveals the rule that

> Whenever there is any plan to adopt a national position or take national action pursuant to a decision as referred to in paragraph 1, information shall be provided by the Member State concerned in time to allow, if necessary, for prior consultations within the Council. The obligation to provide prior information shall not apply to measures which are merely a national transposition of Council decisions.

The *rationale* behind this provision is obvious: it creates a procedure to identify potential conflicting national policies at an early stage. The procedure is in the interest of the member states themselves; it prevents the adoption of national policies which, because of a conflict with a CFSP decision, would run the risk of being in violation of Article 28(2) TEU ("Decisions … shall commit the Member States in the positions they adopt and in the conduct of their activity.").

Member states are not obliged to refer national implementation measures to the Council. On the other hand, when they have major difficulties in implementing a CFSP decision, paragraph

5 stipulates that these should be referred to the Council, which shall discuss them and seek appropriate solutions. The inviolability of adopted joint actions is underlined by the rule, formulated in the last sentence of paragraph 5, that "[s]uch solutions shall not run counter to the objectives of the decision … or impair its effectiveness." While the wording of paragraph 5 is in general quite clear, the question emerges why this procedure is related to "major" difficulties only. What if a member state encounters problems with the implementation of a minor part of the decision only? Obviously, there would be no obligation to refer the case to the Council. On the other hand, we have seen that a decision commits the member states; there is no ground for reading paragraph 2 as "Decisions Actions commit the Member States *to the largest possible extent*." This, together with the loyalty obligation discussed above, leads to the conclusion that the discretion offered to the member states to decide whether or not their implementation problems need to be brought to the attention of the Council is limited. In case of any controversies concerning this issue, it seems to be up to the Council, to seek an appropriate solution.

Does it follow from the fact that CFSP decisions are binding that member states may *never* avoid the obligations laid down in the decision in question? The CFSP provisions in fact include one quite explicit exception (Article 28(4)):

> In cases of imperative need arising from changes in the situation and failing a review of the Council decision as referred to in paragraph 1, Member States may take the necessary measures as a matter of urgency having regard to the general objectives of that decision.

In this case "[t]he Member State concerned shall inform the Council immediately of any such measures." While this provision again comes close to the *rebus sic stantibus* rule in Article 62 of the Vienna Convention on the Law of Treaties, the criteria to be met are strict: (1) there must be a case of *imperative need*; (2) the situation must have been changed; (3) the Council has not (yet) come up with a decision to solve the matter; (4) measures will have to be *necessary*; and (5) must be taken as a *matter of urgency*; (6) the general objectives of the Decision should be taken into consideration; and (7) the Council shall be immediately informed.

Common Security and Defence Policy

The place of common security and defence policy in the treaties

The global ambitions of the European Union are not limited to foreign policy but include a clear security and defense dimension.[19] The "Provisions on the Common Security and Defence Policy" are laid down in Section 2 of Chapter 2 TEU, called "Specific Provisions on the Common, Foreign and Security Policy." Indeed, Article 42(1) provides that "The common security and defence policy shall be an integral part of the common foreign and security policy." Since both CFSP and CSDP deal with "security" and that concept is not defined by the treaty, it has always been unclear where to draw the line. In the 1992 Maastricht Treaty objectives it was implied that there is a difference between the security of the Union and the security of the member states, since the objective originally read "to strengthen the security of the Union and its Member States in all ways." Thus, the objective was aimed at strengthening not only the security of the Union but also the security of individual member states. Nevertheless, the apparent confusion raised by this distinction must have been the reason to delete that reference. These days, the objectives in Article 21(2) TEU simply state that the Union shall "safeguard its values, fundamental interests, security, independence and integrity."

What is meant by "security"? The treaty provisions do not provide reasons to limit this concept to military security. Obviously different dimensions of security are acknowledged, including, for instance, environmental and economic security, international crime, and terrorism. These aspects of security were originally mentioned by the European Council in Lisbon (1992) as well.[20] It may be argued that it is exactly these nonmilitary, or at least *internal*, dimensions of security that are intended in this objective since another objective explicitly deals with the international dimensions: to "preserve peace, prevent conflicts and strengthen international security."[21]

Keeping in mind the assertion of Robert Schuman as reflected in his declaration of 9 May 1950 that the creation of a high authority would "make it plain that any war between France and the Federal Republic of Germany becomes, not merely unthinkable, but materially impossible," a role for the Union as an internal stabilizer should not be ruled out as well. In this interpretation, "security" should at least also be seen as meaning "internal security." Since the first drafts of the TEU, the objectives included a reference to the eventual framing of a defense policy, which strengthens the idea that the security concept is also directed at security between the member states. After all, this security would be ultimately guaranteed when a common defense policy existed. In this context it can be noted that the current treaty unconditionally confirms that

> [t]he Union's competence in matters of common foreign and security policy shall cover … all questions relating to the Union's security, including the progressive framing of a common defence policy that might lead to a common defence. (Article 24(1) TEU)

Although not all concepts are defined by the treaties, practice reveals that CFSP would be linked more to "foreign affairs" whereas CSDP would be the responsibility of the defense ministries. This would also draw a relatively clear line of division between "military security" (CSDP) and other forms of security (CFSP). However, the different provisions on security and defense policy are far from clear. Obviously, they can again be seen as compromises between states in favor of more integration in this area and states that are afraid of losing control.

The specific CSDP provisions

As CSDP can be seen as forming part of CFSP, the decision making takes place along similar lines. Decisions are taken by the Council. Article 42(4) TEU provides that

> [d]ecisions relating to the common security and defence policy, including those initiating a mission as referred to in this Article, shall be adopted by the Council acting unanimously on a proposal from the High Representative of the Union for Foreign Affairs and Security Policy or an initiative from a Member State. The High Representative may propose the use of both national resources and Union instruments, together with the Commission where appropriate.

The "external" nature of this policy is underlined by the first provision in this section, Article 42(1):

> The common security and defence policy shall be an integral part of the common foreign and security policy. It shall provide the Union with an operational capacity drawing on civilian and military assets. The Union may use them on missions outside the Union for peace-keeping, conflict prevention and strengthening international security in accordance with the principles

> of the United Nations Charter. The performance of these tasks shall be undertaken using capabilities provided by the Member States.

Indeed, "the Union may use them on missions outside the Union." The CSDP is thus intended to allow the Union to play its role as a regional and global security actor. This is underlined by Article 43(1), which lays down the other key provision:

> The tasks referred to in Article 42(1), in the course of which the Union may use civilian and military means, shall include joint disarmament operations, humanitarian and rescue tasks, military advice and assistance tasks, conflict prevention and peace-keeping tasks, tasks of combat forces in crisis management, including peace-making and post-conflict stabilisation. All these tasks may contribute to the fight against terrorism, including by supporting third countries in combating terrorism in their territories.

The references to "joint disarmament operations," "military advice and assistance tasks," "post-conflict stabilization," and "the fight against terrorism" in Article 43(1) were introduced by the Lisbon Treaty and allow the Union to further develop its security and defense policy.

Crisis management may also be needed in relation to an attack on the Union itself. However, with regard to the "defence" part of CSDP, the treaty remains ambiguous:

> The common security and defence policy shall include the progressive framing of a common Union defence policy. This will lead to a common defence, when the European Council, acting unanimously, so decides. (Article 42(2) TEU)

Despite the careful wording of this provision in line with earlier versions, the treaty does offer reasons to conclude that something has changed. First of all – and despite the claim that a "common defence" is not yet included in CSDP – Article 42(7) provides the following:

> If a Member State is the victim of armed aggression on its territory, the other Member States shall have towards it an obligation of aid and assistance by all the means in their power, in accordance with Article 51 of the United Nations Charter. This shall not prejudice the specific character of the security and defence policy of certain Member States.

The collective defense obligation does not really differ from Article 5 of the North Atlantic Treaty or Article V of the Western European Union (WEU) Treaty.[22] What is different, however, is that both the North Atlantic Treaty Organization (NATO) and the WEU started their life as collective defense organizations and only started to engage in other security operations later. The European Union seems to follow the reverse path, by concentrating on external crisis management before establishing a mechanism to defend its own member states.

Nevertheless, the feeling that something similar to a collective defense obligation has been created (although somewhat hidden in paragraph 7 of Article 42) becomes stronger when the so-called solidarity clause is taken into account. This clause flowed from the Declaration on Solidarity Against Terrorism,[23] which was issued by the European Council after the Madrid terrorist attacks in March 2004, although the Declaration does not refer to a role for the Union as such but to the "Member States acting jointly." It is somewhat peculiar that this solidarity clause is separated from the collective defense clause and is included in the TFEU (Article 222) rather than together with the CSDP provisions in the

TEU. The clause does not restrict common defense to "armed aggression" but in fact extends the obligation to terrorist attacks:

> The Union and its Member States shall act jointly in a spirit of solidarity if a Member State is the object of a terrorist attack or the victim of a natural or man-made disaster. The Union shall mobilise all the instruments at its disposal, including the military resources made available by the Member States, to:
>
> (a) prevent the terrorist threat in the territory of the Member States;
> protect democratic institutions and the civilian population from any terrorist attack;
> assist a Member State in its territory, at the request of its political authorities, in the event of a terrorist attack;
> (b) assist a Member State in its territory, at the request of its political authorities, in the event of a natural or man-made disaster.

Paragraph 2 adds the following:

> Should a Member State be the object of a terrorist attack or the victim of a natural or man-made disaster, the other Member States shall assist it at the request of its political authorities. To that end, the Member States shall coordinate between themselves in the Council.

Paragraph 3 refers to a coordinating role of the Council as well as the procedure: the arrangements for the implementation of the solidarity clause shall be defined by a decision adopted by the Council acting on a joint proposal by the Commission and the high representative.

While the wording of the solidarity clause leaves room for both the member states and the Council regarding the type and scope of their reaction, it may be seen as an innovation to the previous legal regime, where no obligations for the member states or competences of the Council formed part of the treaties.

The CSDP missions

Both military and civilian missions may be established on the basis of the CSDP provisions. On 1 January 2003, the Union launched the European Union Police Mission in Bosnia and Herzegovina as its first ever civilian crisis management operation within the framework of the CSDP.[24] On 31 March 2003, the Union finally deployed "Operation Concordia," its inaugural military mission, to follow up on NATO's efforts to contribute to a stable and secure environment in the Former Yugoslav Republic of Macedonia.[25] Since 2003, the Union has affirmed its operational capability through the launching of more than twenty CSDP operations, mainly in Africa and in the Western Balkans but also in its eastern neighborhood, the Middle East, and Asia. The European Union has acted as a crisis manager in several guises.

- an honest broker of peace between the parties to a conflict (e.g., Aceh);
- an assistant to border management (e.g., Moldova/Ukraine);
- an adviser in justice reform (e.g., Georgia);
- a trainer of police and prison staff (e.g., Iraq);
- a security sector reformer (e.g., Guinea-Bissau);
- a security guarantor during elections (e.g., Democratic Republic of Congo);
- a peacekeeper on the invitation of a host country (e.g., Former Yugoslav Republic of Macedonia);

- a regional arrangement operating under a mandate by the United Nations Security Council to counter the threat to international peace and security (posed by, e.g., piracy and armed robberies against vulnerable vessels off the Somali coast) and to assist peace-keeping operations carried out by other international organizations (e.g., Chad and, indirectly, Darfur); and
- a component of an international transitional administration (e.g., Pillar IV in UNMIK).

The European Union has never acted in the capacity of enforcer of the peace (like NATO in Kosovo in 1999) nor in defense against an armed attack on its territory.

While most of the early operations were fairly successful, largely thanks to the fact that they were usually short term and limited in both scope and size, they have also revealed shortfalls, bottlenecks as well as broader issues in crisis management. They range from "growing pains," including the creation of the "brand" of EU crisis management as well as the planning and drawing up of appropriate mandates for CSDP missions, to more enduring challenges such as coherence among EU policies, institutions, and instruments, coordination with other international organizations, notably NATO and the United Nations, and consistency of "output."[26] Lessons learned from these operations should be taken to heart now that the European Union is facing its "maturity test" as an international crisis manager.

In spite of the growing pains in the development of CSDP, the European Union has made significant strides in deploying crisis management operations. However, the issue of defining success of the CSDP is no longer measured in terms of merely launching missions, ensuring mission output, and gathering operational experience. CSDP is past its age of innocence. The bar is set much higher now. Not only is greater intra- and interinstitutional coordination and cross-pillar coherence required by EU law and policy,[27] the Union is also expected to conduct several operations at the same time,[28] to carry them out in line with both human rights law and international humanitarian law, to live up to its promises by accomplishing its tasks, to effect positive change on the ground, and to show that it can take the lead among other international and institutional actors. These issues have become more pressing since the Union embarked on bigger and more difficult CSDP operations, for instance in the high-risk theatres of Kosovo, Afghanistan, and Chad. If such crises are managed badly, then the European Union risks losing its recently found confidence and acquired image as a regional and global actor serving the interest of international peace and security, especially if an ill-prepared and/or under-equipped CSDP operation stumbles into another "Srebrenica." In short, the European Union is facing a daunting maturity test in CSDP.

Conclusion

The image of CFSP as a purely "intergovernmental" form of international cooperation is not supported by the treaty provisions. Yet, the nonexclusive nature of CFSP is paramount. The competences of the institutions, the obligations of the member states, and the decision-making procedures all reflect the intention of the states to create a common policy that would not unconditionally *replace* the national policies of the individual states but that would only emerge *where and when possible*. Despite concrete obligations aiming at the establishment of a common policy, a number of vague notions ("important common interests," "general interest," "reasons of national policy") allow for a large margin of appreciation on the part of the member states. Whenever a common policy does not prove possible, member states are free to pursue their own national foreign policies.

Even adopted "decisions" – as the key CFSP legal instruments – do not deprive the member states of all their rights to maintain national policy in the areas covered by the CFSP decisions. Practice reveals that most decisions have a narrow scope only, allowing for parallel national policies in the same issue area. And, even within the scope of the CFSP decisions, it is possible for member states to lay emphasis on certain national preferences and implementation modalities.

The legal outcome of the negotiations on CFSP was the only one possible in situation where member states have a common foreign policy but are not prepared to give up their sovereign rights in favor of an independent common institution. While an analysis of the origins of CFSP and the subsequent negotiations indeed reveal a certain preference for "intergovernmental" cooperation on the part of most member states, the further institutionalization of both CFSP and CSDP indicates serious constraints on the member states in executing their foreign policy as well as on the EU institutions involved.

Notes

1 See more extensively, Bart Van Vooren and Ramses A. Wessel, *EU External Relations Law: Text, Cases and Materials* (Cambridge: Cambridge University Press, 2014).

2 Cf. Aurel Sari, "Between Legalisation and Organisational Development: Explaining the Evolution of EU Competence in the Field of Foreign Policy," in *EU External Relations Law and Policy in the Post-Lisbon Era*, ed. Paul J. Cardwell (The Hague: T.M.C. Asser Press, 2012); Panos Koutrakos, ed., *The European Union's External Relations a Year after Lisbon* (The Hague: CLEER working paper, no. 2011/3); and Ramses A. Wessel, "The Dynamics of the European Union Legal Order: An Increasingly Coherent Framework of Action and Interpretation," *European Constitutional Law Review* 5 (2009).

3 Peter Van Elsuwege, "EU External Action after the Collapse of the Pillar Structure: In Search of a New Balance between Delimitation and Consistency," *Common Market Law Review* 47 (2010).

4 Cf. Marise Cremona, "A Constitutional Basis for Effective External Action? An Assessment of the Provisions on EU External Action in the Constitutional Treaty" (EUI working paper, Law, no. 30 (2006): 17).

5 Ramses A. Wessel, *The European Union's Foreign and Security Policy: A Legal Institutional Perspective* (The Hague: Kluwer Law International, 1999).

6 These exceptions recur in Article 31(2) TEU and apply as follows: when adopting a decision defining a Union action or position on the basis of a decision of the European Council relating to the Union's strategic interests and objectives, as referred to in Article 22(1); when adopting any decision implementing a decision defining a Union action or position; and when appointing a special representative in accordance with Article 33.

7 See also Directorate-General for External Policies of the Union, Policy Department, "The Lisbon Treaty and its Implications for CFSP/ESDP," Briefing Paper, European Parliament, February 2008, 3. Nevertheless, for some member states, resort to the EU budget may remain attractive, even if this means delaying the European Union's response. See Richard Whitman and Ana Juncos, "The Lisbon Treaty and the Foreign, Security and Defence Policy: Reforms, Implementation and the Consequences of (non-)Ratification," *European Foreign Affairs Review* 14 (2009): 39.

8 Ana E. Juncos and Christopher Reynolds, "The Political and Security Committee. Governing in the Shadow," *European Foreign Affairs Review* 12 (2007).

9 The Political Committee was introduced by the Davignon Report in 1970 and gained a legal treaty basis in Article 30, paragraph 10(c) of the Single European Act (1986). The usual abbreviation is CP from the French title for the committee, *Comité politique*.

10 An overview is published by the Council Secretariat. See, for instance, http://register.consilium.europa.eu/pdf/en/12/st05/st05269.en12.pdf.

11 More extensively, see Christine Kaddous, "Role and Position of the High Representative of the Union for Foreign Affairs and Security Policy under the Lisbon Treaty," in *The Lisbon Treaty:*

Constitutionalism without a Constitutional Treaty? ed. Stefan Griller and Jacques Ziller (Vienna: Springer, 2008), 206. Cf. also Whitman and Juncos, "The Lisbon Treaty and the Foreign, Security and Defence Policy," 32; and Jonas Paul, "EU Foreign Policy after Lisbon: Will the New High Representative and the External Action Service Make a Difference?" *Centre for Applied Policy Research (CAP) Policy Analysis*, no. 2 (2008).

12 See Bart Van Vooren, "A Legal-Institutional Perspective on the European External Action Service," *Common Market Law Review* 48 (2011); Steven Blockmans and Marja-Liisa Laasit, "The European External Action Service: Enhancing Coherence in EU External Action?" in Cardwell, *EU External Relations Law and Policy in the Post-Lisbon Era*; and Steven Blockmans, *The European External Action Service One Year On: First Signs of Strengths and Weaknesses* (The Hague: CLEER working paper series, no. 2012/2).

13 Cf. Maja Brkan, "The Role of the European Court of Justice in the Field of Common Foreign and Security Policy after the Treaty of Lisbon: New Challenges for the Future," In Cardwell, *EU External Relations Law and Policy in the Post-Lisbon Era.*

14 A case in point is Case C-91/05 *Commission v. Council* EU:C:2008:288. See Christophe Hillion and Ramses A. Wessel, "Competence Distribution in EU External Relations after *ECOWAS*: Clarification or Continued Fuzziness?" *Common Market Law Review* 46 (2009).

15 It goes without saying that the Court has jurisdiction in relation to restrictive measures not based on a CFSP Decision but on a Council Regulation following the procedure in Article 215 TFEU, even if there is a relation with CFSP (see Case C-130/10 *European Parliament v. Council* (Restrictive measures directed against certain persons and entities associated with Usama bin Laden, the Al-Qaeda network and the Taliban) EU:C:2012:472.

16 See, for instance, European Council Decision 2011/199/EU of 25 March 2011 amending Article 136 of the Treaty on the Functioning of the European Union with regard to a stability mechanism for Member States whose currency is the euro [2011] OJ L 91/1.

17 Ramses A. Wessel, "The Legal Dimension of European Foreign Policy," in *Handbook of European Foreign Policy*, ed. Knud Erik Jørgensen et al. (London: Sage, 2015).

18 Vienna Convention on the Law of Treaties, Article 62, paragraphs 1(a) and (b). The criteria to justifiably invoke this provision include the fundamental change of circumstances was not foreseen by the parties and (a) the existence of those circumstances constituted an essential basis of the consent of the parties to be bound by the treaty; and (b) the effect of the change is radically to transform the extent of obligations still to be performed under the treaty.

19 Steven Blockmans and Ramses A. Wessel, "The European Union and Crisis Management: Will the Lisbon Treaty Make the EU More Effective?" *Journal of Conflict and Security Law* 14 (2009).

20 Lisbon European Council, 26 and 27 June, 1992, Annex 1: Report to the European Council in Lisbon on the likely development of the Common Foreign and Security Policy (CFSP) with a view to identifying areas open to joint action vis-à-vis particular countries or groups of countries, *Bulletin EC* 6–1992.

21 Steven Blockmans and Ramses A. Wessel, "The European Union and Peaceful Settlement of Disputes in its Neighbourhood: The Emergence of a New Regional Security Actor?" in *The European Union and Global Emergencies: A Law and Policy Analysis*, ed. Antonis Antoniadis, Robert Schütze, and Eleanor Spaventa (Oxford: Hart, 2011).

22 Article 5 of the North Atlantic Treaty reads, "The Parties agree that an armed attack against one or more of them in Europe or North America shall be considered an attack against them all and consequently they agree that, if such an armed attack occurs, each of them, in exercise of the right of individual or collective self-defence recognised by Article 51 of the Charter of the United Nations, will assist the Party or Parties so attacked by taking forthwith, individually and in concert with the other Parties, such action as it deems necessary, including the use of armed force, to restore and maintain the security of the North Atlantic area." Article V of the modified Brussels Treaty (WEU) reads, "If any of the High Contracting Parties should be the object of an armed attack in Europe, the other High Contracting Parties will, in accordance with the provisions of Article 51 of the Charter of the United Nations, afford the Party so attacked all the military and other aid and assistance in their power."

23 Brussels European Council, 25–26 March 2004, Presidency Conclusions.

24 See Council Decision 2002/968/CFSP of 10 December 2002 concerning the implementation of Joint Action 2002/210/CFSP on the European Union Police Mission [2002] OJ L 335/1.

25 See Council Decision 2003/202/CFSP of 18 March 2003 relating to the launch of the EU military operation in the Former Yugoslav Republic of Macedonia [2003] OJ L 76/43.

26 These issues are well documented. See, e.g., Frederik Naert, "ESDP in Practice: Increasingly Varied and Ambitious EU Security and Defence Operations," in *European Security Law*, ed. Martin Trybus and Nigel White (Oxford: Oxford University Press, 2007); and Tom Hadden, ed., *A Responsibility to Assist: Human Rights Policy and Practice in European Union Crisis Management Operations* (Oxford: Hart, 2009).

27 For academic analysis and references to relevant case law of the Court of Justice of the European Union, see Panos Koutrakos, "Security and Defence Policy within the Context of EU External Relations: Issues of Coherence, Consistency and Effectiveness," in Trybus and White, *European Security Law*; Sophie Vanhoonacker, "The European Security and Defence Policy and Coherence Challenges in the Council," in *The European Union and Crisis Management: Policy and Legal Aspects*, ed. Steven Blockmans (The Hague: T.M.C. Asser Press, 2008); Kolja Raube, "European Parliamentary Oversight of Crisis Management," in Blockman, *The European Union and Crisis Management: Policy and Legal Aspects*; and Vincent Kronenberger, "Coherence and Consistency of the EU's Action in International Crisis Management: The Role of the European Court of Justice," in Blockmans, *The European Union and Crisis Management: Policy and Legal Aspects.*

28 In its Declaration on Strengthening Capabilities of 11 December 2008, the Council mentioned the following ambitions: "two major stabilisation and reconstruction operations, with a suitable civilian component, supported by up to 10,000 troops for at least two years; two rapid-response operations of limited duration using inter alia EU battle groups; an emergency operation for the evacuation of European nationals (in less than ten days), bearing in mind the primary role of each Member State as regards its nationals and making use of the consular lead State concept; a maritime or air surveillance/interdiction mission; a civilian-military humanitarian assistance operation lasting up to 90 days; around a dozen ESDP civilian missions (inter alia police, rule-of-law, civilian administration, civil protection, security sector reform, and observation missions) of varying formats, including in rapid-response situations, together with a major mission (possibly up to 3000 experts) which could last several years." The declaration is available on the website of the Council of the European Union, among the reference documents about civilian crisis management.

References

Blockmans, Steven, ed. *The European Union and Crisis Management: Policy and Legal Aspects*. The Hague: T.M.C. Asser Press, 2008.

Blockmans, Steven. *The European External Action Service One Year On: First Signs of Strengths and Weaknesses*. The Hague: CLEER working paper series, no. 2012/2.

Blockmans, Steven, and Marja-Liisa Laasit. "The European External Action Service: Enhancing Coherence in EU External Action?" In Cardwell, *EU External Relations Law and Policy in the Post-Lisbon Era*, 135–159.

Blockmans, Steven, and Ramses A. Wessel. "The European Union and Crisis Management: Will the Lisbon Treaty Make the EU More Effective?" *Journal of Conflict and Security Law* 14 (2009): 265–308.

Blockmans, Steven, and Ramses A. Wessel. "The European Union and Peaceful Settlement of Disputes in its Neighbourhood: The Emergence of a New Regional Security Actor?" In *The European Union and Global Emergencies: A Law and Policy Analysis*, edited by Antonis Antoniadis, Robert Schutze, and Eleanor Spaventa, 73–103. Oxford: Hart, 2011.

Brkan, Maja. "The Role of the European Court of Justice in the Field of Common Foreign and Security Policy after the Treaty of Lisbon: New Challenges for the Future." In Cardwell, *EU External Relations Law and Policy in the Post-Lisbon Era*, 97–115.

Cardwell, Paul J., ed. *EU External Relations Law and Policy in the Post-Lisbon Era*. The Hague: T.M.C. Asser Press, 2012.
Cremona, Marise. "A Constitutional Basis for Effective External Action? An Assessment of the Provisions on EU External Action in the Constitutional Treaty." EUI working paper, Law, no. 30 (2006).
Hadden, Tom, ed. *A Responsibility to Assist: Human Rights Policy and Practice in European Union Crisis Management Operations*. Oxford: Hart, 2009.
Hillion, Christophe, and Ramses A. Wessel. "Competence Distribution in EU External Relations after *ECOWAS*: Clarification or Continued Fuzziness?" *Common Market Law Review* 46 (2009): 551–586.
Juncos, Ana E., and Christopher Reynolds. "The Political and Security Committee: Governing in the Shadow." *European Foreign Affairs Review* 12 (2007): 127–147.
Kaddous, Christine. "Role and Position of the High Representative of the Union for Foreign Affairs and Security Policy under the Lisbon Treaty." In *The Lisbon Treaty: Constitutionalism without a Constitutional Treaty?* edited by Stefan Griller and Jacques Ziller, 205–221. Vienna: Springer, 2008.
Koutrakos, Panos. "Security and Defence Policy within the Context of EU External Relations: Issues of Coherence, Consistency and Effectiveness." In Trybus and White, *European Security Law*, 249–269.
Koutrakos, Panos, ed. *The European Union's External Relations a Year after Lisbon*. The Hague: CLEER working paper, no. 2011/3.
Kronenberger, Vincent. "Coherence and Consistency of the EU's Action in International Crisis Management: The Role of the European Court of Justice." In Blockmans, *The European Union and Crisis Management: Policy and Legal Aspects*, 199–211.
Naert, Frederik. "ESDP in Practice: Increasingly Varied and Ambitious EU Security and Defence Operations." In Trybus and White, *European Security Law*, 61–101.
Paul, Jonas. "EU Foreign Policy after Lisbon: Will the New High Representative and the External Action Service Make a Difference?" *Centre for Applied Policy Research (CAP) Policy Analysis*, no. 2 (2008).
Raube, Kolja. "European Parliamentary Oversight of Crisis Management." In Blockmans, *The European Union and Crisis Management: Policy and Legal Aspects*, 181–198.
Sari, Aurel. "Between Legalisation and Organisational Development: Explaining the Evolution of EU Competence in the Field of Foreign Policy." In Cardwell, *EU External Relations Law and Policy in the Post-Lisbon Era*, 59–95.
Trybus, Martin, and Nigel White, eds. *European Security Law*, 61–101. Oxford: Oxford University Press, 2007.
Van Elsuwege, Peter. "EU External Action after the Collapse of the Pillar Structure: In Search of a New Balance between Delimitation and Consistency." *Common Market Law Review* 47 (2010): 987–1019.
Vanhoonacker, Sophie. "The European Security and Defence Policy and Coherence Challenges in the Council." In Blockmans, *The European Union and Crisis Management: Policy and Legal Aspects*, 145–156.
Van Vooren, Bart. "A Legal-Institutional Perspective on the European External Action Service." *Common Market Law Review* 48 (2011): 475–502.
Van Vooren, Bart, and Ramses A. Wessel. *EU External Relations Law: Text, Cases and Materials*. Cambridge: Cambridge University Press, 2014.
Wessel, Ramses A. *The European Union's Foreign and Security Policy: A Legal Institutional Perspective*. The Hague: Kluwer Law International, 1999.
Wessel, Ramses A. "The Dynamics of the European Union Legal Order: An Increasingly Coherent Framework of Action and Interpretation." *European Constitutional Law Review* 5 (2009): 117–142.
Wessel, Ramses A. "The Legal Dimension of European Foreign Policy." In *Handbook of European Foreign Policy*, edited by Knud Erik Jørgensen, Åsne Kalland Aarstad, Edith Drieskens, Katie Laatikainen, Ben Tonra. London: Sage, 2015.
Whitman, Richard, and Ana Juncos. "The Lisbon Treaty and the Foreign, Security and Defence Policy: Reforms, Implementation and the Consequences of (non-)Ratification." *European Foreign Affairs Review* 14 (2009): 25–46.

27

EU Law and International Humanitarian Law

Marco Sassòli and Djemila Carron

Introduction

The European Union is based on law. Any EU action promoting or implementing international humanitarian law (IHL) is therefore grounded in EU law. Article 2 of the Treaty on European Union(TEU) includes among the fundamental values of the European Union the respect of human rights and the rule of law. Article 3(5) states that the Union must uphold these values in its external relations. IHL protects the human rights of those affected by armed conflict. Up to now, the European Union has mainly referred to IHL in its policy and in nonbinding sources, only rarely in binding EU law. EU law referring to IHL is much more advanced on what third states and actors should do than on what the Union and its member states should do. After some thoughts about EU law and IHL in case of armed conflicts within the European Union, we discuss the application of IHL to EU military operations outside of the European Union. Finally, we describe where the Union has performed best: promoting the development, acceptance, and respect of IHL by others.

IHL and EU Law in Case of Armed Conflicts within the European Union

Since the European Community was founded (and certainly also owing to its existence) there have been no armed conflicts between member states. EU law does not deal with such a possibility. Article 347 of the Treaty on the Functioning of the European Union (TFEU) merely requires member states to

> consult each other with a view to taking together the steps needed to prevent the functioning of the internal market being affected by measures a Member State may be called upon to take … in the event of war …

Yet, it is highly improbable that member states would do this if they were involved in an armed conflict against each other. If measures taken according to Article 347 TFEU distort the

A Companion to European Union Law and International Law, First Edition.
Edited by Dennis Patterson and Anna Södersten.

conditions of competition in the internal market, the Commission and any member state may, however, bring the matter before the Court of Justice of the European Union (CJEU).[1]

In case of armed conflict between EU member states, genuine conflicts between IHL provisions and EU law would be rare since EU law does not cover most issues encompassed by IHL (e.g., the conduct of hostilities or the protection of medical personnel). Additionally, IHL never prohibits the European Union or a member state from respecting guarantees of EU law, which offer better protection than IHL. Nevertheless, in the case of an armed conflict between member states, it is unfeasible that belligerents to respect rules of EU law on issues like free movement of persons and goods, judicial and police cooperation, and economic and monetary policy. In cases where norms do not genuinely conflict but IHL allows measures prohibited by EU law (e.g., the internment of civilians for imperative security reasons with only administrative and no judicial control[2]), from the perspective of public international law, IHL might prevail as the *lex specialis* in armed conflicts. However, whether the same would be true from the point of view of EU law is not clear. In the past, the CJEU has concluded that international agreements cannot affect the autonomy of the EU legal system when they conflict with EU constitutional principles, including fundamental rights.[3]

Arguably, non-international armed conflicts (NIACs) have, historically, taken place on EU territory (e.g., in Northern Ireland). Yet, they did not appear to pose major problems regarding the applicable Article 3 common to the Geneva Conventions and its compatibility with EU law. Today, with the considerable development of both the substantive and institutional rules of EU law and of IHL of NIACs, there would certainly be many more areas of overlap (where EU law would normally offer better protection to individuals), but not necessarily of contradiction.

Finally, since 1974 part of the territory of one EU member state, Cyprus, has arguably been occupied by a nonmember state, Turkey.[4] The theoretically interesting question of whether an occupying power must respect EU law in an occupied territory because under IHL it must respect local law and local institutions[5] does not arise in this case. Indeed, this obligation only covers laws and institutions already in force when the occupation starts,[6] while Cyprus joined the European Union only after 1974. In addition, EU law itself prescribes that its application is suspended in the areas in which "the Government of the Republic of Cyprus does not exercise effective control."[7]

EU Law and Provisions of IHL Applicable in Peacetime

Under Article 87 TFEU (at the time Article 30 EU), the Council has adopted rules to facilitate cooperation between member states to investigate war crimes,[8] whereby they must set up national contact points for exchanging information on such investigations.[9] This had an important impact on the willingness and ability of member states to comply with their IHL obligations in this field.[10] Another peacetime obligation under IHL requires that states not involved in an armed conflict ensure that belligerents respect IHL. This obligation will be dealt with hereafter when discussing the European Union as a promoter of IHL.

Is the European Union an Addressee of IHL in its External Action?

International organizations such as the European Union are not among the explicit addressees of IHL. While security has always been a concern for Europe, since the closing years of the twentieth century the European Union has equally grown into a military actor.

Its Common Foreign and Security Policy (CFSP) comprises a Common Security and Defence Policy (CSDP), which was inter alia implemented since 2003 in six EU-led military operations deploying more than ten thousand military personnel. In two operations, Artemis (in the Democratic Republic of Congo) and EUFOR (in Chad/Central African Republic), EU forces had the mandate to use force beyond self-defense. IHL, however, applies based upon the facts on the ground, not on the mandate of the belligerents. On only four occasions did EU forces return fire, and only one member of the EU forces has been killed.[11] If the European Union were a state, it is doubtful whether such incidents would have triggered the applicability of IHL, as EU forces were deployed with the consent of all states concerned. Therefore, the higher threshold of intensity of violence and organization of the insurgent group applicable in NIACs[12] would have to be met to make IHL applicable to the European Union.

Nevertheless, EU forces could easily be involved in an armed conflict. With the TEU, such involvement has a broad legal basis as it authorizes the use of military means, inter alia, for "tasks of combat forces in crisis management, including peace-making and post-conflict stabilisation."[13] Therefore, it is appropriate to inquire whether, when, how, and why IHL would apply to the European Union and its forces. This inquiry has similarities with the question of whether IHL applies to the UN and its peace forces, but EU law and the specificity of the European Union imply many particularities.

An international organization such as the European Union may be bound by IHL either because its internal law says so, because it has undertaken to respect it, or because customary law is the same for states and international organizations.

Attempts by the International Committee of the Red Cross to introduce IHL into the primary EU law have failed.[14] IHL may, however, be introduced through the well-established internal obligation of the European Union to respect human rights.[15] Human rights, which are highly relevant for those affected by armed conflict, are protected by the Charter of Fundamental Rights of the European Union, including the right to life, to physical integrity, to liberty and security, to healthcare, and to an effective remedy. These rights bind EU institutions and agencies equally in their external action[16] as well as member states' implementation of EU law,[17] including in their foreign and defense policy. IHL details, specifies, and modifies those rights to make them more realistic for armed conflicts.

Furthermore, the possible accession of the European Union to the European Convention on Human Rights (ECHR), foreseen in Article 6(2) TEU and Protocol 14 to the ECHR, may make the ECHR applicable to the European Union. To the extent that the ECHR applies extraterritorially, an issue discussed later in this chapter, accession will subject EU operations to the ECHR and to judicial control by the European Court of Human Rights (ECtHR), while the CJEU currently has no such jurisdiction.[18] A final entry point for IHL in EU primary law is Article 21(1) TEU, which mentions the respect for international law among the principles that must guide the external action of the Union.[19]

Another indication of the EU attachment to IHL can be found in its "Guidelines on promoting compliance with IHL."[20] These deal with the promotion of IHL by the EU towards third states and nonstate actors in third states, "in line with the commitment of the EU and its Member States to IHL." The Guidelines mention that "the same commitment extends to measures taken by the EU and its Member States to ensure compliance with IHL in their own conduct, including by their own forces," but stress that

> such measures are not covered by these Guidelines. While the Guidelines do not apply to EU forces, this text contains a non-binding commitment by the EU to comply with IHL.[21]

Concerning EU Treaty obligations, while all of its member states are parties to the Geneva Conventions and their Additional Protocols, the European Union itself is not. Obligations of members do not normally bind an international organization. Presently, the Union is not capable of becoming a party to IHL treaties, and there are a good number of rules that can be respected only by a state having a territory, laws, and criminal tribunals.[22]

As for the possibility that the European Union is bound by IHL through customary law, the majority view in scholarly writings on IHL is that as international organizations have (limited) legal personality, they are bound by the same rules as states if they engage in the same activities as states.[23] Two International Court of Justice (ICJ) Advisory Opinions are invariably quoted to support this claim. In the *Reparations* case, the ICJ writes that the UN is "a subject of international law and *capable* of possessing international rights and duties."[24] In the *WHO–Egypt Agreement* case it states, "international organizations are subjects of international law and as such, are bound by any obligation *incumbent upon them* under general rules of international law."[25] As such, the European Union is a subject of international law and military operations are among its functions under EU primary law.[26] Moreover, the CJEU has consistently reaffirmed that the Union must respect customary international law.[27]

However, in our view, the quoted dicta of the ICJ state only that international organizations *may* have obligations under general international law and not that they have the *same* obligations as states. Whether an international organization is or is not bound by the same rules of customary law as states must be determined by the practice of international organizations and of states in relation to international organizations. For IHL and the UN, this is extremely doubtful. However, as mentioned, EU practice raises less doubt. Although the European Union has not had occasion to apply IHL in an armed conflict, its declarations and those of its member states, which are equally a form of practice, clearly state that it will do so.

Even if the Union is not bound by IHL, those who act for it are bound as individuals (by criminalized rules of IHL) or because they are organs of (contributing) states. States contributing to EU missions are parties to IHL treaties, but it is controversial whether and when they are addressees of IHL obligations if the European Union has command and control. For human rights obligations, an ECtHR judgment suggests that in such a case the sending state will not have jurisdiction for the purposes of its obligations under the ECHR.[28] If this is correct, it is also valid for IHL obligations. In our view, the question of who has command and control must be determined separately for every mission; everything depends on the facts, that is, on who has effective control.[29] Until now, both the European Union and the sending states have exercised command and control over EU missions – the Union keeping the political, military, and operational control, and sending states keeping full command (administrative, disciplinary, and criminal control).[30] As long as the sending state controls respect of IHL by its troops, through its disciplinary and criminal systems, it should ensure that its IHL obligations are fulfilled when they are acting for the European Union.

Finally, under Article 1 common to the Geneva Conventions, EU member states have the obligation to "ensure respect" of IHL by their organization.[31] In addition, they are responsible for activities they entrust to their organization to perform, if such delegation aims to circumvent their own obligations with respect to those activities.[32] The ECtHR requires states that entrust an international organization with a certain task to ensure that persons benefit from human rights protection equivalent to what states are bound to offer. In the relevant cases, the individual was, however, always present on the territory of the respondent state.[33]

Extraterritorial Application of EU Human Rights Law

If IHL applies to EU forces, by definition it applies to them worldwide wherever they fight as parties to an armed conflict. Indeed, it is uncontroversial that parties to an armed conflict have to respect IHL even when fighting outside their own territory. If, however, it applies through provisions on the respect of human rights, the traditional controversy over whether and to what extent human rights apply extraterritorially becomes relevant. This problem is often neglected in very rosy assessments of the human rights obligations of EU missions.[34] At least under Article 1 of the ECHR, states parties must secure the rights listed only to everyone within their jurisdiction. Under the jurisprudence of the ECtHR, which is constantly developing, jurisdiction exists in an occupied territory where a state exercises public powers normally exercised by a sovereign government and when a state exercises control and authority over an individual through its agents abroad, but such jurisdiction does not cover everyone whose rights are violated by a party.[35] Detaining someone abroad is sufficient to establish jurisdiction.[36] May the European Union, however, be considered as "detaining" anyone?

The question arises of whether the references to human rights in EU law concerning its external action imply an extraterritorial application of human rights going beyond that of the ECHR. Article 21 TEU affirms that the "Union's action on the international scene shall be guided by ... the universality and indivisibility of human rights." Does this mean only that the European Union promotes human rights worldwide or, equally, that it must respect human rights worldwide, including towards persons who are not under the jurisdiction of the Union? In our view, when the TEU refers to human rights it necessarily refers not only to its substantive entitlements but also to its rules on who is the beneficiary and in what relations they apply. A solution to the question of the extraterritorial application of human rights could be found through a functional approach, distinguishing the degree of control necessary according to the right to be protected.[37] Also, further thought must be given on the ECHR[38] derogation clause for situations in which a state's security is in jeopardy and how it may be adapted to the European Union.

Specific Problems for the European Union to Respect IHL

Arguably, EU missions have not yet been parties to an armed conflict. When and how they could become parties to an armed conflict and what difficulties could arise in complying with IHL are problems regularly neglected by those painting a rosy picture of the applicability of IHL to EU forces.[39]

Armed conflicts that trigger the application of IHL imply a minimum level of violence, which is different for international armed conflicts (IACs) and NIACs. If EU forces use force against a nonstate armed group with the consent of the territorial state, there must be violence of certain intensity against the group for IHL of NIACs to apply.[40] When the adversary is a state, any act of violence or capture of adversaries directed against the forces of a de facto government of an existing state is arguably covered by IHL of IACs.[41] However, some authors and state practices consider that IACs also require a certain level of violence.[42] Accordingly, IHL would not apply if the violence is not widespread and the states involved maintain normal diplomatic and economic relations. However, if there are hostilities between forces belonging to a state or an organized armed group, then the legal basis of the use of force and the mandate of the EU mission are irrelevant for the applicability of IHL. Besides, IHL only applies to military operations directed at combatants or members of an armed group with a continuous fighting function. Even in an armed conflict, police operations against civilians are subject to human rights law and many more restrictions than hostilities.

An additional difficulty is to define whether the European Union or its member states are party to an armed conflict. Although IHL is not only addressed to the parties to a conflict, many rules mention them. When the Union is party to the conflict, because it has command and control over EU forces, its legislation – EU law –lacks certain rules that IHL requires belligerent parties to apply. For example, there is no EU law on the definition of and jurisdiction over grave breaches,[43] the use of the emblem of the red cross or the red crescent,[44] or criminal legislation applicable to detainees.[45] On the two former issues, we consider that contributing states remain in control even if the European Union has command and control over the operation and their domestic law therefore applies (which raises tricky interoperability problems when persons other than members of the EU forces are addressed, prosecuted, or detained). EU forces have done everything possible to transfer any detainee as soon as possible to the territorial state, to avoid legal proceedings. This may not always be possible under the "non-refoulement" principle. If legal proceedings are necessary, they must respect the guarantees foreseen in EU law but be conducted according to the territorial legislation if an agreement with the territorial state exists. Otherwise, legal proceedings must be conducted according to the national legislation of the detaining contributing state as no EU criminal procedure applicable to such cases exists.

Another question that arises is whether the rules of Geneva Convention IV on military occupation bind hypothetical EU forces administering a territory or an international civil administration.[46] The examples of Kosovo or Mostar are not entirely relevant because international forces were present with the agreement of the (former) territorial state. One could, however, imagine an international civil administration run by the European Union without the agreement of the former government. In that case, in our view, Geneva Convention IV applies, although a UN Security Council mandate may extend the rights of the Union compared with those of an occupying power, allowing it, for example, to change local legislation and institutions. Even if EU forces administer a territory with the consent of the local sovereign, it may be wise to apply IHL by analogy since it provides a framework to address many of the situations with which peacekeepers will be confronted.[47]

The European Union Promoting IHL and its Respect

In 2005, the Council adopted Guidelines on promoting compliance with IHL (hereafter: Guidelines).[48] They deal with efforts by the European Union to obtain the respect of IHL by others. Under EU law they are not binding,[49] which does not mean that they do not have an impact.

Acting on the basis of those Guidelines, the European Union first calls upon third states to adhere to IHL instruments that are not yet universally accepted, such as the 1977 Protocol I, to enact the necessary implementing legislation,[50] and it supports training and education on IHL.[51] The Union and its member states also had a crucial role in developing several IHL instruments. They were among the first to insist on individual criminal responsibility for violations of IHL. Declarations and decisions, which initially concerned the former Yugoslavia, demonstrated in particular an *opinio juris* of states concerning the criminalization of violations of IHL of NIACs.[52] Therefore, it was only logical that the European Union supported both the creation of ad hoc international criminal tribunals and of the International Criminal Court (ICC).[53] In fact, the Union and its member states have done a lot to ensure the integrity of the ICC Statute and the effectiveness of the ICC. In various conclusions and recommendations, the

Council has expressed its support to the ICC, in particular for its action in Sudan, Uganda, and the Democratic Republic of the Congo. In its political dialogue with third states, the Union encourages ratification or accession and implementation of the Statute. It aims at the inclusion of an ICC clause in agreements with third states, and it has signed an agreement on cooperation and assistance with the ICC.[54] Facing recent skepticism by African states towards the concept of universal jurisdiction, the European Union established with the African Union an Expert Group on the Principle of Universal Jurisdiction. The report[55] reaffirmed important principles but remained vague and cautious on operational details, as are European states when they are required to prosecute suspected war criminals found on their territory who allegedly committed war crimes abroad. Governments and national justice systems are fearful of diplomatic complications that may result from such prosecutions and accompanying arrests of (former) officials of third states suspected of war crimes and they adopt, apart from a very conservative position in genuine controversies about the extent of immunities of (even former) officials, various avoidance strategies.

In addition, the European Union strongly supported the adoption of the Laser Weapons Protocol to the 1980 Convention on Certain Conventional Weapons and it influenced the prohibition of antipersonnel mines in the Ottawa Convention.[56] Furthermore, it supported the conclusion of an international treaty regulating the arms trade, which prohibits any transfer in the knowledge that the weapons will be used to commit war crimes and, beyond that, requires an assessment of the risk of IHL violations by the receiving country. The Union has also adopted guidelines on children in armed conflict to promote the respect of IHL in this field by third states and armed nonstate actors.[57]

In addition, the Guidelines allow EU member states to respect their obligation under Article 1 common to the Geneva Conventions to ensure respect of IHL by belligerents worldwide, implementing it through the CFSP. As IHL applies only to armed conflicts, a situation must first be so classified. The Guidelines require EU bodies to determine the applicability of IHL in situations within their area of responsibility.[58] A second step would be an impartial inquiry into alleged violations of IHL. While the EU Guidelines prescribe that consideration should be given to drawing on the services of the International Humanitarian Fact-Finding Commission (IHFFC) established under Article 90 of Additional Protocol I,[59] not all EU member states have accepted the competence of the IHFFC.[60] Further, even when it was competent, no EU member state has asked the IHFFC to undertake an inquiry. Instead of using the IHFFC, in the 2008 conflict between Russia and Georgia, the European Union established an ad hoc fact-finding commission,[61] which was heavily dominated by diplomatic concerns to please the parties. This was a missed opportunity for the IHFFC to leave its involuntary lethargy,[62] allowing it to demonstrate that it can work efficiently and impartially.

The third step to ensure respect of IHL consists of taking action against states and armed groups that violate it. The Guidelines envisage that this may be done through political dialogue, demarches, public statements about specific conflicts, restrictive measures, sanctions, cooperation with other international bodies, and crisis management operations.[63] In this respect, the overall performance, in particular of the Council, vis-à-vis powerful or influential states, such as Russia, the US, or Israel, is less satisfactory than vis-à-vis weaker, mainly African, states.[64] As EU member states were involved, it is not surprising that Afghanistan and Iraq only rarely appeared among the crisis situations where the European Union expressed concern about IHL violations.[65] Common positions on respecting IHL in Afghanistan were much stronger before EU member states became involved in the armed conflict.[66]

EU restrictive measures may be taken in its commercial policy (in the form of nonconcession or withdrawal of trade preferences), its foreign and security policy, and its development cooperation policy. Here again, the Council is more reluctant than the Commission to take restrictive measures against powerful states (beyond UN sanctions). IHL violations have never been the only reason for imposing autonomous EU sanctions.[67]

As for commercial policy, the Commission introduces clauses into commercial agreements with third states, allowing the Union to suspend them if that state violates human rights (which includes, as seen earlier in the chapter, IHL).[68] The CJEU, the Council, and the Commission have furthermore confirmed that goods produced in the Israeli settlements in the West Bank (which are unlawful under IHL), may not benefit from preferential treatment under an Israel–EU free-trade agreement. To enforce this position, the Union requires the postal code of the place of production.[69]

The CJEU has confirmed that the Commission may pursue the elimination of small arms and light weapons in its development cooperation policy.[70] The Court's reasoning could be extended to IHL issues, considering that sustainable development cannot be achieved without the respect of IHL.[71] As for EU assistance, promoting observance of IHL is explicitly mentioned as a possible aim the Commission may pursue under the European Instrument for Democracy and Human Rights.[72] Similarly, measures by third countries supported by the European Union under its Instrument for Stability, must comply with IHL.[73]

The Council may decide, under the CFSP, to take restrictive measures or sanctions against states violating IHL.[74] Diplomatic, economic, or financial sanctions may be aimed at governments, armed nonstate actors, or individuals.[75] Often, EU sanctions merely implement decisions taken by the UN Security Council. Violations of IHL justified measures taken against the Former Republic of Yugoslavia and Indonesia.[76] Without explicitly mentioning IHL, the Council has withdrawn the benefits of the generalized system of preferences for developing countries from Myanmar,[77] and has taken restrictive measures, including arms embargoes or bans on the export of luxury goods and technology that may be used for internal repression, against, among others, Liberia,[78] the Democratic Republic of the Congo,[79] Côte d'Ivoire,[80] and Syria.[81] Furthermore, the Council temporarily withheld the special incentive arrangement for sustainable development and good governance (GSP+) for products originating in Sri Lanka because of the country's failure to implement its obligations under several human rights treaties.[82]

A field in which the European Union may have a direct impact on violations of IHL is the export of arms. However, because of commercial and political interests of member states, EU law and policy on the issue are very flexible.[83] The Guidelines rather cautiously mention that the respect of IHL by the importing country "should be considered,"[84] while the Council's Common Position on arms export mentions the respect of IHL as one of the criteria for deciding upon arms export license applications by member states.[85] A denial is only prescribed if "there is a clear risk that the military technology or equipment to be exported might be used in the commission of serious violations."[86]

Conclusion

After millennia of wars, history had mercy on Europe. Since – and because – the idea of European integration became a reality through what is now the European Union, armed conflicts no longer occur between EU member states or on their territory. EU member states continue to be involved in armed conflicts, but EU law did not govern their involvement. Therefore, the relationship between IHL and EU law is fortunately not (yet) an issue of daily concern for practitioners and EU institutions. In the instances in which the European Union has been a military actor abroad, IHL arguably did not apply because the Union had not become a party to an armed conflict. If the European Union becomes involved in an armed conflict, there will be compelling arguments under EU law, IHL, and public international law in general to subject it to IHL. However, it will face serious legal problems to comply with its rules because the European Union and EU law lack several features IHL presupposes to exist among belligerent states and their legislation. Where the European Union has been most active for IHL is in its promotion abroad, including by fulfilling its member states' obligation to ensure its respect. Compared with other international organizations and most states of other regions, the European Union has been a champion in this respect. However, even the Union, a community governed by law, has not been immune from double standards as soon as the interests of its most powerful members are involved.

Notes

We would like to thank Pieter Jan Kuijper, Professor at the University of Amsterdam, for his thoughtful suggestions concerning an earlier version of this contribution, and Ms. Annie Hylton, LL. M., research assistant at the Geneva Academy on International Humanitarian Law and Human Rights for revising this text.

1 Article 348 TFEU. This is what the Commission did in 1994 when Greece adopted trade restrictions against Macedonia. See Case C-120/94 *Commission of the European Communities v. Hellenic Republic* EU:C:1996:116.
2 See Articles 42, 43, and 78 of Geneva Convention IV relative to the Protection of Civilian Persons in Time of War (1949).
3 See Joined Cases C-402/05 P and C-415/05 P *Yassin Abdullah Kadi and Al Barakaat International Foundation v. Council and Commission* EU:C:2008:461, paras 282–289.
4 *Loizidou v. Turkey* (1997) 23 EHRR 513, paras 16 and 56.
5 See in particular Article 43 of the Hague Regulations concerning the Laws and Customs of War on Land (1907) and Article 64 of Geneva Convention IV, n 2 this chapter.
6 Yoram Dinstein, *The International Law of Belligerent Occupation* (Cambridge: Cambridge University Press, 2009), 108.
7 Act concerning the conditions of accession of the Czech Republic, the Republic of Estonia, the Republic of Cyprus, the Republic of Latvia, the Republic of Lithuania, the Republic of Hungary, the Republic of Malta, the Republic of Poland, the Republic of Slovenia, and the Slovak Republic and the adjustments to the Treaties on which the European Union is founded – Protocol No 10 on Cyprus [2003] OJ L 236/955.
8 Council Decision 2003/335/JHA of 8 May 2003 on the investigation and prosecution of genocide, crimes against humanity and war crimes [2003] OJ L 118/12.
9 Council Decision 2002/494/JHA of 13 June 2002 setting up a European network of contact points in respect of persons responsible for genocide, crimes against humanity and war crimes [2002] OJ L 167/1.
10 Article 88 of Additional Protocol I to the Geneva Conventions relating to the Protection of Victims of International Armed Conflicts (1977).
11 Valentina Falco, "The Internal Legal Order of the European Union as a Complementary Framework for its Obligations under IHL," *Israel Law Review* 42 (2009): 176–178.
12 See *Prosecutor v. Ramush Haradinaj, Idriz Balaj and Lahi Brahimaj*, ICTY, Trial Chamber (3 April 2008), in particular paras 49 and 60.
13 Article 43(1) TEU.
14 Falco, "The Internal Legal Order," 190.
15 See Articles 2 and 3(5) TEU.
16 Article 21(3) TEU.
17 Article 6(1) and (3) TEU; Articles 51–53 of the Charter of Fundamental Rights of the European Union. See, e.g., Thierry Bontick, "L'Effectivité des droits fondamentaux dans le Traité de Lisbonne,"

in *La Charte des droits fondamentaux de l'Union européenne après le Traité de Lisbonne*, ed. Bertrand Favreau (Brussels: Bruylant, 2010), 110–113.

18 Article 275 TFEU. Marise Cremona, "The Union's External Action: Constitutional Perspectives," in *Genesis and Destiny of the European Constitution: Commentary on the Treaty Establishing a Constitution for Europe in the Light of the "Travaux Préparatoires" and Future Prospects*, ed. Giuliano Amato, Hervé Bribosia, and Bruno de Witte (Brussels: Bruylant, 2007), 1191, wonders, however, whether the exception in Article 275(2) includes a Council's decision authorizing an EU operation to use restrictive measures against individuals.

19 Article 21(1) TEU.

20 European Union Guidelines on promoting compliance with international humanitarian law (IHL) 2005/C 327/04 [2005] OJ C 327/4.

21 Ibid., Article 2.

22 United Nations Office of Legal Affairs, "Question of the Possible Accession of Intergovernmental Organizations to the Geneva Conventions for the Protection of War Victims: Memorandum to the Under-Secretary General for Political Affairs," *United Nations Juridical Yearbook* 153 (1972): para 3.

23 See Robert Kolb, Gabriele Porretto, and Sylvain Vité, *L'Application du droit international humanitaire et des droits de l'homme aux organisations internationales: Forces de paix et administrations civiles transitoires* (Brussels: Bruylant, 2005), 121–129; Ian Brownlie, *Principles of Public International Law* (Oxford: Clarendon Press, 1998), 690; Michael Bothe, "Peacekeeping," in *The Charter of the United Nations: A Commentary*, ed. Bruno Simma et al. (Oxford: Oxford University Press, 2012), 1190; Marten Zwanenburg, *Accountability of Peace Support Operations* (Leiden: M. Nijhoff, 2005), 151–158; and Claude Emanuelli, *Les Actions militaires de l'ONU et le droit international humanitaire* (Montréal: Wilson & Lafleur, 1997), 41–43.

24 Reparations for injuries suffered in the service of the United Nations, Advisory Opinion, 1949 ICJ REP. 174, 179 (April 11) (emphasis added).

25 Interpretation of the Agreement of 25 March 1971 between the WHO and Egypt, Advisory Opinion, 1980 ICJ REP. 73, 88–90 (December 20) (emphasis added).

26 Articles 47, 42, and 43 TEU.

27 Falco, "The Internal Legal Order," 186; Case C-162/96 *Racke v. Hauptzollant Mainz* EU:C:1998:293, para 45; Case C-308/06 *The Queen, on the application of International Association of Independent Tanker Owners (Intertanko) and Others v. Secretary of State for Transport* EU:C:2008:312, para 51; Case C-286/90 *Anklagemyndigheden v. Peter Michael Poulsen and Diva Navigation Corp.* EU:C:1992:453, para 10; and Case T-115/94 *Opel Austria GmbH v. Council of the European Union* EU:T:1997:3, paras 77 and 90.

28 *Behrami and Saramati v. France, Germany and Norway* (2007) 45 EHRR SE10, paras 128–152.

29 Article 7, Draft Articles on the Responsibility of International Organizations, International Law Commission, *Report of the International Law Commission on the Work of its 63rd Session* (26 April–3 June, and 4 July–12 August 2011), UN doc A/66/10, para 87. See, for a similar approach, John Cerone, "Human Dignity in the Line of Fire: The Application of International Human Rights Law during Armed Conflict, Occupation, and Peace Operations," *Vanderbilt Journal of Transnational Law* 39 (2006): 1457 and 1508.

30 Falco, "The Internal Legal Order," 181–182; Aurel Sari, "The European Status of Forces Agreement: Continuity and Change in the Law of Visiting Forces," *Military Law and the Law of War Review* 46 (2007): 25–29; Aurélie Claeys Bouuaert, "La Responsabilité pour violation des règles du DIH dans le cadre des opérations de l'UE," in *L'Union européenne et le Droit International Humanitaire*, ed. Anne-Sophie Millet-Devalle (Paris: Pedone, 2010), 120–124 and 135–136; and Frederik Naert, *International Law Aspects of the EU's Security and Defence Policy, with a Particular Focus on the Law of Armed Conflict and Human Rights* (Antwerp: Intersentia, 2010), 515–526.

31 Claude Emanuelli, "Les Forces des Nations Unies et le droit international humanitaire," in *The United Nations and International Humanitarian Law*, ed. Luigi Condorelli, Anne-Marie La Rosa, and Sylvie Scherrer (Paris: Pedone, 1996), 365; Luigi Condorelli, "Conclusions générales," in *The United Nations and International Humanitarian Law*, ed. Luigi Condorelli, Anne-Marie La Rosa, and Sylvie Scherrer (Paris: Pedone, 1996), 472.

32 Article 61, Draft Articles on the Responsibility of International Organizations, International Law Commission, n 29 this chapter.

33 *Waite and Kennedy v. Germany* (1999) 30 EHRR 261, para 10; *Bosphorus Hava Yollari Turizm v. Ticaret Anonim Sirketi v. Ireland* (2006) 42 EHRR 1, para 155.

34 See, e.g., Felix Vacas Fernandez, "International Human Rights Law as Legal Framework Applicable to EU Missions," in *The Integration of the Human Rights Component and International Humanitarian Law in Peace Missions Lead by the European Union*, ed. Marian J. Aznar and Milena Costas (Valencia: Psylicom, 2011), 39–43.

35 For an overview of the jurisprudence, see *Al-Skeini and others v. United Kingdom* (2011) 53 EHRR 18, paras 130–141.

36 *Al-Saadoon v. United Kingdom* (2009) 49 EHRR SE11, para 88.

37 Cerone, "Human Dignity in the Line of Fire," 1494–1507, frames the discussion in terms of a "range" of applicable rights and in terms of the "level of obligation" binding states acting extraterritorially.

38 Article 15 of the ECHR refers to "time of war or other public emergency threatening the life of the nation…"

39 Such as Falco, "The Internal Legal Order," 168–205; and Vacas, "International Human Rights," 38–50.

40 See n 12.

41 Jean S. Pictet, ed., *The Geneva Conventions of 12 August 1949: Commentary, I, Geneva Convention for the Amelioration of the Condition of the Wounded and Sick in Armed Forces in the Field* (Geneva: ICRC, 1952), 32–33.

42 See, for instance, Frits Kalshoven, *Reflections on the Law of War: Collected Essays* (Leiden: M. Nijhoff, 2007), 16; and International Law Association, Use of Force Committee, *Final Report on the Meaning of Armed Conflict in International Law*, The Hague, 2010, 29.

43 See Articles 49, 50, 129, and 146, respectively, of the four Geneva Conventions of August 12, 1949.

44 See, e.g., Articles 44, 53, and 54 of Geneva Convention I for the Amelioration of the Condition of the Wounded and Sick in Armed Forces in the Field (1949).

45 See, e.g., Articles 82 of Geneva Convention III relative to the Treatment of Prisoners of War (1949), Article 64 of Convention IV (n 2 this chapter), and Article 3(1)(2)(d) common to the four Geneva Conventions of 1949 ("regularly constituted courts" must be established by law).

46 See for the traditional discussion, mainly centred on the UN, Siobhan Wills, "Occupation Law and Multi-National Operations: Problems and Perspectives," *British Yearbook of International Law* 77 (2006): 256–332; Kolb, Porretto, and Vité, *L'Application du droit international humanitaire*, 204–227; and Simon Chesterman, *You the People: The United Nations, Transitional Administration and State Building* (Oxford: Oxford University Press, 2004).

47 Marco Sassòli, "Legislation and Maintenance of Public Order and Civil Life by Occupying Powers," *European Journal of International Law* 16 (2005): 689 and 691–693.

48 See Guidelines, n 20 this chapter. The Guidelines were updated without changes relevant to this contribution in 2009 (Updated European Union Guidelines on promoting compliance with international humanitarian law (IHL) 2009/C 303/06 [2009] OJ C 303/12).

49 Eric David, "L'UE et le Droit International Humanitaire," in Millet-Devalle, *L'Union européenne*, 7–8; Andrea Breslin, "Ensuring Respect: The European Union's Guidelines on Promoting Compliance With International Humanitarian Law," *Israel Law Review* 43 (2010): 409–410; Pål Wrange, "The EU Guidelines on Promoting Compliance with International Humanitarian Law," *Nordic Journal of International Law* 78 (2010): 542 and 545; and Falco, "The Internal Legal Order," 192–193.

50 Guidelines, n 48 this chapter, Article 16(a).

51 Ibid., Article 16(b)

52 See, for references, Tristan Ferraro, "Le Droit international humanitaire dans la politique étrangère et de sécurité commune de l'Union européenne," *International Review of the Red Cross* 84 (2002): 447–449.

53 See for details Isabelle Moulier, "L'UE et les juridictions pénales internationales," in Millet-Devalle, *L'Union européenne*.

54 See Council Decision 2006/313/CFSP of 10 April 2006 concerning the conclusion of the Agreement between the International Criminal Court and the European Union on cooperation and assistance [2006] OJ L 115/49.
55 See Council of the European Union, AU–EU Technical Ad hoc Expert Group on the Principle of Universal Jurisdiction, Report, 16 April 2009.
56 See Ferraro, "Le Droit international humanitaire," 451, 452, 455–457, with references.
57 European Union Guidelines on children and armed conflict, http://www.consilium.europa.eu/uedocs/cmsUpload/GuidelinesChildren.pdf; Update of the European Union Guidelines on children and armed conflict, http://www.consilium.europa.eu/uedocs/cmsUpload/10019.en08.pdf.
58 Guidelines, n 48 this chapter, Article 15(a).
59 Ibid.
60 France and Latvia have not yet made a declaration under Article 90 of Protocol I. For a list of States Parties to the IHFFC, see the website of the IHFFC.
61 Council Decision 2008/901/CFSP of 2 December 2008 concerning an independent international fact-finding mission on the conflict in Georgia [2008] OJ L 323/66.
62 David, "L'UE et le Droit International Humanitaire," 10.
63 Guidelines, n 48 this chapter, Article 16(a)–(f).
64 Josiane Auvret-Finck, "L'Utilisation du DIH dans les instruments de la PESC," in Millet-Devalle, *L'Union européenne*, 59–61.
65 Stéphane Kolanowski, "La Cooperation de l'UE et du Comité International de la Croix-Rouge," in Millet-Devalle, *L'Union européenne*, 185–186.
66 See Ferraro, "Le Droit international humanitaire," 453, with references.
67 Morten Knudsen, "Les Lignes directrices de l'Union européenne concernant la promotion du droit humanitaire international," in Millet-Devalle, *L'Union européenne*, 180.
68 Sonja Bolaert-Suominen, "Le Rôle du DIH dans les programmes communautaires et l'aide humanitaire," in Millet-Devalle, *L'Union européenne*, 159.
69 Case C-386/08 *Brita GmbH v. Hauptzollamt Hamburg-Hafen* EU:C:2010:91, paras 53, 56, 64–67, and 73; Council's Reply to Written Question, 1 February 2010, E-6035-2009; Commission's Reply to Written Question, 31 August 2011, E007328/2011; Notice to Importers 2005/C 20/02 Imports from Israel into the Community [2005] OJ C 20/2.
70 Case C-91/05 *Commission v. Council* EU:C:2008:288.
71 Bolaert-Suominen, "Le Rôle du DIH," 161.
72 Regulation (EC) No 1889/2006 of 29 December 2006 on establishing a financing instrument for the promotion of democracy and human rights worldwide [2006] OJ L 386/1, para 2(c)(iv).
73 Regulation (EC) No 1717/2006 of the European Parliament and of the Council of 15 November 2006 establishing an Instrument for Stability [2006] OJ L 327/1, para 4(1)(a).
74 See for an overview Auvret-Finck, "L'Utilisation du DIH," 54–59.
75 Articles 75 and 215 TFEU.
76 See Ferraro, "Le Droit international humanitaire," 459.
77 Council Regulation (EC) No 552/97 of 24 March 1997 temporarily withdrawing access to generalized tariff preferences from the Union of Myanmar [1997] OJ L 85/8; Council Regulation (EC) No 732/2008 of 22 July 2008 applying a scheme of generalized tariff preferences for the period from 1 January 2009 to 31 December 2011 and amending Regulations (EC) No 552/97 (EC) No 1933/2006 and Commission Regulations (EC) No 1100/2006 and (EC) No 964/2007 [2008] OJ L 211/1.
78 Council Decision 2010/129/CFSP of 1 March 2010 amending Common Position 2008/109/CFSP concerning restrictive measures imposed against Liberia [2010] OJ L 51/23.
79 Council Common Position 2010/788/CFSP of 20 December 2010 concerning restrictive measures against the Democratic Republic of the Congo and repealing Common Position 2008/369/CFSP [2010] OJ L 336/30.
80 Council Common Position 2004/852/CFSP of 13 December 2004 concerning restrictive measures against Côte d'Ivoire [2004] OJ L 368/50.

81 Council Regulation (EC) No 509/2012 of 15 June 2012 amending Regulation (EU) No 36/2012 concerning restrictive measures in view of the situation in Syria [2012] OJ L 156/10.
82 Implementing Regulation (EU) No 143/2010 of the Council of 15 February 2010 [2010] OJ L 45/1.
83 See for a detailed analysis Anne-Sophie Millet-Devalle, "L'UE et le droit relative aux moyens de combat," in Millet-Devalle, *L'Union européenne*, 217–246.
84 Guidelines, n 48 this chapter, Article 16(i).
85 Council Common Position 2008/944/CFSP of 8 December 2008 defining common rules governing control of exports of military technology and equipment [2008] OJ L 335/99, Article 2(2).
86 Ibid., Article 2(2)(c).

References

Auvret-Finck, Josiane. "L'Utilisation du DIH dans les instruments de la PESC." In Millet-Devalle, *L'Union européenne*, 45–74.

Bolaert-Suominen, Sonja. "Le Rôle du DIH dans les programmes communautaires et l'aide humanitaire." In Millet-Devalle, *L'Union européenne*, 157–171.

Bontick, Thierry. "L'Effectivité des droits fondamentaux dans le Traité de Lisbonne." In *La Charte des droits fondamentaux de l'Union européenne après le Traité de Lisbonne*, edited by Bertrand Favreau, 101–121. Brussels: Bruylant, 2010.

Bothe, Michael. "Peacekeeping." In *The Charter of the United Nations: A Commentary*, edited by Bruno Simma, Daniel Erasmus Khan, Georg Nolte, and Andreas Paulus, 1171–1199. Oxford: Oxford University Press, 2012.

Bouuaert, Aurélie Claeys. "La Responsabilité pour violation des règles du DIH dans le cadre des opérations de l'UE." In Millet-Devalle, *L'Union européenne*, 119–136.

Breslin, Andrea. "Ensuring Respect: The European Union's Guidelines on Promoting Compliance With International Humanitarian Law." *Israel Law Review* 43 (2010): 381–413.

Brownlie, Ian. *Principles of Public International Law*. Oxford: Clarendon Press, 1998.

Cerone, John. "Human Dignity in the Line of Fire: The Application of International Human Rights Law during Armed Conflict, Occupation, and Peace Operations." *Vanderbilt Journal of Transnational Law* 39 (2006): 1447–1510.

Chesterman, Simon. *You the People: The United Nations, Transitional Administration and State Building*. Oxford: Oxford University Press, 2004.

Condorelli, Luigi. "Conclusions générales." In *The United Nations and International Humanitarian Law*, edited by Luigi Condorelli, Anne-Marie La Rosa, and Sylvie Scherrer, 445–474. Paris: Pedone, 1996.

Council of the European Union. AU–EU Technical Ad Hoc Expert Group on the Principle of Universal Jurisdiction, Report, 16 April 2009.

Cremona, Marise. "The Union's External Action: Constitutional Perspectives." In *Genesis and Destiny of the European Constitution: Commentary on the Treaty Establishing a Constitution for Europe in the Light of the "Travaux Préparatoires" and Future Prospects*, edited by Giuliano Amato, Hervé Bribosia, and Bruno de Witte, 1173–1217. Brussels: Bruylant, 2007.

David, Eric. "L'UE et le Droit International Humanitaire." In Millet-Devalle, *L'Union européenne*, 7–14

Dinstein, Yoram. *The International Law of Belligerent Occupation*. Cambridge: Cambridge University Press, 2009.

Emanuelli, Claude. "Les Forces des Nations Unies et le droit international humanitaire." In *The United Nations and International Humanitarian Law*, edited by Luigi Condorelli, Anne-Marie La Rosa, and Sylvie Scherrer, 345–370. Paris: Pedone, 1996.

Emanuelli, Claude. *Les Actions militaires de l'ONU et le droit international humanitaire*. Montréal: Wilson & Lafleur, 1997.

Falco, Valentina. "The Internal Legal Order of the European Union as a Complementary Framework for its Obligations under IHL." *Israel Law Review* 42 (2009): 168–205.

Ferraro, Tristan. "Le Droit international humanitaire dans la politique étrangère et de sécurité commune de l'Union européenne." *International Review of the Red Cross* 84 (2002): 435–461.

International Law Association, Use of Force Committee. *Final Report on the Meaning of Armed Conflict in International Law*. The Hague, 2010.

Kalshoven, Frits. *Reflections on the Law of War: Collected Essays*. Leiden: M. Nijhoff, 2007.

Knudsen, Morten. "Les Lignes directrices de l'Union européenne concernant la promotion du droit humanitaire international." In Millet-Devalle, *L'Union européenne*, 175–182.

Kolanowski, Stéphane. "La Cooperation de l'UE et du Comité International de la Croix-Rouge." In Millet-Devalle, *L'Union européenne*, 183–188.

Kolb, Robert, Gabriele Porretto, and Sylvain Vité. *L'Application du droit international humanitaire et des droits de l'homme aux organisations internationales: Forces de paix et administrations civiles transitoires*. Brussels: Bruylant, 2005.

Millet-Devalle, Anne-Sophie, ed. *L'Union européenne et le Droit International Humanitaire*. Paris: Pedone, 2010.

Millet-Devalle, Anne-Sophie. "L'UE et le droit relative aux moyens de combat." In Millet-Devalle, *L'Union européenne*, 217–289.

Moulier, Isabelle. "L'UE et les juridictions pénales internationals." In Millet-Devalle, *L'Union européenne*, 271–289.

Naert, Frederik. *International Law Aspects of the EU's Security and Defence Policy, with a Particular Focus on the Law of Armed Conflict and Human Rights*. Antwerp: Intersentia, 2010.

Pictet, Jean S., ed. *The Geneva Conventions of 12 August 1949: Commentary, I, Geneva Convention for the Amelioration of the Condition of the Wounded and Sick in Armed Forces in the Field*. Geneva: ICRC, 1952.

Sari, Aurel. "The European Status of Forces Agreement: Continuity and Change in the Law of Visiting Forces." *Military Law and the Law of War Review* 46 (2007): 9–254.

Sassòli, Marco. "Legislation and Maintenance of Public Order and Civil Life by Occupying Powers." *European Journal of International Law* 16 (2005): 661–694.

United Nations Office of Legal Affairs. "Question of the Possible Accession of Intergovernmental Organizations to the Geneva Conventions for the Protection of War Victims: Memorandum to the Under-Secretary General for Political Affairs." *United Nations Juridical Yearbook* 153 (1972): 153–154.

Vacas Fernandez, Felix. "International Human Rights Law as Legal Framework applicable to EU Missions." In *The Integration of the Human Rights Component and International Humanitarian Law in Peace Missions Lead by the European Union*, edited by Marian J. Aznar and Milena Costas, 38–50. Valencia: Psylicom, 2011.

Wills, Siobhan. "Occupation Law and Multi-National Operations: Problems and Perspectives." *British Yearbook of International Law* 77 (2006): 256–332.

Wrange, Pål. "The EU Guidelines on Promoting Compliance with International Humanitarian Law." *Nordic Journal of International Law* 78 (2010): 541–552.

Zwanenburg, Marten. *Accountability of Peace Support Operations*. Leiden: M. Nijhoff, 2005.

28

Emergence of EU Maritime Law

Barış Soyer

Introduction

The European Union's interest in developing rules concerning maritime law and liabilities has gained momentum, particularly after the *Erika* disaster in 1999.[1] Despite the increase in EU legislation in this area, it is too early to mention the existence of a comprehensive framework for maritime liability and compensation within the EU legal system. The development of EU maritime law has taken place on an incremental basis and to a large extent it is closely associated with various EU institutions' knee-jerk reaction to pollution disasters within EU waters – prompted, no doubt, by the extensive media coverage of public outrage following such oil spills.[2]

Despite the fact that the original driving force behind the development of EU maritime law was the desire to complement and strengthen the international rules by introducing regional standards, recent years have seen a more ambitious agenda which has manifested itself in the Union's implementation of an international liability convention[3] into the EU legal system long before the date when it came into force, perhaps with the intention of leading the way in the international arena. The legal landscape was further muddled when one of the parties succeeded in bringing an EU directive[4] that is remotely relevant to maritime affairs into play in a dispute concerning compensation arising out of an oil pollution incident.

This chapter considers several relevant EU directives and regulations devised particularly since the mid-2000s, with a view to evaluating the effectiveness of these measures in achieving a uniform marine legal regime within the European Union in harmony with the international law. It is hoped that as well as assisting in mapping the relationship between EU legislation and provisions of international conventions, this analysis will provide food for thought as to how the European Union's maritime law could be best developed in future in line with international law.

A Companion to European Union Law and International Law, First Edition.
Edited by Dennis Patterson and Anna Södersten.

Complementing International Rules

On several occasions, the European Union has sought to supplement international liability regimes either by regulating areas that have not received the attention of international regulators or simply by plugging the gaps left by various liability regimes. For instance, in the aftermath of the *Prestige* incident, the international community became concerned about the lack of an international legal framework dealing with the places of refuge for ships in need of assistance. Even though the International Maritime Organization finalized its guidelines to provide member states, shipmasters, shipowners, and salvors with a framework enabling them to respond effectively should a vessel be in distress and in need of assistance,[5] these guidelines do not deal with liability issues that might be critical from the point of view of coastal states receiving ships into a place of refuge. A directive passed on 23 April 2009[6] sought to address concerns with respect to issues concerning financial liability that might arise when a vessel in distress is accepted into a port of refuge. Article 20(a) of the directive requires, as part of the accommodation plan, the financial guarantee and liability procedures to be put in place for ships to be accommodated in a place of refuge. Article 20(b) provides that the competent authorities, when deciding on the acceptance of a ship in a place of refuge, may take into consideration the financial guarantee provided by the shipowner and the available liability procedures. While absence of an insurance certificate shall not in itself be considered a sufficient reason for a member state to refuse to accommodate a ship in distress in a port of refuge,[7] the directive nevertheless encourages member states to concentrate the discussion on insurance matters and enables them to formulate further legislation on issues with regard to financial liability. The directive can, therefore, be viewed as filling a gap arising from lack of international regulation on the matter.

Another piece of legislation that attempts to supplement international liability regimes is Directive 2004/35/EC of 21 April 2004 on environmental liability with regard to the prevention and remedying of environmental damage.[8] The directive imposes strict liability on operators for environmental damage caused when engaged in potentially hazardous occupational activities specified in Annex III and fault-based liability for environmental damage to protected species and natural habitats from all other occupational activities.[9] The environmental damage caused by transport of dangerous goods by sea would come under the scope of the directive but recovery in such cases is limited to the cost of preventive or remedial actions taken by public authorities.[10] The directive does not, therefore, enable private individuals or corporations to claim compensation for damage to property or economic losses. On the other hand, for claims that fall under the scope of the directive the operators would benefit from the limitation of liability which is widely available for shipowners and other players in maritime law.[11]

The directive excludes from its ambit environmental damage arising from incidents covered by some of the major international conventions concerned with liability for marine pollution arising from carriage of goods by sea, namely the International Convention on Civil Liability for Oil Pollution Damage (CLC) 1992, the International Convention on the Establishment of an International Fund for Compensation for Oil Pollution Damage (Fund Convention) 1992, the International Convention on Civil Liability for Bunker Oil Pollution Damage (BOPC) 2001, the International Convention on Liability and Compensation for Damage in Connection with the Carriage of Hazardous and Noxious Substances by Sea (HNS) 1996, and their future amendments as long as these instruments are in force in the member state where the pollution occurs.[12] This is a positive step and demonstrates a commitment to respect the treaty obligations of member states while at the same time complementing the international maritime liability conventions.

However, it should be stressed that on certain occasions difficulties could still arise around whether the liability regime under the directive could be applied in conjunction with the abovementioned international regimes. Let us assume that a tanker laden with oil and hazardous/

noxious substances is grounded causing large-scale marine pollution. Given that the HNS Convention 1996 is yet not in force internationally, one would expect the public authorities to be able to seek the cost of preventive or remedial actions taken under the directive. However, if the source of pollution could also be traced to the oil on board or the vessel's bunkers, there is a case to argue that the directive should be sidestepped by virtue of Article 4(2) and Annex IV.

Leaving this potential legal difficulty aside, it is fair to say that the directive ensures a harmonized approach within the European Union in relation to the assessment of damage and the necessary rules for preventing and remedying environmental damage by stepping in on cases where no international maritime liability regime applies.

The Union's intervention with the objective of complementing existing liability regimes in maritime law has not, however, always been free from controversy; at times, the EU legislation has put the member states in a vulnerable position with regard to their obligations under international treaties. Two examples will suffice to illustrate the legal and political difficulties that could emerge.

Let us start with the Waste Directive,[13] which, at first, was believed to have very little to do with maritime law. The directive requires member states to impose – by way of their national law – liability for the cost of disposing of waste on the "holder" and/or "previous holders" of the waste, and/or the "producer" of the waste or the product from which it came. In the days following the *Erika* disaster, the Commune de Mesquer (municipality of Mesquer) brought proceedings against the Italian company that produced and sold the heavy oil and against the company that chartered the *Erika* for carriage of the oil (both of these companies were part of the Total Group). The basis of the claim was the French legislation that implemented the Waste Directive into French law, and the claimant's case centered on the argument that the cargo on board could be deemed as "waste" within the meaning of the Waste Directive. Once the case reached the Cour de cassation, it was referred to the Court of Justice of the European Union (CJEU) for preliminary ruling[14] on various points including: (1) whether the transported fuel and the spilled residues were covered by the definition of waste in the directive; and (2) whether the Total Group could be regarded as the "producer and/or holder" of the waste even if the discharged substance had been transported by a third party, namely the shipowner.

By framing its claim against Total Group companies in this manner, the claimant's main expectation was to put itself in an advantageous position in the litigation process. Sidestepping the CLC 1992, which channels liability only to the registered owner of the vessel in question, not only increases the number of parties that can be targeted as defendants but also enables the claimant to bypass the financial limits imposed by that international regime. Using the directive as the basis of the claim yields another advantage in that the claimant could seek compensation for pure ecological damage, something which is not available under the CLC 1992.

It is a plausible argument to suggest that by expecting the member states to devise legislation extending the application of the directive to pollution cases, the European Union in a way forces the member states to violate their international treaty obligations and disregard international conventions to which they are party. Furthermore, it can be further argued that the rationale behind the Waste Directive was to ensure that industrial companies pay for the disposal of waste that is the byproduct of their hazardous activities; it is very unlikely that the drafters of the directive contemplated it becoming the legislative source of compensation for damage caused by accidental oil spills at sea.

Despite the robustness of these arguments, the CJEU refused to be drawn into a wide-ranging discussion on whether, and if so to what extent, international law could impose limits on EU legislation.[15] The CJEU was of the view that the European Union was not in contravention of international law by regulating this area mainly because the Union was not bound by the CLC and Fund Convention 1992 as it had not acceded to them and cannot be regarded as having taken the place of its member states if only because not all of them are parties to those conventions.[16] In the view of this stance taken, there was no need to discuss further the compatibility of the provisions of the Waste Directive with the Conventions in question, but the CJEU went on, expressing the view that the provisions of the Waste Directive do not prohibit member states from laying down limitations and exceptions of liability in favor of the registered shipowner in accordance with these international agreements.[17] There would, therefore, be no incompatibility between EU and international law.

Having dealt with the question of compatibility, the CJEU turned its attention to the substantive points. Agreeing with the Opinion of Advocate General Kokott, the CJEU was convinced that the transported heavy fuel oil was a petroleum product and not waste given that it could have been marketed on economically advantageous terms and also that it did not require any processing prior to its use.[18] However, in the CJEU's view a cargo of heavy fuel oil that was accidentally spilled from a ship into the sea constituted "waste" within the meaning of the Waste Directive essentially on the ground that such substances are no longer capable of being exploited or marketed without prior processing.[19] On the matter of whether the producer of the oil and/or the charterer could be regarded as the "producer" and/or "previous holder" of it within the meaning of the Waste Directive, the answer was positive. The Court stressed that the concept of "holder of the waste" in the context of the Waste Directive appears to be much broader than that of "owner" because it is intended to cover all persons likely to discard waste. The CJEU has also drawn analogy from another case, *Paul Van de Walle Daniel Laurent, Thierry Mersch and Texaco Belgium SA.*[20] There, hydrocarbons that had been bought by a service station to meet its operating needs spilled by accident as the result of a leak from the service station's storage facilities. The Court found that an oil company selling hydrocarbons to the service station could, in certain circumstances, be considered as the holder of the hydrocarbons that accidentally leaked from the station's storage tanks even though the oil company did not own them.

Accordingly, it was held that even if it was in principle the shipowner who held the waste, the producer of heavy fuel oil as well as the seller and the tanker charterer could be held liable for waste disposal costs on the grounds that they could be deemed to have contributed in some way to the causal chain that led to the shipwreck at the origin of the accidental spillage.[21] However, the Court was adamant that the seller and/or charterer may only be liable, in accordance with the "polluter pays" principle,[22] insofar as the latter has "contributed by his conduct to the risk that the pollution caused by the shipwreck will occur."[23]

Technically speaking, the CJEU's judgment is defendable and has legal backing.[24] Given that the CLC 1992 has not been integrated into the EU legal regime, the provisions of this convention do not prohibit a rule of secondary law from having its full effects in the light of the guiding policy to which the Waste Directive relates. Furthermore, it is arguably the case that devising legislation that will make parties other than the registered shipowner of a tanker liable for pollution arising out of an oil spill does not mean that the channeling provisions within the CLC Convention 1992 are undermined. The purpose of channeling provisions is to direct liability arising out of the CLC regime to the registered owner of the ship. The Waste Directive does not change this premise. It simply introduces a new liability regime and makes other parties, such as producer and charterer of the ship, liable for the cost of cleaning up expenses to the extent that these parties have contributed to the occurrence of the event that led to the spill. To sum up, it is submitted that the stance taken by the CJEU on this matter is the right one, although it should be added that it is highly unlikely that the framers of this directive had envisaged it playing a role in this context.

Directive 2005/35/EC of 7 September 2005 on ship-source pollution and on the introduction of penalties for infringements[25] is a more controversial secondary EU legislation that has raised questions as to whether the European Union is in breach of international law by taking unilateral action. The objective of the directive is to transpose into the EU law the discharge standards introduced by the International Convention for the Prevention of Pollution from Ships (MARPOL) 73/78 and to require member states to impose adequate penalties on persons responsible for discharge of polluting substances from ships in violation of MARPOL 73/78 if such discharge is "committed with intent, recklessly or by serious negligence."

The directive imposes criminal sanctions on the owner of the vessel, master and crew members, salvors, charterers, and classification societies for discharges at sea, irrespective of whether they are accidental or operational, in cases where the discharge is committed with intent, recklessness, or by serious negligence. The sanctions would apply irrespective of the flag of the vessel and regardless of whether the discharge occurs in territorial seas or even in Exclusive Economic Zones (EEZ) of the member states. The extensive use of criminal sanctions might potentially put the member states in conflict with their obligations under international law in several respects:

1. By virtue of MARPOL Regulations I/4(2) and II/3(2) in cases of accidental discharges resulting from damage to the ship or its equipment, violation of discharge standards set in MARPOL 73/78 will not have any legal consequence unless "the owner and master acted either with intent to cause damage, or recklessly and with knowledge that damage would probably result." The directive, by requiring the imposition of criminal sanctions in cases of accidental discharges caused by serious negligence of those responsible, especially outside the territorial sea of member states, seems to restrict the defense that would have been available to master and crew under MARPOL Regulations. The matter becomes even more complicated as far as EEZs of the member states are concerned. The United Nations Convention on the Law of the Sea (UNCLOS) 1982 provides that the coastal state's prescribed laws in the EEZ must conform to and give effect to "generally accepted international rules and standards."[26] In the context of pollution, such "generally accepted international rules and standards" are commonly understood to refer to MARPOL 73/78 and other International Maritime Organization Conventions. Therefore, deviating from the standards set by MARPOL 73/78 in regulating issues concerning pollution within the EEZ would potentially amount to breach of UNCLOS.

2. Article 230 of the UNCLOS 1982 allows coastal states to impose monetary penalties in respect of violations of national laws or regulations or applicable international rules and standards for the prevention, reduction, and control of pollution of the marine environment committed by foreign vessels beyond the territorial seas. Other penalties can only be imposed for violations committed by foreign vessels in the territorial sea if they are perpetrated with intent. It can, therefore, be forcefully argued that the European Union is in violation of this provision by obliging member states to impose criminal sanctions including imprisonment for violations committed by foreign vessels beyond territorial waters and in the territorial waters even though such violations are not committed with intent.

3. Foreign vessels enjoy a right of innocent passage in the territorial seas of coastal states and this right can only be restricted in cases where the foreign vessel acts willfully creating serious pollution hazard.[27] It can be maintained that in lowering the threshold of liability for violations of MARPOL 73/78 to one of "serious negligence," the directive hampers the right of innocent passage of foreign vessels in territorial seas.

Against this legal background, a number of shipping industry organizations (led by the International Association of Independent Tanker Owners (INTERTANKO)[28]) decided to challenge the validity of the directive on the grounds that it violated MARPOL 73/78 and international law of the sea. A case was brought in the High Court for England and Wales[29] and the Court decided to refer the case for a ruling by the CJEU. Apart from issues relating to the compatibility of the directive with MARPOL 73/78 and UNCLOS 1982, the High Court also asked the CJEU to make a preliminary ruling on whether the standard of liability in the directive of "serious negligence" satisfied the requirement of legal certainty.

The judgment of the CJEU has been a huge disappointment for those who expected a thorough analysis of the relationship between the directive and international law. The CJEU refused to rule on the substance of the matter and upheld the validity of the directive on technical grounds.[30] On issues of compatibility with MARPOL 73/78, the view was that the European Union was not bound by the provisions of this convention when devising secondary legislation since it was not a party to it.[31] It also did not matter that all EU member states were parties to it. As for UNCLOS, the CJEU ruled that even though the European Union was party to that convention, it did not confer on individuals any rights of freedom on which they could rely against states.[32] This ruling made the need for any ruling on the concept of "serious negligence" redundant, but the CJEU, nevertheless, commented on this concept, indicating that its use in the directive did not infringe the Community law requirement of legal certainty because it was well understood in the member states' legal systems and could be defined as such when transposed into national law.[33]

The CJEU's reasoning was adequate to dispose of the case but it falls short of solving the main problem: by implementing this directive into their national laws will the member states be in breach of their international treaty obligations? The case put forward by INTERTANKO and other shipping organizations is a solid one, and it appears that introducing a lower threshold of "serious negligence" might well amount to a violation of the provisions of MARPOL 73/78 and UNCLOS 1982. The truth of the matter is that the validity of the directive might still be challenged before national courts, especially when member states transpose its requirements into their national laws. At that stage, if an interested party brings an action against the implementing legislation on the premise that the legislation is inconsistent with the provisions of the UNCLOS, the court seized in the member state would be required to solve the inconsistency by giving precedence to the UNCLOS, given that it is expected to give priority to the UNCLOS over the secondary EU legislation in case of an inconsistency.[34] Another possibility is that a non-EU state could start a legal action against a member state implementing the directive before another judicial body such as the International Court of Justice or the International Tribunal for the Law of the Sea on the basis that the relevant member state is in breach of its treaty obligations.[35] Admittedly, this is not an option that can easily be put in practice, but one can see a non-member state taking the matter to an international tribunal in a case where crew on board a vessel flying its flag is charged with criminal offences in accordance with the requirements of the directive.

There is a lesson to be learned from this legal battle that has not yet settled. The European Union, when taking unilateral action for the purpose of complementing international rules, should be extremely careful especially if the field that it attempts to regulate has already been the subject of international conventions. One should not lose sight of the fact that international conventions are usually the product of a political compromise. Taking unilateral action by disregarding the underlying philosophies of these conventions and compromises parties made to reach a settlement not only undermines the role of the international law and organizations committed to developing such rules but might also create harmful economic consequences for member states and the EU economic zone altogether.[36]

Implementing International Conventions into EU Law

A new trend within the European Union is to incorporate provisions of international conventions into the EU legal order by duplicating them in EU directives and regulations. The most recent and significant example is the introduction of the Athens Convention 2002[37] by Council Regulation (EC) No 392/2009 of 23 April 2009.[38] By virtue of this regulation the provisions of the Athens Convention 2002[39] have been made effective within the EU legal order from 31 December 2012[40] even though the convention is not yet in force internationally.

This new method not only ensures expansion of the "EU competence" in this field but it also enables the Commission to bring before the CJEU any member state not complying with the regulation and, effectively, provisions of the Athens Convention 2002. Member states might even be obliged to pay lump-sum penalties in case of continued noncompliance.[41] It could, therefore, be tentatively suggested that the regulation ensures the application of a uniform liability regime with regard to passenger claims within the European Union. However, on closer scrutiny it becomes apparent that several difficulties remain that might jeopardize uniformity and also create uncertainty. These will be evaluated next.

First, incorporating the provisions of the Athens Convention 2002 into EU law without attempting to clarify those that are vague or open to misinterpretation means that the ambiguities surrounding the Athens Convention will be made part of EU law. Of course, it is possible to call the CJEU into action to determine the accurate legal position once the regulation is in force, and this will possibly be necessary. However, it would have been a more effective and possibly more economical solution had the drafters of the regulation attempted to clarify the ambiguities inherent in the Athens Convention itself prior to finalizing the text of the regulation. Two examples should suffice to illustrate the legal difficulties that might exercise the CJEU in the years to come.

1. By virtue of Article 3 of the Athens Convention, the carrier is required to compensate a passenger for loss suffered as a result of death or personal injury. The relevant provision makes no attempt to define the meaning of "personal injury" other than stating that "loss shall not include punitive or exemplary damages." An interesting question in this context is whether mental (psychiatric) injury suffered by a passenger could be claimed under the convention regime. This question was answered negatively when considered in the context of the Warsaw Convention 1929[42] both in the United Kingdom[43] and the United States of America.[44] However, when identifying types of claims recoverable, the Warsaw Convention 1929 makes reference to "bodily injury" while in the Athens Convention the term "personal injury" has been used. There is room to argue that the use of the term "personal injury" enables the courts to construe this provision of the Athens Convention in the widest possible way so that it would be possible in pursuance thereof to award compensation for pure mental anguish in addition to physical injury suffered by passengers carried by sea.

2. One of the preconditions for the application of the Athens regime is that the carriage is performed on a ship. Article 1(3) defines the ship for the purposes of the convention as a "sea-going vessel, excluding an air-cushion vehicle." No further definition has been provided in the convention as to the physical attributes a craft should carry to be considered as a "ship." Therefore, one must turn to the general maritime law in search of an appropriate definition of the term "ship." Naturally, the definition of the term "ship" might vary from one member state to another. As far as UK maritime law is concerned, the most general definition of the term can be found in s. 313 of the Merchant Shipping Act 1995, which indicates that the term "ship" includes every description of vessel used in navigation. Based on this definition, it was held in *McEwan v. Bingham (t/a Studland Watersports)*[45] that a seventeen-foot

inflatable banana raft which was towed in a bay by a marine assault craft was not a vessel. It cannot be said with certainty that the French courts would reach the same decision in a similar case. Therefore, there is a genuine possibility that in case of an accident, passengers who purchase a ticket for a ride on an inflatable raft in the United Kingdom will be treated differently from those who decide to enjoy their ride in the Mediterranean coast of France. This anomaly could have been addressed had the regulation contained a definition of "ship" for its purposes.

The second difficulty with the approach adopted by the regulation is that it might put the member states that fail to denounce the 1974 version of the Athens Convention in a difficult position as far as their international treaty obligations are concerned. Let us assume that under a contract of carriage made in a non-EU state that is party to the Athens Convention 1974, passengers are carried from a non-EU state to a member state that is also a party to the Athens Convention 1974. In that case, the member state is under a treaty obligation to apply the liability and limitation regime that is set out in the Athens Convention 1974 by virtue of Article 2 of the Athens Convention 1974. However, given that the place of destination according to the contract of carriage is in a member state, Article 2 of the regulation would require the courts in the member state to apply the liability regime set out in the Athens Convention 2002. Essentially, in this case the member state in question is under a EU law obligation to apply the more stringent liability provisions of the Athens Convention 2002 whereas it is bound under international law to implement the Athens Convention 1974 in relation to other states parties to that convention.

Concluding Remarks

So far, the European Union's desire to regulate maritime matters has yielded mixed results. One can see considerable benefits in implementing international conventions into the EU legal system. However, it would be desirable when this is done to clarify vague or contentious provisions of the relevant international regime in the implementing secondary legislation so that a more harmonized regime could be achieved within the Union. It is evident that this opportunity was missed when implementing the Athens Convention 2002. It is also a positive step to fill the gaps left by international regimes by devising rules that apply throughout the European Union; Directive 2004/35/EC of 21 April 2004[46] on environmental liability is a good example of how this can be done in an effective fashion.

However, taking unilateral action disregarding treaty obligations of member states, which is arguably what the directive on ship-source pollution and on the introduction of penalties for infringements[47] recommends, is a step that might have dramatic consequences. The obvious danger is that unilateral actions might isolate the European region from international standards. A further danger inherent in taking unilateral action is that EU member states might be forced to denounce treaties in order to avoid breaking their international obligations under such treaties. If that were to happen with respect to the international maritime liability regimes, there is a serious possibility that these regimes would collapse. This would undoubtedly be detrimental to other states, and in particular to the victims of marine pollution in developing countries. It is vital that in the wake of pollution disasters affecting the European coastlines, the relevant bodies within the European Union refrain from knee-jerk reactions and take into account the international regimes to which member states and other maritime nations are party.

Notes

1 On 12 December 1999, the *Erika*, a twenty-five-year-old single-hull oil tanker flying the Maltese flag, sank some sixty nautical miles off the Brittany coast, spilling some 20,000 tonnes of heavy fuel which in due course polluted some four hundred kilometers of the French coastline. This has been regarded as the worst environmental disaster to hit France and had catastrophic economic consequences for fishing and tourism sectors.

2 The sinking of another single-hull oil tanker registered in the Bahamas, the *Prestige*, about two hundred and fifty kilometers from the Spanish coast on 19 November 2002, encouraged the Commission to take further drastic action and prompted legal measures with the intention of protecting European waters and coastline from the risk of oil pollution. Prior to the *Erika* and *Prestige* incidents, the European Union's tendency was to rely heavily on international bodies such as the International Maritime Organization for the development of rules and practices to protect the marine environment.

3 The Convention relating to the Carriage of Passengers and their Luggage by Sea of 1974 (Athens Convention) as modified by the Protocol of 2002, commonly known as the Athens Convention 2002.

4 Council Directive 1975/442/EEC of 15 July 1975 on waste [1975] OJ L 194/39. This directive has been replaced by Directive 2008/98/EC of the European Parliament and of the Council of 19 November 2008 on waste and repealing certain Directives [2008] OJ L 312/3, hereinafter referred to as the Waste Directive.

5 International Maritime Organization Resolution A. 949(23), "Guidelines on Places of Refuge For Ships in Need of Assistance," adopted on 5 December 2003.

6 Directive 2009/17/EC of the European Parliament and of the Council of 23 April 2009 amending Directive 2002/59/EC establishing a Community vessel traffic monitoring and information system [2009] OJ L 131/101.

7 Ibid., Article 20(c).

8 Directive 2004/35/EC of the European Parliament and of the Council of 21 April 2004 on environmental liability with regard to the prevention and remedying of environmental damage [2004] OJ L 143/56.

9 The operator is defined as "any natural or legal, private or public person who operates or controls the occupational activity or, where this is provided for in national legislation, to whom decisive economic power over the technical functioning of such an activity has been delegated, including the holder of a permit or authorisation for such an activity or the person registering or notifying such an activity." Ibid., Article 2(6).

10 Ibid., Article 8.

11 Ibid., Article 4(3).

12 Ibid., Article 4(2) and Annex IV.

13 Directive 1975/442/EEC, n 4 this chapter. This directive has been replaced by Directive 2008/98/EC, n 4 this chapter.

14 *Commune de Musquer v. Total Raffinage Distribution SA and Total International Ltd*, 04 12.315, 3ème chamber civile.

15 For a comprehensive analysis of the CJEU's judgment see Nicolas de Sadeleer, "Liability for Oil Pollution Damage versus Liability for Waste Management: The Polluter Pays Principle at the Rescue of the Victims," *Journal of Environmental Law* 21 (2009).

16 Case C-188/07 *Commune de Masquer v. Total France SA* EU:C:2008:359, para 85.

17 Ibid., para 81.

18 Ibid., para 48.

19 Ibid., para 63.

20 Case C-1/03 *Criminal proceedings against Paul Van de Walle, Daniel Laurent, Thierry Mersch and Texaco Belgium SA* EU:C:2004:490.

21 Case C-188/07 *Commune de Masquer*, n 16 this chapter, para 78.

22 This principle has been enshrined in Article 174(2) EC.

23 Case C-188/07 *Commune de Masquer*, n 16 this chapter, para 82. Following the judgment of the CJEU, the Cour de cassation overturned the judgment of the appeal court and held that Total could be considered as "producers" of the product from which the waste had come or as "previous holders" of the waste found on the beaches after the shipwreck. The case was remitted to the Cour d'appeal in Bordeaux in order for it to rule on a single point: namely, whether the Total companies had or not contributed to the risk of pollution occasioned by the shipwreck of the *Erika*. The case was still ongoing at the time of writing of this paper.

24 See Joined Cases C-402/05 P and C-415/05 P *Yassin Abdullah Kadi and Al Barakaat International Foundation v. Council of the European Union and Commission of the European Communities* EU:C:2008:461, paras 299 and 300.

25 Directive 2005/35/EC of the European Parliament and of the Council of 7 September 2005 on ship-source pollution and on the introduction of penalties for infringements [2005] OJ L 255/11 as amended by Directive 2009/123/EC of the European Parliament and of the Council of 21 October 2009 amending Directive 2005/35/EC on ship-source pollution and on the introduction of penalties for infringements [2009] OJ L 280/52.

26 Article 211(5) of the UNCLOS 1982.

27 Article 19(2) of the UNCLOS 1982 and Articles 14–16 of the Convention on the Territorial Sea and the Contiguous Zone of 1958. See also *Corfu Channel Case* (*United Kingdom v. Albania*), Merits, 1949 ICJ REP. 1 (April 9)

28 Other organizations involved in the litigation were: International Association of Dry Cargo Shipowners (Inter Cargo), the Greek Shipping Co-operation Committee, Lloyd's Register, and the International Salvage Union.

29 *Intertanko and others v. Secretary of State for Transport* [2006] EWHC 1577 (Admin).

30 Case C-308/06 *The Queen on the application of International Association of Independent Tanker Owners (Intertanko) and others v. Secretary of State for Transport* EU:C:2008:312.

31 Ibid., paras 42–45 and 50–52.

32 Ibid., paras 64–65.

33 Ibid., paras 69–80. For a comprehensive analysis of the case, see Eileen Denza, "A Note on Intertanko," *European Law Review* 33 (2008); and Alan Khee-Jin Tan, "The EU Ship-Source Pollution Directive and Coastal State Jurisdiction over Ships," *Lloyd's Maritime and Commercial Law Quarterly* (2010).

34 See, Article 9 of Directive 2005/35/EC, n 25 this chapter, as amended by Directive 2009/123/EC, n 25 this chapter.

35 This option would not be available to an EU member state in the light of the judgment in C-459/03 *Commission v. Ireland* EU:C:2006:345. There, it was held that it was impermissible for a member state to proceed against another in an international forum in an area given over to Community competence.

36 For a general discussion on harmful effects of unilateralism see Alan Boyle, "EU Unilateralism and the Law of the Sea," *International Journal of Marine and Coastal Law* 21 (2006).

37 This convention (n 3 this chapter) intends to provide a liability regime for passengers and their luggage carried on international voyages. As of 31 May 2012, this convention has been ratified by eight states (Albania, Belize, Denmark, Latvia, Palau, Saint Kitts and Nevis, Serbia, Syrian Arab Republic) and the European Union and is not yet in force.

38 Regulation (EC) No 392/2009 of the European Parliament and of the Council of 23 April 2009 on the liability of carriers of passengers by sea in the event of accidents [2009] OJ L 131/24.

39 For a comprehensive analysis on the new Athens 2002 Regime, see Barış Soyer, "Sundry Considerations on the Draft Protocol to the Athens Convention Relating to the Carriage of Passengers and Their Luggage by Sea 1974," *Journal of Maritime Law & Commerce* 33 (2002).

40 The application of the regulation in respect of some vessels operating within a single member state can be deferred by virtue of Article 11 of the Regulation (EC) No 392/2009, n 38 this chapter.

41 Article 260 TFEU.

42 The relevant provision, which is now expressed in Article 17(1) of the Convention for the Unification of Certain Rules for International Carriage by Air of 1999 (Montreal Convention), reads, "The carrier is liable for damage sustained in case of death or bodily injury of a passenger upon condition

only that the accident which caused the death or injury took place on board the aircraft or in the course of any of the operations of embarking or disembarking."

43 *King v Bristow Helicopters Ltd, Morris v. KLM Royal Dutch Airlines* [2002] UKHL 7; [2002] 2 AC 628.

44 *Eastern Airlines Inc v. Floyd* (1991) 499 US 530 (Supreme Court).

45 Unreported, decided by the County Court (Howe) on 28 July 2000.

46 See n 8.

47 Directive 2005/35/EC, n 25 this chapter, as amended by Directive 2009/123/EC, n 25 this chapter.

References

Boyle, Alan. "EU Unilateralism and the Law of the Sea." *International Journal of Marine and Coastal Law* 21 (2006): 15–31.

Denza, Eileen. "A Note on Intertanko." *European Law Review* 33 (2008): 870–874.

de Sadeleer, Nicolas. "Liability for Oil Pollution Damage versus Liability for Waste Management: The Polluter Pays Principle at the Rescue of the Victims." *Journal of Environmental Law* 21 (2009): 299–307.

Khee-Jin Tan, Alan. "The EU Ship-Source Pollution Directive and Coastal State Jurisdiction over Ships." *Lloyd's Maritime and Commercial Law Quarterly* (2010): 469–488.

Ringbom, Henrik. "Maritime Liability and Compensation in EU Law." In *Pollution at Sea: Law and Liability*, edited by Barış Soyer and Andrew Tettenborn, 155–171. London: Lloyd's List, 2012.

Soyer, Barış. "Sundry Considerations on the Draft Protocol to the Athens Convention Relating to the Carriage of Passengers and Their Luggage by Sea 1974." *Journal of Maritime Law & Commerce* 33 (2002): 519–541.

Part VI

Human Rights, Social Issues, and the Environment

29

International Human Rights Law

Martin Scheinin

Origins of the Idea of Human Rights

Although the notion of "human rights" made its breakthrough in the aftermath of the Second World War, the idea of the individual human person possessing fundamental rights in relation to the state, or more generally in relation to those who exercise power over him or her is much older.[1] What was new in the emerging post-Second World War order was the recognition of the need of the international community, and of international law, to be concerned over how a state treats *its own nationals*. Previously, international law primarily addressed the question how a territorial state treats nationals of other countries (diplomatic protection),[2] or how a state deals with its national minorities with an ethnic, linguistic, or religious tie to a neighboring country (the protection of national minorities).[3] In the Nuremberg war crimes process, massive crimes committed by a regime against its own citizens were defined as "crimes against humanity." The same relationship between a state and its own subjects was brought under the notion of human rights in the United Nations (UN) Charter (1945) and the Universal Declaration of Human Rights (UDHR) adopted as a resolution by the UN General Assembly (1948).[4] The charter proclaims (in its Article 1(3)) one of the purposes of the UN to be the promotion and encouragement of respect for human rights.[5]

The philosophical origins of human rights, as fundamental and inalienable rights of the individual, can be derived from various religious and secular moral traditions.[6] In the sphere of law, they inspired the French and American revolutions of the late eighteenth century and thereafter the drafting of national constitutions, which routinely came to include a chapter on the "fundamental," "basic," or "civil" rights of the individual.[7]

The UDHR consists of a preamble and thirty articles. It opens with a poetic but somewhat anachronistic (cf. "brotherhood") formulation in Article 1:

> All human beings are born free and equal in dignity and rights. They are endowed with reason and conscience and should act towards one another in a spirit of brotherhood.

A Companion to European Union Law and International Law, First Edition.
Edited by Dennis Patterson and Anna Södersten.

Articles 2 to 27 contain the actual catalogue of human rights that subsequently has been affirmed and refined in a long line of human rights treaties.[8] The rights can be grouped into four categories as follows.

1. Nondiscrimination (Articles 2 and 7).
2. Civil and political rights: rights to life, liberty, and security (Article 3); prohibition against slavery and servitude (Article 4); prohibition against torture (Article 5); right to recognition as person before the law (Article 6); prohibition against arbitrary arrest, detention, or exile (Article 9); right to a fair trial (Article 10); presumption of innocence and the requirement of legality in criminal law (Article 11); protection of privacy, family, home, and correspondence (Article 12); freedom of movement (Article 13); right to seek and enjoy asylum (Article 14); right to a nationality (Article 15); right to marry and to found a family (Article 16); right to property (Article 17); freedom of thought, conscience, and religion (Article 18); freedom of expression (Article 19); right to freedom of association and peaceful assembly (Article 20); right to participation, including through periodic and genuine elections (Article 21).
3. Economic, social and cultural rights: right to social security (Article 22); right to work and just conditions of work, including equal pay for equal work and the right to form and join trade unions (Article 23); right to rest and leisure (Article 24); right to an adequate standard of living, including food, clothing, housing, medical services, and security in situations of risk (Article 25); right to education (Article 26); right to participate in cultural life and intellectual property rights (Article 27).
4. Right to a remedy for human rights violations (Article 8).

Sources of Human Rights Law

International human rights law is a branch of public international law. Consistent with Article 38 of the Statute of International Court of Justice,[9] the primary sources of international human rights law can be identified as treaty, custom, and general principles of law derived from national legal systems.[10] The first two – treaty and custom – are prominent in human rights discourse. In addition, constitutional protections of fundamental rights can be seen as a source of "general principles" that would inform international law.[11] Article 38 of the statute also refers to judicial decisions as a subsidiary source of international law, a matter of high relevance in human rights law owing to the prominence of regional human rights courts, international courts and tribunals, and international expert bodies in refining the understanding of the interpretation of human rights treaties. Treaty provisions in human rights law are often textually fairly open-ended and hence will need to be read in the light of institutionalized practices of interpretation, such as the jurisprudence by regional human rights courts and international human rights treaty bodies.

Treaty

Although there are some older international treaties that would qualify as human rights treaties,[12] the process of codifying the substantive rights of the UDHR into the form of legally binding international treaties between states at UN level started in the mid-1960s with the Convention for the Elimination of Racial Discrimination (CERD)[13] and the twin Covenants of

1966, namely the International Covenant on Economic, Social and Cultural Rights (ICESCR)[14] and the International Covenant on Civil and Political Rights (ICCPR).[15] Today, there are nine conventions categorized as "core" human rights treaties at the UN level, plus a number of regional treaties or treaties emanating from some of the UN specialized agencies including the International Labour Organization (ILO) and the United Nations Educational, Scientific and Cultural Organization (UNESCO).[16]

Besides the two covenants of 1966 and the CERD, the notion of nine core treaties refers to the following six treaties: the Convention on the Elimination of All Forms of Discrimination against Women (1979, CEDAW),[17] the Convention against Torture and Other Cruel, Inhuman or Degrading Treatment or Punishment (1984, CAT),[18] the Convention on the Rights of the Child (1989, CRC),[19] the Convention on the Protection of the Rights of All Migrant Workers and Members of Their Families (1990, CMW),[20] the Convention for the Protection of All Persons from Enforced Disappearance (2006, CED),[21] and the Convention on the Rights of Persons with Disabilities (2006, CRPD).[22] Many of these conventions have been supplemented by optional protocols that either introduce new substantive human rights provisions or new monitoring mechanisms.[23]

In 1948, when the catalogue of human rights was decided through the adoption of the UDHR, the UN was a fairly small club of nations, as decolonization was still at a very early stage and as Germany and its Second World War allies had not yet been admitted to the UN. The UDHR itself was adopted by forty-eight votes to none, with eight abstentions.[24] Today, there are 193 member states in the UN, a vast majority of which were either nonexistent or not present when the UDHR was crafted. At times, human rights law has been accused of being a Northern or Western creation with imperialist proclivities and as failing to sufficiently reflect the diversity of humankind, including so-called Asian or African values.

A closer look at the genesis of the UDHR, however, provides strong arguments in support of a real effort to produce a truly universal instrument. There were important non-Western states and individuals who were among the leading drafters. Additionally, the number of countries from Latin America and Asia that cast affirmative votes was almost equivalent to that of Western nations. Eastern European (socialist) countries dominated among the abstention votes. African voices, however, were by and large missing, except for those of South Africa (abstaining) and Egypt, Ethiopia, and Liberia (voting in favor).

More importantly, through the adoption and voluntary ratification of subsequent human rights treaties, the catalogue of human rights enshrined in the UDHR has been affirmed as universal. Through their voluntary treaty ratification, all states are parties to one or more of the nine core human rights treaties. All except two small Pacific island states (Niue and Palau), that is, 99 percent of all states, are party to at least two of the nine main treaties. And 99.5 percent of all states have through their ratifications accepted in treaty form the full normative catalogue of human rights enshrined in the UDHR.[25] The single exception is the United States of America, which has not joined any of the treaties that pertain to economic and social rights, and hence can be said to have accepted in treaty form only a subset of the rights covered by the UDHR.[26] In short, the UDHR catalogue of human rights has become universally accepted through subsequent treaty ratifications that represent full and free consent by all countries in the world.[27]

When looking at these ratification records, one should keep in mind that many human rights treaties include conditions defining what constitutes a "state" eligible to ratify them. For instance, the ICCPR limits membership by certain formal conditions such as UN membership, whereas the CRC uses an "all states" formula, and the CRPD goes even further by allowing membership by all states and by "regional integration organizations" (such as the European Union, which indeed is a party).

Custom

The universal acceptance of human rights through voluntary treaty ratification gives strong support to the contention that human rights also constitute norms of customary international law.[28] According to one view discussed already for decades, the full catalogue of human rights enshrined in the UDHR would amount to customary international law,[29] binding upon all states irrespective of their treaty ratification practice, except for those few states that would have remained persistent objectors in respect of the emergence of certain specific norms of customary law. While such a generalizing view may have been too generous at the time, there certainly are human rights norms that already by the drafting of major human rights treaties would have emerged as norms of customary law. Subsequent state practice in the form of acceptance of human rights treaties through their voluntary ratification provides good grounds to assert that by 2014 there is universal factual acceptance of, and normative commitment to, the substantive catalogue of human rights enshrined in the UDHR. By and large, there is a customary law norm behind the provisions of various human rights treaties, including the rights that can be found both in one of the twin covenants of 1966 and in the CRC.

The two elements in the formation of a rule of customary international law are consistent state practice and *opinio juris*, that is, an understanding that states are adopting a certain practice not merely at their will but with an acknowledgment of a legal obligation to do so. The two elements may overlap; for instance, in the sense that universal ratification of a human rights treaty at the same time represents a form of state practice and is driven by the recognition of a legal norm that all states must respect. While actual practice on the ground may form a significant type of state practice, there are also situations where actual practice that runs counter to the norm is accompanied by official proclamations of adherence to the norm and denial of allegations of factual noncompliance with the norm.[30] Verbal practice, such as statements by a state's diplomatic representatives at international fora or support to resolutions reflecting a normative position may also contribute towards the formation of norms of customary international law.

As all states in the world have voluntarily ratified one or more human rights treaties, and all except one state, through their treaty ratifications, also accept the full scope of the human rights enshrined in the UDHR, there are good grounds to conclude, as already stated, that by 2014 all human rights covered by the UDHR catalogue have obtained customary law status. That said, it would be wrong to draw a conclusion of substantive identity between human rights treaty law and customary norms of international human rights law. Through institutionalized practices of interpretation, treaties (and their interpretation) may have evolved beyond what could be established as a norm of customary law under the two criteria of state practice and *opinio juris*. While the full catalogue of human rights has reached customary law status, there is still a need for careful assessment of what each customary law norm comprises as compared with the coverage of the treaties and their established interpretation.

Jus cogens

Jus cogens norms constitute a subset of the norms of customary law. They are peremptory norms of international law, legally binding upon all states in the world irrespective of their treaty ratification record and not subject to derogation. As expressed by Article 53 of the Vienna Convention on the Law of Treaties (VCLT),[31] any treaty that would be in conflict with *jus cogens* would be null and void. While a state can remain a *persistent objector* in relation to the formation of an emerging norm of customary international law, hence opting out of its legally binding force, this does not apply to *jus cogens* norms, which allow for no objection or derogation. Examples of norms of human rights law that have been recognized as peremptory are the prohibitions against genocide, torture, slavery, and racial discrimination, and the right of all peoples to self-determination.[32]

Universal Acceptance

As explained in the previous section, all states – or at least 99.5 percent of them – have, through their voluntary ratification of human rights treaties, accepted being legally bound by the internationally recognized catalogue of human rights norms. Hence, there is no justification for invoking the sovereignty of a state or the reference to "domestic jurisdiction" in Article 2(7) of the UN Charter to dismiss other states or international human rights bodies from raising issues concerning violations or enjoyment of human rights in a given state.

By ratifying human rights treaties, states have not only accepted the normative code of human rights as a binding legal obligation and as a legitimate basis for international concern. They have also subjected themselves to the international monitoring mechanisms created by the treaties in question. Each of the nine core human rights treaties establishes an obligation to submit periodic state reports to an expert committee created under the respective treaty. These reports are considered by these committees, which then adopt their concluding observations that may include assessments of treaty compliance and recommendations. Additionally, the treaties provide for other more intrusive – but usually optional – monitoring mechanisms, namely on-site inquiries to the country, interstate complaints, and individual complaints. By the end of 2013, not less than 94 percent of all states in the world, ranging from small island states to the United States or Russia, from the Nordic countries to Sub-Saharan states, have accepted at least one of these more intrusive mechanisms, even if traditionally they would have been seen as interfering in the internal affairs of a state.[33]

At the time of the adoption of the Universal Declaration in 1948, the right of an individual to take his or her case – an alleged violation of human rights by the state – to the UN was seen as Utopian.[34] Today, 74 percent of all states in the world have exercised their sovereignty by voluntarily accepting the right of individual complaint under at least one of the nine core treaties.[35]

Compliance and Domestic Implementation

Even if human rights have been transformed from a universal aspiration to universal acceptance, there remain huge problems in actual compliance. International law – even if legally binding upon states – lacks devices for enforcement similar to those available on the domestic level, and, therefore, there is still a fairly widely held perception that states may comply or fail to comply as they see fit, without actual consequences.

Compliance

Louis Henkin famously wrote, "Almost all nations observe almost all principles of international law and almost all of their obligations almost all of the time."[36] While this statement is true, it is also true that violations of human rights are widespread and the international community is struggling to make states accountable for their action or inaction. Social scientists have debated whether the ratification of human rights treaties actually correlates with compliance or whether states ratify human rights treaties to improve their international reputation, this not necessarily translating to better enjoyment of human rights on the ground.[37] For instance, the Soviet Union and its Eastern European allies were quick to ratify major UN human rights treaties in the 1960s and 1970s, apparently without any intention to bring to an end their practices that would be in violation of the same treaties. Notably, their treaty ratifications were not, before 1989, accompanied by the acceptance of the right of individual complaint to the international monitoring bodies.

Despite the universal acceptance of human rights treaties and the recognition of human rights as norms of customary international law, human rights violations do occur in all parts of the world and are often systematic. Major shortcomings of the international monitoring mechanisms for human rights treaties are their underresourcing, lack of visibility, and ineffectiveness. Governments often fail to submit their periodic reports to the respective UN expert committees in a timely manner. Victims of human rights violations may be unaware of the possibility of submitting an individual complaint or may not see these international procedures as providing a meaningful remedy. When a quasi-judicial expert committee makes a finding of noncompliance or violation, there is no guarantee that the state will swiftly proceed with appropriate action. Even if human rights treaties have become universally accepted, compliance control remains underdeveloped.

Domestic implementation

International law consists mainly in obligations of result, in the sense that individual states will have the obligation to see to it that their internal law and practice does not result in violations of internationally defined human rights. In principle, international law does not regulate what forms and procedures should be in place to secure the effective delivery of practical enjoyment of all human rights to all. This is in line with the general approach public international law takes to the issue of the relationship between domestic and international law. Illustrating this approach, the VCLT on the one hand precludes states from invoking their internal law as a justification for failing to perform a treaty (Article 27), and on the other hand leaves the method of domestic implementation to be determined by each state, as long as the treaty is performed "in good faith" (Article 26). Both dualism, that is, a separation between internal law and the international legal obligations of the state, and monism, that is, automatic incorporation of a state's international obligations also into its domestic law, are compatible with international law, and human rights treaties do not require that the constitution of a country, or other statutory law, include exactly the same rights, as long as a state finds a way to secure that its laws and their implementation are compatible with international human rights law.[38]

One consequence of this flexible approach is that while international human rights treaties are accepted as directly applicable (self-executing) in the courts of many countries, this is not the case for all countries or all human rights treaties. In some countries, courts will apply comparable constitutional or other domestic provisions of law, perhaps seeking interpretive guidance from international sources.[39] There may also exist separate domestic bodies, such as a national human rights commission or an ombudsperson, with the authority to take up alleged violations of international human rights law, even if the treaties in question formally speaking are not a part of the law of the land and would not be applied by courts of law.

Even if not required by international law, incorporation of human rights treaties into the domestic legal system either automatically (monism) or through the enactment of treaty-specific incorporation statute has gradually become more and more common and is seen also by international human rights bodies as a recommended "best practice" as it will allow individuals to invoke human rights treaties before national courts.[40]

International Monitoring and Enforcement

Treaty-based mechanisms

Each of the nine core UN human rights treaties establishes an independent expert body (a Committee) that exercises various functions of international monitoring of state compliance with the treaty.[41] Periodic reports by the states parties are a mandatory monitoring mechanism under all nine treaties. These reports are considered through oral hearings before the respective committee with the presence of a government delegation and resulting in a set of concluding observations that address treaty compliance and include recommendations for action. Individual complaints are considered by the same committees and result in a quasi-judicial decision that establishes whether there was a violation of the human rights of the complainant and what remedies should be offered by the state. These complaint procedures are always optional but have gradually been accepted by a clear majority of states. Most treaties also provide for an interstate complaint mechanism that is mandatory under the CERD and optional in other cases. Some of the treaties provide for an inquiry procedure that may entail on-site visits by the respective committee.[42]

A major shortcoming of the UN human rights treaty system is that even if the treaties themselves are legally binding as a matter of international law, there are no explicit provisions on the authority of the findings made by the expert committees established through the treaties. There are good grounds for taking the position that at least when states have not explicitly distanced themselves from an interpretation arrived at by a human rights court or treaty body, its practice is transformed into "subsequent practice in the application of the treaty which establishes the agreement of the parties regarding its interpretation," as expressed in Article 31(3)(b) of the VCLT. Under regional human rights treaties the main political body of the regional intergovernmental organization in question may have the task of securing the effective implementation of the judgments of a regional human rights court,[43] thereby actively transforming the jurisprudence of the court into state practice. Under UN human rights treaties, the General Assembly usually considers the annual reports by the treaty bodies and could, if states so wished, distance itself from the interpretive practice of those treaty bodies. As this has not happened so far, one may conclude that within the UN framework the practice by treaty bodies is transformed into state practice by acquiescence.

Non-treaty-based mechanisms

Besides the treaty bodies under the nine core treaties, the UN human rights system also includes non-treaty mechanisms, sometimes referred to as charter-based mechanisms. They are established by the Human Rights Council that in 2006 replaced the Commission on Human Rights foreseen in Article 68 of the UN Charter. The Human Rights Council itself is a political body composed of diplomatic representatives of forty-seven states elected for a three-year term.[44] The Council undertakes a universal periodic review of the human rights record of all UN member states. In addition it has created a whole range of thematic or country-specific expert mechanisms (special rapporteurs, independent experts, or working groups) that conduct independent fact finding and produce expert reports to the Human Rights Council and in some cases also to the General Assembly.[45]

Remedies and enforcement

When establishing a human rights violation in an individual case, a treaty monitoring body typically also affirms that the victim has a right to an effective remedy and may specify the particulars of the remedy.[46] Unlike, for example, the European human rights system, intergovernmental UN bodies tend not to supervise the implementation of such remedies, even if they would be well placed to do so – the Human Rights Council in the course of its universal periodic review and the General Assembly as the recipient of the annual reports by the treaty bodies. Also, the UN Security Council could have a more systematic role than until now in the execution of findings by expert bodies. In situations of exceptional crisis, the Security Council does resort to its binding powers under Chapter 7 of the Charter also to address human rights issues and the role of human rights in overcoming the crisis.[47]

Limits of Human Rights Law

Despite a focus on fundamental rights of the individual, most human rights are not absolute in the sense that they would not allow any exception or restriction. In particular in the post-9/11 era of heightened attention to the threat posed by international terrorism, reference is often made to the need to strike a proper "balance" between human rights and other pressing social needs, including individual and public security. Human rights law contains several structural and institutional features capable of responding to this need within its own framework, so that the "balance" can be found within the law rather than between the law and something else.

Derogation

Derogation is a notion used for the right of a state to modify its human rights obligations during a publicly proclaimed state of emergency that threatens the ordinary life of the nation. This is the case, for instance, under the ICCPR and the corresponding regional human rights treaties in Europe and the Americas. This reflects the fact that certain civil and political rights are typically subject to derogation during a state of emergency – for instance, freedom of movement, freedom of assembly, freedom of expression, and even the right of access to courts as a dimension of fair trial rights. That said, the right of derogation does not amount to a blanket suspension of these or other rights as it is subject to clear conditions. Derogation is only allowed during a state of emergency and for the duration of the emergency, only within the exigencies of the situation and in compliance with the state's other international obligations – such as international humanitarian law if the emergency constitutes an armed conflict.[48] Most importantly, even those human rights treaties that allow for derogation declare certain human rights as nonderogable, that is, fully operative even during a state of emergency. The category of nonderogable rights includes absolute human rights that are not subject to exception or limitation in any circumstances and constitute peremptory norms of international law (*jus cogens*). The prohibition against torture is a prime example.[49]

Restrictions or permissible limitations

Restrictions or permissible limitations are allowed with respect to most human rights and do not require special circumstances such as a state of emergency. For instance, in the ICCPR the provisions of freedom of movement (Article 12); freedom of conscience, religion, or belief (Article 18); freedom of expression (Article 19); freedom of peaceful assembly (Article 21); and freedom of association (Article 22) all contain an explicit clause that allows for lawful restrictions. The right to privacy (Article 17) is structured differently but belongs to the same category as it prohibits "unlawful" or "arbitrary" interferences, leaving room for lawful and nonarbitrary restrictions. These provisions, and the General Comments issued by the monitoring body, the Human Rights Committee, have given rise to a permissible limitations test comprising the following elements:

1. Any restrictions must be provided by the law;
2. The essence of a human right is not subject to restrictions;
3. Restrictions must be necessary in a democratic society;
4. Any discretion exercised when implementing the restrictions must not be unfettered;
5. For a restriction to be permissible, it is not enough that it serves one of the enumerated legitimate aims; it must be necessary for achieving the legitimate aim;
6. Restrictive measures must conform to the principle of proportionality; they must be appropriate to achieve their protective function; they must be the least intrusive instrument amongst those which might achieve the desired result; and they must be proportionate to the interest to be protected; and
7. Any restrictions must be consistent with the other rights guaranteed in the Covenant.[50]

Both the category of nonderogable rights and the idea that any restrictions must leave unaffected the essential core of any human right indicate that there are aspects of human rights protection that are beyond the sphere of "balancing."[51]

Reservations

Reservations are unilateral statements made by a state when signing or ratifying an international treaty whereby the state purports to exclude or to modify the legal effect of certain provisions of the treaty in their application.[52] Reservations are permitted also under human rights treaties, unless the treaty prohibits them (as is the case for instance in ILO conventions) or it allows only for certain types of reservations (as is the case under the European Convention on Human Rights) or when a reservation would be contrary to the object and purpose of the treaty. The last-mentioned requirement, expressed also in Article 19 of the VCLT, is of course subject to interpretation but may result in a situation in which a state is bound by a human rights treaty beyond its express consent when an impermissible reservation is treated as having no legal effect.[53]

Withdrawal

Withdrawal is a measure through which a state officially declares its intention no longer to be a party to a treaty. According to Article 54 of the VCLT, withdrawal is possible when a treaty provides for it or even otherwise if all other states parties consent. Further, as reflected in

VCLT Article 56, a right to unilateral withdrawal may not always require an express withdrawal provision in the treaty itself but can also be inferred from the temporary nature of the treaty or the intention of the parties that created it. Many human rights treaties contain an explicit withdrawal clause, allowing a state to leave the treaty regime, usually after a certain period of transition. Such withdrawal will not affect the state's obligations under other human rights treaties or under customary international law but will make inoperable the specific treaty in question, including any monitoring mechanisms under it. Importantly, neither of the twin covenants of 1966 contain a withdrawal clause.

When confronted with a purported withdrawal by North Korea in 1997, the Human Rights Committee issued its General Comment No. 26, where it held that as the ICCPR, together with the ICESCR, codify in treaty form the universal human rights enshrined in the UDHR and were not of a "temporary character," no right of unilateral withdrawal could be inferred. Following its earlier practice established during the dissolution of the Soviet Union and former Yugoslavia, the Committee also held that human rights belong to the population and devolve with territory, irrespective of changes in the exercise of state sovereignty.[54] Hence, withdrawal from the covenants of 1966 would not be permissible even with the consent of all other states parties.

Denial of extraterritorial effect

The international protection of human rights grew from the need to transform it into a legitimate matter of international concern how a state treats its own nationals or residents. Against this background it is understandable that, in their opening clauses, some human rights treaties include a reference to "jurisdiction" as a link between the individual and the state, triggering the human rights obligations of the latter.[55] While such clauses need not be read as a territorial limitation to the scope of human rights, some states have nevertheless taken this view and sought to deny the applicability of their human rights treaty obligations when they act outside their own territory with consequences that deny to individuals their effective enjoyment of human rights (for instance, in issues such as detention and treatment of suspected terrorists or the mass surveillance of any electronic communications that cross the borders of the state). Despite such arguments by some states, international human rights bodies have insisted on a universalistic view according to which human rights belong to everyone and are protected everywhere in respect of any state that engages in action that denies or violates them.[56]

Evolution and Reform

International human rights law is a dynamic and evolving field. Even if its substantive norms can be seen to grow out of the trunk provided by the relatively short catalogue enshrined in the 1948 UDHR, new branches (subsequent human rights treaties) continue to grow and to produce new leaves (state practice) and new fruit (international interpretive practice). Because of the open-ended and morality-based language used in many treaty provisions, human rights law is able to respond to new challenges and changes in the world, such as the emergence of new technologies or new types of risks. The downside of this dynamism is that, at times, evolutive interpretation by regional human rights courts or international expert committees may produce outcomes that were not foreseen by the drafters of the original treaty text. Hence, governments may contest the new interpretations arrived at when a treaty is applied in respect of a new issue or in a new context.

In principle, the VCLT provides a framework for resolving such situations of controversy. According to Article 31 of the VCLT, a treaty shall be interpreted in good faith in accordance with the ordinary meaning to be given to the terms of the treaty in their context and in the light of its object and purpose. Subsequent agreements between the same states, as well as any subsequent practice in the application of the treaty that meets the agreement of states, also fall within the "general rule of interpretation," while the preparatory works of a treaty fall under "supplementary means" of interpretation under VCLT Article 32. There is justification for a contextual and holistic approach that may include a teleological dimension by emphasizing the object and purpose of a treaty. Nevertheless, such considerations would not allow for a deviation from the ordinary meaning of the terms of the treaty or from the requirement that subsequent practice in the application of a treaty needs to meet the general agreement of the states parties in order to be authoritative.

In the nearly seven decades since the adoption of the Universal Declaration, several branches have grown on the tree: the Convention on the Status of Refugees[57] in 1951 and the Racial Discrimination Convention and the two covenants in the mid-1960s, more or less already covering the substantive catalogue of the declaration.[58] Between 1979 and 1990, four more of the current nine core treaties were adopted: the Women's Convention, the Convention against Torture, the Convention on the Rights of the Child, and the Convention on Rights of Migrant Workers. And in 2006 the last two were adopted, the Convention against Disappearances and the Convention on the Rights of Persons with Disabilities. Parallel to these developments, a series of optional protocols have been adopted, often to provide existing treaties with new monitoring mechanisms, including individual complaints.

Human rights law primarily focuses on the relationship between the state and an individual. Here, the role of the international community is to transform what previously was seen as a purely domestic matter into an international concern and to make the state accountable at the international level if it violates human rights. As a normative framework for conduct by states, representing a dimension of substantive constitutionalism that is above the will and consent of an individual state, human rights law, however, has also broader implications for the way the international community functions. Human rights law, including through its provisions on economic and social rights or on the duty of international cooperation or on peoples' rights, has much to contribute also in the field of global justice. For instance, in her analysis of applying international human rights law to assess the obligations of a nonterritorial state in the field of international assistance and cooperation, Margot Salomon applies as criteria the parameters of positive extraterritorial obligations, causation, historical responsibility, and capacity.[59]

The process of globalization is characterized by the relative weakening of the nation-state as other actors increasingly operate transnationally, with the capacity to affect the enjoyment of human rights in another part of the world, unhindered by the laws or other protectionist measures of the territorial state. As an understandable consequence, a discourse has emerged about the human rights responsibilities of international organizations, international financial institutions, and transnational corporations.[60] This discourse seeks to overcome the traditional paradigm of human rights merely being vertical norms between the individual and his or her own state. One of the many proposals that have emerged is the establishment of a World Court of Human Rights that would at the same time transform the universal acceptance of human rights by all states into effective compliance control and extend the binding force of human rights law also to actors other than states, provided they voluntarily accept the legally binding jurisdiction of the World Court.[61]

Notes

1 See, Ed Bates, "History," in *International Human Rights Law*, ed. Daniel Moeckli, Sangeeta Shah, and Sandesh Sivakumaran (Oxford: Oxford University Press, 2010).

2 Annemarieke Vermeer-Künzli, "Diplomatic Protection as a Source of Human Rights Law," in *The Oxford Handbook of International Human Rights Law*, ed. Dinah Shelton (Oxford: Oxford University Press, 2013).

3 Péter Kovács, "The Protection of Minorities under the Auspices of the League of Nations," in Shelton, *The Oxford Handbook of International Human Rights Law*.

4 Adopted by General Assembly Resolution 217 A(III) of 10 December 1948.

5 United Nations Charter, 1 United Nations Treaty Series, xiv. See, also Article 55(c) in Chap. 9 on international cooperation, according to which the UN shall promote "universal respect for, and observance of, human rights and fundamental freedoms for all without distinction as to race, sex, language, or religion."

6 James W. Nickel and David A Reidy, "Philosophy," in Moeckli, Shah, and Sivakumaran, *International Human Rights Law*; Heiner Bielefeldt, "Philosophical and Historical Foundations of Human Rights," in *International Protection of Human Rights: A Textbook*, eds. Caterina Krause and Martin Scheinin (Turku: Åbo Akademi University Institute for Human Rights, 2012); M. Christian Green and John Witte, Jr., "Religion," in Shelton, *The Oxford Handbook of International Human Rights Law*; Paul Gordon Lauren, "The Foundations of Justice and Human Rights in Early Legal Texts and Thought," in Shelton, *The Oxford Handbook of International Human Rights Law*; and Siegfried van Duffel, "Moral Philosophy," in Shelton, *The Oxford Handbook of International Human Rights Law*.

7 Michael O'Boyle and Michelle Lafferty, "General Principles and Constitutions as Sources of Human Rights Law," in Shelton, *The Oxford Handbook of International Human Rights Law*.

8 For an article-by-article commentary of the Universal Declaration, see Gudmundur Alfredsson and Asbjørn Eide, eds., *The Universal Declaration of Human Rights: A Common Standard of Achievement* (The Hague: Kluwer, 1999).

9 The Statute of the International Court of Justice is a part of the UN Charter, see n 5.

10 See Christine Chinkin, "Sources," in Moeckli, Shah, and Sivakumaran, *International Human Rights Law*.

11 For a wide variety of comparative studies on domestic constitutional protections for a range of fundamental rights, see, Mark Tushnet, Thomas Fleiner, and Cheryl Saunders, eds., *Routledge Handbook of Constitutional Law* (London and New York: Routledge, 2013)

12 For instance, the Slavery Convention of 1926 (60 League of Nations Treaty Series 253), and the Forced Labour Convention of 1930 (ILO Convention No. 29).

13 660 United Nations Treaty Series (UNTS) 195.

14 993 UNTS 3.

15 999 UNTS 171.

16 The United Nations Office of the High Commissioner for Human Rights maintains a list of universal human rights instruments: http://www.ohchr.org/EN/ProfessionalInterest/Pages/UniversalHumanRightsInstruments.aspx. In addition to non-treaty instruments (such as the UDHR) and the nine core treaties listed below (with their optional protocols), the list includes ten ILO conventions, the UNESCO Convention against Discrimination in Education, conventions and protocols in international humanitarian law, the Statute of the International Criminal Court, and ten other United Nations treaties that address human rights issues, ranging from slavery, trafficking, and the prostitution of others to refugees and stateless persons, and from marriage to genocide.

17 1249 UNTS 13.

18 1465 UNTS 85.

19 1577 UNTS 3.

20 2220 UNTS 3.

21 2715 UNTS, UN doc. A/61/448.

22 2515 UNTS 3.

23 For the texts of the treaties and their optional protocols, see http://www.ohchr.org/EN/ProfessionalInterest/Pages/CoreInstruments.aspx.

24 General Assembly Official Records, 183rd plenary meeting, 10 December 1948, p. 933.

25 In most cases, the acceptance of the UDHR catalogue has been undertaken by ratifying the twin covenants of 1966. A number of states are not a party to one or both of the covenants but have nevertheless ratified other human rights treaties, including the Convention of the Rights of the Child, which on its own covers the scope of the UDHR and signifies the acceptance of the full normative catalogue of human rights, even if the treaty only applies to the benefit of persons under eighteen years of age, often constituting half of the population.

26 However, even the United States has signed the ICESCR. Further, through its ratification of the CERD it has indirectly endorsed the UDHR catalogue of human rights, as Article 5 of the CERD includes a list of human rights in the enjoyment of which a ratifying state undertakes to eliminate racial discrimination "and to guarantee the right of everyone, without distinction as to race, colour, or national or ethnic origin, to equality before the law, notably in the enjoyment of the following rights." The list includes a fairly comprehensive enumeration of economic, social and cultural rights, including the right to housing, the right to public health and the right to social security.

27 The discussion in the text relates to 195 of the 196 states in the world, including three states that are not members of the United Nations (Cook Islands, the Holy See, and Niue). It does not include the newest UN member state, South Sudan. As of 27 November 2013, the official United Nations Treaty Collection (treaties.un.org) did not contain any record of human rights treaties ratified or acceded to by South Sudan. That said, the doctrine of continuity of obligations would apply, to the effect that the population would continue to enjoy the human rights enshrined in the human rights treaties ratified by Sudan prior to the secession by South Sudan, including both of the covenants of 1966 and the CRC.

28 See Chinkin, "Sources," 110–114.

29 See, *Filartiga v. Pena-Irala*, United States Court of Appeals, Second Circuit, 630 F2d 876 (1980), where it was held that the prohibition against torture was a customary norm of international law (at 882) and the view that the UDHR had become customary law *in toto* was attributed to "several commentators" (at 883).

30 The prohibition against torture can be referred to as an example. While this prohibition represents a norm of customary international law, there may nevertheless be instances of torture actually taking place in many countries. When states proclaim their adherence to the norm and deny the factual allegations of torture nevertheless occurring, this may strengthen rather than weaken the customary law nature of the prohibition.

31 1155 UNTS 331.

32 See, Chinkin "Sources," 113; and Erika de Wet, "Jus Cogens and Obligations Erga Omnes," in Shelton, *The Oxford Handbook of International Human Rights Law*.

33 The list of states that so far have not accepted any of the "intrusive" mechanisms is as follows: Bhutan, Brunei Darussalam, Kiribati, Malaysia, Marshall Islands, Niue, Palau, Sao Tome and Principe, Samoa, Singapore, and Tuvalu (eleven states in addition to South Sudan, discussed in n 27).

34 However, it is worth noting that already in 1948 Australia made a proposal about the establishment of an International Court of Human Rights, see UN document E/CN.4/AC.1/27.

35 In most cases (114 states) the right of complaint is accepted under the Covenant on Civil and Political Rights, i.e., in the sphere of traditional civil and political rights. Another thirty states that have not ratified the Optional Protocol to the ICCPR, creating that complaint avenue, have nevertheless accepted the right of international complaint under at least one other treaty, namely the Convention for the Elimination of Discrimination Against Women (twenty additional states), the CRPD (sixteen states), the Convention Against Torture (four states), or CERD (three states). Further, thirty-nine additional states have accepted at least one of the other "intrusive" mechanisms (on-site inquiries or interstate complaints), in most cases because the interstate complaint mechanism is mandatory under Article 11 of the CERD.

36 Louis Henkin, *How Nations Behave* (New York: Columbia University Press 1979), 47.

37 Participants in the debate include Oona Hathaway and Beth Simmons, and a brief account can be found in Samuel Moyn, "Do Human Rights Treaties Make Enough of a Difference?" in *The Cambridge Companion to Human Rights Law*, ed. Conor Gearty and Costas Douzinas (Cambridge: Cambridge University Press, 2012).

38 See, Andrew Byrnes and Catherine Renshaw, "Within the State," in Moeckli, Shah, and Sivakumaran, *International Human Rights Law*; Ineke Boerefijn, "International Human Rights in National Law," in Krause and Scheinin, *International Protection of Human Rights*; and Nisuke Ando, "National Implementation and Interpretation," in Shelton, *The Oxford Handbook of International Human Rights Law*.

39 The United States Supreme Court case *Lawrence v. Texas* 539 U.S. 558 (2003) demonstrates that such interpretive references to human rights treaties may relate to treaties not even ratified by the state in question.

40 In its General Comment No. 31 (2004) the Human Rights Committee expressed this position in the following terms: "Article 2, paragraph 2, requires that States Parties take the necessary steps to give effect to the Covenant rights in the domestic order. It follows that, unless Covenant rights are already protected by their domestic laws or practices, States Parties are required on ratification to make such changes to domestic laws and practices as are necessary to ensure their conformity with the Covenant. Where there are inconsistencies between domestic law and the Covenant, article 2 requires that the domestic law or practice be changed to meet the standards imposed by the Covenant's substantive guarantees. Article 2 allows a State Party to pursue this in accordance with its own domestic constitutional structure and accordingly does not require that the Covenant be directly applicable in the courts, by incorporation of the Covenant into national law. The Committee takes the view, however, that Covenant guarantees may receive enhanced protection in those States where the Covenant is automatically or through specific incorporation part of the domestic legal order. The Committee invites those States Parties in which the Covenant does not form part of the domestic legal order to consider incorporation of the Covenant to render it part of domestic law to facilitate full realization of Covenant rights as required by article 2." (para 13).

41 The Convention Against Torture has two separate expert bodies, as the Committee Against Torture exercises the usual monitoring functions of, e.g., periodic state reporting and individual complaints, while another body, the Subcommittee on Prevention, is in charge of visiting countries and places of detention.

42 See, Martin Scheinin, "International Mechanisms and Procedures for Monitoring," in Krause and Scheinin, *International Protection of Human Rights*. The volume edited by Gudmundur Alfredsson, Grimhemed, B.G. Ramcharan, and A. De Zayas, eds., *International Human Rights Monitoring Mechanisms: Essays in Honour of Jakob Th. Möller* (Leiden: Martinus Nijhoff, 2009), includes ten chapters on the functioning of the treaty bodies.

43 See, in particular, Article 46 of the European Convention on Human Rights, as amended by Protocols 11 and 14 (Council of Europe Treaty Series 194): "1. The High Contracting Parties undertake to abide by the final judgment of the Court in any case to which they are parties. 2. The final judgment of the Court shall be transmitted to the Committee of Ministers, which shall supervise its execution."

44 See, General Assembly Resolution establishing the Human Rights Council, A/RES/60/251 (2006), para 7.

45 See, Markus Schmidt, "United Nations," in Moeckli, Shah, and Sivakumaran, *International Human Rights Law*, as well as several chapters on the special procedures in Alfredsson, Grimhemed, Ramcharan, and De Zayas, *International Human Rights Monitoring Mechanisms*.

46 See, Martin Scheinin, "The Human Rights Committee's Pronouncements on the Right to an Effective Remedy: An Illustration of the Legal Nature of the Committee's Work under the Optional Protocol," in *Towards Implementing Universal Human Rights: Festschrift for the Twenty-Fifth Anniversary of the Human Rights Committee*, ed. Nisuke Ando (Leiden: Brill, 2004).

47 See, Jan Klabbers, "The Security Council and Human Rights," in Alfredsson, Grimhemed, Ramcharan, and De Zayas, *International Human Rights Monitoring Mechanisms: Essays in Honour of*

Jakob Th. Möller. For a recent example of references by the Security Council to human rights in a Chapter 7 resolution, see S/RES/2127 (2013), Situation in the Central African Republic, preamble and operative paragraphs 12, 14, 17, 18, 21, 24, 26, 27, 33, and 56.

48 These conditions are spelled out in Article 4 of the ICCPR, which also includes a prohibition against discrimination through derogation and a double procedural requirement of public declaration and international notification of the state of emergency.

49 The list of nonderogable rights in Article 4(2) of the ICCPR includes: Article 6 (right to life); Article 7 (prohibition of torture or cruel, inhuman, or degrading punishment, or of medical or scientific experimentation without consent); Article 8, paragraphs 1 and 2 (prohibition of slavery, slave trade, and servitude); Article 11 (prohibition of imprisonment because of inability to fulfil a contractual obligation); Article 15 (the principle of legality in the field of criminal law, i.e., the requirement of both criminal liability and punishment being limited to clear and precise provisions in the law that was in place and applicable at the time the act or omission took place, except in cases where a later law imposes a lighter penalty); Article 16 (the recognition of everyone as a person before the law); and Article 18 (freedom of thought, conscience, and religion). This list has been further elaborated on in General Comment No. 29 (2001) by the respective monitoring body, the Human Rights Committee. According to the General Comment, rights that as such are derogable, may contain elements that are nonderogable, for instance, when they provide essential procedural guarantees for other nonderogable rights or when they reflect other international obligations that are not subject to derogation.

50 This formulation of the permissible limitations test was crafted by the Special Rapporteur on human rights and counter-terrorism in the context of the right to privacy. See, Report of the Special Rapporteur on the promotion and protection of human rights and fundamental freedoms while countering terrorism, Martin Scheinin (A/HRC/13/37, December 2009), para 12. See, also, General Comments No. 27 (freedom of movement) and No. 34 (freedom of expression) by the Human Rights Committee. The Special Rapporteur on freedom of expression has applied the same test in respect of freedom of expression, see Report of the Special Rapporteur on the promotion and protection of the right to freedom of opinion and expression, Frank La Rue (A/HRC/23/40, April 2013), para 29.

51 See Martin Scheinin, "Core Rights and Obligations," in Shelton, *The Oxford Handbook of International Human Rights Law*.

52 For a definition, see, VCLT Article 2(1)(d).

53 The consequences of impermissible reservations have given rise to some controversy. In 1988, the European Court of Human Rights held in the *Belilos* case that a reservation by Switzerland constituted a prohibited "general reservation" and was without legal effect. In 1994, the Human Rights Committee adopted its General Comment No. 24 where it affirmed that reservations that would be contrary to the object and purpose of the ICCPR would "generally" be severable, i.e., that a state would be considered a party to the covenant without the benefit of its impermissible reservations. Although differing views were expressed in the literature (see, Ineta Ziemele, ed., *Reservations to Human Rights Treaties and the Vienna Convention Regime: Conflict, Harmony or Reconciliation* (Leiden: Brill, 2004)), the International Law Commission that had itself drafted the VCLT ultimately affirmed the position taken by the European Court and the UN Committee. See, Guide to Practice on Reservations (2011), in particular paragraphs 3.2, 4.5.1, and 4.5.3.2.

54 Human Rights Committee, General Comment No. 26 (continuity of obligations), 1997, paras 3–5.

55 Notably, article 2(1) of the ICCPR reads: "Each State Party to the present Covenant undertakes to respect and to ensure to all individuals within its territory and subject to its jurisdiction the rights recognized in the present Covenant, without distinction of any kind, such as race, colour, sex, language, religion, political or other opinion, national or social origin, property, birth or other status."

56 In its early Uruguayan cases, the Human Rights Committee took this position in respect of abductions and other human rights violations committed by Uruguayan agents on foreign soil. According to the Committee, the reference to "jurisdiction" was "not to the place where the violation occurred, but rather to the relationship between the individual and the State in relation to a violation of any of the rights set forth in the Covenant, wherever they occurred" (*Lopez Burgos v. Uruguay*, Communication 52/1979). In a subsequent General Comment No. 31, the Committee in 2004

paraphrased ICCPR Article 2(1) as follows: "10. States Parties are required by article 2, paragraph 1, to respect and to ensure the Covenant rights to all persons who may be within their territory and to all persons subject to their jurisdiction." (CCPR/C/21/Rev.1/Add. 13)

57 189 UNTS 137.

58 The right to property constitutes an exception, as it fell victim of the political controversies that resulted in splitting the human rights catalogue into two covenants. At universal level, the right to property is mainly protected through the provisions on nondiscrimination and fair trial. The 1951 Convention on the Status of Refugees is not counted as a "core human rights treaty" and it does not establish an independent expert body for the monitoring of state compliance. As it nevertheless more closely than any of the subsequent core treaties still today covers Article 14 of the Universal Declaration (the right to seek and enjoy asylum), it should be seen as an early phase in the process of codifying the declaration into human rights treaties.

59 Margot E. Salomon, "Deprivation, Causation and the Law of International Cooperation," in *Global Justice, State Duties: The Extraterritorial Scope of Economic, Social and Cultural Rights in International Law*, ed. Malcolm Langford et al. (Cambridge: Cambridge University Press 2013), 278–288.

60 The best-known framework for the aspiration to promote human rights responsibilities of corporations is provided by the so-called Ruggie Principles, see Guiding Principles on Business and Human Rights: Implementing the United Nations "Protect, Respect and Remedy" Framework (2011).

61 Julia Kozma, Manfred Nowak, and Martin Scheinin, *A World Court of Human Rights: Consolidated Statute and Commentary* (Wien: Neuer Wissenschaftlicher Verlag, 2010).

References

Alfredsson, Gudmundur, and Asbjørn Eide, eds. *The Universal Declaration of Human Rights: A Common Standard of Achievement*. The Hague: Kluwer, 1999.

Alfredsson, Gudmundur, J. Grimhemed, B.G. Ramcharan, and A. De Zayas, eds. *International Human Rights Monitoring Mechanisms: Essays in Honour of Jakob Th. Möller*. Leiden: Martinus Nijhoff, 2009.

Ando, Nisuke. "National Implementation and Interpretation." In Shelton, *The Oxford Handbook of International Human Rights Law*, 698–718.

Bates, Ed. "History." In Moeckli Shah, and Sivakumaran, *International Human Rights Law*, 17–38.

Bielefeldt, Heiner. "Philosophical and Historical Foundations of Human Rights." In Krause and Scheinin, *International Protection of Human Rights*, 3–18.

Boerefijn, Ineke. "International Human Rights in National Law." In Krause and Scheinin, *International Protection of Human Rights*, 631–656.

Byrnes, Andrew, and Catherine Renshaw. "Within the State." In Moeckli, Shah, and Sivakumaran *International Human Rights Law*, 498–517.

Chinkin, Christine. "Sources." In Moeckli Shah, and Sivakumaran, *International Human Rights Law*, 103–123.

de Wet, Erika. "Jus Cogens and Obligations Erga Omnes" In Shelton, *The Oxford Handbook of International Human Rights Law*, 541–561.

Green, M. Christian, and John Witte Jr. "Religion." In Shelton, *The Oxford Handbook of International Human Rights Law*, 9–31.

Henkin, Louis. *How Nations Behave*. New York: Columbia University Press 1979.

Klabbers, Jan. "The Security Council and Human Rights." In Alfredsson, Grimhemed, Ramcharan, and De Zayas, *International Human Rights Monitoring Mechanisms: Essays in Honour of Jakob Th. Möller*, 241–247.

Kovács, Péter. "The Protection of Minorities under the Auspices of the League of Nations." In Shelton, *The Oxford Handbook of International Human Rights Law*, 325–341.

Kozma, Julia, Manfred Nowak, and Martin Scheinin. *A World Court of Human Rights: Consolidated Statute and Commentary*. Wien: Neuer Wissenschaftlicher Verlag, 2010.

Krause, Catarina, and Martin Scheinin, eds. *International Protection of Human Rights: A Textbook*. Turku: Åbo Akademi University Institute for Human Rights, 2012.

Lauren, Paul Gordon. "The Foundations of Justice and Human Rights in Early Legal Texts and Thought." In Shelton, *The Oxford Handbook of International Human Rights Law*, 163–193.

Moeckli, Daniel, Sangeeta Shah, and Sandesh Sivakumaran, eds. *International Human Rights Law*. Oxford: Oxford University Press, 2010.

Moyn, Samuel. "Do Human Rights Treaties Make Enough of a Difference?" In *The Cambridge Companion to Human Rights Law*, edited by Conor Gearty and Costas Douzinas, 329–347. Cambridge: Cambridge University Press, 2012.

Nickel, James W., and David A Reidy. "Philosophy." In Moeckli Shah, and Sivakumaran, *International Human Rights Law*, 39–63.

O'Boyle, Michael, and Michelle Lafferty. "General Principles and Constitutions as Sources of Human Rights Law." In Shelton, *The Oxford Handbook of International Human Rights Law*, 194–221.

Salomon, Margot E. "Deprivation, Causation and the Law of International Cooperation." In *Global Justice, State Duties: The Extraterritorial Scope of Economic, Social and Cultural Rights in International Law*, edited by Malcolm Langford, Wouter Vandenhole, Martin Scheinin, and Willem van Genugten, 259–296. Cambridge: Cambridge University Press, 2013.

Scheinin, Martin. "The Human Rights Committee's Pronouncements on the Right to an Effective Remedy: An Illustration of the Legal Nature of the Committee's Work under the Optional Protocol." In *Towards Implementing Universal Human Rights: Festschrift for the Twenty-Fifth Anniversary of the Human Rights Committee*, edited by Nisuke Ando, 101–115. Leiden: Brill, 2004.

Scheinin, Martin. "International Mechanisms and Procedures for Monitoring." In Krause and Scheinin, *International Protection of Human Rights*, 657–677.

Scheinin, Martin. "Core Rights and Obligations." In Shelton, *The Oxford Handbook of International Human Rights Law*, 527–540.

Schmidt, Markus. "United Nations." In Moeckli, Shah, and Sivakumaran, *International Human Rights Law*, 391–432.

Shelton, Dinah, ed. *The Oxford Handbook of International Human Rights Law*. Oxford: Oxford University Press, 2013.

Tushnet, Mark, Thomas Fleiner, and Cheryl Saunders, eds. *Routledge Handbook of Constitutional Law*. London: Routledge, 2013.

van Duffel, Siegfried. "Moral Philosophy." In Shelton, *The Oxford Handbook of International Human Rights Law*, 32–53.

Vermeer-Künzli, Annemarieke. "Diplomatic Protection as a Source of Human Rights Law." In Shelton, *The Oxford Handbook of International Human Rights Law*, 194–221.

Ziemele, Ineta, ed. *Reservations to Human Rights Treaties and the Vienna Convention Regime: Conflict, Harmony or Reconciliation*. Leiden: Brill, 2004.

30

The European Union and Human Rights

Sionaidh Douglas-Scott

Introduction

Human rights have occupied a variety of roles in the course of history of the European Union. They played a negligible role at the outset, overlooked by the original Treaty of Rome and, even today, the Union's formidable associations with free trade, the single market, and regulation might suggest that it cannot be primarily defined as a human rights organization. Yet no organization would ever openly reject or ignore the crucial role of human rights in the contemporary consciousness (not least the European Union, with its roots in postwar attempts to forge peace among nations previously guilty of the greatest atrocities). Events such as the extraordinary rendition of terrorist suspects by the United States via EU member state territory, the mass relocation from France of Roma in 2010, or declining media freedom in Hungary[1] illustrate the ongoing need for vigilance. How then should the European Union seek to ensure respect for human rights at a time when economic crisis, or terrorist threat, are sometimes offered as reasons for their diminution or sidelining?

Since the Lisbon Treaty came into force on 1 December 2009, the European Union has introduced, or enhanced, provisions that should strengthen the protection of fundamental rights. The Charter of Fundamental Rights of the European Union has at last acquired binding force, provision is made for the European Union to accede to the European Convention on Human Rights (ECHR), and the Court of Justice of the European Union (CJEU) is to have greater powers of judicial review in the field of police and judicial cooperation in criminal law[2] – an area of obvious relevance to human rights.

Article 2 of the Treaty on European Union (TEU), as amended, insists that "respect for human rights" is one of the values on which the European Union is founded, including a new reference to "the rights of persons belonging to minorities." Moreover, the Union has also sought to incorporate "the protection of human rights as part of a broader effort to improve governance."[3] In 2010, the European Commission adopted a strategy for the effective implementation of the Charter of Fundamental Rights that seeks

A Companion to European Union Law and International Law, First Edition.
Edited by Dennis Patterson and Anna Södersten.

> to promote a "fundamental rights culture" at all stages of the procedure, from the initial drafting of a proposal within the Commission to the impact analysis, and right up to the checks on the legality of the final text.[4]

In June 2012, the European Union adopted a Strategic Framework and Action Plan on human rights and democracy, as mandated by the Lisbon Treaty, and, at the same time announced an EU special representative for human rights. Such initiatives are intended to ensure that, in the words of former EU High Representative Baroness Ashton, human rights are to be a "silver thread" in every area of EU activity.

A brief note of clarification is necessary here. The European Union has a Charter of *Fundamental* Rights: Article 6(3) TEU makes reference to *fundamental* rights as general principles of law (and the Court uses this term in its jurisprudence) whereas Article 2 TEU refers to "respect for *human* rights," which is also the term used in most bills of rights and international treaties. This difference in terminology can be confusing. It is suggested here that the distinction is not highly significant but that "fundamental" rights in the context of EU law tend to be those which have legal protection in constitutions or treaties whereas "human" rights denote a broader category of rights generally viewed as embodying widely shared values and deserving respect regardless of whether they are given legal protection. While these distinctions are not watertight, this is the usage that will be followed in this chapter.

It should also be noted that fundamental rights protection in contemporary Europe is complex. There are at least three possible judicial avenues for European residents to assert their human rights.[5] First, they may apply in their national courts for enforcement of their rights as protected by national law, for example, under the UK Human Rights Act or the German Basic Law. Second, if this fails, once they have exhausted domestic remedies, they may proceed in the European Court of Human Rights (ECtHR) in Strasbourg. Third, if the matter is one that falls within the competence of the European Union, they may have a claim under EU law, either in their national courts, in the CJEU, or both.

So, from this perspective it might appear that there exists not a lack but possibly a *surfeit* of human rights protection within the European legal space. Is the additional, EU level, necessary? Does it add any value to existing fundamental rights protection, and is it coherent? A pertinent question might be whether fundamental rights are indeed "lost in complexity" in the European Union.[6]

The Growth of Fundamental Rights in the European Union

It has taken over sixty years to produce the current level of protection of fundamental rights within Western European integration. The fact that fundamental rights were not a pressing concern in the early European Economic Community (EEC) may be gleaned from the very little space allotted to this subject in earlier textbooks.[7] The EEC Treaty started out as an economic treaty, of limited ambitions, with the aim of creating a common market. It was originally modest in nature, in part no doubt because of the failure of the draft Political and Defense Union Treaties[8] owing to the refusal of General de Gaulle to countenance perceived attacks on French national sovereignty. There were no sections on fundamental rights or citizenship because the EEC founders did not think this relevant to a treaty with mainly economic aspirations. The European Convention on Fundamental Rights was also, of course, already in existence and probably thought sufficient to operate as a "Bill of Rights" for Europe. The scope of the EU treaties, has, however, come to extend far beyond purely economic matters – as some of the EEC's founders intended.[9]

EU law today covers many fields capable of having a human rights dimension. Cases have been heard by the CJEU concerning the freedom of expression (*Connolly*), the right to property (*Bosphorus*), equal treatment of transsexuals (*Grant*), and, most recently, economic sanctions on possible terrorist activities (*Kadi I* and *Kadi II*),[10] and the issue of whether one has a right to be forgotten online (*Google Spain*).[11] The ever-expanding competence of the European Union into areas traditionally within the remit of state sovereignty has ensured that the issue of the breach of fundamental rights by the Union is not merely a theoretical possibility. However, in spite of this, the European Union only proclaimed its own Charter of Fundamental Rights in December 2000. The Union also continues to lack a general legislative competence in the field of human rights.[12]

The most important references are the following:

Article 6 TEU, as amended by the Lisbon Treaty, is a necessary starting point. The first paragraph stipulates that the European Union's Charter of Fundamental Rights shall have the same legal force as the Treaties themselves. It also stipulates that the Charter shall not extend any of the Union's competences.

Article 6(2) requires the European Union to accede to the ECHR – a task of considerable legal complexity.

Article 6(3) also confirms that the ECHR and the protection of fundamental rights under the constitutional traditions of the member states shall continue to constitute general principles of EU law (which the CJEU cites as a form of legal authority in its rulings).

Article 2 TEU, furthermore, stipulates that "[t]he Union is founded on the values of respect for human dignity, freedom, democracy, equality, the rule of law and respect for human rights, including the rights of persons belonging to minorities."

Article 7 TEU backs up these provisions with a sanctions procedure, whereby a member state's rights may be suspended "if there is a clear risk of a serious breach by a Member State of the values referred to in Article 2."[13]

These are the general references to human rights. Previous attempts have also been made by the political institutions of the European Union to improve the protection of fundamental rights. But, although numerous, they were not legally binding, amounting to little more than declarations of intent from the institutions concerned.

The EU Charter of Fundamental Rights

Owing to the amendments to Article 6 TEU introduced by Lisbon, the charter now constitutes the first point of reference for fundamental rights norms in EU law, as a binding document rather than as a source of inspiration.[14] The charter is a freestanding document – it has not been incorporated into the treaties. The transformation of the charter into a legally binding document with primary law status, and the extension of the Court's jurisdiction in areas such as asylum, immigration, and criminal matters, has already increased the Court's profile in the fundamental rights field, and this chapter will pay especial attention to the role of the Court and to its recent jurisprudence.

The charter was originally drafted by a body referred to as "The Convention," composed of sixty-two members (made up of representatives of heads of state and government, national parliaments, the European Parliament, and the Commission). The name of this body was deliberately significant, given that "Convention" was the term used by those delegates who gathered in Philadelphia to draft the American Constitution. The less evocatively titled Intergovernmental Conference is the body that is used to bring about significant changes in EU law; its name has altogether a different sort of resonance, that of international law, in which sovereign states negotiate through their representatives. The term "convention" makes the EU Charter sound more like a constitutional initiative, and that may partly explain why the charter failed to be integrated into the EU treaties. After the failure of the draft EU constitution (which did incorporate the charter) it was seen as necessary to avoid the appearance of a formal EU constitution.

The Content of the Charter

The fifty rights in the charter are set out in six chapters, with the headings Dignity, Freedoms, Equality, Solidarity, Citizens' Rights, and Justice. Each of the charter's fifty rights are taken from a "precursor" text, such as the ECHR, the European Social Charter, the Community Charter of Social Rights of Workers, common constitutional traditions, rulings of the CJEU and ECtHR, as well as international conventions of the Council of Europe, the United Nations (UN), and the International Labour Organization. Some of the rights are specifically introduced to deal with contemporary problems, such as protection of personal data, given the proliferation of information about persons in the more barrier-free Europe,[15] or new innovations in bioethics.[16] Other provisions are innovative in providing general protection across the European Union where only partial protection previously existed – for example, Article 50 provides a *ne bis in idem* (or double jeopardy) protection across the whole Union rather than merely within state borders (as is the case under Article 4 Protocol 7 ECHR).

The charter is also innovative in containing, in the same instrument, both economic and social rights along with the more traditional civil and political rights, which has never been done before in an international human rights instrument. In this way the charter presents in sharpest relief the *indivisibility* of human rights. This also counters the views of those who believe that economic and social rights are of a singular nature and difficult to incorporate into human rights documents because of the positive action they require of governments.[17]

The Emerging Case Law

The CJEU began to refer to the charter even before the Lisbon Treaty elevated the status of the document to that of primary law. For example, in *BECTU v. Secretary of State for Trade and Industry*, Advocate General Tizzano spoke of the charter as a "substantive point of reference."[18] That being said, it was six years before the CJEU itself, as opposed to its Advocates General or the Court of First Instance (as it then was), even referred to the charter at all – it first being mentioned in *Parliament v. Council* and, even then, merely as a document reaffirming fundamental rights "as they result, in particular, from the constitutional traditions … of the Member States."[19]

Now that the charter is binding, numerous cases are beginning to emerge in which it has been successfully invoked, illustrating the practical ability of a legally binding charter to stimulate the use of fundamental rights arguments. For example, in *N.S. and M.E.* the CJEU stressed the right of asylum seekers to protection from inhuman or degrading treatment, when clarifying EU rules for determining which country should deal with an asylum application.[20] In 2011, the Court ruled in *Test-Achats*[21] that different motor insurance premiums for men and women constituted sex discrimination, and in 2010, in *Volker Schecke*, that the obligation to publish personal data of natural persons who were beneficiaries of EU agricultural funds infringed Articles 7 and 8 of the charter.[22] In *Digital Rights Ireland*,[23] the Court held that the EU legislature had exceeded the limits of the proportionality principle in relation to Articles 7, 8, and 52(1) of the charter by adopting the Data Retention Directive, for the first time declaring not merely individual provisions but an entire legal instrument invalid with immediate effect for violating charter rights. Cases such as *Tests-Achats*, *Schecke*, and *Digital Rights Ireland*, in which the Court took the extremely rare step of annulling EU legislative acts for violating fundamental rights, reveal the potential of the charter to increase the invasiveness of review of EU measures. Much will depend, however, upon any margin of discretion accorded to the EU decision maker which has, in numerous instances, been more generous than that granted to the member states.[24]

The Legal Effect and Scope of the Charter: Applicability, Protocol 30, and Horizontality

Given the effect of Article 6 TEU, the charter now holds the same value as the treaties. Article 6 also stresses that the charter shall not extend any of the European Union's competences[25] – an important proviso, given that the charter includes many rights that concern areas over which the European Union has little or no competence, such as the right to marry and found a family. The charter is not an instrument of limitless general review – Article 51(1) of the charter specifies that it is "addressed to the institutions … of the Union … and to the Member States only when they are implementing Union law." This, in turn, raises the question of what exactly is covered by member states in the act of implementing EU law. A narrow understanding of the phrase "implementing Union law" was suggested by Advocate General Cruz Villalón in *Fransson*,[26] who argued that

> [t]he mere fact that such an exercise of public authority has its ultimate origin in Union law is not of itself sufficient for a finding that there is a situation involving the implementation of Union law.

However, the CJEU[27] decided the issue differently. It ignored the advocate general's argument requiring a specific EU interest and instead repeated its former case law, requiring domestic acts to comply with EU law when they fall within the scope of EU law. *Fransson* has not been universally welcomed, given that it apparently enables EU fundamental rights to apply in a potentially wide range of cases that appear to go beyond the literal wording of Article 51. However, the CJEU's reading accords better with the charter's accompanying explanatory document, which indicates that the charter is "binding on Member States when they act *in the scope* of Union law."[28] This phraseology is certainly broader than that of "implementing" EU law, and would suggest that the charter applies even when member states derogate from EU law. The explanations of the Charter of Fundamental Rights are not legally binding but they are certainly aids to interpretation, and so the disparity of this phraseology could have legal effects. As such, it seems probable that the charter applies to national derogations from EU law but, in the event that it does not, the CJEU will in any case apply the general principles of EU law (as will be discussed), which include respect for fundamental rights.

Article 51(1) also raises salient issues for the European Commission when it is presented with parliamentary questions, petitions, and complaints on issues of fundamental rights in the member states. In such cases, the Commission has tended to apply Article 51(1) cautiously and restrictively, rejecting most such issues as falling outside the scope of EU law.[29] Ultimately, surely the key question across all of these instances is whether there exists a sufficiently specific link between the national act at issue and the concrete norm of EU law applied,[30] an approach which is also in line with the principle of nonexpansion of EU competences by the charter.

There are also some other questions regarding the scope of the charter. Beyond the issue of member state liability there is that of *which* EU and member state bodies are covered by the charter. Regarding member states, there is the question of how to define public authorities. It is suggested that the existing direct effect case law of the CJEU might be applied in this area.[31] Related issues apply in the EU context – in particular the charter's application, not only to formal EU institutions but also to entities established within the framework of the EU context. For instance, the Directorate General for Internal Policies has identified Europol's activities in combating crime, irregular migration, and processing personal data as putting into question aspects of the charter.[32]

A further matter concerning the charter's scope is that of the so-called opt-out for the United Kingdom and Poland created under Protocol 30.[33] Article 1(1) of the protocol stipulates that the charter does not extend the ability of UK and Polish courts (nor the CJEU itself) to find that national laws or provisions are inconsistent with the charter. Article 1(2) states that

> for the avoidance of doubt, nothing in Title IV of the Charter creates justiciable rights … except in so far as Poland and the United Kingdom has provided for such rights in its national law.

Title IV concerns various solidarity rights such as collective action (Article 28) and healthcare (Article 35).

However, it is doubtful that Protocol 30 can function as any substantive opt-out. Indeed, Advocate General Trstenjak rejected such an argument,[34] regarding Article 1(1) of the protocol, as interpreted with its recitals, as simply reaffirming that the Charter "does not have the effect of either shifting powers at the expense of the United Kingdom or Poland or of extending the field of application of EU law."[35] However, even if Protocol 30 did successfully exclude the operation of Title IV in Poland and the United Kingdom, EU general principles of law, under Article 6(3) TEU, might fill that gap. Given that most of the rights in Title IV are already recognized as general principles, an exclusionary effect created by Protocol 30 would be irrelevant – such rights would be applied as general principles.

A final matter of concern is the issue of horizontality: whether the charter can have horizontal direct effect, applying in disputes between private parties, or whether there must be a vertical, state element involved.[36] It is unusual for international human rights documents to bind individuals, although the issue of *drittwirkung* (third-party effect) is complex. Certainly, there are articles within the charter that strongly suggest horizontal direct effect. For example, Article 23 speaks of ensuring equality between men and women "in *all* areas." Likewise, Article 24(2) covers actions relating to children "whether taken by public authorities *or private institutions*."[37] On the other hand, Article 51, as already stated, explicitly states that the Charter of Fundamental Rights applies only to EU institutions and bodies and member states when applying EU law. An argument can also be mounted that if the charter is "addressed to the institutions and bodies of the Union" this includes the CJEU itself. The question of horizontal direct effect is thereby left to the court to decide. Such an approach follows that of the UK's Human Rights Act: to impose obligations on public authorities and to leave it up to the courts, who are themselves public authorities under section 6(3)(a) of the act, to decide whether and how to give horizontal effect.

A lost opportunity to settle the issue of horizontal effect of the charter was *Association de Médiation Sociale*.[38] In this case, Advocate General Cruz Villalon had to determine whether

Article 27 of the charter, which sets out the worker's right to consultation and is implemented through Directive 2002/14, could be applied in a legal dispute between two private parties. The advocate general found that the potential for horizontal effect differed from right to right. Given that Article 27 itself referred to the right being granted "within the undertaking" this would imply at least some legal obligations for companies. He therefore concluded that Article 27 can be relied upon in principle between private parties. However, in its rather short judgment, the CJEU did not follow the complex reasoning of the advocate general and left the law on the horizontal effect of the EU charter somewhat ambiguous and elusive.[39]

Furthermore, there are numerous EU fundamental rights provisions that are already capable of horizontal direct effect. For example, the CJEU recently confirmed in *Kücükdeveci* that general principles of EU law can have horizontal direct effect – even in circumstances in which secondary EU legislation is incapable of generating such effects.[40]

Specific Problems

There also remain other problems and uncertainties with the operation of the charter. The first of these is the often opaque language in which its provisions are drafted. For example, Article 36, which states that "[t]he Union recognizes and respects access to services of general economic interest as provided for in national laws and practices …," or Article 38: "Union policies shall ensure a high level of protection." Both of these provisions are extremely vague and not drafted in terms of rights at all.

A second problem concerns the way in which some of the charter's rights are highly qualified. Article 27, for example, provides for a "Workers' right to information and consultation within the undertaking" but this is only to be "in the cases and under the conditions provided for by Union law and national laws and practices." The wording is similar for Articles 28, 34, 35, and 36. A general limitations clause set out in Article 52[41] also applies to all of the rights in the charter. Therefore, the status of something as a "fundamental" right in EU law is compromised by a myriad of possible limitations on it.

A third problem concerns the messy and unfortunate distinction introduced by Article 52(5) between rights and principles. That article provides that

> [t]he provisions of this Charter which contain principles may be implemented by legislative and executive acts …. They shall only be judicially cognizable in the interpretation of such acts and in the ruling on their legality.

In other words, rights which are "principles" are deemed incapable of creating any directly enforceable rights. Rather unhelpfully, the article does not indicate which provisions are "rights" and which are "principles." It is often suggested that "principles" refer to economic, social, and cultural rights,[42] although only three provisions in the charter explicitly use the word "principle."[43] The charter's accompanying explanations are of little help – especially as they note that some articles may contain both rights and principles.[44] In this respect the charter is a somewhat flawed document and leaves much for the CJEU to resolve in its case law.[45] Indeed, it seems that this distinction was a matter that the drafters of the Charter could not agree upon, and deliberately left to the Court to decide.[46] Although the distinction between rights and principles was an important argument in the *AMS* case, the Court in *AMS* did not follow the reasoning of Advocate General Cruz Villalón who paid significant attention to the question of whether Article 27 should be considered a "right" or "principle" (and concluded that it should be understood as a principle but that did not prevent the invocation of the article). The CJEU, however, did not discuss the distinction between rights and principles at all.

A fourth issue engages the relationship of the charter to national constitutional law. Article 53 of the charter requires that "[n]othing in this Charter shall be interpreted as restricting or adversely affecting human rights and fundamental freedoms as recognised … by the Member States' constitutions." However, in the 2013 *Melloni* case,[47] the European Court held that Spain could not refuse to execute a European Arrest Warrant (EAW) on the basis of Article 53. Mr Melloni had been convicted in Italy in absentia. Spanish constitutional law required that his surrender to Italy be subject to the possibility of judicial review of his conviction. The Spanish Constitutional Court asked the Court whether the EAW Framework Decision allowed the Spanish courts to make this stipulation – it might have seemed that Article 53 of the charter would be applicable. However, the European Court held that to make the surrender of Melloni subject to such a condition, a possibility not provided for under the EAW Decision, would cast doubt on the uniformity of the standard of protection of fundamental rights as defined in the EAW decision, undermine the principles of mutual trust it purported to uphold, and compromise its efficacy. Yet, such a strong insistence on a uniform EU fundamental rights standard as a ceiling – in spite of the explicit protection granted to member states' own standards in Article 53 – threatens the possibility of mutual trust and dialogue between the European Union (including the European Court of Justice) and its member states (including their constitutional courts). Notably, however, when the Spanish Constitutional Court rendered its final judgment in *Melloni*[48] in February 2014, it voted unanimously to amend its doctrine to bring it in line with EU law, thus avoiding any further conflict – at least for the time being.

A further problem concerns the relationship between the charter and the ECHR. Article 52(3) of the charter specifies that, in so far as its rights correspond to those in the ECHR, the meaning and scope of those rights "shall be the same as those laid down by the said convention." In *Dereci*[49] and *J McB*,[50] the CJEU added the proviso that the meaning and scope of those rights should be the same as that interpreted by the case law of the ECtHR. This approach increases the coherence of European fundamental rights law, but there is an issue of which charter rights "correspond" to those of the ECHR. There is a list of corresponding rights contained in the charter's explanations, but that list does not appear to be exhaustive given the preceding statement that the list is "without precluding developments in the law, legislation and the Treaties …. It [also] does not include rights additional to those in the ECHR." No doubt, a degree of uncertainty will continue after the EU's accession, until the CJEU, and possibly Strasbourg itself, have exhaustively concluded which rights correspond. It is to the future accession of the European Union which this chapter now turns.

Accession to the ECHR

All member states of the European Union are already contracting parties to the ECHR. However, before the Treaty of Lisbon, the CJEU concluded in Opinion 2/94 that,[51] under the existing treaty provisions, there was no competence for what was then the Community to accede to the ECHR. So the two institutions continued on their separate ways.

However, as amended by Lisbon, Article 6(2) TEU now places an obligation on the European Union to accede to the ECHR. There are many advantages to such an accession. First, a formal linking of the European Union and ECHR can be seen as underlining Union concern with human rights, given that the ECHR is seen as part of European cultural and political heritage.

Second, the accession will finally answer criticisms of double standards: that the Union requires accession of all member states but not, before Lisbon at least, of itself. Third, and crucially, EU accession to the ECHR would alleviate the situation in which individuals may find themselves when faced by possible breaches of the ECHR by EU institutions. At present, unless EU law has been implemented by a member state act (in which case action would be against that member state) there is no possible action in Strasbourg. This was established in the *CM & Co* case, in which the applicants' application in Strasbourg was held inadmissible as the European Union is not a party to the convention.[52] This leaves a gap in judicial enforcement.

However, there are also major problems with the EU accession to the ECHR. An initial obstacle was the European Union's long and complex process for concluding agreements between the Union and third parties in Article 218 of the Treaty on the Functioning of the European Union (TFEU), which requires unanimity in the Council; a two-thirds majority approval in the Parliament; and ratification of the agreement in all EU and Council of Europe member states. In April 2013, however, a draft revised agreement on accession was agreed between the Council of Europe and the European Commission. Additionally, the CJEU was asked to provide its opinion under Article 218(11) TFEU, on the compatibility of the ECHR accession agreement with the EU treaties. Notably, despite the fact that the three major EU institutions, as well as the Union's twenty-eight member states, submitted at the Court hearing that the draft accession agreement was compatible with EU law, the Court held that it is not.[53] Given this adverse holding, the agreement may not enter into force unless it, or the EU treaties, are revised.

In brief, the Court's judgment was based on five main findings, and overall amounted to a robust declaration of the autonomy of EU law. First, the CJEU found that the draft agreement was liable adversely to affect the specific characteristics and the autonomy of EU law in so far as it did not ensure coordination between Article 53 ECHR and Article 53 of the charter (on the level of protection of fundamental rights), so it did not avert the risk that the principle of member states' mutual trust under EU law might be undermined. It also made no provision to ensure that the new mechanism established by ECHR Protocol No 16 did not compromise the preliminary ruling procedure in Article 267 TFEU. Second, it found that the agreement was liable to affect Article 344 TFEU, in so far as it did not preclude the possibility of disputes concerning the application of the ECHR within the scope *ratione materiae* of EU law being brought before the ECtHR. Third, the CJEU found that the draft accession agreement failed to set up a satisfactory mechanism for a co-respondent procedure. A large part of EU law is implemented by its member states, and, therefore, it will seem logical for the applicant to proceed against the state. Yet member states often have no discretion as to whether, or how, an action emanating from the European Union is implemented. In such cases, the root of the problem lies with the EU measure rather than the member state. In order to address these problems, Article 3 of the draft accession agreement made provision for a co-respondent mechanism to be established, providing that a contracting party could become a co-respondent either by accepting an invitation from the ECtHR or by decision of the ECtHR upon the request of that contracting party. However, carrying out such a review would require the ECtHR to assess the rules of EU law governing the division of powers between the European Union and its member states. The CJEU held that to permit the ECtHR to do this would risk adversely affecting the division of powers between the Union and its member states. Fourth, the CJEU held that the draft agreement failed to provide a satisfactory procedure for the prior involvement of the CJEU and thus damaged the interpretive monopoly of the CJEU in the interpretation of EU law.[54] Finally, the CJEU found that the agreement failed to have regard to the specific characteristics of EU law with regard to judicial review of acts, actions, or omissions on the part of the European Union in the area of its common foreign and security policy, in that it entrusted judicial review of some of those matters exclusively to a non-EU body, namely the ECtHR.

This opinion undoubtedly makes it difficult for the European Union to proceed with accession. The draft agreement was only achieved after tortuous negotiations and redrafts, but the Court's opinion sets out so many objections to accession, some requiring treaty change, that one might think that the Court desired to make accession as difficult as possible. The European Union is required by the terms of its own treaty, Article 6(2) TEU, to accede to the ECHR, and the Commission is open to an infringement action if it fails to do so. The history of EU integration provides many illustrations of ad hoc, pragmatic actions in the face of seemingly impossible practical difficulties. So accession may still be achieved. Nonetheless, the CJEU's opinion makes it highly problematic for the Commission to proceed. There may indeed be little prospect that non-EU ECHR states will acquiesce in renegotiating the agreement to suit the terms of the CJEU's opinion. In such a situation, the Commission could not be blamed if non-EU action made it impossible to fulfill the obligation in Article 6(2).

A further issue with accession is that of the "Bosphorus presumption." This originates in the ECtHR *Bosphorus Airways* judgment, and stipulates that, if an international legal organization "protect(s) fundamental rights … in a manner which can be considered at least equivalent to that for which the Convention provides," then

> the presumption will be that a state has not departed from the requirements of the Convention when it does no more than implement legal obligations flowing from its membership of the organisation.[55]

The presumption is problematic given that it is unclear why the European Union should enjoy such a benefit when ECHR contracting states do not. This disparity is not overcome by the fact that "such [a] presumption can be rebutted … [if] the protection of Convention rights was manifestly deficient."[56]

It is clear, then, that EU accession to the ECHR is by no means inevitable. In the meantime, new cases concerning the charter will steadily emerge. However, prior to these recent developments, the Court had already developed its own fundamental rights case law, which will now be examined.

Human Rights as General Principles of Law

Given the absence of any EU Charter of Rights until 2000, protection of fundamental rights for the first forty years of European integration developed through the case law of the CJEU. The wording of Article 6(3) TEU reflects the earlier case law of the CJEU and provides that "[f]undamental rights, as guaranteed by the ECHR and as they result from the constitutional traditions common to the Member States, shall constitute general principles of the Union's law." This residual system of human rights in the European Union should by no means be underestimated.

The insistence of the German courts that EU law respect fundamental rights, and their veiled threat to ignore the primacy of EU law if it did not, was the original motivation for the protection of fundamental rights in the European Union and was reflected in the CJEU's recognition of fundamental rights as general principles of EU law in the early cases of *Stauder* and *Internationale Handelsgesellschaft*.[57] The late Judge Mancini, writing in 1989, summed up the position in this way: "Reading an unwritten Bill of Rights into [Union] law is indeed the most striking contribution the Court has made to the development of a constitution for Europe." But he continued by qualifying it thus: "this statement was forced on the Court by the outside, by the German and, later, the Italian constitutional courts."[58]

The CJEU has recognized a variety of rights, and has applied its fundamental rights jurisprudence not only against actions of the European Union but also against member states when acting within the scope of EU law.[59] However, constitutional traditions of the member states provide a necessarily incoherent source, given the very different traditions and practices of those states. Where a right is respected only in very few states, or protected in a singular way, the tendency may be to fragment rights protection. The *Omega Spielhallen* case[60] provides an illustration.[61] In *Omega*, Germany had banned a laserdome game that involved simulated homicide on the basis that it infringed the protection of human dignity under the German Constitution. The applicant company, Omega, challenged the ban as contrary to freedom to provide services under EU law as the game had been lawfully produced and marketed in the United Kingdom. If the CJEU had enforced internal market law at the expense of protection of dignity this might have encouraged challenges to the supremacy of EU law from Germany. Therefore, the CJEU upheld the German ban but, while holding that human dignity was also respected by EU law, stated that this outcome did not depend upon "a conception shared by all Member States as regards the precise way in which the fundamental right or legitimate interest in question is to be protected." The Court, therefore, considered the subject matter to belong to a sphere properly left to the member states. In this context, it may be seen that, rather than unifying fundamental rights in the European Union, member state constitutional traditions may in fact separate them, operating not as conditions of legality of EU action, but rather as member state defenses to EU action, justified as furthering the public interest – a rather curious inversion of the normal function of fundamental rights to operate as claims against state action.

Furthermore, Article 6(3) makes it possible for the EU courts to recognize and/or enforce rights that are not to be found in the charter or ECHR, or, significantly, rights in the charter whose impact is limited owing to the existence of protocols, such as that of the United Kingdom and Poland, or by the horizontal, or limitations, clauses. It is, however, an interesting question whether general principles should now be seen as subsidiary to the charter, which now seems to have become the first point of reference for fundamental rights in the European Union.

The *Kücükdeveci* case,[62] controversial in its implications, provides an interesting illustration of possible future directions for general principles of law. Ms Kücükdeveci had worked for a German company from the age of eighteen for some ten years until her dismissal. The employer calculated the notice period based upon three rather than ten years – as permitted under the German Civil Code, which provided that employment before the age of twenty-five should not to be taken into account. It was argued that this was clearly discriminatory on grounds of age and thus contrary to Council Directive 2000/78, which put into effect the Union's principle of equal treatment. The CJEU accepted that argument but held that ineffectively transposed directives do not have horizontal effect.[63] However, the CJEU also held that the directive gave expression to the general principle of equal treatment[64] on grounds of age, and required the national courts to apply this principle as an autonomous ground for judicial review, giving rise to an obligation to set aside conflicting national legislation,[65] in a dispute between *private* parties.

Kücükdeveci illustrates that general principles of EU law can have horizontal direct effect. This development is very important, given that general principles and fundamental rights usually protect individuals from public authorities and not private parties. The Court's holding in *Kücükdeveci* seems to threaten legal certainty, resulting in a situation in which EU law can apply even to matters only incidentally governed by a directive, and even if, owing to the lack of horizontal effect, the directive itself cannot apply. *Kücükdeveci* therefore illustrates the ongoing, far-reaching potential of general principles of law, and their capacity to provoke controversial, multidirectional, new developments. However, more recent holdings – such as *Dominguez* – may imply that the *Kücükdeveci* approach does not extend to all general principles of law.[67]

Further Development of a Fundamental Rights Jurisprudence

This section highlights some significant developments in the Court's fundamental rights jurisprudence.

Any legal regime that deploys a concept of fundamental rights immediately faces the challenge of resolving conflicts between those very rights. In particular, the Court's tendency to give equal weight to economic "fundamental freedoms" of movement in the treaties as to fundamental rights has created problems. The *Omega* case, in which the freedom to provide services and the right to dignity were opposed, has already been discussed.[68] Other key examples concerning such oppositions have arisen in the context of a conflict between the free movement of services and labor law rights. In both *Viking and Laval*[69] it was claimed that the applicant undertakings' market freedoms were restricted by trade union collective action. Although the right to take such collective action was acknowledged by the Court as a "fundamental right" and the Charter was cited as a foundation[70] for this, in both cases it was held to be outweighed by the fundamental market freedom. The Court found that the right to strike had not been exercised proportionately. Yet such reasoning is antithetical to fundamental rights and has been strongly criticized,[71] especially in its application of a proportionality test to the concept of fundamental rights themselves. Normally, as in the test applied by the ECtHR, it is the *restrictions* on fundamental rights that must satisfy a proportionality test.

To some extent one could argue that the Court in *Viking* and *Laval* was caught in a bind. If national labor standards in the host state are too high (in the context of posted workers) this renders market penetration from a posting state with lower labor standards impossible – thus retarding market integration. On the other hand, with degrading labor standards in the host state, the risk of social dumping arises. Therefore, how the CJEU balances economic fundamental rights with social fundamental rights is critical and, with respect, it is submitted that the court failed to achieve that sensitivity in *Viking* owing to its particularly harsh proportionality test.[72]

However, if cases such as *Viking* and *Laval* have given EU fundamental rights enthusiasts pause for thought, the more recent case of *Kadi*[73] has often been seen[74] as a victory for EU human rights. This is a significant case, given the Court's identification of EU fundamental rights as the most normatively powerful form of EU law, but it has also been seriously criticized on the ground that it strains the relationship between the EU and international law. The facts of the case concerned the UN Security Council Resolution 1390 (2002), which required the states of the UN to take action against "Osama bin Laden, members of the Al-Qaida organization and the Taliban." Mr Kadi was one of a number of persons and groups who had been blacklisted as terrorists and had had their assets frozen by this resolution. The European Union, as successor to the member states in this area of foreign policy, took measures to implement the resolution. Kadi argued he was the victim of a miscarriage of justice and that the EU measure violated his fundamental rights to property, the right to a fair hearing, and judicial redress. It was not possible for him to petition the UN Sanctions Committee directly as the committee does not accept direct representations from individuals. Such situations have been characterized as "black holes," with persons finding it very hard to find a forum to challenge their blacklisting, a state of affairs that undermines the more usual perception of international law as a source of protection for human rights. So Kadi approached the Luxembourg courts.

Unlike the Court of First Instance (now General Court)[75] the CJEU found that his rights had been violated. The CJEU proclaimed the constitutional autonomy of the EU legal order, holding that the European Union is a community based on the rule of law and that respect for fundamental rights is an integral part of the EU legal order. International obligations could not prejudice the constitutional principles of the EU Treaty. Thus, it was less concerned than the Court of First Instance about the primacy of the UN Security Council resolutions. From there it was able to go on to review the measure under EU rights standards and to find that Mr Kadi's rights had been violated.[76]

The case generated a deluge of academic commentary. Given that the CJEU asserted the primacy of fundamental rights in the EU legal order, and held Kadi's rights to have been violated, this might seem to be a victory for human rights. That being said, concern was voiced over the apparent disregard shown by the CJEU towards the authority of international law. The Court stipulated that what is now Article 351 TFEU, which requires the Union to respect international agreements entered into by the member states before their accession,

> may in no circumstances permit any challenge to the principles that form part of the very foundations of the [Union] legal order, one of which is the protection of fundamental rights.[77]

The Court also went on to state that

> the Charter of the United Nations … would have primacy over acts of secondary [Union] law … [but] would not, however, extend to primary law, in particular to the general principles of which fundamental rights form part.[78]

Such a downgrading in the normative status of the UN Charter concerned commentators such as de Búrca because it might seem to undermine the self-image of the European Union as a body that respects international law, in contrast to US exceptionalism.[79]

However, although these criticisms are certainly potent, a viable counterposition can be formulated. The beginning of the argument is to utilize a *Solange* type methodology.[80] The CJEU's stipulation that, in essence, it will review the international legal order's compliance with human rights is, fundamentally, no different to the German Constitutional Court's approach in *Solange*. If the superior authority in question will not ensure compliance with human rights then that authority's supremacy claim will be ignored.[81]

Human Rights in the Broader Context

To be sure, the CJEU is not the only EU institution of relevance for human rights. For some time, human rights have been a condition for membership of the European Union. In 1993, the European Council laid down the *Copenhagen criteria* for membership, according to which countries must have achieved "stability of institutions guaranteeing democracy, the rule of law, human rights and respect for and protection of minorities."[82] These were given a treaty basis when the Amsterdam Treaty added a new[83] Article 49 TEU, requiring candidate countries for EU membership to respect the values of Article 2 TEU, which include respect for human rights. Human rights issues have also played a significant role in overseas trade, and foreign trade agreements may be made conditional on the other party's observance of human rights – if they fail to do so, the treaty may be terminated, a practice increasingly used since the early 1990s.

Human rights also play their part in general foreign policy. Article 24(2) TEU imposes a basic obligation on the Union to "define and implement a common foreign and security policy," one of whose specific objectives, under Article 21(2)(b) TEU, is to "consolidate and support democracy, the rule of law, human rights and the principles of international law." So far, the European Union has not produced a satisfactory human rights foreign policy.[84] Part of the problem has been a difference of opinion over human rights foreign policy among its member states. Examples of this are numerous. The Union's response to the 2003 Iraq War may have had a thin outward appearance of some degree of consensus but the member states pursued different objectives at the UN and (for those states that were members) the Security Council level.[85] The European Union's position, or lack of it, on China, provides another example. When the Council of Ministers formalized its position regarding human rights in China, for the purpose of a resolution, it was in fact to announce that the European Union would not be acting in China. This was seen by some as "putting markets before morality"[86] and also involved a "leveling down" of positions that might have been taken individually by the more radical member states of the Union.

Some time ago, Weiler and Alston claimed that what the European Union needed was a viable and coherent human rights policy,[87] rather than overly focusing on the protection of human rights through litigation. They also argued the need for a monitoring center for human rights in the European Union to encourage a more proactive approach to human rights and help coordinate the fundamental rights policies of member states. The idea of a human rights agency gained momentum in the context of the "Austrian crisis" of 2000 and the ensuing report of the Comité des Sages.[88] As a result, the EU Agency for Fundamental Rights was set up[89] in 2007 and is based in Vienna. The agency's main task is to collect and disseminate data on the situation of fundamental rights in all EU countries within the scope of EU law, and to raise awareness about fundamental rights.

However, the agency has no power to examine individual complaints. It has no regulatory or binding decision-making powers, nor any sanctioning powers, nor even any power of systematic monitoring of countries' rights records. Its role is purely supportive and advisory. It was initially viewed with suspicion by the Council of Europe – as unnecessarily duplicating that body's human rights activities – and tension and competition over this area of the European human rights law resulted in the weakening of the agency's mandate.[90]

A recent development has been the European Union's adoption, in 2012, of a Strategic Framework and Action Plan on human rights and democracy. At the same time, the newly created role of EU special representative for human rights was also announced. It is the task of the new special representative to respond to crises around the world, and they have to cooperate with potential allies in international forums, such as the UN's Human Rights Council. Notably, this is the first *thematic* mandate given to an EU special representative. However, successful implementation and enforcement will be the true measure of the package. The special representative will also need the necessary powers to be able to tackle rights violations if the office is to live up to initial expectations.

The Dilemmas of EU Fundamental Rights

In the early twenty-first century, the protection of fundamental rights in the European Union has become ever more complex, and the scope for EU involvement in fundamental rights issues constantly grows. It is to be expected that national courts and authorities will keep a watchful eye on this. The saga of the EU Arrest Warrant and the declaration of invalidity of its national implementing measures in Germany[91] and elsewhere, on grounds of its failure to protect fundamental rights sufficiently illustrate the threat to the CJEU and European Union from national constitutional courts when it is believed that inadequate protection has been given to fundamental rights. The German Constitutional Court's 2009 judgment on the compatibility of the Lisbon Treaty with German law[92] discusses these issues at a more fundamental level. The German Court interpreted the Lisbon Treaty as involving a substantial increase in the powers of the European Union. However, it held that this would not violate German sovereignty if national democratic institutions were able to play a full part in European decision making, given the insufficiently democratic political structures at EU level (in the perception of the German court). The German Court's Lisbon Treaty judgment maintains and elucidates the earlier theory of conditional acceptance of EU law established by the German Court in its *Solange I, Solange II,* and *Maastricht*[93] judgments, according to which Germany only accepts the supremacy of EU law "so long" as EU law guarantees the fundamental rights laid down in the German Basic Law.[94]

This indicates that the national courts will continue to reaffirm their own role in policing the observance of fundamental rights in the European Union, thus ensuring that the multilevel and complex structures of fundamental rights protection in the European Union will continue. This also underlines the need for the Union to accede to the ECHR and for the CJEU to conform its fundamental rights jurisprudence with Strasbourg, or at least to maintain it as a minimum standard, in order to legitimize its own institutional position.

The avowal of strong protection of human rights has been a means for the Luxembourg court to maintain and increase its authority and the primacy and constitutional autonomy of EU law. However, the European Union must make good on this avowal and ensure that its protection of human rights is actually robust. The Lisbon Treaty amendments, especially the now binding nature of the charter, provide resources for a more effective protection of fundamental rights in the Union, but it will also be necessary for the Union, and in particular the CJEU, to move beyond an instrumental, ad hoc, market-led mentality toward a mature conception of fundamental rights as goods in themselves. In these challenging times for the European Union, fundamental rights are essential and must not be diminished or become a casualty of economic or security-driven mentalities.

On the other hand, an increase in fundamental rights monitoring through EU law may be perceived as undesirable, as it might be seen as limiting state autonomy, as well as lacking in democratic legitimacy. A strong justification is needed for the EU institutions to challenge a member state for its fundamental rights situation and performance in order to demonstrate that an additional EU level of protection for fundamental rights is necessary beyond that already provided by national law and the ECHR. The adoption and coming into force of the EU Act in the United Kingdom in 2011, which makes ratification of future amendments to the TEU and TFEU subject to approval by referendum, reveals a suspicion of any potential transfers of power from member states to the European Union – as do the legal challenges and ensuing careful scrutiny by, for example, the German Constitutional Court, of each EU overhaul and transfer of sovereignty brought about by treaty change. The dynamic between Luxembourg and Strasbourg cannot be forgotten either, nor the potential impact on the ECHR of a greater fundamental rights competence for the European Union in the future. These are the quandaries of an EU fundamental rights policy, which will be debated for a long time to come.

Notes

1 See further on these: *Al Nashiri v. Poland*, application no. 28761/2011 lodged in the ECtHR on 6 May 2011, in which it is alleged that Poland hosted a secret CIA prison where the applicant was held incommunicado and tortured; Mark Dawson and Elise Muir, "Individual, Institutional and Collective Vigilance in Protecting Fundamental Rights in the EU: Lessons from the Roma," *Common Market Law Review* 48 (2011); and Human Rights Watch, "Memorandum to the European Union on Media Freedom in Hungary," 16 February 2012.

2 Weak judicial protection mechanisms operated pre-Lisbon within the third pillar.

3 Olivier de Schutter, "The New Architecture of Fundamental Rights Policy in the EU," *European Yearbook on Human Rights* (2011): 107–141.

4 Commission Communication on the "Strategy for the Effective Implementation of the Charter of Fundamental Rights by the European Union," COM(2010) 573 final.

5 I write "at least" because sometimes international law may offer further avenues.

6 See Catherine van der Heyning, "Fundamental Rights in the EU: Lost in Complexity?" (PhD thesis, University of Antwerp Law School, 2011).

7 For example, Paul J.G. Kapteyn and Pieter Verloren van Themaat, *Introduction to the Law of the European Communities after the Coming into Force of the Single European Act* (Deventer: Kluwer, 1989) devoted just 4 pages out of 900, and the first edition of Trevor Hartley, *The Foundations of European Community Law* (Oxford: Clarendon Press, 1981) 7 pages out of 546.

8 In which human rights had a prominent role. See Eric Stein and Joseph Vining, "Citizen Access to Judicial Review of Administrative Action in a Transnational and Federal Context," in *European Law and the Individual*, ed. Francis G. Jacobs (Amsterdam: North Holland, 1976).

9 Indeed, even the original treaty was not restricted to purely economic matters, as the provisions on the health and safety of workers, as well as equal treatment, in the original treaty illustrate. But the absence of any concrete reference to human rights in the EEC Treaty is surprising, given that even the Treaty on Economic, Social and Cultural Collaboration and Collective Self-Defence of 1948 ("The Brussels Treaty"), which is concerned with military cooperation, affirms its signatories' "faith in fundamental human rights, in the dignity and worth of the person." On the other hand, very few international treaties did make such reference. The 1945 Preamble to the UN Charter was almost the first to do so, the first being the German and Polish Convention on Upper Silesia of 1922.

10 Joined Cases T-34/96 and T-163/96 *Connolly v. Commission* EU:T:1999:102, FP II-463; Case C-84/95 *Bosphorus* EU:C:1996:312; Case C-249/96 *Grant v. South West Trains* EU:C:1998:63; Case C-402/05 P *Kadi v. Council and Commission* EU:C:2008:461.

11 Case C-131/12 *Google Spain, Google v. Agencia Española de Protección de Datos* EU:C:2014:317.

12 Although Article 19 TFEU constitutes what is, in essence, a general competence for equality legislation.

13 This provision is only to be used in extreme circumstances and there is a special procedure for determining whether there is a "clear risk of a serious breach" of human rights. Determination of an actual breach under Article 7(2) TEU requires unanimity.

14 For further confirmation that the charter should be seen as the first point of reference for fundamental rights in the European Union, see, e.g., the Opinion of Advocate General Cruz Villalón in Case C-447/09 *Prigge* EU:C:2011:573, para 26, and the Court in Case C-272/09 P *KME* EU:C:2011:810.

15 E.g., under the Schengen Information System.

16 Cloning being a prime example – see, e.g., the European Parliament Resolution of 12 March 1997 on Human Cloning [1997] OJ C 115/92.

17 E.g., CBI submission to the Convention on the Charter of 12 April 2000, CHARTE 4226/00, CONTRIB 101.

18 Case C-173/99 *BECTU v. Secretary of State for Trade and Industry* EU:C:2001:356.

19 Case C-540/03 *Parliament v. Council* (Immigration Policy) EU:C:2006:429, para 38.

20 Joined Cases C-411/10 and C-493/10 *N.S. v. Secretary of State for the Home Department and M.E. and Others v. Refugee Applications Commissioner, Minister for Justice, Equality and Law Reform* EU:C:2011:865.
21 Case C-236/09 *Test-Achats* EU:C:2011:100.
22 Joined Cases C-92/09 and C-93/09 *Volker und Markus Schecke and Eifert* EU:C:2010:662, para 46.
23 Joined Cases C-293/12 *Digital Rights Ireland* and C-594/12 *Kärntner Landesregierung* EU:C:2014:238.
24 See, e.g., Jason Coppell and Aidan O'Neill, "The European Court of Justice: Taking Rights Seriously?" *Common Market Law Review* 29 (1992) for a criticism of this sort.
25 See also Article 51(2) which states, "The Charter does not extend the field of application of Union law beyond the powers of the Union or establish any new power or task for the Union, or modify powers and tasks as defined in the Treaties."
26 Case C-617/10 *Åkerberg Fransson* EU:C:2013:105.
27 Ibid.
28 Emphasis added.
29 The Commission did, however, for example, pursue the fundamental rights issue in the case of the expulsion of the Roma from France (see Commission 2010 report on application of the EU Charter of Fundamental Rights, COM(2011) 160 final, 8) and on the restrictive media law in Hungary.
30 See further Clemens Ladenberger, "Institutional Report on 'Protection of Fundamental Rights post-Lisbon: The Interaction between the Charter of Fundamental Rights, the ECHR and National Constitutions," FIDE 2012, 16. For a case in which the connection seemed to be over stretched, see Case C-60/00 *Carpenter* EU:C:2002:434.
31 See Case C-188/89 *Foster v. British Gas* EU:C:1990:313.
32 Directorate-General for Internal Policies, *Implementation of the EU Charter of Fundamental Rights and its Impact on EU Home Affairs Agencies* (Brussels: European Parliament, 2011), 66.
33 See also Declaration no 53 of the Lisbon Treaty by the Czech Republic on the Charter of Fundamental Rights of the European Union.
34 Case C-411/10 *N.S.*, n 20 this chapter, Opinion of Advocate General Trstenjak, para 167.
35 Ibid., para 169.
36 See, further on this, Paul Craig, *The Lisbon Treaty: Law, Politics, and Treaty Reform* (Oxford: Oxford University Press, 2011), 206 *et seq*.
37 Emphasis added in both cases.
38 Case C-176/12 *Association de Médiation Sociale* EU:C:2014:2.
39 Ibid. See also Case C-356/12 *Wolfgang Glatzel v. Freistaat Bayern* EU:C:2014:350.
40 Case C-555/07 *Seda Kücükdeveci v. Swedex GmbH* EU:C:2010:21, and see further in this chapter.
41 Article 52 of the charter reads as follows: "Any limitation on the exercise of the rights and freedoms recognized by this Charter must be provided for by law and respect the essence of those rights and freedoms. Subject to the principle of proportionality, limitations may be made only if they are necessary and genuinely meet objectives of general interest recognized by the Union or the need to protect the rights and freedoms of others."
42 See, further on this, Sionaidh Douglas-Scott, "The EU and Human Rights after the Treaty of Lisbon," *Human Rights Law Review* 11 (2011): 652.
43 Articles 23, 37, and 47.
44 For instance, Articles 23, 33, and 34 of the charter.
45 At time of writing, the Court had not pronounced on this point. In Case C-282/10 *Dominguez* EU:C:2012:33, Advocate General Trstenjak interpreted Article 31(2) of the Charter of Fundamental Rights on paid annual leave as a right rather than a principle, but the Court did not rule on the matter.
46 Ladenberger, "Institutional Report," 32.
47 Case C-399/11 *Stefano Melloni* EU:C:2013:107.
48 STC 26/2014 *Melloni*.

49 Case C-256/11 *Dereci* EU:C:2011:734, para 70.
50 Case C-400/10 PPU *J McB v. LE* EU:C:2010:582, para 53.
51 Opinion 2/94 EU:C:1996:140.
52 Application 13258/87 of 13 February 1990 in *M & Co v. Germany*.
53 Opinion 2/13 EU:C:2014:2454. Advocate General Kokott, in an opinion delivered on 13 June 2014, had also found the agreement compatible with EU law, albeit in highly qualified terms.
54 Article 1 of Protocol 8 specified that the accession agreement must "make provision for preserving the specific characteristics of the Union and Union law." See further also Articles 2 and 3 Protocol 8.
55 *Bosphorus Hava Yollari Turizm Ve Ticaret Anonim Sirketi v. Ireland* (2006) 42 EHRR 1, paras 155–156.
56 Ibid.
57 Case 29/69 *Stauder v. City of Ulm* EU:C:1969:57; Case 11/70 *Internationale Handelsgesellschaft* EU:C:1970:114.
58 Federico Mancini, "The Making of a Constitution for Europe," *Common Market Law Review* 26 (1989).
59 Case C-260/89 *Elliniki Radiophonia Tileorassi* EU:C:1991:254.
60 Case C-36/02 *Omega Spielhallen* EU:C:2004:614.
61 Another example may be found in the right to life of the unborn child, protected most strongly in only a few states, e.g., Ireland and Poland. See Case C-159/90 *SPUC v. Grogan* EU:C:1991:378, and Protocol No 35 to the Lisbon Treaty on Article 40.3.3 of the Constitution of Ireland.
62 Case C-555/07 *Seda Kücükdeveci*, n 10 this chapter.
63 Ibid., para 46.
64 Rather than equality under Article 21 of the charter which was not in force at the time.
65 Case C-555/07 *Seda Kücükdeveci*, n 40 this chapter, paras 27, 50–51.
66 As did also Case C-144/04 *Mangold v. Helm* EU:C:2005:709.
67 In the *Dominguez* case, the Court refused to transpose the *Kücükdeveci* approach to the right to annual leave in Article 31(2) of the charter on the basis that this social right is of a completely different nature (requiring legislative implementation) to that of the right to equality (see further, Case 282/10 *Dominguez*, n 45 this chapter, Opinion of Advocate General Trstenjak, para 145) which would go beyond the exclusionary effect of *Kücükdeveci* (whereby EU law is used to exclude the application of national law, to an substitutionary one (in which EU law itself is substituted for national law). See also Case C-161/11 *Vino II* EU:C:2011:420, para 39.
68 See also Case C-112/00 *Schmidberger v. Republic of Austria* EU:C:2003:333, for a further example of the conflict between fundamental rights and fundamental freedoms in the EU treaty.
69 Case C-341/05 *Laval* EU:C:2007:809; Case C-438/05 *ITWF v. Viking Line* EU:C:2007:772.
70 See Article 28 of the Charter on the right of collective bargaining and action.
71 See, e.g., Catherine Barnard, "Social Dumping or Dumping Socialism," *The Cambridge Law Journal* 67 (2008); Danny Nicol, "Europe's Lochner Moment," *Public Law* (2011).
72 However, a more nuanced approach was suggested by Advocate General Trstenjak (in Case C-271/08 *Commission v. Germany* (Occupational Pensions) EU:C:2010:426), who was critical of C-341/05 *Laval*, n 69 this chapter, and especially C 438/05 *Viking*, n 69 this chapter, arguing that they "sit uncomfortably alongside the principle of equal ranking for fundamental rights and fundamental freedoms" (para 183). She preferred the test for balancing market and social rights to be symmetrical in nature, although neither she nor the Court actually applied such a test in the case at hand. See also Philip Syrpis, "Reconciling Economic Freedoms and Social Rights: The Potential of *Commission v Germany* (Case C-271/08, Judgment of 15 July 2010)," *Industrial Law Journal* 40 (2011).
73 Case C-402/05 *Kadi*, n 10 this chapter.
74 See, e.g., Takis Tridimas, "Terrorism and the ECJ: Empowerment and Democracy in the EC Legal Order," *European Law Review* 34 (2009).

75 The EU Court of First Instance held that the primacy of the UN and international law prevented review of the measure on the basis of EU standards and the only possible review would be on the basis of *jus cogens*, not autonomous EU fundamental rights standards. The CFI found none of his rights to be violated. See Case T-315/01 *Kadi v. Council and Commission* EU:T:2005:332.

76 Albeit with the caveat that it would continue to have effect for thirty days after the judgment, in order to give the European Union time to respond by implementing a new system, which it duly did. In that respect, Mr Kadi's victory was arguably a pyrrhic one. See further, Case T-85/09 *Kadi v. European Commission* (Kadi II) EU:T:2010:418.

77 Ibid.

78 Ibid., paras 307–308.

79 Gráinne de Búrca, "The European Court of Justice and the International Legal Order after *Kadi*," *Harvard International Law Journal* 51 (2010).

80 The *Solange* principle of the German Constitutional Court is a mechanism whereby one legal order accepts decisions of another "so long as" those decisions do not systematically violate its own understanding of constitutional essentials. It originates in the German Court's *Solange I* decision of 1974 (BVerfGE 37, 327) and has been applied in other cases, including, some would argue, by the ECtHR in the *Bosphorus* decision, n 55 this chapter.

81 For another argument – that *Kadi* can be justified through a paradigm of civil disobedience, see N. Türküler Isiksel, "Fundamental Rights in the EU after *Kadi and Al Barakaat*," *European Law Journal* 16 (2010).

82 Copenhagen European Council, Presidency conclusions, Bull EC 6-1993, pt I.13.

83 Prior to this, the main treaty criterion for entry was that the country concerned be a "European" state.

84 Andrew Williams, *The Ethos of Europe* (Cambridge: Cambridge University Press, 2012), 49–63; and for an earlier critique, see Sionaidh Douglas-Scott, "The Common Foreign and Security Policy: Reinforcing the European Identity?" in *Europe's Other: European Law between Modernity and Postmodernity*, ed. Peter Bergeron and James Henry Fitzpatrick (Aldershot: Ashgate, 1998).

85 David Allen and Michael Smith, "External Policy Developments," *Journal of Common Market Studies* 42 (2004): 96.

86 Amnesty International European Union Association, "Outcome of Wei Jingsheng's Visit to Brussels 12–17 March 1998: Agreement on Seriousness of Human Rights Situation and the Need for a Public Approach: Disagreement on Change in EU Policy," 18 March 1998, cited in Andrew Clapham, "Where is the EU's Human Rights Common Foreign Policy, and How is it Manifested in Multilateral Fora?" in *The EU and Human Rights*, ed. Philip Alston (Oxford: Oxford University Press, 1999), 647.

87 Philip Alston and J.H.H. Weiler, "An 'Ever Closer Union' in Need of a Human Rights Policy: The European Union and Human Rights," in Alston, *The EU and Human Rights*.

88 The "Austrian crisis" in question was the election of a government which included members of the far right "Freedom Party." See Office of the High Commissioner for Human Rights, "Report prepared by Martti Ahtisaari, Jochen Frowein, and Marcelino Oreja, adopted in Paris on 8 September 2000."

89 It was set up by Regulation 168/2007/EC of 15 February 2007 establishing a European Union Agency for Fundamental Rights [2007] OJ L 53/1.

90 See, e.g., Memorandum of Understanding Between the Council of Europe and the European Union adopted at the 117th Session of the Committee of Ministers held in Strasbourg on 10–11 May 2007, COM(2007) 74.

91 For the German Constitutional Court decision see BVerfGE, *Neue Juristische Wochenschrift (NJW)*, 58 (2005), 2289.

92 Bundesverfassungsgericht [BVerfG] [Federal Constitutional Court] 30 June 2009, *Entscheidungen des Bundesverfassungsgerichts*, 210 (F.R.G.). 67.

93 In *Brunner v. European Union Treaty* [1994] I CMLR 57 on the compatibility of the Maastricht treaty with the German Basic Law, the German Constitutional court held that it retained the competence to review EU measures which violate fundamental rights.

94 The German Court's judgment also appears to have inspired the Czech Constitutional Court in its decision of 3 November 2009 – Press Release, "Constitutional Court: The Treaty of Lisbon is in conformity with the Constitutional Order of the Czech Republic and there is nothing to prevent its ratification."

References

Allen, David, and Michael Smith. "External Policy Developments." *Journal of Common Market Studies* 42 (2004): 95–112.

Alston, Philip, ed. *The EU and Human Rights*. Oxford: Oxford University Press, 1999.

Alston, Philip, and J.H.H. Weiler. "An 'Ever Closer Union' in Need of a Human Rights Policy: The European Union and Human Rights." In Alston, *The EU and Human Rights*, 4–66.

Barnard, Catherine. "Social Dumping or Dumping Socialism." *The Cambridge Law Journal* 67 (2008): 262–264.

Clapham. Andrew "Where is the EU's Human Rights Common Foreign Policy, and How is it Manifested in Multilateral Fora?" In Alston, *The EU and Human Rights*, 627–683.

Coppell, Jason, and Aidan O'Neill. "The European Court of Justice: Taking Rights Seriously?" *Common Market Law Review* 29 (1992): 227–239.

Craig, Paul. *The Lisbon Treaty: Law, Politics, and Treaty Reform*. Oxford: Oxford University Press, 2011.

Dawson, Mark, and Elise Muir. "Individual, Institutional and Collective Vigilance in Protecting Fundamental Rights in the EU: Lessons from the Roma." *Common Market Law Review* 48 (2011): 751–775.

de Búrca, Gráinne. "The European Court of Justice and the International Legal Order after *Kadi*." *Harvard International Law Journal* 51 (2010): 1–49.

de Schutter, Olivier. "The New Architecture of Fundamental Rights Policy in the EU." *European Yearbook on Human Rights* (2011): 107–141.

Directorate-General for Internal Policies. *Implementation of the EU Charter of Fundamental Rights and its Impact on EU Home Affairs Agencies*. Brussels: European Parliament, 2011.

Douglas-Scott, Sionaidh. "The Common Foreign and Security Policy: Reinforcing the European Identity?" In *Europe's Other: European Law between Modernity and Postmodernity*, edited by Peter Bergeron and James Henry Fitzpatrick, 131–155. Aldershot: Ashgate, 1998.

Douglas-Scott, Sionaidh. "The EU and Human Rights after the Treaty of Lisbon." *Human Rights Law Review* 11 (2011): 645–682.

Hartley, Trevor. *The Foundations of European Community Law*. Oxford: Clarendon Press, 1981.

Human Rights Watch. "Memorandum to the European Union on Media Freedom in Hungary." 16 February 2012.

Isiksel, N. Türküler. "Fundamental Rights in the EU after *Kadi and Al Barakaat*." *European Law Journal* 16 (2010). 551–577.

Kapteyn, Paul J.G., and Pieter Verloren van Themaat. *Introduction to the Law of the European Communities after the Coming into Force of the Single European Act*. Deventer: Kluwer, 1989

Ladenberger, Clemens. "Institutional Report on 'Protection of Fundamental Rights Post-Lisbon: The Interaction between the Charter of Fundamental Rights, the ECHR and National Constitutions." FIDE 2012, 16.

Mancini, Federico. "The Making of a Constitution for Europe." *Common Market Law Review* 26 (1989): 595–614.

Nicol, Danny. "Europe's Lochner Moment." *Public Law* (2011): 308–329.

Office of the High Commissioner for Human Rights. "Report prepared by Martti Ahtisaari, Jochen Frowein, and Marcelino Oreja, adopted in Paris on 8 September 2000."

Stein, Eric, and Joseph Vining. "Citizen Access to Judicial Review of Administrative Action in a Transnational and Federal Context." In *European Law and the Individual*, edited by Francis G. Jacobs, 113–143. Amsterdam: North Holland, 1976.

Syrpis, Philip. "Reconciling Economic Freedoms and Social Rights: The Potential of *Commission v Germany* (Case C-271/08, Judgment of 15 July 2010)." *Industrial Law Journal* 40 (2011): 222–229.

Tridimas, Takis. "Terrorism and the ECJ: Empowerment and Democracy in the EC Legal Order." *European Law Review* 34 (2009): 103–126.

van der Heyning, Catherine. "Fundamental Rights in the EU: Lost in Complexity?" PhD thesis, University of Antwerp Law School, 2011.

Williams, Andrew. *The Ethos of Europe*. Cambridge: Cambridge University Press, 2012.

31

The European Union and Social Policy

Silvana Sciarra

Dilemmas of Social Integration: A Brief Historical Introduction

This chapter analyzes European social policy as a test case to comment on both the originality and the weakness of a unique supranational legal order, such as the one created in 1957 with the Treaty of Rome.[1] In the years following the end of the Second World War, the choice to construct a common market, without attempting to build a European welfare state, acknowledged the search for identity that each founding member state was at the time pursuing. In laying down their own constitutional foundations, implementing democracy, and respecting the rule of law, member states intended to gain full recognition of their sovereignty while subscribing to common economic objectives.

A diachronic interpretation of major reforms occurred over the years in primary and secondary EU law. This shows that the lack of a coherent supranational system of social norms posed serious challenges to national legislatures and gave rise to controversial results. There was, at that time, an unsolved problem of competing competences, which resulted in the emergence of "semi-sovereign welfare states."[2]

The dramatic effects caused by the most recent financial and economic crisis shed further light on this ambiguity and complicate the enhancement of social measures. Hence, dilemmas of social integration animate the contemporary discussion among institutional and social actors on how to mark the indispensable contribution of national legislatures, especially when fundamental rights are at stake.[3]

Dilemmas in the social field are further exacerbated by other circumstances. First of all, controversial case law of the Court of Justice of the European Union (CJEU), ruling on the right to strike and to collective bargaining in potential collision with fundamental market freedoms, inflicted a wound in the body of social policy which has not yet been fully healed.[4] Following the crisis in some member states, institutional balances within the European Union have also been shaken by the adoption of austerity measures.[5] The legitimacy of the institutions taking responsibility for them has been questioned during this unprecedented emergency, and so have national responses to them, whenever fundamental social rights have been imperiled. For this

A Companion to European Union Law and International Law, First Edition.
Edited by Dennis Patterson and Anna Södersten.

reason, what used to be discussed as a long-standing tension between market freedoms and social rights is now complicated by the reconsideration of states' prerogatives in a much broader sense. Questions of sovereignty now have to do with the reestablishment of political priorities within national boundaries and, at the same time, new institutional connections with the supranational legal order. Obligations originated by the adoption of the Treaty on Stability, Coordination, and Governance in the Economic and Monetary Union (the so-called fiscal compact) are illustrative of the current delicate equilibrium between national and supranational institutions.

For all these reasons, a decline of legislative measures in the last few years, both in quality and in quantity, has disconnected social policy from the fundamental aims and values of the European Union. The priority should now be the search for political consensus around legal measures aimed at reestablishing social rights in the internal market.

The Origins

With the Treaty of Paris, signed in 1951, the European Coal and Steel Community saw the light of day[6] and launched social measures to protect workers affected by the results of major restructuring taking place in coal and steel industries. A policy guaranteeing free movement of workers was promoted during those years, before the formal entry into force of the Treaty of Rome, which created the European Economic Community.[7]

The making of a common market was the explicit priority of the founding fathers. Distortion in competition had consequently to be avoided in the social field while at the same time provision was made for the free movement of workers. Hence, countries, such as France (in which social standards were enshrined in the constitution), worked actively towards the introduction into the treaty of the principle of equal pay for male and female workers performing work of equal value, and of paid holiday schemes.[8]

The unexpected consequences of the equal pay principle came later on as the outcome of an imaginative strategic litigation, advocating the direct effect of the principle itself, responding to inactive national legislatures that had failed to implement it.[9] This field proved to be fertile for the adoption of secondary legislation. Equal treatment expanded to other fields, such as matters of social security, access to employment and vocational training, promotion, and working conditions. The urge to consolidate all such legislative initiatives into one text, taking into account the CJEU's case law, is now confirmed by the adoption of a recast directive.[10]

The Treaty of Rome proved to be equally longsighted in establishing the European Social Fund,[11] which provided financial help to workers who were seeking employment opportunities and were in need of training whenever adaptations to changes in production were necessary. Recourse to the fund has been controversial over the years. As a consequence of restructuring in different productive sectors, and in the midst of the economic and financial crisis, the European Social Fund, together with other specialized structural funds, has been pivotal in fighting unemployment and in promoting social cohesion within the European Union. It is worth noting that the delivery of financial support from EU institutions to member states is a cumbersome and highly complex operation that finds its origins in exceptional circumstances and continues to be governed by specific procedures that are subject to severe mechanisms of control. Notably, a harsh controversy between the Commission and the Parliament took place over the recent reform of the EU budget for the years 2014 to 2020 with regard to the amount to be assigned to social and cohesion policies.[12]

From the "Social Model" to the "Social Chapter"

If we continue to follow a diachronic illustration of EU social policies, we see that in the 1970s, member states were exposed to different waves of economic crises, mainly provoked by factors external to national economies. Secondary legislation enacted in those years included a social dimension that, in retrospect, should be positively evaluated, although not all commentators agree on this.[13]

The Werner Report was published in 1970.[14] It argued that economic and monetary policies should be designed with a view to adopting a single currency and indicated ways ahead for reforms that were later adopted, including the cooperation of management and labor in the lawmaking process.

Following a 1974 Council resolution on the adoption of a social action program, the so-called social model started to take shape. Owing to the fact that a supranational welfare state was inconceivable and there would be no access to resources, the ambiguity of this terminology is self-evident. A social model that could function in a common market yet still respect national competences was an original idea, but one with manifest weakness. However, the evolution of social policy was consistent and uninterrupted for many years.[15]

The principle behind the policy of protecting employees in collective redundancies [16] and in transfers of undertaking[17] was that this should not interfere with the completion of the internal market. In both cases, the employer – without being limited in the exercise of economic prerogatives – is nevertheless obliged to inform and consult workers' representatives with the aim of adopting alternative solutions to dismissals and guaranteeing rights in case of transfers.

Recourse to some form of collective representation on the workers' side was regarded as an essential long-term step for countries in which no such institution existed.[18] Furthermore, the procedural connotation of rights to information and consultation, subject to harmonization, gave rise indirectly to a new floor of individual and collective guarantees, which were later expanded. For example, the Directive on European Works Council[19] adds yet another transnational dimension to information and consultation in European companies and in European groups of companies, which has given rise to interesting developments, even beyond the letter of the law. Finally, a general framework for informing and consulting employees, with the intention of filling in the gaps left open by other sources and expanding such a right to individuals, was also adopted.[20]

From 1985 to 1995 Jacques Delors – an innovator and a promoter of social policy – guided the Commission. His main achievement, as he stated, was the adoption of the Single European Act.[21] Amendments of the treaty, allowing for decisions in the Council to be taken with qualified majority voting, unblocked the otherwise stagnant state of social policies. This major institutional reform applied to legislation related to the protection of health and safety at the place of work, a turning point for the drafting of directives having to do with a broad range of working conditions, including working time.

Delors also favored the inclusion of management and labor in processes of decision making, thus acknowledging a long-established tradition in several member states. From a very feeble and unstructured "social dialogue," relations between management and labor developed over the years into contractual relations, implying different degrees of institutional responsibilities, to which social partners are now more and more exposed.

This was the outcome of yet another institutional battle led by Delors: the insertion into the treaty of a "social chapter." This was much disliked by Margaret Thatcher, who strongly opposed the adoption of European social measures, but in 1992 a solution was found, during the last few hours of the European Council held at Maastricht. The social partners drafted the text of a protocol, which was attached to the treaty, the United Kingdom exercising its right to opt out. The protocol was later incorporated in the treaty and is now part of Title X of the Treaty on the Functioning of the European Union (TFEU).

Its most original contribution to the evolution of social policy has to do with the formal inclusion of management and labor in the process of lawmaking. Following a consultation by the Commission, whenever a proposal in this field is foreseen, the social partners can take the initiative to proceed with their own proposal, and they have nine months to complete the process. If they reach an agreement, this is forwarded to the Commission and, if they so choose, it can be implemented through a Council decision.[22]

There is nothing comparable to this step forward in any other supranational system of norm setting. It acknowledges the – mainly Continental – tradition of including groups representing management and labor in institutional contexts, making them responsible for the implementation of standards of protection.[23]

The Employment Title and New Governance Techniques

The successful story of the "social chapter" was undercut during the 1990s by rising unemployment throughout Europe, which provoked harsh criticism from the Nordic countries (which had themselves campaigned for inclusion of an employment title in the treaty). The underlying idea was to wed together the coordination of broad economic policies (occurring through a binding system of guidelines issued by the European Council) to a comparable system, albeit one not assisted by similarly strong sanctions. This innovation saw the light in 1997 in the Amsterdam Treaty and is now dealt with in Title IX TFEU.

The "open method of coordination," namely the enforcement of treaty provisions via soft law measures, has been subject to criticism. The reluctance of national legislatures to act whenever their sovereignty in matters dealing with employment policies was at stake was not balanced by a sufficiently convincing centralized power to coordinate major labor market reforms. Despite an implied duty of cooperation between EU and member state institutions, it proved difficult to ensure that national technocrats would follow a coherent approach, regardless of changes occurring in governments. Intergovernmental coordination has been progressively losing its credibility, even though a complex exchange of messages continues to be the core of this method. Decisions by the Council addressing guidelines to member states demand the definition of national reform programs and the implementation of the same.[24]

In 2010, ten years after the launching of the "Lisbon strategy" on employment policies, the Commission proposed a critical evaluation of synergies among existing policies. The new agenda, framed in a programmatic document named "Europe 2020," set very ambitious targets, which soon proved unrealistic because of the long-lasting effects of the crisis.[25] This document is still considered the starting point for combined initiatives suggested to national legislatures, although its political impact has declined considerably.

Here again, the balance of powers among EU institutions and member states shows how the lack of centralized redistributive policies makes the choice of priorities very problematic, despite the attempt to issue tailor-made recommendations for each country. The crucial point is to guarantee objective criteria for the evaluation of national reforms.

The Commission, through the adoption of social indicators, should assess all responses offered by member states to the Council's employment guidelines. The attempt to include a scorecard of social indicators within multilateral surveillance mechanisms and macroeconomic imbalance procedures, leading afterwards to specific recommendations to member states, has recently been under the severe scrutiny by the European Parliament.[26] The crisis has revealed areas of poverty and social exclusion that are not easily captured by social indicators, nor can they be subject to broad generalizations. Hence the need to provide a floor of guarantees for groups hard hit by unemployment and social exclusion and to support them with selective financial help.

In an effort to demonstrate the good intentions of EU institutions, despite the many limitations in granting financial help, the European Globalisation Adjustment Fund was introduced in 2007 as an exceptional measure. It initially aimed to support workers made redundant because of the imbalances brought about by globalization in local labor markets but was then extended to include redundancies caused by the crisis. The repeated requests that have been made via national governments in efforts to face employment crises in several sectors of the economy explain the reiteration of this initiative, despite its very limited scope.[27]

In 2011, the Commission proposed that its own monitoring and the coordination of national responses should be brought within the new scheme of the European Semester, formalized through Regulation 1175/2011 belonging to the so-called Six Pack.[28] In January, the overall picture of economic priorities is set and the annual growth survey is presented, where measures to tackle recovery are put forward, having as priorities growth and employment. The joint employment report is, consequently, attached to the survey and supplemented by the points of view expressed in official documents by all social partners. In April, national reforms programs, framed within the agenda of "Europe 2020," are presented together with stability and convergence programs, the latter requested by the reformed Stability and Growth Pact.[29] On this basis, the Commission presents country-specific recommendations in May with a view to their adoption by the Council in June. To complete the picture of this calendar of commitments, euro area countries are required to submit draft budget plans by 15 October in view of the final adoption by December 31.

Beyond a Functionalist Approach

The diachronic analysis offered so far motivates a few comments. Regulatory measures in social policy, related to equal treatment, nondiscrimination, and working conditions were implemented via hard law measures aiming at the harmonization of standards.

Procedural rights, in particular information and consultation, despite the emphasis in the 1970s on market building, were not merely ancillary to business strategies. They too developed into a harmonized system of norms, revitalized from time to time by the progressive interpretation of the CJEU.

It has recently been proposed that all major directives dealing with information and consultation should be consolidated to enhance the better regulation policies and cover a wider audience of companies – in particular small and medium-sized enterprises, public sector undertakings, and seafarers – all previously left out of primary legislation.[30] This attempt to rationalize existing sources can arguably show the lack of political consensus to legislate on broader issues related to restructuring. On the other hand, this document shows that the Commission continues to put information and consultation at the center of its policy making.

In this evolution, one can capture the originality of European social policy and put into question the early functionalist approach, which relied on the leading force of market integration. It can be argued, on the contrary, that social policy emerged with its own body of norms despite the coercing role of the market, finding new forms of expression. One example is the development of antidiscrimination law into a coherent set of norms. Combating discrimination on the ground of racial or ethnic origin[31] and establishing a general framework for equal treatment in employment[32] represent important achievements, albeit not always accompanied by meaningful initiatives to provide concrete entitlements for disadvantaged groups.[33] Another example is the inclusion of the social partners in the lawmaking process and the emergence of their role as specialized interlocutors of European institutions. This option has facilitated the materialization of *sui generis* negotiations, in the so-called sector and inter-sector social dialogue, grown autonomously, albeit with a formal recognition by the Commission.[34] This solution, adopted by the Commission through a legal act, introduces criteria of representativeness of the organizations involved and elements of transparency.

As for the weakness of the legal basis in the treaty, one can argue that challenges to legislation have been unsuccessful, whereas the interpretation of the CJEU has often been innovative, for example granting the full recognition of fundamental rights to health and safety and paid annual leave.[35] Hence, we can envisage a certain stability of what can be described as the unexpected architecture of social policy, standing on pillars that imply the recognition of individual rights and support to sector social dialogue.

However, the positive developments described so far encounter an obstacle when collective fundamental social rights are at stake, as with the already mentioned case law originated with the rulings in *Viking* and *Laval*.[36]

With these observations in mind, we can now turn our attention to the latest innovations in social policy brought about by the Lisbon Treaty.

The Lisbon Treaty

The first thing to notice when examining the Lisbon Treaty[37] is the forward steps that have been taken in the social policy field. Article 3 of the Treaty on European Union (TEU) mentions full employment among the objectives to be pursued in a "social market economy." This is by all means an unfulfilled promise and one that has driven European citizens towards disenchantment in the last few years. It is unfortunate that the Lisbon Treaty came into force when the Greek crisis, the first in a series of national emergencies, began to show its devastating impact on social rights, as well as on more complex institutional balances.

Article 9 TFEU refers to "the promotion of a high level of employment, the guarantee of adequate social protection, the fight against social exclusion" in "defining and implementing" policies and activities of the Union. This horizontal or mainstreaming clause represents a novelty. At the same time, it binds EU institutions and member states in their own initiatives, directing them towards specific outcomes. However, it is difficult to connect this regulatory technique with a specific impulse towards concrete actions. The adoption of legislation can often be very slow and not in tune with needs of EU citizens, particularly when emergency measures have to be given priority.

It has been argued, though, that Article 9 should be interpreted in conjunction with Article 151 TFEU. The mere programmatic function of the latter can be questioned, particularly when taking into account the reference it makes to the 1961 European Social Charter (ESC), revised in 1996.[38] This interpretation may respond to some of the critiques raised by the CJEU's rulings in *Viking* and *Laval*, given the explicit mention of the right to strike in Article 6 ESC. It would also pave the way to more consistent interpretations of international standards, following the European Union's accession to the ECHR. The social charter, while fitted in a separate legal system, constitutes a binding source for national legislatures within the Union when they adopt legal measures and when they comply, as in the Swedish *Lex Laval*, with a CJEU ruling.[39]

In fact, should an extensive interpretation of collective social rights continue to be missing, the relevance of "values" enshrined in Article 2 TEU, above all the value of solidarity, which is such an inherent part of national constitutional traditions, could run the risk to be marginalized. Because of all these uncertainties and weaknesses, it has been suggested that, at present, nothing but a "human developmental" view of labor law can be traced in the Lisbon Treaty.[40] The expansion of social policy is not only limited by the scarcity of resources and redistributive measures but also by the uncertainties of political priorities and the ambiguity of judicial interventions.

As for competences, Article 5 TFEU indicates that the Union "shall" take measures aiming at the coordination of employment policies, through the definition of guidelines, and "may" take initiatives for the coordination of social policies.

Title IX, dealing with employment policies, despite a more assertive tone in Article 5, is constructed on soft law techniques and has been critically discussed before. Title X on social policies is, on the contrary, constructed around hard law measures aimed at the harmonization of standards. It also provides, as previously mentioned, for the inclusion of social partners in the lawmaking process, thus allowing for a certain degree of self-determination and openness to collective representation.

Article 152 TFEU, an important novelty introduced in the Lisbon Treaty, follows this path, since it institutionalizes the practice of social dialogue, informally started by Jacque Delors and now transformed into a recognized procedure, while respecting the "autonomy" of social partners. Furthermore, Article 152 endorses the Council's Tripartite Social Summit for Growth and Employment,[41] which includes representatives of employers and labor. The specific composition of this Council can be seen as an anomaly, when compared with other Council's "configurations," as indicated in Article 16(6) TEU.[42] The Commission now seems to be aware of this and is proposing a more visible role of the tripartite summit within the overall architecture of economic governance.[43] It is, in fact, hard to deny that employment and growth constitute essential elements of macroeconomic strategies.

Article 152 shows that the interplay among large groups representing organized interests and the European institutions developed over the years into a complex method is not comparable to national collective bargaining and not in conflict with it. However, the visibility of collective representation in primary EU law contradicts the explicit exclusion from EU competence of matters such as "pay, the right of association, the right to strike or to impose lock outs" (Article 153(5)).

Hence, the conclusion to be drawn is that despite an uninterrupted plethora of institutional reforms that have occurred over the decades, the problem of clashes among lawmakers at different levels, when exercising their competences in this delicate field, is still unsolved. However, new ways forward are possible if we look at the Charter of Fundamental Rights of the European Union (the Charter), which is now granted "the same legal value as the Treaties" (Article 6 TEU).

Chapter III on "Equality" and Chapter IV on "Solidarity" enshrine a large spectrum of fundamental rights, some of which have already been transposed into secondary legislation (nondiscrimination, equality between men and women, information and consultation, fair and just working conditions, reconciliation of family and professional life, social security).

The recognition of the "right of collective bargaining and action" is found in Article 28. The right of collective action should be interpreted in conjunction with Article 152 and provide a legal basis in the treaty, as recently indicated with regard to the adoption of a legal framework for transnational company agreements.[44] In recent years, large multinational companies, leaving aside the adoption of unilateral codes of conduct, have chosen to sign transnational agreements with European Work Councils and with European trade union federations. Such agreements very often deal with the enforcement of fundamental rights throughout the value chain of production. They also endorse organizational questions, such as labor mobility and the matching of new skills with new jobs. The fact that these autonomous practices, set in place by large and representative bargaining agents, have been spreading in times of crisis is instructive and could exemplify the dissatisfaction of management and labor with the slow evolution of social policy.

Concluding Remarks and Open Questions

As part of a wider reconsideration of social policies within EU macroeconomic governance, social dialogue and workers' involvement are mentioned in a number of documents. The point to make is that there seems to be a transitory scheme of action that should drive the Commission into a new phase. We have already acknowledged the institutional dimension of social dialogue, through the new configuration and functions of the Tripartite Summit. We have also pointed to the decline of legislative initiative. It is worth recalling that, following an initiative of the European Parliament under Article 225 TFEU formally requesting the submission of "any appropriate proposal" on matters relevant for the implementation of the treaty, the failure to adopt legislation on restructuring caused a complaint on the part of the European Trade Union Confederation (ETUC) to the European Ombudsman.[45] This example shows a first attempt made by the ETUC to reestablish an institutional balance using the tool provided in the Lisbon Treaty. This is not enough to show that pluralism is guaranteed and balances of power are reconsidered in the construction of EU social policy.

The economic and financial crisis has accentuated the problems of supranational coordination versus national initiatives and has given rise to exceptional austerity actions that have departed from the "methods" provided for in the treaty.

In the Fiscal Compact[46] references to "governance of the euro area" are connected to measures aimed at strengthening the coordination of economic policies (Article 1). The promotion of a high level of employment, which, as previously mentioned, failed completely, is now presented as one element of the many strategies that should be enforced, in order to enhance a "proper functioning of the euro area" and contribute to "the sustainability of public finances" and to "reinforcing financial stability" (Article 9).

In the Treaty establishing the European Stability Mechanism (ESM),[47] signed by the euro area member states, the mobilization of funding "to provide stability support" can also imply, for countries undergoing serious financial problems, entering into "agreements or arrangements with ESM members, financial institutions or other third parties" (Article 3). Whenever a decision is reached, a memorandum of understanding is signed, reflecting the severity of each case and the measures to be adopted (Article 13.3). These new sources, still to be framed within a clear legal status, have raised criticism and given rise to complaints addressed to international organizations. National collective actors representing organized interests, excluded from the negotiations of memoranda of understanding, have been active in vindicating serious infringements of fundamental rights. One could argue that, following the impact of the crisis (which has imperiled the exercise of fundamental social rights in several countries) coordination in social policy should also take the form of efficient monitoring, addressed to member states, in order to verify compliance with fundamental social rights enshrined in the charter.

Notes

1 Treaty Establishing the European Economic Community, 25 March 1957, 298 U.N.T.S. 11.
2 Stephan Leibfried and Paul Pierson, *European Social Policy* (Washington, DC: The Brookings Institution 1995), 43ff.
3 Mark Dawson and Floris De Witte, "Constitutional Balance in the EU after the Euro-Crisis," *Modern Law Review* 76 (2013): 817ff.
4 Case C-438/05 *International Transport Workers' Federation and Finnish Seamen's Union v. Viking Line ABP and OÜ Viking Line Eesti* EU:C:2007:772; and Case C-341/05 *Laval un Partneri Ltd v. Svenska Byggnadsarbetareförbundet, Svenska Byggnadsarbetareförbundets avdelning 1, Byggettan and Svenska Elektrikerförbundet* EU:C:2007:809. These cases were followed by Case C-346/06 *Dirk Rüffert v. Land Niedersachsen* EU:C:2008:189; and Case C-319/06 *Commission of the European Communities v. Grand Duchy of Luxemburg* EU:C:2008:350. Literature on these cases, the so-called Laval-saga, is immense, and it is therefore impossible here to give full account of them. On 4 December 2013, the Council reached an agreement on the Proposal for a Directive of the European Parliament and of the Council on the enforcement of Directive 96/71/EC concerning the posting of workers in the framework of the provision of services [1997] OJ L 18/1, and on 5 March 2014 the Permanent Representatives Committee of the Council of the European Union approved the compromise text of the directive provisionally agreed between the Greek Presidency of the Council and the European Parliament.
5 Marie-Cécile Escande Varniol, "France," in *Quel droit social dans une Europe en crise?* ed. Marie-Cécile Escande Varniol, Sylvaine Laulom and Emmanuelle Mazuyer (Brussels: Larcier, 2012).
6 Treaty Establishing the European Coal and Steel Community, 18 April 1951, 261 U.N.T.S. 140. The ECSC ceased to exist in 2002, by virtue of Article 97, which provided for its expiry after fifty years from the entering into force of the Treaty of Paris.
7 Otto Kahn-Freund, "Labour Law and Social Security," in *American Enterprise in the European Common Market: A Legal Profile*, vol. 1, eds. Eric Stein and Thomas L. Nicholson (Ann Arbor: The University of Michigan Law School, 1960): 325ff. Article 45 TFEU deals with freedom of movement for workers.
8 Article 119 and Article 120 EEC are now Article 157 and 158 TFEU.
9 Case 43/75 *Gabrielle Defrenne v. Société anonyme belge de navigation aérienne Sabena* EU:C:1976:56.
10 Directive 2006/54/EC of the European Parliament and of the Council of 5 July 2006 on the implementation of the principle of equal opportunities and equal treatment of men and women in matters of employment and occupation (recast) [2006] OJ L 204/23.
11 Articles 162 to 164 TFEU.
12 On 2 December 2013 the Council adopted Council Regulation (EU, Euratom) No 1311/2013 of 2 December 2013 laying down the multiannual financial framework for the years 2014–2020 [2013] OJ L 347/884.
13 Fritz W. Scharpf, "The Asymmetry of European Integration, or Why the EU Cannot Be a 'Social Market Economy,'" *Socio-Economic Review* 8 (2010).
14 Report to the Council and the Commission on the realization by stages of Economic and Monetary Union in the Community – "Werner Report" [8 October 1970], Bulletin of the European Communities, Supplement 11/1970.
15 Stefano Giubboni, *Social Rights and Market Freedom in European Constitution: A Labour Law Perspective* (Cambridge: Cambridge University Press, 2006).
16 Council Directive 98/59/EC of 20 July 1998 [1998] OJ L 225/16, consolidating Council Directive 75/129/EEC of 17 February 1975 [1975] OJ L 048/29.
17 Council Directive 2001/23/EC of 12 March 2001 [2001] OJ L 82/16, amending and codifying Council Directive 77/187 EEC of 14 February 1977 [1977] OJ L 61/26.
18 Cases C-382/92 *European Commission v. United Kingdom* EU:C:1994:233 and C-383/92 *European Commission v. United Kingdom* EU:C:1994:234.
19 Council Directive 97/74/EC [1998] OJ L 10/22, followed by Council Directive 09/38/EC (recast) [2009] OJ L 122.

20 Directive 2002/14/EC of the European Parliament and of the Council of 11 March 2002 [2002] OJ L 80/29.

21 See Jacques Delors, *Mèmoires* (Paris: Plon, 2004), 252ff.

22 Articles 154 and 155 TFEU.

23 Some examples of "framework agreements" signed by the European organizations representing management and labor and then incorporated into directives are: Council Directive 2010/18/EU of 8 March 2010 implementing the revised Framework Agreement on parental leave concluded by BUSINESSEUROPE, UEAPME, CEEP and ETUC and repealing Directive 96/34/EC [2010] OJ L 68/13; Council Directive 1999/70/EC of 28 June 1999 concerning the Framework Agreement on fixed-term work concluded by ETUC, UNICE and CEEP [1999] OJ L 175/43; and Council Directive 97/81/EC of 15 December 1997 concerning the Framework Agreement on part-time work concluded by UNICE, CEEP and the ETUC [1998] OJ L 14/9.

24 Council Decision 2013/208/EU of 22 April 2013 on guidelines for the employment policies of the Member States [2013] OJ L 118/21 maintains stable until 2014 the guidelines adopted in 2010.

25 Communication from the Commission of 3 March 2010, Europe 2020: A Strategy for Smart, Sustainable and Inclusive Growth, COM(2010) 2020 final. Among the many targets indicated, it is worth recalling that governments should set 3 percent of GDP aside for research and development; legislation on climate change, energy, and reduction of emissions should become a leading strategy in order to enhance the economy and employment; the number of early school leavers should have been reduced, whereas the number of people with university degrees should have been increased; and the trap for the "working poor" should have been fought against, by supporting those socially excluded.

26 European Parliament – Employment and Social Affair Committee, meeting of 22–23 January 2014.

27 Report from the Commission to the European Parliament and the Council of 14 November 2013 on the activities of the European Globalisation Adjustment Fund in 2012, COM(2013) 782 final.

28 Regulation 1175/2011/EU of the European Parliament and of the Council of 16 November 2011 [2011] OJ L 306/12. The "Six Pack" is a set of five regulations and one directive aimed at strengthening the preventive and corrective arms of the Stability and Growth Pact.

29 Ibid.

30 Communication from the Commission of 13 December 2013 on EU Quality Framework for anticipation of change and restructuring, COM(2013) 882 final, 15.

31 Council Directive 2000/43/EC of 29 June 2000 [2000] OJ L 180/22.

32 Council Directive 2000/78/EC of 27 November 2000 [2000] OJ L 303/16. Mark Bell, "The Principle of Equal Treatment: Widening and Deepening," in *The Evolution of EU Law*, eds. Paul Craig and Gráinne de Búrca (Oxford: Oxford University Press, 2011).

33 Colm O'Cinneide, "Completing the Picture: The Complex Relationship between EU Anti-Discrimination Law and 'Social Europe,'" in *Resocialising Europe in a Time of Crisis*, eds. Nicola Countouris and Mark Freedland (Cambridge: Cambridge University Press, 2013): 118ff.

34 Commission Decision 1998/500/EC of 20 May 1998 on the establishment of Sectoral Dialogue Committees promoting the Dialogue between the social partners at European level [1998] OJ L 225/27.

35 I have argued this in Silvana Sciarra, "National and European Public Policy: The Goals of Labour Law," in *Boundaries and Frontiers of Labour Law: Goals and Means in the Regulation of Work*, eds. Brian Langille and Guy Davidov (Oxford: Hart, 2006): 251 ff.

36 Case C-438/05 *Viking* and Case C-341/05 *Laval*, n 4 this chapter.

37 Entered into force on 1 December 2009.

38 Franck Lecomte, "Embedding Employment Rights in Europe," *Columbia Journal of European Law* 17 (2011): 19.

39 This is the position taken by the European Committee of Social Rights in Case 85/2012 of 3 July 2013, *Swedish Trade Union Confederation (LO) and Swedish Confederation of Professional Employees (TCO) v. Sweden.*

40 Simon Deakin, "The *Viking* and *Laval* Judgments and the Financial Crisis: In Search of New Foundations for Europe's 'Social Market Economy'," in *The Lisbon Treaty and Social Europe*, ed. Niklas Bruun, Klaus Lörcher, and Isabelle Schömann (Oxford: Hart 2012): 36.

41 Council Decision 2003/174/EC of 6 March 2003 [2003] OJ L 70/31.

42 In European Council Decision 2010/594/EU of 16 September 2010 [2010] OJ L 263/12, amending the configuration of the Council to reflect changes provided for in the Lisbon Treaty; no mention is made of the Tripartite Social Summit.

43 Communication from the Commission to the European Parliament and the Council, Strengthening the Social Dimension of the Economic and Monetary Union, of 2 October 2013, COM(2013) 690 final, 14. The EP Committee on Employment and Social Affairs, in its Motion for a Resolution of 6 January 2014, 2013/0361 (APP) suggests to expand even further the competences of the Summit.

44 European Parliament Resolution of 12 September 2013 on cross-border collective bargaining and transnational social dialogue (2012/2292(INI)). Silvana Sciarra, "Resocialising Collective Deliberations," in Countouris and Freedland, *Resocialising Europe in a Time of Crisis*, 420–426.

45 See http://petition.etuc.org/IMG/pdf/ETUC_complaint_to_EU_Ombudsman_on_European_Commission.pdf.

46 Treaty on Stability, Coordination and Governance.

47 The Treaty to create a European Stability Mechanism was signed on 2 February 2012. The negotiation of the ESM was accompanied by the amendment of Article 136 TFEU, through Council Decision 2011/199/EU of 25 March 2011 [2011] OJ L 91/1, with an explicit authorisation to grant financial assistance to eurozone member states.

References

Bell, Mark. "The Principle of Equal Treatment: Widening and Deepening." In *The Evolution of EU Law*, edited by Paul Craig and Gráinne de Búrca, 611–639. Oxford: Oxford University Press, 2011.

Countouris, Nicola, and Mark Freedland, eds. *Resocialising Europe in a Time of Crisis*. Cambridge: Cambridge University Press, 2013.

Dawson, Mark, and Floris De Witte. "Constitutional Balance in the EU after the Euro-Crisis." *Modern Law Review* 76 (2013): 817–844.

Deakin, Simon. "The *Viking* and *Laval* Judgments and the Financial Crisis: In Search of New Foundations for Europe's 'Social Market Economy.'" In *The Lisbon Treaty and Social Europe*, edited by Niklas Bruun, Klaus Lörcher, and Isabelle Schömann, 19–44. Oxford: Hart 2012.

Delors, Jacques. *Mèmoires*. Paris: Plon, 2004.

Escande Varniol, Marie-Cécile. "France." In *Quel droit social dans une Europe en crise?* edited by Marie-Cécile Escande Varniol, Sylvaine Laulom, and Emmanuelle Mazuyer. Brussels: Larcier, 2012.

Giubboni, Stefano. *Social Rights and Market Freedom in European Constitution: A Labour Law Perspective*. Cambridge: Cambridge University Press, 2006.

Kahn-Freund, Otto. "Labour Law and Social Security." In *American Enterprise in the European Common Market: A Legal Profile*. Vol. 1, edited by Eric Stein and Thomas L. Nicholson, 291–458. Ann Arbor: The University of Michigan Law School, 1960.

Lecomte, Franck. "Embedding Employment Rights in Europe." *Columbia Journal of European Law* 17 (2011): 1–21.

Leibfried, Stephan, and Paul Pierson. *European Social Policy*. Washington, DC: The Brookings Institution, 1995.

O'Cinneide, Colm. "Completing the Picture: The Complex Relationship between EU Anti-Discrimination Law and 'Social Europe.'" In Countouris and Freedland, *Resocialising Europe in a Time of Crisis*, 118–137.

Scharpf, Fritz W. "The Asymmetry of European Integration, or Why the EU Cannot Be a 'Social Market Economy.'" *Socio-Economic Review* 8 (2010): 211–250.

Sciarra, Silvana. "National and European Public Policy: The Goals of Labour Law." In *Boundaries and Frontiers of Labour Law: Goals and Means in the Regulation of Work*, edited by Brian Langille and Guy Davidov, 251–270. Oxford: Hart, 2006.

Sciarra, Silvana. "Resocialising Collective Deliberations." In Countouris and Freedland, *Resocialising Europe in a Time of Crisis*, 414–426.

32

EU Citizenship

Elspeth Guild

Introduction

Citizenship of the European Union is a status that is held by every person who is a national of a member state of the Union. Today, there are twenty-eight member states. The European Union is committed to further enlargement in the Western Balkans and Turkey, though the timetable is not yet certain.

At present, there are approximately 503 million people who are citizens of the European Union. As the composition of the Union changes with each enlargement, the number of EU citizens changes as well. There is no mechanism whereby citizens of member states, irrespective of when the states joined the Union, can be deprived of their Union citizenship unless their underlying nationality is revoked (or their state of nationality leaves the European Union).[1] Equally, there is no mechanism whereby citizenship of the Union can be acquired by an individual otherwise than by virtue of acquisition of the nationality of a member state or accession of the person's state of nationality to the European Union.

In this chapter I will examine the history of Union citizenship, where it came from and how it developed over time. I will then move to the rights and duties of citizenship of the Union, explaining what they are and how they can be accessed. In the third section I look at what citizenship of the Union means and where the issues are regarding its relationship with nationality of the member states. Finally, I comment on some of the current political challenges for this citizenship.

History

While free movement of persons has been an objective of the European Union since the inception of the European Economic Community in 1957, the extension from rights of free movement of persons for economic purposes to the economically self-sufficient has taken some time. Transitional arrangements for free movement of workers were lifted in 1968, but free movement rights for students, pensioners, and the economically self-sufficient

A Companion to European Union Law and International Law, First Edition.
Edited by Dennis Patterson and Anna Södersten.

were not adopted until 1990.[2] The following year with the opening of the negotiations for treaty amendments, some member states, in particular Spain, campaigned for the establishment of the new status of citizen of the Union. These efforts were successful. Citizenship was created by the Maastricht Treaty, which entered into force in 1993.[3]

The idea of a new citizenship was not welcomed by all its beneficiaries. In order to enter into force, the Maastricht Treaty had to be ratified by all member states, some of which were required to poll their citizens in a referendum on their views. When Denmark held its first referendum on the treaty in June 1992, a "no" vote succeeded with 50.7 percent. It is somewhat problematic for the principle of liberal democracy for a state's government to act explicitly contrary to the will of the people after they have been asked their opinion in a referendum. Thus, although a second referendum would be required, before this could take place a compromise that reflected the concerns of the Danish people had to be found. Denmark presented a document to the Edinburgh Council Meeting in December 1992 where it noted seven points central to the negative vote, inter alia citizenship of the Union, on which it sought compromises. The Council adopted a decision that sought to address the Danish issues, stressing that citizenship of the Union in no way takes the place of national citizenship and "the question whether an individual possesses the nationality of a Member State will be settled solely by reference to the national law of the Member State concerned."[4] This decision was supplemented by a declaration by Denmark that commences by saying that

> citizenship of the Union is a political and legal concept which is entirely different from the concept of citizenship within the meaning of the Constitution of the Kingdom of Denmark and of the Danish legal system.

A second Danish referendum held in May 1993 succeeded with 53.2 percent of votes in favor of ratifying the treaty. In November 1993, the Maastricht Treaty came into force and citizenship of the Union came into existence.

After declaring its existence, the EU citizenship provision (as amended) states, "Every person holding the nationality of a Member State shall be a citizen of the Union. Citizenship of the Union shall be additional to and not replace national citizenship" (Article 20 of the Treaty on the Functioning of the European Union (TFEU)). This means that from the entry into force of the Maastricht Treaty, all nationals of the member states have two citizenships – that of their member state and that of the Union. At this point, the difference between citizenship and nationality is important. To what extent is it the same thing to have two citizenships or nationalities? There is no clear answer to this question in international law. In so far as the terms "citizenship" and "nationality" may be used to express the same concept, citizenship of the Union gives every citizen of a member state a second citizenship.

As Aleinikoff and Klusmeyer point out,[5] there is global hostility to dual citizenship. In Europe, this has been expressed in the Council of Europe's[6] Convention on the Reduction of Cases of Multiple Nationality and on Military Obligations in Cases of Multiple Nationality 1963. The principle of the convention is found in Article 1(1):

> Nationals of the Contracting Parties who acquire of their own free will … the nationality of another party shall lose their former nationality. They shall not be authorised to retain their former nationality.

Nonetheless, in February 1993 (slightly more than eight months before the entry into force of the Maastricht Treaty and the creation of citizenship of the Union) the Council of Europe adopted a protocol to the convention reversing the principle against dual nationality. It inserted the following wording into Article 1: "where a national of a Contracting Party acquires the nationality of another Contracting Party on whose territory either he was born and is resident, or has been ordinarily resident for a period of time beginning before the age of 18, each of these Parties may provide that he retains the nationality of origin."

Of the twenty-eight member states, twelve have signed and ratified the convention, one has only signed (Portugal), and fourteen have done nothing. Of the member states that have neither signed nor ratified, twelve acceded to the Union in 2004 or later.[7] The only pre-2004 member states that have not signed are Finland and Greece. Thus, there is a fairly wide consensus among EU member states that had not been in the Soviet Bloc that the convention is valuable.[8] The changes in the shape of the European Union since 2004 have brought in states that have a much greater skepticism regarding the benefits of acceding to international conventions which constrain state sovereignty in the field of citizenship. This fits with the assessment of Aleinikoff and Klusmeyer that even though over recent decades "[n]ew practices that tolerate or foster dual nationality … have often sprung up without close scrutiny or without systematic attention to the full implications of the changed practices" there is no political consensus that this is a beneficial development in Europe.[9]

The rules for acquisition and loss of citizenship of the Union rest firmly with the member states, according to the Edinburgh Declaration of 1992. It stresses that whether an individual possesses the nationality of a member state or not is a matter to be settled exclusively by the state concerned in accordance with its national law. These rules differ substantially among the member states. Systems of "pure" *ius sanguinis*, where the nationality of the parents is the sole factor determining that of any child born to them, and of modified *ius sanguinis*, where the nationality of the parents is tempered by an element of residence and birth on the territory of a state when determining the nationality of a child resident on the territory, are now the norm across the EU member states.[10] In no member state does a child acquire citizenship exclusively by reason of birth on the territory of the state (*ius soli*). While birth on the territory may form an important component of whether or not a child is a citizen, the immigration or nationality status of at least one of the parents is a necessary condition throughout the European Union. However, this does not mean that member states are unencumbered by international obligations in respect of acquisition and loss of citizenship. In fact, the member states have been particularly active in limiting their power to determine acquisition and loss rules through international commitments.

The acquisition and loss of citizenship has troubled the international community, in particular at the end of each of the World Wars. After the First World War, within the context of the League of Nations, two measures were adopted in 1930. First, the Convention on Certain Questions relating to the Conflict of Nationality Laws 1930 sought to resolve a series of outstanding issues, in particular regarding the nationality of women and children. As recognition of an independent legal status for women became widespread, rules on their automatic acquisition and loss of citizenship on marriage became unacceptable. The convention sought to protect the nationality status of women from the negative effects of citizenship laws that confer nationality on them or deprive them of it on the basis of their husband's status. Second, the convention contains provisions to regulate the citizenship of children, whether legitimate or illegitimate, with a view to diminishing their risk of being stateless. A second measure, a protocol relating to a certain case of statelessness in 1930, provides for a child born to a woman with the nationality of the state of birth to acquire that citizenship where the child's father is either without nationality or of unknown nationality.

After the Second World War, statelessness was again an issue, resulting in two conventions within the United Nations, one in 1954 and a second one in 1961. Both aimed at reducing the incidence of statelessness. Married women were the subjects of their own convention in 1957. The common feature of all these measures is that they aim to set a threshold for acquisition and loss of citizenship in the international community. Specific focus on stateless persons resulted from concern about displaced persons who were excluded from participation in any community because of a lack of belonging to any one. Women and children had become the subject of measures as a result of the gradual individualization of members of a family as separate legal entities distinct from the adult male considered to be the head of the family.

The advantages and drawbacks of each of the systems of the EU member states regarding acquisition and loss of citizenship vis-à-vis international law have been incorporated into citizenship of the European Union. While the vast majority of EU citizens acquired that status as the result of a birth right, dependent on the citizenship of their parents (whether born in Estonia or Argentina) according to the national law of the state that claims them as citizens, it is those who do not acquire citizenship automatically whose situation is the most revealing about the meaning of citizenship. The conditions under which a state chooses to accord citizenship or to withdraw it tell much about the underlying meaning of citizenship within state sovereignty in that place. Thus citizenship of the Union, as an amalgam of very different traditions, international obligations, and structures, is quite a patchwork, about which nothing consistent can be said concerning acquisition and loss except that these rules are not currently within EU competence.

Perhaps as a result of this rather complex international and national law framework of citizenship and nationality, the CJEU did not engage centrally with the concept until almost a decade after the creation of Union citizenship. When it did, it did so with a statement of enormous political and legal promise:

> Union citizenship is destined to be the fundamental status of nationals of the member states, enabling those who find themselves in the same situation to enjoy the same treatment in law irrespective of their nationality, subject to such exceptions as are expressly provided for.[11]

This statement has now become standard, available in virtually every judgment that the Court hands down on the issue of Union citizenship. It provides the framework for a teleological approach to the meaning and rights of citizens of the Union.

The Locus of the Rights and Duties of EU Citizenship

The rights that are allocated to European citizenship are formally tied to the act of moving from one member state to another. So long as an individual does not venture forth from his or her member state of nationality, he or she remains the subject of the nationality of his or her member state in so far as the EU status of a citizen of the Union is concerned. This is called the "wholly internal rule": EU rights associated with free movement of persons can only be claimed by those EU citizens who have first exercised their free movement rights.[12] Thus, EU citizens who move to work or live in another member state "activate" their EU citizenship when they are outside their member state of origin and rely on those rights for their residence and other protections while in another member state.[13] The main exception to this wholly internal rule is when an EU citizen, after having exercised a free movement right to live and/or work in another member state, returns to his or her home member state of nationality and seeks to continue to rely on rights acquired by virtue of EU citizenship that are not recognized as rights in the national law of his or her member state. The majority of cases of this type revolve around family reunification with third country national family members where some member states have adopted rules that are more restrictive as regards the admission of third country national family members of their own nationals than EU law provides for as regards EU citizens who exercise free movement rights.[14]

The first right of Union citizenship states,

> Every citizen of the Union shall have the right to move and reside freely within the territory of the member states, subject to the limitations and conditions laid down in this Treaty and by the measures adopted to give it effect.

The right to move and reside presents most clearly the tension inherent in citizenship of the Union. Is it a citizenship of one territory, that of the European Union, or an immigration status that permits the crossing of sovereign borders? The right to move and reside as a territorially bounded right is clearly expressed in international human rights law regarding the interior space of a state. Article 12 International Covenant of Civil and Political Rights 1966 (ICCPR) provides that "everyone lawfully within the territory of a State shall, within that territory, have the right to liberty of movement and freedom to choose his residence." Restrictions are only permissible where provided by law; necessary to protect national security, public order, public health or morals, or the rights and freedoms of others; and are consistent with the other rights contained in the ICCPR. What is a right to everyone lawfully within a territory in international human rights law becomes a right for citizens of the Union within the territory of the member states. Thus, the position of the citizen of the Union is assimilated to the position of any human being, including the foreigner, in international human rights law.

If the territory of the Union is that of all the member states and the nationals of the member states are citizens of the Union, one might argue that a citizen must have an unrestricted right to move and reside within the European Union. This would be consistent with the Human Rights Committee's interpretation of Article 12 ICCPR:

> Everyone lawfully within the territory of a State enjoys, within that territory, the right to move freely and to choose his or her place of residence. In principle, citizens of a State are always lawfully within the territory of that State.[15]

Thus, the scope of permissible restrictions on the movement within a state of its citizens cannot include, at least in principle, a legal regime which permits the citizen's presence to be unlawful per se. Citizenship of the Union may be criticized for lacking a fundamental quality in this regard. From the outset, the right of free movement of persons was qualified by an exception on grounds of public policy, public security, or public health. The jurisprudence on citizenship of the CJEU accepted that the right to enter and remain in any part of the territory of which one is a national is not a right attendant on citizenship of the Union.[16] These citizens can still be expelled from one member state to another on the basis that they are nationals of another member state and have offended against the member state of residence's sensibilities regarding public policy, public security, and public health. This exception is inscribed in the treaty, and thus within the European Union's own legal order it is a permissible exception to the citizenship right.

The right of member states to expel EU citizens from one member state to another on grounds of public policy or public security (the grounds most commonly used) remains problematic from the perspective of citizenship. This continuing power of the member states makes it difficult to gain recognition of citizenship of the Union as a genuine citizenship in international law, where the key international characteristic is the right always to enter the country of citizenship. Only if one considers the European Union as single territory and expulsion of an

EU citizen from one member state to another as an internal matter can one reconcile the two. This issue was rather obliquely addressed by the CJEU in a rather controversial judgment of 2011.[17] Minor children who had been granted Belgian citizenship in Belgium sought recognition of a right (which they claimed was one of Union citizenship) to have their third country national parents reside with them in Belgium and for those parents to be entitled to work. The CJEU found in favor of the children's claim that

> It must be assumed that … a refusal would lead to a situation where those children, citizens of the Union, would have to leave the territory of the Union in order to accompany their parents. (para 44)

Following its creation, there was substantial doubt in the legal community whether citizenship of the Union was capable of having direct effect, the EU legal doctrine whereby provisions of law have direct application in the legal orders of the member states without the need to be incorporated into national law.[18] This debate ended when the CJEU confirmed that the treaty provision establishing the status did have such an effect.[19] As a result of having such effect, once an individual has activated his or her EU citizenship rights, the question arises when (if ever) they are extinguished. Once again, the answer to this question has so far arisen only as regards the EU citizenship right of family reunification with third country nationals. As mentioned above, a number of member states have national rules on family reunification of their citizens with third country national family members that are more restrictive than those which apply to EU citizens who have exercised their right of free movement to live and exercise economic activities in a member state other than that of their underlying nationality.[20] The articulation of the rights accruing to citizens of the Union as a result of their status as citizens of their underlying nationality has been a matter of substantial friction with a number of member states. Two main arguments have arisen before the CJEU:

1. Citizens of the Union may enjoy rights attendant on that status as long as they are not within the territory of their state of nationality. Thus if they are within their state of nationality they are subject, exclusively to the family reunification law of that state (not the more generous EU rules).
2. Citizens of the Union may only enjoy family reunification rights with their third country national family members once they have been admitted as family members at least somewhere in the European Union in accordance with national law (not EU law).

The first argument was presented to the CJEU in 1991 by way of a reference from the United Kingdom. As family reunification rights only come into existence when the principal exercises a right of free movement to live and exercise an economic activity in another member state,[21] in principle they do not apply to nationals of the member states within their own state.[22] When the principal exercises a free movement right (more substantial than service receipt for a couple of days), he or she is entitled to enjoy family reunification in the host member state. On return to his or her country of origin would the principal retain the right to family reunification under Union law or fall back into the embrace of his or her member state of nationality and its national legislation? The case which raised and resolved this question was that of Mr and Mrs Singh.[23] Mrs Singh, a British national, had moved to Germany to work. Her husband, a third country national, joined her there. Subsequently, they decided to return to the United Kingdom, where Mrs. Singh opened a shop. The UK authorities sought to deport Mr Singh on the basis of national law when he stopped living with Mrs Singh. He argued that national law did not apply to him as he was the spouse of a Union worker (now self-employed). The CJEU held that the

United Kingdom could not apply its national law to persons in this situation, as this would constitute an obstacle to free movement of persons. Union citizens (as the status was about to be created) would be discouraged from exercising their free movement right if they feared they would not be able to return to their home state with their family members. Mr Singh was entitled to remain in the United Kingdom so long as he continued to be married to Mrs Singh.

Thus, EU citizens normally retain the family reunification rights acquired under Union law by virtue of their exercise of a free movement right, at least for a period of time after they return to their home member state. So, while an EU state could make family reunification impossible for its nationals at home, it could not stop them going to another member state to enjoy the right and then returning to the home member state with those same family members. This, in fact, became quite common for Dutch, Danish, and UK nationals who, on being refused permission to have their foreign spouses live with them in the home state went to work in another member state, primarily Belgium, Sweden, or Ireland. This informal banishment of the "identity offenders" could not, however, be applied to those lucky EU citizens who were dual nationals holding also the citizenship of another member state as they were entitled to rely on this other identity to enjoy family life under EU rules within the member state without having to migrate.[24] The CJEU, however, raised some doubts about this class as well, where the dual national has been born, lived his or her whole life in the host state, and never exercised any form of economic activity.[25]

When a national of a member state marries a third country national, a second EU passport is not automatically forthcoming, nor is such a person automatically capable of moving to another member state and living there for an extended period before moving back home with the spouse. This was the situation of a British national which came before the CJEU. Mr Carpenter, from the account in the CJEU's judgment,[26] appears to have been quite an ordinary Englishman, living in the United Kingdom. He was a self-employed businessman selling advertising space in medical and scientific journals. He had responsibility for his young children by a previous marriage. Mr Carpenter married a Filipino national, who was irregularly in the United Kingdom having overstayed her permitted visit. The UK authorities refused, as is consistent with national law, to allow Mrs Carpenter to remain in the United Kingdom with her husband. In the face of the rejection of Mr Carpenter's choice to live in the United Kingdom with his Filipino wife, who was centrally engaged in the upbringing of his children by his previous marriage, Mr Carpenter sought to establish this right of residence as a citizenship right at the level of EU law. The UK Government argued that since Mr Carpenter had not exercised his right of free movement by physically moving and residing in another member state, his spouse could not rely on an entitlement to residence in EU law as the matter was wholly internal to the United Kingdom.

The CJEU found as a matter of fact that Mr Carpenter was self-employed selling advertising space, a significant proportion of which was to advertisers in other member states. As a result, he came within the scope of the EU law as a service provider. Once within the scope of Union law, the CJEU "borrowed" Article 8 European Convention on Human Rights, the respect for family life, and applied it to the situation of Mr Carpenter, who was now within the scope of Union law (the case predates the entry into force of the EU Charter of Fundamental Rights). The CJEU found that it was not compatible with Article 8 as protected by Union law that Mrs Carpenter should be required to leave the United Kingdom:

> A decision to deport Mrs Carpenter, taken in circumstances such as those in the main proceedings, does not strike a fair balance between the competing interests, that is, on the one hand, the right of Mr Carpenter to respect for his family life, and, on the other hand, the maintenance of public order and public safety.[27]

Nonetheless, it is noteworthy that the CJEU avoided any mention of Mr Carpenter's capacity as a citizen of the Union. Instead it relied entirely on his identity as an economic actor.

The second argument came before the CJEU when some member states became increasingly insistent, in national legislation, that all third country national family members obtain visas before taking up residence. Belgium was among this group. A Belgian nongovernmental organization, MRAX, challenged this requirement as regards migrant citizens of the Union on the basis of the right of Union citizens to enjoy family reunification. The matter was referred by the national court to the CJEU for an answer as to whether the strict application of the visa requirement in respect of third country national family members of citizens of the Union was consistent with Union law in three situations:[28]

1. Where the third country national family member arrives at the border without the required visa
2. Where the third country national family member has entered and stayed in the member state unlawfully and then marries a migrant Union citizen
3. Where the third country national family member has entered lawfully but stayed beyond his or her permitted period and then seeks to remain on the basis of the family relationship with the migrant Union citizen.

Starting with the first and most difficult question, the CJEU noted that the Union legislature recognized the importance of ensuring protection for the family life of nationals of member states in order to eliminate obstacles to the exercise of the fundamental freedoms guaranteed by the treaty. While the CJEU recognized that the secondary legislation does not, on the face of it, preclude turning such a person back at the border, it noted that the member states are under a duty to facilitate the issue of visas. It found that member states are under a duty to give full effect to this duty of facilitation even to the extent of issuing the visa at the border to such a family member. It added,

> it is in any event disproportionate, and, therefore, prohibited to send back a third country national married to a national of a member state where he is able to prove his identity and the conjugal ties and there is no evidence that he represents a risk to the requirements of public policy, public security or public health.[29]

With respect to the second question, the CJEU noted that it was established case law that the issue of a residence permit cannot be regarded as a measure that gives rise to rights but rather as a measure by a member state that proves the position of the individual. While sanctions for failure to respect administrative requirements as regards residence permits of a member state are permitted, an expulsion order on this basis alone would be manifestly disproportionate. Thus, member states are not permitted solely on this ground to refuse to issue a residence permit and to issue an expulsion order against a third country national who is able to furnish proof of identity and relationship with a migrant Union citizen.

The CJEU then came to the final issue: overstayers. It found that as member states are obliged to grant a right of residence to workers who can produce either a valid identity card or passport, regardless of the document on which they entered the territory, so too must member states issue residence permits to these family members. A member state is precluded from making the issue of a residence permit in Union law conditional upon production of a valid visa. The underlying rationale of the judgment is the obligation on member states to eliminate obstacles to the exercise of fundamental freedoms in the treaty. Of course, the right to family reunification can be defeated by a successful claim by the state that the individual is a threat to public policy, public security, or public health. These terms, however, have been narrowly defined by the CJEU – an interpretation which applies equally to third country national family members as to Union citizens. The right of citizens of the Union to enjoy family reunification with their third country national family members irrespective of the immigration status of the latter was again affirmed in 2008 by the CJEU, correcting a minor deviation in the jurisprudence that had caused some consternation.[30]

While these cases all revolve around the specific situation of third country national family members of EU citizens, they reveal the location of citizenship of the Union in ways that other citizenship disputes do not. Fundamentally, citizenship of the Union, as it currently stands, is a status which protects those who have exercised free movement rights, mainly those who have moved to another member state and spent enough time there no longer to qualify as citizens of their own state only. How much time is enough time? There is no legal answer to this question (yet), but it is the dividing line between a citizen of the Union genuinely exercising a free movement right and one who is abusing the national laws of his or her member state. When does a citizen have the right to hold his or her head high as a citizen of the Union and when does a national of a member state have to sneak around the immigration rules of his or her member state like a thief in the night? This is the locus of citizenship of the Union.

Union Legislation – Where is Citizenship of the Union and What Does it Mean?

Article 20(1) TFEU contains the genesis and determination of the status of citizen of the European Union. It states that citizenship of the Union is hereby established. Every person holding the nationality of a member state shall be a citizen of the Union. Citizenship of the Union shall be additional to and not replace national citizenship.

The rights that attach to citizenship of the Union are contained in Article 20(2) and in Articles 21 to 23 TFEU. Article 20(2) TFEU states that citizens of the Union shall enjoy the rights and be subject to the duties provided for in the treaties. They shall have, inter alia,

- the right to move and reside freely within the territory of the member states;
- the right to vote and to stand as candidates in elections to the European Parliament and in municipal elections in their member state of residence, under the same conditions as nationals of that state;
- the right to enjoy, in the territory of a third country in which the member state of which they are nationals is not represented, the protection of the diplomatic and consular authorities of any member state on the same conditions as the nationals of that state; and
- the right to petition the European Parliament, to apply to the European Ombudsman, and to address the institutions and advisory bodies of the Union in any of the treaty languages and to obtain a reply in the same language.

The rights are specifically stated to be capable of exercise in accordance with the conditions and limits defined by the treaties and by the measures adopted thereunder. Article 21 TFEU provides once again for the right of free movement and residence subject to the conditions laid down thereunder. Article 22 TFEU states that every citizen of the Union residing in a member state of which he or she is not a national shall have the right to vote and to stand as a candidate at municipal elections in the member state in which he resides, under the same conditions as nationals of that State. Finally, Article 23 TFEU provides that every citizen of the Union shall, in the territory of a third country in which the member state of which he is a national is not represented, be entitled to protection by the diplomatic or consular authorities of any member state, on the same conditions as the nationals of that state. Member states shall adopt the necessary provisions and start the international negotiations required to secure this protection. For all the specific rights, powers are granted to the Union institutions to adopt secondary legislation as necessary.

Commencing with the first right, as regards secondary legislation, in 2004 the European Union adopted Directive 2004/38 on the right of citizens of the Union to move and reside in the Union. This directive consolidates a number of earlier directives and extends the rights of citizens of the Union. The following are the key rights:

- The right to move and reside for up to three months on the territory of any member state without formalities; job seekers are entitled to more favorable conditions.
- The right to move and reside on the territory of another member state as a worker, including as a work seeker and as a self-employed person without any financial support or health insurance requirement.
- The right to move and reside on the territory of another member state as a student, retired, or self-sufficient person, subject to having all-risk health insurance and evidence (or merely a declaration for students) of sufficient resources, so as not to become a burden on the social assistance system of the host state.
- The lack of obligation to obtain a residence card of permit unless the member state so determines, for the purpose of registering presence.
- The right to family reunification.
- The right, after five years of continuous residence in a host state, to permanent residence. This is acquired automatically and does not require the citizen to apply for and receive a document.
- The right to equal treatment with the host state's own nationals as regards all social benefits for the economically active and for all on acquisition of permanent residence.
- The right to protection against expulsion (or exclusion), which the state must justify on grounds of public policy, public security, or public health, which have been strictly interpreted by the CJEU. Expulsion must not be the automatic consequence of reliance on social assistance for the economically inactive. Protection against expulsion is enhanced on the acquisition of permanent residence and again after ten years residence in the host member state.

In 2008 the European Commission produced a report on the implementation of the directive.[31] It noted that

> not one Member State has transposed the Directive effectively and correctly in its entirety. Not one article of the Directive has been transposed effectively and correctly by all Member States.

The key problems identified by the Commission were the following:

- Only Denmark, Finland, Malta, and Sweden provide, as required by EU law, for more favorable entry conditions for the first three months for job seekers than for others.
- Malta requires EU citizens to have a work license in order to take up a job.

- Twelve member states have transposed the concept of sufficient resources ambiguously.[32]
- Only ten member states have transposed the provision prohibiting systematic verification of the conditions attached to the right of residence.[33]
- Thirteen member states do not exclude expulsion as an automatic consequence of recourse to the social assistance system.[34]
- Italy and Finland provide for automatic expulsion where a crime of a certain gravity has been committed. Italy also provides for increased detention where an offender is irregularly present on its territory (which the CJEU has held to be unlawful).
- Only Cyprus, Latvia, Spain, and Portugal have correctly transposed the procedural safeguards.

The Commission further noted that since the directive came into force, it has received more than 1,800 individual complaints, forty questions from the European Parliament, and thirty-three petitions about member states' applications. The most persistent problems were about family members who are third country nationals (see the earlier discussion) and member states requiring citizens of the Union to submit applications for residence with additional documents not provided for in the directive.

Turning to voting rights, Directive 93/109 provides for the participation of citizens of the Union in elections of the European Parliament where such persons are living in a member state other than that of their nationality. The objective was to ensure that these citizens had the right to participate in the European Parliament elections which were held in June 1994. The most recent report from the European Commission on the application of the directive is from 2010.[35] It should be noted that for all EU citizens, for the vast majority of citizens who live in their home member state (only approximately 3 percent live in a member state other than that of their underlying nationality according to the Commission), the turn out was 43 percent. For those EU citizens living in a state other than that of their underlying nationality, only 11.6 percent registered to vote in the most recent European Parliament elections of 2009. This is a considerable increase from the 5.9 percent who were registered for the 1994 elections, but it is still an extremely low percentage. This is notwithstanding the fact that according to a Commission initiated survey, 69 percent knew about the right to vote in a member state of residence. The Commission's report points out a number of weaknesses in member states' implementation of the directive and a more general problem that a number of member states apply strict requirements to prevent double voting. These restrictions, while legitimate, may have the effect of inhibiting political participation.

Regarding the Union citizenship right to vote (and stand for election) in municipal elections, Directive 94/80 was adopted to this end. The most recent report of the Commission on the implementation of this directive was published in 2012.[36] Similarly to European Parliament elections (in those member states where voting is not obligatory), participation rates in local elections have dropped, according to the Commission. In more than twenty member states (for which the Commission was able to acquire data), the turn out was between 50 and 60 percent. There are differences between capital cities and other municipalities in favor of the former. While a majority of EU citizens know that they have the right to vote in municipal elections in a host member state, in member states where registration to vote is not automatic, only on average 10 percent of EU citizens living in a member state other than that of their underlying nationality registered to vote. There is no data available on how many of those actually voted. Similarly, there is no reliable available data on how many of these EU citizens stood for office in municipal elections. For some member states, there are derogations still in place regarding access to voting in municipal elections, though this is a small minority. While transposition of the directive, according to the Commission, has been less than ideal in a number of member states, there is evidence of good practices as well. It is hard to avoid the conclusion that, at least for the moment, Union citizens have not been enchanted by their right to vote in a host member state.

The final Union citizenship right, which truly belongs only to Union citizens (unlike the right to petition the European Parliament, the Ombudsman, and to address EU bodies in official languages, which rights actually accrue to anyone, legal or natural, whether in the European Union or outside it), is the right to consular protection. Only in 2009 with the entry into force of the Lisbon Treaty did this right become one in respect of which the Commission has the right to propose legislation. From 1993 until 2009, this right remained one subject to political agreement only. The Commission produced a report entitled "Consular protection for EU citizens in third countries: State of play and way forward."[37] It sets out why there is a need for a legal measure that establishes a minimum level of help that consulates of any member state should provide to any EU citizen whose member state of underlying nationality does not have a representation in the third country in question. The key argument is the large number of EU citizens who travel outside the European Union each year (apparently more than 90 million such trips were taken in 2008). Crises such as those in Libya, Japan, Haiti, and others, have immediate impact on many EU citizens whose countries may or may not be represented in the relevant third country. The Commission insists strongly on the new legal framework in which it has the right to introduce legislation. However, before doing so, it proposes a number of actions, including information programs for EU citizens, seminars for consular officials, and an analysis of the rules and practices of consular authorities. Among the issues that it considers of immediate importance are financial advances to Union citizens who find themselves destitute in third countries and the identification and repatriation of the deceased. There is no immediate timetable, at the time of writing, for EU legislation in this field.

Political Challenges in 2014

Citizenship of the Union became the focus of an important political campaign by the European Commission in 2011/12, which sought to remove obstacles to the exercise of citizens' rights. As a result of a detailed consultation with all interested groups, the Commission identified twenty-five main obstacles that citizens may confront in seeking to exercise their EU citizenship rights. The areas in which these obstacles fall are

- uncertainty regarding the property rights of international couples;
- cumbersome and costly formalities regarding cross-border recognition of civil status documents and difficult cross-border access to justice;
- insufficient protection of suspected and accused persons in criminal proceedings and of victims of crimes;
- taxation in cross-border situations, in particular regarding registration of cars;
- lack of full benefit to EU citizens from cross-border healthcare and health technology;
- consular protection not fully effective as a right for EU citizens in distress in third countries;
- lack of awareness and insufficient enforcement of citizens' rights when buying holidays packages as passengers and as tourists;

- absence of single consumer protection rules, lack of awareness about existing means of redress and insufficient means of redress;
- divergent and incorrect application of EU law and cumbersome administrative procedures hindering to the right to free;
- burdensome and uncertain procedures for recognition of academic diplomas and professional qualifications;
- coexistence of different social security systems challenges workers' mobility;
- low level of political attachment of EU citizens living outside the state of their underlying nationality;
- lack of easily accessible information and assistance to citizens; and
- lack of awareness of the meaning of EU citizenship itself.

The Commission committed itself to an ambitious program to resolve the problems and remove the obstacles, which is tied also to the Commission's Single European Act Communication 2010, thus strengthening the legal and political pressure to produce results. That delivery of the rights of citizens of the Union should constitute such an important political issue in European politics indicates how far practice in the member states strays from the legal obligation to achieve equality of treatment for all EU citizens. Most of the Commission's efforts have focused on better implementation of the rights of EU citizens. However, there has been increasing political concern in some member states, most notably the United Kingdom but also in the Netherlands and Germany, that some EU citizens are engaging in social benefits tourism.[38] While the Commission has investigated the issue intensively and responded frequently to the concerned member states the issue remains politically toxic in some member states.

Notes

1 Case C-135/08 *Rottmann* EU:C:2010:104.
2 Elspeth Guild, *Immigration Law in the European Community* (The Hague: Kluwer Law International, 2001).
3 Elspeth Guild, *The Legal Elements of European Identity: EU Citizenship and Migration Law* (The Hague: Kluwer Law International, 2004).
4 Conclusions of the Presidency: Edinburgh, 12 December 1992, Annex I: Decision of the Heads of State and Government, Meeting within the European Council, Concerning Certain Problems Raised by Denmark on the Treaty on European Union.
5 Alexander Aleinikoff and Douglas Klusmeyer, *Citizenship Policies for an Age of Migration.* Washington (Washington, DC: Carnegie Endowment for International Peace, 2002).
6 The "other" Europe of forty-seven member states parties to the Council of Europe. This institution is based in Strasbourg.
7 Bulgaria, the Czech Republic, Cyprus, Estonia, Hungary, Latvia, Lithuania, Malta, Poland, Romania, Slovakia, and Slovenia.
8 This is notwithstanding the fact that among the states that had signed and ratified are a number which permit multiple nationality without restraint such as Ireland and the United Kingdom.
9 Aleinikoff and Klusmeyer, *Citizenship Policies for an Age of Migration*, 22.
10 See the website: http://eudo-citizenship.eu/ managed by the European University Institute, which maintains information on the citizenship laws of all the member states.
11 Case C-184/99 *Grzelczyk* EU:C:2001:458.
12 Niamh Nic Shuibhne, "Free Movement of Persons and the Wholly Internal Rule: Time to Move on?" *Common Market Law Review* 39 (2003).

13 Michael Dougan, "The Constitutional Dimension to the Case Law on Union Citizenship," *European Law Review* 31 (2006).
14 Helena Wray, *Regulation of Marriage Migration into the UK: A Stranger in the Home* (Farnham: Ashgate, 2011); and Sarah van Walsum. "Transnational Mothering, National Immigration Policy, and European Law," in *Migrations and Mobilities: Gender, Citizenship, Borders*, eds. Seyla Benhabib and Judith Resnik (New York: New York University Press, 2009).
15 UN Human Rights Committee General Comment No 27(67), 2 November 2, 1999.
16 Case C-348/96 *Calfa* EU:C:1999:6.
17 Case C-34/09 *Ruiz Zambrano* EU:C:2011:124.
18 Yolande Prinssen and Annette Schrauwen, *Direct Effect: Rethinking a Classic Of EC Legal Doctrine* (Groningen: Europa Law, 2002).
19 Case C-413/99 *Baumbast* EU:C:2002:493.
20 Guild, *The Legal Elements of European Identity*; and van Walsum, "Transnational Mothering, National Immigration Policy, and European Law."
21 Joined Cases 35/82 and 36/82 *Morson and Jhanjhan* EU:C:1982:368.
22 Nic Shuibhne, "Free Movement of Persons and the Wholly Internal Rule."
23 Case C-370/90 *Singh* EU:C:1992:296.
24 The Commission proposed to extend EU family reunification rules to all Community nationals whether or not they exercised a free movement right. This was included in the proposal for a directive on family reunification (COM(1999) 638 final) but it was among the first provisions to be rejected by the Council.
25 Case C-434/09 *McCarthy* EU:C:2011:277.
26 Case C-60/00 *Carpenter* EU:C:2002:434.
27 The CJEU's reasoning on Article 8 ECHR was quite generous in comparison with the ECtHR's own decision making.
28 Case C-459/99 *MRAX* EU:C:2002:461.
29 Ibid.
30 Case C-127/08 *Metock* EU:C:2008:449.
31 COM(2008) 840, p 3.
32 Bulgaria, Germany, Greece, Finland, Ireland, Italy, Luxembourg, Latvia, the Netherlands, Romania, Sweden, and Slovenia.
33 Belgium, Cyprus, Germany, Greece, Finland, Luxembourg, Malta, the Netherlands, Poland, and Portugal.
34 Austria, Belgium, Bulgaria, Germany, Denmark, Estonia, France, Hungary, Ireland, Italy, Latvia, Romania, and Slovakia.
35 COM(2010) 605 final.
36 COM(2012) 99 final.
37 COM(2011) 149, p 2.
38 Euroactiv, 26 April 2013, http://www.euractiv.com/socialeurope/commission-gets-cold-feet-push-l-news-519366.

References

Aleinikoff, Alexander, and Douglas Klusmeyer. *Citizenship Policies for an Age of Migration*. Washington, DC: Carnegie Endowment for International Peace, 2002.

Dougan, Michael. "The Constitutional Dimension to the Case Law on Union Citizenship." *European Law Review* 31 (2006): 613–660.

Guild, Elspeth. *Immigration Law in the European Community*. The Hague: Kluwer Law International, 2001.

Guild, Elspeth. *The Legal Elements of European Identity: EU Citizenship and Migration Law*. The Hague: Kluwer Law International, 2004.

Nic Shuibhne, Niamh. "Free Movement of Persons and the Wholly Internal Rule: Time to Move On?" *Common Market Law Review* 39 (2003): 731–784.

Prinssen, Yolande, and Annette Schrauwen. *Direct Effect: Rethinking a Classic Of EC Legal Doctrine*. Groningen: Europa Law, 2002.

van Walsum, Sarah. "Transnational Mothering, National Immigration Policy, and European Law." In *Migrations and Mobilities: Gender, Citizenship, Borders*, edited by Seyla Benhabib and Judith Resnik, 228–254. New York: New York University Press, 2009.

Wray, Helena. *Regulation of Marriage Migration into the UK: A Stranger in the Home*. Farnham: Ashgate, 2011.

33

The International Law of Economic Migration

Joel P. Trachtman

Introduction

There is today no multilateral system for liberalization of economic migration. While there are human rights norms that protect the right of exit, and regional systems for liberalization of migration, such as the European Union, there is no general system for commitment to labor market access. And yet, the economic welfare that could be unlocked by such a system, especially to the extent that it allows poor people to move to places where they could be more productive, is enormous. The development potential for the states from which emigration takes place is also substantial.

What are the factors suggesting unmet demand to move? First, wage rate disparities are very large. They are much larger than the differences in prices of goods that provide the motivation for trade. Second, demographic decline in wealthy countries, combined with demographic surge in poor countries, suggests the bilateral need for migration.

Although it seems fairly clear that there are significant potential global gains to be achieved by liberalizing migration, it is also clear that these gains are not distributed evenly. Rather, as is the case with trade in goods or services, there will be winners and there will be losers. The problem for domestic and international politics, and for international institutions, is to establish a method of facilitating policy changes that are Pareto improvements in the sense that even those who might otherwise be losers are better off. The problem for international institutions is to assist in building domestic coalitions that will enable welfare-enhancing policy changes. These policy changes may require careful structuring of liberalization, or linkage of liberalization of emigration to other types of concessions.

I focus here on the implications of economically self-interested behavior by voters and lobbyists, rather than important issues of irredentism, demagoguery, and security.

Between wealthy states, there is little need for international agreements regarding migration. First, there is little demand to migrate, because wages and productivity are relatively homogeneous. Second, wealthy states already autonomously allow immigration of skilled workers from other wealthy states, and unskilled workers have little reason to move. While

A Companion to European Union Law and International Law, First Edition.
Edited by Dennis Patterson and Anna Södersten.

there is little need for such an agreement, and the welfare payoff would be low, there is little reason not to provide commitments and clarification of market access for labor.

The more interesting case is migration between poor and rich countries. Here, the potential welfare gains are very large. However, there are three substantial political problems:

- First, the welfare gains accrue largely to the migrants themselves. The implication of this fact is that neither the home country nor the destination country has strong incentives for liberalization.
- Second, there is little room for reciprocal agreements within the field of migration because migration between poor and rich countries is a "one-way street." That is, generally speaking, there is little demand from rich country citizens for migratation to poor countries. This is because the differences in productivity that give rise to the incentive to migrate from poor to rich countries also give rise to strong disincentives to migrate from rich to poor countries.
- Third, there is concern, although there is no consensus among economists on the empirics, that migration of low-skilled workers into wealthy countries reduces the jobs and employment of native low-skilled workers in wealthy countries.

And yet, the political economy of migration is different from the political economy of trade because producers are generally interested in liberalization of immigration by their own state.

Let us focus on the political problems of liberalizing migration between poor and wealthy states. If productivity differences were not great, it would be possible that reciprocal international agreements for liberalization could assist in forming a pro-liberalization coalition between producers and potential emigrants who seek openness in other states. If productivity differences are great, it may be more difficult to form pro-liberalization coalitions. However, one way to do so is to provide for other concessions by poor states to wealthy states, perhaps along the lines of liberalization of investment or high-value services. This type of reciprocation would be benevolent, with both parts of the bargain improving the welfare of poor states. To the extent that unskilled or other classes of workers are hurt in wealthy states, the wealthy states may need to provide adjustment mechanisms to procure support. Another possible inducement for a pro-liberalization reciprocal agreement might be the alternative strategy that destination state capital can pursue, through use of outsourcing or through employment of illegal workers. From the standpoint of destination state labor, it may be that legal immigration is a superior outcome compared to outsourcing or illegal immigration.

One of the political problems with migration is that most of the benefits accrue to the migrants themselves – the sending state experiences adverse effects of brain drain. Economists often support temporary migration in order to guard against potential adverse effects of brain drain. However, a more attractive option in order to prevent adverse effects of brain drain, and to increase political support of liberalization in the home state, is to support the home state's efforts to recapture its investment in high-skilled emigrants through the ability to charge a tax on some portion of the emigrant's income. Furthermore, to the extent that immigration may harm certain classes of workers in the destination state, or may impose undue pressures on welfare or transfer programs, it may be appropriate to allow some level of discriminatory taxation of migrants by the destination state. These tax arrangements may assist in inducing the development of pro-liberalization coalitions.

A migration fee levied on migrants, perhaps in the form of a tax, might be split, as appropriate, between the host state and the home state. The calculation of this migration fee, and its allocation, should depend on two principal components: (1) the value of the home state contribution to human capital of the migrant, and (2) the value of the increment to productivity, and wages, that the migrant attains simply by moving from the host state to the home state. In a sense these components together measure the societal contribution to the individual's productivity.

The form of any international agreement, and the structure of any international organization, to address international economic migration will result, if at all, from an extensive domestic and international political give-and-take that this chapter cannot anticipate. Different states will have different strategic positions, different economic sectors within these states will have different strategic positions, and even different occupational groups will have different strategic positions. Thus, it is clearly impossible to specify a single arrangement for international cooperation, or even to predict whether international cooperation will occur.

However, we know that in the aggregate, liberalization is expected to provide increased surplus, and, assuming (1) that there are mechanisms that can be devised to overcome the strategic problems that may exist between different domestic constituencies, and between different states, and (2) that the increased surplus exceeds the cost of its capture, we would expect states to move to do so. To move forward, it will be necessary to analyze different states, different sectors within states, and different occupations within those sectors, in order to understand the strategic position of each. Then, we can evaluate which international legal rules, if any, are useful so as to allow for the maximum net payoffs. It is by establishing a framework agreement, and engaging in negotiations, that states will be able to evaluate and reveal whether there are useful transactions that may be effected.

A framework agreement that allows for states to agree on the specific structure of reciprocity, to allow sending states to share in the benefits of a liberalization migration fee, tax, or other mechanism, to make side payments through linkage to other areas of liberalization, and to make side payments through immigration fees, would establish an appropriate institutional framework – would minimize the transaction costs – for states to negotiate optimal arrangements. While such a framework agreement might best be legally binding, it is possible that it might alternatively be best kept informal. In international law, the distinction may have only subtle behavioral implications.

Today there seems to be no regime to address international economic migration, and little law outside of a few regional organizations by which states commit to liberalizing market access for economic migration: states generally make unilateral decisions regarding migration. Should the International Labor Organization (ILO) have been the fourth Bretton Woods institution, alongside the International Monetary Fund, the World Bank, and the General Agreement on Tariffs and Trade (GATT)? After the First World War, France, Italy, Japan, and Poland argued unsuccessfully that the ILO should regulate migration.[1] But after the tightening of immigration restrictions in the interwar period, migration was not addressed at Bretton Woods. To this day, it is striking how liberalization of labor migration seems to have been deemed to fall outside the mandate of each of the existing international organizations, even though some of their formal mandates arguably could be understood to include significantly broader activities in this field.

In order for an assignment of authority to an international organization to be justified, states must first wish to regulate the relevant subject matter under international law. Once it is decided to regulate a subject matter under international law, it is possible that an organization may be useful in order to serve as a secretariat for – to manage, enforce, and develop – a multilateral agreement on migration. Indeed, as in the case of the existing International Organization for Migration (IOM), an international organization might be useful even if there is no need for international law. But where international law is useful, an international organization may serve important complementary functions. It may house adjudication, engage in enforcement or surveillance, or be a forum for decision making. Of course, the type of international organization that will be useful, the desirable structure, and the type of functions that it would perform are dependent upon the type of international legal rules that are determined to be desirable.

The major roles include facilitation of negotiations, research, technical assistance, preparation of new treaty rules, making of new rules other than by treaty, surveillance, dispute settlement, and punishment. And, of course, at least four important multilateral organizations already address economic migration, in at least some dimensions: (1) the IOM, (2) the ILO, (3) the United Nations Conference on Trade and Development (UNCTAD), and (4) the World Trade Organization (WTO). Competing with these multilateral organizational choices are a variety of sub-multilateral structures, including regional integration arrangements such as the European Union or MERCOSUR, as well as bilateral or plurilateral migration partnership arrangements.

States can be expected to establish legal rules or organizations for migration where they expect some benefit from the reciprocal commitments of other states. Otherwise, states would prefer to retain unilateral discretion. The principal type of international arrangement – formal or informal – between states relating to labor migration is the bilateral labor agreement. These agreements are generally, although not exclusively, concluded between labor-sending and labor-receiving countries and contain only the most basic organizational features. Such agreements generally exclude coverage of commitments to accept migrants: they are generally not labor market access agreements. While they do not contain market access commitments, they often have the result of providing privileged labor market access to citizens of the sending-country partner. They therefore raise some issues of most favored nation treatment, and of competition among potential sending countries.

Most bilateral labor agreements deal, often in nonbinding terms, with managerial and collateral issues of recruitment, remittances, and return: they address important issues of management related to migration that will be permitted unilaterally by the home and destination states. Sending countries may be responsible for prescreening migrant workers, including ensuring that they do not have criminal records. These agreements also may provide for measures to ensure return to the home country. These measures may include incentives or sanctions applied to employers or employees to ensure return. Recent agreements have also sought to ensure cooperation to restrict illegal immigration.

There are hundreds of bilateral labor agreements in force. Geronimi lists twenty-four basic elements of an international labor agreement. I have highlighted the provisions that might be expected to be found in an international agreement for labor market access:

the competent government authority
exchange of information
migrants in an irregular situation
notification of job opportunities
drawing up a list of candidates
preselection of candidates
final selection of candidates
nomination of candidates by the employers (possibility for the employer to provide directly the name of a person to be hired)
medical examination
entry documents
residence and work permits
transportation
employment contract
employment conditions
conflict resolution mechanism

the role of trade unions and collective bargaining rights
social security
remittances
provision of housing
family reunification
activities of social and religious organizations
establishment of a joint commission (to monitor the agreements' implementation)
validity and renewal of the agreement
applicable jurisdiction.[2]

These bilateral agreements, while very important to deal with a number of managerial and practical issues, ordinarily do not provide formal commitments to market access or address other important economic issues. The following is a list of additional issues that might be addressed in a labor market access agreement:

market access commitments
national treatment
most favored nation treatment
taxation
professional licensing
transparency and regular procedures
exceptions, including national security and health – coordination with WHO
social security coordination
citizenship, national service, and draft obligations
cooperation in suppression of illegal migration
loyalty and demagoguery
linkage to other types of commitments
dispute settlement
safeguards and compensation.

Some of these issues have been addressed in connection with regional or other plurilateral regimes for labor market liberalization. The European Union, which has extensive liberalization, has addressed most of these issues in extensive terms. Plurilateral arrangements may address all of the same issues as multilateral arrangements, and may address some issues with less difficulty. However, plurilateral arrangements may be unable to provide for multilateral nondiscriminatory (most favored nation) market access and would not provide the transaction cost savings that might come from a single regime. There are some good political and economic reasons why most favored nation might be valuable.[3]

Would an International Organization be Useful?

Not all international law requires an organization. Much, if not most, international law lacks a secretariat, dispute settlement, decision making, surveillance, and other organizational functions. While some type of international law may be useful in the field of economic migration, it is not necessarily clear what, if any, organizational components are suitable. Nor is it clear what relationship international migration law should have with other international law or with existing international organizations. One example of this uncertainty is the relationship between economic migration, on the one hand, and the international legal regime for forced migration, on the other hand. The UN High Commissioner for Refugees holds important expertise regarding migrants, but does not address voluntary migration.

Given the complexity of a likely migration treaty, with many opportunities for uncertainty and defection, it is possible that an organization may provide certain useful services. In particular, we might examine the possibility of strategic behavior. Where states find themselves in a prisoner's dilemma or another strategic setting that could be resolved efficiently by a change in the payoffs effected through legal rules, an international organization might be useful. It would allow states to cooperate where cooperation is beneficial and where it otherwise would not be possible.

Organizations can serve to engage in surveillance, communication, and adjudication in order to enforce rules. In addition, it is necessary to specify bureaucratic, legislative, or dispute resolution methods of completing contracts in order to avoid opportunism: to complete the contemplated transaction as intended. The higher the magnitude of asset specificity, the greater the incentives for opportunism and institutional integration: for the transfer of authority to bureaucratic, legislative, or dispute resolution mechanisms.

Responsibility for international economic migration could be assigned to an existing organization or to a new organization. In this section, I will describe the possible features of a new international organization addressing migration. For purposes of discussion, let us call it the World Migration Organization (WMO).[4] A WMO could have a variety of features beyond substantive treaty obligations, including perhaps the following:

- Purposes. These would include the facilitation of international migration in order to better the welfare of individuals. A focus on the welfare of poor individuals might be appropriate. The purposes may be expressed in broad enough terms to include collateral matters such as social security, healthcare, and other issues to the extent that they would bear on economic migration.
- Membership arrangements and termination. Membership could be open to states willing to accept the obligations of the WMO treaty, including obligations to liberalize immigration.
- Secretariat:
    - Facilitating negotiations. The WMO secretariat could be accorded responsibility for managing negotiations regarding liberalization commitments and other matters. Whether these negotiations would be continuous or focused in particular periods, like GATT/WTO rounds, would be determined by the member states.
    - Facilitating dispute settlement. The WMO secretariat could include a function similar to that of the Legal Affairs Division of the WTO, or like the International Centre for the Settlement of Investment Disputes, in servicing independent dispute settlement tribunals. Alternatively, the WMO could house a specialized permanent tribunal.
    - Surveillance. The secretariat could be tasked with periodic review of member states' systems to evaluate the degree to which they could be improved in order to facilitate migration. This function could be modeled on the WTO's trade policy review mechanism.
    - Technical assistance. Some member states will require technical assistance in support of their negotiation, as well as in support of their implementation, compliance, and dispute settlement activities. The secretariat, or an independent entity, could provide these services.
    - Research. Member states will require research to be performed about many aspects of migration, including especially the economic effects of different types of migration in different contexts.

  - Public relations and transparency. Immigrants can often be scapegoats for economic problems in destination states. If the antiglobalization backlash has been significant with respect to goods, it may become even more active, and more dangerous, with respect to immigration. Therefore, it may be appropriate to develop an effective public relations function for the secretariat. Given the criticism that has been experienced by the European Union, the Organisation for Economic Co-operation and Development (OECD), the WTO, and other international economic organizations, it will be important to develop sufficient transparency to support the perception of legitimacy of a migration organization. Adopting the ILO's tripartite governance structure may also facilitate transparency and the perception of legitimacy between employers as well as workers.[5]
- Substantive expertise and experience. A WMO might contain experience in economic negotiations, including analytical capabilities that could support negotiations and dispute settlement, expertise in the human side of migration, including the capacity of societies to absorb migrants, expertise in labor market conditions and dynamics, expertise in tax policy, expertise in human rights, and experience in multilateral negotiations.
- Treaty making and secondary lawmaking.
  - Committee structure. From a bureaucratic standpoint, it may be useful to divide the work of an organization into committees to prepare for lawmaking of various types. These types of committees may have an important agenda-setting role and should be structured in a way that advances the goals of the organization.
  - Majority voting. It would be highly unlikely that states would agree in the near term to allow significant liberalization or public policy decisions to be made against their individual will by virtue of majority voting. On the other hand, many related issues have been addressed through majority voting within the European Union, so we know that such majority voting is not categorically impossible. After more experience of increased liberalization, and greater commitments for liberalization, states may determine that some matters could be addressed through majority voting. A number of different decision-making structures are possible. One would have the composition of delegates to the WMO take a tripartite structure, similar to the ILO, where representatives of states, employers, and workers are integrated into the decision-making process.[6]
- Dispute settlement. Disputes might arise, for example, over the operation of exceptional mechanisms relating to public health or security, over the operation of safeguards mechanisms, or over arrangements for professional licensing. Dispute settlement can be more or less limited, with more or less "legislative" discretion.
- Remedies. Remedies should be designed to induce an efficient level of compliance with obligations. They may include payment of fines, withdrawal of rights, or requirements of provision of alternative concessions.

Coherence and the Regime Complex for International Labor Migration

The list of functions provided in the prior section is not definitive, nor is it required to be provided by a single organization. So, it is possible that multiple organizations could combine to provide these functions. For example, analytical work or research could be assigned to the OECD, UNCTAD, and perhaps the IOM, while the IOM, ILO, UNCTAD, WTO, or a WMO could perform other functions. Or, dispute settlement for individuals, if they are to have private rights of action, could be assigned to a specialized organization such as the International Centre for the Settlement of Investment Disputes, which would thereupon require a change in name. Negotiations over liberalization commitments could take place at the WTO and could even be addressed in rounds in order to allow package deals to be created that would include all the subjects presently addressed at the WTO, plus migration liberalization.

Indeed, there are no "ideal" answers to these questions, only practical choices to be made based on multiple criteria. I begin by describing the present migration-related functions of the IOM, ILO, and WTO.

The IOM

The IOM has had an operational role in managing specific flows of migrants but has not served to facilitate the development and operation of international law in this field.

> Facilitating the migration of the hundreds of thousands of people in Europe displaced or lacking economic opportunity in the post war period was one of the principal activities of IOM when it was founded in 1951.[7]

Article 1(1)(e) of the IOM Constitution provides that it shall make available a forum for the exchange of views and the "promotion of cooperation and coordination" among states. However, Article 1(3) of the IOM Constitution stipulates that it "shall recognize the fact that the control of standards of admission and number of immigrants to be admitted are matters within the domestic jurisdiction of States …" Thus, the mandate of the IOM does not seem to include the establishment of international legal commitments for admission of migrants. Of course, this is by no means an insuperable barrier: in the same instrument by which states entered into a multilateral agreement to liberalize migration within the context of the IOM, they could modify the IOM Constitution to permit this activity. Furthermore, as a matter of interpretation, the fact that the IOM recognizes that admission is within domestic jurisdiction does not mean that states cannot make international legal commitments to constrain their authority over admission.

However, the IOM has no particular history or institutional commitment relating to liberalization of migration. The IOM contains a great deal of expertise regarding the dynamics of migration and the facilitation and management of migration, especially under dire circumstances. This expertise would no doubt be beneficial in any initiative toward liberalization of migration.

The ILO

The ILO was established in 1919 as part of the League of Nations system, and became a specialized agency of the United Nations in 1946. The ILO, with 179 members, engages in analytical work and in facilitating negotiations relating to labor. It states its goals as follows:

> The ILO is devoted to advancing opportunities for women and men to obtain decent and productive work in conditions of freedom, equity, security and human dignity. Its main aims are to promote rights at work, encourage decent employment opportunities, enhance social protection and strengthen dialogue in handling work-related issues.[8]

While this set of goals does not necessarily include liberalization of migration, there are important connections. Moreover, liberalization of migration may be a critical means to advance opportunities to obtain the kind of decent work described in this statement. Yet, surprisingly, the ILO does not today seem to see facilitation of liberalization of migration in order to make work available as one of its "fields of action." Article 10 of the ILO Constitution states that it shall focus on "international adjustment of conditions of industrial life and labour." The Declaration of Philadelphia, concerning the aims and purposes of the ILO, calls for "the provision … of facilities for … the transfer of labour, including migration for employment and settlement …"

In 2004, the ILO adopted a multilateral framework on labor migration as part of a plan to manage labor migration better. However, none of the activities planned under this framework seem aimed at liberalizing migration. In 2004, it adopted a plan of action with respect to migration, which includes as one component the development of a nonbinding multilateral framework for a rights-based approach to labor migration.

The ILO has produced a number of treaties, mostly addressing issues relating to the conditions of work. However, the rate of ratification of ILO treaties that relate to migration for employment as well as the suppression of illegal employment and trafficking of labor has been low.[9] The ILO also provides technical assistance in areas such as vocational training and rehabilitation, employment policy, labor administration, working conditions, and social security. So it has important experience in many critical areas relating to migration.

The ILO also has some salient governance features. One of the intriguing and attractive features of the ILO for purposes of work on issues of labor migration is its tripartite governance, which includes representatives of states, employers, and workers. Each member state has four representatives at the International Labor Conference, which is held annually: two state delegates, one employers' delegate, and one workers' delegate. Each delegate has one vote, and there is no requirement for the four delegates of each state to vote as a bloc. This tripartite structure and its potential to "catalyz(e) new international norms on worker mobility" has been noted by Charnovitz, who has also recommended that any WMO should consider adopting this structure "to enable the formation of stronger constituencies for lessening barriers to migration."[10]

The WTO

The WTO, formed in 1995, addresses trade in goods, trade in services, and intellectual property rights. Unlike the ILO and the IOM, the WTO's main function is to facilitate and service national commitments, mostly in the area of liberalization of trade in goods and services. The WTO generally makes decisions by consensus, meaning that decisions can generally be adopted if no state objects, although its charter provides for voting on certain issues. But any significant new commitments are made by treaty, where a state is only committed if it actually signs. The WTO has a very highly articulated system of mandatory dispute settlement, which is often used.

The WTO's GATS Mode 4 already addresses movement of natural persons to perform services but has an ambivalent relationship with immigration law in the host state. Perhaps surprisingly, Mode 4 was seen as compensation to developing countries for the inclusion of Mode 3 (commercial presence, which includes investment in services enterprises) at the request of developed countries.[11] This is surprising from an economics standpoint, first, because investment is generally understood to be beneficial to developing countries, and second, because the risk of brain drain makes Mode 4 of uncertain benefit to developing countries, especially because Mode 4 commitments as agreed in 1994 generally did not cover unskilled labor (although there is no a priori reason why they could not have).

Furthermore, the 1994 Uruguay Round commitments in Mode 4 were modest. "Even by the modest standards of Uruguay Round liberalization on trade in services, little was achieved on Mode 4."[12] The GATS is a framework agreement in the sense that it is a positive list in which most obligations only apply to service sectors listed and then only to the extent not excluded. Most countries only made limited commitments. However, this does not mean that greater commitments cannot be made in future, or that the character of GATS as a positive list agreement cannot be modified if states determine to do so.

The basic GATS disciplines include national treatment and market access. But in connection with these disciplines, the GATS is a positive list-based agreement. Therefore, the application of these disciplines is dependent upon scheduling of the relevant service sector in the schedule of commitments of the relevant state. In other words, unless the service sector is scheduled, there is no national treatment or market access obligation. States were permitted to specify limits to their national treatment or market access obligations on the face of their schedules of commitments, and the schedules are replete with such limits. On the other hand, the most favored nation obligation contained in GATS applies regardless of the scheduling of the relevant service sector. This obligation was subject to the much more limited, and degressive, list of Article II Exemptions. Finally, GATS contains rather modest disciplines on domestic regulation.

There are three critical limitations on Mode 4 as agreed in the Uruguay Round. First, GATS does not cover all labor but only labor that is related to the supply of services as specified in Article I:2(d). So, labor related to the production of goods is generally not covered (even though in theoretical terms production of goods results from the application of "services" to raw materials).[13] Second, as mentioned above, GATS is a positive list agreement – meaning that only those service sectors that are scheduled are the subject of commitments, and states negotiate over these schedules. In the 1994 WTO agreement, Mode 4 services commitments did not fare very well. Third, the GATS Annex on Movement of Natural Persons Supplying Services under the Agreement (the "MONP Annex") restricts the scope of application of GATS to immigration measures.

In fact, the commitments were generally limited to high-skill based services. Many commitments were linked to Mode 3 – commercial presence: movement of natural persons as intracorporate transferees in connection with commercial establishments. Most commitments were limited to cases of intracorporate transferees where the transferee had worked for the corporate transferor for a minimum period of time. The requirement of a Mode 3 linkage limits availability to developing countries, which are generally capital-importing, rather than capital-exporting, countries. For commitments relating to independent service providers, most commitments specified that a prior contract would be required: Mode 4 did not open up the domestic market to contract seekers. Many of the commitments still contain economic needs tests or labor market condition tests that are highly discretionary with the destination state.

The WTO has a highly developed and successful system of dispute settlement. While states would be able to make "cross-concessions" – exchanging, for example, liberalization in goods for liberalization in migration – even if migration were not assigned to the WTO, such cross-concessions might be facilitated by inclusion of these subject matters in a single organization.

Any analysis of international cooperation in the field of international labor migration, or of lack of international cooperation, must examine the relationship among the different "regimes." I focus on existing formal organizations. To some extent, examining the IOM, ILO, and WTO, it is striking how liberalization of labor migration seems to have been deemed to fall outside the mandate of each of these organizations, even though their formal mandates arguably could be understood to include significantly broader activities in this field. As Ghosh suggests, "the fragmented institutional set-up inhibits a comprehensive and coherent policy approach to the multi-dimensional problem of migration management."[14]

Yet, as we examine the rationales for international cooperation in this field, it appears that, as many economists have suggested, the greatest payoff from cooperation may come from liberalization of migration. International law, including these international organizations, has done little to address this issue.[15] Presumably, it is the determination of the member states of these organizations to avoid addressing commitments regarding migration that has kept these organizations from moving into this area.

The Global Migration Group was established in order to provide coherence in migration policy. Indeed, the Global Commission on International Migration report suggested the establishment of an interorganizational facility for coherence among international organizations dealing with migration issues.

Which Organization?

As stated above, there would be many parameters to consider in order to determine the organizational structure that would be appropriate to perform the functions useful in connection with international liberalization of migration. But perhaps it would be appropriate here to speculate, or brainstorm, a possible structure.

Of course, it would be straightforward, if not necessarily best, to simply assign liberalization to the WTO, insofar as the WTO is the premier organization for negotiations over international liberalization of goods and services. Cross-sectoral concessions would be facilitated, the WTO's experience with dispute settlement would be made available, and explicit authority for cross-sectoral retaliation in the event of a violation might support compliance. And if this path were followed, the OECD, UNCTAD, IOM, and ILO could keep their current functions and engage in cooperative activities. However, while cross-concessions seem appropriate, these could be facilitated in other ways, as has been discussed in this chapter.

The ILO has broad experience in a variety of labor and migration issues, and its tripartite structure may facilitate negotiations that necessarily will involve the concerns of industry and labor. However, the ILO has little experience in the kinds of distributive negotiations that have been the subject matter of the WTO. The ILO's multilateral Migrant Workers Convention, providing only for rights of migrants, with no corresponding benefits to receiving states, has received little support from receiving states.

None of the other existing agencies seems to have special institutional features that would make them a likely candidate for authority over economic migration. Perhaps if there were thought to be a sufficient relationship between forced migration and economic migration, the expertise of the IOM, or even the UN High Commissioner for Refugees, would be relevant.

On the other hand, a new agency – a WMO – might be designed with an agreement that it would draw specified resources from, and engage in specified joint activities with, the other agencies with relevant responsibilities.

Conclusion

According to a recent World Bank study, the gains from total trade liberalization are estimated at $155 billion annually while the gains from a 3 percent increase in the stock of migrants is $175 billion. Furthermore, these gains would be distributed more greatly to developing countries. No wonder thoughtful observers ask why liberalization of economic migration is not on the global agenda.

If a multilateral framework agreement existed within which states could negotiate specific liberalization commitments regarding immigration, it is likely that states could more easily unlock these welfare increases. It is also possible that enough additional welfare could be generated to compensate any workers in the destination state who are hurt, or to compensate the home state for any brain drain.

Notes

This chapter expands on themes addressed in Joel Trachtman, *The International Law of Economic Migration* (Kalamazoo, MI: The Upjohn Institute Press, 2008).

1 Harold James, *The End of Globalization: Lessons from the Great Depression (Cambridge*, MA: Harvard University Press, 2001).
2 Eduardo Geronimi, "Acuerdos bilaterales de migración de mano de obra: Modo de empleo" (International Migration Papers no. 65S/2004, ILO), 23–26, emphasis added.
3 Trachtman, *The International Law of Economic Migration*.
4 Jagdish Bhagwati, "The World Needs a New Body to Monitor Migration," *Financial Times*, 24 October 24.
5 Steve Charnovitz, "Assessing the ILO's Efforts to Develop Migration Law," *Legal Issues of Economic Integration* 30 (2003): 193–200.
6 Ibid.
7 United Nations High Commissioner for Human Rights, Brunson McKinley, Statement to the High Level Segment, United Nations High Commissioner for Human Rights, 59th Session, 20 March 20, 2003.
8 See their web page: http://www.un.cv/agency-ilo.php.
9 Charnovitz, "Assessing the ILO's Efforts to Develop Migration Law."
10 Ibid., 200.
11 The other modes are cross-border supply (Mode 1) and service consumer travel (Mode 2). Julia Nielson and Daria Taglioni, "A Quick Guide to the GATS and Mode 4," (OECD/World Bank/IOM Seminar on Trade and Migration, Geneva, 12–14 November 2003), 6.
12 See Julia Nielson, "Service Providers on the Move: A Closer Look at Labour Mobility and the GATS" (Paris: OECD papers, 2003). See also WTO Council for Trade in Services, Presence of Natural Persons (Mode 4), Background Note by the Secretariat, S/C/W/75 (8 December 1998), Table 9; and Antonia Carzaniga, "GATS, Mode 4 and the Pattern of Commitments," in *Moving People to Deliver Services*, ed. Antonia Carzaniga and Aaditya Matto (Washington, DC: World Bank and Oxford University Press, 2003), 21–26.
13 The scope of activities that may be included in the word "service" may be determined, in part, by reference to the WTO, Services Sectoral Classification List, MTN.GNS/W/120 (10 July 1991).
14 Bimal Ghosh, "Managing Migration: Towards the Missing Regime," in *Migration Without Borders: Essays on the Free Movement of People*, ed. Antoin Pécoud and Paul de Guchteneire (Paris: UNESCO Publishing and Berghahn Books, 2007), 111.
15 See Trachtman, *The International Law of Economic Migration*

References

Bhagwati, Jagdish. "The World Needs a New Body to Monitor Migration," *Financial Times*, 24 October 2003.

Carzaniga, Antonia. "GATS, Mode 4 and the Pattern of Commitments." In *Moving People to Deliver Services*, edited by Antonia Carzaniga and Aaditya Matto. Washington DC: World Bank and Oxford University Press, 2003.

Charnovitz, Steve. "Assessing the ILO's Efforts to Develop Migration Law." *Legal Issues of Economic Integration* 30 (2003): 193–200.

Geronimi, Eduardo. "Acuerdos bilaterales de migración de mano de obra: Modo de empleo." International Migration Papers no. 65S/2004, ILO.

Ghosh, Bimal. "Managing Migration: Towards the Missing Regime." In *Migration Without Borders: Essays on the Free Movement of People*, edited by Antoin Pécoud and Paul de Guchteneire, 97–118. Paris: UNESCO Publishing and Berghahn Books, 2007.

James, Harold. *The End of Globalization: Lessons from the Great Depression.* Cambridge, MA: Harvard University Press, 2001.

Nielson, Julia. "Service Providers on the Move: A Closer Look at Labour Mobility and the GATS." Paris, OECD papers, 2003.

Nielson, Julia, and Daria Taglioni. "A Quick Guide to the GATS and Mode 4." OECD/World Bank/IOM Seminar on Trade and Migration, Geneva, November 12–14, 2003.

Trachtman, Joel. *The International Law of Economic Migration.* Kalamazoo, MI: The Upjohn Institute Press, 2008.

United Nations High Commissioner for Human Rights. Brunson McKinley, Statement to the High Level Segment, United Nations High Commissioner for Human Rights, 59th Session, 20 March 2003.

34

EU Immigration and Asylum Law

Steve Peers

Introduction

The gradual development of EU immigration and asylum law has been characterized by two related, ongoing tensions: the conflict between EU competence in this field and national sovereignty, and the friction between immigration control and the protection of human rights. The first of these conflicts has manifested itself, in part, in a long-running argument over the institutional framework that should apply to this area. While the Treaty of Lisbon ultimately resolved the argument in favor of applying the "Community method" (the ordinary legislative procedure, including qualified majority voting in the Council and the full jurisdiction of the Court of Justice of the European Union) to this field,[1] concerns about sovereignty are still addressed by some restrictions on the European Union's competence (on which, see below) and the possibility for three member states (the United Kingdom, Ireland, and Denmark) to opt out of most or all of the relevant EU legislation.[2]

The European Union's approach to resolving the two key tensions in this area will be assessed by examining, in turn, the four key subjects addressed by immigration law: visas and border controls; irregular (illegal) migration; legal migration; and asylum.

Visas and Border Controls

The European Union has been more active in the fields of visas and border controls than in any other area of immigration and asylum law owing to the early development of a legal framework, originally in the form of the Schengen Convention.[3] This convention was initially signed in 1990 and was ultimately extended in principle to all member states except the United Kingdom and Ireland, although new member states only fully participate in the Schengen rules several years after joining the Union, when the states already participating in the Schengen rules unanimously agree that the new member states can meet the constraints of participation in the system.[4] Moreover, four non-member states (Norway, Iceland, Switzerland, and

A Companion to European Union Law and International Law, First Edition.
Edited by Dennis Patterson and Anna Södersten.

Liechtenstein) also follow the Schengen rules.[5] Since 1999, pursuant to the Treaty of Amsterdam, the Schengen Convention and measures based upon it (referred to as the Schengen *acquis*) have been integrated into the EU legal order.

The central purpose of the Schengen rules is to abolish internal border controls between all of the participating states and, as a corollary, to strengthen their common external border controls, provide freedom to travel between the Schengen states for any persons who are legally residing in or visiting those states, and to adopt a common short-term visa policy. In order to address the perceived consequences of abolishing internal border controls, the Schengen Convention also included "flanking" rules on the allocation of asylum applications (which were superseded by the Dublin Convention: see this chapter under Asylum), irregular migration, and judicial and police cooperation, including the creation of a database known as the "Schengen Information System" (SIS).[6]

The core of the detailed Schengen rules are now (mostly) set out in a number of EU regulations,[7] in particular those: setting out a "Schengen border code";[8] establishing an EU agency to assist with border controls (known as Frontex);[9] creating a second generation version of the previous Schengen Information System (SIS II);[10] listing the third (i.e., non-EU) countries whose nationals do (or do not) need a visa to enter the European Union; setting out a "visa code"; and establishing a Visa Information System (VIS) concerning visa applicants.

First of all, the Schengen borders code sets out the key rules on the control and surveillance of external borders, as well as the basic obligation to abolish internal border controls between the member states, subject to limited exceptions.[11] Concerns about the ability of some Schengen states to play their role controlling the external borders led to an amendment to the borders code to set out a process by which a state's participation in the Schengen *acquis* could be, in effect, temporarily suspended.[12] While this partial retreat from the principle of free movement met with the approval of member states, they were insistent that any reintroduction of border controls had to remain within the sole control of member states, not (as the Commission had proposed) EU institutions.

The application of the borders code is implemented by the SIS; the second generation of this system became operational in 2013. This provides for a system of issuing alerts for refusal of entry of third-country nationals who should in principle be refused entry into the entire Schengen area.[13]

Furthermore, the Frontex agency has a key role supplementing the member states' border control authorities. Originally established in 2004, its budget has been hugely increased and its powers have been enlarged so that it can play a larger role, for instance, coordinating return flights and sending rapid action teams to assist member states facing particular difficulties controlling their share of the external border. The most recent amendment to the legislation establishing Frontex also aimed to ensure that its activities were compatible with human rights obligations – an increasingly important issue in light of the case law of the European Court of Human Rights.[14]

As for the common visa policy, the original visa list regulation was adopted in 1995, but it only partially harmonized the list of countries whose nationals needed visas to enter the European Union.[15] After the integration of the Schengen *acquis* (which included a more fully harmonized visa policy) within the EU legal order in 1999, the Council adopted a regulation in 2001 which completely harmonized the lists of the countries whose nationals did (or did not) require a visa to cross the external borders.[16] This legislation was subsequently amended a number of times.[17]

The criteria to waive or impose a visa requirement are essentially political, and they take into account foreign policy considerations, security risks, and the prospect of irregular migration.

Within Europe, the EU legislation permits visa-free entry for nationals of the Western Balkan countries and European microstates (e.g., Liechtenstein and Monaco), but it requires visas for nationals of Russia, Ukraine, other ex-Soviet countries, and Turkey. But as a compromise, the visa regime for a number of nearby countries has been softened by means of visa facilitation treaties which simplify the process and reduce the cost of obtaining Schengen visas.[18]

In the Asia/Pacific region, the EU legislation requires visas for nationals of all countries except wealthy countries like Japan, Australia, Korea, Taiwan, and New Zealand. As for the Americas, most countries are exempt from a visa requirement except some Andean countries (nationals of Ecuador and Bolivia need visas). Finally, nationals of all African and Caribbean countries require visas, with the exception of a few small tropical islands such as Mauritius and Bermuda.

The conditions for obtaining a visa are now set out in the European Union's visa code, which also includes provisions on the right to appeal the refusal of a visa.[19] The visa application system is now bolstered by the VIS, which became operational in 2011 and is being rolled out worldwide, with full coverage planned for late 2015.[20]

On the whole, the European Union has gradually stepped up the degree of harmonization of visa and border control policies and increased control of entry to EU territory, in particular by means of technical measures (the SIS and VIS) and the enhanced operational role of Frontex.[21] On the other hand, however, the EU visa regime, which increasingly interacts with the Union's external policies and has even come to resemble its hierarchy of trade preferences, is becoming gradually more liberal, in particular with the waiver of visa requirements for Western Balkan countries in 2009 and 2010. However, the European Union usually insists on a *quid pro quo* for the waiver of visa requirements or the conclusion of visa facilitation treaties, in the form of readmission treaties (see this chapter under Irregular Migration) and further alignment with EU migration control policy. As regards human rights, EU legislation in this field sets out general rules on this issue but does not specify concretely how such rights are to be protected in the context of visas and border controls.[22]

Irregular Migration

Irregular migration (often referred to as "illegal" migration) is a subject of great public concern: so-called illegal immigrants are often demonized as if they were a single category of persons. However, the concept of irregular migration covers many different groups of people, including those who enter in need of protection from persecution or serious harm in their country of origin. So, as with border controls, there are "mixed flows" of irregular migrants, some of whom argue that they need international protection and some who do not.

What has the European Union done to address these issues? As for the legal framework, Article 67(2) of the Treaty on the Functioning of the European Union (TFEU) provides that the European Union "shall frame a common policy on asylum, immigration and external border control, based on solidarity between Member States, which is fair towards third-country nationals." More specifically, Article 79(1) TFEU sets out the Union's objectives as regards immigration:

> The Union shall develop a common immigration policy aimed at ensuring, at all stages, the efficient management of migration flows, fair treatment of third-country nationals residing legally in Member States, and the prevention of, and enhanced measures to combat, illegal immigration and trafficking in human beings.

Article 79(2) TFEU then gives the European Union powers to adopt legislation for these purposes, inter alia on the issues of:

(c) illegal immigration and unauthorised residence, including removal and repatriation of persons residing without authorisation;
(d) combating trafficking in persons, in particular women and children.

Also, Article 79(3) TFEU provides that the European Union may agree readmission treaties with third states.

To achieve these objectives, the European Union has adopted a number of measures concerning the prevention of irregular migration, the treatment of irregular migrants on the territory, and the expulsion of irregular migrants from the territory. The first category of acts applies in addition to the visa and border control measures discussed in the previous section, and includes rules on carrier sanctions (i.e., penalizing private companies that transport irregular migrants),[23] the transfer of passenger data,[24] prohibiting and criminalizing the facilitation of irregular entry and residence,[25] trafficking in persons,[26] and the posting of immigration liaison officers to non-EU countries.[27] The second category of measures comprises rules sanctioning the employers of irregular migrants and rules permitting the stay of victims of trafficking – but on the condition that they help to facilitate criminal prosecutions against their traffickers, and only so long as they are useful for those prosecutions.[28] The third category of measures includes the most important EU measure on irregular migration, the so-called Returns Directive, which regulates the procedure for expelling irregular migrants, including rules on detention, entry bans, and procedural rights.[29] This category also includes legislation on the mutual recognition of expulsion orders,[30] transit for expulsion,[31] and joint expulsion flights,[32] as well as readmission treaties with a number of non-EU countries.[33]

As the growing corpus of legislation indicates, the European Union has been gradually harmonizing national law with regard to control of irregular migration, and moreover it has continually been increasing the degree of control of irregular entry. But, as with its visas and borders legislation, there are countervailing tendencies towards human rights protection, in this case due to the role of the Court of Justice.[34]

Legal Migration

The European Union's involvement in the regulation of legal migration has been more limited than its involvement in other areas of immigration and asylum law. Nevertheless, its role in this area continues to increase, and was facilitated by the switch to qualified majority voting in the Council pursuant to the Treaty of Lisbon. The key elements of EU policy were set out in the conclusions of the Tampere European Council in 1999, which stated that the European Union had to "ensure fair treatment of third country nationals who reside legally on the territory of its Member States," that "[a] more vigorous integration policy should aim at granting them rights and obligations comparable to those of EU citizens," that there was a "need for approximation" of national law "on the conditions for admission and residence of third country nationals," and that "[t]he legal status of third country nationals should be approximated to that of Member States' nationals," with the grant of "uniform rights … as near as possible to those enjoyed by EU citizens" to a person who "has resided legally in a Member State for a period of time to be determined and who holds a long-term residence permit."

Following the entry into force of the Treaty of Lisbon, these objectives are reflected in Article 79(1) TFEU, which provides inter alia that the European Union "shall develop a common immigration policy aimed at ensuring, at all stages … fair treatment of third-country nationals residing legally in Member States." To this end, Article 79(2) TFEU gives the Union power to adopt legislation concerning "(a) the conditions of entry and residence" of third-country nationals, and "(b) the definition of the rights of third-country nationals residing legally in a Member State," including rules on movement between member states. However, these powers are limited by Article 79(5) TFEU, which specifies that Article 79

> shall not affect the right of Member States to determine volumes of admission of third-country nationals coming from third countries to their territory in order to seek work, whether employed or self-employed.

So, while in principle the European Union must aim to establish a "common immigration policy," including rules on the admission, residence, and rights of third-country nationals legally migrating to the Union, member states remain free to regulate the numbers of economic migrants coming from third countries.

For some time, in fact, EU legislation did not regulate economic migration at all, and a Commission proposal for comprehensive regulation of this issue was rejected by member states.[35] Instead, the Commission adopted a "policy plan" on economic migration,[36] which suggested instead a series of piecemeal measures on this issue. This policy was then implemented by means of the adoption of general legislation on the equal treatment and procedural rights of most economic migrants (the "Single Permit" Directive),[37] as well as more detailed legislation concerning the admission of highly skilled migrants, the so-called Blue Card Directive, along with directives on seasonal workers and intracorporate transferees.[38]

As for other categories of legal migrants, the European Union has also adopted legislation concerning admission to carry out a research project,[39] and on the admission of post-secondary students, school pupils, unpaid trainees, and volunteers.[40] EU directives also regulate family reunion with legal migrants,[41] as well as (implementing the Tampere objectives) the acquisition of EU long-term residence status for those who have resided legally for more than five years.[42]

The two key themes of this chapter – the extent of EU harmonization and the tension between human rights protection and immigration control – are clearly reflected in the case law of the Court of Justice concerning this legislation. In fact, the European Parliament sued to annul certain provisions of the family reunion directive,[43] on the ground that human rights were not sufficiently protected by the rules in the directive allowing member states to insist on a three-year wait for family reunion and to exclude certain categories of children from the usual rules.[44] The Court of Justice rejected this argument, assessing the directive particularly in light of the jurisprudence of the European Court of Human Rights on Article 8 of the European Convention on Human Rights (ECHR) concerning the right to family life, which generally does not guarantee a right to admission of family members into the host state.[45] As a general rule, the Court said, the directive sets a higher standard than this case law, as it guarantees a right of admission for spouses and children; but to the extent that it does not guarantee such a right, member states are still bound by their ECHR obligations to admit family members in special situations (for instance, to avoid siblings growing up in different states) and must carry out a case-by-case assessment of any applications for family reunion.

Subsequently, the Court ruled that despite the apparent flexibility which the directive gives to member states as regards conditions for admission,[46]

> Since authorisation of family reunification is the general rule, the faculty provided for in Article 7(1)(c) of the Directive [i.e., the condition relating to social assistance] must be interpreted strictly. Furthermore, the margin for manoeuvre which the Member States are recognised as having must not be used by them in a manner which would undermine the objective of the Directive, which is to promote family reunification, and the effectiveness thereof.

Furthermore,

> the concept of "social assistance system of the Member State" is a concept which has its own independent meaning in European Union law and cannot be defined by reference to concepts of national law,

and

> the provisions of the Directive … must be interpreted in the light of the fundamental rights and, more particularly, in the light of the right to respect for family life enshrined in both the ECHR and [the European Union's Charter of Fundamental Rights].

The Court then ruled that the particular Dutch rule setting a social assistance condition breached the directive.

The Court took a comparable approach as regards the long-term residents' directive. First of all, in the case of *Kamberaj*,[47] the Court ruled on the interpretation of the equal treatment rules in the directive. Although that directive provides in principle for equal treatment of long-term residents, it leaves some discretion to member states by specifying that equal treatment as regards "social security, social assistance and social protection" is "defined by national law"; moreover, it permits member states to "limit equal treatment in respect of social assistance and social protection to core benefits."[48] While the Court accepted that the member states had discretion to define the relevant concepts in their national law, this did not mean that member states are free to "undermine the effectiveness" of the equal treatment rule. Also, the directive had to be interpreted in light of the charter, which

> recognises and respects the right to social and housing assistance so as to ensure a decent existence for all those who lack sufficient resources, in accordance with the rules laid down by European Union law and national laws and practices.[49]

As for the possibility of limiting the application of equal treatment to "core benefits," this also gave only limited discretion to member states in light of the charter, and in principle this concept covered housing benefit (the relevant benefit in this case).

In *Commission v. Netherlands*,[50] the Court was asked to rule on whether the Dutch government had breached the directive by imposing high fees for applications for residence permits made by long-term residents or their family members. Even though the directive did not regulate the issue of application fees, the Court ruled that member states' "discretion" to charge fees "is not unlimited": member states cannot "apply national rules which are liable to jeopardise the achievement of the objectives pursued by a directive and, therefore, deprive it of its effectiveness." It followed that the level of fees being charged in the Netherlands breached the directive.

In light of both the continued adoption of legislation in this field and the dynamic interpretation of that legislation by the Court of Justice, one sees that the European Union's role as regards legal immigration is becoming steadily more significant. The Court has a clear tendency to look for uniform interpretations of EU law, or to constrain member states' activity by means of the principle of effectiveness where the legislation refers to national law or is silent on an issue. In the Court's view, the legislation aims to confer rights on individuals, and exceptions from those rights must be interpreted narrowly. The overriding importance of human rights also has a continuing impact, not only as regards the right to family reunion but also as regards social rights. Taken as a whole, the case law of the Court of Justice has reduced member states' power to restrict the benefits of EU legislation on legal migration only to relatively well-off migrants.

Asylum

The definition and status of refugees is set out in the first place in the 1951 UN Convention on the Status of Refugees (referred to as the Geneva Convention in EU law), along with the 1967 protocol to that convention.[51] This issue is also affected by other international human rights treaties, in particular the ECHR, which, according to the European Court of Human Rights, bans the return of a person to a state in which there is a real risk of suffering torture or other inhuman or degrading treatment as set out in Article 3 ECHR.[52] Since the Geneva Convention does not address all situations in which persons might need some form of protection from return to their country of origin, the concept of "subsidiary protection" (i.e., protection outside the scope of that convention) has been developed. EU law has focused on refugee and subsidiary protection issues: but there are other forms of protection based on national law and practice that are not harmonized by EU law. The Court of Justice has confirmed that member states can establish and retain such nonharmonized forms of protection provided that there is no confusion with refugee status.[53]

Originally, the Treaty of Amsterdam granted the EU powers to set only "minimum standards" as regards asylum law.[54] However, EU leaders soon decided, at the Tampere European Council of 1999, that the European Union should aim to establish a "Common European Asylum System" (CEAS), starting with a first round of legislation in the "short term" (which became known as the "first phase" of the CEAS), with the intention to establish, "in the longer term," a "common asylum procedure and a uniform status for those who are granted asylum valid throughout the Union."

The first phase of legislation to establish the CEAS was adopted between 2003 and 2005, and consisted of a directive on the qualification for and content of refugee and subsidiary protection status (the "Qualification Directive");[55] a directive on procedures for applying for refugee status (the "Procedures Directive");[56] a directive on reception conditions for asylum-seekers (the "Reception Directive");[57] and a regulation setting out rules to allocate responsibility for each asylum-seeker to a single member state (the Dublin Regulation).[58] In order to facilitate the application of the latter regulation, there was also an earlier regulation establishing "Eurodac," a system for storing and comparing asylum-seekers' fingerprints.[59] There is also a directive providing for a ready-made system of EU-wide "temporary protection" in the event of a mass influx of people, but this directive has never been put into practice.[60]

The European Union's next multi-year justice and home affairs agenda, the Hague Programme, then set a deadline of 2010 for completing the second phase of legislation to establish the CEAS.[61] However, it did not set any objectives for this second phase. Subsequently, the European Union set a new deadline of 2012 to establish the second phase and also established the twin objectives of raising the level of protection and reducing the large divergences between member states' recognition rates (i.e., the percentages of persons whose application for refugee or subsidiary protection status are successful).[62] Following the entry into force of the Treaty of Lisbon, the objectives agreed in Tampere are now reflected explicitly in Article 78 TFEU, which first of all requires that

> The Union shall develop a common policy on asylum, subsidiary protection and temporary protection with a view to offering appropriate status to any third-country national requiring international protection and ensuring compliance with the principle of *nonrefoulement*. This policy must be in accordance with the Geneva Convention of 28 July 1951 and the Protocol of 31 January 1967 relating to the status of refugees, and other relevant treaties.

To that end, the European Parliament and the Council can adopt legislation on the issues already addressed by the first-phase legislation.

The European Union adopted all legislation to establish the second phase of the CEAS by the summer of 2013.[63] As a whole, the second-phase measures provide for further harmonization of national law and additional protection of human rights, taking a modest but significant step towards raising standards in this field and potentially reducing the divergences in member states' recognition rates somewhat. Pending the adoption and implementation of this second-phase legislation, the Court of Justice became a significant actor in the field of asylum law, following the removal of the restrictions on its jurisdiction with the entry into force of the Treaty of Lisbon.[64]

The Union's asylum legislation raises a large number of issues, including first of all issues concerning the definition of refugee and subsidiary protection status. As regards both types of protection, a protection need may arise following the applicant's departure from the country of origin (known as protection *sur place*).[65] Also, the "actors of persecution or serious harm" need not be the state but may also be private parties if it can be "demonstrated" that the state, or parties controlling the state, is "unable or unwilling" to provide protection against non-state agents.[66] This rule changed the more restrictive interpretation of the Geneva Convention in several member states, which had traditionally recognized as refugees only those persons fleeing persecution by the state. There is a parallel rule on "actors of protection" which provides that protection can "only" be provided by states or parties, including international organizations, controlling all or a substantial part of a state's territory, provided (inter alia) that such bodies are "willing and able to offer protection."[67]

The core definition of a "refugee" is a person who has "a well-founded fear of being persecuted for reasons of race, religion, nationality, political opinion or membership of a particular social group."[68] The EU directive expands upon both the concept of persecution and the grounds of persecution.[69] For instance, on the first point, the Court of Justice has ruled that persons persecuted on the grounds of their religion could not have been expected to avoid persecution in their country of origin by refraining from proselytizing to believers in the dominant religion there, or otherwise avoiding public displays of their beliefs.[70] On the second point, the 2011 amendments to the directive strengthened the rules relating to gender-based persecution.[71]

As for the definition of subsidiary protection, it must be granted where there are "substantial grounds … for believing" that the person concerned faces a "real risk" of "serious harm," which consists of: (1) the death penalty or execution; or (2) torture or other inhuman or degrading treatment or punishment; or (3) a "serious and individual threat to a civilian's life or person by reason of indiscriminate violence in situations of international or internal armed conflict."[72] While the first two criteria are based on the established case law of the European Court of Human Rights,[73] the meaning of the third criterion was unclear, particularly since it is quite clearly contradictory: how could a person face an "individual" threat by reason of "indiscriminate violence"? The Court of Justice answered this question in a case about Iraqis who feared violent retaliation because they were linked to the American forces then occupying Iraq.[74] In the Court's view, an "individual" threat could include

> harm to civilians irrespective of their identity, where the degree of indiscriminate violence characterising the armed conflict taking place … reaches such a high level that substantial grounds are shown for believing that a civilian, returned to the relevant country or, as the case may be, to the relevant region, would, solely on account of his presence on the territory of that country or region, face a real risk of being subject to the serious threat referred to in Article 15(c) of the Directive.

Once an applicant has been granted refugee or subsidiary protection status, he or she (along with his or her family members) is entitled to the benefits set out in the Qualification Directive, which include a residence permit, access to employment and self-employment, equal treatment with nationals as regards social welfare and healthcare, and equal treatment with legally resident third-country nationals as regards accommodation.[75] While the first-phase directive left member states with an option to give fewer such rights to beneficiaries of subsidiary protection, the second-phase directive only permits lower standards for such persons as regards social welfare and residence permits.[76]

The directive on reception conditions regulates issues such as the employment, healthcare, education, and welfare of asylum seekers during the process of deciding on their application.

Next, the rules on asylum procedures address such issues as legal aid, interviews, the right to an effective remedy (in particular as regards the suspensive effect of appeals), and special procedural rules such as accelerated procedures, the "safe country of origin" concept, and the "safe third country" concept.[77]

Finally, there has been continued controversy concerning the application of the "Dublin" rules on responsibility for asylum applications, in part because the criteria for responsibility (which in turn assign that responsibility based on family reunion, the issue of a visa or a residence permit, or evidence of crossing a border or remaining on the territory illegally) shifted the burden of dealing with asylum applications towards the European Union's external eastern and southern land and sea borders, mostly consisting of poorer member states. Furthermore, there were widespread concerns that some member states were systematically not applying many of the basic standards of the Geneva Convention, the ECHR, and EU law as regards reception conditions, qualification for status, and asylum procedures. Ultimately, the European Court of Human Rights ruled that Greece frequently breached Article 3 ECHR (the ban on torture or other inhuman and degrading treatment) because of its low standards on reception conditions (interpreting the ECHR on this point in light of the Reception Directive) and asylum procedures, and that Belgium breached Article 3 ECHR by returning an asylum seeker to Greece despite its knowledge that such breaches were taking place.[78]

In turn, the Court of Justice ruled that while the EU rules were based on mutual trust that each member state would comply with its human rights obligations, it was possible that the CEAS might

> experience major operational problems in a given member state, meaning that there is a substantial risk that asylum seekers may, when transferred to that Member State, be treated in a manner incompatible with their fundamental rights.

However, the Dublin system could not be suspended following *any* breach of those human rights obligations but rather where there "are substantial grounds for believing that there are systemic flaws in the asylum procedure and reception conditions for asylum applicants," leading to a breach of the ban on torture or other inhuman and degrading treatment set out in

Article 4 of the EU's Charter of Fundamental Rights. So EU law also prevented sending asylum seekers to Greece pursuant to the Dublin rules.[79]

As in other areas, it can be seen that the European Union's role in this area is steadily increasing, and indeed is governed by a political and legal objective of establishing a "common" policy, with a view to both reducing divergences in national policy and increasing standards of human rights protection. Indeed, increasing the role of the European Union was formally built in to the concept of a first and second phase of asylum legislation. The legislation and the case law of the Court of Justice to date both point clearly in the direction of an increasing level of protection and of harmonization, but the European Union will still clearly fall short of establishing a "uniform" concept of asylum law, even following the implementation of the second-phase legislation.

Conclusion

In all four areas of immigration and asylum law, the European Union's role has been steadily growing. It began with the development of visas and borders rules outside the EU framework, which were integrated into the EU legal framework in 1999 and have been developed significantly (VIS, SIS II, Frontex, visa and border codes) since then. Moreover, since 1999 the Union has adopted a first phase of legislation concerning the Common European Asylum System and has begun to develop a second phase. In the area of legal migration, the European Union began by harmonizing the noneconomic aspects of the issue and has subsequently addressed sundry aspects of labor migration. As for irregular migration, the European Union's initial piecemeal approach has been supplemented by the adoption of the fairly comprehensive Returns Directive. And these legislative developments have proceeded in pace with the gradual full extension of the Community method of decision making and judicial control to this area of the law.

The position as regards the tension between human rights protection and immigration control is more mixed. EU legislation and policy on border control and irregular migration, along with technical and operational developments, points clearly towards more control of immigration, but these developments are qualified by human rights exceptions in the borders code, human rights rules in the Frontex legislation, and increased procedural rights for the persons concerned. And the ongoing development of EU legislation on visas, legal migration, and asylum points towards a more liberal approach. There is likely to be a continuing struggle within and between the European Union's political institutions and courts to establish the right balance between migration control and the protection of fundamental rights. This particularly manifested itself in the so-called refugee crisis of 2015, when member states took divergent approaches as to the best policy to respond to the increased flows of migrants across the Mediterranean (most of them going to successfully claim asylum).[80]

Notes

1 On the historical evolution of the institutional framework, see Steve Peers, "EU Justice and Home Affairs Law (Non-Civil)," in *The Evolution of EU Law*, eds. Paul Craig and Gráinne De Búrca (Oxford: Oxford University Press, 2011), 269–297.

2 See previously Cases C-77/05 *UK v. Council* EU:C:2007:803; C-137/05 *UK v. Council* EU:C:2007:805; and C-482/08 *UK v. Council* EU:C:2010:631; and now Cases C-431/11 *UK v. Council* EU:C:2013:589 and C-656/11 *UK v. Council* EU:C:2014:97. On the current opt-outs, see Steve Peers, "In a World of Their Own? Justice and Home Affairs Opt-Outs and the Treaty of Lisbon," *Cambridge Yearbook of European Legal Studies* 10 (2007–2008).

3 Convention implementing the Schengen Agreement [2000] OJ L 239.
4 Croatia, Cyprus, Romania, and Bulgaria do not yet participate in the Schengen system.
5 See the Schengen association treaties with Norway and Iceland [1999] OJ L 176/35; and Switzerland [2006] OJ L 53; and the protocol to the latter treaty as regards Liechtenstein [2008] OJ L 83.
6 On the Convention, see, for instance, David O'Keeffe, "The Schengen Convention: A Suitable Model for European Integration?," *Yearbook of European Law* 11 (1991).
7 The Schengen Convention still sets out the main rules regarding the freedom to travel (Articles 19–21 and 25 of the convention).
8 Regulation (EC) No 562/2006 of the European Parliament and the Council of 15 March 2006 establishing a Community Code on the rules governing the movement of persons across borders (Schengen Borders Code) [2006] OJ L 105/1.
9 Council Regulation (EC) 2007/2004 of 26 October 2004 establishing a European Agency for the Management of Operational Cooperation at the External Borders of the Member States of the European Union [2004] OJ L 349/1, as amended by Regulation (EC) No 863/2007 of the European Parliament and the Council of 11 July 2007 establishing a mechanism for the creation of Rapid Border Intervention Teams and amending [Regulation 2007/2004] as regards that mechanism and regulating the tasks and powers of guest officers [2007] OJ L 199/30, and Regulation (EU) No 1168/2011 of the European Parliament and the Council of 25 October 2011 amending [Regulation 2007/2004], [2011] OJ L 304/1.
10 Regulation (EC) No 1987/2006 of the European Parliament and the Council of 20 December 2006 on the establishment, operation and use of the second generation Schengen Information System (SIS II) [2006] OJ L 381/4.
11 On the extent of member states' remaining power to police the internal borders without infringing the obligation to abolish internal border controls, compare Joined Cases C-188/10 and C-189/10 *Aziz Melki and Selim Abdeli* EU:C:2010:363 to Case C-278/12 PPU *Atiqullah Adil v. Minister voor Immigratie, Integratie and Asiel* EU:C:2012:508.
12 Regulation 1051/2013 of the European Parliament and the Council amending Regulation (EC) No 562/2006 in order to provide for common rules on the temporary reintroduction of border control at internal borders in exceptional circumstances, [2013] OJ L 295/1.
13 See Regulation (EC) No 1987/2006 (n 10 above), which sets out the key rules on alerts for refusal of entry. There are further rules on entry bans in the European Union's Returns Directive (see below). EU free movement law takes priority over the SIS, so entry bans cannot be issued or enforced as regards third-country national family members of EU citizens unless the conditions in the free movement rules for refusing entry to such persons are satisfied. See Case C-503/03 *Commission v. Spain* EU:C:2006:74.
14 See the judgment of that Court of 23 February 2012 in *Hirsi v. Italy*, nyr, in which it found that the policy of stopping ships with asylum-seeking passengers in the high seas and returning those passengers to Libya without considering their asylum claims breached the ECHR.
15 Council Regulation (EC) No 2317/95 of 25 September 1995 determining the third countries whose nationals must be in possession of visas when crossing the external borders of the Member States [1995] OJ L 234/1.
16 Council Regulation (EC) No 539/2001 of 15 March 2001 listing the third countries whose nationals must be in possession of visas when crossing the external borders and those whose nationals are exempt from that requirement [2001] OJ L 82/1.
17 Council Regulations (EC) Nos: 2414/2001 of 7 December 2001 ([2001] OJ L 327/1); 453/2003 of 6 March 2003 ([2003] OJ L 69/10), 851/2005 of 2 June 2005 ([2005] OJ L 141/3); 1791/2006 of 20 November 2006 ([2006] OJ L 363/1); 1932/2006 of 21 December 2006 ([2006] OJ L 405/23); and 1244/2009 of 30 November 2009 ([2009] OJ L 336/1); and Regulations (EU) Nos 1091/2010 of 24 November 2010 ([2010] OJ L 329/1); 1211/2010 of 15 December 2010 ([2010] OJ L 339/9); 1289/2013 of 11 December 2013 ([2013] OJ L 347/74); 259/2014 of 3 April 2014 ([2014] OJ L 105/9); and 509/2014 of 15 May 2014 ([2014] OJ L 149/67) of the European Parliament and the Council, all amending Regulation (EC) No 539/2001 (ibid.).

18 Such treaties are in force with Russia, Georgia, Ukraine, Moldova, Armenia, Cape Verde, and Azerbaijan; one is also being negotiated with Belarus. The countries in the Western Balkans also benefited from such treaties from the start of 2008 until the European Union waived the visa requirement for them.

19 Regulation (EC) No 810/2009 of the European Parliament and the Council of 13 July 2009 establishing a Community Code on Visas (Visa Code) [2009] OJ L 243/1.

20 Regulation (EC) 767/2008 of the European Parliament and the Council of 9 July 2008 concerning the Visa Information System (VIS) and the exchange of data between Member States on short-stay visas (VIS Regulation) [2008] OJ L 218/60.

21 See also Regulation (EU) No 1052/2013 of the European Parliament and of the Council of 22 October 2013 establishing the European Border Surveillance System (Eurosur) [2013] OJ L 295/11.

22 See, for instance, Article 1(2) of the Frontex Regulation, as inserted by Reg. 1168/2011 (n 9 this chapter).

23 Article 26 of the Schengen Convention (n 3 this chapter), as supplemented by Council Directive (EC) 2001/51 of 28 June 2001 supplementing the provisions of Article 26 of the Convention implementing the Schengen Agreement of 14 June 1985 [2001] OJ L 187/45.

24 Council Directive (EC) 2004/82 of 29 April 2004 on the obligation of carriers to communicate passenger data [2004] OJ L 261/24.

25 Council Directive (EC) 2002/90 of 28 November 2002 defining the facilitation of unauthorized entry, transit and residence [2002] OJ L 328/17; and Framework Decision (EU) 2002/946 of 28 November 2002 on the strengthening of the penal framework to prevent the facilitation of unauthorised entry, transit and residence [2002] OJ L 328/1. These rules take priority over the rules in the visa code (n 19 this chapter) on the revocation of visas issued by another member state: Case C-83/12 PPU *Criminal Proceedings against Minh Khoa Vo* EU:C:2012:202.

26 Directive 2011/36 (EU) of the European Parliament and the Council of 5 April 2011 on preventing and combating trafficking in human beings and protecting its victims, and replacing Council Framework Decision 2002/629/JHA [2011] OJ L 101/1.

27 Council Regulation 377/2004/EC of 19 February 2004 on the creation of an immigration liaison officers network [2004] OJ L 64/1.

28 Council Directive 2004/81/EC of 29 April 2004 on the residence permit issued to third-country nationals who are victims of trafficking in human beings or who have been the subject of an action to facilitate illegal immigration, who cooperate with the competent authorities [2004] OJ L 261/19.

29 Directive 2008/115/EC of the European Parliament and the Council of 16 December 2008 on common standards and procedures in Member States for returning illegally staying third-country nationals [2008] OJ L 348/98. Entry bans are entered into the SIS (see under Visas and Border Controls).

30 Council Directive 2001/40/EC of 28 May 2001 on the mutual recognition of decisions on the expulsion of third-country nationals [2001] OJ L 149/34.

31 Council Directive 2003/110/EC of 25 November 2003 on assistance in cases of transit for the purposes of removal by air [2003] OJ L 321/26.

32 Council Decision 2004/573/EC of 29 April 2004 on the organization of joint flights for removals from the territory of two or more Member States, of third-country nationals who are subjects of individual removal orders [2004] OJ L 261/28. See also the role of Frontex in joint expulsions, discussed under Visas and Border Controls.

33 At the time of writing, there were EU readmission treaties in force with Serbia, Bosnia, Macedonia, Montenegro, Albania, Moldova, Russia, Ukraine, Georgia, Pakistan, Sri Lanka, Hong Kong, Macao, Turkey, Cape Verde, Armenia, and Azerbaijan. Negotiations were actively underway with Belarus, Tunisia, and Morocco.

34 See for instance Case C-61/11 PPU *Hassen El Dridi, alias Soufi Karim* EU:C:2011:268; and Case C-329/11 *Alexandre Achughbabian v. Préfet du Val-de-Marne* EU:C:2011:807.

35 Proposal for a Council Directive on the conditions of entry and residence of third-country nationals for the purpose of paid employment and self-employed economic activities, COM(2001) 386.

36 COM(2005) 669; and see the earlier Green Paper (COM(2004) 811).

37 Directive 2011/98/EU of the European Parliament and the Council of 13 December 2011 on a single application procedure for a single permit for third-country nationals to reside and work in the territory of a Member State and on a common set of rights for third-country workers legally residing in a Member State [2011] OJ L 343/1.

38 Council Directive 2009/50/EC of 25 May 2009 on the conditions of entry and residence of third-country nationals for the purposes of highly qualified employment [2009] OJ L 155/17; Directive 2014/36/EU of the European Parliament and of the Council of 26 February 2014 on the conditions of entry and stay of third-country nationals for the purpose of employment as seasonal workers ([2014] OJ L 94/375); and Directive 2014/66/EU of the European Parliament and of the Council of 15 May 2014 on the conditions of entry and residence of third-country nationals in the framework of an intra-corporate transfer ([2014] OJ L 157/1).

39 Council Directive 2005/71/EC of 12 October 2005 on a specific procedure for admitting third-country nationals for the purposes of scientific research [2005] OJ L 289/15.

40 Council Directive 2004/114/EC of 13 December 2004 on the conditions of admission of third-country nationals for the purposes of studies, pupil exchange, unremunerated training, or voluntary service [2004] OJ L 375/12.

41 Council Directive 2003/86/EC of 22 September 2003 on the right to family reunification [2003] OJ L 251/12.

42 Council Directive 2003/109/EC of 25 November 2003 concerning the status of third-country nationals who are long-term residents [2004] OJ L 16/44. This directive was later amended, in order to extend its scope to refugees and persons with subsidiary protection: Directive 2011/51/EU of the European Parliament and the Council of 11 May 2011 amending Council Directive 2003/109/EC to extend its scope to beneficiaries of international protection [2011] OJ L 132/1.

43 Case C-540/03 *European Parliament v. Council* EU:C:2006:429.

44 In fact, few member states apply these rules: see the Commission's report on the implementation of the directive (COM(2008) 610).

45 See the discussion in Steve Peers, "Family Reunion and Community Law," in *Towards an Area of Freedom, Security and Justice*, ed. Neil Walker (Oxford: Oxford University Press, 2004): 145–149.

46 Case C-578/08 *Rhimou Chakroun v. Buitsenlandse Zaken* EU:C:2010:117, para 43.

47 Case C-571/10 *Servet Kamberaj v. Istituto per l'Edilizia sociale della Provincia autonoma di Bolzano (IPES) and Others* EU:C:2012:233.

48 Article 11(1)(d) and (4), Directive 2003/109, n 42 this chapter.

49 Article 34(3). As the Court recognized, the charter, like the directive, refers back to national law.

50 Case C-508/10 *Commission v. Netherlands* EU:C:2012:243.

51 All member states have ratified both measures.

52 See, for instance, Nuala Mole and Catherine Meredith, *Asylum and the European Convention of Human Rights* (Strasbourg: Council of Europe Publishing, 2010).

53 Joined Cases C-57/09 and C-101/09 *Bundesrepublik Deutschland v. B and D* EU:C:2010:661; see also Case C-542/13 *Mohamed M'Bodj v Belgian State*, EU:C:2014:2452.

54 Article 63(1) and (2) EC.

55 Council Directive 2004/83/EC of 29 April 2004 on minimum standards for the qualification and status of third country nationals or stateless persons as refugees or as persons who otherwise need international protection and the content of the protection granted [2004] OJ L 304/12.

56 Council Directive 2005/85/EC of 1 December 2005 on minimum standards on procedures in Member States for granting and withdrawing refugee status [2005] OJ L 326/13.

57 Council Directive 2003/9/EC of 27 January 2003 laying down minimum standards for the reception of asylum seekers [2003] OJ L 31/18.

58 Council Regulation (EC) 343/2003 of 18 February 2003 establishing the criteria and mechanisms for determining the Member State responsible for examining an asylum application lodged in one of the Member States by a third-country national [2003] OJ L 50/1. The regulation replaced the (Dublin) Convention determining the State responsible for examining applications for asylum lodged in one of the member states of the European Communities [1997] OJ C 254/1.

59 Council Regulation 2725/2000/EC of 11 December 2000 concerning the establishment of "Eurodac" for the comparison of fingerprints for the effective application of the Dublin Convention [2000] OJ L 316/1. The Eurodac system began operations on 15 January 2003 ([2003] OJ C 5/2). The regulation also provides for the mandatory storage of the fingerprints of third-country nationals who cross the border without authorization (to compare those fingerprints with persons who apply for asylum later) and for the optional comparison of the fingerprints of irregular migrants with asylum-seekers' fingerprints (to check whether an irregular migrant is the responsibility of another member state).

60 Council Directive 2001/55/EC of 20 July 2001 on minimum standards for giving temporary protection in the event of a mass influx of displaced persons and on measures promoting a balance of efforts between Member States in receiving such persons and bearing the consequences thereof [2001] OJ L 212/12.

61 [2005] OJ C 53.

62 [2010] OJ C 115.

63 The European Union first adopted Directive 2011/95/EU of the European Parliament and the Council of 13 December 2011 on standards for the qualification of third-country nationals or stateless persons as beneficiaries of international protection, for a uniform status for refugees or for persons eligible for subsidiary protection, and for the content of the protection granted (recast) [2011] OJ L 337/9 (Qualification Directive). It also established a European Asylum Support Office: see Regulation (EU) No 439/2010 of the European Parliament and the Council of 19 May 2010 establishing a European Asylum Support Office [2010] OJ L 132/11. Other measures adopted later were: Regulation of the European Parliament and the Council of 26 June 2013 establishing the criteria and mechanisms for determining the member state responsible for examining an application for international protection lodged in one of the Member States by a third-country national or a stateless person (Recast) ([2013] OJ L 180/31); Directive 2013/33 of the European Parliament and the Council of 26 June 2013 laying down standards for the reception of applicants for international protection (Recast) ([2013] OJ L 180/96); Directive 2013/32 of the European Parliament and the Council of 26 June 2013 on minimum standards on procedures in Member States for granting and withdrawing international protection (Recast) ([2013] OJ L 180/60); and Regulation 603/2013 of the European Parliament and the Council of 26 June 2013 concerning the establishment of "Eurodac" for the comparison of fingerprints for the effective application of Regulation (EC) No 604/2013 (Recast) ([2013] OJ L 180/1). The 2001 Temporary Protection Directive was not updated.

64 For an assessment of the Court's impact, see Gabor Gyulai, *The Luxembourg Court: Conductor for a Disharmonious Orchestra? Mapping the National Impact of the Four Initial Asylum-Related Judgments of the EU Court of Justice* (Budapest: Hungarian Helsinki Committee, 2012).

65 Directive 2011/95, n 64 this chapter, Article 5.

66 Ibid, Article 6.

67 Ibid, Article 7. This provision was amended by the 2011 directive to raise the standards of protection and reduce divergences of interpretation. For instance, some member states had argued that protection could be provided for by clans: see the Commission's report on the implementation of Directive 2004/83 (COM(2010) 314, 16 June 2010).

68 Directive 2011/95, note 63 this chapter, Article 2(d), echoing Article 1A(2) of the Geneva Convention.

69 Ibid., Articles 9 and 10.

70 Joined Cases C-71/11 and C-99/11 *Bundesrepublik Deutschland v. Y and Z*, EU:C:2012:518.

71 While the 2004 directive stated that, as regards the concept of "particular social group," that "gender-related aspects can be considered, without by themselves alone creating a presumption," the 2011 directive provides that "[g]ender related aspects, including gender identity, *shall* be given due consideration for the purposes of determining membership of a particular social group or identifying a characteristic of such a group."

72 Directive 2011/95, n 64 this chapter, Articles 2(f) and 15.

73 See Mole and Meredith, *Asylum and the European Convention of Human Rights.*

74 Case C-465/07 *Meki Elgafaji and Noor Elgafaji v. Staatssecretaris van Justitie* EU:C:2009:94.

75 Directive 2011/95, note 64 this chapter, Articles 20–34.

76 Ibid., Articles 24 and 29.
77 The latter two rules permit member states to provide for presumptions that the country an asylum seeker came from or passed through was safe.
78 *MSS v. Belgium and Greece*, judgment of 21 January 2011, nyr.
79 Joined Cases C-411/10 and C-493/10, *N. S. v. Secretary of State for the Home Department et M. E. and Others v. Refugee Applications Commissioner and Minister for Justice, Equality and Law Reform* EU:C:2011:865.
80 For details, see most recently (at time of writing) the Commission Communication "Managing the refugee crisis: State of Play of the Implementation of the Priority Actions under the European Agenda on Migration," COM(2015) 510.

References

Gyulai, Gabor. *The Luxembourg Court: Conductor for a Disharmonious Orchestra? Mapping the National Impact of the Four Initial Asylum-Related Judgments of the EU Court of Justice*. Budapest: Hungarian Helsinki Committee, 2012.

Mole, Nuala, and Catherine Meredith. *Asylum and the European Convention of Human Rights*. Strasbourg: Council of Europe Publishing, 2010.

O'Keeffe, David. "The Schengen Convention: A Suitable Model for European Integration?" *Yearbook of European Law* 11 (1991): 185–219.

Peers, Steve. "Family Reunion and Community Law" In *Towards an Area of Freedom, Security and Justice*, edited by Neil Walker, 143–197. Oxford: Oxford University Press, 2004.

Peers, Steve. "In a World of Their Own? Justice and Home Affairs Opt-Outs and the Treaty of Lisbon." *Cambridge Yearbook of European Legal Studies* 10 (2007–2008): 383–412.

Peers, Steve. "EU Justice and Home Affairs Law (Non-Civil)." In *The Evolution of EU Law*, edited by Paul Craig and Gráinne De Búrca, 269–297. Oxford: Oxford University Press, 2011.

35

International Criminal Law

Roger S. Clark

The Concept

This chapter takes a descriptive and less normative approach to its subject. It tries to explicate what scholars seem to understand about the field. It should, nevertheless, be apparent that I take an expansive view of the subject matter of international criminal law, but not one totally out of the mainstream. No radical new understanding of the field is proposed. The subjects I deal with under this title fit into four, rough-and-ready, categories:

- International aspects of national criminal law
- International criminal law *stricto sensu*
- Suppression conventions/transnational criminal law
- International standards for criminal justice.

I offer a thumbnail sketch of each of these to set the stage. I then turn to some crosscutting issues that are in the forefront of both historical and contemporary discussions in the area, organizing the material under the rubric of "jurisdiction," paying particular attention to how this plays out in a number of suppression conventions. In this context, I mean by "jurisdiction" the competence of the legislative, executive, and judicial organs of a nation-state to deal with crimes having a cross-border aspect. I conclude by introducing a recent international criminal treaty that I regard as the state of the art.

The first category, "international aspects of national criminal law," is the equivalent in criminal theory of the issues discussed on the civil side as "conflict of laws" or "private international law." What happens if two or more bodies of domestic law apply potentially to a particular situation? The answer lies in a mixture of domestic and international law.

I first encountered such issues as a student pondering the implications of the *Lotus* case[1] on the fundamental question of national jurisdiction and its possible limits. The *Lotus* case involved a collision between French and Turkish vessels on the high seas. The Turkish ship sank with loss of life; the French ship limped into Constantinople (as it then was) bearing

A Companion to European Union Law and International Law, First Edition.
Edited by Dennis Patterson and Anna Södersten.

survivors. Turkish prosecutors put the French officer of the watch, M Demons, and the captain of the Turkish ship, Hassan Bey, on trial for manslaughter. France cried foul; it had no objection to the trial of the Turkish sailor but it did claim exclusive jurisdiction over its own national on its own ship. Notice the nature of the crime (although the setting was exotic) – a mundane homicide, a crime in every legal system. More about the *Lotus* case later. Suffice it to say here that the parties went to the Permanent Court of International Justice (PCIJ), predecessor of the present International Court of Justice. The PCIJ held, by a narrow margin,[2] that Turkey could, consistent with international law, do what it did, although there was "concurrent" jurisdiction and France had competence to try the officer too. Neither country had special priority; neither had exclusive jurisdiction. The Court's analysis revealed a fault line that continues to run through the discussion to this day: is the nature of international law such that it was incumbent on Turkey to demonstrate that the rules permitted it to act; or was it necessary for France to show that Turkey was forbidden from acting? The majority settled for the latter position, but there was a powerful dissent.

Closely related to jurisdiction are questions of extradition and mutual legal assistance. If, as is generally asserted, a state will not "enforce" another state's penal law by prosecuting it in its own courts, can it be persuaded to hand over (extradite) alleged criminals for trial elsewhere, or to provide "mutual legal assistance" in developing another state's criminal proceedings (for example, by executing search warrants or interviewing witnesses)? The positive answers to those questions gave rise to an extensive body of bilateral (and more recently multilateral) treaties and some non-treaty practice that provides considerable fodder for courses in international criminal law.

In this first category, then, the issues are mainly about enforcing crimes defined under domestic law within the constraints imposed by public international law or through assistance gained via public international law.

Jurisdiction, extradition, and mutual legal assistance are important features, too, of the second category of topics, international criminal law *stricto sensu*. While I take a wider view, some scholars deem this area the only one worthy of examination as international criminal law.[3] Here, it is said, the crimes *arise under* international law. They are a creature of customary international law, although some have been codified by treaty, most recently for the purposes of the Rome Statute of the International Criminal Court in 1998[4] and in the aggression amendments adopted for that Statute in Kampala in 2010.[5] The crimes in question are usually regarded as having the characteristic of being *jus cogens* or peremptory norms. They may be criminal even if domestic law does not recognize them, or even if they conflict with domestic obligations. They are usually said to represent a select list of examples of extreme evil, especially genocide, crimes against humanity, war crimes, and the crime of aggression. They are associated in particular with the jurisdiction of the Nuremberg and Tokyo Tribunals, the *Ad Hoc* Tribunals for Former Yugoslavia and Rwanda, and, most recently, of the International Criminal Court. A feature of these crimes is, thus, that they are regarded as suitable for trial in an international tribunal, although this does not preclude the possibility of national prosecution on various jurisdictional theories, including "universal jurisdiction." Some would see this latter possibility as the defining characteristic of a crime under international law: that it may be subject to universal jurisdiction in the courts of any state.

Suppression conventions may well be of a different epistemological ilk, although some skepticism is appropriate.[6] Here, the thrust is that states have agreed – either by bilateral or by multilateral treaty – to make the subject of the treaty criminal under domestic law and to assist one another in various ways in enforcement in domestic courts. It is the treaty in question, not some deeper rules of the international system, that are said to render the proscribed activities "criminal." The earliest modern examples I have found dealt with the suppression of land-based assistance to pirates, in the "Jay Treaty" of 1794,[7] and with suppression of the transatlantic slave trade.[8] More recent examples include the series of terrorism treaties beginning in the 1970s. Some writers use the term "transnational criminal law" to describe this material.[9] In modern usage there are always several jurisdictions potentially available concurrently, since the idea is that as many domestic legal systems as possible will be ready to make sure that there are no safe havens for those committing the treaty crimes. The early suppression conventions tended to be bilateral; the most notable of the last century have been negotiated in multilateral forums, especially under the auspices of international organizations such as the League of Nations,[10] the United Nations,[11] the International Civil Aviation Organization,[12] and the International Maritime Organization.[13]

The final category, international standards of criminal justice, is an aspect of the post-1945 ferment on human rights. Much modern human rights law is devoted to setting standards for performance in the domestic criminal law system. Think, for example, of items in the Universal Declaration of Human Rights,[14] the International Covenant on Civil and Political Rights,[15] the European Convention on Human Rights and Fundamental Freedoms,[16] and the Convention against Torture and other Cruel, Inhuman, or Degrading Treatment or Punishment.[17] There is also a plethora of "soft law" instruments in this area, especially those developed under the auspices of the branch of the United Nations Secretariat in Vienna, now known as the United Nations Office on Drugs and Crime. This same office is a focal point for a number of contemporary activities involving the suppression conventions or transnational criminal law activities. The classic example of the work of this nature is the Standard Minimum Rules for the Treatment of Prisoners, adopted in 1955 at the UN Crime Congress that year and later approved by the Economic and Social Council.[18] Another good example of the soft law instruments developed in Vienna is the 1985 UN General Assembly Declaration on Basic Principles of Justice for Victims of Crime and Abuse of Power.[19] In addition to insisting that victims be treated with respect in the domestic criminal justice process, the declaration delineated obligations in respect of reparation and restitution and encouraged a role for victims in criminal proceedings. Some of these fundamental principles have found their way into later treaty obligations as standards for proceedings in international courts[20] or for proceedings in domestic courts exercising jurisdiction over transnational crimes.[21]

Jurisdiction

The appropriateness of domestic court jurisdiction is a fundamental issue in relation to most of the subject matter of the first three of my categories of international criminal law and to significant instruments developed in the fourth. Accordingly, I structure most of this chapter around that question. It is pedagogically helpful to lay out initially two discrete ways of unpacking aspects of jurisdiction, namely "categories" of jurisdiction and "bases" of jurisdiction.

Categories of Jurisdiction

The American Law Institute's *Restatement (Third) of the Foreign Relations Law of the United States*, echoing concepts that are widely accepted elsewhere, draws a very useful distinction between three "categories of jurisdiction":

1. jurisdiction to prescribe, *i.e.*, to make its law applicable to the activities, relations, or status of persons, or the interests of persons or things, whether by legislation, by executive act or order, by administrative rule or regulation, or by determination of a court;

2. jurisdiction to adjudicate, *i.e.*, to subject persons or things to the process of its courts or administrative tribunals, whether in civil or in criminal proceedings, whether or not the state is a party to the proceedings;
3. jurisdiction to enforce, *i.e.*, to induce or compel compliance with its laws or regulations, whether through courts or by use of executive, administrative, police or other nonjudicial action.[22]

It is important to appreciate that, while in some situations all three categories of jurisdiction may be exercised at the same time by the same state, this is not always so. Take the *Lotus* case. Turkey had custody of M Demons. Its executive enforcement authorities were able to bring him before an adjudicator who applied Turkish prescriptive law. Equally, given his presence in Constantinople, Turkey could have taken a different kind of enforcement action, namely surrender M Demons to France. France at least professed an interest in bringing him to trial, thus implicating French adjudicative and prescriptive jurisdiction. The decisive question at the international level was whether it was appropriate for Turkey to exercise its prescriptive jurisdiction and apply the Turkish law of homicide to him.

Think about another kind of enforcement jurisdiction. What if M Demons had not made the fateful entry into Turkish space voluntarily? What if Turkey had arrested him on the high seas? The PCIJ spoke obliquely to this:

> It is certainly true that – apart from certain special cases which are defined by international law – vessels on the high seas are subject to no authority except that of the State whose flag they fly. In virtue of the principle of freedom of the seas, that is to say, the absence of any territorial sovereignty upon the high seas, no State may exercise any kind of jurisdiction over foreign vessels on them. Thus, if a war vessel, happening to be at the spot where a collision occurs between a vessel flying its flag and a foreign vessel were to send on board an officer to make investigations or to take evidence, such an act would undoubtedly be contrary to international law.[23]

If it is illegal "to make investigations or to take evidence" then, in my hypothetical case, it must, *a fortiori*, be illegal to make an arrest. We shall see a little later what the Court must have meant by the "special cases defined by international law." For now, note what the PCIJ said in the next paragraph:

> But it by no means follows that a State can never in its own territory exercise jurisdiction over acts which have occurred on board a foreign ship on the high seas.[24]

This sets up the successful argument that Turkey can prosecute in its own territory one who acts on a floating piece of France and causes damage on a floating piece of Turkey. It emphasizes prescriptive not enforcement jurisdiction.

Bases of Jurisdiction

The literature often asserts that in customary international law there are five recognized "bases of jurisdiction" on which states may exercise prescriptive jurisdiction. The five are certainly the most commonly discussed, but I do not believe that the categories are closed; and the application of each of them may be disputed in particular situations. Treaty provisions are increasingly opening up new possibilities. The five are: territorial; nationality or active personality (offences committed by nationals); passive personality (offences against nationals); protective; and universal. Exercises of the latter four and the "objective territorial" or "effects" version of the first are often characterized as "extraterritorial," that is, concerned with events outside the national territory.

Territorial jurisdiction, the most common, is premised on the place where the crime is committed. The simple case is, for example, where all the elements of a homicide occur in the same state. This is sometimes characterized as "subjective territoriality." The more complicated case is one like the *Lotus* where the carelessness of M Demons on the French vessel resulted in death on the Turkish one. Two conceptual moves are necessary to apply a territorial theory here – and were made by the PCIJ. First, the ships have to be treated as the equivalent of French and Turkish territory, thence the notion of "flag State" jurisdiction. Second, the territory where the "effects" occur must be treated as having a sufficient relationship to found jurisdiction to prescribe. This, sometimes called "objective territoriality," is what the PCIJ upheld in the *Lotus* case. This is not to deny the right of France to apply its laws also to M Demons (on a nationality or territoriality/flag state basis). The system tolerates concurrent jurisdiction and there is no clear "hierarchy" with respect to who may act first. Turkey was able to go first here since it had custody of M Demons. It could have been magnanimous and handed him over to French justice, but it did not; it committed no breach of international law in failing to do so.

Nationality jurisdiction is more typical of civil law countries than of common law ones, but assertions of jurisdiction based on nationality are increasingly common in the Anglo-American system, especially in the case of military personnel and other representatives of the state, and in terrorism cases.

"Passive personality" was also asserted as a theory by Turkey against M Demons. Turkish legislation, based on the Italian Penal Code, made it an offence to commit certain crimes (including homicide) against a Turkish citizen anywhere in the world. The majority of the Court stopped short of upholding Turkey's actions on this basis. Common law countries were long opposed to such assertions of jurisdiction. It is an increasingly asserted ground of jurisdiction, especially as permitting a state's action against those alleged to have committed acts of terrorism against its citizenry elsewhere on the planet.

"Protective jurisdiction" is extraterritorial in its application as well. It relates to actions by persons who are not nationals of the target state directed against its security or related interests. The classic everyday case is the visa applicant who lies abroad on a visa application form and then is prosecuted after arriving in the country concerned. Protective jurisdiction is often an alternative basis to justify jurisdiction in terrorism cases.

Universal jurisdiction is exercised by a state even in a situation where the state itself has no particular connection to the specific offence. It exercises that jurisdiction on behalf of the international community to impose sanctions for a small class of crimes regarded as sufficiently heinous to be punishable under international law. Historically, the paradigm example of such a case was piracy on the high seas. In modern usage, the slave trade is usually regarded as attaining a similar status (although many states have not legislated to that effect) and, of course, the same is true of genocide, crimes against humanity, war crimes, torture, and perhaps the crime of aggression. While it has been suggested that a domestic court could directly apply international law to provide a basis for the punishment of crimes of universal jurisdiction, most legal systems require some action on the part of the legislature to support the exercise of prescriptive and enforcement jurisdiction.

Jurisdiction and the Suppression Conventions

In the piracy and slave-trade bilateral treaties already mentioned, the focus is on the obligatory exercise of jurisdiction to prescribe on certain bases – territoriality against those who aid pirates by land in the Jay Treaty and nationality in the case of Portuguese slavers. There was presumably an implied obligation in both treaties to exercise enforcement jurisdiction also. The implicit Portuguese duty to prosecute was backstopped by an explicit power granted to British warships to board suspected slave ships and free the slaves; but criminal trials would take place in Portugal proper or in its widespread colonies. Thus, the British had a role in enforcement, conferred by treaty.

This division of labor between enforcement and prescription was spelled out in a more sophisticated fashion in a remarkable convention on submarine cables later in the nineteenth century. Invention of the telegraph led to submarine cables circling the globe. Cables are vulnerable to thieves, vandals, and incompetent sailors. Hence the suppression treaty known as the 1884 Convention for the Protection of Submarine Cables.[25] Article II of the convention made it

> a punishable offence to break or injure a submarine cable, willfully or by culpable negligence, in such a manner as might interrupt or obstruct telegraphic communication, either wholly or partially, such punishment being without prejudice to any civil action for damages.

Article XII obligated contracting states to criminalize these offences under domestic law. What about jurisdiction?

Article VIII dealt with prescriptive and adjudicative jurisdiction, decreeing that "[t]he tribunals competent to take cognizance of infractions of the present Convention are those of the country to which the vessel on board of which the offence committed belongs." Flag state jurisdiction is the norm. But article VIII continued,

> It is, moreover, understood that in cases where the provisions of the previous paragraph cannot be carried out, offences against the present Convention will be dealt with by each of the Contracting States in accordance, so far as the subjects and citizens of those States respectively are concerned, with the general rules of criminal jurisdiction prescribed by the laws of that particular State, or by international treaties.

The meaning of "cannot be carried out" is not made explicit but must refer to cases where extradition is not available, either because there is no treaty or other arrangement in place, or the accused has fled to his home state which does not render nationals. This paragraph contemplates nationality jurisdiction, if consistent with the general approach of the state in question. But it stops short of universal prescriptive jurisdiction.

Jurisdiction to enforce is broader. It is universal, or at least shared by all treaty parties. Article X of the convention provided that

> [o]ffences against the present Convention may be verified by all means of proof allowed by the legislation of the country of the court. When the officers commanding ships of war, or ships specially commissioned for the purpose by one of the High Contracting Parties, have reason to believe that an infraction of the measures provided for in the present Convention has been committed by a vessel other than a vessel of war, they may demand from the captain or master the production of the official documents proving the nationality of the said vessel. The fact of such document having been exhibited shall then be endorsed on it immediately. Further, formal statements of the facts may be prepared by the said officers, whatever may be the nationality of the vessel incriminated. These formal statements shall be drawn up in the form and in the language used in the country to which the officer taking them belongs; they may be considered, in the country where they are adduced, as evidence in accordance with the laws of that country. The accused and the witnesses shall have the right to add, or to have added thereto, in their own language, any explanations they may consider useful. These declarations shall be duly signed.

This must be one of the "special cases" referred to in the *Lotus*, that is, there is treaty-based enforcement jurisdiction exercisable by all the parties, namely to board a ship flying another state's flag, check documents, and take statements on behalf of the flag state. So, if M Demons had negligently damaged a cable (whether Turkish or belonging to another treaty partner) instead of negligently killing Turks, the Turkish navy could have boarded *The Lotus* to make enquiries. Turkey and France being parties to the convention, the necessary consent to board could be drawn from Article X. The article does not justify an arrest, but enforcement jurisdiction short of that surely is provided for. Of course, contrary to the situation in the Lotus case, Turkey has no prescriptive jurisdiction under this treaty, that being confined to the flag (or national) state. There is a division of labor among the contracting states of prescriptive and (parts of) enforcement jurisdiction. Do not underestimate the randomness in all of this: one might think that killing someone is worse than damaging a piece of wire (albeit an expensive one), and others ought probably to be able to board and investigate homicides, but the treaty dealt with cables, not dead people.

A further division of labor had been devised by 1929 and appeared in the International Convention for Suppression of Counterfeiting Currency.[26] After requiring the criminalization "as ordinary crimes" of various depredations against currency (Article 3) and requiring that no distinction should be made in the scale of punishments for offences relating to domestic currency on the one hand and foreign currency on the other (Article 5), the convention (Article 8) addressed extradition and jurisdiction as follows:

> In countries where the principle of extradition of nationals is not recognized, nationals who have returned to the territory of their own country after the commission abroad of an offence referred to in Article 3 should be punishable in the same manner as if the offence had been committed in their own territory, even in a case where the offender has acquired his nationality after the commission of the offence.
>
> This provision does not apply if, in a similar case, the extradition of a foreigner could not be granted.

The state of nationality already has the obligation under Article 3 to criminalize, that is, to exercise its prescriptive jurisdiction over the offences, at least territorially. Now it has an obligation to prescribe and enforce the crimes *extra*territorially against its own nationals when it refuses to extradite them (as many states do) on the basis of nationality.

States that extradite their own nationals, or who find themselves with foreigners sought by a third state, have a further enforcement obligation under Article 10. It provides that the offences under the treaty "shall be deemed to be included as extradition crimes in any extradition treaty which has been or may hereafter be included between any of the High Contracting Parties." Parties that "do not make extradition conditional on the existence of a treaty or reciprocity, henceforward recognize the offences referred to in Article 3 as cases of extradition as between themselves." The 1929 extradition provisions do not, in themselves, authorize extradition. They merely amend any existing extradition treaties or arrangements by including the counterfeiting crimes in the list of crimes for which extradition may be granted. In the absence of procedures otherwise in place, through treaty or comity, this aspect of the 1929 convention was a dead letter. The same was true of Article 16 of the convention which sought to encourage the use of what it called "letters of request" or "letters rogatory" relating to convention offences. In later usage, this morphed into an obligation of "mutual legal assistance."

Article 8 of the convention concerning nationals combined with Article 9 concerning foreigners to form the starting point for a dramatic development that bore fruit in 1970 in the Hague Hijacking Convention[27] in the form of "subsidiary" or "fallback" universal jurisdiction, based on the presence of the accused in country. Article 9 of the 1929 convention provided that

> [f]oreigners who have committed abroad any offence referred to in Article 3, and who are in the territory of a country whose internal legislation recognizes as a general rule the principle of the prosecution of offences committed abroad, should be punishable in the same way as if the offence had been committed in the territory of that country.
>
> The obligation to take proceedings is subject to the condition that extradition has been requested and that the country to which application is made cannot hand over the person accused for some reason which has no connection with the offence.
>
> Extradition shall be granted in conformity with the law of the country to which application is made.

We are speaking here about both prescriptive jurisdiction and jurisdiction to enforce against foreigners! I know of no common law country that had such a "general rule" in 1929, but there may have been some civil law countries that did. The important point for this part of the story was the establishment of the principle both that there could be an obligation undertaken by treaty to invoke nationality jurisdiction to punish nationals who could not be extradited (Article 8) and a recognition that it might be possible (even obligatory) to prosecute foreigners who committed their offences abroad (Article 9). Notice in the case of Article 9 that the obligation was triggered only by an extradition request. The rapporteur of the League of Nations Legal Committee that worked on the drafting of the Convention was Mr Vespasian Pella of Romania, one of the giants of international criminal law. He is quoted as saying that the provision that became Article 9 was "a first step towards admitting in the future, without reservations, the principle of universality of justice in the pursuit of criminals."[28] He added, "such proceedings being justified either by the nature of the offence or the interest injured, or on account of the offender's nationality etc."[29] Jurisdiction based on nationality was already covered by Article 8; "universal" jurisdiction based on the "nature of the offence or the interest injured" was a work in progress in 1929 and so it remains.

The Hague Convention on the Suppression of Unlawful Seizure of Aircraft (Hijacking)[30] was adopted in 1970 under the auspices of the International Civil Aviation Organization. Article 1 declares as criminal the acts of a person who, on board an aircraft in flight, "unlawfully, by force or threat thereof, or by any other form of intimidation, seizes or exercises control of, that aircraft, or attempts to perform such act," or "is an accomplice or a person who performs or attempts to perform any such act." In Article 2, each contracting state "undertakes to make the offence punishable by severe penalties."[31] Article 4 considers the various situations and makes concomitant requirements of the participating states:

> 1. Each Contracting State shall take such measures as may be necessary to establish its [prescriptive] jurisdiction over the offence and any other act of violence against passengers or crew committed by the alleged offender in connection with the offence, in the following cases:
>   (a) when the offence is committed on board an aircraft registered in that State;
>   (b) when the aircraft on board which the offence is committed lands in its territory with the alleged offender still on board; when the offence is committed on board an aircraft leased without crew to a lessee who has his principal place of business or, if the lessee has no such place of business, his permanent residence, in that State.
> 2. Each Contracting State shall likewise take suc h measures as may be necessary to establish its jurisdiction over the offence in the case where the alleged offender is present in its territory and it does not extradite him pursuant to Article 8 to any of the States mentioned in paragraph 1 of this Article.[32]

Article 4(2), combined with Article 7 takes the Currency Convention model about nationals to the next stage. Article 7 provides that

> [t]he Contracting State in the territory of which the alleged offender is found shall, if it does not extradite him, be obliged, without exception whatsoever and whether or not the offence was committed on its territory, to submit the case to its competent authorities for the purpose of prosecution. The authorities shall take their decision in the same manner as in the case of any ordinary offence of a serious nature under the law of that State.[33]

Now it is not only nationals (the 1929 model) who must be subject to jurisdiction. The optional part of Article 9 of the 1929 convention is now obligatory and is not contingent upon a request for extradition: it is an obligation owed to all other parties to the treaty.[34] *Anybody* "found" there must be susceptible to prescriptive and enforcement jurisdiction, a regime now widely referred to as "extradite or prosecute" or "*aut dedere aut judicare*." "Prosecute" and "*judicare*" in these phrases, consistent with prosecutorial independence and with the due process requirement that a prosecution be based on adequate evidence, underscore that the obligation is not necessarily to bring the accused to trial. It requires that the prosecutor make an independent determination "in the same manner as in the case of an ordinary offence of a serious nature."[35] Notice that while the "found" jurisdictional theory is often described as universal, this "fallback" or "subsidiary" jurisdiction requires some connection to the forum state at the outset – presence. The "pure" form of universal jurisdiction, like that over pirates, would permit the institution of proceedings in the absence of the accused with the expectation that he might fortuitously turn up later, or, more likely, that extradition proceedings would be instituted.

Article 8 follows the 1929 model of including the convention offences in existing extradition arrangements, treaty or otherwise. But it goes further. It provides that a state that requires a treaty basis for extradition

> may at its option consider this Convention as the legal basis for extradition in respect of the offence. Extradition shall be subject to the other conditions provided by the law of the requested State.

In short, the Hague Treaty may itself be treated as an extradition treaty, with a short list of applicable crimes: hijacking. Extradition is also facilitated in principle by a fiction contained in Article 8. It reads:

> The offence shall be treated, for the purpose of extradition between Contracting States, as if it had been committed not only in the place in which it occurred but also in the territories of the States required to establish their jurisdiction in accordance with Article 4, paragraph 1.

Many older extradition treaties require that the offence be committed in the "territory" of the states concerned. The fiction enables a court (or executive authority) to treat aircraft located somewhere else (and wherever registered) as being within the territory of the homeland.

Article 10 attempts to firm up the assistance provisions of the 1929 model, although its language is very general:

> Contracting States shall afford one another the greatest measure of assistance in connection with criminal proceedings brought in respect of the offence and other acts mentioned in Article 4. The law of the State requested shall apply in all cases.

The Hague Convention was the state of the art in its day and a model for many other conventions.[36]

The New State of the Art? The 2010 Beijing Convention

As should be obvious by now, treaty negotiators build their suppression structures upon what was done in the past, sometimes in quite different substantive areas. The 2010 Beijing Convention on the Suppression of Unlawful Acts Relating to International Civil Aviation[37] is a reworking of the 1971 Montreal Convention of the same name.[38] Articles 1 and 3 contain an obligation to criminalize (i.e., make "punishable by severe penalties") a wide range of offences against aircraft and persons associated with them, including destruction of air navigation facilities, using aircraft for the purpose of causing death or serious bodily injury, other actions involving weapons of mass destruction, and acts of violence at airports. There are expansive principles of liability: threats; attempts; complicity; accessories after the fact; and inchoate conspiracies, including penalties for corporate entities. There is an extensive extradition article and one on mutual assistance.

But it is Article 8, which contains the convention's basic jurisdictional assertions, that is really striking in showing where we have come. It provides as follows:

> 1. Each State Party shall take such measures as may be necessary to establish its jurisdiction over the offences set forth in Article 1 in the following cases:
>   (a) when the offence is committed in the territory of that State;
>   (b) when the offence is committed against or on board an aircraft registered in that State;
>   (c) when the aircraft on board which the offence is committed lands in its territory with the alleged offender still on board;
>   (d) when the offence is committed against or on board an aircraft leased without crew to a lessee whose principal place of business or, if the lessee has no such place of business, whose permanent residence is in that State;
>   (e) when the offence is committed by a national of that State.
> 2. Each State Party may also establish its jurisdiction over any such offence in the following cases:
>   (a) when the offence is committed against a national of that State;
>   (b) when the offence is committed by a stateless person whose habitual residence is in the territory of that State.
> 3. Each State Party shall likewise take such measures as may be necessary to establish its jurisdiction over the offences set forth in Article 1, in the case where the alleged offender is present in its territory and it does not extradite that person pursuant to Article 12 to any of the States Parties that have established their jurisdiction in accordance with the applicable paragraphs of this Article with regard to those offences.
> 4. This Convention does not exclude any criminal jurisdiction exercised in accordance with national law.

Notice the structure of the obligations here:

Paragraph 1 is *obligatory* exercise of prescriptive jurisdiction[39] on the bases there listed: territoriality (including state-of-registration and state-of-leasing); landing state; nationality.

Paragraph 2 envisages *permissive* prescriptive jurisdiction in two instances. The first underscores the ambivalence states still have about passive personality jurisdiction; they are, nevertheless, prepared to concede that other states can lawfully exercise it in respect of these offences, although they may not wish to do so themselves. In terms of the *Lotus* case's basic fault line about whether it is necessary to find an authorizing or a prohibiting rule, this one fits either analysis; it either suggests that there is no prohibition, or, if you prefer, it amounts to an authorization to proceed. The second sub-paragraph in paragraph 2 raises the issue, always a little vague, of who "counts" as a national, by making it possible to include stateless persons as nationals for the purpose of active nationality jurisdiction.[40]

Paragraph 3 presses the *aut dedere aut judicare* button. A state has an obligation to extradite or prosecute an alleged offender present in its territory.

And, yes, paragraph 4! This is a good mystery to end with. Does it mean that anything goes? This language made its first appearance in the 1963 Tokyo Convention on Offences and Certain Other Acts Committed on Board Aircraft.[41] That convention required the state of registration of aircraft to take jurisdiction over events occurring on those craft ("flag state" jurisdiction for aircraft). The United States had argued in the negotiations for the primary form of jurisdiction in aircraft cases to be the place where the aircraft landed. It failed to convince the other parties to that effect, but the language about national law was included in the 1963 treaty to save the possibility of exercising "landing state" jurisdiction.[42] In the 1970 Hague Convention,[43] landing-state jurisdiction was obligatory, so an identical saving provision[44] may well have "saved" nationality jurisdiction (which was not included). Yet, the 2010 treaty itself contains both landing state and nationality jurisdiction (Article 8(1)), which certainly do not now need to be saved. What of a state that now adopts a "pure" form of universal jurisdiction rather than the "fallback" version required by the convention, which depends on the presence of the accused within the territory when proceedings are commenced? Does the broader principle of the *Lotus* case still reign? Does that receive a boost from the saving? Is all permitted unless it is forbidden? Or is paragraph 4 merely mindless repetition of past language?

Notes

1 The case of the *S.S. Lotus* (*France v. Turkey*), PCIJ, Ser. A, No. 10 (1927) 1.

2 The Court being split six to six, the president, acting under the Court's rules, exercised a (second) deciding vote.

3 E.g., Antonio Cassese, *International Criminal Law* (Oxford: Oxford University Press, 2003); and Antonio Cassese, ed., *The Oxford Companion to International Justice* (Oxford, Oxford University Press, 2009). For broad views of the subject, see M. Cherif Bassiouni, ed., *International Criminal Law* (Leiden: Martinus Nijhoff, 2008); Cherif M. Bassiouni, *Introduction to International Criminal Law* (Ardsley, NY: Transnational, 2003); Gerhard O.W. Mueller and Edward M. Wise, *International Criminal Law* (London: Sweet and Maxwell, 1965); Ellen S. Podgor and Roger S. Clark. *Understanding International Criminal Law* (Newark, NJ: LexisNexis, 2008); Sharon A. Williams and J.-G. Castel, *Canadian Criminal Law: International and Transnational Aspects* (Toronto: Butterworths, 1981); and Edward A. Wise, Ellen S. Podgor, and Roger S. Clark, *International Criminal Law: Cases and Materials* (New Providence, NJ: LexisNexis, 2009).

4 Rome Statute of the International Criminal Court, UN Doc. A/CONF. 183/9, revised (1998), Articles 6–8 (genocide, crimes against humanity, and war crimes). Another crime under customary international law is torture, codified in the Convention against Torture and other Cruel, Inhuman, or Degrading Treatment or Punishment, GA Res. 39/46 (1984). Such codifications have "a preventive and deterrent character" and states "commit themselves to co-ordinating their efforts to eliminate any risk of impunity." See Questions Relating to the Obligation to Prosecute or Extradite (*Belgium v. Senegal*), 2012 *ICJ Rep.*, para 75 (discussing Torture Convention). See also ibid., para 99 (torture *jus cogens* under customary law).

5 ICC Resolution RC/Res. 6 (2010), Article 8 *bis* (crime of aggression).

6 The line between what offences fit the *stricto sensu* category as opposed to the "convention" or "transnational" category is both fuzzy and subject to change as state practice develops. A substantial minority of those involved in the creation of the International Criminal Court thought that serious drug crimes and terrorism should join the *stricto sensu* crimes within the jurisdiction of the Court. A consensus could not be found and the matter was left for future consideration. See Final Act of the United Nations Diplomatic Conference of Plenipotentiaries on the Establishment of an International

Criminal Court, Annex, Resolution E, (1998) UN Doc. A/CONF.183, Vol. I, at 71–72. The issue is still under consideration.

7 Treaty of Amity, Commerce and Navigation between Great Britain and the United States, signed at London, 19 November 1794 ("Jay Treaty"), Article 20, 52 *Consolidated Treaty Series* 243 ("bring to condign punishment" those who assist pirates).

8 Additional Convention between Great Britain and Portugal for the Prevention of the Slave Trade, signed at London, 28 July 1817, Article III, 67 *Consolidated Treaty Series* 373 (King of Portugal "shall prescribe the punishment of any of His Subjects who may in the future participate in the illicit traffic of Slaves").

9 E.g., Neil Boister, *Transnational Criminal Law* (Oxford: Oxford University Press, 2012).

10 E.g., Convention for Suppression of Counterfeiting Currency, Geneva, 20 April 1929, 112 *LNTS* 371.

11 Notable ones include the Torture Convention, n 4 this chapter; the Convention against Illicit Traffic in Narcotic Drugs and Psychotropic Substances (1988); the United Nations Convention against Transnational Organized Crime (2000); and the United Nations Convention against Corruption (2003).

12 Hague Convention on the Suppression of Unlawful Seizure of Aircraft (Hijacking), 860 *UNTS* 105 (1970); Montreal Convention for the Suppression of Unlawful Acts against the Safety of Civil Aviation, 974 *UNTS* 177 (1971). See also below at nn 37 and 38 for the modern version of these instruments.

13 Notably the 1988 Convention for the Suppression of Unlawful Acts against the Safety of Maritime Navigation, (1988) 27 *ILM* 668.

14 GA Res. 217A (III), 3(1) UN GAOR, Resolutions 71, UN Doc. A/810 (1948).

15 999 *UNTS* 171 (1966).

16 Available at: http://conventions.coe.int/treaty/en/treaties/html/005.htm.

17 GA Res. 39/46 (1984).

18 ESC Res. 663 (XXIV) C, UN ESCOR, 24th Sess., Supp. No. 1 at 11, UN Doc. E/3048 (1957), amended by ESC Res. 2076 (LXII), UN ESCOR, 62nd Sess., Supp. No. 1 at 35, UN Doc. E/5988 (1977).

19 GA Res. 40/34 (1985).

20 Particularly the Rome Statute of the International Criminal Court, n 4 this chapter, Article 68 ("views and concerns of victims" to be "presented and considered" by the Court, subject to right of accused to a fair trial) and Article 75 (reparations to victims); Statute of the Special Tribunal for Lebanon, SC Res. 1757 (2007), Article 17 (strong provision on views and concerns of victims).

21 UN Convention against Corruption, n 11 this chapter, Articles 32–35 (protection of witnesses and victims); UN Convention against Transnational Organized Crime, n 9 this chapter, Article 26 (involvement of victims and reparations).

22 American Law Institute, *Restatement of the Law, Third, Foreign Relations Law of the United States* (1987), § 401.

23 *The Lotus*, n 1 this chapter at 25.

24 Ibid.

25 Signed in Paris, 14 March 1884. French text in 163 *Consolidated Treaty Series* 391; English Translation in *US Compilation of Treaties in Force*.

26 Convention for Suppression of Counterfeiting Currency, Geneva, 20 April 1929, 112 LNTS 371.

27 See n 12 this chapter.

28 Quoted in, Survey of multilateral conventions which may be of relevance for the work of the International law Commission on the topic "The obligation to extradite or prosecute (*aut dedere aut judicare*)," UN Doc. A/CN.4/630 (2010) at 8.

29 Ibid.

30 See n 12 this chapter. On post-Second World War suppression agreements, see Roger S. Clark, "Offenses of International Concern: State Practice in the Forty Years since Nuremberg," *Nordic Journal of International Law* 57 (1988).

31 The Hague Convention on the Suppression of Unlawful Seizure of Aircraft (Hijacking), Article 2.

32 Ibid., Article 4.

33 Note also the additional obligation in Article 6 to take an offender or alleged offender who is "present" into custody and make a "preliminary enquiry into the facts."

34 See discussion of similar provisions of Torture Convention in *Belgium v. Senegal*, n 4 this chapter, para 94.
35 Ibid., para 90.
36 Notably the Torture Convention, n 4 this chapter, and see the valuable discussion in *Belgium v. Senegal*, ibid.
37 Beijing Convention on the Suppression of Unlawful Acts Relating to International Civil Aviation (not yet in force).
38 See n 12. The Beijing negotiation that produced the "new Montreal" treaty also produced a Protocol Supplementary to the Convention for the Suppression of Unlawful Seizure of Aircraft, updating the 1970 Hague Convention along similar lines, but by way of amendment to the original rather than by replacing it with a wholly new one.
39 See also, on shared enforcement jurisdiction, Article 9 (temporary custody of suspects pending inquiry and extradition request); Article 16(1): "States Parties shall, in accordance with international and national law, endeavor to take all practicable measures for the purpose of preventing the offences set forth in Article 1"; and Article 18: "Any State Party having reason to believe that one of the offences set forth in Article 1 will be committed shall, in accordance with its national law, furnish any relevant information in its possession to those States Parties which it believes would be the States set forth in paragraphs 1 and 2 of Article 8."
40 Are resident aliens (a much broader class than resident stateless persons) nationals for the purpose of active or passive personality jurisdiction?
41 704 *UNTS* 219.
42 See *US v. Georgescu*, 723 F. Supp. 912 (ED NY. 1989).
43 See n 12.
44 Ibid., Article 4(3).

References

Bassiouni, M. Cherif. *Introduction to International Criminal Law*. Ardsley, NY: Transnational, 2003.

Bassiouni, M. Cherif, ed. *International Criminal Law*. 3 vols. Leiden: Martinus Nijhoff, 2008.

Boister, Neil. *Transnational Criminal Law*. Oxford: Oxford University Press, 2012.

Cassese, Antonio. *International Criminal Law*. Oxford: Oxford University Press, 2003.

Cassese, Antonio, ed. *The Oxford Companion to International Justice*. Oxford: Oxford University Press, 2009.

Clark, Roger S. "Offenses of International Concern: State Practice in the Forty Years since Nuremberg." *Nordic Journal of International Law* 57 (1988): 49–188.

Mueller, Gerhard O.W., and Edward M. Wise. *International Criminal Law*. London: Sweet and Maxwell, 1965.

Podgor, Ellen S., and Roger S. Clark. *Understanding International Criminal Law*. Newark, NJ: LexisNexis, 2008.

Williams, Sharon A., and J.-G. Castel. *Canadian Criminal Law: International and Transnational Aspects*. Toronto: Butterworths, 1981.

Wise, Edward A., Ellen S. Podgor, and Roger S. Clark. *International Criminal Law: Cases and Materials*. New Providence, NJ: LexisNexis, 2009.

36

EU Criminal Law

Valsamis Mitsilegas

Introduction

The evolution of the European Union into an Area of Freedom, Security and Justice has been largely reflected in the substantial growth of EU action in the field of criminal law and justice. The development of EU action in the field has not been without controversy: criminal law is still perceived by many (in particular national governments) as inextricably linked with state sovereignty and the exercise of state power. At the same time, the necessity of criminal law action at the level of the European Union has been brought into question. This reticence with respect to EU criminal law has led to tortuous incremental steps towards European integration in criminal matters resulting in turn into a highly complex constitutional framework governing EU action in the field. This chapter will begin with an analysis of this constitutional framework, examining institutional developments brought about by the Maastricht and Amsterdam Treaties and by focusing in particular on the major institutional changes brought about by the entry into force of the Lisbon Treaty. The institutional analysis will inform the remaining sections of this chapter, which have been designed to illustrate how European integration in criminal matters has been organized over time. The chapter will thus examine, in turn, the extent of EU competence to harmonize national legislation in the field of substantive criminal law; European integration in criminal matters via the application of the principle of mutual recognition to criminal law and justice; harmonization of criminal procedure in order to facilitate the operation of mutual recognition; European integration via delegation, by an examination of the powers and interrelationship between various EU bodies and agencies in the field of criminal justice; and last, but not least, the external dimension of EU action in criminal matters. The analysis throughout the chapter is forward looking in that it attempts to capture the potential impact of the Lisbon Treaty on European integration in the field of criminal law.

A Companion to European Union Law and International Law, First Edition.
Edited by Dennis Patterson and Anna Södersten.

The Institutional Framework

The evolution of European integration in criminal matters has been fraught with institutional complexity. This complexity can be explained by the close link of criminal law with the exercise of state power and thus state sovereignty. Fears of loss of sovereignty have led member states to agree to confer powers to the European Union in criminal matters only in a gradual and incremental manner. The institutional framework in the field of EU criminal law has been largely intergovernmental until the entry into force of the Lisbon Treaty. However, as will be seen later in the chapter, even following Lisbon a number of elements of resistance to supranationalism in the field have remained. For the first time, the treaties confirmed express EU powers on criminal law in the three-pillar Maastricht Treaty. The Maastricht third pillar on Justice and Home Affairs contained strong intergovernmental elements: unanimity in the Council and a very limited role for the Parliament, the Court of Justice, and the Commission. EU action in criminal law would take the form of very weak legal instruments, including Joint Actions and Conventions, an instrument reminiscent of public international law. The Amsterdam Treaty retained the pillar structure but revamped the third pillar to focus only on criminal matters. Intergovernmental elements remained prominent in the Amsterdam third pillar. Decision-making took place by unanimity in the Council and consultation of the Parliament. The Commission shared the right to initiative with member states and did not have its first-pillar powers of guardian of the treaties. The Court of Justice had limited jurisdiction, in particular no jurisdiction to rule on infringement proceedings and jurisdiction to give preliminary rulings dependent on member states' declarations. Third-pillar law was strengthened with the exodus of joint actions and the introduction of framework decisions in the treaty. Framework decisions were similar to directives in that they were binding as to the objectives but left member states with leeway as to how to achieve these objectives. However, unlike directives, they did not entail direct effect.[1] The Court of Justice subsequently confirmed in its landmark ruling in *Pupino* that, notwithstanding this limitation, framework decisions do entail "indirect" effect.[2] The applicability of other Community law principles to the third pillar remained contested.[3]

The Lisbon Treaty introduced radical changes to the institutional framework in EU criminal law. First of all, it abolished the three-pillar structure of the Union. EU criminal law measures now form part of a unitary title on the Area of Freedom, Security and Justice (Title V) of the Treaty on the Functioning of the European Union (TFEU). The abolition of the third pillar and the "communautarisation" of EU criminal law it engenders have resulted in a number of significant constitutional changes in the field. The first major change concerns *decision making*, which, for the vast majority of Title V measures will take place under the "ordinary" legislative procedure, that is, codecision between the Council (which will decide by majority voting) and the European Parliament.[4] The second major institutional change involves the role of the Court of Justice, and the "communautarization" of *judicial control*. The Court now has full jurisdiction to rule on infringement proceedings in criminal matters[5] – a move that strengthens the Commission's role as "guardian of the Treaties" to monitor the implementation of EU criminal law by member states. The full jurisdiction of the Court in the field of preliminary rulings now applies.[6] The Court also assumes full jurisdiction to actions for compensation for damages[7] and the review of legality;[8] review the compliance of legislative acts with the principle of subsidiarity;[9] and review the legality of acts of the European Council and bodies, offices, or agencies of the Union intended to produce legal effects vis-à-vis third parties.[10] The third major institutional change concerns the change in the form of the legal instruments, with criminal law being adopted in the form of regulations, directives, and decisions, which are the general EU legal instruments after Lisbon.[11] Direct effect of EU criminal law measures is thus no longer excluded. A further horizontal change with a potentially profound impact on EU action in criminal matters has been the express incorporation of the EU Charter of Fundamental Rights in the EU constitutional framework as well as the expression of the EU commitment to accede to the European Convention on Human Rights.[12]

This move towards supranationalism in EU criminal law has not, however, been absolute. The Lisbon Treaty contains a number of provisions which reveal what I have characterized elsewhere as "resistance to the communautarisation" in EU criminal law.[13] A key aspect of this resistance is reflected in the emphasis placed by the Lisbon Treaty on the need to respect the diversity of national legal systems.[14] Moreover, the treaty stresses mutual recognition as a method of European integration in criminal matters and grants the Union competence in criminal procedure only by subordinating harmonization in the field to mutual recognition. The need to respect national diversity is also reflected in the choice of the form of EU legislative action concerning harmonization of substantive criminal law and criminal procedure: in both cases, harmonization will take place by means of directives.[15] This choice is significant, as directives leave member states a considerable margin of maneuver in the implementation of EU law, being binding as to the result to be achieved but leaving to the national authorities the choice of form and methods.[16] However, the use of directives in EU criminal law (and the prospect of directives being drafted in general terms leaving the detail to member states) may challenge the requirement for legal certainty, which is of particular relevance to criminal law measures. This emphasis on national diversity is also reflected in the prominent place envisaged by the Lisbon Treaty for the control of subsidiarity, which has introduced national elements in the EU legislative and policy process – with national parliaments being granted an enhanced role in subsidiarity monitoring.[17] National diversity is also safeguarded via the introduction of limits to conferral of EU competence in criminal matters. According to Article 72 TFEU, Title V will "not affect the exercise of the responsibilities incumbent upon member states with regard to the maintenance of law and order and the safeguarding of internal security."[18] Moreover, EU action in the field of criminal procedure and the harmonization of substantive criminal law will take the form of minimum rules only.[19]

Resistance to communautarization is also reflected by shifting the interinstitutional balance towards intergovernmentalism during the legislative cycle. The first aspect of this shift concerns the right of initiative, with member states retaining a key role in the initiation of both legislation and strategy in EU criminal law. The European Council has a central role in this context in defining "the strategic guidelines for legislative and operational planning within the area of freedom, security and justice."[20] Initiative remains with governments not only at the stage of the initiation of policy and strategy but also at the stage of the initiation of *legislation*: member states share the right of initiative in criminal matters with the Commission.[21] The prominent role of the European Council seems potentially at odds with the central role of the Commission as a generator of legislation and policy and may challenge the operation of the principle of mutual sincere cooperation between the EU institutions which is a key principle of the Lisbon Treaty.[22] Along with its role as a policy and strategy initiator, the European Council also assumes under Lisbon the role of a mediator: it plays a central part in the "emergency brake" procedure envisaged in cases where member states express concerns about the impact of proposals for EU criminal law on their domestic systems.[23] The second element of intergovernmentalism in decision making concerns exceptions to the ordinary legislative procedure: these involve instances where the treaty allows for the expansion of EU competence via "passerelle" provisions,[24] the establishment of a European Public Prosecutor's Office (EPPO),[25] and legislation involving operational cooperation between member states.[26] Moreover, "communautaire elements" may be sidelined in areas such as the adoption of terrorist sanctions, where the treaty contains an Area of Freedom, Security and Justice legal basis as well as a more intergovernmental foreign policy legal basis if preference is given to the latter.[27] The third element of intergovernmentalism in the legislative cycle is reflected in the limited participation of Denmark,[28] Ireland, and the United Kingdom in EU criminal law. In the case of Ireland and the United Kingdom, the Amsterdam "opt-out" protocols have been refined in Lisbon to allow greater freedom to opt out from the development of the Schengen *acquis* on the one hand[29] and to extend the immigration law opt-out to criminal law on the other.[30] At the insistence of the United Kingdom, third pillar law would retain its effects for a period of five years after the entry into force of the Lisbon Treaty, at which point these measures will be fully "Lisbonized" and the United Kingdom will have the choice of accepting or rejecting the third pillar *acquis* as a whole.[31] The United Kingdom has now declared that it will opt out of the third pillar *acquis* following the Protocol on Transitional Provisions,[32] but it has subsequently expressed its wish to opt back into a list of thirty-five third pillar measures, including the Framework Decision on the European Arrest Warrant. The extent and start of UK participation in third pillar law after the end of the five-year transitional period is still to be decided at the time of writing.

A further dimension of resistance to communautarization involves the configuration of the *ex post* scrutiny of EU criminal law. Limits to judicial control remain: the Court will have no jurisdiction to review the validity or proportionality of operations carried out by the police or other law enforcement services of a member state or the exercise of the responsibilities incumbent upon member states with regard to the maintenance of law and order and the safeguarding of internal security.[33] Moreover, the jurisdiction of the Court in proceedings reviewing the legality of restrictive measures adopted under Title V TEU,[34] the treaty seems to exclude from the Court's jurisdiction the implementing measures adopted by the Council under the foreign policy legal basis of Article 215(2) TFEU. Further limits to communautarization can be discerned at the level of the monitoring of the implementation of EU criminal law. Central to the monitoring architecture of Title V is the establishment of mechanisms for the "objective and impartial evaluation" of the implementation of the Union policies referred to in this Title by national authorities in particular in order to facilitate full application of the principle of mutual recognition.[35] Evaluation is thus an *ex post* scrutiny mechanism containing strong intergovernmental elements: it will be conducted by member states (in collaboration with the Commission) with the European Parliament *and* national parliaments being "informed" of its content and results.[36] A joint interparliamentary involvement (of the European Parliament and national parliaments) is also envisaged with regard to the evaluation of the activities of Eurojust (the EU's Judicial Cooperation Unit).[37] It is unclear how this intergovernmental evaluation mechanism will coexist with the traditional powers of the European Commission as guardian of the treaties. Interinstitutional tensions with regard to the application of the specific Lisbon evaluation provisions have already arisen with respect to the development of the Schengen *acquis*.[38]

Harmonization of Substantive Criminal Law

Although the Treaty of Rome did not envisage express powers for the European Community in the field of criminal justice, European integration has demonstrated that it has been increasingly difficult to disassociate Community action in the main areas of Community competence (including free movement and the completion of the internal market) from criminal justice policy. Interconnections between Community law and criminal law have emerged in a twofold manner. First, by Community law influencing *national* criminal law that needs to be interpreted in a way that ensures the effectiveness of Community law. Second, by Community law *as such* dealing with criminal matters in cases where the Community is called to respond to global security threats. In a consistent line of case law (extending to the post-Lisbon era), the Court has set limits to the freedom of member states to use criminal law when criminalization at national level is detrimental to achieving the effectiveness of Union law.[39] The Court has further recognized (by 1989) the principle of assimilation, obliging national authorities to treat EU interests in an equivalent manner to domestic interests.[40] The absence of an express Community competence to define criminal offences and adopt criminal sanctions did not act as an obstacle to finding a legal basis in the Treaty of Rome to adopt Community anti-money-laundering law.[41]

The third pillar introduced express legal bases enabling the adoption by the European Union of concrete measures defining criminal offences and introducing criminal sanctions. An analysis of harmonization of substantive criminal law today demonstrates that the Union *acquis* is a combination of instruments adopted since Maastricht (e.g., the Fraud[42] and Corruption in the Public Sector Conventions[43]), since Amsterdam (a series of framework decisions addressing security threats such as terrorism,[44] organized crime,[45] and drug trafficking[46]), and since Lisbon (see the recently adopted directives on human trafficking[47] and sexual exploitation[48]). On a number of occasions, such as in the case of human trafficking and sexual exploitation, continuity in EU law has meant that harmonization measures have been evolving substantively and institutionally over time. Overall, the EU legislator has adopted an expansive approach to EU competence in substantive criminal law under the third pillar. Harmonization has not been limited to the fields of crime expressly mentioned in the treaty but has also extended to harmonization in the fields of, inter alia, irregular migration,[49] corruption,[50] and cybercrime.[51] The existence of express harmonization legal bases in the third pillar and the expansive approach to harmonization adopted by member states has not stopped the Commission from arguing that the Community (and not only the Union under the third pillar) also had competence to legislate in the field. Following a number of unsuccessful Commission proposals on first-pillar criminal law,[52] the Commission initiated legal basis litigation in Luxembourg. In two important rulings, the Court of Justice found in favor of the existence of the Community competence to define criminal offences and impose criminal sanctions.[53] Community competence was deemed necessary to ensure the effective protection of the environment, which was viewed as a key Community objective, with criminal law thus viewed not as a separate Union policy but rather as a means to an end towards achieving effectiveness of Community policies[54] However, it was not clear from the Court's case law whether Community competence would extend beyond cases involving the protection of the environment. Moreover, following sustained opposition by member states in the ship-source pollution litigation, the Court limited Community competence in only defining criminal offences and imposing criminal sanctions *in abstracto*, with the concrete levels of sanctions to be established under the third pillar.[55] This case law has led to the adoption of the pre-Lisbon first-pillar criminal law, but with all three measures adopted introducing only very limited harmonization as to penalty levels.[56]

Along with its constitutional dimension, the debate over the existence and extent of Community criminal law competence has raised the key question of criminalization at the EU level and whether criminal law should be adopted not only to address perceived threats of serious cross-border crime but also in order to achieve the effective implementation of Union policies of a predominantly regulatory character (such as transport policy, the protection of the environment, or the completion of the internal market). This dual approach has been espoused by the drafters of the Lisbon Treaty and, in particular, of Article 83 TFEU. The first paragraph of Article 83 confers upon the Union competence to establish *minimum rules* concerning *the definition of criminal offences and sanctions* in the areas of *particularly serious crime with a cross-border dimension* resulting from the nature or impact of such offences or from a special need to combat them on a common basis. These areas of crime are enumerated exhaustively in Article 83(1).[57] Article 83(1) thus affirms the acceptance of the added value of criminalization at EU level in order to address perceived serious security threats. The second paragraph of Article 83 constitutes an attempt to translate the Court's functionalist interpretation of the extent of Community (and now Union) criminal law competence in the environmental crime and ship-source pollution case law. Article 83(2) TFEU thus grants the Union competence to approximate criminal laws and regulations if such approximation *proves essential* to ensure the effective implementation of a Union policy in an area which has been subject to harmonization measures. Rather than assuming the status of a self-standing Union policy, criminal law is thus perceived as a means to an end, the end being the effective implementation of other Union policies.[58] EU competence to define in substantive criminal law after Lisbon includes thus both a paradigm of securitized criminalization under Article 83(1) TFEU – under which the Union can criminalize conduct which is deemed to be a serious security threat – as well as a paradigm of functional criminalization under Article 83(2) TFEU – whereby criminal law is used as a means to the end of achieving the effective implementation of Union policies.[59]

While Article 83 TFEU can be seen as an attempt to clarify and circumscribe clearly EU competence to define criminal offences and criminal sanctions, a number of issues on the extent of EU competence remain unresolved. With regard to Article 83(1), it is not clear whether the European Union can legislate in the fields of crime enumerated therein if these areas of crime are not considered to be serious or cross-border, especially with questions of evaluation of what constitutes serious cross-border crime likely to arise in negotiations on proposals under Article 83(1) in the future. Moreover, the exhaustive enumeration of areas of criminality as a means of limiting EU competence in the field can be deceptive: these areas of crime may actually correspond to a wide range of criminal offences or sanctions. A clear example of the potential to overstretch EU criminal law competence under Article 83(1) involves the use of the concept of "organized crime." Not only is the definition of the concept vague and amorphous at the EU level,[60] it can also be used as a legal basis for harmonization of a wide range of specific criminal offences and sanctions linked to the activities of a criminal organization. Such a broad approach may serve to address some gaps in the Lisbon legal bases for criminal law, whose wording may be narrower than the third pillar legal bases and can thus be seen to exclude prima facie EU action in areas where the European Union has legislated extensively under the third pillar. The recent Commission proposal for a directive on confiscation constitutes a prime example in this context,[61] where the Commission has used Article 83(1) TFEU as a broad legal basis to justify EU action on confiscation and enable confiscation of the proceeds of all offences committed within the framework of organized crime. The directive was eventually adopted on the basis of a joint legal basis consisting of Articles 82(2) and 83(1) TFEU,[62] reflecting the absence of an express decision on whether confiscation constitutes a means of criminal procedure (necessitating a legal basis under Article 82(2) TFEU) or whether it constitutes a sanction (calling for the use of Article 83(1) TFEU). Moreover, the use of Article 83(1) as a legal basis means that confiscation for the purposes of the directive is limited to criminal offences deemed to fall within the list of conduct enumerated in Article 83(1) TFEU.

The extent of Union competence under Article 83(2) TFEU may prove to be even more contested. Article 83(2) establishes a functional legal basis for substantive criminal law by justifying EU intervention when essential to ensure the effective implementation of Union policies. By using the term "essential," the treaty adopts a high threshold for EU intervention. But what kind of action meets this threshold is unclear and demonstrating the essential character of EU intervention under Article 83(2) is prone to litigation. Moreover, it is contested whether Article 83(2) is a sufficient, self-standing legal basis for the adoption of criminal law or whether a dual legal basis (in conjunction with the specific EU sectoral provision) will be necessary in this context. The answer may have implications for the future development of enhanced cooperation in the field. The issue is of particular significance with respect to member states such as the United Kingdom that have been offered the possibility of not opting in to EU criminal law in the future. If a dual legal basis is required, it appears that a member state that has participated in and is bound by the underlying Union policy is also bound by measures adopted under Article 83(2). Otherwise, the effectiveness of Union law may be seriously jeopardized. The other side of the coin is the question of whether Article 83(2) is indeed a required legal basis in cases where a legal basis for the adoption of Union law can be found elsewhere in the treaty. Using a legal basis other than Article 83(2) has significant constitutional consequences: it may enable the adoption of EU substantive criminal law measures in the form of regulations; it deprives member states of the option of using the emergency brake; and it forces the participation of Denmark, Ireland, and the United Kingdom in EU criminal law. A development that may imply that the Union's criminal law competence may extend beyond Article 83(2) TFEU is the deletion of the last sentence of Article 280(4) EC in its reincarnation as Article 325 TFEU in Lisbon. This sentence states that measures to combat fraud (an area which is not expressly listed in Article 83(1) TFEU but may be included in 83(2)) will not concern the application of national criminal law and the national administration of justice.[63] The Commission has opted in favor of exclusively using Article 325 TFEU as a legal basis for its recent proposal for a draft directive on fraud.[64]

A related unresolved issue is the relationship between Article 83(2) TFEU and other treaty provisions in cases where EU measures are being put forward that envisage the adoption of both criminal and noncriminal (administrative) sanctions. Is one instrument under a dual legal basis necessary or should two separate instruments with distinct legal bases be adopted? The Commission has opted in favor of the latter solution in its recent proposals for revised post-Lisbon legislation introducing sanctions for insider dealing and market manipulation.[65] All these examples demonstrate that the extent of EU competence under Article 83(2) is far from clear-cut and that the attempt to translate the Court's case law in treaty provisions may not serve to avoid future legal basis litigation in the field.[66] The debate over the extent of EU competence to criminalize and introduce criminal sanctions under Article 83(2) (but also Article 83(1) TFEU) is inextricably linked with the broader discussion of the substance of the EU criminalization policy. Thus far, the focus has been largely on asserting and using Union competence in the field,[67] without considering the potential overcriminalization impact this framing of the issue may have. The sustained focus on the constitutional aspects of criminalization should not avoid the discussion of the question of whether – irrespective of the existence of EU competence to legislate – criminal law is the most effective way to address security threats or achieve the effective implementation of Union policies.[68]

Mutual Recognition

A key factor contributing to the growth in European criminal law since Amsterdam has been the application of the principle of mutual recognition in criminal matters. Under this principle, decisions issued by a judicial authority of one member state will as a rule be recognized and executed by authorities in other member states. Mutual recognition is based on the dual presumption of, on the one hand, the existence of mutual trust among the authorities of member states and, on the other hand, the presumption of the full respect of fundamental rights by all member states.[69] Proposals to introduce the principle of mutual recognition in EU criminal law can be seen as a balancing act between the need to address concerns with regard to the slow pace of improvement of judicial cooperation in criminal matters in the European Union following Maastricht and the need to reassure member states skeptical of further EU harmonization in criminal matters at a time when ambitious proposals for criminal law uniformity in the Union, such as the *Corpus Juris*, had emerged – with mutual recognition being perceived as advantageous in this context as it would seem that (at least prima facie) it would not lead to changes in member states' domestic substantive criminal law in order to implement Union law.[70] According to the Tampere European Council Conclusions, mutual recognition "should become the cornerstone of judicial co-operation" in criminal matters.[71] This led in 2001 to the adoption by member states of a very detailed program of measures to implement the principle of mutual recognition of decisions in criminal matters.[72] Since then, a raft of third pillar measures has been adopted, establishing, at least on paper, a comprehensive system of mutual recognition extending from the pretrial (recognition of arrest warrants,[73] evidence warrants,[74] freezing orders,[75] decisions on bail[76]) to the posttrial stage (recognition of confiscation orders,[77] decisions on financial penalties,[78] probation orders,[79] and decisions on the transfer of sentenced persons[80]). Although no specific EU framework decision has been adopted in the field, the Court of Justice has addressed additional reflections of mutual recognition by developing detailed case law interpreting the principle of *ne bis in idem* as enshrined in Article 54 of the Schengen Implementing Convention, which was incorporated in the EU constitutional order by the Amsterdam Treaty.[81] The principle of mutual recognition has been constitutionalized following Lisbon, with Article 82(1) TFEU recognizing the close link between mutual recognition and judicial cooperation in criminal matters.

The main features of the application of the principle of mutual recognition in criminal matters are automaticity, speed, and the execution of judicial decisions with a minimum of formality. Based on mutual trust, the system includes very limited grounds to refuse the recognition and execution of a judicial decision or to raise questions regarding the legal system of the member state of the issuing authority. Automaticity has presented a number of challenges, most notably with regard to the protection of the fundamental rights of affected individuals. These challenges have arisen in particular in the context of the Framework Decision on the European Arrest Warrant, which is emblematic of the application of the principle of mutual recognition in the field of criminal law. It is the first measure to be adopted in the field and the only mutual recognition measure that has been implemented fully and in detail at the time of writing.[82] Under the framework decision, surrender (formerly extradition) has been judicialized,[83] applies to a wide range of offences,[84] and targets a wide range of individuals with the option for member states not to surrender their own nationals being abolished. European arrest warrants can be issued with a view to the arrest and surrender by another member state of a requested person for the purposes of conducting a criminal prosecution or executing a custodial sentence and must be executed on the basis of the principle of mutual recognition.[85] Automaticity in the operation of interstate cooperation under the European Arrest Warrant Framework Decision has been introduced at three levels. Firstly, cooperation must take place within a limited timeframe, under strict deadlines, and on the basis of a pro forma form annexed to the framework decision – this means that in practice few questions can be asked by the executing authority beyond what has been included in the form.[86] Secondly, the executing authority is not allowed to verify the existence of dual criminality for a list of thirty-two categories of offence listed in the framework decision[87] – this means that the executing state is asked to deploy its law enforcement mechanism and arrest and surrender an individual for conduct which is not an offence under its domestic law.[88] The third level of automaticity arises from the inclusion of limited grounds of refusal to recognize and execute a European Arrest Warrant under the framework decision. The framework decision includes only three, in their majority procedural, mandatory grounds for refusal,[89] which are complemented by a series of optional grounds for refusal[90] and provisions on guarantees underpinning the surrender process.[91] These grounds for refusal can further be grouped into two categories: grounds for refusal related to limits to prosecution arising from the law of the executing member state;[92] and grounds for refusal related to territoriality, nationality, or residence.[93] Noncompliance with fundamental rights is not, however, included as a ground to refuse to execute a European Arrest Warrant. This legislative choice reflects the view that cooperation can take place on the basis of a high level of mutual trust in the criminal justice systems of member states, premised upon the presumption that fundamental rights are in principle respected fully across the European Union.[94]

A major challenge in the implementation of the framework decision has been reconciliation of the automaticity introduced in the European Arrest Warrant Framework Decision with the protection of fundamental rights. A number of member states added noncompliance of surrender with fundamental rights as an express ground of refusal in their national implementing law.[95] While this implementation choice was initially criticized by the European Commission as being contrary to the framework decision,[96] its most recent implementation report indicates a change of strategy: the Commission now perceives Article 1(3) of the framework decision as constituting a de facto ground for refusal, at least as regards breach of fundamental rights resulting from deficiencies in detention conditions.[97] The Commission also argues in favor of the application of a proportionality test by member states in the operation of the framework decision.[98] The debate on proportionality has been triggered by concerns that European Arrest Warrants are issued for relatively minor offences, resulting in considerable pressure on the criminal justice systems of executing member states and disproportionate results for the requested individuals.[99] Noncompliance with proportionality has thus far been dealt with as a human rights related ground of refusal to execute a warrant,[100] or, alternatively, as a matter to be considered at the issuing stage.[101] The latter approach is also gaining ground with the EU legislator as regards the development of further measures on mutual recognition in criminal matters. The recently adopted Directive on the European Investigation Order (EIO)[102] not only includes noncompliance with fundamental rights as a ground for refusal[103] but also introduces a proportionality test in the issuing state: the issuing authority may only issue an EIO where the issuing of the EIO is necessary and proportionate and where the investigative measures indicated in the EIO could have been ordered under the same conditions in a similar domestic case.[104]

While the introduction of a proportionality check in these terms may serve as a limit to the automaticity of the European Arrest Warrant system, its limits should not be disregarded: a proportionality check is not to be equated with a general check of fundamental rights compliance; the approach currently adopted by the Council does not allow for the examination of the principle by the authorities in the executing state; the framing of the debate – at least in the Council and the Commission – suggests that the primary aim of the proportionality check is to minimize the cost of the operation of the system for member states and not the protection of the rights of requested persons; and a proportionality check may be of limited value if the scope of the European Arrest Warrant Framework Decision remains broad enough to include the majority of criminal offences under national law.[105] The fundamental rights effects of automatic surrender have also been addressed by the adoption of mutual recognition instruments regulating *ex post* the consequences of surrender. The framework decision on the mutual recognition of bail decisions would enable an individual surrendered under a European Arrest Warrant to spend the pretrial period under bail conditions in the executing, and not the issuing, member state. The framework decisions on the mutual recognition of probation decisions and on the transfer of sentenced person could have similar effects at the posttrial stage. However, neither of these instruments addresses directly the automaticity challenges arising from the operation of the European Arrest Warrant as such.

An important development on the issue of automaticity in mutual recognition in criminal matters has arisen from a Luxembourg ruling in the field of asylum law. In the case of *N.S.* and *M.E.* (hereinafter *N.S.*),[106] the Court of Justice was asked to interpret the compatibility of the Dublin Regulation (which is similar to mutual recognition measures in criminal matters in that it introduces an automatic system of interstate cooperation based on negative mutual recognition)[107] with the protection of fundamental rights. In a seminal ruling, the Court found that an application of the Dublin Regulation on the basis of the conclusive presumption that the asylum seeker's fundamental rights will be observed in the member state primarily responsible for his application is incompatible with the duty of the member states to interpret and apply the regulation in a manner consistent with fundamental rights.[108] Were the regulation to require a conclusive presumption of compliance with fundamental rights, it could itself be regarded as undermining the safeguards which are intended to ensure compliance with fundamental rights by the European Union and its member states.[109] Such presumption is rebuttable.[110] The implications of this ruling for the operation of mutual recognition in criminal matters are significant. First, executing authorities are now under a duty to examine, on a case-by-case basis, the *individual* circumstances in each case and the human rights implications of a transfer in each particular case. Second, national authorities are obliged to *refuse* to execute such requests when the transfer of the affected individuals will result in the breach of their fundamental rights within the terms of *N.S.* The ruling in *N.S.* has thus in effect introduced a fundamental rights mandatory ground for refusal that is also applicable to mutual recognition in criminal matters.[111] In its recent case law on the European Arrest Warrant, the Court of Justice appears to have maintained its restrictive approach with regard to the interpretation of the grounds to refuse to recognize and execute a Warrant on the grounds of concerns that such action by the executing authority would result in a breach of fundamental rights.[112] However, it is submitted that the constitutional landscape of EU law since Lisbon necessitates the introduction of clear limits to the automaticity of mutual recognition when the protection of fundamental rights is at stake.[113]

Harmonization for Mutual Recognition

A key question which has arisen from the application of the principle of mutual recognition in criminal matters has been whether mutual recognition should be accompanied by a degree of harmonization of national criminal procedure standards in order to enhance mutual trust in the Area of Freedom, Security and Justice and address the adverse impact of mutual recognition on the rights of affected individuals. In order to address the fundamental rights concerns resulting from the introduction of automaticity in the European Arrest Warrant system, in 2004 the Commission tabled a proposal for a framework decision on procedural rights in criminal proceedings.[114] Both substantive and legal basis concerns by member states resulted in the proposal not being adopted by the Council under the third pillar unanimity requirements.[115] The entry into force of the Lisbon Treaty provided a renewed momentum toward the adoption of EU law on defense rights, with Article 82(2) TFEU now providing an express legal basis for the adoption of minimum standards on the rights of individuals in criminal procedure. This momentum was created during the 2009 Swedish EU presidency, leading to the adoption of a road map for the rights of the defendant.[116] The road map is based upon a step-by-step approach and envisages the adoption of a number of specific EU law instruments each covering specific defense rights. Thus far, three of these measures – a directive on the right to translation and interpretation,[117] a directive on the right of information,[118] and a directive on access to a lawyer[119] have been adopted. These instruments establish minimum standards and apply not only to cross-border cases involving the operation of the European Arrest Warrant but also to cases arising in the context of the domestic criminal justice process.[120]

A key question in the adoption of these measures is whether they will lead to the enhancement of mutual trust in the operation of the system of mutual recognition in criminal matters.[121] The treaty's legal basis – enabling the adoption of minimum rules on the rights of the defense – is a functional legal basis: competence to legislate in the field has been conferred to the European Union only to the extent necessary to facilitate mutual recognition and police and judicial cooperation in criminal matters having a cross-border dimension. EU competence to legislate on the rights of the defense is, thus, not self-standing but conditional upon the need to demonstrate that defense rights are necessary for mutual recognition. Indeed, the two recently adopted directives on defense rights have been justified by linking the adoption of EU measures in the field with the enhancement of mutual trust.[122] However, the use of mutual trust as an element justifying the adoption of EU measures in the field is problematic in two respects. First, it fails to provide a direct and clear link between the defense rights proposed and their necessity for the operation of mutual recognition.[123] Second, it is based on a concept (of mutual trust) which is too subjective for it to meet the criteria set out by the Court of Justice when ascertaining the legality of EU instruments, namely that the choice of legal basis must be based on objective factors which are amenable to judicial review.[124] An alternate way forward could be to justify EU defense rights measures as necessary to address the *effects* of the operation of mutual recognition on the individual. The necessity requirement of Article 82(2) TFEU would thus be viewed from the perspective of the individual – and the need to protect fundamental rights – and not from the perspective of the state or of the authorities which cooperate under mutual recognition.

These concerns over the legal basis should not minimize the significance of the adoption of specific EU law standards on the rights of the defense for the position of the individual in a system of mutual recognition. Article 82(2) TFEU is a clear rebuttal to the view that the application of mutual recognition in criminal matters will have no impact on the domestic criminal law of member states. In this context, the benefits of EU secondary law on procedural safeguards for the affected individuals are manifold. The implementation of these measures by member states will, following Lisbon, be subject to the full scrutiny of EU institutions. The drafting of the rights provisions of the directives adopted thus far indicate that these are concepts which are likely to assume an autonomous EU law meaning in the future (the Court of Justice has already conferred autonomous meaning to provisions in the European Arrest Warrant Framework Decision[125]). Provisions conferring rights on the defendant will be subject to interpretation both by Luxembourg and by national courts, with the provisions granting rights in the directives which have already been adopted being clear, unconditional, and sufficiently precise and thus entailing direct effect.[126] The adoption of specific EU secondary law on defense rights will also serve to concretize and further develop the protection of general fundamental rights included in the charter and the European Convention on Human Rights.

Delegation: Bodies, Offices, and Agencies

Another key element of European integration in criminal matters has been delegation, as reflected by the establishment of a number of EU bodies with powers in the criminal justice field. The first major EU initiative in this context has been the post-Maastricht adoption of a convention establishing the European Police Office (Europol), which has since been replaced by a post-Amsterdam decision.[127] Europol is essentially a criminal intelligence agency, with its main tasks consisting of analysis of data provided to it by national authorities and providing intelligence products to these authorities, as well as producing risk-assessment reports on major areas of criminality. The establishment of Europol was followed by the establishment of Eurojust via a 2002 decision, which was subsequently amended by a decision adopted shortly before the entry into force of the Lisbon Treaty in 2009.[128] The main tasks of Eurojust are to coordinate member states' activities in the field of criminal investigations and prosecutions and to provide advice on conflicts of jurisdiction. The mandate of Europol and Eurojust is largely aligned to cover a wide range of areas of serious crime. Their work is complemented by the work of the European Anti-Fraud Office (OLAF), which was established in 1999 and whose legal framework was revised in 2013.[129] OLAF replaced UCLAF (the Unité de Coordination de La Lutte Anti-Fraude) as a response to the events leading to the resignation of the Santer Commission. Although the OLAF legal framework proclaims its independence, OLAF remains situated within the European Commission. It has a hybrid nature, conducting both external and internal administrative investigations involving alleged fraud in member states.[130]

There are three major, interrelated issues which have arisen from the operation of these bodies thus far: the issue of *their impact on state sovereignty*, and the extent to which member states are willing to transfer powers in the sensitive field of criminal law to EU bodies; the issue of the *accountability and legal responsibility* of these bodies; and the issue of *overlap and competition* between these bodies. As regards the issue of sovereignty, strong intergovernmental elements remain in both the Europol and Eurojust decisions as regards the mandate (with these bodies not allowed to conduct investigations themselves [or in the case of Eurojust also prosecutions] in the territory of member states) and the structure of these bodies (with member states appointing liaison officers in Europol and national members in Eurojust). Crucially, EU bodies in the field cannot compel national authorities to act – most significantly, Eurojust can ask but not currently oblige national authorities to undertake investigations or prosecutions.[131] The strong intergovernmental features of these bodies engender gaps in their accountability and legal responsibility. Limited accountability mechanisms towards the European Parliament are provided.[132] The strengthening of judicial review of the work of these bodies after Lisbon is tempered by the strong element of informality in their work – a key example here being decisions taken within the framework of Eurojust about conflicts of jurisdiction that are taken without any formalized process including the representation of the defendant and without clear, legally binding hierarchical criteria governing such decisions. Similar limits to legal responsibility can be discerned in the work of OLAF, where on a number of occasions – but also with significant exceptions – the Court of Justice has accepted that OLAF actions are mere preparatory acts bearing no direct consequences for the investigated individuals.[133] These gaps in the protection of individuals affected by the work of EU bodies are compounded by the competition and overlap in their work. The proliferation of EU bodies in the field has led to bodies with overlapping functions (especially as regards criminal investigations) and an overlapping mandate. While a number of interinstitutional agreements between these bodies have been concluded, this has not been translated into a coherent framework of cooperation or a coherent vision as to how these bodies fit within EU criminal justice policy.[134]

The entry into force of the Lisbon Treaty may motivate addressing the above-referenced issues. Before Lisbon, state sovereignty and law enforcement concerns led to a system which avoids centralization at EU level and is based upon cooperation between national authorities and EU bodies – with justice ultimately delivered at national level. Lisbon has the potential to shift this balance. Article 85 TFEU on Eurojust grants the potential to Eurojust in the future to compel member states to initiate investigations.[135] More importantly, Article 86 TFEU leaves open the possibility of the establishment of an EPPO "from Eurojust," an initiative which may lead to greater centralization of criminal justice in Europe. The Lisbon momentum generates a number of questions regarding the nature and relationship of EU criminal justice bodies. Key questions in this context relate to the relationship between Eurojust and the EPPO, and the future of Eurojust once an EPPO has been established "from it"; the future of OLAF and whether it will be rendered obsolete by the dual existence of Eurojust and the EPPO; and the position of Europol in this scheme – does it merit an independent existence or is it to be subsumed under a centralized EU EPPO structure? Proposals for the establishment of an EPPO, which reflect various visions for this body,[136] are currently being negotiated in Brussels.[137] The time has come for a detailed discussion on the role, functions, and position of EU criminal justice bodies within the general framework of EU criminal justice policy since Lisbon.

The External Dimension

An analysis of the growing subject of European criminal law cannot be complete without an overview of the external dimension of EU action in the field. In the past decade, the Union has emerged as a strong global actor in criminal matters. Union action in the field has focused on two levels: on the multilateral level, with the EU being increasingly active in the negotiations of regional and global criminal law conventions[138] and on the bilateral level, with the Union and its bodies concluding agreements with third states on criminal matters.[139] A prime example of the latter strand of EU action is the conclusion of a number of agreements between the European Union and the United States of America aimed primarily at counter terrorism.[140] The emergence of the Union as a global actor in a field which has been fraught with heightened internal constitutional complexity has not been an easy task from an institutional perspective.[141] The entry into force of the Lisbon Treaty has largely addressed these issues but has not necessarily addressed the substantive issues arising from EU external action.[142] A key issue in this context concerns coherence. Coherence can be viewed from an EU law perspective (coherence in particular between EU internal policies and values on the one hand and EU external action on the other) as well as from an international law perspective (coherence between EU law and international law). As regards coherence between internal and external EU action, the compatibility of EU external action (in particular the various EU–US counter-terrorism agreements) with the constitutional values of the Union is contested, with securitized external action presenting the danger of undermining European values.[143] As regards coherence between EU and international law, the need to preserve the autonomy and specificity of the EU legal order (as reflected for instance in the insertion of disconnection clauses in a number of international agreements and in the case law of the Court of Justice in judgments such as *Kadi*[144] and *Intertanko*[145]) when viewed from an international law perspective may challenge the unity and lead to the fragmentation of international law.[146]

Conclusion

Notwithstanding its contested nature, EU criminal law has reached a significant level of maturity. European integration in the field has not been limited to the harmonization of substantive criminal law but has also progressed via the parallel use of forms of governance, including the promotion of interstate cooperation via mutual recognition and the establishment of EU bodies in the field of criminal justice. The potentially far-reaching impact of EU criminal law on state sovereignty has meant that European integration in the field has proceeded hand in hand with considerable institutional and constitutional complexity. While the entry into force of the Lisbon Treaty has been decisive in normalizing the EU institutional framework in the field of criminal law, a high level of complexity and an emphasis on intergovernmentalism remains. It is not at the institutional level but rather at the level of the protection of fundamental rights where the most significant impact of Lisbon on EU criminal law may lie. The focus on the proliferation of EU enforcement measures, which in reality have strengthened, and not weakened, state power, is gradually shifting in order to take into account the pressing need to address the impact of EU criminal law on the individual. The need for full compliance of EU criminal law with fundamental rights must be examined when EU criminal law is proposed and negotiated (for instance in proposals to introduce new criminal offences and sanctions or to establish an EPPO) but also when examining the implementation and operation on the ground of EU measures. Not only must fundamental rights be taken into account by national authorities when they implement EU criminal law – in particular by interpreting these provisions consistently with the charter – but they are also promoted by specific, secondary EU legislation in the field. The evolving EU legislative framework on defense rights is a prime example in this context, with EU law producing specific human rights standards which, by virtue of EU constitutional law, may be directly effective in the domestic legal orders of member states. By reconfiguring the relationship between the individual and the state in this manner, EU criminal law since Lisbon may in effect lead to a deeper constitutionalization of the European Union as a whole.

Notes

1 Article 34(2)(b) TEU.
2 Case C-105/03 *Pupino* EU:C:2005:386.
3 For an overview of the institutional evolution of EU criminal law, see Valsamis Mitsilegas, *EU Criminal Law* (Oxford: Hart, 2009), Chap. 1.
4 On the "ordinary" legislative procedure see Articles 289(1) and 294 TFEU.
5 Articles 258–260 TFEU.
6 On the preliminary ruling jurisdiction under Lisbon, see Article 267 TEU. The last paragraph states that such rulings must be given with a minimum of delay in cases involving individuals in custody.
7 Article 268 TFEU.
8 Article 263(4) TFEU.
9 Article 8, Protocol No 2 on the Application of the Principles of Subsidiarity and Proportionality. Further analysis is provided later in the chapter.

10 Article 263(1) TFEU. See also Article 277 TFEU.
11 Article 288(1) TFEU.
12 Article 6 TEU.
13 Valsamis Mitsilegas, "European Criminal Law and Resistance to Communautarisation Post-Lisbon," *New Journal of European Criminal Law* 1 (2010).
14 See Article 67(1) TFEU.
15 Articles 82(2), 83(1) and (2) TFEU respectively.
16 Article 288(3) TFEU.
17 Article 12 TEU. See also Article 5(1) and (3) TEU on the principle of subsidiarity. Protocol No 1 on the Role of National Parliaments in the European Union and Protocol No 2 on the Application of the Principles of Subsidiarity and Proportionality respectively. See also Article 69 TFEU in the specific context of Title V.
18 Article 72 TFEU.
19 Articles 82(2) and 83(1) and (2) TFEU respectively.
20 Article 68 TFEU.
21 Article 76 TFEU.
22 Article 13(2) TEU. Examples of interinstitutional tensions concern the follow-up action plans to the Stockholm Programme and the right of initiative with regard to the Directive on the European Investigation Order. See Mitsilegas, "European Criminal Law and Resistance to Communautarisation Post-Lisbon."
23 See Articles 82(3) and 83(3) TFEU. See also, for a similar role, Articles 86(1) TFEU and 87(3) TFEU and, in the context of assessing the implications of nonparticipation by the United Kingdom and Ireland in Schengen Declaration 47 on Article 5(3), (4), and (5) of the Protocol on the Schengen *acquis*.
24 Articles 82(2) and 83(1) TFEU.
25 Article 86 TFEU.
26 Articles 74, 87(3), and 89 TFEU.
27 The Court of Justice upheld the foreign policy legal basis of these measures in its ruling in Case C-130/10 *Parliament v. Council* EU:C:2012:472.
28 See Protocol No 22 on the position of Denmark, stating that Denmark will not take part in the adoption of all Title V measures (Article 1(1)) and that no Title V measure will be binding upon or applicable to it (Article 2).
29 See Protocol No 19, Article 5. See, in particular, Article 5(3) of the Schengen Protocol and Declaration 47 annexed to the Final Act of the Lisbon Intergovernmental Conference.
30 See Protocol No 21 on the position of the United Kingdom and Ireland in respect of the Area of Freedom, Security and Justice.
31 Protocol No 36 on Transitional Provisions, Article 10(3). It has been indicated that the United Kingdom will choose not to accept the third pillar *acquis* as a whole. See "PM to reclaim 100 powers from EU," *The Sunday Times*, 23 September 2012, p. 2.
32 Council document 12750/13, Brussels, 26 July 2013.
33 Article 276 TFEU. Note also Article 88(3) TFEU on Europol, which states that the application of coercive measures will be the exclusive responsibility of the competent national authorities. For further details, see Mitsilegas, *EU Criminal Law*, Chap. 4.
34 Article 275(2) TFEU. Note also Articles 75(3) and 215(3) TFEU, explicitly referring to the inclusion of provisions on legal safeguards.
35 Article 70 TFEU.
36 Ibid.
37 Article 85(1) TFEU and 12(c) TEU. See also Article 88(2) TFEU and 12(c) TEU with regard to arrangements for the scrutiny of Europol's activities by the European Parliament and national parliaments. For further details on the scrutiny of EU bodies, see Mitsilegas, *EU Criminal Law*, Chap. 4.
38 A recent example of interinstitutional battles in this context has been the negotiation for the adoption of a revised Schengen evaluation mechanism. While the legal basis of the Commission's proposal was

Article 77(2)(e) TFEU, the Justice and Home Affairs Council agreed unanimously to change the legal basis to the more intergovernmental Article 70 TFEU. See Council document 10760/12, p 9.

39 For an affirmation of this case law, see Case C-61/11 PPU *El Dridi* EU:C:2011:268.

40 See, in particular, Case C-68/88 *Commission v. Greece* (Greek maize) EU:C:1989:339.

41 For an analysis, see Valsamis Mitsilegas, *Money Laundering Counter-Measures in the European Union: A New Paradigm of Security Governance versus Fundamental Legal Principles* (The Hague: Kluwer Law International, 2003).

42 OJ C 316/49.

43 OJ C 195/2.

44 See the 2002 Framework Decision 2002/475/JHA of 13 June 2002 on combating terrorism [2002] OJ L 164/3, as amended in 2008 ([2008] OJ L 330/21).

45 Framework Decision 2008/841/JHA of 24 October 2008 on organized crime [2008] OJ L 300/42.

46 Framework Decision 2004/757/JHA of 25 October 2004 on drug trafficking [2004] OJ L 335/8.

47 Directive 2011/36/EU of the European Parliament and of the Council of 5 April 2011 on preventing and combating trafficking in human beings and protecting its victims, and replacing Council Framework Decision 2002/629/JHA [2011] OJ L 101/1.

48 Directive 2011/92/EU of the European Parliament and of the Council of 13 December 2011 on combating the sexual abuse and sexual exploitation of children and child pornography, and replacing Council Framework Decision 2004/68/JHA [2011] OJ L 335/1.

49 See Framework Decision 2002/946/JHA on the facilitation of unauthorised entry, transit, and residence [2002] OJ L 328/1, and more recently Directive 2009/52/EC of 18 June 2009 providing for minimum standards on sanctions and measures against employers of illegally staying third-country nationals [2009] OJ L 168/24.

50 Joint Action 98/742/JHA of 22 December 1998 adopted by the Council on the basis of Article K.3 of the Treaty on European Union [1998] OJ L 358/2.

51 Council Framework Decision 2005/222/JHA of 24 February 2005 on attacks against information systems [2005] OJ L 69/67.

52 See Mitsilegas, *EU Criminal Law*, Chap. 2.

53 Case C-176/03 *Commission v. Council* (environmental crime) EU:C:2005:542, followed by Case C-440/05 *Commission v. Council* (ship-source pollution) EU:C:2007:625.

54 See Valsamis Mitsilegas, "The Transformation of Criminal Law in the Area of Freedom, Security and Justice," *Yearbook of European Law* 26 (2007).

55 Paras 70–71.

56 See the directives on environmental crime, ship-source pollution, and employers' sanctions, all of which contain general references to the introduction of "effective, proportionate and dissuasive sanctions."

57 Terrorism, trafficking in human beings, and sexual exploitation of women and children, illicit drug trafficking, illicit arms trafficking, money laundering, corruption, counterfeiting of means of payment, computer crime, and organized crime. The list of these offences may be expanded "on the basis of developments in crime" by the Council acting unanimously after obtaining the consent of the European Parliament.

58 Mitsilegas, "The Transformation of Criminal Law in the Area of Freedom, Security and Justice."

59 Valsamis Mitsilegas, "EU Criminal Law Competence after Lisbon: From Securitised to Functional Criminalisation," in *EU Security and Justice Law*, eds. Diego Acosta Arcarazo and Cian C. Murphy (Oxford: Hart, 2014).

60 Valsamis Mitsilegas, "Defining Organised Crime in the European Union: The Limits of European Criminal Law in an Area of Freedom, Security and Justice," *European Law Review* 26 (2001); and Mitsilegas, *EU Criminal Law*, Chap. 2.

61 COM(2012) 85 final.

62 Directive 2014/42/EU of the European Parliament and of the Council of 3 April 2014 on the freezing and confiscation of instrumentalities and proceeds of crime in the European Union [2014] OJ L 127/39.

63 A similar clause was deleted from Article 135 EC concerning customs cooperation (this is Article 33 in the TFEU).

64 COM(2012) 363 final. Article 325(4) TFEU.

65 Draft Directive on criminal sanctions for insider dealing and market manipulation, COM(2011) 654 final accompanying a proposal for a Regulation under Article 114 TFEU (COM(2011) 651 final).

66 See the case pending before the Court of Justice with the Commission requesting the annulment of a road traffic directive adopted under Article 87(2) TFEU, with the Commission arguing in favor of the more supranational legal basis of Article 91(1) TFEU. Although the case does not involve the adoption of substantive criminal law, it is a clear indication that the Commission will not hesitate to defend its choices or prerogatives in cases involving the use of Article 83(2) TFEU. Case C-43/12, EU:C:2014:298. Directive 2011/82/EU facilitating the cross-border exchange of information on road safety related traffic offences [2011] OJ L 288/1.

67 Commission Communication "Towards an EU Criminal Policy: Ensuring the Effective Implementation of EU Policies through Criminal Law," COM(2011) final.

68 For a recent discussion, see Valsamis Mitsilegas, "From Overcriminalisation to Decriminalisation: The Many Faces of Effectiveness in European Criminal Law," *New Journal of European Criminal Law* 5 (2014).

69 For an overview of the principle, see Valsamis Mitsilegas, "The Constitutional Implications of Mutual Recognition in Criminal Matters in the EU," *Common Market Law Review* 43 (2006).

70 On the background to EU legislative production in criminal matters following Maastricht and the *Corpus Juris* proposals, see Mitsilegas, *EU Criminal Law*, Chap. 2.

71 Para 33. The reference to mutual recognition as the "cornerstone" of judicial cooperation in criminal matters in the European Union was reiterated five years later in the Hague Programme extending the EU JHA agenda to 2009, para 3.3.1.

72 [2001] OJ C 12, p 10.

73 Framework Decision 2002/584/JHA of 13 June 2002 on the European Arrest Warrant [2002] OJ L 190/1.

74 Framework Decision 2008/978/JHA of 18 December 2008 on the European Evidence Warrant [2008] OJ L 350/72.

75 Framework Decision 2003/577/JHA of 22 July 2003 on the mutual recognition of orders freezing property or evidence [2003] OJ L 196/45.

76 Framework Decision 2009/829/JHA of 23 October 2009 on the application, between Member States of the European Union, of the principle of mutual recognition to decisions on supervision measures as an alternative to provisional detention [2009] OJ L 294/20.

77 Framework Decision 2006/783/JHA of 6 October 2006 on the mutual recognition of confiscation orders [2006] OJ L 328/59.

78 Framework Decision 2005/214/JHA of 24 February 2005 on the mutual recognition of judgments imposing financial penalties [2005] OJ L 76/16.

79 Framework Decision 2008/947/JHA of 27 November 2008 on the application of the principle of mutual recognition to judgments and probation decisions with a view to the supervision of probation measures and alternative sanctions [2008] OJ L 337/102.

80 Framework Decision 2008/909/JHA of 27 November 2008 on the transfer of custodial sentences (sentenced persons) [2008] OJ L 327/27.

81 See the leading judgment in Cases C-187/01 and C-385/01 *Gözütok and Brügge* EU:C:2003:87. For an analysis of the ruling and subsequent case law, see Mitsilegas, *EU Criminal Law*, Chap. 3.

82 On the implementation of the Framework Decision, see Gisèle Vernimmen-van Tiggelen, Laura Surano, and Anne Weyembergh, eds., *The Future of Mutual Recognition in Criminal Matters in the European Union* (Brussels: Éditions de l'Université de Bruxelles, 2009); and Valsamis Mitsilegas, "The Area of Freedom, Security and Justice from Amsterdam to Lisbon: Challenges of Implementation, Constitutionality and Fundamental Rights," in *The Area of Freedom, Security and Justice, Including Information Society Issues*, vol. 3 of *Reports of the XXV FIDE Congress*, ed. Julia Laffranque (Tartu University Press: Tallin, 2012) and national reports included therein.

83 The Framework Decision confirms from the outset that the European Arrest Warrant is a judicial decision (Article 1(1)).

84 A European Arrest Warrant may be issued for acts punishable by the law of the issuing member state by a custodial sentence or a detention order for a maximum period of at least twelve months or, where a sentence has been passed or a detention order has been made, for sentences of at least four months (Article 2(2)).
85 Articles 1(1) and 1(2).
86 See Articles 15, 17, and 23 of the Framework Decision. The Court has confirmed the limited role of the executing authority in examining the content of the European Arrest Warrant in its ruling in, Case C-261/09 *Gaetano Mantello* EU:C:2010:683.
87 Article 3(2).
88 The compatibility of the abolition of the verification of dual criminality with the legality principle has been affirmed by the Court of Justice in Case C-303/05 *Advocaten voor de Wereld* EU:C:2007:261. However, subsequent mutual recognition measures have watered down the abolition of dual criminality requirement. For an overview, see Valsamis Mitsilegas, "The Third Wave of Third Pillar Law: Which Direction for EU Criminal Justice?" *European Law Review* 34 (2009).
89 Article 3.
90 Article 4.
91 Articles 5, 27, and 28.
92 Including, for instance, cases where the offence on which the warrant is based is covered by amnesty or cases involving minors or cases where the prosecution is statute-barred (Article 3(1), 3(3), and 4(4) respectively).
93 See Articles 4(6) and 4(7) of the framework decision. See also Article 5(3) under the provision of guarantees. The Court has now delivered a number of important rulings on the scope of Article 4(6). See Case C-66/08 *Kozłowski* EU:C:2008:437; Case C-123/08 *Wolzenburg* EU:C:2009:616; and Case C-42/11 *Da Silva Jorge* EU:C:2012:517.
94 See also recital 10 of the preamble to the framework decision.
95 For an overview, see, Vernimmen-van Tiggelen, Surano, and Weyembergh, *The Future of Mutual Recognition in Criminal Matters*; and Laffranque, *The Area of Freedom, Security and Justice, Including Information Society Issues*.
96 See COM(2005) 63 final.
97 COM(2011) 175 final.
98 Ibid., p. 8.
99 See Joint Committee on Human Rights, *The Human Rights Implications of UK Extradition Policy*, Fifteenth Report, session 2010–2012, pp. 40–43.
100 See the ruling of the Higher Regional Court of Stuttgart of 25 February 2010, reported by Joachim Vogel, "Introduction to the Ruling of the Higher Regional Court of Stuttgart of 25 February 2010: The Proportionality of a European Arrest Warrant," *New Journal of European Criminal Law* 1 (2010).
101 See the revised version of the European Handbook on how to issue a European Arrest Warrant Council doc 17195/1/10 REV 1; and the *Assange* ruling of the UK Supreme Court [2012] UKSC 22, Lord Phillips in paragraph 90.
102 Directive 2014/41/EU of the European Parliament and of the Council of 3 April 2014 regarding the European Investigation Order in criminal matters [2014] OJ L 130/1.
103 Article 11, optional grounds for nonrecognition or nonexecution: 11(1)(f): where there are substantial grounds to believe that the execution of the investigative measure indicated in the EIO would be incompatible with the executing state's obligations in accordance with Article 6 TEU and the charter.
104 Article 6(1)(a) and (b) respectively.
105 See Article 2(1) of the European Arrest Warrant Framework Decision.
106 Joined Cases C-411/10 *N.S. and others* and C-493/10 *M.E. and others* EU:C:2011:865.
107 See Valsamis Mitsilegas, "The Limits of Mutual Trust in Europe's Area of Freedom, Security and Justice: From Automatic Inter-State Cooperation to the Slow Emergence of the Individual," *Yearbook of European Law* 31 (2012).
108 Para 99.

109 Para 100.
110 Para 104.
111 Mitsilegas, "The Limits of Mutual Trust in Europe's Area of Freedom, Security and Justice."
112 Case C-399/11 *Melloni* EU:C:2013:107; Case C-396/11 *Radu* EU:C:2013:39.
113 See also the recommendations by the European Parliament in this context: Report of 28 January 2014 with recommendations to the Commission on the review of the European Arrest Warrant, Rapporteur: Sarah Ludford, Motion for a Resolution, doc. A7-0039/2014.
114 COM(2004) 328 final.
115 On the negotiating history of the Framework Decision, see House of Lords European Union Committee, *Breaking the Deadlock: What Future for EU Procedural Rights?* 2nd Report, session 2006–2007, HL paper 20.
116 Resolution of the Council of 30 November 2009 on a Roadmap for strengthening procedural rights of suspected or accused persons in criminal proceedings [2009] OJ C 295/1.
117 Directive 2010/64/EU of the European Parliament and of the Council of 20 October 2010 on the right to interpretation and translation in criminal proceedings [2010] OJ L 280/1.
118 Directive 2012/13/EU of the European Parliament and of the Council of 22 May 2012 on the right to information in criminal proceedings [2012] OJ L 142/1.
119 Directive 2013/48/EU of the European Parliament and of the Council of 22 October 2013 on the right of access to a lawyer in criminal proceedings and in European arrest warrant proceedings, and on the right to have a third party informed upon the deprivation of liberty and to communicate with third persons and with consular authorities while deprived of liberty [2013] OJ L 294/1.
120 See, for instance, Article 1(1) of the directive on the right to interpretation and translation.
121 Mitsilegas, "The Limits of Mutual Trust in Europe's Area of Freedom, Security and Justice."
122 See recital 4 in both directives. See also recital 3 of the Commission's draft directive on the right of access to a lawyer.
123 This issue is even more problematic with regard to Commission proposals on the rights of the victim under 82(2) TFEU. See Valsamis Mitsilegas, Evidence submitted to House of Lords EU Committee inquiry on EU criminal procedure, cited in *The European Union's Policy on Criminal Procedure*, 30th Report, Session 2010–2012, HL paper 288.
124 See, inter alia, Case C-300/89 *Commission v. Council* (Titanium Dioxide) EU:C:1991:244.
125 See C-66/08 *Kozłowski*, n 93 this chapter, and C-261/09 *Mantello*, n 86 this chapter.
126 Valsamis Mitsilegas, "European Union Law," in *Blackstone's Criminal Practice 2014*, ed. Sir Anthony Hooper and D. Ormerod QC (Oxford: Oxford University Press, 2014).
127 Council Decision 2009/371/JHA of 6 April 2009 establishing the European Police Office [2009] OJ L 121/37.
128 Council Decision 2002/187/JHA of 28 February 2002 setting up Eurojust with a view to reinforcing the fight against serious crime [2002] OJ L 63/1, as amended by Council Decision 2009/426/JHA [2009] OJ L 138/14.
129 Regulation (EU, Euratom) no 883/2013 of the European Parliament and of the Council of 11 September 2013 concerning investigations conducted by the European Anti-Fraud Office (OLAF) and repealing Regulation (EC) No 1073/1999 of the European Parliament and of the Council and Council Regulation (Euratom) No 1074/1999 [2013] OJ L 248/1
130 For further details on these bodies, see Mitsilegas, *EU Criminal Law*, Chap. 4. On the 2009 developments of the legal framework on Europol and Eurojust, see Mitsilegas, "The Third Wave of Third Pillar Law."
131 Article 7(1) of the Eurojust Decision as it stands after the 2009 amendments.
132 Article 32 of the Eurojust Decision, Article 48 of the Europol Decision. As mentioned earlier in the chapter, the Treaty of Lisbon envisages a prominent role for national parliaments in this context.
133 The very limited judicial protection offered by the Court in Case T-193/04 *Tillack* EU:T:2006:292 was addressed in Case T-48/05 *Franchet et Byk* EU:T:2008:257. However, the Court appears to have limited judicial protection again in the case of *Violetti–Affaire*, T-261/09 P *Commission v. Violetti* EU:T:2010:215.

134 Mitsilegas, *EU Criminal Law*.

135 For the potential of Article 85 TFEU, see Anne Weyembergh, "The Development of Eurojust: Potential and Limitations of Article 85 of the TFEU," *New Journal of European Criminal Law* 2 (2011).

136 For various scenarios on the EPPO, see special issue of *Eucrim* 2 (2012). For an examination of different EPPO models, see, in particular, Simone White, "A Decentralised European Public Prosecutor's Office: Contradiction in Terms or Highly Workable Solution?" special issue, *Eucrim* 2 (2012). For more recent analyses, see Katalin Ligeti and Michele Simonato, 'The European Public Prosecutor's Office: Towards a Truly European Prosecution Service?' and Simone White, 'Towards a *Decentralised* European Public Prosecutor's Office?' *New Journal of European Criminal Law* 4 (2013): 7–21 and 22–39 respectively.

137 See in this context primarily the Commission's original proposal on the EPPO (COM(2013) 534 final) and the draft EPPO Regulation resulting from negotiations under the Greek Presidency of the European Union (document 9834/1/14 REV 1).

138 Valsamis Mitsilegas, "The EU and the Rest of the World: Criminal Law and Policy Interconnections," in *Beyond the Established Orders: Policy Interconnections between the EU and the Rest of the World*, ed. Malcolm Evans and Panos Koutrakos (Oxford: Hart, 2011).

139 Valsamis Mitsilegas, "The External Dimension of EU Action in Criminal Matters," *European Foreign Affairs Review* 12 (2007).

140 See the latest EU–US Agreement on the use and transfer of passenger name records to the United States Department of Homeland Security [2012] OJ L 215/4; the EU–US Agreement on the processing and transfer of Financial Messaging Data from the European Union to the United States for the purposes of the Terrorist Finance Tracking Programme [2010] OJ L 195/3; and the earlier EU–US Agreements on Extradition and Mutual Legal Assistance [2003] OJ L 181/25.

141 Institutional limits were related primarily to the absence of express legal personality for the Union prior to Lisbon and to the very limited mechanisms of transparency and scrutiny of third pillar agreements. See Mitsilegas, "The External Dimension of EU Action in Criminal Matters."

142 Valsamis Mitsilegas, "Transatlantic Counter-Terrorism Cooperation after Lisbon," *Eucrim* 3 (2010).

143 Valsamis Mitsilegas, "Transatlantic Counter-Terrorism Cooperation and European Values: The Elusive Quest for Coherence," in *A Transatlantic Community of Law*, eds. Deirdre Curtin and Elaine Fahey (Cambridge: Cambridge University Press, 2014).

144 Joined Cases C-402/05 P and C-415/05 P *Yassin Abdullah Kadi and Al Barakaat International Foundation v. Council and Commission* EU:C:2008:461. Joined Cases C-584/10 P, C-593/10 P, and C-595/10 P *European Commission v. Kadi* EU:C:2013:518.

145 Case C-308/06 *The Queen, on the application of International Association of Independent Tanker Owners (Intertanko) and Others v. Secretary of State for Transport* EU:C:2008:312.

146 Valsamis Mitsilegas, "The European Union and the Globalisation of Criminal Law," *Cambridge Yearbook of European Legal Studies* 12 (2009–2010).

References

Laffranque, Julia, ed. *The Area of Freedom, Security and Justice, Including Information Society Issues*. Vol. 3 of *Reports of the XXV FIDE Congress*. Tartu University Press: Tallinn, 2012.

Ligeti, Katalin and Michele Simonato. "The European Public Prosecutor's Office: Towards a Truly European Prosecution Service?" *New Journal of European Criminal Law* 4 (2013): 7–21.

Mitsilegas, Valsamis. "Defining Organised Crime in the European Union: The Limits of European Criminal Law in an Area of Freedom, Security and Justice." *European Law Review* 26 (2001): 565–581.

Mitsilegas, Valsamis. *Money Laundering Counter-Measures in the European Union: A New Paradigm of Security Governance versus Fundamental Legal Principles* (The Hague: Kluwer Law International, 2003).

Mitsilegas, Valsamis. "The Constitutional Implications of Mutual Recognition in Criminal Matters in the EU." *Common Market Law Review* 43 (2006): 1277–1311.
Mitsilegas, Valsamis. "The Transformation of Criminal Law in the Area of Freedom, Security and Justice." *Yearbook of European Law* 26 (2007): 1–32.
Mitsilegas, Valsamis. "The External Dimension of EU Action in Criminal Matters." *European Foreign Affairs Review* 12 (2007): 457–497.
Mitsilegas, Valsamis. *EU Criminal Law* (Oxford: Hart, 2009).
Mitsilegas, Valsamis. "The Third Wave of Third Pillar Law: Which Direction for EU Criminal Justice?" *European Law Review* 34 (2009): 523–560.
Mitsilegas, Valsamis. "The European Union and the Globalisation of Criminal Law." *Cambridge Yearbook of European Legal Studies* 12 (2009): 337–407.
Mitsilegas, Valsamis. "European Criminal Law and Resistance to Communautarisation Post-Lisbon." *New Journal of European Criminal Law* 1 (2010): 458–480.
Mitsilegas, Valsamis. "Transatlantic Counter-Terrorism Cooperation after Lisbon." *Eucrim* 3 (2010): 111–117.
Mitsilegas, Valsamis. "The EU and the Rest of the World: Criminal Law and Policy Interconnections." In *Beyond the Established Orders: Policy Interconnections between the EU and the Rest of the World*, edited by Malcolm Evans and Panos Koutrakos, 149–178. Oxford: Hart, 2011.
Mitsilegas, Valsamis. "The Area of Freedom, Security and Justice from Amsterdam to Lisbon: Challenges of Implementation, Constitutionality and Fundamental Rights." General Report, in Laffranque, *The Area of Freedom, Security and Justice*, 21–142.
Mitsilegas, Valsamis. "The Limits of Mutual Trust in Europe's Area of Freedom, Security and Justice: From Automatic Inter-State Cooperation to the Slow Emergence of the Individual." *Yearbook of European Law* 31 (2012): 319–372.
Mitsilegas, Valsamis. "European Union Law." In *Blackstone's Criminal Practice 2014*, edited by Sir Anthony Hooper and David Ormerod QC, 172–182. Oxford: Oxford University Press, 2014.
Mitsilegas, Valsamis. "EU Criminal Law Competence after Lisbon: From Securitised to Functional Criminalisation." In *EU Security and Justice Law: After Lisbon and Stockholm*, edited by Diego Acosta Arcarazo and Cian C. Murphy, 110–129. Oxford: Hart, 2014.
Mitsilegas, Valsamis. "Transatlantic Counter-Terrorism Cooperation and European Values: The Elusive Quest for Coherence." In *A Transatlantic Community of Law*, edited by Deirdre Curtin and Elaine Fahey, 289–315. Cambridge: Cambridge University Press, 2014.
Mitsilegas, Vasamis. "From Overcriminalisation to Decriminalisation: The Many Faces of Effectiveness in European Criminal Law." *New Journal of European Criminal Law* 5 (2014): 415–423.
Vernimmen-van Tiggelen, Gisèle, Laura Surano, and Anne Weyembergh, eds. *The Future of Mutual Recognition in Criminal Matters in the European Union* (Brussels: Éditions de l'Université de Bruxelles, 2009).
Vogel, Joachim. "Introduction to the Ruling of the Higher Regional Court of Stuttgart of 25 February 2010: The Proportionality of a European Arrest Warrant." *New Journal of European Criminal Law* 1 (2010): 145–152.
Weyembergh, Anne. "The Development of Eurojust: Potential and Limitations of Article 85 of the TFEU." *New Journal of European Criminal Law* 2 (2011): 75–99.
White, Simone. "A Decentralised European Public Prosecutor's Office: Contradiction in Terms or Highly Workable Solution?" Special issue, *Eucrim* 2 (2012): 67–75.
White, Simone. "Towards a *Decentralised* European Public Prosecutor's Office?" *New Journal of European Criminal Law* 4 (2013): 22–39.

37

EU Environmental Law

Maria Lee

Introduction

The European Union has developed a vast body of environmental law, relying on a treaty title setting out normatively and descriptively complex environmental principles and approaches, as well as on those parts of the treaties focusing on the internal market. Not only is a comprehensive discussion of EU environmental law in a brief chapter obviously impossible but the diversity and breadth of EU environmental law means a chapter like this might be constructed around many possible themes. In this chapter, I explore a directive that – by any definition – is a central element of EU environmental law and that, moreover, allows us to explore a crucial theme in EU environmental law and governance: the Industrial Emissions Directive (IED).[1] Industrial pollution is a substantively significant aspect of any system of environmental law, although it tends to be regulated in a more piecemeal, less explicit way at the international level.[2] Further, the IED allows us to explore two prominent and closely related themes in EU environmental law. First, we can examine evolving approaches to the continuum between harmonization and decentralization in EU environmental law. Substantively flexible legislation creates a framework of varying flexibility within which environmental norms are generated and applied beyond the legislative process. Second, the IED allows us to examine the way in which EU environmental law creates institutional arrangements for learning and for change in environmental regulation.

When the European Union first turned its attention to environmental problems in the early 1970s, like most governments of the time, it took the central role of "command and control" regulation more or less for granted. The tools in this range of regulatory techniques share the basic characteristic that regulation dictates a particular end or particular methodology, and requires compliance. In the European Union, this implied both command from the center to the member state and its regulators, and command and control of polluters. A greater use of economic instruments of regulation has been one response to the many criticisms of command and control, and while EU legislation sometimes urges the member states to use economic instruments,[3] little use has been made of economic instruments at EU level – subject to the enormous exception of greenhouse gas emissions trading.[4] Another response to the criticisms

A Companion to European Union Law and International Law, First Edition.
Edited by Dennis Patterson and Anna Södersten.

of command and control has been a turn to more flexible and cooperative modes of governance. This we do see in EU environmental law, as in the two themes already set out. Less rigid, less hierarchical approaches to environmental protection respond not only to the complexity of environmental challenges but also to the complex governance features of the Union, in particular the relationship between different levels of governance. Nevertheless, these phenomena are by no means limited to the European Union, or indeed to environmental law. They have received an enormous amount of attention in US administration and scholarship.[5] Providing a framework for cooperation (rather than straightforward standards) on environmental matters is an important feature of environmental law at the international level.[6] We might even categorize the entire international regulatory framework for climate change as a (currently not especially successful) framework within which detailed commitments can be agreed.[7]

The two themes (of (de)centralization and learning) outlined above could usefully be examined through a "new governance" model, which emphasizes flexibility, revisability, and cooperation over fixed hierarchical commands.[8] The phenomena represented by the IED are, however, significant aspects of EU environmental law regardless of any theoretical commitment to a particular governance approach. And few would wish to insist that any particular characteristic of new governance (such as "flexibility") is either empirically universal or universally normatively desirable.[9] Alongside flexibility and cooperation, the IED (like other areas of EU environmental law) certainly contains clearly defined, enforceable legal rules (sometimes in substantive environmental standards, frequently in procedural requirements). Thus, some features of the IED fit within understandings of EU law that are worlds away from new governance, such as "legalism"[10] or "interventionist regulation."[11] We also see a greater emphasis on centralization in the IED than in its predecessors, and a more familiarly "law-like" approach to norm generation and application.[12] Some may see the death of new governance, others "experimentalism" in practice. But one further lesson that the IED has for EU environmental law is that the complexity and diversity of EU environmental law defies categorization. Not only is the command from the center qualified in the IED but also the flexible, cooperative development of the content of the command is of great interest.

In addition to providing some introductory insights into EU environmental law, this chapter makes two key arguments or observations. First, the IED shows the potential of an approach to governance that sets environmental norms in a collaborative, problem-solving forum beyond the face of legislation. Equally, however, it shows the challenges. In particular, "inclusion" can easily privilege particular interests and viewpoints, working to exclude even as it includes. Second, "harmonization" is not a straightforward category in EU environmental law. Much was made of the decentralization and local or national flexibility in the predecessor to the IED. By comparison, the IED places greater emphasis on the mandatory application of EU-wide environmental standards. However, *both* the initial decentralization and the recentralization are highly ambiguous.

The IED: An Introduction

The IED was promulgated in 2010 and replaces the Integrated Pollution Prevention and Control (IPPC) Directive[13] as well as a number of directives applying to specific sectors (large combustion plants, waste incineration and co-incineration plants, installations and activities using organic solvents, and installations producing titanium dioxide). It is the central piece of legislation dealing with the environmental effects of industrial installations. The IED rests on a straightforward, command and control form of regulation: all installations or activities covered by the directive need a permit from the national competent authority (referred to here as the regulator). In this chapter I focus on Chapter II of the IED, which contains the overarching provisions on integrated pollution prevention and control. Chapter II applies to those installations listed in Annex I of the directive. Again, in a fairly conventional manner, these are primarily major industrial activities, such as chemical and energy installations, as well as certain intensive farming operations. While the IED purports to simplify by dealing in one directive with industrial sectors previously dealt with in different pieces of legislation, a number of sectors are now dealt with in separate chapters of the directive. Many of these sectors are also covered by Annex I. This means that the IPPC requirements apply, subject to minimum EU-wide sectoral requirements set out in the directive.[14]

The directive sets out in some detail what must be contained in any permit. Substantively, the most important requirement for the permit is that emission limit values be set for polluting substances that are either listed in the directive or are "likely to be emitted from the installation in significant quantities."[15] Of the principles with which the permit must ensure compliance, the key principle is that the emissions from the installation do not exceed those associated with the use of "best available techniques" (BAT, discussed further in the next section);[16] other principles include the taking of "all the appropriate preventive measures … against pollution"; ensuring that "no significant pollution is caused"; and that "energy is used efficiently."[17] Other requirements that must be contained in the permit include obligations in respect of the protection of soil and groundwater, accident prevention, and waste management.[18] Monitoring and reporting obligations must be imposed, as must requirements in respect of "conditions other than normal operating conditions," including leaks, stoppages, and the decommissioning of the installation.

A further notable element of the IED, shared with many directives, is its foregrounding of questions of procedure. We see this in the discussion of BAT in the next section: rather than detailed rules on environmental standards that must be met, we see detailed rules on *how* environmental standards shall be set, and the circumstances in which those standards do and do not apply. As in the IPPC Directive, a further notable procedural aspect of the IED is around "public participation" at the permitting stage, which predated the well-known United Nations Economic Commission for Europe (UNECE) Aarhus Convention in EU law, but is now framed largely around its requirements.[19] There are many potential motivations and roles for public participation in EU environmental law, sometimes overlapping, sometimes conflicting, and often complex, or even cynical, in their normative claims (such as for democracy or quality of decision making).[20] While this is potentially an enormous topic, the IED seems to bear a largely *instrumental* understanding of public participation in EU environmental law. The presence of "publics" at the permitting stage seems not to be much about claiming a democratic stake in decisions. The ability to influence outcomes is limited both by prior decisions at EU level and by the highly technical and specialist nature of the regulatory questions being asked. Public participation (including access to information and access to courts)[21] in the permitting process seems to be primarily a way of monitoring the national and local application of EU norms.

Best Available Techniques: Norm Generation in EU Environmental Governance

The key principle, and the key substantive environmental norm, in the IED is BAT. BAT is defined in the directive as

> the most effective and advanced stage in the development of activities and their methods of operation which indicates the practical suitability of particular techniques for providing the basis for emission limit values and other permit conditions designed to prevent and, where that is not practicable, to reduce emissions and the impact on the environment as a whole.[22]

It is clear that what amounts to BAT in any particular case requires considerable thought. "Techniques" is expansively defined to include both the technology used "and the way in which the installation is designed, built, maintained, operated and decommissioned." "Best" is "the most effective in achieving a high general level of protection of the environment as a whole," reinforcing the holistic (whole environment) aspirations of BAT. The "integration" of pollution control addresses the environmental media of soil, water, and air together, attempting to overcome the tendency of media-specific regulation to transfer pollution from one environmental medium to another, for example because the stringency of regulation or its enforcement is uneven.[23]

The definition of "best" appears to have a single-mindedly environmental focus. It is striking, however, that the European IPPC Bureau, when it compares potential BAT to identify the "best" technique(s), considers the relationship between cost and environmental benefits.[24] In the directive, "availability" introduces nonenvironmental cost considerations. "Available" techniques are "those developed on a scale that allows implementation in the relevant industrial sector, under economically and technically viable conditions, taking into consideration the costs and advantages." The Commission has insisted that EU-wide, rather than national, sectoral affordability is the issue. A technique is "available" "whether or not the techniques are used or produced inside the Member State in question, as long as they are reasonably accessible to the operator."[25] Impecuniosity on the part of individual operators is not apparently relevant. Annex III provides twelve additional criteria for assessing BAT, including the use of low-waste technology, technological advances, the consumption and nature of raw materials (including water) in the process, and "the need to prevent or reduce to a minimum the overall impact of the emissions on the environment and the risks to it."

The legislative definition of BAT leaves considerable space to decision makers. While BAT prescribes a number of relevant factors, the overall outcome of the decision-making framework remains relatively undetermined, and how the different relevant issues are to be weighed up and traded off is left open. So, for example, which costs and advantages might be relevant and when costs might be too high are left open.[26] Nor is there any direction in the legislation on how to trade off different impacts on different environmental media, which cannot be measured against a single metric. The more detailed methodology on cross-media effects "normalizes" contributions to the different environmental themes of the different techniques against European data.[27] Thus, one technique might lead to 0.01 percent of the total methane emissions to air from the sector in the European Union, together with 1 percent of the total phenol emissions to water; another 0.1 percent methane emissions to air and 0.001 percent phenols to water. Compared to the first technique, the second thus leads to ten times higher relative methane emissions to air but one thousand times lower relative phenol emissions to water.[28] But the numbers, even if they are available and reliable, do not escape a crucial value judgment as to which of these options is "best," whether we prefer, for example, emissions that contribute to climate change or to water pollution, when we prefer increased respiratory problems for children over an increased long-term cancer burden.

We certainly do not see on the face of the legislation the detailed norms that will be applied to operators. The loosely defined nature of BAT meant that, notwithstanding its reliance on the classic "command and control" instrument of the permit, the IPPC Directive became representative of the focus on procedure in EU environmental legislation rather than on clearly defined standards of environmental quality or performance. Instead of setting out clear, immediately implementable and enforceable standards, the IED (and the IPPC Directive before it) provides a governance framework within which those norms can be identified. We see a similar approach in other areas of EU environmental law, most obviously the Water Framework Directive, where the central standard of "good quality" is spelled out in a complex, more or less collaborative process beyond the legislation.[29]

The difference between the IPPC Directive and the IED is not in the legal content of BAT but in the legislative nature of the governance framework within which its detailed and specific content in any particular case is worked out. BAT in IPPC was apparently directed towards the member states, or subnational regulators. Now, BAT is explicitly directed to a process at the EU level. Documents setting out BAT for particular sectors or issues, known as "BAT reference notes" (BREFs) are drawn up, reviewed or updated during an "exchange of information" under Article 13 of the directive. The Commission decides when to draw up and review a BREF in any particular area (taking into account the view of the Forum, below).[30] BREFs were not mentioned in the IPPC Directive. However, BREFs emerged, not in the negotiation of the IED but through the information exchange provisions contained in the IPPC Directive, which required the Commission to report on BAT.[31] The process for drawing up a BREF evolved beyond the terms of the legislation, and it was known as the "Seville process" because of the central role of the European IPPC Bureau, based in Seville.

Both the role of BREFs and the process for their drafting have been formalized by the IED. In most respects, Article 13 IED places the status quo on a legislative basis. The initial "exchange of information," which under Article 13 must include "Member States, the industries concerned, non-governmental organisations promoting environmental protection and the Commission" is the Technical Working Group (TWG). The European IPPC Bureau "coordinates," "leads," and "steers" the work carried out by the TWGs.[32] The Commission must in addition "establish and regularly convene" a forum, also composed of "Member States, the industries concerned, non-governmental organisations promoting environmental protection" but this time not the Commission. In the Commission Implementing Decision establishing the Forum, the membership is limited to "*international* organisations representing industries concerned" and the environmental interest groups "shall have an acceptable degree of European representation."[33] Members of the Forum are responsible for nominating members ("their representatives") to the TWGs, although we should note that this is not apparent on the face of the IED.[34] The forum provides an "opinion" on the content of any BREF proposed by the TWG.[35] The opinion is made public and taken into account by the Commission in its drafting of "BAT conclusions." The most important innovation in the Seville process is that BAT conclusions are now formally adopted through a comitology process rather than simply being published by the Commission. So in addition to involvement during the BREF drafting, member states have an additional opportunity to intervene during the adoption of the BAT conclusions.[36]

There was an effort under IPPC to separate the "technical" TWG from the "political" stage of decision making in what was then known as the Information Exchange Forum,[37] and now comitology introduces an additional political stage to the process. But the technical discussion was never straightforwardly "technical", in the sense of being free from regulatory choices with political consequences. The European Environmental Bureau (EEB), a Brussels-based NGO, criticizes the "political" negotiations in TWGs, and Bettina Lange's study of the BREF decision-making process suggests that interest representation (negotiation and compromise, rather than simple fact finding) can be expected in the BREF committees.[38] It is not at all surprising that BAT turns out to be a mixture of the technical and the political, the evaluative and the factual, as much about private interest bargaining as deliberation in the public interest. The greater concern is that highly political choices (e.g., who bears the costs of a particular level of environmental protection or degradation) might be reconceptualized as technical by a specialist group's shared assumptions about what matters. But it does make process very important, especially who makes the decisions and on the basis of what information.

The Seville process includes industry and environmental groups, and there is a reasonable degree of openness in terms of publishing material on the IPPC Bureau website. The most serious concern about the BREF process is the domination of TWGs by industry. Flexible and nonhierarchical governance mechanisms do not always bring with them greater or wider participation,[39] and they can exclude as well as include. At the crudest level, discussions in TWGs take place in English without translation services.[40] Membership of TWGs has always included environmental interest groups (in fact, often just the EEB), although this inclusion only became mandatory in the IED.[41] Research into membership of the TWGs suggests that member states and the Commission make up around half of the participants, companies and industry associations most of the rest, and research institutes and environmental interest groups around 11 percent.[42] This information is a little dated now, and it is a matter of concern that the European IPPC Bureau no longer routinely makes such information available owing to database protection rules (although the affiliations of participants in TWGs can be made available on request).[43] Knowing who is in the room is a bare minimum, even if not the full picture.

Equally important is what the different participants are actually able to contribute to the decision. "Interests" are complex: sometimes member states might have a distinct "regulatory" interest, at other times their interests overlap with a powerful industry.[44] The EEB points to industry experts increasingly taking on the role of member state representative.[45] And participating in the Seville process is enormously resource intensive,[46] limiting the capacity of environmental interest groups to participate fully. The Commission seems to acknowledge that industry's access to resources of expertise and information gives it considerable influence. In particular, the "most comprehensive information"[47] on BAT comes from industry; more worryingly, industry often does not make economic data available, or if it does, it proves very difficult to cross check.[48]

Methodologies beyond the bare bones of the legislative definition of BAT have been developed within the Seville process. The "key purpose" of the methodologies in the BREF on Economics and Cross-Media Effects is to ensure transparency, "so that any part of the process can be validated or audited."[49] Transparency is a common response to close involvement of private actors in governance mechanisms,[50] and while it is not a solution to unbalanced processes, disclosure of the professional affiliation (if not the names) of participants in TWGs would be a proportionate response to the need for transparency in the lawmaking process. There is a clear role for legal standards to ensure that collaborative modes of governance are exposed to rather than sheltered from external, as well as peer, scrutiny. One of the reasons for the emphasis on transparency in the BREF seems to be a pervasive concern about the quality of data, both costs data and information on environmental effects. Transparency in part is to "warn" users about concerns, and while some of those concerns are about the completeness or adequacy of research and data gathering, others are precisely about the potentially self-interested source of the data. Highly technical assessments of complicated data are crucial, even at the same time as doubts are cast on the ability of the data in all cases to reflect reality. The expectation seems to be that the weight attributed to the data will depend in part on (transparently available) information on its source and reliability. Transparency is apparently directed not at outsiders but at the members of the TWG, the forum, and the comitology committee that supports the Commission in its final decision.[51] No matter whether it is successful in these terms, even the most perfect methodology is no solution to poor data.

To the extent that we are dealing with a participatory or collaborative process, it is also clearly an elite, expert-driven process. There is no more general right to participate in, even to be consulted on, BREF drafting.[52] Whether concerns about balance in BREF drafting can be corrected by the new Article 13 process is doubtful. Indeed, the loss of transparency as to who takes part in TWGs suggests that we are going backwards. The *involvement* of industry is an important, and positive, part of the whole IED system, using industry's expertise and resources to arrive at superior solutions. The difficulty is if there is industry *dominance* and the main reason for any such dominance seems to be precisely their superior resources, especially resources of information. Formalizing the inclusion of environmental interest groups is positive, but the problem is less the fact of their participation than their capacity to match the contributions of industry. In this context, the protected space of comitology, beyond the reach of the "public" (including industry), may be a positive development, although some member states may identify very closely with industry interests. Comitology is not without its own legitimacy issues, in part precisely because of this isolation from public scrutiny, and from the democratic control of Parliament.[53] The European Parliament's right of scrutiny, however, allows it to check whether implementing powers have been overstepped,[54] in principle including disagreement about the application of the legislative requirements on "BAT." Such a detailed technical challenge may seem unlikely at this stage, but it is at least an opportunity to flag political concerns *in extremis*. Along with the role of the member states in committee, Parliament could highlight cases where there is disagreement between industry and outsiders, perhaps revolving around the use of "sound science" to rebut, cynically or naively, nonscientific ethical or political concerns about industrial pollution.[55]

Best Available Techniques: Norm Application in EU Environmental Governance

The process for the adoption of BREFs under the IED has become more important because of their enhanced status in on-the-ground regulatory decision making. Under IPPC, BREFs were not legally binding on member state permitting authorities but were simply a factor to take into account during permitting.[56] BAT conclusions (the part of the BREF setting out conclusions)[57] now provide a mandatory approach to BAT for permit setting in the member states. The divide between IPPC Directive and IED is not, however, as wide as it seems. First, because the mandatory application of the BAT conclusions in IED is subject to important provisos discussed below.

Second, to say that BREFs were not binding under IPPC Directive does not mean that they were without effect. The BREFs were always negotiated within the remit of a "European" body, that is the European IPPC Bureau, and they always carried considerable scientific, if not legal, authority. The Commission even indicated that it would consider challenging the application of lower standards in the absence of justification,[58] although it did not follow through on this threat and any challenge would have required a detailed analysis of the member states' actual determination of BAT. If enforcement of BAT (by the Commission or third parties before national courts) had been a realistic possibility, the difficulty of assessing BAT locally means that BREFs would have provided a tempting refuge. This is particularly the case in member states with fewer resources to devote to environmental regulation, and Koutalakis and his fellow authors do indeed find that in both Romania and Greece BREFs were simply "validated" through command-and-control style government orders, rather than used as a guide.[59]

Notwithstanding the potential authority of BREFs under IPPC, an apparently important motivation for the harder status of the BAT conclusions under the IED was concern about inconsistent implementation of the IPPC Directive. The Commission's 2007 IED Proposal does seem to be concerned about deviation from BREFs: "permits issued for implementing the IPPC Directive often include conditions that are not based on BAT as described in the BREFs with little, if any, justification for such deviation."[60] It is important to be clear. The IPPC Directive was not intended to provide uniform substantive environmental standards. It was built on the principle that varied local conditions require varied local environmental regulation. One might disagree with that principle, or mistrust its implementers. And the precise scale of the "local" (especially between national and local flexibility) was never entirely clear.[61] But mere variation from BREFs did not imply failure of the IPPC Directive in its own terms. That BREFs were not uniformly applied is even, arguably, an indicator of success. Of course, the reference to "justification" in this quotation from the Commission is important.[62] We would indeed have expected deviations from BREFs to be *explicable* in terms of BAT, even if there was no legal requirement for an actual explanation.[63] And the new IED returns to the importance of justification, with reason giving obligations as discussed below.

But, while the BREFs were always "soft," BAT never was; it might have been weakly defined and as much procedural as substantive, but it was always binding.[64] There is a straightforward failure to comply with EU law if BAT is not applied in the member states. The difficulty is in the *enforcement* of BAT, which would in principle require resource-intensive detailed scrutiny of local permitting processes.

Under Article 14(3) IED, the "BAT conclusions" have become "*the* reference" rather than simply one factor for setting permit conditions.[65] That applies to all permit conditions. In addition, Article 15(3) requires that "emission limit values" (ELVs),[66] are at least as strict as those associated with the BAT "laid down in the decisions on BAT conclusions" that have been agreed through comitology. But the BAT conclusions are not the end of the story. First, where there are no relevant BAT conclusions, the regulator determines BAT after consulting the operator.[67] Article 15(3) refers explicitly to those BAT conclusions adopted through comitology, so if there is a BREF, but no comitology decision, Article 15(3) apparently does not apply. Neither Article 14(3), nor the Article 3 definition of "BAT conclusions," however, refers to comitology, so that even if not formally adopted, the conclusions in the BREF are still "the" reference point for permits. So BREFs not (yet) adopted through comitology are not formally binding in respect of ELVs, but they do have authority in the permitting process. Similarly, BREFs adopted by the Commission before the IED applied (without comitology and on the assumption that they would not be binding) "shall apply as BAT conclusions," but not for the purposes of Article 15(3).[68]

Second, member states have simple discretion to set stricter conditions than those required by the BAT conclusions.[69] So there is some scope for (transparent) concerns about the reliability of data used in BREF to feed into the permitting process, if weak data mean that stricter ELVs are required; although the ability of users of BAT conclusions to look behind those conclusions is limited. In addition, the permit *must* contain stricter conditions than those in the BAT conclusions if necessary to meet environmental quality standards (EQSs).[70] The Water Framework Directive and the Air Quality Directive set such maximum levels of specific pollutants in the receiving environment,[71] as might any future legislation on soil. EQSs set a minimum guarantee of environmental quality, while at the same time eating into both flexibility and the principle of integration (these parts of the permit are not subject to the "environment as a whole" analysis). But EQSs are generally thought to be the most flexible form of environmental standard since they control emissions only to the extent "necessary" to protect the environment.[72]

Finally, and most importantly, a regulator may in certain circumstances set ELVs less strict than those associated with the BAT conclusions. Article 15(4) provides for a derogation, if applying the BAT conclusions

> would lead to disproportionately higher costs compared to the environmental benefits, due to
>
> (a) the geographical location or the local environmental conditions of the installation concerned; or
> (b) the technical characteristics of the installation concerned.

The EEB "strongly regretted" the Article 15(4) derogation, seeing it as a "loophole" that will lead to implementation differences and divergence.[73] But equally, Article 15(4) is all that remains of the attention paid to local conditions under the IPPC Directive, of the ethos that divergent conditions may legitimately require divergent responses. A number of pressures pointed to the decentralization of environmental law towards the end of the twentieth century. Successive EU enlargements brought with them ever more diverse environmental conditions, as well as diverse economic conditions and diverse regulatory and institutional traditions. Legitimacy-centered subsidiarity concerns would tend to encourage decisions "closer to the people"; effectiveness-type subsidiarity concerns, which level of government will do the best job, exercise a similar effect in terms of responding to varied conditions. And while the IPPC philosophy was in favor of flexibility and local diversity, flexibility was always highly constrained, by procedural obligations, by EQSs and ELVs as in the IED, and indeed by the scientific authority of BREFs.

The Article 15(4) derogation is subject to both substantive and procedural constraints. As with other areas of EU environmental law, member states are subject not to a simple comply/breach dichotomy but to a set of primary obligations, which need not be met provided that certain secondary requirements are complied with.[74] The first substantive provisos are that EQSs (as above) and minimum harmonized EU ELVs set in the annexes to the directive (currently applying to the sectors covered in Chapters III to VI of the directive) may not be breached. So there are EU-wide harmonized environmental norms spelled out in precise terms in the directive. Article 15(4) also demands that there be "no significant pollution" and "a high level of protection of the environment as a whole." And, as set out above, costs must be "disproportionate." Conceptually speaking, breach of EQSs and ELVs is relatively straightforward, but the other substantive requirements are potentially difficult to pin down and enforce. Local discretion is not just about the local environment, but also about the nature of the plant, and so it is potentially highly individualized.[75] This is all very open ended at the moment. Member states must report to the Commission on the use of Article 15(4), discussed further below, and the Commission will consider whether to issue guidance to "further clarify … the criteria to be taken into account."

Given the vagueness of some of the substantive requirements on the face of Article 15(4), the procedural constraints provide an important control. In addition to periodic reporting to the Commission, obligations of reason giving and publicity mean that the derogation is applied in the knowledge that its application will be subject to scrutiny. The assessment and justification of the use of Article 15(4) must be documented by the regulator in an annex to the permit. The explicit reference to the Article 15(4) derogation in the public participation provisions suggests a special concern that there be external scrutiny of the derogation; EU law has openly relied on individuals and national courts to mitigate the shortcomings of Commission supervision since at least *Van Gend en Loos*.[76] So, while it is important that discretion is available to individual permit writers, it must be exercised transparently. If there were no (good) reasons for not using BREFs before, now the decision maker can only use the derogation if it can find, reflect on, and disclose the reasons. And while no constraints are placed on standards stricter than those found in BREFs, it seems likely that industry, especially industry associations or large well-resourced plants, will fight hard to avoid stricter standards, so that regulators will be forced to explain themselves.

The potential of the Article 15(4) derogation to allow for the export of pollution is also addressed largely through procedural mechanisms. All of the substantive provisos have the potential to speak in some way to transboundary pollution ("no significant pollution" and "high level" of protection are not geographically bounded), including the harmonized ELVs. In addition, the IED, like the IPPC Directive, explicitly requires the permit to contain conditions on the "minimisation of long-distance or transboundary pollution."[77] Furthermore, if a member state is aware that an installation "is likely to have significant negative effects" on the environment of another member state, or if the other member state makes a request, information on the application for a permit has to be provided to that negatively affected member state.[78] There is an opportunity for the member states to consult, and for comments from the public of the other member state. The results of these consultations must be taken into account in the decision making. While not mandating any particular result, these mechanisms are supposed to prompt reflection on transboundary issues, mitigating any problems of decentralization.

The governance framework provided on the face of the IED looks very different from that on the face of the IPPC Directive. And there are some crucial legal differences. The position is, however, more subtle than appearances suggest. The reversion to harmonization raises questions about the degree of flexibility really left to member states under the IPPC Directive, as suggested above. It also requires us to reexamine what we mean by centralization. Yes, we now have prima facie legally binding norms applicable across the European Union. These norms are, however, agreed through a complex, ideally collaborative, process. Moreover, a generous possibility for derogation maintains a focus on local conditions, constrained, but real. Nor is the nature of the harmonized norms entirely straightforward. While they close down discretion in some areas, they are still open-ended in certain respects. So the EEB, for example, criticizes the BREFs on the basis that it is "difficult to derive ELVs for permit writers."[79] Lange talks about "open" and "closed" BAT norms. Though she acknowledges that sharp lines cannot be drawn between them, closed norms are a clear and specific definition of BAT, either for the sector or installation, whereas open norms have no such clear and specific definition. They are largely "descriptive" of the social world, rather than closing down BAT. [80] What these observations mean is that there is not always a simple read-across from BAT conclusions to permit conditions. Their mandatory legal status does not remove national or local regulatory discretion or make the implementation of BAT straightforward. This is confirmed by a close look at one of the first set of BAT conclusions agreed through the IED process, for iron and steel production.[81] There are some clear, quantitative ELVs associated with these techniques, which provide a hard-edged standard for permitters. But even these are expressed as ranges, which

> may reflect the differences within a given type of installation (e.g., differences in the grade/purity and quality of the final product, differences in design, construction, size, and capacity of the installation).

Varied ELVs between member states and installations therefore continue to depend on regulatory judgment. A great deal of qualitative information, for example, as to environmental management within the organization, could be directly incorporated into a permit. But in other cases, for instance, on appropriate energy efficiency techniques, the specific requirement "depends on the scope of the process, the product quality and the types of installation."

So even *with* mandatory BAT conclusions, national regulators still have a crucial and difficult evaluative role. And monitoring compliance with the extensive set of applicable material is still likely to be challenging: the BAT conclusions refer to seven other BREFs that might be relevant. This is emphasized by the different methodologies that might be applied at EU and national level. The BREF on economic and cross-media effects makes it clear that some of its methodologies, useful at the BREF level, are not appropriate at the local level. So for example, in assessing BAT in the EU IPPC Bureau, "average acidification potential" is used, but that is explicitly not appropriate "when the location of the proposal is known."[82] So BAT conclusions using average acidification potential cannot be simply applied but need to be assessed for local applicability. All of this is consistent with the directive. But it demonstrates that setting BAT at EU level by no means renders the national implementation a simple exercise of transposition.

Institutional Learning

One of the IED's important characteristics is its attempt to stimulate thought and learning by those involved in regulation.[83] First of all, decisions are based on a significant amount of data and information, gathered from diverse sources, and potentially subject to contestation. Operators are required to include a wide range of information in applications, including on use of raw materials and on emissions and waste. Some of this information will need to be generated (learned) before it can be shared. For example, the obligation, if certain hazardous substances are produced or released, to produce a "baseline report" on soil and water quality has the potential to enhance quite considerably the understanding of regulators, regulatees, and outsiders. In the absence of an obligation of this type, operators have no incentive to bear the costs of generating information.[84] The operator's information obligations are not limited to permitting. Monitoring provisions, which can be found in the BAT conclusions, have to be included in permits; again the responsibility is on the operator.[85] The operator has to supply information to the regulator during the operation of the permit "at least annually."[86]

Participatory processes are able to provide information and knowledge that simply cannot be found in a single bureaucracy. The BREF process itself involves the provision of information on experience and knowledge from a range of sources outside the bureaucracy, and it opens up the possibility of shared problem solving. This looks like one of those cases where not just solutions, but even "policy aims … cannot be extensively defined in advance of implementation"; they have to be discovered during the course of problem solving.[87] Concerns about industry dominance were raised in the section Best Available Techniques: Norm Generation in EU Environmental Governance. While dominance is a problem, BREF drafting might equally be seen as a process demanding profound industrial involvement. BREF drafting is not simply a regulatory process undermined by the asymmetry of information between industry and others. It is also an effort to overcome that asymmetry, to learn from and to use the information resources of industry. Whether the opportunity to influence BREFs and the various "good faith" type obligations imposed on TWG members[88] are enough to overcome the incentive to leave the costs of generating and sharing information to others must, however, be open to question.[89] The elite process of BAT negotiation is arguably tempered by more extensive participation at the permitting stage, which can add local information, potentially challenging information from the BREF process.

The subsequent stages of the BAT conclusions process, involving the forum and comitology, provide additional, especially political, inputs into the process. They have the potential to feel like overkill. But they are consistent with efforts to encourage deliberation to consensus in EU environmental law.[90] According to the Commission Implementing Decision on drawing up BREFs, "consensus is sought" in the TWG, but "it is not a prerequisite." "Split opinions" are possible in cases of disagreement, and one of the tasks of the forum is to "remove or modify" a split view expressed by "their own" TWG representative.[91]

The dynamic nature of BAT also implies a learning aspect to the IED. BAT changes with time: "new measures and techniques may emerge, science and technologies are continuously developing, and new or emerging processes are being successfully introduced into the industry."[92] Recital 13 to the directive says that the Commission should "aim" to update BREFs "not later than 8 years after the publication of the previous version," although this is not repeated in the legally binding part of the directive. Part of this constant evolution is institutionalized by the obligation for BREFs to consider "emerging" as well as "best available" techniques. An "emerging technique" is a novel technique for an industrial activity that, if commercially developed, could either improve environmental protection or save costs.[93] To be included in the BREF, there needs to be a "good chance that they may become BAT in the (near) future."[94] Regulators can grant a "temporary derogation" of up to nine months to the BAT obligations for the "testing and use" of "emerging techniques."[95]

Certain aspects of the IED enhance incentives for operator reflection on environmental performance. In addition to information gathering for the permit application and for monitoring, the ability of the operator to use any technique to meet its ELVs allows for innovation and experimentation within the regulated installation. Rather than requiring operators to apply BAT (such as a particular type of incinerator operated in a particular way), the permit granted under the IED requires an operator to meet ELVs associated with BAT, but "without prescribing the use of any technique or specific technology."[96] The ability of operators facing different conditions to choose their own method of implementation builds in an incentive for operators (even if most do not use it) to discover cheaper or better ways of achieving regulatory objectives. The IED also attempts to encourage participation in the European Union's Eco-Management and Audit Scheme (EMAS), in which organizations voluntarily commit themselves to internal environmental management, a process intended to encourage self-critical reflection on environmental performance and active engagement with environmental impacts. The IED incentivizes EMAS participation by an innovative approach to national inspection and enforcement, resolving a lengthy debate on the role of EMAS in enforcement. The frequency of site visits "shall be based on a systematic appraisal of the environmental risks of the installations concerned," one factor in the assessment of which is whether the operator participates in EMAS.[97] Regulators also have learning obligations. They are required to follow or be informed of developments in BAT, and that information has to be made available to the public.[98] Article 21 of the IED requires "periodic" reconsideration, and if necessary, updating, of permit conditions, without any requirements for changed circumstances. In addition, there is an obligation for reconsideration of a permit within four years of the adoption of BAT conclusions relating to the "main activity" of an installation.

So the directive demands the generation of diverse information from a range of actors to form the context for decision making. Knowledge is subject to change and criticism is possible. We might go so far as to say that the recasting of IPPC in the IED reflects learning about failure to apply BAT on the ground. Joanne Scott and Jane Holder discuss the importance of the "iterative evaluation and adaptation of Directives" (in their case, environmental impact assessment).[99] A central tool in enabling such adaptation is arrangements for information exchange and reporting, providing an element of peer review as well as important opportunities for mutual learning.[100] The enormous complexity of the "problem" of industrial emissions, in environmental and economic terms, makes this form of learning and iteration crucial if mistakes are to be corrected and minimized. National reporting is now a standard element of environmental directives. The IED requires member states to report to the Commission every three years, including on ELVs and BAT, as well as explicitly on the use of the Article 15(4) derogation and on emerging techniques.[101] The Commission, in response, has to review and report on the operation of the directive and put forward a legislative proposal "where appropriate."[102] Certain specific issues have to be considered for action, including generally an assessment of the need for new EU-wide minimum ELVs and EU rules for the monitoring and compliance of activities within the scope of recent BAT conclusions. EU harmonization remains in the background.[103]

This sort of information and justification exercise is potentially a powerful tool for focusing attention on environmental questions (as well as economic impacts). Joanne Scott has highlighted the removal of a potentially important "learning" obligation in respect of the comparative performance of different regulatory approaches.[104] Specifically, the original IPPC Directive required the Commission to report on the directive's "effectiveness compared with other Community environmental instruments."[105] We might have expected, among other things, a comparison of the effectiveness in combatting climate change of the IED and the EU Emissions Trading Scheme. The reporting obligation has, however, been removed from the directive – and without debate – on the highly contentious ground that its removal is consistent with codification, that is, is not a substantive change. While not written with greenhouse gases in mind, thinking about the absence of a report on this particular controversial issue underlines for us the galvanizing potential of information.

Of course the quality of reports under environmental directives, of the learning and revisiting, may not match the theory. Reports from both member states and the Commission (often produced by external consultants) can seem superficial and hurried, sometimes descriptive rather than evaluative, sometimes plainly self-serving.[106] It sometimes looks as if the "learning" aspect may be no more than a form of delaying compromise for difficult decisions. For example, there was some debate during the drafting of the IED of systematically extending the role of EU-wide ELVs.[107] Instead, the Commission has to revisit this on a three-yearly basis. It might be that additional information will make it clear whether BAT is working or we need harmonized ELVS. More likely, this is a disagreement based on a value judgment about the type of Union, the type of harmonization, we really want, rather than a disagreement amenable to data. But whatever the difficulties, the IED institutionalizes the opportunity to reflect upon legislation, to base decisions upon the fullest information on the values and issues at stake, to revisit decisions.

Conclusion

While EU environmental law is diverse, certain features of the IED are typical of environmental law and governance in the European Union generally. They are not necessarily features that are universally shared, and I would not like to suggest that they capture all that is most interesting and important about EU environmental law. Nor would I want to suggest that all is well with the governance forms that we see in IED, especially in terms of the legal and political accountability of parts of the process. Indeed, the loss of information on who participates in TWGs demonstrates the vulnerability of these governance mechanisms to evolving approaches to the relationship between transparency and privacy.[108] The need to build a system where public values (e.g., as to transparency of participation) are protected in norm generation is enormous. But the phenomena that we see in the IED are significant and pervasive.

The IED demonstrates the complexity and diversity of environmental norms in the European Union, of their generation and their application. Seen from within a paradigm of "new governance," we might focus on the substantive flexibility on the face of the directive (the open-ended, even vague, environmental norm of BAT), the procedural demands in the directive, the collaborative fora for generating norms, the variety of approaches within the directive. Most importantly, sitting behind these open-ended substantive standards is a complex governance framework for the negotiation of more concrete substantive norms. This form of new governance has been formalized in the journey from IPPC to IED, and the final word is firmly with comitology. "Experimentalist" governance[109] focuses our attention on those elements of the directive that work on learning and adaptation. In both cases, decentralization is important. And here we see an ambiguous philosophy at play in the IED. Certainly, there is far greater emphasis on centralization than there was in the IPPC Directive, and much less emphasis on the value of the local. But the scope for local interventions seems not much different in the IED compared with what was *intended* in the IPPC Directive. The binding/nonbinding, law/nonlaw boundary is not a clear one.

Notes

I am grateful to Joanne Scott for her very helpful comments on an earlier draft of this chapter (and for discussions on transparency/data protection) and to James Nierinck for his research assistance.

1 Directive 2010/75/EU of 24 November 2010 on industrial emissions (integrated pollution prevention and control) [2010] OJ L 334/17.

2 For example, Convention on Long Range Transboundary Air Pollution (UNECE, Geneva, 1979), with its protocols on different pollutants. The convention entered into force in the European Union in 1983.

3 For example Directive 2000/60/EC of 23 October 2000 establishing a framework for the Community action in the field of water policy [2000] OJ L 327/1, Article 9.

4 Directive 2009/29/EC of 23 April 2009 amending Directive 2003/87/EC so as to improve and extend the greenhouse gas emission allowance trading scheme of the Community [2009] OJ L 140/63.

5 On some of the common ground, see Gráinne de Búrca, "New Governance and Experimentalism: An Introduction," *Wisconsin Law Review* 2010 (2010).

6 While the theoretical background is distinct, see, for example, Martti Koskenniemi, "The Fate of Public International Law: Between Technique and Politics," *Modern Law Review* 70 (2007): 9–15, "Deformalisation." See also Mark Dawson, "Transforming into What? New Governance in the EU and the 'Managerial Sensibility' in Modern Law," *Wisconsin Law Review* (2010).

7 And the creation of a framework for cooperation is a claimed success of the otherwise weak LRTAP Convention, n 2 this chapter, see http://www.unece.org/env/lrtap/lrtap_h1.html, and Patricia W. Birnie, Alan E. Boyle, and Catherine Redgwell, *International Law and the Environment* (Oxford: Oxford University Press, 2009), 347.

8 See the preliminary description in Gráinne de Búrca and Joanne Scott, "New Governance, Law and Constitutionalism," in *Law and New Governance in the EU and US*, ed. Joanne Scott and Gráinne de Búrca (Oxford: Hart, 2006) of new governance as modes of governing that are "less rigid, less prescriptive, less committed to uniform outcomes, and less hierarchical in nature." On new governance in the environmental field, see especially Joanne Scott, ed., *Environmental Protection: European Law and Governance* (Oxford: Oxford University Press, 2009).

9 Ibid.

10 Daniel Kelemen, *Eurolegalism: The Transformation of Law and Regulation in the European Union* (Cambridge, MA: Harvard University Press, 2011).

11 Katharina Holzinger, Christoph Knill, and Ansgar Schafer, "Rhetoric or Reality? 'New Governance' in EU Environmental Policy," *European Law Journal* 12 (2006): 403–420.
12 On new governance and "not law," see David Trubeck and Louise Trubek, "The World Turned Upside Down: Reflections on New Governance and the Transformation of Law," *Wisconsin Law Review* 2 (2010).
13 Directive 2008/1/EC of 15 January 2008 concerning integrated pollution prevention and control [2008] OJ L 24/8.
14 Note that there is still some debate on this. See European Environmental Bureau (EEB), *New Features under the Industrial Emissions Directive* (2011), although the language of the legislation seems clear in many respects.
15 Article 14(1)(a).
16 Under Article 3(13), "emission levels associated with the best available techniques" are defined as "the range of emission levels obtained under normal operating conditions using a best available technique or a combination of best available techniques, as described in BAT conclusions, expressed as an average over a given period of time, under specified reference conditions."
17 Article 11. Other principles include the application of the waste hierarchy, accident prevention, and decommissioning.
18 Article 14(1).
19 Article 24(1) and Annex IV; UNECE Convention on Access to Information, Public Participation in Decision-Making and Access to Justice in Environmental Matters (Aarhus, 1998). We see similar language elsewhere in EU environmental law, for example Directive 2011/92 of 13 December 2011 on the assessment of the effects of certain public and private projects on the environment (codification) [2012] OJ L 26/2; Directive 2000/60/EC, n 3 this chapter.
20 For more detail and references, see my discussion in Maria Lee, *EU Environmental Law: Challenge Change and Decision Making* (Oxford: Hart, 2005), especially Chap. 5.
21 Article 25.
22 Article 3(10). The definition of BAT and each of its elements in UNECE Guidance document on best available techniques for reducing emissions of persistent organic pollutants from major stationary sources (UNECE, 18 December 2009), and Annex V to the 1998 Aarhus Protocol to the LRTAP Convention on Persistent Organic Pollutants (POPs) is almost identical to the definition in the IED. The definitions in the Stockholm Convention on Persistent Organic Pollutants (UN, 2001) are also very similar.
23 There is no obligation to integrate the national permitting systems.
24 BREF on Economics and Cross-Media Effects (2006). This is consistent with empirical observations that arguments around costs are a crucial and pervasive part of the whole BREF and permitting process, Bettina Lange, *Implementing EU Pollution Control: Law and Integration* (Cambridge: Cambridge University Press, 2008).
25 All Article 3(10).
26 Lange, *Implementing EU Pollution Control*, Chap. 7. See Mark Wilde's discussion of the controversy around flue gas desulphurization versus integrated gasification combined cycle, "Best Available Techniques (BAT) and Coal-Fired Power Stations: Can the Energy Gap be Plugged without Increasing Emissions?" *Journal of Environmental Law* 20 (2008).
27 BREF on Economics and Cross-Media Effects (2006), section 2.6.2.
28 See ibid., section 2.6.3. The BREF suggests comparison between seven themes (human toxicity, global warming, aquatic toxicity, acidification, eutrophication, ozone depletion, photochemical ozone creation potential), plus energy use and waste production: Chap. 2, Guideline 3.
29 For discussion, see Maria Lee, "Law and Governance of Water Protection Policy," in Scott, *Environmental Protection: European Law and Governance.*
30 Commission Implementing Decision 2012/119/EU of 10 February 2012 laying down rules concerning guidance on the collection of data and on the drawing up of BAT reference documents and on their quality assurance referred to in Directive 2010/75/EU of the European Parliament and of the Council on industrial emissions [2012] OJ L 63/1.

31 Directive 2008/1/EC, n 13 this chapter, Article 16.
32 Commission Implementing Decision 2012/119/EU, n 30 this chapter, section 4.5.
33 Commission Decision of 16 May 2011 establishing a forum for the exchange of information pursuant to Article 13 of the Directive 2010/75/EU on industrial emissions [2011] OJ C 146/3, Article 4 (emphasis added).
34 Commission Implementing Decision 2012/119/EU, n 30 above 24, section 4.3.
35 Article 13(4).
36 Regulation 182/2011 of the European Parliament and of the Council of 16 February 2011 laying down the rules and general principles concerning mechanisms for control by Member States of the Commission's exercise of implementing powers [2011] OJ L 55/13. Note that the Commission has established the Industrial Emissions Expert Group (IEEG) (made up of member state representatives) for advice on *delegated* acts under Article 290 TFEU (rather than implementing acts under Article 291, to which comitology applies). See generally Paul P. Craig and Gráinne de Búrca, *EU Law: Text, Cases and Materials* (Oxford: Oxford University Press, 2011).
37 For a detailed discussion, see Lange, *Implementing EU Pollution Control.*
38 Ibid., Chap 5.
39 Stijn Smismans, "New Modes of Governance and the Participatory Myth" (European governance papers no. 06-01, 2006).
40 Lange, *Implementing EU Pollution Control*, 105. There is now an obligation to translate the BAT conclusions into all official languages, Article 13(6).
41 Charalampos Koutalakis, "Regulatory Effects of Participatory Environmental Networks: The Case of the 'Seville Process'" (Brussels: New Modes of Governance Project, 2005) provides data suggesting that national NGOs constitute 57 percent of NGO participation, mainly from Germany.
42 Koutakalis, "Regulatory Effects of Participatory Environmental Networks."
43 Email communication with European IPPC Bureau, 26 June 2012. There is an argument to be made that this blanket approach is overly cautious: "The right to the protection of personal data is not ... an absolute right, but must be considered in relation to its function in society," Joined Cases C-92/09 and C-93/09 *Volker und Markus Schecke and Eifert v. Land Hessen* EU:C:2010:662, para 48. In this case, the need to strike a balance between public interests in transparency and the protection of personal data is emphasized. Limitations to rights to protection of personal data are applied "only in so far as is strictly necessary," para 77. The decision can be interpreted as laying no priority on either transparency or data protection but requiring a balance between the two. See also Michal Bobek, "Case Note: Joined Cases C-92 & 93/09, *Volker und Markus Schecke GbR and Hartmut Eifert*," *Common Market Law Review* 48 (2011).
44 Lange, *Implementing EU Pollution Control*, Chap. 5.
45 EEB, n 14 this chapter, 9. Lange, *Implementing EU Pollution Control*, 110.
46 Koutakalis, "Regulatory Effects of Participatory Environmental Networks" cites an industry association estimate of €1 million for effective participation, footnote 10. A new BREF is expected to take 31–39 months to complete the TWG process, Commission Implementing Decision 2012/119/EU, n 30 this chapter 24, section 1.2.4.
47 Communication from the Commission, On the Road to Sustainable Production: Progress in Implementing Council Directive 96/61/EC Concerning Integrated Pollution Prevention and Control, COM(2003) 354 final, 17. The BREF, n 24 this chapter, outlines a number of sources of cost data but emphasizes the need to "think critically about the validity of the data," section 3.2.1.
48 COM(2003) 354 final, n 47 this chapter.
49 See p. iii, but references to transparency pervade the document.
50 Elizabeth Fisher, "Transparency and Administrative Law: A Critical Evaluation," *Current Legal Problems* 63 (2010).
51 See ibid., on the "end users" of transparency.
52 Environmental interest groups and industry have to be nominated by the forum. Not only is there no "public" participation, but other organized groups, such as trade unions, are also excluded.
53 In the context of post-Lisbon changes to comitology, see Steve Peers and Marios Costa, "Accountability for Delegated and Implementing Acts after the Treaty of Lisbon," *European Law Journal* 18 (3) (2012).

54 The Council also has a right of scrutiny.

55 Applications for authorization of genetically modified organisms (GMOs) have always gone to Council (now to appeal committee) when put to comitology, precisely because of disagreement about political or ethical concerns. For discussion, see Maria Lee, *EU Regulation of GMOs: Law, Decision-Making and New Technology* (Cheltenham: Edward Elgar, 2008).

56 Directive 2008/1/EC, n 13 this chapter, Annex IV.

57 Under Article 3(12) "BAT conclusions" are defined as "a document containing the parts of a BAT reference document laying down the conclusions on best available techniques, their description, information to assess their applicability, the emission levels associated with the best available techniques, associated monitoring, associated consumption levels and, where appropriate, relevant site remediation measures." BREFs have a common format, and Chap. 5 of the sector-specific BREFs contain "BAT Conclusions."

58 Neil Emmott, Stefani Bar, and R. Andreas Kraemer, "Policy Review: IPPC and the Sevilla Process," *European Environment* 10 (2000).

59 Charalampos Koutalakis, Aron Buzogany, and Tanja A. Börzel, "When Soft Regulation is Not Enough: The Integrated Pollution Prevention and Control Directive of the European Union," *Regulation and Governance* 4 (2010): 332. The authors argue that "soft regulation" leads to noncompliance, apparently also with the requirement to consider local conditions. The study also included Hungary and Poland.

60 Proposal for a Directive on industrial emissions (integrated pollution prevention and control) (Recast) COM(2007) 843 final, 9. See also European Commission, Report on the implementation of Directive 2008/1/EC concerning integrated pollution prevention and control and Directive 1999/13/EC on the limitation of emissions of volatile organic compounds due to the use of organic solvents in certain activities and installations COM(2010) 593 final, 4.

61 Joanne Scott, "Flexibility, 'Proceduralization,' and Environmental Governance in the EU" in *Constitutional Change in the European Union*, ed. Joanne Scott and Gráinne de Búrca (London: Hart, 2000). This is not the place for a detailed discussion, but who enjoys any flexibility will depend in part on national constitutional arrangements, and it potentially tells us a lot about subsidiarity. The IED provides the option of "General Binding Rules," set nationally for ("at least") a sector, which can be incorporated directly into permit conditions, Article 3(8) (as did the IPPC Directive, n 13 this chapter, Article 9). This allows the member states to restrict the discretion of their regulators to take account of local conditions in setting permits, as well as providing the possibility of reducing the administrative burden carried by the regulator. On this approach, flexibility seems largely to be for the benefit of the member state, rather than subnational decision makers, or subnational industry or environment.

62 Also COM(2010) 593 final, n 61 this chapter.

63 Although it is not far-fetched to imagine the CJEU imposing a reason giving obligation.

64 See the discussion of hybridity in de Búrca and Scott, "New Governance, Law and Constitutionalism."

65 Article 14(3). A regulator can set permit conditions on the basis of BAT not found in the BAT conclusions without breaching the directive, provided that environmental protection is at least as high as under the BAT conclusions, Article 14(5) and 15.

66 Under Article 3(5), "emission limit value" is defined as "the mass, expressed in terms of certain specific parameters, concentration and/or level of an emission, which may not be exceeded during one or more periods of time."

67 Article 14(6).

68 Article 13(7). See the challenge brought in Case T-158/11 *Magnesitas de Rubián SA v. Parliament and Council*, judgment of 4 February 2013.

69 Article 14(4).

70 Article 14(1) and 18. Under Article 3(6), "environmental quality standard" is defined as "the set of requirements which must be fulfilled at a given time by a given environment or particular part thereof, as set out in Union law." In a reference from a Dutch court, in which an environmental interest group challenged permits granted to three power stations, the CJEU confirmed that the "national emissions ceilings" for nitrogen oxides and sulphur dioxide set by Directive 2001/81 of 23 October 2001 on national

emission ceilings for certain atmospheric pollutants [2001] OJ L 309/22 are not EQSs. EQSs are about the quality of the receiving environment; the national emissions ceilings are about total emissions, Case C-165/09 *Stichting Natuur en Milieu v. College van Gedeputeerde Staten van Groningen* EU:C:2011:348.

71 Directive 2000/60, n 3 this chapter; Directive 2008/50/EC of the European Parliament and of the Council of 21 May 2008 on ambient air quality and cleaner air for Europe [2008] OJ L 152/1. Advocate General Kokott gives this directive as an example in Case C-165/09 *Stichting Natuur*, n 70 this chapter, para 62.

72 However, given that a comprehensive quality standard (soil acidification in Sweden and the ozone layer above the North Pole) is unrealistic, *minimizing* pollution from all installations reduces impacts in a way EQSs cannot. See Gertrude Lubbe-Wolf, "Efficient Environmental Legislation – On Different Philosophies of Pollution Control in Europe," *Journal of Environmental Law* 13 (2001): 79.

73 EEB, n 14 this chapter, p. 7.

74 For example, the Water Framework Directive, n 3 this chapter, discussed in Lee, "Law and Governance of Water Protection Policy." In a very different context, a similar approach applies in Council Directive 1992/43/EEC of 21 May 1992 on the conservation of natural habitats and of wild fauna and flora [1992] OJ L 206/7.

75 Lange's examination of permitting suggests that this reflects the status quo, at least in the United Kingdom and Germany, *Implementing EU Pollution Control*, 195–196.

76 Case 26/62 *Van Gend en Loos* EU:C:1963:1.

77 Article 14(1)(9).

78 Article 26.

79 EEB, n 14 this chapter, 10.

80 Lange, *Implementing EU Pollution Control*, Chap. 6.

81 Commission Implementing Decision 2012/135/EU of 28 February 2012 establishing the best available techniques (BAT) conclusions under Directive 2010/75/EU of the European Parliament and of the Council on industrial emissions for iron and steel production [2012] OJ L 70/63.

82 This chapter, n 24, section 2.5.4. See also section 2.6.4 on general "screening for local effects."

83 Again, the same might be said of Directive 2000/60/EC, n 3 this chapter.

84 In the context of chemicals, see the discussion in Elizabeth Fisher, "The 'Perfect Storm' of REACH: Charting Regulatory Controversy in the Age of Information, Sustainable Development and Globalization," *Journal of Risk Research* 11 (2008): 541.

85 Article 16(1).

86 Article 14(1)(d).

87 Charles F. Sabel and William H. Simon, "Minimalism and Experimentalism in the Administrative State," *The Georgetown Law Journal* 100 (2011): 56.

88 Commission Implementing Decision 2012/119/EU, n 30 this chapter, 24.

89 We might compare the IED with chemicals regulation, where the "privatization" of information generation and provision is linked in with the permitting process – no data, no market. Regulation 1907/2006 of the European Parliament and of the Council of 18 December 2006 concerning the Registration, Evaluation, Authorization, and Restriction of Chemicals (REACH), establishing a European Chemicals Agency [2006] OJ L 396/1. There is a hint of this in the obligation to supply information when applying for the permit, but not in BREF drafting.

90 See, for example, the discussion of GMOs (where this consensus seeking fails) in Maria Lee, "Multi-Level Governance of Genetically Modified Organisms in the EU: Ambiguity and Hierarchy," in *The Regulation of GMOs: Comparative Approaches*, ed. Michael Cardwell and Luc Bodiguel (Oxford: Oxford University Press, 2010).

91 Commission Implementing Decision 2012/119/EU, n 30 this chapter, section 1.3.

92 Ibid., section 1.2.2.

93 Article 3(14).

94 Commission Implementing Decision 2012/119/EU, n 30 this chapter, section 2.3.9.

95 Article 15(5).

96 Article 15(2). "[E]mission limit values may be supplemented or replaced by equivalent parameters or technical measures ensuring an equivalent level of environmental protection," Article 14(2).

97 Article 23.
98 Article 19.
99 de Búrca and Scott, "New Governance, Law and Constitutionalism."
100 Sabel and Simon, "Minimalism and Experimentalism in the Administrative State"; and Charles F. Sabel and Jonathan Zeitlin, "Learning from Difference: The New Architecture of Experimentalist Governance in the European Union," *European Law Journal* 14 (2008).
101 Article 72.
102 Article 73.
103 Article 75(1).
104 Joanne Scott, "The Multi-Level Governance of Climate Change," in *The Evolution of EU Law*, ed. Paul Craig and Gráinne de Búrca (Oxford: Oxford University Press, 2011).
105 Directive 1996/61/EC of 24 September 1996 on Integrated Pollution Prevention and Control [1996] OJ L 257/26, Article 16(3).
106 See the criticism of the IPPC review process in Eberharde Bohne, "The Implementation of the IPPC Directive from a Comparative Perspective and Lessons for its Recast," *Journal for European Environmental and Planning Law* 5 (2008).
107 EEB, n 14 this chapter.
108 See n 43 this chapter.
109 Sabel and Simon, "Minimalism and Experimentalism in the Administrative State" explicitly put experimentalism and new governance in the same category of approaches, 55.

References

Birnie, Patricia W., Alan E. Boyle, and Catherine Redgwell. *International Law and the Environment*. Oxford: Oxford University Press, 2009.

Bobek, Michal. "Case Note: Joined Cases C-92 & 93/09, *Volker und Markus Schecke GbR and Hartmut Eifert*." *Common Market Law Review* 48 (2011): 2005–2022.

Bohne, Eberharde. "The Implementation of the IPPC Directive from a Comparative Perspective and Lessons for its Recast." *Journal for European Environmental and Planning Law* 5 (2008): 319–338.

Craig, Paul P., and Gráinne de Búrca, eds. *EU Law: Text, Cases and Materials*. Oxford: Oxford University Press, 2011.

de Búrca, Gráinne. "New Governance and Experimentalism: An Introduction." *Wisconsin Law Review* (2010): 227–238.

de Búrca, Gráinne, and Joanne Scott. "New Governance, Law and Constitutionalism." In *Law and New Governance in the EU and US*, edited by Joanne Scott and Gráinne de Búrca. Oxford: Hart, 2006.

Dawson, Mark. "Transforming into What? New Governance in the EU and the 'Managerial Sensibility' in Modern Law." *Wisconsin Law Review* (2010): 389–440.

Emmott, Neil, Stefani Bar, and R. Andreas Kraemer. "Policy Review: IPPC and the Sevilla Process." *European Environment* 10 (2000): 204–207.

European Environmental Bureau. *New Features under the Industrial Emissions Directive*. Brussels: European Environmental Bureau, 2011.

Fisher, Elizabeth. "The 'Perfect Storm' of REACH: Charting Regulatory Controversy in the Age of Information, Sustainable Development and Globalization." *Journal of Risk Research* 11 (2008): 541–563.

Fisher, Elizabeth. "Transparency and Administrative Law: A Critical Evaluation." *Current Legal Problems* 63 (2010): 272–314.

Holzinger, Katharina, Christoph Knill, and Ansgar Schafer. "Rhetoric or Reality? 'New Governance' in EU Environmental Policy." *European Law Journal* 12 (2006): 403–420.

Kelemen, Daniel. *Eurolegalism: The Transformation of Law and Regulation in the European Union*. Cambridge, MA: Harvard University Press, 2011.

Koskenniemi, Martti. "The Fate of Public International Law: Between Technique and Politics." *Modern Law Review* 70 (2007): 1–30.

Koutalakis, Charalampos. "Regulatory Effects of Participatory Environmental Networks: The Case of the 'Seville Process.'" Brussels: New Modes of Governance Project, 2005.

Koutalakis, Charalampos, Aron Buzogany, and Tanja A. Börzel. "When Soft Regulation is Not Enough: The Integrated Pollution Prevention and Control Directive of the European Union." *Regulation and Governance* 4 (2010): 329–344.

Lange, Bettina. *Implementing EU Pollution Control: Law and Integration*. Cambridge: Cambridge University Press, 2008.

Lee, Maria. *EU Environmental Law: Challenges, Change and Decision Making*. Oxford: Hart, 2005.

Lee, Maria. *EU Regulation of GMOs: Law, Decision-Making and New Technology*. Cheltenham: Edward Elgar, 2008.

Lee, Maria. "Law and Governance of Water Protection Policy." In Scott, *Environmental Protection: European Law and Governance*, 27–55.

Lee, Maria. "Multi-Level Governance of Genetically Modified Organisms in the EU: Ambiguity and Hierarchy." In *The Regulation of Genetically Modified Organisms: Comparative Approaches*, edited by Michael Cardwell and Luc Bodiguel, 101–122. Oxford: Oxford University Press, 2010.

Lubbe-Wolf, Gertrude. "Efficient Environmental Legislation – On Different Philosophies of Pollution Control in Europe." *Journal of Environmental Law* 13 (2001): 79–87.

Peers, Steve, and Marios Costa. "Accountability for Delegated and Implementing Acts after the Treaty of Lisbon." *European Law Journal* 18 (3) (2012): 427–460.

Sabel, Charles F., and William H. Simon. "Minimalism and Experimentalism in the Administrative State." *The Georgetown Law Journal* 100 (2011): 53–93.

Sabel, Charles F., and Jonathan Zeitlin. "Learning from Difference: The New Architecture of Experimentalist Governance in the European Union." *European Law Journal* 14 (2008): 271–327.

Scott, Joanne. "Flexibility, 'Proceduralization', and Environmental Governance in the EU." In *Constitutional Change in the European Union: From Uniformity to Flexibility?* edited by Joanne Scott and Gráinne de Búrca, 259–280. London: Hart, 2000.

Scott, Joanne, ed. *Environmental Protection: European Law and Governance*. Oxford: Oxford University Press, 2009.

Scott, Joanne. "The Multi-Level Governance of Climate Change." In *The Evolution of EU Law*, edited by Paul Craig and Gráinne de Búrca, 805–836. Oxford: Oxford University Press, 2011.

Smismans, Stijn. "New Modes of Governance and the Participatory Myth." European governance papers no. 06-01, 2006.

Trubek, David, and Louise Trubek. "The World Turned Upside Down: Reflections on New Governance and the Transformation of Law." *Wisconsin Law Review* (2010): 719–726.

Wilde, Mark. "Best Available Techniques (BAT) and Coal-Fired Power Stations: Can the Energy Gap be Plugged without Increasing Emissions?" *Journal of Environmental Law* 20 (2008): 87–114.

Index

A Companion to European Union Law and International Law, First Edition.
Edited by Dennis Patterson and Anna Södersten.

Table of Cases
Alphabetical

A Companion to European Union Law and International Law, First Edition.
Edited by Dennis Patterson and Anna Södersten.

Table of Cases

Numerical

A Companion to European Union Law and International Law, First Edition.
Edited by Dennis Patterson and Anna Södersten.

C-176/03 *Commission v. Council* EU:C:2005:542, 551
C-210/03 *Swedish Match* EU:C:2004:802, 91, 201
C-266/03 *Commission v. Luxembourg* EU:C:2005:341, 379
C-380/03 *Germany v. European Parliament and Council ('Tobacco Advertising II')* EU:C:2006:772, 201
C-411/03 *Sevic Systems AG v. Amtsgericht Neuwied* EU:C:2005:762, 225
C-433/03 *Commission v. Germany* EU:C:2005:462, 379
C-436/03 *Parliament v. Council* EU:C:2006:277, 263
C-459/03 *Commission v. Ireland (MOX plant)* EU:C:2006:345, 52, 173, 432
C-503/03 *Commission v. Spain* EU:C:2006:74, 520
C-540/03 *Parliament v. Council* EU:C:2006:429, 49, 461, 523
C-144/04 *Mangold* EU:C:2005:709, 71-72, 160, 173, 468
C-154/04 and 155/04 *Alliance for Natural Health and Others* EU:C:2005:449, 91
C-158/04 and C-159/04 *Trofo Super Markets* EU:C:2006:562, 210
C-212/04 *Adeneler* EU:C:2006:443, 69
C-234/04 *Kapferer v. Schlank & Schick* EU:C:2006:178, 161
C-295/04 to C-298/04 *Manfredi* EU:C:2006:461, 158, 275
C-317/04 and C-318/04 *Parliament v. Council* EU:C:2006:346, 381
C-354/04 P *Gestoras Pro Amnistía and Others* EU:C:2007:115, 181
C-355/04 P *Segi and Others* EU:C:2007:116, 181
C-372/04 *Watts v. Bedford Primary Care Trust* EU:C:2006:325, 223
C-392/04 and C-422/04 I-21 *Germany and Arcor* EU:C:2006:586, 188
C-434/04 *Leppik v. Virallinen syyttäjä* EU:C:2006:609, 209
C-441/04 *A-Punkt Schmuckhandels GmbH v. Claudia Schmidt* EU:C:2006, 287
C-452/04 *Fidium Finanz AG v. Bundesanstalt für Finanzdienstleistungsaufsicht* EU:C:2006:631, 221
C-503/04 *Commission v. Germany* EU:C:2007:432, 274
C-77/05 *UK v. Council* EU:C:2007:803, 519
C-91/05 *Commission v. Council* EU:C:2008:288, 377, 400, 420
C-110/05 *Commission v. Italy* EU:C:2009:66, 200, 211
C-112/05 *Commission v. Germany* EU:C:2007:623, 221, 236
C-119/05 *Lucchini* EU:C:2007:434, 161
C-137/05 *UK v. Council* EU:C:2007:805, 519
C-142/05 *Mickelson and Roos* EU:C:2009:336, 211
C-168/05 *Mostaza Claro v. Centro Movil Milenium SL* EU:C:2006:675, 275
C-222/05 to C-225/05 *van der Weerd* EU:C:2007:318, 160
C-303/05 *Advocaten voor de Wereld* EU:C:2007:261, 555
C-341/05 *Laval un Partneri* EU:C:2007:809, 63, 122, 173, 217, 247, 469, 479, 484
C-402/05 P and C-415/05 P *Kadi and Al Barakaat International Foundation v. Council and Commission ('Kadi I')* EU:C:2008:461, 42, 44, 47–51, 156, 158, 171, 374, 381, 414, 430, 460, 469, 560
C-403/05 *Parliament v. Commission* EU:C:2007:624, 377
C-432/05 *Unibet (London) Ltd and Unibet (International) Ltd v. Justitiekanslern* EU:C:2007:163, 157
C-438/05 *International Transport Workers' Federation, Finnish Seamen's Union v. Viking Line ABP, O. Viking Line Eesti* EU:C:2007:772, 63, 173, 200, 217, 220, 247, 469, 479, 484
C-440/05 *Commission v. Council* EU:C:2007:625, 551
C-462/05 *Commission v. Portugal* EU:C:2008:337, 160
C-2/06 *Kempter KG* EU:C:2008:78, 161, 188
C-120/06 P and C-121/06 P *FIAMM and Fedon v. Council and Commission* EU:C:2008:476, 46, 52
C-199/06 *Centre d'exportation du livre Français and Ministre de la Culture et de la Communication v. Société internationale de diffusion et d'Edition ('CELF 1')* EU:C:2008:79, 346
C-205/06 *Commission v. Austria* EU:C:2009:118, 59
C-210/06 *Cartesio Oktato es Szolgaltato bt* EU:C:2008:723, 183–184, 224-225, 272
C-244/06 *Dynamic Medien v. Avides Media* EU:C:2008:85, 50
C-249/06 *Commission v. Sweden* EU:C:2009:119, 49
C-268/06 *Impact* EU:C:2008:223, 158
C-308/06 *Intertanko and Others* EU:C:2008:312, 44, 46, 49, 50, 51, 381, 416, 432, 560